Could You Be Their Chaplain?

Since the Royal Air Force was formed in 1918, chaplains have been an integral part of the RAF and today, as then, they represent the Church where it is needed most.

As an RAF chaplain you will be involved in the lives of our personnel, regardless of their rank or religious beliefs. You will serve alongside them, providing vital religious, pastoral and ethical support wherever they go, including deployed Operations. Home-based duties will be equally important, supporting personnel and their families, Reservists, civil servants and the wider RAF community. While exploring innovative ways of engaging with them, you will also fulfil the more traditional role of leading regular worship, including officiating at baptisms, weddings and funerals. Partners and families are well cared for and the RAF provides excellent in-service training and education opportunities.

If you are ready for an exciting, highly-rewarding position, contact us now.

We have vacancies for full-time and spare-time chaplains.

www.raf.mod.uk/chaplains

ⓞ ROYAL
FORCE

467 811 237

i

CHRISTIAN RESOURCES EXHIBITIONS

IS COMING TO A CITY NEAR YOU

CRE SOUTH WEST
Westpoint, Exeter
10 & 11 February 2015

CRE INTERNATIONAL
ExCeL, London
19 – 22 May 2015

CRE MIDLANDS
NEC, Birmingham
7 & 8 October 2015

VISIT US FOR ALL YOUR RESOURCE AND EQUIPMENT NEEDS AND ENJOY SEMINARS, THEATRE, FILM, BOOKS, MULTIMEDIA & MORE ...

For all the latest information and to buy your tickets go to
CREONLINE.CO.UK or call 01793 418218

CRE is part of Bible Society (Charity Reg: No 232759)

SONS AND FRIENDS OF THE CLERGY

WORKING TO SUPPORT THE CLERGY

IN 2014 OVER £2 MILLION WAS AWARDED IN GRANTS FOR A WIDE RANGE OF PURPOSES INCLUDING:

- School uniform, travel and educational trips
- Music lessons and musical instruments
- Sporting activities
- Gap year grants
- Vocational training grants
- University/Diploma maintenance grant
- Bereavement expenses
- Holiday grants
- Clothing

to clergy of the Anglican Communion (stipendiary, self supporting or retired) who work in the United Kingdom, the Crown Dependencies, Eire and the Diocese of Europe and to Anglican clergy missionaries who are working abroad, who are sponsored financially by a UK-based missionary society.

FOR MORE INFORMATION please contact us at:
1 Dean Trench Street, London SW1P 3HB
Tel: 020 7799 3696
Email: enquiries@clergycharities.org.uk
www.clergycharities.org.uk

Sons and Friends of the Clergy **Charity No: 207736**

WITH UP TO

4,000 CARS

YOU'RE SURE TO FIND YOUR PERFECT CAR!

PRICE CHECKED DAILY, COMPREHENSIVELY CHECKED & FULLY GUARANTEED

FINANCE AVAILABLE

NATIONWIDE **DELIVERY** TO YOUR DOOR

PART EXCHANGE WELCOME

BRAND NEW FORD FIESTA 1.25 STUDIO

ONLY **£128**.47 A MONTH*

48 MONTHS (9+47)

Over 35 years experience provinding cars to clergy, charities and the caring profession

autosave ✝ | Call **0845 122 6917** | **autosave**.co.uk

*Contract hire based on 9+47 payment profile. Finance subject to status, a guarantee may be required. Cars for illustration only. Autosave, Trax Park, Doncaster, DN4 5PD

FOLLOW US ON:

x

Leadership development
events across the UK

Patrons to 500+ Church
of England benefices

10,000+ people on vocations
events over 50 years

4,000+ young people
each year on Ventures and
Falcon Camps

Supporting 3,000+ Ventures
and Falcon Camps leaders

Mentor Connect for
leaders and *Mentoring
Matters* for churches

Discover all this plus the *Arrow
Leadership Programme, Growing
Leaders* resources and much more.

www.cpas.org.uk

making disciples, developing leaders, growing churches

Mercy
Ships

Bring Hope and Healing

Will your church help our patients?
Can you help those like Adjovi suffering
from a disfiguring tumour, and thousands
more, who are in desperate need of
medical services?

**Find out more about the inspiring work
of our hospital ship, *Africa Mercy***

† Invite a speaker
† Request information for your congregation
† Medical and other professional volunteers needed
† Make us your charity and mission partner
† Give for Mercy!

e: info@mercyships.org.uk • t: 01438 727800 • www.mercyships.org.uk
Mercy Ships UK, 12 Meadway Court, Stevenage SG1 2EF

Registered Charity Numbers 1053055 and SCO39743 (Scotland)

TOGETHER
WE CAN TACKLE
POVERTY IN ENGLAND

With your help **Gemma** has gone from the despair of not being able to feed her family and the cycle of pay-day loans to hope through employment

Jason has gone from alcoholism and living on the streets to purpose through volunteering and can now dream of settling down

Kirsty has come through a background of neglect and abuse and thanks to you is now able to face her future with confidence

Together we've helped **Calvin** move from the isolation of fear and anxiety to happily volunteering and reaching out to others

Together, churches are transforming the lives of the poorest and most marginalised.

Join us on **Poverty Sunday – 21 June 2015** – as we raise vital funds and awareness. Find resources for your church **services** at **www.cuf.org.uk**

⊕ The Church of England
Mobile app story

APPS

5 Apps so far with more on the way

COUNTRIES

140

Countries have people downloading the apps

DOWNLOADS

100,000

First-time app downloads since October 2011

RATINGS

☆☆☆☆☆ **4.06**

Average rating across all apps (out of 5)

Reflections for Daily Prayer
"This is a great little app ... The first app I turn on each morning"

Lectionary
"With direct access to the readings. It's so easy to use ... at the same time complete."

Sunday Worship
"I think it's great. The C of E has been very good at putting good quality material online."

Daily Prayer
"The most rewarding app I have next to the Bible."

Reflections for Lent
"An excellent resource as well as a bargain."

APPLE OR ANDROID?

 85%   15%

For downloads of comparable apps over same period.

WHEN AND WHERE

Apps used for prayer or Bible study in the following locations:

45%
30%
15%
0%

 Church   Public Transport   Holiday   Home

No.1 Highest position in chart for Reflections for Lent - iTunes UK Book App Chart

 Available on the **App Store**

 ANDROID APP ON **Google play**

For more information visit
www.chpublishing.co.uk/features/our-apps/

The journey continues...

Since its launch last year, Pilgrim has helped thousands of enquirers explore the basics of the Christian faith. Now you can help your small group develop a deeper level of discipleship with the **Pilgrim Grow Stage**.

Get to grips with the core of Christian doctrine in **Pilgrim: The Creeds,** or explore how Christians know and worship God with **Pilgrim: The Eucharist**.

Find out more at **www.pilgrimcourse.org**

THE CHURCH OF ENGLAND

CHURCH HOUSE PUBLISHING

working to create positive futures for young people

XLP stands for '**The eXceL Project**'; an urban youth work charity in London started by Patrick Regan OBE in 1996, after a stabbing in a local school in Peckham.

Today **XLP** serves children, young people and their families in schools and communities across seven inner-London boroughs, working with over **1000 young people** each week and engaging with over **18,000 young people** per year.

If you are interested in getting involved with **mentoring** in your area visit our website:

www.xlm.org.uk

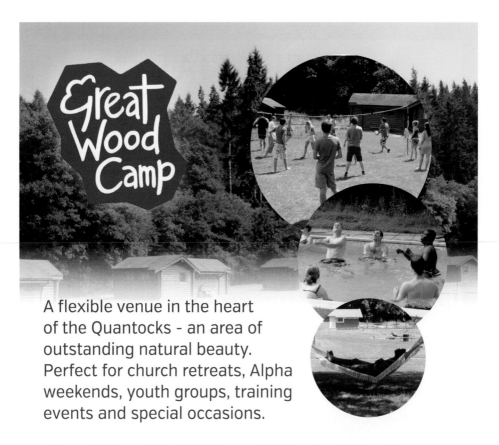

Great Wood Camp

A flexible venue in the heart of the Quantocks - an area of outstanding natural beauty. Perfect for church retreats, Alpha weekends, youth groups, training events and special occasions.

- En-suite log cabins for 70+
- Two large meeting rooms, with sound and projectors (one with WiFi)
- Fully equipped kitchen
- Low-ropes course

- Outdoor heated pool
- Outdoor chapel
- Camp fire area
- Massive scope for mountain biking, walking and exploring

Available at weekends and during half term and Easter holidays.

07759 817496
www.greatwood.org.uk

 Great Wood is owned and managed by the Great Wood Trust; a charity affiliated to Scripture Union. Charity number 1120240. During school holidays, Scripture Union runs activities for children and young people at Great Wood. See www.scriptureunion.org.uk

Contents

INDEX TO ADVERTISEMENTS

Advertisements can be found on the following pages

The inclusion of an advertisement in this book does not imply endorsement by the publisher

THE CHURCH OF ENGLAND

YEAR BOOK

131ST EDITION

2015

A directory of local and national
structures and organizations
and the Churches and Provinces
of the Anglican Communion

SINCE 1883

CHURCH HOUSE
PUBLISHING

Church House Publishing, Church House, Great Smith Street, London SW1P 3AZ

ISBN 978–0–7151–1072–0
ISSN 0069 3987

Typeset by RefineCatch Ltd, Bungay, Suffolk

Printed by Ashford Colour Press, Gosport, Hants

The Church of England Year Book
The official Year Book of the Church of England

131st edition © The Archbishops' Council 2014

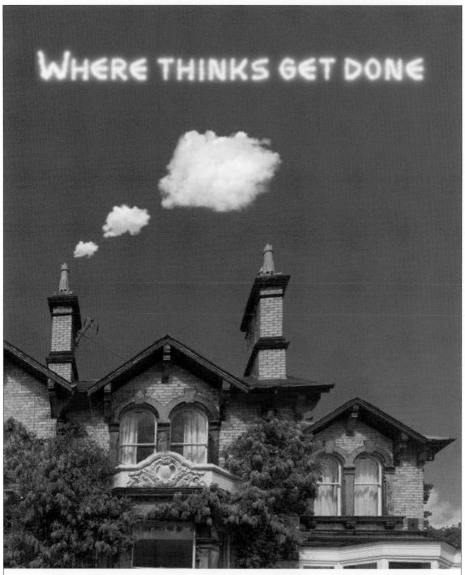

"A wonderful place for a wonderful retirement"

The College of St Barnabas is a residential community of retired Anglican clergy, set in beautiful Surrey countryside. Married couples are very welcome, as are those who have been widowed. Admission is open to licensed Church Workers and Readers; there are facilities for visitors and guests. Occasional quiet days and private retreats can be accommodated.

Residents are encouraged to lead active, independent lives. There is a Nursing Wing, to which both internal and direct admission are possible, providing domiciliary, residential and full nursing care for those who need it. This enables most residents to remain members of the College for the rest of their lives. It is sometimes possible to offer respite care here.

Sheltered 'Cloister flats' all have separate sitting rooms, bedrooms and *en suite* facilities. There are two Chapels; Mass and Evensong are celebrated daily. We have three Libraries and a well equipped Common Room. Meals are served in the Refectory or may be taken privately when necessary.

For further details or to arrange a preliminary visit, please see our website or contact the Warden, Fr Howard Such, at:

The College of St Barnabas, Blackberry Lane, Lingfield, Surrey, RH7 6NJ

Tel. 01342 870260   Fax. 01342 871672
Email: warden@collegeofstbarnabas.com
Website: www.st-barnabas.org.uk

A YEAR IN REVIEW 2013–14

November 2013

- Lambeth Palace announced that it was welcoming members of an international ecumenical community, Chemin Neuf, to 'share in the daily round of prayer that underpins the Archbishop's ministry and to further the ecumenical and international dimensions of his work'.
- The Bishop of Rochester, the Rt Revd James Langstaff, was announced as the next Bishop to Her Majesty's Prisons, the senior church advocate for Christian values in the criminal justice system in England and Wales.
- At the November session of General Synod, a package of legislation to allow women to become bishops was given initial approval for revision in the February sessions.
- The Archbishop of York launched a task group for 're-evangelizing' Britain during a debate on intentional evangelism at Synod. Dr John Sentamu introduced the debate and called on Synod to put evangelism at the top of its agenda, saying that 'next to worship, witness is the primary and urgent task of the Church'.

- More than sixty bishops, led by the Bishop of Aston, the Rt Revd Andrew Watson, supported a White Ribbon campaign to raise awareness of gender-based violence around the world.
- The Archbishops of Canterbury and York published the Report of the House of Bishops Working Group on Human Sexuality (also known as the Pilling Report). In a statement thanking the working group for its report, the Archbishops commented that the report 'is a substantial document proposing a process of facilitated conversations in the Church of England over a period of perhaps two years. The document offers findings and recommendations to form part of that process of facilitated conversations. It is not a new policy statement from the Church of England.'

December 2013

- A scheme for young would-be ordinands was launched in four dioceses. The one-year programme provides theological teaching, practical experience and personal development for young people aged 18–30 who are considering ordained ministry in the church.
- A new app, *Sunday Worship*, was released by Church House Publishing. The app presents the full Bible readings for the main Sunday service, together with the Collect and post-Communion prayers for the week.
- Women participant observers attended their first meeting of the House of Bishops in December. Over its meeting the House covered a wide range of business including discussion of women in the episcopate, the Pilling

Report, the approval of experimental liturgy for baptism, changes to legislative approaches on safeguarding and discussion of the Anglican–Methodist covenant.

- The new Bishop of Bath and Wells was announced as the Rt Revd Peter Hancock. Bishop Peter, whose election was confirmed in March 2014, is the seventy-eighth Bishop of Bath and Wells.

- The Church of England's Communications Office launched their Christmas social media campaign, #Christmasmeans. The Archbishop of Canterbury supported the campaign with a short video message on Instagram. The campaign had a reach of 4.1 million for the more than 7,000 tweets that used the hashtag.

January 2014

- The Church Growth research programme published a report, *From Anecdote to Evidence*, at the Faith in Research conference held in London. The report, supported by the Church Commissioners, looked into aspects of growth and decline in the Church and considered areas including the growth of Fresh Expressions and church planting, and the impact of amalgamations on the numerical growth or decline of congregations.

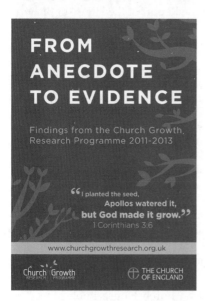

- Sir Hector Sants was announced as Chair of the Archbishop's Task Group on Responsible Credit and Savings, which was set up to develop the Church's ongoing support for local credit unions as part of a more competitive financial sector.
- The College of Bishops issued a statement after their meeting, in which they supported the recommendations of the Pilling Report, including entering a process of 'facilitated [or shared] conversations' within the Church which 'should set the discussion of sexuality within the wider context of human flourishing'.
- The Archbishops of Canterbury and York wrote to the Primates of the Anglican Communion and the Presidents of Uganda and Nigeria, recalling the commitment made by the Primates of the Anglican Communion to the pastoral support and care of everyone worldwide, regardless of sexual orientation.
- The Projects and Developments team for the Archbishops' Council launched the pilot phase of *Grave Talk*, a project in which churches provide venues for people to talk about matters such as death and grief, as part of the Funerals Project.

February 2014

- The Archbishop of Canterbury visited the Provinces of South Sudan, Burundi, Rwanda and the Democratic Republic of Congo as part of his commitment to visiting each province during his first eighteen months in office.

- The Rt Revd Nick Baines, the former Bishop of Bradford, was announced as the first Bishop of Leeds in the new Diocese of West Yorkshire and the Dales.
- The General Synod met in London, and passed the revision stage of legislation to admit women to the episcopate. It also voted to enable a final vote to be taken on the legislation on women bishops in July. Other business at Synod included a vote to affirm work combating gender-based violence after a presentation given by Mandy Marshall from the charity Restored.
- The House of Bishops issued a statement of Pastoral Guidance on Same Sex Marriage in advance of the change in law in March. The statement came as an appendix to a pastoral letter from the Archbishops of Canterbury and York addressed to the clergy and people of the Church of England.
- Church House Publishing launched the *Daily Prayer* app, a free app for iOS and Android providing Morning and Evening Prayer in an easy-to-use interface.
- Statistics on ordained ministry were published showing the growth in the number of young people becoming ordinands, with nearly a quarter of those beginning training coming forward between the ages of 18 and 30.
- Twenty-seven Anglican bishops signed an open letter to the Government from the *End Hunger Fast* campaign. The letter called on the Government to respond to growing concerns over the use of food banks and the increase in food poverty.

March 2014

- The Church of England's Communications Office launched @OurCofE, a one-year social media venture in which members of the Church of England can take over the account for a week and tweet about their life in the church.

- New resources to commemorate the centenary of World War One were published by the Church of England's Liturgical Commission. The pack includes prayers, music, literature and art for parishes and groups, for use over the four years of the centenary commemorations.
- The Church of England Pensions Board announced that it has agreed a 'buy-in' covering 70 per cent of the pensioner liabilities of the Defined Benefit Scheme (DBS) section of the Church Workers' Pension Fund with Prudential.
- The Archbishops' Evangelism Task Group met for the first time at Lambeth Palace. The group, made up of evangelists, mission directors, clergy and bishops, considered how it could bring influence to bear on the Church in the short, medium and long term.

- The Cathedral Fabric Council for England welcomed an announcement of £20 million of funding for repairs to cathedrals for World War One commemorations. The announcement, made in the Government's March budget, stated that the money is to be set aside for Anglican and Roman Catholic cathedrals for necessary repair works.
- The Archbishops' Council's Research and Statistics Office published the Church's annual attendance statistics for 2012, which showed that 1.05 million people attended Church of England churches each week for worship. Over the year the Church conducted over 356,000 services of baptism, weddings and funerals at an average of almost 1,000 per day.

April 2014
- The Archbishop of York hosted Easter baptisms on the steps of York Minster on the Saturday before Easter. Archbishop Sentamu said: 'This is the eighth year of our outdoor baptisms, when people come to make a public commitment to following Jesus Christ. I encountered Jesus Christ when I was ten years old, and I knew I had to follow him whatever the challenges. Faith in the God revealed in

Jesus Christ is always a risk, you never quite know how things will work out but they always do!'
- The Church of England launched its Easter Twitter campaign, #EasterMeans, which ran from Maundy Thursday (17 April) until Easter Day (20 April). The campaign asked people to finish the sentence '#EasterMeans . . .' to share a personal meaning of Easter with pictures, stories and messages. Around 29 million people were reached by the hashtag, with over 20,000 tweets sent over the Easter period.
- The appointment of two new Church Commissioners was confirmed. Poppy Allonby, MD at BlackRock Investment Management (UK) Ltd, and Graham Oldroyd, former Partner at European Private Equity fund manager Bridgepoint, joined the Board of Governors of the Commissioners.
- The new Diocese of West Yorkshire and the Dales came into being on Easter Day, bringing together the Dioceses of Bradford, Ripon and Leeds, and Wakefield.
- The Church of England launched a national initiative to plant poppies as part of the beginning of World War One centenary commemorations.
- A report from the *Turning Up the Volume* group was launched to encourage more UK Minority Ethnic (ME) clergy to consider senior positions within the Church of England.
- The Archbishop of Canterbury welcomed the publication of the report and draft Bill by the Parliamentary Joint Select Committee on Modern Slavery.

May 2014
- The next Bishops of Liverpool and Europe were announced. The Bishop of Hertford, the Rt Revd Paul Bayes, was announced as the next Bishop of Liverpool, and the Revd Canon Dr Robert Innes was announced as the next Bishop of Gibraltar in Europe.
- The Archbishop of Canterbury launched new guidance for church schools on stamping out homophobic bullying.

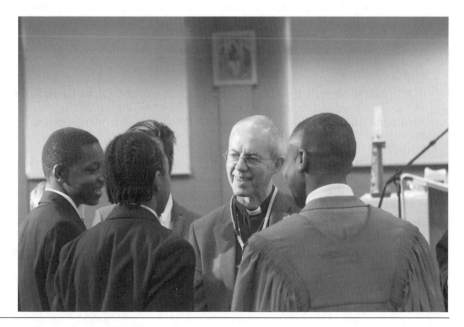

- The Church Commissioners announced their 2013 annual results, posting a 15.9 per cent investment return. The annual report, and accompanying review, gave details of the performance of the Commissioners' investment portfolio and highlighted ways in which the Commissioners support parish life and mission around the country.

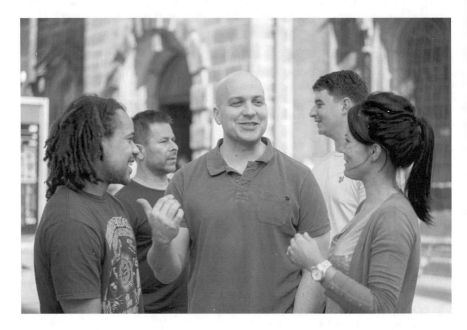

- St Paul's Cathedral held a service to mark the twentieth anniversary of the ordination of women as priests. The Archbishop of Canterbury preached and acted as deacon at the service, with Canon Philippa Boardman presiding. In his sermon, Archbishop Justin said: 'We celebrate today because the good thing that He did twenty years ago is beyond all measure, good for His world as well as good for each woman who has found herself called into this ministry.'
- The House of Bishops met in York, and discussed issues including the progress of legislation on women in the episcopate, the meeting of the General Synod in July, additional liturgical materials for baptism, closer working with the Methodist Church, shared conversations on enabling wider debate of the Pilling Report and the place of bishops in public debate.
- Sir Hector Sants launched the Church Credit Champions Network at an event held at St Martin-in-the-Fields Church in central London.
- The Archbishop of Canterbury condemned the public stoning of a pregnant Pakistani woman while visiting the country. In an article in *The Times*, Archbishop Justin said: 'I was utterly horrified and every Pakistani I have spoken to is also horrified. It [the stoning] was in no sense a punishment, but a revolting lynching.' Archbishop Justin also spoke out against the abduction of Nigerian school girls by members of Boko Haram, and the imprisonment of Meriam Ibrahim in Sudan for charges of apostasy.
- The Head of Investments for the Church Commissioners, Tom Joy, received the Chief Investment Officer/Investment Head of the Year award at aiCIO's European Innovation Awards.

June 2014

- The Archbishops' Council submitted a petition to the Government regarding the plans for HS2, calling for the protection of consecrated ground and churches affected by the route.

- The Dean of Lichfield Cathedral reflected on the role the Church played in a vigil and service for Stephen Sutton, who died at nineteen, four years after being diagnosed with cancer. The Very Revd Adrian Dorber said the Cathedral wanted to create the right atmosphere and 'make the unacceptable fact of Stephen's death beautiful and help people find meaning in it'.
- The Ethical Investment Advisory Group (EIAG) published their annual review, and announced that they were tightening recommendations regarding investment restrictions for the Church's National Investment Bodies (NIBs). The EIAG also announced that during 2013 it instructed votes for the NIBs on over 30,000 resolutions at approximately 3,000 company general meetings. Reflecting wider concern over executive remuneration packages, the EIAG withheld support in over 70 per cent of cases, and in wider corporate engagement, church investors recorded important successes as a result of dialogue in the areas of both alcohol and pornography.
- The Church celebrated at Petertide as nearly 1,000 new clergy were ordained over the year. A social media campaign, #NewRevs, was launched to celebrate and congratulate those being ordained.

July 2014

- The Bishop of Durham, the Rt Revd Paul Butler, lead bishop for safeguarding, called for a wide-ranging inquiry into child abuse. In his statement, Bishop Paul said: 'A full public inquiry into institutional sex abuse needs to take place or the whole truth might not come out.'
- The Church Commissioners confirmed that they had exited their indirect investment into Wonga through a pooled fund, doing so without taking profit or suffering loss.
- The Archbishop of Canterbury wrote about the dangers of assisted suicide prior to a debate in the House of Lords on Lord Falconer's bill, warning that 'this bill suggests that it [assisted suicide] is the only truly compassionate response that a civilised society can make to those who are terminally ill and who wish to end their own lives. This opinion is sincerely held and well-intentioned, but it is both mistaken and dangerous; quite literally, lethally so.'

- The Church of England Pensions Board announced new arrangements for the provision of housing for retired clergy after a consultation process taking place over the previous year.
- The General Synod met in York, and gave its final approval for women to be admitted into the episcopate. The legislation was passed with a necessary two-thirds majority in each of the three houses of the Synod. At the end of the debate, the Archbishop of Canterbury said: 'Today marks the start of a great adventure of seeking mutual flourishing while still, in some cases disagreeing.'
- The Church of England's new website to commemorate World War One (www.churchofengland.org/ww1) was formally launched. The website has been designed to provide resources and information about events over the four years of the commemorations for the centenary.
- The Pensions Board for the Church of England published their annual report for 2013, showing that their two investment pools both outperformed benchmarks. The 'Return Seeking' pool generated an 18.6 per cent return on its investments over 2013, while the 'Liability Matching' pool also outperformed its benchmark with a 0.6 per cent return.
- Church House Publishing announced that downloads of their five apps for mobile devices passed 100,000 in July.
- The next Bishop of Hereford was announced as the Rt Revd Richard Frith, the former Bishop of Hull.
- The Bishop of Ely, the Rt Revd Stephen Conway accepted the invitation to become the lead bishop for Education.

August 2014
- The Church launched *A Harvest Near You*, an addition to the popular *A Church Near You* website (www.achurchnearyou.com) for churches to advertise their harvest services.
- The Church Commissioners sold their holdings in the Pollen Estate, covering areas of Mayfair including Savile Row, for £381 million.

- The Church of England's Research and Statistics Office launched financial statistics for 2012, showing that parishes across the country raised a record amount of £929 million to fund the ministry and mission of the Church.
- The Spending Plans Task Group of the Church Commissioners and Archbishops' Council has awarded £4.6 million to projects from five dioceses from the new stream of Strategic Development Funding.

- The Church of England published a set of resources responding to the Iraq crisis, calling on Christians to 'Pray. Act. Give.' The resources include prayers, a poster to display in solidarity with Iraqi minorities being persecuted, and details of how to give to support the Iraqi church as well as humanitarian relief.
- The Archbishop of Canterbury made a statement in response to the growing crisis in Iraq and Syria. Archbishop Justin said: 'It is extremely important that aid efforts are supported and that those who have been displaced are able to find safety. I believe that, like France, the United Kingdom's doors should be open to refugees, as they have been throughout history.'
- The Archbishop of York held a week-long fast and vigil of 'Hope and Trust for the Peace of the World' at York Minster, praying on the hour each hour between 6am and 6pm. Dr Sentamu also issued a statement calling on the Government to show leadership over the Iraq crisis. He said: 'It is essential that Her Majesty's Government now take a lead both internationally and domestically to respond to the daily unfolding horrors in Iraq.'

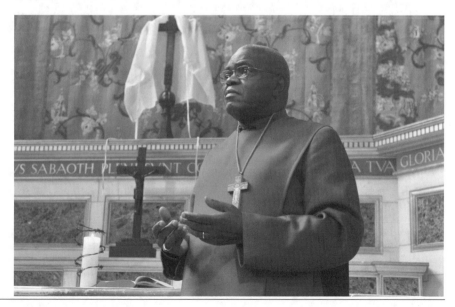

September 2014

- The Church of England became one of twelve global institutional investors backing a new project to study how climate change will impact the investment landscape.
- UNISON, the UK's largest education union, and the National Society, which promotes and resources Church of England schools, reached a landmark agreement to support every Church of England school to gain Living Wage accreditation.
- The Bishop of Salisbury, the Rt Revd Nicholas Holtam, became the Church of England's lead bishop for Environmental Affairs and the Bishop of Worcester, the Rt Revd Dr John Inge, became the Church's lead bishop for cathedrals and church buildings.
- The College of Bishops met, with two of the days devoted to the first of a series of shared conversations in the Church of England on Sexuality, Scripture and Mission.
- Archbishop Justin announced the Community of St Anselm, a new programme for adults aged 20–35 to spend a year living, praying and studying together as a radical new Christian community.

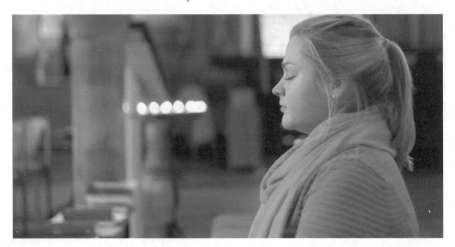

- The Rt Revd Andrew Watson, the Bishop of Aston, was announced as the next Bishop of Guildford.

October 2014

- The Church of England backed Freedom Sunday, a global day of prayer, action and worship, and urged congregations to pray for victims of human trafficking. In a foreword to resources published for Freedom Sunday, Archbishop Justin said that human trafficking is a 'grave crime' against humanity.
- The Archbishop of York, Dr John Sentamu, hailed the success of the Church of England's Pilgrim Course, which launched new books as part of the second stage, entitled *Grow*.
- The Archbishop of Canterbury visited the Church of Ireland, meeting with leaders, congregations and their local communities. Archbishop Justin spent time visiting reconciliation projects in Belfast, Armagh and Dublin as part of making reconciliation one of the priorities of his ministry. Archbishop Justin also visited the provinces of South East Asia and Myanmar, and the province of Ghana.

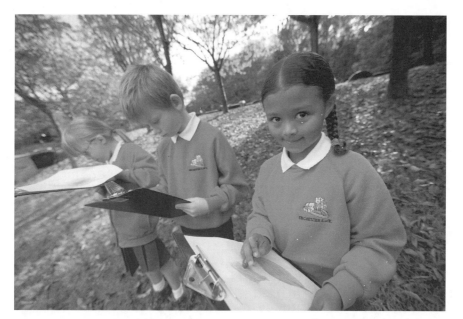

- The Church of England's National Education Office launched *Working Together*, a report into small rural schools. The report says that they must form effective partnerships and collaborations if they are to survive into the future and continue to be a vital part of rural community life.
- It was announced that twenty-five Church of England cathedrals were to receive £8.3 million in grants from the second round of money awarded from the World War One Centenary Cathedral repairs fund, a government-funded scheme to support vital repairs to some of England's most important historic buildings.

CALENDAR 2015–16

According to the Calendar, Lectionary and Collects authorized pursuant to Canon B 2 of the Canons of the Church of England for use from 30 November 1997 until further resolution of the General Synod of the Church of England.

Key
BOLD UPPER CASE – Principal Feasts and other Principal Holy Days
Bold Roman – Sundays and Festivals
Roman – Lesser Festivals
Small Italic – Commemorations
Italic – Other Observances

JANUARY (Year B)

1 **The Naming and Circumcision of Jesus**
2 Basil the Great and Gregory of Nazianzus, bishops, teachers of the faith, 379 and 389
   Seraphim, monk of Sarov, spiritual guide, 1833
   Vedanayagam Samuel Azariah, bishop in South India, evangelist, 1945
4 **The Second Sunday of Christmas**
6 **THE EPIPHANY**
10 *William Laud, archbishop, 1645*
11 **The Baptism of Christ** – *The First Sunday of Epiphany*
12 Aelred of Hexham, Abbot of Rievaulx, 1167
   Benedict Biscop, Abbot of Wearmouth, scholar, 689
13 Hilary, Bishop of Poitiers, teacher of the faith, 367
   Kentigern (Mungo) missionary bishop, 603
   George Fox, founder of the Society of Friends (Quakers), 1691
17 Antony of Egypt, hermit, abbot, 356
   Charles Gore, bishop, founder of the Community of the Resurrection, 1932
18–25 Week of Prayer for Christian Unity
18 **The Second Sunday of Epiphany**
19 Wulfstan, Bishop of Worcester, 1095
20 *Richard Rolle, spiritual writer, 1349*
21 Agnes, child martyr at Rome, 304
22 *Vincent of Saragossa, deacon, martyr, 304*
24 Francis de Sales, bishop, teacher of the faith, 1622
25 **The Conversion of Paul** – *The Third Sunday of Epiphany*
26 Timothy and Titus, companions of Paul
28 Thomas Aquinas, priest, philosopher, teacher of the faith, 1274
30 Charles, king and martyr, 1649
31 *John Bosco, priest, founder of the Salesian Teaching Order, 1888*

FEBRUARY

1 **The Fourth Sunday of Epiphany**
2 **THE PRESENTATION OF CHRIST IN THE TEMPLE** (Candlemas)
3 Anskar, Archbishop of Hamburg, missionary in Denmark and Sweden, 865
4 *Gilbert of Sempringham, founder of the Gilbertine Order, 1189*
6 *Martyrs of Japan, 1597*
   Accession of Queen Elizabeth II, 1952
8 **The Second Sunday before Lent**
10 *Scholastica, sister of Benedict, Abbess of Plombariola, c.543*
14 Cyril and Methodius, missionaries, 869 and 885
   Valentine, martyr at Rome, c.269
15 **The Sunday next before Lent**
17 Janani Luwum, Archbishop of Uganda, martyr, 1977
18 **ASH WEDNESDAY**
22 **The First Sunday of Lent**
23 Polycarp, Bishop of Smyrna, martyr, c.155
27 George Herbert, priest, poet

MARCH

1 **The Second Sunday of Lent**
2 Chad, Bishop of Lichfield, missionary, 672
7 Perpetua, Felicity and companions, martyrs, 203
8 **The Third Sunday of Lent**
15 **The Fourth Sunday of Lent** – *Mothering Sunday*
17 Patrick, bishop, missionary, patron of Ireland, c.460
18 *Cyril, bishop, teacher of the faith, 386*
19 **Joseph of Nazareth**
20 Cuthbert, bishop, missionary, 687
21 Thomas Cranmer, archbishop, Reformation martyr, 1556
22 **The Fifth Sunday of Lent**
24 *Walter Hilton of Thurgarton, Augustinian canon, mystic, 1396*
   Oscar Romero, Archbishop of San Salvador, martyr, 1980
25 **THE ANNUNCIATION OF OUR LORD TO THE BLESSED VIRGIN MARY**
26 *Harriet Monsell, founder of the Community of St John the Baptist, 1883*
29 **Palm Sunday**
30 Monday of Holy Week
31 Tuesday of Holy Week

APRIL

1 Wednesday of Holy Week
2 **Maundy Thursday**

3 **Good Friday**
4 Easter Eve
5 **EASTER DAY**
6 Monday of Easter Week
7 Tuesday of Easter Week
8 Wednesday of Easter Week
9 Thursday of Easter Week
10 Friday of Easter Week
11 Saturday of Easter Week
12 **The Second Sunday of Easter**
16 *Isabella Gilmore, deaconess, 1923*
19 **The Third Sunday of Easter**
21 Anselm, abbot, archbishop, teacher of the faith, 1109
23 **George, martyr, patron of England, c.304**
24 *Mellitus, bishop, 624*
   Seven Martyrs of the Melanesian Brotherhood, 2003
25 **Mark the Evangelist**
26 **The Fourth Sunday of Easter**
27 *Christina Rossetti, poet, 1894*
28 *Peter Chanel, missionary, martyr, 1841*
29 Catherine of Siena, teacher of the faith, 1380
30 *Pandita Mary Ramabai, translator, 1922*

MAY
1 **Philip and James, Apostles**
2 Athanasius, bishop, teacher of the faith, 373
3 **The Fifth Sunday of Easter**
4 English saints and martyrs of the Reformation Era
8 Julian of Norwich, spiritual writer, c.1417
10 **The Sixth Sunday of Easter**
12 *Gregory Dix, priest, mon, scholar, 1952*
14 **ASCENSION DAY**
15 **Matthias the Apostle**
16 *Caroline Chisholm, social reformer, 1877*
17 **The Seventh Sunday of Easter**
19 Dunstan, Archbishop of Canterbury, restorer of monastic life, 988
20 Alcuin, deacon, abbot, 804
21 *Helena, protector of the Holy Places, 330*
24 **PENTECOST (Whit Sunday)**
25 The Venerable Bede, monk at Jarrow, scholar, historian, 735
   Aldhelm, bishop 709
26 Augustine, first Archbishop of Canterbury, 605
   John Calvin, reformer 1564
   Philip Neri, founder of the Oratorians, spiritual guide, 1595
28 *Lanfranc, Prior of Le Bec, Archbishop of Canterbury, scholar, 1089*
30 Josephine Butler, social reformer, 1906
   Joan of Arc, visionary, 1431
   Apolo Kivebulaya, priest, evangelist in Central Africa, 1933
31 **TRINITY SUNDAY**

JUNE
1 **The Visit of the Blessed Virgin Mary to Elizabeth**
3 *Martyrs of Uganda, 1885–7, 1977*
4 **Day of Thanksgiving for the Institution of the Holy Communion (Corpus Christi)**

5 Boniface (Wynfrith), bishop, martyr, 754
6 *Ini Kapuria, founder of the Melanesian Brotherhood, 1945*
7 **The First Sunday after Trinity**
8 Thomas Ken, Bishop of Bath and Wells, non-juror, hymn writer, 1711
9 Columba, Abbot of Iona, missionary, 597
   Ephrem of Syria, deacon, hymn writer, teacher of the faith, 373
11 **Barnabas the Apostle**
14 **The Second Sunday after Trinity**
15 *Evelyn Underhill, spiritual writer, 1941*
16 Richard, Bishop of Chichester, 1253
   Joseph Butler, Bishop of Durham, philosopher, 1752
17 *Samuel and Henrietta Barnett, social reformers, 1913 and 1936*
18 *Bernard Mizeki, apostle of the MaShona, martyr, 1896*
19 *Sundar Singh, sadhu (holy man), evangelist, teacher of the faith, 1929*
21 **The Third Sunday after Trinity**
22 Alban, first martyr of Britain, c.250
23 Etheldreda, Abbess of Ely, c.678
24 **The Birth of John the Baptist**
27 *Cyril, bishop, teacher of the faith, 444*
28 **The Fourth Sunday after Trinity**
29 **Peter and Paul, Apostles** *or* **Peter the Apostle**

JULY
1 *Henry, John, and Henry Venn, priests, evangelical divines, 1797, 1813, 1873*
3 **Thomas the Apostle**
5 **The Fifth Sunday after Trinity**
6 *Thomas More, scholar, and John Fisher, Bishop of Rochester, Reformation martyrs, 1535*
11 Benedict, abbot, c.550
12 **The Sixth Sunday after Trinity**
14 John Keble, priest, Tractarian, poet, 1866
15 Swithun, bishop, c.862
   Bonaventure, friar, bishop, teacher of the faith, 1274
16 *Osmund, Bishop of Salisbury, 1099*
18 *Elizabeth Ferard, deaconess, founder of the Community of St Andrew, 1883*
19 **The Seventh Sunday after Trinity**
20 *Margaret of Antioch, martyr, 4th century*
   Bartolomé de las Casas, apostle to the Indies, 1566
22 **Mary Magdalene**
23 *Bridget of Sweden, Abbess of Vadstena, 1373*
25 **James the Apostle**
26 **The Eighth Sunday after Trinity**
27 *Brooke Foss Westcott, Bishop of Durham, teacher of the faith, 1901*
29 Mary, Martha and Lazarus, companions of Our Lord
30 William Wilberforce, social reformer, Olaudah Equiano and Thomas Clarkson, anti-slavery campaigners, 1833, 1797 and 1846
31 *Ignatius Loyola, founder of the Society of Jesus, 1556*

AUGUST
2 **The Ninth Sunday after Trinity**
4 *Jean-Baptiste Vianney, Curé d'Ars, spiritual guide, 1859*
5 Oswald, king, martyr, 642
6 **The Transfiguration of Our Lord**

7 *John Mason Neale, priest, hymn writer, 1866*
8 Dominic, priest, founder of the Order of Preachers, 1221
9 **The Tenth Sunday after Trinity**
10 Laurence, deacon at Rome, martyr, 258
11 Clare of Assisi, founder of the Minoresses (Poor Clares), 1253
   John Henry Newman, priest, Tractarian, 1890
13 Jeremy Taylor, Bishop of Down and Connor, teacher of the faith, 1667
   Florence Nightingale, nurse, social reformer, 1910
   Octavia Hill, social reformer, 1912
14 *Maximilian Kolbe, friar, martyr, 1941*
15 **The Blessed Virgin Mary**
16 **The Eleventh Sunday after Trinity**
20 Bernard, Abbot of Clairvaux, teacher of the faith, 1153
   William and Catherine Booth, founders of the Salvation Army, 1912 and 1890
23 **The Twelfth Sunday after Trinity**
24 **Bartholomew the Apostle**
27 Monica, mother of Augustine of Hippo, 387
28 Augustine, bishop, teacher of the faith, 430
29 Beheading of John the Baptist
30 **The Thirteenth Sunday after Trinity**
31 Aidan, Bishop of Lindisfarne, missionary, 651

SEPTEMBER
1 *Giles of Provence, hermit, c.710*
2 *Martyrs of Papua New Guinea, 1901, 1942*
3 Gregory the Great, Bishop of Rome, teacher of the faith, 604
4 *Birinus, bishop, 650*
6 **The Fourteenth Sunday after Trinity**
8 The Birth of the Blessed Virgin Mary
9 *Charles Fuge Lowder, priest, 1880*
13 **The Fifteenth Sunday after Trinity**
14 **Holy Cross Day**
15 Cyprian, Bishop of Carthage, martyr, 258
16 Ninian, bishop, c.432
   Edward Bouverie Pusey, priest, 1882
17 Hildegard, Abbess of Bingen, visionary, 1179
19 *Theodore, archbishop, 690*
20 **The Sixteenth Sunday after Trinity**
21 **Matthew, Apostle and Evangelist**
25 Launcelot Andrewes, bishop, spiritual writer, 1626
   Sergei of Radonezh, monastic reformer, teacher of the faith, 1392
26 *Wilson Carlile, founder of the Church Army, 1942*
27 **The Seventeenth Sunday after Trinity**
29 **Michael and All Angels**
30 *Jerome, translator, teacher of the faith, 420*

OCTOBER
1 *Remigius, Bishop of Rheims, apostle of the Franks, 533*
  Anthony Ashley Cooper, Earl of Shaftesbury, social reformer, 1885
3 *George Bell, bishop, ecumenist, peacemaker, 1958*
4 **The Eighteenth Sunday after Trinity**
6 William Tyndale, translator of the Scriptures, Reformation martyr, 1536

9 *Denys, bishop, and companions, martyrs, c.250*
  Robert Grosseteste, bishop, philosopher, scientist, 1253
10 Paulinus, bishop, missionary, 644
   Thomas Traherne, poet, spiritual writer, 1674
11 **The Nineteenth Sunday after Trinity**
12 Wilfrid of Ripon, bishop, missionary, 709
   Elizabeth Fry, prison reformer, 1845
   Edith Cavell, nurse, 1915
13 Edward the Confessor, King of England, 1066
15 Teresa of Avila, teacher of the faith, 1582
16 *Nicholas Ridley and Hugh Latimer, bishops, martyrs, 1555*
17 Ignatius, bishop, martyr, c.107
18 **Luke the Evangelist** – *The Twentieth Sunday after Trinity*
19 Henry Martyn, translator of the Scriptures, missionary in India and Persia, 1812
25 **The Last Sunday after Trinity** – *Bible Sunday*
26 Alfred, king, scholar, 899
   Cedd, abbot, bishop, 664
28 **Simon and Jude, Apostles**
29 James Hannington, Bishop of Eastern Equatorial Africa, martyr in Uganda, 1885
31 *Martin Luther, reformer, 1546*

NOVEMBER
1 **ALL SAINTS' DAY**
2 Commemoration of the Faithful Departed (All Souls' Day)
3 Richard Hooker, priest, Anglican apologist, teacher of the faith, 1600
   Martin of Porres, friar, 1639
6 *Leonard, hermit, 6th century*
  William Temple, archbishop, teacher of the faith, 1944
7 Willibrord, bishop, 739
8 **The Third Sunday before Advent** – *Remembrance Sunday*
9 *Margery Kempe, mystic, c.1440*
10 Leo the Great, Bishop of Rome, teacher of the faith, 461
11 Martin of Tours, bishop, c.397
13 Charles Simeon, priest, evangelical divine, 1836
14 *Samuel Seabury, bishop, 1796*
15 **The Second Sunday before Advent**
16 Margaret, Queen of Scotland, philanthropist, reformer of the Church, 1093
   Edmund Rich of Abingdon, Archbishop of Canterbury, 1240
17 Hugh, Bishop of Lincoln, 1200
18 Elizabeth of Hungary, princess, philanthropist, 1231
19 Hilda, Abbess of Whitby, 680
   Mechtild, béguine of Magdeburg, mystic, 1280
20 Edmund, king, martyr, 870
   Priscilla Lydia Sellon, a restorer of the religious life in the Church of England, 1876
22 **Christ the King** – *The Sunday next before Advent*
23 Clement, Bishop of Rome, martyr, c.100
25 *Catherine, martyr, 4th century*
   Isaac Watts, hymn writer, 1748
29 **The First Sunday of Advent**
30 **Andrew the Apostle**

DECEMBER

1 *Charles de Foucauld, hermit in the Sahara, 1916*
3 *Francis Xavier, missionary, apostle of the Indies, 1552*
4 *John of Damascus, monk, teacher of the faith, c.749*
  Nicholas Ferrar, deacon, founder of the Little Gidding Community, 1637
6 **The Second Sunday of Advent**
7 Ambrose, Bishop of Milan, teacher of the faith, 397
8 The Conception of the Blessed Virgin Mary
13 **The Third Sunday of Advent**
14 John of the Cross, poet, teacher of the faith, 1591
17 *O Sapientia*
  Eglantyne Jebb, social reformer, founder of 'Save the Children', 1928
20 **The Fourth Sunday of Advent**
24 Christmas Eve
25 **CHRISTMAS DAY**
26 **Stephen, deacon, first martyr**
27 **John, Apostle and Evangelist** *or The First Sunday of Christmas*
28 **The Holy Innocents**
29 Thomas Becket, Archbishop of Canterbury, martyr, 1170
31 *John Wyclif, reformer, 1384*

JANUARY 2016

1 **The Naming and Circumcision of Jesus**
2 Basil the Great and Gregory of Nazianzus, bishops, teachers of the faith, 379 and 389
  Seraphim, monk of Sarov, spiritual guide, 1833
  Vedanayagam Samuel Azariah, bishop in South India, evangelist, 1945
3 **The Second Sunday of Christmas**
6 **THE EPIPHANY**
10 **The Baptism of Christ** – *The First Sunday of Epiphany*
12 Aelred of Hexham, Abbot of Rievaulx, 1167
  Benedict Biscop, Abbot of Wearmouth, scholar, 689

13 Hilary, Bishop of Poitiers, teacher of the faith, 367
  Kentigern (Mungo), missionary bishop, 603
  George Fox, founder of the Society of Friends (Quakers), 1691
17 **The Second Sunday of Epiphany**
18–25 Week of Prayer for Christian Unity
19 Wulfstan, Bishop of Worcester, 1095
20 *Richard Rolle, spiritual writer, 1349*
21 Agnes, child martyr at Rome, 304
22 *Vincent of Saragossa, deacon, martyr, 304*
24 **The Third Sunday of Epiphany**
25 **The Conversion of Paul**
26 Timothy and Titus, companions of Paul
28 Thomas Aquinas, priest, philosopher, teacher of the faith, 1274
30 Charles, king and martyr, 1649
31 **The Fourth Sunday of Epiphany**

Other dates

1 February	Education Sunday
6 February	Accession Day
9 February	General Synod meets until 13 February
15 February	Unemployment Sunday
10 May	Christian Aid Week until 16 May
5 July	Day of Prayer for Vocations to Religious Life
10 July	General Synod meets in York until 14 July
12 July	Sea Sunday
13 September	Racial Justice Sunday
4 October	Animal Welfare Sunday
18 October	Hospital Sunday
24 October	United Nations Day
8 November	Prisoners' Sunday
23 November	General Synod meets until 25 November
1 December	World AIDS Day
7 December	Human Rights Day

SELECTED CHURCH STATISTICS

The Church of England today

The Church of England plays a vital role in the life of the nation, proclaiming the Christian gospel in words and actions and providing services of Christian worship and praise.

Its network of parishes covers the country, bringing a vital Christian dimension to the nation as well as strengthening community life in numerous urban, suburban and rural settings. Its cathedrals are centres of spirituality and service, and its network of chaplaincies across continental Europe meets important local needs.

The Church of England plays an active role in national life with its members involved in a wide range of public bodies. Twenty-six bishops are members of the House of Lords and are engaged in debates about legislation and national and international affairs.

The Church of England is part of the worldwide Anglican Communion.

There are a number of interviews relating to the Church of England on Premier Christian Radio, under the title 'Work in Progress'.

Key facts about the Church of England

Church attendance and visits
- **1.5 million** people take part in a Church of England service each month, a level that has reduced slightly since the turn of the millennium. Around one million participate each Sunday.
- Approximately **2.5 million** participate in a Church of England service on Christmas Day or Christmas Eve. **Thirty-three per cent** of the population attend a church service around Christmas, including 22 per cent among those of non-Christian faiths and 13 per cent of those with no religious alignment.
- In 2011, **70 per cent** of adults attended a church or place of worship for a baptism, wedding, or funeral service for someone who has died and **18 per cent** were seeking a quiet space.
- **Eighty-five per cent** of the population visit a church or place of worship in the course of a year, for reasons ranging from participating in worship to attending social events or simply wanting a quiet space.
- Every year, around **10 million** people visit Church of England cathedrals, including over **300,000** pupils on school visits. Three of England's top five historic 'visitor attractions' are St Paul's Cathedral, London, Canterbury Cathedral and Westminster Abbey.

Education
- **Seven in ten** (70 per cent) of the population agree that Church of England schools have a positive role in educating the nation's children.
- **One in four** primary schools and **one in 16** secondary schools in England are Church of England schools. Approaching **one million pupils** are educated in more than 4,600 Church of England schools.

Ministers
- At the end of 2012, there were **18,300** ministers licensed by Church of England dioceses, including clergy, Readers and Church Army officers: one minister for every 2,900 people in England. The total does not include around **1,500** chaplains to prisons, hospitals, the armed forces and in education, nor nearly **6,000** retired ministers with permission to officiate.

Community involvement
- **More people do unpaid work for church organizations than any other organization.** Eight per cent of adults undertake voluntary work for church organizations while 16 per cent belong to religious or church organizations.
- A quarter of regular churchgoers (among both Anglicans and other Christians separately) are involved in voluntary community service outside the church. Churchgoers overall contribute **23.2 million hours** voluntary service each month in their local communities outside the church.

- The Church of England provides activities outside church worship in the local community for over **500,000 children and young people** (aged up to 25 years). **More than 120,000 volunteers** run children/young people activity groups sponsored by the Church of England outside church worship.

Church buildings
- **Nearly half the population** (46 per cent) think that central taxation, local taxation, the National Lottery or English Heritage should be 'primarily' responsible for providing money to maintain churches and chapels. In fact, these churches and cathedrals are largely supported by the efforts and financial support of local communities. Often, they are the focus of community life and service.
- There are 14,500 places of worship in England listed for their special architectural or historic interest, **85 per cent of which belong to and are maintained by the Church of England.**
- Necessary repairs to all listed places of worship in England have been valued at £925 million over the next five years, or £185 million a year.

Sources: *Statistics for Mission* 2012, Finance statistics 2012 and Ministry statistics 2012
    Opinion Research Business national polls 2011.
    English Heritage and Church of England Cathedral and Church Buildings Division joint research.

Tables

The following pages contain a selection of tables as available at the Church of England website, www.churchofengland.org

Table K
Consistent measures of church attendance have been employed from 2000.

Average weekly attendance – the average number of attenders at church services throughout the week typically over a four-week period in October.

Average Sunday attendance – the average number of attenders at Sunday church services typically over a four-week period in October.

Tables N to S
The following definitions apply:

Income

Unrestricted income	income that may be used by the PCC for general church expenses.
Restricted income	income which may not be used for any purpose other than as specified by the donor. (Income which a PCC designates for a specified purpose is considered to be unrestricted, since the PCC and not the donor is determining how it is to be used.)
Recurring income	includes direct giving, other voluntary income and any other recurring income. It may be unrestricted or restricted.
One-off income	includes non-recurring grants, legacies, special appeals, insurance claims and the sale of fixed assets. It may be unrestricted or restricted.
Total voluntary income	direct giving plus income tax on gift aid plus other voluntary income.
Total direct giving	planned giving plus church collections and boxes.
Other voluntary income	all other voluntary income for ordinary expenditure excluding direct giving and income tax on gift aid, e.g. fund-raising events, net profit on magazine/bookstall, sundry donations.

Expenditure
Total charitable donations includes payments to: the recognized missionary societies, or other overseas missions, diocesan associations, Diocesan Mission Councils; Christian organizations primarily concerned with relief and development; home missions and other Church societies and organizations (including the Church Urban Fund); other charities – payments to other charities which are secularly based.

Recurring expenditure	includes donations to charities, parish share/quota, clergy expenses, church running costs, costs relating to trading, salaries and support costs.
Capital expenditure	includes major repairs, redecoration and new building work.

Notes on tables N to S
1. Figures for cathedrals are not included.
2. *i.e. adjusted by the Retail Price Index to reflect 2012 purchasing power.
3. The Diocese in Europe is not included in these tables.

Please also note that:

1. Whilst many figures in these tables have been rounded, totals, percentages and averages were calculated before rounding. Hence row and column totals will not always agree exactly with the sum of the stated amounts.

2. Among the 12,500 parishes of the Church of England there are around 600 Local Ecumenical Projects in roughly half of which there is a congregation and a ministry shared between the Church of England and certain other churches. In such circumstances it is not always possible (or indeed desirable) to isolate the Anglican component of the congregation. The parochial statistics will therefore include a small element which may appear also in the statistics of other churches.

3. Where figures are not available for any reason, 'N/A' appears in these tables.

Selected Church Statistics

A   Church of England Licensed Ministries 2012

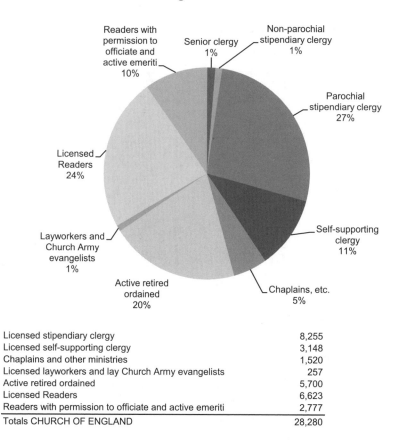

Licensed stipendiary clergy	8,255
Licensed self-supporting clergy	3,148
Chaplains and other ministries	1,520
Licensed layworkers and lay Church Army evangelists	257
Active retired ordained	5,700
Licensed Readers	6,623
Readers with permission to officiate and active emeriti	2,777
Totals CHURCH OF ENGLAND	28,280

The figures for stipendiary clergy (full-time, part-time and including those outside the clergy share system) and for lay workers above are based on statistics derived from the central Church payroll. Details of chaplains and other ministers working outside the parish framework, and of non-stipendiary clergy, are based on statistics derived from the database used to compile Crockford's Clerical Directory. Where possible, they have been cross-referenced with material produced by organizing bodies (Church Army, the Home Office for prison chaplains, and the Hospital Chaplaincies Council for hospital chaplains).

The figure shown for active retired ordained clergy is an estimate of the number of licensed retired clergy who take an active part in ministry. It is based on the number of retired clergy known to have either permission to officiate, licence to officiate or actual appointments. Pension Board records indicated a total of 8,776 retired stipendiary clergy in 2011.

B Summary of Diocesan Licensed Ministers 2012

Provinces of Canterbury and York (including Europe)

Diocese		Full-time stipendiary clergy			Part-time stipendiary clergy			Self-supporting clergy, except ordained local ministers		
		men	women	Total	men	women	Total	men	women	Total
1 Bath & Wells	C	144	53	197	6	8	14	32	25	57
2 Birmingham	C	115	48	163	1	4	5	16	23	39
3 Blackburn	Y	148	20	168	5	6	11	28	24	52
4 Bradford	Y	69	18	87	4	7	11	22	23	45
5 Bristol	C	86	19	105	4	4	8	24	33	57
6 Canterbury	C	105	27	132	2	1	3	23	31	54
7 Carlisle	Y	98	26	124	2	3	5	23	21	44
8 Chelmsford	C	265	89	354	5	8	13	49	45	94
9 Chester	Y	168	56	224	21	10	31	23	43	66
10 Chichester	C	253	22	275	17	6	23	56	43	99
11 Coventry	C	99	18	117	4	6	10	17	25	42
12 Derby	C	104	45	149	1	1	2	31	27	58
13 Durham	Y	132	33	165	4	5	9	17	25	42
14 Ely	C	81	46	127	3	8	11	33	30	63
15 Exeter	C	168	38	206	23	6	29	31	27	58
16 Gloucester	C	93	32	125	4	6	10	42	43	85
17 Guildford	C	136	34	170	7	12	19	24	41	65
18 Hereford	C	57	33	90	0	3	3	17	25	42
19 Leicester	C	95	41	136	6	4	10	16	23	39
20 Lichfield	C	241	51	292	11	13	24	36	39	75
21 Lincoln	C	112	35	147	3	1	4	17	25	42
22 Liverpool	Y	150	56	206	0	2	2	17	19	36
23 London	C	450	80	530	5	8	13	98	52	150
24 Manchester	Y	158	66	224	7	1	8	19	15	34
25 Newcastle	Y	88	28	116	4	3	7	12	23	35
26 Norwich	C	145	37	182	11	7	18	11	15	26
27 Oxford	C	293	98	391	7	4	11	99	93	192
28 Peterborough	C	100	37	137	5	0	5	20	16	36
29 Portsmouth	C	76	22	98	3	6	9	14	32	46
30 Ripon & Leeds	Y	81	40	121	0	1	1	16	19	35
31 Rochester	C	158	42	200	5	7	12	26	36	62
32 St. Albans	C	168	71	239	6	10	16	30	40	70
33 St. Edms & Ipswich	C	94	39	133	4	7	11	18	21	39
34 Salisbury	C	142	50	192	2	1	3	35	68	103
35 Sheffield	Y	107	38	145	4	6	10	14	11	25
36 Sodor & Man	Y	13	2	15	1	1	2	3	3	6
37 Southwark	C	264	82	346	2	4	6	76	83	159
38 Southwell & Nottingham	Y	92	43	135	5	6	11	12	19	31
39 Truro	C	73	21	94	6	5	11	15	23	38
40 Wakefield	Y	100	35	135	1	3	4	26	25	51
41 Winchester	C	137	33	170	3	1	4	70	50	120
42 Worcester	C	86	27	113	1	1	2	12	27	39
43 York	Y	163	36	199	5	3	8	38	37	75
44 Europe	C	110	14	124	0	0	0	23	12	35
Totals Province of Canterbury	C	**4,450**	**1,284**	**5,734**	**157**	**152**	**309**	**1,011**	**1,073**	**2,084**
Totals Province of York	Y	**1,567**	**497**	**2,064**	**63**	**57**	**120**	**270**	**307**	**577**
Totals CHURCH OF ENGLAND		**6,017**	**1,781**	**7,798**	**220**	**209**	**429**	**1,281**	**1,380**	**2,661**

Notes:

1 The above figures include only those ministers who were working within the diocesan framework as at 31 December 2012.

2 The Archbishop of Canterbury and ordained members of his staff at Lambeth Palace are classed as extra-diocesan and are not included in these figures.

B continued

Ordained local ministers among self-supporting clergy			Total clergy (stipendiary and self-supporting)	Readers and Church Army	Total clergy, readers and Church Army	
men	women	Total				
0	0	0	268	219	487	1
0	0	0	207	165	372	2
0	0	0	231	143	374	3
0	0	0	143	89	232	4
8	11	19	189	158	347	5
4	6	10	199	101	300	6
0	1	1	174	126	300	7
1	3	4	465	282	747	8
0	0	0	321	285	606	9
0	0	0	397	136	533	10
2	6	8	177	138	315	11
3	8	11	220	186	406	12
1	4	5	221	142	363	13
0	0	0	201	122	323	14
0	0	0	293	178	471	15
2	1	3	223	147	370	16
25	22	47	301	116	417	17
2	7	9	144	64	208	18
0	0	0	185	131	316	19
23	26	49	440	308	748	20
16	27	43	236	125	361	21
11	16	27	271	290	561	22
0	0	0	693	211	904	23
35	41	76	342	135	477	24
8	8	16	174	85	259	25
20	24	44	270	149	419	26
16	24	40	634	209	843	27
0	0	0	178	156	334	28
0	0	0	153	88	241	29
0	0	0	157	108	265	30
0	0	0	274	226	500	31
0	1	1	326	180	506	32
10	16	26	209	106	315	33
10	12	22	320	93	413	34
0	0	0	180	174	354	35
2	0	2	25	27	52	36
0	0	0	511	192	703	37
0	0	0	177	262	439	38
3	2	5	148	69	217	39
5	13	18	208	88	296	40
0	0	0	294	184	478	41
0	0	0	154	137	291	42
0	1	1	283	189	472	43
0	0	0	159	80	239	
145	196	341	8,468	4,656	13,124	
62	84	146	2,907	2,143	5,050	
207	280	487	11,375	6,799	18,174	

3 Reader and Church Army figures do not include Readers with PTO or emeriti, or ordained Church Army evangelists.

C   Licensed Readers and Church Army 2012

Provinces of Canterbury and York (including Europe)

Diocese		Reader admissions during year m	f	Licensed Readers at 31 Dec 2012 m		f		Readers in training at 31 Dec 2012 m	f	Church Army (lay evangelists) at 31 Dec 2012 m	f
1 Bath & Wells	C	5	6	89	(77)	125	(47)	5	7	5	0
2 Birmingham	C	5	8	76	(19)	88	(23)	14	18	1	0
3 Blackburn	Y	2	9	57	(36)	85	(22)	5	13	1	0
4 Bradford	Y	1	5	36	(26)	47	(19)	9	10	5	1
5 Bristol	C	2	7	63	(24)	94	(29)	6	7	1	0
6 Canterbury	C	8	0	44	(29)	51	(24)	6	8	6	0
7 Carlisle	Y	6	4	65	(12)	59	(7)	3	5	2	0
8 Chelmsford	C	2	5	114	(48)	161	(33)	2	4	4	3
9 Chester	Y	6	8	139	(102)	141	(44)	14	15	2	3
10 Chichester	C	4	7	97	(70)	34	(66)	7	11	3	2
11 Coventry	C	2	5	62	(28)	70	(19)	0	0	4	2
12 Derby	C	1	1	88	(25)	95	(27)	4	11	3	0
13 Durham	Y	0	4	60	(14)	79	(13)	3	13	1	2
14 Ely	C	2	3	57	(32)	62	(17)	5	11	3	0
15 Exeter	C	4	6	85	(55)	88	(52)	8	6	5	0
16 Gloucester	C	5	5	75	(15)	71	(9)	7	16	0	1
17 Guildford	C	0	1	66	(35)	45	(21)	7	4	4	1
18 Hereford	C	3	1	34	(12)	27	(9)	5	5	2	1
19 Leicester	C	6	4	65	(27)	64	(15)	9	8	1	1
20 Lichfield	C	4	11	137	(72)	162	(53)	14	15	6	3
21 Lincoln	C	3	6	45	(30)	78	(19)	10	29	2	0
22 Liverpool	Y	5	7	140	(47)	144	(23)	11	24	3	3
23 London	C	4	5	106	(28)	100	(30)	9	23	3	2
24 Manchester (2008 data)	Y	2	5	62	(32)	69	(22)	7	8	2	2
25 Newcastle	Y	1	3	30	(25)	50	(19)	6	14	2	3
26 Norwich	C	0	4	64	(62)	83	(52)	6	9	1	1
27 Oxford	C	1	8	108	(48)	97	(36)	12	15	2	2
28 Peterborough	C	3	4	79	(24)	75	(11)	7	8	1	1
29 Portsmouth	C	1	1	42	(19)	46	(22)	3	3	0	0
30 Ripon & Leeds	Y	1	7	51	(18)	55	(27)	1	12	2	0
31 Rochester	C	9	3	118	(77)	106	(41)	5	8	0	2
32 St. Albans	C	9	10	90	(57)	87	(44)	18	26	3	0
33 St. Edms & Ipswich	C	1	3	57	(46)	45	(26)	7	10	3	1
34 Salisbury	C	2	3	53	(71)	38	(37)	11	15	1	1
35 Sheffield	Y	2	3	80	(25)	75	(19)	13	16	11	8
36 Sodor & Man	Y	3	2	15	(6)	12	(3)	1	2	0	0
37 Southwark	C	5	5	85	(50)	100	(31)	14	23	4	3
38 Southwell & Nottingham	Y	0	0	114	(32)	142	(29)	7	11	4	2
39 Truro	C	2	3	32	(31)	34	(16)	4	9	2	1
40 Wakefield	Y	2	2	43	(16)	43	(20)	4	10	2	0
41 Winchester	C	6	4	87	(53)	90	(19)	13	9	6	1
42 Worcester	C	1	6	54	(22)	80	(12)	3	10	2	1
43 York	Y	2	2	88	(38)	94	(28)	10	20	4	3
44 Europe	C	5	7	45	(19)	35	(8)	14	16	0	0
Totals Province of Canterbury	**C**	**105**	**142**	**2,217**	**(1,205)**	**2,331**	**(848)**	**235**	**344**	**78**	**30**
Totals Province of York	**Y**	**33**	**61**	**980**	**(429)**	**1,095**	**(295)**	**94**	**173**	**41**	**27**
Totals CHURCH OF ENGLAND		**138**	**203**	**3,197**	**(1,634)**	**3,426**	**(1,143)**	**329**	**517**	**119**	**57**

Comparable figures for 2011:											
Totals Province of Canterbury	**C**	**85**	**148**	**2,323**	**(1,187)**	**2,416**	**(824)**	**262**	**366**	**75**	**32**
Totals Province of York	**Y**	**42**	**74**	**1,017**	**(465)**	**1,100**	**(287)**	**112**	**164**	**42**	**28**
Totals CHURCH OF ENGLAND		**127**	**222**	**3,340**	**(1,652)**	**3,516**	**(1,111)**	**374**	**530**	**117**	**60**

1 Readers figures in brackets refer to the additional number of Readers with Permission to Officiate and active emeriti. These figures have been revised since the publication of 'The Annual Report of the Central Readers Council of the Church of England 2012'.

2 There are a further five Church Army evangelists who are nationally deployed. Ordained Church Army evangelists are counted in the 'Chaplaincy and other ministries' table.

D Ordinations and Reader Admissions 1996 to 2012

	Stipendiary			Self-supporting			Total stipendiary and self-supporting	Readers
	m	f	Total	m	f	Total		
1996	273	67	340	59	74	133	473	566
1997	244	72	316	55	34	89	405	633
1998	201	67	268	46	59	105	373	586
1999	174	67	241	100	127	227	468	608
2000	223	90	313	106	150	256	569	544
2001	190	105	295	92	109	201	496	494
2002	199	112	311	101	128	229	540	494
2003	181	120	301	79	113	192	493	472
2004	143	92	235	94	140	234	469	487
2005	158	103	261	112	139	251	512	435
2006	128	98	226	106	149	255	481	425
2007	163	104	267	128	160	288	555	435
2008	197	124	321	103	150	253	574	375
2009	193	116	309	105	150	255	564	358
2010	173	111	284	100	179	279	563	344
2011	170	94	264	89	151	240	504	349
2012	162	94	256	107	127	234	490	341

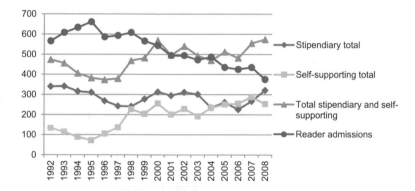

Proportion of ordinations by gender

E Ages of Candidates Recommended for Ordination Training 2000 to 2012

	20-29	30-39	40-49	50-59	60 or over	Total
2000	106	146	148	123	14	537
2001	73	126	160	109	18	486
2002	71	103	149	125	27	475
2003	78	118	159	124	26	505
2004	71	117	166	157	53	564
2005	86	123	173	161	35	578
2006	90	149	174	144	37	594
2007	88	155	174	132	46	595
2008	82	117	133	117	41	490
2009	74	112	136	126	43	491
2010	108	94	140	117	56	515
2011	77	126	138	91	32	464
2012	113	115	126	111	45	510

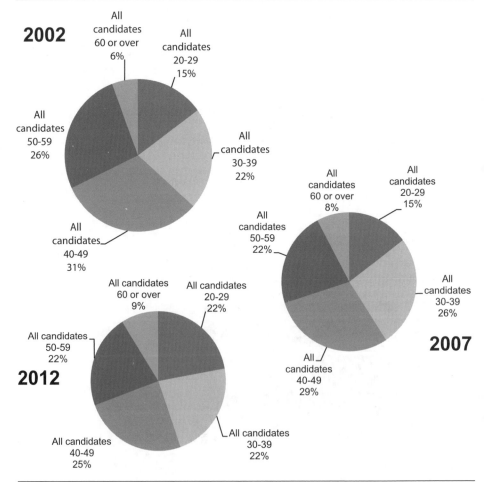

2002
All candidates 60 or over 6%
All candidates 20-29 15%
All candidates 50-59 26%
All candidates 30-39 22%
All candidates 40-49 31%

2007
All candidates 60 or over 8%
All candidates 20-29 15%
All candidates 50-59 22%
All candidates 30-39 26%
All candidates 40-49 29%

2012
All candidates 60 or over 9%
All candidates 20-29 22%
All candidates 50-59 22%
All candidates 30-39 22%
All candidates 40-49 25%

F Parochial Baptisms and Thanksgivings 2012

Provinces of Canterbury and York (including Europe and Cathedrals)

Diocese		Live births	Infants under one year	Infant baptisms per 1,000 live births	Children aged 1 to 12 years	All other persons	Thanksgivings Infants	Thanksgivings Child	Baptisms and Thanks-givings Total
1 Bath & Wells	C	9,900	1,730	174	820	200	110	90	2,950
2 Birmingham	C	23,200	1,660	72	940	250	60	30	2,940
3 Blackburn	Y	16,100	2,730	170	1,240	210	70	30	4,270
4 Bradford	Y	10,400	900	86	410	110	70	30	1,510
5 Bristol	C	13,800	1,090	79	630	130	20	10	1,880
6 Canterbury	C	10,900	1,560	143	1,150	240	70	40	3,050
7 Carlisle	Y	5,000	1,770	356	450	90	30	10	2,340
8 Chelmsford	C	44,600	2,660	60	1,970	680	210	110	5,630
9 Chester	Y	19,100	2,870	150	1,530	300	220	180	5,090
10 Chichester	C	17,800	2,150	120	1,340	280	90	50	3,900
11 Coventry	C	10,600	1,020	96	790	180	90	40	2,120
12 Derby	C	12,300	1,630	133	720	150	140	40	2,670
13 Durham	Y	17,000	3,620	214	1,280	310	150	40	5,400
14 Ely	C	9,300	1,230	132	600	170	30	20	2,060
15 Exeter	C	12,500	1,820	146	940	240	50	20	3,060
16 Gloucester	C	7,300	1,420	194	670	260	40	10	2,400
17 Guildford	C	12,900	1,650	128	1,110	230	60	20	3,060
18 Hereford	C	3,200	1,000	309	320	90	10	10	1,420
19 Leicester	C	12,500	1,200	96	670	170	20	10	2,070
20 Lichfield	C	26,200	3,940	150	1,990	480	290	120	6,820
21 Lincoln	C	11,900	2,900	243	1,170	250	50	30	4,400
22 Liverpool	Y	18,800	2,990	159	1,590	290	100	80	5,060
23 London	C	63,900	2,220	35	1,960	660	110	60	5,010
24 Manchester	Y	30,100	3,100	103	1,920	450	200	90	5,750
25 Newcastle	Y	8,900	1,480	166	620	150	10	0	2,260
26 Norwich	C	9,800	1,400	144	600	180	60	20	2,260
27 Oxford	C	31,000	3,610	116	1,930	460	120	100	6,230
28 Peterborough	C	11,900	1,290	109	650	170	50	20	2,180
29 Portsmouth	C	8,700	1,140	131	660	160	20	10	1,990
30 Ripon & Leeds	Y	10,600	1,180	111	700	180	30	20	2,110
31 Rochester	C	17,200	1,620	95	1,320	290	150	110	3,490
32 St. Albans	C	25,000	2,190	88	1,500	390	90	30	4,210
33 St. Edms & Ipswich	C	7,500	1,040	139	500	90	30	20	1,680
34 Salisbury	C	9,600	1,780	184	1,070	240	70	30	3,190
35 Sheffield	Y	15,400	2,190	142	1,020	320	230	90	3,850
36 Sodor & Man	Y	900	110	124	80	10	0	0	210
37 Southwark	C	43,900	2,210	50	1,830	440	80	60	4,630
38 Southwell & Nottingham	Y	13,500	1,380	102	790	280	50	30	2,530
39 Truro	C	5,700	1,080	189	550	110	10	10	1,770
40 Wakefield	Y	15,200	1,920	126	910	390	160	70	3,440
41 Winchester	C	16,200	2,640	163	1,200	270	140	60	4,310
42 Worcester	C	10,400	1,660	159	820	200	110	40	2,840
43 York	Y	16,500	3,380	205	1,270	350	80	30	5,100
44 Europe	C		320		170	80	60	10	640
Totals Province of Canterbury	C	**499,600**	52,840	**106**	30,590	7,740	2,460	1,220	94,840
Totals Province of York	Y	**197,500**	29,620	**150**	13,810	3,420	1,400	680	48,920
Totals CHURCH OF ENGLAND		**697,100**	82,460	**118**	44,400	11,160	3,850	1,900	143,770
Comparable figures for 2011:									
Totals Province of Canterbury	C	**494,300**	52,920	**107**	30,900	7,290	2,520	1,280	94,910
Totals Province of York	Y	**196,400**	30,160	**154**	13,850	3,220	1,420	620	49,260
Totals CHURCH OF ENGLAND		**690,700**	83,070	**120**	44,750	10,510	3,940	1,900	144,170

1 Live births per diocese are estimates based on statistics obtained from the Office for National Statistics (ONS).
2 The figures for 2011 quoted in the 2014 Yearbook were subsequently revised following publication. The updated figures have been restated above.

G Parochial Marriages and Funerals 2012

Provinces of Canterbury and York (including Europe and Cathedrals)

Diocese		Marriages	Blessings and civil marriages	Total	Funerals Held in church	Held in crematoria/ cemeteries	Total	Number of deaths	Per cent with C-of-E funeral
1 Bath & Wells	C	1,650	70	1,720	2,240	1,490	3,730	9,200	40%
2 Birmingham	C	1,100	60	1,160	1,290	3,220	4,510	12,300	37%
3 Blackburn	Y	1,140	70	1,200	2,240	1,690	3,930	13,600	29%
4 Bradford	Y	670	30	700	960	820	1,780	5,900	30%
5 Bristol	C	830	40	870	990	1,020	2,010	7,600	27%
6 Canterbury	C	1,350	90	1,440	1,270	1,980	3,250	9,000	36%
7 Carlisle	Y	780	40	830	1,830	1,040	2,870	5,400	53%
8 Chelmsford	C	2,340	140	2,480	2,840	3,640	6,480	24,100	27%
9 Chester	Y	1,800	50	1,850	3,400	2,630	6,030	15,900	38%
10 Chichester	C	1,950	150	2,100	2,190	2,420	4,610	17,000	27%
11 Coventry	C	1,050	50	1,090	1,630	930	2,560	7,200	35%
12 Derby	C	1,180	40	1,220	2,380	1,320	3,700	9,800	38%
13 Durham	Y	1,180	50	1,230	3,250	1,880	5,130	15,100	34%
14 Ely	C	1,010	50	1,060	1,440	900	2,340	6,000	39%
15 Exeter	C	1,690	100	1,790	2,720	1,360	4,080	12,700	32%
16 Gloucester	C	1,270	70	1,330	1,970	1,140	3,110	6,000	52%
17 Guildford	C	1,190	60	1,250	1,250	1,710	2,960	8,200	36%
18 Hereford	C	700	40	740	1,350	680	2,030	3,200	63%
19 Leicester	C	1,080	50	1,130	1,770	1,280	3,050	8,100	37%
20 Lichfield	C	2,410	110	2,520	5,270	3,960	9,230	19,700	47%
21 Lincoln	C	1,570	90	1,660	2,440	1,840	4,280	11,000	39%
22 Liverpool	Y	1,130	40	1,180	3,330	2,220	5,550	15,300	36%
23 London	C	1,430	120	1,550	1,420	2,150	3,570	22,100	16%
24 Manchester	Y	1,170	60	1,240	2,200	2,240	4,440	18,000	25%
25 Newcastle	Y	710	30	740	1,190	1,240	2,430	7,900	31%
26 Norwich	C	1,280	70	1,350	2,200	2,020	4,220	9,400	45%
27 Oxford	C	2,920	180	3,100	3,560	3,140	6,700	17,000	39%
28 Peterborough	C	1,120	60	1,180	1,420	790	2,210	7,200	31%
29 Portsmouth	C	1,000	60	1,060	1,140	1,330	2,480	7,500	33%
30 Ripon & Leeds	Y	850	40	890	1,310	720	2,040	7,300	28%
31 Rochester	C	1,200	70	1,270	1,390	3,170	4,560	10,600	43%
32 St. Albans	C	1,660	90	1,750	2,460	2,610	5,070	14,400	35%
33 St. Edms & Ipswich	C	1,110	60	1,170	1,760	990	2,740	6,100	45%
34 Salisbury	C	1,540	100	1,630	2,170	1,470	3,640	9,500	38%
35 Sheffield	Y	1,100	40	1,140	2,090	2,050	4,140	11,700	35%
36 Sodor & Man	Y	130	10	130	220	150	370	800	46%
37 Southwark	C	1,300	70	1,370	1,210	2,630	3,840	16,200	24%
38 Southwell & Nottingham	Y	1,140	70	1,210	2,270	1,580	3,850	9,900	39%
39 Truro	C	1,170	60	1,230	1,540	580	2,130	5,900	36%
40 Wakefield	Y	900	30	930	2,070	1,670	3,740	10,500	36%
41 Winchester	C	1,900	90	1,990	2,150	1,560	3,710	12,000	31%
42 Worcester	C	1,190	50	1,240	1,730	1,590	3,320	8,400	40%
43 York	Y	1,770	80	1,860	2,880	2,030	4,910	14,300	34%
44 Europe	C	100	280	380	270	490	760		
Total Province of Canterbury	**C**	**41,280**	**2,520**	**43,800**	**57,470**	**53,390**	**110,860**	**317,400**	**35%**
Totals Province of York	**Y**	**14,470**	**640**	**15,110**	**29,250**	**21,950**	**51,200**	**151,700**	**34%**
Totals CHURCH OF ENGLAND		**55,750**	**3,160**	**58,910**	**86,720**	**75,340**	**162,050**	**469,100**	**35%**

Comparable figures for 2011

Total Province of Canterbury	**C**	**38,040**	**2,810**	**40,860**	**56,390**	**53,140**	**109,530**	**307,200**	**36%**
Totals Province of York	**Y**	**13,410**	**760**	**14,180**	**29,660**	**21,930**	**51,590**	**147,900**	**35%**
Totals CHURCH OF ENGLAND		**51,460**	**3,580**	**55,040**	**86,050**	**75,070**	**161,120**	**455,100**	**35%**

1 The number of deaths are estimates based on statistics obtained from the Office National Statistics (ONS).

2 The figures for 2011 quoted in the 2014 Yearbook were subsequently revised following publication. The updated figures have been restated above.

3 The figures in this table have been rounded but totals were calculated before rounding. Hence row and column totals will not always agree exactly with the sum of the stated amounts.

Selected Church Statistics

H   Confirmations 2012

Diocese		Males	Females	Total	Number of services
1 Bath & Wells	C	260	204	464	28
2 Birmingham	C	123	202	325	78
3 Blackburn	Y	418	603	1,021	79
4 Bradford	Y	70	107	177	21
5 Bristol	C	96	160	256	18
6 Canterbury	C	166	284	450	44
7 Carlisle	Y	149	207	356	49
8 Chelmsford	C	407	659	1,066	88
9 Chester	Y	269	501	770	99
10 Chichester	C	316	370	686	48
11 Coventry	C	104	183	287	20
12 Derby	C	108	187	295	80
13 Durham	Y	234	296	530	32
14 Ely	C	103	172	275	24
15 Exeter	C	167	244	411	47
16 Gloucester	C	108	187	295	34
17 Guildford	C	279	396	675	36
18 Hereford	C	87	141	228	33
19 Leicester	C	96	135	231	26
20 Lichfield	C	337	460	797	112
21 Lincoln	C	120	212	332	37
22 Liverpool	Y	347	565	912	45
23 London	C	678	879	1,557	185
24 Manchester	Y	348	495	843	82
25 Newcastle	Y	94	169	263	45
26 Norwich	C	97	127	224	35
27 Oxford	C	643	699	1,342	116
28 Peterborough	C	179	245	424	77
29 Portsmouth	C	113	169	282	13
30 Ripon & Leeds	Y	157	274	431	50
31 Rochester	C	268	424	692	57
32 St. Albans	C	300	509	809	70
33 St. Edms & Ipswich	C	120	209	329	33
34 Salisbury	C	253	413	666	31
35 Sheffield	Y	129	224	353	29
36 Sodor & Man	Y	14	23	37	11
37 Southwark	C	384	643	1,027	71
38 Southwell & Nottingham	Y	119	197	316	21
39 Truro	C	53	95	148	27
40 Wakefield	Y	85	196	281	43
41 Winchester	C	428	274	702	56
42 Worcester	C	111	151	262	35
43 York	Y	194	290	484	63
44 Europe	C	103	126	229	37
Totals Province of Canterbury	**C**	**6,607**	**9,159**	**15,766**	**1,596**
Totals Province of York	**Y**	**2,627**	**4,147**	**6,774**	**669**
Totals Church Of England		**9,234**	**13,306**	**22,540**	**2,265**
Comparable figures for 2011:					
Totals Province of Canterbury	**C**	**5,890**	**9,143**	**15,033**	**1,525**
Totals Province of York	**Y**	**2,698**	**4,511**	**7,209**	**635**
Totals CHURCH OF ENGLAND		**8,588**	**13,654**	**22,242**	**2,160**

1 Confirmations in the Armed Forces are not included.

I   Parochial Church Electoral Rolls 1996 to 2012

Provinces of Canterbury and York (including Europe and including Cathedrals from 2002 onwards)

Diocese		2012	2011	2007	2002	1996
1 Bath & Wells	C	35,200	35,300	36,000	38,000	42,700
2 Birmingham	C	16,900	16,900	17,500	18,200	19,300
3 Blackburn	Y	32,800	33,000	34,700	34,300	37,400
4 Bradford	Y	10,800	11,100	11,300	12,300	12,700
5 Bristol	C	15,800	15,900	15,400	16,600	19,000
6 Canterbury	C	20,200	20,100	20,600	21,000	21,000
7 Carlisle	Y	20,600	20,400	20,400	21,600	24,900
8 Chelmsford	C	47,300	46,600	45,300	48,600	50,800
9 Chester	Y	46,000	46,300	42,600	45,700	48,600
10 Chichester	C	53,200	52,600	54,100	51,800	58,200
11 Coventry	C	17,300	17,400	17,300	16,300	17,700
12 Derby	C	17,500	17,900	17,800	20,700	20,100
13 Durham	Y	21,700	23,100	22,800	24,000	27,400
14 Ely	C	19,000	19,200	18,300	19,100	20,900
15 Exeter	C	30,000	30,600	30,800	30,500	33,900
16 Gloucester	C	24,100	24,000	22,100	23,600	26,300
17 Guildford	C	30,000	30,100	28,100	29,500	30,600
18 Hereford	C	16,800	17,100	17,600	18,100	18,900
19 Leicester	C	17,400	17,200	16,400	17,000	16,100
20 Lichfield	C	45,000	44,500	44,600	45,000	52,200
21 Lincoln	C	24,600	25,600	28,400	27,800	31,300
22 Liverpool	Y	28,600	28,700	26,800	28,800	32,500
23 London	C	68,600	77,300	64,400	59,600	52,500
24 Manchester	Y	33,300	33,400	32,600	34,500	38,000
25 Newcastle	Y	15,800	16,300	16,000	16,700	17,500
26 Norwich	C	18,000	18,600	19,800	23,900	25,900
27 Oxford	C	55,600	56,400	52,700	54,600	60,600
28 Peterborough	C	19,400	19,300	18,300	18,000	19,500
29 Portsmouth	C	17,000	16,900	16,400	17,500	18,000
30 Ripon & Leeds	Y	15,600	16,300	15,300	17,600	19,300
31 Rochester	C	29,800	30,100	28,500	29,900	31,300
32 St. Albans	C	38,600	38,700	36,900	39,400	43,100
33 St. Edms & Ipswich	C	22,200	22,800	23,300	24,100	25,300
34 Salisbury	C	40,300	40,800	40,700	42,500	45,900
35 Sheffield	Y	18,000	18,000	17,400	18,600	20,700
36 Sodor & Man	Y	2,300	2,600	2,700	2,400	2,800
37 Southwark	C	48,500	49,900	44,800	44,200	45,400
38 Southwell & Nottingham	Y	19,300	19,400	18,800	18,300	18,700
39 Truro	C	15,100	15,400	15,700	16,900	17,600
40 Wakefield	Y	18,300	18,700	19,800	20,300	23,200
41 Winchester	C	38,200	38,000	37,000	38,500	42,100
42 Worcester	C	17,800	18,400	19,200	20,300	22,400
43 York	Y	33,600	33,900	33,600	35,000	38,200
44 Europe	C	11,000	11,100	10,300	9,300	
Totals Province of Canterbury	**C**	**870,400**	**884,700**	**858,300**	**880,500**	**928,600**
Totals Province of York	**Y**	**316,800**	**321,200**	**314,800**	**330,100**	**361,900**
Totals CHURCH OF ENGLAND		**1,187,200**	**1,206,000**	**1,173,100**	**1,210,600**	**1,290,500**

Notes:

1 Electoral Rolls are revised annually and new rolls are compiled every six years in general. New electoral rolls were compiled in 1996 and 2002 and 2007.

2 Figures for cathedrals are included from 2002 onwards.

3 National electoral roll totals for 1996 do not include the Diocese of Europe.

Selected Church Statistics

J Average Weekly Attendances 2012
Adults, Children and Young People

Provinces of Canterbury and York (including Europe and Cathedrals)

Diocese		Average weekly Adults	Average weekly Children and young people	Average Sunday Adults	Average Sunday Children and young people	Usual Sunday Adults	Usual Sunday Children and young people
1 Bath & Wells	C	20,500	4,100	18,600	2,400	17,700	2,500
2 Birmingham	C	14,100	3,600	12,400	2,300	11,700	2,000
3 Blackburn	Y	21,000	5,600	18,600	4,500	16,800	4,000
4 Bradford	Y	8,100	1,700	7,300	1,200	6,800	1,000
5 Bristol	C	13,200	3,100	11,200	2,100	10,400	1,900
6 Canterbury	C	16,400	4,800	14,100	2,900	13,400	2,700
7 Carlisle	Y	12,800	2,200	11,200	1,300	9,600	1,000
8 Chelmsford	C	32,100	7,800	28,700	5,700	26,400	4,900
9 Chester	Y	28,400	7,100	24,800	4,300	21,700	3,400
10 Chichester	C	35,100	7,600	30,500	5,000	29,100	4,700
11 Coventry	C	12,900	2,700	11,100	1,900	10,600	1,700
12 Derby	C	14,400	3,000	12,700	1,800	11,300	1,500
13 Durham	Y	16,500	3,600	13,300	2,100	11,300	1,700
14 Ely	C	14,200	3,600	13,000	2,100	12,100	2,200
15 Exeter	C	20,900	3,300	19,300	2,200	18,200	1,900
16 Gloucester	C	16,400	3,400	14,300	1,900	13,200	1,800
17 Guildford	C	21,600	6,500	19,200	4,500	17,300	3,700
18 Hereford	C	8,500	1,400	7,400	700	7,500	800
19 Leicester	C	12,700	2,700	11,000	1,700	11,200	1,700
20 Lichfield	C	28,300	7,500	24,200	3,500	22,900	3,300
21 Lincoln	C	13,300	2,500	11,700	1,300	13,400	1,300
22 Liverpool	Y	22,000	6,400	18,300	3,800	16,400	3,100
23 London	C	63,600	17,900	49,800	11,400	48,300	10,500
24 Manchester	Y	23,600	8,400	20,300	5,500	18,200	4,900
25 Newcastle	Y	12,200	2,100	10,100	1,200	8,900	1,000
26 Norwich	C	15,900	2,300	13,700	1,200	13,700	1,000
27 Oxford	C	41,700	9,700	37,200	6,800	36,000	6,900
28 Peterborough	C	13,400	3,400	11,700	2,100	11,300	1,900
29 Portsmouth	C	11,000	2,400	9,900	1,400	9,000	1,200
30 Ripon & Leeds	Y	11,200	2,900	9,900	1,900	9,200	1,700
31 Rochester	C	21,900	5,900	19,500	4,100	17,100	3,600
32 St. Albans	C	27,200	9,100	22,500	4,300	21,100	4,000
33 St. Edms & Ipswich	C	14,300	2,400	12,600	1,500	12,600	1,600
34 Salisbury	C	23,300	4,900	20,600	2,800	19,900	2,600
35 Sheffield	Y	15,900	3,800	12,900	2,200	11,100	1,900
36 Sodor & Man	Y	1,800	300	1,500	200	1,200	200
37 Southwark	C	32,600	10,900	30,100	8,400	28,300	7,700
38 Southwell & Nottingham	Y	13,900	3,200	12,000	2,000	11,400	1,700
39 Truro	C	10,100	1,600	8,900	800	8,100	700
40 Wakefield	Y	12,800	2,600	11,100	1,600	9,700	1,300
41 Winchester	C	25,100	6,700	21,700	3,700	20,300	3,800
42 Worcester	C	11,900	2,800	10,500	1,300	8,800	1,000
43 York	Y	22,500	5,100	19,200	2,900	17,800	2,300
44 Europe	C	9,900	1,400	9,400	1,400	9,300	1,600
Totals Province of Canterbury	C	616,500	149,100	537,700	93,100	510,200	86,600
Totals Province of York	Y	222,800	54,900	190,400	34,600	170,000	29,000
Totals CHURCH OF ENGLAND		839,300	204,000	728,100	127,700	680,200	115,600
Comparable figures for 2011							
Totals Province of Canterbury	C	614,100	150,200	534,400	91,200	513,800	86,400
Totals Province of York	Y	226,000	56,600	193,300	35,700	175,000	29,600
Totals CHURCH OF ENGLAND		840,100	206,800	727,600	126,800	688,800	116,000

1 Children and young people are, for the majority of dioceses, defined as under the age of 16 years.

2 The figures for 2011 quoted in the 2014 Yearbook were subsequently revised following publication. The updated figures have been restated above.

Parochial Church Attendance 2003 to 2012

K   Weekly Church Attendance

Provinces of Canterbury and York (including Europe and Cathedrals)

	Weekly attendance									Monthly
	Adult weekly attendance			Children and young people weekly attendance			All age weekly attendance			All age
Year	Highest (000s)	Average (000s)	Lowest (000s)	Highest (000s)	Average (000s)	Lowest (000s)	Highest (000s)	Average (000s)	Lowest (000s)	(000s)
2003	1,228	905	674	406	218	105	1,602	1,126	805	1,602
2004	1,219	896	664	410	220	104	1,597	1,119	794	1,597
2005	1,224	898	662	415	218	101	1,604	1,119	790	1,604
2006	1,219	894	657	417	217	99	1,602	1,115	782	1,602
2007	1,212	888	651	395	205	92	1,577	1,097	770	1,577
2008	1,197	877	646	416	215	94	1,580	1,094	768	1,580
2009	1,184	867	638	415	211	89	1,567	1,082	754	1,567
2010	1,164	851	622	415	208	84	1,548	1,063	733	1,548
2011	1,148	840	612	421	207	81	1,538	1,050	720	1,538
2012	1,152	839	609	409	204	84	1,529	1,047	723	1,529

L   Sunday Church Attendance

	Sunday attendance									Christmas
	Adult Sunday attendance			Children and young people Sunday attendance			All age Sunday attendance			All age
Year	Highest (000s)	Average (000s)	Lowest (000s)	Highest (000s)	Average (000s)	Lowest (000s)	Highest (000s)	Average (000s)	Lowest (000s)	(000s)
2003	1,088	802	606	259	154	88	1,325	959	721	2,588
2004	1,074	789	595	255	151	85	1,308	942	707	2,594
2005	1,078	791	595	251	147	83	1,307	941	706	2,749
2006	1,072	786	591	250	145	80	1,302	935	698	2,947
2007	1,064	779	585	239	137	75	1,282	919	687	2,662
2008	1,048	768	578	240	139	76	1,267	910	683	2,639
2009	1,036	758	571	234	134	72	1,249	895	670	2,446
2010	1,015	741	557	229	130	69	1,225	874	652	2,329
2011	995	728	546	225	127	67	1,200	858	640	2,642
2012	1,006	728	542	225	128	68	1,212	859	639	2,521

Notes

1 Children and young people are under 16 years of age while adults are 16 years of age or over.
2 Church attendance figures are calculated typically from a four-week count in October.
3 An approximation to monthly attendance can be taken from the highest weekly attendance counted over a typical month.
4 'Highest Sunday/weekly attendance' = the sum of the highest Sunday (weekly) attendances for each church over the four week period.
5 'Lowest Sunday/weekly attendance' = the sum of the lowest Sunday (weekly) attendances for each church over the four week period.
6 'Average Sunday/weekly attendance' = the sum of the average Sunday (weekly) attendances for each church over the four week period.
7 Weekly attendance consists of Sunday attendance plus weekday attendance.

Selected Church Statistics

M   All Age Church Attendance 2003 to 2012

M   continued

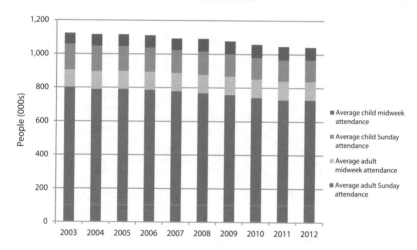

Selected Financial Comparisons 1964 to 2012

N   Total Income of Parochial Church Councils 1964 to 2012

Excluding Europe and Cathedrals

Year	Tax-efficient planned giving				Total unrestricted direct giving			
	Net (£ 000s)		Weekly average per subscriber, £		(£ 000s)		Weekly average per Electoral Roll member, £	
	Actual	Real terms	Actual	Real terms	Actual	Real terms	Actual	Real terms
1964	2,100	35,900	0.30	5.10	15,000	256,400	0.10	1.70
1970	3,300	43,300	0.40	5.20	15,800	207,300	0.10	1.30
1980	17,700	64,200	0.90	3.30	51,500	186,800	0.50	1.80
1992	86,600	151,800	4.10	7.20	164,900	289,000	2.20	3.90
1993	95,300	164,400	4.50	7.80	175,900	303,400	2.30	4.00
1994	103,700	174,700	4.90	8.30	187,500	315,800	2.40	4.00
1995	111,000	180,700	5.30	8.60	197,200	321,000	2.60	4.20
1996	118,100	187,700	5.60	8.90	205,400	326,500	3.10	4.90
1997	124,400	191,700	6.00	9.20	215,600	332,200	3.20	4.90
1998	132,100	196,800	6.40	9.50	244,300	364,000	3.50	5.20
1999	145,800	213,900	6.80	10.00	253,000	371,200	3.60	5.30
2000	157,900	225,000	6.70	9.50	268,500	382,600	3.80	5.40
2001	179,700	251,700	7.00	9.80	282,200	395,200	4.00	5.60
2002	189,900	261,600	7.20	9.90	296,400	408,300	4.70	6.50
2003	201,300	269,500	7.50	10.00	306,700	410,600	4.80	6.40
2004	215,100	279,600	8.00	10.40	323,400	420,400	5.00	6.50
2005	224,600	283,900	8.30	10.50	335,100	423,600	5.10	6.40
2006	236,600	289,900	8.60	10.50	348,700	427,200	5.30	6.50
2007	247,800	291,100	9.30	10.90	368,700	433,100	6.10	7.20
2008	261,400	295,400	9.80	11.10	383,900	433,800	6.30	7.10
2009	267,000	303,200	10.10	11.50	386,700	439,200	6.30	7.20
2010	271,400	294,600	10.40	11.30	389,400	422,700	6.20	6.70
2011	275,700	284,500	10.70	11.00	398,000	410,700	6.30	6.50
2012	282,800	282,800	11.10	11.10	407,800	407,800	6.70	6.70

1   Figures in 'real terms' have been adjusted by the Retail Price Index to reflect 2012 purchasing power.
2   'Total voluntary income' = 'direct giving' plus 'other voluntary income' (see notes and definitions).
3   'Total recurring income' = 'total voluntary income' plus 'other recurring income' (see notes and definitions).
4   Tax-efficient planned giving includes regular Gift Aid donations.

O   Giving 2001 to 2012 (in actual amounts)

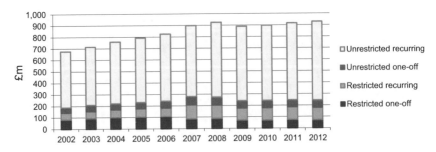

Total unrestricted voluntary income				Unrestricted			Restricted		Total income		
(£ 000s)		Weekly average per Electoral Roll member, £		recurring income (£m)		one off (£m)	recurring income (£m)	one off (£m)	recurring income (£m)	one off (£m)	Total (£m)
Actual	Real terms	Actual	Real terms	Actual	Real terms	Actual	Actual	Actual	Actual	Actual	Actual
20,000	341,800	0.10	1.70	22	378	-	-	-	-	-	-
22,100	289,900	0.20	2.60	26	346	-	-	-	-	-	-
72,800	264,100	0.80	2.90	86	312	-	-	-	-	-	-
230,000	403,000	3.00	5.30	274	479	-	-	-	-	-	-
246,100	424,509	3.20	5.50	287	496	-	-	-	-	-	-
262,900	442,789	3.40	5.70	308	518	-	-	-	-	-	-
275,400	448,287	3.60	5.90	328	533	-	-	-	-	-	-
288,400	458,380	4.30	6.80	345	548	-	-	-	-	-	-
305,300	470,453	4.50	6.90	374	577	-	-	-	-	-	-
314,900	469,200	4.50	6.70	404	602	36	54	63	457	100	557
326,400	478,900	4.60	6.70	419	614	37	55	69	473	106	579
346,900	494,400	4.90	7.00	443	631	39	57	86	499	126	625
365,900	512,400	5.20	7.30	463	648	40	61	88	523	128	652
385,900	531,500	6.20	8.50	487	670	46	61	81	547	128	675
401,600	537,600	6.30	8.40	507	678	54	63	92	570	146	716
423,500	550,500	6.50	8.40	538	699	53	67	101	605	154	759
440,600	556,900	6.70	8.50	561	709	55	73	103	635	158	792
459,800	563,300	7.00	8.60	585	717	59	75	107	661	166	826
485,100	569,900	8.00	9.40	619	728	73	122	84	741	157	898
504,800	570,400	8.30	9.40	651	735	70	117	87	768	158	925
511,700	581,100	8.30	9.40	648	735	65	104	72	752	137	889
515,700	559,800	8.20	8.90	654	710	64	109	70	763	134	897
524,700	541,400	8.40	8.70	671	692	62	110	74	780	136	916
531,000	531,000	8.70	8.70	685	685	65	108	71	793	136	929

5   Unrestricted income is income that may be used by the PCC for general church expenses. Restricted income is income which may not be used for any purpose other than as specified by the donor. (Income which a PCC designates for a specified purpose is considered to be unrestricted, since the PCC and not the donor is determining how it is to be used.)

P   Weekly Average Tax-efficient Planned Giving per Subscriber

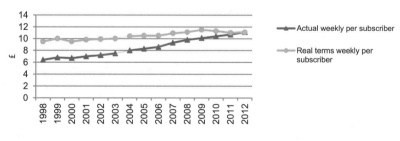

Q   Charitable Giving and Total Expenditure 1964 to 2012

Excluding Europe and Cathedrals

Year	Total charitable donations (£m)		Total recurring expenditure (£m)		Capital expenditure (£m)	Total expenditure (£m)
	Actual	Real terms	Actual	Real terms	Actual	Actual
1964	2.17	37.14	21.71	371.07	-	-
1970	2.59	34.02	28.04	367.83	-	-
1980	8.48	30.76	77.85	282.42	-	-
1992	26.37	46.20	270.37	473.77	-	-
1993	24.99	43.11	289.45	499.28	-	-
1994	25.81	43.48	307.70	518.24	-	-
1995	25.15	40.94	320.20	521.21	-	-
1996	25.36	40.31	338.67	538.28	-	-
1997	26.87	41.41	365.43	563.11	-	-
1998	35.30	52.60	415.20	618.59	103	518
1999	36.95	54.22	437.05	641.31	127	564
2000	37.46	53.39	458.34	653.19	145	603
2001	41.42	58.00	483.12	676.59	145	628
2002	44.40	61.15	513.85	707.78	149	663
2003	41.95	56.15	534.98	716.16	162	697
2004	45.31	58.90	567.93	738.28	159	726
2005	50.80	64.22	600.76	759.40	178	779
2006	46.55	57.02	617.71	756.78	176	793
2007	50.51	59.33	654.13	768.43	184	838
2008	51.72	58.43	694.28	784.46	194	888
2009	48.77	55.38	714.61	811.58	187	901
2010	48.82	52.99	721.38	783.00	197	918
2011	49.03	50.59	728.33	751.55	201	930
2012	46.23	46.23	743.02	743.02	186	929

1   Figures in 'real terms' have been adjusted by the Retail Price Index to reflect 2012 purchasing power.

2   'Total recurring expenditure' = the total of ALL expenditure (including charitable giving) for the ordinary purposes of the PCC i.e. excluding only non-recurring items of capital expenditure and non-revenue items.

3   'Recurring expenditure' includes donations to charities, parish share/quota, clergy expenses, church running costs, costs relating to trading, salaries and support costs. 'Capital expenditure' includes major repairs, redecoration and new building work.

R   Growth in Income and Expenditure

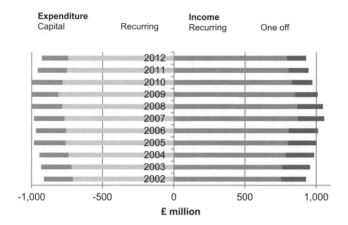

Expenditure
Capital   Recurring

Income
Recurring   One off

2012
2011
2010
2009
2008
2007
2006
2005
2004
2003
2002

-1,000   -500   0   500   1,000

£ million

S   Income and Expenditure 2007 and 2012

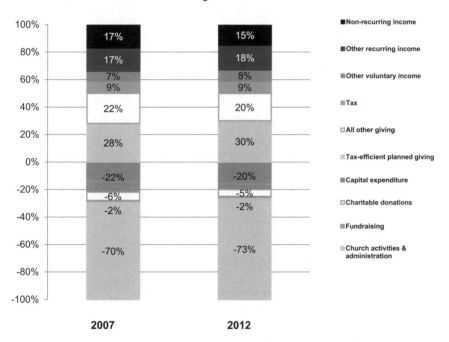

	2007	2012
■ Non-recurring income	17%	15%
■ Other recurring income	17%	18%
■ Other voluntary income	7%	8%
■ Tax	9%	9%
□ All other giving	22%	20%
■ Tax-efficient planned giving	28%	30%
■ Capital expenditure	-22%	-20%
□ Charitable donations	-6%	-5%
■ Fundraising	-2%	-2%
■ Church activities & administration	-70%	-73%

| TABLE OF PAROCHIAL FEES from 1 January 2015

Note: This table sets out the fees prescribed by the Parochial Fees Order 2014 (a Statutory Instrument) and summarizes other relevant information. For legal purposes reference should be made to the Order itself.	Fee Payable towards Diocesan Board of Finance	Fee Payable to Parochial Church Council	Total Fee payable
BAPTISMS	£	£	£
Certificate issued at time of baptism (See Note 1)	—	13.00	13.00
Short certificate of baptism given under section 2, Baptismal Registers Measure 1961	—	13.00	13.00
MARRIAGES			
Publication of banns of marriage	—	28.00	28.00
Certificate of banns issued at time of publication	—	13.00	13.00
Marriage Service (See Note 5. For Marriage certificate see Note 6)	188.00	225.00	413.00
FUNERALS AND BURIALS OF PERSON AGED 16 YEARS OR MORE (See Note 3(i)) **Service in Church**			
Funeral service in church, whether taking place before or after burial or cremation (See Note 5)	96.00	82.00	178.00
Burial of body in churchyard immediately preceding or following on from service in church	12.00	272.00	284.00
Burial or other lawful disposal of cremated remains in churchyard immediately preceding or following on from service in church	12.00	110.00	122.00
Burial of body, or burial or other lawful disposal of cremated remains, in cemetery immediately preceding or following on from service in church	26.00	—	26.00
Cremation immediately preceding or following on from service in church	26.00	—	26.00
Burial of body in churchyard on separate occasion (See Note 3(ii))	38.00	272.00	310.00
Burial of cremated remains in churchyard or other lawful disposal of cremated remains on separate occasion (See Note 3(ii))	38.00	110.00	148.00
Burial of body, or burial or other lawful disposal of cremated remains in cemetery on separate occasion (See Note 3(ii))	50.00	13.00	63.00
No Service in Church			
Funeral service (including burial of body) at graveside in churchyard	96.00	272.00	368.00
Funeral service (including burial or other lawful disposal of cremated remains) at graveside in churchyard	96.00	110.00	206.00
Funeral service at crematorium, or funeral service (including burial of body or burial or other lawful disposal of cremated remains) in cemetery	150.00	28.00	178.00
Burial of body in churchyard (committal only)	38.00	272.00	310.00
Burial of cremated remains in churchyard or other lawful disposal of cremated remains (committal only)	38.00	110.00	148.00
Certificate issued at time of burial (See Note 3(iii))	—	13.00	13.00
MONUMENTS IN CHURCHYARDS			
Permitted in accordance with rules, regulations or directions made by the Chancellor of the diocese, including those relating to a particular churchyard or part of a churchyard (but excluding a monument authorized by a particular faculty, the fee for which is set by the Chancellor)			
Small cross of wood	12.00	29.00	41.00
Small vase not exceeding 305mm × 203mm × 203mm (12" × 8" × 8") or tablet, plaque or other marker commemorating a person whose remains have been cremated	12.00	55.00	67.00
Any other monument (the above fees include the approval of the original inscription by the incumbent)	12.00	116.00	128.00
Additional inscription on existing monument	12.00	13.00	25.00
SEARCHES IN CHURCH REGISTERS			
Searching registers of marriages for period before 1 July 1837 (See Note 4) (for up to one hour)	—	28.00	28.00
for each subsequent hour or part of an hour	—	28.00	28.00
Searching registers of baptism or burials (See Note 4) (including the provision of one copy of any entry therein) for up to one hour	—	28.00	28.00
for each subsequent hour or part of an hour	—	28.00	28.00
Each additional copy of an entry in a register of baptism or burials	—	13.00	13.00
Inspection of instrument of apportionment or agreement for exchange of land for tithes deposited under the Tithe Act 1836	—	—	—
Furnishing copies of above (for every 72 words)	—	13.00	13.00

EXTRAS
The fees shown in this table are the statutory fees payable. It is stressed that the figures do not include any charges for extras such as heating, the services of a verger, music (e.g. organist, choir), bells, and flowers, which are fixed by the Parochial Church Council.

Published by
The Archbishops' Council
Church House, Great Smith Street,
London SW1P 3AZ

NOTES

1 CERTIFICATES OF BAPTISM

The fee for a certificate issued at the time of baptism is for a certified copy of the entry in the register book of baptisms giving the particulars required in Form No 1 in Schedule 1 to the Parochial Registers and Records Measure 1978. The fees payable for a certified copy of the full entry issued at any other time are the fees prescribed for searching registers of baptisms and burials and, if applicable, for each additional copy of an entry in such a register.

2 DEFINITIONS etc.

'*Burial*' includes deposit in a vault or brick grave and the interment or deposit of cremated remains.

'*Churchyard*' includes the curtilage of a church and a burial ground of a church whether or not immediately adjoining such church.

(NOTE: This includes any area used for the interment of cremated remains within such a curtilage or burial ground, whether consecrated or not.)

'*Cemetery*' means a burial ground maintained by a burial authority.

'*Monument*' includes headstone, cross, kerb, border, vase, chain, railing, tablet, plaque, marker, flatstone, tombstone or monument or tomb of any other kind.

'*immediately preceding or following on from service in church*' includes the day before and the day after the service in church.

Where " — " appears in the table no fee is payable to the body indicated.

3 FUNERALS AND BURIALS

i   No fee is payable in respect of a burial of a still-born infant, or for the funeral or burial of a person dying within sixteen years after birth.

ii The fee for a burial in a churchyard on a separate occasion applies when burial does not take place on the same day as, or on the day before or the day after, a service in church.

iii The certificate issued at the time of burial is a certified copy of the entry in the register book of burials kept under the Parochial Registers and Records Measure 1978.

4 SEARCHES IN CHURCH REGISTERS

The search fee relates to a particular search where the approximate date of the baptism, marriage or burial is known. The fee for a more general search of a church register is negotiable.

5 COSTS AND EXPENSES

In the case of a marriage service or a funeral service in church, any costs and expenses incurred in respect of routine administration (including arranging dates and times and the making of entries in registers), making the church available and lighting it are included in the fee prescribed as payable to the Parochial Church Council.

6 FEE FOR MARRIAGE CERTIFICATE

The following fees are currently payable under the Marriage Act 1949 to the Parochial Church Council under the Registration of Births, Deaths and Marriages (Fees) (Amendment) Order 2014: certified copy of entry of marriage register at time of registration £4.00; subsequently £10.00.

Dioceses

PART 1

PART 1 CONTENTS

Every effort has been made to ensure that all details are accurate at the time of going to press.

Provinces of Canterbury and York

The dioceses in the respective Provinces of Canterbury and York are as below:

The Province of Canterbury Bath and Wells, Birmingham, Bristol, Canterbury, Chelmsford, Chichester, Coventry, Derby, Ely, Europe, Exeter, Gloucester, Guildford, Hereford, Leicester, Lichfield, Lincoln, London, Norwich, Oxford, Peterborough, Portsmouth, Rochester, St Albans, St Edmundsbury and Ipswich, Salisbury, Southwark, Truro, Winchester, Worcester.

The Province of York Blackburn, Carlisle, Chester, Durham, Liverpool, Manchester, Newcastle, Sheffield, Sodor and Man, Southwell and Nottingham, West Yorkshire and the Dales (formerly Bradford, Ripon and Leeds, and Wakefield dioceses), York.

Data in this publication correspond to the dioceses before 20 April 2014, therefore refer to the three dioceses in West Yorkshire and the Dales separately.

The entry for each diocese is preceded by a territorial description and a few vital statistics:

Population Derived from the 2011 census statistics published by the Office for National Statistics (source: ONS website www.statistics.gov.uk). Calculations are based on diocesan proportions of Output Area populations.

Area in square miles, as calculated from material supplied by the Office of National Statistics and the Church Commissioners.

Stipendiary clergy Full-time parochial clergy, men and women, working within the diocesan framework in parishes as at 31 December 2012 and counted under the current deployment formula.

Benefices Figures as at December 2012, compiled from information provided by the Church Commissioners. The figure does not include cathedrals or conventional districts.

Parishes / **Churches** are listed in the Parish Register maintained by the Research and Statistics Department of the Archbishops' Council as at 31 December 2012.

In most cases, the Diocesan Secretary/Chief Executive is also the Secretary of the Diocesan Synod.

PROVINCIAL LAY OFFICERS

Canterbury
Dean of the Court of Arches Rt Worshipful Charles George QC

Vicar-General Rt Worshipful Timothy Briden

Registrar Revd Canon John Rees, 16 Beaumont St, Oxford OX1 2LZ
Tel: 01865 297200
Fax: 01865 726274
email: jrees@wslaw.co.uk

York
Official Principal and Auditor of Chancery Court of York Rt Worshipful Charles George QC

Vicar-General of the Province and Official Principal of the Consistory Court Rt Worshipful Peter Collier QC

Registrar Mr Lionel Lennox, Provincial Registry, Stamford House, Piccadilly, York YO1 9PP
Tel: 01904 623487
Fax: 01904 561470
email: lpml@denisontill.com

Joint Registrar (Provincial Elections) Mr Stephen Slack, The Legal Office, Church House, Great Smith St, London SW1P 3AZ   Tel: 020 7898 1366
email: stephen.slack@churchofengland.org

Archbishop of Canterbury's Personal Staff

Lambeth Palace, London SE1 7JU
Tel: 020 7898 1200   *Fax:* 020 7401 9886
Web: www.archbishopofcanterbury.org

CHIEF OF STAFF
Mrs Kay Brock LVO DL
BISHOP AT LAMBETH
Rt Revd Nigel Stock

Archbishop's Senior Executive Assistant
Miss Joanne Scott

Archbishop's Diary Manager
Miss Elise Gallagher

Chaplain
Revd Dr Jo Bailey Wells

Archbishop's Adviser for Evangelism and Witness
Revd Canon Chris Russell

Archbishop's Director for Reconciliation
Canon David Porter

Director of Communications
Mrs Ailsa Anderson LVO

Senior Press Officer
Mr Ed Thornton

Digital Communications Officer
Mr Chris Cox

Correspondence Secretary and CDM Officer
Mr Andrew Nunn

Archbishop's Adviser on Anglican Communion Affairs
Revd Canon Precious Omuku

Anglican Communion Liaison Officer
Miss Fiona Millican

Adviser on Social and Public Affairs
Revd Helen Dawes

Secretary for Inter Religious Affairs
Vacancy: contact Katie Jarman, Inter Religious Affairs Programmes Officer

Finance Officer
Miss Rebecca Pashley

Steward
Colonel Malcolm Croft

Archbishop of York's Personal Staff

Bishopthorpe Palace, Bishopthorpe, York YO23 2GE
Tel: 01904 707021   *Fax:* 01904 772389
email: office@archbishopofyork.org
Web: www.archbishopofyork.org

Chief of Staff
Revd Malcolm Macnaughton
email: malcolm.macnaughton@archbishopofyork.org

Chaplain/Researcher to the Archbishop
Revd Dr Daphne Green
email: daphne.green@archbishopofyork.org

Executive Officer / Researcher
Mrs Margaret Pattinson
email: margaret.pattinson@archbishopofyork.org

Domestic Chaplain to the Archbishop
Revd Richard Carew
email: richard.carew@archbishopofyork.org

Palace and Events Manager
Mrs Sandy Reynard
email: sandy.reynard@archbishopofyork.org

Senior Secretary
Miss Alison Cundiff
email: alison.cundiff@archbishopofyork.org

Communications Office
Elizabeth Addy
email: elizabeth.addy@archbishopofyork.org

DIOCESE OF BATH AND WELLS

Founded in 909. Somerset; north Somerset; Bath; north-east Somerset; a few parishes in Dorset.

Population 916,000   Area 1,610 sq m
Full-time Stipendiary Parochial Clergy 197   Benefices 188
Parishes 465   Churches 564
www. bathandwells.org.uk
Overseas link dioceses: Luapula, Lusaka, Central Zambia,
Northern Zambia and Eastern Zambia.

BISHOP (78th)
Rt Revd Peter Hancock, The Palace, Wells BA5 2PD   *Tel:* 01749 672341
Fax: 01749 679355
email: bishop@bathwells.anglican.org

SUFFRAGAN BISHOP
TAUNTON Rt Revd Peter Maurice, The Palace, Wells BA5 2PD (*Office*) [2006]   *Tel:* 01749 672341
Fax: 01749 679355
email: bishop.taunton@bathwells.anglican.org
Bishops' Senior Chaplain and Adviser Preb Stephen Lynas (*same address, tel and fax nos*)
email: chaplain@bathwells.anglican.org
Bishop's Domestic Chaplain Revd Canon Michael Caddy (*same address, tel and fax nos*)
email: michael.caddy@bathwells.anglican.org

ASSISTANT BISHOPS
Rt Revd Richard Third, La Fontana, Fold Hill Lane, Martock TA12 6PQ   *Tel:* 01935 825519
Rt Revd William Persson, Ryalls Cottage, Burton St, Marnhull, Sturminster Newton DT10 1PS
Tel: 01258 820452
Rt Revd Paul Barber, Hillside, 41 Somerton Rd, Street BA16 0DR   *Tel:* 01458 442916
Rt Revd Barry Rogerson, Flat 2, 30 Albert Rd, Clevedon BS21 7RR   *Tel:* 01275 541964
email: barry.rogerson@blueyonder.co.uk
Rt Revd Roger Sainsbury, Abbey Lodge, Battery Lane, Portishead BS20 7JD   *Tel:* 01275 847082
email: bishoproger@talktalk.net
Rt Revd John Perry, 8 The Firs, Combe Down, Bath BA2 5ED   *Tel:* 01225 833987
email: jperry8@btinternet.com
Rt Revd George Cassidy, Darch House, 17 St Andrew Road, Stogursey, Bridgwater TA5 1TE
Tel: 01278 732625
email: georgecassidy123@btinternet.com

CATHEDRAL CHURCH OF ST ANDREW IN WELLS
Dean of Wells Very Revd John Clarke, The Dean's Lodging, 25 The Liberty, Wells BA5 2SZ [2004]
Tel: 01749 670278
email: thedeanofwells@googlemail.com

Cathedral Offices Chain Gate, Cathedral Green, Wells BA5 2UE   *Tel:* 01749 674483
Fax: 01749 832210
email: office@wellscathedral.uk.net
Web: www.wellscathedral.org.uk
Canons Residentiary
Chancellor Canon Andrew Featherstone, 8 The Liberty, Wells BA5 2SU [2005]   *Tel:* 01749 679587
email: chancellorofwellscathedral@gmail.com
Precentor Canon Nicholas Jepson-Biddle, 4 The Liberty, Wells BA5 2SU [2013]
Tel: 01749 673489
email: nicklb@hotmail.co.uk
Treasurer Canon Dr Graham Dodds, 2 The Liberty, Wells BA5 2SU [2010]   *Tel:* 01749 670607
email: Graham.Dodds@bathwells.anglican.org
Archdeacon Ven Nicola Sullivan, 6 The Liberty, Wells BA5 2SU [2007]   *Tel:* 01749 685147
email: adwells@bathwells.anglican.org
Lay Members
Cathedral Administrator Dr Paul Richards, Cathedral Offices
email: administrator@wellscathedral.uk.net
Preb Adrian I'Anson, Cathedral Offices
Preb Barbara Bates, Cathedral Offices
Preb Gill Hawkings, Cathedral Offices
Registrar Preb Mr Tim Berry, Diocesan Registry, 14 Market Place, Wells BA5 2RE
Tel: 01749 674747
Fax: 01749 834060
email: tim.berry@harris-harris.co.uk
Cathedral Organist Mr Matthew Owens (*based at Cathedral Offices*)
email: musicoffice@wellscathedral.uk.net

ARCHDEACONS
WELLS Ven Nicola Sullivan, 6 The Liberty, Wells BA5 2SU [2007]   *Tel:* 01749 685147
email: adwells@bathwells.anglican.org
BATH Ven Andy Piggott, 56 Grange Rd, Saltford, Bristol BS31 3AG [2005]   *Tel:* 01225 873609
email: adbath@bathwells.anglican.org
TAUNTON Ven John Reed, 2 Monkton Heights, West Monkton, Taunton TA2 8LU [1999]
Tel: 01823 413315
email: adtaunton@bathwells.anglican.org

CONVOCATION (MEMBERS OF THE HOUSE OF CLERGY OF THE GENERAL SYNOD)
Proctors for Clergy
Ven Andy Piggott
Preb Stephen Lynas
Revd James Dudley-Smith
Revd Sue Rose

MEMBERS OF THE HOUSE OF LAITY OF THE GENERAL SYNOD
Mr Edward Armitstead
Mr Tim Hind
Mrs Jenny Humphreys
Miss Fay Wilson Rudd
Ms Christina Baron

DIOCESAN OFFICERS
Dioc Secretary Mr Nick May, Dioc Office, The Old Deanery, Wells BA5 2UG
Tel: 01749 685109
Fax: 01749 674240
email: nick.may@bathwells.anglican.org
Chancellor of Diocese The Worshipful Timothy Briden, 1 Temple Gardens, Temple, London EC4Y 9BB
Registrar of Diocese and Bishop's Legal Secretary Preb Mr Tim Berry, Diocesan Registry, 14 Market Place, Wells BA5 2RE *Tel:* 01749 674747
Fax: 01749 834060
email: tim.berry@harris-harris.co.uk

DIOCESAN ORGANIZATIONS
Diocesan Office The Old Deanery, Wells BA5 2UG
Tel: 01749 670777
Fax: 01749 674240
email: general@bathwells.anglican.org
Web: www.bathandwells.org

ADMINISTRATION
Dioc Synod (Chairman, House of Clergy) Preb Stephen Stuckes, The Vicarage, Manor Road, Alcombe, Minehead TA24 6EJ *Tel:* 01643 703285
email: sstuckes24@btinternet.com
(Chairman, House of Laity) Ms Christina Baron, The Old Vicarage, St Thomas Street, Wells BA5 2UZ *Tel:* 01749 675071
email: baron.christina@googlemail.com
(Secretary) Mr Nick May, Dioc Office *(as above)*
Board of Finance (Chairman) Mr Harry Musselwhite, Highfields, 207 Bailbrook Lane, Bath BA1 7AB *Tel:* 01225 858913
email: harry.musselwhite@btopenworld.com
(Secretary) Mr Nick May, Dioc Office
Finance Group Mr Nick May *(as above)*
Board of Patronage Mr Peter Evans, Dioc Office
email: peter.evans@bathwells.anglican.org
Mission and Pastoral Committee Mr Peter Evans *(as above)*
Designated Officer Mr Peter Evans *(as above)*
Assistant Dioc Secretary Mr Peter Evans *(as above)*

Accountant Vacancy, Dioc Office
Property Officer Mrs Alison Walker, Dioc Office
email: alison.walker@bathwells.anglican.org
Dioc Surveyor Mr Paul Toseland, Dioc Office
email: paul.toseland@bathwells.anglican.org

CHURCHES
Advisory Committee for the Care of Churches (Chairman) Mr Chris Hyldon, Mill Stream Barn, Martin Street, Baltonsborough, Glastonbury BA6 8QT *Tel:* 01458 851641
email: chrishyldon@hotmail.com
(Secretary) Preb Mr Tim Berry, Dioc Registry, 14 Market Place, Wells BA5 2RE
Tel: 01749 674747
Fax: 01749 834060
email: tim.berry@harris-harris.co.uk
(Assistant Secretary) Mrs Sarah Davis, Dioc Registry *(as above)*
email: sarah.davis@harris-harris.co.uk
Association of Change Ringers Revd Tim Hawkings, The Rectory, Cheddar Rd, Axbridge BS26 2DL *Tel:* 01934 732261
email: revhawkings@googlemail.com

EDUCATION
Board of Education Diocesan Office, The Old Deanery, Wells BA5 2UG *Tel:* 01749 670777
Fax: 01749 674240
email: education@bathwells.anglican.org
Dioc Director of Education Mrs Theresa Gale, Dioc Office
email: theresa.gale@bathwells.anglican.org
School Improvement Advisers
Mrs Pauline Dodds, Dioc Office
email: pauline.dodds@bathwells.anglican.org
Mr David Williams, Dioc Office
email: david.williams@bathwells.anglican.org
School Development Advisers
Ms Natalie Paull, Dioc Office
email: natalie.paull@bathwells.anglican.org
Mrs Suzanne McDonald, Dioc Office
email: suzanne.mcdonald@bathwells.anglican.org
Parish Adviser for Young People Mr Tony Cook, Dioc Office
email: tony.cook@bathwells.anglican.org
Parish Adviser for Children Mrs Jane Tibbs, Dioc Office *email:* jane.tibbs@bathwells.anglican.org
Safeguarding Adviser Ms Glenys Armstrong, Dioc Office
email: glenys.armstrong@bathwells.anglican.org

MINISTRY FORUM
Chairman The Bishop of Taunton
Principal of the School of Formation Preb Dr Graham Dodds, Dioc Office
email: graham.dodds@bathwells.anglican.org
Director of Continuing Ministerial Development Revd Simon Hill, Dioc Office
email: simon.hill@bathwells.anglican.org

Education for Discipleship Officer Revd Jennifer Cole, Dioc Office

email: jennifer.cole@bathwells.anglican.org
Diocesan Director of Vocations Vacancy
Adviser in Prayer and Spirituality Revd Jane Eastell, Meadowside, Wild Oak Lane, Trull, Taunton TA3 7JT   *Tel:* 01823 321069

email: jane.eastell@bathwells.anglican.org
Adviser in Care and Counselling of the Clergy and their Families Mrs Sue Yabsley, Prometheus Therapy Centre, Foundry Cottage, Foundry Road, Taunton TA1 1JJ   *Tel:* 01823 251915

email: sue.yabsley@bathwells.anglican.org
Chaplain to the Deaf Mrs Pamela Grottick, 9 Chestnut Close, Baltonsborough, Glastonbury BA6 8PH   *Tel:* 01458 851401

email: pamg@wpci.org.uk
Warden of Readers Ven John Reed, 2 Monkton Heights, West Monkton, Taunton TA2 8LU

Tel: 01823 413315

email: adtaunton@bathwells.anglican.org
Director of Reader Studies Preb Dr Graham Dodds (as above)
Dean of Women Clergy Vacancy

MISSION FORUM

Chairman The Archdeacon of Bath
Executive Officer/Diocesan Missioner Canon Roger Medley, Dioc Office

email: roger.medley@bathwells.anglican.org
Social Justice and Environment Adviser Mr David Maggs, Dioc Office

email: david.maggs@bathwells.anglican.org
World Mission Adviser & Exec Sec Zambia Link Mrs Jenny Humphreys, Dioc Office

email: jenny.humphreys@bathwells.anglican.org
Rural Life Adviser Mr Rob Walrond, The Wagon House, Pitney, Langport TA10 9AP

Tel: 01458 253002

email: rob.walrond@hotmail.com
Healing Adviser Revd Matthew Thomson, The Vicarage, Station Road, Congresbury, Bristol BS49 5DX   *Tel:* 01934 833126

email: revmattthomson@hotmail.com
Renewal Adviser Revd Keith Powell, Homefields House, Paynes Lane, Othery, Bridgwater TA7 0QB   *Tel:* 01823 698619

email: jill.powell3@googlemail.com

STEWARDSHIP GROUP

Chairman The Archdeacon of Bath
Stewardship Adviser Mr Andrew Rainsford, Dioc Office

email: andrew.rainsford@bathwells.anglican.org

BISHOP'S LITURGY GROUP

Chairman Revd Robin Lodge, St Andrew's Vicarage, 118 Kingston Road, Taunton TA2 7SR

Tel: 01823 352471

email: robin.lodge1@btinternet.com

PRESS AND PUBLICATIONS

Diocesan Communications Manager Miss Gillian Buzzard, Dioc Office   *Mobile:* 07848 028798

email: gillian.buzzard@bathwells.anglican.org
Diocesan Communications Officer Mr James Butterworth (currently on secondment)
Diocesan Communications Officer Mrs Helen Hawthorne, Dioc Office   *Mobile:* 07436 090256

email: helen.hawthorne@bathwells.anglican.org
Editor of Directory/Database Manager Mrs Joanne Sleight, Dioc Office   *Tel:* 01749 685130

email: joanne.sleight@bathwells.anglican.org

WIDOWS' OFFICER

Revd Chris Hare, Cuckoo Hill, 61 Packsaddle Way, Frome BA11 2RW   *Tel:* 01373 469788

email: cshare@hotmail.co.uk

RETREAT HOUSE

Abbey House, Glastonbury

Tel: 01458 831112

Fax: 01458 831893

email: director@abbeyhouse.org

DIOCESAN RECORD OFFICE

Somerset County Record Office, Somerset Heritage Centre, Brunel Way, Langford Mead, Norton Fitzwarren, Taunton TA2 6SF   *Tel:* 01823 278805

Fax: 01823 325402

email: archives@somerset.gov.uk

DIOCESAN RESOURCE CENTRE

Old Deanery, Wells BA5 2UG   *Tel:* 01749 685129

Fax: 01749 674240

email: resourcecentre@bathwells.anglican.org

RURAL DEANS
ARCHDEACONRY OF WELLS

Axbridge Revd Tim Hawkings, The Rectory, Cheddar Rd, Axbridge BS26 2DL

Tel: 01934 732261

email: revhawkings@googlemail.com
Bruton and Cary Preb Rose Hoskins, Springfields, Weston Bampfylde, Yeovil BA22 7HZ

Tel: 01963 440026

email: revroseanne@gmail.com
Frome Revd Colin Alsbury, St John's Vicarage, Vicarage Close, Christchurch Street East, Frome BA11 1QL   *Tel:* 01373 472853

email: colin.alsbury@btinternet.com
Glastonbury Revd David MacGeoch, The Vicarage, 24 Wells Road, Glastonbury BA6 9DJ

Tel: 01458 834281

email: vicarabbeyparish@btinternet.com
Ivelchester Revd Bruce Faulkner, 3 The Paddocks, West Street, Ilchester BA22 8PS

Tel: 01935 849441

email: ilchestervicar@aol.com
Yeovil Revd Anthony Perris, St James Vicarage, 1 Old School Close, Yeovil BA21 3UB

Tel: 01935 429398

email: antonyperris@yahoo.com

Shepton Mallet Revd Preb Alastair Wheeler, 3 Orchard Lea, Wells BA5 2LZ   *Tel:* 01749 677810
email: AQHW@aol.com

Bath Revd Martin Lloyd Williams, 71 Priory Close, Combe Down, Bath BA2 5AP
Tel: 01225 835490
email: rector@stmichaelsbath.org.uk
Chew Magna Preb Jan Knott, Rectory, Church Lane, Fanrborough, Bath BA3 1AN
Tel: 01761 479311
email: jpknott@btinternet.com
Locking Revd Richard Taylor, The Rectory, Cecil Rd, Weston Super Mare BS23 2NF
Tel: 01934 623399
email: revrjtaylor@hotmail.com
Midsomer Norton Revd Chris North, The Rectory, The Street, Chilcompton BA3 4HN
Tel: 01761 232219
email: c.north123@btinternet.com
Portishead Revd Noel Hector, The Rectory, All Saints Lane, Clevedon BS21 6AU
Tel: 01275 873257
email: eastcleveub@blueyonder.co.uk

Crewkerne Revd Jonathan Morris, The Rectory, New Street, North Perrott TA18 7ST
Tel: 01460 72356
email: jonbea@cooptel.net
Ilminster Revd Preb Andrew Tatham, Rectory, Broadway, Ilminster TA19 9RE   *Tel:* 01460 52559
email: aftatham@btinternet.com
Exmoor Revd Preb Stephen Stuckes, The Vicarage, Manor Road, Alcombe, Minehead TA24 6EJ
Tel: 01643 703285
email: stephen1962@btinternet.com
Quantock Revd Craig Marshall, The Vicarage, 25 St Mary Street, Nether Stowey, Bridgwater TA5 1LT   *Tel:* 01278 734777
email: craig785@btinternet.com
Taunton Revd Geoff Boucher, The Rectory, West Monkton, Taunton TA2 8QT   *Tel:* 01823 412226
email: geoffboucher@btinternet.com
Tone Revd Revd Hugh Allen, Woodpeckers, Langley Marsh, Wiveliscombe TA4 2UL
Tel: 01984 624166
email: hallenarkwood@yahoo.co.uk
Sedgemoor Revd Chris Keys, The Vicarage, Church Lane, Westonzoyland TA7 0EP
Tel: 01278 691098
email: chris.keys@me.com

DIOCESE OF BIRMINGHAM

Founded in 1905. Birmingham; Sandwell, except for an area
in the north (LICHFIELD); Solihull, except for an area in the east
(COVENTRY); an area of Warwickshire; a few parishes in Worcestershire.

Population 1,514,000   Area 290 sq m
Full-time Stipendiary Parochial Clergy 163   Benefices 141
Parishes 151   Churches 188
www.birmingham.anglican.org
Overseas link dioceses: Lake Malawi, Southern Malawi, Northern Malawi & Upper Shire.

DIOCESES

BISHOP (9th)
Rt Revd David Andrew Urquhart, Bishop's Croft, Old Church Rd, Harborne, Birmingham, B17 0BG [2006]   *Tel:* 0121 427 1163
Fax: 0121 426 1322
email: bishop@birmingham.anglican.org
Domestic Chaplain Revd Kate Stowe, East Wing, Bishop's Croft, Old Church Rd, Birmingham B17 0BE   0121 427 1163 (Office)
email: bishopschaplain@birmingham.anglican.org

SUFFRAGAN BISHOP
ASTON Vacancy

HONORARY ASSISTANT BISHOPS
Rt Revd Michael Humphrey Dickens Whinney, 3 Moor Green Lane, Moseley, Birmingham B13 8NE [1989]   *Tel:* 0121 249 2856
Rt Revd Maurice Walker Sinclair, 55 Selly Wick Drive, Selly Park, Birmingham B29 7JQ [2002]   *Tel:* 0121 4712617
email: mauricewsinclair@blueyonder.co.uk
Rt Revd Mark Santer, 81 Clarence Rd, Moseley, Birmingham B13 9UH [2003]
Rt Revd Iraj Mottadeheh, 2 Highland Rd, Newport TF10 7AE [2005]   *Tel:* 01952 813615

CATHEDRAL CHURCH OF ST PHILIP
Dean Very Revd Catherine Ogle, 38 Goodby Road, Moseley, Birmingham B13 8NJ
Tel: 0121 262 1840
email: dean@birminghamcathedral.com
Cathedral Office Birmingham Cathedral, Colmore Row, Birmingham B3 2QB   *Tel:* 0121 262 1840
Fax: 0121 262 1869
email: enquiries@birminghamcathedral.com
Canons Residentiary
Canon Missioner Revd Canon Nigel Hand, 12 Nursery Drive, Handsworth, Birmingham B20 2SW [2008]   *Tel:* 0121 262 1840
email: canonmissioner@birminghamcathedral.com
Canon Liturgist Revd Canon Janet Chapman, 4 Nursery Drive, Handsworth, Birmingham B20 2SW   *Tel:* 0121 262 1840
email: canonliturgist@birminghamcathedral.com

Director of Operations Ruth Harvey, Cathedral Office   *Tel:* 0121 262 1847
email: administrator@birminghamcathedral.com
Director of Music Canon Marcus Huxley, Cathedral Office   *Tel:* 0121 262 1846
email: music@birminghamcathedral.com

ARCHDEACONS
ASTON Ven Simon Heathfield, c/o Dioc Office [2014]   *Tel:* 0121 426 0437
Fax: 0121 428 1114
email: archdeaconofaston@birmingham.anglican.org
BIRMINGHAM Ven Hayward Osborne, c/o Dioc Office [2001]   *Tel:* 0121 426 0441
Fax: 0121 428 1114
email: archdeaconofbham@birmingham.anglican.org

CONVOCATION (MEMBERS OF THE HOUSE OF CLERGY OF THE GENERAL SYNOD)
Proctors for Clergy
Revd Catherine Grylls
Revd Canon Nigel Hand
Ven Hayward Osborne

MEMBERS OF THE HOUSE OF LAITY OF THE GENERAL SYNOD
Canon Dr Paula Gooder
Dr Rachel Jepson
Mr Geoffrey Shuttleworth

DIOCESAN OFFICERS
Dioc Secretary Mr Andrew Halstead, The Church of England, 1 Colmore Row, Birmingham B3 2BJ
Tel: 0121 426 0402
Fax: 0121 428 1114
email: andrew@birmingham.anglican.org
Chancellor of Diocese Mr Mark Powell QC c/o Diocesan Registrar, SGH Martineau, No. 1 Colmore Square, Birmingham B4 6AA

Registrar of Diocese and Bishop's Legal Secretary Mr Hugh Carslake, SGH Martineau, No. 1 Colmore Square, Birmingham B4 6AA
Tel: 0800 763 1000
Fax: 0800 763 1001
email: hugh.carslake@sghmartineau.com
Web: www.sghmartineau.com
Dioc Surveyor Mr Alan Broadway, Dioc Office
Tel: 0121 426 0409
email: alanb@birmingham.anglican.org

DIOCESAN ORGANIZATIONS
Diocesan Office The Church of England, 1 Colmore Row, Birmingham B3 2BJ   Tel: 0121 426 0400
Fax: 0121 428 1114
Web: www.cofebirmingham.com

ADMINISTRATION
Dioc Synod (Chair, House of Clergy) Revd Canon Martin Stephenson, 33 Paradise Lane, Hall Green, Birmingham B28 0DY   Tel: 0121 777 1935
email: martin.stephenson@cantab.net
(Chair, House of Laity) Mr Stephen Fraser, 47 Wroxton Rd, Yardley, Birmingham B26 1SH
email: stevef_bham@sky.com
(Secretary) Mr Andrew Halstead, Dioc Office
Board of Finance (Chair) Mr Phil Nunnerley
(Secretary) Mr Andrew Halstead (as above)
Parsonages Committee Mr Andrew Halstead (as above)
Dioc Trustees (Secretary) Mr Andrew Halstead (as above)
Pastoral Committee Mr Andrew Halstead (as above)
Designated Officer Mr Hugh Carslake, SGH Martineau (as above)   Tel: 0800 763 1000
Fax: 0800 763 1001
email: hugh.carslake@sghmartineau.com

CHURCHES
Advisory Committee for the Care of Churches (Chair) Dr Jim Berrow, c/o Dioc Office; (Secretary) Mr Adrian Mann, Dioc Office
email: adrianm@birmingham.anglican.org

EDUCATION
Dioc Director of Education Revd Canon Jackie Hughes, Dioc Office
email: jackieh@birmingham.anglican.org
Schools Support Officer Revd Peter French, Dioc Office
email: peterf@birmingham.anglican.org
RE Adviser Mrs Jill Stolberg, Dioc Office
email: jills@birmingham.anglican.org

MINISTRY
Director of Ordinands and Women's Ministry Revd Canon Faith Claringbull, Dioc Office
email: faithc@birmingham.anglican.org

MINISTRIES
Chair Bishop of Birmingham
Bishop's Adviser for Continuing Clergy Ministerial Education Revd Canon Mark Pryce, Dioc Office
email: markp@birmingham.anglican.org
Bishop's Adviser for Lay Adult Education and Training Revd Liz Howlett, Dioc Office
email: lizh@birmingham.anglican.org
Bishop's Adviser for Minority Ethnic Anglicans Revd Joycelyn Lewis-Gregory, Dioc Office
email: revjoycelyn@gmail.com
Bishop's Adviser for Children's Ministry Ms Claire Wesley, Dioc Office
email: claire@birmingham.anglican.org
Bishop's Adviser for Youth Ministry Miss Helen Tomblin, Dioc Office
email: helen@birmingham.anglican.org
Dioc Music Adviser Mr Mick Perrier, c/o Dioc Office   email: mick@mperrier.freeserve.co.uk
Readers' Board (Secretary) Mr Michael Lynch, 57 Fairholme Rd, Hodge Hill, Birmingham B36 8HN
Tel: 0121 242 0534
email: mike4jeannie@blueyonder.co.uk

LITURGICAL
Bishop's Liturgical Advisory Committee Chair Revd Peter Babington, Parish Office, St Francis Centre, Sycamore Rd, Bournville, Birmingham B30 2AA
Tel: 0121 472 7215
email: pgbabington@gmail.com

MISSION AND EVANGELISM
Chair The Bishop of Aston
Director of Mission Revd Rhiannon Jones, Dioc Office   Tel: 0121 426 0420
07595 880584 (Mobile)
email: rhiannon@birmingham.anglican.org
Bishop's Ecumenical Adviser Revd Nick Parker, Vicarage, High Street, Coleshill B46 3BP
Tel: 01675 462188
email: nickthevicparker@outlook.com
Bishop's Adviser for the Environment Revd Patrick Gerard, Rectory, Church Lane, Lapworth, Solihull B94 5NX   Tel: 01564 782098
email: Patrick@gerard.net
Bishop's Adviser for New Religious Movements Revd Paul Cudby, Vicarage, Vicarage Hill, Tanworth-in-Arden, Solihull B94 5EB
Tel: 01564 742565
email: paul@logos.myzen.co.uk
Bishop's Rural Adviser Revd Stephen Banks, Vicarage, 132 Main Road, Austrey, Atherstone CV9 3EB   Tel: 01827 839022
email: stephenbanks132@btinternet.com
Malawi Partnership Officer Revd Richard Tucker, 280 Chester Road North, Sutton Coldfield B73 6RR   Tel: 0121 354 5873
email: malawiofficer@birmingham.anglican.org

HEALTHCARE CHAPLAINCIES
Bishop's Adviser Ven Hayward Osborne, Dioc Office

PRESS AND PUBLICATIONS

Bishop's Director of Communications Mr Steve Squires, Dioc Office   *Tel:* 0121 426 0438
07973 173195 (Mobile)
email: steves@birmingham.anglican.org
Editor of Dioc Newsletter Mr Steve Squires
Editor of Dioc Directory Mr Steve Squires
Assistant to the Director of Communications Mrs Cara Butowski   *Tel:* 0121 426 0439
email: cara@birmingham.anglican.org

CHURCHES AND INDUSTRY GROUP BIRMINGHAM

Industrial Chaplain (CIGB) Revd Peter Sellick, Dioc Office   *Tel:* 0121 426 0425
email: peters@birmingham.anglican.org

RETIREMENT OFFICERS

Revd Barbara Fletcher, 231 Abbey Road, Smethwick B67 5NN   *Tel:* 0121 429 9354
07972 627510 (mobile)
email: bfletcher@talktalk.net
Canon John Nightingale, 19 Berberry Close, Bournville, Birmingham B30 1TB
Tel: 0121 458 6182
07811 128831 (mobile)
*email:*johnnightingale@btinternet.com

DIOCESAN RECORD OFFICES

Birmingham Archives and Heritage, Library of Birmingham, Centenary Square, Broad Street, Birmingham B1 2ND (*For parish records in the City and Diocese of Birmingham*)   *Tel:* 0121 242 4242
email: enquiries@libraryofbirmingham.com
Warwick County Record Office, Priory Park, Cape Rd, Warwick CV34 4JS, *Archive and Historic Environment Manager* Mrs Sam Collenette *Tel:* 01926 738959 (*For parish records in the Metropolitan Borough of Solihull, together with those still in the County of Warwick*)
email: recordoffice@warwickshire.gov.uk
Sandwell Council Community History and Archives Service, Smethwick Library, High St, Smethwick, Warley, W Midlands B66 1AA *Tel:* 0121 558 2561 (*For parish records in the Warley deanery*)
email: archives_service@sandwell.gov.uk

CHRISTIAN STEWARDSHIP

Stewardship Support Mrs Amanda Homer, Dioc Office   *Tel:* 0121 426 0414
email: amandah@birmingham.anglican.org

COMMUNITY REGENERATION

Director Fred Rattley, Faithful Neighbourhoods Centre, 10 Court Rd, Sparkhill, Birmingham B11 4LX   *Tel:* 0121 426 0442
email: f.rattley@birmingham.anglican.org

COMMUNITY PROJECTS COMMITTEE

Chair Revd Nigel Traynor

AREA DEANS
ARCHDEACONRY OF ASTON

Aston Revd Nigel Traynor, 1162 Tyburn Rd, Pype Hayes, Birmingham B24 0TB   *Tel:* 0121 373 3534
email: revnigel@yahoo.co.uk
Coleshill Revd Stuart Carter, Vicarage, Lanchester Way, Castle Bromwich, Birmingham B36 9JG
Tel: 0121 748 5550
email: sccarter5867@hotmail.co.uk
Polesworth Revd Ann Simmons, Vicarage, Watling Street, Dordon, Tamworth B78 1TE
Tel: 01827 892294
email: annbsimmons@aol.com
Solihull Revd Duncan Ballard, Vicarage, 1 High Street, Hampton-in-Arden, Solihull B92 0AE
Tel: 01675 442339
email: duncan.ballard@me.com
Sutton Coldfield Revd Adrian Leahy, 26 All Saints Drive, Four Oaks, Sutton Coldfield B74 4AG   *Tel:* 0121 308 5315
email: revaleahy@gmail.com
Yardley and Bordesley Revd Andrew Bullock, 34 Dudley Park Rd, Acocks Green, Birmingham B27 6QR   *Tel:* 0121 706 9264
email: andrewbullock2@blueyonder.co.uk

ARCHDEACONRY OF BIRMINGHAM

Central Birmingham Revd Ian Harper, St John's Vicarage, Darnley Rd, Ladywood, Birmingham B16 8TF   *Tel:* 0121 454 0973
email: harper-i1@sky.com
Edgbaston Revd Priscilla White, 115 Balden Road, Harborne, Birmingham B32 2EL
Tel: 0121 427 2410
email: priscillawhite.harborne@btinternet.com
Handsworth Revd Philip Calvert, The Clergy House, Bandywood Crescent, Kingstanding, Birmingham B44 9JX   *Tel:* 0121 360 7288
email: frphilipcalvert@aol.com
King's Norton Revd Melusi Sibanda, Vicarage, Edgewood Rd, Rednal, Birmingham B45 8SG
Tel: 0121 453 3347
email: melusi.sibanda@googlemail.com
Moseley Revd Catherine Grylls, 15 Raglan Road, Edgbaston, Birmingham B5 7RA
Tel: 0121 440 1138 (Office)
Tel: 0121 440 2196 (Home)
email: gryllsc@btinternet.com
Shirley Revd Duncan Hill-Brown, 54 Glendon Way, Dorridge, Solihull B93 8SY
Tel: 01564 775652 (Office)
Tel: 01564 772472 (Home)
email: duncan@stphilipsandstjames.org
Warley Revd Ian Shelton, 192 Hanover Road, Rowley Regis B65 9EQ   *Tel:* 0121 559 1251
email: ianshelton232@hotmail.co.uk

DIOCESE OF BLACKBURN

Founded in 1926. Lancashire, except for areas in the east (BRADFORD) and in the south (LIVERPOOL, MANCHESTER); a few parishes in Wigan.

Population 1,318,000   Area 880 sq m
Full-time Stipendiary Parochial Clergy 168   Benefices 183
Parishes 229   Churches 276
www.blackburn.anglican.org
Overseas link dioceses: Free State (South Africa),
Braunschweig (Germany) (Evangelical Lutheran Landeskirche).

BISHOP (8th)
Rt Revd Julian Henderson, Bishop's House, Ribchester Rd, Clayton-le-Dale, Blackburn BB1 9EF   *Tel:* 01254 248234
Fax: 01254 246668
email: bishop@bishopofblackburn.org.uk
Domestic Chaplain Revd Toby Webber, Bishop's House
email: chaplain@bishopofblackburn.org.uk
Bishop's Secretary Mrs Sue Taylor, Bishop's House
email: secretary@bishopofblackburn.org.uk
Assistant Secretary Miss Jill Wall, Bishop's House
email: asstsecretary@bishopofblackburn.org.uk

SUFFRAGAN BISHOPS
LANCASTER Rt Revd Geoffrey S. Pearson, Shireshead Vicarage, Whinney Brow, Forton, Preston PR3 0AE [2006]   *Tel:* 01524 799900
Fax: 01524 799901
email: bishoplancaster@gmail.com
BURNLEY Vacancy

HONORARY ASSISTANT BISHOP
Rt Revd Cyril Ashton, Charis, 17c Quernmore Road, Lancaster LA1 3EB   *Tel:* 01524 848684

CATHEDRAL CHURCH OF ST MARY THE VIRGIN
Dean Very Revd Christopher Armstrong, The Deanery, Preston New Rd, Blackburn BB2 6PS [2001]   *Tel:* 01254 52502 (Home)
email: dean@blackburncathedral.co.uk.
Cathedral Office Cathedral Close, Blackburn BB1 5AA   *Tel:* 01254 503090 (Office)
Fax: 01254 689666
email: cathedral@blackburncathedral.co.uk.
Canons Residentiary
Sacrist Revd Canon Andrew Hindley, 22 Billinge Ave, Blackburn BB2 6SD [1996]
Tel: 01254 261152 (Home)
01254 503099 (Office)
*email:*andrew.hindley@blackburncathedral.co.uk.
Chancellor Revd Canon Dr Ian Stockton, St Francis Vicarage, 1, St Francis Road, Blackburn BB2 2TZ [2011]   *Tel:* 01254 200720 (Home)
01254 503 090 (Office)
email: ian.stockton@blackburncathedral.co.uk

Community Canon Revd Canon Dr Shannon Ledbetter, 20 Buncer Lane, Blackburn BB2 2SE [2011]   *Tel:* 01254 503090 (Office)
email:
shannon.ledbetter@blackburncathedral.co.uk
Diocesan Directory of Ministry Revd Canon Dr Susan Penfold, The Vicarage, Church Lane, Great Harwood BB6 7PU [2008]
Tel: 01254 884039 (Home)
01254 503090 ext. 245 (Office)
email: sue.penfold@blackburn.anglican.org
Honorary Administrator Mr Maurice Maguire, Cathedral Office   *Tel:* 01254 503090
email:
maurice.maguire@blackburncathedral.co.uk
Director of Music Mr Samuel Hudson, Cathedral Office
Tel: 01254 503090 ext. 251 (Office)
email: samuel.hudson@blackburncathedral.co.uk

ARCHDEACONS
BLACKBURN Ven John Hawley, 19 Clarence Park, Blackburn BB2 7FA [2002]   *Tel:* 01254 262571
Fax: 01254 263394
email: john.hawley@blackburn.anglican.org
LANCASTER Ven Michael Everitt, 6 Eton Park, Fulwood, Preston PR2 9NL   *Tel:* 01772 700337
email: michael.everitt@blackburn.anglican.org

CONVOCATION (MEMBERS OF THE HOUSE OF CLERGY OF THE GENERAL SYNOD)
Proctors for Clergy
Revd Canon Dr Susan Penfold
Revd Paul Benfield
Revd Canon Dr Simon Cox
Ven Michael Everitt

MEMBERS OF THE HOUSE OF LAITY OF THE GENERAL SYNOD
Mrs Rosemary Lyon
Mr Gerald Burrows
Mrs Susan Witts
Mrs Vivienne Goddard
Mrs Alison Wynne
Canon Mike Chew

DIOCESAN OFFICERS

Dioc Secretary Canon Graeme Pollard, Church House, Cathedral Close, Blackburn BB1 5AA
Tel: 01254 503070
Fax: 01254 693052
email: graeme.pollard@blackburn.anglican.org
Chancellor of Diocese His Honour Judge John Bullimore, Rectory, 5 Snowgate Head, Norn Lane, New Mill Nr Huddersfield HD9 7HD
Tel: 01484 521025
Registrar of Diocese and Bishop's Legal Secretary Mr Stephen Crossley, Napthens LLP, Greenbank Court, Challenge Way, Greenbank Business Park, Blackburn BB1 5QB *Tel:* 01254 686245
email: registry@napthens.co.uk

DIOCESAN ORGANIZATIONS

Diocesan Office Church House, Cathedral Close, Blackburn BB1 5AA *Tel:* 01254 503070
Fax: 01254 693052
email: diocese@blackburn.anglican.org

ADMINISTRATION

Dioc Synod (*Chairman, House of Clergy*) Revd Canon John Hall, The Vicarage, 49 Mount Road, Fleetwood FY7 6QZ *email:* johnbloem@aol.com (*Chairman, House of Laity*) Mr Jeff Warburton, 6 Chapel Street, Longridge, Preston PR3 3JH
email: jeffpne@aol.com
(*Secretary*) Canon Graeme Pollard, Church House (*as above*)
Board of Finance (*Chairman*) Canon John Dell, 66 Moseley Rd, Burnley BB11 2RF
(*Secretary*) Canon Graeme Pollard (*as above*)
Property Committee (*Chairman*) Revd Canon Andrew Sage; (*Secretary*) Canon Graeme Pollard (*as above*)
Mission and Pastoral Committee Canon Graeme Pollard (*as above*)
Designated Officer Mr Stephen Crossley (*as above*)

CHURCHES

Advisory Committee for the Care of Churches (*Chairman*) Mr John Tillotson, Bonds Farm, Horns Lane, Goosnargh, Preston PR3 2NE
Tel: 01772 783436
(*Secretary*) Canon Graeme Pollard (*as above*)

EDUCATION

Board of Education (*Director*) Vacancy, Church House
email: paul.lock@blackburn.anglican.org
Schools' Adviser Miss Lisa Fenton, Church House
email: lisa.fenton@blackburn.anglican.org
Diocesan Youth Officer Miss Kat Witham, Church House
email: kat.witham@blackburn.anglican.org
Children's Work Adviser Mrs Susan Witts, Church House
email: susan.witts@blackburn.anglican.org

DISCIPLESHIP AND MINISTRY

Director of Ordinands Revd Dr John Darch, 24 Bosburn Drive, Mellor Brook, Blackburn BB2 7PA *Tel:* 01254 813544
Director of Ministry Revd Canon Dr Susan Penfold, Unit 250, Glenfield Park Business Centre, Blakewater Road, Blackburn BB1 5QH *Tel:* 01254 658910
email: sue.penfold@blackburn.anglican.org
Director of IME 1–4 Revd Dr John Darch (*as above*)
Adviser in Women's Ministry Revd Canon Fleur Green, The Rectory, 2 St Peter's Close, Darwen BB3 2EA *Tel:* 01254 702411
email: chauntry1@live.co.uk
Mothers' Union Mrs Beverley Laycock, St Stephen's Vicarage, 154 Todmorden Road, Burnley BB11 3ER *Tel:* 01282 424733
Lay Ministry Development Officer Mrs Mandy Stanton, Unit 250 Glenfield Park Business Centre, Blakewater Road, Blackburn BB1 5AH
Tel: 01254 658910

LITURGICAL

Chairman Very Revd Christopher Armstrong (*as above*)
Secretary Revd Michael Gisbourne, St Thomas' Vicarage, Church St, Garstang, Preston PR3 1PA
Tel: 01995 602162
email: michael.gisbourne@phonecoop.coop

ECUMENICAL

Ecumenical Officer Revd Mike Hartley, Vicarage, Church Rd, Warton, Preston PR4 1BD
Tel: 01772 632227
email: blackburndeo@googlemail.com

PRESS AND PUBLICATIONS

Dioc Communications Manager Mr Ronnie Semley, Church House *Tel:* 01254 503070
email: ronnie.semley@blackburn.anglican.org

DIOCESAN RECORD OFFICES

Diocesan Registry, Napthens LLP
Tel: 01254 686244
Lancashire Record Office, Bow Lane, Preston PR1 8ND *Tel:* 01772 254868

PARISH MISSION SUPPORT

Department Leader Revd David Banbury, Unit 250, Glenfield Business Park, Blakewater Road, Blackburn BB1 5AH *Tel:* 01254 658910
email: david.banbury@blackburn.anglican.org
Social Responsibility Lead Officer Revd Canon Ed Saville Unit 250, Glenfield Business Park, Blakewater Road, Blackburn BB1 5AH *Tel:* 01254 658910
email: ed.saville@blackburn.anglican.org
Parish Development Officer Revd Tim Horobin, The Vicarage, Stopes Brow, Lower Darwen BB3 0QP *Tel:* 01254 53898
email: timhorobin@aol.com

Rural and Environmental Officer Revd Chris Halliwell, Starch Hall Farm, Gallows Lane, Ribchester, Preston PR3 3XX   *Tel:* 01772 653283
    email: chris.halliwell@blackburn.anglican.org
Urban Areas Officer The Archdeacon of Blackburn (*as above*)

AREA DEANS
ARCHDEACONRY OF BLACKBURN
Accrington Revd John Holland, The Vicarage, 29 Mayfield Avenue, Oswaldtwistle BB5 3AA
    Tel: 01254 231038
Blackburn with Darwen Revd Canon Andrew Raynes, Christ Church with St Matthew's Vicarage, Brandy House Brow, Blackburn BB2 3EY   *Tel:* 01254 56292
    email: andrewraynes@btopenworld.com
Burnley Revd Mark Jones, Vicarage, 1 Arbory Drive, Padiham, Burnley BB12 8JS
    Tel: 01282 772442
    email: jones.padiham@btinternet.co.uk
Chorley Revd Tim Wilby, St George's Vicarage, Letchworth Place, Chorley PR7 2HJ
    Tel: 01257 263064
    email: stgeorgeschorley@aol.com
Leyland Revd Alistair McHaffie, St John's Vicarage, Leyland Lane, Leyland PR25 1XB
    Tel: 01772 621646
    email: alistair@mchaffie.com
Pendle Revd Canon Ed Saville, Unit 250, Glenfield Park Business Centre, Blakewater Road, Blackburn BB1 5AH   *Tel:* 01254 658910

Whalley Revd Michael Woods, The Vicarage, Somerset Road, Rishton, Blackburn BB1 4BP
    Tel: 01254 886191
    email: mwoods4@supanet.com

ARCHDEACONRY OF LANCASTER
Blackpool Revd Canon Dr Simon Cox, All Hallows Rectory, 86 All Hallows Rd, Bispham, Blackpool FY2 0AY   *Tel:* 01253 351886
    email: drsjcox@yahoo.co.uk
Garstang Revd Andrew Wilkinson, Vicarage, Vicarage Lane, Churchtown, Garstang, Preston PR3 0HW   *Tel and Fax:* 01995 602294
    email: a.wilkinson703@btinternet.com
Kirkham Revd Ann Wood, 3 Winston Avenue, Lytham St Annes FY8 3NS   *Tel:* 01253 788199
    email: ann.wood6@btopenworld.com
Lancaster and Morecambe Revd Linda Macluskie, St John's Vicarage, 2 St John's Avenue, Heysham, Morecambe LA3 1EU   *Tel:* 01253 411039
    email: lindamacluskie55@gmail.com
Poulton Revd Martin Keighley, Vicarage, 7 Vicarage Rd, Poulton-le-Fylde FY6 3NA
    Tel: 01253 883086
    email: martinkeighley@btconnect.com
Preston Revd Canon Timothy Lipscomb, Rectory, 13 Ribblesdale Place, Preston PR1 3NA
    Tel: 01772 252528
    email: lavish@ermine2.fsnet.co.uk
Tunstall Revd Damian Porter, St Oswald's Vicarage, Warton, Carnforth LA5 9PG
    Tel: 01253 732946

DIOCESE OF BRISTOL

Founded in 1542. Bristol; the southern two-thirds of South Gloucestershire; the northern quarter of Wiltshire, except for two parishes in the north (GLOUCESTER); Swindon, except for a few parishes in the north (GLOUCESTER) and in the south (SALISBURY); a few parishes in Gloucestershire.

Population 979,000   Area 470 sq m
Full-time Stipendiary Parochial Clergy 105   Benefices 111
Parishes 164   Churches 205
www.bristol.anglican.org
Overseas link province: Uganda.

BISHOP (55th)
Rt Revd Michael Hill, 58a High Street, Winterbourne, Bristol BS36 1JQ [2003] *Tel:* 01454 777728
Fax: 01454 777814
email: bishop@bristoldiocese.org

SUFFRAGAN BISHOP
SWINDON Rt Revd Dr Lee Rayfield, Mark House, Field Rise, Swindon SN1 4HP [2005]
Tel: 01793 538654
Fax: 01793 525181
email: bishop.swindon@bristoldiocese.org

CATHEDRAL CHURCH OF THE HOLY AND UNDIVIDED TRINITY
Dean Very Revd Dr David Michael Hoyle, The Deanery, 20 Charlotte Street, Bristol BS1 5PZ [2010] *Tel:* 0117 926 2443
email: dean@bristol-cathedral.co.uk
Cathedral Office Bristol Cathedral, Abbey Gatehouse, College Green, Bristol BS1 5TJ
Tel: 0117 926 4879
Fax: 0117 925 3678
email: dean@bristol-cathedral.co.uk
Canons Residentiary
Canon Precentor Canon Nicola Stanley, 55 Salisbury Road, Bristol BS6 7AS [2014] *Tel:* 0117 926 4879
email: canon.precentor@bristol-cathedral.co.uk
Canon Pastor Canon Robert Bull, 41 Salisbury Road, Bristol BS6 7AR [2011] *Tel:* 0117 909 8910
email: canon.pastor@
bristol-cathedral.co.uk
Capitular Canons
Canon Jon Cannon, Canon John Savage, Canon Sue Topalian
Chapter Clerk Miss Wendy Matthews, Cathedral Office *Tel:* 0117 946 8172
email: wendy.matthews@bristol-cathedral.co.uk
Cathedral Organist Mr Mark Lee, Cathedral Office
Tel: 0117 946 8177
email: organist@bristol-cathedral.co.uk

ARCHDEACONS
MALMESBURY AND ACTING BRISTOL Ven Christine Froude, Diocesan Office, 1st Floor, Hillside House, 1500 Parkway North, Newbrick Road, Stoke Gifford, Bristol BS34 8YU [2011] *Tel:* 0117 906 0100
email: christine.froude@bristoldiocese.org

CONVOCATION (MEMBERS OF THE HOUSE OF CLERGY OF THE GENERAL SYNOD)
Proctors for Clergy
Revd Christopher Dobson
Revd Dr Emma Ineson
Revd Canon Mark Pilgrim

MEMBERS OF THE HOUSE OF LAITY OF THE GENERAL SYNOD
Prof Glynn Harrison
Ian Yemm
Canon David Froude

DIOCESAN OFFICERS
Diocesan Secretary Mr Oliver Home, Diocesan Office, 1st Floor, Hillside House, 1500 Parkway North, Newbrick Road, Stoke Gifford, Bristol BS34 8YU *Tel:* 0117 906 0100
email: oliver.home@bristoldiocese.org
Chancellor of Diocese Revd Justin Gau, 3 Pump Court, Temple, EC4Y 7AJ *Tel:* 020 7353 0711
Registrar of Diocese and Bishop's Legal Secretary Mr Tim Berry, Harris and Harris, 14 Market Place, Wells BA5 2RE *Tel:* 01749 674747
Fax: 01749 676585
email: tim.berry@harris-harris.co.uk
Joint Registrar of Diocese Mr Roland Callaby, Harris and Harris, 14 Market Place, Wells BA5 2RE *Tel:* 01749 674747
Fax: 01749 676585
email: roland.callaby@harris-harris.co.uk

DIOCESAN ORGANIZATIONS
Diocesan Office 1st Floor, Hillside House, 1500 Parkway North, Newbrick Road, Stoke Gifford, Bristol BS34 8YU *Tel:* 0117 906 0100
email: any.name@bristoldiocese.org

ADMINISTRATION
Diocesan Synod (Chairman, House of Clergy) Revd Canon Raymond Adams
(Chairman, House of Laity) Canon David Froude
Board of Finance (Chairman) Mr Andrew Lucas, c/o Diocesan Office; *(Secretary)* Mr Oliver Home, Diocesan Office

Finance Manager Mr Matthew Hall, Diocesan Office
Mission and Pastoral Committee (*Secretary*) Ms Janey Hiller (*as above*)
Diocesan Electoral Registration Officer Ms Lynette Cox (*as above*)
Designated Officer Mr Tim Berry, Harris and Harris, 14 Market Place, Wells BA5 2RE
Tel: 01749 674747
Fax: 01749 676585
Safeguarding Adviser Ms Leanne Smith
Tel: 01179 060100
Tel: 0844 8920104
email: leanne.smith@bristoldiocese.org

CHURCHES

Advisory Committee for the Care of Churches (*Chairman*) Revd Canon James Wilson, St Gregory's Vicarage, Filton Road, Horfield, Bristol BS7 0PD
Tel: 0117 969 2839
email: revjameswilson@aol.com
(*Secretary*) Mr Tim Berry
(*Asst Secretary*) c/o Harris and Harris, 14 Market Place, Wells BA5 2RE
Tel: 01749 674747
Fax: 01749 676585

EDUCATION

Board of Education (*Director*) Mr John Swainston, Diocesan Office
Tel: 0117 906 0100
email: john.swainston@bristoldiocese.org

DIOCESAN LAY MINISTERS' COUNCIL

Secretary Mrs Sue Farrance, 102 Jersey Avenue, Brislington, Bristol, BS4 4QZ
Tel: 0117 971 1629
email: sue.farrance@blueyonder.co.uk

DIOCESAN ECUMENICAL AND GLOBAL DEVELOPMENT OFFICER

Revd Chris Dobson, Diocesan Office

MINISTRY DEVELOPMENT

Adviser for Ministry Development (*DDO*) Revd Canon Derek Chedzey, Diocesan Office
Adviser for Licensed Ministry (*DDO*) Revd Samantha Rushton, Diocesan Office
Administrators Mrs Rachel Miller, Mrs Brenda Greet, Diocesan Office

STRATEGY SUPPORT

Transition Manager Mr George Rendell, Diocesan Office

ADVISER FOR MINISTERIAL SUPPORT

Revd Ian Tomkins, Diocesan Office

DEAN OF WOMEN'S MINISTRY

Revd Judith Ashby, 57 Greywethers Avenue, Lakeside, Swindon SN3 1QG
Tel: 01793 978528
email: judith.ashby@tiscali.co.uk

BISHOP'S ADVISORY GROUP ON HEALING

Chairman Mrs Lorraine Izzard, St Edyth's Vicarage, Avonleaze, Lea Mill, Bristol BS9 2HU
Tel: 0117 9638 1912
email: lorraineizzard.1@googlemail.com

DIOCESAN WORSHIP AND LITURGY COMMITTEE

Chairman Canon Gill Behenna, 1 Saxon Way, Bradley Stoke, Bristol BS32 9AR
Tel: 01454 202483
email: gillbehenna@me.com

PRESS, PUBLICITY AND PUBLICATIONS

Communications Officer and Press Officer Ms Vanesther Rees
Tel: 0117 906 0100
email: vanesther.rees@bristoldiocese.org
Editor of Diocesan Directory Ms Lynette Cox, Diocesan Office

DIOCESAN RECORD OFFICES

Bristol Record Office, 'B' Bond, Smeaton Road, Bristol BS1 6XN *County Archivist* Mr J. S. Williams, *Tel:* 0117 922 4224 (*For parish records in the archdeaconry of Bristol*)
Wiltshire and Swindon History Centre, Cocklebury Road, Chippenham SN15 3QN *County Archivist* Mr John Darcy, *Tel:* 01249 705500 (*For parish records in the archdeaconry of Malmesbury*)

DIOCESAN RESOURCE CENTRE

All Saints Centre, 1 All Saints Court, Bristol BS1 1JN
Tel: 0117 917 5587
And Diocesan Office
email: allsaints@bristoldiocese.org

AREA DEANS
ARCHDEACONRY OF BRISTOL

Bristol South Canon Gwyn Owen, Vicarage, Goslet Road, Stockwood, Bristol BS14 8SP
Tel: 01275 831138
email: christtheservant@blueyonder.co.uk
Bristol West Canon Mark Pilgrim, St Peter's Vicarage, 17 The Drive, Henleaze, Bristol BS9 4LD
Tel: 0117 962 0636
email: markpilgrimis@aol.com
City Revd Rod Symmons, Redland Vicarage, Redland Church Hall, Redland Green Road, Bristol BS6 7HE
Tel: 0117 916 4691
email: rod@redland.org.uk

ARCHDEACONRY OF MALMESBURY

Chippenham Revd Samantha Rushton, 33 Fallowfield Close, Chippenham, Wiltshire SN14 6YA
Tel: 01249 660451
email: sam.rushton@bristoldiocese.org
Kingswood and South Gloucestershire Revd Simon Jones, 119 North Road, Stoke Gifford, Bristol BS34 8PE
Tel: 0117 979 1656
email: simon@st-michaels.org
North Wiltshire Revd Neill Archer, Abbey Vicarage, Holloway, Malmesbury SN16 9BA
Tel: 01666 823126
email: neill@malmesburyabbey.com
Swindon Revd Simon Stevenette, The Vicarage, 26 Cricklade Street, Swindon SN1 3HG
Tel: 01793 529166
email: simonstevenette@tiscali.co.uk

DIOCESE OF CANTERBURY

Founded in 597. Kent east of the Medway, excluding the Medway Towns (ROCHESTER).

Population 923,000   Area 970 sq m
Full-time Stipendiary Parochial Clergy 132   Benefices 139
Parishes 253   Churches 328
www.canterburydiocese.org
Overseas link dioceses: Antananarivo, Antsiranana,
Toamasina, Mahajanga (Madagascar), Arras (Pas-de-Calais), Basel.

ARCHBISHOP (105th)
Most Revd and Rt Hon Justin Portal Welby, *Primate of all England and Metropolitan,* Lambeth Palace, London SE1 7JU *Tel:* 020 7898 1200; *Fax:* 020 7261 9836 and Old Palace, Canterbury, Kent CT1 2EE *Tel:* 01227 459382
[Justin Cantuar:]
Dioc Chaplain Revd Julia Pickles

Matters relating to the Diocese of Canterbury should be referred to the **Bishop of Dover** *(see below)*
For the **Archbishop of Canterbury's Personal Staff** *see page 4*

BISHOP OF DOVER
Rt Revd Trevor Willmott, Old Palace, Canterbury, Kent CT1 2EE, *Tel:* 01227 459382, *Fax:* 01227 784985
PA Mrs Anne Neal *(same address, tel and fax nos)*
PA Mrs Sue Bowles *(same address, tel and fax nos)*
Chaplain Revd Julia Pickles, Old Palace, Canterbury, Kent CT1 2EE, *Tel:* 01227 459382, *Fax:* 01227 784985
Hon Chaplains Canon Alan Duke, Roundways, Derringstone Hill, Barham, Canterbury CT4 6QD, *Tel:* 01227 831812, *email:* mail@alanaduke.com
Canon Roger Martin, 'Kwetu', 23 Tanners Hill Gardens, Hythe CT21 5HY   *Tel:* 01303 237204, *email:* rogmartin@btinternet.com
Ven John Barton, 7 The Spires, Canterbury CT2 8SD   *Tel:* 01227 379688
email: johnbarton@greenbee.net

PROVINCIAL EPISCOPAL VISITORS
EBBSFLEET Rt Revd Jonathan Goodall, Hill House, The Mount, Caversham, Reading RG4 7RE
Tel: 01865 288030
email: office@ebbsfleet.org.uk
RICHBOROUGH Rt Revd Norman Banks, Parkside House, Abbey Mill Lane, St Albans AL3 4HE
Tel: 01727 836358
email: bishop@richborough.org.uk

HONORARY ASSISTANT BISHOPS
Rt Revd Michael Gear, 10 Acott Fields, Yalding, Maidstone ME18 6DQ   *Tel:* 01622 817388
email: bp_mikegear@yahoo.com

Rt Revd Richard Llewellin, 15a The Precincts, Canterbury CT1 2EL   *Tel:* 01227 764645
email: rllewellin@clara.co.uk
Rt Revd Anthony Michael Turnbull, 67 Strand St, Sandwich CT13 9HN   *Tel:* 01304 611389
email: amichaelturnbull@yahoo.co.uk

CATHEDRAL AND METROPOLITICAL CHURCH OF CHRIST
Dean Very Revd Dr Robert Willis, The Deanery, The Precincts, Canterbury CT1 2EP [2001]
Tel: 01227 865200 (Office)
email: dean@canterbury-cathedral.org
Cathedral Office Cathedral House, 11 The Precincts, Canterbury CT1 2EH
Tel: 01227 762862
Fax: 01227 865222
Canons Residentiary
Canon Treasurer Revd Canon Nicholas Papadopulos, 15 The Precincts, Canterbury CT1 2EL [2013]   *Tel:* 01227 865233
email:
nick.papadopulos@canterbury-cathedral.org
Canon Librarian Canon Christopher Irvine, 19 The Precincts, Canterbury CT1 2EP [2007]
Tel: 01227 865226
email:
christopher.irvine@canterbury-cathedral.org
Canon Pastor Canon Clare Edwards, 22 The Precincts, Canterbury CT1 2EP [2004]
Tel: 01227 865227
email: canonclare@canterbury-cathedral.org
Archdeacon Ven Sheila Watson, 29 The Precincts, Canterbury CT1 2EP [2007]   *Tel:* 01227 865238
Fax: 01227 785209
email: archdeacon@canterbury-cathedral.org
Precentor and Sacrist Revd Matthew Rushton, 5 The Precincts, Canterbury CT1 2EE
Tel: 01227 876225
email: matthew.rushton@
canterbury-cathedral.org
Receiver General Brigadier M. J. Meardon, Cathedral House   *Tel:* 01227 865212
email: john.meardon@canterbury-cathedral.org
Cathedral organist Dr David Flood, 6 The Precincts, Canterbury CT1 2EE   *Tel:* 01227 865242
email: david.flood@canterbury-cathedral.org

ARCHDEACONS

CANTERBURY Ven Sheila Watson, 29 The Precincts, Canterbury CT1 2EP [2007]   *Tel:* 01227 865238
Fax: 01227 785209
email: archdeacon@canterbury-cathedral.org
MAIDSTONE Ven Stephen Taylor, The Archdeaconry, 4 Redcliffe Lane, Penenden Heath, Maidstone ME14 2AG [2011]   *Tel:* 01622 200221
email: staylor@archdeaconmaid.org
ASHFORD Ven Philip Down, The Archdeaconry, Pett Lane, Charing, Ashford TN27 0DL [2011]
Tel and fax: 01233 712649
email: pdown@archdeacashford.org

CONVOCATION (MEMBERS OF THE HOUSE OF CLERGY OF THE GENERAL SYNOD)

Dignitaries in Convocation
The Dean of Canterbury
Proctors for Clergy
Revd Canon Clare Edwards
Ven Philip Down
Canon Mark Roberts

MEMBERS OF THE HOUSE OF LAITY OF THE GENERAL SYNOD

Mr David Kemp
Ms Sally Muggeridge
Mrs Caroline Spencer

DIOCESAN OFFICERS

Diocesan House, Lady Wootton's Green, Canterbury CT1 1NQ   *Tel:* 01227 459401
Fax: 01227 450964
Please note that individual Diocesan Officers may be emailed on initialsurname@diocant.org (e.g. jhills@diocant.org)
Dioc Secretary Mr Julian Hills   *Fax:* 01227 787073
email: jhills@diocant.org
Commissary General Miss Morag Ellis QC c/o The Registry, Minerva House, 5 Montague Close, London SE1 9BB   *Tel:* 020 7593 5000
Dioc Registrar and Legal Adviser to the Diocese Mr Owen Carew-Jones, Minerva House, 5 Montague Close, London SE1 9BB
Tel: 020 7593 5110

DIOCESAN ORGANIZATIONS

Diocesan House, Lady Wootton's Green, Canterbury CT1 1NQ   *Tel:* 01227 459401
Fax: 01227 450964
email: reception@diocant.org

ADMINISTRATION (RESOURCE MANAGEMENT AND COMPLIANCE)

Dioc Synod (Chairman, House of Clergy) Vacancy
(Chairman, House of Laity) Mr Andrew Collie, Colwood, Canterbury Road, Lyminge, Folkestone CT18 8HU   *Tel:* 01303 863276
email: andrew@colliefamily.plus.com
(Secretary) Mr Julian Hills, Dioc House

Board of Finance (Chairman) Mr Raymond Harris
(Secretary) Mr Julian Hills *(as above)*
Designated Officer Tbc
Director of Finance Mr Mark Spraggins, Dioc House
HR Adviser Miss Sarah Carruthers, Dioc House
Director of Property Services Mr Philip Bell, Old Palace, The Precincts, Canterbury CT1 2EE
Tel: 01227 478390
email: pbell@diocant.org

COMMUNICATONS

Communications Director and Deputy Diocesan Secretary Mrs Emily Shepherd, Dioc House
IT Manager Mark Binns, Dioc House
Editor of Diocesan Directory Online Marilyn Shrimpton, Dioc House

CHURCHES

Diocesan Advisory Committee for the Care of Churches (Secretary) Mr Ian Dodd, Old Palace, The Precincts, Canterbury CT1 2EE
Tel: 01227 478390
email: idodd@diocant.org
Chairman Dr Richard Morrice, 3 Stafford Rd, Tunbridge Wells TN25 4QZ

CHILDREN, SCHOOLS AND YOUNG PEOPLE
(including the Board of Education)

Chairman Mr Alasdair Hogarth
Director of Education Quentin Roper, Dioc House
Assistant Director of Education (School Effectiveness) Vacancy, Dioc House
Assistant Director of Education (Schools Organisation) Revd Simon Foulkes, Dioc House
Children and Young People's (ChYPs) Ministry Adviser Mr Murray Wilkinson, Dioc House

LICENSED MINISTRY

Chair Mrs Caroline Spencer, Little Eggarton, Godmersham, Canterbury CT4 7DY
Director of Ordinands Reverend Joss Walker, Dioc House
Assistant Directors of Ordinands
Revd Ben Jones   *Tel:* 01303 771637
email: benmarkjones@hotmail.com
Revd Marian Bond   *Tel:* 01622 858251
email: mnhbond@googlemail.com
Revd Philip Brown   *Tel:* 01227 730141
email: filbrown@btinternet.com
Revd Sheila Cox   *Tel:* 01233 501193
email: sheila.m.cox@btopenworld.com
Revd Richard King   *Tel:* 01233 623334
email: richarddking@hotmail.com
Revd Cathy Sigrist   *Tel:* 01304 37395
email: catherine.sigrist@btinternet.com
Ministry Development Officer Mr Neville Emslie, Dioc House
Association of Readers (Wardens) Revd Donald Lawton and Mr Nigel Collins, Dioc House
(Hon Secretary) Mr Nigel Collins, 79 Alfred Rd, Dover CT16 2AD   *Tel:* 01304 204737
email: nigelcollins@cross-links.org.uk

Clergy Retirement and Registration Officers
Ashford Archdeaconry, Canon Gilbert Spencer
Tel: 01233 501774
email: gilbert_spencer@hotmail.com
Canterbury Archdeaconery, Revd Grahame Whittlesea *Tel:* 01227 472536
email: gandawhittlesea@tiscali.co.uk
Maidstone Archdeaconery, Revd Ron Gamble
email: r-gamble@sky.com

LOCAL CHURCH DEVELOPMENT

Chairman Revd Canon Andrew Sewell
Tel: 01622 691926
email: andrew@asewell.plus.com
Mission and Growth Adviser Canon Kerry Thorpe, Dioc House
Mission and Ministry Executive Officer Mrs Emma Sivyer, Dioc House
Local Ministries and Growth Advisor Revd Peter Ingrams, Dioc House
Children's Missioner Captain Graham Nunn, CA
Tel: 01622 672088
email: gnunn@diocant.org
Stewardship Adviser Ms Liz Mullins, Dioc House
Part-time Stewardship Adviser Mrs Jenny Hunt, Dioc House

COMMUNITY AND PARTNERSHIPS

Chairman Amanda Cottrell OBE
Tel: 01580 240973
email: benendenparishmagazine@gmail.com
Community and Partnership Exec Officer and Rural Life Adviser Canon Caroline Pinchbeck, Dioc House

DIOCESAN RECORD OFFICES

Cathedral Archives and Library, The Precincts, Canterbury CT1 2EH (*For parish records in the archdeaconry of Canterbury*) *Tel:* 01227 865330
Kent History Services, Kent History and Library Centre, James Whatman Way, Maidstone ME14 1LQ (*For parish records in the archdeaconries of Maidstone and Ashford*) *Tel:* 08458 247200
email: historyandlibrarycentre@kent.gov.uk

AREA DEANS
ARCHDEACONRY OF ASHFORD

Ashford Canon Timothy Wilson, The Rectory, Great Chart, Ashford, TN23 3AY
Tel: 01233 620371
email: tandcwilson@lineone.net
Dover Revd Sue White, The Vicarage, 20 Alexandra Road, Capel le Ferne, Folkestone CT18 7LD *Tel:* 01304 240539
email: suewhite712@hotmail.com
Elham Revd David Adlington, St Peter's Vicarage, North Street, Folkestone CT19 6AL
Tel: 01303 254472
email: david.adlingto@btinternet.com

Romney and Tenterden Revd Canon Lindsay Hammond, The Vicarage, Church Road, Tenterden TN30 6AT *Tel:* 01580 761591
email: lindsay57@uwclub.net
Sandwich Revd Seth Cooper, Elizabeth House, 32 St Marys Road, Walmer CT14 7QA *Tel:* 01304 375340
email: sethandjen@tinyworld.co.uk

ARCHDEACONRY OF CANTERBURY

Canterbury Revd Barney De Berry, 57 Nunnery Fields, Canterbury CT1 3JN *Tel:* 01227 453777
email: barney.deberry@smb.org.uk
East Bridge Revd Stephen Hardy, The Rectory, The Street, Barham, Canterbury CT4 6PA
Tel: 01227 831340
email: stephenhardy1@mac.com
Reculver Revd Elaine Richardson, The New Vicarage, Herne Street, Herne CT6 7HE
Tel: 01227 370256
email: elaine.longview@virgin.net
Reculver Revd Canon Steve Coneys, The Vicarage, 11 Kimberley Grove, Seasalter, Whitstable CT5 4AY *Tel:* 01227 276795
email: steveconeys@btinternet.com
Thanet Revd Paul Worledge, St Luke's Vicarage, St Luke's Avenue, Ramsgate CT11 7JX
Tel: 01843 592562
email: adthanet@btinternet.com
West Bridge Revd Dr Paul Ratcliff, The Vicarage, 3 Hambrook Close, Chilham CT4 8EJ
Tel: 01227 738720
email: pr.ratcliff@googlemail.com

ARCHDEACONRY OF MAIDSTONE

Maidstone Revd Andrew Sewell, St Paul's Vicarage, 130 Boxley Road, Maidstone ME14 2AH
Tel: 01622 691926
email: andrew@asewell@plus.com
North Downs Revd Steve Hughes, 4 Kingsacre, Downs Wood, Maidstone ME15 8UP
Tel: 01622 862793
email: steven.hughes24@btinternet.com
Ospringe Revd Steve Lillicrap, The Vicarage, 76 Station Road, Teynham ME9 9SN
Tel: 01795 522510
email: steve.lillicrap@btopenworld.com
Sittingbourne Revd John Lewis, Vicarage, School Lane, Borden, Sittingbourne ME9 8JS
Tel: 01795 472986
email: fr.johnlewis@tiscali.co.uk
The Weald Revd Ali Duguid, The Vicarage, High Street, Marden, Tonbridge TN12 9DR
Tel: 01622 831379
email: ali@dogooders.co.uk

BISHOP (67th)

Rt Revd James Newcome, Bishop's House,
Ambleside Road, Keswick, CA12 4DD[2009]
Tel: 01768 773430
email: bishop.carlisle@carlislediocese.org.uk
[James Carliol]
Bishop's Chaplain and Chief of Staff Ven George
Howe, Bishop's House (*as above*)
Tel: 01768 773430 (office)
01768 779168 (home)
email: george.howe@carlislediocese.org.uk

SUFFRAGAN BISHOP

PENRITH Rt Revd Robert Freeman, Holm Croft,
13 Castle Road, Kendal LA9 7AU [2011]
Tel: 01539 727836
email: bishop.penrith@carlislediocese.org.uk

HONORARY ASSISTANT BISHOPS

Rt Revd Ian Macdonald Griggs, Rookings,
Patterdale, Penrith CA11 0NP [1994]
Tel: 01768 482064
email: ian.griggs@virgin.net
Rt Revd George Lanyon Hacker, Keld House,
Milburn, Penrith CA10 1TW [1994]
Tel: 01768 361506
email: bishhack@mypostoffice.co.uk
Rt Revd Andrew Alexander Kenny Graham, Fell
End, Butterwick, Penrith CA10 2QQ [1997]
Tel: 01931 713147
Rt Revd Hewlett Thompson, Low Broomrigg,
Warcop, Appleby CA16 6PT [2000]
Tel: 01768 341281
Rt Revd Robert Hardy, Carleton House, Back
Lane, Langwathby, Penrith CA10 1NB [2002]
Tel: 01768 881210
Rt Revd John Richardson, The Old Rectory,
Bewcastle, Carlisle CA6 6PS [2003]
Tel: 01697 748389
Rt Revd Richard Henderson, Tralispean,
Skibbereen, Co Cork, Republic of Ireland [2011]
Rt Revd Nigel McCulloch, Stonelea, 1 Head's
Drive, Grange over Sands LA11 7DY [2013]
Tel: 01539 536018

CATHEDRAL CHURCH OF THE HOLY AND UNDIVIDED TRINITY

Dean Very Revd Mark Christopher Boyling, The
Deanery, Carlisle CA3 8TZ [2004]
Tel: 01228 523335
Fax: 01228 547049
email: dean@carlislecathedral.org.uk
Cathedral Office 7 The Abbey, Carlisle CA3 8TZ
Tel: 01228 548151
Fax: 01228 547049
email: office@carlislecathedral.org.uk
Web: www.carlislecathedral.org.uk

Canons Residentiary
Revd Canon Jan Elizabeth Kearton, 3 The Abbey,
Carlisle CA3 8TZ [2013]   *Tel:* 01228 521857
email: canonwarden@carlislecathedral.org.uk
Ven Kevin Thomas Roberts, 2 The Abbey, Carlisle,
CA3 8TZ [2009]   *Tel:* 01228 523026
email: archdeacon.north@carlislediocese.org.uk
Revd Canon Michael Alan Manley, 1 The Abbey,
Carlisle CA3 8TZ [2007]   *Tel:* 01228 542790
email: canonmissioner@carlislecathedral.org.uk

Lay Canons
Canon James Westoll, Kirkandrews Tower,
Longtown, Carlisle CA6 5NF [2011]
Canon Alex Barbour, Castlehow Scar, via Shap,
Penrith CA10 3LG [2012]
Canon Bryan Gray, The Chapel, Hunsonby,
Penrith CA10 1PN [2014]
Bursar and Chapter Clerk Mr Ian Burns, Cathedral
Office
Commercial and Administration Co-ordinator Mrs
Wendy Murrell, Cathedral Office
Cathedral Organist Mr Jeremy Suter, 6 The Abbey,
Carlisle CA3 8TZ   *Tel:* 01228 526646
Fax: 01228 547049
email: jeremysuter@hotmail.com

ARCHDEACONS

CARLISLE Ven Kevin Roberts, 2 The Abbey,
Carlisle CA3 8TZ [2009]   *Tel:* 01228 523026
email: archdeacon.north@carlislediocese.org.uk
WEST CUMBERLAND Ven Richard Pratt, 50 Stainburn Rd, Workington CA14 1SN [2009]
Tel: 01900 66190
email: archdeacon.west@carlislediocese.org.uk

WESTMORLAND AND FURNESS Ven Penny Driver, The Vicarage, Windermere Road, Lindale in Cartmel, Grange over Sands LA11 6LB [2012]
Tel: 015395 34717
email: archdeacon.south@carlislediocese.org.uk

CONVOCATION (MEMBERS OF THE HOUSE OF CLERGY OF THE GENERAL SYNOD)
Proctors for Clergy
Revd Ferial Etherington
Ven George Howe
Canon Nigel Davies
Revd Ruth Crossley

MEMBERS OF THE HOUSE OF LAITY OF THE GENERAL SYNOD
Dr Christopher Angus
Dr Charles Hanson
Mr Geoffrey Hine
Mr David Mills

DIOCESAN OFFICERS
Dioc Secretary Mr Derek Hurton, Church House, West Walls, Carlisle CA3 8UE   *Tel:* 01228 522573
01228 815402 (Direct Line)
Fax: 01228 815400
email: diocesan.secretary@carlislediocese.org.uk
Chancellor of Diocese Mr Geoffrey Tattersall, 2 The Woodlands, Lostock, Bolton BL6 4JD
Registrar of Diocese and Bishop's Legal Secretary Mrs Jane Lowdon, Sintons Solicitors, The Cube, Barrack Rd, Newcastle-upon-Tyne NE4 6DB
Tel: 0191 226 7878
Fax: 0191 226 7852
email: j.lowdon@sintons.co.uk

DIOCESAN ORGANIZATIONS
Diocesan Office Church House, West Walls, Carlisle CA3 8UE   *Tel:* 01228 522573
Fax: 01228 815400
email: enquiries@carlislediocese.org.uk
Web: www.carlislediocese.org.uk

ADMINISTRATION
Dioc Synod (*Chairman, House of Clergy*) Canon Nigel Davies, St Oswald's Vicarage, Burneside, Kendal LA9 6QX   *Tel:* 01539 722015
email: canon.nigel@beaconteam.org.uk
(*Chairman, House of Laity*) Mr Michael Bonner, 1 Fell View, Branthwaite, Workington CA14 4SY
Tel: 01900 605536
email: mimbonner@talktalk.net
(*Secretary*) Mr Derek Hurton, Dioc Office
Board of Finance (*Chairman*) Mr John Lee, Millersholme, Lanercost, Brampton CA8 2HL
Tel: 016977 2515
(*Secretary*) Mr Derek Hurton (*as above*)
Assistant Dioc Secretary (*Finance*) Mr Neil Barrett, Dioc Office   *Tel:* 01228 815404
email: finance@carlislediocese.org.uk

Property Manager Mr Neal Andrews, Dioc Office
Tel: 01228 815403
email: property@carlislediocese.org.uk
Pastoral Committee Mr Derek Hurton, Dioc Office
Tel: 01228 815408
Designated Officer Mrs Jane Lowdon (*as above*)

CHURCHES
Advisory Committee for the Care of Churches (*Chairman*) Miss Lilian Hopkins, Rodford House, 58 Gillinggate, Kendal LA9 4JB (*Secretary*) Mr Derek Hurton, Dioc Office

EDUCATION
Board of Education, Church House, West Walls, Carlisle CA3 8UE   *Tel:* 01228 522573
Fax: 01228 815400
email: education@carlislediocese.org.uk
Director of Education Mr Michael Mill, Dioc Office
email: director.education@carlislediocese.org.uk
Deputy Director of Education Revd Bert Thomas, Dioc Office
email: bert.thomas@carlislediocese.org.uk
Church in Schools Officers Mrs Sarah Hulme and Mrs Emma Richardson, Dioc Office
email: sarah.hulme@carlislediocese.org.uk; emma.richardson@carlislediocese.org.uk

MINISTRY AND TRAINING
Ministry Development Adviser Canon Amiel Osmaston, Dioc Office   *Tel:* 01228 815406
email: ministry.dev@carlislediocese.org.uk
Principal, Lancashire and Cumbria Theological Partnership and Adviser for Ministry and Training Vacancy, Dioc Office
Tel: 01228 815405
email: admin@lctp.co.uk
Adviser for Clergy Training Revd Ruth Crossley, Vicarage, Levens, Kendal LA8 8PY
Tel: 01539 560233
email: cme@carlislediocese.org.uk
Director of Ordinands Ven George Howe, Bishop's House (*as above*)   *Tel:* 01768 773430 (office)
01768 779168 (home)
email: george.howe@carlislediocese.org.uk
Adviser for Women's Ministry Revd Gill Hart, The Vicarage, Church Terrace, Netherton, Maryport CA15 7PS   *Tel:* 01900 819886
email: hart.gill@btopenworld.com

LOCAL LEADERSHIP AND MISSION
ACTION PLANNING
Adviser Canon Tim Montgomery, 10 Gowan Crescent, Kendal LA8 9NF   *Tel:* 07584 684305
email: tim.montgomery@carlislediocese.org.uk

SOCIAL RESPONSIBILITY
Churches Social Action Network Ven Richard Pratt, 50 Stainburn Road, Workington CA14 1SN
Tel: 01900 66190
email: archdeacon.west@carlislediocese.org.uk
Industrial Mission Ven Richard Pratt (*as above*)

ECUMENICAL AFFAIRS

Diocesan Ecumenical Officer Revd David Cooper, The Vicarage, 45 Church Hill, Arnside LA5 0DW *Tel:* 01524 761319
email: revdavidcooper@btinternet.com
Churches Together in Cumbria (Ecumenical Development Officer) Revd Ruth Harvey, Croslands, Beacon Street, Penrith CA11 7TZ
Tel: 07882 259631
email: rctic@phonecoop.coop
Rural Officer Revd Sarah Lunn, Rectory, Long Marton, Appleby in Westmorland CA16 6BN
Tel: 01768 361269
email: sarahlunn@care4free.net

PARTNERSHIP IN WORLD MISSION

Officer Mrs Lynne Tembey, Holm Cultram Vicarage, Abbeytown, Wigton CA7 4SP
Tel: 01697 361246
email: lynnetembey@btinternet.com

ENVIRONMENT ADVISER

Revd Prof Ian James, The Rectory, Main Street, Bootle, Millom LA19 5TH *Tel:* 01229 718223
email: dr.i.n.james@btinternet.com

RETIRED CLERGY AND WIDOWS OFFICER

Rt Revd John Richardson, The Old Rectory, Bewcastle, Carlisle CA6 6PS *Tel:* 016977 48389

PRESS AND PUBLICATIONS

Communications Officer Mr Dave Roberts
Tel: 01228 560079
Mobile: 07984 927434
email: carlisledco@gmail.com
Editor of Dioc News Ven Richard Pratt
Dioc Directory Mrs Jean Hardman, Dioc Office
Tel: 01228 815408
email: jean.hardman@carlislediocese.org.uk

DIOCESAN ARCHIVIST

County Archivist Ms A. Rowe *Tel:* 01228 226477

DIOCESAN RECORD OFFICES

Cumbria Archive Centre, Lady Gillford's House, Petteril Bank Road, Carlisle CA1 3AJ
Tel: 01228 227285
email: carlisle.archives@cumbria.gov.uk
Cumbria Archive Centre, County Offices, Kendal LA9 4RQ *Tel:* 01539 713540
email: kendal.archives@cumbria.gov.uk
Cumbria Archive Centre and Local Studies Centre, 140 Duke St, Barrow-in-Furness LA14 1XW *Tel:* 01229 407377
email: barrow.archives@cumbria.gov.uk

Cumbria Archive Centre and Local Studies Centre, Scotch St, Whitehaven CA28 7NL
Tel: 01946 506420
email: whitehaven.archives@cumbria.gov.uk

RURAL DEANS
ARCHDEACONRY OF CARLISLE

Appleby Revd Stewart Fyfe, The Vicarage, Morland, Penrith CA10 3AX
Tel: 01931 714620
email: stewart.fyfe@btinternet.com
Brampton Revd Rod Allon-Smith, The Vicarage, Lanercost, Brampton CA8 2HQ
Tel: 016977 2478
email: lanercostrod@bigfoot.com
Carlisle Canon Michael Manley, 1 The Abbey, Carlisle CA3 8TZ *Tel:* 01228 542790
email: canonmissioner@carlislecathedral.org.uk
Penrith Revd David Sargent, The Rectory, 3 Lamley Gardens, Graham Street, Penrith CA11 9LR *Tel:* 01768 863000
email: revdave.sargent@talk21.com

ARCHDEACONRY OF WESTMORLAND AND FURNESS

Barrow Revd Gary Cregeen, The Rectory, 98 Roose Road, Barrow in Furness LA13 9RL
Tel: 01229 877367
email: GMCregeen@btinternet.com
Furness Canon Alan Bing, 15 Ford Park Crescent, Ulverston LA12 7JR *Tel:* 01229 584331
email: alanbing@live.co.uk
Kendal Revd Angela Whittaker, The Vicarage, Natland, Kendal LA9 7QQ *Tel:* 01539 560355
email: ang.whitt68@googlemail.com
Windermere Revd James Richards, Rectory, Longlands, Bowness on Windermere LA23 3AS
Tel: 01539 443063
email: rector@stmartin.org.uk

ARCHDEACONRY OF WEST CUMBERLAND

Calder Ven Richard Pratt, 50 Stainburn Road, Workington CA14 1SN *Tel:* 01900 66190
email: archdeacon.west@carlislediocese.org.uk
Derwent Canon Wendy Sanders, 23 Lowscales Drive, Cockermouth CA13 9DR
Tel: 01900 823269
email: revdwes@gmail.com
Solway Canon Bryan Rowe, St Michael's Rectory, Dora Crescent, Workington CA14 2EZ
Tel: 01900 602311
email: bryan.rowe50@yahoo.com

DIOCESE OF CHELMSFORD

Founded in 1914. Essex, except for a few parishes in the north (ELY, ST EDMUNDSBURY AND IPSWICH); five East London boroughs north of the Thames; three parishes in south Cambridgeshire.

Population 3,031,000   Area 1,530 sq m
Full-time Stipendiary Parochial Clergy 354   Benefices 320
Parishes 467   Churches 595
www.chelmsford.anglican.org

Overseas link dioceses: Embu, Kirinyaga, Meru, Mbere and Marsabit (Kenya); Trinidad and Tobago; Karlstad; Iaşi (Romania)

BISHOP
Rt Revd Stephen Cottrell, Bishopscourt, Margaretting, Ingatestone CM4 0HD
Tel: 01277 352001
Fax: 01277 355374
email: bishopscourt@chelmsford.anglican.org
Bishop's Chaplain Chantal Mason (*same address*)
Tel: 01277 352001
Fax: 01277 355374
email: cmason@chelmsford.anglican.org
Director of Communications and Bishop's Press Officer Ralph Meloy   *Tel:* 01245 294424 (Office)
07654 382674 (Pager)
email: rmeloy@chelmsford.anglican.org

AREA BISHOPS
BARKING Rt Revd Peter Hill, Barking Lodge, Verulam Ave, London E17 8ES [2014]
Tel: 020 8509 7377
email: b.barking@chelmsford.anglican.org
BRADWELL Rt Revd John Wraw, Bishop's House, Orsett Rd, Horndon-on-the-Hill SS17 8NS [2012]
Tel: 01375 673806
Fax: 01375 674222
email: b.bradwell@chelmsford.anglican.org
COLCHESTER Rt Revd Roger A. B. Morris, 1 Fitzwalter Road, Lexden, Colchester CO3 3SS [2014]   *Tel:* 01206 576648
email: b.colchester@chelmsford.anglican.org

ASSISTANT BISHOPS
Rt Revd Charles Derek Bond, 52 Horn Brook, Saffron Walden, Essex CB11 3JW
Tel: 01799 521308
email: bondd@aol.com
Rt Revd John Martin Ball, 5 Hillview Rd, Chelmsford CM1 7RS   *Tel:* 01245 268296
email: ball_john@onetel.com

ASSISTANT BISHOP AND PROVINCIAL EPISCOPAL VISITOR
Rt Revd Norman Banks, Parkside House, Abbey Mill Lane, St Albans AL3 4HE
Tel: 01727 836358
email: bishop@richborough.org.uk

CATHEDRAL CHURCH OF ST MARY THE VIRGIN, ST PETER AND ST CEDD
Dean Very Revd Nicholas J. Henshall
Cathedral Office 53 New St, Chelmsford CM1 1TY
Tel: 01245 294489
Fax: 01245 294499
email:
nicholas.henshall@chelmsfordcathedral.org.uk
Web: www.chelmsfordcathedral.org.uk

Canons Residentiary
Vice-Dean Revd Canon Ivor Moody, 4 Bishopscourt Gardens, Springfield, Chelmsford CM2 6AZ   *Tel:* 01245 294493 (Office)
01245 267773 (Home)
email: ivor.moody@chelmsfordcathedral.org.uk

Canon Theologian Revd Canon Edward Carter, 2 Harlings Grove, Chelmsford CM1 1YQ
Tel: 01245 294486
email: edward.carter@chelmsfordcathedral.org.uk

Canon Precentor Revd Canon Simon Pothen, 1a Harlings Grove, Chelmsford CM1 1YQ [2007]
Tel: 01245 491599 (Home)
Tel: 01245 294482 (Office)
email: simon.pothen@chelmsfordcathedral.org.uk

Associate Priest Revd Kate Moore, 33 Church Street, Witham CM8 2JP   *Tel:* 01376 501128
email: kate.moore@chelmsfordcathedral.org.uk

Hon Associate Chaplain and Bishop's Chaplain Revd Chantal Mason, Bishopscourt, Margaretting, Ingatestone CM4 0HD   *Tel:* 01277 352001
Fax: 01277 355374

Hon Associate Chaplain and Diocesan Director of Ordinands Revd Canon Philip Need, The Rectory, 25 The Lintons, Sandon, Chelmsford CM2 7UA   *Tel:* 01245 472212
email: ddo@chelmsford.anglican.org

Administrator Vacancy   *Tel:* 01245 294488
Organist and Master of the Choristers James Davy,
1 Harlings Grove, Chelmsford CM1 1YQ
                              Tel: 01245 252429 (Office)
email: james.davy@chelmsfordcathedral.org.uk
Assistant Organist and Director of Girls' Choir
Laurence Lyndon-Jones
                              Tel: 01245 252429 (Office)
                    email: laurence.lydon-jones@
                              chelmsfordcathedral.org.uk
Youth Minister Tim Leeson
                              Tel: 01245 294483 (Office)
email: tim.leeson@chelmsfordcathedral.org.uk
Corporate Events Manager Julie Brown
                              Tel: 01245 294480 (Office)
email: julie.brown@chelmsfordcathedral.org.uk

ARCHDEACONS
BARKING Ven Dr John Perumbalath, 11 Bridge-
fields Close, Hornchurch RM11 1GQ [2013]
                              Tel: 01708 474951
    email: a.barking@chelmsford.anglican.org
CHELMSFORD Ven David Lowman, The Arch-
deacon's Lodge, 136 Broomfield Road, Chelms-
ford CM1 1RN [2001]   *Tel:* 01245 258257
                              Fax: 01245 250845
    email: a.chelmsford@chelmsford.anglican.org
COLCHESTER Ven Annette Cooper, 63 Powers Hall
End, Witham CM8 1NH [2004]
                              Tel: 01376 513130
                              Fax: 01376 500789
    email: a.colchester@chelmsford.anglican.org
HARLOW Ven Martin Webster, Glebe House,
Church Lane, Sheering CM22 7NR [2009]
                              Tel: 01279 734524
                              Fax: 01279 734426
    email: a.harlow@chelmsford.anglican.org
SOUTHEND Ven Mina Smallman, 459 Rayleigh
Road, Thundersley, Benfleet SS7 3TH
[2013]   *Tel:* 01268 779345
    email: a.southend@chelmsford.anglican.org
STANSTED Ven Robin King, The House, The Street,
Bradwell, Braintree CM77 8EL [2013]
                              Tel: 01376 563357
    email: a.stansted@chelmsford.anglican.org
WEST HAM Ven Elwin Cockett, 86 Aldersbrook Rd,
Manor Park, London E12 5DH [2007]
                              Tel: 020 8989 8557
                              Fax: 020 8530 1311
    email: a.westham@chelmsford.anglican.org

CONVOCATION (MEMBERS OF THE HOUSE OF CLERGY OF THE GENERAL SYNOD)
Proctors for Clergy
Ven Annette Cooper
Revd John Dunnett
Revd Steven Saxby
Revd Canon Martin Wood
Revd Canon David Banting
Revd Canon Jenny Tomlinson

MEMBERS OF THE HOUSE OF LAITY OF THE GENERAL SYNOD
Isabel Adcock
Robert Hammond
Mary Durlacher
Kathleen Playle
David G Llewelyn Morgan
Ruth Whitworth
Robin Stevens

DIOCESAN OFFICERS
Chief Executive and Diocesan Secretary John Ball,
Diocesan Office, 53 New St, Chelmsford
CM1 1AT   *Tel:* 01245 294400
Chancellor of Diocese Chancellor George Pulman
QC, Diocesan Registry, 53 New St, Chelmsford
CM1 1NE   *Tel:* 01245 259470
Registrar of Diocese and Bishop's Legal Secretary
Aiden Hargreaves-Smith, Diocesan Registry, 5
Montague Close, London SE1 9BB
                              Tel: 020 7593 5127
Legal Advisers to the Board of Finance Minerva
House, 5 Montague Close, London SE1 9BB
                              Tel: 020 7593 5000

DIOCESAN ORGANIZATIONS
Diocesan Office 53 New St, Chelmsford CM1 1AT
                              Tel: 01245 294400
                              Fax: 01245 294477
    email: reception@chelmsford.anglican.org

ADMINISTRATION
Dioc Synod (Chairman, House of Clergy) Canon
Martin Wood, *Tel:* 01992 672115; *(Chairman,
House of Laity)* Canon Dr Susan Atkin, *Tel:* 01206
854976; *(Secretary)* John Ball, Dioc Office *Tel:*
01245 294400
Board of Finance (Chairman) Percy Lomax. *Tel:*
01245 462824; *(Company Secretary)* John Ball,
Dioc Office   *Tel:* 01245 294400
          email: jball@chelmsford.anglican.org
Senior Property Manager Richard Smith, Dioc
Office   *Tel:* 01245 294420
Designated Officer Aiden Hargreaves-Smith,
Diocesan Registry, 5 Montague Close, London
SE1 9BB   *Tel:* 020 7593 5127
Mission and Pastoral Committee (Chairman) Rt
Revd Stephen Cottrell, Bishopscourt,
Margaretting, Ingatestone CM4 0HD; *(Secretary)*
Nathan Whitehead, Dioc Office
          email: nwhitehead@chelmsford.anglican.org

CHURCHES
*Advisory Committee for the Care of Churches
(Chairman)* Dr James Bettley, The Old Vicarage,
Church Rd, Maldon CM9 8NP *Tel:* 01612 892450;
(Secretary) Sandra Turner, Dioc Office
          email: sturner@chelmsford.anglican.org
Essex Association of Change Ringers Vicki
Chapman, 20 Mews Court, Chelmsford CM2 9PF
                              Tel: 01245 358040
              email: secretary@eacr.org.uk

SAFEGUARDING

Safeguarding Manager Ian Carter, Dioc Office
Tel: 01245 294490
email: icarter@chelmsford.anglican.org

EDUCATION

Director of Education Tim Elbourne, Dioc Office
Tel: 01245 294440
email: telbourne@chelmsford.anglican.org
Deputy Director of Education Jeff Graham
Tel: 01245 294440
email: jgraham@chelmsford.anglican.org
Early Years Adviser Jo Gilkes, Dioc Office
Tel: 01245 294440
email: jgilkes@chelmsford.anglican.org
School and RE Advisers Ann Bard, Revd Lyn Hillier, Mike Dean, Lallie Godfrey, Ruth Everett, Dioc Office
email: abard@chelmsford.anglican.org
lhillier@chelmsford.anglican.org
mdean@chelmsford.anglican.org
lgodfrey@chelmsford.anglican.org
reverett@chelmsford.anglican.org
Children's Work Adviser Stephen Kersys, Dioc Office   *email:* skersys@chelmsford.anglican.org

MISSION AND MINISTRY

Dioc Director of Ordinands and NSM Officer Revd Canon Philip Need, The Rectory, 25 The Lintons, Sandon, Chelmsford CM2 7UA
Tel: 01245 472212
email: ddo@chelmsford.anglican.org
Dean of Mission and Ministry Revd Canon Dr Roger Matthews, Dioc Office   *Tel:* 01245 294455
email: rmatthews@chelmsford.anglican.org
Lay Development Adviser Revd Elizabeth Jordan, Dioc Office   *Tel:* 01245 294449
email: ejordan@chelmsford.anglican.org
Adviser for Women's Ministry Revd Canon Jenny Tomlinson, 17 Borough Lane, Saffron Waldon CB11 4AG   *Tel:* 01799 500947
Interfaith Adviser Ven Elwin Cockett, 86 Aldersbrook Rd, Manor Park, London E12 5DH
Tel: 020 8989 8557
Fax: 020 8530 1311
email: a.westham@chelmsford.anglican.org

COMMUNICATIONS

Communications Director Ralph Meloy, Dioc Office   *Tel:* 01245 294424
07654 382674 (Pager)
email: rmeloy@chelmsford.anglican.org

OTHER COMMITTEES

Readers' Committee Vacancy, Dioc Office
Tel: 01245 294400
Liturgical Committee (Chairman) Ven Elwin Cockett, 86 Aldersbrook Rd, Manor Park, London E12 5DH   *Tel:* 020 8989 8557
email: a.westham@chelmsford.anglican.org

DIOCESAN RECORD OFFICE

Essex Records Office, Wharf Rd, Chelmsford CM2 6YT   *Tel:* 01245 244644
email: ero.enquiry@essexcc.gov.uk

DIOCESAN HOUSE OF RETREAT

Pleshey, Chelmsford CM3 1HA (*Warden* Revd Sheila Coughtrey)   *Tel:* 01245 237251
Fax: 01245 237594
email: retreathouse.pleshey@virgin.net
Web: www.retreathousepleshey.com

RURAL DEANS
ARCHDEACONRY OF BARKING

Barking and Dagenham Revd Julie Fleming, The Vicarage, 191 Valence Wood Road, Dagenham RM8 3AH   *Tel:* 020 8592 2822
email: juliestmary@gmail.com
Havering Revd David Hague, The Good Shepherd Vicarage, 97 Collier Row Lane, Collier Row, Romford RM5 3BA   *Tel:* 01708 753395
email: vicargs@thegoodshepherd.co.uk

ARCHDEACONRY OF WEST HAM

Newham Revd Canon Dave Wade, Vicarage, 16a Ruscoe Rd, Canning Town, London E16 1JB
Tel: 020 7476 2076
email: davenicky@hotmail.com
Redbridge Revd Paul Harcourt, All Saints Vicarage, 4 Inmans Row, Woodford Green IG8 0NH   *Tel:* 020 8504 0266
email: paul@asww.org.uk
Waltham Forest Revd Simon Heathfield, The Rectory, 117 Church Hill, Walthamstow, London E17 3BD   *Tel:* 020 8520 4281
email: simonh@walthamstowchurch.org.uk

ARCHDEACONRY OF HARLOW

Epping Forest and Ongar Revd Dr Joyce Smith, St Lawrence House, 46 Mallion Court, Ninefields, Waltham Abbey EN9 3EQ   *Tel:* 01992 767916
email: joyce.smith@stclarehospice.org.uk
Harlow Revd Martin Harris, 43 Upper Park, Harlow CM20 1TW   *Tel:* 01279 411100
email: martin.harris@messages.co.uk

ARCHDEACONRY OF CHELMSFORD

Brentwood Revd Dr Ian Jorysz, The Vicarage, Wigley Bush Lane, Brentwood CM14 5QP
Tel: 01277 212054
email: ian@jorysz.com
Chelmsford North Canon Carla Hampton, The New Vicarage, 1 Glebe Meadow, Chelmsford CM3 1EX   *Tel:* 01245 364081
email: carla@hamptonc.freeserve.co.uk
Chelmsford South Revd Andrew Griffiths, 450 Beehive Lane, Chelmsford CM2 8RN
Tel: 01245 353922
email: andy.griffiths@yahoo.co.uk
Maldon and Dengie Revd Sandra Manley, The Vicarage, Fambridge Road, Althorne, Chelmsford CM3 6BZ   *Tel:* 01621 772300
email: sandra.manley@btinternet.com

ARCHDEACONRY OF SOUTHEND

Basildon Revd Margaret Shaw, St Andrew's Vicarage, 3 The Fremnells, Basildon, Essex SS14 2QX   *Tel:* 01268 520516
                    email: sh.ma@btinternet.com
Hadleigh Revd David Tudor, St Nicholas' House, Canvey Island SS8 0JR   *Tel:* 01268 682586
                    email: dstudor@tiscali.co.uk
Rochford Revd Mike Lodge, Rectory, Hockley Rd, Rayleigh SS6 8BA   *Tel:* 01268 742151
          email: mike.lodge@parishofrayleigh.org.uk
Southend Revd Canon Stephen Burdett, Southend Rectory, 144 Alexandra Road, Southend-on-Sea SS1 1HB   *Tel:* 01702 342687
    email: stephen@burdett436.orangehome.co.uk
Thurrock Revd Darren Barlow, The Rectory, 10 High View Avenue, Grays RM17 6RU
                    Tel: 01375 377379
          email: revbarlow@talktalk.net

ARCHDEACONRY OF COLCHESTER

Colchester Revd Paul Norrington, The Rectory, 21 Cambridge Road, Colchester CO3 3NS
                    Tel: 01206 563478
          email: paul.nozzer@btinternet.com
Harwich Vacancy

St Osyth Revd Guy Douglas Thorburn, St John's Vicarage, Valley Avenue, Great Clacton CO15 4AR   *Tel:* 01255 423435
          email: revguy.thorburn@virgin.net
Witham Revd Geoff Bayliss, The Vicarage, 37 Church Street, Tolleshunt D'arcy, Maldon CM9 8TS   *Tel:* 01621 869895
          email: g.bayliss41@btinternet.com

ARCHDEACONRY OF STANSTED

Braintree Revd Beth Bendrey, The Rectory, 265C London Road, Black Notley, Braintree CM77 8QQ   *Tel:* 01376 567971
          email: revbethbendrey@hotmail.co.uk
Dunmow Revd Cilla Hawkes, Greenfields, Felstead, Dunmow CM6 3LF   *Tel:* 01371 856480
          email: cilla@hawkesfarming.co.uk
Hinckford Revd Laurie Bond, Vicarage, Queen St, Castle Hedingham, Halstead CO9 3EZ
                    Tel: 01787 460274
          email: revlbond@hotmail.com
Saffron Walden Revd David Tomlinson, St John's Vicarage, 8a Victoria Avenue, Grays RM16 2RP   *Tel:* 01375 372101
          email: rector.saffronwalden@ntlworld.com

DIOCESE OF CHESTER

Founded in 1541. Cheshire; Wirral; Halton, south of the Mersey; Warrington, south of the Mersey; Trafford, except for an area in the north (MANCHESTER); Stockport, except for a few parishes in the north (MANCHESTER) and in the east (DERBY); the eastern half of Tameside; a few parishes in Derbyshire; a few parishes in Manchester; a few parishes in Flintshire.

Population 1,608,000   Area 1,020 sq m
Full-time Stipendiary Parochial Clergy 224   Benefices 226
Parishes 276   Churches 362
www.chester.anglican.org
Overseas link province: Aru and Boga Congo, Melanesia.

BISHOP (40th)

Rt Revd Dr Peter Robert Forster, Bishop's House, Abbey Square, Chester CH1 2JD [1996]
Tel: 01244 350864
Fax: 01244 314187
email: bpchester@chester.anglican.org
[Peter Cestr:]

SUFFRAGAN BISHOPS

BIRKENHEAD Rt Revd (Gordon) Keith Sinclair, Bishop's Lodge, 67 Bidston Rd, Prenton CH43 6TR [2007]
Tel: 0151 652 2741
Fax: 0151 651 2330
email: bpbirkenhead@chester.anglican.org
STOCKPORT Vacancy, Bishop's Lodge, Back Lane, Dunham Town, Altrincham WA14 4SG [2008]
Tel: 0161 928 5611
Fax: 0161 929 0692
email: bpstockport@chester.anglican.org

HONORARY ASSISTANT BISHOPS

Rt Revd William Alaha Pwaisiho, The Rectory, Church Lane, Gawsworth, Macclesfield, SK11 9RJ
Tel: 01260 223201
Rt Revd Colin Frederick Bazley, 121 Bracken-wood Rd, Higher Bebington, Wirral CH63 2LU
Tel: 0151 608 1193
Rt Revd Geoffrey Turner, 23 Lang Lane, West Kirby, Wirral CH48 5HG
Tel: 0151 625 8504
Rt Revd John Hayden, 45 Birkenhead Rd, Hoylake, Wirral CH47 5AF
Tel: 0151 632 0448
Rt Revd Graham Dow, 34 Kimberley Ave, Romiley SK6 4AB
Tel: 0161 494 9148
Rt Revd Glyn Webster (Bishop of Beverley), Holy Trinity Rectory, Micklegate, York YO1 6LE
Tel: 01904 628155

CATHEDRAL CHURCH OF CHRIST AND THE BLESSED VIRGIN MARY

Dean Very Revd Professor Gordon Ferguson McPhate, Deanery, 7 Abbey St, Chester CH1 2JF [2002]
Tel: 01244 500971
email: dean@chestercathedral.com
Cathedral Office 12 Abbey Square, Chester CH1 2HU
Tel: 01244 324756
email: office@chestercathedral.com
Web: www.chestercathedral.com

Vice-Dean
Canon Peter Howell-Jones, 12 Abbey Street, Chester CH1 2HU [2011]
Tel: 01244 500968
email: vice.dean@chestercathedral.com
Canon Precentor
Canon Jeremy Dussek, 9 Abbey St, Chester CH1 2JF [2014]
Tel: 01244 500967
email: precentor@chestercathedral.com
Canon Chancellor Canon Jane Brooke, 12 Abbey Square, Chester CH1 2HU [2010]
Tel: 01244 324756
Canon Residentiary
Canon Dr Peter Jenner, 11 Abbey Street, Chester CH1 2JF [2012]
email: peter.jenner@chestercathedral.com
Lay Reader
Mr Chris Jones, 12 Abbey Square, Chester CH1 2HU
Tel: 01244 500952
email: chris.jones@chestercathedral.com
Executive Director Carolyn Bruce
Tel: 01244 500950
email: finance.director@chestercathedral.com
Director of Music Mr Philip Rushforth, Cathedral Office
Tel: 01244 500974
email: philip.rushforth@chestercathedral.com
Cathedral Architect Mr Tony Barton, Cathedral Office

ARCHDEACONS

CHESTER Ven Michael Gilbertson, Church House, 5500 Daresbury Park, Daresbury, Warrington WA4 4GE
Tel: 01928 718834 ext 258
email: michael.gilbertson@chester.anglican.org
MACCLESFIELD Ven Ian Bishop, Church House, 5500 Daresbury Park, Daresbury, Warrington WA4 4GE
Tel: 01928 718834 ext 258
email: ian.bishop@chester.anglican.org

CONVOCATION (MEMBERS OF THE HOUSE OF CLERGY OF THE GENERAL SYNOD)

Proctors for Clergy
Revd Ian Bishop
Canon David Felix
Revd Robert Munro
Revd Alison Cox
Revd Charles Razzall

MEMBERS OF THE HOUSE OF LAITY OF THE GENERAL SYNOD
Prof Tony Berry
Mr Peter Hart
Dr Graham Campbell
Mrs Jenny Dunlop
Mr John Freeman
Mrs Lois Haslam
Dr John Mason
Canon Elizabeth Renshaw MBE

DIOCESAN OFFICERS
Dioc Secretary Mr George Colville, Church House, 5500 Daresbury Park, Daresbury, Warrington WA4 4GE   *Tel:* 01928 718834
          email: george.colville@chester.anglican.org
Chancellor of Diocese His Honour Judge David Turner, c/o Friars, White Friars, Chester CH1 1XS
Registrar of Diocese and Bishop's Legal Secretary Mrs Helen McFall, Friars, White Friars, Chester CH1 1XS   *Tel:* 01244 321066
          Fax: 01244 312582
          email: helen.mcfall@cullimoredutton.co.uk

DIOCESAN ORGANIZATIONS
Diocesan Office Church House, 5500 Daresbury Park, Daresbury, Warrington WA4 4GE
          Tel: 01928 718834
          email: churchhouse@chester.anglican.org

ADMINISTRATION
Dioc Synod (Vice-President, House of Clergy) Revd Dr Jonathan Gibbs
(Vice-President, House of Laity) Canon Dr John Mason
(Secretary) George Colville, Church House
Board of Finance (Chairman) Canon Elizabeth Renshaw MBE
(Secretary) George Colville *(as above)*
Diocesan Surveyor Mr Peter Gowrley, Church House
Head of Finance Mr Nigel Strange, Church House
Designated Officer and Director of HR Liz Geddes, Church House

CHURCHES
Advisory Committee for the Care of Churches (Chairman) Prof Robert Munn; *(DAC Sec)* Mr Paul Broadhurst, Church House

EDUCATION
Director of Education Mr Jeff Turnbull, Church House
Children Mr David Bell, Church House
Youth Revd Mark Montgomery, Church House

MISSION AND MINISTRY
Director of Ministry Canon Dr Christopher Burkett, Church House
          email: christopher.burkett@chester.anglican.org

Director of Ordinands Revd Magdelen Smith, Church House
          email: magdalen.smith@chester.anglican.org
Director of Studies for Ordinands Revd Gary O'Neill, 10 Neston Close, Helsby WA6 0FH
          Tel: 01928 723327
          email: gary.oneill@chester.anglican.org
Bishop's Officer for NSMs Canon Prof Roger Yates, 3 Racecourse Park, Wilmslow SK9 5LU
          Tel: 01625 520246
Diocesan Dean of Women in Ministry Revd Libby Lane, St Peter's Vicarage, 1 Harrop Rd, Hale, Antrincham WA15 9BU   *Tel:* 0161 928 4182
Director of Studies for Readers Liz Shercliff, Church House
          email: liz.shercliff@chester.anglican.org
Warden of Readers Revd John Knowles, 15 Clare Avenue, Handforth, Wilmslow SK9 3EQ
          Tel: 01625 526531
          email: john.knowles@chester.anglican.org
Clergy Development Officer Revd Canon David Herbert, Church House
          email: david.herbert@chester.anglican.org
Warden of Pastoral Workers Revd Vivien Gisby, 1 Fearndown Way, Tytherington, Macclesfield SK10 2UF   *Tel:* 01625 501449
          email: viviengisby@btinternet.com
Pastoral Worker Training Officer Revd Maureen Pickering, Curzon Cottage, 2A Curzon Park South, Chester CH4 8AB   *Tel:* 01244 677352
          email: mapickering@btinternet.com

PARISH DEVELOPMENT TEAM
Parish Development Officers Revd Richard Burton, Church House
          email: richard.burton@chester.anglican.org
Revd Ian Rumsey, Church House
          email: ian.rumsey@chester.anglican.org
Adviser in Christian Giving Mr Martin Smith, Church House
          email: martin.smith@chester.anglican.org
Diocesan Worship Adviser Revd Colin Randall
          email: colinrandall@mac.com

MISSIONARY AND ECUMENICAL
Partners in World Mission Mr John Freeman, Stable Court, 20A Leigh Way, Weaverham, Northwich CW8 3PR   *Tel:* 01606 852872
County Ecumenical Development Officer Revd Andrew Taylor   *Tel:* 01270 780529
          email: ceo.ctic@googlemail.com
Dioc Ecumenical Officer Canon Mike Lowe, 4 Greenway Rd, Heald Green, Cheadle SK8 3NR
          Tel: 0161 282 3850
          email: mike.lowe@chester.anglican.org

PRESS AND PUBLICATIONS
Dioc Director of Communications Mr Stephen Regan, Church House or 07764 615069 (Mobile)
          email: stephen.regan@chester.anglican.org
Design and Communications Officer Mr Stephen Freeman
          email: stephen.freeman@chester.anglican.org

DIOCESAN RECORD OFFICE

Cheshire Records Office, Duke St, Chester CH1 1RL   *Tel:* 01244 973391

SOCIAL RESPONSIBILITY

Director of Social Responsibility
Mrs Janice Mason, Church House
          email: janice.mason@chester.anglican.org

RURAL DEANS

ARCHDEACONRY OF CHESTER

Birkenhead Revd Dallas Ayling, 10 Cavendish Road, Claughton, Birkenhead CH41 8AX
          Tel: 0151 653 6092
          email: revddallasayling@yahoo.co.uk
Chester Revd Paul Dawson, The Rectory, 10 Lower Park Road, Queens Park, Chester CH4 7BB   *Tel:* 01244 675199
          email: comet411@tiscali.co.uk
Frodsham Revd Peter Rugen, The Vicarage, Pike Lane, Kingsley, Frodsham WA6 8EH
          Tel: 01928 787180
          email: p.rugen@btinternet.com
Great Budworth Revd Alec Brown, The Vicarage, Great Budworth, Northwich CW9 6HF
          Tel: 01606 891324
          email: alec-brown@tiscali.co.uk
Malpas Revd Canon Ian Arthan Davenport, The Rectory, Church Street, Malpas SY14 8PP
          Tel: 01948 860922
          email: malpas.iandavenport@live.co.uk
Middlewich Revd Simon Drew, The Rectory, Poplar Fell, Nantwich Road, Middlewich CW10 9HG   *Tel:* 01606 833440
          email:
simon.drew@middlewichparishchurch.org.uk
Wallasey Revd Canon Graham Cousins, The Rectory, Dawpool Drive, Moreton, Wirral CH46 0PH   *Tel:* 0151 604 0049
          email: rector@christchurchmoreton.org.uk

Wirral North Revd Gillian Rossiter, The Vicarage, 1 Stanley Road, Hoylake, Wirral CH47 1HL
          Tel: 0151 632 3897
          email: stjohnthebaptist@uwclub.net
Wirral South Revd Beth Glover, The Vicarage, 29 Ferry Road, Eastham CH62 0AJ
          Tel: 0151 327 2182
          email: beth.glover@tesco.net

ARCHDEACONRY OF MACCLESFIELD

Bowdon Revd Julian Heaton, St Anne's Vicarage, Church Road West, Sale M33 3GD
          Tel: 0161 973 4145
          email: julian.heaton@talktalk.net
Chadkirk Revd Janet Parker, 35 Martlet Avenue, Disley, Stockport SK12 2JH   *Tel:* 01663 764519
          email: revjanetparker@btinternet.com
Cheadle Revd Rob McLaren, Vicarage, 41 London Road North, Poynton, Stockport SK12 1AF
          Tel: 01625 850524
Congleton Revd Dr David Page, The Vicarage, 2 Taxmere Close, Elworth, Sandbach CW11 1WT
          Tel: 01270 762415
          email: vicar@stpeters-elworth.org.uk
Knutsford Revd Jane Parry, The Vicarage, Church Lane, Alderley Edge SK9 7UZ
          Tel: 01625 583249
          email: vicarontheedge@hotmail.co.uk
Macclesfield Revd Canon Veronica Hydon, The Vicarage, 35a Shrigley Road, Bollington, Macclesfield SK10 5RD   *Tel:* 01625 573162
          email: vhydon@hotmail.com
Mottram Revd Alison Cox, St Mark's Vicarage, 2 Church Square, Railway Street, Dukinfield SK16 4PX   *Tel:* 0161 330 2783
          email: alisoncox19@hotmail.com
Nantwich Revd Canon Helen Chantry, St James Vicarage, 66 Heathfield Road, Little Heath, Audlem, Crewe CW3 0HG   *Tel:* 01270 811543
          email: helenchantry@btopenworld.com
Stockport Revd Canon Diane Cookson, St Saviour's Vicarage, 22 St Saviour's Road, Great Moor, Stockport SK2 2QE   *Tel:* 0161 483 2633
          email: st.saviours@virgin.net

DIOCESE OF CHICHESTER

Founded in 1070, formerly called Selsey (AD 681). West Sussex, except for one parish in the north (GUILDFORD); East Sussex, except for one parish in the north (ROCHESTER); one parish in Kent.

Population 1,621,000   Area 1,460 sq m
Full-time Stipendiary Parochial Clergy 275   Benefices 291
Parishes 368   Churches 489
www.chichester.anglican.org
Overseas link dioceses: IDWAL (Inter-Diocesan West Africa Link) –
Ghana, Sierra Leone, Cameroon, Guinea (West Africa).

BISHOP (103rd)
Rt Revd Dr Martin Warner, The Palace, Chichester PO19 1PY [2012]   *Tel:* 01243 782161
Fax: 01243 531332
email: bishop@chichester.anglican.org
[Martin Cicestr:]
Senior Chaplain and Episcopal Vicar for Ministry
Vacancy, The Palace (*as above*)

SUFFRAGAN BISHOPS
HORSHAM Rt Revd Mark Sowerby, Bishop's House, 21 Guildford Rd, Horsham RH12 1LU [2009]   *Tel:* 01403 211139
Fax: 01403 217349
email: bishop.horsham@chichester.anglican.org
LEWES Rt Revd Richard Jackson, c/o Church House, 211 New Church Road, Hove BN3 4ED
Tel: 01273 421021

HONORARY ASSISTANT BISHOPS
Rt Revd Kenneth Barham OBE, Rosewood, Canadia Road, Battle TN33 0LR
Tel: 01424 773073
Rt Revd Alan Chesters, The College of St Barnabas, Blackberry Lane, Lingfield RH7 6NJ
Tel: 01342 872861
Rt Revd Ralph Farrer, The Vicarage, 26 Maltravers Street, Arundel BN18 9BU
Tel: 01903 885209
Rt Revd Dr Laurence Green, 86 Belle Hill, Bexhill-on-Sea TN40 2AP   *Tel:* 01424 217872
Rt Revd Michael Langrish, 39 The Meadows, Walberton, Arundel BN18 0PB
Tel: 01243 551704
Rt Revd Christopher Morgan, 6 Wellington Court, Grand Avenue, Worthing BN11 5AB
Tel: 01903 246184
Rt Revd Nicholas Reade, 5 Warnham Gardens, Cooden, Bexhill-on-Sea TN39 3SP
Tel: 01424 842673
Rt Revd Geoffrey Rowell, 2 Roman Wharf, Fishbourne Road, Fishbourne, Chichester PO19 3RZ
Tel: 01243 789867
Rt Revd Michael Scott-Joynt, Easter House, Funtington, Chichester PO18 9LJ
Tel: 01243 575762
Rt Revd Henry Scriven, 16 East St Helen Street, Abingdon OX14 5EA   *Tel:* 01235 536607

Rt Revd Lindsay Urwin, Baverstock House, Bridewell Street, Walsingham NR22 6EE
Tel: 01328 820323
Rt Revd David Wilcox, 4 The Court, Hoo Gardens, Willingdon, Eastbourne BN20 9AX
Tel: 01323 506108

CATHEDRAL CHURCH OF THE HOLY TRINITY
Dean Vacancy   *Tel:* 01243 812484 (Office)
Cathedral Office The Royal Chantry, Cathedral Cloisters, Chichester PO19 1PX
Tel: 01243 782595
Fax: 01243 812499
email: enquiry@chichestercathedral.org.uk
Precentor Canon Timothy Schofield, 4 Vicars' Close, Chichester PO19 1PT [2006]
Tel: 01243 813589
Fax: 01243 812499
email: precentor@chichestercathedral.org.uk
Chancellor Canon Dr Anthony Cane, The Residentiary, 2 Canon Lane, Chichester PO19 1PX [2007]   *Tel:* 01243 813594
Fax: 01243 812499
email: chancellor@chichestercathedral.org.uk
Treasurer Vacancy
Communar Vacancy
Cathedral Organist and Master of the Choristers Mr Charles Harrison
email: organist@chichestercathedral.org.uk

ARCHDEACONS
BRIGHTON AND LEWES Vacancy
CHICHESTER Ven Douglas McKittrick, 2 Yorklands, Dyke Rd Ave, Hove BN3 6RW [2002]
Tel: 01273 505330
Fax: 01273 421041
email: archchichester@chichester.anglican.org
HASTINGS Ven Philip Hugh Jones, 27 The Avenue, Lewes BN7 1QT [2005]   *Tel:* 01273 479530
Fax: 01273 476529
email: archlandh@chichester.anglican.org
HORSHAM Ven Roger Combes, 3 Danehurst Crescent, Horsham RH13 5HS [2003]
Tel: 01403 262710
Fax: 01403 210778
email: archhorsham@chichester.anglican.org

Ven Fiona Windsor, 28 Langley Lane, Ifield, Crawley RH11 0NA [2014]
email: archhorsham@chichester.anglican.org

CONVOCATION (MEMBERS OF THE HOUSE OF CLERGY OF THE GENERAL SYNOD)
Proctors for Clergy
Revd Canon Rebecca Swyer
Revd Jonathan Frais
Ven Douglas McKittrick
Revd John Chitham
Revd Richard Poole

MEMBERS OF THE HOUSE OF LAITY OF THE GENERAL SYNOD
Mr John Ashwin
Mrs Lorna Ashworth
Mr John Booth
Mr Justin Brett
Mrs Mary Nagel
Dr Graham Parr
Mr Jacob Vince
Ms Andrea Williams

DIOCESAN OFFICERS
Diocesan Secretary (Interim) Mr Nicholas Taylor, Diocesan Church House, 211 New Church Rd, Hove BN3 4ED   *Tel:* 01273 421021
Fax: 01273 421041
email:
diocesan.secretary@chichester.anglican.org
Chancellor of Diocese Chancellor Mark Hill, Francis Taylor Building, Inner Temple, London EC4Y 7BY
Registrar of Diocese and Bishop's Legal Secretary Mr Matthew Chinery, Winckworth Sherwood LLP, Minerva House, 5 Montague Close, London SE1 9BB   *Tel:* 0207 593 5000
email: chichesterregistery@wslaw.co.uk

DIOCESAN ORGANIZATIONS
Diocesan Office Diocesan Church House, 211 New Church Rd, Hove BN3 4ED   *Tel:* 01273 421021
Fax: 01273 421041
email: enquiry@chichester.anglican.org

ADMINISTRATION
Dioc Synod (Chairman, House of Clergy) Revd Mark Gilbert
(Chairman, House of Laity) Dr B. Hanson
Dioc Fund and Board of Finance (Incorporated) (Chairman) Mr John Booth; *(Secretary)* Mr Nicholas Taylor *(Interim) (as above)*
Governance and Administration Mr David Mason, Dioc Church House   *Tel:* 01273 425794
email: david.mason@chichester.anglican.org

SAFEGUARDING
Safeguarding Advisor Colin Perkins, Dioc Church House   *Tel:* 01273 425792
email: colin.perkins@chichester.anglican.org

PASTORAL AND CHURCH BUILDINGS
Advisory Committee for the Care of Churches (Chairman) Dr Alan Thurlow, c/o Dioc Church House; *(Secretary)* Miss Beth Hale *(as above)*
email: beth.hale@chichester.anglican.org
Pastoral Committee (Secretary) Mr Steven Sleight, Dioc Church House

PRESS AND PUBLICATIONS
Communications Officer Mrs Lisa Williamson, Dioc Church House   *Tel:* 01273 425691
Out of Hours *Tel:* 07775 022461
email: communications@chichester.anglican.org

EDUCATION AND TRAINING
Schools
Director of Education Dr Anne Holt
Schools Support Mr Martin Lloyd, Mrs Rosemary Black, Mrs Ruth Cumming, Dioc Church House
Children and Young People
Children's Officer Revd Irene Smale, Dioc Church House

DISCIPLESHIP AND MINISTRY
Ministry Development Officer Revd Canon Rebecca Swyer, Dioc Church House
email: rebecca.swyer@chichester.anglican.org
Programme Co-ordinator, Initial Ministerial Education 4–7 Revd Canon Rebecca Swyer *(as above)*
Adult Education and Training Officer Ruth Sowerby, Dioc Church House
email: ruth.sowerby@chichester.anglican.org
Diocesan Director of Ordinands Revd Lu Gale, Dioc Church House
Readers Committee (Hon Secretary) Mr Simon Quail

MISSION AND RENEWAL
Adviser Vacancy, Dioc Church House
Parish Resources Officers Mr John Sherlock and Mr Tony Cox, Dioc Church House
World Mission Officer Revd Canon Ian Hutchinson-Cervantes, Dioc Church House

ECUMENICAL
European Ecumenical Committee (Chairman) Vacancy
(Secretary) Mr Jeffrey Stanbridge
Tel: 01243 789305

DIOCESAN RECORD OFFICES
East Sussex Mrs Elizabeth Hughes, *County Archivist*, The Keep, Woollards Way, Brighton BN1 9BP   *Tel:* 01273 482349
West Sussex Mr R. Childs *County Archivist*, County Records Office, County Hall, Chichester PO19 1RN   *Tel:* 01243 533911

RURAL DEANS
ARCHDEACONRY OF BRIGHTON AND LEWES
Brighton Revd Andrew Manson-Brailsford, St George's House, 6 Sussex Mews, Kemp Town, Brighton BN2 1GZ   *Tel:* 01273 279448
email: revmanson-brailsford@hotmail.co.uk

Hove Revd Terence Stratford, Kingston Buci Rectory, Shoreham-by-Sea BN43 6EB
Tel: 01273 592591
email: terry.stratford@yahoo.co.uk
Lewes and Seaford Revd Geoffrey Daw, The Rectory, 14 Lockitt Way, Kingston, Lewes BN7 3LG
Tel: 01273 473665
email: Geoffrey.Daw@btinternet.com

ARCHDEACONRY OF CHICHESTER

Arundel and Bognor Revd Canon Mark Standen, The Rectory, Rectory Lane, Angmering BN16 4JU
Tel: 01903 784979
email: standens@angmering.org.uk
Chichester Revd Mark Gilbert, St Wilfrid's House, 7 Durnford Close, Chichester PO19 3AG
Tel: 01243 783853
email: frmarkssc@msn.com
Westbourne Revd Clive Jenkins, The Vicarage, 271 Main Road, Southbourne PO10 8JE
Tel: 01243 372436
email: admin@stjohnssouthbourne.com
Worthing Revd Colin Kassell, Park House, 3 Madeira Avenue, Worthing BN11 2AT
Tel: 01903 526571
email: c.kassell@virginmedia.com

ARCHDEACONRY OF HASTINGS

Battle and Bexhill Very Revd Canon John Edmondson, The Deanery, Caldbec Hill, Battle TN33 0JY
Tel: 01903 526571
email: dean@johnedmondson.org
Dallington Revd Marc Lloyd, The Rectory, Rookery Lane, Rushlake Green, Heathfield
Tel: 01435 830421
email: marc_lloyd@hotmail.com
Eastbourne Very Revd Jeffrey Gunn, The Vicarage, Spencer Road, Eastbourne BN21 4PA
Tel: 01323 722317
email: jtgunn@tiscali.co.uk

Hastings Revd Michael Coe, 9 St Matthew's Road, St Leonards-on-Sea TN38 0TN
Tel: 01424 425863
email: mike@mikecoe.co.uk
Rotherfield Revd Canon Jeremy James, Vicarage, High St, Wadhurst TN5 6AA *Tel:* 01892 782083
email: jeremy@jrjames.freeserve.co.uk
Rye Revd Canon David Frost, The Rectory, Gungarden, Rye TN31 7HH *Tel:* 01797 222430
email: david@drfrost.org.uk
Uckfield Revd Canon Martin Onions, The Rectory, 1 Sand Ridge, Ridgewood, Uckfield TN22 5ET *Tel:* 01825 370507
email: martin.onions@tiscali.co.uk

ARCHDEACONRY OF HORSHAM

Cuckfield Revd Gary Simmons, The Rectory, Brighton Road, Handcross RH17 6BU
Tel: 01444 400221
email: slaugham@btinternet.com
East Grinstead Revd Canon Julia Peaty, 15 Overton Shaw, East Grinstead RH19 2HN
Tel: 01342 322386
email: julia@peaty.net
Horsham Canon Guy Bridgewater, The Vicarage, The Causeway, Horsham RH12 1HE
Tel: 01403 272919
email: bridgewaters@tiscali.co.uk
Hurst Revd Kevin O'Brien, St John's Rectory, 68a Park Road, Burgess Hill RH15 8HG
Tel: 01444 232582
email: frkevinobrien@me.com
Midhurst Revd Derek Welsman, Northgates, Dodsley Grove, Easebourne, Midhurst GU29 9BE *Tel:* 01730 812655
email: derekwelsman@btinternet.com
Petworth Revd David Twinley, The Vicarage, Church Lane, Bury, Pulborough RH20 1PB
Tel: 01798 839057
email: frdavid@twinley.me.uk
Storrington Revd David Beal, The Rectory, East Street, West Chiltington RH20 2JY
Tel: 01798 813117
email: dm.beal@btconnect.com

DIOCESE OF COVENTRY

Re-founded in 1918. Coventry; Warwickshire, except for small areas in the north (BIRMINGHAM) and south-west (GLOUCESTER) and one parish in the south (OXFORD); an area of Solihull.

Population 829,000   Area 690 sq m
Full-time Stipendiary Parochial Clergy 117   Benefices 130
Parishes 199   Churches 245
www.coventry.anglican.org

BISHOP
Rt Revd Dr Christopher John Cocksworth, Bishop's House, 23 Davenport Rd, Coventry CV5 6PW [2008]   *Tel:* 024 7667 2244
Fax: 024 7610 0535
email: bishop@bishop-coventry.org
Personal Assistant Christine Camfield (*same address*)
email: christine.camfield@bishop-coventry.org
Secretary Mrs Elizabeth Egan (*same address*)
email: elizabeth.egan@bishop-coventry.org

SUFFRAGAN BISHOP
WARWICK Rt Revd John Ronald Angus Stroyan, Warwick House, 139 Kenilworth Rd, Coventry CV4 7AP [2005]   *Tel:* 024 7641 2627
Fax: 024 7641 5254
email: Bishop.Warwick@covcofe.org
Personal Assistant Mrs Kerry Vanston-Rumney
email: kerry.rumney@covcofe.org

CATHEDRAL CHURCH OF ST MICHAEL
Dean Very Revd John Witcombe
Tel: 024 7652 1227
email: john.witcombe@coventrycathedral.org.uk
Cathedral Offices 1 Hill Top, Coventry CV1 5AB
Tel: 024 7652 1200
Fax: 024 7652 1220
Web: www.coventrycathedral.org.uk
Canons Residentiary and Senior Staff
Canon Precentor and Sub Dean Revd Canon Dr David Stone (*same address*) [2010]
Tel: 024 7652 1212
email: david.stone@coventrycathedral.org.uk
Canon Pastor Revd Canon Kathryn Fleming (*same address*) [2014]   *Tel:* 024 7652 1230
email: kathryn.fleming@coventrycathedral.org.uk
Canon for Reconciliation Ministry Revd Canon Dr Sarah Hills (*same address*) [2014]
Tel: 024 7652 1200
email: sarah.hills@coventrycathedral.org.uk
Canon Treasurer Revd Canon Stephen Fielding (*same address*) [2014]   *Tel:* 024 7652 1200
email: stephen.fielding@coventrycathedral.org.uk

Archbishop's Director for Reconciliation and Senior Advisor for Reconciliation to the Bishop of Coventry
Canon David Porter   *Tel:* 024 7652 1200
email: david.porter@coventrycathedral.org.uk *or* david.porter@lambethpalace.org.uk
Canons Theologian
Revd Canon Professor Ben Quash, Department of Theology and Religious Studies, King's College London, The Strand, London WC2R 2LS [2004]
Tel: 020 7848 2339/2073
Canon Professor Richard Farnell
Tel: 024 7652 1200
Canon John Mumford   *Tel:* 024 7652 1200
Clerk to the College of Canons Mr Roger Pascall, 1 The Quadrant, Coventry CV1 2DW
Tel: 024 7663 1212
Director of Music Mr Kerry Beaumont (*same address*)   *Tel:* 024 7652 1219
email: kerry.beaumont@coventrycathedral.org.uk

ARCHDEACONS
Archdeacon Pastor Ven John Green, Cathedral and Diocesan Offices   *Tel:* 024 7652 1337
email: john.green@covcofe.org
Archdeacon Missioner Ven Morris Rodham, Cathedral and Diocesan Offices   *Tel:* 024 7652 1337
email: morris.rodham@covcofe.org
Dean of Women's Ministry Canon Katrina Scott, Willenhall Vicarage, Robin Hood Rd, Coventry CV3 3AY   *Tel:* 024 7630 3266
email: krgscott@hotmail.com
Dean of Self Supporting Ministry: Revd Dr Jill Tucker, The Old House, Oxhill, Warwick CV35 0QN   *Tel:* 01295 680663
email: revjill.tucker@tiscali.co.uk

CONVOCATION (MEMBERS OF THE HOUSE OF CLERGY OF THE GENERAL SYNOD)
Proctors for Clergy
Revd Canon Martin Saxby
Revd Ruth Walker
Revd Charlotte Gale

MEMBERS OF THE HOUSE OF LAITY OF THE GENERAL SYNOD
Mrs Kay Dyer
Mr Samuel Margrave
Dr Yvonne Warren

DIOCESAN OFFICERS

Diocesan Secretary Canon Simon Lloyd, Cathedral and Diocesan Offices, 1 Hill Top, Coventry CV1 5AB   *Tel:* 024 7652 1307
  Fax: 024 7652 1330
  email: simon.lloyd@covcofe.org
Chancellor of Diocese Chancellor Stephen Eyre, St Phillip's Chambers, 55 Temple Row, Birmingham B2 5LS
Deputy Chancellor Glyn Samuel (*same address*)
Registrar of Diocese and Bishop's Legal Secretary Mrs Mary Allanson, Rotherham & Co, 8 The Quadrant, Coventry CV1 2EL   *Tel:* 024 7622 7331

DIOCESAN ORGANIZATIONS

Diocesan Office Cathedral and Diocesan Offices, 1 Hill Top, Coventry CV1 5AB   *Tel:* 024 7652 1200
  Fax: 024 7652 1330
  Web: www.coventry.anglican.org

ADMINISTRATION

Diocesan Synod (*Chairman, House of Clergy*) Revd Ruth Walker
(*Chairman, House of Laity*) Mr Graham Wright
Diocesan Secretary Canon Simon Lloyd, Cathedral and Diocesan Offices
Board of Finance (*Chairman*) Canon Ian Francis, The Firs, Main St, Frankton, Rugby CV23 9NZ
  Tel: 01926 632918
  email: ian@frankton.org
Director of Finance and Administration Mr David Oglethorpe
  email: david.oglethorpe@covcofe.org
Director of Operations Mr Stephen Davenport
  email: stephen.davenport@covcofe.org
Director of Communications Revd Graeme Pringle, Cathedral and Diocesan Offices
  Tel: 024 7652 1336
  email: graeme.pringle@covcofe.org
Senior Property Manager Mrs Nicky Caunt, Cathedral and Diocesan Offices
  email: nicky.caunt@covcofe.org
Diocesan Trustees David Dumbleton MBE, Rotherham & Co, 8 The Quadrant, Coventry CV1 2EL   *Tel:* 024 7622 7331
Diocesan Mission and Pastoral Committee Mr Stephen Davenport (*as above*)
Designated Officer Mr Stephen Davenport (*as above*)
Diocesan Directory Editor Revd Graeme Pringle (*as above*)

CHURCHES

Advisory Committee for the Care of Churches Dr Claire Strachan, Cathedral and Diocesan Offices   *email:* claire.strachan@covcofe.org

EDUCATION

Diocesan Director Canon Linda Wainscot, The Benn Education Centre, Claremont Road, Rugby CV21 3LU   *Tel:* 01788 422800
  email: linda.wainscot@covcofe.org

MINISTRY

Principal of the Diocesan Training Partnership Revd Canon Dr Richard Cooke, Cathedral and Diocesan Offices   *Tel:* 024 7652 1316
  email: richard.cooke@covcofe.org
Diocesan Director of Ordinands Revd Canon Dr Richard Cooke, Cathedral and Diocesan Offices
  Tel: 024 7652 1316
Learning Adviser (*Ministerial Development*) Revd Naomi Nixon, Cathedral and Diocesan Offices
  Tel: 024 7652 1304
  email: naomi.nixon@covcofe.org
Healthy Churches Development Mentor Revd Canon Martin Saxby, Cathedral and Diocesan Offices   *Tel:* 01788 330790 (Home)
  Mobile: 07944 670288
  email: martin.saxby@covcofe.org
Transforming Communities Together Officer Mrs Jet Jones, Cathedral and Diocesan Offices
  Tel: 024 7652 1344
  email: jet.jones@covcofe.org
Warden of Readers Mrs Heidi Cartledge
  Tel: 01926 641751
  email: hcartledge@fightingclose.freeserve.co.uk
Readers (*Hon Registrar*) Mr Paul Mileham
  Tel: 01926 426250
  email: paul@mileham.net

STEWARDSHIP

Diocesan Adviser Mr Graham Wright, 1 Mayfield Drive, Kenilworth CV8 2SW   *Tel:* 01926 864991
  email: grahampjw@aol.com

DIOCESAN RECORD OFFICE

Warwickshire County Record Office, Priory Park, Cape Rd, Warwick CV34 4JS
Archives and Historic Environment Manager Ms Sam Collenette   *Tel:* 01926 738959
  Fax: 01926 738969
  email: recordoffice@warwickshire.gov.uk

AREA DEANS
ARCHDEACONRY OF COVENTRY

Coventry North Revd Robin Trew, Allesley Rectory, Rectory Lane, Coventry CV5 9EQ
  Tel: 024 7640 25006
  email: robintrew@googlemail.com
Coventry South Revd Stephen Burch, St James Vicarage, 395 Tile Hill Lane, Coventry CV4 9DP
  Tel: 024 7646 6262
  email: stephenburch59@gmail.com
Coventry East Revd Clive Hogger, St Margaret's Vicarage, 18 South Avenue, Coventry CV2 4DR   *Tel:* 024 7665 1642
  email: clive.da.rev@googlemail.com
Kenilworth Revd Dr Mark Bratton, The Rectory, Meriden Road, Berkswell, Coventry CV7 7BE
  Tel: 01676 533605
  email: markbratton@berkswellchurch.org.uk
Nuneaton Revd Dr Richard Hare, The Rectory, 1 Linden Lea, Bedworth CV12 8UD
  Tel: 024 7631 0219
  email: thehares@ic24.net

Rugby Revd Canon Peter Watkins, 23 St Margaret's Avenue, Wolston, Coventry CV8 3LJ   *Tel:* 024 7767 5779
email: michaelwatkins@talktalk.net

ARCHDEACONRY OF WARWICK

Alcester Vacancy

Fosse Revd Kate Mier, The Vicarage, Church Street, Wellesbourne, Warwick CV35 9LS
Tel: 01789 840262
email: kate.mier1@gmail.com

Shipston Revd Dr Jill Tucker, The Old House, Oxhill, Warwick CV35 0QN   *Tel:* 01295 688193
email: revjill.tucker@tiscali.co.uk

Southam Revd Craig Groocock, The Rectory, 2 Vicarage Lane, Harbury, Leamington Spa CV33 9HA   *Tel:* 01926 612377
email: kankudai43@aol.co.uk

Warwick and Leamington Revd Charlotte Gale, Lillington Vicarage, Vicarage Road, Leamington Spa CV32 7RH   *Tel:* 01926 330919
email: charlotte.gale@sky.com

DIOCESE OF DERBY

Founded in 1927. Derbyshire, except for a small area in the north (CHESTER); a small area of Stockport; a few parishes in Staffordshire.

Population 1,032,000   Area 1,000 sq m
Full-time Stipendiary Parochial Clergy 149   Benefices 153
Parishes 254   Churches 329
www.derby.anglican.org
Overseas link of Derbyshire Churches (Baptist, Methodist, URC and Anglican): Church of North India.

BISHOP (7th)
Rt Revd Dr Alastair Redfern, The Bishop's House, 6 King St, Duffield, Derby DE56 4EU [2005]
Tel: 01332 840132
email: bishop@bishopofderby.org
[Alastair Derby]

SUFFRAGAN BISHOP
REPTON Rt Revd Humphrey Southern, Repton House, Lea, Matlock DE4 5JP [2007]
Tel: 01629 534644
email: bishop@repton.free-online.co.uk

HONORARY ASSISTANT BISHOPS
Rt Revd Richard Inwood, 43 Whitecotes Park, Chesterfield S40 3RT [2012]   *Tel:* 01246 766288
email: richardinwood@btconnect.com
Rt Revd Jack Nicholls, 75 Rowton Grange Rd, Chapel-en-le-Frith, High Peak SK23 0LD
Tel: 01298 938249
email: jnseraphim@gmx.com

CATHEDRAL CHURCH OF ALL SAINTS
Dean Very Revd Dr John Davies DL, Derby Cathedral Centre, 18–19 Iron Gate, Derby DE1 3GP   *Tel:* 01332 341201
Fax: 01332 203991
email: dean@derbycathedral.org
Cathedral Office Derby Cathedral Centre, 18–19 Iron Gate, Derby DE1 3GP
email: office@derbycathedral.org
Canons Residentiary
Canon Precentor Canon Chris Moorsom, Derby Cathedral Centre, 18–19 Iron Gate, Derby DE1 3GP   *Tel:* 01332 341201
Fax: 01332 203991
email: precentor@derbycathedral.org
Canon Missioner Canon Dr Elizabeth Thomson, Derby Cathedral Centre, 18–19 Iron Gate, Derby DE1 3GP   *Tel:* 01332 341201
Fax: 01332 203991
email: missioner@derbycathedral.org
Canon Chancellor Canon Dr Simon Taylor, Derby Church House, Full Street, Derby DE1 3DR
Tel: 01332 388650
email: simon.taylor@derby.anglican.org

Cathedral and University Chaplain Revd Adam Dickens, University of Derby, Kedleston Rd, Derby DE22 1GB   *Tel:* 01332 591878 (University)
email: adampdickens@hotmail.co.uk
Lay Chapter Members Mr David Legh, Mr Brian Dollamore, Canon Val Grahl, Mr Mark Titterton
Chapter Steward and Chapter Clerk Vacancy
email: andy@derbycathedral.org
Minor Canon Revd Andy Trenier, Derby Cathedral Centre, 18–19 Iron Gate, Derby DE1 3GP
Tel: 01322 341201
Fax: 01332 203991
email: andy@derbycathedral.org
Finance Officer Mr Peter Holdridge, Cathedral Office   *email:* peterh@derbycathedral.org
Visitors' Officer Mr John Armitage, Cathedral Office   *Tel:* 01322 341201
email: visitors@derbycathedral.org
Master of Music and Organist Canon Peter Gould, Cathedral Office   *Tel:* 01322 202231
email: pdgould@derbycathedral.org
Assistant Organist Mr Tom Corfield, Cathedral Office   *Tel:* 01332 202231

ARCHDEACONS
CHESTERFIELD Ven Christine Wilson, The Old Vicarage, Church St, Baslow, Derby DE45 1RY [2009]   *Tel:* 01246 583023
email: archchesterfield@derby.anglican.org

DERBY Ven Dr Christopher Cunliffe, Derby Church House, Full St, Derby DE1 3DR [2006]
Tel: 01332 388676 (Office)
email: archderby@derby.anglican.org

CONVOCATION (MEMBERS OF THE HOUSE OF CLERGY OF THE GENERAL SYNOD)
Proctors for Clergy
Revd Neil Barber
Revd Canon Dr Simon Taylor
Ven Christine Wilson

MEMBERS OF THE HOUSE OF LAITY OF THE GENERAL SYNOD
Mrs Madelaine Goddard
Canon (Mrs) Christine McMullen
Mr Peter Collard

DIOCESAN OFFICERS

Dioc Secretary Mrs Maureen Cole, Derby Church House, 1 Full St, Derby DE1 3DR
Tel: 01332 388650
email: maureen.cole@derby.anglican.org
Chancellor of Diocese His Honour Judge John W. M. Bullimore, 5 Snowgate Head, Horn Lane, New Mill, Holmfirth HD9 7DH
Registrar of Diocese and Bishop's Legal Secretary Mrs Nadine Waldron, Eddowes Waldron Solicitors, 12 St Peter's Churchyard, Derby DE1 1TZ
Tel: 01332 348484
email: ge@ewlaw.co.uk

DIOCESAN ORGANIZATIONS

Diocesan Office Derby Church House, 1 Full St, Derby DE1 3DR
Tel: 01332 388650
email: enquiries@derby.anglican.org
Web: www.derby.anglican.org

ADMINISTRATION

Dioc Synod (*Chairman, House of Clergy*) Revd Peter Davey, The Vicarage, 197 Heanor Rd, Ilkeston DE7 8TA
Tel: 0115 932 5670
email: peterdavey@outlook.com
(*Chairman, House of Laity*) Canon (Mrs) Christine McMullen, Montpelier Farm Cottage, Montpelier Place, Waterswallows Road, Buxton SK17 7EJ
Tel: 01298 73997
(*Secretary*) Mrs Maureen Cole, Derby Church House
Board of Finance (*Chairman*) The Bishop of Derby (*as above*)
(*Executive Chair*) Mr Mark Titterton (*as above*)
(*Secretary*) Mrs Maureen Cole (*as above*)
Parsonages Secretary Nigel Sherratt, Derby Church House
Tel: 01332 388650
Dioc Surveyors
Derby Archdeaconry Bob Spencer, Sir William Baird & Partners, St Michael's House, Queen St, Derby DE1 3DT
Tel: 01332 347203
Fax: 01332 347708
email: mail@sirwilliambaird.co.uk
Chesterfield Archdeaconry Mr G. Steel, Barlow & Associates Ltd, 7 Vernon St, Derby DE1 1FR
Tel: 01332 603000
email: gary@barlow-associates.co.uk
Mission and Pastoral Committee (*Acting Secretary*) Mr Nigel Sherratt (*as above*)
Designated Officer Mrs Nadine Waldron (*as above*)

CHURCHES

Advisory Committee for the Care of Churches (*Chairman*) Mrs Janet Spencer
(*Secretary*) Mrs Helen Powell, Derby Church House
Tel: 01332 388683

EDUCATION

Dioc Education Office Derby Church House, 1 Full St, Derby DE1 3DR
Tel: 01332 388660
Senior Administrator Netta Russell
email: netta.russell@derby.anglican.org

Director David Channon
email: david.channon@derby.anglican.org
Deputy Director and Schools Adviser Mrs Alison Brown
email: alison.brown@derby.anglican.org
Finance Officer Mrs Lizzie Walker
Tel: 01332 388662
email: lizzie.walker@derby.anglican.org
Children's Work Adviser Sara Brown
email: sara.brown@derby.anglican.org
Youth Adviser Mr Alistair Langton
email: alistair.langton@derby.anglican.org

MISSION AND MINISTRY

Director of Mission and Ministry Vacancy
CMD Officer Revd Canon Dr Simon Taylor
Tel: 01332 388671
email: simon.taylor@derby.anglican.org
Church Growth Officers Revd Lee Townend
Tel: 01332 388668 or 01433 639619
email: lee.townend@derby.anglican.org
Revd Jason Kennedy
Tel: 01332 388691
email: jason.kennedy@derby.anglican.org
Community Action Officer Ms Stella Collishaw
Tel: 01322 388685
email: stella.collishaw@derby.anglican.org
Community Projects Development Officer Mr Gareth Greenwood
Tel: 01332 388690
email: gareth.greenwood@derby.anglican.org
Lay Ministry Officer/Warden of Readers Canon Dr Esther Elliott
Tel: 01322 388674
email: esther.elliot@derby.anglican.org
Fresh Expressions Officer Revd Canon Michael Mitton
Tel: 01332 388687
email: michael.mitton@derby.anglican.org
Leadership Development Officer Revd Alison Maddocks
Tel: 01332 388675
email: alison.maddocks@derby.anglican.org

PORTFOLIO HOLDERS AND ADVISERS

Christian Giving/Stewardship Mr Mike Warner
Tel: 01335 346504
email: mike@warnerclan.fsnet.co.uk
Clergy Wellbeing Revd David Railton
Tel: 01332 843017
email: davidrailton@gmail.com
Disability Vacancy
Ecumenical Revd Kevin Ball
Tel: 01246 462192
email: rectoratcalow@hotmail.co.uk
Revd Judy Henderson Smith
Tel: 0115 946 0395
email: jhhs91@hotmail.com
50+ Revd Canon Ian Gooding
Tel: 0115 849 8726
email: ian.e.gooding@googlemail.com
Emergency Mr Alan Winfield
Tel: 07796 560814
email: winfieldalan28@yahoo.co.uk
Environmental Revd Terry Thake
Tel: 01773 821404
email: terry.thake@btinternet.com
Local Government Revd Kevin Ball
Tel: 01246 462192
email: rectoratcalow@hotmail.co.uk

MSE Officer Revd Gillian White   *Tel:* 01298 871317
   email: gillianwhite1@me.com
New Religious Movements Revd William Bates
   Tel: 01332 550224
   *email:*williambates@btconnect.com
Pastoral Care and Counselling Sheila Pigott
   Tel: 01433 629339
   email: contact.sheilapigott@gmail.com
Prayer and Worship Revd Alan Harper
   Tel: 01332 825667
   email: revd.alan8@btinternet.com
Rural Mr Graham Hinds   *Tel:* 01322 602124
   email: grahamhinds@hotmail.com
Science Revd Dr David de Pomerai
   Tel: 01283 711350
   email: ddepomerai@btinternet.com
Spiritual Direction Eirene Palmer
   Tel: 01773 742064
   email: eirene.palmer@googlemail.com
Revd Garrie Griffiths   *Tel:* 01629 630409
   email: ggriffiths787@btinternet.com
Tourism Adviser Mr Bill Bryant   *Tel:* 01629 815225
   email: bryban@msn.com
World Mission and Development Dr Richard
Henderson Smith   *Tel:* 0115 946 0395
   email: r_smith07@btinternet.com
Worship Advisory Group Revd Karen Padley
   Tel: 01773 712097
   email: revpadley@fsmail.net
Director of Ordinands Revd Canon Geraldine
Pond   *Tel:* 01335 343129
   email: ddo@derby.anglican.org
Assistant Directors of Ordinands Revd Philip
Waller   *Tel:* 0115 973 4819
   email: philipstjohn@tiscali.co.uk
Revd John Baines   *Tel:* 01663 743225
   email: vicar@newmillschurch.co.uk
Vocations Adviser Revd Carollyn MacDonald
   Tel: 01335 664132
   email: carollyn4ashbourne@sky.com
Messy Church Revd Christine Rees
   email: revdchristine.rees@btopenworld.com
Wedding Advisor Revd Karen Hamblin
   Tel: 01773 590529 or 07432 705285
   email: khstmarys@gmail.com
Women's Ministry Revd Jean Burgess
   Tel: 01332 223800
   email: jean@stalkmunds.org.uk
Director of Studies Revd Lisa Shemilt
   Tel: 01773 880380
   email: dofsderby@gmail.com
Journey in Faith Dr Stephen Longden
   Tel: 01283 703259
   email: stephenlongden@btinternet.com
Reader MDR Canon Christine McMullen
   Tel: 01298 73997
   email: christine.mcmullen@hotmail.co.uk

PRESS AND COMMUNICATIONS
Office Derby Church House, Full St, Derby DE1
3DR   *Tel:* 01332 388680
   email: communications@derby.anglican.org
Communications Co-ordinator Lucy Harrison

RETIREMENT CHAPLAINCY
Revd Ian Aldersley   *Tel:* 01629 650413
   email: aldersley_ian@yahoo.co.uk

DIOCESAN RECORD OFFICE
Derbyshire Record Office, County Offices,
Matlock DE4 3AG
County Archivist Ms Sarah Chubb
   Tel: 01629 538347
   email: record.office@derbyshire.gov.uk

RURAL DEANS
ARCHDEACONRY OF DERBY
Ashbourne Revd Andy Larkin, The Vicarage,
Smithy Lane, Parwich, Ashbourne DE6 1QD
   Tel: 07758 704452
   email: andy@peakfive.org
Derby North Revd Julian Hollywell, St Werburghs
Vicarage, Gascoigne Drive, Spondon, Derby
DE21 7GL   *Tel:* 01332 673573
   email: fatherjulian@btinternet.com
Derby South Revd Andy Ward, The Rectory, 155
Almond Street, Derby DE23 6LY
   Tel: 01332 760846
   email: rector.walbrook@gmail.com
Duffield Revd Jonathan Page, Christ Church
Vicarage, Bridge Street, Belper DE56 1BA
   Tel: 01773 824974
   email: vicar@christchurchbelper.org.uk
Erewash Revd Peter Davey, The Vicarage, 197
Heanor Road, Ilkeston DE7 8TA
   Tel: 0115 932 5670
   email: peterdavey@outlook.com
Heanor Revd Karen Padley, All Saints Vicarage,
Marlpool, Heanor DE75 7BP   *Tel:* 01773 712097
   email: revpadley@fsmail.net
Longford Revd Andy Murphie, The Vicarage, 28
Back Lane, Hilton, Derby DE65 5GJ
   Tel: 01283 733433
   email: andymurphie@btinternet.com
Melbourne Revd Tony Luke, The Rectory, Rectory
Gardens, Aston-on-Trent, Derby DE72 2AZ
   Tel: 01332 792658
   email: theramsrev@gmail.com
Repton Revd Dr Graham Rutter, The Vicarage,
Church Street, Swadlincote DE11 8LF
   Tel: 01283 214583
   email: gprutter@gmail.com

ARCHDEACONRY OF CHESTERFIELD
Alfreton Revd Philip Brooks, The Vicarage, 19
Coasthill, Crich, Matlock DE4 5DS
   Tel: 01773 852449
   email: philipdbro@aol.com
Bakewell and Eyam Revd Canon Tony Kaunhoven,
The Vicarage, South Church Street, Bakewell
DE45 1FD   *Tel:* 01629 814462
   email: tony.kaunhoven@derby.anglican.org
Bolsover and Staveley Revd Canon Helen Guest,
The Rectory, Sheepcote Road, Killamarsh,
Sheffield S21 1DU   *Tel:* 0114 248 2769
   email: revshmguest@gmail.com

Buxton Revd John Hudghton, The Rectory, 7 Lismore Park, Buxton SK17 9AU
Tel: 01298 77856
email: rectorofbuxton@hotmail.com
Chesterfield Revd Matt Barnes, 674 Chatsworth Road, Chesterfield S40 3NU   *Tel:* 01246 567634
email: rector@st-thomas-brampton.org

Glossop Revd Canon Tony Kaunhoven, The Vicarage, South Church Street, Bakewell DE45 1FD   *Tel:* 01629 814462
email: tony.kaunhoven@derby.anglican.org
Wirksworth Canon David Truby, The Rectory, Coldwell St, Wirksworth, Matlock DE4 4FB
Tel: 01629 822858
email: david.truby@outlook.com

DIOCESE OF DURHAM

Founded in 635. Approximates Durham, except for an area in the south-west (WEST YORKSHIRE AND THE DALES), and Gateshead; South Tyneside; Sunderland; Hartlepool; Darlington and Stockton-on-Tees.

Population 1,468,000   Area 990 sq m
Full-time Stipendiary Parochial Clergy 165   Benefices 190
Parishes 229   Churches 271
www.durham.anglican.org
Overseas link diocese: Lesotho.

BISHOP (74th)
Rt Revd Paul Roger Butler, Bishop's Office, Auckland Castle, Bishop Auckland DL14 7NR [2014] *Tel:* 01388 602576
email: bishop.of.durham@durham.anglican.org
[Paul Dunelm]
Chaplain to the Bishop of Durham and Office Manager Revd Denise Dodd (*same address*)
email: denise.dodd@durham.anglican.org

SUFFRAGAN BISHOP
JARROW Rt Revd Mark Watts Bryant, Bishop's House, 25 Ivy Lane, Low Fell, Gateshead, NE9 6QD [2007] *Tel:* 0191 491 0917
Fax: 0191 491 5116
email: bishop.of.jarrow@durham.anglican.org

HONORARY ASSISTANT BISHOPS
Rt Revd Glyn Hamilton Webster, Holy Trinity Rectory, Micklegate, York YO1 6LE [2013]
Tel: 01904 628155
email: office@seeofbeverley.org.uk
Rt Revd Prof Stephen Whitefield Sykes, Ingleside, Whinney Hill, Durham DH1 3BE [1999]
Tel: 0191 384 6465
email: sandjsykes@tiscali.co.uk

CATHEDRAL CHURCH OF CHRIST, BLESSED MARY THE VIRGIN AND ST CUTHBERT OF DURHAM
Dean Very Revd Michael Sadgrove, The Deanery, Durham DH1 3EQ [2003]
Tel: 0191 384 7500 (Office)
email: michael.sadgrove@durhamcathedral.co.uk
Canons Residentiary (*two vacancies*)
Revd Canon Dr David Kennedy, 7 The College, Durham DH1 3EQ [2001] *Tel:* 0191 375 0242
email: canon.precentor@durhamcathedral.co.uk
Revd Canon Rosalind Brown, 6a The College, Durham DH1 3EQ [2005]
Tel: 0191 386 4266 ext. 235 (Office)
email: nave.canon@durhamcathedral.co.uk
Ven Ian Jagger, 15 The College, Durham DH1 3EQ [2006] *Tel:* 0191 384 7534
email: archdeacon.of.durham@durham.anglican.org

Lay Members (*two vacancies*)
Mr Ivor Stolliday, The Cathedral Office, The College, Durham DH1 3EH [2013]
Tel: 07968 943101
email: ivorstolliday@gmail.com
Chapter Clerk Canon Philip Davies, The Cathedral Office, The College, Durham DH1 3EH [2009]
Tel: 0191 374 4064
Fax: 0191 386 4267
email: philip.davies@durhamcathedral.co.uk
Cathedral Organist (Lay Canon) Canon Dr James Lancelot, 6 The College, Durham DH1 3EQ
Tel: 0191 386 4766
email: james.lancelot@durhamcathedral.co.uk

ARCHDEACONS
DURHAM Ven Ian Jagger, 15 The College, Durham DH1 3EQ [2006] *Tel:* 0191 384 7534
Fax: 0191 386 6915
email:
archdeacon.of.durham@durham.anglican.org
AUCKLAND Ven Nick Barker, Vicarage, 45 Milbank Rd, Darlington DL3 9NL [2007]
Tel: 01325 480444
Fax: 01325 354027
email:
archdeacon.of.auckland@durham.anglican.org
SUNDERLAND Ven Stuart Bain, St Nicholas Vicarage, Hedworth Lane, Boldon Colliery NE35 9JA [2002] *Tel:* 0191 536 2300
Fax: 0191 519 3369
email:
archdeacon.of.sunderland@durham.anglican.org

CONVOCATION (MEMBERS OF THE HOUSE OF CLERGY OF THE GENERAL SYNOD)
Dignitaries in Convocation
The Dean of Durham
Proctors in Convocation
Revd David Brooke
Revd Graeme Buttery
Revd Dr Margaret Gilley
Ven Ian Jagger

MEMBERS OF THE HOUSE OF LAITY OF THE GENERAL SYNOD
Dr Richard Goudie
Canon Frances Wood
Dr James Harrison
Sister Anne Williams

DIOCESAN OFFICERS
Dioc Secretary Mr Andrew Thurston, Cuthbert House, Stonebridge, Durham DH1 3RY
Tel: 01388 660010
email: Diocesan.Secretary@durham.anglican.org
Chancellor of Diocese The Worshipful the Revd Canon Rupert Bursell, Diocesan Registry, Messrs Smith Roddam, 56 North Bondgate, Bishop Auckland DL14 7PG   *Tel:* 01388 603073
Fax: 01388 450483
Deputy Chancellor Vacancy
Registrar of Diocese and Bishop's Legal Secretary Ms H. Monckton-Milnes, Dioc Registry (*as above*)
Deputy Registrar Mr D. Harris, Dioc Registry
Property Manager, Dioc Surveyor and Secretary to Houses Committee Mr M. Galley, Dioc Office
Tel: 01388 660006
email: mike.galley@durham.anglican.org

DIOCESAN ORGANIZATIONS
Diocesan Office Cuthbert House, Stonebridge, Durham DH1 3RY   *Tel:* 01388 604515
email: diocesan.office@durham.anglican.org

ADMINISTRATION
Dioc Synod (*Chairman, House of Clergy*) Canon Robert Lawrance, St Cuthbert's Vicarage, Aykley Court, Durham DH1 4NW   *Tel:* 0191 386 0146
email: robert.lawrance@durham.anglican.org
(*Chairman, House of Laity*) Dr Jamie Harrison, 5 Dunelm Court, South Street, Durham DH1 4QX
Tel: 0191 384 8643
email: dunelm5@btinternet.com
(*Secretary*) Mr Andrew Thurston, Dioc Office
Board of Finance (*Chairman*) Revd Canon Sheila Bamber, 177 Queen Alexandra Road, Sunderland SR3 1XN   *Tel:* 0191 520 2304
email: canonprovost@sunderlandminster.org
(*Secretary*) Vacancy (*as above*)
Glebe Committee (*Chairman*) Canon Sheila Bamber (*as above*); (*Secretary*) Mr Paul Stringer, Dioc Office   *Tel:* 01388 660002
Houses Committee (*Chairman*) Revd S. Pinnington OBE, Rectory, 5 Lingfield, Houghton le Spring DH5 8QA   *Tel:* 0191 584 3487
email: rectorstmichaels@icloud.com
(*Secretary*) Mr M. Galley, Dioc Office
Mission and Pastoral Committee (*Chairman*) Ven Ian Jagger; (*Secretary*) Mr Paul Stringer, Dioc Office   *Tel:* 01388 660002 (Direct line)
email: paul.stringer@durham.anglican.org
Church Buildings Committee (*Chairman*) Mr Geoff Taylor, 14 Academy Gardens, Gainford, Darlington DL2 3EN   *Tel:* 01325 730379
email: geoffandsue@academygardens.fsnet.co.uk

(*Secretary*) Mr Bill Heslop, Dioc Office
Tel: 01388 660001 (Direct line)
email: bill.heslop@durham.anglican.org
Closed Churches Uses Committee (*Chairman*) Mr W. Grant, 6 Sunniside Terrace, Cleadon, Sunderland SR6 7XE   *Tel:* 0191 536 4140
email: wgrant@talktalk.net
(*Secretary*) Mr Bill Heslop, Dioc Office (*as above*)
Designated Officer Mr Paul Stringer, Dioc Office (*as above*)
Administrative Secretary Mr Paul Stringer, Dioc Office (*as above*)
Office Manager Mrs Mandy Blackett, Dioc Office
Tel: 01388 660010
email: mandy.blackett@durham.anglican.org
Pensions Officer Canon Keith Woodhouse, 85 Baulkham Hills, Penshaw, Houghton le Spring DH4 7RZ   *Tel:* and *Fax:* 0191 584 3977
email: keith.woodhouse@durham.anglican.org
Adviser in Women's Ministry Revd Jennifer Bradshaw, Rectory, 2A Park Avenue, Sunderland SR6 9PU   *Tel:* 0191 548 6607
email: jennifer.bradshaw@durham.anglican.org

CHURCHES
Advisory Committee for the Care of Churches (*Chairman*) Ven Nick Barker (*as above*)
(*Secretary*) Mr G. W. Heslop, Dioc Office (*as above*)   *Tel:* 01388 660001

EDUCATION
Director of Education for Durham and Newcastle Mr Jeremy Fitt, Church House, St John's Terrace, North Shields NE29 6HS   *Tel:* 0191 270 4163
email: jeremy.fitt@drmnewcanglican.org
Assistant Director (Primary) Mrs Suzanne Lithgow (*address as above*)   *Tel:* 0191 270 4135
email: suzanne.lithgow@drmnewcanglican.org
Assistant Director (Secondary and FE) Vacancy
Assistant Director (Governance) Ms Rowan Ferguson (*address as above*)
email: rowan.ferguson@drmnewcanglican.org
Tel: 0191 270 4164
Bursar Mrs Eileen Bell (*address as above*)
Tel: 0191 270 4141
email: eileen.bell@drmnewcanglican.org

DIOCESAN RESOURCE TEAM
Director of Ministerial Development and Parish Support Vacancy
Director of Ordinands Revd Richard Collins
Tel: 0191 374 6015
email: ddo@durham.anglican.org
Adviser in Pastoral Care and Counselling Mr Andrew Quarmby   *Tel:* 07746 846317
Youth Ministry Adviser Mr Nicholas Rowark
Tel: 0191 374 6008
email: nick.rowark@durham.anglican.org
Children's Ministry Adviser Mrs Sharon Pritchard
Tel: 0191 374 6019
email: sharon.pritchard@ddemt.co.uk

Ecumenism Resources Officer Revd Sheelagh Aston, 37 Brancepeth Road, Oxclose, Washington NE38 0LA *Tel:* 0191 415 9468
email: sheelaghaston@yahoo.co.uk
Liturgical Committee Chairman Canon David Kennedy, 7 The College, Durham DH1 3EQ
Tel: 0191 375 0242
email: canon.precentor@durhamcathedral.co.uk
Local Church Growth and Development Adviser (Missioner) Canon Judy Hirst *Tel:* 0191 374 6014
email: judy.hirst@durham.anglican.org
Stewardship Development Officer Mr Alistair Jenkins *Tel:* 0191 374 6016
email: alistair.jenkins@ddemt.co.uk
Warden of Reader Ministry, Bishop of Jarrow, Bishop's House, 25 Ivy Lane, Low Fell, Gateshead. NE9 6QD *Tel:* 0191 491 0917
email: bishop.of.jarrow@durham.anglican.org
Archdeaconry Sub-wardens of Reader Ministry (Sunderland Archdeaconry) Mrs Hilary Avent, 19 Brookside, Houghton le Spring DH5 9NW
Tel: 07870 501629
email: hilary.avent@yahoo.co.uk
(Durham Archdeaconry)
Mr Ian Boothroyd, 1 The Paddock, Sunniside, Bishop Auckland DL13 4LN *Tel:* 01388 730443
email: ian.boothroyd@durham.anglican.org
(Auckland Archdeaconry)
Mrs Hylda Hopper, 3 Dorchester Court, Marlborough Drive, Darlington DL1 5YD
Tel: 01325 460999
email: hyldahopper@aol.com

LINDISFARNE REGIONAL TRAINING PARTNERSHIP
Principal Revd Canon Cathy Rowling, Church House, St John's Terrace, North Shields NE29 6HS *Tel:* 0191 270 4143
email: cathyrowling@lindisfarnertp.org
Director of Studies and Tutor for Ordinands Revd Dr David Bryan, Church House, St John's Terrace, North Shields NE29 6HS *Tel:* 0191 270 4150
email: davidbryan@lindisfarnertp.org
Developing Discipleship Officer Vacancy, Church House, St John's Terrace, North Shields NE29 6HS
IME 4–7 Director Revd Rick Simpson, The Rectory, Brancepeth, Durham DH7 8EL
Tel: 0191 380 0440
email: ricksimpson@lindisfarnertp.org
Tutor for Reader Training Revd Dr Michael Beck, Church House, St John's Terrace, North Shields NE29 6HS *Tel:* 0191 270 4138
email: michaelbeck@lindisfarnertp.org
Administrator Jenny Burton, Church House, St John's Terrace, North Shields NE29 6HS
Tel: 0191 270 4144
email: jennyburton@lindisfarnertp.org

PARTNERSHIP BODIES
DFW Adoption (Chairman) Ven Stuart Bain (*as above*); (*Director*) Ms Margaret Bell, Agriculture House, Stonebridge, Durham DH1 3RY
Tel: 0191 386 3719
email: office@dfw.org.uk

Durham-Lesotho Link Executive Officers Revds Rob and Margaret Bianchi, 8 Lindisfarne, Biddick, Washington NE38 7JR *Tel:* 0191 417 0852
email: dleo.bianchi@tiscali.co.uk
Northumbrian Industrial Mission (Chairman) Mr Paul Southgate, NIM Registered Office, Sunderland Minster Church, High St West, Sunderland SR1 3ET *Tel:* 0191 253 6180
email: director@vip-gb.org
(Chaplain Team Leader) Mrs Fiona Usher, 21 Highfield Gardens, Chester-le-Street, Durham DH3 3UL *Tel:* 07850 937236
email: fiona-nim@btconnect.com
(Secretary) Mrs Joan Smith, 64 Cornmoor Rd, Whickham, Newcastle-upon-Tyne NE16 4PY
Tel: 0191 420 1238
Tees Valley Ministry (Chairman) Tony Sacco c/o Churches Regional Commission in the North-East, St James' URC, Northumberland Road, Newcastle upon Tyne NE1 8JF
email: tony.sacco@intrainsolutions.co.uk
(Secretary) Mr P. Etwell, 5 Priors Wood, Guisborough TS14 6LT *Tel:* 01287 632852
email: peteretwell@sky.com
Chaplaincy to the Arts and Recreation (Chairman) Canon Dr J. P. Cassidy, St Chad's College, University of Durham, 18 North Bailey, Durham DH1 3RH *Tel:* 0191 334 3345
email: j.p.cassidy@dur.ac.uk
Secretary Mr Gary Cox, St Chad's College, University of Durham, 18 North Bailey, Durham DH1 3RH *email:* gary.cox@dur.ac.uk

PRESS
Communications Adviser Mr Keith Blundy, Aegies Associates *Tel:* 01325 301220
email: pr@aegies.com *or* communications@durham.anglican.org

DIOCESAN RECORD OFFICE
Archives and Special Collections, University Library (Palace Green Section), University of Durham, Palace Green, Durham DH1 3RN
Archivist Mr Andrew Gray *Tel:* 0191 334 2972
email: pg.library@durham.ac.uk
(For diocesan records)
County Record Office, County Hall, Durham DH1 5UL *Tel:* 03000 267619
email: record.office@ durham.gov.uk
Web: www.durhamrecordoffice.org.uk
(For parochial records for the whole diocese)

AREA DEANS
ARCHDEACONRY OF SUNDERLAND
Chester-le-Street Revd David Glover, The Parish Office, Holy Trinity Church, The Avenue, Washington NE38 7LE *Tel:* 0191 418 7911
email: htcwashington@tiscali.co.uk
Gateshead Revd Alan Raine, St Andrew's Vicarage, Whinbrooke, Gateshead NE10 8HR
Tel: 0191 469 3257
email: alanraine@virginmedia.com

Gateshead West Revd Tom Jamieson, Barmoor House, 64 Main Road, Ryton NE40 3AJ
Tel: 0191 413 4592
email: tomjamiesonryton@hotmail.com
Houghton-le-Spring Revd Libby Wilkinson, The Rectory, Old Durham Road, Gateshead NE8 4BS
Tel: 0191 477 3990
email: libbywilko@virginmedia.com
Jarrow (*Acting*) Canon Raymond Dick, Boldon Rectory, 13 Rectory Green, West Boldon NE36 0QD
Tel: 0191 908 9102
email: raymonddick@btinternet.com
Wearmouth Revd Dick Bradshaw, Rectory, 2A Park Avenue, Sunderland SR5 9PU
Tel: 0191 548 6607
email: rbradshawbradshaw@btinternet.com

ARCHDEACONRY OF DURHAM

Durham Revd Canon Robert Lawrance, St Cuthbert's Vicarage, 1 Aykley Court, Durham DH1 4NW
Tel: 0191 384 7825
email: robert.lawrance@durham.anglican.org
Easington Revd Alan Milne, The Vicarage, Church Lane, Murton, Seaham SR7 9RD
Tel and *Fax:* 0191 526 2410
email: revalan17@yahoo.co.uk
Hartlepool Revd Janet Burbury, The Vicarage, Hart Village, Hartlepool TS27 3AP
Tel: 01429 262340
email: janetb_231@hotmail.co.uk

Lanchester Revd Heather Murray, Collierley Vicarage, Bourne Terrace, Annfield Plain, Stanley DH9 8QS
Tel: 01207 284760
email: revheather@btinternet.com
Sedgefield Revd Keith Lumsdon, St Luke's Vicarage, Church Lane, Ferryhill DL17 8LT
Tel: 01740 651438
email: keithlumsdon@hotmail.com

ARCHDEACONRY OF AUCKLAND

Auckland Canon Neville Vine, 4 Conway Grove, Bishop Auckland DL14 6AF
Tel: 01388 604397
email: neville.vine@btinternet.com
Barnard Castle Revd Alec Harding, Vicarage, Parsons Lonnen, Newgate, Barnard Castle DL12 8ST
Tel: 01833 637018
email: alec.harding@durham.anglican.org
Darlington Revd Lynda Gough, 32 Skeldale Grove, Darlington DL3 0GW
Tel: 01325 282456
email: legough3@btinternet.com
Stanhope Revd Vince Fenton, Rectory, 14 Hartside Close, Crook DL15 9NH
Tel: 01388 760939
email: vincent.fenton@durham.anglican.org
Stockton Revd David Brooke, St John's Church, Morrison Street, Stillington, Stockton on Tees TS21 1JD
Tel: 01740 630810
email: revdbrooke@stocktonsix.org.uk

Founded in 1109. Cambridgeshire, except for an area in the north-west (PETERBOROUGH) and three parishes in the south (CHELMSFORD); the western quarter of Norfolk; one parish in Bedfordshire.

Population 739,000   Area 1,510 sq m
Full-time Stipendiary Parochial Clergy 127   Benefices 180
Parishes 311   Churches 334
www.ely.anglican.org
Overseas link dioceses: Vellore (Church of South India) (Ecumenical),
Nordkirche (Germany) and Kigali (Church of the Province of Rwanda).

BISHOP (68th)
Rt Revd Stephen Conway, The Bishop's House, Ely CB7 4DW   *Tel:* 01353 662749
    email: bishop@ely.anglican.org
Bishop's Lay Chaplain Dr Bridget Nichols (*same address and tel. no.*)
    email: bridget.nichols@ely.anglican.org
Bishop's Personal Assistant (*same address and tel. no.*) Mrs Jane Sansom
    email: janemsansom@ely.anglican.org
Bishop's Secretary Mrs Debbie Swinton (*same address and tel. no.*)
    email: debbie.swinton@ely.anglican.org

SUFFRAGAN BISHOP (seconded to Diocese of St Edmundsbury & Ipswich as Acting Bishop
HUNTINGDON Rt Revd Dr David Thomson, 14 Lynn Rd, Ely CB6 1DA [2008]   *Tel:* 01353 662137
    Fax: 01353 669357
    email: bishop.huntingdon@ely.anglican.org
Bishop's Secretary Mrs Jane Baker (*same address, tel. no. and email*)

CATHEDRAL CHURCH OF THE HOLY AND UNDIVIDED TRINITY
Dean Very Revd Mark Bonney, The Chapter Office, The College, Ely CB7 4DL [2012]
    Tel: 01353 660316
Canon Pastor Vacancy
Canon Missioner Canon Dr Alan Hargrave, The Chapter House, The College, Ely CB7 4DL [2004]
    Tel: 01353 660304
Canon Precentor Canon Dr James Garrard, The Chapter House, The College, Ely CB7 4DL [2008]
    Tel: 01353 660335
Administrator and Chapter Clerk Mr Stephen Bourne, The Chapter House, The College, Ely CB7 4DL
    Tel: 01353 667735
Director of Music Mr Paul Trepte, The Chapter House, The College, Ely CB7 4DL
    Tel: 01353 660336

ARCHDEACONS
CAMBRIDGE Ven Alexander Hughes, St Botolph's Rectory, 1a Summerfield, Cambridge CB3 9HE [2004]   *Tel:* 01353 652719
    Fax: 01223 360929
    email: archdeacon.cambridge@ely.anglican.org
HUNTINGDON AND WISBECH Ven Hugh Kyle McCurdy, Whitgift House, The College, Ely CB7 4DL [2005]   *Tel:* 01353 658404 (Home)
    Tel: 01353 652709 (Office)
    Fax: 01353 652745
    email: archdeacon.handw@ely.anglican.org

CONVOCATION (MEMBERS OF THE HOUSE OF CLERGY OF THE GENERAL SYNOD)
Proctors for Clergy
Canon Timothy Alban Jones
Revd Michael Booker
Ven Hugh McCurdy

MEMBERS OF THE HOUSE OF LAITY OF THE GENERAL SYNOD
Mrs Janet Perrett
Mr Stephen Tooke
Dr Elaine Storkey

DIOCESAN OFFICERS
Dioc Secretary Mr Paul Evans, Bishop Woodford House, Barton Rd, Ely CB7 4DX
    Tel: 01353 652701
    01353 652702 (Direct Line)
    Fax: 01353 652745
    email: paul.evans@ely.anglican.org
Chancellor of Diocese The Hon Judge Leonard QC
Registrar of Diocese Mr Howard Dellar, 1 The Sanctuary, London SW1P 3JT   *Tel:* 020 7222 5381

DIOCESAN ORGANIZATIONS
Diocesan Office Bishop Woodford House, Barton Rd, Ely CB7 4DX   *Tel:* 01353 652701
    Fax: 01353 652745
    email: office@ely.anglican.org

ADMINISTRATION

Dioc Synod (*Chairman, House of Clergy*) Canon Timothy Alban Jones, The Vicarage, Cross Green, Soham, Ely CB7 5DU
Tel: 01353 720423
email: vicar@soham.org.uk
(*Chairman, House of Laity*) Mrs Janet Perrett, 38 Beachampstead Road, Great Staughton PE19 5DX *email:* jrperrett@talktalk.net
(*Secretary*) Mr Paul Evans, Dioc Office
Assistant Secretary (*Pastoral*) Miss Jane Logan, Dioc Office
Finance Committee (*Chairman*) Mr Hugh Duberly; (*Secretary*) Mr Paul Evans, Dioc Office
Diocesan Accountant Mrs Pauline Allin
Dioc Surveyor Mr Stephen Layton, Dioc Office
Board of Patronage (*Secretary*) Miss Jane Logan, Dioc Office
Designated Officer Vacancy

CHURCHES

Advisory Committee for the Care of Churches (*Secretary*) Miss Jane Logan, Dioc Office
Archdeaconry of Cambridge Church Music Society (*Secretary*) Mrs. Suzanne Barton, 239 Lichfield Road, Cambridge CB1 3SH Tel: 01223 505764
email: suzanne_barton@yahoo.com
Ely RSCM Committee (*Secretary*) Mr Ken Diffey, 1 The Maltings, Godmanchester, Cambs PE29 2JR
Tel: 01480 458846
email: diffey@homecall.co.uk

EDUCATION

email: cathy.priestley@ely.anglican.org
Web: www.ely.anglican.org/education
Dioc Board of Education (*Secretary*) Mrs Tricia Pritchard, Dioc Office
Director of Education Mrs Tricia Pritchard (*as above*)
Children's Adviser Vacancy
Youth Officer Vacancy
RE Adviser (*Schools*) Dr Shirley Hall, Dioc Office
Schools Buildings and Finance Officer Mr Richard Bircham

MINISTRY

Director of Ministry Revd Canon Linda Church
Tel: 01353 652733
Fax: 01353 652745
Diocesan Director of Ordinands Revd Anna Matthews Tel: 01353 652730
Fax: 01353 652745
Reader Ministry Contact The Bishop of Huntingdon
Readers' Board (*Chair*) Mr Stephen Mashford, 7a Haggis Gap, Fulbourn, Cambridge CB21 5HD
Tel: 01223 882163
email: sandjmashford@aol.com
Warden Canon Timothy Alban Jones
Tel: 01353 720423
email: vicar@soham.org.uk

LITURGICAL COMMITTEE

Secretary Mr Simon Kershaw, 5 Sharp Close, St Ives, Cambs PE27 6UN Tel: 01480 381471
email: simon@kershaw.org.uk

MISSION AND ECUMENICAL

Director of Mission Revd Peter Wood
Tel: 01353 652723
Council for Mission (*Chair*) Ven Hugh McCurdy
Tel: 01353 658404 (Home)
Tel: 01353 652709 (Office)
Fax: 01353 652745
email: archdeacon.handw@ely.anglican.org
Ecumenical Officer Revd Canon Prof David Thompson, 7 Sherlock Road, Cambridge CB3 0HR Tel: 01223 362500
email: dmt@cam.ac.uk

PRESS AND PUBLICATIONS

Communications Manager Ms Sarah Williams, Dioc Office Tel: 01353 652728
Editor of Dioc Directory Ms Sarah Williams, Dioc Office

DIOCESAN RECORD OFFICES

Dioc Archivist Peter M. Meadows, c/o University Library, West Rd, Cambridge CB3 9DR
Tel: 01223 333141
Cambridgeshire Archives, Shire Hall, Castle Hill, Cambridge CB3 0AP *Collections Archivist* Mr Richard Anderson *Tel:* 01223 699487/ 699399 (*For parishes in the archdeaconry of Cambridge and the deaneries of Ely and March*)
Huntingdonshire Archives, Princes Street, Huntingdon PE29 3PA *Collections Archivist* Mr Richard Anderson *Tel:* 01480 372738 (*For parishes in the former archdeaconry of Huntingdon*)
Cambridge Record Office, Shire Hall, Cambridge (*see above*) (*For parishes in the deaneries of Ely and March*)
Norfolk Record Office, The Archive Centre, Martineau Lane, Norwich NR1 2DQ *County Archivist* Mr Gary Tuson *Tel:* 01603 222599 (*For parishes in the deaneries of Feltwell and Fincham*)
Wisbech and Fenland Museum, Museum Square, Wisbech PE13 1ES *Assistant Curator* Mr J. R. Bell *Tel:* 01945 583817 (*For parishes in the deanery of Wisbech Lynn Marshland*)

SOCIAL RESPONSIBILITY

Cambridgeshire Deaf Association (*Ely Dioc Association for the Deaf*) c/o Ms S. Watt, 8 Romsey Terrace, Cambridge
Mothers' Union (*President*) Mrs Susan Baker, Dioc Office Tel: 01353 652718

RURAL AND AREA DEANS
ARCHDEACONRY OF CAMBRIDGE

Bourn Revd Mike Booker, The Vicarage, 92 Swaynes Lane, Comberton, Cambridge CB23 7EF
Tel: 01223 260095
Cambridge North Canon Nick Moir, 10 Lynfield Lane, Chesterton, Cambridge CB4 1DR
Tel: 01223 303469

Cambridge South Revd Prof Huw Jones, 17 Barrow Road, Cambridge CB2 8AP
Tel: 01223 358458
Fordham and Quy Canon Timothy Alban Jones, The Vicarage, Cross Green, Soham, Ely, Cambs CB7 5DU
Tel: 01353 720423
North Stowe Revd James Blandford-Baker, St Andrew's Vicarage, Church St, Histon CB4 9EP
Tel: 01223 233456
Granta Revd Dr Julie Norris, The Vicarage, 23 Church Lane, Little Abington, Cambridge CB21 6BQ
Tel: 01223 891350
Shingay Revd Andrew O'Brien, The Vicarage, Vicarage Close, Melbourn, Royston SG8 6DY
Tel: 01763 260295

ARCHDEACONRY OF HUNTINGDON AND WISBECH

Ely Revd Howard Robson, 30 Church Lane, Littleport, Ely CB6 1PS
Tel: 01353 864695
Fincham and Feltwell Revd Barbara Burton, The Rectory, High Street, Fincham, King's Lynn PE33 9EL
Tel: 01366 348079

Huntingdon Canon Brian Atling, Blue Cedars, Common Lane, Hemingford Abbots, Huntingdon PE28 9AW
Tel: 01480 493975
March Revd Nigel Whitehouse, Rectory, 9a St Mary's St, Whittlesey, Peterborough PE7 1BG
Tel: 01733 203676
St Ives Revd Canon Fred Kilner, The Old White Lion, 125 High Street, Somersham PE28 3EN
Tel: 01487 842864
St Neots Canon Annette Reed, Vicarage, 24 St James Rd, Little Paxton, Huntingdon PE19 6QW
Tel: 01480 211048
Wisbech Lynn Marshland Canon Matthew Bradbury, The Vicarage, Church, Wisbech St Mary, Cambs PE13 4RN
Tel: 01945 410814
Yaxley Revd Dr Donald McFadyen, The Rectory, 2a The Village, Orton Longueville, Peterborough PE2 7DN
Tel: 01733 371071

DIOCESE IN EUROPE

Founded 1980 by union of the Diocese of Gibraltar (founded 1842) and the (Fulham) Jurisdiction of North and Central Europe. Area, Europe, except Great Britain and Ireland; Morocco; Turkey; the Asian countries of the former Soviet Union.

Licensed Clergy 159 Churches and Congregations 295
www.europe.anglican.org

BISHOP OF GIBRALTAR IN EUROPE (3rd)
Rt Revd Dr Robert Innes, 47 rue Capitaine Crespel boite 49, 1050 Ixelles, Belgium
Tel: 0032 (0)2 213 7480
email: bishop.europe@churchofengland.org
Bishop's Commissary and Chaplain Revd Canon Meurig Williams (*same address and telephone number*)
email: meurig.williams@churchofengland.org

SUFFRAGAN BISHOP
IN EUROPE Rt Revd Dr David Hamid, 14 Tufton St, London SW1P 3QZ [2002]   Tel: 020 7898 1160
Fax: 020 7898 1166
email: david.hamid@churchofengland.org
Bishop's Chaplain and PA Revd Deacon Frances Hiller

HONORARY ASSISTANT BISHOPS
Rt Revd Michael Colclough, 12 Grosvenor Court, Sloane Square, London SW1X 9PF
Tel: 020 3612 3135
email: michaeljcolclough@gmail.com
Rt Revd John Flack, Huddersfield House, 7 Cemetery Road, Whittlesey, Peterborough PE7 1SF   Tel: 01733 202767
email: johnflack67@yahoo.com
Rt Revd Richard Garrard, 26 Carol Close, Stoke Holy Cross, Norwich NR14 8NN [2001]
Tel: 01508 494165
email: garrard.r.a@btinternet.com
Rt Revd Patrick Harris, Apartment B, Ireton House, Pavillion Gardens, The Park, Cheltenham GL50 2SP [1999]   Tel: 01242 231376
email: pandvharris@blueyonder.co.uk
Rt Revd Edward Holland, 37 Parfrey St, London W6 9EW [2002]   Tel: 020 8746 3636
email: ed.holland@uwclub.net
Rt Revd Michael Manktelow, 14 Little London, Chichester, W Sussex PO19 1NZ [1994]
Tel: 01243 531096
Rt Revd Nicholas Reade, 5 Warnham Gardens, Bexhill-on-Sea, Kent TN39 3SP
Tel: 01424 842673
email: nicholas.reade@btinternet.com

Rt Revd Dr José Jorge Pina Cabral, Centro Diocesano, Rua Afonso de Albuquerque No 86, Apartado 392, 4430 Vila Nova de Gaia, Portugal
Tel: 00 351 22 375 4018
email: bispopinacabral@igreja-lusitana.org
Rt Revd David Stancliffe, 15 The Butts, Stanhope, Bishop Auckland, Durham DL13 2UQ
Tel: 01388 526912
email: david.stancliffe@hotmail.com
Rt Revd John Taylor, 22 Conduit Head Rd, Cambridge CB3 0EY [1998]   Tel: 01223 313783
email: john.taylor6529@ntlworld.com
Rt Revd David Smith, 34 Cedar Glade, Dunnington, York YO19 5QZ [2002]   Tel: 01904 481225
email: david@djmhs.force9.co.uk
Rt Revd Dr Stephen Venner, 81 King Harry Lane, St Albans AL3 4AS   Tel: 07980 743628
email: stephen@venner.org.uk
Rt Revd Pierre Whalon, American Cathedral, 23 Avenue George V, 75008 Paris, France [2001]
Tel: 00 33 1 53 23 84 00 (Cathedral)
Fax: 00 33 1 47 23 95 30 (Cathedral)
Tel: 00 33 1 47 20 02 23 (Direct)
Fax: 00 33 1 40 27 03 53 (Home)
email: office@tec-europe.org
Rt Revd Michael Scott-Joynt, Easter House, Funtington, Chichester P018 9LJ [2011]
Tel: 01243 575762
email: michael.scottjoynt11@gmail.com
Rt Revd Michael Turnbull, 67 Strand St, Sandwich CT13 9HN [2003]   Tel: 01304 611389
email: amichaelturnbull@yahoo.co.uk

CATHEDRAL CHURCH OF THE HOLY TRINITY, GIBRALTAR
Dean Very Revd Dr John Paddock, 41 Jumpers Buildings, Rosia Road, Gibraltar [2008]
Tel: 00 350 200 78377 (Deanery)
Fax: 00 350 200 78463
email: deangib@gibraltar.gi

PRO-CATHEDRAL OF ST PAUL, VALLETTA, MALTA
Chancellor Canon Simon Godfrey, Chancellor's Lodge, St Paul's Anglican Pro-Cathedral, Independence Square, Valletta VLT12, Malta [2009]   Tel: 00 356 21 22 57 14
Fax: 00 356 21 22 58 67
email: anglican@onvol.net /
simonhmgodfrey@googlemail.com

PRO-CATHEDRAL OF THE HOLY TRINITY, BRUSSELS, BELGIUM

Chancellor Vacancy, Pro-Cathedral of the Holy Trinity, 29 rue Capitaine Crespel, 1050 Brussels [2005]   *Tel:* 00 32 2 511 71 83
Fax: 00 32 2 511 10 28
email: chaplain@holytrinity.be

ARCHDEACONS

THE EASTERN ARCHDEACONRY Ven Patrick Curran, c/o British Embassy, Jaurèsgasse 12, 1030 Vienna, Austria [2002]   *Tel:* 00 43 1 718 5902 (Home)
Tel: and *Fax:* 00 43 1 714 8900 (Office)
email: office@christchurchvienna.org
NORTH WEST EUROPE (Acting Archdeacon) Revd Canon Meurig Williams
email: meurig.williams@churchofengland.org
FRANCE Ven Ian Naylor, 3 bis rue Pasteur, 64000 Pau, France [201   *Tel:* 00 33 5 59 30 91 84 /
+33 (0)7885 50980
email: if.naylor@orange.fr
GIBRALTAR (Acting Archdeacon) Revd Canon Geoffrey Johnston, Church House, Calle Jilguero 19, Almijara 2 Sur, Nerja 29780, Spain
Tel: 00 34 952 521 339 / +34 608 695 756
email: anglicansnerja@yahoo.com
ITALY AND MALTA Ven Jonathan Boardman, All Saint's Church, Via del Babuino 153, 00187 Rome, Italy [2009]   *Tel and Fax:* 39 06 3600 1881
email: j.boardman@allsaintsrome.org (Personal)
office@allsaintsrome.org (Office)
GERMANY AND NORTHERN EUROPE (Acting Archdeacon) Ven Peter Potter, St Ursula's Church, Jubiläumsplatz 2, CH-3005 Berne, Switzerland
Tel: 0041 31 351 03 43 (Home)
+41 31 352 85 67 (Office)
email: chaplain.berne@anglican.ch
SWITZERLAND Ven Peter Potter, St Ursula's Church, Jubiläumsplatz 2, CH-3005 Berne, Switzerland [2009]   *Tel:* 0041 31 351 03 43 (Home)
+41 31 352 85 67 (Office)
Fax: +41 31 351 05 48
email: chaplain.berne@anglican.ch

CONVOCATION (MEMBER OF THE HOUSE OF CLERGY OF THE GENERAL SYNOD)

Canon Debbie Flach

MEMBERS OF THE HOUSE OF LAITY OF THE GENERAL SYNOD

Lay Canon Mrs Ann Turner
Mrs Madeleine Holmes

DIOCESAN OFFICERS

Dioc Secretary Mr Adrian Mumford, Dioc Office
Chancellor of Diocese The Worshipful Mark Hill, Francis Taylor Building, London EC4Y 7BY (contact via Dioc Office)
Registrar of Diocese and Bishop's Legal Secretary Mr Aiden Hargreaves-Smith, Winkworth

Sherwood, 5 Montague Close, London SE1 9BB *(contact via the Diocesan Office)*
Tel: 020 7898 1155
Fax: 020 7898 1166
email: bron.panter@churchofengland.org

DIOCESAN ORGANIZATIONS

Diocesan Office 14 Tufton St, London SW1P 3QZ
Tel: 020 7898 1155
Fax: 020 7898 1166
email: bron.panter@churchofengland.org

ADMINISTRATION

Dioc Synod (Lay Vice-President) Mrs Celia Paterson, c/o Dioc Office; *(Secretary)* Mr Adrian Mumford, Dioc Office
Board of Finance (Chairman) Mr Michael Hart, c/o Dioc Office; *(Secretary)* Mr Adrian Mumford

CHURCHES

Faculty Committee (Secretary) Mr Adrian Mumford *(as above)*

MINISTRY AND TRAINING

Warden of Readers Rt Revd Dr David Hamid, Dioc Office
Director of Ordinands Revd Canon William Gulliford, Dioc Office
email: william.gulliford@churchofengland.org
or william.gulliford@london.anglican.org
Director of Training Revd Ulla Monberg, Borgmester Jensens Allé 9, 2th, 2100 Copenhagen, ø, Denmark   *Tel:* 00 45 3526 0660
email: ulla.monberg@churchofengland.org

LITURGY

Enquiries to Revd Canon Paul Bradshaw, 367 Pine Valley Drive, Fairview TX 75069 USA
Tel: 001 214 856 0799
email: bradshaw.1@nd.edu

MEDITERRANEAN MISSIONS TO SEAMEN

Administrator Mr Adrian Mumford *(as above)*

PRESS AND PUBLICATIONS

Press and Communications Officer Revd Paul Needle, Dioc Office
Tel: 07712 463806 (Mobile)
email: paul.needle@churchofengland.org
Editor of 'The European Anglican' Revd Paul Needle *(as above)*

DIOCESAN RECORD OFFICE

London Metropolitan Archives, 40 Northampton Road, London EC1R 0HB   *Tel:* 020 7332 3820
email: ask.lma@cityoflondon.gov.uk

ENVIRONMENTAL OFFICER

Mrs Madeleine Holmes, Le Peladis, Route Pommier, 24350 Lisle, France   *Tel:* 0033 5 53 04 85 44
Fax: 0033 5 53 04 85 44
email: madeleine@peladis.plus.com

ARCHBISHOP'S APOKRISARIOI AND REPRESENTATIVES

To the Holy See Rt Revd David Moxon, The Anglican Centre in Rome, Palazzo Doria Pamphilj, Piazza del Collegio Romano 2, 00186 Rome, Italy   *Tel:* 39 06 678 0302
Fax: 39 06 678 0674
email: director@anglicancentre.it
To the Patriarch of Romania, and the Patriarch of Bulgaria Vacancy, British Embassy – Bucharest, Strada Jules Michelet, Nr 22–24, Sector 1, 70154 Bucharest, Romania   *Tel:* 00 40 740 243789
email: resurrectionbucharest@gmail.com

To the Archbishop of Athens and All Greece Canon Malcolm Bradshaw, c/o British Embassy, Ploutarchou 1, Athens 106 75
Tel and *Fax:* 00 30 210 721 4906 (Home)
email: anglican@otenet.gr
To the Patriarch of Moscow and All Russia Revd Clive Fairclough, British Embassy Moscow, Sofiiskaya Naberezhnaya, Moscow 109702
Tel and *Fax:* 007 495 629 0990
email: chaplain@standrewsmoscow.org
To the Patriarch of Serbia Revd Robin Fox, St Mary's Anglican Church, Visegradska 23, 11000 Belgrade, Serbia   *Tel:* 00 381 11 3232 948
email: robin.fox@sbb.co.rs

DEANERIES

The archdeaconry of Germany and Northern Europe has Deanery Synods rather than a single Archdeaconry Synod. The names and addresses of the officers are available from the Diocesan Office.

DIOCESE OF EXETER

Transferred to Exeter in 1050, formerly at Crediton in 909. Devon, except for one parish in the south-east (SALISBURY) and one parish in the west (TRURO); Plymouth; Torbay.

Population 1,141,000   Area 2,580 sq m
Full-time Stipendiary Parochial Clergy 206   Benefices 181
Parishes 494   Churches 614
www.exeter.anglican.org
Overseas link diocese: Cyprus and the Gulf; Thika (Kenya).

BISHOP (70th)
Rt Revd Robert Atwell, Bishop's Office, The Palace Gatehouse, Palace Gate, Exeter EX1 1HX
Tel: 01392 272362
email: bishop.of.exeter@exeter.anglican.org
Episcopal Vicar and Chaplain Revd Dr Adrian Hough, Bishop's Office, The Palace Gatehouse, Palace Gate, Exeter EX1 1HX   *Tel:* 01392 272362
email: adrian.hough@exeter.anglican.org
Personal Assistant Ms Sarah Johnson (*address and phone number as above*)
email: sarah.johnson@exeter.anglican.org
Administrative Secretary Mrs Maria Loe (*address and phone number as above*)
email: maria.loe@exeter.anglican.org

SUFFRAGAN BISHOPS
CREDITON Rt Revd Nicholas McKinnel, 32 The Avenue, Tiverton, Devon EX16 4HW [2012]
Tel: 01884 250002
email: bishop.of.crediton@exeter.anglican.org
PLYMOUTH Vacancy

HONORARY ASSISTANT BISHOPS
Rt Revd Richard Hawkins, 3 Westbrook Close, Whipton, Exeter EX4 8BS [2005] *Tel:* 01392 462622
Rt Revd Martin Shaw, 11 Russell Terrace, Exeter EX4 4HX [2010]   *Tel:* 01392 663511
email: amartinshaw@gmail.com

CATHEDRAL CHURCH OF ST PETER
Dean Very Revd Dr Jonathan Draper, The Deanery, 10 Cathedral Close, Exeter EX1 1EZ [2012]   *Tel:* 01392 273509 (Office)
email: dean@exeter-cathedral.org.uk
Canons Residentiary
Precentor Vacancy
Chancellor and Missioner Canon Anna Norman-Walker, 6 Cathedral Close, Exeter EX1 1EZ [2011]
Tel: 01392 255573
email:
anna.norman-walker@exeter-anglican.org.uk
Treasurer and Pastor Canon Ian Morter, 9 Cathedral Close, Exeter EX1 1EZ [2010]
Tel: 01392 285987 (Office)
Tel: 01392 758172 (Home)
email: pastor@exeter-cathedral.org.uk

SSM Residentiary Canon Revd Canon Dr John Searle, Belle Isle Lodge, Belle Isle Drive, Exeter EX2 4RY [2014]   *Tel:* 01392 432153
email: j.f.searle@btinternet.com
Chapter Canons Mrs Hannah Foster, Mr Jonathan Harris, Ven Canon Clive Cohen
Priest Vicar Revd Alison Turner
Senior Virger and Sacristan Mr Michael Greaves, 6A Cathedral Close, Exeter EX1 1EZ
Tel: 01392 274779 (Office)
Tel: 01392 479237 (Home)
email: virgers@exeter-cathedral.org.uk
Cathedral Offices 1 The Cloisters, Exeter EX1 1HS
Tel: 01392 255573
Fax: 01392 285986
email: reception@exeter-cathedral.org.uk
Web: www.exeter-cathedral.org.uk
Managing Director Mrs Alison Davenport
Tel: 01392 285977
email: alison.davenport@ exeter-cathedral.org.uk
Clerk of Works Mr Christopher Sampson
Tel: 01392 285971
email: clerkofworks@exeter-cathedral.org.uk
Liturgy and Music Dept   *Tel:* 01392 285984
email: liturgy@exeter-cathedral.org.uk
Director of Music Mr Andrew Millington, 11 Cathedral Close, Exeter EX1 1EZ
Tel: 01392 285985 (Office)
Tel: 01392 277521 (Home)
email: music@exeter-cathedral.org.uk
Assistant Director of Music Mr David Davies, Flat 4 Closter Garth, Exeter EX1 1JS
Tel: 01392 270761 (Office)
Tel: 01392 270877 (Home)
email: adom@exeter-cathedral.org.uk
Cathedral Development Director Mr Paul Courtney, Cathedral Development Office, 1 The Cloisters, Exeter EX1 1HS   *Tel:* 01392 285974
email:
developmentdirector@exeter-cathedral.org.uk
Head of Visitor Services Catherine Escott
Tel: 01392 285983
email: visitors@exeter-cathedral.org.uk

ARCHDEACONS
EXETER Ven Christopher Futcher, Emmanuel House, Station Road, Ide, Exeter EX2 9RS [2012]
Tel: 01392 425577
email: archdeacon.of.exeter@exeter.anglican.org

TOTNES (Acting) Ven Clive Cohen, Blue Hills, Bradley Road, Bovey Tracey, Newton Abbot TQ13 9EU *Tel:* 01626 832064
email: archdeacon.of.totnes@exeter.anglican.org
BARNSTAPLE (Acting) Ven Mike Edson, Stage Cross, Sanders Lane, Bishops Tawton, Barnstaple EX32 0BE Tel: 01271 375475
email:
archdeacon.of.barnstaple@exeter.anglican.org
PLYMOUTH Ven Ian Chandler, St Mark's House, 46a Cambridge Road, Ford, Plymouth PL2 1PU
Tel: 01752 202401
email:
archdeacon.of.plymouth@exeter.anglican.org

CONVOCATION (MEMBERS OF THE HOUSE OF CLERGY OF THE GENERAL SYNOD)
Proctors for Clergy
Revd Preb Douglas Dettmer
Revd Canon Andrew Godsall
Revd Preb Samuel Philpott
Revd Preb Roderick Thomas

MEMBERS OF THE HOUSE OF LAITY OF THE GENERAL SYNOD
Mrs Anneliese Barrell
Mrs Anne Foreman
Miss Emma Forward
Mr Jack Shelley

Dioc Synod (*Chairman, House of Clergy*) Revd Preb Douglas Dettmer, Rectory, Thorverton, Exeter EX5 5NR *Tel:* 01392 860332
(*Secretary, House of Clergy*) Revd Gilly Maude, Vicarage, 17 Seafields, Dartmouth Road, Goodrington, Paignton TQ4 6NY *Tel:* 01803 846335
email: gillian.maude@btinternet.com
(*Chairman, House of Laity*) Mrs Marguerite Shapland, Bartley House, 21 Church Street, Braunton EX33 2EL *Tel:* 01271 814082
email: m.shapland07@btinternet.com
(*Secretary, House of Laity*) Mr Graham Lea, 2 Thornyville Close, Oreston, Plymouth PL9 7LE
Tel: 01752 403392
Synod Secretary Mr Mark Beedell, The Old Deanery

DIOCESAN OFFICERS
Dioc Secretary Mr Mark Beedell, The Old Deanery, The Cloisters, Exeter EX1 1HS
Tel: 01392 272686
Fax: 01392 499594
email: mark.beedell@exeter.anglican.org
Chancellor of Diocese Hon Sir Andrew McFarlane, Royal Courts of Justice, Strand, London WC2A 2LL *Tel:* 020 7947 6008
Deputy Chancellor of Diocese Mr Gregory Percy Jones, Francis Taylor Building, Inner Temple, London EC4Y 7BY *Tel:* 020 7353 8415

Registrar of Diocese and Bishop's Legal Secretary Mr Martin Follett, Michelmores, Woodwater House, Pynes Hill, Exeter EX2 5WR
Tel: 01392 687421
email: martin.follett@michelmores.com
Deputy Registrar Mrs Karen Eagle, Michelmores
Tel: 01392 687419
email: karen.eagle@michelmores.com

THE DEPARTMENT FOR SUPPORT SERVICES
Director and Dioc Secretary Mr Mark Beedell (*as above*)
Asst Dioc Secretary Dr Ed Moffatt, The Old Deanery *Tel:* 01392 294928
Fax: 01392 499594
email: ed.moffatt@exeter.anglican.org
Diocesan Office The Old Deanery, The Cloisters, Exeter EX1 1HS *Tel:* 01392 272686
Fax: 01392 499594
email: admin@exeter.anglican.org

ADMINISTRATION
Board of Finance (*Chairman*) David Cain, c/o The Old Deanery *email:* twelvetwentyfive@msn.com
(*Secretary*) Mr Mark Beedell (*as above*)
Parsonages Committee (*Secretary*) Mr Graham Davies, The Old Deanery *Tel:* 01392 294954
Fax: 01392 499594
email: graham.davies@exeter.anglican.org
Dioc Surveyors Mr Graham Davies, Mr Peter Stanton and Mr Mark Lewis, The Old Deanery
Tel: 01392 294952
Fax: 01392 499594
email: graham.davies@exeter.anglican.org *or* peter.stanton@exeter.anglican.org *or* mark.lewis@exeter.anglican.org
Mission and Pastoral Committee (*Secretary*) Mr Alistair Sutherland *Tel:* 01392 294910
email: alistair.sutherland@exeter.anglican.org
Board of Patronage (*Chairman*) Mrs Shirley-Ann Williams, 2 Katherine's Lane, Ridgeway, Ottery St Mary EX11 1FB *Tel:* 01404 811064
Trusts Mr Raymond Twohig, The Old Deanery
Tel: 01392 294913
email: raymond.twohig@exeter.anglican.org
Designated Officer Mr Alistair Sutherland (*as above*)
Director of Human Resources Miss Catherine Allen, The Palace Gatehouse, Palace Gate, Exeter EX1 1HX *Tel:* 01392 345908
email: catherine.allen@exeter.anglican.org

SAFEGUARDING UNIT
Diocesan Safeguarding Adviser Simon Tickner, The Palace Gatehouse, Palace Gate, Exeter EX1 1HX
Tel: 01392 345909
email: safeguarding@exeter.anglican.org
Assistant Safeguarding Adviser Mrs Sarah Miller (*same address*) *Tel:* 01392 345910
email: sarah.miller@exeter.anglican.org

CHURCHES

Church Buildings Office (*Chairman*) Mr Frank Eul; (*Secretary*) Mrs Louise Bartlett, The Old Deanery, *Tel:* 01392 294944, *email:* louise.bartlett@exeter.anglican.org
Church Buildings Strategy Committee (*Secretary*) Miss Eve Van der Steen *Tel:* 01392 294945 *email:* eve@exeter.anglican.org

COMMUNICATIONS

Director of Communications Mrs Rebecca Paveley *Tel:* 01392 294905
email: rebecca.paveley@exeter.anglican.org
Publications Officer Revd Nicky Davies *Tel:* 01392 294915
email: nicky.davies@exeter.anglican.org
Digital Media Officer Mr John Moxon *Tel:* 01392 294904
email: john.moxon@exeter.anglican.org
The Church of England, Devon (Diocesan News) *Tel:* 01392 294905
email: communications@exeter.anglican.org
Web: www.exeter.anglican.org

WORK WITH CHILDREN AND YOUNG PEOPLE

Diocesan Director of Education Mr Philip Mantell, The Old Deanery *Tel:* 01392 294950
Fax: 01392 294966
email: philip.mantell@exeter.anglican.org
Executive Assistant Mrs Lynne Sargeant *Tel:* 01392 294950
email: education@exeter.anglican.org
Diocesan Education Officer Mrs Tatiana Wilson *Tel:* 01392 294941
email: tatiana.wilson@exeter.anglican.org
Revd Richard Maudsley *Tel:* 01392 294961
email: richard.maudsley@exeter.anglican.org
Mrs Penny Burnside *Tel:* 01392 294942
email: penny.burnside@exeter.anglican.org
Dioc Church Schools Liaison Officer Mrs Christina Mabin *Tel:* 01392 294939
e-mail: christina.mabin@exeter.anglican.org
Children's Work Adviser Miss Katherine Lyddon *Tel:* 01392 294936
email: katherine.lyddon@exeter.anglican.org
Dioc Youth Work Adviser Mr Paul Reisbach *Tel:* 01392 294932
email: paul.reisbach@exeter.anglican.org
Dioc Youth Church Adviser Revd James Grier *email:* james.grier@exeter.anglican.org
Church Schools Surveyors Richard Power and Jason Down *Tel:* 01392 294952
Fax: 01392 294967
email: school.premises@exeter.anglican.org *or* richard.power@exeter.anglican.org *or* jason.down@exeter.anglican.org
Church Schools Funding Adviser Raymond Twohig *Tel:* 01392 294952
email: raymond.twohig@exeter.anglican.org
St Christopher's Primary Multi-Academy Trust The Old Deanery, *Lead Executive Officer* Mrs Janine Waring *Tel:* 01392 294923
email: janine.waring@stchristophersmat.org

Director of Finance and Business Mr Adrian Hilliard *Tel:* 01392 294922
email: adrian.hilliard@st christophersmat.org
St Christopher's Secondary Multi-Academy Trust Company Secretary Ms Laura Nias *Tel:* 01271 863427
email: lnias@ilfracombeacademy.org.uk

WORSHIP AND MINISTRY

Director Vacancy
Officer for Non-Stipendiary Ministry and Continuing Ministerial Education Vacancy
Council Administrator Vacancy
Director of Ordinands, Adviser for Vocations Revd Becky Totterdell, The Palace Gatehouse, Palace Gate, Exeter EX1 1HX *Tel:* 01392 477702
email: ddo@exeter.anglican.org
Administrator Miss Louise Spencer, The Palace Gatehouse, Palace Gate, Exeter EX1 1HX *Tel:* 01392 477702
email: louise.spencer@exeter.anglican.org
Adviser for Women's Ministry Revd Canon Jane Wilson, 17 Ashleigh Park, Bampton, Tiverton EX16 9LF *Tel:* 01884 332135
email: janeoffwell@aol.com
Board of Readers (*Secretary*) Mr Peter Colebrook, The Old Deanery *Tel:* 01392 294907
email: peter.colebrook@exeter.anglican.org
Adult Education Adviser Vacancy
Warden of Readers Ven Christopher Futcher, Emmanuel House, Station Road, Ide, Exeter EX2 9RS *Tel:* 01392 425577
email: archdeacon.of.exeter@exeter.anglican.org
Co-ordinator Spiritual Direction Revd Helen Bays, 14 Stockton Hill, Dawlish EX7 9LP *Tel:* 07722 106632
email: hbays@talktalk.net
Mission Community Teams Adviser Vacancy
Local Ministry Teams Adviser Vacancy
Dioc Consultant for Worship and Music Mr Andrew Maries *Tel:* 01884 34389
email: maries@keynotetrust.org.uk
Web: www.exeterdlc.org.uk

MISSION AND UNITY

Director and Diocesan Missioner Revd Canon Anna Norman-Walker, The Old Deanery *Tel:* 01392 294903
email: missioner@exeter.anglican.org
Administrator Vacancy
Mission Community Development Officer Revd Canon Andrew Godsall, The Old Deanery *Tel:* 01392 294902
email: andrew.godsall@exeter.anglican.org
Chaplain with Deaf People Revd Catherine Carlyon, The Old Deanery *Tel:* 01392 294909 (voice and text)
Fax: 01392 294965
07855 098953 (Mobile)
email: catherinecarlyon@btopenworld.com
Ministry of Healing and Deliverance Vacancy
County Ecumenical Officer Revd Sue Macbeth *email:* churchestogetherdevon@gmail.com

Cyprus and the Gulf Link (*Chairman*) Revd Charles Deacon, The Old Deanery   Tel: 01392 294962
        email: charles.deacon@exeter.anglican.org
Thika Link Mrs Jane Inwood (parish links)
        Tel: 01647 252519
        email: thika.link@exeter.anglican.org
World Development Adviser Revd Charles Deacon (*as above*)
Mission Resource Adviser Mrs Katie Roscorla
        Tel: 01392 272686
        email: katie.roscorla@exeter.anglican.org
Administrator Mrs Hannah Cross
        email: hannah.cross@exeter.anglican.org

CHURCH AND SOCIETY
Director Mr Martyn Goss, The Old Deanery
        Tel: 01392 294924
        Fax: 01392 499594
        email: martyn.goss@exeter.anglican.org
Social Responsibility Officer Miss Sally Farrant, The Old Deanery   Tel: 01392 294918
        email: sally.farrant@exeter.anglican.org
Family Life and Marriage Education Coordinator Vacancy
Rural Officer Vacancy

MISCELLANEOUS ORGANIZATIONS
Widows and Dependants Revd Tony Mortimer, 97 Egremont Road, Exmouth EX8 1SA
        Tel: 01395 271390
        email: tpmortimer@googlemail.com
(Exeter Archdeaconry except Kenn Deanery)
Revd Gerry Reilly, 9 Fleming Way, Exeter EX2 4SE   Tel: 01392 420372
        email: grryreilly@yahoo.co.uk
(Barnstaple Archdeaconry and Kenn Deanery)

DIOCESAN RECORDS OFFICE
Devon Heritage Centre, Great Moor House, Bittern Road, Sowton Industrial Estate, Exeter EX2 7NL *Archivist* Mr John Draisey
        Tel: 01392 384253
        email: devrc@devon.gov.uk

RURAL DEANS
ARCHDEACONRY OF EXETER
Aylesbeare Revd Jeremy Clark, The Vicarage, Rockbeare, Exeter EX5 2EG   Tel: 01404 8522883
        email: jemkiwi@aol.com
Cadbury Revd Preb Nigel Guthrie, The Vicarage, Church Street, Crediton EX17 2AQ
        Tel: 01363 772669
        email: rev.guthrie@btinternet.com
Christianity Revd Robin Eastoe, The Rectory, 10 Victoria Park Road, Exeter EX2 4NT
        Tel: 01392 677150
        email: theeastoes@btinternet.com
Honiton Revd Jeremy Trew, The Vicarage, Colyford Road, Seaton EX12 2DF
        Tel: 01297 20391
        email: jeremytrew@hotmail.com

Kenn Revd Martin Wood, The Rectory, Church Lane, Cheriton Bishop, Exeter EX6 6HY
        Tel: 01647 24119
        email: revwood@btinternet.com
Ottery Revd Cate Edmonds, The Rectory, Station Road, Feniton, Honiton EX14 3DF
        Tel: 01404 851401
        email: cateedmonds@aol.com
Tiverton and Cullompton Revd Barry Dugmore, The Vicarage, Bakers Hill, Tiverton EX16 5NE
        Tel: 01884 252526
        email: vicar@tivertonchurch.org

ARCHDEACONRY OF TOTNES
Moreton Revd David Sherwood, The Rectory, Copperwood Close, Ashburton, Newton Abbot TQ13 7JQ   Tel: 01364 652968
        email: revdcs@yahoo.co.uk
Newton Abbot and Ipplepen Revd Mark Smith, The Vicarage, Daws Meadow, Kingsteignton, Newton Abbot TQ12 3UA   Tel: 01626 355127
        email: marksmith487@btinternet.com
Okehampton Revd Dr Ruth Hansford, The Rectory, Hatherleigh, Okehampton EX20 3JY
        Tel: 01837 810314
        email: maggiethecat@waitrose.com
Torbay Revd Paul Jones, The Rectory, 4 Cary Park, Babbacombe, Torquay TQ1 3NH
        Tel: 01803 323002
        email: liberty.hall@btinternet.com
Totnes Revd Julian Ould, The Rectory, Northgate Castle Hill, Totnes TQ9 5NX   Tel: 01803 865615
        email: julian@totnesrectory.co.uk
Woodleigh Revd Daniel French, The Vicarage, Devon Road, Salcombe TQ8 8HJ
        Tel: 01548 842853
        email: cybervicar@gmail.com

ARCHDEACONRY OF BARNSTAPLE
Barnstaple Revd Preb Giles King-Smith, The Vicarage, Springfield Road, Woolacombe EX34 7BX
        Tel: 01271 870467
        email: clareandgiles@aol.com
Hartland Revd Andrew Richardson, La Retraite, 3 Park Avenue, Bideford EX39 2QH
Holsworthy Revd Christopher Hardwick, The Rectory, Pyworthy, Holsworthy EX22 6SU
        Tel: 01409 253547
        email: revchrishardwick@btinternet.com
Shirwell Revd Shaun O'Rourke, The Rectory, Barnstaple Hill, Swimbridge, Barnstaple EX32 0PH   Tel: 01271 830590
        email: revd.shaun@googlemail.com
South Molton Revd Roderick Withnell, The Rectory, Church Lane, Chulmleigh EX18 7BY
        Tel: 01769 580537
        email: roderickwithnell@btinternet.com
Torrington Revd Lawrence MacLean, The Vicarage, Calf Street, Torrington EX38 8EA
        Tel: 01805 622166
        email: lm61@live.co.uk

ARCHDEACONRY OF PLYMOUTH

Ivybridge Revd Freddie Denman, The Vicarage, Sparkwell, Plymouth PL7 5DB
Tel: 01752 837218
email: freddy.sparkwell@hotmail.co.uk

Plymouth City Ven Ian Chandler, St Mark's House, 46a Cambridge Road, Ford, Plymouth PL2 1PU
Tel: 01752 20240
email:
archdeacon of plymouth@exeter.anglican.org

Tavistock Revd Nicholas Law, The Rectory, Bere Alston, Yelverton PL20 7HQ
Tel: 01822 840229
email: nicklaw2@tiscali.co.uk

DIOCESE OF GLOUCESTER

Founded in 1541. Gloucestershire except for a few parishes in the north (WORCESTER); a few parishes in the south (BRISTOL) and one parish in the east (OXFORD); the northern third of South Gloucestershire; two parishes in Wiltshire; a small area in south-west Warwickshire; a few parishes in the southern part of Worcestershire.

Population 640,000   Area 1,140 sq m
Full-time Stipendiary Parochial Clergy 125   Benefices 106
Parishes 301   Churches 386
www.gloucester.anglican.org

BISHOP (41st)
Vacancy
Bishop's Chaplain Revd John Paul Hoskins, The Bishop of Gloucester's Office, 2 College Green, Gloucester GL1 2LR   *Tel:* 01452 410022, ext. 268
email: jphoskins@glosdioc.org.uk
Bishop's Secretary Mrs Diane Best, The Bishop of Gloucester's Office, 2 College Green, Gloucester GL1 2LR   *Tel:* 01452 410022 ext 270
email: dbest@glosdioc.org.uk

SUFFRAGAN BISHOP
TEWKESBURY Rt Revd Martyn Snow, 2 College Green, Gloucester GL1 2LR
Tel: 01452 410022 ext 228
email: bshptewk@glosdioc.org.uk
Home address: Bishop's House, Staverton, Cheltenham GL51 0TW

HONORARY ASSISTANT BISHOPS
Rt Revd David Jennings, Laurel Cottage, East End, Northleach, Cheltenham GL54 3ET
Tel: 01451 860743
Rt Revd Robert Evens, 30 Highland Road, Charlton Kings, Cheltenham GL53 9LT
Tel: 01242 251411
Rt Revd Anthony Priddis, Round Oak Cottage, Bridstow, Ross-on-Wye HR9 6QJ
Tel: 01989 218503
Rt Revd Christopher Hill, Hillview, Westend, Ruardean, Gloucester GL17 9TP
Tel: 01594 541831
Rt Revd Patrick Harris, Apartment B, Ireton House, Pavilion Gardens, The Park, Cheltenham GL50 2SP   *Tel:* 01242 231376

CATHEDRAL CHURCH OF ST PETER AND THE HOLY AND INDIVISIBLE TRINITY
Dean Very Revd Stephen Lake, The Deanery, 1 Miller's Green, Gloucester GL1 2BP [2011]
Tel: 01452 508217
email: dean@gloucestercathedral.org.uk

Executive PA Mrs Fiona Price, The Cathedral Office, 12 College Green, Gloucester GL1 2LX
Tel: 01452 508217
email: fiona.price@gloucestercathedral.org.uk
The Cathedral Office, 12 College Green, Gloucester GL1 2LX   *Tel:* 01452 528095
Fax: 01452 300469
Web: www.gloucestercathedral.org.uk
Canons Residentiary
Precentor Canon Neil Heavisides, 7 College Green, Gloucester GL1 2LX [1993]
Tel: 01452 523987
email:
neil.heavisides@gloucestercathedral.org.uk
Canon Pastor Canon Celia Thomson, 3 Miller's Green, Gloucester GL1 2BN [2003]
Tel: 01452 415824
email:
celia.thomson@gloucestercathedral.org.uk
Ven Jackie Searle, 2 College Green, Gloucester GL1 2LR [2012]   *Tel:* 01452 835594
email: archdglos@glosdioc.org.uk
Canon Nikki Arthy, The Rectory, Hempsted, Gloucester GL2 5LW [2009]   *Tel:* 01452 523808
email: nikkiarthy@btinternet.com
Canon Andrew Braddock, 4 College Green, Gloucester GL1 2LR [2013]   *Tel:* 01452 835549
email: abraddock@glosdioc.org.uk
Acting Chapter Steward Mrs Judith Knight, The Cathedral Office   *Tel:* 01452 508216
email: judith.knight@gloucestercathedral.org.uk
Director of Music Mr Adrian Partington, 7 Miller's Green, Gloucester GL1 2BN
Tel: 01452 229819
email:
adrian.partington@gloucestercathedral.org.uk
Assistant Director of Music Mr Jonathan Hope, 8a College Green, Gloucester GL1 2LX
Tel: 01452 874964
email:
jonathan.hope@gloucestercathedral.org.uk
Singing Development Leader Nia Llewelyn Jones, The Cathedral Office, 2 College Green, Gloucester GL1 2LX   *Tel:* 01452 508212
email: nia.jones@gloucestercathedral.org.uk
Music Department Manager Mrs Helen Sims, The Cathedral Office (*as above*)   *Tel:* 01452 508212
email: helen.sims@gloucestercathedral.org.uk

ARCHDEACONS

GLOUCESTER Ven Jackie Searle, 2 College Green, Gloucester GL1 2LR [2012]   *Tel:* 01452 835594
email: archdglos@glosdioc.org.uk
CHELTENHAM Ven Robert Springett, 2 College Green, Gloucester GL1 2LY [2010]
Tel: 01452 835594
email: archdchelt@glosdioc.org.uk

CONVOCATION (MEMBERS OF THE HOUSE OF CLERGY OF THE GENERAL SYNOD)
Proctors for Clergy
Revd Canon Dr Tudor Griffiths
Revd Canon Dr Michael Parsons
Revd Canon Celia Thomson
Revd Canon Richard Mitchell

MEMBERS OF THE HOUSE OF LAITY OF THE GENERAL SYNOD
Dr William Belcher
Mr Graham Smith
Prof Jenny Tann

DIOCESAN OFFICERS
Diocesan Secretary Mr Benjamin Preece Smith, Church House, College Green, Gloucester GL1 2LY   *Tel:* 01452 410022 ext. 236
email: bpreecesmith @glosdioc.org.uk
Chancellor of Diocese The Worshipful June Rodgers, Gloucester Diocesan Registry, Veale Wasbrough Vizards, Orchard Court, Orchard Lane, Bristol BS1 5WS   *Tel:* 01173 145680
Registrar of Diocese Mr Jos Moule, Gloucester Diocesan Registry, Veale Wasbrough Vizards, Orchard Court, Orchard Lane, Bristol BS1 5WS
Tel: 01179 252020
email: gloucesterregistry@vwv.co.uk

DIOCESAN ORGANIZATIONS
Diocesan Office Church House, College Green, Gloucester GL1 2LY   *Tel:* 01452 410022
email: church.house@glosdioc.org.uk
Web: www.gloucester.anglican.org

ADMINISTRATION
Diocesan Synod (Chair of the House of Clergy) Revd Canon Richard Mitchell. The Vicarage, School Lane, Shurdington, Cheltenham GL51 4TF
Tel: 0242 702911
email: richard.mitchell@talk21.com
(Chair of the House of Laity) Canon Ian Marsh, Mynd House, The Highlands, Painswick GL6 6SL
Tel: 01452 812829
email: iwmarsh21@gmail.com
(Secretary) Mr Benjamin Preece Smith, Diocesan Office
Board of Finance (Chair) Mrs Mary Adlard, The Pippins, Gambles Lane, Woodmancote, Cheltenham GL52 9PU   *Tel:* 01684 850033
(Secretary) Mr Benjamin Preece Smith *(as above)*

Head of Finance Mrs Julie Ridgway, Diocesan Office
Houses Committee (Secretary) Mr David Woolf, Diocesan Office
Pastoral Committee (Secretary) Mr Benjamin Preece Smith *(as above)*
Board of Patronage (Secretary) Miss Rebecca Shorter, Diocesan Office
Trust (Secretary) Head of Finance Mrs Julie Ridgway *(as above)*
Glebe Committee (Secretary) Mr Benjamin Preece Smith *(as above)*
HR Manager Mrs Judith Knight, Diocesan Office

CHURCHES
Advisory Committee on Faculties and Care of Churches (Chairman) Mr Henry Russell, Ley Mary Farmhouse, Windrush, Burford, Oxon OX18 4TS   *Tel:* 01451 844477
(Secretary) Mrs Natalie Fenner (on maternity leave from November 2014), Diocesan Office
Tel: 01452 835593
email: nfenner@glosdioc.org.uk

EDUCATION DEPARTMENT
Director of Education Canon Helena Arnold, 4 College Green, Gloucester GL1 2LR
Tel: 01452 835542
email: harnold@glosdioc.org.uk
Strategic Lead for Christian Distinctiveness in Primary Schools Mrs Shahne Vickery, 4 College Green, Gloucester GL1 2LR
Tel: 01452 410022 ext 259
email: svickery@glosdioc.org.uk
Strategic Lead for Governance Mrs Linda Rolfe, 4 College Green, Gloucester GL1 2LR
Tel: 01452 835536
email: lrolfe@glosdioc.org.uk
Strategic Lead for Buildings Mr Rob Stephens, 4 College Green, Gloucester GL1 2LR
Tel: 01452 410022 ext. 242
email: rstephens@glosdioc.org.uk

MINISTRY
Director of the Department of Mission and Ministry Revd Canon Andrew Braddock, 4 College Green, Gloucester GL1 2LR   *Tel:* 01452 835549
email: abraddock@glosdioc.org.uk
Director of Ordinands and Curate Training Revd Ian Bussell, 4 College Green, Gloucester GL1 2LR   *Tel:* 01452 835545
Associate Director of Ordinands Revd Stephen Ware, 4 College Green, Gloucester GL1 2LR
Tel: 01452 835547
email: sware@glosdioc.org.uk
Mission and Evangelism Officer Revd Cate Williams, 4 College Green, Gloucester GL1 2LR
Young People and Families Officer Vacancy
Warden of Readers Revd Chris Sterry, 4 College Green, Gloucester GL1 2LR   *Tel:* 01452 835582
email: chrisforestedge@aol.com

Self Supporting Ministry Officer Revd Dr Nick Fisher, 4 College Green, Gloucester GL1 2LR
Tel: 01451 861195
email: nick@5fishers.co.uk
Dean of Women Clergy Revd Robbin Clark, 4 College Green, Gloucester GL1 2LR
Tel: 01452 547469
email: rclark@glosdioc.org.uk
Effective Ministry and Vocations Officer Revd Pauline Godfrey, 4 College Green, Gloucester GL1 2LR
Tel: 01452 835548
email: pgodfrey@glosdioc.org.uk
Diocesan Ecumenical Officer Revd Jacqui Hyde
Tel: 01242 234955
email: Jacqui@clanhyde.me.uk
Civil Protection Liaison Officer Revd Peter Cheesman
Tel: 01452 740533
email: peter@the-cheesman.net
Chaplain to the Deaf and Hard of Hearing Community and Advisor on Disability Issues Revd Steve Morris
Tel: 01452 610450
email: spadework@fsmail.net
Diocesan Advisor in Wellbeing and Support Revd Dr Brian Ludlow
Tel: 01452 835551
Accord Mrs Deborah Curram
Tel: 01453 872546
email: deborahcurram@googlemail.com
Diocesan Worship Officer Revd David Deboys, 4 College Green, Gloucester GL1 2LR
Tel: 01452 410022 ext 280
email: ddeboys@glosdioc.org.uk

BISHOP'S WORSHIP, PRAYER AND SPIRITUALITY GROUP
Chair Revd Canon Rob Axford
Tel: 01453 842175
email: rob@robaxford.plus.com
Secretary Revd David Deboys *(as above)*

COMMUNICATIONS
Head of Communications Mrs Lucy Taylor, Diocesan Office (on maternity leave until June 2015); James Butterworth (maternity cover)
Tel: 01452 410022 ext. 250
07811 174125 (Mobile)
email: jbutterworth@glosdioc.org.uk
Communications Officer Mrs Katherine Clamp, Diocesan Office (on maternity leave until Jan 2015)
Tel: 01452 410022 ext. 291
email: kclamp@glosdioc.org.uk
Communications Officer – New Media Mr Ben Evans, Diocesan Office
Tel: 01452 410022 ext. 227
email: bevans@glosdioc.org.uk

DIOCESAN RECORD OFFICE
Gloucestershire Archives, Clarence Row, Alvin Street, Gloucester GL1 3DW *Dioc Archivist* Ms Heather Forbes
Tel: 01452 425295
email: archives@gloucestershire.gov.uk (Office)

DIOCESAN RESOURCE CENTRE
Manager Mrs Hannah Hauxwell, 9 College Green, Gloucester GL1 2LX *Tel:* 01452 835559
email: hhauxwell@glosdioc.org.uk

AREA DEANS
ARCHDEACONRY OF CHELTENHAM
Cheltenham Revd Canon Dr Tudor Griffiths, 38 Sydenham Villas Road, Cheltenham GL52 6DZ
Tel: 01242 234470
email: tudorg@stmstm.org.uk
Cirencester Revd Canon Leonard Doolan, The Vicarage, 1 Dollar Street, Cirencester GL7 2AJ
Tel: 01285 659317
email: vicarcirencester@hotmail.com
North Cotswolds Revd Canon Veronica James, Rectory, Copse Hill Road, Lower Slaughter, Cheltenham GL54 2HY *Tel:* 01451 821777
email: flojoefred@hotmail.com
Tewkesbury and Winchcombe Revd Canon Paul Williams, Abbey House, Abbey Precinct, Church Street, Tewkesbury GL20 5SR *Tel:* 01684 856144
email: vicar@tewkesburyabbey.org.uk

ARCHDEACONRY OF GLOUCESTER
Forest South Revd Canon Philippa Brunt, The Vicarage, Lower Road, Yorkley, Lydney GL15 4TN
Tel: 01594 562828
email: pabrunt@btinternet.com
Gloucester City Revd David Smith, St George's Vicarage, Grange Road, Tuffley, Gloucester GL4 0PE
Tel and Fax: 01452 520851
email: draesmith@blueyonder.co.uk
Severn Vale Revd Canon Richard Mitchell, The Vicarage, School Lane, Shurdington, Cheltenham GL51 4TF *Tel:* 01242 702911
email: richard.mitchell@talk21.com
Stroud Revd Malcolm S. King, The Vicarage, Church Street, Stroud GL5 3EG
Tel: 01453 882289
email: rector@minchchurch.org.uk
Wotton Revd Canon Jane Kenchington, The Vicarage, Horseshoe Lane, Chipping Sodbury, Bristol BS37 6ET *Tel:* 01454 313159
email: jane@kenchington.plus.com

DIOCESE OF GUILDFORD

Founded in 1927. The western two-thirds of Surrey south of the Thames, except for a small area in the north-east (SOUTHWARK); areas of north-east Hampshire; a few parishes in Greater London; one parish in West Sussex.

Population 1,026,000   Area 540 sq m
Full-time Stipendiary Parochial Clergy 170   Benefices 141
Parishes 163   Churches 217
www.cofeguildford.org.uk
Overseas link diocese: IDWAL (Inter-Diocesan West Africa Link) – Nigeria.

BISHOP (9th)
Rt Revd Andrew Watson, Willow Grange, Woking Road, Guildford, Surrey GU4 7QS
Tel: 01483 590500
Fax: 01483 590501
email: bishop.guildford@cofeguildford.org.uk
Bishop's Chaplain Revd Mark Heather
email: mark.heather@cofeguildford.org.uk
Bishop's Personal Assistant Mary Morris
email: mary.morris@cofeguildford.org.uk

SUFFRAGAN BISHOP
DORKING Rt Revd Ian James Brackley, Dayspring, 13 Pilgrim's Way, Guildford GU4 8AD [1996]
Tel: 01483 570829
Fax: 01483 567268
email: bishop.ian@cofeguildford.org.uk
Bishop's Personal Assistant Muriel Mulvany
email: muriel.mulvany@cofeguildford.org.uk

CATHEDRAL CHURCH OF THE HOLY SPIRIT
Dean Very Revd Dianna Gwilliams
Tel: 01483 547861 (Office)
email: dean@guildford-cathedral.org
Dean's Personal Assistant Mrs Cathy Mansell
Tel: 01483 547862 (Office)
email: cathy@guildford-cathedral.org
Cathedral Office Guildford Cathedral, Stag Hill, Guildford, Surrey GU2 7UP   *Tel:* 01483 547860
Fax: 01483 303350
email: reception@guildford-cathedral.org
Canons Residentiary
Sub-Dean and Precentor Revd Canon Dr Nicholas Thistlethwaite, 3 Cathedral Close, Guildford GU2 7TL [1999]   *Tel:* 01483 547865
email: precentor@guildford-cathedral.org
Canon Residentiary and University Chaplain Revd Canon Dr Andrew Bishop, 6 Cathedral Close, Guildford GU2 7TL   *Tel:* 07891 994069
email: a.bishop@surrey.ac.uk
Canon Residentiary Revd Canon Dr Julie Gittoes, 4 Cathedral Close, Guildford GU2 7TL
Tel: 07702 151173
email: julie@guildford-cathedral.org
Canon Residentiary Ven Stuart Beake, Diocesan House, Quarry Street, Guildford GU1 3XG
Tel: 01483 790352
email: stuart.beake@cofeguildford.org.uk

Director of Operations Mr Matt O'Grady
Tel: 01483 547864
email: dops@guildford-cathedral.org
Cathedral Organist and Master of the Choristers Mrs Katherine Dienes-Williams, 5 Cathedral Close, Guildford GU2 7TL   *Tel:* 01483 547866
email: organist@guildford-cathedral.org

ARCHDEACONS
SURREY Ven Stuart Beake, Diocesan House, Quarry St, Guildford GU1 3XG [2005]
Tel: 01483 790352
email: stuart.beake@cofeguildford.org.uk
DORKING Ven Paul Bryer, Diocesan House, Quarry Street, Guildford GU1 3XG [2014]
Tel: 01483 790352

CONVOCATION (MEMBERS OF THE HOUSE OF CLERGY OF THE GENERAL SYNOD)
Dignitaries in Convocation
The Bishop of Guildford
Proctors for Clergy
Revd Robert Cotton
Revd Karen Hutchinson
Revd Philip Plyming
Canon Dr Hazel Whitehead
Revd George Newton

MEMBERS OF THE HOUSE OF LAITY OF THE GENERAL SYNOD
Canon Peter Bruinvels
Mr Keith Malcouronne
Anne Martin
Mr Adrian Vincent

DIOCESAN OFFICERS
Diocesan Secretary Mr Stephen Marriott, Diocesan House, Quarry St, Guildford GU1 3XG
Tel: 01483 790300
Fax: 01483 790333
Chancellor of Diocese Mr Andrew Jordan, 11 Fairlawn Avenue, Chiswick, London W4 5EF
Registrar of Diocese and Bishop's Legal Secretary Mr Howard Dellar, 1 The Sanctuary, London SW1P 3JT   *Tel:* 020 7222 5381
Fax: 020 7222 7502
Deputy Registrars Mr Lee Coley

DIOCESAN ORGANIZATIONS

Diocesan Office Diocesan House, Quarry St, Guildford GU1 3XG   *Tel:* 01483 790300
                                      Fax: 01483 790333

ADMINISTRATION

President The Bishop of Guildford
Dioc Synod (*Vice-President, House of Clergy*) Revd Canon Nick Whitehead, The Rectory, 5 Spinning Walk, Shere GU5 9HN   *Tel:* 01483 202394
(*Vice-President, House of Laity*) Mrs Anne Martin, 8 Woodberry Close, Chiddingfold GU8 4SF
                                      Tel: 01428 683854
(*Secretary*) Mr Stephen Marriott, Diocesan House
   email: diocesan.secretary@cofeguildford.org.uk
Deputy Secretary Mr Nick Edmonds, Diocesan House
   email: nick.edmonds@cofeguildford.org.uk
Board of Finance (*Chairman*) Mr Nigel Lewis, Diocesan House
Accountant Mr Malcolm Twigger-Ross
                                      email:
   malcolm.twigger-ross@cofeguildford.org.uk
Pastoral Committee Mrs Wendy Harris, Diocesan House
   email: wendy.harris@cofeguildford.org.uk
Designated Officer Mr Howard Dellar, 1 The Sanctuary, London SW1P 3JT   *Tel:* 020 7222 5381
                                      Fax: 020 7222 7502

CHURCHES

Advisory Committee for the Care of Churches (*Chairman*) Mr John Alpass, c/o Diocesan House, Quarry St, Guildford GU1 3XG; (*Secretary*) Mrs Wendy Harris, Diocesan House
   email: wendy.harris@cofeguildford.org.uk

COMMUNITIES ENGAGEMENT

Director Canon Chris Rich, Diocesan House
                                      Tel: 01483 790353
   email: chris.rich@cofeguildford.org.uk
Church's Community Care Adviser and Environmental Adviser Tony Oakden, Diocesan House   *Tel:* 01483 790325
   email: tony.oakden@cofeguildford.org.uk
Health and Wellbeing Adviser Suzette Jones, Diocesan House   *Tel:* 01483 790335
   email: suzette.jones@cofeguildford.org.uk
Deaf and Inclusion Coordinator Tracey Wade, Diocesan House   *Tel:* 01483 790327
   email: tracey.wade@cofeguildford.org.uk
Surrey Faith Links Kauser Akhtar, Diocesan House   *Tel:* 01483 790327
   email: kauser.akhtar@cofeguildford.org.uk

COMMUNICATIONS

Director of Communications Mr Nick Edmonds, Diocesan House   *Tel:* 01483 790310
   email: nick.edmonds@cofeguildford.org.uk
Media Officers Mrs Emma Nutbrown, David Green   *Tel:* 01483 790345

Editors of Diocesan Newspaper Mrs Emma Nutbrown, David Green (*as above*)
                                      Tel: 01483 790347
   email: editorial@cofeguildford.org.uk
Information and Web Administrator Mrs Mary Peters   *Tel:* 01483 790355
   email: mary.peters@cofeguildford.org
Out of Hours Emergency no   *Tel:* 07500 042769

DIOCESAN RECORD OFFICE

Surrey History Centre, 130 Goldsworth Rd, Woking GU2 1ND *Team Leader, Heritage Public Services* Mr Julian Pooley; *Special Collections Archivist* Di Stiff   *Tel:* 01483 518737

DISCIPLESHIP, VOCATION AND MINISTRY

Director of Ministerial Training and Co-Chair South Central Regional Training Partnership Revd Canon Dr Hazel Whitehead, Diocesan House
                                      Tel: 01483 790307
   email: hazel.whitehead@cofeguildford.org.uk
Director of Ordinands and IME 4–7 Revd William Challis, Diocesan House   *Tel:* 01483 790322
   email: william.challis@cofeguildford.org.uk
Local Ministry Programme (*Principal*) Revd Dr Steve Summers, Diocesan House   *Tel:* 01483 790319
   email: steve.summers@cofeguildford.co.uk
Warden of Licensed Lay Ministers Mrs Gertrud Sollars, 6 Overbrook, Godalming, Surrey GU7 1LX   *email:* wardenofllms@cofeguildford.org.uk
Senior Tutor for Pastoral Assistants' Foundation Training Mrs Sue Lawrence, Diocesan House
                                      Tel: 01483 790321
   email: sue.lawrence@cofeguildford.org.uk
CMD Tutor for Pastoral Assistants Revd Lynne Bowden   *Tel:* 01483 790300
   email: lynne.bowden@cofeguildford.org.uk
Vocations Officer Revd Laurence Gamlen
                                      Tel: 01483 790300
   email: laurence.gamlen@cofeguildford.org.uk
Assessing the End of Curacy Officer Revd Bev Hunt
                                      Tel: 01483 790300
   email: bev.hunt@cofeguildford.org.uk
Readers' Board (*Registrar*) Dr Stephen Linton, 18 Bridgefield, Farnham GU9 8AN
                                      Tel: 01252 715209
   email: registrarofllms@cofeguildford.org.uk
Adult Education Adviser Vacancy

PARISH DEVELOPMENT AND EVANGELISM

Diocesan Education Centre, Stag Hill, Guildford GU2 7UP
Director Revd Alan Hulme, Education Centre
                                      Tel: 01483 484921
   email: alan.hulme@cofeguildford.org.uk
Parish Resources Adviser Mrs Juliet Evans, Education Centre   *Tel:* 01483 484923
   email: juliet.evans@cofeguildford.org.uk
Local Mission Adviser Revd Stephen Cox, Education Centre   *Tel:* 01483 484922
   email: stephen.cox@cofeguildford.org.uk
Youth Adviser Mr David Welch, Education Centre   *Tel:* 01483 484908
   email: david.welch@cofeguildford.org.uk

Children's Work Adviser Mrs Alison Hendy, Education Centre Tel: 01483 484910
email: alison.hendy@cofeguildford.org.uk
Diocesan Spiritual Growth Facilitator Revd Sarah Hutton
email: sarah.hutton@cofeguildford.org.uk
Spiritual Direction Co-ordinator Revd Canon Andrew Tuck
email: andrew.tuck@cofeguildford.org.uk
Bishop's Adviser on Hospital Chaplaincy Revd Chris Vallins email: chrisvallins@yahoo.com
Healing Adviser Revd Elizabeth Knifton
email: eknifton@acornchristian.org
World Mission Adviser Revd Andrew Wheeler
email: andrew.wheeler@st-saviours.org.uk
Nigeria Link Officer Revd David Minns
email: dkminns@btinternet.com
Sports Ministry Adviser Revd Clive Potter
email: milfordvicarage@gmail.com
Church Heritage and Tourism Adviser Revd Canon Mervyn Roberts email: mervynrob@aol.com

SCHOOLS, COLLEGES AND UNIVERSITIES
Diocesan Education Centre, Stag Hill, Guildford GU2 7UP Tel: 01483 450423
Fax: 01483 450424
Director of Education and Secretary Dioc Board of Education Mr Derek Holbird
email: derek.holbird@cofeguildford.org.uk
Schools Officer RE, Spiritual Development and Christian Distinctiveness of Church Schools Mrs Jane Whittington
School Estates Officer Mr David Hallam
Further Education Adviser Mr Bob Linnell
Centre Manager/PA to Director Mrs Jane Baker
Deputy Director of Education – Schools Mr Michael Hall

RETIRED CLERGY MINISTER
Revd Canon John Salter, 7 Aldershot Road, Guildford GU2 8AE Tel: 01483 511165
email: j.salter@btinternet.com

RURAL DEANS
ARCHDEACONRY OF SURREY
Aldershot Revd George Newton, 2 Cranmore Lane, Aldershot GU11 3AS Tel: 01252 320618
email: g@gjsk.prestel.co.uk

Cranleigh Revd Canon Nick Whitehead, The Rectory, 5 Spinning Walk, Shere GU5 9HN
Tel: 01483 202394
email: nick@nickhaze.demon.co.uk
Farnham Revd Anne Gell, Vicarage, 2 Kings Lane, Wrecclesham GU10 4QB Tel: 01252 716431
email: annegell@lineone.net
Godalming Revd Clive Potter, The Vicarage, Milford Heath Road, Milford GU8 5BX
Tel: 01483 414710
email: milfordvicarage@gmail.com
Guildford Revd Frank Scammell, Stoughton Vicarage, 3 Shepherds Lane, Guildford GU2 9SJ
Tel: 01483 560560
email: frankpippa@hotmail.com
Surrey Heath Revd Bob Peck, The Vicarage, Hampshire Road, Old Dean, Camberley GU15 4DW Tel: 01276 23958
email: vicar@stmartinolddean.com

ARCHDEACONRY OF DORKING
Dorking Revd Alan Jonas, The Vicarage, Guildford Road, Westcott RH4 3QB
Tel: 01306 885309
email: alchasjonas@aol.com
Emly Revd Philip Plyming, The Vicarage, Church Road, Claygate KT10 0JP
Tel: 01372 463603
email:
philipplyming@holytrinityclaygate.org.uk
Epsom Revd Maria Pallis, The Vicarage, 21 Court Road, Banstead SM7 2NQ Tel: 01737 351134
email: mariapallis@hotmail.com
Leatherhead Revd Robert Jenkins, Vicarage, St Andrew's Walk, Cobham, Surrey KT11 3EQ
Tel: 01932 862109
email: er.jenkins@btinternet.com
Runnymede Revd Jeff Wattley, Mauley Cottage, 13 Manorcrofts Road, Egham TW20 9LU
Tel: 01784 432066
email: jeff@stjohnsegham.com
Woking Revd Cathy Blair, St Paul's Vicarage, Pembroke Road, Woking GU22 7ED
Tel: 01483 850489
email: cathy@stpaulswoking.org.uk

DIOCESE OF HEREFORD

Founded c 676. Herefordshire; the southern half of Shropshire; a few parishes in Powys and Monmouthshire.

Population 317,000   Area 1,660 sq m
Full-time Stipendiary Parochial Clergy 90   Benefices 105
Parishes 340   Churches 411
www.hereford.anglican.org
Overseas link dioceses: Masasi and Tanga with Zanzibar,
Dar es Salaam (Tanzania), Kirchenkreis of Nurnberg.

BISHOP
Rt Revd Richard M. C. Frith, The Bishop's House, Hereford HR4 9BN [2014]   *Tel:* 01432 271355
Fax: 01432 373346
email: bishop@hereford.anglican.org

SUFFRAGAN BISHOP
LUDLOW Rt Revd Alistair J. Magowan, Bishop's House, Corvedale Rd, Craven Arms, Shropshire SY7 9BT [2009]   *Tel* and *Fax:* 01588 673571
email: office@bishopofludlow.co.uk

CATHEDRAL CHURCH OF THE BLESSED VIRGIN MARY AND ST ETHELBERT
Dean Very Revd Michael Tavinor, The Deanery, College Cloisters, Hereford HR1 2NG [2002]
Tel: 01432 374203
email: dean@herefordcathedral.org
Cathedral Office 5 College Cloisters, Hereford HR1 2NG   *Tel:* 01432 374200
Fax: 01432 374220
email: office@herefordcathedral.org
Web: www.herefordcathedral.org
Canons Residentiary
Chancellor Canon Christopher Pullin, 2 Cathedral Close, Hereford HR1 2NG [2008]
Tel: 01432 374273
chancellor@herefordcathedral.org
Precentor Canon Andrew Piper, 1 Cathedral Close, Hereford HR1 2NG [2003]
Tel: 01432 374271
email: precentor@herefordcathedral.org
Cathedral Chaplain Vacancy

Additional Members
Canon Sandra Elliott, c/o Cathedral Office
Canon Richard Price, c/o Cathedral Office
Canon Gordon Powell, c/o Cathedral Office
Administrator and Chapter Clerk Group Captain Julian Andrews, Cathedral Office
Tel: 01432 374201
email: julian.andrews@herefordcathedral.org
Director of Music Mr Geraint Bowen, 7 College Cloisters, Hereford HR1 2NG   *Tel:* 01432 374238
email: organist@herefordcathedral.org
Assistant Director of Music Mr Peter Dyke, 1a Cathedral Close, Hereford HR1 2NG
Tel: 01432 374272
email: peter.dyke@herefordcathedral.org

ARCHDEACONS
HEREFORD Ven Paddy Benson, Dioc Office
Tel: 01432 373316
email: archdeacon@hereford.anglican.org
LUDLOW Rt Revd Alistair J. Magowan, Bishop's House, Corvedale Rd, Craven Arms, Shropshire SY7 9BT   *Tel* and *Fax:* 01588 673571
email: office@bishopofludlow.co.uk

CONVOCATION (MEMBERS OF THE HOUSE OF CLERGY OF THE GENERAL SYNOD)
Proctors for Clergy
Preb Brian Chave
Revd Simon Cawdell
Revd Neil Patterson

MEMBERS OF THE HOUSE OF LAITY OF THE GENERAL SYNOD
Dr John Dinnen
Dr Martin Elcock
Canon Rosemary Lording

DIOCESAN OFFICERS
Dioc Secretary Mr John Clark, Diocesan Office, The Palace, Hereford HR4 9BL
Tel: 01432 373300
Fax: 01432 352952
email: diosec@hereford.anglican.org
Chancellor of Diocese Chancellor R. Kaye, Leeds Combined Court Centre, The Court House, 1 Oxford Row, Leeds LS1 3BG   *Tel:* 0113 306 2800
Registrar of Diocese and Bishop's Legal Secretary Mr Howard Dellar, Dioc Registry, 1 The Sanctuary, Westminster, London SW1P 3JT
Tel: 020 7222 5381
Dioc Surveyors Hook Mason Partnership, 41 Widemarsh St, Hereford HR4 9EA   *Tel:* 01432 352299

DIOCESAN ORGANIZATIONS
Dioc Office The Palace, Hereford HR4 9BL
Tel: 01432 373300
Fax: 01432 352952
email: diooffice@hereford.anglican.org
Bishop's Office The Palace, Hereford HR4 9BN
Tel: 01432 271355
Fax: 01432 373346

ADMINISTRATION

Dioc Synod (Chairman, House of Clergy) Preb B. Chave, Vicarage, Vowles Close, Hereford HR4 0DF   *Tel:* 01432 273086
(Chairman, House of Laity) Canon Rosemary Lording, 93 Kings Acre Road, Hereford HR4 0RQ
                                                      Tel: 01432 340050
(Secretary) Mr John Clark, Dioc Office
Board of Finance (Chairman) Mr John Cox, c/o Dioc Office   *Tel:* 01432 373314
(Secretary) Mr John Clark *(as above)*
Financial Secretary Mr Gordon Powell, Dioc Office
Benefice Buildings Committee Mr Stephen Challenger, Dioc Office
Glebe Committee Mr Stephen Challenger *(as above)*
Board of Patronage Mr John Clark *(as above)*
Designated Officer Mr Howard Dellar, 1 The Sanctuary, Westminster, London SW1P 3JT
                                                      Tel: 020 7222 5381
Trusts Mr John Clark *(as above)*

CHURCHES

Advisory Committee for the Care of Churches (Chairman) Mrs Jane Marston, Dioc Office
(Secretary) Mr Stephen Challenger *(as above)*

EDUCATION

Director of Education Mr Philip Sell, Dioc Office (Ludlow), Unit 11, The Business Quarter, Ludlow Eco Park, Sheet Rd, Ludlow, Shropshire SY88 1FD   *Tel:* 01584 838881
           email: p.sell@hereford.anglican.org
Young Peoples Officer Miss Esther Gregory
                                                      Tel: 01584 871078
      email: e.gregory@hereford.anglican.org

LUDLOW CONFERENCE CENTRE

                                              Tel: 01584 873882
                                              Fax: 01584 877945

MINISTRY AND TRAINING

Diocesan Director of Ordinands (DDO) Revd Preb Mary Lou Toop, The New Vicarage, Minsterley, Shropshire SY5 0AA   *Tel:* 01743 791213
           email: ddo@hereford.anglican.org
DDO Administrator Ms Gill Stanley, Ludlow Diocesan Office, Units 8 & 9, The Business Quarter, Ludlow Eco Park, Sheet Road, Ludlow, Shropshire SY8 1FD   *Tel:* 01584 871079
Continuing Ministerial Development Officer Revd Nicholas Helm, c/o Dioc Office (Ludlow)
Lay Development Officer Revd Caroline Pascoe, c/o Dioc Office (Ludlow)
Local Ministry Officer Revd Dr John Daniels, c/o Dioc Office (Ludlow)   *Tel:* 01584 871081
Advisers for Non-Stipendiary Ministry Revd M. D. Vockins, Birchwood Lodge, Storridge, Malvern WR13 5EZ   *Tel:* 01886 884366
Revd J. Edwards, 2 Madeley Wood View, Madeley, Telford TF7 5TF   *Tel:* 01952 583254
Adviser on Women in Ministry Revd Mary Lou Toop *(as above)*   *Tel:* 01743 791213

Readers' Association (Warden) Revd Dr John Daniels, c/o Dioc Office (Ludlow) *(as above)*
Widows and Dependants (Hereford Diocese Clerical Charity) Mr John Clark *(as above)*

WORSHIP

Chairman Canon Andrew Piper *(as above)*
Secretary Vacancy

MISSIONARY AND ECUMENICAL

Ecumenical Committee (Chairman) Very Revd Michael Tavinor
Council for World Partnership and Development (Chairman) Mrs Hazel Gould
Evangelism Committee (Chairman) The Bishop of Ludlow

RETIRED CLERGY OFFICER

Revd Preb Andrew Talbot-Ponsonby
                                                      Tel: 01989 565003

PRESS, PUBLICITY AND PUBLICATIONS

Dioc Communications Officer Ms Anni Holden, The Palace, Hereford HR4 9BL
                                                      Tel: 01432 373342
           email: a.holden@hereford.anglican.org
Editor of Dioc Newspaper 'Reflections' Mr R. Calver, The Palace *(as above)*

DIOCESAN RECORD OFFICE

Hereford Records Office, The Old Barracks, Harold St, Hereford HR1 2QX *Tel:* 01432 260750
(For diocesan records and parish records for Hereford Archdeaconry)
Shrewsbury Records and Research Centre, Castle Gates, Shrewsbury SY1 2AQ *Tel:* 01743 255350
Head of Records and Research Mary McKenzie *(For parish records for Ludlow Archdeaconry)*

STEWARDSHIP

Community Partnership and Funding Officer Mrs Wendy Coombey, c/o Dioc Office (Ludlow) *(as above)*   *Tel:* 01584 871088
      email: w.coombey@hereford.anglican.org

RURAL DEANS
ARCHDEACONRY OF HEREFORD

Abbeydore Revd A. F. Evans, The Rectory, Ewyas Harold, Herefordshire HR2 0EZ
                                                      Tel: 01981 240079
Bromyard Revd A. Seabrook, Penhope House, Balhurst, Bromyard HR7 4EF   *Tel:* 01885 482184
Hereford Preb P. Towner, The Vicarage, 102 Green St, Hereford HR1 2QW   *Tel:* 01432 273676
Kington and Weobley Revd M. J. Small, Church House, Church Road, Eardisley, Hereford HR3 6NN   *Tel:* 01544 327440
Ledbury Revd R. Ward, The Rectory, Cradley, Malvern, Worcestershire WR13 5LQ
                                                      Tel: 01886 880438
Leominster Preb M. C. Cluett, The Vicarage, Brookside, Canon Pyon, Hereford HR4 8NY
                                                      Tel: 01432 830802

Ross and Archenfield Revd M. Johnson, Becket House (The Rectory), Much Birch, Hereford HR2 8HT   *Tel:* 01981 540390

ARCHDEACONRY OF LUDLOW

Bridgnorth Revd N. Armstrong, The Rectory, Alveley, Bridgnorth WV15 6ND
                                      Tel: 01746 780326
Clun Forest Revd N. Morris, The Rectory, Wentnor, Bishop's Castle, Shropshire SY9 5EE
                                      Tel: 01588 650244

Condover Revd R. Hill, The Rectory, Carding Mill Valley, Church Stretton, Shropshire SY6 6JF
                                      Tel: 01694 722585
Ludlow Revd C. Lording, The Vicarage, Church Street, Tenbury Wells, Worcestershire WR15 8BP
                                      Tel: 01584 810811
Pontesbury Revd M. Jones, The Deanery, Pontesbury, Shrewsbury, Shropshire SY5 0PS
                                      Tel: 01743 792221
Telford Severn Gorge Revd I. Naylor, The Rector's House, Paradise, Coalbrookdale, Telford TF8 7NR   *Tel:* 01952 433514

Restored in 1926, Leicestershire; one parish in Northamptonshire; one parish partly in Derbyshire; one parish partly in Warwickshire.

Population 992,000   Area 840 sq m
Full-time Stipendiary Parochial Clergy 136   Benefices 109
Parishes 238   Churches 313
www.leicester.anglican.org
Overseas link dioceses: Mount Kilimanjaro and Kiteto (Tanzania)
and Trichy, Tanjore (India).

BISHOP (6th)
Rt Revd Timothy John Stevens, Bishop's Lodge Annexe, 12 Springfield Rd, Leicester LE2 3BD [1999]   *Tel:* 0116 270 8985
    Fax: 0116 270 3288
[Timothy Leicester]
Bishop's PA Mrs Melanie Freeman *(same address)*
    email: melanie.freeman@leccofe.org
Bishop's Policy Advisor and Chaplain Revd Adrian Jones *(same address)*   *Tel:* 0116 270 3390
    Fax: 0116 270 3288
    email: adrian.jones@leccofe.org
Executive Assistant to the Bishop Mrs Rachel Radford *(same address)*   *Tel:* 0116 270 8985
    email: rachel.radford@leccofe.org
Assistant Bishop Rt Revd Christopher Boyle
    Tel: 0116 261 5326
    email: bishop.boyle@leccofe.org
PA to Assistant Bishop Mrs Carol Gibbons, St Martins House, 7 Peacock Lane, Leicester LE1 5PZ
    Tel: 0116 261 5326
    email: carol.gibbons@leccofe.org
Bishop's Press Officer Ms Liz Hudson, St Martins House, 7 Peacock Lane, Leicester LE1 5PZ
    Tel: 0116 261 5302
    07943 387265 (Mobile)
    email: liz.hudson@leccofe.org

CATHEDRAL CHURCH OF ST MARTIN
St Martins House, 7 Peacock Lane, Leicester LE1 5PZ   *Tel:* 0116 261 5200
    email: leicestercathedral@leccofe.org
Dean Very Revd David Monteith [2013]
    Tel: 0116 261 5356
    email: david.monteith@leccofe.org
Canons Residentiary and Cathedral Clergy
Canon Chancellor Canon Rosy Fairhurst [2014]
    Tel: 0116 261 5345
    email: rosy.fairhurst@leccofe.org
Precentor Canon Dr Johannes Arens [2011]
    Tel: 0116 261 5364
    email: johannes.arens@leccofe.org
Urban Canon and Sub-Dean Canon Barry Naylor [2002]   *Tel:* 0116 261 5371
    email: barry.naylor@leccofe.org
Canon Paul Hackwood (NSM) [2007]
    Tel: 01530 223265
    email: paul.hackwood@me.com

Acting Canon Missioner Revd Pete Hobson [2013]
    Tel: 0116 261 5363
    email: pete.hobson@leccofe.org
Diocese and Cathedral Social Responsibility Enabler Revd Alison Adams (NSM) [2013]
    Tel: 0116 261 5333
    email: alison.adams@leccofe.org
Chaplain Vacancy
Cathedral Administrator Mr Jonathan Kerry
    Tel: 0116 261 5326
    email: jonathan.kerry@leccofe.org
Marketing and Development Officer Ms Claire Recordon   *Tel:* 0116 261 5368
    email: claire.recordon@leccofe.org
Director of Music Dr Christopher Johns [2011]
    Tel: 0116 261 5374
    email: chris.johns@leccofe.org
Assistant Director of Music Mr Simon Headley
    email: simon.headley@leccofe.org
Cathedral Solicitor Mr Trevor Kirkman, Latham & Co., Charnwood House, 2/4 Forest Rd, Loughborough LE11 3NP   *Tel:* 01509 238822

ARCHDEACONS
LEICESTER Ven Timothy Stratford, St Martins House, 7 Peacock Lane, Leicester LE1 5PZ [2002]
    Tel: 0116 261 5319
    email: tim.stratford@leccofe.org
LOUGHBOROUGH Ven David Newman, St Martins House, 7 Peacock Lane, Leicester LE1 5PZ [2009]
    Tel: 0116 261 5321
    email: david.newman@leccofe.org
Secretary to Archdeacons Mrs Wendy Dunnington
    Tel: 0116 261 5309
    email: wendy.dunnington@leccofe.org
Archdeacons Project Officer Miss Gill Tate
    Tel: 0116 261 2353
    email: gill.tate@leccofe.org

CONVOCATION (MEMBERS OF THE HOUSE OF CLERGY OF THE GENERAL SYNOD)
Proctors for Clergy
Revd John Plant
Revd John McGinley
Vacancy

MEMBERS OF THE HOUSE OF LAITY OF THE GENERAL SYNOD

Mr Stephen Barney
Mrs Yvonne Shayne Ardron
Mrs Anne Bloor

DIOCESAN OFFICERS

Dioc Secretary Mr Jonathan Kerry, St Martins House, 7 Peacock Lane, Leicester LE1 5PZ
Tel: 0116 261 5326
email: jonathan.kerry@leccofe.org
Assistant Dioc Secretary Mr Andrew Brockbank
Tel: 0116 261 5312
email: andrew.brockbank@leccofe.org
PA to Dioc Secretary Mrs Carol Gibbons
Tel: 0116 261 5326
email: carol.gibbons@leccofe.org
Chancellor of Diocese Mark Blackett-Ord, 5 Stone Buildings, Lincoln's Inn, London WC2A 3XT
Tel: 020 7421 7510
Fax: 020 7831 8102
Registrar of Diocese and Bishop's Legal Secretary Mr Trevor Kirkman, Latham and Co., Charnwood House, 2 Forest Rd, Loughborough LE11 3NP
Tel: 01509 238822
Fax: 01509 238833
email: TrevorKirkman@lathamlawyers.co.uk

DIOCESAN ORGANIZATIONS

Diocesan Office St Martins House, 7 Peacock Lane, Leicester LE1 5PZ
Tel: 0116 261 5200
Web: www.leicester.anglican.org

ADMINISTRATION

Director of Finance Mr John Orridge, Dioc Office
email: john.orridge@leccofe.org
Management Accountant Miss Caroline Wademan, Dioc Office *email:* caroline.wademan@covlec.org
Management Accountant Mr Jim Pullen, Dioc Office *email:* jim.pullen@covlec.org
Accounts Assistant Mrs Karen Issitt, Dioc Office
email: karen.issitt@leccofe.org
Senior Property Manager Mrs Nicky Caunt, Dioc Office *email:* nicky.caunt@covlec.org
Clergy Housing Officer Mrs Dinta Chauhan, Dioc Office *email:* dinta.chauhan@covlec.org
Property Officer Miss Lesley Whitwell, Dioc Office
email: lesley.whitwell@covlec.org
IT Manager Mr Phil Ash, Dioc Office
email: phil.ash@covlec.org
Dioc Synod (Chair, House of Clergy) Vacancy
Dioc Synod (Chair, House of Laity) Prof David Wilson *email:* djwilson@dmu.ac.uk
Dioc Synod and Bishop's Council (Secretary) Dioc Secretary, Dioc Office
Mission and Pastoral Committee Dioc Secretary *(as above)*
Stipends Officer Mrs Jill Benn, Coventry Cathedral and Diocesan Offices, 1 Hill Top, Coventry CV1 5AB
Tel: 024 7652 1200
Fax: 024 7652 1330
email: jill.benn@covlec.org

Board of Finance (Chair) Mr Stephen Barney, Peartree, 11 Orchard Way, Wymeswold, Loughborough LE12 6SW
Tel: 01509 881160
email: stephen4747@live.co.uk
Board of Finance (Secretary) Dioc Secretary *(as above)*
Finance Committee Dioc Secretary *(as above)*
Property and Glebe Committee Assistant Dioc Secretary *(as above)*
Designated Officer Mr Jonathan Kerry *(as above)*
Director of Parish Funding and Fundraising Mr Andrew Nutter, Dioc Office
Tel: 0116 261 5322
email: andrew.nutter@leccofe.org
Parish Funding Director
Mrs Maxine Johnson, Brook House, Stonton Rd, Church Langton, Market Harborough LE16 7SZ
Tel: 01858 545745
email: mjohnson@resort-solutions.co.uk
Growth Fund Administrator Mr Luke Fogg
Tel: 0116 261 5200
email: luke.fogg@leccofe.org
Child Protection Officer Mr Andrew Brockbank *(as above)*

CHURCHES

Advisory Committee for the Care of Churches (Chair) Revd Richard Curtis, Vicarage, Oakham Road, Tilton on the Hill LE7 9LB
Tel: 07855 746041
Advisory Committee for the Care of Churches (Secretary) Mr Rupert Allen, Dioc Office
Tel: 0116 261 5332
email: rupert.allen@leccofe.org

EDUCATION

Diocesan Board of Education St Martins House, 7 Peacock Lane, Leicester LE1 5PZ
Tel: 0116 261 5350
Fax: 0116 261 5351
Director Mrs Carolyn Lewis *(same address)*
email: carolyn.lewis@leccofe.org
PA to the Director Vacancy *(same address)*
Chief Executive of LACT Ian Jones
email: ian.jones@leccofe.org
Finance/Business Manager for LACT Ian Sharpe
email: ian.sharpe@leccofe.org
Chair Ven David Newman *(as above)*
School Inspections and Conference/Training Manager Mrs Helen Van Roose, Dioc Office
email: helen.vanroose@leccofe.org
School Support Officer Mrs Kerry Miller *(same address)* *email:* kerry.miller@leccofe.org
Senior Education Officer – School Effectiveness Mr Stephen Gleave, Dioc Office
email: stephen.gleave@leccofe.org

INTERFAITH

Director of Interfaith Relations and of the St Philip's Centre for Study and Engagement in a Multi Faith Society Canon Dr John Hall, St Philip's House, 2a Stoughton Drive North, Leicester LE5 5UB
Tel: 0116 273 3459
email: john.hall@stphilipscentre.co.uk

MINISTRY

Director of Mission and Ministry Canon Dr Mike Harrison, Dioc Office   *Tel:* 0116 261 5328
                                        Fax: 0116 261 5220
    email: mike.harrison@leccofe.org
Head of the School for Ministry Revd Dr Stuart Burns, Dioc Office   *Tel:* 0116 261 5354
    email: stuart.burns@leccofe.org
Mission Enabler Revd Barry Hill, Dioc Office
                                        Tel: 0116 261 5335
    email: barry.hill@leccofe.org
Mission and Ministry Consultant Revd Nicky McGinty, Dioc Office   *Tel:* 0116 261 5348
    email: nicky@njmcginty.co.uk
Youth Ministry Officer Mads Morgan, Dioc Office
                                        Tel: 0116 261 5342
    email: mads.morgan@leccofe.org
Dioc Director of Ordinands Canon Sue Field, 134 Valley Rd, Loughborough LE11 3QA
                                        Tel: 01509 234472
    email: sue.field134@gmail.com
Children's and Families Officer Louise Warner, Dioc Office   *Tel:* 0116 261 5313
    email: louise.warner@leccofe.org
Officer for Non-Stipendiary Ministry Revd Louise Corke, The Rectory, 58 Pymm Ley Lane, Groby, Leicester LE6 0GZ   *Tel:* 0116 231 3090
    email: words.th@talktalk.net
Warden of Evangelists Mr Ivan Bennett, 102 Dumbleton Avenue, Rowley, Leicester LE3 2EH
                                        Tel: 0116 223 9730
    email: ivanbennettsaysgodlovesyou@yahoo.com
Warden of Readers Revd Stephen Bailey, St Paul's House, Hamble Road, Oadby, Leicester LE2 4NX
                                        Tel: 0116 271 0519
    email: vicarstpauloadby@gmail.com
Reader Training Officer Revd Dr Stuart Burns (*as above*)
Pastoral Assistants Adviser Revd Liz Rawlings, 2 Cransley Close, Hamilton, Leicester LE5 1QQ
                                        Tel: 0116 274 2088
    email: lizrawlings@btinternet.com
Director of Post-Ordination Training Revd Canon Jane Curtis, Vicarage, Oakham Road, Tilton on the Hill LE7 9LB   *Tel:* 0116 2597244
    email: jcurtis@leicester.anglican.org
Director of Women's Ministry Revd Sharon Constable, 26 Firwood Road, Melton Mowbray LE13 1SA   *Tel:* 01664 481 793
    email: sharonconstable@msn.com
Retired Clergy and Widows Officer Anthony Wessel Esq, The Old Forge, 16 High St, Desford, Leicester LE9 9JF   *Tel:* 01455 822404
                                        Fax: 01455 823545
    email: anthony.wessel@dial.pipex.com

LITURGICAL

Chairman Revd Richard Curtis (*as above*)
Secretary Revd Alison Booker, The Vicarage, Gaulby Road, Billesdon, Leicester LE7 9AG
                                        Tel: 0116 259 6321
    email: abooker@leicester.anglican.org

PRESS AND COMMUNICATIONS

Communications Officer Ms Liz Hudson, Dioc Office   *Tel:* 0116 261 5302
                                        07943 387265 (Mobile)
    email: liz.hudson@leccofe.org
Editor of Dioc Directory Ms Liz Hudson (*as above*)
Editor of 'In Shape' Ms Liz Hudson (*as above*)

SOCIAL RESPONSIBILITY

Rural Officer Revd Dr Peter Hooper, 23 Ferndale Drive, Ratby, Leicester LE6 0LH
                                        Tel: 0116 239 4606
    email: peter@hoopers.orangehome.co.uk
Environment Officer Revd Andrew Quigley, The Vicarage, 49 Ashley Way, Market Harborough, LE16 7XD   *Tel:* 01858 410253
    email: andrew@aquigley.wanadoo.co.uk
Diocesan and Cathedral Responsibility Officer Revd Alison Adams, Dioc Office   *Tel:* 0116 261 5200
    email: alison.adams@leccofe.org

ECUMENICAL

Ecumenical Officer Mr Vic Allsop, Clematis Cottage, 14 Church Lane, Hoby, Melton Mowbray, Leics LE14 3DR

DIOCESAN RECORD OFFICE

Leicestershire Records Office, Long Street, Wigston, Leicester LE18 2AH   *Tel:* 0116 257 1080
                                        Fax: 0116 257 1120

AREA DEANS
ARCHDEACONRY OF LEICESTER

City of Leicester Revd Richard Worsfold, Martyrs Vicarage, 49 Westcotes Drive, Leicester LE3 0QT
                                        Tel: 0116 223 2632
    email: vicar.richard@martyrs.org.uk
Framland Revd Kevin Ashby, The Rectory, 57 Burton Road, Melton Mowbray LE13 1DL
                                        Tel: 01664 410 393
    email: rector@meltonparish.org.uk
Gartree I and Gartree II Revd Richard Brand, The Rectory, Rectory Lane, Little Bowden, Market Harborough LE16 8AS   *Tel:* 01858 462926
    email: brandrs@btinternet.com
Goscote Revd Canon Rob Gladstone, Rothley Vicarage, 128 Hallfields Lane, Rothley, Leicester LE7 7NG   *Tel:* 0116 230 2241
    email: rob@rgladstone.wanadoo.co.uk

ARCHDEACONRY OF LOUGHBOROUGH

Akeley East Revd Dr Tony Edmonds, The Rectory, Presents Lane, Belton, Loughborough LE12 9UN
                                        Tel: 01530 223447
    email: t.e.edmonds@btconnect.com
North West Leicestershire Revd Canon Vivien Elphick, The Vicarage, High Street, Measham, Swadlincote DE12 7HZ   *Tel:* 01530 270354
    email: vivien.elphick@btinternet.com
Guthlaxton Revd David Hebblewhite, The Vicarage, 102 Station Road, Countesthorpe, Leicester LE8 5TB   *Tel:* 0116 278 4442
    email: davidheb@talktalk.net

Sparkenhoe East Revd Dr Peter Hooper, 23
Ferndale Drive, Ratby, Leicester LE6 0LH
Tel: 0116 239 4606
email: peter@hoopers.orangehome.co.uk

Sparkenhoe West Revd Tom Meyrick, Rectory,
6 The Paddock, Newbold Verdon, Leicester
LE9 9NW
Tel: 01455 824986
email: meyrick@ekit.com

DIOCESE OF LICHFIELD

Founded in 664, formerly Mercia (AD 656). Staffordshire, except for a few parishes in the south-east (BIRMINGHAM, DERBY); a few parishes in the south-west (HEREFORD); the northern half of Shropshire; Wolverhampton; Walsall; the northern half of Sandwell.

Population 2,097,000   Area 1,740 sq m
Full-time Stipendiary Parochial Clergy 292   Benefices 269
Parishes 425   Churches 573
www.lichfield.anglican.org
Overseas link dioceses: W. Malaysia, Kuching, Singapore,
Qu'Appelle (Canada), Mecklenburg, Matlosane.

BISHOP (98th)
Rt Revd Jonathan Gledhill, Bishop's House, 22 The Close, Lichfield WS13 7LG [2003]
Tel: 01543 306000
Fax: 01543 306009
email: bishop.lichfield@lichfield.anglican.org
Bishop's Chaplain and Communications Officer Mr Simon Jones (*same address*)
email: simon.jones@lichfield.anglican.org
Bishop's PA Ms Diana Hill   *Tel:* 01543 306000
email: diana.hill@lichfield.anglican.org
Bishop's Secretary Mrs Margaret Wilson
Tel: 01543 306000
email: margaret.wilson@lichfield.anglican.org

AREA BISHOPS
SHREWSBURY Rt Revd Mark Rylands, 68 London Rd, Shrewsbury SY2 6PG [2009]   *Tel:* 01743 235867
Fax: 01743 243296
email: bishop.shrewsbury@lichfield.anglican.org
STAFFORD Rt Revd Geoff Annas, Ash Garth, Broughton Crescent, Barlaston, Stoke-on-Trent ST12 9DD [2005]   *Tel:* 01782 373308
Fax: 01782 373705
email: bishop.stafford@lichfield.anglican.org
WOLVERHAMPTON Rt Revd Clive Gregory, 61 Richmond Rd, Merridale, Wolverhampton WV3 9JH [2007]   *Tel:* 01902 824503
Fax: 01902 824504
email:
bishop.wolverhampton@lichfield.anglican.org

HONORARY ASSISTANT BISHOPS
Rt Revd David Bentley, 19 Gable Croft, Lichfield, WS14 9RY [2004]   *Tel:* 01543 419376
Rt Revd Iraj Mottahedeh, 2 Highland Rd, Newport, TF10 7AE [2005]   *Tel:* 01952 813615

CATHEDRAL CHURCH OF ST MARY AND ST CHAD
Dean Very Revd Adrian Dorber, The Deanery, 16 The Close, Lichfield WS13 7LD [2005]
Tel: 01543 306250 (Office)
email: adrian.dorber@lichfield-cathedral.org
Chapter Office 19a The Close, Lichfield WS13 7LD
Tel: 01543 306100
Fax: 01543 306109
email: enquiries@lichfield-cathedral.org
Web: www.lichfield-cathedral.org

Canons Residentiary
Vice-Dean and Canon for Liturgy and Formation Revd Canon Dr Anthony Moore, 24 The Close, Lichfield WS13 7LD [2013]   *Tel:* 01543 306148
email: anthony.moore@lichfield-cathedral.org
Canon Treasurer/Lichfield Cathedral School Chaplain Revd Canon Andrew Stead, 8 The Close, Lichfield WS13 7LD [2013]
Tel: 01543 306120 (Office)
07932 703032 (Mobile)
email: andrew.stead@lichfield-cathedral.org
Canon Custos Revd Canon Peter Holliday, c/o Chapter Office, 19a The Close, Lichfield WS13 7LD [2013]   *Tel:* 01543 434537
email: peterlholliday@aol.co.uk
Canon for Pastoral Development and Mission Revd Canon Pat Hawkins, 23 The Close, Lichfield WS13 7LD [2014]   *Tel:* 01543 306101 (Office)
email: pat.hawkins@lichfield-cathedral.org
Operations Director Mr Chris Nuttall, Chapter Office, 19a The Close, Lichfield WS13 7LD
Tel: 01543 306105 (Office)
email: chris.nuttall@lichfield-cathedral.org

Members of Chapter
Mrs Margaret Harding
Miss Anne Parkhill
Mr Peter Durrant
Mr Bryan Ramsell

Directors of Music Mr Ben Lamb and Mrs Cathy Lamb, 11 The Close, Lichfield WS13 7LD
Tel: 01543 306200
email: ben.lamb@lichfield-cathedral.org/
cathy.lamb@lichfield-cathedral.org
Organist, Director of Cathedral Chamber Choir Mr Martyn Rawles, 10 The Close, Lichfield WS13 7LD   *Tel:* 07901 946892
email: martyn.rawles@lichfield-cathedral.org
Development and Commercial Director Mr Jason Dyer, Chapter Office, 19a The Close, Lichfield WS13 7LD   *Tel:* 01543 306100
email: jason.dyer@lichfield-cathedral.org
Marketing Officer Miss Abby Wilson, Chapter Office, 19a The Close, Lichfield WS13 7LD
Tel: 01543 306121
email: abby.wilson@lichfield-cathedral.org

Education and Outreach Officer Mr Alex Nicholson-Ward, Chapter Office, 19a The Close, Lichfield WS13 7LD   *Tel:* 01543 306240
email: education@lichfield-cathedral.org
Personal Assistants:
to the Dean: Bernice Alexander; *Tel:* 01543 306250; *email:* bernice.alexander@ lichfield-cathedral.org
to the Vice-Dean and to the Canon for Pastoral Development: Theresa Willmore
Tel: 01543 306101
email: theresa.willmore@lichfield-cathedral.org

ARCHDEACONS
LICHFIELD Ven Simon Baker, 10 Mawgan Drive, Lichfield WS14 9SD [2013]   *Tel:* 01543 306145
email: archdeacon.lichfield@lichfield.anglican.org
SALOP Ven Paul Thomas, Archdeacon's House, Tong Vicarage, Shifnal TF11 8PW [2011]
Tel: 01902 372622
Fax: 01902 374060
email: archdeacon.salop@lichfield.anglican.org
STOKE-UPON-TRENT Ven Matthew Parker, 39 The Brackens,   Clayton,   Newcastle-under-Lyme ST5 4JL [2013]   *Tel:* 01782 663066
Fax: 01782 711165
email: archdeacon.stoke@lichfield.anglican.org
WALSALL Vacancy
email: archdeacon.walsall@lichfield.anglican.org

CONVOCATION (MEMBERS OF THE HOUSE OF CLERGY OF THE GENERAL SYNOD)
Proctors for Clergy
Revd Nigel Irons
Revd Patricia Hawkins
Revd Stephen Pratt
Revd Maureen Hobbs
Revd Mark Ireland
Vacancy

MEMBERS OF THE HOUSE OF LAITY OF THE GENERAL SYNOD
Mr David Beswick
Mrs Penelope Allen
Mr Christopher Corbet
Mrs Joanna Monckton
Mr John Shand
Dr Chik Kaw Tan
Mr John Wilson

DIOCESAN OFFICERS
Dioc Synod (Chairman, House of Clergy) Revd John Allan, Vicarage, Church Rd, Alrewas, Burton-on-Trent DE13 7BT   *Tel:* 01283 790486
email: revdjohnallan@revdjohnallan.plus.com
(Chairman, House of Laity) Mr John Wilson, 49 Oakhurst, Lichfield WS14 9AL   *Tel:* 01543 268678
email: charity.services@btclick.com
Dioc Secretary Mrs Julie Jones, St Mary's House, The Close, Lichfield, Staffs. WS13 7LD
Tel: 01543 306030
Fax: 01543 306039
email: julie.jones@lichfield.anglican.org

Mission and Pastoral Committee (Secretary) Mrs Mithra Tonking, St Mary's House
Tel: 01543 306030
email: mithra.tonking@lichfield.anglican.org
Chancellor of Diocese Mr Stephen Eyre, FBC, Manby Bowdler LLP, Routh House, Hall Court, Hall Park Way, Telford TF3 4NJ
Tel: 01952 292129
Diocesan Registrar and Bishop's Legal Secretary Mr Niall Blackie, Manby Bowdler LLP, Routh House, Hall Court, Hall Park Way, Telford, Shropshire TF3 4NJ   *Tel:* 01952 292129
Fax: 01952 291716
email: n.blackie@fbcmb.co.uk

DIOCESAN ORGANIZATIONS
Diocesan Office, see individual addresses below

ADMINISTRATION
Chairman Mr John Naylor
Team Leader Mrs Julie Jones, St Mary's House, The Close, Lichfield WS13 7LD   *Tel:* 01543 306030
Fax: 01543 306039
Finance Director Mr Jonathan R. L. Hill, St Mary's House
Benefice Buildings and Glebe Committee (Secretary) Mr Andrew Mason, St Mary's House
Diocesan Surveyor Mr Charles Glenn, St Mary's House
Trust (Secretary) Mrs Diane Holt, St Mary's House
Designated Officer Mr Niall Blackie, St Mary's House
Safeguarding Officer Mrs Kim Hodgkins, St Mary's House   *Tel:* 01543 306030
email: kim.hodgkins@lichfield.anglican.org
Diocesan   Communications   Officer Mr   Neill Harvey-Smith, St Mary's House
Tel: 07969 693613
email: neill.harveysmith@lichfield.anglican.org
Editor of Dioc Newspaper 'Spotlight' Mr Neill Harvey-Smith

ECUMENISM
Area Ecumenical Adviser (Black Country) Revd Simon Mansfield, St Gregory's Vicarage, 112 Long Knowle Lane, Wednesfield, Wolverhampton WV11 1JQ   *Tel:* 01902 731667
email: smansfield@toucansurf.com
Area Ecumenical Adviser (Shropshire) Mrs Veronica Fletcher, 67 Derwent Drive, Priorslee, Telford TF2 9QR   *Tel:* 01952 299318
email: veronica.fletcher@telford.gov.uk
Area   Ecumenical   Adviser   (Staffordshire) Revd Graham Gittings, 21 Princetown Close, Meir Park, Stoke-on-Trent ST3 7WN   *Tel:* 01782 388866
email: graham.gittings77@btinternet.com

CHURCHES
Advisory Committee for the Care of Churches (Chairman) Ven John Hall, 16 Mill House Drive, Cheadle, Stoke-on-Trent ST10 1XL
Tel: 01538 750628
email: j.hall182@btinternet.com

(Secretary) Mrs Kristina Williamson, 27 Frederick Road, Sutton Coldfield B73 5QW
Tel: 07805 772626
email:
kristina.williamson@lichfield.anglican.org

EDUCATION
Chair of Board of Education Dr Alison Primrose, Hill House, Vicarage Lane, Bednall, Stafford ST17 0SE
Tel: 01785 748976
email: aprimrose@talktalk.net
Director of Education and Team Leader Mr Colin Hopkins, St Mary's House
Tel: 01543 306040
email: colin.hopkins@lichfield.anglican.org
Schools Advisers Mrs Joan Furlong, 46 Gravelly Drive, Newport TF10 7QS
Tel and *Fax:* 01952 404381
email: joan.furlong@lichfield.anglican.org
Mrs Sue Blackmore, 153 Hockley Rd, Wilnecote, Tamworth B77 5EF
Tel: 01827 707638
email: sue.blackmore@lichfield.anglican.org
Mrs Rosemary Woodward, 151 Porlock Ave, Stafford ST17 0XY
Tel: 01785 665883
email:
rosemary.woodward@lichfield.anglican.org
Diocesan Schools Outreach Adviser, Miss Libby Leech, St Mary's House
email: libby.leech@lichfield.anglican.org
Warden of Diocesan Youth Centre Vacancy
Tel: 01335 350365
Fax: 01335 350441
email: warden@dovedalehouse.org.uk

MINISTRY MISSION AND TRANSFORMING COMMUNITIES
MINISTRY
Director of Ministry Revd Lesley Bentley, St Mary's House, Lichfield
Tel: 01889 508066 (Home)
01543 306227 (Office)
email: lesley.bentley@lichfield.anglican.org
PA to Director of Ministry Miss Jodie Galley
Tel: 01543 306227
email: jodie.galley@lichfield.anglican.org
Ministry Development Dept
Administrator (with responsibility for Ministry Development Review Mrs Jane Instone
Tel: 01543 306228
email: jane.instone@lichfield.anglican.org
Director of Ordinands Revd David Newsome, St Mary's House, Lichfield
Tel: 01543 306192 (Home)
01543 306220 (Office)
email: david.newsome@lichfield.anglican.org
PA to the Director of Ordinands and Vocations Dept Mrs Angela Bruno
Tel: 01543 306220 (Office)
email: angela.bruno@lichfield.anglican.org
Vocational Education Officer Revd Deborah Sheridan, 45 High Grange, Lichfield WS13 7DU
Tel: 01543 264363
email: d.sheridan@postman.org.uk

Vocations and Ministry Development Officer for Minority Ethnic Anglicans, Wolverhampton Revd Pamela Daniel, 33 Reform Street, West Bromwich B70 7PF
Tel: 0121 525 1985
email: pamdaniel@hotmail.com
Director of Lay Development Dr Lindsey Hall, St Mary's House
Tel: 01543 306225 (Office)
email: lindsey.hall@lichfield.anglican.org
Lichfield Director of Reader Training / OLM Tutor, The Queen's Foundation, Birmingham Revd Pauline Shelton, Dray Cottage, Cheadle Road, Draycott in the Moors, Stoke on Trent ST11 9RQ (home) St Mary's House, Lichfield (Office)
Tel: 01782 388834 (Home)
01543 306224 (Office)
email: pauline.shelton@lichfield.anglican.org
Local Ministry Scheme Administrator Miss Rebecca Harrison
Tel: 01543 306223 (Office)
email: becky.harrison@lichfield.anglican.org
Warden of Readers Mr John Maddison, 19 Woodland Avenue, Wolstanton, Newcastle-under-Lyme ST5 8AZ
Tel: 01782 853169
email: john.maddison@lichfield.anglican.org
Chaplain to Deaf People Revd Dr Leonie Wheeler, St Andrew's Rectory, 7 Wallshead Way, Church Aston, Newport TF10 9JG
Tel: 01952 810942
email: leonie.wheeler@btinternet.com
Bishop's Adviser for Pastoral Care and Wellbeing Revd Preb Jane Tillier, 10 Plantation Park, Keele, Newcastle ST5 5NA
Tel: 01782 639720
email: jane.tillier@lichfield.anglican.org

MISSION
Director of Parish Mission Revd George Fisher, The Parish Mission Office, The Small Street Centre, 1a Small Street, Walsall WS1 3PR
Tel: 01922 650063 (Home)
01922 707863 (Office)
email: george.fisher@lichfield.anglican.org
Director of World Mission Revd Philip Swan, The World Mission Office, The Small Street Centre, 1a Small Street, Walsall WS1 3PR
Tel: 01902 621148 (Home)
01922 707860 (Office)
email: philip.swan@lichfield.anglican.org
Parish Mission Research Assistant Mr Richard Barrett, The Parish Mission Office, The Small Street, Centre, 1a Small Street, Walsall WS1 3PR
Tel: 01922 707863 (Office)
email: richard.barrett@lichfield.anglican.org
PA to the Director of World Mission Miss Clare Spooner, The World Mission Office, The Small Street Centre, 1a Small Street, Walsall WS1 3PR
Tel: 01922 707861 (Office)
email: worldmission@lichfield.anglican.org
Youth and Children's Adviser Mr Mark Hatcher, Hillcroft, Stoney Lane, Endon, Stoke-on-Trent, ST9 9BX
Tel: 01782 502822
email: mark.hatcher@lichfield.anglican.org
Spiritual Companions Co-ordinator Revd Christine Polhill, Little Hayes, Beaudesert Park, Cannock Wood, Rugeley WS5 4JJ
Tel: 01543 674474
email: christine@refectiongardens.org.uk

TRANSFORMING COMMUNITIES

Transforming Communities Director Revd David Primrose, Hill House, Vicarage Lane, Bednall, Stafford ST17 0SE   *Tel:* 01785 748976
Transforming Communities Assistant Revd Ruth Brooker, The Small Street Centre, 1a Small Street, Walsall, WS1 3PR   *Tel:* 01922 707864
          email: ruth.brooker@lichfield.anglican.org

DIOCESAN RECORD OFFICES

Staffordshire Record Office, Eastgate St, Stafford ST16 2LZ *Tel:* 01785 278379, *email:* staffordshire.record.office@staffordshire.gov.uk (*For parishes in the archdeaconries of Lichfield and Stoke-on-Trent*)
Lichfield Record Office, The Library, The Friary, Lichfield WS13 6QG *Tel:* 01543 510720, *email:* lichfield.record.office@staffordshire.gov.uk (*For diocesan records and parishes within the City of Lichfield*)
Shropshire Archives, Castle Gates, Shrewsbury SY1 2AQ *Tel:* 01743 255350, *email:* archives@ shropshire.gov.uk (*For parishes in the archdeaconry of Salop*)

RURAL DEANS
ARCHDEACONRY OF LICHFIELD

Lichfield Revd Margaret Mattocks, The Vicarage, Church Road, Burntwood WS7 9EA
          Tel: 01543 304239
          email: margmattocks1@live.co.uk
Penkridge Revd Simon Witcombe, Codsall Vicarage, 48 Church Road, Codsall, Wolverhampton WV8 1EH   *Tel:* 01902 842168
          email: simonwitcombe50@gmail.com
Rugeley Preb Michael Newman, Rugeley Rectory, 20 Church St, Rugeley WS15 2AB
          Tel: 01889 582149
          email: eileennewman20@aol.com
Tamworth Revd Jim Trood, 6 Bamforth St, Glascote, Tamworth B77 2AS   *Tel:* 01827 305313
          email: jimtrood@btinternet.com

ARCHDEACONRY OF STOKE-ON-TRENT

Alstonfield Revd Revd James Forrester, The Vicarage, Gauledge Lane, Longnor, Buxton SK17 0PA   *Tel:* 01298 83742
          email: james@longnorvic.plus.com
Cheadle Revd Sue Goodwin, 2 Lordshire Mews, Armshead Road, Werrington, Stoke-on-Trent ST9 0HJ   *Tel:* 01782 302418
          email: revsuegoodwin@gmx.com
Eccleshall Revd Nigel Clemas, Whitmore Rectory, Snape Hall Rd, Whitmore Heath, Newcastle-under-Lyme ST5 5HZ   *Tel:* 01782 680258
          email: nclemas@hotmail.com
Leek Revd Martin Cannam, The Vicarage, 7 Wrexham Close, Biddulph, Stoke-on-Trent ST8 6RZ   *Tel:* 01782 513247
          email: martin@cannam.fsnet.co.uk
Newcastle-under-Lyme Revd Terry Bloor, 211 Basford Park Road, Basford Park, Newcastle-under-Lyme ST5 0PG   *Tel:* 01782 623668
          email: terry.bloor@btinternet.com

Stafford Revd John Davis, Stockton Croft, 87 Weeping Cross Stafford ST17 0DQ
          Tel: 01785 661382
          email: email: john_davis19@sky.com
Stoke North Revd Preb Will Slater, St James' Vicarage, 32 Pennyfields Road, Newchapel, Stoke-on-Trent ST7 4PN   *Tel:* 01782 782837
          email: willslater@tinyworld.co.uk
Stoke-upon-Trent Preb David Lingwood, Stoke Rectory, 172 Smithpool Rd, Stoke-on-Trent ST4 4PP   *Tel:* 01782 747737
          email: dp.lingwood@btinternet.com
Stone Revd Peter Dakin, 20 Tudor Hollow, Fulford, Stoke-on-Trent ST11 9NP
          Tel: 01782 397073
          email: pdakin@waitrose.com
Tutbury Revd Michael Freeman, St John's Vicarage, 14 Rolleston Road Burton-on-Trent DE13 0JZ   *Tel:* 01283 568613
          email: email: freeman.burton@googlemail.com
Uttoxeter Revd Brian Leathers, The New Vicarage, Lime Kiln Lane, Alton, Stoke-on-Trent ST10 4AR   *Tel:* 01538 702469
          *email:*briantopsey@googlemail.com

ARCHDEACONRY OF SALOP

Edgmond and Shifnal Revd Keith Hodson, Rectory, Beckbury, Shifnal TF11 9DG
          Tel: 01952 750774
          email: keithhodson@talk21.com
Ellesmere Revd Jules Wilson, The Rectory, Nobold, Baschurch, Shrewsbury SY4 2EB
          Tel: 01939 260305
          email: julian@julianwilson.wanadoo.co.uk
Hodnet Vacancy
Oswestry Revd Adrian Bailey, Vicarage, Old Chirk Road, Gobowen, Oswestry SY11 3LL
          Tel: 01691 661226
          email: arb2@totalise.co.uk
Shrewsbury Revd Mark Salmon, Harlescott Vicarage, Meadow Farm Drive, Shrewsbury SY1 4NG   *Tel:* 01743 369784
          email: revmarksalmon@gmail.com
Telford Revd Andrew Smith, St Matthew's Vicarage, St George's Road, Donnington, Telford TF2 7NJ   *Tel:* 01952 291904
          email: andysmith@telfordchristiancouncil.co.uk
Wem and Whitchurch Revd Rob Haarhoff, Vicarage, Shrewsbury Rd, Hadnall, Shrewsbury SY4 4AG   *Tel:* 01939 210241
          email: rob.haarhoff@gmail.com
Wrockwardine Preb David Chantrey, The Rectory, Wrockwardine, Telford TF6 5DD
          Tel: 01952 251857
          email: david.chantrey@surefish.co.uk

ARCHDEACONRY OF WALSALL

Trysull Revd Preb Maureen Hobbs, Vicarage, 20 Dartmouth Avenue, Pattingham, Wolverhampton WV6 7DP   *Tel:* 01902 700257
          email: hobbsmaureen@yahoo.co.uk

Walsall Revd Martin Rutter, St Margaret's Vicarage, Chapel Lane, Great Barr, Birmingham B43 7BD   *Tel:* 0121 357 5813
email: mcrutter@tesco.net
Wednesbury Revd Allan Gwillim, St Mark's Vicarage, Ocker Hill, Tipton DY4 0UT
Tel: 0121 556 0678
email: allan.gwillim@btinternet.com

West Bromwich Revd Andrew Smith, All Saints Vicarage, 90 Hall Green Rd, West Bromwich B71 3LB   *Tel:* 01215 883698
email: vicar.allsaintswestbrom@googlemail.com
Wulfrun Revd Preb Pat Hawkins, The Vicarage, Lymer Road, Oxley, Wolverhampton WV10 6AA
Tel: 01902 783342
email: pathawkins@btinternet.com

DIOCESE OF LINCOLN

Founded in 1072, formerly Dorchester (AD 886), formerly Leicester (AD 680), originally Lindine (AD 678). Lincolnshire; North East Lincolnshire; North Lincolnshire, except for an area in the west (SHEFFIELD).

Population 1,045,000   Area 2,670 sq m
Full-time Stipendiary Parochial Clergy 147   Benefices 213
Parishes 494   Churches 635
www.lincoln.anglican.org

Overseas link dioceses: RC Diocese of Brugge, Härnösands (Sweden), Tirunelveli (CSI), Tuticorin-Nazareth (CSI).

BISHOP (72nd)
Rt Revd Christopher Lowson, The Old Palace, Lincoln LN2 1PU [2011]   *Tel:* 01522 504092
Fax: 01522 504051
email: bishop.lincoln@lincoln.anglican.org
[Christopher Lincoln]
Bishop's Chaplain Revd Sal McDougall (*same address*)
email: bishops.chaplain@lincoln.anglican.org

SUFFRAGAN BISHOPS
GRIMSBY Rt Revd David Court, The Old Palace, Lincoln LN2 1PU [2014]   *Tel:* 01552 504092
Fax: 01522 504051
email: bishop.grimsby@lincoln.anglican.org
GRANTHAM Vacancy

HONORARY ASSISTANT BISHOPS
Rt Revd Timothy Ellis, 8 Mason Grove, Sheffield S13 8LL
Rt Revd David Rossdale, Home Farm, East Keal, Spilsby PE23 4AY
Rt Revd David Tustin, The Ashes, Tunnel Rd, Wrawby, Brigg DN20 8SF [2001]

CATHEDRAL CHURCH OF THE BLESSED VIRGIN MARY
Dean Very Revd Philip Buckler, The Deanery, 11 Minster Yard, Lincoln LN2 1PJ [2007]
Tel: 01522 561611
email: dean@lincolncathedral.com
Visitor Services Office (main switchboard)
Tel: 01522 561600
Fax: 01522 561634
Web: www.lincolncathedral.com
Canons Residentiary
Precentor Canon Gavin Kirk, The Precentory, 16 Minster Yard, Lincoln LN2 1PX [2003]
Tel: 01522 561632
email: precentor@lincolncathedral.com
Chancellor Canon Dr Mark Hocknull, The Chancery, 12 Eastgate, Lincoln LN2 1QG [2009]
Tel: 01522 561633
email: chancellor@lincolncathedral.com
Subdean Canon John Patrick, The Subdeanery, 18 Minster Yard, Lincoln LN2 1PY [2011]
Tel: 01522 561626
email: subdean@lincolncathedral.com

Chapter Clerk and Administrator Mrs Jacqueline Croft, Chapter Office, Lincoln Cathedral, Lincoln LN2 1PX   *Tel:* 01522 561604
email: chapterclerk@lincolncathedral.com
Director of Music and Organist and Master of the Choristers Mr Aric Prentice, Lincoln Minster School, Prior Building, Upper Lindum St, Lincoln LN2 5RW   *Tel:* 01522 551300
email: aric.prentice@church-schools.com
Assistant Director of Music and Sub-Organist Vacancy
Organist Laureate Dr Colin Walsh, Graveley Place, 12 Minster Yard, Lincoln LN2 1PJ
Tel: 01522 561646
email: colinwalsh1@btinternet.com

ARCHDEACONS
LINCOLN Ven Timothy Barker, The Old Palace, Minster Yard, Lincoln LN2 1PU [2009]
Tel: 01522 504050
email: archdeacon.lincoln@lincoln.anglican.org
STOW and LINDSEY Vacancy
BOSTON Ven Dr Justine Allain Chapman, Archdeacon's House, Castle Hill, Welbourn, Lincoln LN5 0NF [2013]   *Tel:* 01400 273335
email:
justine.allainchapman@lincoln.anglican.org

CONVOCATION (MEMBERS OF THE HOUSE OF CLERGY OF THE GENERAL SYNOD)
Canon Christopher Lilley
Canon Gavin Kirk
Ven Timothy Barker

MEMBERS OF THE HOUSE OF LAITY OF THE GENERAL SYNOD
Miss Rachel Beck
Mrs Sylvia Pounds
Mrs Susan Slater
Mrs Carol Ticehurst

DIOCESAN OFFICERS
Diocesan Secretary Angela Sibson OBE, Edward King House, Minster Yard, Lincoln LN2 1PU
Tel: 01522 504032
Fax: 01522 504051
email: diocesan.secretary@lincoln.anglican.org

Asssistant Diocesan Secretary Mr Will Harrison, Edward King House, Minster Yard, Lincoln LN2 1PU   *Tel:* 01522 504033
    email: will.harrison@lincoln.anglican.org
Chancellor of Diocese HHJ Revd Mark Bishop QC, c/o Diocesan Registry
Registrar of Diocese and Bishop's Legal Secretary Mrs Julie Robinson, The Diocesan Registry, Roythornes Solicitors, Enterprise Way, Pinchbeck, Spalding PE11 3YR   *Tel:* 01775 842618
    email: julierobinson@roythornes.co.uk

DIOCESAN ORGANIZATIONS
Diocesan Office Edward King House, Minster Yard, Lincoln LN2 1PU   *Tel:* 01522 504050
                                Fax: 01522 504051
    email: reception@lincoln.anglican.org
    Web: www.lincoln.anglican.org

ADMINISTRATION
Diocesan Synod (Chairman, House of Clergy) Canon John Patrick   *Tel:* 01522 504050
(Chairman, House of Laity) Mr Cameron Watt
                                Tel: 01522 504050
(Secretary) Mr Will Harrison, Diocesan Office
Bishop's Council (Chairman) Rt Revd Christopher Lowson, Bishop of Lincoln
(Secretary) Mr Will Harrison *(as above)*
Board of Finance (Chairman) Mr Trevor Bush, Diocesan Office
Trusts Committee Mr Andrew Gosling, Dioc Office
Assets (and Glebe) Committee Mr Peter Gaskell
Parsonages and Properties Mr Nicholas Turner, Diocesan Office
Board of Patronage Miss Rachel Beck, Diocesan Office
Designated Officer Mrs Julie Robinson, Roythornes Solicitors, Enterprise Way, Pinchbeck, Spalding PE11 3YR   *Tel:* 01755 842618
    email: julierobinson@roythornes.co.uk
Dioc Electoral Registration Officer Mr Will Harrison, Diocesan Office

CHURCHES
Advisory Committee for the Care of Churches (Chairman) Mrs Susan Leadbetter
(Secretary) Mr Keith Halliday, Diocesan Office
                                Tel: 01522 504046
Church Buildings Officer Mr Ben Stoker (Diocesan Office)
Historic Churches Support Officer Mr Matthew Godfrey (Diocesan Office)
Closed Churches Vacancy

EDUCATION
Director of Education Jacqueline Waters-Dewhurst, Diocesan Office   *Tel:* 01522 504010
    email: education@lincoln.anglican.org
Diocesan Board of Education (Chair) Prof Muriel Robinson
    email: muriel.robinson@lincoln.anglican.org

Deputy Director of Education Mr Paul Thompson, Diocesan Office
Diocesan Board of Education Business Manager Mrs Bridget Starling *(same address)*
Schools Adviser Mr David Clements *(same address)*

MINISTRY
Principal of EM3 Revd Sally Myers, Diocesan Office   *Tel:* 01522 504021
Diocesan Director of Ordinands and Vocations Adviser Canon Dr Jeffrey Heskins, Diocesan Office   *Tel:* 01522 504029
Adviser on Women's Ministry Canon Kathryn Windslow, Rectory, Vicarage Lane, Wellingore, Lincoln LN5 0JF   *Tel:* 01522 810246
    email: kathryn.windslow@btinternet.com
Ordinands' Grants Mr Peter Gaskell, Diocesan Office
Warden of Readers Revd Sally Buck
                                Tel: 01427 788251
Readers (Secretary) Mr J. Marshall, 73 Sentance Crescent, Kirton, Boston PE20 1XF
                                Tel: 01205 723097
Clergy Widows Officers Canon and Mrs Michael Boughton, 45 Albion Crescent, Lincoln LN1 1EB
                                Tel: 01522 569653
Clergy Retirement Officer Ven Geoff Arrand

PRESS, PUBLICITY AND PUBLICATIONS
Communications Officer Miss Michelle Lees, Diocesan Office   *Tel:* 01522 504034

LITURGICAL COMMITTEE
Chairman Canon Gavin Kirk *(as above)*

MISSION AND ECUMENICAL CONCERNS
Ecumenical Officer Revd Moira Astin
Churches Together in all Lincolnshire Mr Simon Dean, c/o Diocesan Office   *Tel:* 01522 504071
Lincolnshire Chaplaincy Services (Company No. 6491058)
Chair of Board and Chaplaincy Director Canon Andrew Vaughan   *Tel:* 01522 528266
    email: andrewvaughan@ntlworld.com
Business Manager Miss Alison McNish, Diocesan Office   *Tel:* 01522 504070
Agricultural Chaplain Canon Alan Robson, The Manse, 1 Manor Drive, Wragby, Market Rasen LN8 5SL   *Tel:* 01673 857871
Work with Young People Capt D. Rose CA, Diocesan Office   *Tel:* 01522 504066
Parish Support & Youth Project Worker Suzanne Starbuck, Diocesan Office

PARISH DEVELOPMENT
Parish Development Officer Mr Simon Bland, Diocesan Office

DIOCESAN RECORD OFFICE
Lincolnshire Archives Office, St Rumbold Street, Lincoln LN2 5AB   *Tel:* 01522 526204

AREA DEANS
ARCHDEACONRY OF STOW

North Lincolnshire Revd Moira Astin, The Vicarage, Vicarage Gardens, Frodingham, Scunthorpe DN14 7AZ   *Tel:* 01724 334873
email: moira.astin@ntlworld.com

ARCHDEACONRY OF LINDSEY

North East Lincolnshire Revd Andrew Dodd, The Rectory, 49 Park Drive, Grimsby, N E Lincs, DN32 0EG   *Tel:* 01472 358610
email: andrew.dodd@grimsbyminster.co.uk

RURAL DEANS
ARCHDEACONRY OF STOW

Isle of Axholme Revd Jonathan Thacker, St George's Vicarage, 87 Ferry Road, Scunthorpe, North Lincolnshire DN15 8LY   *Tel:* 01724 843328
Corringham Revd Philip Wain, The Rectory, 18 Gainsborough Road, Lea DN21 5HZ
Tel: 01427 613188
email: phillip.wain@btinternet.com
Lawres Revd Richard Crossland, Manor Farm, Battleby, Lincoln LN1 2SQ   *Tel:* 01522 730535
email: rcrossland@voxhumana.co.uk
Manlake Revd Jonathan Thacker, St George's Vicarage, 87 Ferry Road, Scunthorpe, North Lincolnshire DN15 8LY   *Tel:* 01724 843328
email: jon@han195.freeserve.co.uk
West Wold Canon Ian Robinson, The Vicarage, 3 Spa Top, Caistor, Lincoln LN7 6UH
Tel: 01472 851339
email: revianrobinson@tiscali.co.uk
Yarborough Revd David Rowett, The Vicarage, Beck Hill, Barton on Humber, North Lincolnshire DN18 5EY   *Tel:* 01652 632202
email: davidrowett@aol.co

ARCHDEACONRY OF LINDSEY

Bolingbroke Canon Peter Coates, The Vicarage, Church Street, Spilsby PE23 5DU
Tel: 01790 752526
email: peter.coates@onetel.net
Grimsby and Cleethorpes Vacancy
Haverstoe Vacancy
Horncastle (Acting) Revd Mark Holden, The Vicarage, Church Street. Wragby. LN8 5RA
Tel: 01673 857825
email: wragbygroup@aol.com

ARCHDEACONRY OF BOSTON

Stamford (Formerly Aveland and Ness with Stamford) Very Revd Mark Warrick, All Saints Vicarage, Casterton Road, Stamford PE9 2YL
Tel: 01780 756942
email: mark.warrick@stamfordallsaints.org.uk
Beltisloe Revd Christopher Atkinson, The Vicarage, Church Walk, Bourne PE10 9UQ
Tel: 01778 422412
email: chris_atk@yahoo.com
Elloe East Revd Rosamund Seal, Vicarage, 34 Church Lane, Moulton, Spalding PE12 6NP
Tel: 01406 370791
email: rosamund.seal@btinternet.com
Elloe West Revd Philip Brent, The Rectory, 13 Church Street, Market Deeping, PE6 8DA
Tel: 01778 342237
email: candpbrent@btinternet.com
Grantham Revd Christopher Boland, The Vicarage, Edinburgh Road, Harrowby, Grantham NG31 9QZ   *Tel:* 01476 564781
email: cpboland@btinternet.com
Loveden Revd Alan Littlewood, The Rectory, 117 Ermine Street, Ancaster, Grantham NG32 3QL
Tel: 01400 231145
email: ancaster.rectory@btinternet.com

ARCHDEACONRY OF LINCOLN

Calcewaithe and Candleshoe Canon Terry Steele, The Rectory, Glebe Rise, Burgh le Marsh, Skegness PE24 5BL   *Tel:* 01754 810216
email: father.terry@btclick.com
Christianity Canon David Osbourne, Rectory, 2A St Helen's Avenue, Boultham, Lincoln LN6 7RA
Tel: 01522 682026
email: davidosbourne@hotmail.co.uk
Graffoe Canon Nicholas Buck, Rectory, 11 Torgate Lane, Bassingham, Lincoln LN5 9HF
Tel: 01522 788383
email: nick_buck@tiscali.co.uk
Holland Revd Simon Dowson, Holy Trinity Vicarage, 64 Spilsby Road, Boston PE21 9NS
Tel: 01205 363657
email:
rev.simondowson@holytrinityboston.org.uk
Lafford Revd Christine Pennock, The Rectory, 2 All Saints Close, Manor Street, Ruskington, Sleaford NG34 9FP   *Tel:* 01526 832463
email: revpennock77@btinternet.com
Louthesk Revd Susan Allison, The Rectory, Peppin Lane, Fotherby, Louth LN11 0UW
Tel: 01507 602312
email: susan.333allison@btinternet.com

DIOCESE OF LIVERPOOL

Founded in 1880. Liverpool; Sefton; Knowsley; St Helens; Wigan, except for areas in the north (BLACKBURN) and in the east (MANCHESTER); Halton, north of the river Mersey; Warrington, north of the river Mersey; most of West Lancashire.

Population 1,567,000   Area 390 sq m
Full-time Stipendiary Parochial Clergy 206   Benefices 170
Parishes 206   Churches 248
www.liverpool.anglican.org
Overseas link dioceses: Akure (Nigeria) and Virginia (USA).

BISHOP (8th)

Rt Revd Paul Bayes, Bishop's Lodge, Woolton Park, Woolton, Liverpool L25 6DT [2014]
Bishop's Personal Assistant Vacancy (*same address*)
Tel: 0151 421 0831 (Office)
Fax: 0151 428 3055
email: bishopslodge@liverpool.anglican.org

SUFFRAGAN BISHOP

WARRINGTON Rt Revd Richard Blackburn, St James' House, 20 St James Rd, Liverpool L1 7BY
Tel: 0151 705 2140
email:
bishopofwarrington@liverpool.anglican.org
Bishop's Personal Assistant Mrs Nerys Cooke, St James' House, 20 St James Rd, Liverpool L1 7BY
Tel: 0151 705 2140
email: nerys.cooke@liverpool.anglican.org

HONORARY ASSISTANT BISHOPS

Rt Revd Cyril Ashton, 'Charis', 17c Quernmore Rd, Lancaster LA1 3EB
Tel: 01524 848684
email: bpcg.ashton@btinternet.com
Rt Revd Glyn Webster, Holy Trinity Rectory, Micklegate, York YO1 6LE
Tel: 01904 628155
email: office@seeofbeverley.org

CATHEDRAL CHURCH OF CHRIST

Dean Very Revd Dr Pete Wilcox
Tel: 0151 702 7220
email: dean@liverpoolcathedral.org.uk
Canons Residentiary
Canon Precentor Canon Myles Davies [2008]
Tel: 0151 702 7203
email: myles.davies@liverpoolcathedral.org.uk
Dwelly Raven Vacancy
Chancellor Canon Cynthia Dowdle [2008]
Tel: 0151 702 7287
email: cynthia.dowdle@liverpoolcathedral.org.uk
Canon for Mission and Evangelism Canon Richard White [2009]
Tel: 0151 702 7243
email: richard.white@liverpoolcathedral.org.uk
Canon for Discipleship Canon Paul Rattigan [2013]
Tel: 0151 702 7233
email: paul.rattigan@liverpoolcathedral.org.uk
Cathedral Curate Revd Tim Watson
Tel: 0151 702 7284
email: tim.watson@liverpoolcathedral.org.uk

Mission Pastor Mr Mike Prescott
Tel: 0151 702 7235
email: mike.prescott@liverpoolcathedral.org.uk
Director of Operations Mr Mike Eastwood, St James' House, 20 St James Rd, Liverpool L1 7BY
Tel: 0151 705 2112
email: mike.eastwood@liverpool.anglican.org
Director of Music Mr David Poulter, The Cathedral
Tel: 0151 702 7291/7240
email: david.poulter@liverpoolcathedral.org.uk
Assistant Director of Music Mr Stephen Mannings
Tel: 0151 702 7234
Organist Titulaire Prof Dr Ian Tracey, The Cathedral
email: ian.tracey@liverpoolcathedral.org.uk

ARCHDEACONS

LIVERPOOL Ven Ricky Panter, St James' House, St James Road, Liverpool L1 7BY
Tel: 0151 705 2154
email: ricky.panter@liverpool.anglican.org
WARRINGTON Ven Peter Bradley, St James' House, St James Road, Liverpool L1 7BY
Tel: 0151 705 2154
email: peter.bradley@liverpool.anglican.org

CONVOCATION (MEMBERS OF THE HOUSE OF CLERGY OF THE GENERAL SYNOD)

Proctors for Clergy
Revd Canon Christopher Cook
Revd Canon Roger Driver
Revd Canon Malcolm Rogers
Revd Canon Peter Spiers
Revd Amanda Fairclough

MEMBERS OF THE HOUSE OF LAITY OF THE GENERAL SYNOD

Mr Paul Hancock
Mr Mark Stafford
Mrs Debra Walker
Mr Christopher Pye
Canon Margaret Swinson

DIOCESAN OFFICERS

Dioc Secretary Mr Mike Eastwood, St James' House, 20 St James Rd, Liverpool L1 7BY
Tel: 0151 705 2112
Fax: 0151 709 2885

Chancellor of Diocese Sir Mark Hedley
Registrar of Diocese and Bishop's Legal Secretary Howard Dellar, Lee Bolton Monier-Williams, 1 The Sanctuary, London SW1P 3JT
Tel: 020 7222 5381

DIOCESAN ORGANIZATIONS
Diocesan Office St James' House, 20 St James Rd, Liverpool L1 7BY
Tel: 0151 709 9722
Fax: 0151 709 2885
Web: www.liverpool.anglican.org

ADMINISTRATION
Dioc Synod (Chair, House of Clergy) Revd Canon Joan Matthews, 8 The Parchments, Newton-le-Willows, Warrington WA12 0DY
Tel: 01925 270795
(Chair, House of Laity) Canon Margaret Swinson, 46 Glenmore Ave, Liverpool L18 4QF
Tel: 0151 724 3533
(Secretary) Mr Mike Eastwood, Dioc Office
(Asst Secretary) Mr Ultan Russell, Dioc Office
Board of Finance (Chair) Mr David Greensmith, Dioc Office
(Secretary) Mr Mike Eastwood *(as above)*
Mission and Pastoral Committee (Chair) Rt Revd Richard Blackburn; *(Secretary)* Mrs Sandra Holmes; *(Bishop's Planning Officer)* Revd David Burrows, Dioc Office
email: davidmacburrows@msn.com
(Assistant Bishop's Planning Officer) Revd Robert Williams *email:* robw49@tiscali.co.uk
Clergy Housing and Glebe Committee (Chair) Mr David Burgess, Dioc Office; *(Surveyor)* Mr Alan Gayner, Dioc Office
Support Mrs Claire Evans, Dioc Office
Tel: 0151 705 2129
email: claire.evans@liverpool.anglican.org
Human Resources Adviser Miss Sharon Townson
Tel: 0151 705 2143
email: sharon.townson@liverpool.anglican.org
Designated Officer Revd David Burrows, Dioc Office

CHURCHES
Advisory Committee for the Care of Churches (Chair) Revd Canon Cllr Stephen Parish, 1a Fitzherbert St, Warrington WA2 7QG
Tel: 01925 631781

EDUCATION
Tel: 0151 705 2190
Chair Bishop of Warrington
Director of Education Dr Jon Richardson, Dioc Office
Asst Director Mr Stuart Harrison, Dioc Office
Senior Diocesan Schools Adviser Mr David Thorpe Dioc Office
Diocesan Schools Adviser Mrs Joan Stein, Dioc Office

MINISTRY
Director of Ordinands Revd Canon David Parry, Vicarage, St Michael's Church Rd, Liverpool L17 7BD
Tel: 0151 286 2411
email: david.parry@liverpool.anglican.org
Dean of Women's Ministry Canon Cynthia Dowdle, Dioc Office
Tel: 0151 702 7287
email: cynthia.dowdle@liverpool.anglican.org
Readers' Association (Warden) Mr Spen Webster
email: spen.webster@liverpool.anglican.org
Diocesan Liturgy and Worship Forum (Chair) Revd Jeremy Fagan, 27 Shakespeare Ave, Kirkby L32 9SH
Tel: 0151 547 2133
email: faganj@mac.com

LEARNING AND STEWARDSHIP
Director Revd Steve Pierce
Learning Managers Mrs Suzanne Matthews, Revd Bob Banton
Director of Studies Revd Simon Chesters
Vocations Officer: Mrs Debbie Ellison
email: lifelonglearning@liverpool.anglican.org
Resources Officer Gordon Fath, Cath Gaskell
email: resources.team@liverpool.anglican.org

CHURCH GROWTH TEAM
Tel: 0151 705 2148
email: warren.hartley@liverpool.anglican.org
Director Canon Linda Jones, Dioc Office
Tel: 0151 705 2109
email: linda.jones@liverpool.anglican.org
Mission and Pastoral Officer Mrs Sandra Holmes
Tel: 0151 705 2142
Children and Families Missioner Mrs Sue Mitchell
Tel: 0151 705 2167
email: sue.mitchell@liverpool.anglican.org
Diocesan Ecumenical Adviser Canon Linda Jones, Dioc Office

COMMUNICATIONS
Director Revd Stuart Haynes, Dioc Office
Tel: 0151 705 2150, 07534 218122
email: stuart.haynes@liverpool.anglican.org
Communications Officer Mrs Sarah Doyle, Dioc Office
Tel: 0151 705 2131
email: sarah.doyle@liverpool.anglican.org

DIOCESAN RECORD OFFICE
For further information apply to Mr Howard Dellar, Lee Bolton Monier-Williams, 1 The Sanctuary, London SW1P 3JT *Tel:* 020 7222 5381 *or* The Lancashire Record Office, Bow Lane, Preston PR1 2RE

CHURCH AND SOCIETY
Tel: 0151 705 2130
Fax: 0151 705 2215
email: churchandsociety@liverpool.anglican.org
Director Mr Ultan Russell
email: ultan.russell@liverpool.anglican.org
Departmental Chair Canon Angela White
email: angela.white@seftoncvs.org.uk

Deputy Chair Revd Canon Cynthia Dowdle
email: cynthia.dowdle@liverpool.anglican.org
Disability Awareness and Vulnerable Adults Officer
Sister Ruth Reed
email: ruth.reed@liverpool.anglican.org
Child Protection Adviser Mrs Su Foster
email: su.foster@liverpool.anglican.org
Domestic Abuse Adviser Mrs Helen Clarey
email: helen.clarey@talktalk.net
Chair, Anglican Partnerships and Links Revd
Canon Malcolm Rogers
email: malrogers@blueyonder.co.uk
Team Leader, Pastoral Services for the Deaf Community Revd Dr Hannah Lewis
email: hannah.lewis@liverpool.anglican.org
Heritage Support Officer Mr Ian Simpson
email: ian.simpson@liverpool.anglican.org
Development Officer (Together Liverpool) Revd John
Davis
email: john.davis@togetherliverpool.org.uk
Chair, Arts and Culture Network Revd Canon Ellen
Loudon
email: ellen@ellenloudon.com
Adviser on Elderly Person Issues Mrs Mary Kessler
email: marykessler@idnet.com

**MERSEYSIDE AND REGION CHURCHES
ECUMENICAL ASSEMBLY**
Ecumenical Development Officer Revd Ian Smith
(URC), Quaker Meeting House, 22 School Lane,
Liverpool L1 3BT   *Tel:* 0151 709 0125
email: office@ctmr.org.uk

MISSION IN THE ECONOMY (MitE)
Team Coordinator Revd Jean Flood, Quaker
Meeting House, 22 School Lane, Liverpool
L1 3BT   *Tel:* 0151 709 6908
email: missionintheeconomy@hotmail.com

AREA DEANS
ARCHDEACONRY OF LIVERPOOL
Bootle Canon Roger Driver, The Vicarage, 70
Merton Rd, Bootle L20 7AT   *Tel:* 0151 922 3316
email: rogerdriver@btinternet.com
Huyton Canon John Taylor, The Vicarage,
Vicarage Place, Prescot L34 1LA
Tel: 0151 426 6719
email: john.taylor@huytondeanery.org
Liverpool North Canon Kate Wharton, St George's
Vicarage, 40 Northumberland Terrace, Liverpool
L5 3QG   *Tel:* 0151 263 6005
email: katewharton@btinternet.com

Liverpool South – Childwall Canon Roland
Harvey, 49 Harbour Drive, Garston, Liverpool
L19 8AB   *Tel:* 0151 345 7475
email: rolandharvey86@gmail.com
Sefton Canon Peter Spiers, St Luke's Vicarage,
71 Liverpool Road, Great Crosby, Liverpool
L23 5SE   *Tel:* 0151 924 1737
email: pete@spiersfamily.eclipse.co.uk
Toxteth and Wavertree Canon Guy Elsmore, 7
Crossley Drive, Liverpool L15 8AJ
Tel: 07932 543900
email: guy.elsmore@gmail.com
Walton Canon Ellen Loudon, 25 Stuart Road,
Walton L4 5QS   *Tel:* 0151 521 1344
email: ellen@ellenloudon.com
West Derby Canon Steve McGanity, St Andrew's
Vicarage, 176 Queen's Drive, Liverpool L13 0AL
Tel: 0151 287 2887
email: smcganity@blueyonder.co.uk

ARCHDEACONRY OF WARRINGTON
North Meols Canon Phil Green, The Vicarage,
Rufford Road, Crossens, Southport PR9 8JH
Tel: 01704 227662
email: revphilgreen@talktalk.net
Ormskirk Canon Nick Wells, 28b Willow Hay,
Maghull, Liverpool L31 3DL
Tel: 0151 531 8972
email: nick.the-vic@blueyonder.co.uk
St Helens Canon David Eastwood, The Rectory,
51a Rainford Road, St Helens WA10 6BZ
Tel: 01744 27446
email: davideastwood86@gmail.com
Warrington Canon Stephen Boyd, St
Margaret's Vicarage, 2 St Margaret's Ave,
Orford, Warrington WA2 8DT
Tel: 01925 631937
email: stephen.boyd@liverpool.anglican.org
Widnes Canon Janice Collier, The Vicarage, 2
Vicarage Close, Hale Village L24 4BH
Tel: 0151 425 3195
email: janice.collier@hotmail.co.uk
Wigan Canon Margaret Sherwin, 3 Green Lane,
Hindley Green, Wigan WN2 4HN
Tel: 01942 255833
email: mjsherwin@btinternet.com
Winwick Canon Joan Matthews, 8 The Parchments, Newton-le-Willows WA12 0DY
Tel: 01925 270795
email: revjoan@hotmail.com

DIOCESE OF LONDON

Founded in 314. The City of London; Greater London north of the Thames, except five East London boroughs (CHELMSFORD) and an area in the north (ST ALBANS); Surrey north of the Thames; a small area of southern Hertfordshire.

Population 4,054,000   Area 280 sq m
Full-time Stipendiary Parochial Clergy 530   Benefices 409
Parishes 398   Churches 489
www.london.anglican.org
Overseas link dioceses: Niassa and Lebombo (Mozambique), Angola.

BISHOP (132nd)
Rt Revd and Rt Hon Dr Richard John Carew Chartres KCVO, The Old Deanery, Dean's Court, London EC4V 5AA [1995]   *Tel:* 020 7248 6233
Fax: 020 7248 9721
email: bishop@londin.clara.co.uk
[Richard Londin:]
Personal Jurisdiction Cities of London and Westminster (*Archdeaconries of London and Charing Cross*)
Matters relating to the other Areas should be referred to the appropriate Area Bishop
Personal Assistant Janet Laws
Diary Assistant Frances Charlesworth

AREA BISHOPS
STEPNEY Rt Revd Adrian Newman, 63 Coborn Road, London E3 2DB [2011]   *Tel:* 020 7932 1140
email: bishop.stepney@london.anglican.org
KENSINGTON Rt Revd Paul Williams, Dial House, Riverside, Twickenham, TW1 3DT [2009]
Tel: 020 7932 1180
email: bishop.kensington@london.anglican.org
EDMONTON Vacancy
WILLESDEN Rt Revd Peter Broadbent, 173 Willesden Lane, London NW6 7YN [2001]
Tel: 020 8451 0189
07957 144674 (Mobile)
Fax: 020 8451 4606
email: bishop.willesden@btinternet.com

SUFFRAGAN BISHOP
FULHAM Rt Revd Jonathan Baker, Bishop of Fulham's Office, The Old Deanery, Dean's Court, London EC4V 5AA   *Tel:* 020 7932 1130
email: bishop.fulham@london.anglican.org
Assists the Diocesan in all matters not delegated to the Areas and pastoral care of parishes operating under the London Plan.

HONORARY ASSISTANT BISHOPS
Rt Revd Michael Colclough, 12 Grosvenor Court, Sloane Street, London SW1X 9PF
Tel: 07809 149581
email: michaeljcolclough@gmail.com
Rt Revd Edward Holland, 37 Parfrey Street, London W6 9EW   *Tel:* 020 8746 3636
email: ed.holland@uwclub.net

Rt Revd Robert Ladds, Christ Church House, 76 Brent Street, London NW4 2ES
Tel: 020 8202 8123
email: episcopus@ntworld.com
Most Revd Walter Makhulu, 16 Downside, 8–10 St John's Avenue, London SW15 2AE
Tel: 020 8704 1220
email: makhulu@btinternet.com
Rt Revd Michael Marshall, 53 Oakley Gardens, London SW3 5QQ   *Tel:* 020 7351 0928
email: sebastian97@hotmail.co.uk
Rt Revd Preb Sandy Millar, 37 Alde Lane, Aldeburgh IP15 5DZ   *Tel:* 01728 452926
email: sandy.millar@techademic.net
Rt Revd Stephen Platten, St Michael's Rectory, St Michael's Alley, London ECV3 9DS
Tel: 0207 283 3121
email: kay@st-michaels.org.uk

CATHEDRAL CHURCH OF ST PAUL
Dean Very Revd Dr David Ison, 9 Amen Court, London EC4M 7BU   *Tel:* 020 72367 2827
Fax: 020 7332 0298
email: dean@stpaulscathedral.org.uk
Canons Residentiary
Canon Pastor Canon Tricia Hillas, 2 Amen Court, London EC4M 7BU [2014]   *Tel:* 020 7236 0199
Fax: 020 7489 8579
email: pastor@stpaulscathedral.org.uk
Chancellor Canon Mark Oakley, 6 Amen Court, London EC4M 7BU [2012]   *Tel:* 020 7248 8572
Fax: 020 7489 8579
email: chancellor@stpaulscathedral.org.uk
Treasurer Canon Philippa Boardman, 3 Amen Court, London EC4M 7BU [2013]
Tel: 020 7248 2559
email: treasurer@stpaulscathedral.org.uk
Precentor Canon Michael Hampel, 1 Amen Court, London EC4M 7BU [2011]   *Tel:* 020 7248 1817
Fax: 020 7489 8579
email: precentor@stpaulscathedral.org.uk
Lay Canons
Ms Pim Baxter, Chapter House, St Paul's Churchyard, London EC4M 8AD
Tel: 020 7246 8350
Fax: 020 7248 3104
email: pbaxter@stpaulscathedral.org.uk

Mr Gavin Ralston, Chapter House, St Paul's Churchyard, London EC4M 8AD
Tel: 020 7246 8350
Fax: 020 7248 3104
email: gavin@stpaulscathedral.org.uk
Minor Canons
Sacrist Revd Nigel Dawkins, 8a Amen Court, London EC4M 7BU
Tel: 020 7246 8331
Fax: 020 7246 8336
email: sacrist@stpaulscathedral.org.uk
Succentor Vacancy
Tel: 020 7246 8338
email: succentor@stpaulscathedral.org.uk
Chaplain Revd Sarah Eynstone, 7b Amen Court, London EC4M 7BU [2009]
Tel: 020 7246 8323
Fax: 020 7246 8336
email: chaplain@stpaulscathedral.org.uk
Headmaster of the School Mr Neil Chippington, St Paul's Cathedral School, New Change, London EC4M 9AD
Tel: 020 7248 5156
Fax: 020 7329 6568
email: admissions@spcs.london.sch.uk
Registrar Nicholas Cottam CB OBE, The Chapter House, St Paul's Churchyard, London EC4M 8AD
Tel: 020 7246 8311
Fax: 020 7248 3104
email: registrar@stpaulscathedral.org.uk
Dean's Virger Mr Charles Williams, 4b Amen Court, London EC4M 7BU
Tel: 020 7246 8320
Fax: 020 7248 3104
email: deansvirger@stpaulscathedral.org.uk
Solicitor to the Foundation at St Paul's Cathedral Mr Owen Carew-Jones, Winckworth Sherwood, Minerva House, 5 Montague Close, London SE1 9BB
Tel: 020 7593 5034
Fax: 020 7248 3221
email: ocj@winckworths.co.uk
Surveyor to the Fabric Mr Oliver Caroe, The Chapter House, St Paul's Churchyard, London EC4M 8AD
Tel: 020 7236 4128
email: oliver@caroe.com
Director of Music Mr Andrew Carwood, 5 Amen Court, London EC4M 7BU
Tel: 020 7651 0899
Fax: 020 7248 2817
email: andrewc@stpaulscathedral.org.uk
Organist Mr Simon Johnson, 4a Amen Court, London EC4M 7BU
Tel: 020 7236 6883
email: organist@stpaulscathedral.org.uk
Sub-Organist Mr Peter Holder, The Chapter House, St Paul's Churchyard, London EC4M 8AD
Tel: 020 7236 6883
Fax: 020 7248 2871
email: suborganist@stpaulscathedral.org.uk

ARCHDEACONS
LONDON Vacancy
email: archdeacon.london@london.anglican.org
CHARING CROSS Vacancy
email:
archdeacon.charingcross@london.anglican.org
HACKNEY Ven Rachel Treweek, St Andrew's House, 35 St Andrew's Hill, London EC4V 5DE
Tel: 020 7932 1145
email: archdeacon.hackney@london.anglican.org

MIDDLESEX Ven Stephan Welch, 98 Dukes Ave, London W4 2AF [2006]
Tel: 020 8742 8308
email:
archdeacon.middlesex@london.anglican.org
HAMPSTEAD Ven Luke Miller, 39 Bounds Green Road, London N22 8HE
Tel: 020 7932 1190
email:
archdeacon.hampstead@london.anglican.org
NORTHOLT Ven Duncan Green, London Diocesan House, 36 Causton Street, London SW1P 4AU
Tel: 020 7932 1274
email: archdeacon.northolt@london.anglican.org

CONVOCATION (MEMBERS OF THE HOUSE OF CLERGY OF THE GENERAL SYNOD)
Dignitaries in Convocation
The Bishop of London
The Bishop of Willesden
Revd Prof Richard Burridge
Proctors for Clergy
Revd Canon Philippa Boardman
Revd Stephen Coles
Revd Clare Herbert
Revd Christopher Hobbs
Revd Preb David Houlding
Revd Preb Charles Marnham
Revd Jane Morris
Revd Preb Alan Moses
Revd Philip North
Ven Rachel Treweek

MEMBERS OF THE HOUSE OF LAITY OF THE GENERAL SYNOD
Mrs Mary Chapman
Ms Susan Cooper
Mrs Sarah Finch
Mr Aiden Hargreaves-Smith
Mrs Mary Johnston
Dr Lindsay Newcombe
Dr Phillip Rice
Mr Anirban Roy
Mrs Alison Ruoff
Mr Clive Scowen
Mr John Ward

DIOCESAN OFFICERS
General Secretary and Chief Executive Mr Andy Brookes, London Diocesan House, 36 Causton St, London SW1P 4AU
Tel: 020 7932 1100
Chancellor of Diocese Chancellor The Worshipful Nigel Seed QC, Winckworth Sherwood, Minerva House, 5 Montague Close, London SE1 9BB
Tel: 020 7593 5110
Fax: 020 7248 3221
Registrar of Diocese and Bishop's Legal Secretary Mr Paul Morris (*same address*)
Official Principal of the Archdeaconry of Hackney His Honour David Smith QC, Beachcroft, Beach, Bitton, Bristol BS30 6NP

Official Principal of the Archdeaconry of Hampstead
Dean Sheila Cameron, 2 Harcourt Bldgs, Temple,
London EC4Y 9DB
Official Principal of the Archdeaconry of Northolt
Mr Paul Morris (*as above*)

DIOCESAN ORGANIZATIONS
CHAIR
London Dioc Fund (*Dioc Board of Finance*) The
Bishop of London
Vice Chair Mr James Normand and Preb Alan
Moses
Finance Committee Ven Dr William Jacob
Dioc Synod (*House of Clergy*) Preb Alan Moses
(*House of Laity*) Mr James Normand
Dioc Board for Schools Ven Stephan Welch

ADMINISTRATION
Diocesan Office London Diocesan House, 36
Causton St, London SW1P 4AU
Tel: 020 7932 1100
Fax: 020 7932 1110
Web: www.london.anglican.org
Director of Finance and Operations Mr Richard
Gough
Human Resources Manager Colette Black
Director of Property Mr Michael Bye
Synodical Secretary Mrs Monica Bolley
Communications Manager Mr Robert Hargrave
Dioc Advisory Committee (*Chair*) The Baroness
Wilcox; (*Secretary*) Mr Geoffrey Hunter

EDUCATION
Senior Chaplain for Higher Education Revd
Stephen Williams, University Chaplaincy Office,
30B Torrington Square, London WC1E 7JL
Tel: 020 7580 9812
Fax: 020 7631 3219
email: chaplaincy@lon.ac.uk
Director, London Diocesan Board for Schools Mr
Inigo Woolf, London Diocesan House
Tel: 020 7932 1165
email: inigo.woolf@london.anglican.org

MINISTRY
*Director of Ministry, Warden of Licensed Lay
Ministry* Revd Dr Neil Evans, 23 St Albans
Avenue, London W4 5LL   *Tel:* 020 8987 7332
email: neil.evans@london.anglican.org
*Vicar General to the London College of Bishops,
Dioc Director of Ordinands,* Preb Nick Mercer,
The Old Deanery, Dean's Court, London
EC4V 5AA   *Tel:* 020 7489 4274
email: nick.mercer@london.anglican.org
Two Cities
Area Director of Training and Development Revd
Dr Neil Evans (*as above*)
Dean of Women's Ministry Revd Rosemary Lain-
Priestley, 13d Hyde Park Mansions, Cabell St,
London NW1 5BD   *Tel:* 020 7723 5352
email: rosemarylainpriestley@btopenworld.com

Stepney
Area Director of Training and Development Revd
Irena Edgcumbe, The Centre for Training &
Development, St Anne's Community Hall,
Hemsworth Street London N1 5LF
Tel: 020 7033 3446
email: irena.edgcumbe@london.anglican.org
Dean of Women's Ministry Vacancy
Kensington
Area Director of Ministry Revd Martin Breadmore,
207 London Road, Twickenham TW1 1EJ
Tel: 020 8891 0324
email: martin.breadmore@london.anglican.org
Dean of Women's Ministry Revd Anna Brooker,
Butterfield House, 63 Church Street, Isleworth
TW7 6BE   *Tel:* 020 8476 0033
email: anna.brooker@allsaints-isleworth.org
Edmonton
Area Director of Training and Development Caulene
Herbert, 27 Thurlow Rd, Hampstead, London
NW3 5PP   *Tel:* 020 7431 6827
email: caulene.herbert@london.anglican.org
Willesden
Area Director of Training and Development Revd
Andrew Corsie, St Edwards House, 12a Medway
Drive, Perivale UB6 8LN   *Tel:* 020 8991 9571
email: andrew.corsie@london.anglican.org
Dean of Women's Ministry Revd Jane Manley, St
Paul's Vicarage, Thurlstone Road, Ruislip
Manor, Ruislip HA4 0BP   *Tel:* 01895 633499
email: jane.e.manley@btinternet.com

MISSION
Children's Ministry Adviser Sam Donoghue,
London Diocesan House   *Tel:* 020 7932 1255
email: sam.donoghue@london.anglican.org
Diocesan Community Ministry Adviser Vacancy

LITURGICAL
Chairman Very Revd Dr David Ison

PRESS AND COMMUNICATIONS
Press, media and public affairs
Tel: 020 7618 9106 (24 hours)
email: dioceseoflondon@luther.co.uk
Communications Manager Mr Robert Hargrave,
London Diocesan House   *Tel:* 020 7932 1227
email: robert.hargrave@london.anglican.org

ENVIRONMENT
Head of Environment and Sustainability Mr Brian
Cuthbertson, London Diocesan House
Tel: 020 7932 1229
email: brian.cuthbertson@london.anglican.org

DIOCESAN RECORD OFFICES
London Metropolitan Archive, 40 Northampton
Rd, London EC1R 0HB
Enquiry team Tel: 020 7332 3820, *email:* ask.lma@
cityoflondon.gov.uk (*All parishes except City and
Westminster*)

Guildhall Library, Aldermanbury, London EC2V 7HH *Tel:* 020 7332 1868/1870, *email:* guildhall. library@cityoflondon. gov.uk (*City parishes*)
City of Westminster Archives Centre, 10 St Ann's St, London SW1P 2DE *Tel:* 020 7798 2180, *email:* archives@westminster.gov.uk (*Westminster parishes*)

AREA DEANS

ARCHDEACONRY OF LONDON

City Revd Oliver Ross, St Olave's Rectory, 8 Hart St, London EC3R 7NB *Tel:* 020 7488 4318
email: areadeantothecity@gmail.com

ARCHDEACONRY OF CHARING CROSS

Westminster (Paddington) Revd Jeremy Allcock, St Stephen's Vicarage, 25 Talbot Road, London W2 5JF *Tel:* 020 7792 2283
email: jeremyallcock@ststephenschurch.info
Westminster (St Margaret) Revd Philip Chester, St Matthew's House, 20 Great Peter St, London SW1P 2BU *Tel:* 020 7222 3704
email: office@stmw.org
Westminster (St Marylebone) Preb Alan Moses, 7 Margaret St, London W1W 8JG
Tel: 020 7636 1788
email: alanmoses111@gmail.com

ARCHDEACONRY OF HACKNEY

Hackney Revd Rob Wickham, The Rectory, 11 Clapton Square, London E5 8HP
Tel: 020 8985 5374 ext 221
email: rectorofhackney@aol.com
Islington Revd Jonathan Brewster, Christ Church Vicarage, 155 Highbury Grove, London N5 1SA
Tel: 020 7226 4544
email: vicar@christchurchhighbury.com
Tower Hamlets Revd Andy Rider, The Rectory, 2 Fournier Street, London E1 6QE
Tel: 020 7247 0790
email: arider@ccspitalfields.org

ARCHDEACONRY OF MIDDLESEX

Chelsea Revd Canon David Reindorp, 2 Old Church Street, London SW3 5DQ
Tel: 020 7352 5627
email: david.reindorp@talk21.com
Hammersmith and Fulham Revd Canon Guy Wilkinson CBE, 31 Lilyville Road, London SW6 5DP *Tel:* 07515 327757
email: guy@gwilkinson.org.uk
Hampton Revd Joe Moffatt, The Vicarage, 11 Twickenham Road, Teddington TW11 8AQ
Tel: 020 8977 2767
email: stmarywithstalban.org
Hounslow Revd Derek Simpson, Rectory, 3 The Butts, Brentford TW8 8BJ (until 04/15)
Tel: 020 8568 7442
email: derek.simpson@parishofbrentford.org.uk
Revd Richard Frank, 295 St Margaret's Road, Twickenham, TW1 1PN (from 04/15)
Tel: 020 8891 6820
email: richardfrank@allsoulschurch.org.uk

Kensington Revd David Walsh, 2 Pembroke Road, London W8 6NT *Tel:* 020 7603 4420
email: vicar@specr.org
Spelthorne Vacancy, c/o Archdeacon of Middlesex, 98 Dukes Avenue, London W4 2AF
Tel: 020 8742 8308
email: jane.bezant@london.anglican.org

ARCHDEACONRY OF HAMPSTEAD

Central Barnet Revd Paul Walmsley-McLeod, The Rectory, 147 Friern Barnet Lane, London N20 0NP *Tel:* 020 8445 7844
email: pawm_friernbarnet@hotmail.com
West Barnet Revd Canon Christopher Chivers, John Keble Vicarage, 142 Deans Lane, Edgware HA8 9NT *Tel:* 020 8959 1312
email: chrischivers01@msn.com
Revd Rex Morton (Auxiliary Area Dean of West Barnet), The Vicarage, 3 St Albans Close, London NW11 7RA *Tel:* 020 8455 1873
email: rex@gg-pc.co.uk
North Camden (Hampstead) Revd Stephen Tucker, The Vicarage, 14 Church Row, London NW3 6UU
Tel: 020 7435 0553
email: vicar@hampsteadparishchurch.org.uk
South Camden (Holborn and St Pancras) Revd Andrew Meldrum, St Anne's Vicarage, 106 Highgate West Hill, London N6 6AP
Tel: 020 8340 5190
email: javintner@aol.com
Enfield Revd Dr Richard James, Christ Church Vicarage, 2A Chalk Lane, Cockfosters, Herts EN4 9QJ *Tel:* 020 8441 1230
email: richard.j.ccc@btconnect.com
Revd Christopher Mitchell (*Auxiliary Area Dean*), The Vicarage, St Peter's Road, London N9 8JP *Tel:* 020 8807 7431
email: fatherchris@btinternet.com
East Haringey Revd Dr Olubunmi Fagbemi, Holy Trinity, Vicarage, Philip Lane, London N15 4GZ
Tel: 020 8801 3021
email: bunmif@btinternet.com
West Haringey Revd Philip Sudell, 163 Colney Hatch Lane, London N10 1HA
Tel: 020 8442 0276
email: philip.sudell@gracech.org.uk

ARCHDEACONRY OF NORTHOLT

Brent Revd Graham Noyce, 26 Ashburnham Road, London NW10 5SD *Tel:* 020 8960 6211
email: graham@noycefamily.co.uk
Ealing Revd Christopher Ramsay, 1 Lancaster Road, Southall UB1 1NP *Tel:* 020 8574 1876
email: christopher.ramsay@btinternet.com
Harrow Revd Philip Barnes, St Edmund's Vicarage, 2 Pinner Road, Northwood HA6 1QS
Tel: 020 8866 9230
email: frphilipbarnes@btinternet.com
Hillingdon Revd Desmond Banister, All Saints' Vicarage, Ryefield Avenue, Hillingdon, Uxbridge UB10 9BT *Tel:* 01895 239457
email: ppash@uk2.net

DIOCESE OF MANCHESTER

Founded in 1847. Manchester, except for a few parishes in the south (CHESTER); Salford; Bolton; Bury; Rochdale; Oldham; the western half of Tameside; an area of Wigan; an area of Trafford; an area of Stockport; an area of southern Lancashire.

Population 2,084,000   Area 420 sq m
Full-time Stipendiary Parochial Clergy 224   Benefices 203
Parishes 259   Churches 325
www.manchester.anglican.org
Overseas link dioceses: Lahore, Namibia, Tampere.

BISHOP (11th)
Rt Revd David Walker, Bishopscourt, Bury New Rd, Salford M7 4LE [2013]
Tel: 0161 792 2096 (Office)
Fax: 0161 792 6826
email:
bishop@bishopscourt.manchester.anglican.org
[David Manchester]
Bishop's Senior Chaplain Revd Canon Dr Christopher Bracegirdle (*same address*)
email:
chaplain@bishopscourt.manchester.anglican.org

SUFFRAGAN BISHOPS
BOLTON Rt Revd Chris Edmondson, Bishop's Lodge, Walkden Rd, Worsley, Manchester M28 2WH [2008]
Tel: 0161 790 8289
Fax: 0161 703 9157
email: bishopchris@manchester.anglican.org
MIDDLETON Rt Revd Mark Davies, The Hollies, Manchester Rd, Rochdale OL11 3QY [2008]
Tel: 01706 358550
Fax: 01706 354851
email: bishopmark@manchester.anglican.org

CATHEDRAL AND COLLEGIATE CHURCH OF ST MARY, ST DENYS AND ST GEORGE
Dean Very Revd Rogers Govender, Manchester Cathedral, Victoria St, Manchester M3 1SX [2006]
Tel: 0161 833 2220
email: dean@manchestercathedral.org
Cathedral Office Manchester Cathedral, Victoria St, Manchester M3 1SX
Tel: 0161 833 2220
Fax: 0161 839 6218
email: office@manchestercathedral.org
Web: www.manchestercathedral.org
Canons Residentiary
Canon for Theology and Mission Canon David Holgate, 3 Booth Clibborn Court, Park Lane, Manchester M7 4PJ [2014]
Tel: 0161 833 2220
Fax: 0161 839 6218
email: canon.holgate@manchestercathedral.org
Sub Dean and Canon Precentor Canon Philip Barratt, 2 Booth Clibborn Court, Park Lane, Manchester M7 4PJ [2012]
Tel: 0161 833 2220
email: precentor@manchestercathedral.org

Archdeacon of Manchester
Ven Mark Ashcroft 14 Moorgate Avenue, Withington, Manchester M20 1HE
email:
archmanchester@manchester.anglican.org
Cathedral Pastor Canon Alma Servant, c/o Cathedral Office
email: alma.servant@manchestercathedral.org
Cathedral Chaplains
Revd Peter Bellamy-Knights (Retired)
email:
peter.bellamyknights@manchestercathedral.org
Canon Adrian Rhodes
email: office@manchestercathedral.org
Cathedral Curate
Revd Jane Walker, c/o Cathedral Office
email: curate@manchestercathedral.org

Lay Members of Chapter
Canon David Howe
Canon Barrie Cheshire
Canon Philip Blinkhorn
Canon Dr Adanna Lazz-Onyenobi

Cathedral Administrator and Chapter Clerk Mr Stuart Shepherd, c/o Cathedral Office (tel. ext. 229)
email: cathedral.administrator@
manchestercathedral.org
Education Officer Mrs Pam Elliott, c/o Cathedral Office (tel. ext. 236)
email: pam.elliott@manchestercathedral.org
Organist and Master of the Choristers Mr Christopher Stokes, c/o Cathedral Office (tel. ext. 225)
email:
christopher.stokes@manchestercathedral.org
Sub-Organist Mr Jeffrey Makinson, c/o Cathedral Office (tel. ext. 225)
email:
jeffrey.makinson@manchestercathedral.org
Dean's PA Mrs Alison Rowland, c/o Cathedral Office (tel. ext. 220)
email:
alison.rowland@manchestercathedral.org
Administrative Secretary: Miss Joanne Hooper, c/o Cathedral Office (tel. ext. 221)
email: joanne.hooper@manchestercathedral.org

Worship and Music Administrator Miss Lucy Shepherd c/o Cathedral Office (tel. ext. 238)
email: worship-music.admin@manchestercathedral.org
Secretary to the Development Project Miss Grace Timperley, c/o Cathedral Office (tel. ext. 237)
email: grace.timperley@manchestercathedral.org
Office Assistant Miss Jade Newbury, c/o Cathedral Office (tel. ext. 235)
email: jade.newbury@manchestercathedral.org
Senior Verger Mr Derrick May, c/o Cathedral Office
email: derrick.may@manchestercathedral.org
Vergers Mr Martin Taylor, c/o Cathedral Office
email: martin.taylor@manchestercathedral.org
Mr Gareth Screeton, c/o Cathedal Office
email: gareth.screeton@manchestercathedral.org
Cathedral Architect Mr John Prichard, Lloyd Evans Prichard, No 5 The Parsonage, Manchester, M3 2HS   *Tel:* 0161 834 6251
email: john.prichard@lep-architects.co.uk
Cathedral Accountant Mr John Atherden, c/o Cathedral Office (tel. ext 234)
accountant@manchestercathedral.org
Finance Assistant Mrs Joanne Hodkin, c/o Cathedral Office (tel. ext. 224)
email: joanne.hodkin@manchestercathedral.org
Director of Fundraising and Development Mr Anthony O'Connor, c/o Cathedral Office (tel. ext. 233)
email: anthony.o'connor@manchestercathedral.org
Logistics Officer and Cathedral Centre Facilities Manager Mr Peter Mellor, c/o Cathedral Office (tel. ext 219)
Tel: 0161 835 4030
email: peter.mellor@manchestercathedral.org
Volunteer Programme Manager Mrs Lauren Bailey-Rhodes, c/o Cathedral Officer (tel. ext 242)
email: lauren.bailey-rhodes@manchestercathedral.org
Visitor Services Manager Mrs Dympna Gould, c/o Cathedral Office (tel. ext 227)
email: dympna.gould@manchestercathedral.org

ARCHDEACONS
MANCHESTER Ven Mark Ashcroft, 14 Moorgate Avenue, Withington, Manchester M20 1HE
Tel: 0161 448 1976
email: archmanchester@manchester.anglican.org
ROCHDALE Ven Cherry Vann, 57 Melling Rd, Oldham OL4 1PN   *Tel:* 0161 678 1454
Fax: 0161 678 1455
email: archrochdale@manchester.anglican.org
SALFORD Ven David Sharples, 2 The Walled Gardens, Ewhurst Avenue, Swinton M7 0FR
Tel: 0161 794 2331 / 0161 708 9366
Fax: 0161 794 2411
email: archsalford@manchester.anglican.org

BOLTON Ven David Bailey, 14 Springside Road, Bury BL9 5JE   *Tel:* 0161 761 6117
Fax: 0161 763 7973
email: archbolton@btinternet.com

CONVOCATION (MEMBERS OF THE HOUSE OF CLERGY OF THE GENERAL SYNOD)
Proctors for Clergy
Ven Dr John Applegate
Revd Marcia Wall
Revd Canon Sharon Jones
Canon Simon Killwick
Revd Canon Andy Salmon
Ven Cherry Vann

MEMBERS OF THE HOUSE OF LAITY OF THE GENERAL SYNOD
Canon Dr Peter Capon
Mr John Barber
The Worshipful Canon Geoffrey Tattersall QC
Mr Michael Heppleston
Canon Dr Adanna Lazz-Onyenobi
Canon Phillip Blinkhorn

DIOCESAN OFFICERS
Diocesan Secretary Canon Martin Miller, Diocesan Office, Church House, 90 Deansgate, Manchester M3 2GH   *Tel:* 0161 828 1412
Fax: 0161 828 1480
Chancellor of Diocese The Worshipful Canon G. F. Tattersall QC, Diocesan Registry, Church House, 90 Deansgate, Manchester M3 2GH
Tel: 0161 834 7545
Deputy Chancellor Ms C. Otton-Goulder, Diocesan Registry, Church House, 90 Deansgate, Manchester M3 2GH   *Tel:* 0161 834 7545
Registrar of Diocese and Bishop's Legal Secretary Mrs Jane Monks, Diocesan Registry, Church House, 90 Deansgate, Manchester M3 2GH
Tel: 0161 839 0093
Fax: 0161 839 0093
Diocesan Surveyor Vacancy

DIOCESAN ORGANIZATIONS
Diocesan Office Diocesan Church House, 90 Deansgate, Manchester M3 2GH
Tel: 0161 828 1400
Fax: 0161 828 1480

ADMINISTRATION
Diocesan Synod (*Chairman, House of Clergy*) Revd Canon Andy Salmon
(*Chairman, House of Laity*) Canon Peter Capon
Board of Finance (*Chairman*) Canon Phillip Blinkhorn, 1 Blundell Close, Unsworth, Bury BL9 8LH   *Tel:* 0161 766 6301
(*Secretary*) Canon Martin Miller (*Head of Finance and IT*) Mr Richard O'Connell (*Legal Secretary*) Mrs Jane Monks, Diocesan Registry, Church House   *Tel:* 0161 834 7545
Property Committee (*Property Secretary*) Vacancy, Diocesan Office (*Chairman*) Ven David Bailey

Mission Pastoral Committee (Secretary) Canon
Martin Miller (*Chairman*) Rt Revd Mark Davies
Designated Officer Mrs Jane Monks, Diocesan
Registry, Church House   *Tel:* 0161 834 7545

CHURCHES

Advisory Committee for the Care of Churches
(*Chairman*) Mr Richard Byrom, 3 Hawkshaw
Lane, Hawkshaw, Bury BL8 4JZ (*DAC Secretary*)
Mr Alan Simpson, Diocesan Office

EDUCATION

Chairman Rt Revd Mark Davies
Director of Education Canon Maurice Smith,
Diocesan Church House, 90 Deansgate,
Manchester M3 2GH   *Tel:* 0161 828 1400
                       Fax: 0161 828 1484
Education Officers
*Assistant Director of Education and School
Improvement* Mr Malcolm Finney (*same address*)
School Buildings Officer and Office Manager Mr
Ian Tomkin (*same address*)
Children's Work Officer Revd Steve Dixon (*same
address*)
Youth Work Officer Miss Susie Mapledoram (*same
address*)

MISSION AND MINISTRY

*There are currently interim governance arrangements
for the Mission and Ministry function pending a
review of diocesan governance by the Bishop's
Council.*
Head of Department Mrs Deborah Dalby,
Diocesan Office   *Tel:* 0161 828 1400
Diocesan contact for environmental issues Mrs
Deborah Dalby
*Deputy Head of Department and Director of
Ministry and Learning* Revd Peter Reiss, Diocesan
Office
Parish Development Officer Mr Colin Barson,
Diocesan Office
Mission Planning Officer Ms Alison Peacock,
Diocesan Office
Heritage and Archdeaconry Resources Adviser Ms
Heather Ford, Diocesan Office
Training Officer (CME and Laity) Revd Julia Babb,
Diocesan Office
Local Ministry Officer Revd Stephen Tranter,
Diocesan Office   *Tel:* 0161 828 1400
Diocesan Director of Ordinands and OLM Officer
Ven David Sharples, Bishopscourt, Bury New Rd,
Manchester M4 4LE   *Tel:* 0161 708 9366

PRESS AND PUBLICATIONS

*Editor of Diocesan Year Book / Editor of Diocesan
Magazine / Communications and Events Manager*
Mrs Ann Mummery, Diocesan Office
                       Tel: 0161 828 1470
                       07836 224444 (Mobile)
email: amummery@manchester.anglican.org

DIOCESAN RECORD OFFICE

For further information apply to The Archivist, The
Central Library, St Peter's Square, Manchester
M2 5PD   *Tel:* 0161 234 1980

RETIRED CLERGY

Retired Clergy and Widows Officer Ven Alan
Wolstencroft, The Bakehouse, 1 Latham Row,
Bolton BL6 6QZ   *Tel:* 01204 469985
email: wolstencroftalan@gmail.com

AREA DEANS
ARCHDEACONRY OF MANCHESTER

Ardwick Revd Ian Gomersall, St Chrysostom's
Rectory, 38 Park Range, Manchester M14 5HQ
                       Tel: 0161 224 6971
                       Fax: 0161 870 6197
email: ian.gomersall@btinternet.com
Heaton Revd Marcus Maxwell, St John's Rectory,
15 Priestnall Road, Stockport SK4 3HR
                       Tel: 0161 442 1932
email: marcus.maxwell@ntlworld.com
Hulme Revd Ken Flood, The Rectory, 6 Edge
Lane, Chorlton-cum-Hardy, Manchester M21 9JF
                       Tel: 0161 881 3063
email: k.flood@stclement-chorlton.org.uk
North Manchester Revd Mike McGurk, The
Rectory, 95 Church Lane, Harpurhey,
Manchester M9 5BG   *Tel:* 0161 205 4020
email: rev.mikemcgurk@hotmail.co.uk
Stretford Revd John Hughes, St John's Rectory,
1 Lindum Ave, Old Trafford, Manchester
M16 9NQ   *Tel:* 0161 872 0500
email: john_dhughes@yahoo.co.uk
Withington Revd Stephen Edwards, William
Temple Vicarage, Robinswood Road, Wythen-
shawe, Manchester M22 0BU   *Tel:* 0161 437 3194
email: revdstephenedwards@yahoo.co.uk

ARCHDEACONRY OF BOLTON

Bolton Canon Rodger Petch, 101 Cloister St,
Bolton BL1 3HA   *Tel:* 01204 842627
email: rodgerpetch@yahoo.co.uk
Bury Revd Gordon Joyce, 1a Pimhole Road,
Bury BL9 7EY
email: gordonjoyce@gordonjoyce.eclipse.co.uk
Deane Revd T. Clark, Deane Rectory, 234 Wigan
Road, Bolton BL3 5QE   *Tel:* 01204 61819
email: clark@clark.cc
Radcliffe and Prestwich Revd Alison Hardy, Stand
Rectory, 32 Church Lane, Whitfield, Manchester
M45 7NF   *Tel:* 0161 766 2619
email: alison.hardy@waitrose.com
Rossendale Revd Martin Short, St Paul's Vicarage,
Hollin Lane, Rossendale BB4 8HU
                       Tel: 01706 215585
email: martin.short1@btopenworld.com
Walmsley Revd Wendy Oliver, Harwood Vicarage,
Stitch-mi-Lane, Bolton BL2 4HU
                       Tel: 01204 525196
email: wendyloliver@googlemail.com

ARCHDEACONRY OF ROCHDALE

Ashton-under-Lyne Revd Roger Farnworth, St James Vicarage, Union St, Ashton-under-Lyne OL6 9NQ *Tel:* 0161 330 2771
email: rogerfarnworth@aol.com

Heywood and Middleton Revd Canon Philip Miller, The Rectory, Wood St, Langley, Middleton M24 5GL *Tel:* 0161 643 5013
email: canonphil@hotmail.co.uk

Oldham East Vacancy

Oldham West Revd David Penny, St Matthew's Vicarage, Mill Brow, Chadderton OL1 2RT
Tel: 0161 624 8600
email: revdpenny@btinternet.com

Rochdale Revd Canon Sharon Jones, St Andrew's Vicarage, Arm Rd, Dearnley, Littleborough OL15 8NJ *Tel:* 01706 378466
email: sharon@dearnleyvicarage.plus.com

ARCHDEACONRY OF SALFORD

Eccles Revd Andrew Young, St Paul's Vicarage, 3 Egerton Road, Monton, Eccles M30 9LR
Tel: 0161 789 2420
email: andrew.young66@ntlworld.com

Leigh Revd Jonathan Carmyllie, St Stephen's Vicarage, 7 Holbeck, Astley, Manchester M29 7DU *Tel:* 01942 883313
email: j.carmyllie@btinternet.com

Salford Revd Lisa Battye, St Paul's Rectory, 1 Moorside Road, Kersal, Salford M7 3PJ
Tel: 0161 792 5362
email: lisabattye@stpaulsparish.org.uk

DIOCESE OF NEWCASTLE

Founded in 1882. Northumberland; Newcastle upon Tyne; North Tyneside; a small area of eastern Cumbria; four parishes in northern County Durham.

Population 802,000   Area 2,110 sq m
Full-time Stipendiary Parochial Clergy 116   Benefices 134
Parishes 172   Churches 236
www.newcastle.anglican.org
Companion link dioceses: Winchester, More (Norway), Botswana (Africa).

BISHOP (11th)
Vacancy, Bishop's House, 29 Moor Road South, Gosforth, Newcastle upon Tyne NE3 1PA
Tel: 0191 285 2220
email: bishop@newcastle.anglican.org
[Martin Newcastle]
Bishop's Chaplain Revd Ian Flintoft, Bishop's House, 29 Moor Road South, Gosforth, Newcastle upon Tyne NE3 1PA   *Tel:* 0191 285 2220
email: i.flintoft@newcastle.anglican.org

ASSISTANT BISHOP
Rt Revd Frank White, (Home) The Vicarage, Riding Mill NE44 6AT [2010]   *Tel:* 01434 682120
email: bishopfrank@newcastle.anglican.org
(Office) Bishop's House, 29 Moor Road South, Gosforth, Newcastle upon Tyne NE3 1PA
Tel: 0191 285 2220

PROVINCIAL EPISCOPAL VISITOR
BEVERLEY Rt Revd Glyn Webster, Holy Trinity Rectory, Micklegate, York YO1 6LE
Tel: 01904 628155
email: office@seeofbeverley.org.uk

HONORARY ASSISTANT BISHOPS
Rt Revd John Packer, Devonshire House, Alma Place, Whitley Bay NE26 2EQ [2014]
Tel: 0191 253 4321
Rt Revd Stephen Pedley, The Blue House, Newbrough NE47 5AN [2005]   *Tel:* 01434 674238
Rt Revd John Henry Richardson, Old Rectory, Bewcastle, Carlisle CA6 6PS [2003]
Tel: 01697 748389

CATHEDRAL CHURCH OF ST NICHOLAS
Dean Very Revd Christopher Charles Dalliston, 26 Mitchell Avenue, Jesmond, Newcastle upon Tyne NE2 3LA [2003]   *Tel:* 0191 281 6554
0191 232 1939
email: dean@stnicholascathedral.co.uk
Chapter Office Cathedral House, 42/44 Mosley Street, Newcastle upon Tyne NE1 1DF
Tel: 0191 232 1939
email: office@stnicholascathedral.co.uk

Canons Residentiary
Ven Geoffrey Vincent Miller, 80 Moorside North, Newcastle upon Tyne NE4 9DU [1999]
Tel: 0191 273 8245
email: g.miller@newcastle.anglican.org
Canon John Robert Sinclair, 16 Towers Avenue, Newcastle upon Tyne NE2 3QE [2011]
Tel: 0191 281 0714
email: johnsinclair247@aol.com
Canon Kevin Hunt, 55 Queens Terrace, Newcastle upon Tyne NE2 2PL [2012]
Tel: 0191 281 0181
email: kevin.hunt@stnicholascathedral.co.uk
Canon Steven Harvey, 2a Holly Avenue, Newcastle upon Tyne NE2 2PY [2013]
Tel: 0191 281 5790
email: steven.harvey@stnicholascathedral.co.uk
Director of Music Mr Michael Stoddart
Tel: 0191 261 4505
email: directorofmusic@stnicholascathedral.co.uk
Director of Girl's Choir Mr James Norrey
email: jamesnorrey@stnicholascathedral.co.uk
Cathedral Secretary Ms Elspeth Robertson, Cathedral House   *Tel:* 0191 232 1939
email: office@stnicholascathedral.co.uk
Cathedral Administrator Mr Julian Haynes, Cathedral House   *Tel:* 0191 232 1939
email: julianhaynes@stnicholascathedral.co.uk
Finance Administrator Mr David Dawe, Cathedral House   *Tel:* 0191 232 1939
email: d.dawe@stnicholascathedral.co.uk

ARCHDEACONS
NORTHUMBERLAND Ven Geoffrey Vincent Miller, 80 Moorside North, Newcastle upon Tyne NE4 9DU [2005]   *Tel:* 0191 273 8245
email: g.miller@newcastle.anglican.org
LINDISFARNE Ven Peter John Alan Robinson, 4 Acomb Close, Morpeth NE61 2YH [2008]
Tel: 01670 503810
Fax: 01670 503469
email: p.robinson@newcastle.anglican.org

CONVOCATION (MEMBERS OF THE HOUSE OF CLERGY OF THE GENERAL SYNOD)
Proctors for Clergy
Revd Janet Appleby

Canon John Sinclair
Canon Dr Dagmar Winter

MEMBERS OF THE HOUSE OF LAITY OF THE GENERAL SYNOD
Canon Prof John Bull
Mrs Margaret White
Canon Carol Wolstenholme

DIOCESAN OFFICERS
Diocesan Secretary Mr Shane Waddle, Church House, St John's Terrace, North Shields NE29 6HS
Tel: 0191 270 4114
07775 037121 (mobile)
email: s.waddle@newcastle.anglican.org
Chancellor of Diocese Mr Euan Duff, Broad Chare Chambers, 33 Broad Chare, Newcastle upon Tyne NE1 3DQ   *Tel:* 0191 2320541
Registrar of Diocese and Bishop's Legal Secretary Mrs Jane Lowdon, Sintons Solicitors, The Cube, Barrack Road, Newcastle upon Tyne NE4 6DB
Tel: 0191 226 7878
Fax: 0191 226 7850
email: j.lowdon@sintons.co.uk

DIOCESAN ORGANIZATIONS
Diocesan Office Church House, St John's Terrace, North Shields NE29 6HS   *Tel:* 0191 270 4100
Fax: 0191 270 4101
email: info@newcastle.anglican.org
Web: www.newcastle.anglican.org
Facebook: www.facebook.com/newcastlediocese
Twitter: @NwcastleDiocese

ADMINISTRATION
Diocesan Synod (Chair, House of Clergy) Canon John Robert Sinclair, 16 Towers Avenue, Newcastle upon Tyne NE2 3QE   *Tel:* 0191 281 9375
email: johnsinclair247@aol.com
Diocesan Synod (Chair, House of Laity) Canon Carol Wolstenholme, Church House   *Tel:* 0191 274 5144
email: cawol43@aol.com
(Secretary) Mr Shane Waddle, Church House
Board of Finance (Chair) Canon Simon Harper, Church House
(Secretary) Mr Shane Waddle *(as above)*
Accountant Mr John Hall, Church House
Tel: 0191 270 4130
email: j.hall@newcastle.anglican.org
Property Manager Mr Ian Beswick, Church House
Tel: 0191 270 4125
email: i.beswick@newcastle.anglican.org
Diocesan Society (Chair) Canon Gilfrid Baker-Cresswell, Church House
Mission and Pastoral Committee (Chair) Revd Paul Malcolm Scott
(Secretary) Mr Nigel Foxon, Church House

CHURCHES
Advisory Committee for the Care of Churches (Chair) Canon Dr Geoffrey Purves, Hawthorn House, Kirkwhelpington NE19 2RT   *Tel:* 01830 540395
(Secretary) Mr Nigel Foxon, Church House

Closed Churches Committee Mr Nigel Foxon, Church House

EDUCATION
Chair of Newcastle Diocesan Education Board Ven Peter Robinson, Church House
Joint Education Team (Joint working with Diocese of Durham)
Director of Education Mr Jeremy Fitt, Church House
PA to Director Mrs Susie Taylor, Church House
Assistant Director of Education Primary Vacancy
Assistant Director of Education Secondary/FE Vacancy
Assistant Director of Education Governance Ms Rowan Ferguson, Church House
PA to Assistant Directors Mrs Colleen Miller, Church House
Bursar Mrs Eileen Bell, Church House
Administrator Mrs Lisa Padgett, Church House
Administrator Mrs Suzanne Keenan, Church House

MINISTRY AND TRAINING
Director of Ordinands Canon Ian Flintoft, Bishop's House, 29 Moor Road South, Gosforth, Newcastle upon Tyne NE3 1PA   *Tel:* 0191 285 2220
email: i.flintoft@newcastle.anglican.org
Adviser for Retired Clergy Canon Colin Gough, 44 Tyelaw Meadows, Shilbottle, Alnwick NE66 2JJ
Tel: 01665 58110
email: canoncolin@gmail.com
Continuing Ministerial Education Adviser Vacancy
Bishop's Adviser for Women's Ministry Canon Dr Dagmar Winter, Church House
Development Officer for Children's Work Vacancy
Development Officer for Youth Work Team Leader Vacancy
Diocesan Environment Officer Vacancy
Lindisfarne Regional Training Partnership
Chair Ven Peter Robinson, Church House
Principal Canon Cathy Rowling, Church House
Director of Studies and Formational Tutor for Clergy IME 1–3 Revd Dr David Bryan, Church House
Formational Tutor for Clergy IME 4–7 Revd Rick Simpson, Church House
Formational Tutor for Readers, Revd Dr Michael Beck, Church House
Director of Discipleship Development Vacancy
Administrator Mrs Jenny Burton, Church House
Tel: 0191 270 4144
email: jennyburton@lindisfarnertp.org
Secretary, Association of Readers Canon Sue Hart, 73 Monkseaton Drive, Whitley Bay NE26 3DQ
Tel: 0191 2523941
Retreat House (Warden) Jane Easterby, Shepherds Dene Retreat House, Riding Mill, Hexham NE44 6AF   *Tel:* 01434 682212
email: enquiry@shepherdsdene.co.uk
Sons of Clergy Society Mrs Gwenda Gofton, 4 Crossfell, Ponteland NE20 9EA
Tel: 01661 820344
Diocesan Widows Officer Mrs Marjorie Craig, 5 Springwell Meadow, Alnwick NE66 2NY
Tel: 01665 602806

LITURGICAL

Chair Rt Revd Frank White, Bishop's House, 29 Moor Road South, Gosforth, Newcastle upon Tyne NE3 1PA *Tel:* 0191 285 2220
email: bishopfrank@newcastle.anglican.org

ADVISERS

Adviser in Local Evangelism Canon John Sinclair, 16 Towers Avenue, Newcastle upon Tyne NE2 3QE *Tel:* 0191 281 9375
email: johnsinclair247@aol.com
Church and Church Society Revd Dr Nicholas Buxton, The Vicarage, 3 Crossway, Newcastle upon Tyne NE2 3QH
Tel: 0191 212 0181
email: buxton.nicholas@gmail.com
Ecumenical Officer Revd Janet Appleby, The Vicarage, Berwick Drive, Wallsend NE28 9ED
Tel: 0191 262 7518
email: janetappleby@yahoo.com
Inter-Faith and Ethnic Relations Adviser Mrs Lesley Hillary, Church House *Tel:* 0191 270 4148
email: l.hillary@newcastle.anglican.org
Local Ministry Development Officer Revd Rachel Wood, St Hilda's Vicarage, Marden, North Shields NE29 9QB *Tel:* 0191 257 3901
email: r.wood@newcastle.anglican.org
Partners Development Officer Revd Frances Wilson, Church House *Tel:* 0191 270 4147
email: f.wilson@newcastle.anglican.org
Pastoral Care and Counselling Adviser Canon Peter Kenney, 7 Spring Gardens Court, North Shields NE29 0AN *Tel:* 0191 257 9512
email: peter.kenney5@btinternet.com
Rural Affairs Adviser Canon Dr Dagmar Winter, The Vicarage, Kirkwhelpington, Newcastle upon Tyne NE19 2RT *Tel:* 01830 540260
email: dagmar.winter@btinternet.com
Spirituality and Spiritual Direction Adviser Canon Alison White, The Vicarage, Riding Mill, NE44 6AT *Tel:* 01434 682120
email: alisonmarywhite@btinternet.com

PRESS, PUBLICITY AND PUBLICATIONS

Development Officer for Communications Mr Martin Sheppard, Church House *Tel:* 0191 270 4139
07544 803160 (mobile)
email: m.sheppard@newcastle.anglican.org
Editor of 'Link' (as above)
Editor of Diocesan Year Book Mr Shane Waddle, Church House

DIOCESAN RECORD OFFICE

For further information apply to Northumberland Collections Service, Woodhorn, Queen Elizabeth II Country Park, Ashington NE63 9YF
Tel: 01670 624455
email: collections@woodhorn.org.uk

DIOCESAN RESOURCE CENTRE

Contact Karenza Passmore, Church House, St John's Terrace, North Shields NE29 6HS
Tel: 0191 270 4161
Fax: 0191 270 4101
email: k.passmore@resourcecentreonline.co.uk

SAFEGUARDING

Diocesan Safeguarding Officer Ms Ruth Rogan, Church House *Tel:* 07825 167016 (mobile)
*email:*r.rogan@newcastle.anglican.org

STEWARDSHIP

Parish Giving Officer Mr Richard Gascoyne, Church House *Tel:* 0191 270 4136
email: r.gascoyne@newcastle.anglican.org

AREA DEANS
ARCHDEACONRY OF NORTHUMBERLAND

Bedlington Revd Philip Hughes, Seghill Vicarage, Mare Close, Seghill, Cramlington NE23 7EA
Tel: 0191 298 0925
email: phil.hughes@pobroadband.co.uk
Newcastle Central Revd Allan Marks, The Vicarage, 11 Gibson Street, Newcastle upon Tyne NE1 6PY *Tel:* 0191 232 0516
email: fatherallan@sky.com
Newcastle East Revd Martin Lee, The Vicarage, 3 Station Road, Benton, Newcastle upon Tyne NE12 8AN *Tel:* 0191 266 1921
email: martinlee903@btinternet.com
Newcastle West Canon Nicholas Darby, St James and St Basil Vicarage, Fenham, Newcastle upon Tyne NE4 9EJ *Tel:* 0191 274 5078
email: npdarby@gmail.com
Tynemouth Revd Jane Wood, St Peter's Vicarage, 6 Elmwood Road, Whitley Bay NE25 8EX
Tel: 0191 253 1055
email: jane.wood14@btinternet.com

ARCHDEACONRY OF LINDISFARNE

Alnwick Canon James Robertson, Whittingham Vicarage, Alnwick NE66 4UP
Tel: 01665 574704
email: canjamesrobertson@virginmedia.com
Bamburgh and Glendale Canon Brian Hurst, Vicarage, 7 The Wynding, Bamburgh NE69 7DB
Tel: 01668 214748
email: brian.hurst1@btopenworld.com
Bellingham Revd Dr Susan Ramsaran, Rectory, Bellingham, Hexham NE48 2JS
Tel: 01434 220019
email: SMRamsaran@aol.com
Corbridge Revd David Hewlett, Vicarage, Greencroft Avenue, Corbridge NE45 5DW
Tel: 01434 632128
email: david.hewlett3@btinternet.com
Hexham Revd Jon Russell, The Rectory, 16 Forstersteads, Allendale NE47 9AS
Tel: 01434 618607
email: jon.russell@allendalechurch.co.uk
Morpeth Revd John Park, Bothal Rectory, Longhirst Road, Pegswood, Morpeth NE61 6XF
Tel: 01670 510793
email: johnp2910@gmx.co.uk
Norham Revd Dr George Robert Joseph (Rob) Kelsey, Vicarage, Norham Berwick upon Tweed TD15 2LF *Tel:* 01289 382325
email: robert.josephkelsey@live.com

DIOCESE OF NORWICH

Founded in 1094, formerly Thetford (AD 1070), originally Dunwich (AD 630) and Elmham (AD 673). Norfolk, except for the western quarter (ELY); an area of north-east Suffolk.

Population 878,000   Area 1,800 sq m
Full-time Stipendiary Parochial Clergy 182   Benefices 186
Parishes 566   Churches 640
www.dioceseofnorwich.org
Overseas link provinces: Luleå (Sweden), Papua New Guinea.

BISHOP (71st)
Rt Revd Graham Richard James, Bishop's House, Norwich NR3 1SB [1999]   *Tel:* 01603 629001
email: bishop@dioceseofnorwich.org
[Graham Norvic:]
Bishop's Chaplain Revd James Stewart (*same address*)   *Tel:* 01603 614172
email: bishops.chaplain@dioceseofnorwich.org
Bishop's PA Mrs Coralie Nichols (*same address*)   *Tel:* 01603 629001
email: coralie.nichols@dioceseofnorwich.org

SUFFRAGAN BISHOPS
THETFORD Rt Revd Dr Alan Winton, The Red House, 53 Norwich Rd, Stoke Holy Cross, Norwich NR14 8AB [2009]   *Tel:* 01508 491014
email: bishop.thetford@dioceseofnorwich.org
Bishop's PA Graham Cossey (*same address*)
email: graham.cossey@dioceseofnorwich.org
LYNN Rt Revd Jonathan Meyrick, The Old Vicarage, Castle Acre, King's Lynn PE32 2AA (2011)   *Tel:* 01760 755553
email: bishoplynn@dioceseofnorwich.org
Bishop's PA Mrs Jessica Hirst (*same address*)
email: jessica.hirst@dioceseofnorwich.org

HONORARY ASSISTANT BISHOPS
Rt Revd Norman Banks, Parkside House, Abbey Mill Lane, St Albans AL3 4HE [2012]
Tel: 01727 836358
email: bishop@richborough.org.uk
Rt Revd Anthony Foottit, Ivy House, Whitwell St, Reepham NR10 4RA [2004]   *Tel:* 01603 870340
email: acfoottit@hotmail.com
Rt Revd Peter Fox, Vicarage, Harwood Rd, Norwich NR1 2NG [2008]   *Tel:* 01603 625679
email: peterandangiefox@yahoo.co.uk
Rt Revd Richard Garrard, 26 Carol Close, Stoke Holy Cross, Norwich NR14 8NN [2003]
Tel: 01508 494165
email: garrard.r.a@btinternet.com
Rt Revd David Gillett, 10 Burton Close, Diss IP22 4YJ [2008]   *Tel:* 01379 640309
email: dkgillett@btinternet.com
Rt Revd David Leake, The Anchorage, Lower Common, East Runton, Cromer NR27 9PG [2003]
Tel: 01263 513536
email: david@leake8.wanadoo.co.uk

Rt Revd Malcolm Menin, 32c Bracondale, Norwich NR1 2AN [2000]   *Tel:* 01603 627987
Rt Revd John Salt, 5 Common Place, Walsingham NR22 6BW [2011]   *Tel:* 01328 820823
email: jsalt@ogs.net
Rt Revd Lindsay Urwin, The College, Walsingham NR22 6EF [2009]   *Tel:* 01328 824204
email: pr.adm@olw-shrine.org.uk

CATHEDRAL CHURCH OF THE HOLY AND UNDIVIDED TRINITY
Dean Very Revd Jane Hedges, The Deanery, The Close, Norwich NR1 4EG [2014]
Tel: 01603 218308
email: dean@cathedral.org.uk
Cathedral Office The Chapter Office, 65 The Close, Norwich NR1 4DH   *Tel:* 01603 218300
email: reception@cathedral.org.uk
Web: www.cathedral.org.uk
Canons Residentiary
Canon Pastor and Custos Vacancy, 52 The Close, Norwich NR1 4EG [2005]
Tel: 01603 218331 (Office)
email: canonpastor@cathedral.org.uk
Precentor and Vice-Dean Canon Jeremy Haselock, 34 The Close, Norwich NR1 4DZ [1998]
Tel: 01603 619169 (Home)
01603 218314 (Office)
email: precentor@cathedral.org.uk
Canon Librarian Canon Dr Peter Doll, 56 The Close, Norwich NR1 4EG [2009]
Tel: 01603 666758 (Home)
01603 218336 (Office)
email: canonlibrarian@cathedral.org.uk
Chapter Steward Mr Neil Parsons, The Chapter Office, 65 The Close   *Tel:* 01603 218304
email: chaptersteward@cathedral.org.uk
Master of the Music Mr Ashley Grote, The Chapter Office, 65 The Close   *Tel:* 01603 218319
email: masterofmusic@cathedral.org.uk
Sacrist Mr Roger Lee, The Chapter Office, 65 The Close   *Tel:* 01603 218325
email: sacrist@cathedral.org.uk

ARCHDEACONS
NORWICH Ven Jan McFarlane, 31 Bracondale, Norwich NR1 2AT [2009]   *Tel:* 01603 620007
email:
archdeacon.norwich@dioceseofnorwich.org

Archdeacon's PA Mrs Coralie Nichols (*as above*)
LYNN Ven John Ashe, Holly Tree House, Whitwell Rd, Sparham, Norwich NR9 5PN [2009]
Tel: 01362 688032
email: archdeacon.lynn@dioceseofnorwich.org
Archdeacon's PA Mrs Sharon Costello (*same address*)
email: sharon.costello@dioceseofnorwich.org
NORFOLK Ven Steven Betts, 8 Boulton Rd, Thorpe St Andrew, Norwich NR7 0DF [2012]
Tel: 01603 559199
email:
archdeacon.norfolk@dioceseofnorwich.org.org
Archdeacon's PA Mr Graham Cossey (*as above*)

CONVOCATION (MEMBERS OF THE HOUSE OF CLERGY OF THE GENERAL SYNOD)
Proctors for Clergy
Ven Steven Betts
Ven Jan McFarlane
Revd Charles Read
Revd Dr Patrick Richmond

MEMBERS OF THE HOUSE OF LAITY OF THE GENERAL SYNOD
Mr Robin Back
Mrs Susan Johns

DIOCESAN OFFICERS AND ADMINISTRATION
Diocesan Office
Diocesan House, 109 Dereham Rd, Easton, Norwich NR9 5ES   *Tel:* 01603 880853
email: diocesan.house@dioceseofnorwich.org
Dioc Secretary Mr Richard Butler MBE DL, Dioc House   *Tel:* 01603 880853
email: richard.butler@dioceseofnorwich.org
Director of Operations Mr David Broom, Dioc House   *Tel:* 01603 882367
email: david.broom@dioceseofnorwich.org
Chancellor of Diocese Mrs Ruth Arlow c/o Registrar of the Diocese
Registrar of Diocese and Bishop's Legal Secretary Mr Stuart Jones, Birketts LLP, Kingfisher House, 1 Gilders Way, Norwich NR3 1UB
Tel: 01603 756501
email: stuart.jones@dioceseofnorwich.org
Diocesan Record Office Norfolk Record Office, Archive Centre, County Hall, Martineau Lane, Norwich NR1 2DO   *Tel:* 01603 222599

Diocesan Synod
Chair, House of Clergy Canon Sally Theakston, The Rectory, Vicarage Meadows, Dereham NR19 1TW   *Tel:* 01362 693680
email: stheakston@aol.com
Chair, House of Laity Miss Cynthia Wake, 71 Burgh Lane, Mattishall NR20 3QT   01362 850434
Secretary and Dioc Electoral Registration Officer Mr David Broom (*as above*)
Designated Officer Diocesan Secretary (*as above*)

Board of Finance
President The Bishop of Norwich (*as above*)
Chair Mr Bill Husselby, c/o Dioc House
email: bill.husselby@cogent.co.uk
Secretary Diocesan Secretary (*as above*)
Director of Finance Miss Susan Bunting, Dioc House   *Tel:* 01603 882377
email: susan.bunting@dioceseofnorwich.org
Property Committee
Chair Mr David Richardson, c/o Dioc House
email: david.richardson@arnolds.uk.com
Surveyor Mr Michael Marshall, Dioc House
Tel: 01603 882364
email: michael.marshall@dioceseofnorwich.org
Board of Patronage
Chair Canon Stuart Nairn, Rectory, Main Rd, Narborough, King's Lynn PE32 1TE
Tel: 01760 338552
email: nairn.nvgrectory@btinternet.com
Secretary Mrs Jennifer Vere, Southlands, Church Corner, North Lopham, Diss IP22 2LP
Tel: 01379 687679
email: jennyvere@btinternet.com
DAC (*Diocesan Advisory Committee for the Care of Churches*)
Chair Mr Alan Kefford, c/o Dioc House
email: akeff@aol.com
Secretary Mr Matthew McDade, Dioc House
Tel: 01603 882350
email: matthew.mcdade@dioceseofnorwich.org
Board of Education
Chair Canon Mr Mark Allbrook, c/o Dioc House
email: markallbrook@btconnect.com
Director of Education Mr Andy Mash, Dioc House
Tel: 01603 881352
email: andy.mash@dioceseofnorwich.org
Children, Youth and Families
Coordinator Mr Mark Heybourne, Dioc House
Tel: 01603 882362
email: mark.heybourne@dioceseofnorwich.org
Administrator Mrs Liz Dawes, Dioc House
Tel: 01603 882354
email: liz.dawes@dioceseofnorwich.org
The Horstead Centre (*Residential Activity Centre*), Rectory Rd, Horstead, Norwich NR12 7EP
Web: www.horsteadcentre.org.uk
Manager Josie Barnett, c/o Horstead Centre
Tel: 01603 737215
email: josie.barnett@dioceseofnorwich.org
Discipleship and Ministry Forum
Chair The Bishop of Thetford (*as above*)
Bishop's Officer for Ordinands and Initial Training Revd David Foster, Dioc House   *Tel:* 01603 882337
email: david.foster@dioceseofnorwich.org
Reader Training Coordinator Revd Charles Read, Dioc House   *Tel:* 01603 882331
email: charles.read@dioceseofnorwich.org
Continuing Ministerial Development Officer Revd Tim Dean, Dioc House   *Tel:* 01603 882339
email: tim.dean@dioceseofnorwich.org
Lay Development Officer Revd Dr Paul Overend, Dioc House   *Tel:* 01603 882336
email: paul.overend@dioceseofnorwich.org

Dioc Officer for NSMs Revd Roger MacPhee, 8 Lawn Close, Knapton, North Walsham NR28 0SD   *Tel:* 01263 720045
email: rmacphee4@aol.com
Readers' Committee
Chair and Warden of Readers The Archdeacon of Lynn (*as above*)
Hon. Secretary Mrs Sharon Costello (*as above*)
Communications
Director of Communications Ven Jan McFarlane (*as above*)   *Tel:* 07818 422395 (Mobile)
Marketing and Communications Manager Mr Gordon Darley, Dioc House   *Tel:* 01603 882349
email: gordon.darley@dioceseofnorwich.org
County Ecumenical Officer Vacancy
Diocesan Ecumenical Officer Revd Dale Gingrich, Church Bungalow, Gayton Rd, Gaywood, King's Lynn PE30 4DZ   *Tel:* 01508 765167
email: dale.gingrich@dioceseofnorwich.org
Bishop's Officer for Retired Clergy and Widows Canon Patrick Foreman, Seorah, 7 Mallard's Close, Fakenham NR21 8PU   *Tel:* 01328 853691
email: patrick@pandmforeman.eclipse.co.uk
Mission The Archdeacon of Norwich (*as above*)
Liturgical Adviser Canon Jeremy Haselock (*as above*)
Chair of Liturgical Committee Revd Charles Read (*as above*)
Social and Community Concerns Coordinator Revd James Stewart (*as above*)
Urban Affairs and Church Urban Fund Canon Peter Howard, St Francis Vicarage, Rider Haggard Rd, Norwich NR7 9UQ   *Tel:* 01603 702799
email: plhoward@btinternet.com
Tourism The Archdeacon of Norfolk (*as above*)
Diocesan Environmental Officer Vacancy

RURAL DEANS
ARCHDEACONRY OF NORWICH
Norwich East Revd Captain Darren Thornton, St Giles Rectory, 44 Heigham Road, Norwich NR2 3AU   *Tel:* 01603 623724
email: d.thornton@uea.ac.uk
Norwich North Revd Paul Mackay, St Catherine's Vicarage, Aylsham Road, Mile Cross, Norwich NR3 2RJ   *Tel:* 01603 426767
email: vicarstcaths@hotmail.co.uk
Norwich South Canon Alan Strange, Rectory, 17 Essex Street, Norwich NR2 5BL
Tel: 01603 622225
email: rector@trinitynorwich.org

ARCHDEACONRY OF NORFOLK
Blofield Revd Paul Cubitt, The Rectory, 10 Oak Wood, Blofield, Norwich NR13 4JQ
Tel: 01603 713160
email: revp@cubitt.karoo.co.uk
Depwade Revd Michael Kingston, The Rectory, The Street, Hempnall NR15 2AD   *Tel:* 01508 498157
email: hempnallgroup.office@btinternet.com

Great Yarmouth Canon Chris Terry, Ludham House, 55 South Beach Parade, Great Yarmouth NR30 1DJ   *Tel:* 01493 842915
email: gyteamrector@btinternet.com
Humbleyard Canon Christopher Davies, Vicarage, 5 Vicar St, Wymondham, NR18 0PL
Tel: 01953 602269
email: vicar@wymondhamabbey.org.uk
Loddon Revd Robert Parsonage, Rectory, Rectory Lane, Poringland, Norwich NR14 7SL
Tel: 01508 492215
email: rector@poringland-benefice.org.uk
Lothingland Revd Jeremy Bishop, The Rectory, Rectory Road, Carlton Colville NR33 8UB
Tel: 01502 565217
email: jbishop771@aol.com
Redenhall Canon Tony Billett, Rectory, 26 Mount St, Diss IP22 3QG   *Tel:* 01379 642072
email: disschurch2@btconnect.com
St Benet at Waxham and Tunstead Revd Simon Lawrence, The Rectory, Campingfield Lane, Stalham NR12 9DT   *Tel:* 01692 580250
email: simon.stalham@btinternet.com
Thetford and Rockland Revd Matthew Jackson, The Rectory, Surrogate Street, Attleborough NR17 2AW   *Tel:* 01953 453185
email: therectory@me.com

ARCHDEACONRY OF LYNN
Breckland Canon Stuart Nairn (*as above*)
Burnham and Walsingham Vacancy
Dereham in Mitford Revd Robert Marsden, Bittering Street, Gressenhall NR20 4EB
Tel: 01362 860102
email: robert@camelhome.co.uk
Heacham and Rising Revd Jonathan Riviere, The Rectory, Sandringham PE35 6EH
Tel: 01485 540587
email: jonathan@riviere.co.uk
Holt Revd Jeremy Sykes, The Vicarage, Grange Close, Briston, Melton Constable NR24 2LY
Tel: 01263 860280
email: Jeremy@Sykes-UK.com
Ingworth Revd Andrew Beane, The Vicarage, Cawston Road, Aylsham NR11 6NB
Tel: 01263 732686
email: andrew.beane@btinternet.com
Lynn Revd James Nash, Wootton Rectory, Castle Rising Road, South Wootton PE30 3JA
Tel: 01553 671381
email: jamesnash8@talktalk.net
Repps Revd Christian Heycocks, The Vicarage, 10 North Street, Sheringham NR26 8LW
Tel: 01263 822089
email: rev.heycocks15@btinternet.com
Sparham Revd Tim Dean, The Rectory, 26 Station Road, Reepham NR10 4LJ   *Tel:* 01603 871062
email: timdean@cnet.org

DIOCESE OF OXFORD

Founded in 1542. Oxfordshire; Berkshire; Buckinghamshire; one parish in each of Hampshire and Hertfordshire.

Population 2,292,000   Area 2,220 sq m
Full-time Stipendiary Parochial Clergy 391   Benefices 289
Parishes 619   Churches 815
www.oxford.anglican.org
Overseas link dioceses: Vaxjo (Sweden), Kimberley and Kuruman (Southern Africa), Nandyal (South India).

BISHOP (42nd)
Vacancy, Diocesan Church House, North Hinksey, Oxford OX2 0NB [2007]
Tel: 01865 208200 (Office)
Fax: 01865 790470
email: bishopoxon@oxford.anglican.org
Bishop's Domestic Chaplain Revd Graham Sykes (*same address*) *Tel:* 01865 208200 (Office)
Fax: 01865 790470

AREA BISHOPS
READING Rt Revd Andrew Proud, Bishop's House, Tidmarsh Lane, Tidmarsh, Reading RG8 8HA [2011] *Tel:* 0118 984 1216
Fax: 0118 984 1218
email: bishopreading@oxford.anglican.org
BUCKINGHAM Rt Revd Dr Alan Wilson, Sheridan, Grimms Hill, Gt Missenden HP16 9BG [2003]
Tel: 01494 862173
Fax: 01494 890508
email: bishopbucks@oxford.anglican.org
DORCHESTER Rt Revd Colin Fletcher, Arran House, Sandy Lane, Yarnton, Oxford OX5 1PB [2000] *Tel:* 01865 375541
Fax: 01865 379890
email: bishopdorchester@oxford.anglican.org

PROVINCIAL EPISCOPAL VISITOR
EBBSFLEET Rt Revd Jonathan Goodall, Hill House, The Mount, Caversham, Reading RG4 7RE
Tel: 01865 288030
email: office@ebbsfleet.org.uk

HONORARY ASSISTANT BISHOPS
Rt Revd Keith Arnold, 9 Dinglederry, Olney MK46 5ES [1997] *Tel:* 01234 713044
Rt Revd Bill Down, 54 Dark Lane, Witney OX28 6LX [2001] *Tel:* 01993 706615
Rt Revd Ronald Gordon, Garden Flat B, St Katherine's House, Ormond Road, Wantage OX12 8EA [1991] *Tel:* 01235 760766
Rt Revd David Jennings, Laurel Cottage, East End, North Leach, Gloucestershire GL54 3ET
Tel: 01451 860743
Rt Revd James Johnson, St Helena, 28 Molyneux Drive, Bodicote, Banbury OX15 4AP [2005]
Tel: 01295 255357
Rt Revd Peter Nott, Westcot House, Westcot, Sparsholt, Wantage OX12 9QA [1999]
Tel: 01235 751233

Rt Revd Henry Richmond, 39 Hodges Court, Marlborough Rd, Oxford OX1 4NZ [1999]
Tel: 01865 790466
Rt Revd Anthony Russell, Lye Hill House, Holton, Oxford OX33 1QF [2011]
Tel: 01865 876415
Rt Revd Henry Scriven, 16 East St Helens St, Abingdon, Oxford, Oxon OX14 5EA
Tel: 01235 536607
Rt Revd John Went, Latimer Rectory, Latimer, Chesham, Bucks HP5 1UA *Tel:* 01494 765586

CATHEDRAL CHURCH OF CHRIST
Dean Very Revd Prof Martyn Percy, The Deanery, Christ Church, Oxford OX1 1DP [2014]
Tel: 01865 276161
Dean's PA Miss Rachel Perham (*same address*)
Tel: 01865 276161
Fax: 01865 276238
email: rachel.perham@chch.ox.ac.uk
Sub-Dean Revd Canon Dr Edmund Newey, Christ Church, Oxford OX1 1DP [2013]
Tel: 01865 276278
email: subdean@chch.ox.ac.uk
Canons Residentiary
Canon Prof Graham Ward, Christ Church, Oxford OX1 1DP [2012] *Tel:* 01865 286334
email: graham.ward@chch.ox.ac.uk
Canon Prof Nigel Biggar, Christ Church, Oxford OX1 1DP [2007] *Tel:* 01865 276219
email: nigel.biggar@chch.ox.ac.uk
Canon Prof Sarah Foot, Christ Church, Oxford OX1 1DP [2007] *Tel:* 01865 286078
email: sarah.foot@chch.ox.ac.uk
Canon Angela Tilby, Christ Church, Oxford OX1 1DP [2011] Tel: 01865 208760/276876
email: angela.tilby@chch.ox.ac.uk/
angela.tilby@oxford.anglican.org
Precentor Revd John Paton, Christ Church, Oxford OX1 1DP [2003] *Tel:* 01865 276214
email: john.paton@chch.ox.ac.uk/
precentor@chch.ox.ac.uk
Liturgy Assistant Mr David Bannister, Christ Church, Oxford OX1 1DP
Tel: 01865 276214
email: david.bannister@chch.ox.ac.uk
Cathedral Registrar Mr John Briggs, Christ Church, Oxford OX1 1DP *Tel:* 01865 286846
email: john.briggs@chch.ox.ac.uk

Cathedral Office Manager Mrs Eileen Head, Christ Church, Oxford OX1 1DP   *Tel:* 01865 276155
    email: eileen.head@chch.ox.ac.uk
Cathedral Organist Dr Stephen Darlington, Christ Church, Oxford OX1 1DP   *Tel:* 01865 276195
    email: stephen.darlington@chch.ox.ac.uk
Organist's PA Miss Florence Maskell, Christ Church, Oxford OX1 1DP   *Tel:* 01865 276195
    email: florence.maskell@chch.ox.ac.uk
Dean's Verger Mr Matthew Power, Christ Church, Oxford OX1 1DP   *Tel:* 01865 286002/276154
    email: matthew.power@chch.ox.ac.uk
Canons' Verger and Sacristan Mr Christopher Waterhouse, Christ Church, Oxford OX1 1DP
    Tel: 01865 276154/286002
    email: christopher.waterhouse@chch.ox.ac.uk
Visitors Officer Mr Jim Godfrey, Christ Church, Oxford OX1 1DP   *Tel:* 01865 286003
    email: jim.godfrey@chch.ox.ac.uk

ARCHDEACONS

OXFORD Ven Martin Gorick, Diocesan Church House, North Hinksey, Oxford OX2 0NB [2007]
    Tel: 01865 208200 (Office)
    Fax: 01865 790470
    email: archdoxf@oxford.anglican.org
BERKSHIRE Ven Olivia Graham, Foxglove House, Love Lane, Donnington, Newbury RG14 2JG [2013]   *Tel:* 01635 552820
    Fax: 01635 522165
    email: archdber@oxford.anglican.org
BUCKINGHAM Ven Karen Gorham, Rectory, Stone, Aylesbury HP17 8RZ [2007]   *Tel:* 01865 208264
    email: archdbuc@oxford.anglican.org
DORCHESTER Ven Judy French, 11 Broadfield Road, Yarnton, Kidlington, Oxon OX5 1UL
    Tel: 01865 208245
    email:
    archdeacon.dorchester@oxford.anglican.org

CONVOCATION (MEMBERS OF THE HOUSE OF CLERGY OF THE GENERAL SYNOD)
Proctors for Clergy
The Bishop of Oxford
Revd Jonathan Beswick
Canon Dr Judith Maltby
Canon Susan Booys
Revd Dr Mark Chapman
Revd Hugh Lee
Revd John Cook
Ven Karen Gorham
Canon Rosie Harper
Canon Christopher Sugden
Canon John Wynburne

MEMBERS OF THE HOUSE OF LAITY OF THE GENERAL SYNOD
Mrs Julie Dziegiel
Mr Robert Hurley
Miss Prudence Dailey
Dr Philip Giddings
Mrs Victoria Russell

Mr Brian Newey
Mr Gavin Oldham
Dr Anna Thomas-Betts

DIOCESAN OFFICERS
Dioc Secretary Canon Rosemary Pearce, Diocesan Church House, North Hinksey Lane, Oxford OX2 0NB   *Tel:* 01865 208200
    Fax: 01865 790470
    email: diosec@oxford.anglican.org
Chancellor of Diocese Revd Alexander McGregor QC, Diocesan Registry, 16 Beaumont St, Oxford OX1 2LZ   *Tel:* 01865 297200
    Fax: 01865 726274
    email: oxford@winckworths.co.uk
Registrar of Diocese and Bishop's Legal Secretary Canon John Rees (*same address*)
Registrar of the Archdeaconries Canon John Rees (*as above*)

DIOCESAN ORGANIZATIONS
Diocesan Office Diocesan Church House, North Hinksey Lane, Oxford OX2 0NB
    Tel: 01865 208200
    Fax: 01865 790470

ADMINISTRATION
Dioc Synod (*Vice-President, House of Clergy*) Canon Sue Booys, The Rectory, Manor Farm Road, Dorchester, Wallingford, Oxon OX10 7HZ
    Tel: 01865 340007
    email: rector@dorchester-abbey.org.uk
(*Vice-President, House of Laity*) Mrs Judith Scott, Quakers Hat, 38 Wellington Road, Wokingham, Berks RG40 2AG   *Tel:* 0118 977 1656
    email: judithscott762@btinternet.com
(*Secretary*) Canon Rosemary Pearce, Diocesan Church House, North Hinksey Lane, Oxford OX2 0NB   *Tel:* 01865 208200
    Fax: 01865 790470
Board of Finance (*Chairman*) Revd John Tattersall, Abingdon House, Park Lane, Swalcliffe, Banbury, Oxon OX15 5EU   *Tel:* 01295 780283
    email: jhtatters@aol.com
(*Secretary*) Canon Rosemary Pearce (*as above*)
Director of Glebe and Buildings Mr David Mason Diocesan Church House, North Hinksey, Oxford OX2 0NB   *Tel:* 01865 208230
    email: david.mason@oxford.anglican.org
Dioc Trustees (*Oxford*) *Ltd* Canon Rosemary Pearce (*as above*)
Pastoral Committee (*Secretary*) *and Electoral Roll Officer* Mr Howard Cattermole, Diocesan Church House, North Hinksey, Oxford OX2 0NB
    Tel: 01865 208243
    email: howard.cattermole@oxford.anglican.org
Designated Officer Canon John Rees (*as above*)

CHURCHES
Advisory Committee for the Care of Churches (*Chairman*) Mr Charles Baker
    email: cb@charlesbaker.org

(*Secretary*) Miss Natalie Merry, Diocesan Church House, North Hinksey, Oxford OX2 0NB
Tel: 01865 208229
email: natalie.merry@oxford.anglican.org
Sites Advisory Committee (*Secretary*) Mr Howard Cattermole (*as above*)

MISSION

Director Canon Dr Michael Beasley, Diocesan Church House, North Hinksey, Oxford OX2 0NB
Tel: 01865 208251
email: michael.beasley@oxford.anglican.org
Parish Development Advisers
Buckingham Mr Andrew Gear, Diocesan Church House, North Hinksey, Oxford OX2 0NB
Tel: 01865 208256
email: andrew.gear@oxford.anglican.org
Dorchester Revd Preb Charles Chadwick, Diocesan Church House, North Hinksey, Oxford OX2 0NB
Tel: 01865 208246
email: charles.chadwick@oxford.anglican.org
Berkshire Revd Catharine Morris, Diocesan Church House, North Hinksey, Oxford OX2 0NB
Tel: 01865 208296
email: catharine.morris@oxford.anglican.org
Children's Work Mrs Yvonne Morris, Diocesan Church House, North Hinksey, Oxford OX2 0NB
Tel: 01865 208255
email: yvonne.morris@oxford.anglican.org
Safeguarding Adviser Mr Stephen Barber, Diocesan Church House, North Hinksey, Oxford OX2 0NB
Tel: 01865 208290
email: stephen.barber@oxford.anglican.org
Christian Giving and Funding Adviser Mr Robin Brunner-Ellis, Diocesan Church House, North Hinksey, Oxford OX2 0NB
Tel: 01865 208254
email: robin.brunner-ellis@oxford.anglican.org
Director of Local Ministry Training Revd Dr Keith Beech-Gruneberg, Diocesan Church House, North Hinksey, Oxford OX2 0NB
Tel: 01865 208282
email: keith.gruneberg@oxford.anglican.org
Deputy Warden of Readers and Director of Postgraduate Studies Revd Phillip Tovey, Diocesan Church House, North Hinksey, Oxford OX2 0NB
Tel: 01865 208212
email: phillip.tovey@oxford.anglican.org
Youth Work Mr Ian Macdonald, Diocesan Church House, North Hinksey, Oxford OX2 0NB
Tel: 01865 208253
email: ian.macdonald@oxford.anglican.org
Director of Initial Ministerial Education (Part 2) Revd Beren Hartless Diocesan Church House, North Hinksey, Oxford OX2 0NB
Tel: 01865 208258
email: beren.hartless@oxford.anglican.org
Diocesan Director of Ordinands Revd Jules Cave Bergquist, Diocesan Church House, North Hinksey, Oxford OX2 0NB
Tel: 01865 208260
Directors of Ordinands
Oxfordshire and Dorchester Revd Jules Cave Bergquist (*as above*)

Berkshire Revd Dr Amanda Bloor (*as above*)
Tel: 01865 208261
Buckingham Revd Caroline Windley, Diocesan Church House, North Hinksey, Oxford OX2 0NB
Tel and *Fax:* 01296 432921
email: caroline.windley@oxford.anglican.org
Vocation Network Chair Revd Jules Cave Bergquist (*as above*)

EDUCATION

Director of Education Ms Anne Davey, Diocesan Church House, North Hinksey, Oxford OX2 0NB
Tel: 01865 208236
email: anne.davey@oxford.anglican.org

MISSIONARY AND ECUMENICAL

Partnership in World Mission (*Secretary*) Vacancy
Diocesan Ecumenical Advisor Revd David Knight, 12 Bankside, Headington, Oxford
Tel: 01865 761476
email: david.knight@bethere.co.uk

COMMUNICATIONS

Director of Communications Ms Sarah Meyrick, Diocesan Church House, North Hinksey, Oxford OX2 0NB
Tel: 01865 208224
Editor of Dioc Newspaper 'The Door' Miss Joanne Duckles, Diocesan Church House, North Hinksey, Oxford OX2 0NB
Tel: 01865 208227
email: joanne.duckles@oxford.anglican.org

DIOCESAN RECORD OFFICES

County Archivist, St Luke's Church, Temple Rd, Cowley, Oxford OX4 2EN *Tel:* 01865 398200
email: archives@oxfordshire.gov.uk (*For records of the diocese, and parish records in the archdeaconry of Oxford*)
Berkshire Record Office, 9 Coley Ave, Reading RG1 6AF *Tel:* 0118 901 5132 (*For parish records in the archdeaconry of Berkshire*)
Buckinghamshire Record Office, County Hall, Aylesbury, Bucks. HP20 1UA *Tel:* 01296 382587 (*For parish records in the archdeaconry of Buckingham*)

SOCIAL RESPONSIBILITY

Social Responsibility Adviser (*Secretary*) Ms Alison Webster, Diocesan Church House, North Hinksey, Oxford OX2 0NB
Tel: 01865 208213
email: alison.webster@oxford.anglican.org
PACT (Parents and Children Together) Council for Social Work Mrs Jan Fishwick, 7 Southern Court, South St, Reading RG1 4QS
Tel: 0118 938 7600
email: info@pactcharity.org
Council for the Deaf (*Chairman*) Revd Tim Edge, 27 Burford Road, Witney OX28 6DP
Tel: 01993 773438
email: tim.edge@talk21.com

AREA DEANS
ARCHDEACONRY OF OXFORD

Cowley Revd Tim Stead, The Vicarage, 46 Quarry Road, Headington, Oxford OX3 8NU
Tel: 01865 762931
email: tim_stead@btinternet.com

Oxford Revd Dr Mark Butchers, 1 Mere Road, Wolvercote, Oxford OX2 8AN
Tel and *Fax:* 01865 515640
email: mark.butchers@dsl.pipex.com

ARCHDEACONRY OF DORCHESTER

Abingdon Revd Richard Zair, 41 North Street, Marcham, Abingdon, Oxon OX13 6NQ
Tel: 01865 391319
email: r_zair@yahoo.co.uk
Aston and Cuddesdon Revd Alan Garratt, Thame Rectory, 3 Fish Ponds, Thame, Oxon OX9 2BA
Tel: 01844 212225
email: alan.garratt@hotmail.co.uk
Bicester and Islip Revd Stephen Griffiths, 3 Larson Road, Upper Heyford, Bicester, Oxon OX25 5TA
Tel: 01869 233249
email: steph78griff@hotmail.com
Chipping Norton Revd Jan Fielden, The Vicarage, Church Lane, Charlbury, Oxon OX7 3PX
Tel: 01608 810286
email: jan@charlburyvicarage.co.uk
Deddington Revd Jeff West, c/o St Mary's Church Centre, Horsefair, Banbury, Oxon, OX16 0AA
Tel: 01608 811136
email: curate@stmaryschurch-banbury.org.uk
Henley Revd Kevin Davies, The Rectory, Checkendon, Reading RG8 0SR
Tel: 01491 680252
email: revkevdavies-langtree@yahoo.co.uk
Witney Revd Toby Wright, Witney Rectory, 13 Station Lane, Witney, Oxon OX28 4BB
Tel: 01993 704441
email: toby-wright@btconnect.com
Woodstock Revd David Tyler, The Rectory, Swan Lane, Long Hanborough, Witney, Oxon OX29 8BT
Tel: 01993 881270
email: revdavidtyler@gmail.com
Vale of White Horse Revd Charles Draper, The Vicarage, Coach Lane, Faringdon, Oxon SN7 8AB
Tel: 01367 240106
email: charlesdraper@btinternet.com
Wallingford Revd Jason St John Nicolle, The Rectory, Church End, Blewbury OX11 9QH
Tel: 01235 850267
email: office@churnchurches.co.uk
Wantage Revd Jason St John Nicolle, The Rectory, Church End, Blewbury OX11 9QH
Tel: 01235 850267
email: office@churnchurches.co.uk

ARCHDEACONRY OF BERKSHIRE

Bracknell Revd David Uffindell, The Vicarage, Sidbury Close, Sunningdale, Ascot, Berks SL5 0PD
Tel: 01344 621886
email: daviduffindell@holytrinitysunningdale.co.uk

Bradfield Revd William Watts, The Vicarage, Pangbourne Road, Upper Basildon RG8 8LS
Tel: 01491 671714
email: willwatts@f2s.com
Maidenhead and Windsor Revd Margaret Bird, The Vicarage, 73 Alma Road, Windsor, Berks SL4 3HD
Tel: 01753 315397
email: Margaret.bird@talktalk.net
Newbury Canon Rita Ball, Rectory, High Street, Hermitage, Berks RG18 9ST
Tel: 01635 202967
email: rita.e.ball@btinternet.com
Reading Vacancy
Sonning Revd Julie Ramsbottom, The Rectory, The Village, Finchampstead, Wokingham RG40 4JX
Tel: 0118 973 6374
email: d.j.ramsbottom@btinternet.com

ARCHDEACONRY OF BUCKINGHAM

Amersham Revd Camilla Walton, 3 St Michael's Green, Beaconsfield HP9 2BN
Tel: 01494 673464
email: camillawalton@googlemail.com
Aylesbury, Revd Andrew Blyth, The Rectory, 42 Redwood Drive, Aylesbury HP21 9RJ
Tel: 01296 394906
email: andrew.blyth@htaylesbury.org
Buckingham Revd Ron Bundock, 1 Holton Road, Buckingham MK18 1PQ
Tel: 01280 813887
email: jandrb@bundock.com
Burnham Revd Rod Cosh, St Thomas House, The New Vicarage, Mill Street, Colnbrook SL3 0JJ
Tel: 07771 527141
email: rod.cosh@oxford.anglican.org
Claydon Revd David Meakin, The Rectory, 1 Greenacres Close, Whitchurch, Aylesbury HP22 4JP
Tel: 01296 641606
email: d.meakin@btinternet.com
Milton Keynes Revd Tim Norwood, 3 Daubeney Gate, Shenley Church End, Milton Keynes MK5 6EH
Tel: 01908 505812
email: tim@mkdeanery.org
Mursley Vacancy
Newport Revd Richard Caddell, The Rectory, High Street, Haversham, Milton Keynes MK19 7DT
Tel: 01908 312136
email: caddells@holtspur.plus.com
Wendover Revd Mark Dearnley, Vicarage, 34a Dobbins Lane, Wendover HP22 6DH
Tel: 01296 622230
email: markdearnley@ntlworld.com
Wycombe Revd Simon Cronk, The Vicarage, Valley Road, Hughenden Valley, Bucks HP14 4PF
Tel: 01494 563439
email: simon.cronk@talktalk.net

DIOCESE OF PETERBOROUGH

Founded in 1541. Northamptonshire, except for one parish in the west (LEICESTER); Rutland; Peterborough, except for an area in the south-east; one parish in Lincolnshire.

Population 865,000   Area 1,150 sq m
Full-time Stipendiary Parochial Clergy 137   Benefices 133
Parishes 348   Churches 377
www.peterborough-diocese.org.uk
Overseas link diocese: Bungoma (Kenya), Seoul (Korea).

BISHOP (37th)
Rt Revd Donald Spargo Allister, Bishop's Lodging, The Palace, Peterborough PE1 1YA
Tel: 01733 562492
email: bishop@peterborough-diocese.org.uk
Bishop's Chaplain Revd Canon Julie Hutchinson (*same address*)   Tel: 01733 887014
email:
julie.hutchinson@peterborough-diocese.org.uk
Bishop's Personal Assistant Miss Alex Low (*same address*)   Tel: 01733 887015
email: alex.low@peterborough-diocese.org.uk
Bishop's Secretary Mrs Cheryl Craggs (*same address*)   Tel: 01733 887037
email:
cheryl.craggs@peterborough-diocese.org.uk

SUFFRAGAN BISHOP
BRIXWORTH Rt Revd John Holbrook, Orchard Acre, 11 North Street, Mears Ashby, Northampton NN6 0DW [2011]   Tel: 01604 812328
email:
bishop.brixworth@peterborough-diocese.org.uk
Bishop's Secretary Mrs Cheryl Craggs (*contact details as for Bishop Donald's office above*)

HONORARY ASSISTANT BISHOPS
Rt Revd John Flack, Huddersfield House, 7 Cemetery Road, Whittlesey, Peterborough PE7 1SF [2003]   Tel: 01733 202767
email: johnflack67@yahoo.com
Right Revd Lindsay Urwin, The College, Walsingham, Norfolk NR22 6EF [2011]
Tel: 01328 824204
email: l.urwin@olw-shrine.org.uk

CATHEDRAL CHURCH OF ST PETER, ST PAUL AND ST ANDREW
Dean Very Revd Charles Taylor, The Deanery, Minster Precincts, Peterborough PE1 1XS [2007]
Tel: 01733 355308
email: dean.pa@peterborough-cathedral.org.uk
Precentor Canon R. Bruce Ruddock, Precentor's Lodging, 14A Minster Precincts, Peterborough PE1 1XX [2004]   Tel: 01733 355310
email:
bruce.ruddock@peterborough-cathedral.org.uk

Canons Residentiary
Missioner Canon Jonathan Baker, Canonry House, Minster Precincts, Peterborough PE1 1XX [2004]
Tel: 01733 897335 (Home)
01733 355300 (Office)
email:
jonathan.baker@peterborough-cathedral.org.uk
Canon Ian Black, 26 Minster Precincts, Peterborough PE1 1XZ [2012]   Tel: 01733 873064 (Home)
email: canonianblack@btinternet.com
Lay Members of Chapter
Mr John Henniker-Major, Linden House, Brook Lane, Great Easton, Market Harborough LE16 8SJ   Tel: 01604 608211 (Office)
01536 770320 (Home)
email: john.henniker-major@carterjonas.co.uk
Hon Treasurer Sir John Parsons, Old Rectory, Eydon, Daventry NN11 3QE   Tel: 01327 260745
email: jparsoneydon@btopenworld.com
Mr Mike Opperman, Littleworth Mission, Main Rd, Deeping St Nicholas, Spalding, Lincs PE11 3EN   Tel: 01775 630497
email: jenny@littleworthmission.com
Mrs Maria Steele, 55 Thorpe Road, Peterborough PE3 6AN   Tel: 07880 585624
Chapter Administrator Mrs Maria Elsey, Cathedral Office, Minster Precincts, Peterborough PE1 1XS   Tel: 01733 355308
email: dean.pa@peterborough-cathedral.org.uk
Dean's Assistant Revd Canon Richard Cattle, Cathedral Office, Minster Precincts, Peterborough PE1 1XS   Tel: 01733 35531
email:
richard.cattle@peterborough-cathedral.org.uk
Director of Music Mr Steven Grahl, The Music Office, 28 Minster Precincts, Peterborough PE1 1XS   Tel: 01733 355318
email:
music.director@peterborough-cathedral.org.uk

ARCHDEACONS
NORTHAMPTON Ven Richard Ormston, Westbrook, The Drive, Northampton NN1 4RZ [2014]
Tel: 01604 0887074
email:
archdeacon.northampton@peterborough-diocese.org.uk

OAKHAM Ven Gordon Steele, The Diocesan Office, The Palace, Peterborough PE1 1YB [2012]
Tel: 01733 887017
Fax: 01733 555271
email:
archdeacon.oakham@peterborough-diocese.org.uk

CONVOCATION (MEMBERS OF THE HOUSE OF CLERGY OF THE GENERAL SYNOD)
Proctors for Clergy
Vacancy
Canon William Croft
Revd Dr Guli Francis-Dehqani
Revd Stephen Trott

MEMBERS OF THE HOUSE OF LAITY OF THE GENERAL SYNOD
Vacancy
Mrs Veronica Heald
Canon Liz Holdsworth
Mr Andrew Presland

DIOCESAN OFFICERS
Dioc Secretary Mr Andrew Roberts, Diocesan Office, The Palace, Peterborough PE1 1YB
Tel: 01733 887000
Fax: 01733 555271
email: diosec@peterborough-diocese.org.uk
Deputy Dioc Secretary Vacancy
Chancellor of Diocese Chancellor David Pittaway QC, c/o Diocesan Registrar, 35 Thorpe Road, Longthorpe, Peterborough PE3 6AG
Deputy Chancellor Mr George Pulman, c/o Diocesan Registrar (*as above*)
Registrar of Diocese and Bishop's Legal Secretary Miss Anna Spriggs, 35 Thorpe Road (*as above*)
Tel: 01733 882800
email: anna.spriggs@hcsolicitors.co.uk

DIOCESAN ORGANIZATIONS
Diocesan Office The Palace, Peterborough PE1 1YB
Tel: 01733 887000
Fax: 01733 555271
email: office@peterborough-diocese.org.uk
Web: www.peterborough-diocese.org.uk

ADMINISTRATION
Dioc Synod (*Vice-President, Clergy*) Canon Margaret Johnson, 13 Booth Lane North, Northampton NN3 6JE
Tel: 01604 648974
email: revmahj@gmail.com
(*Vice-President, Laity*) Mr John MacMahon, 12 Westminster Croft, Brackley NN13 7ED
Tel: (01280) 703791
email: j2macmahon@o2.co.uk
(*Secretary*) Mr Andrew Roberts, The Palace, Peterborough PE1 1YB
Board of Finance (*Chairman*) Mr Michael Truman, Diocesan Office, The Palace, Peterborough PE1 1YB
Tel: 01733 887000
email: m.j.truman@unicombox.co.uk

(*Secretary*) Mr Andrew Roberts (*as above*)
Houses Committee (*Chairman*) Mr Robert Purser, Diocesan Office, The Palace, Peterborough PE1 1YB
Tel: 01733 887000
Property Officer Mrs Sandra Allen, Dioc Office
Safeguarding Officer Mr Garry Johnson, Dioc Office
Mission and Pastoral Committee Mr Andrew Roberts (*as above*)
Board of Patronage Mr Andrew Roberts (*as above*)
Designated Officer Mr Andrew Roberts (*as above*)

CHURCHES
Advisory Committee for the Care of Churches (*Chairman*) Mr John White, c/o DAC, Diocesan Office, The Palace, Peterborough PE1 1YB
Tel: 01733 887007
Fax: 01733 555271
email: dac@peterborough-diocese.org.uk

EDUCATION
Board of Education (*Schools*) (*Director of Education* (*Schools*) *and Secretary*) Mrs Miranda Robinson, Bouverie Court, The Lakes, Bedford Rd, Northampton NN4 7YD
Tel: 01604 887006
Fax: 01604 887077
email: education@peterborough-diocese.org.uk
Deputy Director of Education (*Schools*) Mr Peter Goringe, Bouverie Court, The Lakes, Bedford Rd, Northampton NN4 7YD
Tel: 01604 887006
email: education@peterborough-diocese.org.uk

MINISTRY
Dioc Vocations Adviser and Director of Ordinands Revd Canon Steve Benoy, Bouverie Court, The Lakes, Bedford Rd, Northampton NN4 7YD
Tel: 01604 887047
Fax: 01604 887077
Coordinator of Adult Education and Training Canon Liz Holdsworth, Bouverie Court (*as above*)
Tel: 01604 887042
Fax: 01604 887077
email:
liz.holdsworth@peterborough-diocese.org.uk
Continuing Ministerial Education Officer and Licensed Lay Minister Officer Revd Quentin Chandler, Bouverie Court (*as above*)
Tel: 01604 887042
Fax: 01604 887077
email:
quentin.chandler@peterborough-diocese.org.uk
Continuing Ministerial Education Officer Revd Hannah Jeffery, Bouverie Court (*as above*)
Tel: 01604 887000
Fax: 01604 887077
email:
hannah.jeffery@peterborough-diocese.org.uk
Curates' Training Coordinator Revd Dr Guli Francis-Dehqani, The Vicarage, Vicarage Rd, Oakham, Rutland LE15 6EG
Tel: 01572 722108
or 01604 887054
email: guli.francis-dehqani@peterborough-diocese.org.uk

SELF SUPPORTING MINISTRY OFFICERS

Revd Elizabeth Pelly, Home Farm, Wakefield Lodge, Potterspury, Towcester, Northamptonshire NN12 7QX   *Tel:* 01327 811218
Fax: 01327 811326
email: lulu.pelly@farming.co.uk

Revd Jo Saunders, Mellstock, Bourne Road, Essendine, Stamford, Lincolnshire PE9 4LH
Tel: 01780 480479
email: revjosaunders@live.co.uk

Warden of Readers Revd John Hall, Irthlingborough Rectory, 79 Finedon Road, Irthlingborough NN9 5TY   *Tel:* 01933 650278
email: fr.john@nenecrossings.org.uk

Warden of Pastoral Assistants Revd David Kirby, Rectory, Church Way, Weston Favell, Northampton NN3 3BX   *Tel:* 01604 413218
email: kirbydg@gmail.com

Warden of Parish Evangelists Revd Melvyn Pereira, 20 Ribble Close, Wellingborough, Northants NN8 5XJ   *Tel:* 01933 673437
email: melvyn.pereira@gleneagleschurch.co.uk

MISSION

Diocesan Mission Enabler Revd Miles Baker, Bouverie Court, The Lakes, Bedford Rd, Northampton NN4 7YD   *Tel:* 01604 887043
Fax: 01604 887077
email: miles.baker@peterborough-diocese.org.uk

Children's Missioner Mrs Rona Orme, Bouverie Court (*as above*)   *Tel:* 01604 887045
Fax: 01604 887077
email: rona.orme@peterborough-diocese.org.uk

Youth Officer (Interns) Mr Peter White, Bouverie Court, The Lakes, Bedford Rd, Northampton NN4 7YD   *Tel:* 01604 887044
Fax: 01604 887077
email: peter.white@peterborough-diocese.org.uk

Mission in Society Officer Revd Robert Hill, Bouverie Court, The Lakes, Bedford Rd, Northampton NN4 7YD   *Tel:* 01604 887046
Fax: 01604 887077
email: robert.hill@peterborough-diocese.org.uk

Urban Priority Areas Link Officer and Church Urban Fund Officer Vacancy

Ecumenical Officer Revd Sam Randall, Sundial House, 57 Main Street, Yarwell, Northamptonshire PE8 6PR   *Tel:* 01780 784684
email: sam.randall@peterborough-diocese.org.uk

Hospital Chaplaincy Adviser Canon Lesley McCormack, Barnbrook, Water Lane, Chelveston, Wellingborough NN9 6SP
Tel: 01933 492609
email: lesley.mccormack@kgh.nhs.uk

Rural Officer Vacancy

LITURGICAL

Officer Vacancy

COMMUNICATIONS

Bishop's Media Adviser Revd Derek Williams (c/o Dioc Office)   *Tel:* 01858 432709/07770 981172

Communications Officer Mr Nick Clarke (c/o Dioc Office)   *Tel:* 01733 887012
Fax: 01733 555271
email:
communications@peterborough-diocese.org.uk

DIOCESAN RECORD OFFICES

Wootton Park, Northampton NN4 9BQ *County Archivist* Miss Sarah Bridges   *Tel:* 01604 762129
email: archivist@northamptonshire.gov.uk
(*For all parishes in Northants. and the former Soke of Peterborough*)

Leicestershire Record Office, Long St, Wigston Magna, Leicester LE18 2AH *County Archivist* Mr Carl Harrison *Tel:* 0116 257 1080 (*For all parishes in Rutland*)

RURAL DEANS

ARCHDEACONRY OF NORTHAMPTON

Brackley Revd Simon Dommett, The Rectory, Croughton Road, Aynho, Banbury, Northamptonshire OX17 3BD   *Tel:* 01869 810903
email: the.revd.simon@gmail.com

Brixworth Revd Mary Garbutt, Rectory, 35 Main St, Great Oxenden, Market Harborough LE16 8NE   *Tel:* 01858 461992
email: mary@familygarbutt.plus.com

Daventry Revd Sarah Brown, The Rectory, High Street, Braunston, Daventry, Northamptonshire NN11 7HS   *Tel:* 01788 890298
email: vicar@allsaintsbraunston.org.uk

Northampton Revd Canon David Wiseman, Christ Church Vicarage, 3 Christ Church Rd, Northampton NN3 2LE   *Tel:* 01604 633254

Towcester Revd Paul McLeod, St Michael's Vicarage, High Street, Silverstone, Towcester, Northamptonshire NN12 8US   *Tel:* 01327 858101
email: RevPaulMcLeod@aol.com

Wellingborough Revd Tony Lynett, Vicarage, 154 Midland Rd, Wellingborough NN8 1NF
Tel: 01933 227101
email: tartleknock@aol.com

ARCHDEACONRY OF OAKHAM

Corby Revd Ian Pullinger, St Columba's Vicarage, 157 Studfall Avenue, Corby, Northamptonshire NN17 1LG
Tel: 01536 400225
email: ianpullinger@btinternet.com

Higham Revd Stephen Prior, The Rectory, Rectory Road, Rushden NN10 0HA
Tel: 01933 312554
email: sprior@toucansurf.com

Kettering Revd Brian Withington, Rectory, Gate Lane, Broughton, Kettering NN14 1ND
Tel: 01536 791373
email: brian.andco@virgin.net

Oundle Revd Stephen Webster, 41 Hillfield Road, Oundle PE8 4QR   *Tel:* 01832 275631
email: stephen.webster@yahoo.co.uk

Peterborough Revd Gillian Jessop, The Rectory, 236 Fulbridge Road, Paston, Peterborough PE4 6SN
Tel: 01733 578228
email: rev.gill@tesco.net

Rutland Revd Canon Lee Francis-Dehqani, Vicarage, Vicarage Rd, Oakham, Rutland LE15 6EG
Tel: 01572 722108
email: lee.fd@btinternet.com

DIOCESE OF PORTSMOUTH

Founded in 1927. The south-eastern third of Hampshire; the Isle of Wight.

Population 766,000   Area 410 sq m
Full-time Stipendiary Parochial Clergy 98   Benefices 127
Parishes 142   Churches 173
www.portsmouth.anglican.org
Overseas link diocese: IDWAL (Inter-Diocesan West Africa Link) – Ghana,
Gambia, Liberia (West Africa).

BISHOP (8th)
Rt Revd Christopher Foster, Bishopsgrove, 26 Osborn Road, Fareham PO16 7DQ
Tel: 01329 280247
Fax: 01329 231538
email: bishports@portsmouth.anglican.org
Bishop's Chaplain Revd Jenny Gaffin
email: jenny.gaffin@portsmouth.anglican.org
Secretaries Claire Holland/Rachel Houlberg

HONORARY ASSISTANT BISHOPS
Rt Revd Michael Adie, Greenslade, Froxfield, Petersfield GU32 1EB [2005]   *Tel:* 01730 827266
Rt Revd Timothy Bavin, Alton Abbey, Abbey Road, Beech, Alton GU34 4AP   *Tel:* 01420 562145
Rt Revd John Hind, 1 Stanley Road, Emsworth, PO10 7BD   *Tel:* 01243 430305
email: john@hind.org.uk

CATHEDRAL CHURCH OF ST THOMAS OF CANTERBURY
Dean Very Revd David Brindley, The Deanery, 13 Pembroke Rd, Portsmouth PO1 2NS [2002]
Tel: 023 9282 4400 (Home)
email: david.brindley@portsmouthcathedral.org.uk
Tel: 023 9289 2963 (Personal Assistant)
email: liz.snowball@portsmouthcathedral.org.uk
Cathedral Office Cathedral House, 63–67 St Thomas's St, Old Portsmouth PO1 2HA
Tel: 023 9282 3300
Web: www.portsmouthcathedral.org.uk
Canons Residentiary
Canon with responsibility for Music and Liturgy Revd Canon Michael Tristram, 51 High St, Old Portsmouth PO1 2LU [2003]   *Tel:* 023 9273 1282 (Home)
023 9282 3300 (Office)
email:
michael.tristram@portsmouthcathedral.org.uk
Canon with responsibility for Discipleship, Growth and Community Outreach Revd Canon Peter Leonard, 32 Woodville Drive, Pembroke Park, Portsmouth PO1 2TG [2014]
Tel: 023 9282 3300 ext 229 (Office)
07817 722219 (Mobile)
email: peter.leonard@portsmouth.anglican.org
Revd Canon Nick Ralph, 101 St Thomas's Street, Old Portsmouth PO1 2HE [2009]
Tel: 023 9289 9674 (Office)
email: nick.ralph@portsmouth.anglican.org

Precentor Revd Canon Dr Anthony Rustell, 1 Pembroke Close, Old Portsmouth PO1 2NX [2014]   *Tel:* 023 9289 9654
email: anthony.rustell@portsmouth.anglican.org
Assistant Curate Revd Dawn Banting, Cathedral Offices, St Thomas's Street, Old Portsmouth PO1 2HA
Cathedral Administrator, Chapter Clerk and Clerk to Cathedral Council Peter Sanders
Tel: 023 9289 2961
email:
peter.sanders@portsmouthcathedral.org.uk
Cathedral Organist and Master of Choristers Dr David Price, Cathedral Offices, St Thomas's Street, Old Portsmouth PO1 2HA
Tel: 023 9282 3300 ext 228 (Office)
email: david.price@portsmouthcathedral.org.uk
Cathedral Sub-Organist Oliver Hancock, Flat 1, Cathedral House, St Thomas's Street, Old Portsmouth PO1 2EZ   *Tel:* 023 9282 3300 ext 237
email: oliver.hancock@portsmouthcathedral.org.uk
Head Verger Jessica-Louise Hallion, Cathedral Offices, St Thomas's Street, Old Portsmouth PO1 2HA   *Tel:* 023 9289 2969
email:
jessica.hallion@portsmouthcathedral.org.uk

ARCHDEACONS
PORTSDOWN Ven Dr Joanne Grenfell, 313 Havant Road, Farlington, Portsmouth PO6 1DD
Tel: 023 9289 9650
Fax: 023 9289 9651
email: adportsdown@portsmouth.anglican.org
THE MEON Ven Gavin Collins, Victoria Lodge, 36 Osborn Road, Fareham PO16 7DB
Tel: 01329 608895
email: admeon@portsmouth.anglican.org
ISLE OF WIGHT Ven Peter Sutton, 5 The Boltons, Kite Hill, Wootton Bridge, Isle of Wight PO33 4PB
Tel: 01983 884432
email: adiow@portsmouth.anglican.org

CONVOCATION (MEMBERS OF THE HOUSE OF CLERGY OF THE GENERAL SYNOD)
Proctors for Clergy
Revd Clive Leach
Ven Gavin Collins
Revd Canon Bob White

MEMBERS OF THE HOUSE OF LAITY OF THE GENERAL SYNOD
Mrs Lucy Docherty
Canon Susan Rodgers
Canon Deborah Sutton

DIOCESAN OFFICERS
Dioc Secretary Revd Wendy Kennedy, First Floor, Peninsular House, Wharf Rd, Portsmouth PO2 8HB   Tel: 023 9289 9664
Fax: 023 9289 9651
email: wendy.kennedy@portsmouth.anglican.org
Deputy Dioc Secretary Jenny Hollingsworth
Tel: 023 9282 9664
Fax: 023 9289 9651
email:
jenny.hollingsworth@portsmouth.anglican.org
PAS to Dioc and Deputy Dioc Secretaries and DAC Secretaries David Cain and Catherine Gray
Tel: 023 9282 9664
Fax: 023 9289 9651
email:
executive.assistant@portsmouth.anglican.org
Chancellor of Diocese His Honour Judge Phillip Waller, 49 Woodstock Road North, St Albans AL1 4QD   Tel: 01727 839668
email: hhjudgephilip.waller@judiciary.gsi.gov.uk
Deputy Chancellor His Honour Judge Keith Cutler, Woodacre, West Gomeldon, Salisbury SP4 6LS   Tel: 01980 611710
Registrar of Diocese and Bishop's Legal Secretary Miss Hilary Tyler, Messrs Brutton & Co., West End House, 288 West St, Fareham PO16 0AJ
Tel: 01329 236171
Fax: 01329 289915
email: hilary.tyler@brutton.co.uk
Bishop's Council/Board of Finance/Pastoral Committee (*Chairman*) Rt Revd Christopher Foster (*as above*)
(*Secretary*) Revd Wendy Kennedy (*as above*)

DIOCESAN ORGANIZATIONS
Diocesan Office First Floor, Peninsular House, Wharf Rd, Portsmouth PO2 8HB
Tel: 023 9289 9650
Fax: 023 9289 9651
email: admin@portsmouth.anglican.org

ADMINISTRATION
Dioc Synod (*Secretary*) Revd Wendy Kennedy (*as above*)
Dioc Synod (*Chairman House of Clergy*) Revd Canon Bob White, St Mary's Vicarage, Portsmouth PO1 5PA   Tel: 023 9282 2687 (Home)
023 9282 2990 (Office)
email: revrcwhite@aol.com
(*Chairman, House of Laity*) Mrs Lucy Docherty, 33 Southampton Rd, Fareham PO16 7DZ
Tel: 01329 233602
07952 780108 (Mobile)
email: lucy@docherty1.co.uk

MISSION AND DISCIPLESHIP
Head of Department Revd Canon David Isaac, Dioc Office   Tel: 023 9289 9654
Fax: 023 9289 9651
email: david.isaac@portsmouth.anglican.org
Dioc Director of Ordinands Canon Robin Coutts, Vicarage, Church Lane, Hambledon, Waterlooville PO7 4RT   Tel: 023 9263 2717
email: robin.coutts@portsmouth.anglican.org
Dioc IME Ven Peter Sutton, 5 The Boltons, Kite Hill, Wootton Bridge, Isle of Wight PO33 4PB
Tel: 01983 884432
email: adiow@portsmouth.anglican.org
CME adviser Revd Belinda Davies, 8 Queen Street, Portsea, Portsmouth PO1 3HL
Tel: 023 9273 6097
email: belinda.davies@portsmouth.anglican.org
Youth and Children's Work Adviser Ben Mizen, Dioc Office   Tel: 023 9289 9652
email: ben.mizen@portsmouth.anglican.org
Spirituality Adviser Revd Dr Ruth Tuschling, Dioc Office   Tel: 023 9289 9682
email: ruth.tuschling@portsmouth.anglican.org
Healing Advisor Dr David Pearson, 27 Livingstone Road, Southsea PO5 1RS   Tel: 023 9275 3260
email: david.pearson@portsmouth.anglican.org
Stewardship Adviser Victoria James, Dioc Office
Tel: 023 9289 9655
email: victoria.james@portsmouth.anglican.org

MISSION AND EDUCATION
Director of Education, Portsmouth and Winchester Revd Jeff Williams, Dioc Office
Tel: 023 9289 9658
Fax: 023 9289 9651
email: jeff.williams@portsmouth.anglican.org
Head of Department Revd Jeff Williams (*as above*)
Assistant Director of Education, Portsmouth and Winchester Miss Emily Fletcher, Dioc Office
Tel: 023 9289 9680
Fax: 023 9289 9651
email: emily.fletcher@portsmouth.anglican.org

MISSION AND RESOURCES
Head of Department Mrs Jenny Hollingsworth, Dioc Office (*as above*)
Diocesan Property Manager and Surveyor and Secretary to Property Committee Mr Barry Fryer, Dioc Office   Tel: 023 9289 9663
email: B.Fryer@portsmouth.anglican.org
Synod and Office Support Manager Mrs Jane Dobbs, Dioc Office   Tel: 023 9289 9661
email: jane.dobbs@portsmouth.anglican.org
Safeguarding Adviser Mr Ian Berry, Dioc Office
Tel: 023 9289 9665
email: ian.berry@portsmouth.anglican.org

MISSION AND SOCIETY
Chair (*appointed by the Bishop*) Revd Canon Bob White, St Mary's Vicarage, Fratton Road, Portsmouth PO1 5PA   Tel: 023 9282 2687
email: revrcwhite@aol.com

Head of Mission and Society Section and Social Responsibility Adviser Canon Nick Ralph, First Floor, Peninsular House, Wharf Rd, Portsmouth, Hants PO2 8HB   Tel: 023 9289 9674
          email: nick.ralph@portsmouth.anglican.org
Social Responsibility Co-ordinator Mrs Nicky Pybus, Dioc Office   Tel: 023 8289 9670
          email: nicky.pybus@portsmouth.anglican.org
Chair of the Council for Social Responsibility Steering Group Mrs Lucy Docherty
Chaplain to the Deaf and Hard of Hearing Revd Robert Sanday, The Vicarage, 1 Tangmere Drive, Lord's Hill, Southampton SO16 8GY
          Tel: 023 8026 5897
          email: robertsanday@aol.com
Communications Adviser Mr Neil Pugmire, First Floor, Peninsular House, Wharf Rd, Portsmouth, Hants PO2 8HB   Tel: 023 9289 9673
          email: neil.pugmire@portsmouth.anglican.org
Communications Assistant Julie Minter, First Floor, Peninsular House, Wharf Rd, Portsmouth, Hants PO2 8HB   Tel: 023 9289 9675
Disability Adviser Revd Mary Tillman, 3 Fareham Road, Gosport PO13 0XL   Tel: 023 9286 5488
Environment Adviser Vacancy
Ecumenical Adviser Revd Simon Sayers, Rectory, 20 Church Path, Emsworth PO10 7DP
          Tel: 01243 371324
          email: simonsayers@hotmail.com
Good Neighbours Support Service (Co-Ordinator) Elizabeth Foulds GNSS, Peninsular House, Wharf Rd, Portsmouth PO2 8HB
          Tel: 023 9289 9671
          email:
          elizabeth.foulds@portsmouth.anglican.org
Good Neighbours Group Development Advisor Mrs Angela Smith (as above)
          Tel: 07827 925327 (Mobile)
          email: angela.smith@portsmouth.anglican.org
Interdiocesan West Africa Link (Chair) Revd Canon Graham Morris, The Vicarage, 14 Argyll Street, Ryde, Isle of Wight PO33 3BZ   Tel: 01983 716435
          email: revcanongraham@gmail.com
Interfaith Adviser Revd Andy Marshall, Oasis Suite, Nuffield Centre, St Michael's Road, University of Portsmouth PO1 2ED
          Tel: 023 9284 3030
Mental Health Adviser Revd J. Hair, Fareham and Gosport Adult Mental Health Service, 219 West Street, Fareham PO16 0ET   Tel: 01329 825231
          email: James.Hair@southernhealth.nhs.uk
New Religious Movements Adviser Vacancy
Port Chaplain Revd Philip Hiscock, 36 Gomer Lane, Alverstoke, Gosport, Hants PO12 2SA
          Tel: 02392 346881
          email: philip.hiscock@ntlworld.com
Porvoo Adviser Vacancy
Diocesan Rural Officer and Rural Affairs Adviser (Mainland) Vacancy
Rural Affairs Adviser (IOW) Revd Graham Morris, The Vicarage, 14 Argyll Street, Ryde PO33 3BZ   Tel: 01983 716435
          email: graham.morris@btinternet.com

Urban Ministry Adviser Revd Canon Bob White, St Mary's Vicarage, Fratton Rd, Portsmouth PO1 5PA   Tel: 023 9282 2990
          email: revrcwhite@aol.com
World Development Adviser Canon Marion Mort, Rivendell, High St, Shirrell Heath, Southampton SO32 3JN   Tel: 01329 832178
          email: marion.mort@portsmouth.anglican.org
Evangelism Canon Deborah Sutton, 2 Taswwell Road, Southsea PO5 2RG   Tel: 023 9275 6926
          email: debtas@hotmail.com
The Mothers' Union Mrs Marion Wendon, 1 Maple Road, Southsea PO5 2JH   Tel: 023 9229 4869
          email: marion.wendon@ntlworld.com

CHURCHES
Dioc Advisory Committee for the Care of Churches (Chair) Very Revd David Brindley; (Secretary) Miss Catherine Gray
          email: catherine.gray@portsmouth.anglican.org
Closed Churches for Regular Worship Committee (Chair) Revd Wendy Kennedy (as above); (Secretary) Mrs Jenny Hollingsworth
          email: jenny.hollingsworth@portsmouth.anglican.org

MINISTRY
Widows Officers (Mainland) Revd Canon Peter Kelly 16 Rosedale Close, Titchfield, Fareham, Hants PO14 4EL   Tel: 01329 849567
          email: peterkelly@swanmore.net

DIOCESAN RECORD OFFICES
Portsmouth History Centre, Central Library, Portsmouth PO1 2DX   Tel: 023 9268 8046
          email: portsmouthhistorycentre@portsmouth.gov.uk
(For Gosport, Fareham, Havant and Portsmouth deaneries)
Hampshire Record Office, Sussex St, Winchester SO23 8TH   Tel: 01962 846154; Fax: 01962 878681; email: enquiries.archives@hants.gov.uk   (For Bishop's Waltham and Petersfield deaneries)
Isle of Wight County Record Office, 26 Hillside, Newport, Isle of Wight PO30 2EB Archivist Mr R. Smout   Tel: 01983 823821
          email: record.office @iow.gov.uk
(For the Isle of Wight deaneries)

AREA DEANS
ARCHDEACONRY OF THE MEON
Bishop's Waltham Revd Gregg Mensingh, The Rectory, 46 High Street, Botley, Southampton SO30 2EA   Tel: 01489 780 994
          email: gregg.mensingh@gmail.com
Fareham Revd Susan Allman, The Vicarage, 24 Frog Lane, Titchfield, Fareham, Hants PO14 4DU
          Tel: 01329 842324
          email: susanrev@hotmail.co.uk
Gosport Revd John Draper, The Rectory, Rowner Lane, Gosport PO13 9SO   Tel: 023 9258 7934
          email: stmrowner174@btinternet.com

Petersfield Revd Will Hughes, The Vicarage, 12 Dragon Street, Petersfield GU31 4AB
Tel: 01730 260213
email: revwillhughes@btinternet.com

ARCHDEACONRY OF PORTSDOWN

Havant Revd Jonathan Jeffrey, The Vicarage, Riders Lane, Leigh Park, Havant PO9 4QT
Tel: 023 9247 5276
email: stfrancis@lineone.net

Portsmouth Revd Canon Bob White, St Mary's Vicarage, Fratton Road, Portsmouth PO1 5PA
Tel: 023 9282 2687
email: revrcwhite@aol.com

ARCHDEACONRY OF THE ISLE OF WIGHT

East Wight Revd Chris Feak, 10 Elmbank Gardens, Sandown, Isle of Wight PO36 9SA
Tel: 01983 402548
email: c.feak123@btinternet.com

West Wight Revd Kath Abbott, The Rectory, Church Road, Wootton, Isle of Wight PO33 4PX
Tel: 01983 882213
email: abbott.kath@googlemail.com

DIOCESE OF ROCHESTER

Founded in 604. Kent west of the Medway, except for one parish in the south-west (CHICHESTER); the Medway Towns; the London boroughs of Bromley and Bexley, except for a few parishes (SOUTHWARK); one parish in East Sussex.

Population 1,299,000   Area 540 sq m
Full-time Stipendiary Parochial Clergy 200   Benefices 189
Parishes 217   Churches 266
www.rochester.anglican.org
Overseas link dioceses: Estonia, Harare, Kondoa, Mpwapwa.

BISHOP (106th)

Rt Revd James Langstaff, Bishopscourt, St Margaret's St, Rochester ME1 1TS
Tel: 01634 842471
Fax: 01634 831136
email: bishop.rochester@rochester.anglican.org
Chaplain Revd Lindsay Llewellyn-MacDuff
Tel: 01634 814439
email: bishops.chaplain@rochester.anglican.org

SUFFRAGAN BISHOP

TONBRIDGE Rt Revd Dr Brian Castle, Bishop's Lodge, 48 St Botolph's Rd, Sevenoaks TN13 3AG [2002]
Tel: 01732 456070
Fax: 01732 741449
email: bishop.tonbridge@rochester.anglican.org

HONORARY ASSISTANT BISHOPS

Rt Revd Dr Michael Nazir-Ali, c/o 70 Wimpole Street, London W1G 8AX   *Tel:* 020 3327 1130
email: oxtrad@gmail.com
Rt Revd Michael Turnbull, 67 Strand Street, Sandwich CT13 9HN   *Tel:* 01304 611389

CATHEDRAL CHURCH OF CHRIST AND THE BLESSED VIRGIN MARY

Dean Very Revd Dr Mark Beach [2012]
Chapter Office Garth House, The Precinct, Rochester ME1 1SX   *Tel:* 01634 843366
Fax: 01634 401410

Canons Residentiary
Revd Canon Dr Philip Hesketh, East Canonry, The Precinct, Rochester ME1 1TG [2005]
Tel: 01634 202898 (Home)
01634 810077 (Office)
email: canonpastor@rochestercathedral.org
Ven Simon Burton-Jones, The Archdeaconry, The Precinct, Rochester ME1 1TG [2010]
Tel: 01634 813533 (Home)
01634 560000 (Office)
email: archdeacon@rochestercathedral.org
Revd Canon Neil Thompson, Easter Garth, The Precinct, Rochester ME1 1TG [2008]
Tel: 01634 405265 (Home)
01634 810063 (Office)
email: precentor@rochestercathedral.org

Revd Canon Jean Kerr, Prebendal House, King's Orchard, The Precinct, Rochester ME1 1TG [2005]
Tel: 01634 844508 (Home)
email: jean.kerr@rochester.anglican.org
Chapter Clerk – Executive Director Mrs Gilly Wilford, Chapter Office
Tel: 01634 810060 (Office)
email: chapterclerk@rochestercathedral.org
Cathedral Organist and Director of Music Mr Scott Farrell, Chapter Office   *Tel:* 01634 810061
email: dom@rochestercathedral.org

ARCHDEACONS

BROMLEY AND BEXLEY Ven Dr Paul Wright, The Archdeaconry, The Glebe, Chislehurst BR7 5PX [2004]   *Tel:* 020 8467 8743
email: archdeacon.bromley@rochester.anglican.org
ROCHESTER Ven Simon Burton-Jones, The Archdeaconry, The Precinct, Rochester ME1 1TG [2010]   *Tel:* 01643 560000
email: archdeacon.rochester@rochester.anglican.org
TONBRIDGE Ven Clive Mansell, 3 The Ridings, Blackhurst Lane, Tunbridge Wells TN2 4RU [2002]   *Tel:* 01892 520660
email: archdeacon.tonbridge@rochester.anglican.org

CONVOCATION (MEMBERS OF THE HOUSE OF CLERGY OF THE GENERAL SYNOD)

Proctors for Clergy
Revd Mark Barker
Revd Julie Conalty
Revd Angus MacLeay
Ven Clive Mansell
Vacancy

MEMBERS OF THE HOUSE OF LAITY OF THE GENERAL SYNOD

Vacancy
Brig Ian Dobbie
Mr Philip French
Mr Gerald O'Brien
Mrs Angela Scott

DIOCESAN OFFICERS

Diocesan Secretary Geoff Marsh, St Nicholas Church, Boley Hill, Rochester ME1 1SL
　　　　　　　　　Tel: 01634 560000
　　email: geoff.marsh@rochester.anglican.org
Chancellor of Diocese Mr John Gallagher, Hardwicke Building, New Square, Lincoln's Inn, London WC2A 3SB　　　*Tel:* 020 7242 2523
Registrar of Diocese and Bishop's Legal Secretary Mr Owen Carew-Jones, Minerva House, 5 Montague Close, London SE1 9BB
　　　　　　　　　Tel: 020 7593 5110
　　　　email: a.harrison@wslaw.co.uk

DIOCESAN ORGANIZATIONS

Diocesan Office St Nicholas Church, Boley Hill, Rochester ME1 1SL　　　*Tel:* 01634 560000
　　email: enquiries@rochester.anglican.org
　　　　Web: www.rochester.anglican.org

ADMINISTRATION

Diocesan Synod (*Chair, House of Clergy*) Revd Canon Jim Stewart
　　email: jim.stewart@diocese-rochester.org
(*Chair, House of Laity*) Mr Philip French
　　email: philip.c.french@btinternet.com
(*Secretary*) Mr Geoff Marsh, Diocesan Office
Board of Finance (*Chair*) Rt Revd James Langstaff
(*Secretary*) Mr Geoff Marsh (*as above*)
(*Assistant Diocesan Secretary (Finance)*) Mr Martyn Burt, Diocesan Office
　　email: martyn.burt@rochester.anglican.org
(*Assistant Diocesan Secretary (Property)*) Mr Mark Trevett, Diocesan Office
　　email: mark.trevett@rochester.anglican.org
Director of Strategy and Implementation Mr Matthew Girt, Diocesan Office
　　email: matthew.girt@rochester.anglican.org
Pastoral Committee Mrs Suzanne Rogers, Diocesan Office
　　email: suzanne.rogers@rochester.anglican.org
Board of Patronage Mrs Suzanne Rogers (*as above*)
Designated Officer Mr Owen Carew-Jones, (*as above*)
Trusts Mr Geoff Marsh (*as above*)
Stewardship Adviser Mr Alan Strachan, Diocesan Office
　　email: alan.strachan@rochester.anglican.org

CHURCHES

Advisory Committee for the Care of Churches (*Chair*) Mr Derek Shilling, Ivy Bank, Shoreham Rd, Otford, Sevenoaks TN14 5RP　*Tel:* 01959 522059
(*DAC Secretary*) Mrs Sarah Anderson, Diocesan Office
　　email: sarah.anderson@rochester.anglican.org
Closed Churches Mr Geoff Marsh (*as above*)

EDUCATION

All at Diocesan Office unless otherwise stated
　　email: education@rochester.anglican.org
Board of Education (*Acting Chair*) Ven Clive Mansell (*as above*)

Secretary and Director Mr Alex Tear
　　email: alex.tear@rochester.anglican.org
Deputy Director Mr John Constanti
　　email: john.constanti@rochester.anglican.org
Assistant Director (*Schools*) Mrs Virginia Corbyn
　　email: virginia.corbyn@rochester.anglican.org
Diocesan Children's Work Adviser Mr Nick White
　　email: nick.white@rochester.anglican.org
Diocesan Youth Work Adviser Mrs Cheryl Trice
　　email: cheryl.trice@rochester.anglican.org
Rochester Diocesan Academy Trust Director Mr Ayub Khan
　　email: ayub.khan@rochester.anglican.org

FORMATION AND MINISTRY

Director Canon Christopher Dench, Diocesan Office
　　email: chris.dench@rochester.anglican.org
Assistant Director Revd Trevor Gerhardt, Diocesan Office
　　email: trevor.gerhardt@rochester.anglican.org
Training Officer Mrs Alison Callway, Diocesan Office
　　email: alison.callway@rochester.anglican.or
Directors of Ordinands Revd Glyn Ackerley, Vicarage, Butchers Hill, Shorne, Gravesend DA12 3EB　　　　　　*Tel:* 01474 822239
Revd Canon Elizabeth Walker, Vicarage, Comp Lane, Platt, Sevenoaks TN15 8NR
　　　　　　　　　Tel: 01732 885482
Warden of Lay Ministry Mrs Karen Senior, Diocesan Office
　　email: readers@rochester.anglican.org
Diocesan Co-ordinator of Spirituality Revd Susanne Carlsson, Diocesan Office
　　email: susanne.carlsson@rochester.anglican.org
Diocesan Vocations Adviser Revd Mark Griffin, St Luke's Vicarage, 30 Eardley Road, Sevenoaks TN13 1XT　　　　　*Tel:* 01732 452462
　　email: revd.mark.griffin@talk21.com

MISSION AND COMMUNITY ENGAGEMENT

Director Revd Canon Jean Kerr (*as above*)
Interfaith Adviser Ven Dr Paul Wright (*as above*)

COMMUNICATIONS

Director Lindy Mackenzie MBE, Diocesan Office
　　　　　　　　　Tel: 01634 560000
　　　　　　　07901 670257 (Mobile)
　　email: lindy.mackenzie@rochester.anglican.org
Communications Assistant Mrs Katerina Gerhardt, Diocesan Office　　　*Tel:* 01634 560000
　　　　　　　　　　　　email:
　　katerina.gerhardt@rochester.anglican.org

DIOCESAN RECORD OFFICES

Kent History and Library Centre, James Whatman Way, Maidstone ME14 1LQ
　　　　　　　　　Tel: 03000 413131
　　email: historyandlibrarycentre@kent.gov.uk

Medway Archives and Local Studies Centre, Gun Wharf, Dock Road, Chatham ME4 4TR
Tel: 01634 332714
email: malsc@medway.gov.uk
Bexley Local Studies and Archive Centre, Central Library, Townley Rd, Bexleyheath DA6 7HJ
Tel: 020 8301 1545
(*For the deaneries of Erith and Sidcup in the Archdeaconry of Bromley*)
Bromley Local Studies and Archives, Central Library, High St, Bromley, Kent BR1 1EX
Tel: 020 8460 9955
(*For the deaneries of Beckenham, Bromley and Orpington in the Archdeaconry of Bromley*)

AREA/RURAL DEANS
ARCHDEACONRY OF BROMLEY AND BEXLEY
Beckenham Revd Leon Carberry, The Vicarage, 15 St James' Avenue, Beckenham BR3 4HF
Tel: 020 8650 0420
email: leoncarberry@gmail.com
Bromley Revd Canon Katrina Barnes, St Augustine's Vicarage, Southborough Lane, Bromley BR2 8AT *Tel:* 020 8467 1351
email: katrina.barnes@diocese-rochester.org
Erith Revd Canon Antony Lane, Rectory, 1 Claremont Crescent, Dartford DA1 4RJ
Tel: 020 8301 5086
email: antony.lane@diocese-rochester.org
Orpington Revd Jay Colwill, The Vicarage, 165 Charterhouse Road, Orpington BR6 9EP
Tel: 01689 870923
email: jay.colwill@diocese-rochester.org
Sidcup Revd Colin Terry, The Vicarage, 64 Days Lane, Sidcup DA15 8JR *Tel:* 020 8300 0383
email: colin.terry.49@btinternet.com

ARCHDEACONRY OF ROCHESTER
Cobham Revd Jim Fletcher, The Rectory, 3 St John's Lane, Hartley, Longfield DA3 8ET
Tel: 01474 703819
email: jim.fletcher@diocese-rochester.org

Dartford Revd Ken Clark, Stone Rectory, Church Road, Stone, Greenhithe DA9 9BE
Tel: 01322 382076
email: kenofkent@tiscali.co.uk
Gillingham Revd Bonnie Appleton, The Rectory, 4 Drewery Drive, Wigmore, Gillingham ME8 0NX
Tel: 01634 231071
email: rector@stmattswigmore.org.uk
Gravesend Revd Sue Brewer, The Vicarage, 48 Old Road East, Gravesend DA12 1NR
Tel: 01474 352643
email: suec@brewer86.plus.com
Rochester Revd Penny Foreman, 28 Kingsway, Chatham ME5 7HT *Tel:* 01634 571220
email: penny.foreman@btinternet.com
Strood Revd David Green, The Vicarage, 3 Central Road, Strood, Rochester ME2 3HF
Tel: 01634 719052
email: revdavidgreen@blueyonder.co.uk

ARCHDEACONRY OF TONBRIDGE
Malling Revd Matthew Buchan, The Rectory, 73 Rectory Lane North, Leybourne, West Malling ME19 5HD *Tel:* 01732 842187
email: matthew.buchan@diocese-rochester.org
Paddock Wood Revd Bryan Knapp, The Vicarage, 169 Maidstone Road, Paddock Wood, Tonbridge TN12 6DZ *Tel:* 01892 833917
email: bryan@standrewspw.org.uk
Sevenoaks Revd Mark Griffin, St Luke's Vicarage, 30 Eardley Road, Sevenoaks TN13 1XT
Tel: 01732 452462
email: revd.mark.griffin@talk21.com
Shoreham Revd Stephen Jones, The Rectory, Bates Hill, Ightham, Sevenoaks TN15 9BG
Tel: 01732 886827
email: srjones49@greenbee.net
Tonbridge Revd Mark Brown, Vicarage, Church St, Tonbridge TN9 1HD *Tel:* 01732 770962
email: mark@tonbridgeparishchurch.org.uk
Tunbridge Wells Revd Brian Senior, St Philip's Vicarage, Birken Rd, Tunbridge Wells TN2 3TE
Tel: 01892 512071
email: brian@bsenior.fsnet.co.uk

BISHOP (10th)
Rt Revd Dr Alan Gregory Clayton Smith, Abbey Gate House, Abbey Mill Lane, St Albans AL3 4HD   *Tel:* 01727 853305
                    Fax: 01727 846715
        email: bishop@stalbans.anglican.org
Chaplain Capt Andrew Crooks, CA
                    Tel: 01727 853305
        email: chaplain@stalbans.anglican.org
Secretaries Mrs Mary Handford, Mrs Rosamund Adlard, Mrs Claire Wood
        email: bishop@stalbans.anglican.org

SUFFRAGAN BISHOPS
BEDFORD Rt Revd Richard Atkinson, Bishop's Lodge, Bedford Rd, Cardington MK44 3SS [2003]
                    Tel: 01234 831432
                    Fax: 01234 831484
        email: bishopbedford@stalbans.anglican.org
HERTFORD Vacancy
        email: bishophertford@stalbans.anglican.org

HONORARY ASSISTANT BISHOPS
Rt Revd Robin J. N. Smith, 7 Aysgarth Rd, Redbourn, St Albans AL3 7PJ [2002]
                    Tel: 01582 791964
Rt Revd J. W. Gladwin, The White House, 131A Marford Road, Wheathampstead, St Albans AL4 8NH [2010]   *Tel:* 01582 834223
Rt Revd N. Banks, Parkside House, Abbey Mill Lane, St Albans AL3 4HE [2013]   *Tel:* 01727 836358
Rt Revd Dr S. Venner, 81 King Harry Road, St Albans AL3 4AS [2013]   *Tel:* 01727 831704

CATHEDRAL AND ABBEY CHURCH OF SAINT ALBAN
Dean Very Revd Dr Jeffrey John, The Old Rectory, Sumpter Yard, St Albans AL1 1BY [2004]
                    Tel: 01727 890202
        email: dean@stalbanscathedral.org
Cathedral Office The Chapter House, Sumpter Yard, St Albans AL1 1BY   *Tel:* 01727 890200
                    Fax: 01727 850944
        email: mail@stalbanscathedral.org
        Web: www.stalbanscathedral.org

Canons Residentiary
Canon Richard Watson (*Sub-Dean*), Deanery Barn, Sumpter Yard, St Albans AL1 1BY [2011]
                    Tel: 01727 890201
        email: subdean@stalbanscathedral.org
Canon Kevin Walton (*Canon Chancellor*), 2 Sumpter Yard, St Albans AL1 1BY [2008]
                    Tel: 01727 890242
        email: canon@stalbanscathedral.org
Canon John Kiddle (*Director of Mission*), 19 Stanbury Avenue, Watford WD17 3HW [2010]
                    Tel: 01727 818146
        email: john.kiddle@stalbans.anglican.org
Canon Dr Tim Bull (*Director of Ministry and Ministry Development Officer*), 43 Holywell Hill, St Albans AL1 1HE [2013]   *Tel:* 01727 841116
        email: dome@stalbans.anglican.org
Minor Canons
Young People Revd Sally Jones, 2 Dean Moore Close, St Albans AL1 1DW [2014]
                    Tel: 01727 890206
        email: chaplain@stalbanscathedral.org
Precentor Revd Paul Arbuthnot, 1 The Deanery, Sumpter Yard, St Albans AL1 1BY [2012]
                    Tel: 01727 890207
        email: precentor@stalbanscathedral.org
Cathedral Administrator and Clerk to the Chapter Ms Heather Smith, Cathedral Office
                    Tel: 01727 890208
        email: admin@stalbanscathedral.org
Master of the Music Mr Andrew Lucas, 31 Abbey Mill Lane, St Albans AL3 4HA
                    Tel: 01727 890245
        email: music@stalbanscathedral.org
Assistant Master of the Music and Director of the Abbey Girls Choir Mr Tom Winpenny, 34 Orchard St, St Albans AL3 4HL
                    Tel: 01727 890245
        email: amom@stalbanscathedral.org
Cathedral Education Officer Steve Clarke, Education Centre, Sumpter Yard, St Albans AL1 1BY   *Tel:* 01727 890262
        email: education@stalbanscathedral.org
Cathedral Architect Mr Richard Griffiths
Archaeological Consultant Prof Martin Biddle

ARCHDEACONS

ST ALBANS Ven Jonathan Smith, 6 Sopwell Lane, St Albans AL1 1RR [2002]   *Tel:* 01727 847212
                                          Fax: 01727 848311
    email: archdstalbans@stalbans.anglican.org
BEDFORD Ven Paul Hughes, 17 Lansdowne Rd, Luton LU3 1EE [2003]   *Tel:* 01582 730722
                                          Fax: 01582 877354
    email: archdbedf@stalbans.anglican.org
HERTFORD Ven Dr Trevor Jones, Glebe House, St Mary's Lane, Hertingfordbury, Hertford SG14 2LE [1997]   *Tel:* 01992 581629
                                          Fax: 01992 558745
    email: archdhert@stalbans.anglican.org

CONVOCATION (MEMBERS OF THE HOUSE OF CLERGY OF THE GENERAL SYNOD)
Proctors for Clergy
Revd Canon John Kiddle
Revd Canon Richard Hibbert
Ven Jonathan Smith
Revd Anne Hollinghurst
Revd Dr Joan Spreadbury

MEMBERS OF THE HOUSE OF LAITY OF THE GENERAL SYNOD
Mr Samuel Follett
Mr Simon Baynes
Dr Edmund Marshall
Mr William Seddon
Canon Philip McDonough
Mrs Christina Rees

DIOCESAN OFFICERS
Dioc Secretary Miss Susan Pope, Holywell Lodge, 41 Holywell Hill, St Albans AL1 1HE
                                          Tel: 01727 854532
                                          Fax: 01727 844469
    email: mail@stalbans.anglican.org
Chancellor of Diocese His Honour the Worshipful Roger G. Kaye QC, Holywell Lodge, 41 Holywell Hill, St Albans AL1 1HD   *Tel:* 01727 865765
Registrar of Diocese and Bishop's Legal Secretary Mr Lee Coley LLB (Hons), LLM (Canon Law), 1 The Sanctuary, Westminster, London SW1P 3JT
    Tel: 0207 2225371 *Fax:* 0207 799 2781 (day);
                                          0207 222 7502 (night)
    email: stalbans.registry@1thesanctuary.com
Deputy Registrar Mr Clifford Woodroffe
Surveyor Mr Alastair Woodgate, c/o 41 Holywell Hill, St Albans AL1 1HE   *Tel:* 01727 854516

DIOCESAN ORGANIZATIONS
Diocesan Office Holywell Lodge, 41 Holywell Hill, St Albans AL1 1HE   *Tel:* 01727 854532
                                          Fax: 01727 844469
    email: mail@stalbans.anglican.org
    Web: www.stalbans.anglican.org

ADMINISTRATION
Dioc Synod (Chairman, House of Clergy) Revd Jo Loveridge

(Chairman, House of Laity) Mr John Wallace, 14 Church St, Leighton Buzzard LU7 7BT
                                          Tel: 01525 375133
(Secretary) Miss Susan Pope, Dioc Office
Board of Finance (Chairman) Canon David Nye
(Secretary) Miss Susan Pope *(as above)*
Financial Secretary Mr Martin Bishop, Dioc Office
Estates Secretary Mrs Michèle Manders, Dioc Office
Board of Patronage Mrs Emma Critchley, Dioc Office
Designated Officers (Joint) Mr Lee Coley and Miss Susan Pope *(as above)*
Mission and Pastoral Committee Mrs Emma Critchley *(as above)*
Trusts Mr Nigel Benger, Dioc Office

CHURCHES
Advisory Committee for the Care of Churches (Chairman) Dr Christopher Green, Dioc Office; *(Secretary)* Mrs Emma Critchley *(as above)*

EDUCATION
Dioc Education and Resources Centre Dioc Office
                                          Tel: 01727 854532
                                          Fax: 01727 844469
Director of Education Canon Jon Reynolds *(as above)*
Deputy Director of Education Mr David Morton *(as above)*
RE Adviser Mrs Jane Chipperton *(as above)*

MINISTRY
Director of Ordinands Revd Canon Susan Groom
                                          Tel: 01727 833777
Ministerial Development Officer/Director of Ministry Revd Canon Dr Tim Bull
Parish Development Officer Revd Jeanette Gosney
                                          Tel: 01727 818141
Officer for IME 4–7 Revd Ysmena Pentalow, Dioc Office   *Tel:* 01727 818154
Reader Ministry Officer Ms Lauryn Awbrey, Dioc Office   *Tel:* 01727 818154
Associate Director of Ordinands Revd Emma Coley
Board of Readers' Work Mrs Margaret Tinsley, 145 The Ridgeway, St Albans AL4 9XA
                                          Tel: 01727 859528
Mr Richard Osborn, 41 Tiverton Rd, Potters Bar EN6 5HX   *Tel:* 01707 657491
Youth Officer Mr Dean Pusey, Dioc Office
Children's Work Adviser Revd Ruth Pyke, Dioc Office

MISSIONARY AND ECUMENICAL
Ecumenical Officers
Bedford Archdeaconry Revd Stephen Toze
                          email: s@steve777.plus.com
Hertford Archdeaconry Revd Paul Seymour
                  email: revpaulseymour@btinternet.com
St Albans Archdeaconry Revd Charmaine Sabey-Corkingdale
                  email: csabeycorkingdale@btinternet.com
Board for Church and Society Mr Simon Best *(Chairman)*, The Hollies, Kimpton Rd, Peters Green LU2 9QW

International Mission Council Revd Ray Porter, 24 Bevington Way, Eynesbury, St Neots PE19 2HQ
Tel: 01480 211839
Workplace Matters Revd Dr John Scott, 41 Holywell Hill, St Albans AL1 1HE
Tel: 01727 869461

PRESS AND PUBLICATIONS
Dioc Communications Officer Mr Arun Kataria, Dioc Office
Tel: 01727 818110
Fax: 01727 844469
email: comms@stalbans.anglican.org
Editor of Dioc Directory Miss Susan Pope (*as above*)
Dioc Leaflet Mrs Claudia Ashley-Brown (*as above*)

DIOCESAN RECORD OFFICES
County Hall, Hertford SG13 8DE *Tel:* 01992 555105 (*For diocesan records and parish records for St Albans and Hertford archdeaconries*)
County Hall, Bedford MK42 9AP *County Archivist* Mr Kevin Ward *Tel:* 01234 63222 Ext 277 (*For parish records for Bedford archdeaconry*)

CHURCH AND SOCIETY
Director of Mission Canon John Kiddle, Dioc Office
Tel: 01727 851748
Church and Community Officer Mr Christopher Neilson

STEWARDSHIP
Mission Resourcing Officer Mr Chris Wainman Dioc Office
Tel: 01727 854532

RURAL DEANS
ARCHDEACONRY OF ST ALBANS
Berkhamsted Revd Jonathan Gordon, St Mary's Rectory, 80 High Street, Northchurch, Berkhamsted HP4 3QW
Tel: 01442 871547
Hemel Hempstead Revd Canon David Lawson, St Mary's Vicarage, 7 Belswain's Lane, Hemel Hempstead HP3 9PN
Tel: 01442 261610
Hitchin Revd Ann Pollington, The Vicarage, Stevenage Road, St Ippolyts, Hitchin SG4 7PE
Tel: 01462 457552
Rickmansworth Revd Deborah Snowball, The Vicarage, Bury Lane, Rickmansworth WD3 1ED
Tel: 01923 772627
St Albans Revd Canon David Ridgeway, St Stephen's Vicarage, 14 Watling Rd, St Albans AL1 2PX
Tel: 01727 862598
Watford Revd Canon David Middlebrook, St Luke's Vicarage, Devereux Drive, Watford WD17 3DD
Tel: 01923 246161

Wheathampstead Revd Will Gibbs, The Vicarage, 49 Church End, Redbourn, St Albans AL3 7DU
Tel: 01582 791669

ARCHDEACONRY OF BEDFORD
Ampthill and Shefford Revd Canon Lynda Klimas, The Rectory, Clophill Road, Maulden, Bedford MK45 2AA
Tel: 01525 403139
Bedford Revd Canon Richard Hibbert, Christ Church Vicarage, 115 Denmark Street, Bedford MK40 3TJ
Tel: 01234 359342
Biggleswade Revd Lindsay Dew
Tel: 01462 743617
Dunstable Revd Bernard Minton, St Barnabas' Vicarage, Vicarage Road, Linslade, Leighton Buzzard LU7 2LP
Tel: 01525 372149
Luton Revd Janet Mackenzie, St Augustine's Vicarage, 215 Icknield Way, Luton LU3 2JR
Tel: 01582 572415
Sharnbrook Revd Robert Evens, The Rectory, 81 High Street, Sharnbrook, Bedford MK44 1PE
Tel: 01234 782000

ARCHDEACONRY OF HERTFORD
Barnet Revd Canon Michael Burns, The Vicarage, 8 Dugdale Hill Lane, Potters Bar EN6 2DW
Tel: 01707 661266
Bishop's Stortford (Interim) Revd Anthony Giles, The Rectory, 1 Dovedale, High Wych, Sawbridgeworth CM21 0DT
Tel: 01279 726476
Buntingford Revd Canon Richard Morgan, The Rectory, Church Lane, Therefield, Royston SG8 9QD
Tel: 01763 287364
Cheshunt Revd Rachel Phillips, The Vicarage, 58 Hill Rise, Cuffley, Potters Bar EN6 4RG
Tel: 01707 874126
Welwyn and Hatfield Revd Dr David Munchin, The Rectory, 2 Ottway Walk, Welwyn AL6 9AS
Tel: 01438 714150
Hertford and Ware (Joint Rural Dean) Revd Canon Pauline Higham, Hertford Hundred House, 1 Little Berkhamsted Lane, Little Berkhamsted Hertford SG13 8LU
Tel: 01707 875940
Hertford and Ware (Joint Rural Dean) Revd Nick Sharp, Little Amwell Vicarage, 17 Barclay Close, Hertford Heath, Hertford SG13 7RW
Tel: 01992 589147
Stevenage Revd Timothy Horlock, St Peter's Vicarage, 1 The Willows, Broadwater, Stevenage SG2 8AN
Tel: 01438 221024

DIOCESE OF ST EDMUNDSBURY AND IPSWICH

Founded in 1914. Suffolk, except for a small area in the north-east (NORWICH); one parish in Essex.

Population 656,000   Area 1,440 sq m
Full-time Stipendiary Parochial Clergy 133   Benefices 129
Parishes 446   Churches 478
www.stedmundsbury.anglican.org
Overseas link dioceses: Hassalt (Belgium),
Kagera (Tanzania).

BISHOP
Vacancy Bishop's House, 4 Park Road, Ipswich IP1 3ST   *Tel:* 01473 252829
email: bishops.office@cofesuffolk.org

ACTING BISHOP
Rt Revd Dr David Thomson, Bishop of Huntingdon
Bishop's Chaplain Revd Mary Sokanovic (*same address and telephone*)
email: mary.sokanovic@cofesuffolk.org
Bishop's Secretary Mrs Denise Rudland (*same address and telephone*)
email: denise.rudland@cofesuffolk.org
Assistant Secretary Mrs Julia Venmore-Rowland (*same address and telephone*)
email: juliavenmore-rowland@cofesuffolk.org
Assistant Secretary Vacancy (*same address and telephone*)

SUFFRAGAN BISHOP
Vacancy

CATHEDRAL CHURCH OF ST JAMES AND ST EDMUND, BURY ST EDMUNDS
Dean Very Revd Dr Frances Ward, The Deanery, Bury St Edmunds IP33 1RS [2010]
Tel: 01284 748722
email: dean@stedscathedral.org
Cathedral Office Abbey House, Angel Hill, Bury St Edmunds IP33 1LS   *Tel:* 01284 748720
Fax: 01284 768655
email: cathedral.secretary@stedscathedral.org
Canons Residentiary
Precentor Revd Canon Philip Banks, 1 Abbey Precincts, Bury St Edmunds IP33 1RS [2012]
Tel: 01284 748724
email: precentor@stedscathedral.org
Sub-Dean and Canon Pastor Revd Canon Matthew Vernon, 2 Abbey Precincts, Bury St Edmunds IP33 1RS [2009]   *Tel:* 01284 701472
email: canon.pastor@stedscathedral.org
Administrator Justine Horseman Sewell
Tel: 01284 748728
email:
cathedral.administrator@stedscathedral.org
PR, Pilgrimage and Visits Manager Mrs Sarah Friswell, Cathedral Office   *Tel:* 01284 748726
email: pr.manager@stedscathedral.org

Head of Finance Mrs Elizabeth Gibson, Cathedral Office   *Tel:* 01284 748727
email: finance.manager@stedscathedral.org
Children's Education Officer Mrs Helen Woodroffe, Cathedral Office   *Tel:* 01284 747467
email: discoverycentre@stedscathedral.org
Director of Music Mr James Thomas, Cathedral Office   *Tel:* 01284 748379
email: dom@stedscathedral.org
Assistant Director of Music Mr Dan Soper, Cathedral Office   *Tel:* 01284 748737
email: adom@stedscathedral.org
Head Verger Mr Duncan Withers, Cathedral Office
Tel: 01284 748729
email: head.verger@stedscathedral.org

ARCHDEACONS
SUDBURY Ven Dr David Jenkins, Sudbury Lodge, Stanningfield Rd, Great Whelnetham, Bury St Edmunds IP30 0TL [2010]
Tel and *Fax:* 01284 386942
email: archdeacon.david@cofesuffolk.org
SUFFOLK Ven Ian Morgan, Glebe House, The Street, Ashfield cum Thorpe, Stowmarket IP14 6LX [2012]   *Tel:* 01728 685497
Fax: 01728 685969
email: archdeacon.ian@ cofesuffolk.org

CONVOCATION (MEMBERS OF THE HOUSE OF CLERGY OF THE GENERAL SYNOD)
Proctors for Clergy
Revd Canon Jonathan Alderton-Ford
Revd Andrew Dotchin
Revd Tony Redman

MEMBERS OF THE HOUSE OF LAITY OF THE GENERAL SYNOD
Canon Tim Allen
Mrs Margaret Condick
Mr Peter Smith

DIOCESAN OFFICERS
Diocesan Secretary Canon Nicholas Edgell, Diocesan Office, St Nicholas Centre, 4 Cutler St, Ipswich IP1 1UQ   *Tel:* 01473 298589
Fax: 01473 298501
email: diocesan.secretary@cofesuffolk.org

Chancellor of Diocese Mr David Etherington QC, 20–32 Museum St, Ipswich IP1 1HZ
Deputy Chancellor of Diocese His Honour Judge Anthony Leonard (*as above*)
Registrar of Diocese and Bishop's Legal Secretary Mr James Hall, 20–32 Museum St, Ipswich IP1 1HZ
Tel: 01473 232300
Fax: 01473 230524
email: james-hall@birketts.co.uk
Deputy Registrar Stuart Jones *Tel:* 01603 756501
email: stuart-jones@birketts.co.uk

DIOCESAN ORGANIZATIONS
Diocesan Office St Nicholas Centre, 4 Cutler St, Ipswich IP1 1UQ *Tel:* 01473 298500
Fax: 01473 298501
email: dbf@cofesuffolk.org

ADMINISTRATION
Diocesan Secretary Canon Nicholas Edgell, Dioc Office
Deputy Diocesan Secretary Ms Nicola Andrews, Dioc Office
Assistant Diocesan Secretaries Revd Canon Graham Hedger, Dioc Office, Mr Gavin Stone, Dioc Office
Pastoral and DAC Secretary Mr James Halsall
Diocesan Accountant Mrs Katy Reade
Diocesan Surveyor Mr Paul Edwards MRICS, 31 Lower Brook Street, Ipswich IP4 1AQ
Tel: 01473 235674
email: pjbe@ews-eastanglia.co.uk
Designated Officer Revd Canon Graham Hedger Dioc Office
Diocesan Synod (*Chairman, House of Clergy*) Revd Canon Jonathan Alderton-Ford; (*Chairman, House of Laity*) Canon Michael Wilde; (*Secretary*) Canon Nicholas Edgell, Dioc Office

CHURCHES
Advisory Committee for the Care of Churches (*Chairman*) Canon Tim Allen, Bell House, Quay St, Orford, Woodbridge IP12 2NU *Tel:* 01394 450789
(*Secretary*) Mr James Halsall, Dioc Office

COUNSELLING
Adviser in Pastoral Care and Counselling Revd Canon Harry Edwards, Dunwich View, The Green, Walberswick, Southwold IP18 6TP
Tel: 07748 986022
email: harry@psalm23.demon.co.uk

MINISTRY
Vocations Adviser (*Sudbury*) Vacancy
Vocations Adviser (*Suffolk*) Revd Betty Mockford, 10 Castle Brooks, Framlingham IP13 9SF
Tel: 01728 724193
Diocesan Director of Ordinands and New Ministers Vacancy
Diocesan Director of Mission Revd Dave Gardner, Dioc Office *Tel:* 01473 298521
email: dave.gardner@cofesuffolk.org

Diocesan Director of Ministry, Education and Training Revd Dr John Parr, Dioc Office
Tel: 01473 298553
email: john.parr@cofesuffolk.org
Lay Training Officer Revd David Herrick, Dioc Office *Tel:* 01473 298552
email: david.herrick@cofesuffolk.org
Warden of Readers and Licensed Lay Ministers Officer, Revd David Herrick, Dioc Office
Tel: 01473 298552
email: david.herrick@cofesuffolk.org
Diocesan Children's Officer and Cathedral Education Officer Mrs Helen Woodroffe, The Discovery Centre, St Edmundsbury Cathedral, Angel Hill, Bury St Edmunds IP33 1LS
Tel and *Fax:* 01284 748731
email: helen@discoveryc.fsnet.co.uk
Diocesan Widows Officers Vacancy
Clergy Retirement Officer Revd Ian Hooper, 26 Drake Close, Stowmarket IP14 1UP
Tel: 01449 770179
email: ianavrilhooper126@btinternet.com

SCHOOLS
Dioc Director of Education Mrs Jane Sheat, Dioc Office *Tel:* 01473 298570
email: jane.sheat@cofesuffolk.org
Deputy Dioc Director of Education Mr Alister Gourlay, Dioc Office *Tel:* 01473 298570
email: alister.gourlay@cofesuffolk.org
Dioc Schools Adviser Mrs Helen Matter, Dioc Office
email: helen.matter@cofesuffolk.org

MISSION AND PUBLIC AFFAIRS
Community Affairs Adviser Mrs Kathleen Ben Rabha, Dioc Office
kathleen.benrabha@cofesuffolk.org
Agricultural Chaplain Revd Canon Sally Fogden, Meadow Farm, Sapiston, Bury St Edmunds IP31 1RX *Tel:* 01359 268923
email: sallyfogden@tiscali.co.uk
Church Heritage and Tourism Officer Ms Marion Welham, Dioc Office *Tel:* 07879 634525
email: marion.welham@cofesuffolk.org
Bishop's Ecumenical Adviser Revd Canon Dr Peter Mortimer, 20 Leggart Drive, Bramford, Ipswich IP8 4ET *Tel:* 01473 747419
email: peter.mortimer@hotmail.co.uk
Bishop's Inter Faith Adviser Revd Canon Charles Jenkin, The Vicarage, 18 Kingsfield Avenue, Ipswich IP1 3TA *Tel:* 01473 289001
e mail: c.jenkin@tiscali.co.uk
Chaplain to the Deaf Community Vacancy

COMMUNICATIONS
Diocesan Communications Officer Vacancy, Dioc Office
Bishop's Press Officer John Howard, Dioc Office
email: john.howard@cofesuffolk.org

DIOCESAN RECORD OFFICES

77 Raingate St, Bury St Edmunds IP33 2AR
Tel: 01284 352352 Ext 2352 (*For parish records for Sudbury archdeaconry and Hadleigh deanery*)
Gatacre Rd, Ipswich IP1 2LQ *Tel:* 01473 264541
(*For parish records for Ipswich and Suffolk archdeaconries*)
The Central Library, Lowestoft NR32 1DR
Tel: 01502 405357 (*For parish records for NE Suffolk parishes*)

SPIRITUALITY

Diocesan Spiritual Director for Cursillo Revd Chris Ramsey
        email: revchrisramsey@googlemail.com
Lay Director for Cursillo Mrs Gwen Runnacles, The Bungalow, Church Hill, Burstall, Ipswich IP8 3DU   *Tel:* 01473 652494
        email: gwen.runnacles@virgin.net

RURAL DEANS
ARCHDEACONRY OF IPSWICH

Bosmere Revd Diane Williams, 10 Meadow View, Needham Market, Ipswich IP6 8RH
        Tel: 01449 720316
        email: diane.rev@btinternet.com
Colneys Vacancy
Hadleigh Very Revd Martin Thrower, The Deanery, Church Street, Hadleigh IP7 5DT
        Tel: 01473 822218
        email: martin.thrower@btinternet.com
Ipswich Revd Canon Charles Jenkin, The Vicarage, 18 Kingsfield Ave, Ipswich IP1 3TA
        Tel: 01473 289001
        email: c.jenkin@tiscali.co.uk
Samford Revd Don Mehen, 19 The Link, Bentley, Ipswich IP9 2DJ   *Tel:* 01473 310383
        email: donmehen@googlemail.com
Stowmarket Revd Canon Barbara Bilston, Boy's Hall, Ward Green, Old Newton, Stowmarket IP14 4EY   *Tel:* 01449 781253
        email: b.b.bilston@open.ac.uk
Woodbridge Revd Canon Clare Sanders, The Rectory, Woodbridge Road, Grundisburgh, Woodbridge IP13 6UF   *Tel:* 01473 735183
        email: revclaresanders@tiscali.co.uk

ARCHDEACONRY OF SUDBURY

Clare Revd Cheryl Collins, The Rectory, New Road, Chevington, Bury St Edmunds IP29 5QL
        Tel: 01284 850843
        email: revcherylc@aol.com
Ixworth Revd John Fulton, Rectory, Church Lane, Hepworth, Diss IP22 2PU   *Tel:* 01359 250285
        email: jwfulton@ukonline.co.uk
Lavenham Revd Stephen Earl, The Rectory, Church Street, Lavenham, Sudbury CO10 9SA
        Tel: 01787 247244
        email: earls2222@btinternet.com
Mildenhall Revd Canon Stephen Mitchell, All Saints Vicarage, The Street, Gazeley, Newmarket CB8 8RB   *Tel:* 01638 552630
        email: smitch4517@aol.com
Sudbury Revd Canon Greg Webb, The Rectory, Christopher Lane, Sudbury CO10 2AS
        Tel: 01787 372611
        email: gregorywebb@btinternet.com
Thingoe Revd Mark Haworth, The Rectory, 59 Bennett Avenue, Bury St Edmunds IP33 3JJ
        Tel: 01284 755374
        email: rectornorthburyteam@btinternet.com

ARCHDEACONRY OF SUFFOLK

Hartismere Vacancy
Hoxne Revd Susan Loxton, The Rectory, Doctor Lane, Stradbroke IP21 5HU
        Tel: 01379 388493
        email: revsusan95@gmail.com
Loes Revd Canon Deirdre Parmenter, Avalon, Marlesford Road, Campsea Ash, Woodbridge IP13 0QQ   *Tel:* 01728 748145
        email: deirdreparmenter@gmail.com
Saxmundham Revd Canon Christine Redgrave, 1 Oakwood Park, Yoxford, Saxmundham IP17 3JU
        Tel: 01728 667095
        email: redgrave460@btinternet.com
Waveney and Blyth Revd Simon Pitcher, The Vicarage, Gardner Road, Southwold IP18 6HJ
        Tel: 01502 725424
        email: revsimon@talktalk.net

Founded in 1075, formerly Sherborne (AD 705) and Ramsbury (AD 909). Wiltshire, except for the northern quarter (BRISTOL); Dorset, except for an area in the east (WINCHESTER); a small area of Hampshire; a parish in Devon.

Population 927,000   Area 2,050 sq m
Full-time Stipendiary Parochial Clergy 192   Benefices 146
Parishes 452   Churches 572
www.salisbury.anglican.org
Overseas link provinces and dioceses: Episcopal Church of the Sudan, Evreux (France).

BISHOP (78th)
Rt Revd Nicholas Holtam, South Canonry, 71 The Close, Salisbury SP1 2ER [2011]
Tel: 01722 334031
Fax: 01722 413112
email: bishop.salisbury@salisbury.anglican.org
[Nicholas Sarum]

SUFFRAGAN BISHOPS
SHERBORNE Rt Revd Dr Graham Kings, Sherborne Office, St Nicholas' Church Centre, 30 Wareham Road, Corfe Mullen, Wimborne BH21 3LE [2009]
Tel: 01202 659427
Fax: 01202 691418
email: g.sherborne@salisbury.anglican.org
RAMSBURY Rt Revd Edward Condry, Diocesan Office, Church House, Crane Street, Salisbury, SP1 2QB [2012]
Tel: 01722 438662
Fax: 01722 411990
email: e.ramsbury@salisbury.anglican.org

CATHEDRAL CHURCH OF THE BLESSED VIRGIN MARY
Dean Very Revd June Osborne, The Deanery, 7 The Close, Salisbury SP1 2EF [2004]
Dean's Office 6 The Close, Salisbury SP1 2EF
Tel: 01722 555110
Fax: 01722 555155
email: thedean@salcath.co.uk
Web: www.salisburycathedral.org.uk
Canons Residentiary
Precentor Canon Tom Clammer, Hungerford Chantry, 54 The Close, Salisbury SP1 2EL [2012]
Office Dept of Liturgy and Music, Ladywell, 33 The Close, Salisbury SP1 2EJ   *Tel:* 01722 555125
Fax: 01722 555117
email: precentor@salcath.co.uk
Chancellor Canon Edward Probert, 24 The Close, Salisbury SP1 2EH [2004]   *Tel:* 01722 555193
Office: Chapter Office, 6 The Close, Salisbury SP1 2EF
Tel: 01722 555189
Fax: 01722 555109
email: chancellor@salcath.co.uk
Treasurer Canon Sarah Mullally, 23 The Close, Salisbury SP1 2EH [2012]   *Tel:* 01722 555177
Office: Chapter Office, 6 The Close (*as above*)
Tel: 01722 555186
Fax: 01722 555109
email: treasurer@salcath.co.uk

Vicar of the Close Canon Ian Woodward, 68a The Close, Salisbury SP1 2ES   *Tel:* 01722 555192
email: voc@salcath.co.uk
Chapter Clerk Mrs Katie Sporle, Chapter Office, 6 The Close, Salisbury SP1 2EF
Tel: 01722 555105
Fax: 01722 555109
email: chapterclerk@salcath.co.uk
Visitors Dept Mr David Coulthard, Ladywell, 33 The Close, Salisbury SP1 2EJ   *Tel:* 01722 555120
Fax: 01722 555116
email: d.coulthard@salcath.co.uk
Education Centre Mrs Susan Hayter (*Administrator*), Wren Hall, 56c The Close, Salisbury SP1 2EL   *Tel:* 01722 555180
email: wrenhall@salcath.co.uk
Director of Music Mr David Halls, Dept of Liturgy and Music (*as above*)   *Tel:* 01722 555127
email: d.halls@salcath.co.uk

ARCHDEACONS
SHERBORNE Ven Paul Taylor, Aldhelm House, West Stafford, Dorchester DT2 8AB [2004]
Tel: 01202 659427
Fax: 01202 691418
email: adsherborne@salisbury.anglican.org
DORSET Ven Stephen Waine, 28 Merriefield Drive, Broadstone, BH18 8BP [2010]   *Tel:* 01202 659427
Fax: 01202 691418
email: addorset@salisbury.anglican.org
WILTS Ven Ruth Worsley, Southbroom House, London Road, Devizes SN10 1LT [2013]
Tel: 01722 438662
Fax: 01722 411990
email: adwilts@salisbury.anglican.org
SARUM Ven Alan Jeans, Herbert House, 118 Lower Rd, Lower Bemerton, Salisbury SP2 9NW [2003]
Tel: 01722 438662
Fax: 01722 411990
email: adsarum@salisbury.anglican.org

CONVOCATION (MEMBERS OF THE HOUSE OF CLERGY OF THE GENERAL SYNOD)
Proctors for Clergy
Canon Jane Charman
Canon Richard Franklin
Canon Nigel LLoyd

Ven Alan Jeans
Revd Christopher Strain

MEMBERS OF THE HOUSE OF LAITY OF THE GENERAL SYNOD
Mr Paul Boyd-Lee
Dr Ian Bromilow
Mrs Christine Corteen
Mr Christopher Fielden
Mr Robert Key
Mrs Deborah McIsaac

DIOCESAN OFFICERS
Dioc Secretary Mrs Lucinda Herklots, Church House, Crane St, Salisbury SP1 2QB
Tel: 01722 411922
Fax: 01722 411990
Chancellor of Diocese His Honour Judge Samuel Wiggs, c/o Dioc Office
Registrar of Diocese and Bishop's Legal Secretary Mr Andrew Johnson, Minster Chambers, 42–44 Castle St, Salisbury SP1 3TX
Tel: 01722 411141
Fax: 01722 411566

DIOCESAN ORGANIZATIONS
Diocesan Office Church House, Crane St, Salisbury SP1 2QB *Tel:* 01722 411922
Fax: 01722 411990
email: enquiries@salisbury.anglican.org
Web: www.salisbury.anglican.org

ADMINISTRATION
Dioc Secretary Mrs Lucinda Herklots, Dioc Office
Deputy Dioc Secretary Mr Stephen Dawson, Dioc Office
Dioc Synod (Chairman, House of Clergy) Canon Antony MacRow-Wood, St George's Rectory, 99 Darby's Lane, Oakdale, Poole BH15 3EU
Tel: 01202 660612
(Chairman, House of Laity) Mr Robert Key, 4 Old Street, Salisbury SP2 8JL *Tel:* 01722 326622
(Secretary) Mrs Lucinda Herklots, Dioc Office
Board of Finance (Chairman) Mr Gil Williams, Princes Farm, Ryme Intrinseca, Sherborne DT9 6JX *Tel:* 01935 873580
(Secretary) Mrs Lucinda Herklots, Dioc Office
Diocesan Accountant Mr Phil Musselwhite, Dioc Office *Tel:* 01722 411955
Diocesan Surveyor Vacancy, Dioc Office
Tel: 01722 411933
Pastoral Committee (Secretary) Mrs Siobhan Forster, Dioc Office
Designated Officer Mr Andrew Johnson, Minster Chambers, 42–44 Castle St, Salisbury SP1 3TX
Tel: 01722 411141

CHURCHES
Advisory Committee for the Care of Churches (Chairman) Rt Revd David Hallatt, Flat 10, St Nicholas Hospital, St Nicholas Road, Salisbury SP1 2SW; *(Secretary)* Mrs Sue Cannings, Dioc Office *Tel:* 01722 438654

Re-Use of Closed Churches Working Group and Furnishings Officer Mr Simon Ferris, Dioc Office
Tel: 01722 411933
Ringers' Association Mr Anthony Lovell-Wood, 11 Brook Close, Tisbury, Salisbury
Tel: 01747 871121

EDUCATION
Acting Director of Education Mrs Joy Tubbs, Diocesan Education Centre, The Avenue, Wilton, Wilts SP2 0AG *Tel:* 01722 428420
Fax: 01722 328010
Board of Education (Chairman) Canon Harold Stephens *(same address)*
Acting Deputy Director of Education Mr Giles Pugh *(same address)*
Finance Mr Giles Pugh *(same address)*
Buildings Officer Mr Martyn Kemp *(same address)*
Adviser for School Development Mr Mark Stratta *(same address)*
Youth and Children's Officers Youth and Children's Ministry Team *(same address)*
Tel: 01722 428427

MINISTRY
Director of Learning for Discipleship and Ministry Canon Jane Charman, Dioc Office
Tel: 01722 411944
email: ldmt@salisbury.anglican.org
Co-ordinator for Vocations and Spirituality Revd Ian Cowley, Dioc Office
Co-ordinator for Initial Ministerial Education/Director of Ordinands Revd Charlie Allen, Dioc Office
Co-ordinator for Learning for Discipleship Revd Duncan Strathie, Dioc Office
Co-ordinator for Ministry for Mission Ven Alan Jeans, Dioc Office
Adviser for Women's Ministry Vacancy
Tel: 01980 610305
Warden of Licensed Lay Ministers The Bishop of Sherborne *(as above)*
Lay Pastoral Assistant Officers: (Sarum) Mrs Pip Symonds, *Tel:* 01980 670782; *(Wilts)* Mrs Liz Giles, *Tel:* 01793 852643; *(Dorset)* Mrs Penny Haigh, *Tel:* 01929 471768; *(Sherborne)* Mrs Beth Buchan *Tel:* 01258 450771
Clergy Retirement Officers: (Wilts) Revd Ann Philp *Tel:* 01722 555178; *(Dorset)* Ven Alan Woods *Tel:* 01305 264877

MISSION COUNCIL
Chairman Rt Revd Dr Graham Kings
Secretary Mrs Debbie Albery, Sherborne Office
Tel: 01202 659427

MISSIONARY AND ECUMENICAL
Mission and Stewardship Advisers: (Dorset) Mr Ian Bromilow, The Old School, Hilton, Blandford Forum DT11 0DB *Tel:* 01258 880044; *(Wilts)* Mr John Kilbee, Downs View, Goatacre, Calne SN11 9HY *Tel:* 01249 760776
County Ecumenical Officers: (Wiltshire) Vacancy; *(Dorset)* Mrs Katja Babei

European Affairs Officer Canon Richard Franklin, Holy Trinity Vicarage, 7 Glebe Close, Weymouth, DT44 9RL   *Tel:* 01305 760354
Chaplain to Travelling People Revd Adrian Brook, 21 Durweston, Blandford Forum DT11 0QE
Tel: 01258 268738
International Development and World Mission Canon Ian Woodward, Vicarage, West St, Bere Regis, Wareham BH20 7HQ   *Tel:* 01929 471262

SOCIAL JUSTICE
Social Justice Programme Manager Mr Colin Brady, 23 Bagber Farm Cottages, Milton Rd, Milborne St Andrew, Blandford Forum DT11 0LB
Tel: 01258 839140
Officers for Rural Areas: (*Wiltshire*) Vacancy; (*Dorset*) Revd Canon Dr Jean Coates, Three Gables, Colesbrook, Gillingham, Dorset SP8 4HH
Tel: 01747 229168
Diocesan Environment Officer Mr David Morgan, 12 St John's Hill, Wimborne BH21 1DD
Tel: 01202 883504

PRESS AND PUBLICATIONS
Director of Communications Mr Gerry Lynch, Dioc Office   *Tel:* 01722 438650
07779 780739 (Mobile)
email: comms@salisbury.anglican.org
Editor of Dioc Directory Mrs Miriam Longfoot, Dioc Office   *Tel:* 01722 411922

DIOCESAN RECORD OFFICES
Diocesan Record Office and Wiltshire Parochial Records, Wiltshire and Swindon History Centre, Cocklebury Rd, Chippenham SN15 3QN *Tel:* 01249 705500 and ask for the Duty Archivist (*For diocesan records and parishes in the archdeaconries of Wiltshire and Sarum*)
Dorset History Centre, Bridport Rd, Dorchester DT1 1RP *County Archivist* Mr Hugh Jacques *Tel:* 01305 250550 (*For parishes in the County of Dorset*)
Hampshire Record Office, Sussex Street, Winchester SO23 8TH *Tel:* 01962 846154 (*For the few Salisbury diocesan parishes situated in the County of Hampshire*)

RURAL DEANS
ARCHDEACONRY OF SHERBORNE
Dorchester Canon Janet Smith, Vicarage, Mill Lane, Charminster, Dorchester DT2 9QP
Tel: 01305 262477
Lyme Bay Revd Janet Delaney, Vicarage, Loders, Bridport DT6 3SA   *Tel:* 01308 538118

Sherborne Revd Vivian Enever, Rectory, Trent, Sherborne DT9 4SL   *Tel:* 01935 851118
Weymouth and Portland Revd Tim West, Rectory, Sutton Road, Preston, Weymouth DT3 6BX
Tel: 01305 833142

ARCHDEACONRY OF DORSET
Blackmore Vale Canon Revd David Seymour, Vicarage, Church St, Sturminster, Newton DT10 1DB   *Tel:* 01258 471276
Milton and Blandford Revd John Simmons, Fourways, Frog Lane, Iwerne Courtney, Blandford Forum DT11 8QL   *Tel:* 01747 860515
Poole Revd Jean de Garis, Vicarage, Lytchett Minster, Poole BH16 6JQ   *Tel:* 01202 622253
Purbeck Canon John Wood, Rectory, 12 Church Hill, Swanage BH19 1HU   *Tel:* 01929 422916
Wimborne Canon Chris Tebbutt, Rectory, Canford Magna, Wimborne BH21 3AF *Tel:* 01202 883382

ARCHDEACONRY OF SARUM
Alderbury Revd David Bacon, The Rectory, Bramshaw, Lyndhurst SO43 7JF
Tel: 01794 390256
email: davidbramrec@aol.com
Chalke Revd Stephen Morgan, The Rectory, Semley, Shaftesbury SP7 9AU   *Tel:* 01747 830174
Salisbury Revd Paul Taylor, The Vicarage, 52 Park Lane, Salisbury SP1 3NP
Tel: 01722 333762
email: plaj.taylor52@btopenworld.com
Stonehenge Revd Mark Zammitt, Rectory, Church Street, Durrington, Salisbury SP4 8AL
Tel: 01980 653953

ARCHDEACONRY OF WILTS
Bradford Revd Andrew Evans, Rectory, Ham Green, Holt, Trowbridge BA14 6PZ
Tel: 01225 782289
Calne Ven Ruth Worsley, Southbroom House, London Road, Devizes SN10 1LT
Tel: 01380 738097
Devizes Revd Jonathan Triffitt, Vicarage, 31 Fruitfields Close, Devizes SN10 5JY
Tel: 01380 721441
Heytesbury Revd Jonathan Burke, Vicarage, Bitham Lane, Westbury BA13 3BU
Tel: 01373 822209
Marlborough Canon Andrew Studdert-Kennedy, Rectory, Rawlingswell Lane, Marlborough SN8 1AU   *Tel:* 01672 512357
Pewsey Revd Gerald Osborne, Lower Farm House, Milton Lilbourne, Pewsey SN9 5LQ
Tel: 01672 563459

DIOCESE OF SHEFFIELD

Founded in 1914. Sheffield; Rotherham; Doncaster, except for a few parishes in the south-east (SOUTHWELL AND NOTTINGHAM); an area of North Lincolnshire; an area of south-eastern Barnsley; a small area of the East Riding of Yorkshire.

Population 1,246,000   Area 580 sq m
Full-time Stipendiary Parochial Clergy 145   Benefices 151
Parishes 176   Churches 212
www.sheffield.anglican.org
Overseas link dioceses: Argentina, Hattingen Witten (Germany).

BISHOP (7th)
Rt Revd Dr Steven John Lindsey Croft, Bishops-croft, Snaithing Lane, Sheffield S10 3LG [2009]
Tel: 0114 230 2170
Fax: 0114 263 0110
email: bishop@sheffield.anglican.org
Domestic Chaplain Revd Canon Geoffrey Harbord, Bishopscroft, Snaithing Lane, Sheffield S10 3LG
Tel: 0114 230 2170
Fax: 0114 263 0110
email: geoffrey.harbord@sheffield.anglican.org

SUFFRAGAN BISHOP
DONCASTER Rt Revd Peter Burrows, Doncaster House, Church Lane, Fishlake, Doncaster DN7 5JW [2012]
Tel: 01302 846610
email: bishoppeter@bishopofdoncaster.org.uk

PROVINCIAL EPISCOPAL VISITOR
BEVERLEY Rt Revd Glyn Webster, Holy Trinity Rectory, Micklegate, York YO1 6LE
Tel: 01904 628155
email: office@seeofbeverley.org.uk

CATHEDRAL CHURCH OF ST PETER AND ST PAUL
Dean Very Revd Peter Bradley, The Cathedral, Church St, Sheffield S1 1HA   *Tel:* 0114 263 6060
email: dean@sheffield-cathedral.org.uk
Cathedral Office Sheffield Cathedral, Church St, Sheffield S1 1HA
Tel: 0114 275 3434
Fax: 0114 279 7412
email: enquiries@sheffield-cathedral.org.uk
Web: www.sheffieldcathedral.org
Canons Residentiary
Vice Dean and Precentor Canon Christopher Burke
Tel: 0114 263 6066
email:
christopher.burke@sheffield-cathedral.org.uk
Canon Missioner Canon Keith Farrow
Tel: 0114 263 6065
email: keith.farrow@sheffield-cathedral.org.uk
Director of Operations and Chapter Clerk Mr Mark Ford
Tel: 0114 275 3434
email: mark.ford@sheffield-cathedral.org.uk
Director of Music Mr Neil Taylor, The Cathedral
Tel: 0114 263 6069
email: musicians@sheffield-cathedral.org.uk

Assistant Director of Music Mr Joshua Hales
Tel: 0114 263 6070
email: musicians@sheffield-cathedral.org.uk
Cathedral Archer Project Manager Tim Renshaw, The Cathedral
Tel: 0114 321 2314
email: tim.renshaw@sheffield-cathedral.org.uk

ARCHDEACONS
SHEFFIELD AND ROTHERHAM Ven Malcolm Chamberlain, 34 Wilson Road, Sheffield S11 8RN
email:
malcolm.chamberlain@sheffield.anglican.org
Office Diocesan Church House, 95–99 Effingham St, Rotherham S65 1BL
Tel: 01709 309110
Fax: 01709 309107
DONCASTER Ven Stephen Wilcockson, Fairview House, 14 Armthorpe Lane, Doncaster DN2 5LZ
Tel: 01302 325787
email: steve.wilcockson@sheffield.anglican.org
Office Diocesan Church House, 95–99 Effingham St, Rotherham S65 1BL
Tel: 01709 309110
Fax: 01709 309107

CONVOCATION (MEMBERS OF THE HOUSE OF CLERGY OF THE GENERAL SYNOD)
Proctors for Clergy
Revd Canon Simon Bessant
Revd Canon Geoffrey Harbord
Revd Jeffrey Stokoe

MEMBERS OF THE HOUSE OF LAITY OF THE GENERAL SYNOD
Dr Jacqueline Butcher
Canon Elizabeth Paver
Miss Jane Patterson

DIOCESAN OFFICERS
Dioc Secretary Mr Malcolm Fair, Diocesan Church House, 95–99 Effingham St, Rotherham S65 1BL
Tel: 01709 309117
Fax: 01709 309158
email: malcolm.fair@sheffield.anglican.org
Chancellor of Diocese Her Honour Judge Sarah Singleton QC, Wake Smith LLP, 68 Clarkehouse Road, Sheffield S10 2LJ   *Tel:* 0114 266 6660
Registrar of Diocese and Bishop's Legal Secretary Mr Andrew Vidler, Wake Smith LLP, 68 Clarkehouse Road, Sheffield S10 2LJ   *Tel:* 0114 266 6660
email: andrew.vidler@wake-smith.com

DIOCESAN ORGANIZATIONS

Diocesan Office Diocesan Church House, 95–99 Effingham St, Rotherham S65 1BL
Tel: 01709 309100
Fax: 01709 512550
email: reception@sheffield.anglican.org
Web: www.sheffield.anglican.org

ADMINISTRATION

Dioc Secretary Mr Malcolm Fair, Dioc Office
Tel: 01709 309117
Director of Finance Mr Chun Tsang, Dioc Office
Tel: 01709 309142
Buildings and Ecclesiastical Surveyor Mr Paul Beckett, Dioc Office   *Tel:* 01709 309122
Diocesan Surveyor Vacancy
Board of Finance (*Chair*) Lay Canon Sandra Newton, 50 Broomgrove Rd, Sheffield S10 2NA
Tel: 0114 266 1079
Diocesan Mission and Pastoral Committee (*Chair*) Rt Revd Peter Burrows, Doncaster House, Church Lane, Fishlake, Doncaster DN7 5JW
Tel: 01302 846610
email: bishoppeter@bishopofdoncaster.org.uk
(*Secretary*) Mr Malcolm Fair, Dioc Office
Tel: 01709 309117
Redundant Churches Uses Committee (*Chair*) Vacancy
(*Secretary*) Mr Paul Beckett (*as above*)
Board of Patronages (*Chair*) Rt Revd Steven Croft, Bishopscroft, Snaithing Lane, Sheffield S10 3LG
Tel: 0114 230 2170
(*Secretary*) Mr Malcolm Fair, Dioc Office
Tel: 01709 309117
DAC Chair Revd Canon Peter Ingram, The Vicarage, 80 Millhouses Lane, Sheffield S7 2HB
Tel: 0114 236 2838
DAC Secretary Dr Julie Banham, Diocesan Church House, 95–99 Effingham Street, Rotherham S65 1BL   *Tel:* 01709 309121
Designated Officer Revd Canon Geoffrey Harbord, Bishopscroft, Snaithing Lane, Sheffield S10 3LG
Tel: 0114 230 2170
Fax: 0114 263 0110
email:
geoffrey.harbord@sheffield.anglican.org.uk
Communications Manager Miss LJ Buxton, Dioc Office   *Tel:* 01709 309125
email: lj.buxton@sheffield.anglican.org

DIOCESAN SYNOD

(*Chair, House of Clergy*) Canon Ian Smith, Warmsworth Rectory, 187 Warmsworth Road, Doncaster DN4 0TW   *Tel:* 01302 853324
(*Chair, House of Laity*) Canon Elizabeth Paver, 113 Warning Tongue Lane, Bessacarr, Doncaster DN4 6TB   *Tel:* 01302 530706
(*Secretary*) Mr Malcolm Fair (*as above*)

CHURCHES

Advisory Committee for the Care of Churches (*Chair*) Canon Peter Ingram, Holy Trinity Vicarage, 80 Millhouses Rd, Sheffield S7 2LL
Tel and Fax: 0114 236 2838

(*Secretary*) Dr Julie Banham, Diocesan Church House, 95–99 Effingham Street, Rotherham S65 1BL   *Tel:* 01709 309121

EDUCATION

Dioc Board of Education (*Chair*) Rt Revd Peter Burrows (*as above*); (*Secretary*) Mr Huw Thomas, Dioc Office   *Tel:* 01709 309123
Director of Education Mr Huw Thomas, Dioc Office

CHURCH TOURISM

Malcolm Fair, Dioc Office (*as above*)

MINISTRY AND MISSION

Director of Formation for Ministry Dr Christine Gore [2015], Dioc Office
Director of Parish Support Canon Mark Cockayne, Dioc Office   *Tel:* 01709 309132
Mission Development Adviser (*Doncaster*) Canon Mark Wigglesworth, Dioc Office
Tel: 01709 309130
Mission Development Adviser (*Sheffield and Rotherham*) Revd John Hibberd, Dioc Office
Tel: 01709 309134
Children and Young People's Adviser Mr Mike North, Dioc Office   *Tel:* 01709 309146
Director of Ordinands Revd Stephen Hunter, Overhill, Townhead Road, Dore, Sheffield S17 3GE   *Tel:* 0114 236 9978
Director of IME4–7 Vacancy
Assistant POT Officers Revd Gary Schofield, The Vicarage, Manor Rd, Wales, Sheffield S26 5PD (SMs)   *Tel:* 01909 771 111
Revd Jan Foden, The Vicarage, Stainforth Rd, Barnby Dun, Doncaster DN3 1AA (NSM)
Tel: 01302 882 835
Discipleship Development Officer Revd Alan Isaacson, The Rectory, High Bradfield, Sheffield S6 6LG   *Tel:* 0114 285 1225
Bishop's Adviser on Women in Ministry Revd Mary Gregory, The Rectory, 31 Doncaster Road, Kirk Sandall, Doncaster DN3 1HP   *Tel:* 01302 882861
Bishop's Adviser on Music and Worship Revd Helen Bent, The Vicarage, 61 Whitehill Lane, Brinsworth, Rotherham S60 5JR   *Tel:* 01709 363 850
Bishop's Adviser on Spirituality Revd Philip Roderick, 23 Hill Turrets Close, Sheffield S11 9RE
Tel: 01709 2620655
Bishop's Adviser on Self Supporting Ministry Vacancy
Bishop's Adviser on Church Army Ministry Revd Jane Truman, Wilson Carlile College of Evangelism, 50 Cavendish Street, Sheffield S3 7RZ   *Tel:* 0114 209 6201
Warden of Readers Ms Imogen Clout, Ivy Bank, 327 Fulwood Road, Sheffield S10 3BJ
Tel: 0114 2686645
Readers' Board (*Secretary*) Miss Joan Robinson, 4 Kelvin Grove, Wombwell, Barnsley S73 0DL
Ecumenical Officer Revd Frances Ecclestone, The Vicarage, 1 Barnfield Road, Crosspool, Sheffield S10 5TD   *Tel:* 0114 230 2531

PRESS AND PUBLICATIONS
Communications Manager Miss LJ Buxton, Dioc Office

DIOCESAN RECORD OFFICES
Sheffield City Archives, 52 Shoreham St, Sheffield S1 4SP   *Tel:* 0114 273 4756
(For parishes in the archdeaconry of Sheffield)
Doncaster Archives, King Edward Rd, Balby, Doncaster DN4 0NA   *Tel:* 01302 859811
(For parishes in the archdeaconry of Doncaster)

FAITH AND JUSTICE
Chair The Archdeacon of Sheffield and Rotherham, Dioc Office
Secretary Director of Parish Support, Dioc Office
Bishop's Adviser on Black Concerns Mrs Carmen Franklin   *Tel:* 0114 245 7160
Bishop's Representative for Child Protection Ms Sue Booth   *Tel:* 0113 275 5266
Bishop's Rural Adviser Revd Keith Hale, Tankersley Rectory, 9 Chapel Road, Pilley, Barnsley S75 3AR   *Tel:* 01226 744140

STEWARDSHIP
See Parish Support *under* Ministry and Mission

AREA DEANS
ARCHDEACONRY OF SHEFFIELD
Attercliffe Revd Dave Fry, Heeley Vicarage, 151 Gleadless Rd, Sheffield S2 3AE
          Tel: 0114 255 7718
Ecclesall Revd Toby Hole, St Chad's Vicarage, 9 Linden Avenue, Sheffield S8 0GA
          Tel: 0114 2749302

Ecclesfield Revd Rick Stordy, St John's Vicarage, 23 Housley Park, Chapeltown, Sheffield S35 2UE
          Tel: 0114 257 0966
Hallam Revd Phil Batchford, The Vicarage, 115 Upperthorpe Road, Sheffield S6 3EA
          Tel: 0114 276 7130
Laughton Revd Gary Schofield, The Vicarage, Manor Road, Wales, Sheffield S26 5PD
          Tel :01909 771 111
Rotherham Revd Lyn Wortley, The Vicarage, 16 Church Street, Greasbrough, Rotherham S61 4DX
          Tel: 01709 279 192

ARCHDEACONRY OF DONCASTER
Adwick-le-Street Revd Stephen Gardner, All Saints Vicarage, 9 Great North Road, Woodlands, Doncaster DN6 7RB   *Tel:* 01302 700404
Doncaster Revd Jan Foden, The Vicarage, Stainforth Rd, Barnby Dun, Doncaster DN3 1AA
          Tel: 01302 882 835
Hickleton Revd W. Jeffrey Stokoe, St Hugh's Vicarage, Levet Road, New Cantley, Doncaster DN4 6JQ   *Tel:* 01302 371256
Snaith and Hatfield Revd Canon Elizabeth Turner-Loisel, The Vicarage, 2 Vicarage Close, Hatfield, Doncaster DN7 6HN   *Tel:* 01302 459110
Tankersley Revd Keith Hale, Tankersley Rectory, 9 Chapel Rd, Pilley, Barnsley S75 3AR
          Tel: 01226 744 140
Wath Revd Andrew Brewerton, The Vicarage, Highthorn Road, Kilnhurst, Mexborough S64 5TX   *Tel:* 01709 589674
West Doncaster Revd Neil Redeyoff, The Rectory, Rectory Lane, Finningley, Doncaster DN9 3DA
          Tel: 01302 770 240

DIOCESE OF SODOR AND MAN

Founded in 447. The Isle of Man.

Population 85,000   Area 220 sq m
Full-time Stipendiary Parochial Clergy 15   Benefices 18
Parishes 18   Churches 45
www.sodorandman.im
Overseas link dioceses: Cashel, Ferns and Ossory (Ireland).

BISHOP
Rt Revd Robert M.E. Paterson, Thie Yn Aspick, 4
The Falls, Douglas, Isle of Man IM4 4PZ [2008]
Tel: 01624 622108
email: bishop@sodorandman.im
[+Robert Sodor as Mannin]
Bishop's Chaplain Revd Canon Margaret Burrow
email: chaplain@sodorandman.im
Bishop's Secretary Miss Rosemary Bannan
email: secretary@sodorandman.im

CATHEDRAL CHURCH OF ST GERMAN, PEEL
Dean Very Revd Nigel Godfrey, The Deanery,
Albany Rd, Peel, Isle of Man IM5 1HH
Tel: 01624 842608
email: dean@sodorandman.im
Canons
Canon Ian Brady, St Thomas's Vicarage,
Marathon Ave., Douglas, Isle of Man IM2 4JA
[2013]
Canon Margaret Burrow, Thie yn Aspick, 4 The
Falls, Douglas, Isle of Man IM4 4PZ [2014]
Canon Philip Frear, 37 Hutchinson Square,
Douglas, Isle of Man IM2 4HW [2005]
Canon Dr Jules Gomes, The Vicarage, Arbory Rd.
Castletown, Isle of Man IM9 1ND [2012]

ARCHDEACON
Ven Andrew Brown, St George's Vicarage, 16
Devonshire Rd, Douglas, Isle of Man IM2 3RB
[2011]
Tel: 01624 675430
email: archdeacon@sodorandman.im

YORK CONVOCATION (MEMBER OF THE HOUSE OF CLERGY OF THE GENERAL SYNOD)
Proctor for the Clergy Ven Andrew Brown

MEMBER OF THE HOUSE OF LAITY OF THE GENERAL SYNOD
Miss Laura Davenport

DIOCESAN OFFICERS
Vicar-General and Chancellor of Diocese The
Worshipful Clare Faulds, The Lynague, German,
IM5 2AQ   *Tel:* 01624 842045

*Diocesan Registrar and Bishop's Legal Secretary
and Bishop's Legal Adviser* Mr Lionel Lennox,
The Registry, Stamford House, Piccadilly, York
YO1 9PP   *Tel:* 01904 623487
email: registrar@sodorandman.im
lionel.lennox@lf-dt.com
Diocesan Synod Secretary Mrs Michelle Barwood,
4 Oak Road, Ballawattleworth Estate, Peel, Isle
of Man IM5 1WN   *Tel:* 01624 673477
email: synod@sodorandman.im

CHURCH COMMISSIONERS FOR THE ISLE OF MAN
The Bishop (*Chair*)
The Archdeacon
Revd Clive Burgess
Revd Canon Margaret Burrow
Mr Peter Cowell
Revd Brian Evans-Smith
Mr Stephen Hamer
Mrs Susan Kennaugh
Mrs Susan Kinrade
(*Secretary*) Mrs Michelle Barwood (*as above*)

DIOCESAN ORGANIZATIONS
DIOCESAN SYNOD
Chairman, House of Clergy Revd John Coldwell
email: stninians@manx.net
Chairman, House of Laity Mr Kenneth Gumbley
email: kfwg@gumbley.net

BOARD OF FINANCE
Chairman Rt Revd Robert M.E. Paterson
(*Secretary*) Mrs Michelle Barwood (*as above*)
Diocesan Treasurer Mrs Lisa Johnson, 21 Brighton
Terrace, Douglas, Isle of Man IM1 4AP
Tel: 01624 677512
email: treasurer@sodorandman.im

CHURCH BUILDINGS
Advisory Committee for the Care of Churches
(*Secretary*) Mrs Michelle Barwood
email: synod@sodorandman.im

SECTOR MINISTERS AND ADVISERS
*Contact via the Bishop's Office, Thie yn Aspick, 4
The Falls, Douglas, Isle of Man IM4 4PZ*
Tel: 01624 622108
email: chaplain@sodorandman.im

SOCIAL RESPONSIBILITY

Access and Disability Mr Guy Thompson
Church and Society Adviser Revd Canon Cyril Rogers
Environment Advisers Revd Brian and Mrs Mary Evans-Smith
Rural Life Adviser Revd Tony Butler

EDUCATION, FAMILIES, CHILDREN AND YOUNG PEOPLE

Children's Work Adviser Mrs Nancy Clague
Church School Liaison Revd James McGowan
Mothers' Union President Mrs Patricia Costain
Youth Work Adviser Vacancy
Safeguarding Officer Revd Jo Dudley

COMMUNICATION

Media and Communications Officer Revd John Coldwell Coldwell
email: media@sodorandman.im
Data Protection Officer Mr Charles Flynn
Manx Radio Canon Miss Judith Ley
Webmaster Revd John Coldwell (*as above*)

MISSION AND CHURCH LIFE

Ecumenical Adviser Mr Howard Connell
Healing and Deliverance Adviser Revd Canon Philip Frear (*as above*)
Leisure, Sport and Tourism Adviser Very Revd Nigel Godfrey (*as above*)
Mission Adviser Miss Gillian Poole
email: mission@sodorandman.im
Spiritual Life Adviser Revd David Shirtliff
World Mission Co-ordinators Revd Canon Malcolm and Mrs Valerie Convery (*as above*)
Christian Giving Adviser Revd Diane Marchment
C.M.E.A.C. Link Vacancy

PUBLIC MINISTRY

Director of Vocation and Training (*DDO*) Very Revd Nigel Godfrey (*as above*)
Director of Studies IME 1–3 Revd John Gulland
Director of Ministerial Development (CMD & IME 4–7) Revd Canon Dr Jules Gomes
Warden of Readers Canon Mr Colin Finney

CHAPLAINS

Bishop's Chaplain Revd Canon Margaret Burrow
P.T.O. Ministers (*lay and ordained*) Revd Leslie Lawrinson
Bishop's Visitors Dr Paul and Mrs Barbara Bregazzi
Widows and Widowers of Public Ministers Mrs Brenda Willoughby
King William's College Revd Erica Scott
IOM Prison, Jurby Revd Brian Evans-Smith (*as above*)
Hospice Isle of Man Revd Lynda Brady
The Isle of Man College Revd Daniel Richards
IOM Constabulary (ecumenical) Revd Jo Dudley
Mothers' Union Chaplain Mr Nigel Cretney
Noble's General Hospital Revd Canon Philip Frear (*as above*)
Ramsey Cottage Hospital Revd Brian Evans-Smith
To the Speaker of the House of Keys Revd William Martin

ARCHIVED DIOCESAN RECORDS

Archivist Miss Wendy Thirkettle, The Manx Museum Library, Kingswood Grove, Douglas, Isle of Man IM1 3LY   *Tel:* 01624 64800

MISSION PARTNERSHIP LEADERS

North Revd Canon Cyril Rogers
South Revd Dr Joe Heaton
East Revd Clive Burgess
West Very Revd Nigel Godfrey

DIOCESE OF SOUTHWARK

Founded in 1905. Greater London south of the Thames, except for most of the London Boroughs of Bromley and Bexley (ROCHESTER), and a few parishes in the south-west (GUILDFORD); the eastern third of Surrey.

Population 2,718,000   Area 320 sq m
Full-time Stipendiary Parochial Clergy 346   Benefices 260
Parishes 292   Churches 364
www.southwark.anglican.org

Overseas link dioceses: Manicaland, Central Zimbabwe, Matabeleland, Masvingo (Zimbabwe).

BISHOP

Rt Revd Christopher Chessun, Bishop's House, 38 Tooting Bec Gardens London SW16 1QZ
Tel: 020 8769 3256
Fax: 08432 906894
email: bishop.christopher@southwark.anglican.org
Bishop's Office, Trinity House, 4 Chapel Court, Borough High Street, London SE1 1HW
Tel: 020 7939 9420
Fax: 0843 2906894
Bishop's Chaplain Revd Mark Steadman (Bishop's Office, *same address*)
email: mark.steadman@southwark.anglican.org
Bishop's Personal Assistant Ms Winsome Thomas (Bishop's Office, *same address*)
email: winsome.thomas@southwark.anglican.org
Secretary Mrs Penny Lochead (Bishop's Office, *same address*)
email: penny.lochead@southwark.anglican.org
Bishop's Press Officer Canon Wendy Robins (Bishop's Office, *same address*)
email: wendy.robins@southwark.anglican.org

AREA BISHOPS

CROYDON Rt Revd Jonathan Clark, Croydon Episcopal Area Office, St Matthew's House, 100 George St, Croydon CR0 1PE [2012]
Tel: 020 8256 9630
Fax: 020 8256 9631
email: bishop.jonathan@southwark.anglican.org
KINGSTON Rt Revd Dr Richard Cheetham, Kingston Episcopal Area Office, 620 Kingston Rd, Raynes Park, London SW20 8DN [2002]
Tel: 020 8545 2440
Fax: 020 8545 2441
email: bishop.richard@southwark.anglican.org
WOOLWICH Rt Revd Dr Michael Ipgrave OBE, Woolwich Episcopal Area Office, Trinity House, 4 Chapel Court, London SE1 1HW [2012]
Tel: 020 7939 9400
Fax: 020 7939 9465

HONORARY ASSISTANT BISHOPS

Rt Revd Dr David Atkinson, 6 Bynes Road, South Croydon CR2 0PR [2009] *Tel:* 020 8406 0895
email: davidatkinson43@virginmedia.com

Rt Revd Jonathan Baker (Bishop of Fulham), The Old Deanery, Dean's Court, London EC4V 5AA [2013] *Tel:* 020 7932 1130
email: bishop.fulham@london.anglican.org
Rt Revd Michael Doe, 405 West Carriage House, Royal Carriage Mews, London SE18 6GA [2006]
Tel: 020 3259 3841
email: michaeldd@btinternet.com
Rt Revd and Rt Hon Lord Harries of Pentregarth, 41 Melville Road, Barnes, London SW19 9RH [2006] *Tel:* 020 8288 6053
email: richard.d.harries@googlemail.com
Rt Revd Peter Selby, 57 Girton Road, London SE26 5DJ [2011] *email:* peter.selby@onetel.com
Rt Revd Nigel Stock, Lambeth Palace, London SE1 7JU [2013] *Tel:* 020 7898 1200
Rt Revd Peter Wheatley, 27 Thurlow Road, London NW3 5PP *Tel:* 020 7435 5890

CATHEDRAL AND COLLEGIATE CHURCH OF ST SAVIOUR AND ST MARY OVERIE

Dean Very Revd Andrew Nunn [2011] (*All correspondence to be addressed to the Cathedral Office*) *Tel:* 020 7367 6727 (Office)
Tel: 020 7928 3336 (Home)
Fax: 020 7367 6725 (Office)
Cathedral Office Montague Chambers, London Bridge, London SE1 9DA *Tel:* 020 7367 6700
Fax: 020 7367 6725/6730
email: cathedral@southwark.anglican.org
Canons Residentiary
Pastor and Sub Dean Vacancy
Precentor Canon Gilly Myers, Cathedral Office [2012] *Tel:* 020 7367 6731 (Office)
020 7735 5991 (Home)
email: gilly.myers@southwark.anglican.org
Chancellor and Director of Ministerial Education Canon Mandy Ford, Diocesan Office [2014]
Tel: 020 7939 9449
email: mandy.ford@southwark.anglican.org
Missioner Canon Dr Stephen Hance, Diocesan Office [2012] *Tel:* 020 7939 9417
email: stephen.hance@southwark.anglican.org
Treasurer and Diocesan Director of Ordinands Canon Leanne Roberts, Diocesan Office [2011]
Tel: 020 7939 9458
email: leanne.roberts@southwark.anglican.org

Succentor Revd Stephen Stavrou, Cathedral Office [2013]   *Tel:* 020 7367 6705
  email: stephen.stavrou@southwark.anglican.org
Priest Assistant Canon Wendy Robins [2002]
                            Tel: 020 7939 9436
  email: wendy.robins@southwark.anglican.org
Comptroller Mr Matthew Knight, Cathedral Office
                            Tel: 020 7367 6726
  email: matthew.knight@southwark.anglican.org
Education Officer Mrs Alexandra Carton, Cathedral Office   *Tel:* 020 7367 6715
  email: edcentre@southwark.anglican.org
Cathedral Organist Mr Peter Wright, Cathedral Office   *Tel:* 020 7367 6703
  email: peter.wright@southwark.anglican.org

ARCHDEACONS

CROYDON Ven Christopher Skilton, Croydon Episcopal Area Office, St Matthew's House, 100 George St, Croydon CR0 1PE [2013]
                            Tel: 020 8256 9630
                            Fax: 020 8256 9631
  email: chris.skilton@southwark.anglican.org
LAMBETH Ven Simon Gates, Kingston Episcopal Area Office, 620 Kingston Rd, Raynes Park, London SW20 8DN [2013]
                            Tel: 020 8545 2440
                            Fax: 020 8545 2441
  email: simon.gates@southwark.anglican.org
LEWISHAM AND GREENWICH Ven Alastair Cutting, Diocesan Office, Trinity House, 4 Chapel Court, Borough High Street, London SE1 1HW [2013]
                            Tel: 020 7939 9408
                            Fax: 020 7939 9465
  email: alastair.cutting@southwark.anglican.org
REIGATE Ven Daniel Kajumba, St Matthew's House (*as above*) [2001]   *Tel:* 020 8256 9630
                            Fax: 020 8256 9631
  email: daniel.kajumba@southwark.anglican.org
SOUTHWARK Ven Dr Jane Steen, Diocesan Office (*as above*) [2013]   *Tel:* 020 7939 9408
                            Fax: 020 7939 9465
  email: jane.steen@southwark.anglican.org
WANDSWORTH Ven Stephen Roberts, Kingston Episcopal Area Office (*as above*) [2005]
                            Tel: 020 8545 2440
                            Fax: 020 8545 2441
  email: stephen.roberts@southwark.anglican.org

CONVOCATION (MEMBERS OF THE HOUSE OF CLERGY OF THE GENERAL SYNOD)

Proctors for Clergy
Revd Canon Simon Butler
Revd Canon Giles Goddard
Ven Christine Hardman
Revd Canon Gary Jenkins
Revd Dr Rosemarie Mallett
Very Revd Andrew Nunn
Revd Rupert Shelley
Revd Mark Steadman

MEMBERS OF THE HOUSE OF LAITY OF THE GENERAL SYNOD

Mrs April Alexander
Miss Vasantha Gnanadoss
Mr Adrian Greenwood
Mr Peter Haddock
Mr Robin Hall
Mr Tom Sutcliffe
Mr Brian Wilson

DIOCESAN OFFICERS

Diocesan Secretary Vacancy, Diocesan Office, Trinity House, 4 Chapel Court, Borough High St, London SE1 1HW   *Tel:* 020 7939 9400
                            Fax: 020 7939 9468
Deputy Diocesan Secretary Mr Andrew Lane, Diocesan Office (*as above*)
  email: andrew.lane@southwark.anglican.org
Chancellor of Diocese Mr Philip Petchey, Francis Taylor Building, Inner Temple, London EC4Y 7BY
                            Tel: 020 7353 8415
Registrar of Diocese and Bishop's Legal Secretary Mr Paul Morris, Minerva House, 5 Montague Close, London SE1 9BB   *Tel:* 020 7593 5000
                            Fax: 020 7593 5099

DIOCESAN ORGANIZATIONS

Diocesan Office Trinity House, 4 Chapel Court, Borough High St, London SE1 1HW
                            Tel: 020 7939 9400
                            Fax: 020 7939 9468
  email: trinity@southwark.anglican.org
  Web: www. southwark.anglican.org

ADMINISTRATION

Dioc Synod (Chairman, House of Clergy) Canon Simon Butler
(*Chairman, House of Laity*) Mr Adrian Greenwood; (*Secretary*) The Diocesan Secretary, Dioc Office
South London Church Fund and Diocesan Board of Finance (Chairman) Mr John Kempsell; (*Secretary*) The Diocesan Secretary, Dioc Office
Parsonages Board (Secretary) Mr Eric Greber, Dioc Office
  email: eric.greber@southwark.anglican.org
Mission and Pastoral Committee (Secretary) Mr Andrew Lane, Dioc Office
  email: andrew.lane@southwark.anglican.org
Redundant Churches Uses Committee (Secretary) Mr Eric Greber, Dioc Office
Designated Officer Mr Paul Morris, Minerva House, 5 Montague Close, London SE1 9BB
                            Tel: 020 7593 5000
                            Fax: 020 7593 5099

CHURCHES

Advisory Committee for the Care of Churches (Chairman) Mr Paul Parkinson c/o Dioc Office (*as above*); (*Secretary*) Mr Andrew Lane (*as above*)

ECUMENICAL

Chair of Ecumenical Sub-Group Revd Peter Hart, Vicarage, 70 Marksbury Ave, Richmond TW9 4JF
Tel: 020 8392 1425
email: Pwhart1@aol.com

EDUCATION

Board of Education (*Director*) Mr Colin Powell, 48 Union St, London SE1 1TD   *Tel:* 020 7234 9200
email: colin.powell@southwark.anglican.org

PARISH DEVELOPMENT AND CHURCH GROWTH

Chair The Bishop of Croydon (*as above*)
Canon Missioner Revd Canon Dr Stephen Hance (*as above*)
Mission Support Officer Revd Dr Sharon Prentis c/o Dioc Office

PUBLIC POLICY GROUP

Bishop of Southwark's Adviser on Urban and Public Policy Terry Drummond CA, Bishop's House, 38 Tooting Bec Gardens, London SW16 1QZ
Chair Vacancy: contact Capt Terry Drummond CA, c/o Dioc Office
Regeneration Adviser: Revd Andrew Wakefield
Tel: 020 8542 6566
Environmental Officer Mrs Sue Mallinson, c/o Dioc Office

OTHER OFFICERS

Dioc Safeguarding Adviser Kate Singleton, c/o Dioc Office   *Tel:* 020 7939 9400
email: kate.singleton@southwark.anglican.org
Dean of Women's Ministry Revd Canon Alyson Peberdy   *Tel:* 020 8690 2499
email: alysonpeberdy@aol.com
Minority Ethnic Anglican Concerns Officer Ms Lola Brown, Dioc Office   *Tel:* 020 7939 9418
email: lola.brown@southwark.anglican.org
Spiritual Formation Adviser Mr Chris Chapman, Dioc Office
Inter Faith Relations Co-ordinator Siriol Davies
Tel: 020 7201 4854
email: sirioldavies@yahoo.co.uk
Ecumenical Projects Officer John Richardson
Tel: 01462 422502
email: john@ctslondon.org.uk
Retirement Officer Revd Nicky Tredennick
Tel: 01342 843570
email: rev.nicky@btinternet.com
Faith in the Countryside Link Officer Revd Carol Coslett   *Tel:* 01737 842102
email: ccoslett@btinternet.com
Southwark Dioc WelCare Anna Khan (*Director*), St John's Community Centre, 19 Frederick Crescent, London SW9 6XN   *Tel:* 020 7820 7910
email: anna.khan@welcare.org

MINISTRY AND TRAINING COMMITTEE

Director of Ministerial Education Revd Canon Mandy Ford   *Tel:* 020 7939 9449
email: mandy.ford@southwark.anglican.org

Diocesan Director of Ordinands Revd Canon Leanne Roberts   *Tel:* 020 7939 9458
email: leanne.roberts@southwark.anglican.org
Assistant Diocesan Director of Ordinands Revd Andrew Zihni   *Tel:* 020 7939 9472
email: andrew.zihni@southwark.anglican.org
Warden of Readers Rt Revd Dr Michael Ipgrave
Tel: 020 7939 9407
email: bishop.michael@southwark.anglican.org
Southwark Pastoral Auxiliary Training Officer Mr Chris Chapman   *Tel:* 020 7939 9474
email: chris.chapman@southwark.anglican.org
Officer for Lay Mission and Ministry Vacancy

COMMUNICATIONS

Director of Communications and Resources and Bishop's Press Officer Revd Canon Wendy Robins, Dioc Office   *Tel:* 020 7939 9400 (Office)
email: wendy.robins@southwark.anglican.org
Communications Officer Mr Steve Harris, Dioc Office   *Tel:* 020 7939 9437
email: steve.harris@southwark.anglican.org

DIOCESAN RECORD OFFICES

London Metropolitan Archives, 40 Northampton Rd, London EC1R 0HB *Tel:* 020 7332 3820 *Fax:* 020 7833 9136 (*Parish records for Inner London Boroughs except Lewisham*)
Lewisham Local Studies and Archives Centre, Lewisham Library, 199–201 Lewisham High St, London SE13 6LG *Tel:* 020 8297 0682 *Fax:* 020 8297 1169 (*Parish records for East and West Lewisham deaneries*)
Bexley Local Studies and Archive Centre, Central Library, Townley Road, Bexleyheath DA6 7HJ *Tel:* 020 8301 1545 (*For Parishes in the London Borough of Bexley*)
Surrey History Centre, 130 Goldsworth Rd, Woking GU21 1ND *Tel:* 01483 594594 *Fax:* 01483 594595 (*County of Surrey and Surrey London Boroughs*)
London Borough of Sutton Local Studies Centre, St Nicholas Way, Sutton SM1 1JN *Tel:* 020 8770 5000 (*London Borough of Sutton*)

STEWARDSHIP

Director of Communications and Resources Revd Canon Wendy Robins, Dioc Office
Tel: 020 7939 9400
email: wendy.robins@southwark.anglican.org.uk
Stewardship Resources Officer Mrs Jackie Pontin, Dioc Office   *Tel:* 020 7939 9461
email: jackie.pontin@southwark.anglican.org

AREA DEANS
ARCHDEACONRY OF SOUTHWARK

Bermondsey Revd Canon Mark R. Nicholls, St Mary's Rectory, 72A St Marychurch Street, London SE16 4JE   *Tel:* 020 7394 3394
email: mmarini2001@aol.com
Camberwell Vacancy
Dulwich Vacancy

Southwark and Newington Revd Andrew Moughtin-Mumby, St Peter's Rectory, 12 Villa Street, London SE17 2EJ   *Tel:* 020 7703 3139
email: rector@stpeterswalworth.org

ARCHDEACONRY OF LAMBETH

Merton Revd Richard Lane, Christ Church Vicarage, 16 Copse Hill, London SW20 0HG
Tel: 020 8946 4491
email: westwimbledon@btinternet.com
Lambeth North Revd Deborah Matthews, St Paul's Vicarage, Rectory Grove, London SW4 0DX   *Tel:* 020 7622 2128
email: revdebmatthews@waitrose.com
Lambeth South Revd David Stephenson, All Saints' Vicarage, 165 Rosendale Road, London SE21 8LN   *Tel:* 020 8670 0826
email: vicar@all-saints.org

ARCHDEACONRY OF REIGATE

Caterham Revd Duncan Swan, The Rectory, 5 Whyteleafe Road, Caterham, Surrey CR3 5EG
Tel: 01883 373083
email: duncpen@hotmail.com
Godstone Revd Canon Peter Moseling, The Rectory, Outwood Lane, Bletchingley, Surrey RH1 4LR   *Tel:* 01883 743252
email: frp.moseling@tiscali.co.uk
Reigate Revd Andrew Cunnington, 27 Ridgeway Road, Redhill, Surrey RH1 6PQ
Tel: 01737 761568
email: andrew@stmatthews-redhill.org.uk

ARCHDEACONRY OF LEWISHAM AND GREENWICH

Charlton Revd Canon Kim Hitch, St James Rectory, 62 Kidbrooke Park Rd, London SE3 0DU
Tel: 020 8856 3438
email: k.w.hitch@btinternet.com
Deptford Revd Paul Butler, St Pauls Rectory, Mary Ann Gardens, Deptford, London SE8 3DP
Tel: 020 8692 7449
email: stpaulsdeptford@btinternet.com
East Lewisham Revd Jane L. Kustner, St Swithun's Vicarage, 191 Hither Green Lane, London SE13 6QE   *Tel:* 020 8852 5088
email: janekustner@btconnect.com
Eltham and Mottingham Revd Brett Ward, Holy Trinity Vicarage, 59 Southend Crescent, London SE9 2SD   *Tel:* 020 8850 1246
email: fr.brett@ht-e.org.uk
Plumstead Revd Clive Welham, The Vicarage, 42 Jago Close, London SE18 2TY
Tel: 020 8854 3395
email: clive@plumsteadcommonbenefice.org.uk

West Lewisham Revd Michael Kingston, St Bartholomew's Vicarage, 4 Westwood Hill, Sydenham, London SE26 6QR
Tel: 020 8778 5290
email: michaelkingston@btinternet.com

ARCHDEACONRY OF WANDSWORTH

Battersea Revd Geoffrey Owen, Christ Church Vicarage, Candahar Road, London SW11 2PU
Tel: 020 7228 1225
*email:*geoffrey-owen@o2.co.uk
Kingston Revd Simon Coupland, St Paul's Vicarage, 33 Queen's Road, Kingston-upon-Thames, Surrey KT2 7SF   *Tel:* 020 8549 8597
email: vicar@stpaulskingston.org.uk
Richmond and Barnes Revd Canon Tim Marwood, The Vicarage, Bute Avenue, Petersham, Richmond, TW10 7AX   *Tel:* 020 8940 8435
email: timmarwood@yahoo.co.uk
Tooting Revd Wilma Roest, St Mary's Vicarage, 218a Balham High Road, London, SW12 9BS
Tel: 020 8673 1188
email: vicar@stmarybalham.org.uk
Wandsworth Revd Gregory Prior, Wandsworth Vicarage, 11 Rusholme Road, London SW15 3JX
Tel: 020 8788 7400
email: gregp@wandsworthparish.co.uk

ARCHDEACONRY OF CROYDON

Croydon Addington Revd Stephen Knowers, The Vicarage, 49 Shirley Church Road, Shirley, Surrey CR0 5EF   *Tel:* 020 8654 1013
email: frstiiv@hotmail.com
Croydon Central Revd Canon Trevor Mapstone, 33 Hurst Way, South Croydon, Surrey CR2 7AP
Tel: 020 8688 6676
email: tmapstone@emmanuelcroydon.org.uk
Croydon North Revd Leonard Marsh, The Vicarage, 49 Chevening Road, London SE19 3TD
Tel: 020 8653 2820
email: leonard.marsh@yahoo.co.uk
Croydon South Revd Christine Spurway, St James' Vicarage, 1b St James' Rd, Purley CR8 2DL   *Tel:* 020 8660 5436
email: christinespurway@uwclub.net
Sutton Revd Darren Miller, The Rectory, 33 Mickleham Gardens, Cheam, Surrey SM3 8QJ
Tel: 030 0330 1456
email: rector@cheamparish.org.uk

CHAPTER OF MINISTERS IN SECULAR EMPLOYMENT

Chapter Dean for Kingston Revd Peter King, 49 Leinster Ave, East Sheen, London SW14 7JW
Tel: 020 8876 8997
email: kingpd@hotmail.com

DIOCESE OF SOUTHWELL AND NOTTINGHAM

Founded in 1884. Nottinghamshire; a few parishes in South Yorkshire.

Population 1,103,000   Area 850 sq m
Full-time Stipendiary Parochial Clergy 135   Benefices 158
Parishes 257   Churches 306
www.southwell.anglican.org
Overseas link diocese: Natal (South Africa)

BISHOP (ACTING)
Rt Revd Richard Inwood, c/o Jubilee House, Westgate, Southwell NG25 0JH
Tel: 01636 817996
email: bishop@southwell.anglican.org
Chaplain Revd Lucy Cleland
email: chaplain@southwell.anglican.org
Personal Assistant Mrs Jackie Davies
email: jackie@southwell.anglican.org

SUFFRAGAN BISHOP
SHERWOOD Rt Revd Anthony Porter, Jubilee House, Westgate, Southwell NG25 0JH [2006]
Tel: 01636 819133
email: bishopsherwood@southwell.anglican.org
Personal Assistant Miss Jenny Andrews
email: jenny@southwell.anglican.org

PROVINCIAL EPISCOPAL VISITOR
BEVERLEY Rt Revd Glyn Webster, Holy Trinity Rectory, Micklegate, York YO1 6LE
Tel: 01904 628155
email: office@seeofbeverley.org.uk

HONORARY ASSISTANT BISHOPS
Rt Revd John Finney, Greenacre, Crow Lane, South Muskham, Newark NG23 6DZ [1998]
Tel: 01636 679791
Rt Revd Richard Inwood, c/o Jubilee House, Westgate, Southwell NG25 0BG [2012]
Tel: 01636 817996
Rt Revd Martyn Jarrett, 91 Beaumont Rise, Worksop S80 1YG [2013]   *Tel:* 01909 477847
Rt Revd Ronald Milner, 7 Crafts Way, Southwell NG25 0BL [1994]   *Tel:* 01636 816256
Rt Revd Roy Williamson, 30 Sidney Rd, Beeston, Nottingham NG9 1AN [1998]
Tel: 0115 925 4901

CATHEDRAL AND PARISH CHURCH OF THE BLESSED VIRGIN MARY
Dean Vacancy
Acting Dean Canon Nigel Coates (Canon Pastor)   *Tel:* 01636 812782
email: dean@southwellminster.org.uk

Office The Minster Office, The Minster Centre, Church St, Southwell NG25 0HD
Tel: 01636 812649/817810
Fax: 01636 817284
email: office@southwellminster.org.uk
Web: www.southwellminster.org.uk
Canons Residentiary
Precentor Canon Jacqueline (Jacqui) D. Jones, 2 Vicars' Court, Southwell NG25 0HP [2003]
Tel: 01636 817295
email: jacquijones@southwellminster.org.uk
Canon Pastor Canon Nigel Coates, 3 Vicars' Court, Southwell NG25 0HP [2005]   *Tel:* 01636 817296
email: nigelcoates@southwellminster.org.uk
Chapter Clerk Mrs Caroline Jarvis, The Minster Office, The Minster Centre, Church St, Southwell NG25 0HD   *Tel:* 01636 817285
email: chapterclerk@southwellminster.org.uk
Rector Chori Mr Paul Hale, 4 Vicars' Court, Southwell NG25 0HP   *Tel:* 01636 812228/817297
email: RectorChori@diaphone.clara.net
Head Verger Mr Andrew Todd, The Vestry, Southwell Cathedral   *Tel:* 01636 817290
email: vergers@southwellminster.org.uk

ARCHDEACONS
NOTTINGHAM Ven Sarah Clark, 4 Victoria Crescent, Sherwood, Nottingham NG5 4DA [2014]   *Tel:* 01636 817206 (Office)
email: archdeacon-nottm@southwell.anglican.org
NEWARK Ven David Picken, 22 Rufford Road, Edwinstowe, Mansfield, Notts NG21 9HY [2012]
Tel: 01636 817206 (Office)
email:
archdeacon-newark@southwell.anglican.org

CONVOCATION (MEMBERS OF THE HOUSE OF CLERGY OF THE GENERAL SYNOD)
Proctors for Clergy
Vacancy
Revd Canon Tony Walker
Revd Sally Baylis

MEMBERS OF THE HOUSE OF LAITY OF THE GENERAL SYNOD
Mrs Pamela Bishop
Mr Nick Harding
Mr Colin Slater

DIOCESAN OFFICERS

Chief Executive Canon Nigel Spraggins, Jubilee House, Westgate, Southwell NG25 0JH
Tel: 01636 817206 (Office)
07887 538682 (Mobile)
01636 816445 (Home)
Fax: 01636 815084
email: ce@southwell.anglican.org
Executive Personal Assistant to the Chief Executive and Archdeacons Mrs Jo Padmore
Tel: 01636 817206
email: archdeaconspa@southwell.anglican.org
Chancellor of Diocese The Worshipful Mrs Linda Mary Box, Diocesan Office   Tel: 01636 817209
Deputy Chancellor Mrs Jacqueline Humphreys
Registrar of Diocese and Bishop's Legal Secretary Mrs Amanda J. Redgate   Tel: 01636 817209
Deputy Registrar Mr Charles John George

DIOCESAN ORGANIZATIONS

Diocesan Office Jubilee House, 8 Westgate, Southwell NG25 0JH   Tel: 01636 814331
email: mail@southwell.anglican.org
Web: www.southwell.anglican.org

ADMINISTRATION

Diocesan Synod (Vice-president and Chair, House of Clergy) Revd Canon Phil Williams
(Chair, House of Laity) Mrs Pam Bishop
(Secretary) Mr Nigel Spraggins, Chief Executive
Tel: 01636 817204

FINANCE

Director of Finance Mrs Rebecca Bowes
Tel: 01636 817202

PARISH SUPPORT

(Includes Property, DAC and Stewardship)
Director of Parish Support Mr Fraser McNish
Tel: 01636 817244
*email:*fraser@southwell.anglican.org

PARISH SUPPORT (PROPERTY)

Building Surveyor Mr Ian Greaves
Tel: 01636 817214

CARE OF CHURCHES

Advisory Committee for the Care of Churches (Chairman) Revd Canon Keith Turner, Rectory, Main St, Linby, Nottingham NG15 8AE
Tel: 0115 963 2346
email: k.h.turner@btopenworld.com
Web (Church History Project):
www.southwellchurches.nottingham.ac.uk
DAC Secretary and GIS Manager, Mr Jonathan Pickett   Tel: 01636 817210
email: jonathan.pickett@southwell.anglican.org
Web: http://southwell.anglican.org/church-life/churches/your-church-building/

EDUCATION

Diocesan Office, Jubilee House, 8 Westgate, Southwell NG25 0JH

Director of Education Mrs Claire Meese
Tel: 01636 817238
01636 814504 (Education Department)
Deputy Director (Schools) Mrs Liz Youngman
Tel: 01636 817247
email: liz.youngman@southwell.anglican.org
Assistant Director (Schools) Mrs Sheila Barker
Tel: 01636 817235
email: sheila.barker@southwell.anglican.org
Youth Ministry Adviser (Support and Partnerships) Mrs Angela Brymer   Tel: 07887 530751
email:
youthministryadviser@southwell.anglican.org
Youth Ministry Adviser (Growth and Development) Mr David Keetley   Tel: 07720 511192
email:
youthministryadviser2@southwell.anglican.org
Children's Ministry Adviser Mr Nick Harding
Tel: 01636 817234
email: nick@southwell.anglican.org

DEPARTMENT FOR DEVELOPMENT

Diocesan Office, Jubilee House, Westgate, Southwell NG25 0JH
Director, Ministry and Mission Revd Canon Dr Nigel Rooms   Tel: 01636 817231
email: nigel.rooms@southwell.anglican.org
Director, Partnerships & Mission Revd David McCoulough   Tel: 01636 817246
email: davidmcc@southwell.anglican.org
Vocations Adviser and Diocesan Director of Ordinands Revd Sue Hemsley Halls   Tel: 01636 817212
email: suehh@southwell.anglican.org
Dean of Women's Ministry Ven Sarah Clark
email: saraheclark@ntlworld.com
Ministry Development Advisers Revd Alison Cox
Tel: 01636 817226
email: alison.cox@southwell.anglican.org
Revd Jackie Johnson
Tel: 01636 817208
email: jackie.johnson@southwell.anglican.org
Warden of Readers Mr Christopher Perrett, Harvest Barn, Grassthorpe, Newark, Nottingham NG23 5QZ   Tel: 01636 822426
email: chris.perrett@southwell.anglican.org
Sport Ministry
Sport Ambassador Mr Rob Taylor
Tel: 07775 687682
email: rob.taylor@southwell.anglican.org
Chaplain to Retired Clergy/Clergy Widows Officer Revd David Edinborough   Tel: 0115 9251066
email: david.edinborough@googlemail.com
Workplace Chaplain Revd Rachel Shock
email:
rachel@nottinghamworkplacechaplaincy.org.uk
Equality and Diversity Officer and Rainbow Project Co-ordinator Ms Dianne Skerritt   Tel: 07917 674680
email: dskerritt@southwell.anglican.org
Diocesan Ecumenical Officer Revd Jonathan Smithurst, Vale Cottage, 19 Church Lane, Attenborough, Nottingham NG9 6AS
Tel: 0115 952 9602
email: jonathansmithurst@gmail.com

World Church Link Officer Vacancy

PRESS AND PUBLICATIONS
Director of Communications Richard Ellis, Jubilee House, Westgate, Southwell NG25 0JH
　　email: richard.ellis@southwell.anglican.org

DIOCESAN RECORDS OFFICE
Nottinghamshire Archives, County House, Castle Meadow Rd, Nottingham NG1 1AG *Principal Archivist* Ms Ruth Imeson　　*Tel:* 0115 950 4524

AREA DEANS
ARCHDEACONRY OF NEWARK
Bassetlaw and Bawtry Revd Simon Cash, 11 Poplar Close, Water Meadows, Worksop S30 3BZ
　　Tel: 01909 472069
　　email: s.cash@tiscali.co.uk
Mansfield Revd Mark Adams, St John's Vicarage, St John Street, Mansfield NG18 1QH
　　Tel: 01623 625999
　　email: vicar@stjohnswithstmarys.org.uk
Newark and Southwell Revd David Milner, The Rectory, Marsh Lane, Farndon, Newark NG24 3SS　　*Tel:* 01636 650063
　　email: wd.milner55@gmail.com

Newstead Revd Dr Richard Kellett, Vicarage, Mansfield Rd, Skegby, Sutton-in-Ashfield NG17 3ED　　*Tel:* 01623 558800
　　email: richard@skegbyparish.org.uk

ARCHDEACONRY OF NOTTINGHAM
East Bingham Canon Jim Wellington, The Rectory, Nottingham Rd, Keyworth, Nottingham NG12 0UB　　*Tel:* 0115 937 2017
　　email: jhcwelli@btinternet.com
West Bingham Canon John Bentham, 51 Chatsworth Rd, West Bridgford, Nottingham NG2 7AE
　　Tel: 0115 846 1054
　　email: john.bentham@nottingham.ac.uk
Gedling Canon Phil Williams, St James' Vicarage, Marshall Hill Drive, Mapperley, Nottingham NG3 6FY　　*Tel:* 0115 960 6185
　　email: phil.stjames@virgin.net
Nottingham North Revd Elizabeth Snowden, Emmanuel Vicarage, 10 Church View Close, Warren Hill, Arnold NG5 9QP
　　Tel: 0115 920 8879
　　email: revesnowden@yahoo.co.uk
Nottingham South Revd Karen Rooms, The Vicarage, 17 Robin Hood Close, St Ann's, Nottingham NG3 4EY　　*Tel:* 0115 950 4571
　　email: roomskaren@googlemail.com

DIOCESE OF TRURO

Founded in 1877. Cornwall; the Isles of Scilly; one parish in Devon.

Population 541,000   Area 1,390 sq m
Full-time Stipendiary Parochial Clergy 94   Benefices 128
Parishes 222   Churches 307
www.truro.anglican.org
Overseas link dioceses: Strängnas, Sweden and Umzimvubu, South Africa.

BISHOP (15th)
Rt Revd Tim Thornton, Lis Escop, Feock, Truro
TR3 6QQ [2008]   *Tel:* 01872 862657
                                  Fax: 01872 862037
          email: bishop@truro.anglican.org
[Timothy Truro]
Domestic Chaplain Revd Jem Thorold
          email: chaplain@truro.anglican.org
Bishop's Secretaries Mrs Karen Madeley, Lis Escop
          email: office@truro.anglican.org
Mrs Lesley Rogers, Lis Escop
          email: office@truro.anglican.org

SUFFRAGAN BISHOP
ST GERMANS Rt Revd Chris Goldsmith, Vounder,
Tresillian, Truro TR2 4BW [2013]
                                  Tel: 01872 862657
email: bishopofstgermans@truro.anglican.org

CATHEDRAL CHURCH OF THE BLESSED VIRGIN MARY IN TRURO
Dean Very Revd Roger Bush   *Tel:* 01872 245006
Cathedral Office 14 St Mary's St, Truro TR1 2AF
                                  Tel: 01872 276782
                                  Fax: 01872 277788
          email: dean@trurocathedral.org.uk
Canons Residentiary
Precentor Canon Perran Gay, St Michael's House,
52 Daniell Rd, Truro TR1 2DA [1994]
                                  Tel: 01872 245003
          email: perran@trurocathedral.org.uk
Chancellor Canon Alan Bashforth, Cathedral
Office   *Tel:* 01872 245018
          email: alan@trurocathedral.org.uk
Pastor Canon Lynda Barley, Cathedral Office
                                  Tel: 01872 245016
          email: lynda@trurocathedral.org.uk
Chapter Canons
Mr Robert Foulkes [2001]
Mrs Bridget Hugh-Jones [2001]
Director of Music Christopher Gray, Cathedral
Office   *email:* chris@trurocathedral.org.uk

ARCHDEACONS
BODMIN Ven Audrey Elkington, 4 Park Drive,
Bodmin PL31 2QF [2011]
          Tel and *Fax:* 01208 892811
          email: audrey@truro.anglican.org

CORNWALL Ven Bill Stuart-White, 10 The Hayes,
Bodmin Road, Truro TR1 1FY [2012]
                                  Tel: 01872 242374
          email: bill@truro.anglican.org

CONVOCATION (MEMBERS OF THE HOUSE OF CLERGY OF THE GENERAL SYNOD)
Proctors for Clergy
Revd Alan Bashforth
Very Revd Roger Bush
Revd Canon Perran Gay

MEMBERS OF THE HOUSE OF LAITY OF THE GENERAL SYNOD
Mrs Susannah Leafe
Mrs Sheri Sturgess
Gp Capt Paul Terrett

DIOCESAN OFFICERS
Dioc Secretary Mrs Esther Pollard
                                  Tel: 01872 274351
          email: esther.pollard@truro.anglican.org
Deputy Dioc Secretary Mr Julian Briscoe, Dioc
Office   *Tel:* 01872 274351
          email: julian.briscoe@truro.anglican.org
Assistant Dioc Secretary Mrs Lesley Fusher, Dioc
Office   *email:* lesley.fusher@truro.anglican.org
                    Web: www.truro.anglican.org
Chancellor of Diocese The Worshipful Timothy
Briden, Lamb Chambers, Lamb Building,
Temple, London EC4Y 7AS   *Tel:* 020 7797 8300
                                  Fax: 020 7707 8308
          email: info@lambchambers.co.uk
Registrar of Diocese and Bishop's Legal Secretary Mr
Martin Follett, Truro Diocesan Registry,
Michelmores LLP, Woodwater House, Pynes Hill,
Exeter EX2 5WR   *Tel:* 01392 687415
                                  Fax: 01392 360563
          email: mjf@michelmores.com
Dioc Surveyor Mr Matthew Williams, Dioc House,
Kenwyn, Truro TR1 1JQ   *Tel:* 01872 241507
                                  Fax: 01872 222510
          email: matthew.williams@truro.anglican.org

DIOCESAN ORGANIZATIONS
Church House, Woodlands Court, Truro Business
Park, Truro TR4 9NH   *Tel:* 01872 274351
          email: info@truro.anglican.org

ADMINISTRATION
Dioc Synod and Bishop's Council (Acting Secretary)
Mrs Esther Pollard, Dioc Office
Dioc Synod (Chairman, House of Clergy) Revd Alan
Bashforth, Vicarage, 6 Penwinnick Parc, St Agnes
TR5 0UQ   *Tel:* 01872 553391
(Chairman, House of Laity) Mrs Sheri Sturgess
Board of Finance (Vice Chairman) Dr Mike Todd;
(Secretary) Mrs Esther Pollard *(as above)*
Parsonages Committee Mrs Esther Pollard *(as above)*
Mission and Pastoral Committee Mrs Esther Pollard
Glebe Committee Mrs Clare Jones, Dioc Office
Board of Patronage Dr Mike Todd
Designated Officer Mrs Esther Pollard *(as above)*

CHURCHES
*Advisory Committee for the Care of Churches
(Chairman)*Dr John Kidman, Trepenal Barn,
Blisland, Bodmin PL30 4HS   *Tel:* 01208 821525
                    email: john@tavas.co.uk
(Secretary) Mrs Sue Thorold
Truro Diocesan Guild of Ringers (President) Mr
Michael Wycherley, 34 St Gluvias St, Penryn
TR10 8BJ *Tel:* 01326 374119; *(Gen Secretary)* Mr
Robert Perry, 11 Trevaylor Close, Truro TR1 1RP,
Tel: 01872 277117
Churches Uses Committee (Secretary) Mrs Sue
Thorold *(as above)*

EDUCATION AND TRAINING
Director and Secretary of Education Revd Simon
Cade, Dioc Office   *Tel:* 01872 247214
          email: simon.cade@truro.anglican.org
Project Officer Mrs Sarah Welply *(same address)*
          email: sarah.welply@truro.anglican.org
Discipleship Project Officer Mrs Shelley Porter,
4 Park Drive, Bodmin PL31 2QF
                    Tel: 01208 892811
  email: shelley.porter@truro.anglican.org

MINISTRY
Director of Ministerial Formation and Development
Revd Paul Arthur, Rectory, 16 Trelavour Rd, St
Dennis, St Austell PL26 8AH   *Tel:* 01726 822317
          email: kpaularthur@googlemail.com
Director Accompanied Ministry Development Dr
Jonathan Rowe, Dioc Office   *Tel:* 01872 274351
          email: jonathan.rowe@truro.anglican.org
Director of Ordinands Revd Jane Vaughan-Wilson,
4 Tolver Road, Penzance TR18 2AG
                    Tel: 01736 351825
          email: jvaughanwi@hotmail.co.uk
South-west Ministry Training Course (Principal) Dr
Christopher Southgate, Amory Building,
University of Exeter, Rennes Drive, Exeter EX4
4RJ   *Tel:* 01392 264403
          email: principal@swmtc.org.uk
               Web: www.swmtc.org.uk
Warden of Readers Rt Revd Chris Goldsmith *(as above)*
Deputy Warden of Readers Revd Paul Arthur *(as above)*

Clergy Retirement and Widows Officer Revd Brian
McQuillen, 7 Bonython Drive, Grampound, Truro
TR2 4RL   *Tel:* 01726 883184
          email: revmcq.looe@btinternet.com

EVANGELISM AND UNITY
Chairman Revd Angela Butler, 22 Esplanade
Road, Pentire, Newquay TR7 1QB
                    Tel: 01637 859238
          email: angelambutler@btinternet.com
Officer for Unity Revd Elizabeth Foot, St Johns
in the Fields Vicarage, Hellesvean, St Ives
TR26 2HG   *Tel:* 01736 794899
          email: guenolesenara@hotmail.co.uk
World Church Committee (Chairman) Revd Andrew
Gough

KINGDOM GROUP
Social Responsibility Officer Revd Andrew Yates,
Dioc Office
          email: andrew.yates@truro.anglican.org

PRESS AND PUBLICATIONS
Dioc Communications Officer Kelly Rowe, Dioc
Office   *Tel:* 01872 274351
          email: kelly.rowe@truro.anglican.org
Editor of Dioc News Leaflet Kelly Rowe *(as above)*
Editor of Online Dioc Directory Mrs Clare Jones *(as above)*

DIOCESAN RECORDS
Diocesan Records Officer Mr David Thomas,
County Hall, Truro TR1 3AY   *Tel:* 01872 323127
          email: cro@cornwall.gov.uk
          website: cornwall.gov.uk/cro

STEWARDSHIP
Mrs Rebecca Evans, Dioc House
                    Tel: 01872 274351
          email: rebecca.evans@truro.anglican.org

RURAL DEANS
ARCHDEACONRY OF CORNWALL
St Austell Revd Marion Barrett, The Rectory, St
Mewan, St Austell PL26 7DP   *Tel:* 01726 72679
          email: marionstmewan@btinternet.com
Carnmarth North Revd Olive Stevens, Hideaway,
The Square, Portreath, Redruth TR16 4LA
                    Tel: 01209 842372
          email: olivestevens@aol.com
Carnmarth South Revd Geoffrey Bennett, The
Vicarage, Merry Mit Meadow, Budock Water,
Falmouth TR11 5DW   *Tel:* 01326 376422
          email: rev.bennett@talk21.com
Kerrier Revd Lesley Walker, The Rectory, St
Martin, Helston TR12 6BU   *Tel:* 01326 231971
          email: walker53@btopenworld.com
Penwith Revd David Stevens, Bede House,
Primrose Hill, Goldsithney, Penzance TR20 9JR
                    Tel: 01736 719090
          email: djstevens121@btinternet.com

Powder Revd Ken Boullier, 16 Waterloo Close, St Mawes, Truro TR2 5BD   *Tel:* 01326 270248
                    email: revkjb@hotmail.co.uk
Pydar Revd Christopher Malkinson, The Vicarage, 46 Treverbyn Rd, Padstow PL28 8DN
                              Tel: 01841 533776
                email: chrismalk@hotmail.com

ARCHDEACONRY OF BODMIN

East Wivelshire Revd Michael Goodland, The Vicarage, Millbrook, Torpoint PL10 1BW
                              Tel: 01752 822264
          email: michaelgoodland07@gmail.com

Stratton Revd Robert Thewsey, The Rectory, Boscastle PL35 0DJ   *Tel:* 01288 250359
          email: robert.thewsey@btinternet.com
Trigg Major Revd David Jasper, East Barton, North Petherwin, Launceston PL15 8LR
                              Tel: 01566 785996
      email: davidjasper5dy@btinternet.com
Trigg Minor and Bodmin Canon Dave Elkington, 4 Park Drive, Bodmin PL31 2QF   *Tel:* 01208 892811
                email: djelk@btinternet.com
West Wivelshire Revd Philip Sharp, The Rectory, Barbican Road, East Looe PL13 1NX
                              Tel: 01503 263070
              email: rev.sharp@btinternet.com

Founded in 2014. West Yorkshire, Yorkshire Dales, areas of Barnsley,
east Lancashire and south-western County Durham

Population 2,660,000   Area 2,840 sq m
Full-time Stipendiary Parochial Clergy 496   Benefices 332
Parishes 470   Churches 656
www.westyorkshiredales.anglican.org
Overseas link dioceses: Colombo and Kurunagala (Sri Lanka), Erfurt (Germany),
Faisalabad (Pakistan), Mara, Rorya and Tarime (Tanzania), Skara (Sweden),
South Western Virginia (USA), Sudan.

BISHOP (1st)
Rt Revd Nicholas Baines, Hollin House,
Weetwood Avenue, Leeds LS16 5NG [2014]
Tel: 0113 284 4300
email:
bishop.nick@westyorkshiredales.anglican.org
lyndsay.horsman@
westyorkshiredales.anglican.org
Bishop's Chaplain Revd Lynn Thorius, Hollin
House, Weetwood Avenue, Leeds LS16 5NG
Tel: 0113 284 4304
email:
lynn.thorius@westyorkshiredales.anglican.org

AREA BISHOPS
BRADFORD Rt Revd Toby Howarth
email:
bishop.toby@westyorkshiredales.anglican.org
HUDDERSFIELD Rt Revd Jonathan Gibbs
email: bishop.jonathan@
westyorkshiredales.anglican.org
LEEDS Rt Revd Nicholas Baines, Hollin House,
Weetwood Avenue, Leeds LS16 5NG
Tel: 0113 284 4300
email:
bishop.nick@westyorkshiredales.anglican.org
RIPON Rt Revd James Bell, Thistledown, Main
Street, Exelby, Bedale DL8 2HD   *Tel:* 01677 423525
email:
bishop.james@westyorkshiredales.anglican.org
WAKEFIELD Rt Revd Tony Robinson, Pontefract
House, Manygates Lane, Sandal, Wakefield WF2
7DR   *Tel:* 01924 250781
email:
bishop.tony@westyorkshiredales.anglican.org

HONORARY ASSISTANT BISHOPS
Rt Revd Dr Colin Buchanan, 21 The Drive,
Alwoodley, Leeds LS17 7QB [2004]
Tel: 0113 267 7721
Rt Revd Dr Tom Butler, Overtown Grange
Cottage, The Balk, Walton, Wakefield WF2 6JX
Tel: 01924 256018
email: tom.butler5340@gmail.com
Rt Revd Clive Handford, Wayside, 1 The
Terrace, Kirkby Hill, Boroughbridge YO51 9DQ
Tel: 01423 325406
email: gchandford@gmail.com

Rt Revd David Jenkins, Ashbourne, Cotherstone,
Barnard Castle DL12 9PR [1994]
Tel: 01833 650804
Rt Revd Glyn Webster, Holy Trinity Rectory,
Micklegate, York YO1 6LE   *Tel:* 01904 628155
email: office@seeofbeverley.org

CATHEDRAL CHURCH OF ST PETER, BRADFORD
Dean Very Revd Jerry Lepine, The Deanery,
1 Cathedral Close, Bradford BD1 4EG [2013]
Tel: 01274 777720 (Office)
email: jerry.lepine@bradfordcathedral.org

Canons Residentiary
Canon Samuel Corley, 3 Cathedral Close,
Bradford BD1 4EG [2010]   *Tel:* 01274 777720
Mobile: 07966 524683
email: sam.corley@bradfordcathedral.org
Vacancy, 2 Cathedral Close, Bradford BD1 4EG
Curate Revd Catherine Thatcher, Bradford
Cathedral, Stott Hill, Bradford BD1 4EH [2014]
Tel: 01274 77721
email: cat.thatcher@bradfordcathedral.org
Cathedral Office Bradford Cathedral, Stott Hill,
Bradford BD1 4EH   *Tel:* 01274 777720
Fax: 01274 777730
email: julie.bowyer@bradfordcathedral.org
Director of Strategic Development and Operations
Ms Amanda Anderson, Bradford Cathedral, Stott
Hill, Bradford BD1 4EH   *Tel:* 01274 777726
email: amanda.anderson@bradfordcathedral.org
Education and Visitor Officer Mrs Gillian Davis,
Bradford Cathedral, Stott Hill, Bradford BD1 4EH
Tel: 01274 777734
email: gillian.davis@bradfordcathedral.org
Director of Music Mr Alexander Woodrow,
Bradford Cathedral, Stott Hill, Bradford BD1 4EH
Tel: 01274 777720
email: alex.woodrow@bradfordcathedral.org
Assistant Director of Music Mr Jonathan Eyre,
Bradford Cathedral, Stott Hill, Bradford BD1 4EH
Tel: 01274 777720
email: jonathan.eyre@bradfordcathedral.org
Cathedral Organist Mr Paul Bowen, Bradford
Cathedral, Stott Hill, Bradford BD1 4EH
email: paul.bowen@bradfordcathedral.org

Head Verger Mr Jon Howard, Bradford Cathedral, Stott Hill, Bradford BD1 4EH   *Tel:* 01274 777724
email: jon.howard@bradfordcathedral.org
PA to the Dean and to the Director of Strategic Development and Operations Mrs Sandra Howard, Bradford Cathedral, Stott Hill, Bradford BD1 4EH   *Tel:* 01274 777723
email: sandra.howard@bradfordcathedral.org

CATHEDRAL CHURCH OF ST PETER AND ST WILFRID, RIPON

Dean Very Revd John Dobson, Minster House, Bedern Bank, Ripon HG4 1PE
Tel: 01765 602609
email: deanjohn@riponcathedral.org.uk
Dean's Secretary Mrs Judith Bustard
Tel: 01765 603462
email: judithbustard@riponcathedral.org.uk
Cathedral Office Liberty Courthouse, Minster Rd, Ripon HG4 1QS   *Tel:* 01765 603462
Fax: 01765 690398
email: judithbustard@riponcathedral.org.uk
Canon Precentor Canon Paul Greenwell, St Wilfrid's House, Minster Close, Ripon HG4 1QP
Tel: 01765 600211
email: canonpaul@riponcathedral.org.uk

Canons Residentiary
Canon Keith Punshon, St Peter's House, Minster Close, Ripon HG4 1QR [1996]   *Tel:* 01765 604108
email: keith.punshon@riponcathedral.org.uk
Canon Elizabeth Sewell, 16 Primrose Drive, Ripon HG4 1QR   *Tel:* 01765 608545
email: canonelizabeth@riponcathedral.org.uk
Director of Operations Miss Julia Barker, Cathedral Office, Liberty Courthouse, Minster Road, Ripon HG4 1QS   *Tel:* 01765 603462
email: juliabarker@riponcathedral.org.uk
Director of Music Mr Andrew Bryden, c/o Ripon Cathedral, Ripon HG4 1QT   *Tel:* 01765 603496
email: andrewbryden@riponcathedral.org.uk

CATHEDRAL CHURCH OF ALL SAINTS, WAKEFIELD

Cathedral Centre 8–10 Westmorland St, Wakefield WF1 1PJ   *Tel:* 01924 373923
email: admin@wakefield-cathedral.org.uk
Web: www.wakefield-cathedral.org.uk
Dean Very Revd Jonathan Greener, The Deanery, 1 Cathedral Close, Margaret St, Wakefield WF1 2DP   *Tel:* 01924 373923 (Office)
01924 239308 (Home)
email:
jonathan.greener@wakefield-cathedral.org.uk
Administrator and Chapter Clerk Mr Ashley Ellis
Tel: 01924 371802
email:
ashley.ellis@westyorkshiredales.anglican.org
Dean's PA Mr Neil Holland   *Tel:* 01924 373923
email: neil.holland@wakefield-cathedral.org.uk
Cathedral Secretary: Mrs Karn Dyson
Tel: 01924 373923
email: karn.dyson@wakefield-cathedral.org.uk

Head Verger Mrs Julie Lovell
Tel: 01924 434486 (Direct Line)
Canons Residentiary
Sub Dean and Canon Pastor Canon Michael Rawson, 3 Cathedral Close, Margaret St, Wakefield WF1 2DP [2007]
Tel: 01924 373923 (Office)
01924 379743 (Home)
email:
michael.rawson@wakefield-cathedral.org.uk
Canon Precentor Canon Andrea Hofbauer, 4 Cathedral Close, Margaret St, Wakefield WF1 2DP [2009]   *Tel:* 01924 373923 (Office)
01924 200191 (Home)
email: andi.hofbauer@wakefield-cathedral.org.uk
Canon Librarian Canon Dr John Lawson, 7 Belgravia Rd, St John's, Wakefield WF1 3JP [2005]
Tel: 01924 380182
email:
john.lawson@westyorkshiredales.anglican.org
Canon Missioner Canon Tony Macpherson, 14 Belgravia Rd, St John's, Wakefield WF1 3JP [2007]   *Tel:* 07780 990354
email: canontonymac@gmail.com
Priest Vicar Revd June Lawson
email: jlawson@mirfield.org.uk
Education Officer Ms Ali Bullivent
email: ali.bullivent@wakefield-cathedral.org.uk
Director of Music Mr Tom Moore, Cathedral Office
email: tom.moore@wakefield-cathedral.org.uk
Assistant Director of Music Mr Simon Earl, Cathedral Office
email: simonearl249@btinternet.com

ARCHDEACONS

BRADFORD Ven Dr David Lee, 47 Kirkgate, Shipley, West Yorkshire BD18 3EH [2004]
Tel: 01274 200698
Fax: 01274 200698
email:
david.lee@westyorkshiredales.anglican.org
LEEDS Ven Paul Hooper, Hollin House, Weetwood Avenue, Leeds LS16 5NG   *Tel:* 0113 2690594
email:
paul.hooper@westyorkshiredales.anglican.org
HALIFAX Ven Dr Anne Dawtry, 2 Vicarage Gardens, Rastrick, Brighouse HD6 3HD
Tel: 01484 714553
email: archdeacon.halifax@
westyorkshiredales.anglican.org
PONTEFRACT Ven Peter Townley, The Vicarage, Kirkthorpe, Wakefield WF1 5SZ
Tel: 01924 896327
Tel: 01924 434459 (Church House Direct Line)
Fax: 01924 364834 (Church House)
email: archdeacon.pontefract@
westyorkshiredales.anglican.org
RICHMOND AND CRAVEN Ven Paul Slater, Woodlands, Netherghyll Lane, Cononley, Keighley BD20 8PB [2005]   *Tel:* 01535 635113 (Home)
01535 650533 (Office)
email:
paul.slater@westyorkshiredales.anglican.org

CONVOCATION (MEMBERS OF THE HOUSE OF CLERGY OF THE GENERAL SYNOD)
Proctors for Clergy
Revd Canon James Allison
Revd Paul Ayers
Revd Paul Cartwright
Revd Jonathan Clark
Canon Kathryn Fitzsimons
Revd Ruth Hind
Revd Canon Joyce Jones
Revd Canon Maggie McLean
Ven Paul Slater
Revd Ruth Yeoman

MEMBERS OF THE HOUSE OF LAITY OF THE GENERAL SYNOD
Mr David Ashton
Dr John Beal
Mr Malcolm Halliday
Mrs Alison Fisher
Mr Ian Fletcher
Mr Nigel Greenwood
Mrs Mary Judkins
Mrs Zahida Mallard
Dr Richard Mantle
Mr Paul Neville

DIOCESAN OFFICERS
Diocesan Secretary and Programme Director
Mr John Tuckett, Leeds Office, St Mary's Street, Leeds LS9 7DP   *Tel:* 0113 2000 567
email: john.tuckett@westyorkshiredales.anglican.org
Chief Officers
Mrs Debbie Child, Kadugli House, Elmsley St, Steeton, Keighley BD20 6SE
Tel: 01535 650555
Fax: 01535 650550
email: debbie.child@westyorkshiredales.anglican.org
Mr Ashley Ellis, Church House, 1 South Parade, Wakefield WF1 1LP   *Tel:* 01924 371802
Fax: 01924 364834
email: ashley.ellis@westyorkshiredales.anglican.org
Chancellor of Diocese The Worshipful John Bullimore, c/o Diocesan Registry, Yorkshire House, East Parade, Leeds LS1 5BD
Tel: 0113 280 2000
Registrar of Diocese and Bishop's Legal Secretary Mr Peter William Foskett, Diocesan Registry, Yorkshire House, East Parade, Leeds LS1 5BD
Tel: 0113 280 2000
email: peter.foskett@lf-dt.com

DIOCESAN ORGANIZATIONS
ADMINISTRATION
Programme Office St Mary's Street, Leeds LS9 7DP
Tel: 0113 2000 567
email: jane.butterfield@westyorkshiredales.anglican.org

Synodical Office St Mary's Street, Leeds LS9 7DP
Tel: 0113 2000 542
email: peter.mojsa@westyorkshiredales.anglican.org
Bradford Office Kadugli House, Elmsley St, Steeton, Keighley BD20 6SE   *Tel:* 01535 650555
email: office.bradford@westyorkshiredales.anglican.org
Leeds Office St Mary's Street, Leeds LS9 7DP
Tel: 0113 200 0540
email: reception.leeds@westyorkshiredales.anglican.org
Wakefield Office Church House, 1 South Parade, Wakefield WF1 1LP   *Tel:* 01924 371802
email: reception.wakefield@ westyorkshiredales.anglican.org
Chair of Board of Finance (Bradford) Mrs Sharron Arnold, 42 Effingham Rd, Harden, Bingley BD16 1LQ   *Tel:* 01535 272894
email: sharron.arnold99@hotmail.com
Chair of Board of Finance (Leeds) Mr Simon Baldwin, 4 Boundary Close, Colton, Leeds LS15 9HX
email: s.baldwin@leedsmet.ac.uk
Chair of Board of Finance (Wakefield) Revd Martin Macdonald, Wakefield Office
Secretary of Board of Finance (Bradford) Mrs Debbie Child, Bradford Office
Secretary of Board of Finance (Wakefield) Mr Ashley Ellis, Wakefield Office
Finance Manager (Bradford) Mr Shaun Birch, Bradford Office
Finance Manager (Huddersfield, Wakefield) Mr Bryan Lewis, Wakefield Office
Property Manager and Diocesan Surveyor (Bradford) Mr David Meadows, Bradford Office
Property Manager and Diocesan Surveyor (Leeds, Ripon) Mr Michael Lindley, Leeds Office
Property Manager and Diocesan Surveyor (Huddersfield, Wakefield) Mr Kevin Smith, Wakefield Office
Secretary of Mission and Pastoral Committee (Bradford) Mrs Debbie Child, Bradford Office
Secretary of Mission and Pastoral Committee (Leeds, Ripon) Mr Peter Mojsa, Leeds Office
Secretary of Mission and Pastoral Committee (Huddersfield, Wakefield) Mr Ashley Ellis, Wakefield Office

CHURCHES
Acting Chair of Diocesan Advisory Committee Ven Dr David Lee, 47 Kirkgate, Shipley BD18 3EH
Tel: 01274 200698
email: david.lee@westyorkshiredales.anglican.org
Secretary Mrs Debbie Child, Bradford Office

COMMUNICATIONS
Head of Communications Ian Bustin, Programme Office   *Tel:* 07526 139995
email: ian.bustin@westyorkshiredales.anglican.org

EDUCATION

Chair of Board of Education (Bradford, Leeds, Ripon)
Revd Barry Miller, Beechcroft, 32 Nab Lane, Shipley BD18 4HH   *Tel:* 01274 590630
email:
barry.miller@westyorkshiredales.anglican.org
Chair of Board of Education (Huddersfield, Wakefield) Ven Peter Townley, Wakefield Office
Chief Education Officer (Bradford, Leeds, Ripon) Mr Richard Noake, Windsor House, Cornwall Rd, Harrogate HG1 2PW   *Tel:* 01423 817553
07903 326053 (Mobile)
email:
richard.noake@westyorkshiredales.anglican.org
Chief Education Officer (Huddersfield, Wakefield)
Revd Canon Ian Wildey, Wakefield Office

MINISTRY AND MISSION

Bishop's Officer (Bradford) The Revd Canon Denise Poole, 23 Leylands Lane, Heaton, Bradford BD9 5PX   *Tel:* 01274 401679
email:
denise.poole@westyorkshiredales.anglican.org
Director of Mission Resourcing (Leeds, Ripon)
Canon Adrian Alker, Leeds Office
Chair, Bishop's Advisory Group on Theology and Society (Huddersfield, Wakefield) Revd Roy Clements
Canon Missioner (Huddersfield, Wakefield) Canon Tony Macpherson, 14 Belgravia Road, Wakefield WF1 3JP   *Tel:* 01924 275274
email: canontonymac@gmail.com
Children and Young People (Bradford) Mr Steve Grasham, Bradford Office
Youth Work Adviser (Leeds, Ripon) Capt Canon Nic Sheppard, 7 Loxley Grove, Wetherby LS22 7YG   *Tel:* 01937 585440
email:
nic.sheppard@westyorkshiredales.anglican.org
Team Co-ordinator and 11–18yrs Adviser (Huddersfield, Wakefield) Mrs Liz Morton, Wakefield Office
Under 5s Adviser (Huddersfield, Wakefield) Adviser Mrs Ellie Wilson, Wakefield Office
Ecumenical Officer Revd Glenn Coggins, The Vicarage, 1 Church Lane, East Ardsley, Wakefield WF3 2LJ   *Tel:* 01924 822184
email: glenn.coggins@ely.anglican.org
Environment Officer (Bradford) Revd Canon Rod Anderson, 40 Low Wood, Wilsden, Bradford BD15 0JS   *Tel:* 07900 675350
email: environment@bradford.anglican.org
Environment Officer (Leeds, Ripon) Mrs Jemima Parker   *Tel:* 01423 569121
email:
jemima.parker@westyorkshiredales.anglican.org
Director of Ordinands (Bradford) Canon Ann Turner, The Rectory, 7 Roundell Drive, West Marton, Skipton BD23 3UL   *Tel:* 01282 842332
email: canonannturner@gmail.com

Director of Ordinands (Leeds, Ripon) Revd Peter Clement, The Parish House, 16 Orchard Close, Sharow, Ripon HG4 5BE   *Tel:* 01765 607017
email:
peter.clement@westyorkshiredales.anglican.org
Director of Ordinands (Huddersfield, Wakefield) Revd Canon Stephen Race, St John's Vicarage, Green Rd, Dodworth, Barnsley S75 3R
Tel: 01226 206276
email:
stephen.race@westyorkshiredales.anglican.org
Development Officer (Bradford) Revd Uell Kennedy, Bradford Office
Stewardship Adviser (Leeds, Ripon) Mr Paul Winstanley, Leeds Office
Development Officer (Huddersfield, Wakefield) Susan Parker, Wakefield Office
Warden of Readers (Bradford) Revd Adrian Cragg, 6 Vicarage Close, Wyke, Bradford BD12 8QW
Tel: 01274 676059
email:
adrian.cragg@westyorkshiredales.anglican.org
Warden of Readers (Leeds, Ripon) Canon Ann Hemsworth, 12 Kelmscott Grove, Cross Gates, Leeds LS15 8HH   *Tel:* 0113 293 7494
email: annhemsworth01@btinternet.com
Warden of Readers (Huddersfield, Wakefield) Ven Dr Anne Dawtry, 2 Vicarage Gardens, Rastrick, Brighouse HD6 3HD   *Tel:* 01484 714553
email: archdeacon.halifax@
westyorkshiredales.anglican.org
Rural Ministry Officer (Bradford) Revd David Houlton, The Vicarage, Church Lane, Gargrave, Skipton BD23 3NQ   *Tel:* 01756 748468
email: david.houlton@bradford.anglican.org
Rural Ministry Officer (Leeds, Ripon) Mr Andrew Ryland, 12 Linton Falls, Linton in Craven, Skipton BD23 6BQ   *Tel:* 07771 797073
email:
andy.ryland@westyorkshiredales.anglican.org
Rural Ministry Officer (Huddersfield, Wakefield) Revd Canon James Allison   *Tel:* 01422 202292
email: canonallison@btinternet.com
Safeguarding Adviser Mrs Jenny Price, Wakefield Office   *Tel:* 01924 371802
Mobile: 07800 740001
email:
jenny.price@westyorkshiredales.anglican.org
Director of School of Ministry (Laity) (Bradford) Revd Canon Steve Davie, Tong Vicarage, Holme Wood Road, Bradford BD4 9EJ
Tel: 01274 682100
email: steve.davie@bradford.anglican.org
IME 4–7 (Bradford) Revd Jill Perrett, The Rectory, Low Mill Lane, Addingham, Ilkley LS29 0QP
Tel: 01943 831382
email: jill.perrett@bradford.anglican.org
CME (Bradford) Revd Louise Taylor-Kenyon, The Vicarage, 21 Shires Lane, Embsay, Skipton BD23 6SB   *Tel:* 01756 798057
email: louise.taylor-
kenyon@westyorkshiredales.anglican.org

Director of Lay Training (Leeds, Ripon) Revd
Andrew Tawn, Leeds Office   *Tel:* 0113 200 0557
    email:
andrew.tawn@westyorkshiredales.anglican.org
Director of Clergy Training (Leeds, Ripon) Revd
Andrew Tawn, Leeds Office (*as above*)
Director of Training (Huddersfield, Wakefield) Revd
Canon Dr John Lawson, Wakefield Office
    Tel: 01924 380182
    email:
john.lawson@westyorkshiredales.anglican.org
CME (Huddersfield, Wakefield) Canon Stephen
Kelly, The Vicarage, Woolley, Wakefield WF4 2JU
    Tel: 01226 382550
    email:
stephen.kelly@westyorkshiredales.anglican.org
Urban Ministry Officer (Leeds, Ripon) Canon
Kathryn Fitzsimons, 52 Newton Court, Leeds
LS8 2PH   *Tel:* 0113 248 5011
    email: kathrynfitzsimons@hotmail.com
Urban Ministry Officer (Huddersfield, Wakefield)
Revd Martine Crabtree, St George's Vicarage,
23c Broadway, Lupset WF2 8AA
    Tel: 01924 787801
    email: martinecrabtree@aol.com
Urban Ministry Officer (Huddersfield, Wakefield)
Revd Tracy Ibbotson, Holy Cross Vicarage, The
Mount, Airedale, Castleford WF10 3JN
    Tel: 01977 553157
    email: ibbotson457@btinternet.com

DIOCESAN RECORD OFFICES
Bradford Metropolitan District Archives,
Former Central Library, Princes Way, Bradford
BD1 1NN
    email: bradford@wyjs.org.uk
Calderdale Metropolitan District Archives,
Central Library, Northgate House, Northgate,
Halifax HX1 1UN   *Tel:* 01422 392636
    email: calderdale@wyjs.org.uk
Durham Record Office, County Hall, Durham
DH1 5UL   *Tel:* 0191 386 4411
Kirklees Council Archives, Huddersfield Library
and Art Gallery, Princess Alexandra Walk,
Huddersfield HD1 2SU   *Tel:* 01484 221966
    email: kirklees@wyjs.org.uk
Lancashire County Archives, Bow Lane, Preston
PR1 2RE   *Tel:* 01772 533039
    email: record.office@ed.lancashire.gov.uk
Leeds District Archives, PO Box 5, Nepshaw
Lane, Morley, Leeds LS27 0QP
    Tel: 0113 393 9771
    email: leeds@wyjs.org.uk
North Yorkshire County Record Office,
County Hall, Northallerton DL7 8DF
    Tel: 01609 777585
    email: archives@northyorks.gov.uk
Wakefield Council Archives, Registry of Deeds,
Newstead Road, Wakefield WF1 2DE
    Tel: 01924 305980
    email: wakefield@wyjs.org.uk

AREA DEANS
ARCHDEACONRY OF BRADFORD
Airedale Revd Canon Gary Hodgson, St
Michael's Vicarage, 81 Littlelands, Cottingley,
Bingley BD16 1AL   *Tel:* 01274 560761
    email: gshodgson@sky.com
Bowling and Horton Revd Vaughan Pollard,
The Vicarage, Clayton Lane, Clayton, Bradford
BD14 6AX   *Tel:* 01274 880373
    email: vaughan.pollard@bradford.anglican.org
Bradford North Revd Canon Steve Davie, Tong
Vicarage, Holme Wood Road, Bradford BD4 9EJ
    Tel: 01274 682100
    email: steve.davie@bradford.anglican.org
Ilkley Revd Canon Philip Gray, St Margaret's
Vicarage, The Lodge, Wells Road, Ilkley LS29 9JH
    Tel: 01943 607210
Keighley Revd Susan Griffiths, The Vicarage,
Briggate, Silsden, Keighley BD20 9JS
    Tel: 01535 652204

ARCHDEACONRY OF RICHMOND AND CRAVEN
Bowland Revd Ian Greenhalgh, The Vicarage,
Austwick, Lancaster LA2 8BE
    Tel: 01524 251313
    email: ian.greenhalgh@bradford.anglican.org
Ewecross Revd Ian Greenhalgh, The Vicarage,
Austwick, Lancaster LA2 8BE   *Tel:* 01524 251313
    email: ian.greenhalgh@bradford.anglican.org
Harrogate Revd Brendan Giblin, Wetherby
Vicarage, 3 Lazenby Drive, Wetherby LS22 6WL
    Tel: 01937 520951
    email: bgiblin@me.com
Richmond Revd John Richards, The Rectory,
Barningham, Richmond DL11 7DW
    Tel: 01833 621259
    email: johnmr1953@talk21.com
Ripon Revd Matthew Evans, The Vicarage, Dacre
Banks, Harrogate HG3 4ED   *Tel:* 01423 780262
    email: matthew.dhdt@btinternet.com
Skipton Canon Ann Turner, The Rectory,
7 Roundell Drive, West Marton, Skipton
BD23 3UL   *Tel:* 01282 842332
    email: canonannturner@gmail.com
Wensley Revd Michael Hepper, The Vicarage,
I'Anson Close, Leyburn DL8 5LF
    Tel: 01969 622251
    email: revmichael@btinternet.com

ARCHDEACONRY OF LEEDS
Allerton Revd David Stevens, St Martin's
Vicarage, 2a St Martin's View, Leeds LS7 3LB
    Tel: 0113 2624271
    email: revdstevens@aol.com
Armley Revd Arani Sen, 22 Hill End Crescent,
Leeds LS12 3PW   *Tel:* 0113 263 8788
    email: revaranisen@gmail.com
Headingley (acting) Revd Richard Dimery, St
James' Vicarage, 1 Scotland Close, Horsforth,
Leeds LS18 5SG   *Tel:* 0113 228 2902
    email: richard@dimery.com

Whitkirk Revd Mike Benwell, St Luke's Vicarage, Stanks Lane North, Leeds LS14 5AS
Tel: 0113 273 1302
email: benwell@ndirect.co.uk

ARCHDEACONRY OF HALIFAX
Almondbury Revd Richard Steel, Rectory, Church Lane, Kirkheaton, Huddersfield HD5 0BH
Tel: 01484 532410
email: rector@kirkheatonchurch.org.uk
Brighouse and Elland Canon David Burrows, All Saints' Vicarage, Charles St, Elland HX5 0JF
Tel: 01422 373184
email: rectorofelland@btinternet.com
Calder Valley Revd Owen Page, The Vicarage, 7 Fern Valley Chase, Todmorden OL14 7HB
Tel: 01706 813180
email: owen@todvic55.orangehome.co.uk
Halifax Revd Stephen Bradberry, 129 Paddock Lane, Norton Tower, Halifax HX2 0NT
Tel: 01422 358282
email: sbradberry@tiscali.co.uk
Huddersfield Revd Mary Railton-Crowder, The Vicarage, 4 Brendon Drive, Birkby, Huddersfield HD2 2DF   *Tel:* 01484 546966
email: revmrc@yahoo.com

Kirkburton Canon Joyce Jones, Oakfield, 206 Barnsley Road, Denby Dale, Huddersfield HD8 8TS   *Tel:* 01484 862350
email: joycerjones@aol.com

ARCHDEACONRY OF PONTEFRACT
Barnsley Revd Stephen Race, St John's Vicarage, Green Road, Dodworth, Barnsley S75 3RT
Tel: 01226 206276
email: stephen.race@westyorkshiredales.anglican.org
Birstall (acting) Revd Capt Paul Knight, St Peter's Vicarage, King's Drive, Birstall, Batley WF17 9JJ   *Tel:* 01924 473715
email: vicar@stpetersbirstall.co.uk
Dewsbury Revd Canon Kevin Partington, The Rectory, 16A Oxford Road, Dewsbury WF13 4JT
Tel: 01924 465491/457057
email: kevin.partington@btinternet.com
Pontefract Canon Bob Cooper, St Giles Vicarage, 9 The Mount, Pontefract WF8 1NE
Tel: 01977 706803
email: robert_cooper@msn.com
Wakefield Canon Stephen Kelly, The Vicarage, Woolley, Wakefield WF4 2JU   *Tel:* 01226 382550
email: stephen.kelly@westyorkshiredales.anglican.org

DIOCESE OF WINCHESTER

Founded in 676. Hampshire, except for the south-eastern quarter (PORTSMOUTH), an area in the north-east (GUILDFORD), a small area in the west (SALISBURY) and one parish in the north (OXFORD); an area of eastern Dorset; the Channel Islands.

Population 1,352,000   Area 1,220 sq m
Full-time Stipendiary Parochial Clergy 170   Benefices 182
Parishes 261   Churches 402
www.winchester.anglican.org
Overseas link provinces: Province of Uganda, Province of Myanmar, Provinces of Rwanda, Burundi and Republic of Congo (formerly Zaïre).

BISHOP

Rt Revd Timothy John Dakin, Wolvesey, Winchester SO23 9ND [2012]   *Tel:* 01962 854050
Fax: 01962 897088
Bishop's Chaplain Revd Gavin Foster (*same address*)
Tel: 01962 897082
email: gavin.foster@winchester.anglican.org
Bishop's Secretary Miss Joyce Cockell (*same address*)   *Tel:* 01962 854050
email: joyce.cockell@winchester.anglican.org

SUFFRAGAN BISHOPS

BASINGSTOKE Rt Revd David Williams, Bishop's Lodge, Colden Lane, Old Alresford SO24 9DH
Tel: 01962 737330
email: bishop.david@winchester.anglican.org
SOUTHAMPTON Rt Revd Jonathan Frost, Bishop's House, St Mary's Church Close, Wessex Lane, Southampton SO18 2ST   *Tel:* 023 8055 3627
email: bishop.jonathan@winchester.anglican.org

HONORARY ASSISTANT BISHOPS

Rt Revd Simon Hedley Burrows, 8 Quarry Rd, Winchester, SO23 0JF [1994]   *Tel:* 01962 853332
Rt Revd John Dennis, 7 Conifer Close, Winchester SO22 6SH [1999]   *Tel:* 01962 868881
Rt Revd John Ellison, The Furrow, Evingar Rd, Whitchurch RG28 7EU [2008]
Tel: 01256 892126
Rt Revd Christopher Herbert, 1 Beacon Close, Boundstone, Farnham GU10 4PA [2010]
Tel: 01252 795600
Rt Revd H. Scriven, 16 East St Helen Street, Abingdon OX14 5EA   *Tel:* 01235 536607/787500
Dom Timothy Bavin OSB, Alton Abbey, Abbey Road, Beech, Alton GU34 4AP   *Tel:* 01420 562145
Rt Revd Trevor Willmott, The Old Palace, The Precincts, Canterbury CT1 2EE   *Tel:* 01277 784985
email: trevorwillmott@bishcant.org

CATHEDRAL CHURCH OF THE HOLY TRINITY, AND OF ST PETER, ST PAUL AND OF ST SWITHUN

Dean Very Revd James Edgar Atwell, Cathedral Office, 9 The Close, Winchester SO23 9LS [2006]
Tel: 01962 857203
Fax: 01962 857264
email: the.dean@winchester-cathedral.org.uk

Cathedral Office 9 The Close, Winchester SO23 9LS
Tel: 01962 857200
Fax: 01962 857201
email: cathedral.office@winchester-cathedral.org.uk
Web: www.winchester–cathedral.org.uk

Canons Residentiary
Vice Dean and Canon Chancellor Canon Roland Riem, Cathedral Office, 9 The Close, Winchester SO23 9LS [2005]
Tel: 01962 857216
email: roland.riem@winchester-cathedral.org.uk
Canon Precentor Canon Sue Wallace, Cathedral Office, 9 The Close, Winchester SO23 9LS [2014]
Tel: 01962 857211
email: sue.wallace@winchester-cathedral.org.uk

Lay Canons
Receiver General and Canon Treasurer Mrs Annabelle Boyes, Cathedral Office, 9 The Close, Winchester SO23 9LS   *Tel:* 01962 857206
Fax: 01962 857201
email: annabelle.boyes@ winchester-cathedral.org.uk
Professor Lord Raymond Plant, Cathedral Office, 9 The Close, Winchester SO23 9LS
Tel: 01962 857200
Mr George Medd, Cathedral Office, 9 The Close, Winchester SO23 9LS   *Tel:* 01962 857200
Mrs Debbie Thrower, Cathedral Office, 9 The Close, Winchester SO23 9LS   *Tel:* 01962 857200
Close Vicar Revd Gregory Clifton-Smith, Cathedral Office, 9 The Close, Winchester SO23 9LS   *Tel:* 01962 857231
email: gregory.clifton-smith@winchester-cathedral.org.uk
Clerk at Law Mr Julian Hartwell, Cathedral Office, 9 The Close, Winchester SO23 9LS
Tel: 01962 857200
Director of Music Mr Andrew Lumsden, Cathedral Office, 9 The Close, Winchester SO23 9LS   *Tel:* 01962 857218
email: andrew.lumsden@winchester-cathedral.org.uk
Assistant Director of Music Mr George Castle, Cathedral Office, 9 The Close, Winchester SO23 9LS   *Tel:* 01962 857213
email: george.castle@winchester-cathedral.org.uk

ARCHDEACONS

BOURNEMOUTH Ven Dr Peter Rouch, Glebe House, 22 Bellflower Way, Chandlers Ford SO53 4HN [2011]   *Tel:* 023 8026 0955
          email: peter.rouch@winchester.anglican.org
WINCHESTER Ven Michael Harley, 22 St John's St, Winchester SO23 0HF [2009]   *Tel:* 01962 869442
          email: michael.harley@winchester.anglican.org
MISSION DEVELOPMENT Ven Paul Moore, Wolvesey, Winchester SO23 9ND
          email: paul.moore@winchester.anglican.org

CONVOCATION (MEMBERS OF THE HOUSE OF CLERGY OF THE GENERAL SYNOD)

Dignitaries in Convocation
The Bishop of Winchester
The Bishop of Basingstoke
Proctors for Clergy
Very Revd Bob Key
Ven Michael Harley
Canon Clive Hawkins
Revd Rosalind Rutherford

MEMBERS OF THE HOUSE OF LAITY OF THE GENERAL SYNOD

Mr John Davies
Dr Tony Bennett
Mrs Christine Fry
Mr Ken Shorey
Miss Priscilla Hungerford
Channel Islands
Mrs Jane Bisson
Mr David Robilliard

DIOCESAN OFFICERS

Chief Executive Mr Andrew Robinson, Old Alresford Place, Alresford SO24 9DH
          Tel: 01962 737305
          Fax: 01962 737358
          email: andrew.robinson@winchester.anglican.org
Chancellor of Diocese Worshipful His Honour Christopher Clark QC, c/o Dioc Office
Registrar of Diocese and Bishop's Legal Secretary Mr Andrew Johnson, Batt Broadbent, Minster Chambers, 42/44 Castle Street, Salisbury SP1 3TX
          Tel: 01722 411141
          email: aj@battbroadbent.co.uk

DIOCESAN ORGANIZATIONS

Diocesan Office Old Alresford Place, Alresford SO24 9DH   *Tel:* 01962 737300
          Fax: 01962 737358
          Web: www.winchester.anglican.org

DIOCESAN OFFICE

Head of Operations and Chief of Staff Mr Colin Harbidge, Old Alresford Place   *Tel:* 01962 737307
          email: colin.harbidge@winchester.anglican.org
Head of Finance Mr Malcolm Twigger-Ross, Old Alresford Place   *Tel:* 01962 737336
          email:
malcolm.twigger-ross@winchester.anglican.org

Head of Resource Development Mr Anthony Smith, Old Alresford Place   *Tel:* 01962 737342
          email: anthony.smith@winchester.anglican.org
Dioc Synod (Chairman, House of Clergy) Vacancy
(Chairman, House of Laity) Mr Ian Newman, Meadow View, 15 Bowerwood Rd, Fordingbridge SP6 1BL   *Tel:* 01425 653269
          email: ian@innewman.co.uk
(Secretary) Mr Andrew Robinson, *(as above)*
Board of Finance (Chairman) Rt Revd Timothy John Dakin, Wolvesey, Winchester SO23 9ND
          Tel: 01962 854050
          Fax: 01962 897088
Mission and Pastoral Committee (Secretary) Mrs Catherine Roberts, Old Alresford Place
          Tel: 01962 737306
Electoral Registration Officer Miss Jayne Tarry, Old Alresford Place   *Tel:* 01962 737348
          email: jayne.tarry@winchester.anglican.org
Editor of Diocesan Directory Miss Jayne Tarry *(as above)*

COMMUNICATIONS

Communications Office Luther Pendragon (Mr Ben Frankel)   *Tel:* 01962 737325
          Out of Hours: 020 7618 9197
          email: dioceseofwinchester@luther.co.uk

CHURCHES

Advisory Committee for the Care of Churches (Chairman) Canon Michael Anderson, Old Alresford Place
(Secretary) Mrs Catherine Roberts
          Tel: 01962 737306
          email: catherine.roberts@winchester.anglican.org

EDUCATION

Director of Education Revd Jeff Williams *(Joint working with Diocese of Portsmouth)*, First Floor, Peninsular House, Wharf Rd, Portsmouth PO2 8HB   *Tel:* 023 9289 9681
          email: jeff.williams@portsmouth.anglican.org

DISCIPLESHIP AND MINISTRY (School of Mission)

Director of the School of Mission Archdeacon for Mission Development *(as above)*
Vocations, Recruitment and Selection Officer (including ordinands) Revd Julia Mourant, Wolvesey, Winchester SO23 9ND
          Tel: 01962 710984
          email: julia.mourant@winchester.anglican.org
Ministry Training Adviser Preb Paul Dunthorne
          email: paul.dunthorne@winchester.anglican.org
Evangelism and Fresh Expressions Adviser Revd Phil Dykes, Wolvesey, Winchester SO23 9ND
          Tel: 01962 710973
Diocesan Children and Families Adviser Mr Andy Saunders, Wolvesey, Winchester SO23 9ND
          Tel: 01962 710972
          email: andy.saunders@winchester.anglican.org

Diocesan Youth Adviser Mr Pete Maidment, Wolvesey, Winchester SO23 9ND
Tel: 01962 710971
email: pete.maidment@winchester.anglican.org

ADVISERS
Stewardship Adviser Revd Gordon Randall, Old Alresford Place *Tel:* 01962 737323
email: gordon.randall@winchester.anglican.org
Human Resources Adviser Ms Susan Beckett, Old Alresford Place *Tel:* 01962 737353
email: susan.beckett@winchester.anglican.org
Diocesan Environmental Officer Revd Gordon Randall, Old Alresford Place *Tel:* 01962 737323
email: gordon.randall@winchester.anglican.org

CLERGY RETIREMENT OFFICERS
Archdeaconry of Bournemouth Revd Canon Peter Doores *Tel:* 01420 88794
email: peter@doores.myzen.co.uk
Archdeaconry of Winchester Revd Michael Kenning *Tel:* 01256 87989
email: michael.kenning@telorycoed.co.uk

CLERGY WIDOWS' AND WIDOWERS' OFFICERS
Archdeaconry of Bournemouth Revd Barry Kent *Tel:* 01425 616670
email: barrykent@minister.com
Archdeaconry of Winchester Revd Canon Graham Trasler *Tel:* 01264 359843
email: costadelanton@gamil.com

DIOCESAN RECORD OFFICES
Hants. Record Office, Sussex St, Winchester SO23 8TH *Archivist* Janet Smith *Tel:* 01962 846154; *email:* enquiries.archives@hants.gov.uk *(For diocesan records and parishes in Hampshire [except Southampton], Bournemouth and Christchurch)*
Southampton City Record Office, Civic Centre, Southampton SO14 7LY *Archivist* Mrs Sue Woolgar *Tel:* 023 8083 2251
email: city.archives@southampton.gov.uk
(For parishes in Southampton)
Guernsey Island Archives, St Barnabas, Cornet St, St Peter Port, Guernsey GY1 1LF
Tel: 01481 724512
Fax: 01481 715814
email: archives@gov.gg
Jersey Archive Service, Clarence Rd, St Helier, Jersey JE2 4JY *Archivist* Linda Romeril
Tel: 01534 833300
Fax: 01534 833301
email: archives@jerseyheritagetrust.org

SAFEGUARDING AND INCLUSION
Safeguarding Adviser Ms Jane Fisher, Old Alresford Place *Tel:* 01962 737347
email: jane.fisher@winchester.anglican.org

AREA DEANS
ARCHDEACONRY OF BOURNEMOUTH
Bournemouth Revd Andy McPherson, Vicarage, 53a Holdenhurst Avenue, Iford, Bournemouth BH7 6RB *Tel:* 01202 425978
email: parish.office@stsaviours.f2s.com
Christchurch Revd Gary Philbrick, The Rectory, 71 Church Street, Fordingbridge SP6 1BB
Tel: 01425 839622
email: gary.philbrick@dsl.pipex.com
Eastleigh Canon Peter Vargeson, The Vicarage, School Road, Bursledon, Southampton SO31 8BW *Tel:* 023 8040 2821
email: peter.vargeson@bursledonparish.org
Lyndhurst Revd Peter Salisbury, The Vicarage, Grove Road, Lymington SO41 3RF
Tel: 01590 673847
Romsey Revd Tim Sledge, The Vicarage, Church Lane, Romsey SO51 8EP *Tel:* 01794 513125
email: vicarofromsey@gmail.com
Southampton Revd Jane Bakker, The Vicarage, 41 Station Road, Southampton SO19 8FN
Tel: 023 8044 8337
email: jjbakker@tiscali.co.uk

ARCHDEACONRY OF WINCHESTER
Alresford Revd Phil Collins, The Rectory, 37 Jacklyns Lane, Alresford SO24 9LF
Tel: 01962 732105
email: nortoncollins@yahoo.co.uk
Alton Revd Howard Wright, The Vicarage, 22 Lymington Bottom, Four Marks, Alton GU34 5AA *Tel:* 01420 563344
email: howardwright@xalt.co.uk
Andover Canon John Harkin, St Mary's Vicarage, Church Close, Andover, SP10 1DP
Tel: 01264 362268
email: harkin12@btinternet.com
Basingstoke Revd Arthur Botham, The Vicarage, 25 Tewkesbury Close, Popley, Basingstoke RG24 9DU *Tel:* 01256 324734
email: arthur.botham@btinternet.com
Odiham Revd Peter Dyson, The Vicarage, Church Street, Upton Grey RG25 2RB
Tel: 01256 861750
email: pwdyson@onetel.com
Whitchurch Revd Kelvin Inglis, The Vicarage, Church Street, Whitchurch RG28 7AS
Tel: 01256 892535
email: kelvin.inglis@tiscali.co.uk
Winchester Revd Paul Kennedy, The Rectory, 19 Petersfield Road, Winchester SO23 0JD
Tel: 01962 853777
email: rectoreastwinchester@googlemail.com

CHANNEL ISLANDS
Dean of Jersey Very Revd Bob Key, The Deanery, David Place, St Helier, Jersey, CI JE2 4TE
Tel: 01534 720001
email: robert_f_key@yahoo.com
Dean of Guernsey Vacancy

The Channel Islands

The Channel Islands were formerly part of the Diocese of Coutances, Normandy, but were transferred in 1499/1500 to the Diocese of Winchester by Papal Bull, confirmed in a letter from Henry VII to Thomas Langton, the Bishop of Winchester. After some years in which the Bishops of Coutances continued to exercise *de facto* jurisdiction over the Islands, the transfer to the Diocese of Winchester was put beyond doubt by a letter from Elizabeth I in 1568 and an Order in Council dated 11 March 1569. The Order in Council directed that Henry VII's letter should not henceforth be brought into question and that the Islands and the Diocese were 'perpetually united'. The physical remoteness of the Channel Islands meant that bishops from England did not visit the Islands until 1818, although improved communications and travel in recent times have enabled a more normal relationship between the Deaneries in the Islands and the Diocese. The Deans of Jersey and Guernsey are members of the Diocesan Synod and the Bishop's Council, and the Bishops of Winchester, Basingstoke and Southampton frequently minister in the Islands.

The Channel Islands fall under the Ordinary jurisdiction of the Bishop of Winchester. They are, however, unusual in a number of ways. Jersey has its own Canons, originally promulgated in 1623 and revised extensively in 2011, which recognize the Bishop of Winchester's Ordinary jurisdiction. Guernsey has no written Canons, but follows the English Canons closely. Measures of the General Synod do not automatically apply in the Channel Islands but may be applied, with or without variation, by a scheme made by the Bishop of Winchester under the Measure in accordance with the Channel Islands (Church Legislation) Measure 1931, following consultation with the Islands. In some limited circumstances (e.g. where a Measure affects the formularies of the Church of England) a Measure may be extended to the Channel Islands by express provision in the Measure itself.

The Deans of Jersey and Guernsey hold Commissary powers from the Bishop of Winchester and may institute, collate or license clergy in the Islands at the Bishop's request. They are also Commissioned as presidents of the Ecclesiastical Courts and may grant marriage licences, including special licences and faculties. The Guernsey Ecclesiastical Court retains its jurisdiction in matters concerning probate and may issue Letters of Administration in matters of personalty.

The Deans of Jersey and Guernsey are recognized in a number of ways in civic society by virtue of their office. The Dean of Jersey is an *ex officio* member of the States, the Island's Parliament, although he does not have a vote. The Dean of Guernsey is not a member of the States of Deliberation (the Island's Parliament) but he is a member of the States of Election which appoints Jurats to the Royal Court.

Since 1875 the Dean of Jersey has always been Rector of St Helier. The Dean of Guernsey has usually been Rector of the Town Church in St Peter Port, but this has not always been the case. In addition to the twelve ancient parishes in Jersey and ten in Guernsey which form the basis of local life and government, there are five newer congregations in Jersey and three in Guernsey.

DIOCESE OF WORCESTER

Founded in 679. Worcestershire, except for a few parishes in the south (GLOUCESTER) and in the north (BIRMINGHAM). Dudley; a few parishes in Wolverhampton, Sandwell and in northern Gloucestershire.

Population 865,000   Area 670 sq m
Full-time Stipendiary Parochial Clergy 113   Benefices 97
Parishes 170   Churches 285
www.cofe-worcester.org.uk
Overseas link diocese: Peru (Province of Southern Cone), Morogoro (Province of Tanzania) and Propstei Stendal-Magdeburg (EMD-EKD).

BISHOP (113th)
Rt Revd John Geoffrey Inge, The Bishop's Office, The Old Palace, Deansway, Worcester WR1 2JE [2007]   *Tel:* 01905 731599
Fax: 01905 739382
email: bishop.worcester@cofe-worcester.org.uk
[John Wigorn]

SUFFRAGAN BISHOP
DUDLEY Rt Revd Graham Usher, Bishop's House, Bishop's Walk, Cradley Heath B64 7RH
Tel: 0121 550 3407
Fax: 0121 550 7340
email:
bishopsofficedudley@cofe-worcester.org.uk

HONORARY ASSISTANT BISHOPS
Rt Revd Michael Hooper, 6 Avon Drive, Eckington, Pershore, Worcs WR10 3BU
Tel: 01386 751589
Rt Revd Christopher Mayfield, Harwood House, 54 Primrose Crescent, St Peter's, Worcester WR5 3HT [2002]   *Tel:* 01905 764822
Rt Revd Mark Santer, 81 Clarence Rd, Moseley, Birmingham B13 9UH [2002]   *Tel:* 0121 441 2194
Rt Revd Humphrey Taylor, 10 High St, Honeybourne, Evesham WR10 7PQ [2003]
Tel: 01386 934846
Rt Revd Anthony Priddis, Round Oak Cottage, Bridstow, Ross-on-Wye HR9 6QJ [2014]
Tel: 01989 218503
Rt Revd Jonathan Goodall, Hill House, Treetops, The Mount, Caversham, Reading RG4 7RE [2013]   *Tel:* 0118948 1038

CATHEDRAL CHURCH OF CHRIST AND THE BLESSED MARY THE VIRGIN OF WORCESTER
Dean Very Revd Peter Gordon Atkinson, The Deanery, 10 College Green, Worcester WR1 2LH [2007]   *Tel:* 01905 732939
Tel: 01905 732909 (Office)
email: peteratkinson@worcestercathedral.org.uk
Canons Residentiary
Canon Dr Alvyn Pettersen, 2 College Green, Worcester WR1 2LH [2002]   *Tel:* 01905 732942
email:
alvynpettersen@worcestercathedral.org.uk

Canon Dr Georgina Byrne, 15B College Green, Worcester WR1 2LH [2009]   *Tel:* 01905 732900
email:
georginabyrne@worcestercathedral.org.uk
Canon Dr Michael Brierley, 15A College Green, Worcester WR1 2LH [2014]   *Tel:* 01905 732940
email:
michaelbrierley@worcestercathedral.org.uk

Lay Canons
Mrs Vanessa Godfrey, Chapter Office
Dr Janet Harvey, Chapter Office
Dr David Bryer, Chapter Office
Cathedral Steward Mr Les West, Chapter Office
Tel: 01905 732907
email: leswest@worcestercathedral.org.uk
Chapter Office 8 College Yard, Worcester WR1 2LA   *Tel:* 01905 732900
email: info@worcestercathedral.org.uk
Organist and Director of Music Dr Peter Nardone, 5A College Yard, Worcester WR1 2LA
Tel: 01905 732916
email: peternardone@worcestercathedral.org.uk

ARCHDEACONS
WORCESTER Ven Robert Jones, The Archdeacon's House, Walker's Lane, Whittington, Worcester WR5 2RE [2014]   *Tel:* 01905 773301
email: kjones@cofe-worcester.org.uk
DUDLEY Ven Nikki Groarke, 15 Worcester Rd, Droitwich WR9 8AA [2014]   *Tel:* 01905 773301
Fax: 0871 813 3256
email: kjones@cofe-worcester.org.uk

CONVOCATION (MEMBERS OF THE HOUSE OF CLERGY OF THE GENERAL SYNOD)
Proctors for Clergy
Revd Canon Stuart Currie
Revd Canon Matthew Baynes
Revd Eva McIntyre

MEMBERS OF THE HOUSE OF LAITY OF THE GENERAL SYNOD
Canon Prof Michael Clarke
Mrs Jennifer Barton
Mr Robin Lunn

DIOCESAN OFFICERS

Dioc Secretary Mr Robert Higham, The Old Palace, Deansway, Worcester WR1 2JE
Tel: 01905 20537
Chancellor of Diocese Dr Charles Mynors, Francis Taylor Building, Inner Temple, London EC4Y 7BD *Tel:* 020 7353 8415
Registrar of Diocese and Bishop's Legal Secretary Mr Stuart Ness, Messrs Stallard, March & Edwards, 8 Sansome Walk, Worcester WR1 1LN
Tel: 01905 723561
Fax: 01905 723812
Deputy Diocesan Registrar Vacancy, Messrs Stallard, March & Edwards, 8 Sansome Walk, Worcester WR1 1LN
Dioc Surveyor Mr Mark Wild, Dioc Office
Tel: 01905 20537

DIOCESAN ORGANIZATIONS

Diocesan Office The Old Palace, Deansway, Worcester WR1 2JE *Tel:* 01905 20537
Fax: 01905 612302

ADMINISTRATION

Dioc Secretary Mr Robert Higham, Dioc Office
Asst Dioc Secretary (Finance) Mr Stephen Lindner, Dioc Office
DAC Secretary Mr John Dentith, Dioc Office
Dioc Synod (Chair, House of Clergy) Revd Canon Stuart Currie
(Chair, House of Laity) Mr David Hawkins, Dioc Office
(Secretary) Mr Robert Higham, Dioc Office

DIOCESAN BOARD OF FINANCE

(Chair of DBF) Canon Alastair Findlay; *(Company Secretary)* Mr Robert Higham

DIOCESAN MISSION, PASTORAL AND RESOURCES COMMITTEE

(being the Diocesan Mission Pastoral Committee)
Secretary Mr Robert Higham *(as above)*
Parsonages Committee (Chair) Mr Robert Pearce, via Dioc Office
(Secretary) Mr Stephen Lindner *(as above)*
Investment and Glebe Committee (Chair) Mr Peter Seward *(Vice chair of DBF until 30/6/15) (as above)*
(Secretary) Mr Stephen Lindner *(as above)*
Glebe Agent Mr Anthony Champion, Halls, 4 Foregate St, Worcester WR1 1DB *Tel:* 01905 611066
Mission & Pastoral Committee Mr Robert Higham *(as above)*
Board of Patronage Mr Robert Higham *(as above)*
Designated Officer Mr Robert Higham *(as above)*
Diocesan Trustees Mr Stuart Ness, Messrs Stallard, March & Edwards, 8 Sansome Walk, Worcester WR1 1LN *Tel:* 01905 723561
Fax: 01905 723812

CHURCHES

Advisory Committee for the Care of Churches (Chair) Mr Ian Stainburn, via Dioc Office; *(Secretary)* Mr John Dentith, Dioc Office
Change Ringers Association Mr D. Andrews

EDUCATION

Board of Education (Chair) Revd Canon Stuart W. Currie, St Stephen's Vicarage, 1 Beech Ave, Worcester WR3 8PZ *Tel:* 01905 452169
Director of Education Mrs Ann Mundy, Dioc Office

TRAINING AND MINISTRY

Director of Development Vacancy, Dioc Office
Dioc Director of Ordinands Revd Canon Georgina Byrne, Dioc Office
Dean of Women's Ministry Revd Canon Georgina Byrne, Dioc Office
Children's Officer Mrs Emma Pettifer, Dioc Office
Youth Officer Mr Simon Hill, Dioc Office
Mission Development Officers Revd Doug Chaplin, Dioc Office
email: dchaplin@cofe-worcester.org.uk
Revd Phillip Jones, 7 Egremont Gardens, Worcester WR4 0QH *Tel and Fax:* 01905 755037
email: phillip.jones@cofe-worcester.org.uk
Miss Margaret Rutter, Dioc Office
email: mrutter@cofe-worcester.org.uk
Association of Readers
Secretary Miss E. R. Tomlin, 4 Lambourne Avenue, Malvern Link, Worcestershire WR14 1NL
Tel: 01684 578500
Registrar Dr M. J. Robinson, 5 Park Dingle, Bewdley DY12 2JY *Tel:* 01299 403080
email: mikejrobinson@fsmail.net
Retired Clergy
Dean of Retired Clergy Rt Revd Christopher Mayfield *(as above)*

SAFEGUARDING OFFICE

Diocesan Safeguarding Officer Mrs Maria Johnson, via Dioc Office *Tel:* 01886 889216
email: maria.johnson@cofe-worcester.org.uk

MISSION AND UNITY

Ecumenical Officer Revd David Ryan; Dioc Office

SOCIAL RESPONSIBILITY

Commission for Social Responsibility (Chairman) Professor Michael Taylor, via Dioc Office

PRESS AND PUBLICATIONS

Dioc Communications Officer and Bishop's Press Office Samantha Setchell, Dioc Office
Tel: 07852 302516
Editor of the Dioc Directory Mrs Alison Vincent, Dioc Office

DIOCESAN RECORD OFFICES

County Archivist, The Hive, Sawmill Walk, The Butts, Worcester WR5 3PA *Tel:* 01905 766530; *Fax:* 01905 766363 *(For diocesan records and most parish records)*
Dudley Archives and Local History Dept, Tipton Rd, Dudley, West Midlands DY1 4SQ *Archivists* Helen Donald and Robert Bennett *Tel:* 01384 812770 *(For parish records for the deaneries of Kingswinford (formerly Himley), Dudley and Stourbridge)*

RURAL DEANS

ARCHDEACONRY OF WORCESTER

Evesham Revd Richard Court, The Vicarage, High Street, Badsey, Evesham WR11 7EJ
Tel: 01386 834550
email: richard.court@btinternet.com
Malvern Revd P. J. Knight, St Matthias Vicarage, 12 Lambourne Avenue, Malvern WR14 1NL
Tel: 01684 566054
email: revpeterknight@googlemail.com
Martley and Worcester West Revd David Sherwin, The Rectory, Martley, Worcester WR6 6QA
Tel: 01886 888664
Pershore Revd Susan Renshaw, The Vicarage, Drakes Bridge Road, Eckington, Pershore WR10 3BN
Tel: 01386 750203
email: revsusan@btinternet.com
Upton Revd Christopher Moss, Longdon Vicarage, Tewkesbury GL20 6AT
Tel: 01684 833038
email: cmoss.lcbq@gmail.com
Worcester East Revd S. W. Currie, St Stephen's Vicarage, 1 Beech Avenue, Worcester WR3 8PZ
Tel: 01905 452169
email: sw.currie@virgin.net

ARCHDEACONRY OF DUDLEY

Bromsgrove Revd Garth Nathaniel, St Peter's Church Office Ipsley, Church Lane, Redditch, Worcs B98 0AJ
Tel: 01905 5616351
email: garth_ipsley@btinternet.com
Droitwich Canon Sheila Banyard, Rectory, 205 Worcester Road, Droitwich, Worcs WR9 8AS
Tel: 01905 773134
email: sk.banyard@virgin.net
Dudley Revd Dominic Melville, Halas Rectory, 506 Bromsgrove Road, Hunnington, Halesowen B62 0JJ
Tel: 0121 550 7426
email: domelville@orange.net
Kidderminster Revd Hugh Burton, The Rectory, 30 Leswell Street, Kidderminster DY10 1RP
Tel: 01562 824490
email: hugh.burton@kidderminstereast.org.uk
Kingswinford Revd Colin Jones, The Rectory, 13 Dunsley Drive, Wordsley, Stourbridge DY8 5RA
Tel: 01384 400709
email: paxarana@msn.com
Stourbridge Revd Paul Harrison, The Rectory, 5 Mill Lane, Blakedown, Kidderminster DY10 3ND
Tel: 01562 700144
email: p.g.harrison@btinternet.com
Stourport Revd Mark Turner, 14 Dunley Road, Stourport-on-Severn DY13 0AX
Tel: 01299 829557
email: revmturner@tiscali.co.uk

DIOCESE OF YORK

Founded in 627. York; East Riding of Yorkshire, except for an area in the south-west (SHEFFIELD); Kingston-upon-Hull; Redcar and Cleveland; Middlesbrough; the eastern half of North Yorkshire; Stockton-on-Tees, south of the Tees; an area of Leeds.

Population 1,418,000   Area 2,660 sq m
Full-time Stipendiary Parochial Clergy 199   Benefices 256
Parishes 455   Churches 598
www.dioceseofyork.org.uk
Overseas link dioceses: Cape Town (South Africa), Mechelen-Brussels (Belgium).

ARCHBISHOP (97th)
Most Revd and Rt Hon Dr John Tucker Mugabi Sentamu, *Primate of England and Metropolitan*, Bishopthorpe Palace, Bishopthorpe, York YO23 2GE [2005]   *Tel:* 01904 707021/2
Fax: 01904 709204
email: office@archbishopofyork.org
Web: www.bishopthorpepalace.co.uk
[Sentamu Ebor]
Chaplain and Researcher Revd Dr Daphne Green
email: daphne.green@archbishopofyork.org
Domestic Chaplain Revd Richard Carew
email: richard.carew@archbishopofyork.org
Chief of Staff Revd Malcolm Macnaughton
Tel: 01904 772362
email:
malcolm.macnaughton@archbishopofyork.org

SUFFRAGAN BISHOPS
SELBY Rt Revd Dr John Bromlow Thomson, The Vicarage, York Road, Barlby, Selby YO8 5JP [2014]
email: bishopofselby@yorkdiocese.org
HULL Vacancy, Hullen House, Woodfield Lane, Hessle HU13 0ES [1998]   *Tel:* 01482 649019
Fax: 01482 647449
WHITBY Rt Revd Paul John Ferguson, 21 Thornton Road, Stainton, Middlesbrough TS8 9DS [2014]
Tel: 01642 593273
email: bishopofwhitby@yorkdiocese.org

PROVINCIAL EPISCOPAL VISITOR
BEVERLEY Rt Revd Glyn Webster Holy Trinity Rectory, Micklegate, York YO1 6LE
Tel: 01904 628155
bishop@seeofbeverley.org.uk

HONORARY ASSISTANT BISHOPS
Rt Revd Nicholas Baines, Bishopscroft, Ashwell Road, Bradford BD9 4AU
Rt Revd Clifford Condor Barker, Flat 29 Dulverton Hall, The Esplanade, Scarborough YO11 2AR [1991]   *Tel:* 01723 340129
Rt Revd Gordon Bates, 19 Fernwood Close, Brompton, Northallerton DL6 2UX
Tel: 01609 761586
Rt Revd Graham Cray, The Dovecote, Main Street, Kirby Misperton, Malton YO17 6XL
email: grahamcray@btconnect.com

Rt Revd Michael Henshall, Brackenfield, 28 Hermitage Way, Eskdaleside, Sleights, Whitby YO22 5HG [1996]   *Tel:* 01947 811233
Rt Revd David Charles James, 7 Long Lane, Beverley HU17 0NH   *Tel:* 01482 871240
email: davidjames43@karoo.co.uk
Rt Revd James Stuart Jones, Mount Pleasant Cottage, Main Street, Burythorpe, Malton YO17 9LJ
Rt Revd David Smith, 34 Cedar Glade, Dunnington, York YO19 5QZ [2002]   *Tel:* 01904 481225
email: david@djmhs.force9.co.uk
Rt Revd Martin Wallace, 28 Alexandra Court, Bridlington YO15 2LB   *Tel:* 01262 670265
email: mdw28@btinternet.com

CATHEDRAL CHURCH OF ST PETER
Dean Very Revd Vivienne Faull, Church House, 10–14 Ogleforth, York YO1 7JN [2012]
Tel: 01904 557202 (Office)
email: viviennef@yorkminster.org
Chapter Office Church House, 10–14 Ogleforth, York YO1 7JN   *Tel:* 01904 557200
email: info@yorkminster.org
Canons Residentiary
Precentor Revd Canon Peter Moger, 2 Minster Court, York YO1 7JJ [2010]
Tel: 01904 557265 (Home)
01904 557205 (Office)
email: precentor@yorkminster.org
Canon Chancellor Revd Canon Dr Christopher Collingwood, 3 Minster Court, York YO1 7JJ [2013]   *Tel:* 01904 557267 (Home)
01904 557207 (Office)
email: christopherc@yorkminster.org
Canon Pastor Revd Canon Michael Smith, 4 Minster Yard, York YO1 7JD [2013]
Tel: 01904 557264 (Home)
01904 557211 (Office)
email: michaels@yorkminster.org
Ven David Butterfield, 2A Minster Court, York YO1 7JJ [2014]   *Tel:* 01904 557278 (Home)
01904 557218 (Office)
email: archdeacondavid@yorkminster.org
Ven Richard Seed c/o Chapter Office [2011]
Lay Canons
Canon Dr Andrew Green, Normanby House, Normanby, Sinnington, York YO62 6RH [2008]
email: andrewgreen@bpipoly.com

Canon Dr Julia Winkley, St Catherine's, 11 Clifton, York YO30 6AA [2011]   *Tel:* 07740 779766
email: juleswinkley@gmail.com
Canon Neil Harkin, c/o Chapter Office [2014]
email: neil.harkin@what-group.co.uk
Chapter Steward Kathryn Blacker, Chapter Office
Tel: 01904 557212
email: kathrynb@yorkminster.org
Finance Director Mr Peter Avis, Chapter Office
Tel: 01904 557213
email: petera@yorkminster.org
Superintendent of Works Rebecca Thompson, The Works Department, 4 Deangate, York YO1 7JA
Tel: 01904 559525
email: rebeccat@yorkminster.org
Communications Director Sharon Atkinson, Chapter Office   *Tel:* 01904 557248
email: sharona@yorkminster.org
Director of Visitor Experience Jessica Monaghan, Chapter Office   *Tel:* 01904 559518
email: jessicam@yorkminster.org
Learning Manager Kate Whitworth, Chapter Office   *Tel:* 01904 559543
email: katew@yorkminster.org
Director of Music Mr Robert Sharpe, Chapter Office   *Tel:* 01904 557205
email: roberts@yorkminster.org
CEO of York Minster Revealed Hon Michael Benson, Chapter Office   *Tel:* 01904 557200
email: mbymf@yorkminster.org
Director, York Minster Fund Dr Peter Spence, Chapter Office   *Tel:* 01904 557245
email: peters@yorkminster.org
Headmaster Mr Alex Donaldson, The Minster School, York YO1 7JP   *Tel:* 0844 939 0000
email: hm@yorkminster.org
Chapter Clerk Mr Andrew Oates, Chapter Office
Tel: 01904 557210
email: chapterclerk@yorkminster.org

ARCHDEACONS

YORK Ven Sarah Bullock, 1 New Lane, Huntington, York YO32 9NU
email: adyk@yorkdiocese.org
EAST RIDING Ven Andy Broom, Brimley Lodge, 27 Molescroft Rd, Beverley HU17 7DX [2007]
Tel and *Fax:* 01482 881659
email: ader@yorkdiocese.org
CLEVELAND Vacancy, 48 Langbaurgh Rd, Hutton Rudby, Yarm TS15 0HL [2001]   *Tel:* 01642 706095
Fax: 01642 706097
email: adcl@yorkdiocese.org

CONVOCATION (MEMBERS OF THE HOUSE OF CLERGY OF THE GENERAL SYNOD)

Dignitaries in Convocation
The Bishop of Hull
Proctors for Clergy
Revd Paul Hutchinson
Revd Jane Nattrass
Revd Christian Selvaratnam
Canon Suzanne Sheriff
Revd Rowan Williams

MEMBERS OF THE HOUSE OF LAITY OF THE GENERAL SYNOD

Canon Linda Ali
Mrs Heather Black
Mr Martin Dales
Canon Jennifer Reid
Mrs Rosalind Brewer
Mr Jon Steel

DIOCESAN OFFICERS

Dioc Secretary Canon Peter Warry, Diocesan House, Aviator Court, Clifton Moor, York YO30 4WJ   *Tel:* 01904 699500
Fax: 01904 699501
Chancellor of Diocese The Worshipful Peter Collier QC, 12 St Helen's Rd, Dringhouses, York YO24 1HP
Registrar of Diocese and Archbishop's Legal Secretary Mrs Caroline F. Mockford, The Registry, Stamford House, Piccadilly, York YO1 9PP   *Tel:* 01904 623487
Fax: 01904 611458

DIOCESAN ORGANIZATIONS

Diocesan Office Diocesan House, Aviator Court, Clifton Moor, York YO30 4WJ   *Tel:* 01904 699500
Fax: 01904 699501
email: office@yorkdiocese.org
Web: www.dioceseofyork.org.uk

ADMINISTRATION

Dioc Synod (*Chairman, House of Clergy*) Vacancy
(*Chairman, House of Laity*) Dr Nick Land, Low Farm House, Ingleby Greenhow, Great Ayton, Middlesbrough TS9 6RG
email: drnickland@aol.com
(*Secretary*) Canon Peter Warry, Dioc Office
Assistant Dioc Secretary Ms Shirley Davies, Dioc Office
Board of Finance (*Chairman*) Mrs Maureen Loffill Dioc Office; (*Secretary*) Mrs Catherine Evans
Finance Manager Mrs Catherine Evans, Dioc Office
Diocesan Surveyor and Estates Manager Mr Graham Andrews, Dioc Office
Pastoral & Mission Committee Ms Shirley Davies (*as above*)
Designated Officer Canon Peter Warry, Dioc Office
Property Sub-Committee Mr Graham Andrews, Dioc Office
Dioc Communications Officer Eleanor Course, Dioc Office

CHURCHES

Advisory Committee for the Care of Churches (*Chairman*) Canon David Hodgson, The Ascension Vicarage, Penrith Rd, Berwick Hills, Middlesbrough TS3 7JR   *Tel:* 01642 244857
(*Secretary*) Mr Philip Thomas, Dioc Office
Furnishings Officer Mr David Haddon-Reece, Vicarage, Egton, Whitby YO21 1UT
Tel: 01947 895315
Closed Churches Ms Shirley Davies (*as above*)

EDUCATION

Board of Education (Director) Vacancy
Deputy Director of Education Mrs Claire Graham-Brown
Asst Director of Education Mrs Viv Todd (*Educational Services and Schools Support*)
School Buildings Officer Simon Quartermaine
Schools Development Advisers Mrs Olivia Seymour, Mrs Katherine Humpleby and Ms Helen Wren
School Effectiveness Adviser Mrs Alison Smith

CHILDREN AND YOUTH

East Riding Adviser Jon Steel, 2 Appin Close, Bransholme, Hull HU7 5BB   *Tel:* 01482 828805
07736 378051 (Mobile)
York Adviser Revd Nigel Chapman, Vicarage, Coxwold, York YO61 4AD   *Tel:* 01347 868287
email: nigel.chapman@yorkdiocese.org
Cleveland Advisers Revd Andrew and Mrs Jo Bowden, Chapel House, Back Lane, West Lutton, Malton YO17 8TF   *Tel:* 07544 705064
email: andy@woldsvalley.plus.com

MINISTRY AND MISSION

Director of Training for Missional Ministry Revd Dr Gavin Wakefield, Dioc Office   *Tel:* 01904 699504
email: gavin.wakefield@yorkdiocese.org
Diocesan Adviser on Vocations Revd David Mann, 64 Strensall Road, Huntington, York YO32 9SH
Tel: 01904 768668
email: david.mann@yorkdiocese.org
Dean of Self Supporting Ministry Revd Dr Julie Watson, 25 Fox Lane, Thorpe Willoughby, Selby YO8 9NA   *Tel:* 01757 703123
julie301watson@btinternet.com
Dean of Women's Ministry Canon Elaine Bielby, St Helen's Vicarage, Welton, Brough HU15 1ND
Tel: 01482 666677
email: ebielby@ebielby.karoo.co.uk
Warden of Readers Vacancy
Ecumenical Advisers
York Archdeaconry Revd Andrew Clements, Vicarage, 80 Osbaldwick Lane, York YO10 3AX
Tel: 01904 416763
email: andrew@ozmurt.freeserve.co.uk
East Riding Archdeaconry Vacancy
Cleveland Archdeaconry Revd Paul Hutchinson, The Rectory, Leven Close, Stokesley, Middlesbrough TS9 5AP   *Tel:* 01642 710405
email: paul.hutchinson5@btinternet.com

LITURGICAL

York Diocesan Worship and Liturgical Group Canon Peter Moger (*as above*)

PRESS AND PUBLICATIONS

Archbishop's Media Adviser (*National*) Kerron Cross   *Tel:* 01904 707021
Communications Officer (*Diocese*) Eleanor Course, Dioc Office   *Tel:* 01904 699530
07946 748702 (Mobile)
email: comms@yorkdiocese.org

Diocesan Tourism Group (Chair) Revd Dr Gavin Wakefield (*as above*)
Editor of Dioc Magazine (*as above*)

DIOCESAN RECORD OFFICES

The Borthwick Institute of Historical Research, University of York, Heslington, York YO10 5DD *Director and Diocesan Archivist* Christopher C. Webb   *Tel:* 01904 321166
Web: www.york.ac.uk/inst/bihr
(*For parish records in the Archdeaconry of York*)
East Riding of Yorkshire Archive Office, County Hall, Beverley HU17 9BA *Archivist* Mr Ian Mason *Tel:* 01482 392790
email: ian.mason@eastriding.gov
Web: www.eastriding.gov.uk/learning
(*For parish records in the Archdeaconry of the East Riding*)
North Yorkshire County Record Office, Malpas Rd, Northallerton DL7 8PB *Acting County Archivist* Mrs Judith A. Smeaton *Tel:* 01609 777585 (*For parish records in the Archdeaconry of Cleveland**)
*Parishes within the present county boundaries of Cleveland may, if they so wish, deposit their records in the Cleveland County Archives Dept, Exchange House, 6 Marton Rd, Middlesbrough TS1 1DB *Archivist* Mr D. Tyrell   *Tel:* 01642 248321

SOCIAL RESPONSIBILITY

Social Responsibility Council Vacancy

RURAL DEANS
ARCHDEACONRY OF YORK

Derwent Revd Andrew Clements, The Vicarage, 80 Osbaldwick Lane, York YO10 3AX
Tel: 01904 416763
email: Andrew@ozmurt.freeserve.co.uk
Easingwold Rev Liz Hassall, The Rectory, Church Hill, Crayke, York YO61 4TA   *Tel:* 01347 822809
*email:*revliz@trundlebug.co.uk
New Ainsty Canon Chris Coates, The Vicarage, 48 Church Lane, Bishopthorpe, York YO23 2QG
Tel: 01904 707840
email: chriscoates@hotmail.co.uk
Selby Revd Chris Wilton, Vicarage, 2 Sir John's Lane, Sherburn in Elmet, Leeds LS25 6BJ
Tel: 01977 682122
South Wold Revd Fran Wakefield, The Rectory, 8 Viking Road, Stamford Bridge, York YO41 1BR
Tel: 01759 371264
email: fran.wakefield@btopenworld.com
Southern Ryedale Revd Rachel Hirst, Norton Vicarage, 80 Langton Road, Norton, Malton YO17 9AE   *Tel:* 01653 699222
Mobile: 07896 204121
email: rachel.hirst40@googlemail.com
York Revd Terence McDonough, Fulford Vicarage, 1 Fulford Park, York YO10 4QE
Tel: 01904 633261
email: tmcd@st-oswalds-fulford.org.uk

ARCHDEACONRY OF THE EAST RIDING

Beverley Revd Jeremy Fletcher, The Minster Vicarage, Highgate, Beverley HU17 0DN
Tel: 01482 881434
email: vicar@beverleyminster.org.uk

Bridlington Revd Glyn Owen, The Vicarage, Rudston, Driffield YO25 4XA   *Tel:* 01262 420313
email: revglynowen@btinternet.com

Central and North Hull Revd Paul Smith, The Rectory, Hallgate, Cottingham HU16 4DD
Tel: 01482 847668

Harthill Revd David Fletcher, The Vicarage, Wetwang, Driffield YO25 9XT
Tel: 01377 236189
email: de.fletcher@hotmail.co.uk

Holderness North Revd James Grainger-Smith, The Rectory, 11 Glebe Gardens, Beeford, Driffield YO25 8BF   *Tel:* 01262 48804
email: j.grainger-smith@sky.com

Holderness South Revd Susan Walker, The Vicarage, Main Street, Thorngumbald, Hull HU12 9NA   *Tel:* 01964 601381

Howden Revd James Little, The Minster Rectory, Market Place, Howden DN14 7BL
Tel: 01430 432056
email: RevJLittle@aol.com

Scarborough Revd David Pynn, 6 Stepney Drive, Scarborough YO12 5DH   *Tel:* 01723 369687
email: Davidpynn12@aol.com

East Hull Revd Margaret Jeavons, St Michael's Vicarage, 751 Marfleet Lane, Hull HU9 4TJ
Tel: 01482 374509
email: jeavons2951@jeavons2951.karoo.co.uk

West Hull Revd Tim Boyns, All Saints Vicarage, 4 Chestnut Avenue, Hessle HU13 0RH
Tel: 01482 648555
email: timboyns@timboyns.karoo.co.uk

ARCHDEACONRY OF CLEVELAND

Guisborough Revd Rachel Harrison, St Peter's Vicarage, 66 Aske Road, Redcar TS10 2BP
Tel: 01642 490700
email: rachelhere@hotmail.com

Middlesbrough Revd Dominic Black. The Vicarage, James Street, North Ormesby, Middlesbrough TS3 6LD   *Tel:* 01642 961898
email: Dominic.Black@trinitycentre.org

Mowbray Revd Ian Houghton, Leake Vicarage, Knayton, Thirsk YO7 4AZ   *Tel:* 01845 537277
email: ian.houghton@tiscali.co.uk

Northern Ryedale Revd Tim Robinson, The Vicarage, Baxtons Road, Helmsley YO62 5HT
Tel: 01439 770983
email: revtimrobinson@gmail.com

Stokesley Revd Canon John Ford, The Rectory, 6 Westgate, Yarm TS15 9QT   *Tel:* 07805 792824
email: revjohn.ford@ntlworld.com

Whitby Revd Barry Pyke, The Rectory, Hinderwell, Saltburn by the Sea TS13 5JH
Tel: 01947 840249

National Structures

PART 2

PART 2 CONTENTS

Every effort has been made to ensure that all details are accurate at the time of going to press.

NATIONAL STRUCTURES

THE GENERAL SYNOD OF THE CHURCH OF ENGLAND

Office

Church House, Great Smith St, London SW1P 3AZ
Tel: 020 7898 1000 *Fax:* 020 7898 1369
email: synod@churchofengland.org
Web: www.churchofengland.org

Dates of Sessions

The following periods have been set aside for Groups of Sessions of the General Synod:

2015: 9 February – 13 February
10 July – 14 July
23 November – 25 November

2016: 15 February – 19 February
8 July – 12 July
21 November – 23 November

Composition of the General Synod

	Canterbury	York	Either	Totals
House of Bishops				
Diocesan Bishops	30	12		42
Suffragan Bishops ...	6	3		9
including the				
Bishop of Dover				
ex officio and				
Bishop to the				
Armed Forces			1	1
	36	15	1	52
House of Clergy				
Deans	3	2		5
Armed Forces Synod				
and Chaplain-				
General of				
Prisons		7		7
Elected Proctors				
and the Dean of				
Guernsey or				
Jersey	129	55		184
University Proctors ..	4	2		6
Religious				
Communities			2	2
Co-opted places				
(maximum)	3	2		5
	139	61	9	209

	Canterbury	York	Either	Totals
House of Laity				
Elected Laity	136	59		195
Religious				
Communities			2	2
Lay Armed Forces			3	3
Services				
Co-opted places			5	5
(maximum)........			2	2
Ex officio	136	59	12	207
House of				
Bishops, House of				
Clergy or House of				
Laity				
Ex officio (Dean of the				
Arches, the two				
Vicars General, the				
Third Church				
Estates				
Commissioner, the				
Chairman of the				
Pensions Board				
and six Appointed				
Members of the				
Archbishops'				
Council)			11	11
Maximum totals	311	135	33	479

NATIONAL STRUCTURES

The General Synod consists of the Convocations of Canterbury and York, joined together in a House of Bishops and a House of Clergy, and having added to them a House of Laity.

The House of Bishops is made up of the Upper Houses of the Convocations of Canterbury and York. It consists of the archbishops and all other diocesan bishops and the Bishop of Dover as *ex officio* members, four bishops elected by and from the suffragan bishops (and certain other bishops) of the Province of Canterbury (other than the Bishop of Dover), three bishops elected by and from the suffragan bishops (and certain other bishops) of the Province of York, and any other bishops residing in either Province who are members of the Archbishops' Council.

The House of Clergy is made up of the Lower Houses of the Convocations of Canterbury and York. It consists of clergy (other than bishops) who have been elected, appointed or chosen in accordance with Canon H 2 and the rules made under it (including deans, proctors from the dioceses and university constituencies and clerical members of religious communities) together with *ex officio* members.

The House of Laity consists of members from each diocese of the two Provinces elected by lay members of the deanery synods (or annual meetings of the chaplaincies in the case of the Diocese in Europe) or chosen by and from the lay members of religious communities, together with *ex officio* members.

Representatives of other Churches, the Church of England Youth Council, and Deaf Anglicans Together are invited to attend the Synod and under its Standing Orders enjoy speaking but not voting rights.

OFFICERS OF THE GENERAL SYNOD
Presidents
The Archbishop of Canterbury
The Archbishop of York

Prolocutor of the Lower House of the Convocation of Canterbury Ven Christine Hardman

Prolocutor of the Lower House of the Convocation of York Ven Cherry Vann

Chair of the House of Laity Dr Philip Giddings

Vice-Chair of the House of Laity Mr Tim Hind

Secretary General Mr William Fittall

Clerk to the Synod Dr Jacqui Philips

Chief Legal Adviser and *Joint Registrar of the Provinces of Canterbury and York (Registrar of the General Synod)* Mr Stephen Slack

Deputy Legal Adviser Revd Alexander McGregor

Standing Counsel Mr Christopher Packer

OFFICERS OF THE CONVOCATIONS
Synodical Secretary of the Convocation of Canterbury Revd Stephen Trott, Rectory, 41 Humfrey Lane, Boughton, Northampton NN28RQ
email: revstrott@btinternet.com

Synodal Secretary of the Convocation of York Ven Alan Wolstencroft, The Bakehouse, 1 Latham Row, Horwich, Bolton BL6 6QZ
email: wolstencroftalan@gmail.com

NON-DIOCESAN MEMBERS
The following are non-diocesan members of General Synod:
Bishop to the Forces
Rt Revd Nigel Stock

Suffragan Bishops in Convocation
CANTERBURY
The Bishop of Dover (*ex officio*)
The Bishop of Dorchester
The Bishop of Huntingdon
The Bishop of Lynn
The Bishop of Willesden

YORK
Vacancy
Vacancy
The Bishop of Knaresborough

Deans in Convocation
CANTERBURY
The Dean of Canterbury
The Dean of St Paul's
The Dean of Portsmouth

YORK
Vacancy
The Dean of Sheffield
The Dean of Carlisle

Chaplain-General of Prisons and Archdeacon of Prisons Revd Canon Michael Kavanagh

Armed Forces Synod
Ven Ian Wheatley
Ven Peter Eagles
Ven Jonathan Chaffey
Lt Gemma Winterton
AVM Malcolm Brecht
Vacancy

University Representatives in Convocation
CANTERBURY
Oxford
Revd Canon Dr Judith Maltby

Cambridge
Revd Duncan Dormor

London
Professor the Revd Dr Richard Burridge

Other Universities (Southern)
Vacancy

YORK
Durham and Newcastle
Revd Dr Hannah Cleugh

Other Universities (Northern)
Vacancy

Representatives of Religious Communities in Convocation
CANTERBURY
Revd Sister Rosemary Howorth CHN

YORK
Revd Thomas Seville CR

Lay Representatives of Religious Communities
Sister Anita Smith OHP
Brother Thomas Quin OSB

Ex officio **Members of the House of Laity**
Dean of the Arches
Rt Worshipful Charles George QC
Vicar-General of the Province of Canterbury
Timothy Briden
Vicar-General of the Province of York
Rt Worshipful Peter Collier QC

First Church Estates Commissioner Mr Andreas Whittam Smith

Second Church Estates Commissioner Sir Tony Baldry MP

Third Church Estates Commissioner Mr Andrew Mackie

Chairman of the Church of England Pensions Board
Dr Jonathan Spencer CB

Representatives who have been appointed to the Synod under its Standing Orders with speaking but not voting rights

Ecumenical Representatives
Very Revd David Arnott (Church of Scotland)
Very Revd Archimandrite Vassilios Papavassiliou (Orthodox Church)
Revd Graham Maskery (United Reformed Church)
Revd Jan Mullin (Moravian Church)
Revd Dr Roger Walton (Methodist Church)
Revd Prof Paul Fiddes (Baptist Union)
Bishop Dr Joe Aldred (Black-led Churches)
Vacancy (Roman Catholic Church)
His Grace Bishop Angaelos (Coptic Orthodox Church)

Church of England Youth Council Representatives
Miss Charlotte Cook
Mr Samuel Maggorian
Miss Heather Pritchard

Deaf Anglicans Together Representatives
Revd Catherine Nightingale
Mrs Patricia Callaghan
Susan Myatt

Appointed Members of the Archbishops' Council
Canon John Spence
Vacancy
Mr Philip Fletcher
Mrs Mary Chapman
Revd Dr Rosalyn Murphy
Miss Rebecca Swinson

House of Bishops

Chairman The Archbishop of Canterbury

Vice-Chairman The Archbishop of York

Secretary Mr William Fittall
Tel: 020 7898 1361
email: william.fittall@churchofengland.org

Theological Consultant Revd Canon Dr Jeremy Worthen Tel: 020 7898 1488
email: jeremy.worthen@churchofengland.org

The House of Bishops meets separately from sessions of the General Synod twice a year, in private session. It has a special responsibility for matters relating to doctrine and liturgy under Article 7 of the Constitution of General Synod. Its agendas nevertheless range more widely, reflecting matters relating to the exercise of *episcope* in the Church. Each year the College of Bishops – consisting of all diocesan and suffragan bishops – also meet, as do diocesan bishops with the archbishops.

The following committees or panels work under the umbrella of the House:

THE STANDING COMMITTEE OF THE HOUSE OF BISHOPS

Chairman Most Revd and Rt Hon John Sentamu (*Archbishop of York*)

Secretary Mr William Fittall
The Standing Committee consists of the Archbishops of Canterbury and York and the Bishops of Coventry, Dover, London, Rochester and Sheffield (plus one vacant post to be filled in September 2014). Its principal role is to prepare the agendas for the House's meetings, but it also deals with other matters on the House's behalf.

CONTINUING MINISTERIAL DEVELOPMENT COMMITTEE

Chairman Rt Revd Stephen Conway (*Bishop of Ely*)

Secretary Ms Christina Hedderly
Tel: 020 7898 1098
email: christina.hedderly@churchofengland.org

House of Clergy

Joint Chairs The Prolocutors of the Convocations

Secretary Mr Jonathan Neil-Smith
Tel: 020 7898 1373
email: jonathan.neil-smith@churchofengland.org

Membership of the House of Clergy comprises the Lower House of the Convocation of Canterbury and the Lower House of the Convocation of York joined into one House.

The Standing Committee of the House of Clergy consists of the Standing Committee of the Lower House of the Canterbury Convocation (the Prolocutor, Pro-Prolocutors, elected members of the Archbishops' Council, and four elected members) and the Assessors of the York Convocation (the Prolocutor, Deputy Prolocutors, elected members of the Archbishops' Council, and two elected assessors).

House of Laity

Chair Dr Philip Giddings

Vice-Chair Mr Tim Hind

Secretary Mr Nicholas Hills   *Tel:* 020 7898 1363
email: nicholas.hills@churchofengland.org

The Standing Committee of the House of Laity consists of the Chair and Vice-Chair and the members elected by the House to the Archbishops' Council (2 members), the Business Committee (3 members) and the Appointments Committee (3 members).

Principal Committees

THE BUSINESS COMMITTEE

Chair Revd Canon Sue Booys

Revd Canon Simon Butler, Mrs Anne Foreman, Revd Mark Ireland, Mrs Sue Johns, Rt Revd James Langstaff (*Bishop of Rochester*) Mr Gerry O'Brien, Revd Charles Razzall, Mrs Christina Rees.

Secretary Dr Jacqui Philips (*Clerk to the Synod*)
Tel: 020 7898 1385
email: jacqui.philips@churchofengland.org

The Committee is responsible for organizing the business of the Synod, enabling it to fulfil its role as a legislative and deliberative body.

THE LEGISLATIVE COMMITTEE

Ex officio Members
The Archbishop of Canterbury
The Archbishop of York
The Prolocutors of the Convocations
The Chair and Vice-Chair of the House of Laity
The Dean of the Arches
The Second Church Estates Commissioner
Elected Members
Canon Peter Bruinvels, Revd Canon David Felix, Rt Revd James Langstaff (*Bishop of Rochester*), Mr Clive Scowen, Revd Mark Steadman, Mr Geoffrey Tattersall QC

Secretary Mr Stephen Slack (*Chief Legal Adviser to the General Synod*)
Tel: 020 7898 1366
email: stephen.slack@churchofengland.org

THE STANDING ORDERS COMMITTEE
Chair Mr Geoffrey Tattersall QC

Ex officio Members
The Prolocutors of the Convocations
The Chair and Vice-Chair of the House of Laity

Appointed Members
Revd Canon Sue Booys, Revd Canon Simon Killwick, Canon Elizabeth Paver, Mr David Robilliard, Mr Clive Scowen

Secretary Mr Sion Hughes Carew
Tel: 020 7898 1371
email: sion.hughes-carew@churchofengland.org

PRINCIPAL COMMISSIONS
The Clergy Discipline Commission

Chair Rt Hon Lord Justice McFarlane
Deputy Chair Sir Mark Hedley

Secretary Mr Sion Hughes Carew

Office Church House, Great Smith St, London SW1P 3AZ
Tel: 020 7898 1371
Fax: 020 7898 1718/1721
email: sion.hughes-carew@churchofengland.org

MEMBERS
Revd Canon Moira Astin, Mr Martin Follett, Rt Revd Dr Peter Forster (*Bishop of Chester*), Rt Revd Dr Jonathan Gibbs (*Bishop of Huddersfield*), Dr Jamie Harrison, Rt Revd Christopher Lowson (*Bishop of Lincoln*), Mr David Mills, Ven Jane Sinclair, Dr Anna Thomas-Betts, Revd Canon Celia Thomson

The Clergy Discipline Commission is constituted under the Clergy Discipline Measure 2003. Under that Measure the Commission is required to give general advice to disciplinary tribunals, the courts of the Vicars-General, bishops and arch-bishops as to the penalties which are appropriate in particular circumstances; to issue codes of practice and general policy guidance to persons exercising functions in connection with clergy discipline; and to make annually to the General Synod through the House of Bishops a report on the exercise of its functions during the previous year.

Under the 2003 Measure the Commission is also required to compile and maintain 'provincial panels' of persons available for appointment as members of a disciplinary tribunal or a Vicar-General's Court for the purposes of dealing with cases under it, and to formulate guidance for the purposes of the 2003 Measure generally and to promulgate it in a Code of Practice approved by the Dean of the Arches and the General Synod.

The Commission also monitors the exercise of discipline, highlights and encourages best practice, and builds up casework experience in disciplinary matters.

The Crown Nominations Commission

Secretary to the Commission Ms Caroline Boddington, Archbishops' Secretary for Appointments

Office The Wash House, Lambeth Palace, London SE1 7JU
Tel: 020 7898 1876/7
Fax: 020 7898 1899
email: caroline.boddington@churchofengland.org

MEMBERS

Ex officio
The Archbishop of Canterbury
The Archbishop of York
Elected Members

Three members of the House of Clergy
Revd John Dunnett
Revd Canon Judith Maltby
Very Revd Andrew Nunn

Three members of the House of Laity
Mrs April Alexander
Mr Aiden Hargreaves-Smith
Miss Jane Patterson
Six members of the Vacancy-in-See Committee of the diocese whose bishopric is to become, or has become, vacant

Ex officio non-voting members
Sir Paul Britton (*The Prime Minister's Appointments Secretary*)

Ms Caroline Boddington (*Archbishops' Secretary for Appointments*)

The Commission was established by the General Synod in February 1977. Its function is to consider vacancies in diocesan bishoprics in the Provinces of Canterbury and York, and candidates for appointments to them. At each meeting the Chair is taken by the Archbishop in whose Province the vacancy has arisen. The Commission agrees upon two names for nomination to the Prime Minister by the appropriate Archbishop or, in the case of the Archbishopric of Canterbury or York, by the chairman of the Commission. The names submitted are given in an order of preference voted upon by the Commission. The Prime Minister accepts the first name and reverts to the second name should the first be unable to take up the post.

The Dioceses Commission

Chairman Canon Prof Michael Clarke

Vice-Chair Vacancy

Secretary Mr Jonathan Neil-Smith

Office Church House, Great Smith St, London SW1P 3AZ   *Tel:* 020 7898 1373
  email: jonathan.neil-smith@churchofengland.org

MEMBERS
Revd Canon Jonathan Alderton-Ford (St Edmundsbury & Ipswich), Revd Paul Benfield (Blackburn), Rt Revd Chris Foster (*Bishop of Portsmouth*), Mr Robert Hammond (Chelmsford), Mr Keith Malcouronne (Guildford), Mrs Lucinda Herklots, Revd Canon Sarah Mullally DBE, Canon Prof Hilary Russell

A Dioceses Commission was set up in 1978 under the Dioceses Measure 1978. In 2008 it was replaced by a new body of the same name, established under the Dioceses, Pastoral and Mission Measure 2007. Part II of that Measure makes provision for such matters as the reorganization of diocesan boundaries, the creation and revival of suffragan sees, and the delegation of episcopal functions by diocesan bishops to suffragan and assistant bishops.

The Commission's duties are laid down by the Measure. Its primary duty is to keep under review the provincial and diocesan structure of the Church of England and in particular the size, boundaries and number of provinces; the size, boundaries and number of dioceses and their distribution between the provinces; the number and distribution of bishops and the arrangements for episcopal oversight. The Commission may make reorganization schemes either of its own volition or in response to proposals from diocesan bishops. Schemes require the approval of the diocesan synods concerned (other than in exceptional circumstances) and that of the General Synod. The Commission also gives advice on good practice regarding diocesan administration and responds to requests for advice on particular issues. It comments on proposals to change the names of episcopal sees. Diocesan bishops are obliged to seek the views of the Commission if they propose to fill a vacant suffragan see.

Further information about the Commission and its work may be found on the Church of England website at www.churchofengland.org/about-us/structure/dioceses-commission

The Faith and Order Commission

Chairman Rt Revd Christopher Cocksworth (*Bishop of Coventry*)

Secretary Vacancy

Office Church House, Great Smith St, London SW1P 3AZ   *Tel:* 020 7898 1471

MEMBERS
Revd Canon Prof Loveday Alexander, Rt Revd Donald Allister (*Bishop of Peterborough*), Rt Revd Jonathan Baker (*Bishop of Fulham*), Rt Revd Dr Brian Castle (*Bishop of Tonbridge*), Rt Revd Dr Tim Dakin (*Bishop of Winchester*), Revd Dr Carolyn Hammond, Dr Mike Higton, Revd Dr David Hilborn, Rt Revd Dr John Inge (*Bishop of Worcester*), Revd Canon Dr Charlotte Methuen, Revd Dr Jeremy Morris, Revd Dr John Muddiman, Revd Prof Oliver O'Donovan, Dr Cathy Ross, Revd Thomas Seville CR

The Faith and Order Commission consists of not more than sixteen persons appointed by the Archbishops. The Commission advises the Archbishops, House of Bishops and the Council for Christian Unity on matters of ecumenical, theological and doctrinal concern. The Commission also gives advice on occasion to the General Synod.

The Fees Advisory Commission

Chair Mr John Alpass

Secretary Mr Sion Hughes Carew

Office Church House, Great Smith St, London
SW1P 3AZ   *Tel:* 020 7898 1371
                    Fax: 020 7898 1718/1721
    email: sion.hughes-carew@churchofengland.org

MEMBERS
Rt Revd Colin Fletcher (*Bishop of Dorchester*), Mr
Howard Dellar, Mrs Madelaine Goddard, Revd
Canon Joyce Jones, Mr Geoffrey Tattersall QC,

Canon Elizabeth Renshaw MBE, Revd Canon
John Rees, Revd Stephen Trott.

The Fees Advisory Commission is constituted
under Part II of the Ecclesiastical Fees Measure
1986, as amended. It makes recommendations as
to certain fees to be paid to ecclesiastical judges,
legal officers and others, and embodies those
recommendations in Orders which are laid
before the General Synod for approval. If
approved, the Orders take effect unless annulled
by either House of Parliament, and are published
as Statutory Instruments.

The Legal Advisory Commission

Chair Revd Canon and Worshipful Dr Rupert
Bursell QC

Secretary Revd Alexander McGregor
                    Tel: 020 7898 1748

Administrative Secretary Mr Sion Hughes Carew
                    Tel: 020 7898 1371

Office The Legal Office, Church House, Great
Smith St, London SW1P 3AZ
                    Fax: 020 7898 1718/1721

MEMBERS
Ex officio members
Rt Worshipful Charles George QC (Dean of the
Arches and Auditor)
Rt Worshipful Timothy Briden (Vicar-General of
Canterbury)
Rt Worshipful Peter Collier QC (Vicar-General
of York)
Revd Canon John Rees (Provincial Registrar of
Canterbury) (Vice-Chairman of the Commission)
Mr Lionel Lennox (Provincial Registrar of York)
Mr Stephen Slack (Chief Legal Adviser to the
Archbishops' Council and Official Solicitor to
the Church Commissioners)
Mr Christopher Packer (Legislative Counsel to
the General Synod

Appointed and co-opted members
Revd and Worshipful Dr Rupert Bursell QC,
Worshipful Professor David McClean CBE QC

DCL FBA, Worshipful Mark Hill QC, Sir Mark
Hedley, Rt Revd Christopher Lowson (*Bishop
of Lincoln*), Worshipful Dr Charles Mynors,
Worshipful Nigel Seed QC, Mr Peter Beesley,
Ms Jane Monks, Mr Andrew Johnson, Ven
Christine Hardman, Revd Canon Gavin Kirk,
Revd Mark Steadman, Rt Hon Sir John
Mummery, Ms Francesca Quint, Mr Edward
Nugee TD QC, Mr Robert Higham, Dr Sheila
Cameron CBE QC DCL

The Commission gives legal opinions to the
General Synod and to senior officers of the Church
of England, including diocesan chancellors and
registrars, upon questions generally affecting
the Church of England and advises the General
Synod upon the revision of ecclesiastical statutes,
measures and canons when so requested. The
Commission cannot accept requests for advice
from private individuals or secular bodies and
does not normally give opinions on contentious
matters.

The opinions of the Commission and its pre-
decessor, the Legal Board, on matters of general
interest are published by Church House Publishing in a loose-leaf form under the title *Legal
Opinions Concerning the Church of England*. The
8th edition was published in May 2007. Opinions
issued by the Commission since that date can be
accessed at http://www.churchofengland.org/
about-us/structure/churchlawlegis/guidance

The Legal Aid Commission

Chairman His Honour Judge Andrew Rutherford

Secretary Mr Stephen York

Office Church House, Great Smith St, London
SW1P 3AZ   *Tel:* 020 7898 1703
                          Fax: 020 7898 1718/1721
email: stephen.york@churchofengland.org

MEMBERS
Mrs Isabel Adcock, Revd Christine Allsopp,
Revd Paul Benfield, Mrs Rosalind Brewer,
Mrs Jennifer Dunlop, Revd Geoffrey Harbord,
Mr Aiden Hargreaves-Smith, Revd Canon
Joyce Jones, Rt Revd Alistair Magowan (*Bishop
of Ludlow*), Ven Clive Mansell (*Archdeacon of
Tonbridge*)

The Legal Aid Commission operates under the
Church of England (Legal Aid) Measure
1994 and the Church of England (Legal Aid)
Rules 1995, and administers the Legal Aid Fund
which was originally set up under the Ecclesiastical Jurisdiction Measure 1963 and is continued by the 1994 Measure and the 1995 Rules.

Legal aid under the 1994 Measure may be
granted at the discretion of the Commission,
subject to various conditions, for certain types
of proceedings before Ecclesiastical Courts and
tribunals; details of eligibility for legal aid and
the Commission's procedures, together with an
application form for legal aid, are obtainable
from the Secretary, on request, or at
www.churchofengland.org/about-us/structure/
churchlawlegis/clergydiscipline/legalaid.aspx

The Liturgical Commission

Chair Rt Revd Robert Atwell (*Bishop of Exeter*)

Secretary and Worship Development Officer Tim
Hone   *Tel:* 020 7898 1365
email: tim.hone@churchofengland.org

Assistant Secretary Sue Moore   *Tel:* 020 7898 1376
email: sue.moore@churchofengland.org

Office Church House, Great Smith St, London
SW1P 3AZ   Tel: 020 7898 1376

MEMBERS
Rt Revd Robert Paterson (*Bishop of Sodor and
Man*), Revd Dr Anders Bergquist, Ven Dr Anne
Dawtry, Revd Canon Perran Gay (Truro), Revd
Mark Earey, Mrs Sarah Finch (London), Revd
Canon Christopher Irvine, Revd Dr Simon Jones,
Revd Timothy Lomax, Revd Dr Rosemarie
Mallett (Southwark), Canon Christine McMullen
(Derby), Dr Bridget Nichols, Revd Philip North
(London), Revd Canon Gavin Kirk (Lincoln),
Revd Paul Thomas, Revd Gary Waddington,
Revd Dr Jo Spreadbury
In response to resolutions by the Convocations

in October 1954, the Archbishops of Canterbury
and York appointed a standing Liturgical Commission 'to consider questions of a liturgical
character submitted to them from time to time
by the Archbishops of Canterbury and York
and to report thereon to the Archbishops'.
In 1971 the Commission became a permanent
Commission of the General Synod. Its functions
are:

1 to prepare forms of service at the request of the
House of Bishops for submission to that House in
the first instance;
2 to advise on the experimental use of forms of
service and the development of liturgy;
3 to exchange information and advice on liturgical matters with other Churches both in the
Anglican Communion and elsewhere;
4 to promote the development and understanding of liturgy and its use in the Church.

Further information about the Commission's
work and its Transforming Worship initiative
may be found on the Transforming Worship website at www.transformingworship.org.uk

General Synod Publications

Printed copies of General Synod publications
can be purchased from Church House Bookshop.
The *Report of Proceedings* is now only available in
electronic format and is available to download,

along with the texts of many other papers, on the
General Synod section of the Church of England
website.

THE CONVOCATIONS OF CANTERBURY AND YORK

CONSTITUTION

Each of the Convocations consists of two Houses, an Upper House and a Lower House. The Upper House consists of all the diocesan bishops in the Province, the Bishop of Dover (in the case of the Convocation of Canterbury), bishops elected by and from amongst suffragan bishops of the Province, and any other bishops residing in the Province who are members of the Archbishops' Council. The Archbishop presides. The Lower House comprises clergy (other than bishops) who have been elected, appointed or chosen in accordance with Canon H 2 and the rules made under it (including deans, proctors from the dioceses and university constituencies and clerical members of religious communities) together with *ex-officio* members. The Prolocutor is the chair and spokesperson of the House.

MEMBERS OF THE CONVOCATIONS

	Canterbury	York	Either Province
Upper House			
Diocesan Bishops.....	30	12	
Bishop of Dover	1		
Bishop to the Forces..	1		
Elected Suffragan			
Bishops	4	3	
	—	—	
	36	15	
	—	—	
Lower House			
Deans.................	3	2	
Dean of Jersey or			
Guernsey	1		
Armed Services.......	3		
Chaplain-General of			
Prisons.............	1		
Elected Proctors	128	55	
University Proctors ..	4	2	
Religious			2
Co-opted Clergy......	0	0	
	—	—	—
	140	59	2
	—	—	

OFFICERS

Convocation of Canterbury

President The Archbishop of Canterbury

Prolocutor of the Lower House Ven Christine Hardman

Other Officers
Pro-Prolocutors
Revd Preb David Houlding, Revd Preb Stephen Lynas

Standing Committee of the Lower House
The Prolocutor
The Pro-Prolocutors
Revd Simon Cawdell, Revd Canon Robert Cotton, Revd Stuart Currie, Revd Anne Hollinghurst, Revd Mark Ireland, Revd Hugh Lee

Registrar Mr Stephen Slack

Synodical Secretary, Actuary and Editor of the Chronicle of Convocation
Revd Stephen Trott, Rectory, 41 Humfrey Lane, Boughton, Northampton NN2 8RQ
Tel: 01604 845655
email: revstrott@btinternet.com

Ostiarius Mr Clive McCleester, Hospital of St Cross, St Cross Rd, Winchester SO23 9SD

Convocation of York

President The Archbishop of York

Prolocutor of the Lower House Ven Cherry Vann (*Archdeacon of Rochdale*)

Other Officers
Deputy Prolocutors
Revd Dr Meg Gilley, Revd Canon Simon Killwick

Assessors (Standing Committee)
Vacancy, Revd Canon Suzanne Sheriff

Registrar Mr Lionel Lennox

Synodal Secretary and Treasurer and Editor of the Journal of Convocation
Ven Alan Wolstencroft, The Bakehouse, 1 Latham Row, Horwich, Bolton BL6 6QZ
Tel and *Fax:* 01204 469985
email: wolstencroftalan@gmail.com

Apparitor Mr Alex Carberry, Head Verger of York Minster

ACTS AND PROCEEDINGS

For the Acts and Proceedings of the Convocations, readers are referred to *The Chronicle of the Convocation of Canterbury* and to the *York Journal of Convocation*. Back numbers are available from Wm Dawson & Sons Ltd, Cannon House, Folkestone, Kent.

THE ARCHBISHOPS' COUNCIL

The Archbishops' Council
Charity Registration no: 1074857

Tel: 020 7898 1000
Fax: 020 7898 1369

Purpose and work
The objects of the Archbishops' Council under the National Institutions Measure 1998 are to *'co-ordinate, promote, aid and further the work and mission of the Church of England'*. It aims to further its statutory object by:

• providing an informed Christian view in public debate;
• promoting the views of the Church of England to parliament and government;
• overseeing the delivery of services and support to dioceses and parishes; and
• ensuring that policy and resources are considered together.

The Archbishops' Council works closely with the Offices of the Archbishops of Canterbury and York, the House of Bishops and the General Synod, the Church Commissioners and the Church of England Pensions Board. It is supported in its wide-ranging brief by the staff and members of its Divisions:

• Education
• Cathedral and Church Buildings – which includes the Church Buildings Council and the Cathedrals Fabric Commission for England
• Central Secretariat – which includes the Council for Christian Unity and Research and Statistics
• Church House Publishing
• Ministry
• Mission and Public Affairs – which includes the Committee for Minority Ethnic Anglican Concerns

The work of the Council is described in more detail in its annual report. Its mission is to support the Church in her worship of God and her preparation in:

• proclaiming the Good News of the kingdom
• teaching, baptising and nurturing new believers;
• responding to human need by loving service;
• seeking to transform unjust structures in society; and
• striving to safeguard the integrity of creation and sustaining and renewing the life of the earth.

The Council's objectives are:
1. To enhance the Church's mission by
   • promoting spiritual and numerical growth;
   • enabling and supporting the worshipping Church and encouraging and promoting new ways of being Church; and
   • engaging with social justice and environmental stewardship.
2. To sustain and advance the Church's work in education, lifelong learning and discipleship;
3. To enable the Church to select, train and resource the right people, both ordained and lay, to carry out public ministry and to encourage lay people in their vocation to the world; and
4. To encourage the maintenance and development of the inherited fabric of Church buildings for worship and service to the community.

It engages on behalf of the Church with Government on a wide range of issues of concern to the Church of England and its mission to the nation.

Its programme of work for the new quinquennium, in collaboration with the House of Bishops, is set out in GS 1815, *Challenges for the New Quinquennium*. This seeks to build on the following three main themes set out by the Archbishop of Canterbury in his Presidential Address to General Synod in November 2010:
(i) To take forward the spiritual and numerical growth of the Church of England – including the growth of its capacity to serve the whole community of this country;
(ii) To re-shape or reimagine the Church's ministry for the century coming, so as to make sure that there is a growing and sustainable Christian witness in every local community; and
(iii) To further the Common Good.

MEMBERS
Joint Presidents
Most Revd and Rt Hon Justin Welby, Archbishop of Canterbury
Most Revd and Rt Hon Dr John Sentamu, Archbishop of York
Officers of the General Synod
Ven Christine Hardman, Prolocutor of the Lower House of the Convocation of Canterbury
Ven Cherry Vann, Prolocutor of the Lower House of the Convocation of York
Dr Philip Giddings, Chair of the House of Laity
Mr Tim Hind, Vice-Chair of the House of Laity

Elected by the General Synod:
Rt Revd Dr Steven Croft, Bishop of Sheffield
Rt Revd Trevor Willmott, Bishop of Dover
Revd Canon Robert Cotton
Revd Mark Ireland
Mr Paul Boyd-Lee
Mrs Christina Rees

A Church Estates Commissioner
Mr Andreas Whittam Smith, First Church Estates
Commissioner

Appointed by the Archbishops
Canon John Spence, former Managing Director,
Lloyds TSB plc
Mrs Mary Chapman, former Chief Executive, the
Chartered Institute of Management
Mr Philip Fletcher, former Chairman, Water
Services Regulation Authority
Revd Dr Rosalyn Murphy, priest-in-charge of
St Thomas's Church, Blackpool
Miss Rebecca Swinson, Medical Researcher

Staff
William Fittall, *Secretary General*
Tel: 020 7898 1360
email: william.fittall@churchofengland.org
Nigel Genders, *Education/National Society*
Tel: 020 7898 1500
email: nigel.genders@churchofengland.org

Revd Dr Malcolm Brown, *Mission and Public
Affairs*   *Tel:* 020 7898 1468
email: malcolm.brown@churchofengland.org

Revd Arun Arora, *Communications*
Tel: 020 7898 1462
email: arun.arora@churchofengland.org

Janet Gough, *Cathedral and Church Buildings*
Tel: 020 7898 1887
email: janet.gough@churchofengland.org

Ven Julian Hubbard, *Ministry*
Tel: 020 7898 1390
email: julian.hubbard@churchofengland.org

Vacancy, *Human Resources*   *Tel:* 020 7898 1565
email: name.name@churchofengland.org

Stephen Slack, *Legal Adviser*   *Tel:* 020 7898 0366
email: stephen.slack@churchofengland.org

Dr Jacqui Philips, *Clerk to the Synod and Director of
Central Secretariat*   *Tel:* 020 7898 1559
email: jacqui.philips@churchofengland.org

Nicholas Hills, *Assistant Secretary*
Tel: 020 7898 1363
email: nicholas.hills@churchofengland.org

Archbishops' Council: key working relationships

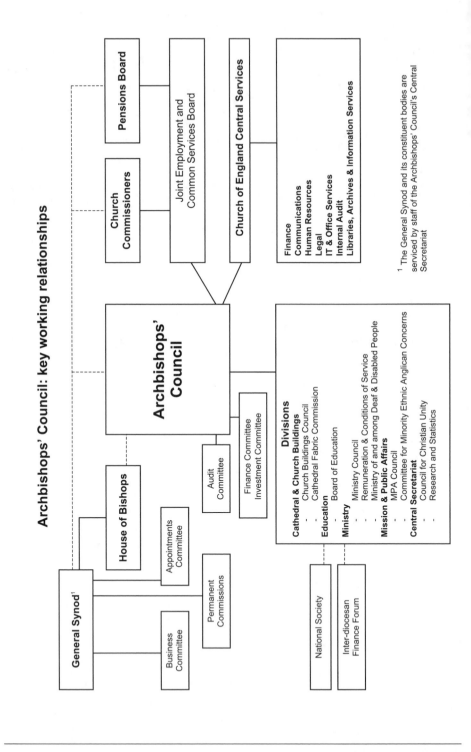

Archbishops' Council

General Synod[1]
- Business Committee
- Permanent Commissions

House of Bishops
- Appointments Committee

Audit Committee

Finance Committee
Investment Committee

National Society
Inter-diocesan Finance Forum

Divisions

Cathedral & Church Buildings
- Church Buildings Council
- Cathedral Fabric Commission

Education
- Board of Education

Ministry
- Ministry Council
- Remuneration & Conditions of Service
- Ministry of and among Deaf & Disabled People

Mission & Public Affairs
- MPA Council
- Committee for Minority Ethnic Anglican Concerns

Central Secretariat
- Council for Christian Unity
- Research and Statistics

Pensions Board

Church Commissioners

Joint Employment and Common Services Board

Church of England Central Services
- Finance
- Communications
- Human Resources
- Legal
- IT & Office Services
- Internal Audit
- Libraries, Archives & Information Services

[1] The General Synod and its constituent bodies are serviced by staff of the Archbishops' Council's Central Secretariat

ARCHBISHOPS' COUNCIL BUDGET

The 2015 Budget, agreed by the General Synod in July 2014 (available on the C-of-E website – paper GS 1959), is the fifth to be prepared within the framework established by the Financial Strategy Review (also available on the website – paper GS 1731) which set spending priorities for 2010–2015. The 2015 expenditure budget of £30.7 million, as summarized in the table overleaf, represents a year-on-year increase of £1.0 million (3.4%) over 2014 budget levels. The dioceses are funding a total of £29.2 million via the apportionment – representing a year-on-year increase of £0.4 million (1.3%) – with the balance (£1.5 million) being met either from the Council's own funds (Designated & Restricted), Reserves, or from the generosity of the Corporation of the Church House via their decision to waive rent liability for 2015.

The Appointments Committee of the Church of England

Chairman Mrs Margaret Swinson

Secretary Mr Nicholas Hills   *Tel:* 020 7898 1363

Four members appointed by the Archbishops' Council
Dr Philip Giddings, Ven Christine Hardman, Revd Dr Rosalyn Murphy, Ven Cherry Vann

Seven elected Members
Ven Dr John Applegate, Ven Annette Cooper, Ms Susan Cooper, Mrs Sarah Finch, Rt Revd Richard Frith (*Bishop of Hereford*), Revd Canon Giles Goddard, Mr Aiden Hargreaves-Smith.

A joint committee of the General Synod and the Archbishops' Council, the Appointments Committee is responsible for making appointments and/or recommendations on appointments to synodical and other bodies as the Archbishops, the Synod or the Archbishops' Council require. It published its guidelines for best practice in the making of such appointments in 2010 as GS Misc 963, copies of which can be obtained from its Secretary.

Audit Committee

MEMBERS
Chair Mary Chapman. Appointed by the Archbishops' Council

Secretary Michael Cole
Membership Keith Malcouronne (elected by General Synod); Paul Boyd-Lee (Archbishops' Council member and appointee); John Neilson (appointed by the Archbishops' Council); Susan Cooper (elected by General Synod); Jonathan Evans OBE (appointed by the Archbishops' Council).

The Committee provides independent oversight of the Archbishops' Council's framework of corporate governance, risk management and internal control. It oversees the discharge of the Council's responsibilities relating to financial statements, external and internal audit and internal control systems, and reports to the Council thereon with recommendations as appropriate.

ARCHBISHOPS' COUNCIL BUDGET

	2015	
	£	£
TRAINING FOR MINISTRY (Vote 1)		
Expenditure	13,437,760	**13,437,670**
Financed by:		
Income	(20,000)	
Corporation of CH Rent Relief	(315,000)	
Diocesan Apportionment	(13,102,670)	**(13,477,670)**
NATIONAL CHURCH RESPONSIBILITIES (Vote 2)		
Central Secretariat	2,075,933	
Ministry	1,537,580	
Mission & Public Affairs	1,349,131	
Cathedral & Church Buildings	908,608	
Education	753,134	
Projects & Developments	376,008	
Church House Publishing (incl Crockford)	(10,973)	
Communications	414,274	
Human Resources	377,051	
Legal	674,940	
Internal Audit	77,168	
Records	210,591	
Finance & Resources	847,834	
IT & Office Services	491,614	
ITC Infrastructure Project	50,000	
Accommodation & Depreciation	1,170,413	
Contingency & Vacancy Provision	(200,000)	**11,103,305**
Financed by:		
Income	(20,000)	
Corporation of CH Rent Relief	(222,000)	
AC Designated & Restricted Funds	(667,703)	
Movement from Reserves	(296,603)	
Diocesan Apportionment	(9,987,000)	**(11,103,305)**
GRANTS (Vote 3)		
Anglican Communion Office	517,840	
Churches Together in England	230,000	
Church Urban Fund	203,000	
World Council of Churches	108,000	
Conference of European Churches	90,474	
Fresh Expressions	40,000	
Expenses of Representatives & Minor Grants	40,000	
Legal Costs Fund	20,000	
Churches Together in Britain & Ireland	15,000	**1,264,314**
Financed by:		
Diocesan Apportionment	(1,264,314)	**(1,264,314)**
MISSION AGENCIES CLERGY PENSION CONTRIBUTIONS (Vote 4)		
Expenditure	772,500	**772,500**
Financed by:		
Diocesan Apportionment	(772,500)	**(722,500)**
CLERGY RETIREMENT HOUSING – CHARM (Vote 5)		
Expenditure	4,151,591	**4,151,591**
Financed by:		
Diocesan Apportionment	(4,151,591)	**(4,151,591)**
TOTAL EXPENDITURE		**30,729,380**
Financed by:		
Diocesan Apportionment	(29,188,075)	
AC Designated & Restricted Funds	(667,703)	
Corporation of CH Rent Relief	(537,000)	
Movement from Reserves	(296,603)	
Income	(40,000)	**(30,729,380)**

FINANCE COMMITTEE

MEMBERS

Chair appointed by Archbishops' Council
Canon John Spence

Three members elected by the General Synod:
Mr Richard Mantle (Ripon and Leeds), Revd
Canon Andrew Salmon (Manchester) and Mrs
Sheri Sturgess (Truro)

*Three members appointed by the Archbishops'
Council on the recommendation of the Appointments
Committee*:
Ven Annette Cooper (*Archdeacon of Colchester*),
Canon Sandra Newton (Sheffield), one vacancy

*Three members elected by the Inter-Diocesan Finance
Forum*:
Canon Michael Arlington (Southwell and
Nottingham), Mr Andy Brookes (London), Mrs
Elizabeth Renshaw (Chester))

Secretary David White   *Tel*: 020 7898 1684
          email: david.white@churchofengland.org

Terms of reference

1. To advise the Archbishops' Council and the
dioceses on all financial aspects of the
Archbishops' Council's work, including its
investment, stewardship and trustee
responsibilities, on the effects of the public
financial policy and on the overall financial
needs and resources of the Church.
2. To make recommendations to the Archbishops' Council as to its annual budget and on
mechanisms for monitoring and controlling the
expenditure of the Council.
3. To consult with the dioceses on financial
matters, and to make recommendations thereon
as appropriate to the Archbishops' Council and
the dioceses.
4. To carry out such other work as may be
entrusted to it by the Archbishops' Council.

INVESTMENT COMMITTEE

MEMBERS

Appointed by the Finance Committee

Canon Michael Arlington (Chair), Mr John
Booth, Mr Stephen Marriott, Mrs Emma
Osborne, Mr Glyn Owen and Canon John Spence

Secretary David White   *Tel*: 020 7898 1684
          email: david.white@churchofengland.org

Summary of Terms of Reference

Responsibility for setting investment policy lies
with the Archbishops' Council with advice from
its Finance Committee.

Within that policy, the Investment Committee
has responsibility for implementing the invest-

ment strategy, and reporting regularly on progress. The Investment Committee's responsibilities include:

1. to select and review the appointment of
investment managers;
2. to set the strategy for the Council's investment
managers including setting performance
objectives, investment guidelines and benchmarks to meet the investment policy set by
Council;
3. to decide the most appropriate investment
strategy for each of the Council's charitable
settlements.

CENTRAL SECRETARIAT

The Central Secretariat supports a number of
different aspects of the Church's institutional role
and functions. This includes the Research and
Statistics Department, the Ecumenical team, the
Safeguarding team and various other groups,
such as the Churches' Funerals Group. The Central
Secretariat also includes staff supporting the
General Synod and its related bodies and com-
mittees, including the three Houses of the Synod
(House of Bishops, House of Clergy and House of
Laity), the Dioceses and Liturgical Commissions
and the Business and Appointments Committees.
The Secretariat for the Archbishops' Council is
also based in the Central Secretariat.

The Clerk to the Synod is also the Director of
the Central Secretariat, acts as Secretary to the
Business Committee and provides advice and
assistance as necessary to synodical bodies and
members of Synod.

Clerk to the Synod and Director Central Secretariat
Dr Jacqui Philips   *Tel*: 020 7898 1385
          email: jacqui.philips@churchofengland.org
*PA to Clerk to the Synod and Administrative
Secretary* Dr Emma Arbuthnot
                              Tel: 020 7898 1560
          email: emma.arbuthnot@churchofengland.org

Senior Administrative Staff and their teams

Research and Statistics
email: statistics.unit@churchofengland.org
Dr Bev Botting (Head of Research and Statistics)
Tel: 020 7898 1542
email: bev.botting@churchofengland.org

Council for Christian Unity
Dr Jeremy Worthen (Secretary for Ecumenical Relations and Theology)   *Tel:* 020 7898 148
email: jeremy.worthen@churchofengland.org
Dr Roger Paul (National Ecumenical Officer for England)   *Tel:* 020 7898 1479
email: roger.paul@churchofengland.org
Dr Leslie Nathaniel (Archbishop's International Ecumenical Secretary and Council for Christian Unity European Secretary)   *Tel:* 020 7898 1474
email: leslie.nathaniel@churchofengland.org
Francis Bassett (Assistant Secretary, Council for Christian Unity)   *Tel:* 020 7898 1481
email: francis.bassett@churchofengland.org
Caroline Kim (Team Administrator, Council for Christian Unity)   *Tel:* 020 7898 1471
email: caroline.kim@churchofengland.org
Angeline Leung (Team Administrator, Council for Christian Unity)   *Tel:* 020 7898 1473
email: angeline.leung@churchofengland.org

Synod Office
Andrew Brown (Head of Events – General Synod and House of Bishops)   *Tel:* 020 7898 1374
email: andrewjbrown@churchofengland.org

Jonathan Neil-Smith (*Secretary:* Dioceses Commission, House of Clergy, Standing Committee of the House of Clergy)   *Tel:* 020 7898 1373
email: jonathan.neil-smith@churchofengland.org
Nicholas Hills (*Secretary:* Appointments Committee, House of Laity, Standing Committee of the House of Laity; *Assistant Secretary:* Archbishops' Council)   *Tel:* 020 7898 1363
email: nicholas.hills@churchofengland.org
Tim Hone (Secretary to the Liturgical Commission and Worship Development Officer*)*
Tel: 020 7898 1365
email: tim.hone@churchofengland.org
Sue Moore (*Secretary:* Churches' Funerals Group [www.christianfunerals.org]; *Assistant to Jonathan Neil-Smith*)   *Tel:* 020 7898 1376
email: sue.moore@churchofengland.org
Jennifer Hornby (Synod Office *Executive Officer*)
Tel: 020 7898 1372
email: jennifer.hornby@churchofengland.org
Diane Bradford (Assistant Secretary to the Dioceses Commission)   *Tel:* 020 7898 1643
email: diane.bradford@churchofengland.org

Safeguarding Team
Vacancy (National Safeguarding Adviser – Child and Adult Protection for the Church of England)
Tel: 020 7898 1330
Simon Payne (Safeguarding Officer – Child and Adult Protection*)*   *Tel:* 07931 281318
email: simon.payne@churchofengland.org
Jill Sandham (Safeguarding Officer – Child and Adult Protection)
email: jill.sandham@churchofengland.org

The Council for Christian Unity

Secretary for Ecumenical Relations and Theology
Revd Canon Dr Jeremy Worthen
Tel: 020 7898 1488

European Secretary Revd Canon Dr Leslie
Nathaniel   *Tel:* 020 7898 1474
email: leslie.nathaniel@churchofengland.org

National Ecumenical Officer for England Revd Dr
Roger Paul   *Tel:* 020 7898 1479
email: roger.paul@churchofengland.org

Assistant Secretary Mr Francis Bassett
Tel: 020 7898 1481
email: francis.bassett@churchofengland.org

Office Church House, Great Smith St, London
SW1P 3AZ   *Tel:* 020 7898 1470
Fax: 020 7898 1483
Web: http://www.churchofengland.org/
about-us/work-other-churches/ccu.aspx

MEMBERS
Chairman Rt Revd Donald Allister (*Bishop of Peterborough*)

Membership Elected: Revd Janet Appleby, Dr Rachel Jepson, Ven George Howe, Canon Elizabeth Paver. Appointed: Revd Dr William Adam, Rt Revd Tim Thornton (*Bishop of Truro*), Revd Peter Anthony, Mrs Margaret Swinson

The Council was established as an advisory committee of the General Synod on 1 April 1991 to continue and develop the ecumenical work formerly undertaken by the Board for Mission and Unity. That Board, set up on 1 January 1972, had inherited the responsibilities of the Missionary and Ecumenical Council of the Church Assembly (MECCA) and the Church of England Council on Foreign Relations (CFR).

FUNCTIONS OF THE COUNCIL
(*Adapted from the Constitution*)
(a) To stimulate and encourage theological reflection in consultation with the Faith and Order Commission and to advise the Archbishops' Council and the General Synod on unity issues and proposals in the light of the Christian understanding of God's purposes for the world.
(b) To advise the House of Bishops on matters referred to it by the House.
(c) To foster ecumenical work in the Church nationally and in the dioceses.
(d) In conjunction with the Archbishops' Council to promote unity and ecumenical concerns in the work of all the Boards, Councils, Divisions, etc.
(e) In ecumenical concerns on behalf of the

Archbishops' Council to be the principal link between the General Synod and

(i)   The Anglican Consultative Council;
(ii)   individual provinces and dioceses of the Anglican Communion and the United Churches incorporating former Anglican dioceses.

(f) On behalf of the Archbishops' Council to be the principal channel of communication between the General Synod and

(i)   The World Council of Churches;
(ii)   The Conference of European Churches;
(iii) Churches Together in Britain and Ireland;
(iv)   Churches Together in England;
(v)   all other Christian Churches in the British Isles and abroad.

(g) To service committees and commissions engaged in ecumenical discussions with other Churches.

COMMITTEE FOR ROMAN CATHOLIC RELATIONS
Chairman Rt Revd Tim Thornton (*Bishop of Truro*)

The Committee for Roman Catholic Relations consists of not more than fifteen persons appointed by the Archbishops after consultation with the Council. This Committee promotes relations between the Church of England and the Roman Catholic Church in this country and it meets twice a year with the equivalent Roman Catholic body. The two bodies form the English Anglican Roman Catholic Committee.

MEISSEN COMMISSION – ANGLICAN COMMITTEE
Chairman Rt Revd Nicholas Baines (*Bishop of Leeds*)
The Meissen Commission (the Sponsoring Body for Church of England EKD Relations) was established in 1991 to oversee the implementation of the Meissen Declaration and encourage relationships with the Evangelical Church in Germany. It comprises Anglican and German committees.

ECUMENICAL INSTRUMENTS
Contact is maintained with the World Council of Churches, the Conference of European Churches, Churches Together in Britain and Ireland, and Churches Together in England, where members and staff represent the Church of England at various levels. The Council is

particularly concerned with helping the Church of England to relate effectively at every level to the ecumenical instruments.

PANELS OF THE CCU

The CCU has two subsidiary panels:

Methodist-Anglican Panel for Unity in Mission
Co-Chairman (Anglican) Rt Revd Paul Bayes (*Bishop of Liverpool*)
Porvoo Panel
Chairman Rt Revd David Hamid (*Suffragan Bishop in Europe*)

Research and Statistics

Head of Research and Statistics Dr Bev Botting
Tel: 020 7898 1542
Fax: 020 7390 1591
email: statistics.unit@churchofengland.org
Web: www.churchofengland.org/about-us/ facts-stats/research-statistics
Office: Church House, Great Smith St, London SW1P 3AZ

While the gathering of parochial statistics for mission and finance statistics remains at the heart of the Research and Statistics department's work, the department has broadened the range of statistics it maintains and has diversified so that it is now providing a statistical and research consultancy service to the central Church, dioceses and beyond. It is also working to develop the department's role as a central resource to colleagues in the National Church Institutions, and with academic institutions. It is based within the Archbishops' Council where it forms part of the Central Secretariat. Working closely with the Archbishops' Council, the Mission and Public Affairs Division, and the Church Commissioners Strategy and Development Division, the department continues to develop the annual church attendance and participation statistics. This aims to provide a range of statistics and research resources to be a tool for mission and to monitor progress on the Archbishops' quinquennial objectives.

The Research and Statistics department is seeking to better understand the needs of users of church statistics and to establish any issues for those (largely volunteers) who provide the data to them. They recognize that the parish data are a valuable resource for parishes in their planning for mission, outreach and growth, and to evaluate the impact of any initiatives. Therefore they are working hard to provide accessible information to parishes. Recently they have provided a Parish Spotlight to every parish in the country. This gives parish information from the 2011 Census, government statistics and parish returns in a range of charts, pictures, words and tables. Feedback to

date has been very positive. The department is developing a web-based mapping system which allows dioceses and parishes to visually show particular characteristics of their ecclesiastical area, both demographic and church statistics. Some of the information presently held on the department's database includes social deprivation, diversity, and population profiles. This system is very user-friendly and it is possible to use the centrally provided information together with local information to create bespoke maps.

The department maintains strong links with the Cathedral and Church Buildings Division regarding the use of cathedral and church buildings, with the Ministry Division in the preparation and production of *Statistics of Licensed Ministers*, and with the Church Commissioners. They also work closely with others funding research, so have been working closely with the Church Growth Programme funded by the Church Commissioners. They are supporting several research projects led by the Ministry Division on the experience of ministry. The collection by General Synod of Statistics of Ethnic Origin in 2002 established the principle of ongoing diversity monitoring across the Church of England and this was done most recently in 2007. The department is now preparing for a Congregational Diversity Survey (Everyone Counts) in October 2014 to continue to monitor diversity, age and gender profiles and levels of disability across the Church. Continued efforts are being made, in conjunction with the Communications Unit, to improve how the research and statistical information is communicated more widely, with reports now being developed for the web primarily, and being published in a more timely way.

The department maintains links with other denominations on statistical and research matters and works closely with the Methodist Church to help analyse and publish their annual mission statistics. It is developing its role across the Church as a source of reliable research information regarding the place of the Church in modern society.

MINISTRY DIVISION

Chairman of Ministry Council Rt Revd Dr Steven Croft (*Bishop of Sheffield*)   *Tel:* 0114 230 2170
    email: bishop@sheffield.anglican.org

Director of Ministry Ven Julian Hubbard
    Tel: 020 7898 1390
    email: julian.hubbard@churchofengland.org

Finance and Administration Mr John Jackson
    Tel: 020 7898 1392
    email: john.jackson@churchofengland.org

Senior Selection Secretary Revd Stephen Ferns
    Tel: 020 7898 1399
    email: stephen.ferns@churchofengland.org

Theological Education and Training Dr David Way
    Tel: 020 7898 1405
    email: david.way@churchofengland.org

National Deaf Ministry Adviser Revd Canon Gill Behenna   *Tel:* 07715 707135
    email: gill.behenna@churchofengland.org
National Disability Adviser Mr Roy McCloughry
    Tel: 07974 768935
    email: rkml@me.com

Selection Secretaries
Mr Kevin Diamond   *Tel:* 020 7898 1402
    email: kevin.diamond@churchofengland.org

Revd Dr Carys Walsh   *Tel:* 020 7898 1406
    email: carys.walsh@churchofengland.org

Revd Catherine Williams (also *Vocations Officer*)
    Tel: 020 7898 1395
    email: catherine.williams@churchofengland.org

Revd Hilary Ison (also *Adviser on Training Pathways*)   *Tel:* 020 7898 1424
    email: hilary.ison@churchofengland.org

Revd Liz Boughton (also *Adviser for Young Vocations*)   *Tel:* 0207 898 1593
    email: liz.boughton@churchofengland.org

Miss Joy Gilliver   *Tel:* 020 7898 1439
    email: joy.gilliver@churchofengland.org

National Continuing Ministerial Development Adviser Dr Tim Ling   *Tel:* 020 7898 1408
    email: tim.ling@churchofengland.org

Grants Officer Dr Mark Hodge   *Tel:* 020 7898 1396
    email: mark.hodge@churchofengland.org

Finance and Statistics Officer Ms Sarah Evans
    Tel: 020 7898 1394
    email: sarah.evans@churchof england.org

Quality Assurance Assistance and Policy Adviser Mr David Hanson   *Tel:* 020 7898 1413
    email: david.hanson@churchofengland.org

Office Church House, Great Smith St, London SW1P 3AZ   *Tel:* 020 7898 1416

Secretary of the Central Readers' Council Dr Alan Wakely   *Tel:* 01353 775132
    email: crcsec@hallam.com
    Web: www.readers.cofe.anglican.org

MINISTRY COUNCIL
Chair Rt Revd Dr Steven Croft

Revd Prof Loveday Alexander, Rt Revd Stephen Conway, Mrs Mary Chapman, Mrs Vivienne Goddard, Revd Vanessa Herrick, Revd Canon Dr Judith Maltby, Canon John Spence, Rt Revd Robert Paterson, Rt Revd David Walker

The Ministry Council oversees the work of the Division. The committee meets three times a year and consists of members appointed by the Archbishops on the advice of the House of Bishops Standing Committee and the Appointments Committee of the Church of England and elected from the Houses of Clergy and Laity by the General Synod.
    The Ministry Council is supported by panels responsible for Candidates, Research Degrees, Quality in Formation, Finance and by its Deployment Task Group. In addition the work of the Remuneration and Conditions of Service Committee and the Committee for Ministry of and Among Deaf and Disabled People is conducted in liaison with the Council. The Chair of the Central Readers' Council is a member of the Ministry Council and the CRC Secretary attends Council.

QUALITY in FORMATION PANEL
Chair Professor Michael Wright

Revd Dr Ruth Ackroyd, Ven Sheila Watson, Dr Paula Gooder, Revd Paul Goodliff

Terms of reference
1 To oversee the transition to a single quality framework for inspection, validation, moderation and Reader moderation and to carry out the current processes of inspection, validation, moderation and Reader moderation as required.
2 To provide training and support for reviewers involved in the current and future processes.

FINANCE PANEL
Chair Prof John Craven

Mr John Butler, Mrs Julie Dziegiel, Mr Richard Finlinson, Ven Christine Froude

Terms of reference
The responsibility of the Finance Panel is to advise the Ministry Council on all aspects of its financial responsibility regarding the cost of ordinand training funded from Central Church Funds. It prepares and administers the Training Budget, and advises on the financial support of candidates.

CANDIDATES PANEL
Chair Rt Revd Mark Bryant (*Bishop of Jarrow*)

Canon Katrina Barnes, Sr Edith Margaret CHN, Canon Sam Corley, Revd Dr James Gardom, Miss Caulene Herbert, Professor Joyce Hill, Mrs Susan Knowles, Revd Preb Dr Brian Leathard, Revd Canon Gary Renison, Canon James Stewart, Revd Margi Walker, Revd Canon Alison White

Terms of reference
1 To advise sponsoring bishops on:
(1) the reduction or lengthening of candidates' training
(2) the transferral of candidates from one training institution to another
(3) the return of candidates to training after a break of more than three months
(4) the suitability of candidates for transfer of category of ministry or change of focus of ministry
(5) the suitability of ministers from other denominations to be ministers in the Church of England
(6) candidates' potential to be theological educators
2 To undertake other work in relation to recruitment and selection

RESEARCH DEGREES PANEL
Chair Canon Dr Judith Maltby

Revd Prof Ben Quash, Prof Andrew Wright, Revd Prof Simon Oliver

Terms of reference
1 To give permission to ordinands seen as potential theological educators to study for research degrees (MPhil, PhD etc) outside of Bishops' Regulations for Training as part of pre-ordination training.
2 To allocate its budget to pay for, or contribute to, the additional costs of such training.

DEPLOYMENT TASK GROUP
Chair Rt Revd Julian Henderson (*Bishop of Blackburn*)
Ven Ian Jagger, Mrs Julie Jones, Ms Ros McCool, Rev Canon Phil Potter, Ven Rachel Treweek

Terms of reference
1 To consider matters related to the deployment of ministry resources in dioceses and across the Church of England in order to encourage mission and growth.
2 To contribute to the development of a framework for national deployment policy.
3 To provide data and information about ministry resources to dioceses and bishops.
4 To consider questions on deployment issues from bishops and diocese.

COMMITTEE FOR MINISTRY OF AND AMONG DEAF AND DISABLED PEOPLE
Chair Rt Revd Nicholas Holtam (*Bishop of Salisbury*)

Vice Chair Ven Cherry Vann
Mrs Penny Beschizza, Revd Catherine Carlyon, Revd David Huntley, Revd Eva McIntrye, Mrs Gail Robinson, Revd Bob Shrine, Mrs Alison Wynne, Revd Ruth Yeoman

The functions of the Committee include:
1 To monitor and advise on the progress of sector and chaplaincy ministries among deaf and disabled people within the total ministry of the Church, in consultation with those responsible for specific areas.
2 To encourage and strengthen the participation of deaf people in the life and witness of the Church, to represent the views of deaf people to the Church and of the Church to deaf people, and to support the work of the chaplains.
3 To report regularly to the Archbishops' Council on the work of the Committee.
4 To advise the Central Bodies and the dioceses on matters related to disability, especially the implementation of the Equality Act as it applies to the Church.

BISHOPS' REGULATIONS FOR TRAINING FOR ORDAINED MINISTRY
Bishops' Regulations for Ordination Training can be found from this page of the Church of England website: https://www.churchorengland.org/clergy-office-holders/ministry/ministerial-education-and-development/initial-ministerial-education/policies.aspx

GRANTSFOR MINISTERIAL EDUCATION
Details about grants can be obtained on the Ministry pages of the Church of England website or from the Grants Officer, Ministry Division, Church House, Great Smith St, London SW1P 3AZ.

For **Theological Colleges** *and* **Regional Courses** *see also* pages 229–230.

The Central Readers' Council

Patron HRH The Duke of Edinburgh

Presidents The Archbishops of Canterbury and York

Chair Rt Revd Robert Paterson (*Bishop of Sodor and Man*)

Vice-Chair Mrs Gertrud Sollars

Secretary Dr Alan Wakely   *Tel:* 01353 775132
email: crcsec@hallarn.com

Associate Secretary Jeff Heaton
Tel: 020 7898 1401
email: jeffrey.heaton@churchofengland.org

National Consultant for Reader Formation Mrs Rosemary Walters   *Tel:* 01227 768891
email: ra.walters@btinternet.com

National Consultant for Reader CMD Ms Lynn Comer   *Tel:* 01904 656295
*email:*lynncomer@yorkdiocese.org

Editor of 'The Reader' Revd Heather Fenton
Tel: 01490 412169
email: reader.editor@btconnect.com

MEMBERS
The CRC Executive Committee is elected for a five-year term co-terminous with General Synod. In addition to the Chair, Vice-Chair and all the officers listed above, the Committee consists of:

Two Wardens
Ven John Reed, Revd Dr Christopher Bracegirdle

Reader representatives
Dr Marion Gray, Mrs Julie Shield, Miss Gloria Cadman, Mr Andy Lie, Mrs Angela Mirani

Treasurer
Mrs Carol Lidgett

The Central Readers' Council (CRC) works to enhance the contribution of Readers to the overall ministry of the Church, particularly to encourage the most effective integration with other forms of ministry, ordained and lay. It works in cooperation with the Ministry Division which moderates and coordinates the training of Reader candidates. CRC arranges national conferences for Readers, provides a forum for the exchange of ideas between dioceses on Reader matters and publishes a quarterly magazine, *The Reader*.

CRC is a registered charity, which derives its income mostly from capitation grants made by diocesan Readers' boards. It has its origins in the revival of Reader ministry in the Church of England in 1866 and particularly in the Central Readers' Board, which was granted a constitution by the Archbishops in 1921. CRC today is the immediate successor to the Central Readers' Conference, under a new constitution adopted in 2002, and revised in 2007 and 2010.

CRC has three representatives from each diocese, including the Warden and Secretary of Readers, and one representative from each of the Armed Forces. Any Reader appointed to a Ministry Division committee is *ex officio* a member of CRC. A non-voting observer is invited from the Deaf Readers and Pastoral Assistants Association, the Church of Ireland, the Scottish Episcopal Church and each of the dioceses of the Church in Wales. The annual general meeting is held in March/April each year.

MISSION AND PUBLIC AFFAIRS DIVISION
Mission and Public Affairs Council

Chairman Mr Philip Fletcher

Vice-Chairs: Rt Revd Michael Hill (*Bishop of Bristol*); Rt Revd Richard Atkinson (*Bishop of Bedford*)

Director Revd Canon Dr Malcolm Brown
Tel: 020 7898 1468
email: malcolm.brown@churchofengland.org

MISSION AND PUBLIC AFFAIRS COUNCIL

FUNCTIONS OF THE COUNCIL
The functions of the Council shall be:
(a) To advise the Archbishops' Council, the General Synod and the House of Bishops on matters within the Council's remit;
(b) To work with dioceses, relevant diocesan networks and the Church's voluntary societies on matters within its remit;
(c) To relate to and cooperate with appropriate bodies within the churches of Britain and Ireland and the ecumenical instruments of CTBI and CTE;
(d) To take lead responsibility in relating to other Churches of the Anglican Communion and the Anglican Consultative Council, its Commissions and Networks, on issues relating to the Church's mission and role in public life;
(e) To relate to government departments and voluntary bodies relevant to its work.

In discharging its functions, the MPA Council shall include within its remit the following areas:
(i) the Church's engagement with social, ethical, political, environmental issues and work for justice and peace at local, national and international levels;
(ii) mission and evangelism; the Church of England's responsibilities for world mission and development; inter faith relations; and theological and missiological reflection on them;
(iii) the Church's mission and ministry (in liaison with Ministry Division) in urban and rural areas;
(iv) the Church's responsibility to confront the reality of racism in its own life and in society;
(v) the support of minority ethnic Christians in the Church of England, and their contribution to its life and witness;
(vi) the work of Hospital Chaplaincy and the Church's relation to the Department of Health, the National Health Service and Trusts and the provision of professional training and Continuing Professional Education for Chaplains.

MEMBERS
The Council is constituted of:

Chair Mr Philip Fletcher
Vice Chairs Rt Revd Richard Atkinson, Rt Revd Michael Hill
General Synod elected members:
Revd Duncan Dormor, Revd Canon Richard Hibbert, Dr Lindsay Newcombe, Mr Clive Scowen, Dr Anna Thomas-Betts, Revd Canon Dr Dagmar Winter
Revd Dr Victoria Johnson (Appointed)
Ven Daniel Kajumba (Chair of CMEAC, Co-opted)
Canon Mark Russell (Co-opted)

STAFF
Director Revd Canon Dr Malcolm Brown
Tel: 020 7898 1468
email: malcolm.brown@churchofengland.org
Parliamentary Secretary Mr Richard Chapman
Tel: 020 7898 1438
email: richard.chapman@churchofengland.org

Deputy Parliamentary Secretary Mr Simon Stanley
Tel: 020 7898 1478
email: simon.stanley@churchofengland.org

Home Affairs Revd Martin Kettle
Tel: 020 7898 1531
email: martin.kettle@churchofengland.org

International and Development Affairs Dr Charles Reed
Tel: 020 7898 1533
email: charles.reed@churchofengland.org

Marriage and Family Policy Mr Jack Palmer
Tel: 020 7898 1472
email: jack.palmer@churchofengland.org

Medical Ethics, Health and Social Care Policy Revd Dr Brendan McCarthy
Tel: 020 7898 1523
*email:*brendan.maccarthy@churchofengland.org

Economic and Social Affairs Mr Tom Sefton
Tel: 020 7898 1446
email: tom.sefton@churchofengland.org

Adviser for Minority Ethnic Anglican Concerns Dr Elizabeth Henry
Tel: 020 7898 1442
email: elizabeth.henry@churchofengland.org

World Mission Policy Adviser Canon Janice Price
Tel: 020 7898 1328
email: janice.price@churchofengland.org

Adviser for Mission Theology, Alternative Spiritualities and New Religious Movements Dr Anne Richards
Tel: 020 7898 1444
email: anne.richards@churchofengland.org

National Adviser for Mission and Evangelism Dr Rachel Jordan   *Tel:* 020 7898 1436
       email: rachel.jordan@churchofengland.org

National Inter Faith Relations Adviser Revd Dr Toby Howarth   *Tel:* 020 7898 1477
       email: toby.howarth@churchofengland.org

National Rural Officer Canon Dr Jill Hopkinson
                                 Tel: 024 7685 3073
                                 Fax: 024 7669 6460
       email: jillh@arthurrankcentre.org.uk

Hospital Chaplaincies Administrator Miss Mary Ingledew   *Tel:* 020 7898 1895
       email: mary.ingledew@churchofengland.org

All staff are based in Church House, Westminster with the following exception: the office of the National Rural Officer is at the Arthur Rank Centre, Stoneleigh Park, Warwickshire CV8 2LZ. The National Inter Faith Relations Adviser is based at Lambeth Palace.

COMMITTEE FOR MINORITY ETHNIC ANGLICAN CONCERNS
Chair Ven Daniel Kajumba
Adviser Dr Elizabeth Henry
The principal tasks of the Committee are to monitor and make recommendations about issues which arise or which ought to arise in the context of the work of the Archbishops' Council and its Divisions and of the General Synod itself, as far as they have policy implications for minority ethnic groups within the Church and the wider community; and to assist the Bishops and their dioceses in developing diocesan-wide strategies for combating racial bias within the Church and in society, encouraging them to make the problem of racism a priority concern in their programmes and to circulate the best analyses of racism, including theological analyses.

GROUPS AND PANELS OF THE MPA COUNCIL
The Council currently has the following working groups or panels. Those which are ecumenical or formally constituted with other agencies, are described in greater detail.

CofE: World Mission and Anglican Communion Panel
Chairman Rt Revd Andrew Watson (*Bishop of Aston*)

Secretary Canon Janice Price   *Tel:* 020 7898 1328
       email: janice.price@churchofengland.org

The CofE: World Mission and Anglican Communion Panel is a partnership between the General Synod and the World Mission Agencies of the Church of England drawing its members from the General Synod, the Mission Agencies, representatives of Diocesan Companion Links, Associate Members and our ecumenical partners. There are ten full partner Agencies: Church Army, the Church's Ministry among Jewish People (CMJ), Church Mission Society (CMS), Church Pastoral Aid Society (CPAS), Crosslinks, Intercontinental Church Society (ICS), The Mission to Seafarers, The Mothers' Union, the Society for Promoting Christian Knowledge (SPCK) and the United Society (Us). There are over 20 Associate Members.

Its main tasks are concerned with the Church of England's role in furthering partnership in mission within the Anglican Communion; supporting the work of Diocesan Companion Links; and with providing a central focus for the Church of England's World Mission Agencies. It has an advisory role in enabling English dioceses and General Synod to see their way more clearly towards their participation in world mission as members of the Anglican Communion and ecumenically.

Mission Theological Advisory Group (MTAG)
Co-Chairman (with Revd Prof John Drane) Rt Revd Dr Brian Castle (*Bishop of Tonbridge*)
Secretary Dr Anne Richards   *Tel:* 020 7898 1444
       email: anne.richards@churchofengland.org
The ecumenical Mission Theological Advisory Group is composed of nominees from the Mission and Public Affairs Division of the Archbishops' Council and the Global Mission Network (GMN) of Churches Together in Britain and Ireland (CTBI). It is concerned with the theology of mission as a resource for the churches' engagement with the world, and deals with theological issues referred to it by the participating bodies.

Presence and Engagement Task Group
Chairman Rt Revd Tony Robinson (*Bishop of Pontefract*)
Secretary Revd Dr Toby Howarth
                                 Tel: 020 7898 1477
       email: toby.howarth@churchofengland.org

Rural Affairs Group
Chair Rt Revd James Bell (*Bishop of Knaresborough*)

Secretary Canon Dr Jill Hopkinson
Office The Arthur Rank Centre, Stoneleigh Park, Warwickshire CV8 2LZ   *Tel:* 024 7685 3073
                                 Fax: 024 7669 6460
       email: jillh@arthurrankcentre.org.uk

EDUCATION DIVISION

Transforming Church and Community through Education and Learning

The Board of Education

The Board of Education's Constitution (as laid down by General Synod) sets out three main functions: to advise the General Synod and the Archbishops' Council on all matters relating to education; to advise the dioceses similarly; to take action in the field of education (in the name of the Church of England, the Archbishops' Council and the General Synod) on such occasion as is required.

The Board of Education meets twice a year, in April and October. Agendas cover the full range of education contexts within which the Church is active, developing policy and strategy and managing ingoing projects and work. Board members, diocesan education staff and Church of England secondary schools and academies receive a regular electronic bulletin about the issues being addressed by the Education Division staff providing regular reports and seeking responses to consultations.

Chair Rt Revd Stephen Conway (*Bishop of Ely*)

EDUCATION DIVISION STAFF

Chief Education Officer and Head of the Education Division Revd Nigel Genders   *Tel:* 020 7898 1500
        email: nigel.genders@churchofengland.org

National Adviser for Higher Education and Chaplaincy Revd Duncan Myers   *Tel:* 020 7898 1513
        email: duncan.myers@churchofengland.org

National Further Education and post 16 Adviser Revd Garry Neave   *Tel:* 020 7898 1517
        email: garry.neave@churchofengland.org

Head of School Effectiveness Mrs Nicola Sylvester
        Tel: 020 7898 1490
        email: nicola.sylvester@churchofengland.org

Head of School Policy Vacancy   *Tel:* 020 7898 1789
        email: tbc

National Research and Policy Officer Mr James Townsend   *Tel:* 020 7898 1515
        email: james.townsend@churchofengland.org

National Going for Growth (Children and Youth) Adviser Revd Mary Hawes   Tel: 020 7898 1504
        email: mary.hawes@churchofengland.org

National Adult Education and Lay Development Adviser Miss Joanna Cox   *Tel:* 020 7898 1511
        email: joanna.cox@churchofengland.org

Business and Support Manager Mrs Cheryl Payne
        Tel: 020 7898 1501
        email: cheryl.payne@churchofengland.org

Office Church House, Great Smith St, London SW1P 3AZ   *Tel:* 020 7898 1501
        Fax: 020 7898 1520

THE WORK OF THE EDUCATION DIVISION

The work of the Education Division embraces four main aspects which support activity at national, diocesan, parish and school level. The four aspects are:

- **Engaging with national institutions** through ensuring a high profile and working closely with Government and key organizations.
- **Growing the Church's mission** by increasing the opportunities for children, young people and students to encounter the Christian faith.
- **Professional support and nurture** by supporting high professional standards, providing high quality support and advice and achieving the best quality outcomes for the people the Division serves.
- **Research, development and evaluation** through a co-ordinated research programme and maintaining databases which inform the work.

The Division operates in four main areas, with overall leadership provided by the Chief Education Officer.

1. developing the Church's presence and witness in **higher education** by:

- developing, implementing and monitoring policy for the Church of England in relation to higher education
- stimulating and developing practical concern in student and university affairs – a concern both for the life of higher education institutions, their ethical, social, spiritual and religious concerns, and for the individuals who work and study in the sector
- liaison and partnership with national bodies, including the Department for Business, Innovation, and Skills, the Higher Education

Funding Council, representative university groups, ecumenical and other faith bodies

• supporting and developing the network of chaplains in higher education by providing training and ongoing communication.

2. In **further education** the key role is strategic support and development with the aim of developing the Church's presence and witness within FE colleges and the wider post-16 sector by:

• engaging with the Government's programme of reform by monitoring policy and contributing to improvement strategies

• increasing the Church's involvement through establishing and supporting chaplaincy and college/faith partnerships

• helping to shape the sector's understanding of spiritual and moral development for staff and students, fostering shared human values and dialogue and promoting a more holistic educational experience for all students

• working with a range of ecumenical and interfaith partners

• resourcing and supporting the growing number of chaplains in schools.

The Division is involved in the work of the eleven **Universities** founded as a direct result of the Church's role as first provider of mass schooling. All are highly diverse organizations which retain a commitment to teacher education alongside a wide portfolio of courses, including (for most) significant departments of theology and religious studies. *The Anglican Identity of Church Higher Education Institutions* was published in September 2012. The Report draws on a year's research into the understanding and expression of Anglican identity with recommendations for the central support of universities as they develop their practice.

3. Informal learning and nurture of **children, young people** and **adults** is guided by *Going for Growth*, the formally adopted framework now entering the second phase of national work. *Going for Growth* provides three focuses of work at national level:

• working towards every child and young person having a life-enhancing encounter with the Christian faith and the person of Jesus Christ

• working for the transformation of communities, recognizing and enabling the capacity of children and young people to be the agents of change for themselves and for others

• professional support and challenge of all those working with children and young people in the name of the church.

Areas of work flowing from *Going for Growth* include developing materials for parishes to help

them listen to children and make changes; research and data to help identify successful mission activities with children and young people; integrating and strengthening the Church of England Youth Council within the work of the Church.

Support and development of the diocesan youth and children's officers is provided through training and ongoing communication, principally through the *Going for Growth* website and the *Child in the Midst* mailing.

The work with **lay discipleship and shared ministry** involves consultancy, support, research and development to enhance the capacity and provision of adult Christian formation and lifelong leaning in the Church. The work seeks to:

• promote the development of theological education for lay people

• provide guidance on developing volunteer, lay and shared ministry, and to resource new diocesan developments in formal lay ministry and patterns of integrated training, in association with the Ministry Division

• improve the quality of adult and lifelong learning through training the trainers, promoting partnerships, researching and disseminating good practice and developing new initiatives encouraging Christian discipleship in the Church and the world.

4. Work with **schools** is carried out by both the Board and the National Society, furthering the development and effectiveness of the Church's 4,700 academies, primary and secondary schools in the light of far-reaching changes to the education system in England.

The ongoing work of the Division includes:

• increasing the number of Church of England schools especially through the Academies programme

• enabling DBEs to grow their provision through professional support and guidance, releasing and accessing funds for new developments

• support for governors and employers of the school workforce

• supporting the implementation of succession strategies for school leadership and research into the performance and characteristics of church schools

• identifying, disseminating and sharing the best practice within the diverse national family of Anglican schools

• developing and maintaining the Statutory Inspection of Anglican Schools (SIAS) Section 48 framework, training and quality assuring inspectors

• providing training and research for school improvement in church schools

• resourcing high quality Religious Education

and collective worship, including developing a new scheme of work for Church schools in the teaching of Christianity
- developing the whole curriculum for church schools and for the spiritual, moral, social

and cultural development and wellbeing of children and young people.
- monitoring the impact of legislation, capital programmes and the various programmes for expanding and changing the school system.

CATHEDRAL AND CHURCH BUILDINGS DIVISION

This area of the Archbishops' Council's responsibilities relates to the Church's concern with cathedral and church buildings and related matters.

Cathedral and Church Buildings Division

Chairman Rt Revd Dr John Inge (*Bishop of Worcester*)

Director Janet Gough

The Cathedral and Church Buildings Division is the national resource supporting the conservation and development of the Church of England's 42 cathedrals and 16,000 parish churches for worship, mission and community engagement. The Church of England has responsibility for 12,500 listed buildings (including 45 per cent of England's Grade I listed buildings and three world heritage sites), while many churchyards are an important ecological resource.

We provide the secretariat for three statutory bodies: the Church Buildings Council (CBC), the Council's Statutory Advisory Committee (SAC) on Closed and Closing Churches and the Cathedrals Fabric Commission for England (CFCE).

We campaign on behalf of cathedral and church buildings, with the Government, Church, English Heritage and other heritage bodies to keep church buildings in their vision and to ensure church buildings' interests are taken into account.

We aim to be strategic, to add value to the work of cathedrals, dioceses and parishes where national initiatives can make a significant difference and always to be outward-looking and service-orientated. We develop new approaches to opening churches to their communities and create models that can be used across the country. Our campaigns raise awareness of conservation issues and threats to church buildings (e.g. schemes such as HS2) and have been highly influential in lobbying government and other national bodies.

Our events have reached more than 500 people over the last year, with specialist topics such as lighting, improving visitor experience, protecting war memorials, and training for clergy on managing church buildings. Promoting good design and improving the presentation of church buildings are other areas where we made a significant impact.

ChurchCare, www.ChurchCare.co.uk, is the Division's website and name for the department's non-statutory functions. ChurchCare provides a comprehensive source of information for everyone involved in managing church and cathedral buildings and maintaining them for the enjoyment of future generations.

It also includes information from *Shrinking the Footprint*, the Church's national campaign working with dioceses to reduce their carbon footprint by 80 per cent and raise awareness of environmental issues. *Shrinking the Footprint* is a cross-divisional campaign involving Cathedral and Church Buildings Division and Mission and Public Affairs. The Chairman is the Rt Revd Nicholas Holtam (*Bishop of Salisbury*).

A list of the Diocesan Environmental Officers can be found on: http://www.churchcare.co.uk/churches/church-buildings-council/who-s-who/deos/deo-contact-details

ChurchCare can be followed on Twitter @CofE_Churchcare and Facebook.

Key achievements of the year include:
- Faculty Simplification: The group, chaired by Mrs Anne Sloman OBE, is working with the Dean of Arches to simplify the Faculty process. The Faculty process is an essential safeguard to ensure that necessary alterations and repairs to our church buildings are of the highest quality. After extensive consultation the Faculty Simplification Group produced a report endorsed by the Archbishops' Council. The first step was changes to the Rules which came in on 1 January 2014. The revision stage of The Amendments to the Care of Churches and Ecclesiastical Jurisdiction Measure (1991) which will implement the core of the reforms was passed unanimously by Synod in July 2014. As part of the simplification project work on creating a user-friendly Online Faculty System is well under way, and it is expected to be rolled out to Dioceses in 2015. This will speed up and simplify the faculty process, relieving the administrative burden on both parishes and dioceses.
- Helping and encouraging churches to keep and celebrate their treasures: Our 100 Church Treasures campaign is a £3 million appeal to protect 100 artworks identified as most in need of conservation. This has raised £270,000 in

donations and pledges so far, enabling 16 projects to get under way. Recently, the Court of Arches delivered a landmark judgement that will restrict the ability of many churches to sell their treasures. In response, ChurchCare released new security guidance to help churches protect their treasures.

- The Always Welcome initiative seeks to increase the number of visitors to churches and to improve the quality of welcome they receive. The development of cycle trails as well as the launch of #TheSpotWhere (celebrating 20 churches that were the site of an extraordinary event) will attract new visitors.
- The policy underlying all our activities is to keep church buildings open, serving the worshipping community and wider society. Following the Division's involvement, the Diocese of Norwich is to launch a new Diocesan Trust to support rural churches with little or no community, which will assist with repairs and maintenance whilst enabling churches to stay open. The initiative is a new arm to the Division's Open and Sustainable Churches campaign which encourages congregations, dioceses and archdeacons to share their buildings and engage with community, cultural, and commercial groups, thereby gaining more financial and social capital to further mission and maintain the Church's priceless heritage. In addition we are carrying out further work on the important use of church buildings for social engagement and expanding guidance on ChurchCare on food banks, night shelters and community banks.

- In 2014 the Division successfully campaigned for the Government's £20 million First World War Centenary Cathedral Repairs Fund. This was in recognition of the huge heritage value of cathedrals and their importance for tourism along with the major role they play in civic life, local regeneration, and local economies. This fund is for two years only and supports urgent and necessary works which will keep the buildings safe, open to worshippers and visitors, and playing their key civic and religious roles. The Division administers this grant fund and the final round closes on 23 January 2015 (full details of eligibility can be found at www.churchcare.co.uk/cathedrals). The Division also raises funds for distribution to cathedrals and church buildings for the conservation of fabric and treasures in church buildings. Two funds, the Anglican Parish Churches Fund (charity number 1148066) and the English Cathedrals Fund (charity number 1148698), act as vehicles for charitable donations to support these programmes. Since 2000 we have distributed over £9 million for church buildings projects.

For more information on the work of the Division, see the ChurchCare Annual Review 2014 http://www.churchcare.co.uk/images/AnnualReview_2014_low_res_web.pdf which provides an update to the ChurchCare Impact Review 2013 (http://www.churchcare.co.uk/images/Churchcare_Impact_Review_digital_15.05.13.pdf)

The Church Buildings Council

Chairman Rt Hon Sir Tony Baldry MP

Vice Chairman Revd Canon Michael Ainsworth

MEMBERS
Mr Tim Allen, Ms Louise Bainbridge, Ven Tim Barker, Dr John Beal, Mr Quinton Carroll, Mr Marcus Chantrey, Revd Nigel Cooper, Ven Michael Everitt, Mr Brian Foxley, Mr Geoffrey Hunter, Mrs Sylvia Johnson, Ms Polly Meynell, Dr Neil Moat, Ms Geraldine O'Farrell, Mrs Valerie Owen, Mrs Sarah Quail, Revd Tony Redman, Mr Henry Russell OBE, Revd Canon Steven Saxby, Dr Hilary Taylor and Dr Alan Thurlow

The Church Buildings Council (CBC) advises Chancellors and Diocesan Advisory Committees on faculty applications, and clergy, churchwardens, architects and others responsible for church buildings on their care, use and development. It considers proposals that have a high impact on significant buildings, parts of buildings or their contents that are or may become the subject of faculty applications (e.g. the construction of church extensions, re-ordering schemes, the sale of church furnishings, the partial demolition of churches, the conservation of significant furnishings and related archaeological work). The CBC also acts on the Archbishops' Council's behalf in contacts with Government and in negotiations with professional bodies over church inspection and repair; it assists in the review of legislation relating to church buildings and their contents.

The CBC maintains contact with Diocesan Advisory Committees through regular circulation of information, by an annual meeting for Chairmen, Secretaries and other members, and by visits. The Chair of the CBC and Director of the Division have regular meetings with the Dean of the Arches and the Chair of the Ecclesiastical Judges Association and contribute to their biennial conferences.

The CBC's specialist committees offer expert advice on conservation matters. They consist of experts from leading institutions including the V&A, Royal Collection and Cambridge University

Annually about 20 churches are closed nationally under the Mission and Pastoral Measure. The CBC, through its Statutory Advisory Committee, advises the Church Commissioners and the Churches Conservation Trust on the interest, quality and importance of closed and closing churches and their contents, and the alteration and conversion of churches for alternative use, working closely with government and local authorities of Church and State. The CBC provides Diocesan Mission and Pastoral Committees with detailed reports about the architectural and historic qualities of churches considering closure for regular worship which also include additional advice about ways the building could be adapted to stay in use in the parish system.

The Cathedrals Fabric Commission for England

Chairman Rt Hon Frank Field MP

Vice-Chairman Ms Jennie Page CBE

MEMBERS
Mr Tim Allen, Very Revd James Atwell, David Baker OBE, Very Revd Mark Beach, Canon Peter Bruinvels, Mr Richard Carr-Archer, Mr John Carter RA, Mr Geoffrey Clifton, Ms Nicola Coldstream, Canon Jeremy Davies, Mrs Mary Durlacher, Revd Canon Perran Gay, Revd Canon Christopher Irvine, Mrs Ulrike Knox, Mrs Judith Leigh, Dr William McVicker, Dr Robyn Pender, Rt Revd Stephen Platten, Mrs Carol Pyrah, Mr Nicholas Rank, Mr Dickon Robinson, Revd Canon Celia Thomson.

The Cathedrals Fabric Commission acts as a planning authority to cathedrals, overseeing the Church's own system of controls under the Care of Cathedrals Measure 2011. Cathedral Chapters are required to get permission from the CFCE, or in some cases their own Fabric Advisory Committee, before implementing any proposals which would materially affect the character and heritage significance of a cathedral building, its setting, or archaeological remains within its precinct, or an object of artistic, archaeological, architectural or historic interest owned by the Chapter. The Commission also offers free, expert advice on the architecture, archaeology, conservation and history of cathedrals and their precincts, landscape and environment, publishes a range of guidance and advisory notes (available on www.ChurchCare.co.uk) and runs seminars and conferences for Fabric Advisory Committees and cathedral chapters and their professional advisers.

Staff of the Cathedral and Church Buildings Division
Director Janet Gough   Tel: 020 7898 1887
          email: janet.gough@churchofengland.org

Senior Cathedrals Officer and Deputy Secretary CFCE
Becky Clark   Tel: 020 7898 1888
          email: becky.clark@churchofengland.org

Cathedrals Officer Anne Locke   Tel: 020 7898 1862
          email: anne.locke@churchofengland.org

Church Buildings Officer, Closed Churches Dr Gabriel Byng   Tel: 020 7898 1871
          email: gabriel.byng@churchofengland.org

Church Buildings Officer Catherine Townsend
          Tel: 020 7898 1885
email: catherine.townsend@churchofengland.org

Senior Church Buildings Officer Dr David Knight
          Tel: 020 7898 1874
          email: david.knight@churchofengland.org

Church Buildings Officer Christina Emerson
          Tel: 020 7898 1886
          email: christina.emerson@churchofengland.org

Church Buildings Officer Lisa McIntyre
          Tel: 020 7898 1864
          email: lisa.mcintyre@churchofengland.org

Major Project Officer Dr Joseph Elders
          Tel: 020 7898 1875
          email: joseph.elders@churchofengland.org

Faculty Online Project Officer Julie Patenaude
          Tel: 020 7898 1860
          email: julie.patenaude@churchofengland.org

Senior Conservation Officer Dr Pedro Gaspar
          Tel: 020 7898 1889
          email: pedro.gaspar@churchofengland.org

Grants Officer Emily Greenaway
          Tel: 020 7898 1863
          email: emily.greenaway@churchofengland.org

Environmental Policy Officer Ruth Knight
          Tel: 020 7898 1865
          email: ruth.knight@churchofengland.org

The ChurchCare library works in conjunction with Lambeth Palace Library and the Church of England Record Centre, housing books, conservation records and photographic archives covering cathedral and church architecture in England. It is open to the public by appointment (ccblibrary@church of england.org).

CHURCH HOUSE PUBLISHING

Church House Publishing (CHP) is the official publisher to the Archbishops' Council and the General Synod. In addition to publishing *Common Worship*, CHP publishes resources to further the mission and enhance the reputation of the Church of England, notably the *Pilgrim* Course. Reference publications include *Crockford's Clerical Directory* and *The Church of England Year Book*. Both these publications are continually updated and you are welcome to send corrections to the addresses below. For up-to-date information visit our online catalogue at www.chpublishing.co.uk

The Council continues to publish a range of print and digital resources to support the ministry and mission of the Church under its Church House Publishing imprint, with Hymns Ancient & Modern (HA&M) acting as its production and marketing arm under an agreement signed on 30 June 2009.

Director of Communications Revd Arun Arora
email: arun.arora@churchofengland.org

Publishing Manager Dr Thomas Allain-Chapman
Tel: 020 7898 1450
email: thomas.allain-chapman@churchof;england.org

General Enquiries *Tel:* 01603 785923
Fax: 01603 785915
email: publishing@churchofengland.org

The Church of England Year Book
email: yearbook@churchofengland.org

Crockford's Clerical Directory
The Compiler, Crockford, Church House, Great Smith St, London SW1P 3AZ *Tel:* 020 7898 1012
Fax: 020 7898 1769
email: crockford@churchofengland.org

PROJECTS AND DEVELOPMENTS

Head of Projects and Developments Revd Dr Sandra Millar
email: sandra.millar@churchofengland.org

Projects Officer Suzanne Gray
email: suzanne.gray@churchofengland.org

The Projects and Developments team looks at how to help churches make the most of mission and ministry opportunities arising from contact with people at times of transition in their lives – weddings, baptism of a child and funerals. Through the approximately 6,500 occasional services held each week throughout the Church of England, the Church encounters around 500,000 people who come as guests as well as the key participants at these services.

Weddings
www.yourchurchwedding.org continues to be a very popular and successful website, and work continues in encouraging local churches to be involved in local wedding fairs as well as engaging with Wedding Shows nationally.

Baptisms
Between February 2013 and June 2014, extensive and wide-ranging research was conducted with families and clergy and this has informed the development of new resources to support church ministry to parents wanting to have younger children baptized. These resources are being trialled with four dioceses and will be rolled out nationally from mid-2015.

Funerals
Research with bereaved people, funeral directors, and clergy has helped to shape the approach to funeral ministry. The Church of England is still the leading provider of funeral 'services' and Projects and Developments are working with four pilot dioceses on new approaches to communicating what we offer effectively, strengthening the relationship with funeral directors, and encouraging churches to help people talk with confidence about death, dying and funerals through a programme called *GraveTalk*.

CHURCH OF ENGLAND CENTRAL SERVICES

From 1 April 2014 all central support functions of the NCIs were transferred to a new NCI – Church of England Central Services. This NCI is owned jointly by the Archbishops' Council, Church Commissioners and Pensions Board and the directors of the Company comprise the members of the JECSB. Day-to-day management of the different functions rests with the Chief Executives of the Archbishops' Council, Church Commissioners and Pensions Board.

ChECS comprises the following departments:

FINANCE AND RESOURCES

Chief Finance Officer: Mr Ian Theodoreson
Tel: 020 7898 1795
email: ian.theodoreson@ian.theodoreson@ churchofengland.org

Finance and Resources is a shared service function providing five levels of support to the NCIs and wider Church generally:

1. The Accounting Services Section is responsible for processing, recording and maintaining the prime books of account, banking, payments, payroll, (including Clergy Pay), management reporting, statutory financial reporting, budgeting and forecasting, securing assets and ensuring the bodies are legally compliant in terms of statutory reporting, tax and charity law.

2. The Financial Policy and Planning section provides financial analysis and advice to help inform management decisions across the NCIs,

3. The SAP support team is responsible for managing the use of and controls within the NCIs SAP system.

4. The Strategy and Development Unit advises on resource allocation, evaluating the effectiveness of spending plans and measuring impact.

5. The National Stewardship and Resources Officer supports parishes and dioceses in developing mechanisms for effective giving and manages the National Procurement team negotiating purchasing contracts which are available for parishes, cathedrals and dioceses to participate in.

Accounting Services

Director of Accounting Services: Mr Paul Burrage
Tel: 020 7898 1677
email: paul.burrage@churchofengland.org

The Accounting Services Section provides accounting services principally for (the three largest NCIs) the Archbishops' Council, the Church Commissioners and the Church of England Pensions Board. It is responsible for payroll (including clergy pay), cash and treasury, processing, tax expertise (principally property and VAT related), and for the largest NCIs provides statutory financial accounting, management accounting, and support for budget setting and forecasts.

Financial Policy and Planning

Head of Financial Policy and Planning Mr David White
Tel: 020 7898 1684
email: david.white@churchofengland.org

The Financial Policy Section provides financial analysis and advice to support decision-making in the Archbishops' Council, Church Commissioners and Pensions Board, and in the monitoring and management of their finances. It calculates and communicates the apportionment of the Council's budget to dioceses.

The section supports the development of spending plans from the Church Commissioners' fund, including liaison with their actuaries. It seeks to ensure that the General Synod (through a Financial Memorandum) is aware of the significant financial implications of proposals before decisions are taken and contributes to the development of policy on financial matters across the Church. It also produces a financial overview of Church finances.

National Structures

The department provides secretariat support for the Council's Finance Committee which is responsible for the management of the Council's financial business and advice and coordination on financial matters over the Church as a whole, its Investment Committee and the Inter-Diocesan Finance Forum. The latter, which comprises three representatives of each diocese, provides a twice-yearly opportunity for consultation and discussion on issues of mutual interest including remuneration policy, conditions of service, pensions policy, the Council's budget and apportionment.

The section supports the work of the Church Commissioners' Assets Committee and its staff level Assets Management Group. Key roles include oversight of the production of coordinated investment performance statistics and financial forecasts in respect of income, cashflow and longer term actuarial projection. It assists the Pensions Board in the financial management of the CHARM clergy retirement housing scheme.

SAP Support

Service Delivery Manager Sarah Jowett
Tel: 020 7898 1600
email: sarah.jowett@churchofengland.org

The SAP support team is responsible for managing the use of the NCIs SAP system, supporting the core modules of finance, real estate, purchasing, loans management and plant maintenance. The team works to ensure that users obtain maximum benefit from the opportunities SAP provides whilst at the same time maintaining the integrity of controls within the system.

The SAP team provides a helpdesk service for the Archbishops' Council, Church Commissioners, Church of England Pensions Board and Church of England Central Services, dealing with technical changes to the system and user queries in relation to all modules.

Strategy and Development Unit

Head of Unit Mr Philip James   *Tel:* 020 7898 1671
email: philip.james@churchofengland.org

The role of the (Resource) Strategy and Development Unit is to undertake research, analysis and strategy development on behalf of the Church of England in respect of its ministry and mission (principally relating to those resources held at national level). One key part of the role is to ensure that the funds of the Church Commissioners are being used effectively to advance the spiritual and numerical growth of the Church. The other key part of the Unit's work is to provide support to diocesan senior leadership teams in developing their growth, change management and resource allocation strategy. The Unit is also responsible for administering the Church and Community Fund.

Stewardship and Resources

National Stewardship and Resources Officer
Dr John Preston   *Tel:* 020 7898 1540
email: john.preston@churchofengland.org

Through its Christian Stewardship Committee, the Archbishops' Council affirms the principles and practice of Christian stewardship as a part of discipleship. Stewardship advisers encourage church people to respond to God's love and generosity and resource God's mission through the Church by the discovery and use of human and financial resources. This is often focused on the giving of money – regularly, tax-effectively and in proportion to income.

Initiatives are promoted, support given and ideas exchanged between the diocesan members of the Christian stewardship network. There is a particular focus on identifying, documenting and resourcing elements of good practice, so that other dioceses and parishes can benefit from what is proven to be effective.

A national website to resource all those concerned with Christian giving, stewardship and parish finances is available at www.parishresources.org.uk. This contains a wide range of resources for parish-giving officers, treasurers, gift-aid secretaries and those who preach and teach on stewardship and generosity.

Through the Parish Buying initiative, all parts of the church are able to access national contracts which pool the Church's purchasing power. This not only aims to save money, but to save time and enable parishes and others to buy with confidence. This is supervised by a National Procurement Group, and can be accessed at www.parishbuying.org.uk

RISK MANAGEMENT AND INTERNAL AUDIT DEPARTMENT

Director of Risk Management and Internal Audit
Mr Michael Cole   *Tel:* 020 7898 1658
email: michael.cole@churchofengland.org

The Risk Management and Internal Audit Department provides internal audit services to the Church Commissioners, the Church of England Pensions Board, the Archbishops' Council and the other National Church Institutions.

The department carries out risk-based internal audit assignments in accordance with the annual internal audit plan, approved by the Audit Committee, and also investigates particular issues that might arise from time to time.

The department coordinates and facilitates the risk management process and works with management to update operational and strategic risk registers. In addition, it provides consultancy support to managers on matters of governance, risk and internal control.

INFORMATION TECHNOLOGY AND OFFICE SERVICES

Head of Information Technology and Office Services
Yasmin Thompson   *Tel:* 020 7898 1640

Office Church House, Great Smith St, London SW1P 3AZ

The Information Technology department provides and maintains the IT and Telecommunications infrastructure for the National Church Institutions, including IT systems implementation, integration and maintenance, as well as all aspects of PC desktop and network support and training. The department also provides central purchasing of IT equipment for the NCIs and some bishops' offices. Office Services includes reprographics, telephony, some central buying facilities across the NCIs and coordinates central meeting room bookings and catering.

LIBRARIES AND ARCHIVES

Director of Libraries and Archives Mr Declan Kelly
Tel: 020 7898 1432

Address Church of England Record Centre, 15 Galleywall Rd, South Bermondsey, London SE16 3PB   *Tel:* 020 7898 1030
email: archives@churchofengland.org
Web: www.lambethpalacelibrary.org

Open: 1000–1600 hours Tues–Thurs
Closed Public Holidays

The Record Centre, which is a central service operated by the Church Commissioners, houses the non-current records of the Church Commissioners, the Archbishops' Council, the Church of England Pensions Board, the General Synod and the National Society, together with those of some ecumenical bodies. Its main purposes are to provide records management advice and low-cost off-site storage for the business records of the Central Church Bodies as well as to preserve, develop and promote access to its archival and printed collections in support of the work of the Church and the wider public. Enquiries are welcome; archive material can be seen at our Reading Room by prior appointment.

HUMAN RESOURCES DEPARTMENT

The Human Resources (HR) department aims to facilitate the National Church Institutions (NCIs) and diocesan bishops in achieving their mission and business objectives by delivering efficient and cost-effective HR services, including support for recruitment, in relation to the 470 staff employed by the NCIs and the 141 staff of diocesan bishops. It also contracts with the Corporation of Church House for services in relation to their 33 staff. It works with the Ministry Division, the Legal Office and dioceses to design, develop and implement the Church's strategy in relation to parochial clergy and their conditions of service.

How we do this in relation to the NCIs
- Establishing a partnership culture and collaborative working between the employers and their people
- Creating a high-performance working environment where employees have role clarity and focus on delivery, learning and development
- Sustaining a diverse workforce and a fair and just workplace
- Maximizing opportunities for employees and the organizations through strategic resourcing, succession planning and talent management

- Engaging with our customers to assist their articulation and our understanding of their needs and expectations to facilitate the successful delivery of their service
- Promoting a safe and healthy working environment
- Enabling, with others (particularly diocesan HR Advisers), bishops and dioceses to better support and develop their parochial clergy.

STAFF

Director of Human Resources Vacancy

HR Senior Staff
Miss Leann Dawson *Senior HR Manager*
Tel: 020 7898 1411
email: leann.dawson@churchofengland.org
Miss Kristal Clark *HR Manager*
Tel: 020 7898 1747
email: kristal.clark@churchofengland.org
Ms Pavlina Wilkin *Secretary, Remuneration and Conditions of Service Committee*
Tel: 020 7898 1651
email: pavlina.wilkin@churchofengland.org

Remuneration and Conditions of Service Committee

Chair Rt Revd David Walker (Bishop of Manchester)

Miss Imogen Clout, Revd Canon David Froude, Revd Mary Gregory, Ven Ian Jagger, Revd Canon Sandra Newton, Revd Dr Philip Plyming, Mrs Susan Pope, Mr Nigel Spraggins, Mr Brian Wilson

The Remuneration and Conditions of Service Committee meets four times a year and advises the Archbishops' Council and the House of Bishops on a strategy for ministry, with particular reference to the remuneration and conditions of service of those in authorized ministry. The Committee works in collaboration with dioceses, the Church Commissioners and the Church of England Pensions Board, and with ecumenical partners on the following matters:

(a) To produce, in partnership with dioceses, a framework of national policy for stipends

and other related matters, and to advise dioceses as appropriate on such matters.

(b) To develop policy relating to pensions in collaboration with the Church of England Pensions Board and, where appropriate, the Church Commissioners.

(c) To promote, in partnership with dioceses, clear conditions of work for all licensed ministers.

(d) To make recommendations about the scope, structure and level of parochial fees.

(e) To monitor and advise in consultation with interested parties on sector and chaplaincy ministries within the total ministry of the Church.

(f) To work in collaboration with dioceses and, as far as possible, with ecumenical partners in the provision and development of continuing ministerial education for and review of accredited ministers, ordained and lay.

(g) To report regularly to the Archbishops' Council on its work.

THE LEGAL OFFICE

The Legal Office of the National Institutions of the Church of England is responsible for providing legal advice and other services to the National Church Institutions. Its principal functions are:

- responsibility for the legislative programme of the General Synod;
- giving advice to the National Church Institutions and their respective committees and staff; and
- undertaking some transactional work for the National Church Institutions, especially the Church Commissioners and the Pensions Board.

Head of the Legal Office, Chief Legal Adviser to the Archbishops' Council, Registrar and Chief Legal Adviser to the General Synod and Official Solicitor to the Church Commissioners
Mr Stephen Slack *Tel:* 020 7898 1366
email: stephen.slack@churchofengland.org

Deputy Legal Adviser to the Archbishops' Council and the General Synod Revd Alexander McGregor
Tel: 020 7898 1748
email: alexander.mcgregor@churchofengland.org

Deputy Official Solicitor Ms Saira Salimi
Tel: 020 7898 1717
email: saira.salimi@churchofengland.org

Legislative Counsel to the General Synod Mr Christopher Packer

Office Church House, Great Smith St, London, SW1P 3AZ *Fax:* 020 7898 1718/1721
email: legal@churchofengland.org
DX: 148403 WESTMINSTER 5
Web: www.churchofengland.org/about-us/structure/churchlawlegis

COMMUNICATIONS OFFICE

Communication is central to the mission of the Church as a Christian presence in every community. The Communications Office provides media support and advice in a digital age to a wide range of people and organizations. The media team works across a broad portfolio ranging from archbishops to assistant curates, investment managers to inner city academies, social justice projects to social media.

The Office serves all the National Church Institutions (including the Archbishops' Council, Church Commissioners and Pensions Board), the General Synod and the House of Bishops, and works closely with Lambeth and Bishopthorpe. It also supports and shares best practice with diocesan communicators around the country, working closely with them on national campaigns and issues.

The team operate a 24-hour media cover and provides a Daily Digest of CofE news while working on a range of proactive good news stories about the Church. In the past year, these have ranged from promoting campaigns run by the Archbishop's Task Group on Responsible Credit and Savings to a responsive campaign providing ways for churches to respond to the Iraq crisis. The office has developed a new training programme of communications and media courses alongside bespoke courses and specialized media training for all bishops.

The Church of England website, www.churchofengland.org is run by the team and continues to be the first port of call for many wanting to find out more about the Christian faith and the Church of England, with over 2.3 million unique users last year. The popular Twitter feed @c_of_e has more than 41,000 followers and its #EasterMeans campaign was nominated for the 2014 Jerusalem Trust awards.

Director of Communications Revd Arun Arora
email: arun.arora@churchofengland.org

Deputy Director of Communications Rachel Harden
email: rachel.harden@churchofengland.org

Senior Media Officer (Broadcast) Jillian Moody
email: jillian.moody@churchofengland.org

Senior Media Officer Martha Linden
email: martha.linden@churchofengland.org
Media Officer Tim Mayo
email: tim.mayo@churchofengland.org

Digital Officer Tallie Proud
email: talitha.proud@churchofengland.org

Marketing Officer Nardine Soloman
email: nardine.soloman@churchofengland.org

Office Church House, Great Smith St, London SW1P 3AZ   *Tel:* 020 7898 1326
07774 800212 (out of hours)

THE CHURCH COMMISSIONERS FOR ENGLAND

Office Church House, Great Smith St, London
SW1P 3AZ   *Tel:* 020 7898 1000
                  Fax: 020 7898 1131
          email: commissioners.enquiry@
                   churchofengland.org

Chairman The Archbishop of Canterbury

Secretary Mr Andrew Brown   *Tel:* 020 7898 1134
     email: andrew.brown@churchofengland.org

Chief Finance Officer for the National Church Institutions Mr Ian Theodoreson
                  Tel: 020 7898 1795
     email: ian.theodoreson@churchofengland.org

Director of Investments Mr Tom Joy
                  Tel: 020 7898 1115
          email: tom.joy@churchofengland.org

Pastoral and Closed Churches Secretary and Bishoprics and Cathedrals Secretary Mr Paul Lewis (Pastoral reorganization, closed churches, clergy housing and glebe)   *Tel:* 020 7898 1741
          email: paul.lewis@churchofengland.org

Director of Libraries and Archives Mr Declan Kelly
                  Tel: 020 7898 1432
     email: declan.kelly@churchofengland.org

LEGAL DEPARTMENT
Official Solicitor Mr Stephen Slack
                  Tel: 020 7898 1704
     email: stephen.slack@churchofengland.org
Deputy Official Solicitor Ms Saira Salimi
                  Tel: 020 7898 1717
     email: saira.salimi@churchofengland.org

MEMBERS
The Archbishops of Canterbury and York

First Church Estates Commissioner Mr Andreas Whittam Smith
Second Church Estates Commissioner Sir Tony Baldry MP

Third Church Estates Commissioner Mr Andrew Mackie

Four bishops elected by the House of Bishops of the General Synod Rt Revd and Rt Hon Richard Chartres (*Bishop of London*), Rt Revd David Walker (*Bishop of Manchester*), Rt Revd Michael Hill (*Bishop of Bristol*), Rt Revd Martin Warner (*Bishop of Chichester*)

Two deans or provosts elected by all the deans and provosts Very Revd Jonathan Greener (*Dean of Wakefield*), Very Revd John Clarke (*Dean of Wells*)

Three clergy elected by the House of Clergy of the General Synod Revd Canon Bob Baker, Revd Amanda Fairclough, Revd Stephen Trott

Four lay persons elected by the House of Laity of the General Synod Mrs April Alexander, Canon Peter Bruinvels, Miss Sally Muggeridge, Mr Jacob Vince

Three persons nominated by Her Majesty the Queen Mr Harry Hart, Mr Ian Watmore, Mr John Wythe

Three persons nominated by the Archbishops of Canterbury and of York acting jointly Mr Mark Woolley, Mr Jeremy Clack, Mr Simon Picken QC

Three persons nominated by the Archbishops acting jointly after consultation with others including the Lord Mayors of the cities of London and York and the Vice-Chancellors of Oxford and Cambridge Mr Graham Oldroyd, Ms Poppy Allonby, Mr Hywel Rees-Jones

Six State Office Holders The First Lord of the Treasury; the Lord President of the Council; the Lord Chancellor; the Speaker of the House of Lords; the Secretary of State for Culture, Media and Sport; and the Speaker of the House of Commons.

FUNCTIONS
The Church Commissioners' main tasks are to manage their assets, and make money available in accordance with the duties laid upon them by Acts of Parliament and Measures of the General Synod and former Church Assembly, and to discharge other administrative duties entrusted to them.

These duties include financial support for mission and ministry in parishes, particularly in areas of need and opportunity, clergy pensions for service before 1998 and other legal commitments such as those in relation to bishops and cathedrals, and the administration of the legal framework for pastoral reorganization and settling the future of churches closed for worship.

CONSTITUTION

The Church Commissioners were formed on 1 April 1948, when Queen Anne's Bounty (1704) and the Ecclesiastical Commissioners (1836) were united.

The full body of Commissioners meets once a year to consider the Report and Accounts and the allocation of available money. The management of the Commissioners' affairs is shared between the Board of Governors, the Assets Committee, the Bishoprics and Cathedrals Committee, the Pastoral Committee, the Church Buildings (Uses and Disposals) Committee and the Audit and Risk Committee.

The National Institutions Measure 1998 created the Archbishops' Council, with consequential amendment to the Church Commissioners' functions and working relationships. The Measure also transferred their former function and powers as Central Stipends Authority to the Council on 1 January 1999.

As from 2010 the Church Commissioners are a registered charity and regulated by the Charity Commission.

Functions of the Board of Governors and the Commissioners' Committees

BOARD OF GOVERNORS

The Board is responsible for overall policy matters and there are individual committees covering policy in the following specific areas. All Commissioners are Board Members except for the six Officers of State.

ASSETS COMMITTEE

Chairman Mr Andreas Whittam Smith
Rt Revd Michael Hill (*Bishop of Bristol*), Revd Amanda Fairclough, Mr Graham Oldroyd, Canon Peter Bruinvels, Ms Poppy Allonby, Mr Harry Hart, Mr John Wythe, Mr Mark Woolley
Secretary Mr Andrew Brown

Exclusive responsibility for managing the Commissioners' assets, for investment policy and for advising the Board on the maximum amount of money available for distribution each year. The Committee is assisted by two sub-groups working on the Commissioners' stock exchange and property portfolios.

AUDIT AND RISK COMMITTEE

Chairman Mr Hywel Rees-Jones
Mrs April Alexander, Mr Stephen East, Mr George Lynn, Ian Ailles, Jeremy Clack
Secretary Mr Michael Cole

Responsible for all matters relating to the audit of the Commissioners' accounts and related matters.

BISHOPRICS AND CATHEDRALS COMMITTEE

Chairman Mr Andrew Mackie
Rt Revd Martin Warner (*Bishop of Chichester*), Rt Revd Richard Blackburn (*Bishop of Warrington*), Very Revd Jonathan Greener (*Dean of Wakefield*), Very Revd John Clarke (*Dean of Wells*), Revd Mary Bide, Mr Jacob Vince, Canon Betty Renshaw MBE, Mrs Rosemary Butler (representative of bishops' wives)
Secretary Mr Paul Lewis

Responsible for the costs of episcopal administration, the provision and management of suitable housing for diocesan bishops, assisting by grants and loans with the housing of suffragan and assistant bishops, and some assistance in respect of cathedral clergy and lay staff.

PASTORAL COMMITTEE

Chairman Mr Andrew Mackie
Rt Revd David Walker (*Bishop of Manchester*), Very Revd Jonathan Greener (*Dean of Wakefield*), Ven Penny Driver, Revd Canon Bob Baker, Revd Canon Stephen Evans, Canon Peter Bruinvels, Mrs Julia Flack, Mr Simon Picken QC, two vacancies
Secretary Mr Paul Lewis

Responsible for matters concerning pastoral reorganization, parsonages and glebe property.

CHURCH BUILDINGS (USES AND DISPOSALS) COMMITTEE

Chairman Mr Andrew Mackie
Revd Stephen Trott, Revd Canon Bob Baker, Revd Canon Peter Cavanagh, Revd Simon Talbott, Mr Ian Watmore, Mrs April Alexander, Miss Sally Muggeridge, Mr John Steel, Mrs Margaret Davies
Secretary Mr Paul Lewis

Responsible for the Commissioners' work relating to closed church buildings.

The Commissioners draw no income from the State.

CHARITABLE EXPENDITURE IN 2013

The Commissioners' charitable expenditure falls under two main headings:
1 Provision of non-pensions support – £86.3 million in 2013 – to the Church including parish mission and ministry support of £40.9 million which was mainly targeted towards areas of greatest financial need.

2 Payment of clergy pensions and pensions to their widows – £121.5 million in 2013. The Church of England Pensions Board authorizes pensions, but much of the money is provided and paid by the Church Commissioners. The Commissioners are responsible for pensions earned on service before 1 January 1998 and dioceses and parishes for pensions earned after that date.

MANAGEMENT OF ASSETS
The total return on the Commissioners' assets in 2013 was 15.9 per cent and their return over the twenty years to 2013 averaged 9.6 per cent per annum (industry benchmark 7.1 per cent per annum).

MISSION AND PASTORAL MEASURE RESPONSIBILITIES
The Commissioners are responsible for preparing schemes for pastoral reorganization based on proposals put forward by Bishops under the Mission and Pastoral Measure 2011. This includes the consideration of any representations made in response to consultation on draft schemes. Those making representations have the opportunity to address the relevant Commissioners' Committee.

The Commissioners also deal with objections to certain personage and glebe transactions.

CLOSED CHURCH BUILDINGS
The Mission and Pastoral Measure 2011 sets out the process for closing a church building which is no longer needed for public worship. The Commissioners will prepare a draft scheme to give effect to the proposals, consult locally and hear any representations received in respect of them.

The Commissioners also determine the future use of closed church buildings. Under the Measure, dioceses are charged with seeking an alternative use for closed church buildings and the Commissioners determine the suitability of such uses, publishing draft schemes to enable their disposal and considering any representations.

Buildings of high heritage value for which no suitable alternative use can be found may be vested in the Churches Conservation Trust, an independent body jointly funded by the Church and State to care for such closed church buildings.

FURTHER INFORMATION
Further information is available in the Commissioners' Annual Report and Accounts, which is available free of charge from the Commissioners and via the Church of England website at https://www.churchofengland.org/about-us/structure/churchcommissioners/annual-reports.aspx

THE CHURCH OF ENGLAND PENSIONS BOARD

Office 29 Great Smith Street, London SW1P 3PS
Tel: 020 7898 1000
Pensions Helpline 020 7898 1802
email: pensions@churchofengland.org
Housing Helpline 020 7898 1824
email: housing@churchofengland.org

Chairman Dr Jonathan Spencer CB

Chief Executive Bernadette Kenny
Tel: 020 7898 1806
email: bernadette.kenny@churchofengland.org

Pensions Manager Peter Dickinson
Tel: 020 7898 1810
email: peter.dickinson@churchofengland.org

Head of Housing Loraine Miller
Tel: 020 7898 1852
email: loraine.miller@churchofengland.org

Customer Insight and Strategy Director Linda
Ferguson
Tel: 020 7898 1833
email: linda.ferguson@churchofengland.org

Chief of Staff Lee Marshall
Tel: 020 7898 1681
email: lee.marshall@churchofengland.org

Chief Investment Officer Pierre Jameson
Tel: 020 7898 1122
email: pierre.jameson@churchofengland.org

MEMBERS

The 20 members of the Board represent a balance
of skills and expertise and are drawn from a wide
range of constituencies, as specified in the
Church of England Pensions Regulations 1997.

*Appointed Chair by the Archbishops with the
approval of the General Synod*
Dr Jonathan Spencer CB

*Appointed by the Archbishops of Canterbury and
York after consultation with the representatives of
dioceses*
Canon David Froude *(Chairman of the Audit and
Risk Committee)*

Appointed by the Archbishops of Canterbury and York
Roger Mountford *(Chairman of the Pensions
Committee)*
Appointed by the Church Commissioners
Jeremy Clack

Elected by the House of Bishops
Rt Revd Richard Blackburn

Elected by the House of Clergy
Revd Fr Paul Benfield, Revd Paul Boughton,
Revd Nigel Bourne, Revd Canon Ian Gooding
Elected by the House of Laity
Simon Baynes, Jane Bisson, Dr Graham
Campbell, Alan Fletcher, *(Chairman of the
Housing Committee)*, Nicolete Fisher, Brian Wilson

*Elected by Members of the Church Workers Pension
Fund*
Ian Boothroyd, Ian Clark

*Elected by Members of the Church Administrators
Pension Fund*
John Ferguson

*Elected by the Employers participating in the Church
Workers Pension Fund and Church Administrators
Pension Fund*
Clive Hawkins *(Deputy Vice Chairman; Chairman
of the Investment Committee)*, Canon Sandra
Newton *(Vice Chairman)*

CO-OPTIONS

The Board has co-opted the following, who bring
a particular expertise, to serve on its committees:
James Archer *(Audit and Risk Committee)*;
James Berrington *(Housing Committee)*;
Debbie Clarke *(Investment Committee)*;
Jeremy Gray *(Housing Committee)*;
Jon Head *(Housing Committee)*;
David Hunt *(Audit and Risk Committee)*;
Peter Parker *(Investment Committee)*;
Henrietta Podd *(Housing Committee)*
Mark Powell *(Investment Committee)*;

INTRODUCTION

The Church of England Pensions Board provides
retirement services for those who have worked
for or served the Church. These include the
administration of various pension schemes for
the stipendiary clergy and lay workers and the
provision of retirement housing for the retired
clergy.

In doing so, it assists over 35,000 people across
over 250 employers, and manages funds in excess
of £1.5 billion.

Vision and Values

The Board's vision is to deliver a professional,
high-quality and efficient service to our customers, respecting the needs of those who provide us with the money to do this.

In our decision-making and operations we are
guided by the following values:

- We are part of the Church of England.
- We understand our customers and their
needs.

- We work closely with employers, dioceses and all our partners and take careful account of their views.
- We behave with openness and integrity.
- We take pride in doing a good job.
- We value our people and the contribution they make.

Pensions

The Board administers three main pension schemes.

- The Church of England Funded Pension Scheme (CEFPS) provides pensions and other benefits for clergy and others in stipendiary ministry, for service from 1 January 1998. Benefits arising from service prior to 1998 are financed by the Church Commissioners. The CEFPS held assets of £1,113.5 million at the end of 2013. The actuarial valuation as at 31 December 2012 was completed during 2013; the next actuarial valuation will take place as at 31 December 2015.
- The Church Worker's Pension Fund (CWPF) is a centralized pension scheme for employers connected with the ministry and mission of the Church of England. At the end of 2013, it held assets of £384.6 million. The actuarial valuation as at 31 December 2013 will be completed towards the end of 2014.
- The Church Administrators Pension Fund (CAPF) provides pensions and other benefits to the staff employed by the National Church Institutions. At the end of 2013, it held assets of £93 million. The next actuarial valuation will take place as at 31 December 2014.

Retirement Housing

Around one in four clergy retiring from the stipendiary ministry seeks our assistance in the provision of retirement housing.

The purpose of the retirement housing scheme – the Church Housing Assistance for the Retired Ministry (CHARM) – is to assist those stipendiary clergy who have been unable to make their own provision for somewhere to live in retirement. CHARM is a discretionary facility and its operation is subsidized partly by the wider Church of England through Vote 5 of the Archbishops' Council's Budget. Property is available either to rent from the Board, or to purchase in partnership with the Board through a shared ownership scheme. The Board announced changes to the rental arm of CHARM at the General Synod's July 2014 Group of Sessions. The changes are due to take effect from 1 April 2015.

In total, the Board assists around 2,500 retired clergy households with their housing needs.

Supported Housing, Nursing and Dementia Care

The Board maintains seven Christian retirement communities to house Church pensioners who want to live as independently as possible but with access to support services. In addition, there is a care home and two specialist dementia care units at Manormead, Surrey.

At the centre of each community is the liturgical and spiritual life of the Church of England. As well as a self-contained flat, residents enjoy use of dining facilities, a library, communal grounds and a chapel.

Publications

The Board's Annual Report and Summary Report for 2013, together with various publications including information about the pension and housing schemes, are available to download from www.cepb.org.uk.

OTHER BOARDS, COUNCILS, COMMISSIONS, ETC. OF THE CHURCH OF ENGLAND

The Advisory Board for Redundant Churches

Function transferred to the Statutory Advisory Committee of the Church Buildings Council.

The Churches Conservation Trust
(formerly the Redundant Churches Fund)

Chief Executive Mr Crispin Truman, 4th Floor, Society Building, 8 All Saints Street, London N1 9RL
Tel: 0845 303 2760
Fax: 020 7841 0434
email: central@thecct.org.uk
Web: www.visitchurches.org.uk

Deputy Chief Executive and Director of Conservation Ms Sarah Robinson

Director, West Mr Colin Shearer

Director, North Ms Rosi Lister

Director, South East Mr Peter Aiers

Director of Income Generation Ms Melanie Knight

Head of Finance, Mr Stuart Popple

Head of Regeneration Mr Matthew McKeague

Head of Resources Ms Tanya Bunney

BOARD OF TRUSTEES

Mr Loyd Grossman OBE FSA (*Chairman*), Ms Jane Weeks (*Deputy Chair*), Rev Duncan Dormor, Lady Lucy French, Mr Keith Halstead, Mr Christopher Knight, Revd Brian McHenry CBE, Mr Nick Thompson, Mr Duncan Wilson OBE, Mr Humphrey Welfare

The Churches Conservation Trust is the national charity protecting historic churches at risk. We've saved over 340 unique buildings which attract almost 2 million visitors a year. With our help and your support they are kept open, in use and free to all – living once again at the heart of their communities.

Trust churches host occasional services as well as concerts, exhibitions and lectures. The Trust, which is a registered charity, depends upon statutory funding from the Church Commissioners (21 per cent) and the Department for Culture, Media and Sport (45 per cent) and charitable grants and voluntary donations (34 per cent).

CCLA Investment Management Limited

Registered Office Senator House, 85 Queen Victoria Street, London, EC4V 4ET
Company Registration No 2183088
Authorized and regulated by the Financial Conduct Authority
Tel: 0844 561 5000
Fax: 0844 561 5128
Web: www.ccla.co.uk

Executive Directors
Chief Executive Mr Michael Quicke
email: michael.quicke@ccla.co.uk

Chief Investment Officer Mr James Bevan
email: james.bevan@ccla.co.uk

Investment Director Mr Colin Peters
email: colin.peters@ccla.co.uk
Director of Market Development Mr Andrew Robinson *email:* andrew.robinson@ccla.co.uk
Chief Financial Officer Mr Adrian McMillan
email: adrian.mcmillan.ccla.co.uk
Non Executive Directors
Mr James Dawnay (*Chairman*), Mr Richard Fitzalan Howard, Mr Trevor Salmon, Revd John Tattersall, Mr Richard Williams
Company Secretary Mrs Jacqueline Fox

CCLA Investment Management Limited (CCLA) is a specialist investment management company serving charities, churches and local authorities. It is the largest manager of charitable funds in the UK, both by the value of funds managed and the number of individual investing charities. It aims to provide good quality investment management services at reasonable cost. It is the manager, registrar and administrator of the CBF Church of England Funds, the trustee of which is CBF Funds Trustee Limited and to which CCLA is accountable. Six Funds are offered to Church of England investors: the Investment Fund, a mixed fund invested mainly in equities, the UK Equity Fund, the Global Equity Income Fund, the Fixed Interest Securities Fund, the Deposit Fund and the Property Fund. CCLA also manages several segregated charity portfolios. CCLA is owned 56 per cent by the CBF Church of England Investment Fund, 23 per cent by the COIF Charities Investment Fund (part of which is non voting), 14 per cent by the Local Authorities Mutual Investment Trust and 7 per cent by the Executive Directors. CCLA is authorized and regulated by the Financial Conduct Authority (FCA) under the Financial Services and Markets Act 2000 (FSMA). Under the FSMA, the CBF, in its role as Trustee, is not considered to be operating the Funds 'by way of business'. In consequence, it is not required to be regulated by the FCA. Deposits taken by the CBF Church of England Deposit Fund are exempted from the FSMA by virtue of the Financial Services and Markets Act (Exemption) Order 2001.

The CBF Church of England Funds

Established under the Church Funds Investment Measure 1958, these open-ended funds aim to meet most of the investment needs of a church trust and are used by diocesan boards of finance and trusts, cathedrals, diocesan boards of education, theological colleges, church schools and educational endowments, church societies and many PCCs.

Investment Fund
The main CBF Church of England Fund for capital that can be invested for the long term. A widely spread portfolio mainly of UK and overseas equities but also including some bond and property investments. Aims to provide steady and rising income and capital growth. Weekly share dealings. The Fund targets an attractive and rising level of income.

UK Equity Fund
This Fund provides church trustees with a means of obtaining investment solely in a specialist UK equity portfolio. Weekly share dealings. The Fund targets an attractive and rising level of income.

Fixed Interest Securities Fund
Invested only in UK fixed interest stocks. Recommended only for a small proportion of long-term capital as it offers little protection from inflation over the longer term. Weekly share dealings.

Deposit Fund
This money Fund is for cash balances which need to be available at short notice and with minimal risk of capital loss. Accounts in the Fund obtain a rate of interest close to money market rates even on small sums. Daily deposit and withdrawal facilities. The Fund is rated AAA/VI by Fitch Ratings.

Property Fund
Invests directly in UK commercial property. Fund is intended primarily for long-term investment by large church trusts. Month end share dealings but periods of notice may be imposed. The Fund provides a high level of income.

Global Equity Income Fund
This fund targets a high and growing income from a portfolio of international shares including the UK. Weekly share dealings.

Risk Warnings: The value of the Investment, UK Equity, Fixed Interest Securities, Global Equity Income and Property Funds and their income can fall as well as rise and an investor may not get back the amount invested. Past performance is no guarantee of future returns. The Funds are intended for long term investment and are not suitable for money liable to be spent in the near future. Guarantees regarding repayment of deposits in the Deposit Fund cannot be given.

Brochures and Reports and Accounts are available from CCLA Investment Management Limited at the address above and on its website, www.ccla.co.uk

31 May 2014	Investment Fund	Fixed Interest Securities Fund	Deposit Fund	Property Fund	UK Equity Fund	Global Equity Income Fund
Value of Fund	£952 million	£53 million	£650 million	£147 million	£51 million	£99 million
Net Asset Value per share	1267.15p	157.45p	–	16.45p	44.47p	154.74p
Income Yield %	3.92	4.19	0.50	6.72	3.97	4.30
Gross Redemption Yield %	–	2.69	–	–	–	–

The Church and Community Fund

Chairman Very Revd Peter Bradley
Grants Manager Mr Andrew Hawkings

Formerly known as the Central Church Fund, the Church and Community Fund (CCF) aims to grow the Church of England and develop its capacity to engage with the whole community by making grants to the national church and local projects.

The Archbishops' Council (registered charity number 1074857) is trustee of the CCF but has delegated management to a CCF Committee whose members are the administrative trustees of the Fund.

By making grants the CCF assists the Church of England to:

a) develop its capacity to engage with the whole community through supporting innovative use of resources;
b) help transform areas of greatest need and opportunity, and
c) grow spiritually and numerically.

In 2012 to 2015 the CCF will support projects that:
1 significantly expand the Church's engagement with neighbourhood renewal;
2 seek innovative ways of developing established community projects so that they help grow the church, and
3 replicate models of successful community engagement across the wider church.

The CCF awarded around £430,000 to church community projects in 2012. It also gave £280,000 as a direct grant to the Archbishops' Council in support of the national work of the Church.

The CCF welcomes legacies and donations to help increase the number of grants awarded so that more churches can reach out to their communities and respond to real local needs. Please contact the Grants Manager to find out more about how to make a donation, leave a legacy or apply for a grant.

The Church and Community Fund, Church House, Great Smith St, London SW1P 3AZ
Tel: 020 7898 1541
email: ccf@churchofengland.org
Web: www.ccfund.org.uk
Twitter: @CCF_CofE

The Corporation of the Church House

Presidents The Archbishop of Canterbury; The Archbishop of York

Chairman of Council Michael Chamberlain OBE

Treasurer David Barnett

Secretary Chris Palmer CBE   *Tel:* 020 7898 1311
                email: chris.palmer@churchofengland.org

Office Church House, Great Smith St, London SW1P 3AZ
                Tel: 020 7898 1311
                Fax: 020 7898 1321

The Corporation owns and maintains Church House, Westminster which is the administrative headquarters of the national institutions of the Church of England.

The original Church House was built in the early 1890s as the Church's memorial of Queen Victoria's Jubilee, to be the administrative headquarters of the Church of England, and was replaced by the present building to a design by Sir Herbert Baker. The foundation stone was laid in 1937 by Queen Mary and on 10 June 1940 King George VI, accompanied by the Queen, formally opened the new House and attended the first Session of the Church Assembly in the great circular hall. The building was almost immediately requisitioned by the Government and for the rest of the war became the alternative meeting place of both Houses of Parliament; the Lords sat in the Convocation Hall and the Commons in the Hoare Memorial Hall. Oak panels in these halls commemorate this use.

By October 1946 some administrative offices of the Church Assembly returned to Church House and the Church Assembly was able to return for its Autumn Session in 1950. The building is now the headquarters of the Archbishops' Council, the Church Commissioners and the Church of England Pensions Board, as well as being the venue for the General Synod in the spring and (if it meets) in the autumn. A large-scale refurbishment carried out in 2006 has provided sufficient open-plan office space to accommodate nearly all staff of the Central Church Institutions, who moved into Church House during the early part of 2007.

Church House has also become an important national centre for conferences and meetings, the income from which contributes significantly to the maintenance costs of the building.

The business of the Corporation is vested in its Council of 9 (of whom 3 are nominated by the Appointments Committee, 2 are elected by the membership of the Corporation and 4 are co-opted by the Council).

The National Society (Church of England) for Promoting Religious Education
Leading Education with Christian Purpose

Patron Her Majesty The Queen

President The Archbishop of Canterbury

Vice Presidents The Archbishop of York and the Archbishop of Wales

Chairman of the Council Rt Revd Stephen Conway (*Bishop of Ely*)

General Secretary Revd Nigel Genders

Honorary Treasurer Revd Canon Peter Ballard

Deputy General Secretary Mrs Nicola Sylvester
Tel: 020 7898 1490
email: nicola.sylvester@churchofengland.org

Deputy General Secretary Vacancy
Tel: 020 7898 1789
email: tbc

Deputy General Secretary (*Wales*) Revd Edwin Counsel

National Research and Policy Officer Mr James Townsend *Tel:* 020 7898 1515
email: james.townsend@churchofengland.org

Business and Support Manager Mrs Cheryl Payne
Tel: 020 7898 1501
email: cheryl.payne@churchofengland.org

Executive Assistant Mr Peter Churchill
Tel: 020 7898 1518
email: peter.churchill@churchofengland.org

Executive Assistant Vacancy *Tel:* 020 7898 1491
email: tbc

Founded in 1811, the Society was chiefly responsible for setting up, in cooperation with local clergy and others, the **nationwide network of Church schools** in England and Wales; it was also, through the Church colleges, a pioneer in teacher education. The original purpose of the Society was '*The Promotion of the Education of the Poor in the Principles of the Established Church*'. It works in close association with the Education Division (*see* page 182), sharing the main objectives focused particularly on schools work.

The Society co-sponsored the *Church School of the Future Review* published in March 2012. The main areas of recommendation in the Report include: supporting and enabling Diocesan Education teams to meet the challenges of the new environment; a renewed focus on church school performance through skilled and supported leadership; additional resources for church school RE and the development of a distinctive approach to the whole curriculum; streamlining internal organization and developing a new approach to membership.

A Diocesan Board of Education for the Future was launched at Lambeth Palace in July 2013 and provides a tool kit for diocesan senior teams in reviewing and upgrading their education provision.

The Society provides the following services to dioceses and Church schools:
- support to diocesan education teams in the development of academies
- revision and development of the nationally authorized framework for the denominational inspection of Anglican and Methodist schools
- training and accreditation for inspectors for Church schools under Section 48 of the Education Act 2005 (Statutory Inspection of Anglican Schools)
- sample contracts and associated policies for appointment of staff in church schools
- funded developmental work in recruitment and training of leaders and governors of church schools
- support for RE and collective worship in dioceses and schools through the work of the

RE Development Officer and the Worship Workshop website
- an advisory service for dioceses and schools
- links to courses accredited by the church universities and university colleges
- presentation scrolls available to mark significant anniversaries in the life of Church of England and Church in Wales schools signed by the Archbishop of Canterbury and the General Secretary.

Archive material

After nearly two centuries of close association with Church schools and colleges, the National Society has built up an impressive collection of documents in its archives. These include about 15,000 files of correspondence with schools throughout England and Wales founded in association with the National Society and many published works, including the Society's own. Access is available to *bona fide* researchers by appointment at the Church of England Record Centre.

Applications for membership and donations to The National Society from individuals, schools and other bodies wishing to support the Society's work and share its resources are welcomed (*see membership form on the website or contact Cheryl Payne*).

THE ECCLESIASTICAL COURTS

The Ecclesiastical Courts consist of (1) the Diocesan or Consistory Courts, (2) the Provincial Courts, and for both Provinces (3) the Court of Ecclesiastical Causes Reserved and, when required, (4) a Commission of Review. In certain faculty cases an appeal lies from the Provincial Courts to the Judicial Committee of the Privy Council. The jurisdiction of the Archdeacons' Courts is now confined to the visitations of archdeacons. The Ecclesiastical Courts are in the main now regulated by the Ecclesiastical Jurisdiction Measure 1963. The Court of Faculties is the Court of the Archbishop of Canterbury through which the legatine powers transferred to the Archbishop of Canterbury by the Ecclesiastical Licences Act 1533 are exercised.

The personnel of the Diocesan Courts is given in the diocesan lists. The personnel of the Court of Faculties and of the Provincial and some of the other Courts is as follows:

THE COURT OF ARCHES
Dean of the Arches Rt Worshipful Charles George QC

Registrar Revd Canon John Rees
16 Beaumont St, Oxford OX1 2LZ
Tel: 01865 297200
Fax: 01865 726274
email: jrees@wslaw.co.uk

THE COURT OF THE VICAR-GENERAL OF THE PROVINCE OF CANTERBURY
Vicar-General Rt Worshipful Timothy Briden

Registrar Revd Canon John Rees (*as above*)

THE CHANCERY COURT OF YORK
Auditor Rt Worshipful Charles George QC

Registrar Mr Lionel Lennox
The Provincial Registry, Stamford House, Piccadilly, York YO1 9PP   *Tel:* 01904 623487
Fax: 01904 561470
email: lpml@denisontill.com

THE COURT OF THE VICAR-GENERAL OF THE PROVINCE OF YORK
Vicar-General Rt Worshipful Peter Collier QC

Registrar Mr Lionel Lennox (*as above*)

THE COURT OF ECCLESIASTICAL CAUSES RESERVED
Judges

(five vacancies)

Registrar for the Province of Canterbury Revd Canon John Rees (*as above*)

Registrar for the Province of York Mr Lionel Lennox (*as above*)

THE COURT OF FACULTIES
Master of the Faculties Rt Worshipful Charles George QC

Registrar Mr Peter Beesley
1 The Sanctuary, London SW1P 3JT
Tel: 020 7222 5381
Fax: 020 7222 7502
email: faculty.office@1Thesanctuary.com

Disciplinary Tribunals constituted under the Clergy Discipline Measure 2003

President of Tribunals Rt Hon Lord Justice McFarlane

Deputy President of Tribunals Sir Mark Hedley
c/o The Legal Office, Church House, Great Smith St, London SW1P 3AZ

'Legally qualified' members of the provincial panels of Canterbury and York (the same ten are appointed to each panel) from which the chair of a disciplinary tribunal will be appointed by the President of Tribunals if the President or Deputy President is not to chair the tribunal.

Chancellor Linda Box
His Honour the Worshipful Dr Rupert Bursell QC
Mr David Cheetham MBE
His Honour Judge Simon Grenfell
Canon Christopher Hodson
His Honour the Worshipful Roger Kaye QC
His Honour Judge John Lodge
Mr Geoffrey Tattersall QC
His Honour Judge David Turner QC
His Honour Judge Samuel Wiggs

Registrar of Tribunals for the Province of Canterbury Revd Canon John Rees (*as above*)

Registrar of Tribunals for the Province of York Mr Lionel Lennox (*as above*)

Designated Officer Mr Adrian Iles, The Legal Office, Church House, Great Smith St, London SW1P 3AZ

Appeal Panels

APPEAL PANEL CONSTITUTED UNDER SCHEDULE 4 MISSION AND PASTORAL MEASURE 2011
(Tribunals to settle compensation claims of

clergy dispossessed under a Pastoral Scheme or Order)

Chair The Dean of the Arches

Deputy Chairs
The Vicar-General of Canterbury
The Vicar-General of York

In addition to the Chair, a tribunal comprises three members of the Lower House of the relevant Province and one member of the House of Laity drawn from the following panels:

Convocation of Canterbury, Lower House
Ven Annette Cooper (Chelmsford)
Revd Canon Robert Cotton (Guildford)
Revd Canon Stuart Currie (Worcester)
Revd Prebendary Maureen Hobbs (Lichfield)
Very Revd Robert Key (Winchester, Channel Islands)
Revd Prebendary Stephen Lynas MBE (Bath and Wells)
Ven Clive Mansell (Rochester)
Revd Prebendary Sam Philpott MBE (Exeter)
Revd Dr Philip Plyming (Guildford)
Revd Mark Steadman (Southwark)
Revd Canon Dr Hazel Whitehead (Guildford)
Ven Christine Wilson (Derby)

Convocation of York, Lower House
Revd Paul Ayers (Bradford)
Revd Ferial Etherington (Carlisle)
Revd Canon Geoffrey Harbord (Sheffield)
Ven Ian Jagger (Durham)
Revd Canon Joyce Jones (Wakefield)
Revd Canon Susan Penfold (Blackburn)
Revd Canon Suzanne Sheriff (York)
Revd Canon John Sinclair (Newcastle)
Revd Canon Peter Spiers (Liverpool)
Ven Cherry Vann (Manchester)
Revd Canon Tony Walker (Southwell and Nottingham)

House of Laity of the General Synod
Mr Martin Dales (York)
Mrs Jenny Dunlop (Chester)
Ms Mary Johnston (London)
Mrs Mary Judkins (Wakefield)
Mr Aiden Hargreaves-Smith (Europe)
Mr Clive Scowen (London)
Mr Geoffrey Tattersall QC (Manchester)
Mr John Ward (London)
Ms Frances Wood (Durham)
(three vacancies)

Secretary Vacancy

APPEAL PANEL CONSTITUTED UNDER STANDING ORDER 120(f)(i)
(Tribunals to hear appeals in internal General Synod elections)

House of Bishops
Rt Revd Paul Butler (*Bishop of Durham*)
Rt Revd Dr Peter Forster (*Bishop of Chester*)
Rt Revd Graham James (*Bishop of Norwich*)
(three vacancies)

House of Clergy
Revd Canon Jonathan Alderton-Ford (St Edmundsbury and Ipswich)
Revd Preb Philippa Boardman MBE (London)
Ven Annette Cooper (Chelmsford)
Revd Prebendary David Houlding (London)
Ven Clive Mansell (Rochester)
Revd Stephen Trott (Peterborough)
(six vacancies)

House of Laity
Mr Martin Dales (York)
Miss Prudence Dailey (Oxford)
Mrs Jenny Dunlop (Chester)
Mrs Sarah Finch (London)
Dr Philip Giddings (Oxford)
Mrs Christina Rees (St Albans)
Mrs Caroline Spencer (Canterbury)
Mr Geoffrey Tattersall QC (Manchester)
Dr Anna Thomas-Betts (Oxford)
Mr John Ward (London)
(two vacancies)

Secretary Vacancy

APPEAL PANEL APPOINTED PURSUANT TO RULE 44(8) OF THE CHURCH REPRESENTATION RULES AS AMENDED BY THE NATIONAL INSTITUTIONS MEASURE 1998 (SCHEDULE 5, PARAGRAPH 2(c))
(Tribunals to hear appeals in elections to the House of Laity of the General Synod)

The Dean of the Arches
The Vicar-General of Canterbury
The Vicar-General of York
Miss Prudence Dailey (Oxford)
Mr Martin Dales (York)
Mrs Jenny Dunlop (Chester)
Mrs Sarah Finch (London)
Dr Philip Giddings (Oxford)
Mrs Christina Rees (St Albans)
Mrs Caroline Spencer (Canterbury)
Mr Geoffrey Tattersall (Manchester)
Dr Anna Thomas-Betts (Oxford)
Mr John Ward (London)
(two vacancies)

Secretary Vacancy

APPEAL PANEL APPOINTED PURSUANT TO RULE 25(5) OF THE CLERGY REPRESENTATION RULES 1975 TO 2004
(Tribunals to hear appeals in elections to the Convocations)

The Dean of the Arches
The Vicar-General of Canterbury
The Vicar-General of York
Revd Jonathan Alderton-Ford (St Edmundsbury and Ipswich)
Revd Prebendary Philippa Boardman MBE (London)

Revd Canon Simon Butler (Southwark)
Revd Canon David Felix (Chester)
Revd Prebendary David Houlding (London)
Ven Clive Mansell (Rochester)
(six vacancies)

Secretary Vacancy

GENERAL SYNOD LEGISLATION AND CONSTITUTION

Legislation passed 2003–2014 together with commencement dates

Dates in brackets are the dates of legislation coming into force. Items of legislation no longer in force are omitted.

MEASURES

Synodical Government (Amendment) Measure 2003 (1 January 2004)

Church of England (Pensions) Measure 2003 (1 May 2003)

Clergy Discipline Measure 2003 (in force 1 October 2003: sections 3, 39, 45 and 48; in force 1 June 2005: sections 44(3) and (4); in force 8 September 2005: sections 4, 5 and 21; remainder in force 1 January 2006)

Stipends (Cessation of Special Payments) Measure 2005 (1 July and 31 December 2005)

Church of England (Miscellaneous Provisions) Measure 2005 (1 June and 1 September 2005)

Church of England (Miscellaneous Provisions) Measure 2006 (all in force 1 October 2006 except section 1 and Schedule 1; section 1 and schedule 1 in force 1 December 2007)

Dioceses, Pastoral and Mission Measure 2007 (in force 1 January 2008: sections 1, 51, 62(1)–(3), 63(1) (so far as it relates to paragraph 7(b) of Schedule 5), 63(5) and 66 and paragraph 7(b) of Schedule 5; in force 1 February 2008: sections 52, 61, 62(5), 64 and 65 (so far as it relates to the repeals in Schedule 7 coming into force on the same date), Schedules 3 and 6 and the repeals in Schedule 7 of section 1 and Schedules 1 and 5 of the Pastoral Measure 1983, section 11(e) of the Church of England (Miscellaneous Provisions) Measure 1995 and sections 2(4) and (5) of the Synodical Government (Amendment) Measure 2003; in force 31 March 2008: sections 47–50 and 63(4); in force 1 May 2008: sections 13–16, 22, 63(7) and 65 (so far as it relates to the repeals in Schedule 7 coming into force on the same date) and the repeals in Schedule 7 of sections 10–15 of the Dioceses Measure 1978, sections 8 and 10 of the Church of England (Miscellaneous Provisions) Measure 1983, section 11(2) of the Bishops (Retirement) Measure 1986, section 2 of the Clergy (Ordination) Measure 1990 and section 12 of the Church of England (Miscellaneous Provisions) Measure 1995; in force 11 June 2008: sections 23–46, 53–60, 62(4) and (6), 63(1) (so far as it is not already in force), (2) and (3) and 65 (so far as it relates to the repeals in Schedule 7 coming into force on the same date) and Schedules 4 and 5 (so far as it is not already in force) and the repeals in Schedule 7 of section 15 of the Faculty Jurisdiction Measure 1964, sections 2, 41, 45 and 87(1) of and paragraphs 1–4 of Schedule 5 to the Pastoral Measure 1983, section 20(1) of the Care of Cathedrals Measure 1990, section 31(1) of the Care of Churches and Ecclesiastical Jurisdiction Measure 1991, section 1 of the Pastoral (Amendment) Measure 1994, section 6(1) of the Care of Places of Worship Measure 1999, section 2(3) of the Synodical Government (Amendment) Measure 2003 and paragraphs 10 and 13 to Schedule 4 to the Church of England (Miscellaneous Provisions) Measure 2005; in force 1 September 2008: section 2, 3(5) and (6), 4, 5, 6((1)–(2) and (4)–(8), 7–11, 18–21, 63(6) and 65 (so far as it relates to the repeals in Schedule 7 coming into force on the same date) and the repeals in Schedule 7 of the words after "being" to "any other diocese" in rule 34(1)(c) in Schedule 3 to the Synodical Government Measure 1969, sections 1–9, 16–17 and 18(1)(a) and (2)–(4), the words "and the report of the Commission thereon" in sections 18(5) and (7) and sections 19–25 of and the Schedule to the Dioceses Measure 1978, section 6 of the Church of England (Legal Aid and Miscellaneous Provisions) Measure 1988, paragraph 18 of Schedule 3 to the Church of England (Miscellaneous Provisions) Measure 1992, paragraph 7 of Schedule 2 to the Cathedrals Measure 1999 and section 18 of the Church of England (Miscellaneous Provisions) Measure 2000; in force 1 February 2009: sections 3(1) to (4) and section 6(3); the remainder in force 1 January 2011)

Church of England Marriage Measure 2008 (1 October 2008)

Ecclesiastical Offices (Terms of Service) Measure 2009 (in force 1 July 2009: sections 2, 10 and 13; in force 24 November 2009: section 8; in force 31 January 2011: all those provisions which have not previously been brought into force, except paragraphs 6, 10, 12 and 13 of Schedule 2; the remainder to come into force on a date or dates yet to be determined)

Church of England Pensions (Amendment) Measure 2009 (2 April 2009)

Vacancies in Suffragan Sees and Other Ecclesiastical Offices Measure 2010 (in force 1 June 2010: sections 1 and 3; in force 11 June 2010: section 4 (so far as not already in force); in force 1 January 2011: section 2)

Church of England (Miscellaneous Provisions) Measure 2010 (in force 1 July 2010: sections 3, 4, 9, 10(1) and (3), and 13; in force 1 September 2010: all remaining provisions except section 8 (to come into force on a date yet to be determined))

Crown Benefices (Parish Representatives) Measure 2010 (1 January 2011)

Ecclesiastical Fees (Amendment) Measure 2011 (in force 1 July 2011: Part 1, Sections 4, 5(2) and (3) and Schedules 1 and 2; the remainder in force 1 October 2011)

Care of Cathedrals Measure 2011 (1 September 2011)

Mission and Pastoral Measure 2011 (1 July 2012)

Church of England Marriage (Amendment) Measure 2012 (in force 19 December 2012: sections 2 and 3; in force 1 June 2013: section 1)

Clergy Discipline (Amendment) Measure 2013 (in force 1 July 2013: section 9(1); the remainder to come into force on a date or dates yet to be determined)

Diocese in Europe Measure 2013 (in force 1 July 2013: sections 2 and 3; in force 1 January 2014: section 1)

Miscellaneous Provisions Measure 2014 (in force 19 May 2014: sections 1, 3–6, 8–11, 13–20; in force 30 July 2014: paragraph 19(4) and (5) of Schedule 2)

STATUTORY INSTRUMENTS

Church Representation Rules (Amendment) Resolution 2004 SI 2004 No. 1889 (1 August 2004, 1 January 2005 and 15 February 2005)

Clergy Discipline Rules 2005 SI 2005 No 2022 (1 January 2006)

Clergy Discipline Appeal Rules 2005 SI 2005 No 3201 (1 January 2006)

Church of England (Legal Aid) (Amendment) Rules 2006 SI 2006 No 1939 (1 August 2006)

Care of Cathedrals Rules 2006 SI 2006 No 1941 (1 January 2008)

Parsonages Measure (Amendment) Rules 2007 SI 2007 No 862 (1 May 2007)

National Institutions of the Church of England (Transfer of Functions) Order 2007 SI 2007 No 1556 (1 January 2008)

Ecclesiastical Offices (Terms of Service) Regulations 2009 SI 2009 No 2108 (1 January 2011)

Church of England Pensions (Amendment) Regulations 2009 SI 2009 No 2109 (1 January 2010)

Church Representation Rules (Amendment) Resolution 2009 SI 2009 No 2129 (1 January 2010)

Church of England Pensions (Amendment) Regulations SI 2010 No 1922 (1 January 2011)

Ecclesiastical Offices (Terms of Service) Directions 2010 SI 2010 No 1923 (1 January 2011)

Ecclesiastical Offices (Terms of Service) (Amendment) Regulations 2010 SI 2010 No 2407 (1 January 2011)

Ecclesiastical Offices (Terms of Service) (Consequential and Transitional Provisions) Order 2010 SI 2010 No 2847 (31 January 2011)

Ecclesiastical Offices (Terms of Service) (Amendment) (No.2) Regulations 2010 SI 2010 No 2848 (31 January 2011)

Church of England Pensions (Sodor and Man) (Amendment) Regulations 2011 SI 2011 No 1717 (10 July 2011)

Payments to the Churches Conservation Trust Order 2011 SI 2011 No 1729 (1 April 2012)

Ecclesiastical Offices (Terms of Service) (Consequential Provisions) Order 2012 SI 2012 No 992 (1 July 2012)

Faculty Jurisdiction Rules 2013 SI 2013 No 1916 (1 January 2014)

Clergy Discipline (Amendment) Rules 2013 SI 2013 No 1917

Clergy Discipline Appeal (Amendment) Rules 2013 SI 2013 No 1921

Parochial Fees and Scheduled Matters Amending Order 2014 SI 2014 No 813 (1 January 2015)

Legal Officers (Annual Fees) Order 2014 SI 2014 No 895 (1 January 2015)

Legal Officers (Annual Fees) (Amendment) Order 2014 SI 2014 No 896 (20 April 2014)

Church of England (Miscellaneous Provisions) Measure 2014 (Appointed Day No. 1) Order 2014 SI 2014 No 1369 (19 May 2014)

Ecclesiastical Judges, Legal Officers and Others (Fees) Order 2014 SI 2014 No 2072 (1 January 2015)

Church of England (Miscellaneous Provisions) Measure 2014 (Appointed Day No. 2 and Transitional and Saving Provisions) Order 2014 SI 2014 No 2077 (30 July 2014)

Ecclesiastical Offices (Terms of Service) (Amendment) Regulations 2014 SI 2014 No 2083 (30 November 2014)

Church Representation Rules (Amendment) Resolution 2014 SI 2014 No 2113

Copies of the above legislation as originally enacted may be obtained from TSO (details below) or from the Office of Public Sector Information website: http:www.legislation.gov.uk/ukcm. The consolidated text of the Church Representation Rules (as at 1 January 2011) is published by Church House Publishing (£7.99) and is available on the Church of England website: http://www.churchofengland.org/about-us/structure/churchlawlegis/church-representation-rules.

Further Details

Lists of Church of England Measures which have received the Royal Assent from 1920 onwards and of Statutory Instruments to date which are still in force are available the Legal Office website at: http://www.churchofengland.org/

about-us/structure/churchlawlegis/legislation/ measures/list. Recently passed Measures and Rules made pursuant to Measures are sold by TSO and may be obtained from (TSO) Orders, PO Box 29, Norwich NR3 1GN (*telephone enquiries:* 0870 600 5522, *email:* customer.services@tso.co.uk *online ordering:* www.tsoshop.co.uk). TSO or the Legal Office will advise on obtaining copies of Measures that are out of print. All requests should quote as a reference the title and year of the Measure. Church of England legislation in up to date form may also be found on the UK Statute Law Database at: www.statutelaw.gov.uk.

Constitution

1 The General Synod shall consist of the Convocations of Canterbury and York joined together in a House of Bishops and a House of Clergy and having added to them a House of Laity.

2 The House of Bishops and the House of Clergy shall accordingly comprise the Upper and the Lower Houses respectively of the said Convocations, and the House of Laity shall be elected and otherwise constituted in accordance with the Church Representation Rules.

3 (1) The General Synod shall meet in sessions at least twice a year, and at such times and places as it may provide, or, in the absence of such provision, as the Joint Presidents of the Synod may direct.

(2) The General Synod shall, on the dissolution of the Convocations, itself be automatically dissolved, and shall come into being on the calling together of the new Convocations.

(3) Business pending at the dissolution of the General Synod shall not abate, but may be resumed by the new Synod at the stage reached before the dissolution, and any Boards, Commissions, Committees or other bodies of the Synod may, so far as may be appropriate and subject to any Standing Orders or any directions of the Synod or of the Archbishops of Canterbury and York, continue their proceedings during the period of the dissolution, and all things may be done by the Archbishops or any such bodies or any officers of the General Synod as may be necessary or expedient for conducting the affairs of the Synod during the period of dissolution and for making arrangements for the resumption of business by the new Synod.

(4) A member of the General Synod may continue to act during the period of the dissolution as a member of any such Board, Commission, Committee or body:

Provided that, if a member of the Synod who is an elected Proctor of the clergy or an elected member of the House of Laity does not stand for re-election or is not re-elected, this paragraph shall cease to apply to him with effect from the date on which the election of his successor is announced by the presiding officer.

4 (1) The Archbishops of Canterbury and York shall be joint Presidents of the General Synod, and they shall determine the occasions on which it is desirable that one of the Presidents shall be the chairman of a meeting of the General Synod, and shall arrange between them which of them is to take the chair on any such occasion:

Provided that one of the Presidents shall be the chairman when any motion is taken for the final approval of a provision to which Article 7 of this Constitution applies and in such other cases as may be provided in Standing Orders.

(2) The Presidents shall, after consultation with the Appointments Committee of the Church of England, appoint from among the members of the Synod a panel of no fewer than three or more than eight chairmen, who shall be chosen for their experience and ability as chairmen of meetings and may be members of any House; and it shall be the duty of one of the chairmen on the panel, in accordance with arrangements approved by the Presidents and subject to any special directions of the Presidents, to take the chair at meetings of the General Synod at which neither of the Presidents takes the chair.

[(3) Under the Synodical Government Measure the Provincial Registrars are Joint Registrars of the General Synod but since 1980 the responsibility has been exercised by the Legal Adviser to the General Synod whom each Archbishop appointed as his Joint Registrar for this purpose.]

5 (1) A motion for the final approval of any Measure or Canon shall not be deemed to be carried unless, on a division by Houses, it receives the assent of the majority of the members of each House present and voting:

Provided that by permission of the chairman and with the leave of the General Synod given in accordance with Standing Orders this requirement may be dispensed with.

(2) All other motions of the General Synod shall, subject as hereinafter provided, be determined by a majority of the members of the Synod present and voting, and the vote may be taken by a show of hands or a division:

Provided that, except in the case of a motion relating solely to the course of business or procedure, any 25 members present may demand a division by Houses and in that case the motion shall not be deemed to be carried unless, on such a division, it receives the assent of the majority of the members of each House present and voting.

(3) This Article shall be subject to any provision of this Constitution or of any Measure with respect to special majorities of the Synod or of each House thereof, and where a special majority of each House is required the vote shall be taken on a division by Houses, and where a special majority of the whole Synod is required, the motion shall, for the purposes of this Article, be one relating solely to procedure.

(4) Where a vote is to be taken on a division by Houses, it may be taken by an actual division or in such other manner as Standing Orders may provide.

6 The functions of the General Synod shall be as follows:

(a) to consider matters concerning the Church of England and to make provision in respect thereof –

  (1) by Measure intended to be given, in the manner prescribed by the Church of England Assembly (Powers) Act 1919, the force and effect of an Act of Parliament, or

  (2) by Canon made, promulged and executed in accordance with the like provisions and subject to the like restrictions and having the like legislative force as Canons heretofore made, promulged and executed by the Convocations of Canterbury and York, or

  (3) by such order, regulation or other subordinate instrument as may be authorized by Measure or Canon, or

  (4) by such Act of Synod, regulation or other instrument or proceeding as may be appropriate in cases where provision by or under a Measure or Canon is not required;

(b) to consider and express their opinion on any other matters of religious or public interest.

7 (1) A provision touching doctrinal formulae or the services or ceremonies of the Church of England or the administration of the Sacraments or sacred rites thereof shall, before it is finally approved by the General Synod, be referred to the House of Bishops, and shall be submitted for such final approval in terms proposed by the House of Bishops and not otherwise.

(2) A provision touching any of the matters aforesaid shall, if the Convocations or either of them or the House of Laity so require, be referred, in the terms proposed by the House of Bishops for final approval by the General Synod, to the two Convocations sitting separately for their provinces and to the House of Laity; and no provision so referred shall be submitted for final approval by the General Synod unless it has been approved, in the terms so proposed, by each House of the two Convocations sitting as aforesaid and by the House of Laity.

(3) The question whether such a reference is required by a Convocation shall be decided by the President and Prolocutor of the Houses of that Convocation, and the Prolocutor shall consult the Standing Committee of the Lower House of Canterbury or, as the case may be, the Assessors of the Lower House of York, and the decision of the President and Prolocutor shall be conclusive:

  Provided that if, before such a decision is taken, either House of a Convocation resolves that the provision concerned shall be so referred or both Houses resolve that it shall not be so referred, the resolution or resolutions shall be a conclusive decision that the reference is or is not required by that Convocation.

(4) The question whether such a reference is required by the House of Laity shall be decided by the Prolocutor and Pro-Prolocutor of that House who shall consult the Standing Committee of that House, and the decision of the Prolocutor and the Pro-Prolocutor shall be conclusive:

  Provided that if, before such a decision is taken, the House of Laity resolves that the reference is or is not required, the resolution shall be a conclusive decision of that question.

(5) Standing Orders of the General Synod shall provide for ensuring that a provision which fails to secure approval on a reference under this Article by each of the four Houses of the Convocations or by the House of Laity of the General Synod is not proposed again in the same or a similar form until a new General Synod comes into being, except that, in the case of objection by one House of one Convocation only, provision may be made for a second reference to the Convocations and, in the case of a second objection by one House only, for reference to the Houses of Bishops and Clergy of the General Synod for approval by a two-thirds majority of the members of each House present and voting, in lieu of such approval by the four Houses aforesaid.

(6) If any question arises whether the requirements of this Article or Standing Orders made thereunder apply to any provision, or whether those requirements have been complied with, it shall be conclusively determined by the Presidents and Prolocutors of the Houses of the Convocations and the Prolocutor and Pro-Prolocutor of the House of Laity of the General Synod.

8 (1) A Measure or Canon providing for permanent changes in the Services of Baptism or Holy Communion or in the Ordinal, or a scheme for a constitutional union or a permanent and substantial change of relationship between the Church of

England and another Christian body, being a body a substantial number of whose members reside in Great Britain, shall not be finally approved by the General Synod unless, at a stage determined by the Archbishops, the Measure or Canon or scheme, or the substance of the proposals embodied therein, has been approved by a majority of the dioceses at meetings of their Diocesan Synods, or, in the case of the Diocese in Europe, of the Bishop's Council and Standing Committee of that diocese.

(1a) If the Archbishops consider that this Article should apply to a scheme which affects the Church of England and another Christian body but does not fall within paragraph (1) of this Article, they may direct that this Article shall apply to that scheme, and where such a direction is given this Article shall apply accordingly.

(1b) The General Synod may by resolution provide that final approval of any such scheme as aforesaid, being a scheme specified in the resolution, shall require the assent of such special majorities of the members present and voting as may be specified in the resolution, and the resolution may specify a special majority of each House or of the whole Synod or of both, and in the latter case the majorities may be different.

(1c) A motion for the final approval of a Measure providing for permanent changes in any such Service or in the Ordinal shall not be deemed to be carried unless it receives the assent of a majority in each House of the General Synod of not less than two-thirds of those present and voting.

(2) Any question whether this Article applies to any Measure or Canon or scheme, or whether its requirements have been complied with, shall be conclusively determined by the Archbishops, the Prolocutors of the Lower Houses of the Convocations and the Prolocutor and Pro-Prolocutor of the House of Laity of the General Synod.

9 (1) Standing Orders of the General Synod may provide for separate sittings of any of the three Houses or joint sittings of any two Houses and as to who is to take the chair at any such separate or joint sitting.

(2) The House of Laity shall elect a Chairman and Vice-Chairman of that House who shall also discharge the functions assigned by this Constitution and the Standing Orders and by or under any Measure or Canon to the Prolocutor and Pro-Prolocutor of that House.

10 (1) The General Synod shall appoint a Legislative Committee from members of all three Houses, to whom shall be referred all Measures passed by the General Synod which it is desired should be given, in accordance with the procedure prescribed by the Church of England Assembly (Powers) Act 1919, the force of an Act of Parliament; and it shall be the duty of the Legislative Committee to take such steps with respect to any such Measure as may be so prescribed.

(2) The General Synod may appoint or provide by their Standing Orders for the appointment of such Committees, Commissions and bodies (in addition to the Committees mentioned in Section 10 of the National Institutions Measure 1998), which may include persons who are not members of the Synod, and such officers as they think fit.

(3) Each House may appoint or provide by their Standing Orders for the appointment of such Committees of their members as they think fit.

11 (1) The General Synod may make, amend and revoke Standing Orders providing for any of the matters for which such provision is required or authorized by this Constitution to be made, and consistently with this Constitution, for the meetings, business and procedure of the General Synod.

(1a) Provision may be made by Standing Order that the exercise of any power of the General Synod to suspend the Standing Orders or any of them shall require the assent of such a majority of the members of the whole Synod present and voting as may be specified in the Standing Order.

(2) Each House may make, amend and revoke Standing Orders for the matter referred to in Article 10 (3) hereof and consistently with this Constitution and with any Standing Orders of the General Synod, for the separate sittings, business and procedure of that House.

(3) Subject to this Constitution and to any Standing Orders, the business and procedure at any meeting of the General Synod or any House or Houses thereof shall be regulated by the chairman of the meeting.

12 (1) References to final approval shall, in relation to a Canon or Act of Synod, be construed as referring to the final approval by the General Synod of the contents of the Canon or Act, and not to the formal promulgation thereof:

Provided that the proviso to Article 4 (1) shall apply both to the final approval and to the formal promulgation of a Canon or Act of Synod.

(2) Any question concerning the interpretation of this Constitution, other than questions for the determination of which express provision is otherwise made, shall be referred to and determined by the Archbishops of Canterbury and York.

(3) No proceedings of the General Synod or any House or Houses thereof, or any Board, Commission, Committee or body thereof, shall be invalidated by any vacancy in the membership of the body concerned or by any defect in the qualification, election or appointment of any member thereof.

13 Any functions exercisable under this Constitution by the Archbishops of Canterbury and York, whether described as such or as Presidents of the General Synod, may, during the absence abroad or incapacity through illness of one Archbishop or a vacancy in one of the Sees, be exercised by the other Archbishop alone.

Full details of the Proceedings of the General Synod are available online at: www.churchofengland.org

General | **PART 3**

PART 3   CONTENTS

GENERAL INFORMATION

How to Address the Clergy

In offering the advice below, we do not intend to imply that other practices are necessarily to be discouraged. A good deal depends on circumstances, and, where a personal preference is known, it is usually good practice to follow it.

The following notes show acceptable current usage:

(a) on an envelope or formal listing
(b) in starting a social letter or in speech, and
(c) when referring to a member of the clergy.

Category (a) is not open to much variation, owing to the formality of the context, but categories (b) and (c) will often vary according to circumstances. It is always acceptable to use the appropriate Christian name in place of initials (for example, the Revd Alice Smith). In the absence of any style or title conferred by a post, all deacons and priests are styled 'The Reverend', and all who have been consecrated bishop are styled 'The Right Reverend'.

1 **Deacons and Priests**
   (a) The Reverend A. B. Smith
   (b) Mr/Mrs/Miss/Ms Smith (unless it is known that some other style is preferred)
   (c) The Reverend A. B. Smith at the first mention, and Mr/Mrs/Miss/Ms Smith thereafter

2 **Prebendaries**
   (a) The Reverend Prebendary A. B. Smith
   (b) Prebendary Smith
   (c) Prebendary Smith

3 **Canons (both Residentiary and Honorary)**
   (a) The Reverend Canon A. B. Smith
   (b) Canon Smith
   (c) Canon Smith

4 **Archdeacons**
   (a) The Venerable the Archdeacon of X
   (b) Archdeacon, *or more formally* Mr/Madam Archdeacon
   (c) The Archdeacon of X at the first mention, and the Archdeacon thereafter

5 **Deans**
   (a) The Very Reverend the Dean of X
   (b) Dean, *or more formally* Mr/Madam Dean
   (c) The Dean of X at the first mention, and the Dean thereafter

6 **Bishops, Diocesan and Suffragan**
   (a) The Right Reverend the Bishop of X, *or* The Right Reverend the Lord/Lady Bishop of X[1,2]
   (b) Bishop, *or more formally* My Lord/Lady[1,2]
   (c) The Bishop of X at the first mention, and the Bishop thereafter

7 **Assistant and Retired Bishops**
   (a) The Right Reverend A. B. Smith
   (b) Bishop
   (c) Bishop Smith

8 **Archbishops of Canterbury and York**
   (a) The Most Reverend and Right Honourable the Lord Archbishop of X
   (b) Archbishop, *or more formally* Your Grace
   (c) (His Grace) the Archbishop of X at the first mention, and the Archbishop thereafter

9 **Chaplains to the Armed Services**
   (a) The Reverend A. B. Smith RN (*or* CF *or* RAF)
   (b) Padre, *or* Padre Smith
   (c) The Padre, *or* Padre Smith

10 **Academics**
   When a member of the clergy holds more than one title, the ecclesiastical one is normally used.

Professor also Canon	(a)	The Reverend Canon A. B. Smith
	(b)	Canon Smith, *or* Professor Smith, according to context
	(c)	Canon Smith, *or* Professor Smith, according to context
Canon also Doctor	(a)	The Reverend Canon A. B. Smith (degree)
	(b)	Canon Smith, *or* Dr Smith, according to context
	(c)	Canon Smith, *or* Dr Smith, according to context

Notes 1 It is a matter of individual preference whether the title 'Lord' or 'Lady' should be used.
2 The Bishop of London is a Privy Councillor, and has the style 'The Right Reverend and Right Honourable the Lord Bishop of London'.

Archbishops of Canterbury and York

CANTERBURY
597 Augustine
604 Laurentius
619 Mellitus
624 Justus
627 Honorius
655 Deusdedit
668 Theodore
693 Beorhtweald
731 Tatwine
735 Nothelm
740 Cuthbeorht
761 Breguwine
765 Jaenbeorht
793 Æthelheard
805 Wulfred
832 Feologild
833 Ceolnoth
870 Æthelred
890 Plegmund
914 Æthelhelm
923 Wulfhelm
942 Oda
959 Ælfsige
959 Beorhthelm
960 Dunstan
c988 Athelgar
990 Sigeric Serio
995 Ælfric
1005 Ælfheath
1013 Lyfing
1020 Æthelnoth
1038 Eadsige
1051 Robert of Jumièges
1052 Stigand
1070 Lanfranc
1093 Anselm
1114 Ralph d'Escures
1123 William de Corbeil
1139 Theobald
1162 Thomas Becket
1174 Richard [of Dover]
1185 Baldwin
1193 Hubert Walter
1207 Stephen Langton
1229 Richard le Grant
1234 Edmund Rich
1245 Boniface of Savoy
1273 Robert Kilwardby
1279 John Peckham
1294 Robert Winchelsey
1313 Walter Reynolds
1328 Simon Mepeham
1333 John Stratford
1349 Thomas Bradwardine
1349 Simon Islip
1366 Simon Langham
1368 William Whittlesey
1375 Simon Sudbury

1381 William Courtenay
1396 Thomas Arundel[†]
1398 Roger Walden
1414 Henry Chichele
1443 John Stafford
1452 John Kemp
1454 Thomas Bourchier
1486 John Morton
1501 Henry Dean
1503 William Warham
1533 Thomas Cranmer
1556 Reginald Pole
1559 Matthew Parker
1576 Edmund Grindal
1583 John Whitgift
1604 Richard Bancroft
1611 George Abbot
1633 William Laud
1660 William Juxon
1663 Gilbert Sheldon
1678 William Sancroft
1691 John Tillotson
1695 Thomas Tenison
1716 William Wake
1737 John Potter
1747 Thomas Herring
1757 Matthew Hutton
1758 Thomas Secker
1768 Frederick
   Cornwallis
1783 John Moore
1805 Charles Manners
   Sutton
1828 William Howley
1848 John Bird Sumner
1862 Charles Thomas
   Longley
1868 Archibald Campbell
   Tait
1883 Edward White
   Benson
1896 Frederick Temple
1903 Randall Thomas
   Davidson
1928 Cosmo Gordon Lang
1942 William Temple
1945 Geoffrey Francis
   Fisher
1961 Arthur Michael
   Ramsey
1974 Frederick Donald
   Coggan
1980 Robert Alexander
   Kennedy Runcie
1991 George Leonard
   Carey
2002 Rowan Douglas
   Williams
2013 Justin Portal Welby

YORK
BISHOPS
625 Paulinus
[vacancy for 30 years]
664 Ceadda
669 Wilfrith I
678 Bosa[‡]
705 John of Beverley
718 Wilfrith II

ARCHBISHOPS
c734 Ecgbeorht
767 Æthelbeorht
780 Eanbald I
796 Eanbald II
c812 Wulfsige
837 Wigmund
854 Wulfhere
900 Æthelbeald
c928 Hrothweard
931 Wulfstan I
958 Oscytel
971 Edwaldus
972 Osweald
992 Ealdwulf
1003 Wulfstan II
1023 Ælfric Puttoc
1041 Æthelric[§]
1051 Cynesige
1061 Ealdred
1070 Thomas I
1100 Gerard
1109 Thomas II
1119 Thurstan
1143 William Fitzherbert
1147 Henry Murdac*
1154 Roger of Pont
   l'Eveque
1191 Geoffrey Plantagenet
1215 Walter de Gray
1256 Sewal de Bovill
1258 Godfrey Ludham
1266 Walter Giffard
1279 William Wickwane
1286 John le Romeyn
1298 Henry Newark
1300 Thomas Corbridge
1306 William
   Greenfield
1317 William Melton
1342 William Zouche
1352 John Thoresby
1374 Alexander Neville
1388 Thomas Arundel
1396 Robert Waldby
1398 Richard le Scrope
1407 Henry Bowet
1426 John Kemp
1452 William Booth

1465 George Nevill
1476 Lawrence Booth
1480 Thomas Rotherham
   (or Scot)
1501 Thomas Savage
1508 Christopher
   Bainbridge
1514 Thomas Wolsey
1531 Edward Lee
1545 Robert Holgate
1555 Nicholas Heath
1561 Thomas Young
1570 Edmund Grindal
1577 Edwin Sandys
1589 John Piers
1595 Matthew Hutton
1606 Tobias Matthew
1628 George Montaigne
1629 Samuel Harsnett
1632 Richard Neile
1641 John Williams
1660 Accepted Frewen
1664 Richard Sterne
1683 John Dolben
1688 Thomas Lamplugh
1691 John Sharp
1714 William Dawes
1724 Lancelot Blackburn
1743 Thomas Herring
1747 Matthew Hutton
1757 John Gilbert
1761 Robert Hay
   Drummond
1777 William Markham
1808 Edward Venables
   Vernon Harcourt
1847 Thomas Musgrave
1860 Charles Thomas
   Longley
1863 William Thomson
1891 William Connor
   Magee
1891 William Dalrymple
   Maclagan
1909 Cosmo Gordon Lang
1929 William Temple
1942 Cyril Foster Garbett
1956 Arthur Michael
   Ramsey
1961 Frederick Donald
   Coggan
1975 Stuart Yarworth
   Blanch
1983 John Stapylton
   Habgood
1995 David Michael
   Hope
2005 John Tucker Mugabi
   Sentamu

[†] On 19 October 1399 Boniface IX annulled Arundel's translation to St Andrews and confirmed him in the see of Canterbury.
[‡] Wilfrith was restored to office in 686 and Bosa in 691.
[§] Ælfric Puttoc was restored in 1042.
* William Fitzherbert was restored in 1153.

Bishops in the House of Lords

The Archbishops of Canterbury and York and the Bishops of London, Durham and Winchester always have seats in the House of Lords. The twenty-one other seats are filled by diocesan bishops in order of seniority. In the case of bishops awaiting seats, the order of seniority is shown (1), (2), (3), etc.

The Bishop of Sodor and Man and the Bishop of Gibraltar in Europe are not eligible to sit in the House of Lords.

	Election as Diocesan Bishop confirmed	Translated to present See	Entered House of Lords
Canterbury (Most Revd & Rt Hon J. P. Welby)	2011	2013	2012
York (Most Revd & Rt Hon J. T. M. Sentamu)	2002	2005	2006
London (Rt Revd & Rt Hon R. J. C. Chartres)	1995		1996
Durham (Rt Revd P. R. Butler)	2009	2014	2014
Winchester (Rt Revd T. J. Dakin)	2012		2012
Bath and Wells (Rt Revd P. Hancock)	2014		(6)
Birmingham (Rt Revd D. A. Urquhart)	2006		2010
Blackburn (Rt Revd J. T. Henderson)	2013		(4)
Bristol (Rt Revd M. A. Hill)	2003		2009
Carlisle (Rt Revd J. W. S. Newcome)	2009		2013
Chelmsford (Rt Revd S. G. Cottrell)	2010		2014
Chester (Rt Revd P. R. Forster)	1996		2001
Chichester (Rt Revd M. C. Warner)	2011		(3)
Coventry (Rt Revd C. J. Cocksworth)	2008		2013
Derby (Rt Revd A. L. J. Redfern)	2005		2010
Ely (Rt Revd S. D. Conway)	2010		2014
Exeter (Rt Revd R. R. Atwell)	2014		(7)
Gloucester (Vacancy)			
Guildford (Vacancy)			
Hereford (Rt Revd R. M. C. Frith)	2014		(9)
Leeds (Rt Revd N. Baines)	2011		2014
Leicester (Rt Revd T. J. Stevens)	1999		2003
Lichfield (Rt Revd J. M. Gledhill)	2003		2009
Lincoln (Rt Revd C. Lowson)	2011		(2)
Liverpool (Rt Revd P. Bayes)	2014		(8)
Manchester (Rt Revd D. S. Walker)	2013		(5)
Newcastle (Vacancy)			
Norwich (Rt Revd G. R. James)	1999		2004
Oxford (Vacancy)			
Peterborough (Rt Revd D. S. A. Allister)	2010		2014
Portsmouth (Rt Revd C. R. J. Foster)	2010		2014
Ripon and Leeds (Vacancy)			
Rochester (Rt Revd J. H. Langstaff)	2010		2014
St Albans (Rt Revd A. G. C. Smith)	2009		2013
St Edmundsbury and Ipswich (Vacancy)			
Salisbury (Rt Revd N. R. Holtam)	2011		(1)
Sheffield (Rt Revd S. J. L. Croft)	2009		2013
Southwark (Rt Revd C. T. J. Chessun)	2011		2014
Southwell and Nottingham (Vacancy)			
Truro (Rt Revd T. M. Thornton)	2008		2013
Worcester (Rt Revd J. G. Inge)	2007		2012

Chaplains

Chaplains in Her Majesty's Services

ROYAL NAVY

The Royal Navy employs chaplains of all denominations. The majority serve in a full-time capacity but there are a growing number of Reserve Chaplains who exercise a valuable and effective ministry as Royal Naval Chaplains in addition to their civilian ministry. Chaplains are employed in many parts of the world, ashore and afloat in capital ships, frigates and destroyers, Royal Marine Commando Units, hospitals, Royal Naval Air Stations, HM Naval Bases and Training Establishments. Apart from conducting the customary services in their ships, units or establishments, for which all the necessary facilities are provided, chaplains find numerous opportunities for extending the work of the Church through pastoral contacts with families and dependants, as well as being 'friend and adviser of all on board'. In-Service training for all Royal Naval Chaplains is carried out at the Armed Forces Chaplaincy Centre, Amport House, Andover, Hants. SP11 8BG. Christian Leadership Courses for all service personnel are provided at the centre during the year. The Anglican Church in the Royal Navy is served by 45 priests and is very much a part of the Church of England with the Single Service and Tri-Service Synodical structures. The Senior Anglican Chaplain in the Royal Navy is granted the ecclesiastical dignity of Archdeacon by the Archbishop of Canterbury. The Archbishop is the Ordinary for all service chaplains and grants ecclesiastical licences to all Anglican chaplains on the Active List. The Royal Navy is an Equal Opportunities employer and applications for entry from both male and female priests up to the age of 49 are always welcome. Full particulars concerning the entry of Anglican Chaplains can be obtained from NCS, Navy Command HQ, MP 1.2, Leach Building, Whale Island, Portsmouth PO2 8BY. *Tel:* 023 9262 5508 *Fax:* 023 9262 5134 *email:* lee.king211@mod.uk

ARMY

Army chaplains serve wherever soldiers serve, including the front line in Afghanistan, providing spiritual, moral and pastoral support to soldiers and their families. Army chaplains are non-combatants and do not bear arms. They are ordained men and women recommended for this ministry by the Sending Churches: Church of England, Church of Scotland, Roman Catholic, Methodist and United Board (United Reformed Church and Baptist), Elim Pentecostal and Assemblies of God. They provide an 'all-souls' ministry to all in their care but ensure that soldiers have access to a chaplain of a particular denomination or faith group when required. Chaplains of all denominations are administered by the Chaplain General. The Chaplain General's post may be filled by a chaplain from any of the Sending Churches. The appointment is currently held by a Baptist Minister, Revd Jonathan Woodhouse CF QHC. The Archdeacon for the Army is Ven Peter Eagles: Ministry of Defence Chaplains (Army), Army Headquarters, Ramillies Building, Marlborough Lines, Monxton Road, Andover SP11 8HJ *Tel:* 01264 381841 *Fax:* 01264 381824 *email:* peter.eagles330@mod.uk

ROYAL AIR FORCE

From the foundation of the Royal Air Force, chaplains have been proud to minister to the needs of servicemen and women and their families, in peace and war. The Chaplains' Branch of the Royal Air Force offers a real challenge and a rewarding ministry to young priests who have the necessary qualities, initiative and enthusiasm. The Royal Air Force is a large body of men and women drawn from every corner of Britain and from every stratum of society. There is a continuing need for clergy to minister to these men and women, through prayer, presence and proclamation, and the Royal Air Force understands and supports this ministry. Chaplains are commissioned by Her Majesty the Queen to provide for the pastoral and spiritual needs of all Service personnel and their families. This care is unlimited, and extends wherever members of the Royal Air Force are called to serve. Clergy may apply for a position in either a full-time or reserve capacity. Further details concerning chaplaincy in the Royal Air Force can be obtained from: Chaplaincy Services (RAF), Valiant Block, RAF High Wycombe HP14 4UE *Tel:* 01494 494469 *email:* AirChapServs-StaffChaplain@mod.uk *Web:* www.raf.mod.uk/chaplains

For a list of **Chaplains to Her Majesty's Services** *see Crockford.*

Armed Forces Synod

President The Archbishop of Canterbury

Senior Vice-President Rt Revd Nigel Stock (*The Archbishop of Canterbury's Episcopal Representative to Her Majesty's Forces*)

Lay Vice-President Vacancy

Secretary Revd Martyn Gough RN, Naval Chaplaincy Service, Naval Command HQ, MP 1.2, Leach Building, Whale Island, Portsmouth PO2 8BY   *email:* martyn.gough656@mod.uk

On the direction of the Secretary of State for Defence and the Archbishop of Canterbury in the 1980s, the Forces Synodical Council (now known as the Armed Forces Synod) was first convened in 1990 in London. It consists of thirty-six elected members (six clergy and six laity from each of the Royal Navy, Army and Royal Air Force) and up to ten *ex officio* members: the elected Service members of General Synod (currently one clergy and one laity from each Service), the three Service Archdeacons and the Bishop to HM Forces. However, the clergy members of General Synod are currently the three Service Archdeacons.

The Council is chaired by the Bishop to HM Forces but has no fiscal or Armed Service command authority. It gives the Anglican clergy and laity of the whole Armed Services the opportunity to contribute to General Synod, to the Armed Services Chain of Command and to the Ministry of Defence. They can also make decisions pertinent to the life and ministry of the Anglican Church within the Armed Forces, and although members are not drawn exclusively from the Church of England, all ministers hold the Licence of the Archbishop of Canterbury.

Until 2009, each Service was required to convene an Archdeaconry Synod and, below this level, Chaplaincy Councils. Under the new Representation Rules, however, this formal requirement has been dispensed with, although the Army still maintains this structure and the Royal Navy an Archdeacon's Council.

Chaplains in Higher Education

The Church of England supports chaplains in universities across the country including the Church Universities. The National Adviser for Higher Education, based in the Education Division at Church House, Westminster, is the officer of the Board of Education leading on the Church's policy and ministry in higher education.

The National Adviser advises the Board on policy relating to HE; resources dioceses, universities and chaplains; coordinates conferences, induction and training for HE chaplains (with ecumenical cooperation through the Churches' Higher Education Liaison Group (CHELG)); acts as consultant to chaplains and ecumenical chaplaincy teams; and advises enquirers considering ministry in this sector of education. In general, organized events are open to chaplains throughout Great Britain as well as to ecumenical partners and diocesan staff. The National Adviser and the Board of Education's Higher Education Panel are available to advise the government and Church at all levels when required.

The role of chaplain includes ministry to staff and students, and to institutions as a whole, their leaders and structures. Chaplains are also a point of contact for people of other faiths. The university student experience has changed dramatically in recent years; the sector is undergoing further changes at present, with new funding arrangements and priorities set by government. A key focus for chaplaincy is enlarging an understanding of faith and the Church's ministry in the higher education sector. This is a challenging ministry in the context of mission, in the face of continuing change and increasing student numbers, with all the pressures on people, finance and structures that these bring. It is increasingly carried out in a multi-faith context and is seen as bringing a major contribution to community cohesion. It requires wisdom and understanding. A range of materials reflecting the church's work in Higher Education can be found at: www.churchofengland.org or obtained from the National Adviser for Higher Education, Education Division, Church House, London SW1P 3NZ.   *Tel:* 020 7898 1513
        email: duncan.myers@churchofengland.org

For a list of **Educational Chaplains** *see Crockford.*
For **Church Universities and Colleges of Higher Education** *see* page 215.

Chaplains in Schools and Further Education

Chaplaincy to Further Education colleges and schools is one of the most vital and challenging forms of ministry among young people today. For many – staff and students alike – it is through the work of a chaplaincy team that faith is encountered and experienced. Chaplaincy takes many forms but there is a common commitment to providing for the spiritual and moral needs of the whole community, of any faith or none.

For those working in FE, one of the most striking features is the sector's enormous size, scale and rich diversity. Almost twice as many 16–18 year olds study at colleges than in sixth forms and this includes high proportions of learners from disadvantaged areas and from ethnic minority groups.

Within colleges, roughly 80 per cent have some form of chaplaincy provision, usually in ecumenical and multi-faith teams, with a mix of ordained and lay members contributing time on a part-time and often voluntary basis to support a regular presence and activities in their local college. Although full-time posts are comparatively rare, unless the chaplain also serves as a counsellor or tutor, there are many examples of imaginative collaboration between faith groups, colleges and local communities, especially as resources are increasingly constrained in the present economic climate.

Colleges continue to respond to major changes in the curriculum, the examinations and assessment which their students undergo and the impact of new funding models, as well as seeking to embrace the opportunities offered through greater local autonomy, the need to increase their engagement with their community and the expansion of new approaches to training and skills, notably through Apprenticeships. In such testing conditions, chaplaincies can offer support to staff and students, as well as making their contribution to the wider curriculum and their help with the exploration of values and ethos during a time of such radical change.

School chaplaincy has long been a familiar form of Anglican ministry and in recent years there has been a significant increase in the number of schools choosing to offer chaplaincy provision, especially in secondary schools and academies, not all of which have a designated religious character. This is testimony to the importance of pastoral and other support for students and staff which takes matters of faith and belief seriously and enables people to develop an appreciation and sensitive awareness of the spiritual dimension to human flourishing, alongside a deeper understanding of the values of faiths and beliefs which the school and wider community embody. A flavour of this work can be gained from our most recent research report *The Public Face of God*, about chaplaincy in Church of England secondary schools and academies.

Alongside the 400 or so chaplains who have a formal role in their school, parish clergy and lay volunteers also provide an enormous amount of support which is, in effect, a form of chaplaincy, especially to local primary schools.

At a national level, the Education Division is working to increase the profile and effectiveness of chaplaincy provision in schools and in FE colleges and to influence the development of new forms of training for these roles, to influence policy making in key areas such as SMSC, inspection, equality and diversity and working with multi-faith communities. Through its partnerships with other bodies, including the Methodist and Roman Catholic churches, the National Union of Students, SCALA (the School Chaplains and Leaders Association) the All Faiths and None network and the National Council for Faiths and Beliefs in FE, the team are helping make available an increasing range of curriculum materials to support college and school staff, who are trying to explore sensitive issues in imaginative and fruitful ways.

All who are interested in supporting or learning more about this work may contact:

The National Further Education and Post-16 Adviser, Education Division, Church House, London SW1P 3AZ   *Tel:* 020 7898 1517
Web: www.churchofengland.org/education

Chaplains in the Prison Service

The Prison Service Chaplaincy, in partnership with faith communities through a network of national Faith Advisers, provides chaplains for all HM Prisons in England and Wales. It works within the Prison Service which is part of the National Offender Management Service (NOMS) in the Ministry of Justice. The responsibilities of the Chaplain General and his headquarters colleagues include the giving of advice to ministers and officials about policy decisions with a religious or ethical dimension. The multi-faith team at HQ also visit every establishment on a yearly basis to provide assurance that chaplaincy services are being delivered to a high standard in accordance with Prison Service Instructions and the expectations of Her Majesty's Inspectorate of Prisons.

Chaplains are recruited, trained, deployed and supported in their work of providing for the religious needs of prisoners, giving opportunities for worship, formation and instruction, and offering a pastoral ministry at times of crisis and opportunity. Chaplains are also involved in enabling the observance of all faith traditions as part of multi-faith teams. Their ministry is always available to staff. The Chaplain General has responsibility for all faith traditions.

It is an exciting and privileged ministry and the Chaplain General is available if anyone is interested in taking through becoming a prison chaplain – contact details as below.

The Bishop to Prisons Rt Revd James Langstaff (*Bishop of Rochester*)

Chaplain General
Canon Michael Kavanagh, Chaplaincy HQ, 4th Floor – Red Zone, Post Point 4.08, Clive House, 70 Petty France, London SW1H 9EX
Tel: 0300 047 5182/07807 509720
Fax: 0300 047 5182
email: michael.kavanagh@noms.gsi.gov.uk
For a list of **Prison Chaplains** see *Crockford*.

Chaplains to the Police

Apart from a handful of chaplains who are paid full-time or half-time with the Police, the majority of chaplains are ordinary clergy, both men and women working in parishes or local churches and giving their time and energy as volunteers. Most, but not all, chaplains are from the mainstream Christian denominations, but there are a growing number of chaplains of other faiths and belief systems. The services of police chaplains are available to all police officers and staff, and are not dependent upon membership of a faith community. Chaplains can be contacted at local police stations, or privately by telephone or email.

The National Association of Chaplains to the Police advances and supports the work of chaplains to the police in the United Kingdom. Further information is available through the website at www.police-chaplains.org.uk
President Baroness Harris of Richmond
Vice-President Matthew Baggott (*Chief Constable, Police Service in Northern Ireland*)
National Chaplain Revd David Wilbraham (*Force Chaplain, Thames Valley Police*)
Deputy National Chaplain Revd Adrian Gatrill (*Force Chaplain, Durham Constabulary*)
National Secretary Revd Viv Baldwin, 20 Castle Rd, Woodford Halse, Northants NN11 3RS
email: secretary@police-chaplains.org.uk

Church Universities and University Colleges

Bishop Grosseteste University, Newport, Lincoln LN1 3DY   *Tel:* 01522 527347
Vice Chancellor Professor Peter Neil
Chaplain Revd Dr Peter Green   *Tel:* 01522 583607
email: peter.green@bishopg.ac.uk

Canterbury Christ Church University, North Holmes Rd, Canterbury, Kent CT1 1QU
Tel: 01227 767700
Vice Chancellor Mr Rama Thirunamachandran
Dean of Chapel Revd Dr Jeremy Law
Tel: 01227 782747
email: j.law@canterbury.ac.uk
Chaplains
Revd David Stroud
email: david.stroud@canterbury.ac.uk
Revd Sally Womersley
email: sally.womersley@canterbury.ac.uk
Revd Sally-Ann Apokis
email: sally-medwaychaplain@gre.ac.uk

University of Chester, Parkgate Rd, Chester CH1 4BJ   *Tel:* 01244 511000
Vice Chancellor Professor Tim Wheeler
Chester Campus
Chaplains
Revd Dr Peter Jenner
email: p.jenner@chester.ac.uk

Chaplaincy Assistant
Mrs Alison Upton   *email:* a.upton@chester.ac.uk
Warrington Campus
Chaplain Fr Ian Delinger   *Tel:* 01925 534361
email: i.delinger@chester.ac.uk

University of Chichester, Bishop Otter Campus, College Lane, Chichester PO19 4PE
Tel: 01243 816000
Vice Chancellor Professor Clive Behagg
Chaplain Revd John Dane   *Tel:* 01243 816036
email: j.dane@chi.ac.uk
University of Gloucestershire, Francis Close Hall, Swindon Rd, Cheltenham, Gloucestershire GL50 2QF   *Tel:* 01242 532700
Vice Chancellor and Principal Mr Stephen Marston
Chaplain Revd Bruce Goodwin   *Tel:* 01242 532735
email: bgoodwin@glos.ac.uk

Liverpool Hope University, Hope Park, Liverpool L16 9JD   *Tel:* 0151 291 3000
Liverpool Hope is an ecumenical Roman Catholic / Church of England institution.
Vice Chancellor Professor Gerald Pillay
Chaplain Revd Stephen Pritchard
email: pritchs@hope.ac.uk

University of St Mark and St John, Derriford Rd, Plymouth PL6 8BH   *Tel:* 01752 636700

Vice Chancellor Professor Cara Aitchison
　　　　　　Tel: 01752 636700 Ext 6528
Chaplain Vacancy

University of Cumbria, Fusehill Street, Carlisle, Cumbria CA1 2HH
Vice Chancellor Prof Peter Strike
Fusehill Street Campus
Chaplain Revd Matthew Firth　　Tel: 01524 385689
　　　　　email: matthew.firth@cumbria.ac.uk
Lancaster Campus　　　　　Tel: 01524 384260
Co-ordinating Chaplain Revd Alexandra Logan
　　　　　email: alexandra.logan@cumbria.ac.uk

Whitelands College, Roehampton University, Parkstead House, Holybourne Avenue, Roehampton, London SW15 4JD　　Tel: 020 8392 3500
Vice Chancellor Professor Paul O'Prey

Principal Dr Mark Garner
Chaplain Revd Dr Daniel Eshun
　　　　　　　　　　Tel: 020 8392 3516
　　　　　email: d.eshun@roehampton.ac.uk

University of Winchester, Sparkford Rd, Winchester SO22 4NR　　Tel: 01962 841515
Vice Chancellor Professor Joy Carter
　　　　　　　　　　Tel: 01962 827063
Chaplain Revd Dr Peter Waddell
　　　　　　　　　　Tel: 01904 624624
　　　　　email: chaplaincy@winchester.ac.uk
York St John University, Lord Mayor's Walk, York YO3 7EX　　　　　Tel: 01904 624624
Vice Chancellor Professor David Fleming
Interim Chaplain Annie Borthwick
　　　　　　email: a.borthwick@yorkj.ac.uk

Church Urban Fund

President
The Archbishop of Canterbury

Chairman of Trustees
Canon Paul Hackwood

Other Trustees
Mr Derek Twine (Deputy Chair), Rt Revd Christopher Chessun, Mr Brian Caroll, Mr Patrick Coldstream CBE, Mr Andrew Dorton, Mr Michael Eastwood, Canon Denise Poole, Rt Revd David Walker, Marnie Woodward FCMA

Office Church House, Great Smith St, London SW1P 3AZ　　　　　Tel: 020 7898 1647
　　　　　　　　　Fax: 020 7898 1601
　　　　　email: enquiries@cuf.org.uk
　　　　　　Web: www.cuf.org.uk

Church Urban Fund (CUF) raises money to change lives in the poorest communities in England. Working with the Church of England, CUF's mission is to serve people of faith who put their faith into action in the community. Working in collaboration with dioceses and partner organizations, CUF funds faith-based social action in the most economically and socially deprived areas of England, but its support also extends to advocacy and practical advice, working to create sustainable, relevant and local solutions to deeprooted issues. The projects CUF partners with work in a broad range of areas, including community development, support for vulnerable and marginalized groups, housing and homeless, and interfaith dialogue. CUF is also closely involved in wider debate, both inside and outside the Church, representing faith-based social action and enabling the voices of faith communities and practitioners to be heard at a national level. Our vision is to see all local churches and Christians in England empowered to work to end poverty in their communities.

Established in 1987 following the landmark report *Faith in the City*, CUF has supported nearly 5.500 projects across England. Our experience over the last 25 years has been that a combination of money and capacity building is the best way to sustainably support projects. This explains CUF's shift from an endowed fund towards an active, fundraising foundation model. We are now a development organization that provides advice, money and guidance to local churches and activists who share our passion to see lives changed. This change marks an important stage in the charity's development and maturation.

CUF's work has been made possible by the continuing support of individuals, parishes and dioceses, which have contributed to the Fund's work through time, money and prayers.

CUF is about Christians working together to tackle poverty, transforming the lives of society's poorest and most marginalized in England.

We recognize the inherent worth of all human beings, made, as they are, in the image of God, and believe in an inclusive society that values each and every individual.

We embrace and embody the Church's calling to respond to poverty in England. We want to see all Christians, in every church and every community, tackling the problem together through the giving of time, money, action and prayer.

We believe that the most effective response to poverty happens at the local, personal level, from people working within the community and sensitive to its needs. With an established presence in every community in England, the Church is uniquely placed to deliver such a response, touching areas that other agencies simply cannot reach.

Many Christians, both clergy and lay people,

are already building transformative relationships with the poor and vulnerable. Living sacrificially, they achieve miracles but they can often feel isolated in challenging circumstances.

Nurturing them is part of CUF's work, but there is much more to be done. That's why we are moving from offering short-term funding to developing local partnerships with Anglican dioceses which will provide long-term, sustainable support.

In partnership with dioceses throughout England, we are expanding our networks to re-inforce the efforts of those working in deprived areas, by improving their access to resources, in the form of money, information and expertise.

Whilst continuing to educate people about the problem of poverty in England, we need to share the many stories of lives being turned around and the once desperate being given back their future.

We need the solidarity and commitment of Christians everywhere. Then, together, we can really tackle poverty in England.

For further information on the resources available please visit our website, www.cuf.org.uk.

Clergy Appointments Adviser

The adviser has been appointed by the Archbishops of Canterbury and York to assist clergy, in England and from overseas, to find suitable new appointments and to assist patrons and others responsible for making appointments to find suitable candidates. The adviser has a responsibility for beneficed and unbeneficed clergy, together with stipendiary deacons. A list of vacancies for incumbencies, team posts and specialized ministries is available on-line. For further information please contact: Revd John Lee, Clergy Appointments Adviser, Church House, Great Smith Street, London SW1P 3AZ

Tel: 020 7898 1898
Fax: 020 7898 1899
email: admin.caa@churchofengland.org
Web:
www.churchofengland.org/clergy-office-holders/clergy-appointments-adviser.aspx

Conference Centres and Retreat Houses

CONFERENCE CENTRES

ASHBURNHAM PLACE

Ashburnham Place, Battle, E Sussex TN33 9NF (*Administrator:* Revd Andrew Wooding-Jones)
Tel: 01424 892244 *Fax:* 01424 894200
email: bookings@ashburnham.org.uk
Web: www.ashburnham.org.uk

BELSEY BRIDGE CONFERENCE CENTRE

Ditchingham, Bungay, Suffolk NR35 2DZ (*Manager:* Erica Strange) *Tel:* 01986 892133   *Fax:* 01986 895765
email: belseybridge@cct.org.uk
web: www.cct.org.uk

HAYES CONFERENCE CENTRE

Hayes Conference Centre, Swanwick, Derbyshire DE55 1AU (*Manager:* Mr Peter Anderson)
Tel: 01773 526000 *Fax:* 01773 540841
email: office@cct.org.uk *Web:* www.cct.org.uk

HIGH LEIGH CONFERENCE CENTRE

High Leigh Conference Centre, Lord St, Hoddesdon, Herts EN11 8SG (*Manager:* Mr Ian Andrews)
Tel: 01992 463016 *Fax:* 01992 446594
email: highleigh@cct.org.uk *Web:* www.cct.org.uk

LEE ABBEY

Lee Abbey Fellowship, Lynton, Devon EX35 6JJ (*Warden:* David Rowe) *Tel:* 0800 389 1189
Fax: 01598 752619
email: publicity@leeabbey.org.uk
Web: www.leeabbey.org.uk

RETREAT HOUSES

The following is a list of diocesan conference centres and retreat houses including some run by religious communities. For details of accommodation for individual retreats *see* Religious Communities page 237, or contact the Retreat Association, Clare Charity Centre, Wycombe Road, Saunderton, Buckinghamshire HP14 4BF *Tel:* 01494 569056 *email:* info@retreats.org.uk, *Web:* www.retreats.org.uk

BATH AND WELLS

Abbey House, Chilkwell St, Glastonbury, Som. BA6 8DH (*Retreat House*) (*The Warden*) *Tel:* 01458 831112

BLACKBURN

Whalley Abbey, Whalley, Clitheroe, Lancs. BB7 9SS (*Warden*: Canon Andrew Sage)
Tel: 01254 828400 *Fax:* 01254 825519

BRADFORD

Parcevall Hall, Appletreewick, Skipton, N Yorks. BD23 6DG
Tel: 01756 720213 *Fax:* 01756 720656

CARLISLE

Carlisle Diocesan Conference and Retreat Centre, Rydal Hall, Ambleside, Cumbria LA22 9LX (*General Manager:* Jonathan Green) *Tel:* 01539 432050 *Fax:* 01539 434887
email: mail@rydalhall.org

CHELMSFORD

Diocesan House of Retreat, Pleshey, Chelmsford, Essex CM3 1HA (*Warden:* Revd Sheila Coughtrey)
Tel: 01245 237251

CHESTER

Chester Diocesan Conference Centre, Foxhill, Tarvin Road, Frodsham, Cheshire WA6 6XB (*Wardens:* Mr & Mrs Ian Cameron) *Tel:* 01928 733777 *Fax:* 01928 551041
email: foxhill@chester.anglican.org
Web: foxhillconferences. co.uk

CHICHESTER	Monastery of the Holy Trinity, Crawley Down, Crawley, W Sussex RH10 4LH *Tel:* 01342 712074
DURHAM	*See* entry for NEWCASTLE
ELY	Bishop Woodford House, Barton Road, Ely, Cambs. CB7 4DX (*Warden*: Peggie Banks) *Tel:* 01353 663039
GUILDFORD	St Columba's House, Maybury Hill, Woking, Surrey GU22 8AB (*Director:* Fr Owen Murphy) *Tel:* 01483 766498
	House of Bethany, 7 Nelson Rd, Southsea, Hants. PO5 2AR *Tel:* 023 9283 3498
HEREFORD	Ludlow Conference Centre, Lower Galdeford, Ludlow, Shropshire SY8 1RZ *Tel:* 01584 873882 *Fax:* 01584 877945 *email:* info@ludlowconferencecentre.co.uk
LEICESTER	Launde Abbey, East Norton, Leicestershire LE7 9XB (*Warden*: Revd Tim Blewett) *Tel:* 01572 717254 *Fax:* 01572 717454 *email:* laundeabbey@leicester.anglican.org *Web:* www.launde.org.uk
LICHFIELD	Lichfield Diocesan Retreat and Conference Centre, Shallowford House, Shallowford, Stone, Staffs. ST15 0NZ (*Director*: Simon Hudson) *Tel:* 01785 760233 *Fax:* 01785 760390
LONDON	The Royal Foundation of Saint Katharine, 2 Butcher Row, London E14 8DS (*Master:* Preb David Paton) *Tel:* 0300 111 1147 *Fax:* 020 7702 7603 *email:* info@rfsk.org.uk
NEWCASTLE/DURHAM	Shepherd's Dene, Riding Mill, Northumberland NE44 6AF *Tel:* 01434 682212
NORWICH	Horstead Centre, Norwich NR12 7EP (*Manager:* Mark Heybourne) *Tel:* 01603 737215 (*Office*); 01603 737674 (*Guests*)
	All Hallows Convent, Ditchingham, Bungay NR35 2DT *Tel:* 01986 892840
OXFORD	St Mary's Convent, Wantage OX12 9DJ *Tel:* 01235 763141 / 01235 774075
SALISBURY	Sarum College, 19 The Close, Salisbury SP1 2EE *Tel:* 01722 424800 *Fax:* 01722 338508 *email:* hospitality@sarum.ac.uk
	Society of St Francis, The Friary, Hilfield, Dorchester DT2 7BE *Tel:* 01300 341345
SOUTHWARK	Wychcroft, Bletchingley, Redhill, Surrey RH1 4NE *Tel:* 01883 743041
	The Community of Sisters of the Church, St Michael's Convent, 56 Ham Common, Richmond TW10 7JH *Tel:* 020 8940 8711/8948 2502

GENERAL

SOUTHWELL	Sacrista Prebend Retreat House, 4 Westgate, Southwell, Notts NG25 0JH *Tel:* 01636 816 833
TRURO	Epiphany House, Kenwyn, Church Rd, Truro, Cornwall TR1 3DR *Tel:* 01872 272249
WAKEFIELD	Community of the Resurrection, Stocksbank Road, Mirfield, W Yorks. WF14 0BN *Tel:* 01924 483348 *Fax:* 01924 490489 *email:* guests@mirfield.org.uk
	Community of St Peter, Horbury, W Yorks. WF4 6BB *Tel:* 01924 272181 *Fax:* 01924 261225
WINCHESTER	Old Alresford Place, Winchester Retreat and Conference Centre, Old Alresford, Hants. SO24 9DH *Tel:* 01962 737360 *Fax:* 01962 737300 *email:* ian.knight@winchester.anglican.org
	Alton Abbey, King's Hill, Beech, Alton, Hants. GU34 4AP (*Abbot:* Rt Revd Dom Giles Hill osb) *Tel:* 01420 562145/563575
WORCESTER	Holland House, Cropthorne, nr Pershore, Worcs. WR10 3NB (*Warden:* Ian Spenser) *Tel:* 01386 860330 *email:* enquiries@hollandhouse.org
YORK	Wydale Hall, York Diocesan Retreat and Conference Centre, Brompton-by-Sawdon, Scarborough, N Yorks. YO13 9DG (*The Warden*) *Tel:* 01723 859270 *Fax:* 01723 859702 *email:* admin@wydale.org *Web:* www.wyedale.org
	St Oswald's Pastoral Centre, Woodlands Drive, Sleights, Whitby, N Yorks. YO21 1RY *Tel:* 01947 810496
	Sneaton Castle Centre, Whitby, N Yorks. YO21 3QN (*Centre Manager:* Linda Antill) *Tel:* 01947 600051 *Fax:* 01947 603490 *email:* sneaton@globalnet.co.uk *Web:* www.sneatoncastle.co.uk

Evangelism

Evangelism is one of the three stated priorities of the Archbishop of Canterbury. This work is led by the Archbishop's Adviser in Evangelism and Witness, Revd Chris Russell, and the Mission and Evangelism Adviser of the Archbishops' Council, Dr Rachel Jordan. A new Evangelism Task Group was commissioned by Synod in February 2014; its key slogan is 'use words'. The aim of the task group is to focus the Church of England on intentional evangelism.

In addition, the advisers work closely with Diocesan Missioners, Diocesan Evangelism Enablers, Fresh Expressions Enablers and Parish Development Officers to identify and share good practice in mission, evangelism and church growth across the Church. These people together make up the Mission Network. They work in the dioceses to enable local churches to reach many more people with the love and message of Jesus Christ.

Along with this network is a wider network of mission agencies and denominational leaders who also work in close collaboration. Important partners are the Fresh Expressions team, CMS (Church Missionary Society) and Church Army. Together this group continue to work to promote and support pioneering and the creation of fresh expressions of church. These new forms of church are reaching new people in new ways with the love and message of Jesus Christ. To aid this there has been new legislation in the form of bishops' mission orders to authorize new churches, and there is an official pathway for the training and ordaining of pioneers. Yet the majority of fresh expressions across the dioceses are led by lay pioneers. Some of the lay pioneers have been trained and licensed by their dioceses but the majority have just started a new contextual congregation in their local community on their own initiative.

This year is also HOPE2014 and Dr Rachel Jordan has been working with this organization to mobilize the Church across the denominations in 'word and action' mission. This has included HOPE Revolution, a young people's stream, that is releasing and equipping young people in mission and evangelism amongst their peers through Mission Academies.

The advisers also work in partnership with colleagues across the NCIs to help the Church grow and make mission and evangelism in the twenty-first century a focus for the whole church.

Fresh Expressions

Changing Church for Changing World

Fresh Expressions encourages new forms of church for a fast-changing world, working with Christians from a variety of denominations and traditions. It was initiated by the Archbishops of Canterbury and York with the Methodist Council and now includes the United Reformed Church, Church of Scotland, The Salvation Army, CWM, Congregational Federation, Ground Level Network, Church Army, CMS, ACPI and 24/7 Prayer as formal partners. The initiative has resulted in hundreds of new congregations being formed alongside more traditional churches.

Tel: 0300 3650563
email: contact@freshexpressions.org.uk
Web: www.freshexpressions.org.uk

Archbishops' Missioner and Team Leader of the Fresh Expressions Team Canon Phil Potter

Names and contact details for team members can be found on the website.

Faculty Office and Special Marriage Licences

The Faculty Office of the Archbishop of Canterbury, otherwise known as The Court of Faculties, exercises on behalf of the Archbishop the dispensing powers that he has by virtue of the Ecclesiastical Licences Act of 1533. These comprise the appointment of Notaries Public, the granting of degrees, and the granting of marriage licences. The right to grant a Special Licence for marriage at any convenient time or place in England or Wales is unique to the Archbishop, and this jurisdiction is sparingly exercised and good cause must always be shown why a more normal preliminary to Anglican marriage cannot be used. At the time of writing, marriage with any other ecclesiastical preliminary must by law be solemnized between 8.00 a.m. and 6.00 p.m., and although a Special Licence could omit this requirement, that will only in practice be done in a case of serious illness.

The more common need for a Special Licence is the parties' desire to marry in a building not normally authorized for Anglican marriage, or in a parish where they do not have a legal qualification. Even in the last case cause must be shown, normally in the form of a real connection with the parish or church in question; the *Special Licence procedure is not intended to enable parties to choose a church building on aesthetic or sentimental grounds.*

More detailed guidance on the grounds that may be considered sufficient for the granting of a Special Licence may always be sought from the Faculty Office by letter or telephone.

Special arrangements may sometimes be made in a genuine emergency. In such cases the clergy or the couple concerned should first contact the Diocesan Registrar, archdeacon, or diocesan or area bishop. If unable to resolve the difficulty himself he will make arrangements for the Faculty Office to be approached.

Orders made by the Master of the Faculties prescribe from time to time fees which are to be charged for applications for Special Licences. The fee is currently £310.00 (until 31 March 2015).

The Faculty Office is open to telephone and personal callers between 10.00 a.m. and 4.00 p.m. Monday to Friday, except on public holidays and certain days around Easter and Christmas.

The Faculty Office 1 The Sanctuary, Westminster, London SW1P 3JT   *Tel:* 020 7222 5381 Ext 7162
Fax: 020 7222 7502
email: faculty.office@1thesanctuary.com
Web: www.facultyoffice.org.uk

Hospice Movement

The word 'Hospice' was first used from the fourth century onwards when Christian orders welcomed travellers, the sick and those in need. It was first applied to the care of dying patients by Mme Jeanne Garnier who founded the Dames de Calvaire in Lyon, France in 1842. The modern hospice movement, however, with its twin emphases on medical and psychosocial intervention, dates from the founding of St Christopher's Hospice by Dame Cicely Saunders in 1967. Since 1967, 'hospice' has become a worldwide philosophy adapting to the needs of different cultures and settings – hospital, hospice and community – and is established in six continents.

Hospice and palliative care is the active, total care of patients whose disease no longer responds to curative treatment, and for whom the goal must be the best quality of life for them and their families. Palliative medicine is now a distinct medical speciality in the UK. It focuses on controlling pain and other symptoms, easing suffering and enhancing the life that remains. It integrates the psychological and spiritual aspects of care, to enable patients to live out their lives with dignity. It also offers support to families, both during the patient's illness and their bereavement. It offers a unique combination of care in hospices and at home.

Hospice and palliative care services mostly help people with cancer, although increasingly patients with other life-threatening illnesses may also be supported; this includes HIV/AIDS, motor neurone disease, heart failure and kidney disease. Hospice and palliative care is free of charge to the patient regardless of whether it is provided by an independent charitable hospice, Macmillan Service, Marie Curie Cancer Care, Sue Ryder Palliative Care Centre or by an NHS service. The criteria for admission are based on medical, social and emotional need. Referral to a hospice or palliative care service (including inpatient and home care nursing services) is normally arranged by the patient's own GP or hospital doctor. Further information about hospice care in the UK and overseas, including the facility to find your local hospice and resources for health professionals, is available from The Hospice Information Service (*see below*). This is a partnership between Help the Hospices and St Christopher's Hospice and provides an enquiry service for the public and professionals. Publications include UK and International Directories of Hospice and Palliative Care.

Tel: 020 7520 8222
email: info@helpthehospices.org.uk
Web: www.helpthehospices.org.uk

Together for Short Lives

Together for Short Lives is the leading UK charity for all children with life-threatening and life-limiting conditions and all those who support, love and care for them. We support families, professionals and services, including children's hospices. Our work helps to ensure that children can get the best possible care, wherever and whenever they need it. From the moment of diagnosis, for whatever life holds, we help to ensure that families make the most of their precious time together.

There are an estimated 49,000 children and young people in the UK living with a life-

threatening or life-limiting condition that may require palliative care services. We are there for every single one of these children, and their families, so they know where to go for help and are aware of the support available to them. With the right kind of information, it can become easier to access care and support, as well as practical and emotional help for the whole family when it's needed most. We help families get this information so they know what to expect at different stages throughout their journey.

We also work closely with the organizations and professionals that provide an important lifeline to children and families. We raise funds for children's hospices and a range of other voluntary organizations to enable them to sustain the vital work they do. We offer resources and training to help them maintain consistent, high quality care from the moment a child is diagnosed until their eventual death, and to continue supporting families for as long as they need it.

Our work also involves campaigning for equal coverage of specialized services for children with life-threatening and life-limiting conditions and families across the UK; and better co-ordination of health, social care and education. By working nationally we give a powerful voice to children, families and the organizations that support them, ensuring their views are heard by the government and that they influence policy. To realize our vision we have developed four strategic objectives to guide our work over the next three years. Our strategy is designed to lead change to make life better for every child and young person with a life-threatening or life-limiting condition. These children and families are at the heart of everything we do.

We want every child and their family to have:

- the right information from the moment of diagnosis so they can make choices about the care they receive
- easy access to services so that they can spend more time together
- the best quality care
- reliable support now and throughout their journey.

Our free Together for Families Helpline provides information and support for families, carers and professionals who look after a child with a life-threatening illness. Lines are open 7am–midnight, 7 days a week.

Together for Families Helpline *Tel:* 0808 8088 100
Together for Short Lives general enquiries
Tel: 0117 989 7820
email: info@togetherforshortlives.org.uk
Web: www.togetherforshortlives.org.uk

Together for Short Lives is a registered charity in England and Wales (1144022) and Scotland (SC044139) and a company limited by guarantee (7783702).

Marriage: Legal Aspects

The comprehensive statement of the law and information on related matters published by the Faculty Office of the Archbishop of Canterbury, *Anglican Marriage in England and Wales – A Guide to the Law for Clergy*, was revised and updated in 2010 and copies were sent to incumbents and licensed clergy of the Church of England and the Church in Wales. Further copies are available by post, price £7.50, from: The Faculty Office, 1 The Sanctuary, Westminster, London SW1P 3JT (cheques are to be made payable to 'The Faculty

Office'). An electronic update to the Guide (known as the 'First Supplement'), to cover changes in the law since 2010, was issued in July 2013 to diocesan offices for distribution to parish clergy. Further copies of the First Supplement can be obtained from the Faculty Office or downloaded from its website (www.facultyoffice.org.uk).

For details of **Special Marriage Licences** *see* the entry for the Faculty Office, page 221.

Services Authorized and Commended

Public worship in the Church of England is a matter governed by law.

Canon B 2 provides that the General Synod may approve forms of service with or without time limit. Services thus approved are alternative to those of *The Book of Common Prayer*. The power given to General Synod under Canon B 2 derives from the Worship and Doctrine Measure 1974.

Canon B 4 provides that the convocations, the archbishops in their provinces or the bishops in their dioceses may approve forms of service for use on occasions for which *The Book of Common Prayer* or *Authorized Alternative Services* do not provide.

Canon B 5 (paragraph 2) allows discretion to any minister where no other provision has been made under Canons B 1 or B 4, to use other forms of service that are considered suitable. If questions are raised as to whether such forms of service are suitable the decision rests with the bishop.

Authorized Alternative Services are those approved by the General Synod under Canon B 1 (for fuller details *see* below).

Commended Services are those that the bishops corporately have judged to be 'suitable' either for approval under Canon B 4 or for use in the contexts envisaged in Canon B 5 (for fuller details *see* page 225).

AUTHORIZED SERVICES ALTERNATIVE TO THE BOOK OF COMMON PRAYER
APPROVED BY THE GENERAL SYNOD PURSUANT TO CANON B 2
As at 1 January 2013

Published in *Common Worship: Services and Prayers for the Church of England* **and** *Common Worship: Collects and Post Communions*

1   A Service of the Word
2   Schedule of permitted variations to *The Book of Common Prayer* Orders for Morning and Evening Prayer where these occur in *Common Worship*
3   Prayers for Various Occasions
4   The Litany
5   Authorized Forms of Confession and Absolution
6   Creeds and Authorized Affirmations of Faith
7   The Lord's Prayer
8   The Order for the Celebration of Holy Communion also called The Eucharist and The Lord's Supper
9   Collects and Post Communions
10 Rules for Regulating Authorized Forms of Service
11 The Lectionary
12 Opening Canticles at Morning and Evening Prayer; Gospel Canticles; Other Canticles; A Song of Praise (Epiphany); Te Deum Laudamus

Published in *Common Worship: Initiation Services*

13 Holy Baptism
14 Emergency Baptism
15 Holy Baptism and Confirmation
16 Seasonal Provisions and Supplementary Texts
17 Affirmation of Baptismal Faith
18 Reception into the Communion of the Church of England

Published in *Common Worship: Pastoral Services*

19 Wholeness and Healing
20 The Marriage Service with prayers and other resources
21 Thanksgiving for the Gift of a Child
22 The Funeral Service with prayers and other resources
23 Series One Solemnization of Matrimony
24 Series One Burial Services

Published in *Common Worship: Ordination Services*

25 Ordination Services

Published in *Common Worship: Daily Prayer (Fourth Impression 2010)*

26 The Calendar

Published separately

27 Public Worship with Communion by Extension (*NB explicit permission must be obtained from the bishop for the use of this rite.*)
28 Weekday Lectionary
29 An Order of Marriage for Christians from Different Churches
30 Additional Weekday Lectionary
31 Additional Eucharistic Prayers *with guidance for celebrating the Eucharist with children*

The above are all authorized for use until further resolution of the Synod.

Form of Service authorized by the Archbishops of Canterbury and York without time limit for use in their respective Provinces

A Service for Remembrance Sunday (included in *Common Worship: Times and Seasons – see* below)

COMMENDED SERVICES AND RESOURCES
(Material commended by the House of Bishops as being suitable for use by ministers in exercise of their discretion under Canon B 5)
As at 1 January 2012

Published in *Common Worship: Services and Prayers for the Church of England*
1   Introduction to Morning and Evening Prayer on Sunday
2   Introduction to Holy Baptism
3   Short Prefaces for the Sundays before Lent and after Trinity
4   Additional Canticles

Published in the President's Edition of *Common Worship*
5   Additional Blessings

Published in *Common Worship: Christian Initiation*
6   Rites Supporting Disciples on the Way of Christ
7   Admission of the Baptized to Communion
8   Celebration after an Initiation Service outside the Parish
9   Thanksgiving for Holy Baptism
10   A Corporate Service of Penitence
11   The Reconciliation of a Penitent

Published in *Common Worship: Pastoral Services*
6   An Order for Prayer and Dedication after a Civil Marriage
7   Thanksgiving for Marriage
8   Ministry at the Time of Death
9   Receiving the Coffin at Church before the Funeral
10   Funeral of a Child: Outline Orders and Resources
11   At Home after the Funeral
12   Memorial Services: Outline Orders and Sample Services
13   Prayers for Use with the Dying and at Funeral and Memorial Services
14   Canticles for Marriages, Funerals and Memorial Services

Published separately
15   Material contained in *New Patterns for Worship*
16   Material contained in *Common Worship: Times and Seasons*
17   Material contained in *Common Worship: Times and Seasons – President's Edition for Holy Communion*
18   Material contained in *Common Worship: Festivals*
19   *Common Worship: The Admission and Licensing of Readers*
20   Material contained in: *Common Worship: Holy Week and Easter*
21   Material contained in: *Common Worship: A Pastoral Ministry Companion*

SERVICES WHICH COMPLY WITH THE PROVISIONS OF A SERVICE OF THE WORD
(see Authorized Services, no. 2)
As at 1 January 2013

Published in *Common Worship: Services and Prayers for the Church of England*
1   An Order for Morning Prayer on Sunday
2   An Order for Evening Prayer on Sunday
3   An Order for Night Prayer (Compline)
4   An Order for Night Prayer (Compline) in Traditional Language

Published separately
5   Sample services contained in *New Patterns for Worship*
6   Services contained in *Common Worship: Daily Prayer*

PUBLICATIONS

The material is published in the following volumes:

- *Common Worship: Services and Prayers for the Church of England*
- *Common Worship: President's Edition*
- *Common Worship: Collects and Post Communions*
- *Common Worship: Christian Initiation*
- *Common Worship: Pastoral Services*
- *Common Worship: Daily Prayer*
- *Common Worship: Times and Seasons*
- *Common Worship: Festivals*
- *Common Worship: Ordination Services (Study Edition)*
- *Common Worship: Times and Seasons – President's Edition for Holy Communion*
- *Common Worship: Holy Week and Easter*
- *Common Worship: Additional Eucharistic Prayers*
- *Common Worship: A Pastoral Ministry Companion*
- *New Patterns for Worship*
- *Public Worship with Communion by Extension*
- *Common Worship: The Admission and Licensing of Readers*
- *An Order of Marriage for Christians from Different Churches*
- annual editions of the Common Worship Lectionary

It may also be found in the Common Worship area of the Church of England website at www.cofe.anglican.org/worship/liturgy/commonworship/

VERSIONS OF THE BIBLE AND OF THE PSALMS

The following may be used in Book of Common Prayer services (with the permission of the Parochial Church Council) instead of the Authorized Version of the Bible and the Psalter in *The Book of Common Prayer:*

Revised Version
Revised Standard Version
New English Bible
The Revised Psalter
The Liturgical Psalter (The Psalms
  in a new translation for worship)

Jerusalem Bible
Good News Bible
(Today's English Version)

Any version of the Bible or Psalter not prohibited by lawful authority may be used with Alternative Services and Commended Services.

A leaflet entitled *A Brief Guide to Liturgical Copyright* deals with the procedures for local reproduction. It provides guidance on preparing local texts and information about copyright requirements. The third edition (2000) is available at £1.50 from Church House Publishing and in the *Common Worship* area of the Church of England website at www.cofe.anglican.org/worship/liturgy/commonworship/copyright/

Media

CHURCH TIMES

Established 1863. The best-selling, award-winning independent weekly newspaper and website, reporting on the worldwide Christian Church and Anglicanism in particular. As well as its wide news coverage, the paper contains reflection on current affairs, general features, reviews of books, music and arts, a comprehensive gazette, and the biggest selection of church job advertisements. Goes to press on Wednesday; published on Friday; advertisements to be placed on Friday for the following week; price £1.95; subscription £75. *Editor* Mr Paul Handley. *Office* 3rd Floor, Invicta House, 108–114 Golden Lane, London EC1Y 0TG   *Tel:* 020 7776 1089
Fax: 020 7490 7093
Subscriptions: *Tel:* 01603 785911
email: editor@churchtimes.co.uk
Web: www.churchtimes.co.uk

CHURCH OF ENGLAND NEWSPAPER

A weekly newspaper which aims to provide a full, objective and lively coverage of Christian news from Britain and overseas. Contents include general features, book, music, film and art reviews, the latest clergy appointments and an ongoing focus on how the Church can improve its mission. Goes to press on Tuesday; published Friday; deadline for advertisements 10.00am Monday; price £1.35 (annual subscription UK £65, Eur £90, Rest of world £110; Online £25; other rates on application). *Editor* C. M. Blakely. *Office* The Church of England Newspaper, 14 Great College St, London SW1P 3RX   *Tel:* 020 7222 8700
email: cen@churchnewspaper.com
Web: www.churchnewspaper.com

STANDING CONFERENCE ON RELIGION AND BELIEF

The Standing Conference on Religion and Belief meets biannually to provide a forum for the BBC and its audience to discuss issues of religion and belief. Its membership is drawn from the major Christian traditions, along with other world faiths and humanist groups represented in the United Kingdom. The Standing Conference is chaired by Rt Revd Stephen Cottrell, Bishop of Chelmsford and Dilwar Hussein, and the secretariat is provided by the Church and Media Network. Contact Andrew Graystone
Tel: 07772 710090
email: andrew.graystone1@btinternet.com

CHURCH AND MEDIA NETWORK

The Church and Media Network is an ecumenical body with charitable status. It was formed in 2009, succeeding the Churches' Media Council. The Network aims to build bridges of understanding between the Christian community and the media. The Church and Media Network also runs *theMediaNet*, which encourages vocations to the media and also offers support, encouragement and discipleship to Christians working in the media. *Acting Chair* Revd Tony Miles *Director* Andrew Graystone   *Tel:* 0845 6520027
07772 710090 (Mobile)
email: info@churchandmedia.net
Web: www.churchandmedia.net *or*
www.themedianet.org

CTVC

Television, radio and new media production company founded by the British film pioneer, Lord Rank. CTVC specializes in making documentaries on religious, ethical and moral issues. The company has produced documentaries for the BBC, Channel 4 and ITV as well as radio programmes for BBC Radio 3, 4 and the World Service. In the last few years CTVC has been awarded the prestigious Sandford St Martin religious broadcasting award. CTVC also hosts TrueTube, an award-winning website for secondary schools that provides interactive resources for films for RE, PSHE and Citizenship lessons. Alongside filmmaking, CTVC also runs Things Unseen, a podcast with its own website engaging both people of faith and those who 'believe but don't belong'.

CTVC has one of the largest film and tape archive of any independent production company in Britain, covering the hundreds of films and programmes we have made over the past 80 years.

Chief Executive Officer Mr Peter Weil, CTVC, 9–10 Copper Row, Tower Bridge Piazza, London SE1 2LH   *Tel:* 020 7940 8480
Fax: 020 7940 8490
email: info@ctvc.co.uk
Web: www.ctvc.co.uk and www.truetube.co.uk

OFFICE OF COMMUNICATIONS (Ofcom)

Ofcom is the independent regulator and competition authority for the UK communications industries, with responsibilities across television, radio, telecommunications, postal services and the airwaves over which wireless devices operate. *Chairman* Dame Patricia Hodgson DBE *Deputy Chairman* The Baroness Noakes DBE *Chief Executive* Ed Richards, Ofcom, Riverside House, 2a Southwark Bridge Rd, London SE1 9HA.
Tel: 0300 123 3000
Textphone: 020 7981 3043
Fax: 020 7981 3333
email: contact@ofcom.org.uk
Web: www.ofcom.org.uk

INDEPENDENT CHRISTIAN BROADCASTERS

A range of independent Christian broadcasters operate in the UK, including:

Premier   *Web:* www.premier.org.uk
United Christian Broadcasting (UCB)
     Web: www.ucb.co.uk
God TV   *Web:* http://uk.god.tv/
Eternal World Television Network
     Web: http://www.ewtn.com/
For a full list of Christian Digital Satellite Channels, visit: http://www.christiantv.org.uk/

SANDFORD ST MARTIN (CHURCH OF ENGLAND) TRUST

Established in 1978, the Trust's initial purpose was to recognize and promote excellence in religious broadcasting, and to encourage Christian involvement in television and radio at both national and local levels. Founded through the vision of the late Sir David Wills, its origins were Anglican, but reflecting the multi-faith nature of contemporary Britain, it currently seeks not only to promote high-quality programmes inspired by any of the major world religions but to develop a higher profile in advocating the importance of religious broadcasting. In 2013 it was represented at the Festival of Religion at Media City, Salford and in 2014 it sponsored and hosted a discussion on the significance of religious broadcasting at the Guardian Edinburgh International Festival of Television.

Recognizing that greater involvement in the media and wider recognition and promotion of the Trust's aims and activities would need additional funding, the Trustees agreed to realize up to £100k a year for the next three years. The Strategy Group completed its work and in fulfilling its recommendations, the Trustees appointed an Executive Secretary for a period of three years. The Awards Advisory Group, a PR Strategy Group, PR Strategy Group and Finance Group have met to implement the proposed developments in Trust activity.

As in previous years, the Trust held its broadcast media awards ceremony at Lambeth Palace on 3 June 2014, when the Chairman, the Rt Revd Nick Baines, Bishop of Leeds, presented the prizes.

Introduced by the editor, Ben Preston, the prestigious *Radio Times* Readers' Award went to Simon Schama's series *The Story of the Jews* (Oxford Film and Television for BBC2). The 2014 Trustees Award was awarded posthumously to Sir John Tavener for his contribution to the importance of religion through music. Presenting it, Sir Nick Kenyon reflected how honoured Sir John would be at its recognition of the religious influence of his composition. A personal Award was made to Lord Bragg for his public recognition of the significance of religion in intellectual debate through a long career in broadcasting.

Chaired by writer and broadcaster, Ed Stourton, the panel in the television category also recognized Simon Schama's *History of the Jews: Over the Rainbow* (Oxford Film and Television for BBC2) as the winning programme. The runner-up Award was shared by *A Very British Ramadan* (Watershed Productions for Channel 4) and *Hillsborough – Never Forgotten* (BBC Religion and Ethics for BBC2).

Novelist Patrick Gale chaired the Radio panel, which awarded *I Have a Dream* (BBC Scotland Features for BBC Radio 4) its top prize, while the runner-up was *Married for a Minute*, an investigation of the custom of temporary marriage (Nikah Mut'ah) in Islam (BBC Asian Network).

Reflecting the developing media opportunities, a new award for Local Community and Online Programming was awarded to *Sounds Jewish: The Jewish Revival in Poland* which was made by JW3 as a podcast on theguardian.com.

Chairman Rt Revd Nicholas Baines, Bishop of Leeds. *Awards Administrator* Gill Macdonald, *Executive Secretary* Ms Anna Macnamee, Room 202, Church House, Great Smith St, London SW1P 3AZ   *Tel:* 020 7898 1796
Fax: 020 7898 1797
email: SandfordSMT@churchofengland.org.uk
Web: www.sandfordawards.org.uk

WORLD ASSOCIATION FOR CHRISTIAN COMMUNICATION (WACC)

WACC is an organization of corporate and individual members who wish to give high priority to Christian values in the world's communication and development needs. It is not a council or federation of churches. The majority of members are communication professionals from all walks of life. Others include partners in different communication activities, and representatives of churches and agencies. It funds communication activities that reflect regional interests, and encourages ecumenical unity among communicators. As a professional organization, WACC serves the wider ecumenical movement by offering guidance on communication policies, interpreting developments in communications worldwide, discussing the consequences that such developments have for churches and communities everywhere but especially in the global South. WACC publishes *Media Development*, an online quarterly journal; *Media and Gender Monitor*, a bi-annual bulletin; and occasional publications. It has 1600 members and partners in 120 countries. UK members and affiliates include the Anglican Communion Office, Leeds Trinity University College, Feed the Minds, and SPCK. Contact WACC UK, 16 Tavistock Crescent, London W11 1AP

Tel: 07985 276515
email: info@waccglobal.org
Web: www.waccglobal.org

Theological Colleges and Regional Courses

Address and Telephone Number	Principal or Warden
All Saints Centre for Mission and Ministry (formerly SNWTP), Aiken Hall, University of Chester, Crab Lane, Warrington WA2 0BD *Tel:* 01925 534303 *email:* snwtpprincipal@chester.ac.uk	Ven Dr John Applegate
Cranmer Hall (St John's College), Durham DH1 3RJ *Tel:* 0191 334 3924 *Fax:* 0191 334 3866 *email:* enquiries@cranmerhall.com	Revd Mark Tanner
College of the Resurrection, Stockbank Road, Mirfield WF14 0BW *Tel:* 01924 490441 *Fax:* 01924 492738 *email:* principal@mirfield.org.uk	Revd Fr Peter Allan CR
Eastern Region Ministry Course, Westcott House, Jesus Lane, Cambridge CB5 8BJ *Tel:* 01223 366378 *Fax:* 01223 741027 *email:* mcintosh@ermc.cam.ac.uk	Revd Canon Dr Ian McIntosh
Lancashire and Cumbria Theological Partnership, Church House, West Walls, Carlisle, Cumbria CA3 8UE *Tel:* 01228 815405 *Fax:* 01228 815400 *email:* admin@lctp.co.uk	Revd Roger Latham (Acting Principal)
Lincoln School of Theology, Edward King House, Minster Yard LN2 1PU *Tel:* 01522 504050 *email:* sally.myers@lincoln.anglican.org	Revd Sally Myers
Lindisfarne Regional Training Partnership, Church House, St John's Terrace, North Shields NE29 6HS *Tel:* 0191 270 4144 *email:* cathyrowling@lindisfarnertp.org	Revd Canon Cathy Rowling
Local Ministry Programme: Guildford, Diocesan House, Quarry St, Guildford GU1 3XG *Tel:* 01483 790319 *email:* steve.summers@cofeguildford.org.uk	Revd Dr Stephen Summers
Oak Hill Theological College, Chase Side, Southgate, London N14 4PS *Tel:* 020 8449 0467 *Fax:* 020 8441 5996 *email:* mike@oakhill.ac.uk	Revd Dr Michael Ovey
Oxford Local Ministry Programme, Diocesan Church House, North Hinksey Lane, Oxford OX2 0NB *Tel:* 01865 208282 *Fax:* 01865 790470 *email:* keith.beech-gruneberg@oxford.anglican.org	Revd Dr Keith Beech-Gruneberg
The Queen's Foundation for Ecumenical Theological Education, Somerset Rd, Edgbaston, Birmingham B15 2QH *Tel:* 0121 454 1527 *Fax:* 0121 454 8171 *email:* enquire@queens.ac.uk	Revd Canon Dr David Hewlett
Ridley Hall, Ridley Hall Road, Cambridge CB3 9HG *Tel:* 01223 741060 *Fax:* 01223 746581 *email:* ridleypa@hermes.cam.ac.uk	Revd Canon Andrew Norman
Ripon College, Cuddesdon, Oxford OX44 9EX including Oxford Ministry Course and West of England Ministerial Training Course *Tel:* 01865 874404 *Fax:* 01865 875431 *email:* enquiries@ripon-cuddesdon.ac.uk	Revd Mark Chapman (Acting Principal)

GENERAL

St John's College, Chilwell Lane, Bramcote, Nottingham NG9 3DS *Tel:* 0115 925 1114 *Fax:* 0115 943 6438 *email:* enquiries@stjohns-nottm.ac.uk	Revd Dr David Hilborn
St Mellitus College , 24 Collingham Road, London SW5 0LX including NTMTC *Tel:* 020 7052 0573 *email:* info@stmellitus.ac.uk	Revd Dr Graham Tomlin
St Stephen's House, 16 Marston St, Oxford OX4 1JX *Tel:* 01865 613500 *Fax:* 01865 613513 *email:* enquiries@ssho.ox.ac.uk	Revd Canon Dr Robin Ward
South East Institute for Theological Education, Room Hf17, Hepworth Building, Canterbury Christ Church University, North Holmes Road, Canterbury CT1 1QU *Tel:* 01227 471120 *email:* administrator@seite.co.uk (*office*); principal@seite.co.uk (*Principal*)	Revd Dr Alan Gregory
Southern Theological Education and Training Scheme, 19 The Close, Salisbury SP1 2EE *Tel:* 01722 424820 *email:* acthomasson-rosingh@stets.ac.uk	Revd Dr Anne Claar Thomasson-Rosingh (Acting Principal)
South West Ministry Training Course, Suite 1.3, Renslade House, Bonhay Road, Exeter EX4 3AY *Tel:* 01392 272544 *email:* principal@SWMTC.org.uk	Dr Christopher Southgate
Trinity College, Stoke Hill, Bristol BS9 1JP *Tel:* 0117 968 2803 *Fax:* 0117 968 7470 *email:* principal@trinity-bris.ac.uk	Revd Dr Emma Ineson
Westcott House, Jesus Lane, Cambridge CB5 8BP *Tel:* 01223 741000 *Fax:* 01223 741002 *email:* info@westcott.cam.ac.uk	Revd Canon Martin Seeley
Wycliffe Hall, 54 Banbury Road, Oxford OX2 6PW *Tel:* 01865 274200 *Fax:* 01865 274215 *email:* enquiries@wycliffe.ox.ac.uk	Revd Dr Michael Lloyd
Yorkshire Ministry Course, The Mirfield Centre, Stocks Bank Rd, Mirfield WF14 0BW *Tel:* 01924 481 925 *email:* principal@ymc.org.uk	Vacancy
Theological Institute of the Scottish Episcopal Church, TISEC, Forbes House, 21 Grosvenor Crescent, Edinburgh EH12 5EE *Tel:* 0131 225 6357 *Fax:* 0131 346 7247 *email:* tisec@scotland.anglican.org	Revd Canon Dr Michael Fuller
St Michael's College, 54 Cardiff Road, Llandaff, Cardiff CF5 2YJ *Tel:* 029 2056 3379 *Fax:* 029 2083 8008 *email:* via website	Revd Mark Clavier (Acting Principal)

ROYAL PECULIARS, THE CHAPELS ROYAL, ETC.

Westminster Abbey

Description of Arms. Azure, a cross patonce between five martlets or; on a chief or France and England quarterly on a pale, between two roses, gules, seeded and barbed proper.

COLLEGIATE CHURCH OF ST PETER
The Collegiate Church of St Peter in Westminster, usually called Westminster Abbey, is a Royal Peculiar, and, as such, it is extra-provincial as well as extra-diocesan and comes directly under the personal jurisdiction of Her Majesty The Queen, who is the Visitor.

Throughout medieval times it was the Abbey Church of a great Benedictine Monastery, which was in existence at Westminster before the Norman Conquest. After the dissolution of the monastery in 1540 it became increasingly a great national shrine, where famous writers, poets, statesmen and leaders in the Church and State are buried. It is the Coronation Church, and in it also take place from time to time Royal weddings and many services on great occasions of a National or Commonwealth character. Daily, the Holy Communion is celebrated and Morning and Evening Prayers are said or sung.

THE VISITOR
The Sovereign

DEAN
Very Revd Dr John R. Hall, The Deanery, Westminster SW1P 3PA [2006]   *Tel:* 020 7654 4801
Fax: 020 7654 4883
email: john.hall@westminster-abbey.org
Web: www.westminster-abbey.org

CANONS OF WESTMINSTER
Sub-Dean, Archdeacon and Canon Rector of St Margaret's Church, Revd Andrew Tremlett, 5 Little Cloister SW1P 3PL [2010]
Tel: 020 7654 4806
Fax: 020 7654 4811
email: andrew.tremlett@westminster-abbey.org

Canon Theologian Revd Prof Vernon P. White, 3 Little Cloister, London SW1P 3PL [2011]
Tel: 020 7654 4808
Fax: 020 7654 4811
email: vernon.white@westminster-abbey.org

Canon Treasurer and Almoner Revd David Stanton, 1 Little Cloister, London SW1P 3PL [2013]   *Tel:* 020 7654 4804
Fax: 020 7654 4811
email: david.stanton@westminster-abbey.org

Canon Steward Revd Jane Sinclair, 2 Little Cloister, London SW1P 3PL [2014]   *Tel:* 020 7654 4815
Fax: 020 7654 4811
email: jane.sinclair@westminster-abbey.org

MINOR CANONS
Precentor Revd Dr James D. T. Hawkey, 7 Little Cloister, London SW1P 3PL [2010]
Tel: 020 7654 4850
email: james.hawkey@westminster-abbey.org
Sacrist Revd Christopher B. Stoltz, 6 Little Cloister, London SW1P 3PL [2014]   Tel. 020 7654 4855
email: christopher.stoltz@westminster-abbey.org

CHAPLAIN
Revd Tony Kyriakides-Yeldham, The Chapter Office, 20 Dean's Yard, London SW1P 3PA
Tel: 020 7654 4957

PRIESTS VICAR
Revd Paul Bagott
Revd Alan Boddy
Revd Laura Jørgensen
Revd Philip Chester
Revd Chris Chivers
Revd Dr Alasdair Coles
Revd Dominic Fenton
Revd Ralph Godsall
Rt Revd Jonathan Goodall
Revd Alan Gyle
Revd Dr Sarah Hartley
Revd Rose Hudson-Wilkin
Rt Revd Graeme Knowles
Revd Peter McGeary
Revd Jonathan Osborne
Revd Dr Fiona Stewart-Darling
Very Revd Dr Victor Stock
Revd Garry Swinton
Revd Gavin Williams

LAY OFFICERS
Receiver General and Chapter Clerk Sir Stephen Lamport KCVO DL, The Chapter Office, 20 Dean's Yard, London SW1P 3PA   *Tel:* 020 7654 4861
Fax: 020 7654 4914
email: stephen.lamport@westminster-abbey.org
Web: www.westminster-abbey.org

Organist and Master of the Choristers Mr James O'Donnell (*same address*)   *Tel:* 020 7654 4854
email: music@westminster-abbey.org

Registrar Sir Stephen Lamport KCVO DL (*same address*)

Press and Communications Office (*same address*)
Tel: 020 7654 4923
email: press@westminster-abbey.org

Head of Communications Mr Duncan Jeffery (*same address*)
Tel: 020 7654 4888
Fax: 020 7654 4891
email: duncan.jeffery@westminster-abbey.org

Surveyor of the Fabric Mr Ptolemy Dean (*same address*)

Head of the Abbey Collection Dr Tony Trowles, The Muniment Room and Library, Westminster Abbey, London SW1P 3PL   Tel: 020 7654 4829
email: tony.trowles@westminster-abbey.org

Keeper of the Muniments Mr Matthew Payne (*same address*)
Tel: 020 7654 4829
email: matthew.payne@westminster-abbey.org

Headmaster of the Choir School Mr Jonathan Milton, Dean's Yard, London SW1P 3NY
Tel: 020 7654 4918
email: jonathan.milton@westminster-abbey.org

Legal Secretary Mr Christopher Vyse, The Chapter Office, 20 Dean's Yard, London SW1P 3PA
Tel: 020 7654 4885
email: chris.vyse@westminster-abbey.org

Auditor Mr Andrew McIntyre, Ernst & Young, 1 More London Place, London SE1 2AF
Tel: 020 7951 2068

Windsor

Description of Arms. The shield of St George, argent a cross gules, encircled by the Garter

THE QUEEN'S FREE CHAPEL OF ST GEORGE WITHIN HER CASTLE OF WINDSOR

A ROYAL PECULIAR
Founded by Edward III in 1348 and exempt from diocesan and provincial jurisdictions, the College of St George is a self-governing secular community of priests and laymen, the first duty of which is to celebrate Divine Service daily on behalf of the Sovereign, the Royal House and the Order of the Garter. Its present Chapel was founded by Edward IV in honour of Our Lady, St George and St Edward in 1475 and, with the cloisters and buildings annexed, is vested in the Dean and Canons. In it the Eucharist, Mattins and Evensong are sung or said daily and are open to all.

The Order of the Garter has its stalls and insignia in the Quire, where Knights and Ladies Companions are installed by the Sovereign. Beneath the Quire – the scene of many Royal funerals – are vaults in which lie the bodies of six monarchs. Elsewhere in the Chapel are the tombs of four others.

The College has its own school of 400 children, where it maintains twenty-four choristerships. It also awards an organ scholarship. A house for conferences has been established under the name of St George's House.

THE VISITOR
The Sovereign

DEAN
Rt Revd David Conner KCVO, The Deanery, Windsor Castle, Windsor, Berkshire SL4 1NJ [1998]   Tel: 01753 865561

CANONS
Chaplain in the Great Park Canon Martin Poll, Chaplain's Lodge, Windsor Great Park, Windsor, Berkshire SL4 2HP [2012]   Tel: 01784 432434

Warden, St George's House and Canon Treasurer Canon Dr Hueston Finlay, 8 The Cloisters, Windsor Castle, Windsor, Berkshire SL4 1NJ [2004]   Tel: 01753 848887

Steward Canon Dr James Woodward, 6 The Cloisters, Windsor Castle, Windsor, Berkshire SL4 1NJ [2009]   Tel: 01753 848709

MINOR CANONS
Chaplain to St George's School Vacancy
Tel: 01753 848710

LAY OFFICERS
Chapter Clerk Miss Charlotte Manley LVO OBE, Chapter Office, 2 The Cloisters, Windsor Castle, Windsor, Berkshire SL4 1NJ [2003]
Tel: 01753 848888

Director of Music Mr James Vivian, 23 The Cloisters, Windsor Castle, Windsor, Berkshire SL4 1NJ [2013]   Tel: 01753 848747

Assistant Director of Music Mr Richard Pinel, 3 The Cloisters, Windsor Castle, Windsor, Berkshire SL4 1NJ

Clerk of Accounts Mr Nick Grogan, 2 The Cloisters, Windsor Castle, Windsor, Berkshire SL4 1NJ   Tel: 01753 848720

Clerk of Works Mr Darren Cave, 11a The Cloisters, Windsor Castle, Windsor, Berkshire SL4 1NJ [2014]   *Tel:* 01753 848766

Archivist and Chapter Librarian Dr Clare Rider FSA, The Vicars' Hall Undercroft, Windsor Castle, Windsor, Berkshire SL4 1NJ   *Tel:* 01753 848724

Virger Mr Vaughn Wright, 22 Horseshoe Cloister, Windsor Castle, Windsor, Berkshire SL4 1NJ   *Tel:* 01753 848727

Head Master, St George's School Mr Christopher McDade, St George's School, Windsor Castle, Windsor, Berkshire SL4 1QF   *Tel:* 01753 865553

Domestic Chaplains to Her Majesty the Queen

Buckingham Palace Revd Paul Wright
Windsor Castle The Dean of Windsor

Sandringham Revd Jonathan Riviere

Chapels Royal

The Chapel Royal is the body of Clergy, Singers and Vestry Officers appointed to serve the spiritual needs of the Sovereign – in medieval days on Progresses through the Realm as well as upon the battlefields of Europe, as at Agincourt. Its ancient foundation is first century with the British Church: its latter day choral headquarters have been at St James's Palace since 1702 along with the Court of St James. Since 1312 the Chapel Royal has been governed by the Dean who, as the Ordinary, also exercises, along with the Sub-Dean, jurisdiction over the daughter establishments of Chapels Royal at the Tower of London and at Hampton Court Palace. Members of the public are welcome to attend Sunday and weekday services as advertised.

The Chapel Royal conducts the Service of Remembrance at the Cenotaph in Whitehall, with a Forces Chaplain in company, and combines with the choral establishment of the host abbey or cathedral on the occasion of Royal Maundy, under the governance of the Lord High Almoner and Sub-Almoner. Each Member of the College of thirty-six Chaplains to Her Majesty the Queen, headed by the Clerk and Deputy Clerk of the Closet, is required by Warrant to preach in the Chapel Royal once a year, and is visibly distinguished, along with the Chapel Royal, Forces and Mohawk Chaplains, by the wearing of a royal scarlet cassock.

Dean of the Chapels Royal
The Bishop of London

Sub-Dean
Revd Paul Wright
Chapel Royal, St James's Palace, London SW1A 1BL   *Tel:* 020 7024 5576

CHAPEL ROYAL AND THE QUEEN'S CHAPEL, ST JAMES'S PALACE
Priests in Ordinary
Revd Richard Bolton
Revd William Whitcombe

Deputy Priests
Canon Roger Hall
Canon Dennis Mulliner
Canon Mark Oakley
Revd Dr Stephen Young

HAMPTON COURT PALACE
Chapel Royal, Hampton Court, East Molesey, Surrey KT8 9AU   *Tel:* 020 3166 6515

Chaplain
Canon Denis Mulliner

HM TOWER OF LONDON
The Chaplain's Residence, London EC3N 4AP   *Tel:* 020 3166 6796
(includes the Chapels Royal of St John the Evangelist and St Peter ad Vincula)

Chaplain
Canon Roger Hall

THE ROYAL CHAPEL OF ALL SAINTS, WINDSOR GREAT PARK
This is a Private Chapel and the property of the Crown within the grounds of the Royal Lodge. Attendance is restricted to residents and employees of the Great Park.

Chaplain
Ven Martin Poll, Chaplain's Lodge, Windsor Great Park, Windsor, Berkshire SL4 2HP   *Tel:* 01784 432434

College of Chaplains

The position of Royal Chaplain is a very ancient one. The College of Chaplains, the members of which as such must not be confused with the Priests in Ordinary, preach according to a Rota of Waits in the Chapels Royal. The College comprises the Clerk of the Closet (who presides), the Deputy Clerk of the Closet, and thirty-six Chaplains. When a vacancy in the list of chaplains occurs, the Private Secretary to Her Majesty the Queen asks the Clerk of the Closet to suggest possible names to Her Majesty. The duties of the Clerk of the Closet include the presentation of bishops to Her Majesty when they do homage before taking possession of the revenues of their Sees; and he also examines theological books whose authors desire to present copies to Her Majesty the Queen. He preaches annually in the Chapel Royal, St James's Palace.

CLERK OF THE CLOSET
Rt Revd James Newcome (*Bishop of Carlisle*)

DEPUTY CLERK OF THE CLOSET
Revd Paul Wright

CHAPLAINS TO HER MAJESTY THE QUEEN
Canon Christopher Andrews
Canon Gavin Ashenden
Preb Paul Avis
Revd Hugh Bearn
Revd Mary Bide

Canon John Byrne
Canon Gillian Calver
Canon Andrew Clitherow
Canon Richard Cooper
Canon Ann Easter
Preb Kathleen Garlick
Canon Jeremy Haselock
Canon Roger Hill
Revd Rose Hudson-Wilkin
Canon Robert Innes
Canon George Kovoor
Revd John Lee
Revd Edward Lewis
Preb Paul Locke
Canon Kevan McCormack
Canon Bill Matthews
Canon Paul Miller
Canon George Moffat
Revd David Nicholson
Ven William Noblett
Canon John Ovenden
Rev Hugh Palmer
Canon Stephen Palmer
Revd Jonathan Riviere
Canon Bruce Ruddock
Canon Anthony Shepherd
Preb Pippa Thorneycroft
Ven Ruth Worsley

Extra Chaplains
Canon Anthony Caesar
Revd John Robson

Royal Almonry

The Royal Almonry dispenses the Queen's charitable gifts and is responsible for the Royal Maundy Service each year, at which Her Majesty distributes Maundy money to as many men and as many women pensioners as the years of her own age.

HIGH ALMONER
Rt Revd John Inge (*Bishop of Worcester*)

SUB-ALMONER
Revd Paul Wright
Chapel Royal, St James's Palace, London SW1A 1BL

The Queen's Chapel of the Savoy

Savoy Hill, Strand, London WC2R 0DA
Tel: 020 7379 8088 (Chaplain) *or* 020 7836 7221 (Steward)
email: chapel@duchyoflancaster.com
web: www.royalchapelsavoy.org

CHAPEL OF THE ROYAL VICTORIAN ORDER
The Queen's Chapel of the Savoy was built as the principal chapel of a hospital for 'pouer, nedie people' founded by King Henry VII and finished in 1512 after his death. It is a private

Chapel of Her Majesty the Queen in right of her Duchy of Lancaster, and Her Majesty appoints the chaplain. It is, therefore, a 'free' Chapel not falling within any diocese or episcopal jurisdiction.

On the occasion of his Coronation in 1937, King George VI commanded that the chapel of the Savoy should become the chapel of the Royal Victorian Order, an honour in the personal gift of the Sovereign, and the Chaplain of the Queen's Chapel is ex officio Chaplain of the Order. An ante-chapel (now renamed the Lancaster Hall), chaplain's office and robing room were constructed in 1958 to provide additional accommodation.

A new three-manual Walker organ was presented to the Chapel by Her Majesty the Queen in 1965. Further work in 2011–12 included the installation of a new stained glass window to mark the Diamond Jubilee of the Queen's reign, an extension of the royal robing room, the creation of a new sunken courtyard on the north side of the Lancaster Hall, the construction of a new chaplain's study and an office for the Steward, and the development of new facilities for receptions.

Members of the public are welcome to attend services which are held on Sundays (11 am) and weekdays (except August and September)

with the exception of those for special or official occasions. The Chapel has a particularly fine musical tradition with a choir of men and boys. The Chapel is normally open to the public between 1 October and 31 July from 9am to 4pm Monday to Thursday.

CHAPLAIN
Revd Prof Peter Galloway JP OBE

STEWARD
Sqn Ldr Thomas Leyland BSC RAF (rtd)

MASTER OF MUSIC
Mr Philip Berg MVO FRCO ARCM

CHAIRMAN OF THE COUNCIL
The Lord Shuttleworth KCVO

Royal Memorial Chapel Sandhurst

Camberley, Surrey GU15 4PQ   *Tel:* 01276 412543
                             Fax: 01276 412097

The Royal Memorial Chapel Sandhurst is the Chapel of the Royal Military Academy Sandhurst. It is also the Memorial Chapel of the officers of the British Army.

The present building was erected after the First World War as a memorial to those trained at Sandhurst who gave their lives in that conflict. Their names are inscribed on the Chapel's pillars. A memorial book contains the names of all officers of the Commonwealth Armies who died in the Second World War, and a page of this book is turned at the beginning of principal services.

A Book of Remembrance containing the names of all officers who have been killed in service since 1947 is kept in the South Africa Chapel.

The main Sunday service is at 1030. The forms of service include the *Book of Common Prayer, Common Worship*, and special services within the

Academy's calendar. Services are open to the public, and passes may be obtained by contacting the Chapel Office.

SENIOR CHAPLAIN
Revd Mike Parker CF

ASSISTANT CHAPLAIN
Revd Keith Barry CF

CHOIRMASTER AND ORGANIST
Mr Peter Beaven

CONSTITUTION OF THE CHAPEL COUNCIL
Maj-Gen P. C. Marriot (*Chairman*); Canon J. R. B. Gough (*Deputy Chairman*); Maj J. M. Watkinson (*Secretary*); Ven Peter Eagles (*Chaplain General*); Maj-Gen Sir Simon Cooper; Maj Gen R. L. Kirkland; Brig M. Owen

The Royal Foundation of St Katharine

2 Butcher Row, London E14 8DS
                    Tel: 0300 111 1147
                    Fax: 0300 777 1147
                 email: info@rfsk.org.uk
                  Web: www.rfsk.org.uk

St Katharine's, founded by Queen Matilda in 1147 originally adjacent to the Tower of London, is a charitable conference and retreat centre at Limehouse in East London, between the City and Canary Wharf. It serves the Church of England, other churches and charities, offering an attractive setting for day or residential group meetings, seminars or retreats. It is also an excellent place to stay for business or pleasure in London. There are excellent facilities with residential en suite accommodation for 44 people and a choice of 7 meeting rooms. Daily worship is held in the peaceful chapel.

Her Majesty Queen Elizabeth II is Patron of the Foundation.

MEMBERS OF THE COURT
Revd John Tattersall (*Chairman*)
Mr David Swanney (*Treasurer*)
Rt Revd and Rt Hon Richard Chartres (*Bishop of London*)
Mr Ian Graham
Mr Andrew Grigson
Mr Simon Martin
Sir Stephen Lamport
Mrs Elizabeth Marshall
Revd Mark Aitken (*Master*)

MASTER
Revd Mark Aitken

Deans of Peculiars

The few present-day Deans of Peculiars are the residue of some 300 such office-holders in the medieval period, when the granting of 'peculiar' status, fully or partially exempting a jurisdiction from episcopal control, was commonly employed by popes and others to advance the interests of a particular institution, or limit the power of the bishops. Unlike the Royal Peculiars, the deaneries had little in common, and the privileges and duties of the individual posts ranged from nominal to significant. Most of the special provisions were brought to an end in the nineteenth century. But each Peculiar has interesting light to throw on a phase of Anglican or national history.

Battle
Very Revd Canon Dr John Edmondson, The Deanery, Caldbec Hill, Battle, E. Sussex TN33 0JY [2005]   *Tel* and *Fax:* 01424 772693
            email: dean@johnedmondson.org

Bocking
Vacancy, The Deanery, Bocking, Braintree, Essex CM7 5SR (Bocking, Essex) [1996]
            Tel: 01376 324887
            01376 553092 (Office)
Very Revd Martin Thrower, The Deanery, Church St, Hadleigh, Ipswich IP7 5DT (Hadleigh, Suffolk) [2009]   *Tel:* 01473 822218
            email: martin.thrower@btinternet.com

Stamford
Very Revd Mark Warrick (*Vicar of Stamford All Saints with St John the Baptist*)
            email: mark.warrick@stamfordallsaints.org.uk

Preachers at the Inns of Court

THE TEMPLE
Master Revd Robin Griffith-Jones, The Master's House, Temple, London EC4Y 7BB
            Tel: 020 7353 8559
            email: master@templechurch.com

Reader Revd A. H. Mead, 11 Dungarvan Ave, London SW15 5QU   *Tel:* 020 8876 5833

LINCOLN'S INN
Very Revd Derek Watson, 29 The Precincts, Canterbury CT1 2EP   *Tel:* 01227 865238

GRAY'S INN
Rt Revd Michael Doe, 405 West Carriage House, Royal Carriage Mews, Royal Arsenal, Woolwich SE18 6GA   *Tel:* 020 3259 3841

RELIGIOUS COMMUNITIES

Anglican Religious Communities

The roots of the Religious Life can be traced back to the Early Church in Jerusalem, and the subsequent traditions such as the Benedictines, Franciscans, etc., were flourishing in England until the Reformation when all were suppressed.

Most Anglican Communities were founded in the nineteenth century as a result of the Oxford Movement. There are over eighty different Communities in the British Isles and throughout the Anglican Communion. Some are very small. Some have over 100 members worldwide.

Religious Communities are formed by men and women who feel called to seek God and live out their baptismal vows in a particular way under vows. There are some 400 Anglican men and women living this life in the United Kingdom.

PRAYER AND WORK

Each Community has its own history and character; some follow one of the traditional Rules, and others those written by more recent founders, but all have one thing in common: their daily life based on the work of prayer and living together centred in their Daily Office and the Eucharist. The work grows from the prayer, depending on the particular Community and the gifts of its members.

Some Communities are 'enclosed'. The members do not normally go out, but remain within the convent or monastery and its grounds, seeking and serving God through silence and prayer, study and work. Other Communities share the basic life of prayer and fellowship and are involved in a variety of work in society at large.

HOSPITALITY

Most Community houses offer a place where people can go for a time of Retreat, either alone or with a group, for a day, several days, or occasionally for longer periods of time. They offer a place of quiet to seek God, grow in prayer and find spiritual guidance.

THE CALLING

People who feel called to the Religious Life and who wish to apply to a Community need to be over 21. They normally need to be physically and psychologically robust. Academic qualifications are not essential. There is a training period of about three years before any vows are taken.

Those who are considering a vocation are advised to visit Community houses to experience their particular ethos: further information is available from the houses or general enquiries may be made to Anglican Religious Communities at the address below. Details of Communities may be found in *Anglican Religious Life*, published by Canterbury Press, or, in an abbreviated form, via the following web address: www.arcie.org.uk

Advisory Council on the Relations of Bishops and Religious Communities

This Council, to serve the two Provinces, is responsible to the Archbishops and the House of Bishops. Its functions are (1) to advise bishops upon (a) questions arising about the charters, constitutions and rule of existing Communities, (b) the establishment of new Communities, (c) matters referred to it by a diocesan bishop; (2) to advise existing Communities or their Visitors in any matters that they refer to it; (3) to give guidance to those who wish to form Communities. The Chairman and Convenor of the Council must be a diocesan bishop appointed by the Archbishops of Canterbury and York. The Council consists of at least thirteen members, three of whom are nominated by the bishops and ten elected by the Communities. Up to five additional members may be co-opted. The present membership is: *Chair* Rt Revd David Walker (*Bishop of Manchester*); *three members nominated by the House of Bishops* Rt Revd John Pritchard (*Bishop of Oxford*), Rt Revd Anthony Robinson (*Bishop of Pontefract*), Rt Revd Humphrey Southern (*Bishop of Repton*); *ten members elected by the Communities* Sister Anita csc, Sister Elizabeth Pio ssb, Sister Joyce csf, Sister Mary Julian Gough chc, Sister Mary Stephen osb, Sister Rosemary chn, Mother Winsome csmv, Abbot Stuart Burns osb, Father Colin Griffiths ssm, Brother Damian ssf, Father Peter Allan cr; *Co-opted* Rt Revd Jonathan Clark, Revd Canon Christopher Neal cms, Revd Ian Mobsby; *ARC Representative* Dom Simon Jarratt osb; *Roman Catholic Observer* Sister Catherine McGovern osf; *Secretary* Father Colin cswg.

Correspondence in relation to the Advisory Council should be addressed to: The Bishop of Manchester, Bishopscourt, Bury New Road, Salford, Manchester M7 4LE   *Tel:* 0161 792 2096
email:
bishop@bishopscourt.manchester.anglican.org

Anglican Religious Communities in England

ARC is an umbrella body of all members of Anglican Religious Communities, Monks and Nuns, Brothers and Sisters living in community under vows of poverty, chastity and obedience. The communities range from large monastic houses to small groups of two or three brothers or sisters living and working in urban areas. It acts to support its members by encouraging cooperation and the exchange of ideas and experiences which are relevant to Religious Life.

The ARC Committee has members elected from four constituent groups: Leaders, General Synod Representatives, Novice Guardians and Professed Religious. An annual conference is held.

Contact The Secretary, Anglican Religious Communities, Church House, Great Smith St, London SW1P 3AZ

email: info@arcie.org.uk
Registered Charity no. 1097586

Communities for Men

**BENEDICTINE COMMUNITY OF
ST BENEDICT'S PRIORY**
19a The Close, Salisbury, SP1 2EB
email: salisbury.priory@gmail.com

Conventual Prior Dom Simon Jarratt OSB

Visitor Rt Revd Dominic Walker OGS

Founded 1914. 1926–87 Nashdom Abbey, 1987–2010 Elmore Abbey, from 2010 St Benedict's Priory, Salisbury. Resident community four monks. Oblate confraternity of around 300. The community receives day guests.

**BENEDICTINE COMMUNITY AT
MUCKNELL ABBEY**
See **Mixed Communities** page 247.

COMMUNITY OF OUR LADY AND ST JOHN
Alton Abbey, Abbey Road, Alton, Hants. GU34 4AP   *Tel:* 01420 562145
email: giles@altonabbey.org.uk
Web: www.altonabbey.org.uk

Abbot Rt Revd Dom Giles Hill OSB

Visitor Rt Revd Michael Scott-Joynt

Founded 1884. A community of Benedictine monks which undertakes retreats. Guest accommodation for 18 people. Other work includes the manufacture of altar wafers and incense. The Seamen's Friendly Society of St Paul is managed from the Abbey. Day conference facilities and residential groups welcome: contact the Guestmaster.

**COMMUNITY OF THE GLORIOUS
ASCENSION**
The Priory, 26 Helmers Way, Chillington, Kingsbridge, Devon TQ7 2EZ   *Tel:* 01548 580127
email: ascensioncga@fsnet.com

Prior Br Simon CGA

Visitor Rt Revd Richard Hawkins

Founded in 1960 – the brothers are based in Devon and continue the monastic pattern of a common-life, prayer and worship; together with their work of hospitality and ministry. The Sisters have established a priory in the nearby village of Chillington.

COMMUNITY OF THE RESURRECTION
House of the Resurrection, Mirfield WF14 0BN
Tel: 01924 494318
Fax: 01924 490489
email: www.community@mirfield.org.uk
Web: mirfieldcommunity.org.uk

Superior Fr George Guiver CR   *Tel:* 01924 483301

Visitor Rt Revd Graham James (*Bishop of Norwich*)

Founded 1892, it undertakes teaching (theological college), retreats, missions and missionary works.

Theological College College of the Resurrection, Mirfield WF14 0BW   *Tel:* 01924 481900
Fax: 01924 492738
email: registrar@mirfield.org.uk
Web: http://college.mirfield.org.uk

The Mirfield Centre offers a programme of day and evening events and small conferences as well as offering a meeting place for about 50 people. *Address* Mirfield Centre, College of the Resurrection, Mirfield WF14 0BW
Tel: 01924 481920
Fax: 01924 492738
email: centre@mirfield.org.uk
Web: www.mirfieldcentre.org.uk

**COMMUNITY OF THE SERVANTS OF THE
WILL OF GOD**
See **Mixed Communities** page 247.

COMPANY OF MISSION PRIESTS

Secretary Fr Philip North, The Rectory, 191 St Pancras Way, London NW1 9NH

Tel: 020 7485 5791
email: philip.north@mac.com

Visitor Bishop Lindsay Urwin OGS

Warden Fr Beresford Skelton CMP

Founded 1940. A society of apostolic life, a dispersed community of male priests of the Anglican Communion who, wishing to consecrate themselves wholly to the Church's mission, keep themselves free from the attachments of marriage and family, and endeavour to encourage and strengthen one another by mutual prayer and fellowship, sharing the vision of St Vincent de Paul of a priesthood dedicated to service, and in association with the whole Vincentian family.

ORATORY OF THE GOOD SHEPHERD

Web: www.ogs.net

Superior Revd Prof Peter Hibbert OGS, 2 Blossom Road, Erdington, Birmingham B24 0UD
email: phibbert@ogs.net

European Provincial Revd Peter Walker OGS, 38 Glynde Crescent, Felpham, West Sussex PO22 8HT
email: pwalker@ogs.net

Founded in 1913 at Cambridge University. The Oratory is a society of celibate priests and laymen of the Anglican Communion who are endeavouring, under the direction of the Rule, to live a life of devotion and service. Members of the Oratory work in four provinces: Europe, Australia, North America and Southern Africa. They are bound together by a common Rule and discipline. They do not normally live together in community but meet for Chapter and are resident regularly for an annual Oratory Retreat and for Provincial Chapter (annual) and General Chapter (triennial). Members include bishops, parish priests, lecturers and missionaries. A two-year period of probation precedes profession, and after ten years of profession, life vows may be taken. The Rule of the Oratory requires celibacy, the daily offices, where possible daily Eucharist, and a regular account of spending and direction of life. In addition, 'Labour of the Mind' is a characteristic of the Oratory and members are expected to spend time in study. Attached to the Oratory are Companions and Associates, lay, ordained, married and single, who keep a Rule of Life and are part of the Oratory family.

THE SOCIETY OF ST FRANCIS

The Society comprises a First Order for men (Society of St Francis) and women (*see* Community of St Francis, page 241), called to the

Franciscan life under the vows of poverty, chastity and obedience; a Second Order of enclosed sisters (*see* Community of St Clare, page 241); and the Third Order for ordained and lay people, pledged to the spirit of the vows (*see* Third Order, Society of St Francis, page 248).

The Brothers of the First Order, founded in 1921, live a life of community centred on prayer and engage in active work especially in the areas of the poor and underprivileged. The three large Friaries in this province (at Hilfield, Glasshampton and Alnmouth) have a ministry with guests and retreatants. The other centres of work are principally within a city context from which the brothers engage in various active ministries. Some work with educational institutions, conducting retreats and with parishes continues.

There are five Provinces: Europe, Province of the Divine Compassion, Papua New Guinea, the Solomon Islands, and the Americas.

Minister General Brother Clark Berge SSF, Little Portion Friary, PO Box 399, Mt Sinai, NY 11766/0399
Tel: (+1) 631 473 0553
email: clarke.berge@s-s-f.org

European Province

Minister Brother Benedict SSF, St Matthias' Vicarage, 45 Mafeking Road, Canning Town, London E16 4NS
Tel: 020 7511 7848
email: ministerssf@franciscans.org.uk
Web: www.franciscans.org.uk

Assistant Minister Brother Philip Bartholomew SSF (Canning Town)

Bishop Protector Rt Revd Stephen Cottrell (*Bishop of Chelmsford*)

Houses
All SSF-UK houses can be emailed using [*name of the house*] ssf@franciscans.org.uk *e.g.* hilfieldssf@franciscans.org.uk
Friary of St Francis, *Alnmouth* *Tel:* 01665 830213/830660
Fax: 01665 830580
The Master's Lodge, 58 St Peter's Street, *Canterbury* CT1 2BE *Tel:* 01227 479364
St Anthony's Friary, Enslin Gardens, *Newcastle upon Tyne* NE6 3ST
St Mary at the Cross, *Glasshampton*, Shrawley, Worcester WR6 6TQ *Tel:* 01299 896345
Friary of St Francis, *Hilfield*, Dorchester, Dorset, DT2 7BE *Tel:* 01300 341345
Fax: 01300 341293
25 Karnac Road, *Leeds* LS8 5BL *Tel:* 0113 226 0647
House of the *Divine Compassion*, 42 Balaam Street, Plaistow, London E13 8AQ
Tel: 020 7476 5189

St Matthias' Vicarage, 45 Mafeking Road, *Canning Town*, London E16 4NS *Tel:* 020 7511 7848

Province of the Divine Compassion
Minister Brother Christopher John ssf. *Houses:* Brisbane (QLD), Stroud (NSW), Kirikiriroa/Hamilton (NZ), Gangchon (Korea)

Papua New Guinea Province
Minister Brother Oswald Dumbari ssf. Houses: Haruro, Dipoturu, Koki, Popondetta: Ukaka

Province of the Solomon Islands
Minister, Brother Clifton Henry ssf. *Houses:* Auki, Busa, Hautambu: La Verna, Hautambu: Little Portion, Honiara, Kira Kira, Kohimarama, Honiara Temotu

Province of the Americas
Minister Brother Jude ssf. *Houses:* Long Island, Los Angeles, San Francisco, São Paulo (Brazil)

Communities for Women

EDGWARE ABBEY
Anglican Benedictine Community of St Mary at the Cross, 94A Priory Field Drive, Edgware, Middx HA8 9PU

Tel: 020 8958 7868
Fax: 020 8958 1920
email: info@edgwareabbey.org.uk

Abbess Mother Mary Therese Zelent osb

Visitor Rt Revd Peter Wheatley

The Community was founded by Revd Henry Daniel Nihill and Mother Monica Skinner in 1866 in Shoreditch, London. Living under the Rule of St Benedict, the Community's primary objective is prayer at the heart of the Church through the offering of the Divine Office and Eucharist, and through the service of hospitality, especially in caring for the sick and poor as Christ Himself.

From the beginning, under the dedication of St Mary at the Cross, the vocation of the Community has been to stand with Mary, the Mother of Jesus beside those who suffer. The care given in those early days to the sick and poor and disabled children of the local area grew and developed through the years, and continues today in Henry Nihill House in the beautiful grounds of the abbey, providing high-quality care and nursing for disabled people and frail elderly people.

Edgware Abbey is seen as a haven of peace which enfolds many visitors. All are offered Benedictine hospitality with space for rest and renewal. The small comfortable guest wing provides short-stay accommodation and a small centre for Parish Group Quiet Days and Meetings. All visitors are welcome to share in the Community's offering of the Divine Office and Eucharist, which remains central to its life.

Chapel Service times are subject to change: please check with Edgware Abbey.

BENEDICTINE COMMUNITY OF ST MARY'S ABBEY
52 Swan St, West Malling, Kent ME19 6JX

Tel: 01732 843309
Fax: 01732 849016
Web: www.mallingabbey.org

Abbess Sister Mary David Best osb

Visitor Rt Revd Laurie Green

We are a monastic community of women following the Rule of St Benedict. Our home is a Benedictine Abbey that flourished from c. 1090 to 1538. Our priorities are prayer, community life and hospitality to those who stay at our guest house and who wish to share in our worship and silence.

BENEDICTINE COMMUNITY AT MUCKNELL ABBEY
See **Mixed Communities** page 247.

COMMUNITY OF ALL HALLOWS
All Hallows Convent, Ditchingham, Norfolk

Postal Address Bungay, Suffolk NR35 2DT
Tel: 01986 892749
Fax: 01986 895838
email: allhallowsconvent@btinternet.com
Web: www.allhallows.org

Leaders Sister Rachel and Sister Sheila cah

Visitor Rt Revd Graham James (*Bishop of Norwich*)

Founded 1855. Augustinian Visitation Rule.

Work and Houses at Ditchingham:
The Convent (*as above*)
Lavinia House, Ditchingham
Guests, retreats and spiritual direction
Tel: 01986 892840

All Hallows House, Rouen Rd, Norwich NR1 1QT
Tel: 01603 624738
Guests, retreats and spiritual direction

All Hallows Country Hospital and All Hallows Nursing Home: the hospital and nursing home have now been combined under the management of the All Hallows Health Care Trust.

Ditchingham Day Nursery: the childcare provision has transferred ownership and is now managed by The Benjamin Foundation.

COMMUNITY OF ST ANDREW

St Mary's Convent and Nursing Home, Burlington Lane, Chiswick W4 2QE
Tel: 020 8747 0001 (Mother Lillian)
Tel: 020 7221 4604 (Sr Teresa)
email: teresajoan@btinternet.com
Superior Revd Mother Lillian csa
Visitor Rt Revd Richard Chartres (*Bishop of London*)
Founded 1861. Full membership of the Community consists of professed sisters who are Deaconesses or Distinctive Deacons or Priests. Present number is five.

The fundamental ministry is the offering of prayer and worship, evangelism and pastoral work now through retirement ministries.

The Community celebrated its 150th anniversary at St Andrewstide 2011 with the (private) publication of *The Deaconess Community of St Andrew 1861–2011*, 225pp and photos (available from Sr Teresa).

The 150th anniversary of the reception of Deaconess Licence No.1 by Elizabeth Ferard, on 18 July 1862 was celebrated by members of the Deaconess Order of the Church of England at Lambeth Palace in July 2012.

COMMUNITY OF ST CLARE

St Mary's Convent, Freeland, Witney, Oxon. OX29 8AJ
Tel: 01993 881225
email: damien@oscfreeland.co.uk
Web: www.oscfreeland.org.uk

Abbess Sister Damien osc

Bishop Protector Rt Revd Stephen Cottrell (*Bishop of Chelmsford*)

Founded in 1950 to be the Second Order of the Society of St Francis, we are a small community of women living a vowed, contemplative, enclosed life. Like St Clare, our life/work is dependence on God in prayer. We pray for the whole world and in particular for our sisters and brothers after the example of Francis and Clare. We have a determination for a simple life, earning our living by the production of Communion wafers and by designing and printing greetings cards. We have a large garden where we grow vegetables, fruit and flowers and look after hens.

We share our life in hospitality to those who visit or come to stay at the Old Parsonage, and all who wish may come to our chapel for the daily celebration of the Eucharist and four-fold Office.

COMMUNITY OF ST DENYS

c/o Stephen Hutton, Clerk to the Trustees, 59 Barley Close, Warminster BA12 9LX
Tel: 01985 216486
email: communitystdenys@gmail.com

Leader Mrs June Watt (oblate)

Visitor Rt Revd Nicholas Holtam (*Bishop of Salisbury*)

Christian mission at home and overseas through prayer and intercession, mission work and by giving counsel and help where needed through the award of charitable grants for religious or educational purposes.

COMMUNITY OF ST FRANCIS

Founded in 1905, the sisters of the First Order of the Society of St Francis, in the European Province (now including a Region in South Korea) and in the Province of the Americas, seek to live the gospel for today through lives of prayer, study and work. Prayer, together and alone, with the Eucharist having a central place, is the heart of each house and each sister's life. Six sisters are priests, and three live the solitary life. Study nurtures each sister's spiritual life and enables and enriches ministries. Work (voluntary or salaried) includes practical domestic tasks and a wide range of ministries. Currently these include hospitality, spiritual direction, leading retreats and quiet days, preaching, parish work and missions, cathedral chaplaincy, speaking and writing, administration, teaching computer skills, being a presence in poor urban areas, work with deaf and blind people, befriending and support of people with particular vulnerabilities, ministerial development and mentoring, running an after school project for children, assisting in care for homeless people and providing a short-term residential facility for families of those with a life-threatening illness. In all this the sisters seek to follow Christ in the footsteps of Francis and Clare of Assisi, and in the spirit of humility, love and joy.

Minister General Sister Helen Julian csf, Budby, Newark
email: ministergeneralcsf@franciscans.org.uk

Minister Provincial, European Sister Sue csf, Southwark
Tel: 020 7928 7121
email: ministercsf@franciscans.org.uk
Web: www.franciscans.org.uk

Bishop Protector Rt Revd Stephen Cottrell (*Bishop of Chelmsford*)

Houses St Alphege Clergy House, Pocock St, London SE1 0BJ   *Tel:* 020 7898 8912
email: southwarkcsf@franciscans.org.uk

San Damiano, 38 Drury Street, Metheringham, Lincoln LN4 3EZ
Tel: 01526 321115
email: metheringhamcsf@franciscans.org.uk

The Vicarage, 11 St Mary's Rd, Plaistow, London E13 9AE   *Tel:* 020 8552 4019
email: stmaryscssf@franciscans.org.uk

St Francis House, 113 Gillott Rd, Birmingham B16 0ET   *Tel:* 0121 454 8302
email: birminghamcsf@franciscans.org.uk

St Matthew's House, 25 Kamloops Crescent, Leicester LE1 2HX   *Tel:* 0116 253 9158
email: leicestercsf@franciscans.org.uk

Korean Region: 44–23, Suryu-gil, Haepyeong-myeon, Gumi-si, Gyeongsangbukdo 730–872, Republic of Korea
Tel: 054 451 2317; *email:* csfkorea@gmail.com

Deputy Bishop Protector for Korean Region Rt Revd Onesimus Park (*Bishop of Busan*)

Minister Provincial, Province of the Americas Sister Pamela Clare CSF, St Francis House, 3743 Cesar Chavez St, San Francisco CA 94110-4316 USA
email: pamelaclarecsf@aol.com
Web: www.communitystfrancis.org

Bishop Protector Rt Revd Bevi Edna (Nedi) Rivera, (*Bishop of Eastern Oregon*)

COMMUNITY OF ST JOHN BAPTIST
c/o Ripon College, Cuddesdon, Oxford OX44 9EX   *Tel:* 01865 877400
email: enquiries@rcc.ac.uk

Community Leader Sr Jane Olive CSJB

Visitor Rt Revd John Pritchard (*Bishop of Oxford*)

Chaplain Very Revd Lister Tonge (*Dean of Monmouth*)

Founded 1852 to honour and worship Almighty God and to serve him in works of charity. Undertakes mission and parish work, group quiet days, private retreats and spiritual direction.

COMMUNITY OF ST JOHN THE DIVINE
St John's House, 652 Alum Rock Rd, Birmingham, W Midlands B8 3NS   *Tel:* 0121 327 4174
email: csjdivine@btconnect.com
Web: www.csjd.org.uk

Leaders of the Community Sister Christine CSJD and Sister Margaret Angela CSJD

Visitor Rt Revd David Urquhart (*Bishop of Birmingham*)

The Community was founded in 1848. The underpinning of our life and work is a spirituality based on St John the Apostle of Love. Today, as we continue to welcome people to test their vocation in the Religious Life, we have considered the challenge of change. The small core group of the Community has become the centre for a growing circle of Associates and Alongsiders who share much of our life. Our vision is to be a centre of prayer within the diocese, to exercise a ministry of hospitality to individuals and groups, to offer a ministry of spiritual accompaniment and to be open to new ways in which God might use us here, for example building friendships with our Muslim neighbours.

COMMUNITY OF ST LAURENCE
Convent of St Laurence, 4a Westgate, Southwell, Nottinghamshire NG25 0JH   *Tel:* 01636 815005

Warden Very Revd David Leaning
Founded 1874 in Norwich and moved to Belper in Derbyshire in 1877. Moved to Southwell in September 2001. Accommodation for visitors is available in the Sacrista Prebend Retreat House next door. (*See* **Retreat Houses** page 218.)

COMMUNITY OF ST MARY THE VIRGIN
St Mary's Convent, Challow Rd, Wantage, Oxon. OX12 9DJ   *Tel:* 01235 763141
email: conventsisters@csmv.co.uk
guestwing@csmv.co.uk
Web: www.csmv.co.uk

Superior Mother Winsome CSMV

Visitor Rt Revd John Pritchard

The Community of St Mary the Virgin (CSMV) was founded in 1848. We are called to respond to our vocation in the spirit of the Blessed Virgin Mary: 'Behold, I am the handmaid of the Lord. Let it be to me according to your word.' Our common life is centred in the worship of God through the Eucharist, the daily Office and personal prayer, from which all else flows. The strong musical tradition of CSMV continues to enrich our worship. The work of the Community is inspired by Mary's words, 'Whatever He says to you, do it.' It may take the form of outgoing ministry in neighbourhood and parish or in living alongside those in inner city areas. For others, it will be expressed in hospitality, spiritual direction, preaching and retreat giving, or in creative work in studio and press. Sisters also live and work among the elderly at St Katharine's House, a large Care Home for the elderly in Wantage. An extensive new area of mission has opened up for us since the launch of our interactive website in September 2009. In addition to a daily update, we offer weekly meditations and retreats on line. We are able to receive requests for prayer through our website, and we also stream all our Offices live. The Community has had a share in the nurturing and training of a small indigenous Community in Madagascar, and continues to maintain links with the sisters there. The Community also lived and worked in India and South Africa for many years. Involvement with both these countries remains through 'Wantage Overseas'. Our links with South Africa are also maintained by groups of Oblates and Associates living there. There are larger groups of Oblates and Associates in England. At St Mary's Convent there is a Guest Wing for those who wish to spend time in rest, retreat and silence within the setting of a religious community.

366 High St, Smethwick B66 3PD
Tel: 0121 558 0094
email: smethwick.sisters@btinternet.com

116 Seymour Rd, Harringay, London N8 0BG
Tel and *Fax:* 020 8348 3477
email: wanatage-os@fireflyuk.net

St Katharine's House, Ormond Rd, Wantage OX12 8EA (Home for the Elderly)
Tel: 01235 767380
email: sisters.stkatharines@gmail.com

COMMUNITY OF ST PETER
St Columba's House, Maybury Hill, Woking, Surrey GU22 8AB   *Tel:* 01483 750739
email: reverendmother@stpetersconvent.co.uk
Web: stcolumbashouse.org.uk

Superior Mother Lucy Clare csp

Visitor Rt Revd David Walker (*Bishop of Manchester*)

Founded in 1861 for mission work and nursing. The Sisters are dispersed, but meet together at least monthly. The sisterhood is now five in number. Reverend Mother Lucy Clare lives at Church of England Supported Housing, Fosbrooke House, Flat 33, 8 Clifton Drive, Lytham, Lancs FY8 5RQ. Her responsibility is to keep in touch with sisters regularly by email or telephone or other modern technology. Sister Angela lives in Woking and works within St Columba's House retreat and conference centre. Sisters Margaret Paul, Rosamond and Georgina Ruth live at St Mary's Nursing Home and Convent, Burlington Lane, Chiswick, London.

COMMUNITY OF ST PETER, HORBURY
St Peter's Convent, 14 Spring End Road, Horbury, Wakefield, West Yorkshire WF4 6DB
Tel: 01924 272181
email: stpetersconvent@btconnect.com

Reverend Mother Mother Robina csph

Visitor Rt Revd Stephen Platten

Benedictine in spirit. Undertakes a variety of pastoral ministries and retreat work.

COMMUNITY OF THE COMPANIONS OF JESUS THE GOOD SHEPHERD
c/o Ripon College, Cuddesdon, Oxford OX44 9EX   *Tel:* 01865 877400
email: enquiries@rcc.ac.uk

Superior Sister Ann Verena cjgs

Visitor Rt Revd Dominic Walker ogs

Founded 1920. Undertakes work with the elderly, lay and ordained ministry training, quiet days, retreats and spiritual direction.

COMMUNITY OF THE HOLY CROSS
Holy Cross Convent, Highfields, Nottingham Rd, Costock, Nr Loughborough LE12 6XE
Tel: 01509 852761
Fax: 01509 853051
Web: www.holycrosschc.org.uk
email: mother@holycrosschc.org.uk / sisters@holycrosschc.org.uk

Mother Superior Revd Mother Mary Luke chc

Visitor Rt Revd Dr David Hope

Founded in 1857 for mission work but later adopted the Rule of St Benedict. All the work, centred on the daily celebration of the Divine Office and the Eucharist, is done within the Enclosure.

The Sisters contribute articles on spirituality and Christian unity to various publications and disseminate these via their website and Facebook page. A variety of prayer and greeting cards are also produced by the Sisters. The Community provides for Quiet Days for individuals and groups, and there is limited residential accommodation for those wishing to make longer retreats.

COMMUNITY OF THE HOLY NAME
Convent of the Holy Name, Morley Rd, Oakwood, Derby DE21 4QZ   *Tel:* 01332 671716
Fax: 01332 669712
email: bursarsoffice@tiscali.co.uk
web: www.chnderby.org

Superior Sr Pauline Margaret chn

Visitor Rt Revd John Inge

Founded 1865. Undertakes mission and retreat work. Guests received.

Branch Houses
64 Allexton Gardens, Welland Estate, Peterborough PE1 4UW   *Tel:* 01733 352077
St John's Rectory, St John's Rd, Longsight,
Manchester M13 0WU   *Tel:* 0161 224 4336

Overseas
Lesotho Convent of the Holy Name, PO Box 22,
Ficksburg 9730, RSA   *Tel:* 00266 22400249

Zululand Convent of the Holy Name, P/B 806,
Melmoth 3835, RSA   *Tel:* 00273 54502892

COMMUNITY OF THE SACRED PASSION
Mother House: Convent of the Sacred Passion, 22
Buckingham Rd, Shoreham-by-Sea, W Sussex
BN43 5UB   *Tel:* 01273 453807
          email: communitysp@yahoo.co.uk

Superior Mother Philippa CSP

Visitor Rt Revd Ian Brackley (*Bishop of Dorking*)

Founded 1911. An order which combines prayer
and mission work in varying forms. In England
the sisters continue their life of prayer at the
Mother House and a house in Clapham. Their
active work is a response to the needs of the
people among whom they live and so keeps
developing. The Community withdrew from
Tanzania in June 1991, leaving behind a community of more than ninety Tanzanian women
known as the Community of St Mary. This
community is still given support by CSP, as is
the Kwamkono Polio Hostel which was founded
by CSP.

COMMUNITY OF THE SERVANTS OF THE CROSS
Rustington Hall, Station Road, Rustington
BN16 3AY   *Tel:* 01903 777501
Sadly Mother Angela died earlier this year and
there is only Sister Jane left.
Visitor Rt Revd Martin Warner (*Bishop of
Chichester*)
Warden and Chaplain Revd J. Lyon

Augustinian Rule. The sisters are now in
retirement.

COMMUNITY OF THE SERVANTS OF THE WILL OF GOD
See **Mixed Communities** page 247.

COMMUNITY OF THE SISTERS OF THE CHURCH
St Michael's Convent, 56 Ham Common,
Richmond, Surrey TW10 7JH   *Tel:* 020 8940 8711
          email: info@sistersofthechurch.org.uk
          Web: www.sistersofthechurch.org.uk

UK Provincial Sister Susan CSC
          email: provincial@sistersofthechurch.org.uk

Visitor Rt Revd Christopher Chessun (*Bishop of
Southwark*)
Founded 1870 and has a modern rule, based on
the original, expressing a life rooted in prayer
and worship, which flows into an active ministry
through hospitality, pastoral and social justice
work, spiritual direction and counselling.
Other Houses in the UK
82 Ashley Rd, St Paul's Bristol BS6 5NT
          Tel: 0117 941 3268
112 St Andrew's Rd North, St Annes-on-Sea,
Lancs. FY8 2JQ   *Tel:* 01253 728016
10 Furness Rd, West Harrow, Middx HA2 0RL
          Tel: 020 8423 3780

Novitiate
St Gabriel's, 27a Dial Hill Rd, Clevedon, North
Somerset BS21 7HL   *Tel:* 01275 544 471

Main Houses of Overseas Provinces
Sister Linda Mary CSC, Mother Superior and
Australia Provincial

29 Lika Drive, Kempsey, NSW 2440, Australia
send all correspondence to: PO Box 1105, Glebe,
NSW2037, Australia
          email: cscaust@hotmail.com

Sister Margaret CSC, Canadian Provincial
CSC c/o Sr Margaret Hayward, 1003/6 John
Street, Oakville, ON L6K 3T1
          email: sistersofthechurch@sympatico.ca

Sister Kathleen CSC, Solomon Islands Provincial,
Box 510, Honiara, Solomon Islands
          email: kkapei@yahoo.com.au

COMMUNITY OF THE SISTERS OF THE LOVE OF GOD
Convent of the Incarnation, Fairacres, Parker St,
Oxford OX4 1TB   *Tel:* 01865 721301
          Fax: 01865 250798
          email: sisters@slg.org.uk
          Guest Sister guests@slg.org.uk
          Web: www.slg.org.uk

Reverend Mother Sister Margaret Theresa SLG

Visitor Rt Revd Michael Lewis (*Bishop of Cyprus
and the Gulf*)

A contemplative community with a strong
monastic tradition founded in 1906, which seeks
to witness to the priority of God and to respond
to the love of God – God's love for us and our
love for God. We believe that we are called to live
a substantial degree of withdrawal, in order to
give ourselves to a spiritual work of prayer
which, beginning and ending in the praise and
worship of God, is essential for the peace and
well-being of the world. Through offering our
lives to God within the Community and through
prayer and daily life together, we seek to deepen
our relationship with Jesus Christ and one

another. The Community has always drawn upon the spirituality of Carmel; life and prayer in silence and solitude is an important dimension in our vocation. The Community also draws from other traditions, and our Rule is not specifically Carmelite. Another important ingredient is an emphasis on the centrality of Divine Office and Eucharist together in choir, inspired partly by the Benedictine way of life.

SLG Press publishes pamphlets on spirituality and prayer.

SLG Press, Convent of the Incarnation, Fairacres, Parker St, Oxford OX4 1TB   *Tel:* 01865 241874
Fax: 01865 241889
email: editor@slgpress.co.uk
Web: www.slgpress.co.uk

ORDER OF THE HOLY PARACLETE
St Hilda's Priory, Sneaton Castle, Whitby YO21 3QN   *Tel:* 01947 602079
Fax: 01947 820854
email: ohppriorywhitby@btinternet.com
Web: www.ohpwhitby.org

Prioress Sister Dorothy Stella OHP

Visitor Most Revd John Sentamu (*Archbishop of York*)
Founded in 1915 and based on the Rule of St Benedict. Main undertaking: prayer, pastoral work, retreats, conferences, missions and parish work.

Residential Conference Centre Sneaton Castle Centre, Whitby YO21 3QN   *Tel:* 01947 600051
Fax: 01947 603490
email: sneaton@globalnet.co.uk
Web: www.sneatoncastle.co.uk
Accommodation (100 beds) for large and small groups for parish activities, conferences and school visits. Day visits, including tea, talk and tours.

Branch Houses
St Oswald's Pastoral Centre, Woodlands Drive, Sleights, Whitby YO21 1RY   *Tel:* 01947 810496
Fax: 01947 810759
email: ohpstos@globalnet.co.uk
IGRs, retreats, parish groups, individual guests.

1 Minster Court, York YO1 7JJ
Tel: 01904 557276
email: sistersohp@googlemail.com
Work in York Minster.

3 Acaster Lane, Bishopthorpe YO23 2SA
Tel: 01904 777294
email: ohpbishopthorpe@archbishopofyork.org
On the staff of Bishopthorpe Palace.

All Saints House, South Avenue, Dormanstown TS10 5LL   *Tel:* 01642 486424
email: sisteranita@btinternet.com

Work in parishes and schools.

Chaplain Revd Graham Weir

Overseas
Convent of the Holy Spirit, PO Box AH 9375, Ahinsan, Kumasi, Ashanti, Ghana
Tel: 00233 242 203 432
*email:*abbaotoo498@yahoo.com

Eye clinic, pastoral work, craft and sewing.

Anglican Sisters OHP, Resurrection House, PO Box 596, Sunyani, Brong Ahafo Ghana
Tel: 00233 243 7068
email: nyamebekyere2010@yahoo.com

Fostering vocations, Bishop's Secretary, wafer making, vocational school.

PRIORY OF OUR LADY, WALSINGHAM
Priory of Our Lady, Walsingham, Norfolk NR22 6ED   *Tel:* 01328 820340 (Reverend Mother);
01328 820901 (Sisters and Guest Sister)

Superior Vacancy

Sister Administrator Sister Mary Angela CSWG
email: bursar@prioryofourlady.uk.com

Visitor Rt Revd Peter Wheatley
Autonomous house of the Society of St Margaret. Sisters are involved in the ministry of healing and reconciliation in the Shrine, the local parishes and the wider Church. They are also available to pilgrims, visitors and others, and offer spiritual direction. They work in the Shrine, the Shrine Shop and the Welcome Centre, and join in the life of the village and local parishes whenever possible. Short retreats and quiet days can be arranged on request. The Guest House offers periods of rest, relaxation and retreat. All bookings to be made through the Guest Sister.

ST SAVIOUR'S PRIORY
18 Queensbridge Rd, London E2 8NS
Tel: 020 7739 6775 (Guest bookings)
020 7739 9976 (Sisters)
email: ssmpriory@aol.com
Web: www.stsaviourspriory.org.uk

Superior Revd Sr Judith Blackburn SSM

Visitor Rt Revd Jonathan Clark

Autonomous convent of the Society of St Margaret, working as staff members (lay or ordained) in various parishes, dance workshops, complementary therapy, with the homeless, etc.; retreats and individual spiritual direction. The Priory has a few guest rooms and facilities for individual private retreats as well as excellent facilities for small group meetings.

SISTERS OF BETHANY

7 Nelson Rd, Southsea PO5 2AR
Tel: 023 9283 3498
email: ssb@sistersofbethany.org.uk
Web: www.sistersofbethany.org.uk

Superior Mother Rita-Elizabeth, ssb

Visitor Rt Revd Trevor Willmott (*Bishop of Dover and Bishop in Canterbury*)

Founded 1866 for hospitality, retreat work and prayer for Christian Unity. The Sisters are available for leading quiet days and retreats, as spiritual directors, and also to give talks on prayer. People are welcome to come individually or as groups to spend time in silence and prayer. It is possible to accommodate a few residential guests, or groups of up to 24 for the day. A reference is required for guests applying to stay for the first time.

SISTERS OF CHARITY

83 Fore Street, Plympton, Plymouth PL7 2HP
Tel: 01752 336112
email: plymptonsisters@gmail.com

Superior Revd Mother Elizabeth Mary sc

Visitor Vacancy
Founded 1869. The Rule is based on that of St Vincent de Paul. We assist as required in parish work and in intercessory prayer, and maintain a nursing home.
Morning Prayer 9 am. Most convenient time to telephone 5.30–7.00 pm.

Branch Houses
St Vincent's Nursing Home, Plympton, Plymouth PL7 1NE
Tel: 01752 336205
Carmel, 7a Gress, Isle of Lewis HS2 0NB
Tel: 01851 820734

SOCIETY OF ALL SAINTS SISTERS OF THE POOR

All Saints Convent, 15A Magdalen Road, Oxford OX4 1RW
Tel: 01865 249127
email: admin@socallss.co.uk
Guests' email: guestsister@socallss.co.uk
Web: asspoxford.org

Community Leader Sister Jean Raphael assp

Visitor Rt Revd Bill Ind

Founded in London 1851. Works of the Society: St John's Residential Home for the Elderly, St Mary's Rd, Oxford OX4 1QE
Tel: 01865 247725
email: admin@st-johns-home.org

Guest House (single, twin and double accommodation available). Also conference facilities for groups of up to about 12, weekdays, daytime only. Enquiries regarding visits, private retreats and conferences welcomed. Telephone as shown above for All Saints' Convent.

The Society is associated with:
Helen and Douglas House; The Porch Steppin' Stone Centre.

SOCIETY OF ST MARGARET

St Margaret's Convent, Hooke Hall, 250 High St, Uckfield RN22 1EN
Tel: 01825 766808
Fax: 01825 763474
email: egmotherssm@hotmail.com

Superior Sister Cynthia Clare ssm

Visitor Rt Revd Martin Warner (*Bishop of Chichester*)

Founded 1855 and undertakes nursing and parish work. Sisters available for spiritual guidance. A residential home for elderly retired ladies and nursing home for those needing full-time nursing care.

Branch House St Mary's Convent and Nursing Home, Burlington Lane, Chiswick, London W4 2QE (guest house for elderly ladies and nursing home for geriatric and handicapped ladies)
Tel: 020 8994 4641
Fax: 020 8995 9796
Superior Sister Jennifer Anne ssm

Visitor Rt Revd Martin Warner (*Bishop of Chichester*)

Overseas St Margaret's Convent (*semi-autonomous*), 157 St Michael's Rd, Polwatte, Colombo 3, Sri Lanka

A home for the aged and a retreat house.

Sister Superior Sister Chandrani ssm
Tel: 00 94 11 2320692
Visitor Rt Revd Dhiloraj Canagasaby (*Bishop of Colombo*)

Branch House
St John's Home, 133 Galle Rd, Moratuwa, Sri Lanka (children's home).
Tel: 00 94 11 2645304

Independent Convents of the Society St Margaret
St Saviour's Priory, 18 Queensbridge Rd, London E2 8NS
Leader Sister Judith ssm
Tel: 020 7739 6775
email: ssmpriory@aol.com
Priory of Our Lady, Walsingham, Norfolk, NR22 6ED
Superior Vacancy
Tel: 01328 820340

St Margaret's Convent, 50 Harden Hill Road, Box C, Duxbury MA 02331-0605, USA

Superior Sister Adele Marie ssm

Tel: 00 1 781 934 9477
email: ssmconvent@ssmbos.com

SOCIETY OF THE PRECIOUS BLOOD

Burnham Abbey, Lake End Rd, Taplow, Maidenhead, Berks. SL6 0PW   Tel: 01628 604080
email: burnhamabbey@btinternet.com
Web: www.burnhamabbey.org

Superior The Revd Mother spb

Visitor Rt Revd Stephen Cottrell (*Bishop of Chelmsford*)

Founded 1905 and based on Rule of St Augustine. Contemplative and exists for the purpose of perpetual intercession for the Church and for the world.

SOCIETY OF THE SACRED CROSS

Tymawr Convent, Lydart, Monmouth, Gwent NP25 4RN   Tel: 01600 860244
email: tymawrconvent@btinternet.com
Web: www. tymawrconvent.org

Superior Sister Gillian Mary ssc

Visitor Rt Revd Dominic Walker ogs

We are an Anglican Contemplative Community living a life of prayer, based on silence, solitude and learning to live together, under monastic vows. The Daily Offices and other times of shared and private prayer span each day, together with a common life which includes study, recreation and work in the house and grounds of the Convent.

At the heart of the corporate life of the community is the Eucharist and the crucified and risen Lord is the focus of its life and the source of the power to live it.

Our purpose is to pray, and to offer an environment of prayer and hospitality to guests, visitors, those on retreat, parishes and clergy. We welcome people from all denominations and those who are simply seeking to widen their spiritual horizons.

The Tymawr Community is at the centre of the family of The Society of the Sacred Cross – people who link in with our life through prayer, work and mutual support. Some commit to a personal rule of life to form a structure for a life of prayer in their own circumstances.

Our own dedication to a life of prayer includes praying for others and supporting the ministry of other Christians.

If you would like to visit us or to come for a quiet day, or longer, you would be very welcome.

It is possible for men and women, married or single, to experience the contemplative life by living alongside the community and sharing in our work and prayer for periods longer than the usual guest stay. This has proved a very creative and worthwhile experience for many people.

SOCIETY OF THE SACRED MISSION

See **Mixed Communities** page 247.

Mixed Communities

BENEDICTINE COMMUNITY AT MUCKNELL ABBEY

Mucknell Abbey, Mucknell Farm Lane, Stoulton, Worcestershire WR7 9RB   Tel: 01905 345900
email: abbot@mucknellabbey.org.uk

Abbot Rt Revd Stuart Burns osb
email: abbot@mucknellabbey.org.uk

Visitor Rt Revd John Inge

By a common life of prayer, manual work and study the Community tries to create an atmosphere of stillness and silence in which the Community and its guests are enabled to be open and receptive to the presence of God.

While the recitation of the Office and celebration of the Eucharist constitute the principal work of the Community, the ministry of hospitality, the care of the grounds (which comprise a large organic kitchen garden in 40 acres of orchard, meadow and woodland), and the income-generating crafts of incense-making, icon writing and block-mounting provide a variety of manual work for the members of the Community and those guests who wish to share in it.

The monastery seeks to be a place of encounter and reconciliation. The early concern of the Community was to pray for Christian unity, and the Community enjoys links with Baptist, Lutheran, Old Catholic, Orthodox and Roman Catholic communities, and is particularly committed to the furthering of the Covenant between the Church of England and the Methodist Church. This ecumenical concern has broadened to include dialogue with people of other faiths, particularly those with a monastic tradition, and those who are seeking a spiritual way, either within or outside an established religious tradition.

COMMUNITY OF THE SERVANTS OF THE WILL OF GOD

Monastery of the Holy Trinity, Crawley Down, Crawley, W Sussex RH10 4LH   Tel: 01342 712074
email: brother.andrew@cswg.org.uk

Father Superior Revd Fr Colin cswg
Visitor Rt Revd John Hind

Founded 1953 for men (clerical and lay). Women are now received also. Contemplative. Retreats and conferences. The Community has also founded a charitable trust for promoting the Christian tradition of contemplative life and prayer within the Church.

SOCIETY OF ST FRANCIS, THIRD ORDER

One of the three Orders of the Society of St Francis (see also Communities for Men, page 238; Communities for Women, page 240). The Third Order is made up of women and men, lay and ordained, single and married, seeking to live out Franciscan ideals in the ordinary walks of life. There are just under 2000 Tertiaries in the European Province; there are four other Provinces: Africa, the Americas, Australia with Papua New Guinea and East Asia and Aotearoa – New Zealand and Polynesia with Melanesia.

Minister General Ken E. Norian TSSF, 45 Malone Street, Hicksville NY 11801 USA

Tel: +1 917 416 9579
email: ken@tssf.org

Minister Provincial European Province Averil E. Swanton, 11, The Grange, Fleming Way, Exeter EX2 4SB   *Tel:* 01392 430355
email: ministertssf@tssf.org.uk
Web: www.tssf.org.uk

SOCIETY OF THE SACRED MISSION

Founded 1893. A religious community engaged in educational, pastoral and missionary work.
    The Society is divided into Provinces:
Web: www.sacredmission.org

Province of Europe
Visitor Rt Revd John Pritchard

Provincial Fr Colin Griffiths ssm
The Well, Newport Rd, Willen MK15 9AA
Tel: 01908 300552
email: ssmeprovincial@gmail.com
Houses
St Antony's Priory, 74 Claypath, Durham DH1 1QT   *Tel:* 0191 384 3747
email: info@stantonyspriory.co.uk
The Well, Newport Rd, Willen MK15 9AA
Tel: 01908 242190
email: info@thewellatwillen.org.uk
1 Linford Lane, Milton Keynes, Bucks. MK15 9DL
Tel: 01908 663749

Australian Province
Visitor Rt Revd Garry Weatherill (*Bishop of Ballarat*)
Provincial Fr Christopher Myers ssm
St John's Priory, 14 St John's Street, Adelaide, South Australia 5000
email: ssm.s.province@esc.net.au
Houses
St John's Priory, 14 St John's St, Adelaide, S Australia 5000

Southern African Province
Visitor Most Revd Thabo Makgoba (*Archbishop of Cape Town*)
Provincial Fr Tanki Mofana ssm
St Stephen's, Mohale's Hoek, Lesotho
email: mofanatanki@yahoo.com
Houses
SSM Priory, PO Box 1579, Maseru 100, Lesotho, Southern Africa   *email:* ssmaseru@tlmail.co.ls

Healing of Memories Institute
Fr Michael Lapsley
SSM House, 33 Elgin Rd, Syband Park, Cape Town 7700, RSA
email: michaelssm@gmail

Organizations PART 4

Classified List of Organizations Included in this Section

Animal Welfare
Anglican Society for the Welfare of Animals

Art, Architecture
Art and Christianity Enquiry
Art and Sacred Places
Christian Arts
Church Monuments Society
Ecclesiological Society
Friends of Friendless Churches
York Glaziers' Trust

Bell-ringing
Ancient Society of College Youths
Central Council of Church Bell Ringers
Society of Royal Cumberland Youths

Bible Study
BRF
Bible Society
Lord Wharton's Charity
SASRA
Scripture Union
SGM Lifewords (formerly Scripture Gift Mission International)
Summer Biblical Study in Cambridge

Blind People
Guild of Church Braillists
RNIB (Royal National Institute of Blind People)
St John's Guild

Church Buildings
Friends of Friendless Churches
Greater Churches Network
Marshall's Charity
Vergers, Church of England Guild of

Church Societies – General
Additional Curates Society
Affirming Catholicism
Association of English Cathedrals
Cathedral and Church Shops Association
Cathedral Libraries and Archives Association
Cathedrals Administration and Finance Association
Catholic Group in General Synod
Church of England Flower Arrangers Association
Church Society
Church Union
Churches' Advertising Network
Modern Church
Open Synod Group
Parish and People
Society for the Maintenance of the Faith
Society of the Faith (Inc)
Unitas – The Catholic League

Church Societies – Specific
Anglican Fellowship in Scouting and Guiding
Anglican Mainstream
Association of Diocesan Registry Clerks (Southern Province)
Baptismal Integrity
Christian Evidence Society
CHRISM
Church House Deaneries Group
Church of England Record Society
College of Readers
Community of Aidan and Hilda
Day One Christian Ministries
Diocesan Clergy Chairs' Forum
Ecumenical Society of the Blessed Virgin Mary
Forward in Faith
Foundation for Church Leadership
Guild of St Leonard
Guild of Servants of the Sanctuary
Reform
Royal Martyr Church Union
Society of King Charles the Martyr
Society of Mary
Third Province Movement

Clergy Associations
Anglo-Catholic Ordination Candidates' Fund
Association of Black Clergy
Association of Hospice and Palliative Care Chaplains
Association of Ordinands and Candidates for Ministry
College of Health Care Chaplains
English Clergy Association
Federation of Catholic Priests
Fellowship of Word and Spirit
Industrial Mission Association
Retired Clergy Association
Society of Catholic Priests
Society of Ordained Scientists
Society of the Holy Cross
Unite Clergy and Faith Workers
See also **Professional Groups**

Consultancy
CTBI Christians Abroad
Grubb Institute
Living Stones

Coordinating Bodies
Church of England Evangelical Council
Churches' Funerals Group
Churches' Legislation Advisory Service
Evangelical Alliance
National Association of Diocesan Advisers for Women's Ministry

Religious Education Council of England and Wales
Universities and Colleges Christian Fellowship

Counselling
Anglican Pastoral Care
Lesbian and Gay Christian Movement
Relate
True Freedom Trust

Deaf People
British Deaf Association
Deaf Anglicans Together
Deaf People, Royal Association for
RNID

Defence, Disarmament, Pacifism
Anglican Pacifist Fellowship
Commonwealth War Graves Commission
Council on Christian Approaches to Defence and
   Disarmament

Diocesan Associations *see* pages 311–313

Drama
Actors' Church Union
Radius

Ecumenism
Anglican and Eastern Churches Association
Anglican–Lutheran Society
Churches' Funeral Group
Fellowship of St Alban and St Sergius
International Ecumenical Fellowship
Nikaean Club
Nikaean Ecumenical Trust
Order of Christian Unity
Society of Archbishop Justus Ltd
Society of St Willibrord

Education
Archbishop's Examination in Theology
Association of Church College Trusts
Awareness Foundation
Christian Education
Culham St Gabriel's Trust
Lincoln Theological Institute
Mirfield Centre
RE Today Services
Religious Education Council of England and
   Wales
Royal Alexandra and Albert School
Royal Asylum of St Ann's Society
St George's College, Jerusalem
St Hild and St Bede Trust
SCALA (School Chaplains and Leaders
   Association)
Scripture Union
United Church Schools Trust
Woodard Corporation, the (Woodard Schools)

Evangelism
Church Army
College of Evangelists

Family
CARE
Family Action
Fellowship of St Nicholas
Mothers' Union
St Michael's Fellowship

Finance
Ecclesiastical Insurance Office PLC
Ecumenical Council for Corporate
   Responsibility
Number 1 Trust Fund

Grant-Making Bodies
All Saints Educational Trust
Bristol Clerical Education Society
Church of England Clergy Stipend Trust
Church Pastoral Aid Society Ministers in
   Training Fund
Cleaver Ordination Candidates' Fund
Culham St Gabriel's Trust
Elland Society Ordination Fund
Foundation of St Matthias
Hockerill Educational Foundation
Keswick Hall Trust Charity
Newton's Trust
Ordination Candidate Funds (General)
Pilgrim Trust
Queen Victoria Clergy Fund
Revd Dr George Richards' Charity
Sarum St Michael Educational Charity
St Christopher's Educational Trust
St Luke's College Foundation
St Mary's College Trust
St Peter's Saltley Trust
See also **Welfare**

Health, Healing and Medicine
Acorn Christian Foundation
Association of Hospice and Palliative Care
   Chaplains
Burrswood
Christian Healing Mission
Christian Medical Fellowship
College of Health Care Chaplains
Guild of Health
Guild of Pastoral Psychology
Guild of St Raphael
Harnhill Centre of Christian Healing
Pilsdon at Malling Community
Richmond Fellowship
St Luke's Healthcare for the Clergy

Inter Faith, Religions
Council of Christians and Jews
INFORM
Inter Faith Network
World Congress of Faiths

Internet
COIN: Christians on the Internet
Society of Archbishop Justus Ltd

Organizations

Libraries and Archives *see* pages 313–318

Marriage
Anglican Marriage Encounter
Broken Rites
Relate

Ministry
CHRISM
Diaconal Association of the Church of England
Diakonia
Distinctive Diaconate
MODEM

Ministry, Women
Li Tim-Oi Foundation
WATCH

Mission
Aim International
Bible Society
Christian Witness to Israel
Church's Ministry Among Jewish People
Greenbelt Festivals
London City Mission
Mersey Mission to Seafarers, The
Mission to Seafarers, The
SASRA
Scripture Union
SGM Lifewords (formerly Scripture Gift Mission International)
Society for Promoting Christian Knowledge
Student Christian Movement
Trinitarian Bible Society
Universities and Colleges Christian Fellowship

Mission Overseas
All Nations Christian College
Church Mission Society
Crosslinks
Feed the Minds
Highbury Centre, The
Intercontinental Church Society
Interserve
Korean Mission Partnership
Leprosy Mission
Melanesian Mission
Mid-Africa Ministry
Mozambique and Angola Anglican Association (MANNA)
New England Company
OMF International (UK)
Overseas Bishoprics Fund
Oxford Mission
Papua New Guinea Church Partnership
Reader Missionary Studentship Association
Southern Africa Church Development Trust
Tearfund
Us. (Formerly USPG: Anglicans in World Mission)
World Vision

Music
Archbishops' Certificate in Church Music
Choir Benevolent Fund
Choir Schools Association
Church Music Society
Guild of Church Musicians
Hymn Society of Great Britain and Ireland
Jubilate Group
Morse-Boycott Bursary Fund
Plainsong and Medieval Music Society
Royal College of Organists
Royal School of Church Music

Overseas
Christian Aid
CTBI Christians Abroad
Farnham Castle International Briefing and Conference Centre
United Nations Association (UNA–UK)
Womenaid International
World Vision

Patronage Trusts *see* pages 318–320

Prayer, Meditation, Retreats
Archway
Association for Promoting Retreats
Confraternity of the Blessed Sacrament
Friends of Little Gidding
Guild of All Souls
Guild of St Leonard
Julian Meetings, The
Julian of Norwich, Friends of
Pilsdon at Malling Community
Retreat Association
Sarum College
Servants of Christ the King
Society of Retreat Conductors
Women's World Day of Prayer

Professional Groups
Actors' Church Union
Association of Christian Teachers
Association of Christian Writers
Association of Ordinands and Candidates for Ministry
Christian Arts
Christians at Work
Christians in Library and Information Services
Church House Deaneries' Group
Church Schoolmasters' and School Mistresses' Benevolent Institution
Deans' Conference
Deans' Vergers' Conference
Ecclesiastical Law Society
Guild of Pastoral Psychology
Homes for Retired Clergy
Industrial Mission Association
National Association of Diocesan Advisers in Women's Ministry
Society of Retreat Conductors
Unite Clergy and Faith Workers

Vergers, Church of England Guild of
See also **Clergy Associations**

Publishing, Print Media
BRF
Feed the Minds
Rebecca Hussey's Book Charity
Scripture Union
Society for Promoting Christian Knowledge
Trinitarian Bible Society

Renewal
Keswick Convention
Sharing of Ministries Abroad (SOMA)

Research
Arthur Rank Centre
CARE
Centre for the Study of Christianity and
    Sexuality
Christian Research
Churches' Fellowship for Psychical and
    Spiritual Studies
Latimer Trust
Rural Theology Association
St George's House, Windsor
Urban Theology Unit
William Temple Foundation

Rural Affairs
Arthur Rank Centre
Rural Theology Association

Scholarship and Science
Alcuin Club
Canterbury and York Society
Christian Evidence Society
Ecclesiastical Law Society
Faith and Thought
Henry Bradshaw Society
Latimer Trust
National Archives, The
Philip Usher Memorial Fund
Pusey House
Society for Liturgical Study
Society for Old Testament Study
Society of Ordained Scientists
Summer Biblical Study in Cambridge

Social Concern
Age UK
Changing Attitude
Christians on the Left (formerly the Christian
    Socialist Movement)
Church Housing Trust
English Churches Housing Group
Lesbian and Gay Christian Movement
Livability
Mediawatch–uk
National Council for Social Concern
Order of Christian Unity
Pilsdon at Malling Community

St Pancras and Humanist Housing Association
Samaritans

Training
Anglican Marriage Encounter
Association of Church Fellowships
Bridge Pastoral Foundation
Christian Education
Christians at Work
College of Preachers
Girls Friendly Society in England and Wales
Industrial Christian Fellowship
Paradox Ministries
RE Today Services
Student Christian Movement
William Temple Foundation

Travel, Pilgrimage
Accueil, Rencontre, Communauté UK
British Isles and Eire Airport Chaplains'
    Network
Cathedrals Plus
Journeying
Walsingham, Shrine of Our Lady of

Welfare
Almshouse Association
Beauchamp Community
Bromley and Sheppard's Colleges
Came's Charity for Clergymen's Widows
Catch 22 (formerly Rainer)
Church of England Soldiers', Sailors' and
    Airmen's Clubs
Church of England Soldiers', Sailors' and
    Airmen's Housing Association
Church Schoolmasters' and School Mistresses'
    Benevolent Institution
Church Welfare Association
College of St Barnabas
Community Housing and Therapy
Compassionate Friends, The
Corporation of the Sons of the Clergy
Diocesan Institutions of Chester, Manchester,
    Liverpool and Blackburn
Elizabeth Finn Care
Family Action
Frances Ashton Charity
Friends of the Clergy Corporation
Friends of the Elderly
Homes for Retired Clergy
Keychange
Langley House Trust
Livability
Pyncombe Charity
Revd Dr George Richards' Charity
St Michael's Fellowship
Samaritans
Seamen's Friendly Society of St Paul
Society for the Assistance of Ladies in
    Reduced Circumstances
Society for the Relief of Poor Clergymen
Society of Mary and Martha

Together (formerly MACA – Mental After Care Association)
YMCA
Young Women's Trust

Worship
Alcuin Club
Praxis
Prayer Book Society

Youth
Accueil, Rencontre, Communauté UK
Barnardo's
Boys' Brigade
Campaigners England and Wales
Catch 22 (formerly Rainer)

Children's Society
Church Lads' and Church Girls' Brigade
Fellowship of St Nicholas
Frontier Youth Trust
Girlguiding UK
Girls' Brigade
Girls Friendly Society in England and Wales
Lee Abbey Household Communities
Lee Abbey International Students' Club
St Christopher's Fellowship
Scout Association
Shaftesbury Homes and 'Arethusa'
Urban Saints (formerly Crusaders)
William Temple House

ORGANIZATIONS

The following list of societies and organizations with importance for the Church of England includes many that are specifically Anglican, others that are inter-denominational, and others without religious affiliation.

The inclusion of an organization is for the purposes of information and is not to be taken as implying acceptance of the objects of the organization by the Editor and Publishers of the *Year Book* or by the General Synod.

A classified list of organizations is provided in the preceding pages. **Diocesan Associations** (in support of overseas provinces and dioceses), **Libraries and Archives**, and **Patronage Trusts** are grouped together at the end of the section. *See also* Part 3 (General Information).

Accueil, Rencontre, Communaute UK (ARC UK)

ARC UK is a charity that organizes summer projects in which young people from across Europe give guided tours in their native language to visitors to churches. In so doing we seek to turn tourists into pilgrims through devotional tours in which visitors have the chance to engage, question and wonder. Our projects aim to enable churches in their ministry of welcome and education, ecumenical links and youth involvement. ARC UK is part of a network of associated organizations which organizes such projects throughout Europe. We are always interested to hear from those who might like to participate on one of our projects, or churches who might be interested in hosting a project. We are supported in our work by our Patron, the Bishop of Southwark, the Rt Revd Christopher Chessun. *President:* Nik Myers. *Secretary:* Matt Cooper. *Recruitment Officer:* Eleanor Perkins. *Treasurer:* Matthew Howson

Tel: 07817 830 244 (Mobile)
email: president.arcuk@gmail.com
Web: www.encounterarc.org.uk

Acorn Christian Foundation

Founded originally as the Acorn Christian Healing Trust in 1983 by Bishop Morris Maddocks and his wife Anne to see the Church and nation renewed in the service of Christ the Healer, believing that every person has the right to receive the best care and attention that will enable them to grow into wholeness. Acorn offers all Christian churches a variety of teaching and training resources in Christian healing. Many of these are conducted at Whitehill Chase, Acorn's resource centre in Hampshire, where a weekly open day is held every Tuesday (except August) in conjunction with a service of healing. Quiet Days are held bi-monthly, normally on Thursdays, and include three devotional talks and a midday service with the opportunity for personal prayer and reflection. 'Deeper Healing Days' are also run bi-monthly and these are days of prayer for inner healing concluding with a communion service. The well-established Christian Listener courses range from a short introductory unit through to a twelve-session course, taught by trained tutors. There are 500 Acorn trained voluntary tutors throughout the country who teach listening skills to local church members. They in turn offer these resources in their church, home, workplace, local schools and wider community. Acorn has identified priority listening areas for rural and inner city deprived areas, a schools programme for youth, listening to Aids in Africa and reconciliation in Northern Ireland. Whitehill Chase is also available as a retreat centre and for church groups to hold meetings and conferences. Registered Charity no. 1080011. *Patron:* The Archbishop of Canterbury. *Director:* Revd Dr Russ Parker, Whitehill Chase, High St, Bordon, GU35 0AP

Tel: 01420 478121
Fax: 01420 478122
email: info@acornchristian.org
Web: www.acornchristian.org

Actors' Church Union

Founded 1899, members and associates serve those engaged in the performing arts through their interest, their action – often in association with other related bodies – and their prayers. Additionally, more than two hundred honorary chaplains serve all members of the profession in theatres, studios and schools at home and overseas. As well as spiritual counsel and practical advice, material help is given when possible. Through the Children's Charity, for example, funds are available for theatrical parents facing difficulties with the costs of their children's education. *President:* Rt Revd Jack Nicholls. *Senior Chaplain:* Revd Lindsay Meader, St Paul's Church, Bedford St, Covent Garden, London, WC2E 9ED *Tel and Fax:* 020 7240 0344

email: actorschurchunion@gmail.com
Web: www.actorschurchunion.org

Additional Curates Society

Founded in 1837 to help maintain additional curates in poor and populous parishes and especially in new areas. The Society also fosters vocations to the priesthood. *General Secretary:* Revd Darren Smith. *Chairman:* Canon J. Winston. *Vice Chair:* Rt Revd A. Robinson. *Treasurer:* Revd M.

Lane, Gordon Browning House, 8 Spitfire Rd, Birmingham, B24 9PB   *Tel:* 0121 382 5533
Fax: 0121 382 6999
email: info@additionalcurates.co.uk
Web: www.additionalcurates.co.uk

Affirming Catholicism

A movement within the Church of England and the Anglican Communion, formed in 1990. 'The object of the Foundation shall be the advancement of education in the doctrines and the historical development of the Church of England and the Churches of the wider Anglican Communion, as held by those professing to stand within the catholic tradition' (extracted from the Trust Deed). Its purposes are to promote theological thinking about the contemporary implications of Catholic faith and order; to further the spiritual growth and development of clergy and laity; to organize or support lectures, conferences and seminars; to publish or support books, tracts, journals and other educational material; and to provide resources for local groups meeting for purposes of study and discussion. *Chair:* Revd Dr Rosemarie Mallett. *Administrator:* Mark Perrett, St Mary's Parish Office, Stoke Newington Church St, London, N19 9ES   *Tel:* 079 9185 1722
email: administrator@affirmingcatholicism.org.uk
Web: www.affirmingcatholicism.org.uk

Age UK (formerly Age Concern England)

Age UK cares about all older people and believes later life should be fulfilling and enjoyable. For too many this is impossible. As the leading charitable movement in the UK concerned with ageing and older people, Age UK finds effective ways to change that situation. Nationally, we take a lead role in campaigning, parliamentary work, policy analysis, research, specialist information and advice provision, publishing and training in the care of older people. Where possible we enable older people to solve problems themselves, providing as much or as little support as they need. Locally, Age UK provides community-based services such as lunch clubs, day centres and home visiting. These services are made possible through the work of many thousands of volunteers. Innovative programmes promote healthier lifestyles and provide older people with opportunities to give the experience of a lifetime back to their communities. Age UK is dependent on donations and legacies. The helpline is open seven days a week from 8 a.m. to 7 p.m. *Director General:* Mr Gordon Lishman CBE, Astral House, 1268 London Rd, London, SW16 4ER   *Tel:* 0800 169 6565 (Helpline)
020 8765 7200 (Reception)
email: contact@ageuk.org.uk
Web: www.ageuk.org.uk

AIM International

AIM International is the largest evangelical Christian mission agency with purely an African focus, working in more than twenty countries in Africa and ministering to the African diaspora living around the world. Founded in 1895, it has nearly a thousand mission partners working together to see Christ-centred churches established amongst all Africa's peoples. With a priority for church planting, AIM International is also involved in long- and short-term ministries of leadership training, education and healthcare. *International Director:* Dr Luke Herrin. *UK Director:* Revd Andrew Chard MA, AIM International, Halifax Place, Nottingham, NG1 1QN
Tel: 0115 983 8120
email: admin.eu@aimint.net
Web: www.aimint.org

Alcuin Club

Founded in 1897 to promote the study of liturgy, the Alcuin Club has a long and proud record of publishing both works of scholarship and practical manuals. Publications include collections, tracts and a new series of liturgy guides designed to accompany Common Worship. It also publishes, in conjunction with GROW, a series of Joint Liturgical Studies which has won wide acclaim. Members pay an annual subscription and receive new titles on publication. *President:* Rt Revd Michael Perham. *Chairman:* Canon Donald Gray. *Treasurer:* Mr John Collins. *Secretary:* Revd Gordon Jeanes. *Editorial Secretary:* Revd Dr Ben Gordon Taylor, 5 Saffron St, Royston, Herts, SG8 9TR   *Tel:* 01763 248678
email: alcuinclub@gmail.com
Web: www.alcuinclub.org.uk

All Nations Christian College

All Nations came into existence in 1971 following the merger of three Bible colleges. Whilst interdenominational in character, around 20 per cent of its students are members of the Anglican Communion. The College exists to train students primarily for cross-cultural ministries. With up to 120 international students of about 30 nationalities, as well as a respected international team of tutors, the community studying and socializing life is vibrant and challenging. Students can follow a ten-week (en route), one-year or two-year biblical and intercultural studies course with a profound missiological emphasis. In addition to the popular Cert HE, Dip HE and BA (Hons) programmes, there are now validated specialist pathways in the Arts, Leadership and Development Studies. The College also offers a thirteen-week online programme (en route explore) and a five-day short course for groups heading out on to short term mission trips (en route express). This can be accessed as a residential or on line course. The All Nations Masters programme in Contemporary Mission Studies was the first to be taught in the UK and has attracted leaders from around the world. There are five exit awards to choose from: MA in Contemporary Mission Studies, MA in Development

ORGANIZATIONS

with Mission, MA in Leadership with Mission, MTh in Contextual Theology with Mission, MTh in Messianic Jewish Theology and Intercultural Studies. The College has a good mix of married and single students. There are number of facilities to help such as childcare on site, wifi access, multi-gym, sports ground and beautiful surroundings, to name a few. All Nations, Easneye, Ware, SG12 8LX *Tel:* 01920 443500
Fax: 01920 462997
email: info@allnations.ac.uk
Web: www.allnations.ac.uk

All Saints Educational Trust
Home/EU applicants: personal scholarships for intending teachers in degree-level education and/or professional training, particularly teachers of religious education, home economics and other subjects; those studying dietetics, food and nutrition, and public health promotion. Postgraduate qualifications relevant to continuing professional development may be considered. Financial constraint must in all cases be demonstrated. Not assisted: school pupils, students of counselling, engineering, law, medicine, ordination, social work, commercial hospitality. Overseas applicants: scholarships for full-time, taught postgraduate study in the UK only (taught Masters programmes favoured; doctorates and PGCE programmes will not normally be funded). Corporate awards: given for imaginative new projects that will support the classroom teacher and build up the profession, preference being given to those aimed at enhancing the Church's contribution to education. Member of the Association of Church College Trusts (*see separate entry*). *Clerk to the Trust:* Mr K. D. Mitchell, Knightrider House, 30–32 Knightrider Street, London, EC4V 5JT *Tel:* 020 7256 9360
020 7248 8380
email: clerk@aset.org.uk
Web: www.aset.org.uk

Almshouse Association (National Association of Almshouses)
Supports 1,700 member almshouse charities in providing good quality housing for those in need, many of whom are elderly. This is achieved through advising on best practice in almshouse management as well as advising and lobbying on regulatory matters relating to almshouses. The Association also provides grants and loans to enable almshouse charities to carry out essential repairs and refurbishments to what, in many cases, are ancient, listed buildings. Its other key role is to promote and encourage new building of almshouses. A number of these almshouse trusts have Anglican chaplains or appoint Anglican clergy as Master or Custos of the foundation. *Chairman:* Mr Blair Gulland. *Director:* Mr Anthony De Ritter. *Deputy Director:* Mr Julian Marczak. *Assistant Director:* Mrs S. Turner, Bill-

ingbear Lodge, Maidenhead Rd, Wokingham, RG40 5RU *Tel:* 01344 452922
Fax: 01344 862062
email: naa@almshouses.org
Web: www.almshouses.org

Ancient Society of College Youths
Established 1637. An international bell-ringing society based in the City of London, the College Youths seeks to recruit leading ringers from any part of the world in which English style change-ringing is practised. Members are active in supporting ringing for church services throughout the world. The Society maintains a charitable fund for the maintenance of bells, fittings and towers of churches where it has a current or historic association. *Secretary:* Mr David E. House, 28 Waldegrave Road, Brighton, Sussex, BN1 6GE *Tel:* 01273 507077
07710 085403
email: secretary@ascy.org.uk
Web: www.ascy.org.uk

Anglican and Eastern Churches Association
Founded 1864 to promote mutual understanding of, and closer relations between, the Orthodox, Oriental and Anglican Churches. Patrons: the Archbishop of Canterbury and the Patriarch of Constantinople. *Presidents:* The Lord Bishop of London and Archbishop Gregorios of Thyateira and Great Britain. *Chairman:* Revd Dr William Taylor. *General Secretary:* Ms Janet Laws, c/o The Old Deanery, Dean's Court, London, EC4V 5AA *Tel:* 020 7248 6233
email: janet.laws@btopenworld.com

Anglican Fellowship in Scouting and Guiding
Founded in 1983 at the request of Guiders, Scouters and clergy. Its aims are to support leaders and clergy in the religious aspect of the Promise and Law and other training programmes in Scouting and Guiding, and to maintain links with other Guide/Scout religious guilds and fellowships in order to foster ecumenical understanding. The Anglican Fellowship is a national Scout 'Active Support Unit' and is recognized in a support role by the Guide Association, the Church of England and the Church in Wales. Membership is open to Scout Groups (which do not have to be church sponsored), individuals aged 18 years or over who are members of the Scout or Guiding movement, and others (e.g. clergy) who are sympathetic to the aims of Guiding or Scouting. *Chairman:* Mrs June Davies. *Vice-Chairman:* Vacancy. *Secretary:* Miss Joan Taylor. *Treasurer:* Miss Sandra Bendall, 31 Loseley Rd, Farncombe, Godalming, GU7 3RE *Tel:* 01483 428876
email: nanniejune@btinternet.com
Web: www.anglicanfellowship.org.uk

Anglican Mainstream
Anglican Mainstream is a movement of organizations, churches, dioceses and individuals within

the Anglican Communion worldwide, dedicated to teaching and preserving the Scriptural truths on which the Anglican Church was founded. It seeks to nurture, support and provide a network for orthodox Anglicans throughout the Communion. It published *Repair the Tear* as a response to the Windsor Report and *God, Gays and the Church*. Its Marriage, Sex and Culture group seeks, through bi-annual conferences, to support Christian marriage as a calling. It has a website, www.anglican-mainstream.net, as an information resource for orthodox Anglicans. *Convenor:* Dr Philip Giddings. *Executive Secretary:* Revd Andrew Symes, 21 High St, Eynsham, OX29 4HE   *Tel:* 01865 883388
email: sugdenmainstream@googlemail.com
Web: www.anglicanmainstream.org

Anglican Marriage Encounter
Anglican Marriage Encounter is a voluntary organization which offers residential programmes for married and engaged couples to review and deepen their relationship by developing a compelling vision for their marriage, and providing the communication skills to support this. *Lay Executive Couple:* Nigel and Tracey Burt, Taliesin, 1 Chillerton, Netley Abbey, Southampton, SO31 5GU
Tel: 023 8056 1342
email: mail@marriageencounter.org.uk
Web: www.marriageencounter.org.uk /
www.engagedencounter.org.uk

Anglican Pacifist Fellowship
Founded 1937. Members pledged to renounce war and all preparation to wage war and to work for the construction of Christian peace in the world. Quarterly newsletter *The Anglican Peacemaker*. *Chairperson:* Mrs Mary Roe. *Hon Secretary:* Dr Tony Kempster, 11 Weavers End, Hanslope, Milton Keynes, MK19 7PA   *Tel:* 01908 510642
email: ajkempster@aol.com
Web: www.anglicanpeacemaker.org.uk

Anglican Pastoral Care (Anglican Association of Advisers in Pastoral Care and Counselling)
To support the work of Bishops' and Diocesan Advisers in Pastoral Care and Counselling or their equivalents; to encourage the appointment of an adviser in every diocese; to promote good practice in pastoral care and counselling of those in ministry, within the structures of the Church of England. Full membership is open to Bishops' and Diocesan Advisers or their equivalents. Associate membership is open to those holding similar appointments in other denominations and those interested in furthering the work of the Association. Anglican Pastoral Care, 68 John Street, Hinckley, Leicestershire, LE10 1UY
Web: www.pastoralcare.org.uk

Anglican Society for the Welfare of Animals
Founded 1972, for the purpose of including the whole creation in the redemptive love of Christ and especially for prayer, study and action on behalf of animals. Registered Charity no. 1087270. Promotes Animal Welfare Sunday each October and offers a free information pack to all churches. *President:* Rt Revd Dominic Walker OGS. *Chairman:* Revd Dr Helen Hall. *Treasurer:* Mrs Jenny White, PO Box 7193, Hook, RG27 8GT
Tel and Fax: 01252 843093
email: AngSocWelAnimals@aol.com
Web: www.aswa.org.uk

Anglican–Lutheran Society
Founded in 1984 to pray for the unity of the Church and especially the Anglican and Lutheran Communions; to encourage opportunities for common worship, study, friendship and witness; to encourage a wider interest in and knowledge of the Anglican and Lutheran traditions and contemporary developments within them. The Society publishes a newsletter, *The Window*, and organizes conferences, lectures and other events. *Co-Presidents:* Very Revd Dr J. Arnold (Anglican); Rt Revd J. Johannesdotter (Lutheran). *Co-Moderators:* Rt Revd Michael Ipgrave (Anglican); Revd Dr Jaako Rusama (Lutheran). *Secretary:* Revd Canon Dick Lewis, Rectory Farm, Rectory Road, Retford, DN22 7AY
Tel: 01601777 719200 (Secretary)
email: Dick@ccwatford.u-net.com
Web: www.anglican-lutheran-society.org

Anglo-Catholic Ordination Candidates' Fund
Secretary: Revd J. F. H. Shead SSC, 57 Kenworthy Rd, Braintree, CM7 1JJ   *Tel:* 01376 321783
email: j.shead@tiscali.co.uk

Archbishop's Examination in Theology
Until 2007 the Archbishop's Examination in Theology comprised the Diploma of Student in Theology (the Lambeth Diploma) and the Degree of Master of Arts (the Lambeth MA). The Lambeth Diploma was instituted in 1905 by Archbishop Randall Davidson. It provided an opportunity for women to study theology, principally so that they could teach religious education in schools and churches. It was then extended to both men and women and the means of study was either by thesis or examination. The Lambeth MA was inaugurated by Dr Runcie in 1990 in order to provide an opportunity for theological study at a more advanced level. In 2007 the Archbishop's Examination in Theology was revised and now offers the Lambeth MPhil research degree, with the opportunity to extend to a Lambeth PhD. (The Lambeth Diploma and Lambeth MA are no longer options.) *For more information about the MPhil/PhD research degrees please contact:* Executive Assistant: Patronage and Awards, Archbishop's Examination in Theology, Lambeth Palace, London, SE1 7JU
email: ruth.ruse@lambethpalace.org.uk

Archbishops' (Canterbury, Wales and Westminster) Certificate in Church Music
See Guild of Church Musicians, page 283.

Archway
Retreat and Conference House Wardens' Association. Promotes the use of retreat and conference houses as a vital contribution to the life and development of Church and community. Is available to advise trustees/management committees and diocesan boards on issues concerning the running of retreat houses. *President:* Rt Revd Christopher Edmondson, Bishop of Bolton. *Chairperson:* Liz Pearson. *Secretary:* Janet Haynes. *Administrator:* Mr Jeff Witts, Norlands, Norwich Road, Edgefield, Norfolk, NR24 2RL
Tel: 01263 587661
email: jeffwitts@hotmail.com
Web: www.archwaywardens.org.uk

Art and Christianity Enquiry (ACE)
ACE is the leading UK organization in the field of visual arts and religion. ACE offers stimulating educational projects and publications, advice, information and skills. The ACE awards for religious art, architecture and literature are given biennially. The quarterly journal *Art and Christianity* is available by membership; complimentary copy available on request. *Director:* Laura Moffatt, St John's Church, Pitfield Street, London, N1 6NP
Tel: 020 7033 9481
email: enquiries@acetrust.org
Web: www.acetrust.org

Art and Sacred Places (ASP)
ASP promotes interaction between religion and art, largely by siting specially commissioned contemporary art in sacred places. It engages new audiences by exploring the relationship between art and spirituality, encouraging debate and understanding. ASP's work is based on the conviction that art and religion share fundamental concerns and explore similar territory, albeit in significantly different ways. ASP's portfolio of projects includes inspirational permanent commissions, innovative temporary commissions and mutually beneficial interfaith projects. ASP was founded under the auspices of Bishop John Gladwin in 1999 and became a charity in 2001. Charity Registration no. 1086739. Enquiries welcome. *Project Director:* Angela Peagram, Bakerswell, Meonstoke, Southampton, SO32 3NA
Tel: 01489 878725
Fax: 01489 878737
email: angela@artandsacredplaces.org
Web: www.artandsacredplaces.wordpress.com (blog); www.artandsacredplaces.org

Arthur Rank Centre
The ARC is an ecumenical charity serving rural churches, providing a vast range of resources online, covering worship, discipleship, evangelism, buildings, community engagement and examples of good practice, amongst other things. We offer training for clergy recently appointed to rural areas, lay and clergy training in creative leadership, and consultations at local, diocesan and national levels. The Diocesan Rural Officers meet annually with the Church of England National Rural Officer, who is a member of staff at the ARC and offers advice, information and support. We publish the magazine *Country Way: Life and Faith in Rural Britain*, and a monthly newsletter with information on the latest resources for rural churches. *CEO:* Jerry Marshall. *National Rural Officer, Mission and Public Affairs Division, Abps' Council:* Canon Dr Jill Hopkinson, The Arthur Rank Centre, Stoneleigh Park, Warwickshire, CV8 2LG
Tel: 024 7685 3060
Fax: 024 7641 4808
email: info@arthurrankcentre.org.uk
Web: www.arthurrankcentre.org.uk

Association for Promoting Retreats (APR)
The APR celebrated its centenary year in 2013, having been founded in 1913 to foster the growth of the spiritual life in the Anglican Communion by the practice of retreats. Welcomes as members all Christians in sympathy with this aim. Membership by subscription for individuals, parishes and retreat houses. The APR is one of the retreat groups which form the Retreat Association (*see* separate entry). *Administrator and Secretary to the Executive Committee:* Mrs Julia Reading, PO Box 10248, Newark, NG24 9LQ
Tel: 01636 555085
email: promoting.retreats@gmail.com
Web: www.promotingretreats.org

Association of Black Clergy
Founded 1982 to bring together the minority ethnic clergy and lay ministers of the Christian Church in the United Kingdom, to provide support for all minority ethnic clergy and lay ministers, to encourage good practice and challenge racism individually, institutionally and structurally in particular in the Christian Church in the United Kingdom and to promote theological education and training that is relevant to minority ethnic Christian leadership. *Chairman:* Revd Jennifer Thomas. *Vice-Chair:* Revd Karowei Dorgu. *Facilitators (South):* Revd Yvonne Clarke, Revd Charles Lawrence. *Facilitator (North):* Very Revd Rogers Govender. *Secretary:* Revd Smitha Prasadam, Sherwood Park Vicarage, Sherwood Park Rd, Mitcham, CR4 1NJ
Tel: 020 8764 1258
Fax: 020 8764 8369

Association of Christian Teachers
ACT is a non-denominational Christian membership organization which provides professional and spiritual support to Christians engaged in pre-school, primary, middle, secondary, special, college and university education in England.

ACT encourages Christians to apply their faith to their work and provides opportunities for them to share together in prayer and fellowship. ACT strives to influence policy makers, politicians, the media and the Church by speaking from a professionally well-informed standpoint with a loving, Christian voice on behalf of Christians working in education. *Director (Strategy):* Mr Clive Ireson. *Office Manager:* Mrs Carol Horne, Suite 7 Rowan House, 23 Billing Road, Northampton, NN1 5AT   *Tel:* 01604 632046
email: act@christians-in-education.org.uk
Web: www.christians-in-education.org.uk

Association of Christian Writers
The Association of Christian Writers aims to encourage, equip and inspire its members to use their talents with integrity, and to produce excellent material which comes from a Christian world view. We hold two writers' days per year, and local writing groups meet regularly. We also produce a quarterly magazine for members. *Chair:* Revd Philip S. Davies. *Vice-Chair:* Marion Osgood. *Administrator:* Mandy Johnson, 7 Eversley Walk, Nottingham, NG5 5NL
Tel: 07970 198556
Fax: 0115 926 7229
email: admin@christianwriters.org.uk
Web: www.christianwriters.org.uk

Association of Church College Trusts
In 1979 the Association of Church College Trusts was established as a loosely knit organization to facilitate an exchange of information and co-operation. It meets every six months. The Church College Trusts were formed following the closure of their respective Colleges of Education. They are autonomous, answerable only to the Charity Commission; their financial management policies are such that they are required both to sponsor present work from their income and also to ensure that their capital is maintained at a level that can finance similar levels of work in the future. In the last 30 years they have been involved in helping individual teachers, students and others, sponsoring corporate projects in part or in total, and aiding school, college and church educational activities. The individual Trusts are: All Saints Educational Trust, Culham St Gabriel's Trust, Foundation of St Matthias, Hockerill Educational Foundation, Keswick Hall Charity, St Christopher's Educational Trust, St Hild and St Bede Trust, St Luke's College Foundation, St Mary's College Trust, St Peter's Saltley Trust, Sarum St Michael Educational Charity (*see separate entries*). Please note that applications have to be made to the individual Trusts concerned and not centrally through the Association. *Secretary:* Dr Mark Chater, 15 Norham Gardens, Oxford, OX2 6PY   *Tel:* 01865 284885
Fax: 01865 284886
email: enquiries@cstg.org.uk
Web: www.cstg.org.uk

Association of Church Fellowships
Founded 1963. Sponsored by clergy and laity to meet a growing need in this country and overseas to encourage and enable the laity to take their full part in the life and work of the Church in open groups and in cooperation with existing groups. *National Chairman:* Revd Andrew Bullock, 34 Dudley Park Rd, Acocks Green, Birmingham, B27 6QR   *Tel:* 0121 706 9764
email: andrewbullock2@blueyonder.co.uk

Association of Diocesan Registry Clerks
The Association was established in 1999 to support and assist clerks and assistant staff in the furtherance of their professional roles in the diocesan and provincial registries and the Faculty Office of the Church of England by encouraging and sharing knowledge of ecclesiastical law, practice and procedures, imparting and exchanging information, and promoting discussion relevant to their roles. A day conference is organized for members, alternating biannually with a two-day residential conference; a lively group email correspondence provides an invaluable resource and a semi-regular newsletter keeps members informed. *President:* The Right Worshipful Charles George QC, Dean of the Arches and Auditor. *Chair:* Mrs Elisabeth Crouch. *Communications Officer:* Gini Hunt, Chattertons 2 Lower Moor Road, off Doddington Road, Lincoln, LN6 3JY   *Tel:* 01522 814600
DX: 700679NORTHHYKEHAM
Fax: 01522 813601
email: gini.hunt@chattertons.com

Association of English Cathedrals
Established in 1990 and authorized by the Administrative Chapters of the Anglican Cathedrals as their representative organization, the AEC deals with governmental agencies, the General Synod and its constituent bodies and the Churches' Legislation Advisory Service on behalf of the English cathedrals, provided only that it cannot commit any individual cathedral chapter to a specific decision. Membership consists of one representative of each Administrative Chapter. *Chairman:* Very Revd Vivienne Faull. *Coordinator:* Mrs Sarah King, PO Box 53506, London, SE19 1ZL   *Tel:* 020 8761 5130
email: sarah.king@englishcathedrals.co.uk
Web: www.englishcathedrals.co.uk

Association of Hospice and Palliative Care Chaplains (AHPCC)
The AHPCC is the professional organization for health care chaplains whose primary role is to provide spiritual and religious care in hospices and other palliative care settings. Hospice and Palliative Care Chaplains seek to work as members of a multidisciplinary team committed to providing holistic care. They have primary responsibility for the spiritual and religious care of patients, carers, staff and volunteers,

regardless of faith or life stance. They provide an informed ethical, theological and pastoral resource for individuals and for their employing organizations, and offer training and pastoral support to staff.

The AHPCC aims to identify and promote good practice, to provide support and training opportunities to its members, to collaborate with other palliative care professionals and to promote links with church bodies and faith communities. The AHPCC offers information and advice about appointments, induction, and training courses, keeps members up to date with current issues by means of its website, and organizes a three-day conference and training event in May each year. The AHPCC is happy to liaise with religious bodies, training institutions and individuals interested to know more about palliative care chaplaincy. Many hospices offer placements and courses which form part of pre- and post-ordination training.

The AHPCC monitors professional developments within the constituency of palliative care, and works to its own professional Standards, Competencies and Code of Conduct. It collaborates closely with other Chaplaincy bodies e.g. the College of Health Care Chaplains, the Scottish Association of Chaplains in Healthcare, and the UK Board for Healthcare Chaplaincy to further the professionalism of healthcare chaplaincy throughout the UK. The membership fee is currently £35, and individuals interested in becoming members should consult the website for information. *President:* Revd Judy Davies. *Website Editor:* Mike Rattenbury, Sue Ryder – Duchess of Kent House, 22 Liebenrood Road, Reading, RG30 2DX
email: president@ahpcc.org.uk
2nd email: editor@ahpcc.org.uk
Web: www.ahpcc.org.uk

Association of Ordinands and Candidates for Ministry

Founded in 1968, AOCM represents ordinands from the Church of England, Church in Wales, Episcopal Church of Scotland and Church of Ireland as well as trainee Church Army evangelists. AOCM holds regional and national conferences during the year, to which every theological college, course and OLM scheme may send a representative. These conferences allow ordinands to share fellowship, and also for information and questions to pass between AOCM and the Ministry Division. AOCM publishes an annual handbook, *Together in Training*, which is provided free of charge to all ordinands, bishops and DDOs. *Chairman:* Alan Maxwell. *Treasurer:* Ian Robinson. *Secretary:* John Allister
email: secretary@aocm.org.uk
Web: www.aocm.org.uk

Awareness Foundation

The Awareness Foundation is an international ecumenical institution committed to fostering community harmony through education. The Foundation's teaching programme, the Awareness Course, is designed and written by Bishop Michael Marshall and Revd Nadim Nassar to educate Christians for life in the twenty-first century. Each course module is written from a Christian viewpoint, teaching Christians about their own faith and that of their neighbours, so that they can respect the differences and live in a diverse society without fear and without compromising their faith. The Course considers Islamic and Jewish perspectives to build an awareness of 'the other' and to go deeper into the Christian faith. It is designed to be taught in churches, parish halls or any appropriate space, and is suitable for regular or occasional churchgoers, Christians outside the Church, seekers and the undecided. New courses are published each year. *President:* Rt Revd Michael Marshall. *Director:* Revd Nadim Nassar. *Chair of Trustees:* Charles Longbottom. *Chief Executive Officer:* Helen Carey. *Education Director:* St John Wright, Holy Trinity Church, Sloane St, London, SW1X 9BZ   *Tel:* 020 7730 8830 (Office)
020 7259 0619 (Education)
Fax: 020 7730 9287
email: tfcc@tfccinternational.com
Web: www.tfccinternational.com

Baptismal Integrity (BI)

BI has four aims: to bring to an end the indiscriminate administration of infant baptism; to demonstrate that baptism is the sacrament instituted by Christ for those becoming members of the visible church; to seek the reform of the Canons and rules of the Church of England in line with the above stated aims; and to promote within the Church of England debate and review of the biblical, theological, pastoral and evangelistic aspects of Christian initiation. BI affirms the propriety of baptizing the infants of practising Christian believers and also of deferring baptism until later years. It also affirms the relevance and value of the Service of Thanksgiving for the Gift of a Child. BI publishes its magazine *Update* at intervals. Membership is £10 per annum (or concession) – more information via website or Chairman. *President:* Rt Revd Colin Buchanan. *Acting Chairman:* Revd Stephen Corbett. *Vice-Chairman:* Mr Roger Godin. *Secretary:* Revd John Hartley. *Treasurer:* Ms Sallie Bassham, The Stables, Capland Lane, Hatch Beauchamp, Taunton, LA6 3AT   *Tel:* 01823 480606
email: roger.godin@baptism.org.uk
Web: www.baptism.org.uk

Barnardo's

Founded in 1866, Barnardo's is the UK's largest children's charity, whose inspiration and values derive from the Christian faith. It runs more than 400 projects nationwide and each year helps more than 100,000 children, young people and their families to overcome severe disadvantage. Barnardo's believes in children and works with them over the long term to tackle the effects of disadvantage and to ensure they can fulfil their potential. Children are helped to address problems such as abuse, homelessness and poverty and to tackle the challenges of disability. Barnardo's also campaigns for better care for children and their families in the community and champions the rights of every child. The charity no longer runs orphanages and now concentrates on working with children and their families in the community. *President:* HRH The Duchess of Cornwall. *Chief Executive:* Javed Khan, Barnardo's, Tanners Lane, Barkingside, Ilford, IG6 1QG

Tel: 020 8550 8822
Fax: 020 8551 6870
email: supportercare@barnardos.org.uk
Web: www.barnardos.org.uk

Beauchamp Community

Situated near Malvern, we are a Christian Almshouse Charity providing unfurnished single and double flats for retired clergy and laity at reasonable cost. Aged from 60 years upwards, applicants should be in good health. Daily Eucharist in a caring community. Apply to the Administrator. *Warden:* Mrs Lesley Lewis. *Chaplain:* Fr Roger Watson, Newland, Malvern, WR13 5AX *Tel:* 01684 562100
email: bcomadmin@btconnect.com
Web: www.beauchamp150.co.uk

Bible Reading Fellowship

At the heart of BRF's ministry is the desire to help people of all ages – children, adults and families – to explore Christianity and to grow in faith. We're passionate about helping people to engage with the Bible and prayer, and about resourcing Christian discipleship. These aims are fulfilled through the following ministries and resources:

- Barnabas in Churches – visit www.barnabas inchurches.org.uk. Includes free resources to use with under 11s and much more.
- Barnabas in Schools – visit www.barnabas inschools.org.uk. Working with primary schools to help children and their teachers explore Christianity creatively.
- Bible Reading Notes – visit www.biblereading notes.org.uk. Four different series to choose from.
- Bible Reading Notes Resource Pack – visit www.biblereadingnotes.org.uk. Discover all you need to know about promoting daily reading notes in church.
- BRF publishing – visit www.brfonline.org.uk. Church resources, prayer and spirituality, group study books and more.
- Church accounts – receive discount off BRFs books to help you encourage reading in your church. Contact Rebecca Fillis on 01865 319714 to find out more.
- Faith in Homes – visit www.faithinhomes. org.uk. Helping churches to support families to develop faith in the home. Free ideas, resources and more.

- Electronic books – visit www.brfonline.org/ ebooks. New BRF titles available for the Kindle.
- Foundations21 – visit www.foundations21.net. BRFs free online discipleship resource for groups and individuals.
- Messy Church – visit www.messychurch. org.uk. BRFs dynamic fresh expression of church based around welcome, crafts and art celebration, and eating together. Active in 14 countries.
- Who Let The Dads Out – visit www.wholet thedadsout.org. A way of reaching dads and their young children in your community.

BRF is a registered charirty (no. 233280). *Chair of Trustees:* Rt Revd Colin Fletcher, Bishop of Dorchester. *Chief Executive:* Mr Richard Fisher. *Deputy Chief Executive:* Mrs Karen Laister, 15 The Chambers, Vineyard, Abingdon, Oxfordshire OX14 3FE *Tel:* 01865 319700
Fax: 01865 319701
email: enquiries@brf.org.uk
Web: www.brf.org.uk

Bible Society

Bible Society is working towards a day when the Bible's life-changing message is shaping lives and communities everywhere. We aim to show how the Bible connects with life. We make Scriptures available where there are none. And we work with the Church to help it live out the Bible's message in its daily life and witness. *Chief Executive:* James Catford. *Executive Director of Charity:* Paul Woolley. *Executive Director of Finance:* Julie Fletcher, Stonehill Green, Westlea, Swindon, SN5 7DG *Tel:* 01793 418100
Fax: 01793 418118
email: contactus@biblesociety.org.uk
Web: www.biblesociety.org.uk

Boys' Brigade

Week by week the Boys' Brigade reaches out to children and young people, both girls and boys. We are passionate about partnering with churches to build bridges into local communities and engage a generation of children and young people with a message of hope rooted in Jesus. *Director for England:* Eric Hudson, Felden Lodge, Felden Lane, Hemel Hempstead, HP3 0BL

Tel: 01442 231681
Fax: 01442 235391
email: enquiries@boys-brigade.org.uk
Web: www.boys-brigade.org.uk

Bridge Pastoral Foundation (formerly the Clinical Theology Association)

Founded in 1962. The core activity of the Association is seminars in pastoral care and pastoral counselling, which are directed by authorized tutors and widely available in the UK. Seminars are designed to promote self-awareness, which is needed for effective pastoral work, and to teach the theory and practice of pastoral counselling

with reference to the assumptions, values and meanings of the Christian faith. Further information about Bridge Pastoral Foundation education and training may be obtained from the Administrator. 2 Gar Street, Winchester, SO23 8GQ
Tel: 01962 843040
email: admin@bridgepastoral.org.uk
Web: www.bridgepastoral.org.uk

Bristol Clerical Education Society
Grants of up to 250 to ordinands and, occasionally, to clergy undertaking CME, for specific and practical needs. *Secretary:* Mrs S. J. Clover, The Croft, Cox's Hill, Ashton Keynes Wiltshire, SN6 6NY
Tel: 01285 861199
email: sueclover.clover@googlemail.com

British Deaf Association
The British Deaf Association (BDA) is the largest national organization run by Deaf people with Deaf people. We represent the UK's Deaf community and campaign for the official recognition of British Sign Language (BSL). Our vision is 'Deaf people fully participating and contributing as equal and valued citizens in the wider society'. Our Mission is to ensure a world in which the language, culture, community, diversity and heritage of Deaf people in the UK is respected and fully protected, ensuring that Deaf people can participate and contribute as equal and valued citizens in the wider society. This will be achieved through:
• Improving the quality of life by empowering Deaf individuals and groups;
• Enhancing freedom, equality and diversity;
• Protecting and promoting BSL.

Patron: HRH The Duke of York. *Chair:* Terry Riley. *Chief Exec:* David Buxyon, BDA Head Office, 18 Leather Lane, London, EC1N 7SU
Tel: 020 7405 0090
email: bda@bda.org.uk
Web: www.bda.org.uk

British Isles and Eire Airport Chaplains' Network
The British Isles and Eire Airport Chaplains' Network meets twice a year for a day or two-day conference and is working towards seeing airport chaplaincy established at every international or regional airport in the UK and Ireland. In 2005 there were chaplaincies at 35 airports, with others being negotiated. Of these, full-time chaplains or chaplaincy teams are at: Heathrow, Gatwick, Manchester, Luton and East Midlands. All airport chaplains are on call and are pleased to be able to assist those travelling through airports in any way. They can be contacted via the airport information desk. Some airport chaplaincies have web pages on their particular airport websites; for a list of sites visit the address given below. *Coordinator:* Revd Roy Monks. *General Secretary:* Vacancy, East Midlands Air-

port Chaplaincy Team, Chaplains' Office, East Midlands Airport, Castle Donington, Derby, DE74 2SA
Tel: 01332 818407 ext 6407
email: roy.monks@talk21.com
Web: www.aoa.org.uk/ourmem/index.asp

Broken Rites
Formed in 1983, Broken Rites is an interdenominational and independent association for the divorced and separated spouses/partners of Anglican clergy, ministers and Church Army officers living in the United Kingdom, the Republic of Ireland and the geographical area covered by the Diocese in Europe. It welcomes the support of everyone who is in sympathy with its aims: to support one another with compassion, understanding and practical help where possible; to continue to draw the attention of the Churches to the problems of former clergy spouses/partners; and, while affirming the Christian ideal of lifelong marriage, to promote a more vivid awareness among Christian people of the increasing incidence of clergy marriage/partnership breakdown. *Hon Secretary:* Sue Atack
Tel: 01257 423893
email: enquiry@brokenrites.org
Web: www.brokenrites.org

Bromley and Sheppard's Colleges
Bromley College was founded in 1666 to provide houses for clergy widows and Sheppard's College in 1840 to provide houses for unmarried daughters of clergy widows who had lived with their mothers at Bromley College. Houses in both colleges have been converted into flats and widows/widowers of clergy, retired clergy and their spouses, divorced and separated spouses of clergy or retired clergy of the Church of England, the Church in Wales, the Scottish Episcopal Church or the Church of Ireland may now be admitted. Contact the Chaplain/Clerk to the Trustees. *Clerk and Chaplain:* Revd Christopher Boulton, Chaplain's Office, Bromley and Sheppard's Colleges, London Road, Bromley, BR1 1PE
Tel: 020 8460 4712
Fax: 020 8464 3558
email: bromleysheppardscolleges@btconnect.com
Web: www.bromleycollege.org

Burrswood
Burrswood is a Christian hospital and place of healing founded in 1948 by Dorothy Kerin, who received a commission from God to 'heal the sick, comfort the sorrowing and give faith to the faithless'. The Dorothy Kerin Trust is a registered charity, administered by a board of trustees and has a non-surgical hospital with 40 beds for short-term inpatient care supported by an interdisciplinary team of resident doctors, nurses, physiotherapists and counsellors; a church with resident chaplains, which is fully integrated within the hospital and has healing services open to the public twice a week; a guest/retreat

house with single and twin rooms, sleeping 9; a physio- and hydrotherapy complex for inpatients and outpatients and a medical and counselling outpatient facility. Additional public facilities include a Christian bookshop and tea room on-site and a charity shop in nearby Crowborough. Profits from these trading operations go into Burrswood's 'Access to Care' bursary fund which assists financially disadvantaged patients to receive care. *Chief Executive Officer:* John Ashelford. *Senior Chaplain:* Revd Christine Garrard. *Senior Physician:* Dr Paul Worthley, Groombridge, Tunbridge Wells, TN3 9PY

Tel: 01892 863637 (Enquiries)
01892 865988 (Admissions)
email: enquiries@burrswood.org.uk
Web: www.burrswood.org.uk

Came's Charity for Clergymen's Widows

Founded to provide small annual grants to benefit clergy widows who are wanting. Apply to the Clerk. Worshipful Company of Cordwainers, Dunster Court Mincing Lane, London, EC3R 7AH   *Tel:* 020 7929 1121
Fax: 020 7929 1124
email: office@cordwainers.org

Campaigners England and Wales,The

Founded 1922, The Campaigners England and Wales is a national youth movement working in partnership with local churches. The Campaigners England and Wales trains and resources local leaders, enabling them to operate an exciting and relevant relational and holistic programme of evangelism and Christian discipleship for boys and girls between 4 and 18. It is recognized by UK government education departments and is a member of the Evangelical Alliance. *Executive Director:* Mr John Radcliffe. *Resources Director:* Mr Tony Etherington, 7 Frankpledge Road, Cheylesmore, Coventry, CV3 5GT   *Tel:* 0247 650 5758
Web: www.campaignersew@weebly.com

Canterbury and York Society

Founded 1904 for the printing of bishops' registers and other ecclesiastical records. *Joint Presidents:* The Archbishops of Canterbury and York. *Chairman:* Dr P. Zutshi. *Secretary:* Dr C. Fonge. *Treasurer:* Dr R. Hayes. *Editor:* Dr P. Hoskin, c/o Borthwick Institute, University of York Heslington, York, YO10 5DD

email: charles.fonge@york.ac.uk
Web: http://www.canterburyandyork.org

CARE (Christian Action Research and Education)

CARE is a registered charity seeking to combine practical caring initiatives, at national and community level, with public policy on social and ethical issues. CARE campaigns, provides resources, undertakes caring work and helps to bring Christian insight and experience to matters of public policy, education and practical caring initiatives, particularly on the behalf of the needy. *Chairman:* Revd Lyndon Bowring. *Chief Executive:* Mrs Nola Leach. *Director of Parliamentary Affairs:* Dr Dan Boucher, 53 Romney St, London, SW1P 3RF   *Tel:* 020 7233 0455
08453 100 244 (supporter helpline)
Fax: 020 7233 0983
email: mail@care.org.uk
Web: www.care.org.uk

Catch 22 (formerly Rainer)

A national voluntary organization, founded in 1788, working primarily with young people at risk, through over 60 community-based projects, some in partnership with local authorities and other voluntary organizations. Particular services include leaving care projects and bail support schemes, accommodation and support to young people on release from young offender institutions or who are homeless, youth training and employment schemes. *Chief Exec:* Mrs Joyce Moseley, Churchill House, 142–146 Old Street, London, EC1V 9BW   *Tel:* 020 7336 4800
Fax: 020 7336 4801
email: information@catch-22.org.uk
Web: www.catch-22.org.uk

Cathedral and Church Shops Association

The Association provides a forum for the exchange of information, and arranges an annual conference and trade fair for its members. We sponsor meetings of shop staff in several areas of the country each spring, giving advice and assistance for the setting up and running of church shops from experienced shop managers. Membership is open to any cathedral/church-/abbey/religious house which is under sole control, or operated by a trading company for the sole benefit, of its chapter, parochial church council or religious house. *Chairman:* Hugh Fearnall JP. *Hon Secretary:* Ann Waller, Stable Cottage, Aydon, Corbridge Northumberland, NE45 5PL

Tel: 07779 346150
email: via website
Web: www.cathedralandchurchshops.com

Cathedral Libraries and Archives Association

The CLAA supports the work of the cathedral and capitular libraries and archives in the Anglican churches of the United Kingdom and Ireland. It seeks to advance education by the promotion, preservation and protection of those collections and provides a forum for cooperation and the exchange of information among those who care for them. *Chairman:* Very Revd Peter Atkinson. *Hon Secretary:* Judith Curthoys. *Hon Treasurer:* Dr Michael Stansfield, c/o Christ Church Archives, Oxford, OX1 1DP   *Tel:* 01865 276171
Fax: 01603 766032
email: library@cathedral.org.uk
Web: http://www.cofe.anglican.org/about/
librariesandarchives/cathanddioceseslibs/

ORGANIZATIONS

Cathedrals Administration and Finance Association (CAFA)

In 1975 cathedral administrators and treasurers began, as a body, to exchange information on all matters touching on best practice and the most effective administration of the English Anglican cathedrals. The association now enjoys a valued link with the Association of English Cathedrals for which organization it undertakes research as needed. There is an annual conference and regular regional meetings. *Chairman:* Mrs Caroline Jarvis. *Admin Secretary:* Miss Casey Chick. *Treasurer:* Mrs Caroline Robinson, Church House, Great Smith St, London, SW1P 3NZ

Tel: 020 7898 1058
email: casey.chick@churchofengland.org

Cathedrals Plus

Founded in 1981, Cathedrals Plus, formerly known as The Pilgrims' Association, provides a forum in which those responsible for the care and welcome of pilgrims, visitors and tourists to our cathedrals, abbeys, churches, shrines and chapels can meet and exchange ideas and experiences. It is also responsible for bringing together those in cathedrals and churches who deliver education outside the classroom both to schools and adults.

Originally a Trust, it is now a fully democratic institution governed by a Council of 15 members elected at the annual general meeting. Membership is both ecumenical and international, consisting of the great majority of Church of England cathedrals, four Roman Catholic cathedrals and several of the most visited parish churches, abbeys, priories and chapels from Anglican, Roman Catholic and Free Church denominations in England, Wales, the Republic of Ireland and Belgium. It operates mainly through an annual conference and periodic newsletters and through its website. It is consulted regularly by government and VisitBritain on tourism and educational matters relating to cathedrals and churches and is currently absorbing the work of CPAL, Cathedrals as Partners in Adult Education, into its remit. *Chairman:* Very Revd Charles Taylor, Dean of Peterborough. *Secretary:* Mrs Judy Davies. *Hon Treasurer:* Barry Palmer, 1 St John's Rd, Queen's Park, Chester, CH4 7AL

Tel and Fax: 01244 677991
email: secretary@cathedralsplus.org.uk
Web: www.cathedralsplus.org.uk

Catholic Group in General Synod

The Catholic Group consists of those on General Synod committed to the catholic, traditional and orthodox voice in the Church of England. It seeks to make a positive contribution to all debates and especially where Catholic faith and order are involved. It welcomes both the ARCIC discussions and dialogue with the Orthodox churches. The group maintains that ethical teaching which scripture and tradition have consistently upheld. *Chairman:* Canon Simon Killwick. *Secretary:* Mrs

Mary Nagel, Aldwick Vicarage, 25 Gossamer Lane, Bognor Regis, PO21 3AT

Tel: 01243 262049
email: mary@nagel.me.uk

Central Council of Church Bell Ringers

Founded 1891. Its aims are to promote the ringing of church bells, to represent the ringing exercise to the world at large and to provide expert information and advice to ringers, church authorities and the general public on all matters relating to bells and bell-ringing. *President:* Mrs Kate Flavell. *Hon Secretary:* Mrs Mary Bone, 11 Bullfields, Sawbridgeworth, CM21 9DB

Tel: 01297 726159
email: secretary@cccbr.org.uk
Web: www.cccbr.org.uk

Centre for the Study of Christianity and Sexuality

Launched in 1996, CSCS provides opportunities for issues of sexuality and gender identity to be discussed honestly and openly, and aims to help others in the churches to provide similar opportunities. CSCS is a unique, UK-based, ecumenical network specifically engaged in this task. It is associated with the international journal *Theology & Sexuality* and publishes *CSCS News* three times a year. It also organizes an annual conference. Patrons and Matron: Rt Revd John Gladwin (formerly Bishop of Chelmsford), Revd David Gamble (Chair of The Methodist Council), Revd Roberta Rominger (former URC General Secretary). *Chair:* Mr Martin Pendergast. *Secretary:* Revd Canon Jane Fraser. *Acting Treasurer:* Mr Michael Egan. *Newsletter Editor:* Mr Anthony Woollard, PO Box 24632, London, E9 6XF

email: info@christianityandsexuality.org
Web: www.christianityandsexuality.org

Changing Attitude

Working for lesbian, gay, bisexual and transgender affirmation within the Anglican Communion, Changing Attitude is a network of lesbian, gay, bisexual, transgendered and heterosexual members of Anglican churches founded in 1995. In England local groups meet regularly in eight dioceses to offer encouragement and support and provide educational and training resources. We have a network of contacts in over thirty-three dioceses and supporters in every English diocese. Changing Attitude has groups in Australia, Ireland, Kenya, New Zealand, Nigeria, Scotland and Wales. We work alongside Integrity USA and Canada and with many international groups and networks campaigning for equality. *Director:* Revd Colin Coward. *Hon Administrator:* Brenda Harrison, 6 Norney Bridge, Mill Rd Worton, Devizes, SN10 5SF

Tel: 01380 724908
07770 844302
email: ccmcoward@aol.com
Web: www.changingattitude.org.uk

Children's Society, The

The Children's Society has helped change children's stories for over a century. We expose injustice and address hard truths, tackling child poverty and neglect head-on. We fight for change based on the experiences of every child we work with and the solid evidence we gather. Through our campaigning, commitment and care, we are determined to give every child in this country the greatest possible chance in life. We transform children's lives by pressurizing central and local government to protect them, and we challenge attitudes that perpetuate harm and injustice. We are inspired by Christian values and work in close partnership with churches. In hard times, children are among the hardest hit. We don't just help them survive – we help them flourish. *Chair of Trustees:* Rt Revd Tim Thornton, Bishop of Truro. *Chief Executive Officer:* Revd Matthew Reed, Edward Rudolf House, 69–85 Margery St, London, WC1X 0JL   *Tel:* 020 7841 4400 (Switchboard) 0845 300 1128 (Supporter Action Line) *email:* supportercare@childrenssociety.org.uk *Web:* www.childrenssociety.org.uk

Choir Benevolent Fund

Founded 1851. A registered Friendly Society for subscribing cathedral and collegiate lay clerks and organists. *Trustees:* The Deans of St Paul's, Westminster and Windsor. *Secretary:* Mr Roland Tatnell, Foxearth Cottage, Frittenden, Cranbrook, TN17 2AU   *Tel:* 01580 712825

Choir Schools Association

Founded in 1918 to promote the welfare of children in cathedral, collegiate and parish church choir schools. In 1985 it set up a bursary trust to help children from low income families become choristers. *Chairman:* Mr Tim Cannell. *Administrator:* Mrs Susan Rees, 39 Grange Close, Winchester, SO23 9ND   *Tel:* 01962 890530 *email:* info@choirschools.org.uk *Web:* www.choirschools.org.uk

CHRISM (CHRistians In Secular Ministry)

Formed in 1984, CHRISM is the national association for all Christians who see their secular employment as their primary Christian ministry and for those who support that vision. CHRISM welcomes members, both lay and ordained, from all Christian denominations, encourages them to be active within their own faith communities and to champion ministry in and through secular employment. A journal is published quarterly, as well as occasional papers. We hold an open annual conference and also a members' reflective weekend. *Presiding Moderator:* Lyn Page, Willow Bank, Hawkley, Nr Liss, Hants, GU33 6NF *Tel:* 01730 827334 *email:* lynpage@btconnect.com *Web:* www.chrism.org.uk

Christian Aid

Christian Aid is an agency of the British and Irish churches and as such is one of the largest church-related international relief and development agencies in Europe. It works largely in the developing world providing support wherever the need is greatest, irrespective of race or religion. A substantial amount of its voluntary income is received through the annual Christian Aid Week collections led by churchgoers. It funds projects in more than 50 countries, standing by poor communities whether they are digging wells or fighting the consequences of debt, unfair trade or climate change, learning to read or articulating human rights abuses, healing the wounds of war or tackling the spread of preventable illnesses. Money spent overseas is passed to local partner organizations as Christian Aid believes that poor communities are best placed to devise and run their own projects and solve their own problems. Channelling money in this way is seen as an effective and respectful way of giving poor people the means to help themselves.

Prevention of the causes of poverty is better than cure, but Christian Aid remains active in emergencies, sending immediate help and capacity to cope with emergencies and disaster mitigation including food, shelter, medicine and transport when flood, famine, earthquake or war strike. The agency's charitable work includes campaigning and education work in the UK and Ireland, which accounts for up to 11 per cent of its income. This is because Christian Aid believes it must also tackle the structures and systems that keep people poor. It puts great emphasis on the involvement of individuals to address the root causes of poverty and encourage action by politicians and international institutions that will lead to their removal. *Director:* Loretta Minghella OBE. *Chair of the Board:* Dame Anne Owers, Inter-Church House, 35–41 Lower Marsh, London, SE1 7RL   *Tel:* 020 7620 4444 *Fax:* 020 7620 0719 *email:* info@christian-aid.org.uk *Web:* www.christian-aid.org.uk

Christian Arts

An association of artists, architects, designers, craftsmen and craftswomen all involved in the arts who are committed Christians and wish to explore and deepen the relationship between their faith and the arts. Its activities include holding exhibitions, study days and an annual conference. An illustrated magazine is published twice a year, with interim newsletters. Many members are available to accept commissions. Information may be found on the website detailed below. *Secretary:* Paula Widdicombe, 16 Belcombe Place, Bradford-on-Avon, Wiltshire, BA15 1NA   *Tel:* 01225863726 *email:* widdicombebutton@btinternet.com *Web:* www.christianartists.org.uk

Christian Education (incorporating International Bible Reading Association and RE Today Services)

Christian Education provides advice, resources and opportunities for teaching and learning in the school, the church and the family group, carrying forward the work of the National Christian Education Council and the Christian Education Movement. *Chief Executive:* Peter Fishpool, 1020 Bristol Rd, Selly Oak, Birmingham, B29 6LB   *Tel:* 0121 472 4242
Fax: 0121 472 7575
email: admin@christianeducation.org.uk
Web: www.christianeducation.org.uk

Christian Evidence Society

Founded in 1870, its principal object is 'to give instruction in evidences of Christianity'. Initially it produced tracts, sponsored lectures and arranged open-air work at Tower Hill and Hyde Park Corner. Later it organized annual Drawbridge Lectures by distinguished names. Nowadays its literature is on its website, available for free download by all and it sponsors broadcasts on Premier Radio. To mark the Darwin anniversary, in 2009 the Revd Professor Alister McGrath delivered a Drawbridge Lecture on 'Belief in God'. *President:* The Archbishop of Canterbury. *Chairman:* Revd Prof Richard Burridge. *Administrator:* Mr Christopher Garman, Springers, The Street, Coney Weston Bury St Edmunds, IP31 1HG   *Tel:* 01359 221600
email: admin@christianevidence.org
Web: www.christianevidencesociety.org.uk

Christian Healing Mission

The Christian Healing Mission (CHM) seeks to bring people into the presence of Jesus and to find the healing that flows from him. There are two main strands to the work: taking the exciting message of the person of Jesus the healer to as many churches and groups as possible and providing places where people can safely find Jesus and his healing touch. The Mission has a non-residential healing centre in London and a number of link centres and churches throughout the country. It offers training for those who are, or wish to be, involved in prayer ministry. Although rooted in the Church of England, the CHM is keen to work with people and churches of all denominations. The Director is an Anglican priest with many years' experience of parish ministry and is also the Bishop of Kensington's Adviser for Healing. *Director:* Revd John Ryeland. *Chaplain:* Revd Sarah Swift, 8 Cambridge Court, 210 Shepherds Bush Rd, London, W6 7NJ
Tel: 020 7603 8118
email: chm@healingmission.org
Web: www.healingmission.org

Christian Medical Fellowship

CMF has four aims:
- Discipleship – to unite Christian doctors and medical students in Christ, and to encourage them to deepen their faith, live like Christ, and serve him obediently, particularly through acting competently and with compassion in their medical practice;
- Evangelism – to encourage Christian doctors and medical students to be witnesses for Christ among all those they meet;
- Mission – to mobilize and support all Christian doctors, medical students and other healthcare professionals, especially members, in serving Christ throughout the world;
- Values – to promote Christian values, especially in bioethics and healthcare, among doctors and medical students, in the Church and in society.

Chief Executive: Dr Peter Saunders. *Head of Communications:* John Martin, 6 Marshalsea Rd, London, SE1 1HL   *Tel:* 020 7234 9660
email: mail@cmf.org.uk
Web: www.cmf.org.uk

Christian Research

Using a full range of Qualitative and Quantitative research methodologies, we help organizations identify and maximize opportunities to grow God's kingdom numerically, strategically and in depth. Our ongoing projects include ChurchCheck, Faith Journeys and Religious Trends, and we also conduct bespoke research for clients such as Bible Society, Tearfund, Alpha and Evangelical Alliance. Members receive *Quadrant*, a bi-monthly publication and *Research Brief*, a monthly email digest of trends in church and society. Forums and seminars help leaders apply the findings to their own context. Please ask for details. *Exec Director:* Mrs Benita Hewitt, Stonehill Green, Westlea, Swindon, SN5 7DG
Tel: 01793 418 264
Fax: 01793 418 100
email: admin@christian-research.org.uk
Web: www.christian-research.org.uk

Christian Witness to Israel

To a people of promise – the message of Messiah. Working alongside local churches, Christian Witness to Israel has been sharing the message of Messiah with the Jewish people for over 150 years. It is a non-denominational, international and evangelical organization with workers in seven countries worldwide. We believe that the Jewish people's greatest need is to know Jesus their Messiah. In order to help meet this need, we provide appropriate literature and run an evangelistic website. We also host outreach events and provide training for Christians who wish to share the gospel with their Jewish friends, neighbours and colleagues. *General*

Secretary: Mr Mike Moore, 166 Main Rd, Sundridge, Sevenoaks, TN14 6EL   *Tel:* 01959 565955
Fax: 01959 565966
email: comms@cwi.org.uk
Web: www.cwi.org.uk

Christians at Work

Christians at Work seeks to encourage, support and equip Christian fellowship, evangelism and witness in the workplace. It does this by seeking to unite Christian men and women at work in order to promote a sense of unity in the gospel. The organization produces resources, fact sheets and Bible study material; organizes conferences and seminars for local churches; and coordinates a network of around 200 workplace groups and around 200 individual members committed to the extension of Christ's kingdom in the working world. It was founded in 1942 to bring together Christians to pray and work for the extension of Christ's kingdom in the world of business and industry; to encourage active evangelism and fellowship; to provide information, literature and other facilities; to help Christians who stand alone in their place of work and to provide a means whereby young Christians starting work may be strengthened in their faith. *Director:* Revd Brian Allenby, Suite 10, Hubbway House, Bassington Lane, Cramlington Northumberland, NE23 8AD   *Tel:* 01670 700908
email: brianallenby@caw.uk.net
Web: www.caw.uk.net

Christians in Library and Information Services

Constituted 1976 under the original name of Librarians' Christian Fellowship to provide opportunities for Christians working in library and information services to consider issues in their professions from a Christian standpoint, and to promote opportunities for presenting the Christian faith to people working in libraries and information services of all kinds. *Hon Secretary:* Graham Hedges, 34 Thurlestone Ave, Ilford, IG3 9DU   *Tel:* 020 8599 1310
email: secretary@christianlis.org.uk
Web: www.christianlis.org.uk

Christians on the Left (formerly the Christian Socialist Movements)

Christians on the Left seeks to be the Christian conscience of the Labour Party and a voice to churches on social and political issues. We have a tradition stretching back 150 years, believing that the teachings of Jesus – justice, equality and love for one another – are inextricably linked to the foundations and continuation of the Labour Party. Newsletter and other booklets are published throughout the year. We also organize events, such as hustings for the leadership of the Labour Party, and have a presence at the Labour Conference; where we run fringe events with other major organizations, well known journalists and prominent political figures. Details of membership rates are available on our website. *Director:* Dr Andy Flannagan. *Chair:* Rt Hon Stephen Timms MP, PO Box 65108, London, SW1P 9PQ   *Tel:* 020 7783 1590
email: info@christiansontheleft
Web: www.christiansontheleft

Church Army

Church Army is a mission community of people who are transforming lives and communities through the work of commissioned evangelists, staff and community members. We are committed to sharing the Christian faith through words and action in a variety of contexts across the United Kingdom and Ireland. We work beyond church buildings with those on the margins of society: the elderly, the homeless, those living on deprived housing estates and many more. We have more than 300 evangelists who are trained and licensed and we support, resource and enable others to engage in evangelism locally. For more information and to find out about our projects, including Xplore for young people, please visit www.churcharmy.org.uk. *President:* Most Revd Desmond Tutu. *Chief Executive:* Canon Mark Russell. *Guardian of Vocations and Volunteers:* Sean Andrews, Wilson Carlile Centre, 50 Cavendish St, Sheffield, S3 7RZ
Tel: 0300 123 2113
email: info@churcharmy.org.uk
Web: www.churcharmy.org.uk/
http://twitter.com/churcharmy

Church House Deaneries' Group – The National Deaneries Network

The Church House Deaneries' Group – The National Deaneries Network – exists to stimulate local and national consideration of the developing role of the deanery, to encourage an informal network for the exchange of information about deanery thinking and deanery initiatives, and to promote the mission opportunities of deaneries. Every two years since 1988 it has held a national conference about deaneries. *Contact:* The Vicarage, Station Road, Benton, Newcastle upon Tyne, NE12 8AN   *Tel:* 0191 266 1921
email: secretary@chdg.org
Web: www.chhdg.org

Church Housing Trust

Church Housing Trust is committed to changing the lives of homeless people, providing the help and services they would otherwise be denied. Our principal objective is to raise funds to benefit homeless people and those in housing need, and in particular those cared for by Riverside ECHG (formerly English Churches Housing Group). Our funds support residents in more than 80 projects throughout England, including hostels, women's refuges, projects for young people, supported housing for ex-Service people, accommodation for vulnerable young parents and children, specialist supported housing for people with drug, alcohol and mental health

Organizations

problems, and projects for ex offenders. Our funds help turn hostels into homes and prepare homeless people for independent living through life skills and education and training programmes. Charity no. 802801. PO Box 50296, London, EC1P 1WF   *Tel:* 020 7269 1630
Fax: 020 7404 2562
email: info@churchhousingtrust.org.uk
Web: www.churchhousingtrust.org.uk

Church Lads' and Church Girls' Brigade

The Brigade is the Anglican Church's only uniformed youth organization, welcoming children and young people of all faiths and none, from ages 5 years to 21 years, engaging in 'fun, faith and friendship', equipping them to cope with the demands that society places upon them. The Brigade creates a caring and safe environment in which friendships between young people, children and adults can be established; helping children and young people to grow in confidence, developing their individual skills and abilities to work together, showing concern for others and the environment, exploring their spirituality and developing moral values. Operating in four age groups: 5–7 years, 7–10 years, 10–13 years and 13–21 years, there are appropriate training and activity programmes for all leaders and members to be engaged in. *Patron:* HM The Queen. *President:* The Archbishop of Canterbury. *Governor:* Anthony Baker. *Brigade Chaplain:* Rt Revd Jack Nicholls. *Brigade Secretary:* Alan Millward, National Headquarters, Saint Martin's House, 2 Barnsley Rd, Wath-Upon-Dearne, Rotherham, South Yorkshire S63 6PY   *Tel:* 01709 876535
Fax: 01709 878089
email: brigadesecretary@clcgb.org.uk
Web: www.clcgb.org.uk

Church Mission Society

We are a community of people in mission who want the world to know Jesus. Founded in 1799 in the crucible of the anti-slavery movement, CMS has some 350 people currently serving through our mission programmes internationally, sharing Jesus and changing lives in Africa, Asia, Europe, the Middle East and Latin America. The 2,500 members of the CMS mission community aspire to live a life shaped by God's mission wherever they are. CMS Pioneer Mission Leadership Training is a unique course for pioneer mission leaders working in many contexts, including those training to be ordained pioneer ministers in the Church of England. CMS is committed to working in networks, especially with CMS Africa and AsiaCMS, and is a founder member of the Faith2Share mission movements network. Registered Charity no. 1131655. Company no. 6985330. *Patron:* The Archbishop of Canterbury. *Episcopal Visitor:* Rt Revd Dr Christopher Cocksworth, Bishop of Coventry. *Chair of Trustees:* John Ripley. *Executive Leader:*

Revd Canon Philip Mounstephen, Watlington Rd, Oxford, OX4 6BZ
Tel: 01865 787 400 (Switchboard)
Fax: 01865 776 375
email: info@cms-uk.org
Web: www.cms-uk.org

Church Monuments Society

Founded in 1979 to encourage the appreciation, study and conservation of monuments. The Society promotes a biennial symposium, excursions, study days, a twice-yearly newsletter and an annual refereed journal. It also offers a programme of visits to locations throughout the country, a series of occasional lectures and an opportunity for people to meet and exchange views on a subject which spans many disciplines. It is the only society to cover all periods and all types of monument, and is the sponsor of the National Ledger Stone Survey. *President:* Dr Phillip G. Lindley. *Secretary:* Dr Amy L. Harris. *Treasurer:* Dr John Brown. *Membership Secretary:* Mr Clive Easter. *Publicity:* Dr John Bromilow, c/o Society of Antiquaries of London, Burlington House, Piccadilly, London, W1J 0BE
Tel: 01752 773634 (Membership)
01837 851483 (Publicity)
Fax: 01837 851483
email: churchmonuments@aol.com
Web: www.churchmonumentssociety.org

Church Music Society

Founded 1906. The society is a leading publisher of all types of Church music, and has consistently served the Church of England by this means. An annual lecture and other events for members pursue further aims of advancing knowledge of the art and science of Church music. Although much of the society's focus is on music specifically for liturgy, CMS publications are also in world-wide use by choirs of all types for concerts, recitals and recordings. *Te Deum Laudamus*, a CD of CMS publications, is now available. Details of membership and activities are available from the Secretary. *President:* The Dean of Hereford. *Chairman:* MrTimothy Byram-Wigfield. *Hon Secretary:* Dr Simon Lindley. *Hon General Editor:* Mr Richard Lyne, 17 Fulneck, Pudsey, LS28 8NT   *Tel and Fax:* 0113 255 6143
email: cms@simonlindley.org.uk
Web: www.church-music.org.uk

Church of England Clergy Stipend Trust

Founded 1952 to augment stipends of parochial clergy, normally through Diocesan Boards of Finance. *Chairman:* Mr J. W. Parkinson FCA, 3 Bunhill Row, London, EC1Y 8YZ
Tel: 020 7423 8000
Fax: 020 7423 8001

Church of England Evangelical Council

Founded in 1960 to promote effective consultation between Anglican evangelical leaders, in order that the evangelical heritage, as expressed in the Basis of Faith, may be better applied to contemporary problems in church and nation. CEEC seeks to interact with and encourage diocesan evangelical fellowships, societies, and other groups working within the evangelical constituency, and is a channel for establishing and maintaining relationships with the Church of England as a whole, and with evangelicals in other churches. It acts as the English agent of the Evangelical Fellowship in the Anglican Communion. *President:* Rt Revd Julian Henderson. *Chairman:* Revd Hugh Palmer. *Secretary:* Vacancy (Acting Secretary Revd Andrew Symes). *Treasurer:* Revd George Curry, All Souls Church, 2 All Souls' Place, London, W1B 3DA

Tel: 020 7580 3522
email: via website
Web: www.ceec.info

Church of England Flower Arrangers Association

The Church of England Flower Arrangers Association (CEFAA) was founded in 1981 to help and encourage all those who tend flowers in churches and link them in fellowship and friendship. It is open to all those baptized in the Christian faith. The aims are to expand interest in church flower arranging, to use talent to enrich places of worship and to support what theology and creation try to teach. CEFAA is a voluntary charity whose constitution covers the work members do in churches, church buildings and at church events. The Association is not sponsored and is non-competitive. Registered Charity no. 514372. *President:* Revd Noel Michell. *Chairman:* Mrs Ada Fawthrop. *Treasurer:* Mrs Naomi Hadden. *Secretary:* Mr Roger Brown, 25B Church Road, Hale Village, Liverpool, L24 4AY

Tel: 0151 425 2823
email: cefaa@btinternet.com
Web: www.cefaa.org.uk

Church of England Record Society

Founded in 1991 with the object of promoting interest in and knowledge of the history of the Church of England from the sixteenth century onwards, the Society publishes primary material of national significance for Church history. It aims to produce one volume each year, set against an annual subscription of 25 (individuals), and 38 (institutions). *Hon Secretary:* Dr Michael Snape, Dept of Modern History, University of Birmingham, Edgbaston, Birmingham, B15 2TT   *email:* m.f.snape@bham.ac.uk
Web: www.coers.org

Church of England Soldiers', Sailors' and Airmen's Clubs (1891)

A registered charity which, since its foundation in 1891, has maintained clubs at home and abroad for HM Forces and their dependants, whatever their religious denomination. The work of the association now encompasses rented housing for elderly ex-Service people or their widows/widowers. The association also helps other charities to build sheltered housing for ex-Service people, working in parallel with its sister organization, CESSA Housing Association. Donations always welcomed. *General Secretary:* Cdr Martin Marks. *Assistant Secretary:* Cdr Mike Pearce, CESSAC, 1 Shakespeare Terrace, 126 High St, Portsmouth, PO1 2RH

Tel: 023 9282 9319
Fax: 023 9282 4018
email: martin.marks@ntlbusiness.com

Church of England Soldiers', Sailors' and Airmen's Housing Association Ltd (1972)

A charitable Housing Association, registered with the Homes and Communities Agency (L0104) to provide low-cost rented sheltered accommodation for over-60s ex-Service people and/or their partners regardless of belief. Construction costs were provided partly by government grants, but donations are always welcome to help fund modernization. *Chief Exec:* Cdr Patrick Keefe. *Director of Housing:* Chris Wren, CESSA H. A., 1 Shakespeare Terrace, 126 High St, Portsmouth, PO1 2RH   *Tel:* 023 9282 9319
Fax: 0239282 4018
email: patrick.keefe@cessaha.co.uk
Web: www.cessaha.co.uk

Church Pastoral Aid Society Ministers in Training Fund

The Church Pastoral Aid Society administers the Ministers in Training Fund. This fund gives grants to evangelical Anglican students for personal maintenance (not fees) who have been recommended for training for ordained ministry following a Bishop's Advisory Panel or an accredited lay ministry selection process and are facing financial difficulties. *Ministers in Training Administrator:* Miss Joanna Coleman, Ministers in Training Fund, CPAS, Sovereign Court One (Unit 3), Sir Williams Lyons Road, Coventry, CV4 7EZ   *Tel:* 0300 123 0780 (ext. 4374)
email: jcoleman@cpas.org.uk
Web: www.cpas.org.uk

Church Schoolmasters and School Mistresses' Benevolent Institution

Founded in 1857 to provide assistance for Church of England teachers in England and Wales in times of temporary affliction or misfortune, or upon retirement or permanent disablement, and assistance towards the maintenance and education of their orphans. The CSSBI runs Glen Arun Care Home which has a strong Christian ethos and is set in a semi-rural location. The home provides residential and nursing care accommodation. It has 35 single rooms where residents can benefit from 24 hour nursing care. *Patron:* HM The Queen. *President:* The Bishop of London. *Chairman:* Miss Diana Bell. *Patient Care*

Manager: Mrs Sue Green. *Company Secretary:* Mrs Marie di Cara, Glen Arun, 9 Athelstan Way, Horsham, RH13 6HA *Tel:* 01403 253881 (Admin) 01403 255749 (Nursing Office) *Fax:* 01403 254971 *email:* glenarun@hotmail.com

Church Society
Formed in 1950 by the amalgamation of the Church Association and National Church League, which was founded in 1835, the Church Society continues to seek to maintain the evangelical and reformed faith of the Church of England, based upon the authority of Holy Scripture (see Canon A 5) and the foundational doctrines of the Thirty-nine Articles and the Book of Common Prayer. Publishes a journal, *Churchman*, and a quarterly broadsheet, *Cross+Way*. The Society publishes books, booklets and leaflets on current issues and organizes conferences and public meetings. Patronage is administered through the Church Society Trust. (*See also* Patronage Trusts.) *President:* The Viscount Brentford. *Chairman:* Mr James Crabtree, Dean Wace House, 16 Rosslyn Rd, Watford, WD18 0NY *Tel:* 01923 235111 *Fax:* 01923 800362 *email:* admin@churchsociety.org *Web:* www.churchsociety.org

Church Union
Founded in 1859 at the time of the Oxford Movement, to promote catholic faith and order, it continues this work today by providing support and encouragement to those lay people and priests who wish to see catholic faith, order, morals and spirituality maintained and upheld, and who wish to promote catholic unity. The Union publishes books and tracts and produces an in-house magazine, the *Church Observer*. *President:* Prebendary David Houlding SSC. *Chairman:* Mr David Morgan. *Treasurer:* Revd Owen Higgs. *Membership Secretary:* Mrs Jenny Miller, 2a The Cloisters, Gordon Square, London, WC1H 0AG
Tel: 020 7388 3588 01884 34563 (Membership) *email:* secretary@churchunion.co.uk *2nd email:* membership@churchunion.co.uk *Web:* www.churchunion.co.uk

Church Welfare Association (Incorporated)
(formerly the Church Moral Aid Association) Founded 1851. Gives financial aid to Church projects assisting and supporting women and children in need of residential care and/or moral support. We can also support Day Care projects designed to assist and support women and children, particularly single-parent families. *Honorary Secretary:* Mrs Bridget Trump, Portway Place, The Portway Stratford sub Castle, Salisbury, SP1 3LD *email:* secretary@churchwelfareassociation.org.uk *Web:* www.churchwelfareassociation.org.uk

Church's Ministry Among Jewish People
Founded 1809 as London Society for Promoting Christianity Among the Jews, to take the Christian gospel to Jewish people. *President:* Rt Revd David Evans. *Chair:* Mr Ben Salter. *CEO:* Revd Alex Jacob, Eagle Lodge, Hexgreave Hall Business Park, Farnsfield, Notts, NG22 8LS
Tel: 01623 883960 *Fax:* 01623 884295 *email:* enquiries@cmj.org.uk *Web:* www.cmj.org.uk

Churches Visitor and Tourism Association
A charitable ecumenical organization committed to promoting the daily openness of church buildings to visitors and tourists as a contributory component of the Church's mission, and to the significance of church buildings as places of worship, repositories of architectural heritage and locations for community engagement. In addition to its own resources CVTA, through its website, signposts organizations which specialize in offering literature and training in ministry to visitors and tourists. A newsletter is published approximately bi-monthly. Charity Registration No. 1101254. *Chair:* Canon John D. Brown. *Administrator:* Mrs Carol Roast, c/o 556 Galleywood Road, Chelmsford, Essex, CM2 8BX
Tel: 01245 358185 *email:* canonjbrown@mac.com *Web:* www.churchestourismassociation.info

Churches' Advertising Network (also known as ChurchAds. Net)
A professional group of Christians from all traditions cooperating to develop the professional use of advertising as part of the Churches' communication and outreach. CAN seeks free or low cost poster space and radio airtime from leading media owners, which it uses on behalf of the Churches. All members give their services free. Charity Registration no. 1096868. *Chair:* Mr F. Goodwin. *Secretary & Treasurer:* Revd Tony Kinch. *Asst Treasurer:* Mrs Karen Gray. *Trustee:* Mr Michael Elms, The Methodist Centre, 24 School St, Wolverhampton, WV1 4LF *Tel:* 01902 422100 *Fax:* 01902 313301 *email:* churchads@methodist.fsnet.co.uk *Web:* www.churchads.org.uk

Churches' Fellowship for Psychical and Spiritual Studies
Founded 1953 to study the psychic and spiritual and their relevance to Christian faith and life. *President:* Very Revd Alexander Wedderspoon. *Chair:* Mrs Davina Thomas. *General Secretary:* Mr Julian Drewett, The Rural Workshop, South Rd, North Somercotes, Louth, LN11 7PT
Tel and Fax: 01507 358845 *email:* gensec@churchesfellowship.co.uk *Web:* www.churchesfellowship.co.uk

Organizations

Churches' Funerals Group

The Churches' Group on Funeral Services at Cemeteries and Crematoria was formed as an advisory group in 1980 by the mainstream Churches in England and Wales to co-ordinate their policies in connection with the pastoral and administrative aspects of funeral services at cemeteries and crematoria, and to represent the Churches at national level in joint discussions with public and private organizations on any matters relating to ministry at such funerals. The Group keeps in close touch with the main organizations concerned with funeral provision and bereavement counselling.

To reflect its involvement in the wider aspects of all concerned with funerals and death in our society, the Group shortened its working title in 2002 to 'The Churches' Funerals Group'. Publications sponsored by the Group include *The Role of the Minister in Bereavement: Guidelines and Training Suggestions* (Church House Publishing, 1989); *Guidelines for Best Practice of Clergy at Funerals* (Church House Publishing, 1997); and two joint funeral service books (The Canterbury Press, Norwich), one for use in England (1986, 1994, 2001 and 2009), the other for use in Wales (1987). Three previous conference reports have been published: *The Role of a Minister at a Funeral* (1991), *Bereavement and Belief* (1993) and *Clergy and Cremation Today* (1995). An information leaflet entitled *Questions Commonly Asked about Funerals* (2nd edition, 2007) is also available free of charge from the Secretary. *Chairman:* Rt Revd James Langstaff, Bishop of Rochester. *Secretary:* Ms Sue Moore, Church House, Great Smith St, London, SW1P 3AZ   *Tel:* 020 7898 1376
Fax: 020 7898 1369
email: enquiries@christianfunerals.org
Web: www.christianfunerals.org

Churches' Legislation Advisory Service

Founded 1941 (as the Churches Main Committee), and first registered as a charity in 1966, CLAS exists to advance the religious and other charitable work of its member Churches by furthering their common interests in those secular issues (such as property matters, finance, tax and charitable status) which help underpin and deliver that work. Registered Charity No. 256303. *Chairman:* Rt Revd Alastair Redfern. *Secretary:* Frank Cranmer, Church House, Great Smith St, London, SW1P 3AZ   *Tel:* 020 7222 1265
email: frank.cranmer@centrallobby.com
Web: www.clas.org.uk

Cleaver Ordination Candidates' Fund

The Cleaver Ordination Candidates Fund exists for the support and encouragement of Anglican ordinands committed to a traditional Catholic understanding of the priesthood and episcopate, and to urge the importance of continuing sound theological learning among the clergy. Book grants are awarded to eligible ordinands, and applications may be considered from clergy in respect of university fees for post-graduate theological study. *Clerk to the Cleaver Trustees:* Revd John Hanks, 50 Thames Street, Oxford, OX1 1SU   *email:* clerk@cleaver.org.uk
Web: www.cleaver.org.uk

COIN: Christians on the Internet

An interdenominational group of Christians throughout Britain and Ireland working together since 1995 to advise, help and encourage the Church in its use of the Internet. It functions both as a group of individuals able to offer their particular expertise, and also, through email, as a lively online community discussing in depth a wide variety of issues affecting Christians, including specialist lists discussing Church of England issues, and Common Worship. Further details of COIN and its activities can be found on its website. *Chair:* Andrew Foulsham. *Secretary:* Jill Wright. *Treasurer:* Revd Peter Muir. *Membership Secretary:* Revd Alan Jesson
email: jill@woodchipcomputers.co.uk
Web: www.coin.org.uk

College of Evangelists

The national College of Evangelists was founded in 1999 to support and give the accreditation of the Archbishops of Canterbury and York to evangelists in the Church of England. To be admitted as a member of the College, evangelists will be involved in active evangelistic ministry (not just training or teaching about evangelism) and will be operating nationally or regionally, beyond their diocesan boundaries. Potential candidates should contact their diocesan bishop in the first instance. *Chairman:* The Bishop of Worcester. *Enquiries to:* Jenny Lowery, The Bishop of Worcester's Office, Old Palace, Deansway, Worcester, WR1 2JE   *Tel:* 01226 891213
email: jennyl@blueyonder.co.uk

College of Health Care Chaplains

The College of Health Care Chaplains (CHCC) is the largest professional body representing chaplaincy within healthcare and an autonomous section of Unite the Union (Britain and Ireland's biggest trade union with 1.5 million memberships), which negotiates terms and conditions for all chaplains (irrespective of College membership) on a national basis; members also receive professional support on employment issues. Founded in 1992, the College is a multi-faith, interdenominational professional association open to all recognized health care chaplaincy staff, full-time and part-time, including voluntary and support workers, and others with an interest in health care chaplaincy. With around 800 members throughout the United Kingdom, it provides peer support, advice and fellowship for members nationally and in ten regional branches

with a focus on professional development, good practice and training. The College publishes two issues a year of *The Journal of Health Care Chaplaincy* (available on subscription to non-members). The College exists to promote the professional standing of healthcare chaplaincy and that of its members both nationally and within health and social care organizations. 'We work as a part of the healthcare team to care for the whole person.' *President:* Revd Mark Burleigh. *Vice-President:* Revd Gareth Rowlands. *Registrar:* Revd William Sharpe, Unite Health Sector, 128 Theobald's Rd, London, WC1X 8TN
Tel: 020 3371 2004
Fax: 0870 731 5043
email: william.sharpe@unitetheunion.org
Web: www.healthcarechaplains.org

College of Preachers
An ecumenical network of preachers, ordained and lay, dedicated to preaching which is faithful and fresh, biblical and relevant, and to helping one another to develop preaching skills through seminars, conferences, a journal and guided study. *Chairman:* Rt Revd Stephen Cottrell. *Administrator:* Miss Helen Skinner, 16 Exeter Road, West Bridgford, Nottingham, NG2 6FA
email: administrator@collegeofpreachers.co.uk
Web: www.collegeofpreachers.co.uk

College of Readers
An independent membership organization providing fellowship and support for Readers of the Anglican Communion in the British Isles, especially to those Readers who subscribe to the authority of scripture, the grace of the sacraments and the traditional understanding of the ordained ministry of the bishop, priest and deacon. The College is establishing a network of local circles and chaplains, and publishes a quarterly magazine, *Blue Scarf*, which keeps all members in touch. Distance learning packages are available, as are a series of publications on aspects of Reader ministry. Regional and national meetings are organized each year. *Chairman:* Mr Barry Barnes. *Registrar/Treasurer:* Mrs Mary E. Snape, 1 Soames Crescent, Stoke-on-Trent, ST3 5UE
email: mary@college-of-readers.org.uk
Web: www.college-of-readers.org.uk

College of St Barnabas
Set in idyllic Surrey countryside, the College is a residential community of retired Anglican clergy, including married couples and those who have been widowed. Admission is also open to licensed Church Workers and Readers. There are facilities for visitors and guests, and occasional quiet days and private retreats can be accommodated. Residents lead active, independent lives for as long as possible. There is a Nursing Wing providing domiciliary, residential and full nursing care for those who need it, to which direct admission is possible. This enables most residents to remain members of the College for the rest of their lives. Respite care for patients and/or carers can occasionally be offered here. Sheltered flats in the Cloisters all have separate sitting rooms, bedrooms and en suite facilities. There are two chapels, daily Eucharist and Evensong, three libraries, a well-equipped common room and refectory, a snooker table and a nine-hole putting green. The College is easily accessible by road and is also next to Dormans Station on the line from London to East Grinstead. For further details or to arrange a preliminary visit, please see our website or contact the Warden. *Warden:* Fr Howard Such. *Bursar:* Paul G. F. Wilkin, The College of St Barnabas, Blackberry Lane, Lingfield, Surrey RH7 6NJ
Tel: 01342 870260
Fax: 01342 871672
email: warden@collegeofstbarnabas.com
Web: www.st-barnabas.org.uk

Commonwealth War Graves Commission
Founded 1917. Responsible for marking and maintaining in perpetuity the graves of those of Commonwealth Forces who fell in the 1914–18 and 1939–45 Wars and for commemorating by name on memorials those with no known grave. *President:* HRH The Duke of Kent. *Chairman:* Secretary of State for Defence in the UK. *Enquiries:* Director Legal Services, 2 Marlow Rd, Maidenhead, Berkshire, SL6 7DX
Tel: 01628 507 138
Fax: 01628 507 134
email: legal@cwgc.org
Web: www.cwgc.org

Community Housing and Therapy
CHT provides group and individual psychotherapy in residential settings to clients who are experiencing mental health and emotional difficulties. The care of each client is planned through an individual Care Plan which is reviewed every three to six months. Reviews are interdisciplinary and CHT therapists with social workers and psychiatrists, together with others, review progress and set goals together with the client. These goals focus on key areas in the life of each client, for example, housing needs, relationships, medication and re-training for work. *Chief Exec:* Mr John Gale. *Chief Operating Officer:* Ms Inma Vidana. *Deputy Director, Clinical Services:* Miss Beatriz Sanchez. *Senior Managers:* Mr Terry Saftis, Mrs Yin Ping Leung, 24/5–6 The Coda Centre, 189 Munster Rd, London, SW6 6AW
Tel: 020 7381 5888/0800 018 1261 (Freephone)
Fax: 020 7610 0608
email: co@cht.org.uk
Web: www.cht.org.uk

Community of Aidan and Hilda

A dispersed, ecumenical and international body of Christians who journey with God, and re-connect with the Spirit and the Scriptures, the saints and the streets, the seasons and the soil. The Community seeks to cradle a Christian spirituality for today which renews the Church and brings healing to fragmented people and communities. It welcomes people of all back-grounds and countries who wish to be wholly available to God the Holy Trinity, and to the way of Jesus as revealed in the Bible. In the earthing of that commitment members draw particular inspiration from Celtic saints such as Aidan and Hilda.

Members follow a Way of Life based on a rhythm of prayer and study, simplicity, care for creation, and mission, seeking to weave together the separated strands of Christianity. Each shares their journey with a spiritual companion known as a Soul Friend. The work of the Community is the work of each member and can be expressed individually and corporately in many ways, such as through link houses, churches, monastic experiments, and indigenous national branches. Its mother house and spirituality centre is The Open Gate, Holy Island, Berwick-upon-Tweed, TD15 2SD. *Community Soul Friend (Episcopally endorsed visitor):* Canon Godfrey Butland. *International Guardian:* Revd Ray Simpson. *Secretary:* Naomi Ackland. *Retreat House Wardens:* Revd Graham and Dr Ruth Booth, Lindisfarne Retreat, Holy Island, Berwick-upon-Tweed, TD15 2SD
Tel: 01289 389249 (International Office)
01289 389222 (Holy Island Retreat
House Bookings)
email: admin@aidanandhilda.org.uk
Web: www.aidanandhilda.org

Compassionate Friends, The

The Compassionate Friends is an organization of bereaved parents, siblings and grandparents offering support and mutual understanding to others after the loss of a child, of any age, from any cause. We have a National Telephone Help-line, with calls taken only by bereaved parents, which is available for support and information 365 days a year. We also have a comprehensive website which includes a Members Forum which enables those who join up to speak electronically to others similarly bereaved. Our helpline and website are the best ways to get contact us initially and we will then put you in touch with our local support volunteers, local groups, weekend gatherings and meetings, information leaflets, bereavement support publications and postal library. Support specifically for siblings is also available. Helpline hours: daily from 10.00–16.00 and 19.00–22.00. *Tel:* 0845 123 2304 (Helpline)
email: helpline@tcf.org.uk
Web: www.tcf.org.uk

Confraternity of the Blessed Sacrament

Founded 1862 to honour Jesus Christ our Lord in the Blessed Sacrament; to make mutual eucharistic intercession and to encourage eucharistic devotion. Registered Charity no. 1082897. *Superior-General:* Revd Christopher Pearson. *Secretary General:* Canon Lawson Nagel, Aldwick Vicarage, 25 Gossamer Lane, Bognor Regis, PO21 3AT *Tel:* 01243 262049
*email:*cbs@confraternity.org.uk
Web: www.confraternity.org.uk

Corporation of the Sons of the Clergy and Friends of the Clergy Corporation

The two charities work together and are able to assist Anglican clergy and their widows/ widowers and dependants in times of financial need or distress. Grants are made for a wide range of purposes including holidays and resettlement, school clothing and school trips, university maintenance for undergraduate chil-dren, clerical clothing, heating and home main-tenance for the retired, bereavement expenses and some of the expenses arising from separation and divorce. Book grants can be considered for ordinands in training. The Corporation of the Sons of the Clergy also administers the Clergy Orphan Corporation. *Registrar and Secretary:* Robert Welsford, 1 Dean Trench St, Westminster, London, SW1P 3HB *Tel:* 020 7799 3696
Fax: 020 7222 3468
email: enquiries@clergycharities.org.uk
Web: www.clergycharities.org.uk

Council of Christians and Jews

Founded 1942 to combat all forms of religious and racial intolerance, to promote mutual under-standing and goodwill between Christians and Jews, and to foster cooperation in educational activities and in social and community service. Forty local branches in the UK. Presidents: Arch-bishop of Canterbury; Cardinal Archbishop of Westminster; Moderator of the Free Churches; Moderator of the General Assembly of the Church of Scotland; Archbishop of Thyateira and Great Britain; Chief Rabbi of the United Hebrew Congregations of the Commonwealth; Senior Rabbi to the Movement for Reform Judaism; Spiritual Head, Spanish and Portuguese Jews' Congregation; Chief Executive, Liberal Judaism. *Patron:* HM The Queen. *Chair:* Rt Revd Nigel McCulloch. *Chief Executive:* Dr Jane Clements, 21 Godliman Street, London, EC4V 5BD
Tel: 020 7015 5160
email: cjrelations@ccj.org.uk
Web: www.ccj.org.uk

Council on Christian Approaches to Defence and Disarmament

CCADD was established in 1963 by the Rt Revd Robert Stopford, then Bishop of London, to study problems relating to defence and disarmament within a Christian context. The British Group

of CCADD comprises Christians of different traditions, varying vocations and specializations and political views, with a range of responsibilities, governmental and non-governmental. CCADD seeks to bring an ethical viewpoint to bear on disarmament and arms control and related issues and to this end the British Group has always stressed the importance of dialogue between official and non-official bodies. *President:* Rt Revd Richard Harries. *Chairman:* Mr Brian Wicker. *Admin Secretary:* Mrs Liza Hamilton, 5 Cubitts Meadow, Buxton, Norwich, NR10 5EF   *Tel and Fax:* 01603 279939
email: ccadd@lineone.net
Web: http://website.lineone.net/ccadd

Crosslinks

Crosslinks is an international mission society with its roots in the Bible, working largely within the worldwide Anglican Communion. Our strapline is 'God's word to God's world'. Our business is making Christ known through the proclamation of the gospel and training those who will train others for gospel ministry. We do this by organizing gospel partnerships across cultural boundaries. *President:* Mr David Mills. *General Secretary:* Revd Canon Andy Lines. *Chairman:* Revd James Poole, 251 Lewisham Way, London, SE4 1XF   *Tel:* 020 8691 6111
Fax: 020 8694 8023
email: info@crosslinks.org
Web: www.crosslinks.org

CTBI Christians Abroad

CTBI Christians Abroad is a project of the Churches Together in Britain and Ireland. CTBI Christians Abroad provides self-funded opportunities for men and women of any age to work overseas in development or mission in Africa, Asia, South America and the Caribbean for short periods in projects associated with local Christian communities. Using a team of six experienced consultants CTBI Christians Abroad also provides, to national and local churches in Britain and Ireland, support and consultancy services to mission partners working overseas, to the personnel function of the church and to development projects overseas. For further information and travel, health and accident or medical insurance for overseas travellers, visit www.cabroad.org.uk For Volunteer opportunities contact David Brett, recruit@cabroad.org.uk For Consultancy services contact Colin South, support@cabroad.org.uk c/o 22 Ebenezer Close, Witham, Essex, CM8 2HX   *Tel:* 03000 121 201
email: recruit@cabroad.org.uk
2nd email: insurance@cabroad.org.uk
Web: www.cabroad.org.uk

Culham St Gabriel's Trust

Culham St Gabriel's is an endowed charitable trust dedicated to educational work in support of religious education (RE). We are committed to excellence in religious education for all learners. We support teachers by helping them to offer the best, high-quality learning experiences in RE, school worship and spiritual and moral development. We also support work that promotes the links between school ethos, values, leadership and school improvement. Culham St Gabriel's is formed of the union of two church college trusts, Culham Educational Foundation and St Gabriel's Trust, both of which have shared a long-term commitment to supporting religious education. We provide individual and corporate grants to support research, development and innovation in RE in the UK. We run an extensive programme of conferences, professional development opportunities and websites for teachers of RE, supported by our national network of consultants and collaborative projects. Current collaboration includes work with the Jerusalem Trust and the National Society to improve the teaching of Christianity in primary and secondary schools, and work with the Association of Church College Trusts and other partners to redevelop RE online. *Director:* Dr Mark Chater FRSA. *Chair of Trustees:* Dr Priscilla Chadwick FRSA, 62 Banbury Road, Oxford, OX2 6PN   *Tel:* 01865 612035
Fax: 01865 284886
email: enquiries@cstg.org.uk
Web: www.cstg.org.uk

Day One Christian Ministries

Day One Publications produces Christian books and cards, and Day One Prison Ministry works to supply prisons with evangelistic items. We now offer tours to Israel, Egypt, Greece and Turkey, with more places to follow. We have a new dedicated youth work offering bespoke on-site training and resources to churches. *President:* Mr John Roberts. *Managing Director:* Mr Mark Roberts, Ryelands Rd, Leominster, HR6 8NZ
Tel: 01568 613740
Fax: 01568 611473
email: sales@dayone.co.uk
Web: www.dayone.co.uk

Deaf Anglicans Together (DAT) (formerly National Deaf Church Conference)

This is the members' organization for deaf people in the Church of England, and it welcomes members of other churches and hearing people as well. DAT provides fellowship and training through conferences and other events, and promotes British Sign Language and deaf culture by means of workshops and festivals, exploring the use of drama, storytelling. signed hymns and poems. DAT also acts as a forum for exploring relevant issues, and encourages the participation of deaf people in the structures of the Church. DAT has three representatives on General Synod and three representatives on the Committee for Ministry of and among Deaf and Disabled People (CMDDP). DAT also works closely with other organizations involved with deaf Christians,

including Go! Sign (Christian Deaf Link UK), Signs of God and the Christian Interpreters Network. *Contact:* Revd Bob Shrine, 7 Russell Hall Lane, Queensbury, Bradford, BD13 2AJ
email: deafanglicans@gmail.com
Web: www.deafanglicanstogether.org

Deaf People, Royal Association for

RAD promotes the welfare and interests of deaf people, working with the Deaf Community, Deaf Clubs, deaf individuals and the parents of deaf children. Most of RAD's work is in London, Essex and the south-east of England. RAD is organized around the following services:
• Deaf Community Development;
• Advice and Advocacy;
• Learning Disability;
• Mental Health;
• Sign Language Interpreting;
• Training.

Chief Executive: Mr Tom Fenton, 18 Westside Centre, London Rd, Stanway, Colchester, CO3 8PH   *Tel:* 0845 688 2525/0845 688 2527 (Text)
Fax: 0845 688 2526
email: info@royaldeaf.org.uk
Web: www.royaldeaf.org.uk

Deans' Conference

The Deans' Conference is the meeting together (three times annually) of those who preside over their Cathedral Chapters to reflect upon cathedral issues of particular concern to Deans in their public and cathedral roles. *Chairman:* The Dean of Canterbury. *Treasurer:* The Dean of Exeter. *Secretary:* The Dean of St Albans, Cathedral Office, New St, Chelmsford, CM1 1TY
Tel: 01245 294492
Fax: 01245 294499
email: dean@chelmsfordcathedral.org.uk

Deans' Vergers' Conference

Founded in 1989 to bring together Head Vergers who are employed in that capacity by a Dean and Chapter of the Church of England. The Conference enables members to communicate with one another, exchange and discuss ideas of common interest and to have regular contact with the Deans' Conference. The Head Vergers of the forty-two English cathedrals, Westminster Abbey and St George's Windsor are eligible for membership. *Chairman:* Alex Carberry. *Treasurer:* Clive McCleester. *Secretary:* Glynn Usher, Head Verger and Sub-Sacrist, Bristol Cathedral, College Green, Bristol BS1 5TJ
Tel: 0117 946 8179 (Direct)
0117 926 4879 (Cathedral Office)
Fax: 0117 925 3678
email: glynn.usher@bristol-cathedral.co.uk

Diaconal Association of the Church of England

DACE is a professional association for diaconal ministers (deacons, accredited lay workers and Church Army officers) working in the Church of England, established in 1988 to succeed the Deaconess Committee and the Anglican Accredited Lay Workers Federation. Associate membership is also open to those who support diaconal ministry, and diaconal ministers working in other provinces in the UK. DACE exists to promote the distinctive (permanent) diaconate and other diaconal ministries in the Church of England, support all nationally recognized diaconal ministers, and to consider the theological and practical implications of diaconal ministry within the total ministry of the Christian Church, in partnership with other agencies and denominations. DACE is a member of the Diakonia World Federation of Diaconal Associations and Diaconal Communities. A registered charity. *President:* Revd David Rogers. *Secretary:* Revd Ann Wren. *Treasurer:* Revd Christopher Wren, St Peter's Bourne, 40 Oakleigh Park South, London, N20 9JN   *Tel:* 0208 4455 535
email: secretary@dace.org
Web: www.dace.org

Diakonia

Founded in 1947 to link the various European deaconess associations, it is now a 'World Federation of Diaconal Associations'. It concerns itself with the nature and task of 'Diakonia' and encourages deaconesses, deacons, and lay people doing diaconal work. It also furthers ecumenical relations between the diaconal associations in other countries. The Diaconal Association of the Church of England is a member. There is a Diakonia UK Liaison Group which also includes representatives from the Methodist Diaconal Order, the Church of Scotland Diaconate and the Deaconesses of the Presbyterian Church in Ireland. *Secretary:* Sr Traude Leitenberger
email: secretary@diakonia-world.org
Web: www.diakonia-world.org

Diocesan Clergy Chairs' Forum

The Forum is a voluntary group, allowing the elected chairs of the houses of clergy in each diocese to share ideas and experience, to address together various issues affecting the Church of England, to offer mutual support, and to develop principles of best practice in fulfilling this role in each diocese. Guidelines for best practice have been agreed with the House of Bishops. *Chair:* Rt Revd Jonathan Gibbs. *Hon. Secretary:* Revd Canon Steve Parish, 1A Fitzherbert St, Warrington, WA2 7QG   *Tel:* 01925 631781
email: s.parish17@ntlworld.com

Diocesan Institutions of Chester, Manchester, Liverpool and Blackburn

For the relief of widows and orphans of clergymen who have officiated in their last sphere of duty in the Archdeaconries of Chester, Macclesfield, Manchester, Rochdale, Liverpool, Warrington or Blackburn. *Chair:* Canon Michael

S. Finlay, 40 Chatteris Park, Sandymoor, Cheshire, WA7 1XE   *Tel:* 01928 579354
email: finlay289@btinternet.com

Distinctive Diaconate
An unofficial Church of England centre which serves to promote the diaconate as one of the historic orders of the Church's ministry with manifold potential for ministry today. From 1981 to 2012 it produced *Distinctive Diaconate News* and, from 1994–2012, *Distinctive News of Women in Ministry*. A *History of the Community of St Andrew: 1861–2011* was produced for its sesquicentennial, 30 November 2012. A commemorative booklet, *Our 150th*, was prepared for the 150th anniversary of the Deaconess Order of the Church of England which was celebrated at Lambeth Palace in July 2012. Writings on the history of women's diaconate are in preparation. *Editor:* Revd Dr Sr Teresa CSA, St Andrew's House, 16 Tavistock Crescent, Westbourne Park, London, W11 1AP   *Tel:* 020 7221 4604
email: teresajoan@btinternet.com

Ecclesiastical Insurance Office PLC
Ecclesiastical is an independent UK-owned insurer and investment management organization that donates a significant proportion of its profits to charity. Ecclesiastical has been providing a range of personal insurances, financial advice and investment services for the Church and community for more than 125 years. Today Ecclesiastical provides a range of personal insurances and financial services, including home insurance, savings and investments and funeral plans through their partner company. They also offer specialist commercial insurance for churches, church halls, charities, historic buildings, schools and care sector organizations. Ecclesiastical is owned by a registered charity, Allchurches Trust, and is one of the UK's Top 10 Company Donors to charity according to the Directory of Social Change. *Chairman:* Mr Will Samuel. *Group Chief Executive:* Mr Mark Hews, Beaufort House, Brunswick Rd, Gloucester, GL1 1JZ   *Tel:* 0845 777 3322
Fax: 01452 304818
email: information@ecclesiastical.com
Web: www.ecclesiastical.com

Ecclesiastical Law Society
Founded in 1987 to promote the study of ecclesiastical law, through the education of office bearers and practitioners in the ecclesiastical courts, the enlargement of knowledge of ecclesiastical law among clergy and laity of the Anglican Communion, and assistance in matters of ecclesiastical law to the General Synod, Convocations, bishops and church dignitaries. It is open to all with an interest in ecclesiastical law. *President:* Dr Sheila Cameron QC CBE. *Chairman:* Rt Revd Christopher Hill. *Secretary:* Mr Howard

Dellar. *Deputy Secretary:* Mr Stephen Borton, 1 The Sanctuary, London, SW1P 3JT
Tel: 020 7222 5381
Fax: 020 7799 2781
email: info@ecclawsoc.org.uk
Web: www.ecclawsoc.org.uk

Ecclesiological Society
For those who love churches. Studies the arts, architecture and liturgy of the Christian Church through meetings, tours and publications. *President:* David Stancliffe. *Chairman of the Council:* Trevor Cooper. *Honorary Membership Secretary:* Valerie Hitchman, PO Box 287, New Malden, KT3 4YT   *Tel:* 020 8942 2111
07718 155541
email: admin@ecclsoc.org
Web: www.ecclsoc.org

Ecumenical Council for Corporate Responsibility (ECCR)
ECCR, founded in 1989, is a church-based investor coalition and membership organization working for economic justice, human rights, environmental stewardship, and corporate and investor responsibility. It undertakes research, advocacy and dialogue with companies and investors and seeks to influence company policy and practice and to raise awareness of corporate and investor responsibility issues among the British and Irish churches, the investor community and the general public. It is a Body in Association with Churches Together in Britain and Ireland and a company limited by guarantee, registered in England and Wales. *Researcher:* Suzanne Ismail. *Executive Director:* John Arnold. *Administrator:* Binia Nightingale. *Church and Membership Relations Officer:* Helen Boothroyd, PO Box 500, Oxford, OX1 1ZL
Tel: 01865 245 349 (Admin)
075 0393 1172 (Membership)
email: info@eccr.org.uk
Web: www.eccr.org.uk

Ecumenical Society of the Blessed Virgin Mary
Founded in London in 1967, 'to advance the study at various levels of the place of the Blessed Virgin Mary in the Church under Christ and to promote ecumenical devotion'. Patrons include the Archbishop of Canterbury, Cardinal Kurt Koch (President of the Pontifical Council for Promoting Christian Unity), the Bishop of London, the Cardinal Archbishop Emeritus of Westminster, Archbishop Gregorios of Thyateira, Revd Dr John Newton, the Revd Dr Frances Young and the Bishop of Brentwood. *Hon General Secretary:* Father Bill OSM. *Hon Treasurer:* Vacancy. *Membership Secretary:* Mrs A. J. Gate. *Constitution Secretary:* Revd Victor Cassam. *Website Secretary:* Revd Giles Pinnock, 11 Belmont Rd, Wallington, SM6 8TE   *Tel:* 020 8647 5992
email: gensec@esbvm.org.uk
2nd email: membership@esbvm.org
Web: www.esbvm.org.uk

Elizabeth Finn Care

Elizabeth Finn Care gives grants and support to people struggling to cope with sudden or unexpected changes in their circumstances. We provide a financial and supportive safety net for people from over 120 occupations. Elizabeth Finn Care helps by providing both one-off and ongoing financial help, tailored to individual circumstances, as well as emotional support through our experienced caseworkers and national volunteer network. In 2007 we founded Turn2us, a charity offering website and helpline services designed to help people in financial need, and those who support them, access the welfare benefits and grants available to them. Turn2us and EFC joined together as a single charity with effect from October 2009. *Chief Exec:* Matthew Sykes. *Director of Income Generation and Communications:* Malcolm Tyndall, Hythe House, 200 Shepherds Bush Rd, London, W6 7NL

Tel: 020 8834 9200/ 0800 413 220 (helpline)
Fax: 020 7396 6739
email: info@elizabethfinn.org.uk
Web: www.elizabethfinncare.org.uk/
www.turn2us.org.uk

Elland Society Ordination Fund

Grants are made to applicants who are evangelical in conviction and who are in either residential or non-residential training for ordination in the Church of England. Priority is given to ordinands who are sponsored by dioceses in the Province of York or who intend to serve their title in that Province. Grants are usually to help those with unexpected or special financial needs which were not included in their main Church grant (if any). *Secretary/Treasurer:* Revd Colin Judd, 57 Grosvenor Road, Shipley, BD18 4RB

Tel: 01274 584775
email: thejudds@saltsvillage.wanadoo.co.uk
Web: www.ellandsociety.co.uk

English Churches Housing Group

In 2006 ECHG merged with Riverside Housing to become their specialist provider of sheltered and supported housing services. ECHG has gone on to win national awards for its work and each year provides housing and support for over 10,000 people across 170 local authorities. *Chair:* Mr Philip Raw. *Managing Director:* Derek Caren, 2 Estuary Boulevard, Estuary Commerce Park, Liverpool, L24 8RF *Tel:* 0345 111 0000
email: info@riverside.org.uk
Web: www.riverside.org.uk

English Clergy Association

Founded 1938, the Association seeks to sustain in fellowship all Clerks in Holy Orders in their vocation and ministry within the Church of England, promoting in every available way the good of English parish and cathedral life and the welfare of clergy. Related Trustees give discretionary clergy holiday grants upon applica-tion to the Hon Almoner. The Association seeks to foster the independence within the Established Church of all clergy whether in freehold office or not, and broadly supports the patronage system. Publishes twice-yearly *Parson and Parish* magazine. Lay members may be admitted. Subscription £10 p.a. (£5 retired/ordinands). *Patron:* The Bishop of London. *Chairman:* Revd John Masding. *Deputy Chairman:* Dr Peter Smith. *Vice-Chairman:* Revd Jonathan Redvers Harris, Office Address: The Old School, Norton Hawkfield, Bristol, BS39 4HB

Tel: 01275 830017/01983 565953/
Fax: 01275 830017
email: benoporto-eca@yahoo.co.uk
Web: www.clergyassoc.co.uk

Evangelical Alliance

Founded in 1846 as a representative body with denominational, congregational, organizational and individual supporters, its vision is to unite evangelicals and to provide an evangelical voice in the public square. Also aims to encourage action among evangelicals leading to spiritual and social transformation in the UK. Operates in England, Northern Ireland, Scotland and Wales. *General Director:* Mr Steve Clifford. *Executive Director – England and Churches in Mission:* Dr Krish Kandiah. *Executive Director – Finance and Operations:* Miss Helen Calder. *Advocacy Director:* Dr David Landrum, 176 Copenhagen Street, London, N1 0ST *Tel:* 020 7520 3830
Fax: 020 7520 3850
email: info@eauk.org
Web: www.eauk.org

Faith and Thought (the operational name of the Victoria Institute or Philosophical Society of Great Britain)

Founded 1865 to enquire into the relationship between the Christian revelation and modern scientific research. Publishes *Faith and Thought new series* in succession to *The Journal of the Transactions of the Victoria Institute* (JTVI); from 1958 *Faith and Thought*; from 1989 *Faith&Thought Bulletin*. Jointly with Christians in Science, since 1989 it sponsors the publication of *Science and Christian Belief*. Charity Registration no. 285871. *President:* Professor Sir Colin J. Humphreys CBE. *Chairman:* Revd Dr Robert Allaway. *Hon. Treasurer and Membership Secretary:* Revd John Buxton. *Editor and Meetings Secretary:* Reginald S. Luhman. *Administrator:* Dr Alan Kerry, 110 Flemming Avenue, Leigh on Sea, SS9 3AX

Tel: 01279 422661 (Hon Treasurer
and Membership Secretary)
01702 475110 (Editor and Meeting Secretary)
email: drapkerry@gmail.com
Web: www.faithandthought.org.uk

Family Action

Family Action has been the leading provider of services to disadvantaged and socially isolated

families since its foundation in 1869. We work with over 45,000 children and families a year by providing practical, emotional and financial support through over 100 services based in communities across England. Family Action works with the whole family and helps to tackle some of the most complex and difficult issues facing families today – including domestic abuse, mental health problems, learning disabilities and severe financial hardship. 501–505 Kingsland Rd, Dalston, London, E8 4AU   *Tel:* 020 7241 6251
email: info@family-action.org.uk
Web: www.family-action.org.uk

Farnham Castle International Briefing and Conference Centre
Farnham Castle, the former palace of the bishops of Winchester, offers a unique and special location for church weekend retreats. Several London churches are regular visitors. The castle has 31 en suite bedrooms, including some family rooms, all with television. Facilities include two historic consecrated chapels, a wide choice of conference rooms and five acres of beautifully maintained gardens. Farnham Castle has an excellent dining room and bar. It overlooks the town of Farnham and is only seven minutes by taxi from the railway station. Farnham is 30 miles west of London, with good rail connections to Waterloo station (55 minutes). Special weekend rates are available for groups of over 30 adults. Please contact Teresa Clue, Events Manager, for further information. A video tour is available on the website. *Chief Executive:* Mr James Twiss. *Director of Marketing & Client Services:* Mr Jeff Toms. *Conference Manager:* Mrs Barbara Milam. *Events Manager:* Teresa Clue, Farnham Castle, Farnham, GU9 0AG   *Tel:* 01252 721194
email: info@farnhamcastle.com
Web: www.farnhamcastle.com

Federation of Catholic Priests
A federation of priests in communion with the See of Canterbury who have undertaken to live in accordance with Catholic doctrine and practice. It exists for mutual support in propagating, maintaining and defending such doctrine and practice and for the deepening of the spiritual life of members. *Chairman:* Canon James Southward. *Secretary General:* Preb Brian Tubbs, 58 Dorset Avenue, Exeter, EX4 1ND
Tel: 01392 200506
email: fathertubbs@aol.com
Web: www.priests.org.uk

Feed the Minds
Feed the Minds believes that education saves lives, reduces poverty and builds community. Working in partnership worldwide, Feed the Minds funds a wide variety of innovative, indigenous educational projects. By improving access to knowledge and learning, Feed the Minds helps give people the opportunity to experience life in all its fullness. Registered Charity no. 291333 in England and Wales, and in Scotland, No SC041999. *President:* Revd David Cornick. *Chair of Trustees:* Dr David Goodbourn. *Director:* Ms Josephine Carlsson, Feed the Minds, Park Place, 12 Lawn Lane, London, SW8 1UD
Tel: 08451 21 21 02/
+44(0) 20 7582 3535 (International)
Fax: +44(0)20 7735 7617
email: info@feedtheminds.org
Web: www.feedtheminds.org

Fellowship of St Alban and St Sergius
Founded 1928. An unofficial body which fosters understanding and friendship between Eastern Orthodox and Western Christians. *Patrons:* Archbishop Gregorios of Thyateira and Great Britain; Lord Williams of Oystermouth; the Bishop of London; Archbishop Elisey of Sourozh; Metropolitan Kallistos of Diocletia; Bishop Angaelos; Dr Sebastian Brock FBA. *General Secretary:* Very Revd Stephen Platt, 1 Canterbury Rd, Oxford, OX2 6LU
Tel: 01865 552991
email: gensec@sobornost.org
Web: www.sobornost.org

Fellowship of St Nicholas (FSN)
FSN uses its resources to offset the disadvantage, deprivation and abuse of children in need in Sussex. Our current services include two centre-based family support and day care services including mobile and outreach, UK on-line centres, youth clubs, nurseries, children's bereavement project and family support. *Chairman:* Mrs Mollie Green. *Chief Executive:* Ms Christine Unsworth, The St Nicholas Centre, 66 London Rd, St Leonards-on-Sea, TN37 6AS
Tel: 01424 423683/01424 855222
Fax: 01424 460446
email: enquiries@fellowshipofstnicholas.org.uk
Web: www.fsncharity.co.uk

Fellowship of Word and Spirit
Anglican evangelical organization comprising 300 clergy and lay people committed to empowering, equipping and encouraging evangelicals through the development of thoughtful biblical theology for the 21st century using publications, conferences and a network of supportive fellowship. *Honorary President:* Rt Revd Wallace Benn. *Chairman:* Revd Simon Vibert, c/o 86 All Hallows Rd, Bispham, Blackpool, FY2 0AY   *email:* admin@fows.org
Web: www.fows.org

Forward in Faith
Founded in November 1992, Forward in Faith exists to proclaim the catholic faith and uphold catholic order and the catholic doctrine of the

sacraments. Through a national and local network it supports all who in conscience are unable to accept the ordination of women to the priesthood or the episcopate. It is working, through the Society under the patronage of St Wilfrid and St Hilda, for an ecclesial structure with a ministry and sacraments in which its members can have confidence, so that they can flourish within the Church of England and make their full contribution to its life and mission. It is governed by a council elected by the members of its National Assembly, which meets annually. It publishes the monthly journal *New Directions* and the catechetical weekly Pew Sheet *Forward!* and, with other leading catholic societies, a quarterly newspaper. *Chairman:* The Bishop of Fulham. *Director:* Dr Colin Podmore, 2A The Cloisters, Gordon Square, London, WC1H 0AG

Tel: 020 7388 3588
Fax: 020 7387 3539
email: FiF. UK@forwardinfaith.com
Web: www.forwardinfaith.com

Foundation for Church Leadership

The Foundation for Church Leadership (FCL) is an endowed charitable trust: its aims are to facilitate the support and development of emerging and senior church leaders, faith representatives and organizations for the benefit of leadership across the church. The Foundation primarily delivers its objectives through the provision of a series of consultancy and research initiatives. *Chair:* Dame Janet Trotter. *Director:* Julie Farrar, 16 Sycamore Business Park, Copt Hewick, Ripon, HG4 5DF   *Tel:* 01765 609167
Fax: 01765 709168
email: director@churchleadershipfoundation.org
Web: www.churchleadershipfoundation.org

Foundation of St Matthias

Considers applications for personal and corporate grants with preference given to higher and further education; applicants from the dioceses of Bath and Wells, Bristol and Gloucester. This does not preclude applicants from elsewhere. Applications should show how the chosen subject will contribute to the advancement of the Church of England. Examples of personal study not considered: medicine, veterinary science, engineering, law. Corporate applications should promote projects for the educational training of others and show how the Church's contribution to higher and further education will be enhanced. Closing dates for applications: 31 May and 30 September each year. The Trust is a member of the Association of Church College Trusts (*see separate entry*). *Correspondent:* Miss L. Cox, Hillside House, First Floor, 1500 Parkway North Newbrick Road, Stoke Gifford Bristol, BS34 8YU
Tel: 0117 906 0100
Fax: 0117 969 1530
email: stmatthiastrust@bristoldiocese.org
Web: www.stmatthiastrust.org.uk

Frances Ashton Charity

Supports serving or retired members of the Church of England clergy, or the widows/widowers thereof, who are in need. The trustees will consider almost any kind of financial hardship so long as the applicant falls within these categories. Where the applicant has an exceptional and urgent need, the trustees will consider applications quickly and at any time. Any urgent applications should be discussed with the adminstrator before applying. For holiday applications the deadline is 1 March of the year in which the holiday is to be taken. All other applications are ongoing throughout the year. Please seek the new applicant form from the administrator. *Administrator:* Georgina Fowle, Beech House, Woolston North Cadbury, Somerset, BA22 7BJ   *Tel:* 07775 717 606
email: francesashton@hotmail.co.uk

Friends of Friendless Churches

Founded 1957 to preserve churches and chapels of architectural or historic interest. Now owns 47 redundant places of worship, half in England and half in Wales. Also administers the Cottam Will Trust, which gives grants for the introduction of works of art into ancient Gothic churches. *President:* The Marquess of Salisbury. *Chairman:* Mr Roger Evans. *Director:* Mr Matthew Saunders. *Asst Director:* Mrs Alison Du Cane, St Ann's Vestry Hall, 2 Church Entry, London, EC4V 5HB
Tel: 020 7236 3934
email: office@friendsoffriendlesschurches.org.uk
Web: www.friendsoffriendlesschurches.org.uk

Friends of Julian of Norwich

The cell of Julian of Norwich, a chapel attached to St Julian's Church, Norwich, stands on the site where the 14th-century anchoress wrote her book *Revelations of Divine Love*. The Julian Centre, beside the church, houses a small bookshop and a library of works on Julian and spirituality and welcomes visitors and pilgrims (open Monday to Saturday 10.30 a.m. to 3.30 p.m.). Large parties should book in advance (office hours as above). Accommodation is often available in the small convent beside the church. Quiet days can be arranged. Please contact the Sister in Charge, All Hallows House. The Julian Centre, Rouen Rd, Norwich, NR1 1QT
Tel: 01603 767380 (group bookings)
01603 624738 (accommodation, quietdays)
email: centre@friendsofjulian.org.uk
Web: www.friendsofjulian.org.uk

Friends of Little Gidding, The

Little Gidding is rightly called a 'thin place'. From the seventeenth-century Ferrar family community to T. S. Eliot's visit in 1936 and up to the present time, many have experienced the presence of God at Little Gidding. The Friends (founded in 1947) take a practical and active involvement in the care of the historic church and the old farmhouse – now a retreat centre. It co-ordinates, with the T. S. Eliot Society, an annual Eliot Festival; arranges an annual pilgrimage in May; commemorates Nicholas Ferrar's life on his feast day, 4 December; and supports the provision of accommodation and hospitality for visitors and pilgrims. *Chair:* Simon Kershaw. *Secretary:* Neil McKittrick, c/o Ferrar House, Little Gidding, Huntingdon, PE28 5RJ

Tel: 01832 275343
email: friends@littlegidding.org.uk
Web: www.littlegidding.org.uk

Friends of the Clergy Corporation
See Corporation of the Sons of the Clergy

Friends of the Elderly
Friends of the Elderly has been helping older people since 1905. Our vision is that all older people should retain their independence, dignity and peace of mind. We offer high quality residential and nursing care in 14 care homes, some with dementia units. We support older people to stay living in their own homes with a range of community services including welfare grants for those in financial need, day care, home support, home visiting and telephone befriending. Registered Charity no. 226064 *Patron:* HM The Queen. *Chief Executive:* Richard Furze, 40–42 Ebury St, London, SW1W 0LZ

Tel: 020 7730 8263
Fax: 020 7259 0154
email: enquiries@fote.co.uk
Web: www.fote.org.uk

Frontier Youth Trust
Frontier Youth Trust (FYT) works with young people at risk towards justice, equality and community. Motivated by the Christian faith and informed by its principles, we work with people of all faiths and none. Based upon our youth work experience and research we also support, resource, inform, advise and train those working with and on behalf of disadvantaged young people. FYT works through a diverse range of projects including StreetSpace, Out4Good, Alongside and AIMCommunity. *Chief Executive:* Dr Alastair Jones, 202 Bradford Court, 123/131 Bradford Street, Birmingham, B12 0NS

Tel: 0121 771 2328
email: frontier@fyt.org.uk
Web: www.fyt.org.uk

Fulcrum
A network for evangelical clergy and laity. Launched in 2003 at the National Evangelical Anglican Congress in Blackpool, Fulcrum seeks to renew the evangelical centre by giving a voice to a nourishing orthodoxy. It provides support, theological exploration and encouragement for evangelical Anglicans and creates a space in which genuine debate can take place in a spirit of non-defensiveness and gracious disagreement, acknowledging that the clash of ideas can be creative and worthwhile. It has a website with regularly updated articles from leading evangelical theologians. *President:* Dr Elaine Storkey. *Chair:* Revd John Watson. *Theological Secretary:* Rt Revd Graham Kings. *General Secretary:* Revd Rachel Marszalek, All Saints Vicarage, Elm Grove Road, Ealing London, W5 3JH

email: admin@fulcrum-anglican.org.uk
Web: www.fulcrum-anglican.org.uk

Girlguiding UK
Founded 1910. Open to all girls and women between 5 and 65 years regardless of race, faith or any other circumstance. Its purpose is to enable girls to mature into confident, capable and caring women determined, as individuals, to realize their potential in their career, home and personal life, and willing as citizens to contribute to their community and the wider world. Rainbows age 5–7; Brownies age 7–10; Guides age 10–14; Senior Section age 14–25; Leaders age 18 plus. *Chief Guide:* Gill Slocombe. *Chief Executive:* Julie Bentley, 17/19 Buckingham Palace Rd, London, SW1W 0PT *Tel:* 0800 169 5901/020 7834 6242

Fax: 020 7828 8317
email: join.us@girlguiding.org.uk
Web: www.girlguiding.org.uk

Girls Friendly Society in England and Wales, The (Campaign name GFS Platform)
Established in 1875, GFS Platform works with girls and young women aged 7+. The work focuses on two specific areas, namely four community projects that work with young women between the ages of 14 and 25 who are either pregnant or who have children, and 40 parish-based youth work branches throughout England and Wales that run voluntary youth groups for girls and young women aged 7+. Main activities include reducing social exclusion and building self-esteem by providing social, formal educational and health awareness sessions and generic support in a single gender and non-judgemental environment. GFS Platform offers young women and girls the opportunity to explore their own personal and social development. This enables them to acquire new skills and knowledge, gain confidence, make informed choices and take responsibility for their own lives. *Director:* Joy Lauezzari, Unit 2 Angel Gate, 326 City Rd, London, EC1V 2PT

Tel: 020 7837 9669
Fax: 020 7837 4107
email: annualreport@gfsplatform.org.uk
Web: www.gfsplatform.org.uk

Girls' Brigade England and Wales
Girls' Bridge (GB) works with churches and schools to develop tailored outreach groups which enable children and young people to

belong, achieve and discover Jesus. GB is an international, interdenominational children's and youth organization. *National Director:* Miss Ruth Gilson, Cliff Colllege, Calver, Hope Valley Derbyshire, S32 3XG   *Tel:* 01246 582322
email: gbco@gb-ministries.org
Web: www.girlsb.org
Twitter: @GilsbrigadeEW

Greater Churches Network

The Greater Churches Group (now 'Network') was founded in 1991 as an informal association of non-cathedral churches, which, by virtue of their great age, size and of their historical, architectural or ecclesiastical importance, display many of the characteristics of a cathedral and also fulfil a role which is additional to that of a normal parish church. Its aims are to provide help and mutual support in dealing with the special challenges of running a 'cathedral-like' church within the organizational and financial structure of a parish church; to enhance the quality of parish worship in such churches; and to promote wider recognition of the unique position and needs of churches in this category. The group also serves as a channel of communication for other organizations wishing to have contact with churches of this type. *Hon Secretary:* Ms Philippa Shaw, Tewkesbury Abbey Office, Church Street, Tewkesbury, Gloucestershire, GL20 5RZ
Tel: 01684 856141
email: philippa.shaw@tewkesburyabbey.org.uk

Greenbelt Festivals

Greenbelt Festival takes place annually over the August Bank Holiday weekend, gathering together artists, musicians, speakers and performers, alongside 14,000 festivalgoers at Boughton House near Kettering. Its 41–year history is firmly rooted within a Christian tradition which is politically and culturally engaged. The festival is a family-friendly celebration, inclusive and accepting of all, regardless of ethnicity, gender, sexuality, background or belief. *Chair:* Andy Turner. *CEO:* Beccie D'Cunha, Greenbelt Festivals Ltd, 1B Snowhill Court, London, EC1A 2EJ   *Tel:* 020 7374 2755 (office)
020 7874 2760 (ticket line)
email: info@greenbelt.org.uk
Web: www.greenbelt.org.uk

Grubb Institute, The

The Grubb Institute seeks to contribute to the repair, healing and transformation of the world, which we have all contributed to creating both consciously and unconsciously. It enables leaders to work with their experience of human systems, institutions and personal relations in the context of Christ's activity, using insights and concepts developed from the human sciences and Christian theology and values. It provides consultancy, action research and learning events for people of all faiths or of none, from voluntary organizations, education, health, social care, criminal justice agencies, and business. As a Christian foundation, it has worked since 1969 with leaders in churches and dioceses, religious orders and agencies worldwide. *Executive Director:* Bruce Irvine, The Grubb Institute, 49–51 East Road, London, N1 6AH   *Tel:* 020 7250 8434
email: info@grubb.org.uk
Web: www.grubb.org.uk

Guild of All Souls

Founded 1873 as an intercessory guild, caring for the dying, the dead and the bereaved. Open to members of the Church of England and Churches in communion with her and any who share the objects of the Guild. Chantry chapel at Walsingham and at St Stephen's Church, Gloucester Road, London W8 5PU. Patron of forty-one livings of the Catholic tradition. *President:* The Bishop of Richborough. *General Secretary:* David Llewelyn Morgan. *Warden:* Louis A. Lewis. *Hon Treasurer:* Revd Paul E. Jones, St Alban's Centre, 18 Brooke Street, London, EC1N 7RD
Tel: 0207 404 8422
email: contact@guildofallsouls.org.uk
Web: www.guildofallsouls.org.uk

Guild of Church Braillists

The Guild consists of a group of people who give their services to help blind readers by transcribing a variety of religious literature into Braille. Requests are welcome from individual readers for books, special services, etc. All other productions are sent to the National Library for the Blind or the Library of the RNIB. For further details contact the Secretary. *Secretary:* Mary Hazlewood, Farthings, Pennymoor, Tiverton Devon, EX16 8LF   *Tel:* 01727 845183
email: info@gocb.org
Web: www.gocb.org

Guild of Church Musicians

Patrons: The Archbishop of Canterbury; the Archbishop of Westminster. Founded in 1888, but since 1961 has administered the Archbishops' Certificate in Church Music (ACert. CM) on behalf of the Archbishops of Canterbury and Westminster. This Certificate is a minimum qualification for church organists, choir trainers, cantors, choristers and leaders of instrumental groups and is fully ecumenical. The Archbishops' Award in Church Music is available for those who wish to be examined in practical skills only and the Guild's Preliminary Certificate in Church Music is aimed at young people and those starting in church music. Since 2002 the new qualification of Archbishops' Certificate in Public Worship (ACert. PW), for all who lead public worship, both clerical and lay, has been established. There is also a Fellowship examination (FGCM). *President:* Dame Mary Archer. *Warden:*

Revd Canon Dr Jeremy Haselock. *Administrative Secretary and General Secretary Emeritus:* John Ewington OBE. *Chairman of Academic Board:* Dr Hugh Benham. *Examinations Secretary:* Dr Helen Burrows, Tally Ho, Toys Hill, Westerham Kent, TN16 1QG
email: JohnMusicsure@orbixmail.co.uk
Web: www.churchmusicians.org

Guild of Health
The Guild of Health is an ecumenical Christian society serving the Healing Ministry which was founded (in 1904) to bring together doctors and clergy, in the first instance, to work together for health and wellbeing. We have a long history of the practice of meditation and intercessory prayer within the Christian tradition. More than a century later, we are still seeking to offer resources for healing in a variety of settings, through retreats, seminars and prayer groups. We are proud to be supporting the work of three organizations, sympathetic to our mission, who are engaged in specific aspects of healing and health: the Durham Project for Spirituality, Theology and Health; Saint Marylebone Healing and Counselling Centre; and Burrswood Christian Hospital (with particular regard to those suffering from ME). For further information please contact us or visit our website. *President:* Rt Revd John Pritchard. *Chair:* Revd Roger Hoath. *Vice-Chair:* Revd Stanley Baxter. *CEO:* Alex Scott. *Membership Secretary:* Mrs Rosie Press, c/o St Marylebone Parish Church, 17 Marylebone Rd, London, NW1 5LT
Tel: 020 7563 1389
email: guildofhealth@stmarylebone.org
2nd email: enquiries@gohealth.org.uk
(membership)
Web: www.gohealth.org.uk

Guild of Pastoral Psychology
The Guild offers a meeting ground for all interested in the relationship between religion and depth psychology, particularly the work of C. G. Jung and his followers. Depth psychology has contributed many new insights into the meaning of religion and its symbols and their relevance to everyday life. The Guild has monthly lectures in central London, a day conference in London in the spring and a three-day summer conference at Oxford. Further information and details of membership available from the Administrator. *Administrator:* Val Nurse, KVT BusinessCare, GPP Administration, Unit 1, Chapleton Lodge, East Winch Road, Blackborough End, Kings Lynn, PE32 1SF   *email:* administration@guildofpastoralpsychology.org.uk
Web: www.guildofpastoralpsychology.org.uk

Guild of Servants of the Sanctuary
Founded 1898 to raise the spiritual standard of Servers, to promote friendship among them and to encourage attendance at Holy Communion in addition to times of duty. *Warden:* Revd David Moore. *Secretary General:* Mr Terry Doughty, 7 Church Ave, Leicester, LE3 6AJ
Tel: 0116 262 0308
email: secretary@gssonline.org.uk
Web: www.gssonline.org.uk

Guild of St Leonard
The Guild was founded by the Revd John Sankey. Its object is to pray for all prisoners, those on licence or probation and for all who care for them. The Guild publishes a quarterly Intercession Paper. *Warden:* Rt Revd Lloyd Rees. *Secretary:* Revd Andrew Nichols, The Chaplain's Office, HMP Ford, Arundel, BN18 0BX
Tel: 01903 663000

Guild of St Raphael
Founded 1915 to work for the restoration of the Ministry of Healing as part of the normal function of the Church, by preparing the sick for all ministries of healing, by teaching the need of repentance and faith, by making use of the Sacraments of Healing and by Intercession. *Organizing Secretary:* Mrs Hanna Hart. *Warden:* Rt Revd N. Reade. *Sub-Warden:* Canon Paul Nener. *Editor of Chrism:* Prof Helen Leathard, 1a Snaetell Ave, Tuebrook, Liverpool, L13 7HA
Tel: 0151 228 3193/0151 228 2023
Fax: 0151 228 3193
email: office@guildofstraphael.org.uk
Web: www.guildofstraphael.org.uk

Harnhill Centre of Christian Healing
A retreat centre for the ministry of Christian Healing through prayer ministry, prayer, quiet days, teaching courses and Christian Healing Services. The Centre provides residential accommodation. *Chairman:* Dr David Wells. *Director:* Revd Kate Picot, Harnhill Manor, Cirencester, GL7 5PX   *Tel:* 01285 850283
Fax: 01285 850519
email: office@harnhillcentre.org.uk
Web: www.harnhillcentre.org.uk

Henry Bradshaw Society
Founded 1890 for printing liturgical texts from manuscripts and rare editions of service books, etc. For available texts, please consult the Society's website. *Secretary:* Dr Nicolas Bell, Music Collections, The British Library, 96 Euston Rd, London, NW1 2DB
email: nicolas.bell@bl.uk
Web: www.henrybradshawsociety.org

Highbury Centre
Christian guesthouse on quiet private road with ample free on-street parking. Reductions for missionaries/clergy. *Manager:* Mrs S. Scalora, 20–26 Aberdeen Park, Highbury, London, N5 2BJ
Tel: 020 7226 2663
email: enquiries@thehighburycentre.org
Web: www.thehighburycentre.org

Hockerill Educational Foundation

The Foundation makes personal awards to teachers, intending teachers and others in further or higher education, with a priority for the teaching of Religious Education in our schools. It does not make awards to those training for ordination, mission, social work or counselling, or to children at school. The Foundation makes corporate grants to support the development of religious education, particularly in the Dioceses of Chelmsford and St Albans. Full details of eligibility for awards can be found on our website at www.hockerillfoundation.org.uk. The applications deadline is 31 March each year. Working with NATRE it provides the Hockerill NATRE Prize for Innovation in the teaching of Religious Education. Available in both the Primary and Secondary sectors, this annual award gives a monetary prize to the school and an educational bursary to the teacher. It is a member of the Association of Church College Trusts (*see separate entry*), and the RE Council, and it part funds the APPG on Religious Education as well as the RE Quality Mark. *Correspondent/ Secretary:* Mr Derek J. Humphrey, 3 The Swallows, Harlow, Essex, CM17 0AR
Tel: 01279 420855
Fax: 0560 3140931
email: info@hockerillfoundation.org.uk
Web: www.hockerillfoundation.org.uk

Holy Rood House, Centre for Health and Pastoral Care

Opened in 1993, the Centre is a friendly house with a residential community. The house offers a gentle and holistic approach in a Christian environment where individuals or groups, of all ages and backgrounds, can work towards their own healing and explore their spiritual journey within an atmosphere of acceptance, love and openness. Professional counsellors and therapists, working closely with the medical profession, offer support at times of bereavement, abuse, addiction, relationship breakdown or illness, and creative arts and stress management play an important role in the healing process. Holy Rood House ministers within an awareness of justice and peace to daily or residential guests, and is also the home of the Centre for the Study of Theology and Health. *Patrons:* Lord Williams of Oystermouth; Prof Mary Grey. *Executive Director:* Revd Elizabeth Baxter. *Director,Therapeutic Care:* Jane Younger. *Director of Mission:* Revd Stanley Baxter, Holy Rood House 10 Sowerby Rd, Sowerby, Thirsk, YO7 1HX
Tel: 01845 522580/01845 522004
Fax: 01845 527300
email: enquiries@holyroodhouse.org.uk
Web: www.holyroodhouse.freeuk.com

Homes for Retired Clergy

See separate entries for Beauchamp Community *and* College of St Barnabas.

Hymn Society of Great Britain and Ireland

Founded in 1936 to encourage study and research into hymns, both words and music; to promote good standards of hymn singing and to encourage the discerning use of hymns and songs in worship. The Society publishes a quarterly magazine and there is a three-day annual conference. Further information and details of membership from the Secretary. *Secretary:* Revd Robert A. Canham, Windrush, Braithwaite, Keswick, CA12 5SZ
Tel: 01768 778054
email: robcanham.causeypike@gmail.com
Web: www.hymnsocietygbi.org.uk

Industrial Christian Fellowship

Founded in 1918 as a successor to the Navvy Mission (1877) and incorporating the Christian Social Union, ICF is a nationwide ecumenical network that provides support for Christians who want to apply their faith in fresh and creative ways in the everyday working world. A recent new initiative to make links between the local church and working life is the 'Take your Minister to Work' project. ICF provides resources, including liturgy and prayers for personal and corporate use, reflections and services related to work; a newsletter and occasional papers; and the quarterly journal *Faith in Business* (in association with the Ridley Hall Foundation). Close links with other groups and agencies involved with faith and work are maintained. Membership is open to individuals and organizations. *Chair:* Revd Phil Jump. *Secretary:* Mrs Ann Wright. *Treasurer:* Revd Jeremy Brown, PO Box 414, Horley, RH6 8WL
Tel: 01293 821322
email: wright@btinternet.com
Web: www.icf-online.org

Industrial Mission Association

The Industrial Mission Association (IMA) is a national and ecumenical association, mainly, though not exclusively, comprised of chaplains appointed to places of work throughout the UK. *Moderator:* Randell Moll, Penn Cottage, Green End, Granborough MK18 3NT
email: info@industrialmission.org.uk
Web: www.industrialmission.org.uk

INFORM

Inform is an independent charity founded in 1988 with funding from the British Home Office and mainstream Churches with the aim of obtaining and making available accurate, balanced and up-to-date information about alternative spirituality and new religious movements or 'cults'. It has a large collection of data on computer and in various other forms (books, articles, cuttings, videos and cassettes), and is in touch with an international network of scholars and other specialists. People with questions or concerns about new religious movements or alternative spirituality should contact the Inform office, which is based at the London School of

ORGANIZATIONS

Economics, between 10 a.m. and 4.30 p.m., Mondays to Fridays. *Chair of the Board of Governors:* Prof Eileen Barker. *Director:* Nicholas Parke; Deputy Director Dr Amanda van Eck Duymaer van Twist. *Research Officers:* Sarah Harvey and Dr Suzanne Newcombe. *Assistant Research Officers:* Silke Steidinger and Adviya Khan. *Administrative Officer:* Sibyl Macfarlane, LSE, Houghton St, London, WC2A 2AE
Tel: 020 7955 7654 (Information line)
email: INFORM@LSE.ac.uk
Web: www.inform.ac

Inter Faith Network for the UK
Established in 1987 to encourage contact and dialogue between different faith communities in the United Kingdom. It aims to advance public knowledge and mutual understanding of the teaching, traditions and practices of the different faith communities in Britain, including an awareness of their distinctive features and of their common ground, and to promote good relations between persons of different faiths. Its member organizations include national faith community representative bodies; national, regional and local inter faith bodies; and academic institutions and educational bodies concerned with inter faith issues. *Director:* Dr Harriet Crabtree. *Co-Chairs:* Rt Revd Richard Atkinson and Mr Vivian Wineman, 2 Grosvenor Gardens, London, SW1W 0DH
Tel: 020 7730 0410
Fax: 020 7730 0414
email: ifnet@interfaith.org.uk
Web: www.interfaith.org.uk

Intercontinental Church Society
Founded in 1823, ICS is an Anglican mission agency ministering to English-speaking people worldwide; it is engaged in church planting, growth and outreach to tourists and is a patronage society (nominating chaplains for international Anglican churches abroad). *President:* Viscount Brentford. *Mission Director:* Revd Richard Bromley, Unit 11, Ensign Business Centre, Westwood Way, Westwood Business Park, Coventry CV4 8JA
Tel: 024 7646 3940
email: enquiries@ics-uk.org
Web: www.ics-uk.org

International Ecumenical Fellowship – British Region
IEF is a community of Christians both lay and ordained, with regional groups in Belgium, Czech Republic, France, Germany, Great Britain, Hungary, Poland, Romania, Slovak Republic and Spain. It also has individual members in various other countries. Through annual international gatherings and smaller regional groups, Christians from Catholic, Orthodox and Protestant traditions meet to worship, pray, study and enjoy fellowship together. IEF tries to strengthen the spirit of ecumenism and international friendship. IEF practises eucharistic hospitality as far as church discipline and individual conscience permit. *President of British Region:* Revd Richard Orchard. *Secretary:* Revd C. R. Hardiman. *Treasurer:* Mr G. Morton, 20 Kent Place, South Shields, NE34 6PU
Tel: 0191 456 1943
email: cynthiahardiman@blueyonder.co.uk
Web: www.ief-oecumenica.org

Interserve
Interserve is an interdenominational, evangelical mission agency with over 800 full-time Christian professionals working across Asia, the Arab World, and among ethnic groups in England and Wales. Interservers work in many different ministries, seeking to share the love of Christ through everything they say and do. All Christians with a burden to respond to Jesus commission and make disciples of all nations are welcomed for both long and short term periods of service, with the aim of seeing lives and communities transformed through encounter with Jesus Christ. *National Director:* Steve Bell, 5/6 Walker Avenue, Wolverton Mills, Milton Keynes, MK12 5TW
Tel: 01908 552700
Fax: 01908 552779
email: info@interserve.org.uk
Web: www.interserve.org.uk

Journeying
Journeying is an ecumenical organization which takes small groups of people on holiday in an informal Christian ambience to the more remote and not-so-remote parts of Britain and Ireland. What we offer is almost certainly unique in Britain. Its origins lie in Celtic spirituality and most of our trips still reflect that approach. Pilgrimage too has been part of our story from the earliest days and that aspect continues to form a thread woven through all that we do. Journeying, formerly known as Pilgrim Adventure, was founded in 1988, *Patron:* Rt Revd John Pritchard, Bishop of Oxford. *Co-ordinators:* David Gleed and Paul Heppleston, 18 Holyland Road, Pembroke, Pembrokeshire, SA71 4BL
Tel: 01646 279478
email: info@journeying.co.uk
Web: www.journeying.co.uk

Jubilate Group
An association of authors and musicians formed in 1974 for the purpose of publishing material for contemporary worship: *Hymns for Today's Church, Church Family Worship, Carols for Today, Carol Praise, Let's Praise!* 1 and 2, *Prayers for the People, Psalms for Today, Songs from the Psalms, The Dramatised Bible, The Wedding Book, Hymns for the People, World Praise* 1 and 2 and *Sing Glory. Chairman:* Dr Noel Tredinnick. *Secretary:* David Peacock. *Copyright Managers:* Mrs Cathy Davis. *Editorial*

Organizations

Coordinator: Mr Roger Peach. Resound Coordinator: Mr Joel Payne   Tel: 01803 607754
Fax: 01803 605682
email: copyrightmanager@jubilate.co.uk
2nd email: roger@jubilate.co.uk /
joelresound@gmail.com
Web: www.jubilate.co.uk

Julian Meetings, The
A network of Christian contemplative prayer groups, begun in Britain in 1973. There are now about 350 groups in Great Britain and some in Australia, Canada, Ireland, Southern Africa and the USA. Ecumenical. Magazine three times a year. Contact: Deidre Morris, 263 Park Lodge Lane, Wakefield, WF1 4HY   Tel: 01924 369437
email: gb@julianmeetings.org
Web: www.julianmeetings.org

Keswick Convention
The Keswick Convention is the main event organized annually by Keswick Ministries and has been taking place since 1875. It offers something for everyone – life-changing Bible teaching, uplifting worship and great fellowship combined with the chance to relax and enjoy a holiday in the wonderful setting of the Lake District. Chairman: Mr John Risbridger. General Director: Mr David Bradley. Operations Manager: Mr Simon Overend, Keswick Convention Trust, Skiddaw St, Keswick, CA12 4BY   Tel: 01768 780075
Fax: 01768 775276
email: info@keswickministries.org
Web: www.keswickministries.org

Keswick Hall Trust Charity
The Trustees' spending gives priority to their own local initiatives, but they also have limited funds and give grants in response to personal or corporate applicants for research or study in religious education. Within this field, they give priority to students studying for a PGCE in RE. Applications are welcomed from students attending universities throughout the UK. Member of the Association of Church College Trusts (see separate entry). Applications should be made online only at our website www.keswickhalltrust.org.uk Executive Officer: Malcolm Green, Keswick Hall Trust, PO Box 307, Woodbridge, IP13 6WL
Tel: 07760 433 409
email: admin@keswickhalltrust.org.uk
Web: www.keswickhalltrust.org.uk

Keychange Charity (formerly Christian Alliance)
Established 1920. Offers care, acceptance and Christian community to people in need through the provision of residential care for frail elderly people and supported accommodation for young homeless people. Chief Executive: Graham Waters, 5 St George's Mews, 43 Westminster Bridge Rd, London, SE1 7JB   Tel: 020 7633 0533
Fax: 020 7928 1872
email: info@keychange.org.uk
Web: www.keychange.org.uk

Korean Mission Partnership
Founded in 1889 by Edward White Benson, Archbishop of Canterbury, as the Church of England Mission to Korea, the name was changed in 1993 when the Province of Korea was inaugurated. The name reflects the two-way nature of our mission today. Support goes to Korea by way of prayer, interest and funding. The Province has sent a priest from Seoul to run the Korean Chaplaincy in the Diocese of London, ministering to Korean people who live mainly in and around the Home Counties. President: The Primate of Korea. Chairman: Revd Mark Williams. Hon Admin Secretary: Revd Martin Fletcher. Hon Treasurer: Mrs Lucille West, St John the Divine Vicarage, 92 Vassall Road, London, SW9 6JA
Tel: 020 7735 9340
email: fr_mark@yahoo.com
Web: www.koreanmission.org

Langley House Trust
Founded in 1958, the Langley House Trust is national Christian charity that provides support and care to offenders (and those at risk of offending), enabling individuals to live independent and crime-free lives. Langley enables offenders to address their needs, including support for mental health and substance misuse issues and the provision of a safe and stable home. Langley currently runs a number of residential projects across England, including care homes and projects for women. Langley works with a wide variety of people, with the belief that no one's history should define their destiny, achieving an exceptional reoffending rate of just 3 per cent. Langley bases its services on Christian beliefs and values but is open to men and women of any or no faith. Chairman: Anthony Howlett-Bolton. Chief Exec: Tracy Wild. Corporate Operations Director: David Reynolds. Corporate Services Director: Ken Brown. Corporate Development Director: Andrew Lerigo, PO Box 181, Witney, OX28 6WD   Tel: 01993 774075
Fax: 01993 772425
email: info@langleyhousetrust.org
Web: www.langleyhousetrust.org

Latimer Trust
The Latimer Trust is dedicated to providing a biblical and considered response to the issues facing today's Anglican Communion. Through a range of resources it is continuing and developing the work of Latimer House, founded in Oxford in the 1960s. Reg. Charity no. 1084337. Chairman of the Council: Revd Dr Mark Burkill.

Director of Research: Revd Dr Gerald Bray, c/o Oak Hill College, Chase Side, London, N14 4PS   *Tel:* 020 8449 0467 ext. 227   *email:* administrator@latimertrust.org   *Web:* www.latimertrust.org

Lee Abbey Household Communities
There are two household communities based in Urban Priority Areas in Birmingham and Bristol. Community members live under a common rule of life and seek to be involved in their local community and church. *Contact:* Gill Arbuthnot, 101 Dorridge Rd, Dorridge, Solihull, B93 8BS   *Tel:* 0121 327 0095/01567 776558   *Web:* www.leeabbey.org.uk/households/

Lee Abbey International Students' Club
Founded in 1964 by the Lee Abbey Fellowship as a ministry to students of all nationalities, the Club provides long- and short-term hostel accommodation for students of all faiths or none and is served by a Christian community, which consists of young people from all over the world. Applications are invited from anyone interested in joining the community, residing as a student or staying as a holiday-maker. *Warden:* Canon Trevor Hubble, 57–67 Lexham Gardens, London, W8 6JJ   *Tel:* 020 7373 7242   *Fax:* 020 7244 8702   *email:* personnel@leeabbeylondon.com   *2nd email:* accommodation@leeabbeylondon.com   *Web:* www.leeabbeylondon.com

Leprosy Mission, The
We are an international Christian development organization. Inspired by our Christian values, we work in equal partnership with people affected by leprosy and with other stakeholders. As partners, together we transform lives through advocacy and the enablement of physical, social, economic and spiritual development of individuals and communities affected by leprosy and other disabilities. *National Director:* Peter A. Walker, Goldhay Way, Orton Goldhay, Peterborough, PE2 5GZ   *Tel:* 01733 370505   *Fax:* 01733 404880   *email:* post@tlmew.org.uk   *Web:* www.leprosymission.org.uk

Lesbian and Gay Christian Movement
LGCM has four principal aims: to encourage fellowship, friendship and support among lesbian and gay Christians through prayer, study and action; to help the whole Church examine its understanding of human sexuality and to work for positive acceptance of gay relationships; to encourage members to witness to their Christian faith within the gay community and to their convictions about human sexuality within the Church; and to maintain and strengthen links with other lesbian and gay Christian groups both in Britain and elsewhere. An extensive network of local groups exists and a wide range of resources are available. *Chief Executive:* Revd Richard Kirker, Oxford House, Derbyshire St, Bethnal Green, London, E2 6HG   *Tel and Fax:* 020 7739 1249   *email:* lgcm@lgcm.org.uk   *Web:* www.lgcm.org.uk

Li Tim-Oi Foundation
2014 was the seventieth anniversary of the priesting of the first Anglican woman, Florence Li Tim-Oi, on 25 January 1944. In 2007, the centenary year of her birth, the Trustees adopted the mantra: 'it takes one woman'. Since it was launched twenty years ago, the Foundation has allocated more that 750,000 in bursaries to empower over 380 Anglican women in the Two-thirds World of the 'South' to become agents for change in church and society. Celebrations of the twentieth anniversary of the first Church of England women preists yielded more that 7,500 and raised our profile. New requests for help, particularly from Africa, continue to outstrip available funds. Every donation from parishes and individuals is put to effective use. Celebrations of the twentieth anniversary, significant birthdays, wedding anniversaries, Christmas or memorial services are opportunities for requesting donations. Bequests, especially from women in gratitude for their own priesting, are particularly welcome. *Patrons:* Lord Williams of Oystermouth, the Archbishop of Hong Kong, the Archbishop of Kenya, the Archbishop of the Congo, Rt Revd Victoria Matthews, Baroness Perry of Southwark and Mrs Jane Williams. *Chair:* Canon Pamela Wilding MBE. *Secretary:* Canon Christopher Hall, The Knowle, Deddington, Banbury, OX15 0TB   *Tel:* 01869 338225   *email:* info@ittakesonewoman.org   *Web:* www.ittakesonewoman.org

Librarians' Christian Fellowship
See Christians in Library and Information Services.

Liddon Trust
See Society of the Faith (Incorporated).

Lincoln Theological Institute
Inaugurated in 1997 and based at the University of Manchester, the Institute's primary aim is to undertake, promote and support theological enquiry into contemporary society and thereby to practise theology in the fullest sense. It focuses on postgraduate and postdoctoral research, working closely with colleagues in the Department of Religions and Theology. Core areas for research include: (1) place, locality, habitation and ecology; (2) global threats and powers; (3) religion and civil society; (4) technology, limits and transformation; (5) power and institutions (including the church); (6) liberation, political, ecologial and public theologies; (7) culture – includng religious cultures – and resources of

hope; and (8) theologies of education. Students wishing to study under the auspices of the Institute may enrol through the University of Manchester for Masters and Doctoral degree programmes. Formal and informal enquiries from prospective students are encouraged. The Lincoln Theological Institute originated from Lincoln Theological College, founded in 1874 as an ordination training college. Since 2003 the Institute has been a fully integrated research unit within the University of Manchester. For further information please contact the Director. *Director:* Prof Peter M. Scott. *Research Associate:* Dr Benjamin J. Wood, School of Arts, Histories and Cultures, University of Manchester, Oxford Rd, Manchester, M13 9PL

> *Tel:* 0161 275 3064 0161 275 3736
> *email:* peter.scott@manchester.ac.uk
> *Web:* http://www.lincolntheologicalinstitute.com

Livability (formerly known as the Shaftesbury Society)
Livability is a new charity, formed by the merger of the Shaftesbury Society and John Grooms. Livability creates choices for disabled people and brings life to local communities. We offer a wide range of services to around 8,000 disabled people and their families, including residential care, supported living, education and accessible holidays. We also provide community organizations with the resources, advice and confidence to transform their neighbourhoods. *Chief Executive:* Mary Bishop, 50 Scrutton St, London, EC2A 4XQ

> *Tel:* 020 7452 2000
> *Fax:* 020 7452 2001
> *email:* info@livability.org.uk
> *Web:* www.livability.org.uk

Liverpool Seafarers Centre
See Mersey Mission to Seafarers, The.

Living Stones (formerly Church and Community Trust)
An independent charitable trust offering friendly guidance and support at both diocesan and individual church level on building a future by making the most effective use of resources – buildings, money, people – for worshipping God and serving the community. *Administrator:* Roger Munday, Cally Hall, Blackshawhead, Hebden Bridge, HX7 7JP   *Tel:* 07971 378 533

> *email:* info@living-stones.org.uk
> *Web:* www.living-stones.org.uk

London City Mission
For over 175 years, LCM has been working with churches to bring the Christian message to the people of London. Today, in the workplace, out on the streets and in the various communities of London, over 300 workers and volunteers are actively seeking to bring Christian values and hope to those they meet. *Chairman:* Mark Harding. *Chief Executive:* Revd Dr John Nicholls,

Nasmith House, 175 Tower Bridge Rd, London, SE1 2AH   *Tel:* 020 7407 7585

> *Fax:* 020 7403 6711
> *email:* enquiries@lcm.org.uk
> *Web:* www.lcm.org.uk

Lord Wharton's Charity
Founded 1696 to distribute Bibles and other religious books to children and young people of all denominations in all counties of the United Kingdom and Northern Ireland. *Clerk to the Trustees:* Mrs B. Edwards, Magnolia Cottage, Harrowbeer Lane, Yelverton, PL20 6EA

> *Tel and Fax:* 01822 852636
> *email:* edwardsbobbarbara@btinternet.com

Marshall's Charity
Founded 1627. Makes grants for (1) building, purchasing or modernizing parsonages of the Church of England or the Church in Wales, (2) repairs to churches in Kent, Surrey and Lincolnshire. *Clerk to the Trustees:* Mrs Catherine Dawkins, Marshall House, 66 Newcomen St, London, SE1 1YT   *Tel:* 020 7407 2979

> *Fax:* 020 7403 3969
> *email:* grantoffice@marshalls.org.uk
> *Web:* www.marshalls.org.uk

Mediawatch-UK (formerly the National Viewers' and Listeners' Association)
Mediawatch-UK is a voluntary association which campaigns for family values in the media. We believe that the media we consume inevitably shapes the moral, ethical, social and political values of our culture and we champion the rights of the public to socially responsible broadcasting. Our campaigns include fighting for meaningful protection for children from premature sexualization by the media and from potentially harmful material online. The organization was founded in 1965 by Mary Whitehouse and her associates who were concerned that that television was attacking and undermining family life. Benefits of membership include representation at the highest levels, regular newsletters and updates and assistance to enable members to make their voices heard. *Director:* Miss Vivienne Pattison, 3 Willow House, Kennington Rd, Ashford, TN24 0NR   *Tel:* 01233 633936

> *Fax:* 01233 633836
> *email:* info@mediawatchuk.org
> *Web:* www.mediawatchuk.org

Melanesian Mission
The Melanesian Mission was established in 1854 to buy the first 'Southern Cross' ship for Bishop Selwyn to use for mission work in the islands of Melanesia. Today the Mission supports the Church of Melanesia (including the religious orders) through money, prayer and people – helping the church to fulfil its priorities and work through this vast and isolated region. *Chairman:* Rt Revd Nigel Stock. *Hon. Treasurer:* Mrs Helen

Miller. *Executive Officer:* Mrs Katie Drew, 21 The Burlands, Feniton, Honiton, Devon, EX14 3UN
email: mission@melanesia.anglican.org
Web: www.melanesia.anglican.org

Mersey Mission to Seafarers, The

Founded 1856 to 'promote the spiritual and temporal welfare of seafarers' from around the world who visit the ports of the River Mersey, Manchester Ship Canal and the Isle of Man. We will also respond to any emergency within the geographical area, Holyhead to Scottish Borders. *Chairman:* Mrs Pamela Brown MBE, JP, DL. *Chief Executive:* John P. Wilson, Liverpool Seafarers Centre, 20 Crosby Rd South, Liverpool, L22 1RQ   *Tel:* 0300 800 8080
07973 824154 (Mobile)
Fax: 0871 900 3223
email: admin@liverpoolseafarerscentre.org
Web: www.liverpoolseafarerscentre.org

Mid-Africa Ministry (CMS)

Mid-Africa Ministry (MAM), founded in 1921, now forms part of the Church Mission Society. *See* Church Mission Society.

Mirfield Centre

Offers a meeting place for about 60 people. Small residential conferences are possible in the summer vacation. Day and evening events are arranged by the Centre management team. *Director:* Revd June Lawson. *Centre Administrator:* Mrs Rachael Salmon. *Centre Brothers:* Father Thomas Seville, Father Simon Holden, Father Dennis Berk, The Mirfield Centre, Stocks Bank Road, Mirfield, WF14 0BW   *Tel:* 01924 481920
email: centre@mirfield.org.uk
Web: www.mirfieldcentre.org.uk

Mission to Seafarers, The

Founded in 1856, and entirely funded by voluntary donations, today's Mission to Seafarers offers emergency assistance, practical support, advocacy services, access to legal advice and family liaison to seafarers in need in over 260 ports in 71 countries around the world, through its global network of chaplains and volunteers who offer a warm Christian welcome. In many ports it works in close cooperation with Christian societies of other denominations, and it is a member of the International Christian Maritime Association. *President:* HRH The Princess Royal. *Secretary General:* Revd Andrew Wright. *Director of Justice and Public Affairs:* Revd Canon Ken Peters, St Michael Paternoster Royal, College Hill, London, EC4R 2RL   *Tel:* 020 7248 5202
Fax: 020 7248 4761
email: info@missiontoseafarers.org
Web: www.missiontoseafarers.org

MODEM

MODEM is a network/association whose mission is to lead and enable authentic dialogue between exponents of Christian leadership, management and organization, and spirituality, theology and ministry. MODEM is an ecumenical membership organization, open to all Christians irrespective of age, gender, race, culture or nationality, and welcoming dialogue with all comers of all faiths. In association with SCM/Canterbury Press, MODEM has published three ground-breaking books, *Management and Ministry* – appreciating contemporary issues; *Leading, Managing, Ministering* – challenging questions for church and society; and *Creative Church Leadership* – on the challenge of making a difference through leadership, the latter edited by Dr John Adair and John Nelson. The fourth and latest book *How to Become a Creative Leader* was published in February 2008, and is essentially the 'how to' book following the previous three. See website for further information and details of special introductory membership offer to include some or all of the books. *Chairman:* Revd Elizabeth Welch. *Secretary:* John Nelson. *Contact:* Peter J. Bates, Carselands, Woodmancote, Henfield, BN5 9SS
Tel and Fax: 01273 493172
email: info@modem-uk.org
2nd email: membership@modem-uk.org
Web: www.modem-uk.org

Modern Church (formerly Modern Churchpeople's Union)

Modern Church promotes liberal theology and offers Christian debate and discussion on religious issues. It embraces the spirit of freedom and informed enquiry and seeks to involve the Christian faith in an ongoing search for truth by interpreting traditional doctrine in the light of present day understanding. It was founded at the end of the nineteenth century as a Church of England society but now welcomes all who share its ethos. It holds an annual conference on contemporary issues. Membership includes subscription to the journal *Modern Believing*. *General Secretary:* Revd Guy Elsmore, Modern Church Office, 7 Crossley Drive, Liverpool, L15 8AJ   *Tel:* 0845 345 1909
email: office@modernchurch.org.uk
Web: www.modernchurch.org.uk

Montgomery Trust Lectures

This endowment by Sir Alexander Montgomery of Albury, Surrey supports public lectures particularly for theological societies and religious education teachers on the results of modern scholarship on the Bible, with an emphasis on Christian apologetics. Hosts include: University departments; Further Education colleges; organizations providing ministerial support; ordinand and preacher training; theological societies; local groupings of Religious Education teachers; Standing Advisory Councils for

Religious Education, churches and cathedrals. Host organizations should contact the Administrator to identify a lecturer/theme. An interactive catalogue is available on our website http://www.montgomerytrust.org.uk/. Printed copies of the catalogue are available by post. The Administrator arranges the booking with an available lecturer. The host organization gathers an audience in excess of 30 people and provides the venue. After the Lecture the host organization completes and returns to the Trust a straightforward report pro forma. Then the Trust provides the Lecturer direct with an honorarium and reimburses their travel expenses. The Advisory committee meets in the summer when amongst other duties they approve new additions to the list of Montgomery Lecturers. Suggestions for new additions to this list are invited to our Administrator Mark Clarke in Birmingham. *Advisers:* Revd Prof Richard Burridge, Dean of King's College London, Very Revd David Ison, Dean of St Paul's Cathedral and Very Revd Dr John Hall, Dean of Westminster. *Administrator:* Mark Clarke, Christian Education, 1020 Bristol Road, Selly Oak, Birmingham, B29 6LB *Tel:* 0121 472 4242 *Fax:* 0121 472 7575 *email:* professionalservices@christianeducation.org.uk *Web:* http://www.montgomerytrust.org.uk/

Morse-Boycott Bursary Fund (formerly St Mary-of-the-Angels Song School Trust)
Founded in 1932 originally as a parochial Choir School but from 1935 to 1970 served the Church at large. Now provides financial assistance to the parents of boy choristers at cathedral choir schools throughout the UK. The Fund depends entirely on donations and legacies to build the capital from which bursaries can be provided to the needy. *Trustees:* Dean and Chapter of Chichester. *Administrator:* The Communar, The Royal Chantry, Cathedral Cloisters, Chichester, PO19 1PX *Tel:* 01243 782595 01243 812 92 *Fax:* 01243 812499 *email:* admin@chichestercathedral.org.uk *Web:* www.chichestercathedral.org.uk

Mothers' Union
A Christian organization devoted to promoting marriage and the well-being of families worldwide. The Vision of Mothers' Union is 'A world where God's love is shown through loving, respectful and flourishing relationships'. This means that Mothers' Union invests in relationship. Through programmes, policy work, community outreach, Christian fellowship and prayer, Mothers' Union supports and nurtures relationships in the belief that this brings about stable families and benefits society. To do this, Mothers' Union takes positives steps to encourage marriage and family life. Projects tackle the most urgent needs threatening relationships and communities, and work towards fostering strong families and independent, cohesive communities.

Mothers' Union is not a mission-sending organization, or a development charity, although mission and development are strong characteristics of its work. Rather, it is a network of 3.6 million people, each serving Christ in their local community at the grassroots level. It has a subscribers magazine, *Families First* and a magazine for members, *Families Worldwide* which includes the prayer diary material. Further information and resources are available from the charity's website. *Worldwide President:* Mrs Lynne Tembey. *Chief Exec:* Mr Reg Bailey, Mary Sumner House, 24 Tufton St, London, SW1P 3RB *Tel:* 020 7222 5533 *Fax:* 020 7227 9737 *email:* mu@themothersunion.org *Web:* www.themothersunion.org

Mozambique and Angola Anglican Association (MANNA)
Founded by 1906, MANNA was formed to support the Diocese of Lebombo in southern Mozambique; it has now developed into supporting work within both the former Portuguese Territories, which are among the poorest in the world. While two world wars and lengthy civil wars hindered the work, since peace was established in both countries the church is growing at a great rate, predominantly through indigenous clergy who need support for their work. There are now three dioceses with well over 200 clergy. Registered Charity no. 262818. *Chair:* Ven Christopher Cunliffe, Archdeacon of Derby. *General Secretary:* Elizabeth Thomas, 1 The Green, Marcham, Oxfordshire, OX13 6NE *Tel:* 07801 523461 *email:* elizabeth@maninga.org *Web:* www.manna-anglican.org

National Archives, The
Records of central government and courts of law from the Norman Conquest (Domesday Book) to the recent past (for example, the Suez Campaign). Kew, Richmond-upon-Thames, TW9 4DU *Tel:* 020 8876 3444 *email:* via website *Web:* www.nationalarchives.gov.uk

National Association of Diocesan Advisers in Women's Ministry
NADAWM is a national network of diocesan advisers, appointed by their Bishop, for the purpose of advising in relation to the ministry of ordained women in the Church of England. This work involves monitoring the culture in which women clergy exercise their roles, consultng with those women, supporting them in their work, celebrating their ministry, acting as advocates of ordained women in a wide range of ways and contexts and advising bishops accordingly.

Chair: Revd Rosemary Lain-Priestly. *Treasurer:* Revd Hilary Jones. *Secretary:* Revd Robbin Clark, 15b College Green, Worcester, WR1 2LH
email: rclark@glosdioc.org.uk

National Churches Trust

The National Churches Trust is the only national independent charity dedicated to promoting and supporting church buildings of historic, architectural and community value across the UK. The successor to the Historic Churches Preservation Trust (HCPT), the Trust offers grants mainly for structural repairs, new facilities and improved access, promotes the benefit to communities of church buildings and inspires everyone to value and enjoy them. Registered charity no. 1119845. *Patron:* HM The Queen. *Chairman of Trustees:* Luke March. *Chief Executive:* Claire Walker. *Grants Manager:* Alison Pollard. *Communications Manager:* Eddie Tulasiewicz, 7 Tufton Street, London, SW1P 3QB
Tel: 020 7222 0605
email: info@nationalchurchestrust.org
Web: www.nationalchurchestrust.org

National Council for Social Concern

The charity (also known by the short titles 'Concern' and 'Social Concern') has promoted a wide range of activities in connection with the Church of England, but in recent years has had a particular interest in aspects of the criminal justice system and in issues arising from addictions. It works closely with the Church of England Board for Social Responsibility. Details from the Secretary. *Presidents:* The Archbishops of Canterbury and York. *Chairman:* Rt Revd Colin Docker. *Secretary:* Mr Francis Mac Namara, 3 Vinson Rd, Liss, GU33 7NE
Tel: 01730 300974/07958 425927
email: info@socialconcern.org
Web: www.socialconcern.org

New England Company

A charity founded 1649. It is the senior English missionary society. *Governor:* Mr T. C. Stephenson. *Treasurer:* D. M. F. Scott. *Secretary:* Nikki Johnson, Flinders Cottage, The Street, Bolney, West Sussex RH17 5QW   *Tel:* 01444 882898
email: johnsonnikki@yahoo.co.uk
Web: www.newenglandcompany.org

Newton's Trust

Established to provide assistance to widows, widowers, separated or divorced spouses and unmarried children of deceased clergy and to divorced or separated wives of clergy of the Church of England, the Church in Wales and the Scottish Episcopal Church. Applications are considered by the Trustees, and one-off cash grants are made at their discretion. The Trustees meet four times a year. *Chairman:* Ven George Frost. *Treasurer:* Mr John Allen. *Secretary:* Mr

D. E. Wallington, Secretary to Newton's Trust, 1 Tudor Close, Lichfield, Staffordshire WS14 9RX
Tel: 01543 302924 (Evenings)
email: d.wallington@ntlworld.com

Nikaean Club

Founded in 1925 as an association of Anglican clergy and laity. It provides the ecumenical ministry of the Archbishop of Canterbury with a network of ecumenical expertise and the capacity to offer hospitality to visiting Christian leaders, heads of non-Anglican churches and international ecumenical bodies. *Chair:* Mr Colin Menzies OBE. *Guestmaster:* Rt Revd Nigel Stock. *Hon Secretary:* Mr Christopher Austen. *Hon Treasurer:* Revd Martin Macdonald, Lambeth Palace, London, SE1 7JU   *Tel:* 020 7898 1221
Fax: 020 7401 9886
email: christopher.austen@lambethpalace.org.uk

Nikaean Ecumenical Trust

Founded in 1992 and relaunched in 2002, the Trust exists to support ecumenical links between the Church of England and Christian churches overseas. It acts as the charitable wing of the Nikaean Club (*see separate entry*) and receives support from its members as well as from other Anglican bodies and individuals. It has also acquired the assets of the former Harold Buxton Trust, thanks to the generous co-operation of the SPCK. The Trust's principal activity at present is to provide grants to scholars from needy, non-Anglican Churches overseas (particularly the Orthodox and Oriental Orthodox Churches) who wish to study at colleges in the UK which are specifically Anglican or have strong Anglican connections. As the funds are still relatively modest, donations towards the work of the Trust are welcome. *Chair:* Rt Revd Dr Geoffrey Rowell. *Hon Secretary:* Mrs Margery Roberts, 7 Nunnery Stables, St Albans, AL1 2AS   *Tel:* 01727 856626
email: robertssopwellnunnery@btopenworld.com

Number 1 Trust Fund

Founded 1909 for holding property and investments for the promotion of catholic practice and teaching within the Church of England, reformed by the Fidelity Trust Act 1977, and incorporated by the Charity Commissioners in 1996. One trustee is appointed by each of the Abbot of Elmore, the Superior of the Community of the Resurrection, the President of the Church Union, the President of the Society for the Maintenance of the Faith, the Master of the Guardians of the Shrine at Walsingham, the Principal of Pusey House, Oxford and the Principal of St Stephen's House, Oxford. *Chairman:* Revd Canon R. Ward. *Trustees:* Rt Revd J. M. R. Baker, Revd A. A. Mayoss, Mr J. D. Hebblethwaite, Revd P. J. North, Dr B. J. T. Hanson, Canon Dr P. E. Ursell. *Secretary:* Revd W. E. P. Davage, 7 Hampstead Square, London, NW3 1AB   *Tel:* 07821 108769
email: william.davage@stx.ox.ac.uk

OMF International (UK) (formerly China Inland Mission)

We serve the church and seek to bring the gospel to all the peoples of East Asia. We help place Christians with professional skills in China and other Asian countries, and share the love of Christ with East Asians worldwide. *National Directors:* Peter and Christine Rowan, Station Approach, Borough Green, Sevenoaks, TN15 8BG

Tel: 01732 887299
Fax: 01732 887224
email: omf@omf.org.uk
Web: www.omf.org.uk

Open Synod Group

The Open Synod Group provides a safe space in which Christians of all persuasions can meet and discuss any issues without fear of censure. The meetings are a mixture of interactive meetings about matters of concern and social events to foster friendships. The magazine attracts articles from a wide range of contributors of all shades of churchmanship. *President:* The Bishop of Ripon and Leeds. *Chairman:* Mrs Caroline Spencer. *Secretary:* Mrs Debbie McIsaac. *Treasurer:* Mr John Freeman. *Membership Secretary:* Mr Stephen Barney, 5 Brook Street, Burton-on-the-Wolds, Leicester, LE12 5AB

email: stephen4747@live.co.uk
Web: www.opensynodgroup.org.uk

Order of Christian Unity/Christian Projects

Christians from all denominations who care about Christian values in the family, medical ethics, Christian education and the media, and run an annual Schools Bible Project for secondary schools across Britain. *Chairman:* Mrs Joanna Bogle. *Treasurer:* Mr Andrew Pollock. *Vice-Chairman:* Lady Elizabeth Benyon, 24 Smith Terrace, London, SW 4DL

email: auntiejoanna@yahoo.co.uk
Web: www.christianprojects.org.uk

Ordination Candidate Funds (General)

See separate entries for Anglo-Catholic Ordination Candidates' Fund, Bristol Clerical Education Society, Church Pastoral Aid Society Ministers in Training Fund, Cleaver Ordination Candidates' Fund, Elland Society Ordination Fund.

Overseas Bishoprics' Fund

Founded in 1841 to assist towards the endowment and maintenance of bishoprics in any part of the world and to act as trustees of episcopal endowment funds. *Chairman:* Dr Charles Mynors. *Secretary:* Mr Stephen Lyon. *Clerk:* Mr Paul Burrage, Finance Division Church House, Great Smith St, London, SW1P 3NZ

Tel: 020 7803 1677
email: paul.burrage@churchofengland.org

Oxford Mission

Founded 1880. The Oxford Mission consists of two Religious Communities, the Brotherhood of St Paul and the Christa Sevika Sangha. Has houses in India and Bangladesh. Their work is pastoral, medical and educational and is carried on in the Dioceses of Kolkata and Dhaka. India: Col Subir Ghosh (Administrator); Bangladesh: Father Francis Pande SPB, Sister Superior, Sister Jharna *General Secretary:* Mrs Mary K. Marsh, 18 Market Place, Romsey, SO51 8NA

Tel and Fax: 01794 515004
email: oxfordmission@aol.com
Web: www.oxford-mission.org

Papua New Guinea Church Partnership

PNGCP is the voluntary agency through which the Anglican Church of Papua New Guinea and the Church of England relate to each other. In 2007 ACPNG celebrated 30 years as an independent province in the Anglican Communion. Registered as a charity in 1960, the New Guinea Mission was founded in 1891 to give support to the then Diocese of New Guinea in prayer, by sending staff and raising money. In 1977, when the Province was inaugurated with five dioceses, the agency name was changed to Papua New Guinea Church Partnership in order to reflect the reciprocal nature of the work: giving and receiving. ACPNG continues to request people with skills and experience for governmentally approved support posts, mainly in health and administration. Most years see a steady trickle of 'gap year' students and medical and nursing electives travelling to PNG to gain never-to-be-forgotten experience in the poorest, most populous Pacific nation. An annual grant goes to the provincial budget, money is raised for provincially approved projects, and audited accounts are sent to the UK. *President:* Rt Revd Dr David M. Hope. *Chairman:* Revd Paul Bagott. *General Secretary:* Miss Louise Ewington

Tel: 020 7313 3918
email: holyredeemerstmark@tiscali.co.uk
Web: www.pngcp.com

Paradox Ministries

Paradox Ministries encourages Christians to understand and pray about the Israeli–Palestinian Conflict, seeing it through the eyes of both people groups involved, and taking the needs, fear and pain of both sides seriously. Its director, who was Rector of a church in the Old City of Jerusalem for a number of years, circulates a free email newsletter, speaks at seminars and encourages support of indigenous reconciliation ministry in Jerusalem. The website contains background material, advice to clergy and regular news updates, together with a blog. *Directors (Chairman):* Revd Tony Higton. *(Executive):* Mrs Patricia Higton, 17 Church View, Marham, King's Lynn, PE33 9HW

Tel: 01760 338342
email: tony@higton.info
Web: www.prayerforpeace.org.uk

Parish and People

Parish and People decided that the Deanery Resource Unit mailing would cease at the end of 2013. To replace that mailing the committee of the National Deaneries Network is providing an email-based newsletter that is being sent free of charge to all deaneries. If you want to make sure you receive this newsletter send an email headed 'Newsletter' to subscriptions@parishand people.org.uk. The Parish and People website will remain live, and our publications, mainly concerned with helping deaneries to work better, ministry and mission, in particular the involvement of the laity, will be available for download free of charge at www.parishandpeople.org.uk. We are continuing our work on lay ministry and leadership, and if you would like to encourage this work you can sign up to our Charter for Total Ministry by sending an email to secretary@ parishandpeople.org.uk. Any queries can be addressed to the Secretary, Jimmy Hamilton-Brown at the above email address.

Philip Usher Memorial Fund

Founded 1948. Grants annual scholarships to Anglican priests, deacons or ordinands, preferably under 35 years of age, to study in a predominantly Orthodox country. *Chairman:* Rt Revd Dr Geoffrey Rowell. *Administrator:* Janet Laws, c/o The Old Deanery, Dean's Court, London, EC4V 3AA   *Tel:* 020 7248 6233
Fax: 020 7248 9721
email: janet.laws@londin.clara.co.uk

Pilgrim Trust, The

The Pilgrim Trust considers applications from charities and exempt public bodies. The Trust operates two programmes: Social Welfare and Preservation and Scholarship. More details on the programme themes can be found in the Trust's guidelines which are available on the website. The Pilgrim Trust makes large annual block grants to the Church Buildings Council and the National Churches Trust. Church of England churches seeking grants for the conservation of items of church furniture e.g. repairs to bells/ organs/monuments etc. should apply directly to the Church Buildings Council. Applications for repairs to the fabric of a building should be directed towards the National Churches Trust. *Director:* Miss Georgina Nayler, Clutha House, 10 Storeys Gate, London, SW1P 3AY
Tel: 020 7222 4723
email: info@thepilgrimtrust.org.uk
Web: www.thepilgrimtrust.org.uk

Pilsdon at Malling Community

The Pilsdon Community in Dorset established a new community in 2004, taking over the former Ewell Monastery site next to St Mary's Abbey, West Malling, Kent. The community is dedicated to the same ideals of the Christian Gospel as the original community in Dorset, offering community living, sustainable self-sufficient lifestyle and open hospitality, particularly to those who are homeless, recovering from addiction, mental illness or breakdown. The community consists of four to five community members (leadership) and resident volunteers, up to twelve long-stay resident guests and up to two visitors and wayfarers/asylum seekers. The six acres of land and two large glasshouses are used for livestock and horticulture. The 16th-century barn chapel is used for daily offices, and the Eucharist is celebrated twice weekly. Enquiries are always welcome. Please see our website for more details and also the Pilsdon Community entry. Registered Charity no. 1123682. Company no. 6218667. *Guardian:* Revd Pam Rink. *Treasurer:* Mr Albert Granville. *Admissions:* The Guardian. *Enquiries:* Any community member, 27 Water Lane, West Malling, ME19 6HH   *Tel:* 01732 870279
Fax: 01732 870434
email: pilsdon@pilsdonatmalling.org.uk
Web: www.pilsdonatmalling.org.uk

Pilsdon Community

The Pilsdon Community is dedicated to the ideals of the Christian gospel in the context of community living and open hospitality. The Community at any one time will comprise between five to seven community members (leadership) and their children, about twenty guests (staying from one month to several years), up to six visitors (staying one day to a week) and up to ten wayfarers (staying up to three days). Many of the guests have experienced a crisis in their lives (e.g. mental breakdown, alcoholism, drug addiction, marital breakdown, abuse, homelessness, prison, etc.). Pilsdon provides an environment of communal living, manual work, creative opportunities (pottery, art, crafts, music, etc.) recreation, worship and pastoral care, to rebuild peoples' lives, self-respect, confidence and faith. Founded in 1958 by an Anglican priest, the Community occupies an Elizabethan manor house and its outbuildings and smallholding of thirteen acres, seven miles from the sea near Bridport. The community life is inspired by the monastic tradition and the Little Gidding Community. The worship and spirituality is Anglican at its root and sacramental, but ecumenical in its practice. Pilsdon welcomes guests of all faiths and none as well as all races and cultures. are welcome. Membership enquiries should be made to the Warden, enquiries from guests and respite visitors should be directed to the Admissions Officer. More information and application forms are available on our website. *Warden:* Revd Michael Deegan. *Administrator:* Alan Frost, Pilsdon Manor, Pilsdon, Bridport, DT6 5NZ
Tel: 01308 868308
Fax: 01308 868161
email: pilsdon@btconnect.com
Web: www.pilsdon.org.uk

Plainsong and Medieval Music Society

The Plainsong and Medieval Music Society, founded in 1888, exists to promote the performance and study of liturgical chant and medieval polyphony, through the publication of editions, facsimiles and scholarly articles, and through educational and liaison events. New members are always welcome and membership includes a subscription to the Society's twice-yearly journal, *Plainsong and Medieval Music*, invitations to the Society's events and discounts on many of the Society's publications. *Chair:* Dr Emma Hornby. *Administrator:* Emma Hembry, School of Music, Bangor University College Road, Bangor Gwynedd, LL57 2DG

email: admin@plainsong.org.uk
Web: www.plainsong.org.uk

Praxis

Founded in 1990, Praxis is sponsored by the Liturgical Commission, the Alcuin Club and the Grove Group for the Renewal of Worship. Its aims are to enrich the practice and understanding of worship in the Church of England; to serve congregations and clergy in their exploration of God's call to worship; and to provide a forum in which different worshipping traditions can meet and interact. Praxis events include day meetings on a whole variety of subjects related to liturgy. Full details are always available on the website. *Chair:* Revd Jo Spreadbury. *Secretary:* Revd Richard Curtis. *Administrator:* Revd Peter Furber, c/o 19 The Close, Salisbury, SP1 2EB

Tel: 01202 296886
email: praxis@praxisworship.org.uk
Web: www.praxisworship.org.uk

Prayer Book Society

The Prayer Book Society exists to promote the use of the Book of Common Prayer and to defend the worship and doctrine contained therein. Diocesan branches provide members with regular meetings, Prayer Book services and advice on church matters. It runs the yearly Cranmer Awards for young people. It has a popular mail order book company stocking a wide range of religious books and Christmas cards. Donations and memberships are appreciated and needed. Membership form from 0118 984 2582 or from any Secretary shown on the website. *Patron:* HRH The Prince of Wales. *Ecclesiastical Patron:* The Bishop of London. *Chairman:* Miss Prudence Dailey, The Studio, Copyhold Farm, Goring Heath, RG8 7RT
Tel: 0118 984 2582
Fax: 0118 984 5220
email: pbs.admin@pbs.org.uk
Web: www.pbs.org.uk

Pusey House, Oxford

Founded 1884 to continue the work of Dr Pusey, academic and pastoral, in Oxford. *Principal:* Revd Dr George Westhaver. *Librarian:* Vacancy, Pusey House, Oxford, OX1 3LZ

Tel: 01865 278415/01865 288024
email: chapter@puseyhouse.org.uk
Web: www.puseyhouse.org.uk

Pyncombe Charity

Income about £10,000 p.a. applied to assist needy serving ordained clergy in financial difficulties due to illness, or occasionally other special circumstances, within the immediate family. Applications must be made through the diocesan bishop. *Secretary:* Mrs Rita Butterworth, Wingletye, Hagleys Green Crowcombe, Taunton, TA4 4AQ *email:* joeandrita@waitrose.com

Queen Victoria Clergy Fund

Founded 1897 to raise money towards the support of Church of England parochial clergy. All the Fund's income is disbursed annually in block grants to dioceses specifically for the help of the clergy. Requests for assistance should be directed to the diocese. *Chairman:* John Booth. *Secretary:* Chris Palmer CBE, Church House, Great Smith St, London, SW1P 3AZ

Tel: 020 7898 1311
email: chris.palmer@churchofengland.org

Radius

Radius (The Religious Drama Society of Great Britain). Founded in 1929 to promote drama which throws light on the human condition and to support people who create and use drama as a means of Christian understanding. Organizes training events, publishes a magazine and a small number of plays, offers a playwrights' assessment service and holds a collection of photocopiable typescripts suitable for use in churches and by church groups. *Patron:* Dame Judi Dench. *Patron:* Rt Revd Rowan Williams. *President:* Rt Revd Graeme Knowles. *Magazine/General Enquiries/Council Vice-Chair:* Margaret Hunt, 7 Lenton Rd, The Park, Nottingham, NG7 1DP
Tel: 0115 941 3922
email: office@radius.org.uk
Web: www.radius.org.uk

RE Today Services

RE Today Services is wholly owned by the charity Christian Education, and is committed to the teaching of the major world faiths in religious education, and to an accurate and fair representation of their beliefs, values and practices in all its teaching materials. It carries forward the work of the Christian Education Movement (CEM). *Chief Executive:* Peter Fishpool. *Professional Team Director:* Rosemary Rivett, 1020 Bristol Rd, Selly Oak, Birmingham, B29 6LB *Tel:* 0121 472 4242
Fax: 0121 472 7575
email: retoday@retoday.org.uk
Web: www.retoday.org.uk

ORGANIZATIONS

Reader Missionary Studentship Association

Founded 1904 to offer financial assistance to Readers training as priests for service in the Church overseas. *Chairman:* Mr G. E. Crowley. *Hon Treasurer:* Mr Ron Edinborough. *Hon Secretary:* Dr Ann Whitfield, 30 Balmoral Drive, Methley, Leeds, LS26 9LE   *Tel:* 01977 602176
email: secretary@rmsa.org.uk
Web: www.rmsa.org.uk

Rebecca Hussey's Book Charity

Established 1714 to give grants of religious and useful books to institutions in the United Kingdom. *Clerk to the Trustees:* Elizabeth LeMoine, 29 Hearnshaw Street, London, E14 7BU
email: elizabethlemoine@gmail.com

Reform

Established in 1993, Reform is a network of individuals and churches within the Church of England. Reform is committed to reforming the Church of England from within according to the Holy Scriptures. *Chairman:* Rod Thomas. *Director:* Susie Leafe. *Administrators:* Jonathan Lockwood, PO Box 1183, Sheffield, S10 3YA *Tel:* 0114 230 9256
email: administrator@reform.org.uk
Web: www.reform.org.uk

Relate

Relate is the country's largest relationship counselling organization, providing help and support for couples, singles, families and in schools. Also the national organisation for sex therapy and a leading source of information and advice online. Help is available at around 600 locations nationwide and by calling 0300 100 1234 or visit the website: www.relate.org.uk *Chief Executive Officer:* Ruth Sutherland, Premier House, Lakeside, Doncaster, DN4 5RA
Tel: 0300 100 1234 (Helpline)
Web: www.relate.org.uk

Religious Education Council of England and Wales

The Religious Education Council of England and Wales seeks to represent the collective interests of a wide variety of organizations and communities in deepening and strengthening provision for religious education in schools and colleges. The Council was formed in 1973 and is open to national organizations which have a special interest in the teaching of religious education. The present membership of more than 45 organizations includes representation from the main Christian denominations, the world faiths, the British Humanist Association and the main educational bodies with professional and academic RE interests. *Chair:* Dr Joyce Miller. *Deputy Chair:* Helen Harrison. *Treasurer:* Rosemary Rivett. *Company Secretary:* Deborah Weston, CAN Mezzanine, 49–51 East Road, London, N1 6AN   *Tel:* 020 7250 8166
email: info@religiouseducationcouncil.org.uk
Web: www.religiouseducationcouncil.org.uk

Retired Clergy Association

Founded 1927 to act as a bond of friendship in prayer and mutual help to retired clergy. Membership at 31 July 2014 was 3,454. The Association works closely with Bishops' and Diocesan Retirement Officers throughout the Church of England to encourage local groups of retired clergy for fellowship and support. It is often consulted by the Church of England Pensions Board on housing issues and other matters of mutual concern. *President:* The Bishop of Exeter. *Chairman:* Rt Revd David Jennings. *Secretary and Treasurer:* Revd David Phypers, 15 Albert Road, Chaddesden, Derby, DE21 6SL
Tel: 01332 239134
email: david@phypers.co.uk

Retreat Association

Comprising these Christian retreat groups: Association for Promoting Retreats, Baptist Union Retreat Group, Catholic Network for Retreats and Spirituality, Reflect (Methodists supporting spirituality and retreats) and Affiliates of the Retreat Association. Offers information and resources about retreats to both would-be and seasoned retreatants, facilitates spiritual direction, promotes the work of retreat houses and coordinates training opportunities and regional activity. *Retreats*, an ecumenical journal listing retreat houses and their programmes in the UK and beyond, is published annually (2015 edition £10.50 incl p+p). Other literature available; send for publications list. *Director:* Alison MacTier, Clare Charity Centre, Wycombe Road, Saunderton, Bucks, HP14 4BF   *Tel:* 01494 569056
Fax: 0871 715 1917
email: info@retreats.org.uk
Web: www.retreats.org.uk

Revd Dr George Richards' Charity

Founded 1837 to provide financial assistance to clergy of the Church of England forced to retire early owing to ill-health. Widows, widowers and dependants can also apply for assistance. *Secretary:* Dr P. D. Simmons, 96 Thomas More House, Barbican, London, EC2Y 8BU   *Tel:* 020 7588 5583

Richmond Fellowship

Established in 1959, Richmond Fellowship (RF) currently operates over 100 services for people with mental health problems throughout England. These include supported housing, registered care homes and care homes with nursing support, employment and training services, individual self-directed packages of care and community and day services. For further information contact us or visit our website *Chief Executive:* Derek Caren. *PA to Chief Executive:* Marise Willis, 80 Holloway Rd, London, N7 8JG
Tel: 020 7697 3300
Fax: 020 7697 3301
email:
communications@richmondfellowship.org.uk
Web: www.richmondfellowship.org.uk

RNIB (Royal National Institute of Blind People)

RNIB (Royal National Institute of Blind People) is a charity which supports blind and partially sighted people to remain independent by: giving you free advice about your eye condition, the benefits you're entitled to, and the specialist and local support that's available; providing employment services and practical help for children and their families; suggesting ideas on how you can continue to enjoy your hobbies and leisure time; recommending everyday items and gadgets to make your life easier; and offering a listening ear. *President:* Dame Gail Ronson DBE. *Chairman:* Kevin Carey. *Chief Executive:* Lesley-Anne Alexander, 105 Judd St, London, WC1H 9NE
Tel: 0303 123 999 9 (Helpline) 020 7388 1266
email: helpline@rnib.org.uk
Web: www.rnib.org.uk

RNID (formerly the Royal National Institute for Deaf People)

RNID is the largest charity representing the 9 million deaf and hard of hearing people in the UK. It offers a range of services for deaf and hard of hearing people, and provides information and support on all aspects of deafness, hearing loss and tinnitus. As a membership charity, it aims to achieve a radically better quality of life for deaf and hard of hearing people. RNID's work involves campaigning and lobbying, providing services, training, products and equipment, and undertaking medical and technical research. It works throughout the UK. *Chairman:* Mr James Strachan. *Chief Executive:* Dr John Low, 19–23 Featherstone St, London, EC1Y 8SL
Tel: 0808 808 0123 (Voice)
0808 808 9000 (Textphone)
email: informationline@rnid.org.uk
Web: www.rnid.org.uk

Royal Alexandra and Albert School

A large coeducational state boarding school for pupils aged 7–18, situated in 260 acres of park on Reigate Hill just outside the M25. Bursaries are available for applicants who are without one or both parents or who would benefit from boarding education because of their home circumstances. Bursaries of two-thirds of the fees are also available for children of clergy and the full fees for 2014–15 are only £4,640 per term. In exceptional circumstances, further bursary support can be provided. The school has excellent boarding and sports facilities and a successful Sixth Form of almost 200 pupils. Contact: Headmaster for further details. *Patron:* HM the Queen. *President:* HRH the Duchess of Gloucester. *Headmaster:* Paul D. Spencer Ellis. *Foundation Secretary:* Diana Bromley. *Admissions Secretary:* Fiona Newport, Gatton Park, Reigate, RH2 0TW
Tel: 01737 649001
Fax: 01737 649000
email: headmaster@gatton-park.org.uk
Web: www.raa-school.co.uk

Royal Asylum of St Ann's Society

The Society, founded in 1702, offers grants towards the expenses of educating children, from the age of 11, at boarding or day schools. Most, but not all, of those aided are children of clergy of the Church of England; however, in the first instance clergy should approach the Corporation of the Sons of the Clergy. The Society welcomes collections, donations and legacies towards this purpose. *President:* The Dean of Westminster. *Chairman:* Mr Peter Ashby. *Secretary:* Mr David Hanson, King Edward's School, Witley, Petworth Rd, Wormley, GU8 5SG

Royal College of Organists

Founded 1864, incorporated by Royal Charter 1893, 'to promote the art of organ-playing and choir training'. Holds lectures, recitals and master-classes nationwide. Examinations for Certificate, Associateship, Fellowship, Licentiateship in Teaching and Diploma in Choral Directing. Holds a large specialist library and archive, and publishes a scholarly journal every year. Membership open to all who take an interest in the work and profession of the organist and in organ music. *Patron:* HM The Queen. *President:* James O'Donnell. *General Manager:* Kim Gilbert, PO Box 56357, London, SE16 7XL
Tel: 05600 767208
email: admin@rco.org.uk
Web: www.rco.org.uk

Royal Martyr Church Union

Founded 1906: (1) Ever to cherish the sacred remembrance of Charles the First, King and Martyr, both in public worship and private devotion, and to this end to promote the restoration of his name to its proper place in the calendar of the worldwide Anglican Communion, and the observance of 30 January, the day of his martyrdom, by suitable services in the Book of Common Prayer and elsewhere. (2) To maintain the principles of faith, loyalty and liberty for which the King died – the faith of the Church, loyalty to the Crown, and the ancient liberties of the people. Holds annual commemorative eucharists in London and Edinburgh. Subscription £15.00 p.a.to include *Royal Martyr Annual. Chairman:* Tom Kerr. *Hon Secretary and Treasurer:* David Roberts, 7 Nunnery Stables, St Albans, AL1 2AS
Tel: 01727 856626

Royal School of Church Music

The Royal School of Church Music (RSCM) is the leading organization promoting and supporting church music. It is an educational charity dedicated to raising standards and promoting the best use of music in every style of Christian worship and in every denomination. It is funded through membership subscriptions, publication sales, course fees and the charitable support of individuals and institutions. It provides musical and educational resources to train, develop and inspire clergy, music leaders, musicians, singers and congregations. Its *Voice for Life* programme is a training scheme for singers of all ages that can be used by individual churches and schools, and *Church Music Skills* provides practical training for those leading music in worship. These programmes are complemented by workshops, festivals and short residential courses, and a network of volunteers runs events to meet local needs in the UK and five overseas branches. The RSCM publishes music through the RSCM Press, including musical resources for *Common Worship*, and RSCM Music Direct provides a fast and efficient mail-order service for music from all publishers. Affiliated churches and schools and individual members receive *Church Music Quarterly*, a highly informative and interesting magazine for all those concerned with church music, and *Sunday by Sunday*, an essential liturgy planner aiding those who plan and lead worship to enhance it through music appropriate to the day. Appointed the official music agency for the Church of England from April 1996. *President:* The Archbishop of Canterbury. *Chairman:* Lord Brian Gill. *Director:* Mr Andrew Reid, 19 The Close, Salisbury, SP1 2EB

Tel: 01722 424848/01722 424841 (membership)
Fax: 01722 424849
email: enquiries@rscm.com
Web: www.rscm.com

Rural Theology Association
Founded in 1981 to provide a forum for the rural churches and to focus for the Church at large the distinctive ways, needs and contributions of the rural. Its aims are to study the gospel and develop theology in a rural setting, to encourage the development of patterns of ministry and mission appropriate to the countryside today, and to discover ways of living in the countryside which embody a Christian response to the world. It publishes the journal *Rural Theology* twice yearly. *President:* Revd Prof Leslie Francis. *Chairman:* Rt Revd Mark Rylands. *Secretary:* Canon Stephen Cope. *Treasurer:* Revd Dr Christine Brewster, Vicarage, 28 Park Ave, Withernsea, HU19 2JU   Tel: 01964 611426
email: secretary@rural-theology.org.uk
Web: www.rural-theology.org.uk

Saint George's Trust
The Trust exists to give grants to individuals to further the work of the Church of England. The Fellowship of Saint John (UK) Trust Association is the sole trustee. The funds at the Trust's disposal do not permit large grants for restoration projects, or any long-term financial support. The wide remit enables it to help a large number of individuals for sabbaticals, gap years and the like to a maximum of 350. All applications should be sent, together with a stamped addressed envelope, to the Trust with as much supporting

documentation as possible. St Edward's House, 22 Great College St, London, SW1P 3QA

Samaritans
Samaritans exists to provide confidential emotional support to any person, irrespective of race, creed, age or status who is in emotional distress or at risk of suicide; and to increase public awareness of issues around suicide and depression. *Chief Exec:* Mr Dominic Rudd, The Upper Mill, Kingston Rd, Ewell, Surrey, KT17 2AF
Tel: 020 8394 8300 (admin)
08457 909090 (helpline)
Fax: 020 8394 8301
email: admin@samaritans.org
Web: www.samaritans.org

Sarum College
Sarum College is an ecumenical study and research centre based in Salisbury's Cathedral Close. The College is housed in Grade I listed buildings in Salisbury Cathedral Close and offers an extensive and varied programme of short residential and day courses, as well as four postgraduate programmes with options to gain a PG Certificate, Diploma or Masters degree. The College has bedrooms for short or long-term stays and some overlook the Cathedral. There is also a range of meeting and conference rooms, a 19th-century chapel, common room/bar, and a dining room seating up to 120. On-site parking is usually available. Residential conferences, parish groups, training events, board meetings and individual guests are all welcome. The College also houses a fine theological library with more than 40,000 volumes, and Salisbury's only independent theological bookshop, both of which offer postal/mail order services. *Principal:* Canon Keith Lamdin. *Bursar/Deputy Principal:* Mark Manterfield. *Director of Learning Resources:* Jenny Monds. *Residential Services Manager:* Linda Cooper. *Director of Development and Marketing/Deputy Principal:* Christine Nielsen-Craig, 19 The Close, Salisbury, SP1 2EE   Tel: 01722 424800
Fax: 01722 338508
email: info@sarum.ac.uk
Web: www.sarum.ac.uk

Sarum St Michael Educational Charity
Personal grants may be awarded for further or higher education, to those who live, work or study within the Salisbury or adjacent dioceses (also to former students of the college). Bursaries may be awarded to those who live or study within the Salisbury diocese or adjacent dioceses, who intend to train to teach RE. Grants may be made to local schools, mainly for RE and worship resources. Grants may be made to parishes within the Salisbury diocese, for work with children and young people. Corporate grants may be made, where funds permit, to certain projects within the Salisbury diocese and adjacent dioceses. The governors meet four times a year to

consider applications. Grants are not awarded retrospectively. Please consult our website for closing dates for applications, and to download application forms. Member of the Association of Church College Trusts (*see separate entry*). First Floor, 27A Castle St, Salisbury, SP1 1TT

Tel: 01722 422296
Fax: 0870 135 9943
email: clerk@sarumstmichael.org
Web: www.sarumstmichael.org

SASRA (The Soldiers' and Airmen's Scripture Readers Association)

Founded in 1838 to present the claims of Christ to the men and women serving in the Army and later the RAF, to promote interdenominational Christian fellowship among them and to encourage individual serving Christians to witness to their comrades. *Chairman:* Brigadier Ian Dobbie. *General Secretary:* Sqdn Ldr Colin Woodland, Havelock House, Barrack Rd, Aldershot, GU11 3NP

Tel: 01252 310033
Fax: 01252 341804
email: admin@sasra.org.uk
Web: www.sasra.org.uk

SCALA (School Chaplains and Leaders Association) (formerly the Bloxham Project/School Chaplains Association)

Founded in 1967, charged with developing an understanding of Christian faith and values in education. Offering a spiritual, inspirational and practical resource for schools and educators, helping to develop spirituality, pastoral care, Christian leadership and ethos and values. Providing a forum for debate and the exchange of best practice. Offers consultancy services and tailor-made training, day events, regional meetings, a termly publication and some other materials. A network of schools across denominations and sectors. A resource for headteachers, leadership teams, chaplains, teaching and pastoral staff. *Chair of Trustees:* Dr Priscilla Chadwick. *Director:* Revd Gordon Parry. *Administrator:* Paul Hansford, SCALA, University of Chichester, Bognor Regis Campus, Upper Bognor Road, Bognor Regis, West Sussex, PO21 1HR

Tel: 01243 812134
email: admin@scala.uk.net
Web: www.scala.uk.net

Scout Association, The

Scouting exists to actively engage and support young people in their personal development, empowering them to make a positvie contribution to society. Scouting is open to all from six years onwards. Membership 500,000. *Chief Scout:* Lt Cdr (Hons) Bear Grylls RN. *Chief Executive:* Matt Hyde, Gilwell Park, Bury Rd, Chingford, London, E4 7QW

Tel: 0845 300 1818 0208 433 7100
Fax: 020 8433 7103
email: info.centre@scouts.org.uk
Web: www.scouts.org.uk

Scripture Union

Scripture Union seeks to make the Christian faith known to children, young people and families and to support the Church through resources, Bible reading and training. SU's work in Britain includes schools work, Bible ministries, digital and conventional publishing, training, evangelism, holidays, missions and family ministry. Scripture Union is active in more than 100 countries. *National Director:* Revd Tim Hastie-Smith. *Development Director:* Mr Terry Clutterham. *Managing Director:* Mr David Thorpe, 207–209 Queensway, Bletchley, Milton Keynes, MK2 2EB

Tel: 01908 856000
Fax: 01908 856111
email: info@scriptureunion.org.uk
Web: www.scriptureunion.org.uk

Seamen's Friendly Society of St Paul

Trust administered by Alton Abbey, able to offer financial assistance to merchant sailors. *Contact:* Rt Revd Dom Giles Hill OSB, Alton Abbey, Abbey Rd, Beech, Alton, Hampshire, GU34 4AP

Tel: 01420 562145 / 01420 563575
email: giles@altonabbey.org.uk

Servants of Christ the King

Founded 1942 by Canon Roger Lloyd of Winchester. A movement of groups or 'Companies' of Christians who seek to develop a corporate life by praying together in silence, with disciplined discussion. They actively wait upon God to be led by the Holy Spirit, and undertake to do together any work which they are given by him to do. *Enquirers' Correspondent:* Dr Pauline Waters, Swallowfield, Wheelers Lane, Linton, Maidstone, ME17 4BN

Tel: 01622 743392
Web: www.sck.org.uk

SGM Lifewords (formerly Scripture Gift Mission)

SGM LIfewords creates Bible resources to help people communicate God's word to today's generation. A new, research-based range uses up-to-date Bible versions and contemporary graphics. SGM publishes materials in over 200 languages for use worldwide. 75 Westminster Bridge Rd, London, SE1 7HS

Tel: 020 7730 2155
Fax: 020 7401 9070
email: uk@sgmlifewords.com
Web: www.sgmlifewords.com

Shaftesbury Homes and 'Arethusa'

Founded 1843 to house and educate homeless children in London, the charity is now the leading voluntary sector provider of residential care for children in London. In London and Suffolk the charity also provides services for young people leaving care, and supported housing for the young homeless. Personal development is promoted through venture activities at the Arethusa Venture Centre on the Medway.

Chairman: Gerri McAndrew. *Chief Exec:* Karen Wright, The Chapel, Royal Victoria Patriotic Building, Trinity Rd, London, SW18 3SX
Tel: 020 8875 1555
Fax: 020 8875 1954
email: info@shaftesbury.org.uk
Web: www.shaftesbury.org.uk

Sharing of Ministries Abroad (SOMA)

Founded in 1978 to serve the renewal of the Church throughout the world, particularly in the Anglican Communion, SOMA has eleven centres across the world. SOMA works for the transformation of individuals and churches, and the healing of communities and their lands through the renewing power of the Holy Spirit by intercession and sending and receiving teams worldwide on short-term mission across the Anglican Communion. A newsletter, *Sharing*, is published three times a year. *SOMA International Chairman:* Most Revd Ben Kwashi. *SOMA UK National Director:* Revd Stephen Dinsmore. *SOMA UK Finance Administrator:* Steve Fincher. *SOMA UK Administrator:* Zena Durrant, PO Box 69, Merriott, TA18 9AP
Tel: 01460 279737
email: info@somauk.org
Web: www.somauk.org

Social Responsibility Network, The

The Network (developed from the Anglican Association for Social Responsibility) aims to share good practice, ideas and information on a wide range of issues and provide peer support and encouragement for Christian practitioners in social responsibility and related fields in England and Wales. We do this by meeting together in local and regional groups, holding an annual conference on key issues, making resources available to one another, and sharing ideas, needs and resources via our discussion e-net. Open to all Christian practitioners. *Chair:* Revd Robert Hill. *Treasurer:* Tony Oakden. *Secretary:* Mrs Ann Wright, PO Box 414, Horley, RH6 8WL
email: wright@btinternet.com
Web: www.srnet.org.uk

Society for Liturgical Study

Founded in 1978, this ecumenical Society for the UK and Ireland promotes liturgical study and research, particularly amongst younger scholars. The Society works through postgraduate study days and a biennial conference, and through its peer-reviewed journal, *Anaphora*, published twice a year. Membership of the Society is open to anyone, lay and ordained, with a scholarly interest in the history, development and practice of Christian worship in all its various and diverse forms. *Secretary:* Mr Harvey Howlett, 88 Gainsborough Road, New Malden, KT3 5NX
email: secretary@studyliturgy.org.uk
Web: www.studyliturgy.org.uk

Society for Old Testament Study

Founded 1917 as a society for OT/HB scholars in Britain and Ireland. Scholars not resident in the British Isles may also become members. Two meetings to hear and discuss papers are arranged annually. The Society also publishes its annual Book List and is involved in other publishing activities. It maintains links with OT/HB scholars throughout the world, particularly the Dutch-Flemish OT Society with which it holds joint meetings every three years. Candidates for membership must be proficient in biblical Hebrew and be proposed by two existing members. *Hon Secretary:* Dr David Shepherd, Assistant Professor of Hebrew Bible/Old Testament, Loyola Institute, Sch of Religions, Theology & Ecumenics, Old Physiology Building Trinity College, Dublin 2 Ireland
Tel: 00 353(0)1 896 4796
email: shepherd@tcd.ie
Web: www.sots.ac.uk

Society for Promoting Christian Knowledge

SPCK was founded in 1698 to help people to understand – and to grow in – the Christian faith. It works to support and develop the knowledge of Christians and to interest and inform others. Throughout its history SPCK has been associated with the spread of education and informative literature in all its forms. It is an Anglican foundation but supports a diversity of Christian traditions.

The Society has been involved in publishing since its foundation, and currently publishes around 100 new titles each year. Its output includes Christian books, websites and digital items across a broad spectrum of church traditions for a wide readership from the most popular level to the highly academic. The range includes liturgy, theology, science and religion, biblical studies and spirituality, with resources for clergy, parishes and study groups.

SPCK Worldwide's International Study Guides programme is aimed particularly at those training for ministry in the global south, including many for whom English is not a first language. It depends entirely upon donations from individuals, churches and charitable trusts. The Assemblies website (www.assemblies.org.uk) provides teachers with regularly updated materials for school assemblies which they can download free of charge.

SPCK's Diffusion programme aims to make fruitful contact with those who are searching for meaning but find Christian vocabulary or churches unfamiliar, difficult or off-putting, through projects that seek to reach out to a wider audience. *President:* The Archbishop of Canterbury. *Chairman of the Governing Body:* Rt Revd John Pritchard. *Chief Executive:* Mr Sam

Richardson. *Executive Administrator:* Mrs Pat Phillips, 36 Causton St, London, SW1P 4ST

Tel: 020 7592 3900
Fax: 020 7592 3939
email: spck@spck.org.uk
Web: www.spck.org.uk/www.assemblies.org.uk

Society for the Assistance of Ladies in Reduced Circumstances

Founded by the late Miss Edith Smallwood in 1886. Assistance is given to ladies living alone in their own home (either owned or rented) on a low income and domiciled in the United Kingdom, irrespective of age or social status. Registered Charity no. 205798. Enquiries welcome by telephone (calls cost the same as to a number beginning 01 or 02). Donations and legacies gratefully received. *Patron:* HM The Queen. *Apply:* The Secretary, Lancaster House, 25 Hornyold Rd, Malvern, WR14 1QQ

Tel: 0300 365 1886
email: info@salrc.org.uk
Web: www.salrc.org.uk

Society for the Maintenance of the Faith

Founded in 1873, the Society presents, or shares in the presentation of, priests to over 80 benefices. As well as its work as a patronage body the Society aims to promote Catholic teaching and practice in the Church of England at large. *President:* Dr Brian Hanson. *General Secretary:* Revd John Hanks, Pusey House, Oxford, OX1 3LZ

email: secretary@smftrust.org.uk

Society for the Relief of Poor Clergy (SRPC)

The Committee of Trustees, which conducts the Society's affairs, may consider applications for assistance from: evangelical clergy of the Church of England, the Church in Wales, the Church of Ireland and the Scottish Episcopal Church; evangelical Accredited Lay workers (those who have been nationally selected, trained and licensed for Anglican ministry; Church Army Officers who have been commissioned and hold the Bishop's licence); widows and widowers of the above. Grants are made to help meet the following categories of need, and the Committee has the discretionary power to consider other circumstances, but only where these are giving rise to exceptional hardship. The Society's resources are limited and grants may therefore have to be refused, even where the required conditions may have been fulfilled: bereavement; illness; removals; family support to enable young people to participate in a 'ministry experience' during a gap year before university; family support to enable children/young people of evangelical ministers to attend Christian camps, for their spiritual benefit and to develop leadership potential; other special needs (at the Committee's discretion). For further details, including an application form, please contact the Secretary. *Secretary:* Mrs Pauline Walden, c/o CPAS

Sovereign Court One (Unit 3), Sir William Lyons Road, Coventry, CV4 7EZ   *Tel:* 07962 227959

Fax: 01926 458459
email: secretary@srpc-aid.com
Web: www.srpc-aid.com

Society of Archbishop Justus Ltd

The Society, named after the fourth Archbishop of Canterbury, was formed in 1996 and incorporated in 1997 as a non-profit corporation in New York, USA for the purpose of using the Internet to foster and further unity among Christians, especially Anglicans. It focuses on internet information services: web and email servers that help Anglicans to be one body. Members help install, operate and maintain the computers and networks that enable online communication, and help educate the Anglican public about how best to use those computers. Directors include both Church of England and ECUSA members. The Society sponsors the Anglicans Online website and, on behalf of the International Anglican Domain Committee, administers the anglican.org internet domain. More information is available on the website. *Director:* Simon Sarmiento, 22 Rodney Avenue, St Albans, AL1 5SX

email: directors@justus.anglican.org
Web: www.justus.anglican.org/soaj.html

Society of Catholic Priests

Founded in 1994, with around 700 members in the UK and Ireland, an inclusive society of priests who 'believe in one, holy, catholic and apostolic church ordaining men and women to serve as deacons, priests and bishops in the Church of God'. The objects of the Society are to promote the formation and support of priestly spirituality and catholic evangelism. *Visitor General:* The Bishop of Truro. *Rector General:* Very Revd Andrew Nunn. *Provincial Secretary:* Revd Michael Skinner. *Membership Secretary:* Revd John Joyce, 3 Wolstonbury Road, Hove, East Sussex, BN3 6EJ

Tel: 01273 773150/07798 941095
email: membership@scp.org.uk
Web: www.scp.org.uk

Society of King Charles the Martyr

Founded 1894 to promote observance of January 30, the day of the martyrdom of King Charles I in 1649, and uphold the traditional Anglican Catholic principles for which he died. Publishes various material including the journal *Church and King*. *Chairman:* Mr Robin Davies, 22 Tyning Rd, Winsley, Bradford on Avon, BA15 2JJ

Tel: 01225 862965
email: robinjbdavies@talktalk.net
Web: www.skcm.org

Society of Mary

Founded 1931 to promote devotion to Our Lady. Originally an Anglican Society and now an ecumenical Society welcoming all practising Catholics. Organizes pilgrimages to Marian

Shrines, in particular Lourdes and Nettuno. *Superior General:* Rt Revd Robert Ladds. *Chaplain General:* Revd G. C. Rowlands. *Secretary:* Mrs Celia Bush, 169 Humber Doucy Lane, Ipswich, IP4 3PA *Tel:* 01473 423750
email: secretary@societyofmary.net
Web: www.societyofmary.net

Society of Mary and Martha
An independent ecumenical charity run by a mixed lay Community providing confidential support for clergy and/or spouses, especially at times of stress, crisis, burnout or breakdown. Resources exclusively for people in ministry include the famous 12,000–mile Service weeks, Family Holiday week, and Linhay Lodges: well-appointed, self-contained accommodation for private retreats, sabbaticals, safe place, emergency bolt-hole or battery re-charge. Programme events open to everyone include retreat and training resources for personal and spiritual growth. Hen Runs and Pig Pens available for private retreats, open to everyone. The Sheldon Centre is a beautifully converted farm with lovely views across the Teign Valley, just ten miles from the M5 and main line railway at Exeter. £1m upgrade completed in 2011 – all rooms now en-suite. Also available for self-catering hire for groups of 10–50 (cell groups, leadership training, parish retreats, etc.) *Warden:* Sarah Horsman. *Lay Chaplain:* Sarah Horsman. *Administrator:* Hilary Todd, Sheldon, Dunsford, Exeter, EX6 7LE
Tel: 01647 252752
Fax: 01647 253900
email: smm@sheldon.uk.com
Web: www.sheldon.uk.com

Society of Ordained Scientists
Founded 1987. A dispersed order for ordained scientists, men and women. Members aim to offer to God, in their ordained role, the work of science in the exploration and stewardship of creation, to express the commitment of the Church to the scientific enterprise and their concern for its impact on the world, and to support each other in their vocation. Associate membership is available to those who are not ordained but are interested in the work of the Society. *Visitor:* Rt Revd David Walker, Bishop of Manchester. *Secretary:* Revd Colin Brockie. *Warden:* Revd Dr Keith Suckling *Tel:* 01563 559960
email: revcol@revcol.demon.co.uk
Web: www.ordainedscientists.org

Society of Retreat Conductors
Founded in 1923 for the training of retreat conductors, the running of retreat houses and the conducting of retreats. *Chairman:* Revd A. Walker. *Company Secretary:* Mrs Kathryn Redington, c/o St Mary Woolnoth Vestry, Lombard St, London, EC3V 9AN *Tel:* 07979 157603
email: admin.src@btconnect.com

Society of Royal Cumberland Youths
Bell-ringing society founded in 1747. Its headquarters are at St Martin-in-the-Fields and the Society is responsible for ringing at a number of London churches. The society has a worldwide membership, promoting high standards among proficient change-ringers. *Master:* Mrs Shirley McGill. *Secretary:* Mr John Ford, 28 Villiers Street, Hertford, SG13 7BW *Tel:* 01992 550280
email: secretary@srcy.org.uk
Web: www.srcy.org.uk

Society of St Willibrord
(The Anglican and Old Catholic Society of St Willibrord)
Founded 1908 to promote friendly relations between the Anglican and Old Catholic Churches, including the fullest use of the full Communion established between them in 1931. Membership of the society is open to members of churches in full communion with Canterbury and/or Utrecht. *President:* Vacancy. *Patrons:* The Archbishops of Canterbury and Utrecht. *Hon Secretary:* Mtr Ariadne van den Hof. *Chairman:* Rt Revd Michael Burrows, Bishop of Cashel and Ossory, 1 Craigholm, Shooters Hill, London, SE18 3RR *Tel:* 020 8856 5858
email: honsecssw@gmail.com
Web: www.willibrord.org.uk

Society of the Faith (Incorporated)
The objects of the Society are to act as an Association of Christians in communion with the See of Canterbury for mutual assistance in the work of Christ's Church and for the furtherance of charitable undertakings, especially for the popularization of the Catholic Faith. We have occupied Faith House in Westminster since 1935 and formerly ran the Faith Press and Faithcraft. We manage Faith House as a resource for the Church, promote charitable activities, hold the annual Liddon Lecture and sponsor publications which promote the Society's objects. The restricted Liddon Fund provides two or three grants per year for young Anglicans (under 25 years old) who are engaged in advanced theological study, for example for a second degree. *Principal:* Dr Julian Litten. *Vice-principal:* Canon Robert Gage. *Secretary and Treasurer:* Mrs Margery Roberts, Faith House, 7 Tufton St, London, SW1P 3QB *Tel:* 01727 856626
Web: www.societyofthefaith.org.uk

Society of the Holy Cross (SSC)
Founded 1855 for priests (1100 members) 'to maintain and extend the Catholic faith and discipline and to form a special bond of union between Catholic clergy'. Provinces: European Union, Australasia, Canada, Africa, USA. *Master General:* Preb Dr David Houlding ssc. *Provincial Master (for England):* Fr Nicolas Spicer ssc. *Secretary General:* Fr Colin Ames ssc. *Treasurer General:* Fr David Lawson ssc. *Registrar:* Fr

Trevor Buxton ssc, All Hallows House, 52 Courthope Rd, London, NW3 2LD

Tel: 020 7267 7833 (Home)
020 7263 6317 (Office)
Fax: 020 7267 6317
email: sscmaster@lineone.net

South American Mission Society
Merged in 2010 with the Church Mission Society. *See* Church Mission Society.

Southern Africa Church Development Trust
Founded 1960 to inform, encourage concern for and involvement in the Church in Southern Africa. Supports churches, community centres and schools, primary and secondary education through scholarships, clergy and lay training, and medical work. Publishes a quarterly bulletin of information and projects which is sent to all subscribers and supporters. *President:* Mr Martin Kenyon. *Director:* Dr Jack Mulder. *Chairperson:* Canon David Cook. *Hon Treasurer:* Stuart Barley, 43 Cranham Avenue, Billingshurst, RH14 9EN
Tel: 01403 581066
email: director@sacdtrust.org
Web: www.sacdtrust.org

St Christopher's Educational Trust
Small grants to promote Christian religious education by improving practice in teaching, by developing new programmes of education and nurture for adults and young people and by support for individual study or research. The Trustees meet twice a year. Member of the Association of Church College Trusts (*see separate entry*). *Clerk to the Trustees:* Mrs Lindsey Anderson-Gear, 5 Windmill Avenue, Bicester, Oxon, OX26 3DX
email: stchristopherstrust@hotmail.co.uk
Web: www.churchofengland.org/education

St Christopher's Fellowship
St Christopher's is a charity and housing association providing care, accommodation, education, training and support to children, young people and vulnerable adults. We run children's homes, fostering services, supported housing and hostels, along with education, employment and outreach services. *Chairman:* Mr Anthony Hickinbotham. *Chief Exec:* Mr Jonathan Farrow, 1 Putney High St, London, SW15 1SZ
Tel: 020 8780 7800
Fax: 020 8780 7801
email: info@stchris.org.uk
Web: www.stchris.org.uk

St George's College, Jerusalem
St George's College is a unique centre of continuing education in the Anglican Communion, offering short-term courses as well as facilities for individual reflection and study. It is open to both clergy and laity. Since its founding in 1962, the College has hosted participants from 92 countries and 96 Christian traditions. Course members engage with a wide range of biblical texts in the context of the land; encounter Jewish, Christian and Muslim faith as it is exercised today; and come to appreciate anew the rich fabric of faith and spirituality that this environment offers to the pilgrim. The College is situated 500 metres north of the Damascus Gate of the Old City of Jerusalem, and set in its own grounds adjacent to the Anglican Cathedral of St George the Martyr. Full details of courses can be obtained from the website or the Secretary of the British Regional Committee. *Secretary of the British Regional Committee:* Revd Paul Conder, St George's College Jerusalem, Post Office Box 1248, Jerusalem 91000, Israel
Tel: 1 972 2 626 4704
Fax: 1 972 2 626 4703
email: genia@sgcjerusalem.org
Web: www.sgcjerusalem.org

St George's House, Windsor Castle
Founded 1966. A residential consultation centre within Windsor Castle, and part of the fourteenth-century College of St George. Apart from ecumenical clergy conferences, the House also hosts a range of other consultations. Some are internally organized, while others are instigated by external groups under the guidance of House staff. The range of themes is wide but all share a concern for greater human well-being. Accommodation for up to 33 people. *Chairman, Board of Trustees and Council:* Rt Revd David J. Conner, Dean of Windsor. *Warden:* Revd Canon Dr Hueston Finlay. *Programme Director:* Mr Gary McKeone. *Clergy Consultation Administrator:* Mrs Patricia Birdseye. *Warden's Administrator:* Miss Jenna Tyer, St George's House, Windsor Castle, Windsor, Berkshire SL4 1NJ
Tel: 01753 848848
Fax: 01753 848849
email: jenna.tyer@stgeorgeshouse.org
Web: www.stgeorgeshouse.org

St Hild and St Bede Trust
The Trust's annual income is restricted to the advancement of higher and further education in the Dioceses of Durham and Newcastle, and is presently committed to supporting the North East Religious Learning Resources Centre based in the City of Durham and in Newcastle, the chaplaincies of the College of St Hild and St Bede and of the University of Newcastle. The Trust gives scholarships for theology and music within the colleges of St Hild and St Bede and supports aided status Church of England Schools in both dioceses. Member of the Association of Church College Trusts (*see separate entry*). *Correspondent:* Mr W. Hurworth. *Home:* 16 Tempest Court, Wynyard Park, Billingham TS22 5TD, c/o College of St Hild and St Bede, Pelaw Leazes Lane, Durham, DH1 1SZ
Tel: 01740 644 274
email: w.hurworth@btinternet.com

St John's Guild

Founded in 1919 to assist the spiritual well-being of blind people, as well as to ease the isolation and loneliness in which some of them lived. Since that time both needs and society have changed. St John's Guild has developed to meet those changes. The Guild supports ten branches, which are located in different parts of the country and meet to provide worship, fellowship and friendship. Regular publications in Braille and audio are produced and widely distributed. *Chairman:* Mrs Judith Dunk. *Finance Officer:* Mrs Patricia Richards, Guild Office, 8 St Raphael's Court, Avenue Rd, St Albans, AL1 3EH

Tel: 01727 864076
email: stjohnsaccounts@btconnect.com
2nd email: r.mcewan1@btinternet.com
Web: www.stjohnsguild.org

St Luke's College Foundation

The Foundation's object is the advancement of further and higher education in religious education and theology. Grants are awarded to individuals for research and taught postgraduate qualifications in these fields; and to eligible organizations for related initiatives and facilities. The Foundation does not finance buildings, or provide bursaries for institutions to administer; and it is precluded from the direct support of schools (although it supports teachers who are taking eligible studies). Member of the Association of Church College Trusts (*see separate entry*). *Director:* Dr David Benzie, 15 St Maryhaye, Tavistock, Devon, PL19 8LR

email: director@st-lukes-foundation.org.uk
Web: www.st-lukes-foundation.org.uk

St Luke's Healthcare for the Clergy

Providing appropriate physical and psychological healthcare services to the clergy, their spouses, widows, and dependent children, monks and nuns, deaconesses, ordinands, Church Army staff, and overseas missionaries. To find out more or to access these services please contact the Medical Secretary at the email address below. *President:* The Archbishop of Canterbury. *Chairman:* Mr Edward Martineau. *Chief Executive:* Dr Claire Walker, Room 201, Church House, Great Smith Street, London, SW1P 3AZ

Tel: 020 7898 1700
email: medical@stlukeshealthcare.org.uk
Web: www.stlukeshealthcare.org.uk

St Mary's College Trust

The Trust's annual income is normally committed to supporting the Welsh National Centre for Religious Education, WNCRE at Gladstone's Library, Hawarden, Flint, and the Anglican Chaplaincy at the University of Wales, Bangor. As a result, grants to individuals and other institutions are only awarded in very exceptional circumstances. Member of the Association of Church College Trusts (*see separate entry*). *Contact:* Clerk to the Trustees, St Mary's College Trust,

Eifionydd, Normal Site (UWB), Holyhead Road, Bangor, Gwynedd, LL57 2PX. *Joint Chairmen:* The Bishops of Bangor and St Asaph

Tel: 01248 382934

St Michael's Fellowship

Runs four residential family assessment centres and one community assessment service in South London working in partnership with parents to enable them to meet the needs of their child. Works with adolescent mothers, one- or two-parent families where parents may have learning disabilities, psychiatric illness, a history of abuse, domestic violence and where there are child protection concerns. Offers assessed and supervised contact in a child-friendly 'homely' environment. Runs one supported housing scheme for vulnerable families, with self-contained flats and low support. Through Sure Start Children's Centres offers community support to teenage parents and young fathers in the Borough of Lambeth. *Director:* Mrs Sue Pettigrew, 136 Streatham High Road, London, SW16 1BW   *Tel:* 020 8835 9570

Fax: 020 8677 4883
email: admin@stmichaelsfellowship.org.uk
Web: www.stmichaelsfellowship.org.uk

St Pancras and Humanist Housing Association

Founded 1924 by the Revd Basil Jellicoe, this charitable association provides housing and support for families, single people and those with special needs in nearly 4,500 flats and houses in N London and Hertfordshire. c/o Origin Housing, St Richards, 110 Eversholt St, London, NW1 1BS   *Tel:* 020 7209 9287

Fax: 020 7209 9223
email: enquiries@originhousing.org.uk
Web: www.sph.org.uk

St Peter's Saltley Trust

The Trust's annual income is committed to supporting, developing and evaluating creative, innovative, locally-based project work in adult Christian learning and discipleship, the churches' work in further education and religious education in schools. The Trust's area of benefit comprises the region covered by the Anglican dioceses of Birmingham, Coventry, Hereford, Lichfield and Worcester. The Trust does not make grants towards capital projects or ongoing core costs (e.g., to fund building works or subsidize ongoing staff salaries) or to individuals for personal research or continuing education purposes. Member of the Association of Church College Trusts (*see separate entry*). *Director:* Dr Ian Jones. *Bursar and Clerk to the Trustees:* Mrs Lin Brown, Grays Court, 3 Nursery Rd, Edgbaston, Birmingham, B15 3JX   *Tel:* 0121 427 6800

email: director@saltleytrust.org.uk
Web: www.saltleytrust.org.uk

Student Christian Movement

SCM is a student-led community passionate about faith and justice. We have a long history

of bringing students together to explore how to live out a radical faith in today's world. The national network is made up of university links, individual members, friends and subscribers. The movement holds regular conferences and produces a variety of resources, including the termly magazine *Movement*. It is affiliated to the World Student Christian Federation. *National Coordinator:* Hilary Topp. *Links Worker:* Rosie Venner. *Administrator:* Lisa Murphy, 308F The Big Peg, 120 Vyse St, Hockley, Birmingham, B18 6ND
Tel: 0121 200 3355
email: scm@movement.org.uk
Web: www.movement.org.uk

Summer Biblical Study in Cambridge
Summer Biblical Study in Cambridge is a residential Summer School run by the Vacation Term for Biblical Study (Registered Charity no. 1125494) which takes place at Robinson College, Cambridge, during the first two weeks in August. It is particularly suitable for theology students and any ordained and lay people with an interest in critical biblical study. Participants can take part for one or both weeks; non-residents are also welcome. Lectures are given by professional biblical scholars, specializing in Old and New Testament studies and related subjects. There is also the opportunity (optional) for tuition in biblical Greek or Hebrew at absolute beginner, intermediate or advanced level. Participants have time to enjoy the attractions of Cambridge and the surrounding countryside. A limited number of bursaries towards the cost of accommodation are available. The programme and application form are available from the website from about mid-January. Contact the Treasurer for further details. *Chairman:* Professor Keith Elliott. *Secretary:* Miss Gillian Glenn. *Treasurer:* Mr Richard Garner, 45 Souldern Street, Watford, Hertfordshire, WD18 0EU
Tel: 01923 229306
email: jrmgarner@btinternet.com
Web: www.vtbs.org.uk

Tearfund
Tearfund is an evangelical Christian relief and development charity working with the local church around the world to bring physical, emotional and spiritual transformation to people living in poverty. Responding to natural disasters and emergencies, engaging in longer-term community development and speaking out to challenge injustice, Tearfund aims to make the fullness of life promised by Christ a reality for people in need. With support from individuals and churches in the UK and Ireland, Tearfund is in active partnership with local Christians in more than 60 countries. *Chief Executive:* Mr Matthew Frost, 100 Church Rd, Teddington, TW11 8QE
Tel: 0845 355 8355
Fax: 020 8943 3594
email: enquiry@tearfund.org
Web: www.tearfund.org

Third Province Movement
The object of the Third Province Movement, which was started in November 1992, is to advocate, and eventually secure, the establishment within the Church of England of an autonomous province for all those, whatever their churchmanship, who in conscience cannot accept the ordination of women to the priesthood, the episcopate and other liberal developments. It also advocates a realignment on the same principle within the whole Anglican Communion. *Chairman:* Mrs Margaret Brown, Luckhurst, Mayfield, TN20 6TY
Tel: 01435 873007
Web: www.thirdprovince.org.uk

Together (Mental After Care Association, formerly MACA)
Together is a leading national charity providing a wide range of quality community- and hospital-based services for people with mental health needs and their carers, including: advocacy, assertive outreach schemes, community support, employment schemes, forensic services, helplines/information, respite for carers, social clubs, supported accommodation with 24–hour care. *Chief Executive:* Liz Felton, 12 Old Street, London, EC1V 9BE
Tel: 020 7780 7300
Fax: 020 7780 7301
email: contact-us@together-uk.org
Web: www.together-uk.org

Traditional Choir Trust, The
The Traditional Choir Trust was started in 2002 by Dr John Sanders in Gloucester to: 'give grants, bursaries and scholarships to boys otherwise unable to attend recognized choir schools. To encourage and financially assist choir schools, cathedrals, Chapels Royal, collegiate churches, university chapels, parish churches and other choral foundations to maintain the ancient tradition of the all male choir.' Upon Dr Sanders' death in 2003, the Trusteeship was handed over to the Dean and Chapter of Chichester Cathedral. The Trust relies solely upon donations and legacies to build capital from which bursaries can be provided. *Trustees:* Dean and Chapter of Chichester. *Patron:* Very Revd Michael Tavinor, Dean of Hereford. *Administrator:* The Communar, The Royal Chantry, Cathedral Cloisters, Chichester, West Sussex, PO19 1PX
Tel: 01243 782595
01243 812492
Fax: 01243 812499
email: admin@chichestercathedral.org.uk
Web: www.chichestercathedral.org.uk

Trinitarian Bible Society
Founded in 1831 for the circulation of Protestant or uncorrupted versions of the Word of God. The Society will only circulate the Authorized Version in English, and foreign language scriptures translated from the same Greek and Hebrew texts with comparable accuracy. *Office*

ORGANIZATIONS

Manager: Mr J. M. Wilson, Tyndale House, Dorset Rd, London, SW19 3NN   *Tel:* 020 8543 7857
Fax: 020 8543 6370
email: tbs@trinitarianbiblesociety.org
Web: www.trinitarianbiblesociety.org

True Freedom Trust
An interdenominational support and teaching ministry for people struggling with same-sex attraction and related issues, and for their church leaders, families and friends. It supports people who experience same-sex attraction but who choose not to embrace a gay identity or be involved in same-sex relationships because of convictions of faith. It supplies resources, speakers and organizes conferences to help the Church overcome fear and prejudice and act with understanding and love in a biblical and Christlike way. *Chairman:* Mr Stefan Cantore. *Director:* Mr Jonathan Berry, PO Box 357, Birkenhead, Wirral, CH25 9EP   *Tel:* 0151 653 0773
email: info@truefreedomtrust.co.uk
Web: www.truefreedomtrust.co.uk

Unitas – The Catholic League
Founded in 1913, the special objects of this ecumenical society are the reunion of all Christians with the See of Rome, the spread of the Catholic faith, the promotion of fellowship among Catholics and the deepening of the spiritual life. It is governed by a Priest Director and six elected members. Further details from the Secretary. *The Secretary:* Mr David Chapman, Lower Flat, 293 Ordnance Road, Enfield, EN3 6HB
Tel: 01992 763 893
email: nomadyane@btinternet.com
Web: www.unitas.org.uk

Unite Clergy and Faith Workers
Unite Faith Workers is the union for those who work for religious organizations as ministers, clergy and lay staff. Membership is open to all faiths and denominations. Set up in 1994, it is now part of Unite, which has more than 1.5 million members, following the merger of Amicus with TGWU.

Unite Faith Workers provides its members with a professional association of their own, with access to all the facilities and support of a modern union. Unite is recognized by the Church of England for staff in the National Church Institutions, and by some of the largest church-related charities, including Action for Children and The Children's Society. A growing number of diocesan office staff and others working for church organizations and agencies are members.

Unite Faith Workers has its own Executive, and a national network of local representatives providing support for members, and belongs to the specialist Community, Youth Workers and Non-Profit Sector within Unite, in partnership with a number of national agencies, professional associations and charities. It works to bring about fairness and dignity at work for all its members, whatever their situation, and is currently leading the campaign for modern conditions of service for those who serve as ministers. A wide range of benefits is provided for members in good standing, including legal representation and professional advice on many issues affecting work and pensions, equal opportunities, harassment and bullying at work, and much more. *Chair of Church of England Section:* Revd Pete Hobson. *Unite National Officer:* Sally Kosky. *Communications:* Maureen German, Unite the Union, Unite House, 128 Theobald's Road London, WC1X 8TN
Tel: 020 337 2028 0333 123 0021 (Faith Workers' Helpline)
Fax: 0870 731 5043
email: maureen.german@unitetheunion.org
Web: www.unitetheunion.org

United Church Schools Trust (formerly Church Schools Company)
Founded as an educational charity in 1883 to create schools that offer pupils a good academic education based on Christian principles with particular reference to the Church of England. The Company's council has developed the concept of offering a broad and challenging education. To achieve this it has invested in the provision of excellent buildings and facilities including extensive ICT at each school. This ideal of strong schools embraces not just academic learning to high standards, but also the development of skills that will be essential throughout life both at work and socially. Teamwork, leadership, an enthusiastic response to challenge and an active concern for others are all attributes which are valued. Schools at Blackpool, Guildford, Surbiton, Caterham, Ashford, Hampshire near Romsey, Hull, Lincoln, Sunderland, Bournemouth and Claygate. Clergy bursaries available. A subsidiary charity, the United Learning Trust, was founded in 2002 to manage a number of City Academies spread across the country. Twenty Academies and one City Technology College are currently open, mainly in inner city areas, with more to be added. *Chairman:* Rt Revd and Rt Hon The Lord Carey of Clifton. *Chief Executive:* Jon Coles, Fairline House, Nene Valley Business Park, Oundle, Peterborough, PE8 4HN   *Tel:* 01832 864444
Fax: 01832 734760
email: admin@unitedlearning.org.uk
Web: www.unitedlearning.org.uk

United Nations Association of Great Britain and Northern Ireland (UNA-UK)
The UNA-UK is the UK's leading source of independent information and analysis on the United Nations, and a UK-wide grassroots movement. UNA-UK is committed to a strong, credible and effective UN. We believe that a strengthened UN

is in the UK's national interest. We advocate strong government support for the UN, and seek to demonstrate why the UN matters to people everywhere. *Executive Director:* Natalie Samarasinghe. *Administrative Assistant:* Natalie Saad, 3 Whitehall Court, London, SW1A 2EL

Tel: 020 7766 3454
Fax: 020 7000 1381
email: saad@una.org.uk
Web: www.una.org.uk

Universities and Colleges Christian Fellowship

UCCF: The Christian Unions exists to give every student in Great Britain an opportunity to hear and respond to the gospel of Jesus. We are full-time staff, volunteers, supporters and students all working together to make disciples of Christ in the student world. Visit www.uccf.org.uk to find out more. UCCF: The Christian Unions, Blue Boar House 5 Blue Boar Street, Oxford, OX1 4EE

Tel: 01865 253678
email: email@uccf.org.uk
Web: www.uccf.org.uk

Urban Saints

Since 1906 Urban Saints (formerly known as Crusaders) has been reaching out to children and young people with the good news of Jesus Christ. We are passionate about working with all children and young people, helping them to realize their full God-given potential as they journey from childhood to adulthood. Young people (aged 5 to 18+) connect with the movement in a variety of ways, including weekly youth groups, special events, holidays, community projects and training programmes. These activities are led by thousands of volunteers who are comprehensively trained and supported in order to help them work effectively and achieve the highest possible standards of youth work practice. Whilst much of our work is in the UK and Ireland, increasingly we are helping indigenous churches within countries in the developing world to set up and run outreach work among un-churched children and young people. *Exec Director:* Matt Summerfield. *Volunteers Director:* Mark Arnold. *Marketing and Income Development Director:* Lorne Campbell. *Ministry Development Director:* John Fudge. *HR Manager:* Liz Dore, Kestin House, 45 Crescent Rd, Luton, LU2 0AH

Tel: 01582 589850
Fax: 01582 721702
email: email@urbansaints.org
Web: www.urbansaints.org /
www.crusadersreunited.org.uk /
www.urbansaints.org/energize

Urban Theology Unit

Ecumenical educational charity offering academic programmes engaging with contextual theology, ministerial practice, and urban realities. Academic programmes include Foundation Degree, MA in Theology and Ministry and MA in Urban Theology (York St John University), and M Phil/Ph D in Contextual, Urban and Liberation Theology and Ministerial Practice (University of Birmingham). There are UTU publications on British Liberation Theology, urban ministry, and contextual Bible readings. *Chairperson:* Revd Eileen Sanderson. *Acting Director:* Revd Dr Ian K. Duffield. *Support Services Manager:* Mrs Kate Thompson, 210 Abbeyfield Rd, Sheffield, S4 7AZ

Tel: 0114 243 5342
Fax: 0114 243 5356
email: office@utusheffield.org.uk
Web: www.utusheffield.org.uk

Us. (also known as United Society, formerly USPG)

We are called Us., and are also known as United Society. We changed our name from USPG in 2012. We are an Anglican mission agency working in partnership with churches around the world. Together, we work alongside local communities to improve health, put children in school, tackle discrimination, nurture leaders, give a voice to women, and much more. We also work closely with the Churches in Britain and Ireland, inviting people to share in our mission through friendship, prayer and financial support, and encouraging congregations to receive the riches that the global church offers.

One of our key aims is to inspire churches and Christians in Britain and Ireland to enjoy closer connections with their brothers and sisters around the world through friendship, prayer and financial support.

Our work in more detail: (1) We support church-based development programmes that empower people and communities to draw upon their faith, skills and resources to tackle poverty and speak out for justice. We want to see lives transformed through healthier living, better education, more food security, safety for children, an end to gender-based violence, justice for all, and freedom to worship. (2) We support programmes that train leaders and build the capacity of churches so they are better equipped to reach out to local communities. (3) We support the long-term relief and rehabilitation work of Anglican churches in response to emergencies and natural disasters. (4) We provide opportunities for volunteers from Britain and Ireland to take up placements with the world church, including a special programme for clergy and ordinands.

We also produce a range of publications for readers in Britain and Ireland, including a magazine, prayer diary and a range of free resources for study and worship at Advent, Lent and Harvest.

We were founded in 1701 as the Society for the Propagation of the Gospel in Foreign Parts (SPG), making us one of the oldest Anglican mission agencies. In 1965 we merged with the Universities' Mission to Central Africa (UMCA) and

then with the Cambridge Mission to Delhi to become USPG. *President:* The Archbishop of Canterbury. *Chair:* Revd Canon Chris Chivers. *General Secretary:* Janette O'Neill, Harling House, 47–51 Great Suffolk Street, London, SE1 0BS
Tel: 020 7921 2200
email: info@weareUs.org.uk
Web: www.weareUs.org.uk

Vergers, Church of England Guild of
Founded in 1932 to promote Christian fellowship and spiritual guidance among the vergers of the cathedrals and parish churches of England. The Guild is divided into branches which meet locally every month and nationally several times throughout the year. The Guild provides a comprehensive training course which students can study from home with the help of an area tutor and mentor. The course works alongside the well-established Annual Training Conference. The Guild Diploma is awarded to successful students. Advice concerning appointments, job descriptions and contracts is available through the Welfare Officer. Contact can be made through the General Secretary. *General Secretary:* Stephen Stokes, Box 4485, 6 Slington House Rankin Road, Basingstoke, RG24 8PH   *Tel:* 01223 322860
email: cevgensec@gmail.com
Web: www.cofegv.org.uk

Walsingham, Shrine of Our Lady of
Founded in 1061 in response to a vision, destroyed in 1538, restored in 1922 by Revd A. Hope Patten, Vicar of Walsingham. Since 1931, when it was moved from the parish church, the Shrine has contained the image of Our Lady of Walsingham together with the Holy House, representing the house of the Annunciation and the home in Nazareth of the Holy Family. Nowadays Walsingham is England's premier place of pilgrimage. It is administered by a College of Guardians. Special facilities include accommodation for people of all ages and those with special needs, an Education Department for school visits, and retreat and conference facilities. Information is available from the Administrator. *Administrator:* Rt Revd Lindsay Urwin OGS. *Assistant Administrator and Youth Missioner:* Revd S. Gallagher, The College, Walsingham, NR22 6EF   *Tel:* 01328 824204
Fax: 01328 824209
email: pr.adm@olw-shrine.org.uk
Web: www.walsingham.org.uk

WATCH (Women and the Church)
Founded in 1996, WATCH promotes the ministry of women in the Church of England. It is based on a vision of the Church as a community of God's people where justice and equality prevail, regardless of gender. WATCH works for an inclusive church in which women and men work together as laypeople, deacons, priests and bishops. Other priorities shaping our work are to achieve honesty and openness in church appointments and better support for women in ministry, and to challenge barriers which impede the full expression of a woman's vocation and gifts. The ministry of both lay and ordained women is fostered through local diocesan WATCH branches, and members receive the magazine *Outlook. Chair:* Hilary Cotton. *Secretary:* Gill Gould, St John's Church, Waterloo Rd, London, SE1 8TY   *Tel:* 07815 729565
01993 832514
Fax: 01763 848774
email: admin@womenandthechurch.org
Web: www.womenandthechurch.org

William Temple Foundation
Founded in 1947, as a research organization focusing on the links between theology, the economy and urban mission practice. The Foundation's current programme reflects theologically and strategically on the evolving relationship between religion and public space, including the mission and identity of the church in postsecular society, urban societies and the contribution of Christianity and other religions to current wellbeing and happiness agendas, public policy and social welfare. This agenda also encompasses mapping and analyzing the ongoing contribution of religion to ethics and economics, including the regulation of business and financial institutions.

The Foundation continues its research into the work and identity of faith-based organizations in civil society across the UK, using the concept of religious and spiritual capital, and completed a major Leverhulme Trust programme in this area (2007–10). The Foundation works with a wide variety of partners including several community and grassroots organizations in the UK and across Europe. Emerging from this research, the Foundation is contributing teaching at postdoctoral level at the University of Chester, with whom it has signed a research partnership, including the creation of a Centre for Faiths and Public Policy. The Centre produces research, publications and offers MA and doctoral level opportunities in the field. Its most recent project is a partnership with the University of Liverpool entitled *Philosophy and Religious Practice (2013–14)* which explores the ongoing impact of religious and philosophical ideas on public life and policy. *Director of Research:* Dr Chris Baker, Centre for Faiths and Public Policy, University of Chester, Parkgate Road, Chester, CH1 4BJ
Tel: 01244 511074
email: chris.baker@wtf.org.uk
Web: www.wtf.org.uk

William Temple House
William Temple House is a residence for 49/50 students from overseas and the United Kingdom in full-time education. The male and female students are of all faiths and nationalities. The

House is under the management of The International Students' Club (C of E) Ltd, a registered charity. Enquiries to the Warden. International Students Club (C of E) Ltd, William Temple House, 29 Trebovir Rd, London, SW5 9NQ
Tel: 020 7373 6962
Fax: 020 7341 0003
email: office@williamtemplehouse.co.uk
Web: www.williamtemplehouse.co.uk

Women's World Day of Prayer
Founded in America in 1887 (Britain 1930–34) to unite Christian women in prayer by means of services held on the first Friday in March each year, by fostering local interdenominational prayer groups meeting throughout the year and to give financial support to Christian charities throughout the world. *President:* Mrs Mimi Barton. *Chairperson:* Mrs Margaret Pickford. *Administrator:* Mrs Mary Judd, WWDP, Commercial Rd, Tunbridge Wells, TN1 2RR
Tel: 01892 541411
Fax: 01892 541745
email: office@wwdp.org.uk
Web: www.wwdp.org.uk

Womenaid International
A humanitarian aid and development agency run by volunteers in the UK, which provides relief and assistance to women and children suffering distress caused by war, disasters or poverty. It seeks to empower women through education, training, provision of credit, and also campaigns against violations of women's human rights. An implementing partner of the European Community Humanitarian Office (ECHO), the British Government and several UN agencies, it has provided over 30,000 tonnes of food, medical supplies and clothing to more than 1.5 million refugees in the former Yugoslavia, the Caucasus and Central Asia. Development assistance globally has ranged from building and repairing schools, supporting rescue centres for street children, repairing hospitals and providing medical equipment/supplies to micro-credit support and water/sanitation projects. *Founder:* Ms Pida Ripley, 3 Whitehall Court, London, SW1A 2EL
Tel: 020 7839 1790
Fax: 020 7839 2929
email: womenaid@womenaid.org
Web: www.womenaid.org

Woodard Schools
Founded by Canon Nathaniel Woodard in 1848 to promote Christian education informed by the doctrines and principles of the Church of England. Woodard now owns some sixteen schools and a further eighteen schools are linked to Woodard through formal agreements of affiliation or association. Woodard also sponsors five academies. *President:* Rt Revd Dr Anthony Russell. *Senior Provost:* Canon Brendan Clover. *Chairman:* Mr Tom Fremantle. *Director of Educa-*

tion: Mr Christopher Wright. *Director of Finance and Company Secretary:* Mr Michael Corcoran, High St, Abbots Bromley, Rugeley, WS15 3BW
Tel: 01283 840120
Fax: 01283 840893
email: jillshorthose@woodard.co.uk
Web: www.woodard.co.uk

World Congress of Faiths
Founded in 1936 to promote mutual understanding and a spirit of fellowship between people of different religious traditions. WCF works to explain and reconcile religious conflict and the tensions between the different communities. Conferences and lectures are arranged. The journal *Interreligious Insight* is published two or three times a year, jointly with the Interreligious Engagement Project, and has its own website. *President:* Revd Marcus Braybrooke and Rabbi Jacqueline Tabick. *Chairman:* Revd Dr Alan Race. *Hon Treasurer:* Pejman Khojasteh. *Editor:* Revd Dr Alan Race. *Secretary:* Revd Feargus O'Connor, London Interfaith Centre, 125 Salusbury Rd, London, NW6 6RG
Tel: 01935 864055
email: admin@worldfaiths.org
Web: www.worldfaiths.org

World Vision
Formed in London in 1979, World Vision UK is part of the international World Vision partnership and is a major UK relief and development agency. World Vision is at work in over 100 countries in Africa, Asia, Eastern Europe, Latin America and the Middle East. It is involved in partnering churches and other non-governmental organizations in projects which range from relief work in Africa to income generation projects in Bangladesh. *Chief Exec Officer:* Charles Badenoch. *Church Relations Manager:* Alistair Metcalfe, World Vision House, Opal Drive, Fox Milne, Milton Keynes, MK15 0ZR
Tel: 01908 841000
Fax: 01908 841001
email: church@worldvision.org.uk
Web: www.worldvision.org.uk/church

YMCA
Founded 1844 to promote the physical, intellectual and spiritual well-being of young people. *President:* The Archbishop of York. *Chief Executive:* Denise Hatton, YMCA England, 29–35 Farringdon Road, London, EC1M 3JF
Tel: 020 7186 9500
email: enquiries@ymca.org.uk
Web: www.ymca.org.uk

Young Women's Trust
The Young Women's Trust is a force for change for women facing discrimination and inequalities of all kinds. Our principal aims are to enable young women who are experiencing particular disadvantage to identify and realize their full potential, to influence public policy in order to

achieve equality and social justice for young women, and to provide opportunities for participation in a worldwide women's movement. CAN Mezzanine, 49–51 East Road, London, N1 6AH   *Tel:* 020 7250 8339
email: via website
Web: www.youngwomenstrust.org

York Glaziers' Trust
Established 1967 by the Dean and Chapter of York and the Pilgrim Trust (1) to conserve and restore the stained glass of York Minster; (2) to conserve, restore and advise on all stained glass or glazing of historic or artistic importance, in any building whether religious or secular, public or private; (3) to establish and maintain within the City of York a stained glass workshop dedicated to the training and employment of conservators and craftsmen specializing in the preservation of glass of historic and artistic importance; and (4) to encourage public interest in the preservation of stained glass, to collaborate with educational institutions and to assist with scientific and art historical research into stained and painted glass. Advice should always be sought when considering treatment of glass of artistic or historic value. The Trust welcomes enquiries from all sources. It offers a full advisory service and will compile comprehensive condition reports. *Director:* Mrs Sarah E. Brown FSA. *Senior Conservator:* Nick Teed MA. *Business Manager:* Trevor Lawson MRICS, MAPM, 6 Deangate, York, YO1 7JB
Tel: 01904 557228
email: info@yorkglazierstrust.org
Web: www.yorkglazierstrust.org

Diocesan Associations

Association of the Dioceses of Singapore and West Malaysia
Mrs Jane Sheard
Ivy Cottage
9 Queen Street
Kirton-in-Lindsey
Gainsborough
Lincolnshire DN21 4NS
email: jane_ivycottage@
btinternet.com

Belize Church Association
Mrs Michele Orio
email: elleorio@
hotmail.co.uk
Web:
www.belizechurch
association.org.uk

Church of Ceylon Association
Revd Preb Dr Brian
Leathard
Parish Office
St Luke's Crypt,
Sydney Street,
London SW3 6NH
Tel: 020 7351 7365
email: brianleathard@
chelseaparish.org

Congo Church Association
Mrs Rosemary Peirce
8 Burwell Meadow
Witney
Oxford OX28 5JQ
Tel: 01993 200103
email: rosemary.peirce@
ntlworld.com

Egypt Diocesan Association
Mr Joseph Wasef
88 Chichester Road
Croydon CR0 5NB
Tel: 020 8686 4159
email: edasecretary@
gmail.com

Fellowship of the Maple Leaf
(*Provides grants to further mutual learning between the Church in Canada and the UK*)
Preb David Sceats
Nether Dalgleish
Ettrick
Selkirk
TD7 5HZ
Tel: 01750 62269
email:
dsceats@gmail.com
Web:
www.mapleleaf.org.uk

Friends of the Church in India
Chair: Revd Jessie
Anand
All Saints Vicarage
100 Prince of Wales
Drive
Battersea
London SW11 4BD
Tel: 020 7622 3809
Mobile: 07760 252655
email: jessieanand@
yahoo.co.uk

Friends of the Diocese of Cyprus and the Gulf
Mrs Sally Milner
123 Barnett Wood
Lane
Ashtead
Surrey KT21 2LR
Tel: 01372 270263
email:
friends@cypgulf.org

Friends of the Diocese of Iran
Mr John Clark
32 Weigall Rd
Lee
London SE12 8HE
email: john@mclark32.
freeserve.co.uk

Friends of the Diocese of Uruguay
N. J. Roberts
2 Upland Rise
Walton
Chesterfield S40 2DD
Tel: 01246 233590
Mobile: 07896 162461
email: nick.roberts@
bcs.org
Web: www.friends-of-
the-diocese-of-
uruguay.org.uk

Guyana Diocesan Association
Chairman: Mrs Marlene
Edwards
68 Waddon Way
Croydon CR0 4HW
Tel: 020 8688 3930
Mobile: 07944 052255
email: mpchambers@
sky.com

Secretary: Mrs Jane
Garner
Flat 2, Hill House
38 Park Street
Old Hatfield AL9 5AZ
Tel: 01707 275974
Mobile: 07761 96767
email: janemgarner@
yahoo.co.uk

Jerusalem and the Middle East Church Association	Ms Shirley Eason 1 Hart House The Hart Farnham Surrey GU9 7HJ *Tel and fax:* 01252 726994 *email:* secretary@ jmeca.eclipse.co.uk *Web:* www.jmeca.org.uk	**Province of the Indian Ocean Support Association**	*Hon. Secretary:* Vacancy *Chair:* Canon Hall Speers The Rectory 38 Manor Rd Barnet EN5 2JJ *Tel:* 020 8449 3894 *email:* hall.speers@ talk21.com *Hon. Treasurer:* Revd
Kenya Church Association	Mr James Ireri 48 Parkside Road Addlestone KT15 3AW *Tel:* 07590 697595 *email:* james@safi- shine.co.uk		Hilary C. Jones St Martin's Rectory Horn St Folkestone CT20 3JJ *Tel:* 01303 238509 *email:* revhilaryjones@ btinternet.com
Lesotho Diocesan Association	Sister Jean Mary CHN Convent of the Holy Name Morley Road Oakwood Derby DE21 4QZ *Tel:* 01332 671 716 *email:* chnjmary@ yahoo.co.uk	**St Helena Association**	Canon Patricia Ann Turner 7 Roundell Drive West Marton Skipton BD23 3UL *Tel:* 01282 842332 *email:* canonannturner@ gmail.com
MANNA Mozambique and Angola Anglican Association	Elizabeth Thomas 1 The Green Marcham Oxfordshire OX13 6NE *Tel:* 07801 523461 *email:* elizabeth@ maninga.org *Web:* www.manna- anglican.org	**Sudan Church Association**	Mrs Sara Taffinder 69 Poynders Rd Clapham London SW4 8PL *Tel* and *Fax:* 020 8671 1974
		TZABA Trans-Vaal, Zimbabwe and Botswana Association	Mrs Liz Martin 120 Church Lane East Aldershot Hampshire GU11 3SS *Tel* and *Fax:* 01252 320108 *email:* elizmmartin@ yahoo.co.uk *Web:* www.TZABA.org
Nigeria Fellowship	*Chair:* Dr Anne Phillips 33 Cliffe Road Sheffield S6 5DR *Tel:* 0114 233 8529 *email:* annephillips2@ hotmail.co.uk	**Uganda Church Association**	Revd Dr Michael Hunter 18 Linnet Grove Kendal Cumbria LA9 7RP *Tel:* 01539 725093 *email:* mutagwok@aol.com

Zululand Swaziland Association	The Zululand Swaziland Association has ceased to exist as an independent charity. The Zululand Swaziland Trusteeship has now passed to the trustees of United Society (also known as Us., formerly USPG), and donations to its	ongoing work can be made by cheque payable to 'United Society', earmarked 'Zululand Swaziland Trust'. Us. (formerly USPG) Harling House 47–51 Great Suffolk Street London SE1 0BS

Libraries and Archives

Canterbury

Cathedral Archives and Library
The Precincts
Canterbury
Kent CT1 2EH

Cathedral Librarian
Mrs Karen Brayshaw

Cathedral Archivist
Mrs Cressida Williams

Information about the Archives and Library, and links to their separate online catalogues, are available on the Cathedral website at www.canterbury-cathedral.org

Tel: 01227 865330 (Archives); 01227 865287 (Library)
Fax: 01227 865222
email: archives@canterbury-cathedral.org; library@canterbury-cathedral.org

Library collections: 52,000 printed volumes, 15th century to present. The Howley-Harrison Collection (16,000 books and pamphlets) includes anti-slavery and Oxford Movement material. Also cathedral printed music, and scores of Canterbury Catch Club. Three parish libraries: Crundale, Elham and Preston-next-Wingham, in a Dr Bray cabinet. The collections include substantial holdings on national and local history, including the English Civil War, travel, botany, English and foreign literature.

Archive collections: 2km of collections of manuscripts and archives, 9th century to present, including the Dean and Chapter's archives; records of the Diocese of Canterbury; parish records; records of Canterbury City Council and other organizations, businesses, administrations and individuals in the Canterbury area.

Crowther Library

Crowther Centre for Mission Education
Church Mission Society
Watlington Rd
Oxford
OX4 6BZ

Librarian Ken Osborne

Tel: 01865 787552
Fax: 01865 776375
email: ken.osborne@cms-uk.org
Web: www.cms-uk.org/heritage/default.htm
Open: 0900–1700 hours Mon–Fri
Closed public holidays.

30,000 volumes, 250 current periodicals. Successor to the Partnership House Mission Studies Library that incorporated the post-1945 collections of the former Church Missionary Society and United Society for the Propagation of the Gospel Stock focuses on the work of the Church worldwide, missiology, history of mission, church history, African and Asian Christianity and interfaith relations. Also houses CMS's pre-1945 collection entitled the Max Warren Collection. Reference only.

ORGANIZATIONS

Durham

Durham Cathedral Library
The College
Durham
DH1 3EH

Canon Librarian Canon Rosalind Brown
Head of Collections Gabriel Sewell

Tel: 0191 386 2489
email: Library@
durhamcathedral.co.uk

Open: 0900–16.45 hours
Mon–Fri

Chapter Library of 375 medieval manuscripts from the 7th century onwards, including Northumbrian, Norman and scholastic material. 1000 post-medieval manuscripts. Manuscript and printed music 16th cent–early 19th cent. Archival collections include historical collections for County Durham and the NE of England, with much of wider interest, formed by local antiquaries, 17th–20th cent; papers and correspondence of 19th–20th cent. bishops and churchmen. Printed books include 70 incunabula, 11,000 books printed pre-1851 and modern works of church history, local interest and the arts. Archdeacon Sharp Library of modern theology of approx. 10,000 books in English. Meissen Library of theology in German of approx. 20,000 books donated by EKD inaugurated 1998. Catalogue at its website www.meissenlibrarydurham.co.uk.

Exeter

Exeter Cathedral Library
   and Archives
c/o Cathedral Office,
1 The Cloisters,
Exeter
EX1 1HS

Cathedral Librarian Peter Thomas
Assistant Librarian Stuart Macwilliam
Cathedral Archivist Ellie Jones

Tel: 01392 421423
email: library@exeter-cathedral.org.uk
archive@exeter-cathedral.org.uk
Web: http://www.exeter-cathedral.org.uk/Admin/Library/html

Open: 1000–1600 hours Mon–Fri. Closed on public holidays.
(Archives, by appointment only, closed on public holidays).

20,000 items (Library); 50,000 (Archives), Manuscripts include Exeter Book and Exon Domesday; special collections include cathedral manuscripts and archives, early printed books in medicine and science, Cook Collection (16th–19th c., early linguistics), printed tracts (mainly Civil War period), Harington Collection (16th–19th c., theology, ecclesiastical history, history). Pre-2001 accessions included in online catalogue of Exeter University Library at www.ex.ac.uk/library/. Medical and scientific collections also catalogued in *Medicine and science at Exeter Cathedral Library*, compiled by Peter W. Thomas (University of Exeter Press, 2003). See also *The library and archives of Exeter Cathedral*, by L. J. Lloyd and Audrey M. Erskine, 3rd edn (Exeter 2004).

Gladstone's Library

Gladstone's Library
Church Lane
Hawarden
Flintshire
CH5 3DF

Warden Revd Peter Francis

Tel: 01244 532350
Fax: 01244 520643
email: enquiries@
gladlib.org
Web:
www.gladstoneslibrary.org

Extensive holdings in Theology and Religious Studies. Main subject areas include: contextual theologies, Christian doctrine, biblical studies, ethics, spirituality, liturgy, church history plus Islamic Collection, Liberal/Radical Theology Archive, Bishop Moorman Franciscan Collection and excellent holdings in nineteenth-century history, art and literature. Twenty-six bedrooms, four conference rooms and chapel. Subsidised rates for clergy and students. Bursaries and scholarships available.

Hereford

Hereford Cathedral Library and
   Archives
Hereford Cathedral
Hereford
HR1 2NG

Canon Chancellor Canon Christopher Pullin
Archivist Mrs Rosalind Caird
Librarian Dr Rosemary Firman
Cataloguer Tessa Smart
Library and Archives Assistant Lucy Barrell
Photographer Gordon Taylor MBE LRPS

Tel: 01432 374225/6
email: library@
herefordcathedral.org
Web:
www.herefordcathedral.org

Open: Tues–Thurs 1000–1600 hours. Other times by prior appointment. Closed in January for essential conservation and maintenance work.

The Library cares for the Mappa Mundi (*c.* 1300), Chained Library and All Saints' Chained Library. The collection includes 227 medieval manuscripts from the 8th to the early 16th centuries, over 3,000 pre-1801 printed books including 56 incunabula, 10,000 books published post-1800 (many borrowable) and manuscript and printed music (18th to 20th centuries). There are also 30,000 archives of the Dean and Chapter, dating from the 9th to 21st centuries. Photographic service available.

Lambeth

Lambeth Palace Library
London
SE1 7JU

Librarian and Archivist Giles Mandelbrote

Tel: 020 7898 1400
email: archives@
churchofengland.org
Web: www.
lambethpalacelibrary.org
Facebook: https://
www.facebook.com/
LambethPalaceLibrary
Follow us on Twitter:
@lampallib

Open: 1000–1700 hours Tues–Fri (Thursday evening opening until 19.30). Closed Mondays, public holidays and ten days at Christmas and Easter.

Main library for the history of the Church of England, open for public use since 1610. 200,000 printed books and pamphlets, 4,900 manuscripts 9th–20th centuries. Registers and correspondence of Archbishops of Canterbury 12th–20th centuries. Records of Province of Canterbury, the Faculty Office, Lambeth Conferences up to 1968, Bishops of London, and papers of churchmen, statesmen and organizations within the Church of England. Also holds the manuscripts and printed books earlier than 1850 from Sion College Library.

Pusey House

Pusey House
Oxford
OX1 3LZ

Principal Revd Dr George
Westhaver
Librarian Vacancy
Chaplain Revd Mark Stafford

Tel: 01865 278415
email: chapter@
puseyhouse.org.uk
Web: www.puseyhouse.org.uk

Open: 0930–1230, 1400–1630
Mon–Fri; 0930–1230 Sat (by
appointment only) during
full term (weeks 0–8)
During vacation the library is
open Monday to Friday by
appointment only. The
library is closed during
August and at the beginning
of September until after the
St Giles' Fair.

Contact the Custodian for
vacation opening times

80,000 volumes. A theological
library specializing in
patristics, Church history and
liturgy. An extensive archive of
Oxford Movement and related
material.

St Paul's

The Library
St Paul's Cathedral
London
EC4M 8AE

Librarian Mr Jo Wisdom

Tel: 020 7246 8345
Fax: 020 7248 3104
email: library@
stpaulscathedral.org.uk

Re-established after the Great
Fire of 1666, the library is strong
in theology, ecclesiastical history,
and sermons, especiallyof 17th
and 18th centuries. Special
collections include early printed
Bibles; St Paul's Cross sermons;
19th-century tracts. The archive
of Dean and Chapter is deposited
at London Metropolitan Archives,
40 Northampton Road, London
EC1R 0HB
email:
ask.lma@cityoflondon.gov.uk

Sarum College

Sarum College Library
19 The Close
Salisbury
SP1 2EE

Director of Learning Resources
Jennifer Monds
Librarian Jayne Downey

Tel: 01722 424803
email: library@sarum.ac.uk
web: www.sarum.ac.uk/
library

Open: 0900–1700 Mon–Fri
and some evenings during
term time

Fees: £30 per annum for
reading rights; £40 per
annum for reading and
borrowing rights; £5 per day
or £10 per week for visitors
(subject to revision)

Founded 1860. More than
40,000 volumes mostly on
academic theology, church
history, ethics and Christian
spirituality. Rare book
collection including 274 bound
volumes of mainly 20th-century
tracts, sermons, charges and
letters. About 1000 volumes are
added each year.

Fifty journals are taken, with
back numbers available for
reference use. Inter-library loan
services offered. Internet and
Wi-Fi. Archive of the Christian
Socialist Movement. Catalogue
accessible from the library home-
page at the above web address.
Accommodation available.
Researchers and sabbaticals
welcome. Quiet space. Coffee, tea
and lunches may be purchased.
There is also a bookshop selling
academic theology.

Sarum College Bookshop

19 The Close
Salisbury
SP1 2EE

Director of Learning Resources
Jennifer Monds
Assistant Manager Emily
Button

Tel: 01722 326899
email:
bookshop@sarum.ac.uk
Web:
www.sarumcollege
bookshop.co.uk

Open: 0900–1645 Mon–Fri,
1000–1600 Sat, and Tues
evenings during term time

Excellent selection of new
and second-hand academic
theology, church history,
ethics, Christian spirituality,
etc. Mail order facility. Out-of-
print and hard to find title
search facility. Church supplies
and cards for all church events
(ordination, confirmation,
baptism, etc.) Clergy discount.
Online shop – www.sarum
collegebookshop.co.uk

Sion College

The library has closed. The
older books (–1850) were
transferred to Lambeth Palace Library. The bulk of the
balance of the collection is in
the library of King's College,
London. Both collections are
freely available for study and
research.

Biblical studies, philosophy,
Anglican theology, church
history, biography and liturgy.
Special collections include Sion
College Port Royal Library,
Industrial Christian Fellowship
Library, and extensive
pamphlet collections.

**United Society for the
Propagation of the Gospel**

The Bodleian Library
Weston Library
Broad Street
Oxford OX1 3BG

Archivist Miss Lucy McCann

Tel: 01865 277150
email:
specialcollections.enquiries@
bodleian.ox.ac.uk
Web: www.bodleian.ox.
ac.uk/bodley/finding-
resources/special
Bodleian reader's ticket
required – details at
www.bodleian.ox.ac.uk/
bodley/using-this-library/
getting-a-readers-card

The Society's library to 1944
and archival material circa
1701–1965. Extensive
collections from the 19th
century, back holdings of
missionary journals.

Westminster Abbey

Westminster Abbey Muniment
Room and Library
London
SW1P 3PA

Librarian Dr Tony Trowles

Keeper of the Muniments Mr
Matthew Payne

Tel: 020 7654 4830
email: library@westminster-
abbey.org
Web: www.westminster-
abbey.org

Open: 1000–1300, 1400–1645
hours Mon–Thurs;
appointments required

Library and archives of the
Dean and Chapter of
Westminster. Library includes
manuscripts, early printed
books (16,000), and modern
collections (5,000) concerned
with the history of Westminster
Abbey and associated subjects.
Extensive archive of the
medieval monastery and its
estates together with post-
Reformation Abbey records to
the present day.

York Minster

York Minster Historic
Collections
The Old Palace
Dean's Park
York
YO1 7JQ

Librarian
Ms Sarah Griffin

Archivist Mr Peter Young
Collections Manager Miss
Victoria Harrison

Tel: 01904 557250
email: Library:
library@yorkminster.org
Archives:
petery@yorkminster.org
Collections:
vickyh@yorkminster.org
Web: (Library catalogue)
http://yorsearch.york.ac.uk/
(Guide to Historic
Collections) http://
www.yorkminster.org/
treasures-and-collections/
historic-collections.html

Open: 0900–1700 hours
Mon–Fri for general use.
Archive, Special Collections
and artefacts by appointment
only
Closed on public holidays

Library: 120,000 volumes.
Theology; church history, art,
architecture and stained glass;
extensive collections of pre-1801
books; incunables; special
collections of Yorkshire history
and Yorkshire Civil War tracts.

Archives: music and
photographic collections;
Yorkshire topographical prints;
archives of Dean and Chapter
from medieval times;
manuscripts.

Collections: Cathedral and
Parish Plate; Textiles; Historic
Furnishings inc. ornaments,
furniture and adornments;
Monuments; Displaced Glass;
Worked Stone; Archaeology;
Treasures.

Patronage Trusts

**Church Pastoral Aid Society
Patronage Trust**

Secretary Revd John Fisher
CPAS, Unit 3, Sovereign
Court One
Sir William Lyons Road
Coventry CV4 7EZ
Tel: 0300 123 0780 extn
4387/4388
email: jfisher@ cpas.org.uk /
patronage@cpas.org.uk

A Trust holding Rights of
Presentation to a number of
benefices. Administered by the
Church Pastoral Aid Society.

Church Patronage Trust

Secretary Preb Charles
Marnham
4 Chester Square
London SW1W 9HH
Tel: 020 7730 8889
email: charles@stmichaels
church.org.uk
Web: www.churchpatronage
trust.co.uk

A Trust holding the Rights of
Presentation to a number of
benefices. Evangelical tradition.

Church Society Trust	*Chairman* Revd Dick Farr Dean Wace House 16 Rosslyn Rd Watford, Herts. WD18 0NY *Tel:* 01923 235111 *Fax:* 01923 800362 *email:* admin@churchsociety.org	Patron of more than 100 livings.
Church Trust Fund Trust	*Secretary* Revd John Fisher CPAS, Unit 3, Sovereign Court One Sir William Lyons Road Coventry CV4 7EZ *Tel:* 0300 123 0780 extn 4387/4388 *email:* jfisher@ cpas.org.uk / patronage@cpas.org.uk	A Trust holding Rights of Presentation to a number of benefices. Administered by the Church Pastoral Aid Society.
Guild of All Souls	*General Secretary* David G. Llewelyn Morgan Guild of All Souls 2 St Andrew's Road Willesden Green London NW10 2QS *Tel:* 020 8459 3813 *Web:* www.guildofallsouls.org.uk	Patron of 41 livings of Catholic tradition.
Hulme Trustees	*Secretary* Mr Jonathan Shelmerdine, Butcher and Barlow Solicitors 31 Middlewich Rd Sandbach Cheshire CW11 1HW *Tel:* 01270 762521	A Trust holding the Rights of Presentation to a number of benefices.
Hyndman's (Miss) Trustees	*Executive Officer* Mrs Ann Brown 6 Angerford Ave Sheffield S8 9BG *Tel:* 0114 255 8522 *email:* ann.brown@ hyndmans.org.uk	Patronage Trust. Varied churchmanship.
Intercontinental Church Society	Unit 11 Ensign Business Centre Westwood Way Westwood Business Park Coventry CV4 8JA *Tel:* 024 7646 3940 *Web:* www.ics-uk.org *email:* enquiries@ics-uk.org	ICS is an Anglican mission society to English-speakers of any nationality who live, work or holiday abroad by planting and growing churches and through seasonal ministry to tourists.
Martyrs Memorial and Church of England Trust	*Secretary* Revd John Fisher CPAS, Unit 3, Sovereign Court One Sir William Lyons Road Coventry CV4 7EZ *Tel:* 0300 123 0780 extn 4387/4388 *email:* jfisher@ cpas.org.uk / patronage@cpas.org.uk	A Trust holding Rights of Presentation to a number of benefices. Administered by the Church Pastoral Aid Society.

ORGANIZATIONS

Peache Trustees	*Secretary* Canon Roger Salisbury 6 Church Street Widcombe Bath BA2 6AZ *Tel:* 01225 489076 *email:* patronage@btinternet.com	A Trust holding the Rights of Presentation to a number of benefices. Evangelical tradition.
Simeon's Trustees	*Executive Officer* Mrs Ann Brown 6 Angerford Ave Sheffield S8 9BG *Tel:* 0114 255 8522 *email:* ann.brown@simeons.org.uk	Holds and administers the patronage of those livings in the Church of England which belong to the Trust on the principles laid down in Charles Simeon's Charge.
Society for the Maintenance of the Faith	*President* Dr Brian Hanson *Secretary* Revd John Hanks Pusey House Oxford OX1 1SU *Web:* www.smftrust.org.uk	Founded in 1873, the Society presents, or shares in the presentation of, priests to over 80 benefices. As well as its work as a patronage body the Society aims to promote Catholic teaching and practice in the Church of England at large.

Anglican and Porvoo Communions

PART 5

PART 5   CONTENTS

THE ANGLICAN COMMUNION

INTRODUCTION

The Anglican Communion comprises 38 self-governing *Member Churches* or *Provinces* that share several things in common including doctrine, ways of worshipping, mission, and a focus of unity in the Archbishop of Canterbury. Formal mechanisms for meeting include the Lambeth Conference, the Anglican Consultative Council, and the Primates' Meeting, together with the Archbishop, known as the *Instruments of Communion*.

Most Communion life, however, is found in the relationships between Anglicans at all levels of church life and work around the globe; dioceses linked with dioceses, parishes with parishes, people with people, all working to further God's mission. There are around 85 million people on six continents who call themselves Anglican (or Episcopalian), in more than 165 countries. These Christian brothers and sisters share prayer, resources, support and knowledge across geographical and cultural boundaries.

As with any family, the Anglican Communion's members have a range of differing opinions. The Anglican Christian tradition has long valued its diversity, and has never been afraid to tackle publicly the hard questions of life and faith.

HISTORY

In continuity with the ancient Celtic and Saxon churches of the British Isles, and Britain's place within Catholic Europe, Anglicanism found its distinctive identity in the sixteenth and seventeenth centuries. At the Reformation national Churches emerged in England, Ireland and Scotland. With the American Revolution an autonomous Episcopal Church was founded in the United States and later Anglican or Episcopal Churches were founded across the globe as a result of the missionary movements of the eighteenth and nineteenthth centuries. Many of these Churches became autonomous Provinces in the course of the nineteenth and twentieth centuries. In South Asia, the United Churches formed between Anglican and Protestant denominations joined the Anglican Communion, as did Churches elsewhere such as the Spanish Episcopal Reformed Church and the Lusitanian Church of Portugal.

OFFICIAL STRUCTURES

It was in 1867 that Lambeth Palace hosted the first conference for Anglican bishops from around the world. From 1948 each Archbishop of Canterbury has called a *Lambeth Conference* every ten years. The last, in 2008, saw more than 800 bishops from around the world invited to Canterbury. The Conference has no authority of itself: rather it is a chance for bishops to meet and explore aspects of Anglican Communion life and ministry.

Bishops attending the 1968 Lambeth Conference called for a body representative of all sections of the churches – laity, clergy and bishops – to co-ordinate aspects of international Anglican ecumenical and mission work. The resulting body was the *Anglican Consultative Council*. This council comprising elected and appointed members from around the globe meets approximately every three years.

Since 1979 the Archbishop of Canterbury has also regularly invited the chief bishops of the Provinces (known as *Primates*) to join him in a meeting for consultation, prayer and reflection on theological, social and international matters. These *Primates' Meetings* take place approximately every two years.

These Instruments of Communion are served by a secretariat with staff based at the Anglican Communion Office in London, England, as well as in New York, Geneva and Lusaka (see below for more information on the Anglican Communion Office).

BELIEFS

There can be many differences between individual Anglican churches, but all uphold and proclaim the Catholic and Apostolic faith, proclaimed in the Scriptures, interpreted in the light of tradition and reason. Anglicans hold these things in common:

- the Holy Bible, comprising the Old and New Testaments, as a basis of our faith;
- the Nicene and Apostles' Creeds as the basic statements of Christian belief;
- recognition of the Sacraments of Baptism and Holy Communion; and
- the Historic Episcopate – ours is a Christian tradition with bishops.

This *quadrilateral*, drawn up in the nineteenth century, is one of the definitions of Anglican faith and ministry. Another is a style of worship which has its roots in the Book of Common Prayer and the Services of Ordination (the Ordinal). Anglicans also celebrate the Eucharist (also known as the Holy Communion, the Lord's Supper or the Mass), the Sacrament of Baptism and other rites including Confirmation, Reconciliation, Marriage, Anointing of the Sick, and Ordination.

Anglicanism rests on the three pillars of Scripture, Tradition and Reason as it seeks to chart 'a middle way' among the other Christian traditions.

MISSION

Following the teachings of Jesus Christ, Anglicans are committed to proclaiming the good news of the gospel to all creation as expressed in the Marks of Mission:

- to proclaim the Good News of the Kingdom;
- to teach, baptize and nurture new believers;
- to respond to human need by loving service;
- to seek to transform unjust structures of society, to challenge violence of every kind and to pursue peace and reconciliation; and
- to strive to safeguard the integrity of creation and sustain and renew the life of the earth.

These Marks are to be expressed in all areas of a Christian's life: their words and their actions. Therefore, members of the Anglican Communion around the world are involved with a range of life-changing activities that include evangelism and church growth; providing food, shelter and clothing to those in need; speaking out with and for the oppressed; and setting up schools, hospitals, clinics and universities.

PROVINCES

The Anglican Church in Aotearoa, New Zealand and Polynesia
The Anglican Church of Australia
The Church of Bangladesh
Igreja Episcopal Anglicana do Brasil
The Anglican Church of Burundi
The Anglican Church of Canada
The Church of the Province of Central Africa
Iglesia Anglicana de la Region Central de America
Province de L'Eglise Anglicane Du Congo
The Church of England
Hong Kong Sheng Kung Hui
The Church of the Province of the Indian Ocean
The Church of Ireland
The Nippon Sei Ko Kai (The Anglican Communion in Japan)
The Episcopal Church in Jerusalem and The Middle East
The Anglican Church of Kenya
The Anglican Church of Korea
The Church of the Province of Melanesia
La Iglesia Anglicana de Mexico
The Church of the Province of Myanmar (Burma)
The Church of Nigeria (Anglican Communion)
The Church of North India (United)
The Church of Pakistan (United)
The Anglican Church of Papua New Guinea
The Episcopal Church in the Philippines
L'Eglise Episcopal au Rwanda
The Scottish Episcopal Church
Church of the Province of South East Asia
The Church of South India (United)
Anglican Church of Southern Africa
Iglesia Anglicana del Cono Sur de America

The Episcopal Church of South Sudan and Sudan
The Anglican Church of Tanzania
The Church of the Province of Uganda
The Episcopal Church
(Founded in the USA, it includes overseas dioceses in Taiwan, Haiti, Columbia, Honduras, Dominican Republic, Ecuador and continental Europe)
The Church in Wales
The Church of the Province of West Africa
The Church in the Province of the West Indies

EXTRA-PROVINCIAL CHURCHES AND OTHER DIOCESES

The Church of Ceylon (Extra-Provincial to Canterbury)
Iglesia Episcopal de Cuba
Bermuda (Extra-Provincial to Canterbury)
The Lusitanian Church (Extra-Provincial to Canterbury)
The Reformed Episcopal Church of Spain (Extra-Provincial to Canterbury)
Falkland Islands (Extra-Provincial to Canterbury)

CHURCHES IN COMMUNION

The Mar Thoma Syrian Church
The Old Catholic Churches of the Union of Utrecht
The Philippine Independent Church
NB: Anglicans/Episcopalians in certain parts of the Communion are in full communion with some Lutheran Churches.

THE ANGLICAN COMMUNION OFFICE

The permanent secretariat (the Anglican Communion Office) serves the Anglican Communion and is responsible for facilitating all meetings of the conciliar Instruments of Communion as well as the commissions, working groups and networks of the Communion. Anglican Communion Office staff from countries including Canada, Zambia, Colombia and Wales also maintain the Anglican Communion website where visitors can find the official prayer cycle (daily prayer intentions for the dioceses of the Communion), vast amounts of official information and documentation about the Anglican Communion's Instruments and its ministries, plus the very latest news from around the Anglican world via the Anglican Communion News Service. Most of the funding for the work of the office comes from the Inter-Anglican budget supported by all Member Churches according to their means. The Secretary General of the Anglican Communion is Canon Kenneth Kearon.

Anglican Communion Office: St Andrew's House, 16 Tavistock Crescent, London W11 1AP
Tel: +44 (0)207 313 3900
Fax: +44 (0)207 313 3999
email: aco@anglicancommunion.org
Web: www.anglicancommunion.org

The Anglican Centre in Rome

The Anglican Centre in Rome was established in April 1966, endorsed by the Metropolitans of the Anglican Communion. This followed consultations among representatives of the several Churches of the Anglican Communion on action for the furtherance of Christian unity and the prospects for renewed fellowship and cooperation between Anglicans and Roman Catholics held out by the Second Vatican Council and by the historic visit of the Archbishop of Canterbury to Rome in March 1966. The Anglican Centre celebrated the fortieth anniversary of its foundation in 2006.

The Anglican Centre:

1. Provides a meeting place where clergy and laity, Anglican, Roman Catholic, and those of other Christian denominations, may come together for discussion, worship and prayer for the achievement of Christian unity.
2. Sponsors courses, lectures, seminars and discussions to enable a deeper understanding of the Roman Catholic Church, Anglicanism and the whole Western Christian tradition.
3. Is a welcoming reference point for visitors to Rome from member churches of the Anglican Communion, helping tourists in becoming pilgrims.
4. Holds a growing library of Anglican history, theology and liturgy, and of ecumenism, for the use of students and scholars of all Christian denominations.
5. Offers assistance to visiting Anglican scholars who wish to work in Rome, where possible putting them in touch with resident scholars in their field.
6. Offers a focal point for Anglican collaboration with the various agencies of the Roman Catholic Church and seeks to promote joint mission in terms of the justice and peace imperatives of the gospel.
7. Works ecumenically in liaison with the Pontifical Council for the promotion of Christian Unity.
8. Publishes a magazine, *CENTRO*, both online and in paper form, twice a year.

At the heart of the Centre's life is the chapel. Here the Eucharist is celebrated weekly on Tuesdays, at which the congregation is a microcosm of Christianity: Anglicans from around the world, Lutherans, Methodists, Roman Catholics and others. Visitors are welcome at the Eucharist and the lunch that follows.

The Centre's library is open from 9 a.m. to 1 p.m. Monday to Friday and by arrangement at other times. The Centre itself is normally open from 9 to 5 Monday to Friday, but it is advisable to ring ahead. It is closed in August and on public holidays. There is a governing body, and a director.

Director and Archbishop of Canterbury's Representative to the Holy See Archbishop David Moxon, The Anglican Centre in Rome, Palazzo Doria Pamphilj, Piazza del Collegio Romano 2, 00186 Rome, Italy   *Tel:* 39 06 678 0302
Fax: 39 06 678 0674
director@anglicancentre.it
Web: http://anglicancentre.churchinsight.com

PA to the Director and Course Administrator Jan Hague
email: pa-courses@anglicancentre.it

Centre Receptionist and Librarian Melanie Giannolo
email: anglicancentre@anglicancentre.it

Development Officer UK Revd Bill Snelson
email: developmentUK@anglicancentre.it

FRIENDS OF THE ANGLICAN CENTRE IN ROME
Founded in 1984 to enlist support through both prayer and financial assistance for the work of the Centre.

President The Archbishop of Canterbury

Chairman Rt Revd Edward Holland

Chairman, English Friends Rt Revd Edward Holland, 37 Parfrey St, London W6 9EW

Secretary Miss Virginia Johnstone, 127 Cranmer Court, Whiteheads Grove, London SW3 3HE
Tel: 020 7589 0697

ANGLICAN AND PORVOO COMMUNIONS

CHURCHES AND PROVINCES OF THE ANGLICAN COMMUNION

AUTONOMOUS CHURCHES AND PROVINCES IN COMMUNION WITH THE SEE
OF CANTERBURY

Note: In the following directory section most provinces correspond to a specific country. In the postal addresses given, the name of the country is included only if some dioceses in the province are outside the country indicated by the name of the province.

Anglican Church in Aotearoa, New Zealand and Polynesia

Members 564,892
Formerly known as the Church of the Province of New Zealand, the Church covers 106,000 square miles and includes the countries of Aotearoa, New Zealand, Fiji, Tonga, Samoa and the Cook Islands. It was established as an autonomous Church in 1857. A revised constitution adopted in 1992 reflects a commitment to bicultural development that allows freedom and responsibility to implement worship and mission in accordance with the culture and social conditions of the Maori (Tikanga Maori), European (Tikanga Pakeha) and Polynesian (Tikanga Pasefika) membership. The Church has a strong and effective Anglican Missions Board.

Primates/Archbishops
Most Revd William Brown Turei (*Tikanga Maori*), PO Box 568, Gisborne 4040, New Zealand
Tel: 64 6 868 7028
Fax: 64 6 867 8859
email: browntmihi@xtra.co.nz
Web: www.anglican.org.nz

Most Revd Dr Winston Halapua (*Tikanga Pasefika*), PO Box 35, Suva, Fiji Islands   *Tel:* 679 330 4716
Fax: 679 330 2687
email: bishoppolynesia@connect.com.fj
Web: www.anglican.org.nz

Most Revd Philip Richardson (*Tikanga Pakeha*), PO Box 547, New Plymouth 4621, New Zealand
Tel: 64 6 759 1178
Fax: 64 6 759 1180
email: bishop@taranakianglican.org.nz
Web: www.anglican.org.nz

General Secretary and *Treasurer* Revd Michael Hughes, PO Box 87188 Meadowbank, Auckland 1742, New Zealand   *Tel:* 64 9 521 4439
email: gensec@anglicanchurch.org.nz
Web: www.anglican.org.nz

THEOLOGICAL COLLEGES
The College of St John the Evangelist, Private Bag 28907 Remuera, Auckland 1541, New Zealand (serves both Anglicans and Methodists) *Manukura/Principal* Revd Canon Anthony Gerritsen; *Tikanga Pakeha* Vacancy; *Tikanga Maori* (Acting Dean) Dr Moeawa Callaghan; *Tikanga Polynesia* Revd Dr Frank Smith
Tel: 64 9 521 2725
Fax: 64 9 521 2420
Web: www.stjohnscollege.ac.nz

Theology House, PO Box 6728 Upper Riccarton, Christchurch 8442, New Zealand (*Director* Revd Dr Peter Carrell)   *Tel:* 64 3 341 3399
Fax: 64 3 355 6140
email: director@theologyhouse.ac.nz
Web: www.theologyhouse.ac.nz

Selwyn College, 560 Castle St, North Dunedin 9016, New Zealand (*Warden* Dr Neil Rodgers)
Tel: 64 3 477 3326
email: warden.selwyn@otago.ac.nz
Web: www.selwyn.ac.nz

The two last named cater for pre-ordination or post-graduate studies.

AOTEAROA
Bishop of Aotearoa Most Revd William Brown Turei (*Primate/Archbishop*), PO Box 568, Gisborne 4040, New Zealand   *Tel:* 64 6 868 7028
Fax: 64 6 867 8859
email: browntmihi@xtra.co.nz

Bishop of Te Manawa o Te Wheke Rt Revd Ngarahu Katene, PO Box 146, Rotorua 3040, New Zealand
Tel: 64 7 348 4043
Fax: 64 7 348 4053
email: bishop@motw.org.nz

Bishop of Te Tairawhiti Most Revd William Brown Turei, PO Box 568, Gisborne 4040, New Zealand
Tel: 64 6 868 7028
Fax: 64 6 867 8859
email: browntmihi@xtra.co.nz

Bishop of Te Tai Tokerau Rt Revd Te Kito Wiremu Pikaahu, PO Box 25 Paihia, Bay of Islands 0247, New Zealand Tel: 64 9 402 6788
email: tkwp@xtra.co.nz

Bishop of Te Upoko o Te Ika Rt Revd Muru Walters, 14 Amesbury Drive, Churton Park, Wellington 6037, New Zealand Tel: 64 4 478 3549
Fax: 64 4 472 8863
email: muru.walters@xtra.co.nz

Bishop of Te Waipounamu Rt Revd John Robert Kuru Gray, PO Box 10086, Phillipstown, Christchurch 8145, New Zealand
Tel: 64 3 389 1683
Fax: 64 3 389 0912
email: bishopgray@hawaipounamu.co.nz

NEW ZEALAND
Bishop of Auckland Rt Revd Ross Graham Bay, PO Box 37242, Parnell, Auckland 1151, New Zealand Tel: 64 9 302 7201
Fax: 64 9 302 7217
email: bishop@auckanglican.org.nz
Web: www.auckanglican.org.nz

Assistant Bishop of Auckland Rt Revd James Andrew White, PO Box 37242, Parnell, Auckland 1151, New Zealand Tel: 64 9 302 7201
Fax: 64 9 302 7217
email: jwhite@auckanglican.org.nz
Web: www.auckanglican.org.nz

Bishop of Christchurch Rt Revd Victoria Matthews, PO Box 4438, Christchurch 8140, New Zealand Tel: 64 3 348 6701
Fax: 64 3 379 5954
email: bishop@anglicanlife.org.nz
Web: www.anglicanlife.org.nz

Bishop of Dunedin Rt Revd Dr Kelvin Peter Wright, PO Box 13170, Green Island, Dunedin 9052, New Zealand Tel: 64 3 488 0820
Fax: 64 3 488 2038
email: bishop@calledsouth.org.nz
Web: www.calledsouth.org.nz

Bishop of Nelson Rt Revd Victor Richard Ellena, PO Box 100, Nelson 7040, New Zealand
Tel: 64 3 548 3124
Fax: 64 3 548 2125
email: bprichard@nelsonanglican.org.nz
Web: www.nelsonanglican.org.nz

Bishop of Waiapu Rt Revd Andrew Hedge, PO Box 227, Napier 4140, New Zealand
Tel: 64 6 835 8230
Fax: 64 6 835 0680
email: bishopandrew@waiapu.com
Web: www.waiapu.com

Bishop of Waikato Rt Revd Dr Helen-Ann Hartley, PO Box 21, Hamilton 3240, New Zealand
Tel: 64 7 857 0020
Fax: 64 7 836 9975
email: hah@waikatoanglican.org.nz
Web: www.waikatotaranakianglican.org.nz

Bishop of Taranaki Most Rt Revd Philip Richardson (Primate/Archbishop), PO Box 547, Taranaki Mail Centre, New Plymouth 4340, New Zealand
Tel: 64 6 759 1178
Fax: 64 6 759 1180
email: bishop@taranakianglican.org.nz
Web: www.waikatotaranakianglican.org.nz

Bishop of Wellington Rt Revd Justin Charles Hopkins Duckworth, PO Box 12046, Wellington 6144, New Zealand Tel: 64 4 472 1057
Fax: 64 4 449 1360
email: justin@wn.ang.org.nz
Web: www.wn.anglican.org.nz

POLYNESIA
Bishop of Polynesia Most Revd Dr Winston Halapua (Primate/Archbishop), PO Box 35, Suva, Fiji Islands Tel: 679 330 4716
Fax: 679 330 2152
email: bishoppolynesia@connect.com.fj

Bishop in Viti Levu West and Vanua Levu and Taveuni Rt Revd Apimeleki Nadoki Qiliho, PO Box 117, Lautoka, Fiji Islands
Tel: 679 666 0124
email: qiliho@gmail.com

On Study Leave Rt Revd Gabriel Mahesh Prasad Sharma email: gabsharma@yahoo.com

Anglican Church of Australia

Members 3,881,162 (2001)
The Church came to Australia in 1788 with the 'First Fleet', which was made up primarily of convicts and military personnel. Free settlers soon followed. A General Synod held in 1872 formed the Australian Board of Missions. The Church became fully autonomous in 1962 and in 1978 published its first prayer book. A second Anglican prayer book was published in 1995. Women were first ordained to the Diaconate in 1985 and to the Priesthood in 1992. There are 23 dioceses of which 19 ordain women as priests and chaplains. The Anglican Church of Australia is part of the Christian Conference of Asia and of the Council of the Church of East Asia. Links with Churches of New Guinea, Melanesia, and Polynesia are strong especially through the Anglican Board of Mission – Australia.

Primate of the Anglican Church of Australia Most Revd Dr Philip Freier (*Archbishop of Brisbane*)

General Secretary of the General Synod Mr Martin Drevikovsky

Hon Treasurer Mr Allan Perryman

General Synod Office Suite 4, Level 5, 189 Kent Street, Sydney, NSW 2000   *Tel:* 61 2 8267 2700
Fax: 61 2 8267 2727
email: gsoffice@anglican.org.au
Web: www.anglican.org.au

THE ANGLICAN THEOLOGICAL COLLEGES
Moore Theological College, 1 King St, Newtown, NSW 2042 (*Principal* Revd Dr Mark Donald Thompson)   *Tel:* 61 2 89577 9999
Fax: 61 2 9577 9988
email: info@moore.usyd.edu.au
Web: www.moore.edu.au

Nungalinya College, PO Box 40371, Casuarina, NT 0811 (*Principal* Dr Judith Long)
Tel: 61 8 8920 7500
Fax: 61 8 8927 2332
email: info@nungalinya.edu.au
Web: www.nungalinya.edu.au

Ridley College, 170 The Avenue, Parkville, VIC 3052 (*Principal* Dr Brian Rosner)
Tel: 61 3 9207 4800
Fax: 61 3 9387 5099
email: registrar@ridley.unimelb.edu.au
Web: www.ridley.unimelb.edu.au

St Barnabas Theological College, 34 Lipsett Terrace, Brooklyn Park, SA 5032 (*Principal* Revd Dr Matthew Anstey)   *Tel:* 61 8 8340 0411
Fax: 61 8 8416 8450

email: admin@sbtc.org.au
Web: http://ehlt.flinders.edu.au/theology/information

St Francis Theological College, 233 Milton Rd, PO Box 1261, Milton QLD 4064 (*Principal* The Revd Dr Steven Ogden)   *Tel:* 61 7 3514 7411
Fax: 61 7 3369 4691
email: stfran@ministryeducation.org.au
Web: www.stfran.qld.edu.au

St Mark's National Theological Centre, 15 Blackall St, Barton, ACT 2600 (*Director* Revd Dr Andrew Cameron)   *Tel:* 61 2 6272 6252
Fax: 61 2 6273 4067
email: stmarks@csu.edu.au
Web: www.stmarksntc.org.au

Trinity College Theological School, Royal Parade, Parkville, VIC 3052 (*Dean* Revd Dr Dorothy Lee)
*Tel:*61 3 9348 7127
Fax: 61 3 9348 7460
email: tcts@trinity.unimelb.edu.au
Web: www.trinity.unimelb.edu.au/theolog

The John Wollaston Theological College, Wollaston Rd, Mt Claremont, WA 6010
Tel: 61 8 9286 0270
Fax: 61 8 9385 3364
email: info@wollastoncollege.com.au
Web: www.wollastoncollege.com.au

CHURCH PAPERS
The Adelaide Church Guardian Monthly newspaper containing wide news coverage from the diocese, province and nationally. *Editorial Offices* 26 King William Road, North Adelaide, SA 5006. *email:*
communications@adelaide.anglican.com.au

The Melbourne Anglican Large monthly diocesan newspaper contains extensive news, comment locally and from around the world; with colour pictures. *Director/Editor* The Anglican Centre, 209 Flinders Lane, Melbourne, VIC 3000.
email: media@melbourne.anglican.com.au
Web: www.melbourne.anglican.com.au

Anglican Encounter Monthly newspaper of Newcastle Diocese, containing diocesan and Australian news. *Editorial Offices* PO Box 817, Newcastle, NSW 2302.
email: editor@angdon.com
Web: www.angdon.com

Tasmanian Anglican Monthly small newspaper format, from Tasmania Diocese, containing wide comment. *Editorial Offices* PO Box 748, Hobart, TAS 7001.   *email:* editor@anglicantas.org.au
Web: www.anglicantas.org.au

Southern Cross Large monthly newspaper of Sydney Diocese, containing diocesan, national, world news and comment, Archbishop's letter in both English and Chinese translation. Extensive use of colour. *Editorial Offices* PO Box W185 Parramatta Westfield NSW 2150.

> *email:* newsroom@anglicanmedia.com.au
> *Web:* www.anglicanmedia.com.au

Anglican Messenger Monthly newspaper of the Anglican Province of Western Australia, includes news from Perth, North West Australia and Bunbury. *Editorial Offices* GPO Box W2067, Perth, WA 6846. *email:* messenger@perth.anglican.org
> *Web:* www.anglicanmessenger.com.au

Market Place A monthly independent Anglican newspaper, includes national and international Anglican news and comment. *Editorial Offices* PO Box 335, Orange, NSW 2800.

> *email:* market@ix.net.au

Focus Monthly newspaper based in Brisbane, containing diocesan and national news. *Editorial Offices* GPO Box 421, Brisbane, QLD 4001.

> *email:* focus@anglicanbrisbane.org.au
> *Web:* www.anglicanbrisbane.org.au

All diocesan newspapers contain a letter from the Archbishop or Bishop of the Diocese. The Dioceses of Armidale, Ballarat, Bathurst, Bendigo, Canberra and Goulburn, Gippsland, Grafton, Murray, Northern Territory, Riverina, Rockhampton, Wangaratta, and Willochra also produce magazines/Bishop's newsletters, with mainly diocesan and parochial news.

PROVINCE OF NEW SOUTH WALES
Metropolitan Most Revd Dr Glenn Davies (*Archbishop of Sydney*)

ARMIDALE
Bishop Rt Revd Richard Lewers, PO Box 198, Armidale, NSW 2350   *Tel:* 61 2 6772 4491
Fax: 61 2 6772 9261
email: office@armidaleanglicandiocese.com
Web: www.armidaleanglicandiocese.com

BATHURST
Bishop Rt Revd Ian Palmer, PO Box 23, Bathurst, NSW 2795   *Tel:* 61 2 6331 1722
Fax: 61 2 6332 2772
email: registrar@bathurstanglican.org
Web: www.bathurstanglican.org.au

CANBERRA AND GOULBURN
Bishop Rt Revd Stuart Robinson, GPO Box 1981, Canberra, ACT   *Tel:* 61 2 6248 0811
Fax: 61 2 6247 6829
Web: www.anglicands.org.au

Assistant Bishops
Rt Revd Genieve Blackwell, PO Box 8605, Wagga Wagga, NSW 2650   *Tel:* 61 2 6926 4226
Fax: 61 2 6926 4226
*email:*genieve.blackwell@anglicands.com.au

Rt Revd Trevor W. Edwards, 28 McBryde Crescent, Wanniassa, ACT 2903   *Tel:* 61 2 648 0811
Fax: 61 2 6247 6829
email: trevor.edwards@anglicands.org.au

Rt Revd Stephen Pickard, c/o GPO Box 1981, Canberra, ACT
> *email:* s.k.pickard@gmail.com

GRAFTON
Bishop Rt Revd Sarah Macneil, Bishopsholme, PO Box 4, Grafton, NSW 2460   *Tel:* 61 2 6642 4122
Fax: 61 2 6643 1814
email: angdiog@nor.com.au
Web: www.graftondiocese.org.au

NEWCASTLE
Bishop Rt Revd Greg Thompson, Bishop's Registry, PO Box 817, Newcastle, NSW 2300
Tel: 61 2 4926 3733
Fax: 61 2 4926 1968
email: bishop@angdon.com
Web: www.angdon.com

Assistant Bishop Rt Revd Peter Stuart, PO Box 817, Newcastle, NSW 2300   *Tel:* 61 2 4926 3733
Fax: 02 4926 1968
email: BishopPeter@angdon.com

RIVERINA
Bishop Rt Revd Allan Gillion, PO Box 10, Narrandera, NSW 2700   *Tel:* 61 2 6959 1648
Fax: 61 2 6959 2903
email: rivdio@dragnet.com.au
Web: www.anglicanriverina.com

SYDNEY
Archbishop Most Revd Dr Glenn Davies (*Metropolitan of the Province of NSW*), PO Box Q190, QVB Post Office, NSW 1230
Tel: 61 2 9265 1555
Fax: 61 2 9261 1170
email: registry@sydney.anglican.asn.au
Web: www.sydneyanglicans.net

Assistant Bishops
Vacancy (*Bishop of Liverpool & Georges River Region*) (*same address*)   *Tel:* 61 2 9265 1530
Fax: 61 2 9265 1543
Rt Revd Chris Edwards (*Bishop of Northern Region*) (*same address*)   *Tel:* 61 2 9265 1533
Fax: 61 2 9265 1543
Rt Revd Robert C. Forsyth (*Bishop of South Sydney*) (*same address*)   *Tel:* 61 2 9265 1501
Fax: 61 2 9265 1543
email: robforsyth@sydney.anglican.asn.au

Rt Revd Peter L. Hayward (*Bishop of Wollongong*), 74 Church St, Wollongong, NSW 2500
Tel: 61 2 4201 1800
Fax: 61 2 4228 4296
email: phayward@wollongong.anglican.asn.au
Rt Revd Ivan Yin Lee (*Bishop of Western Sydney*), PO Box 129, Parramatta, NSW 2124
Tel: 61 2 8023 6700
Fax: 61 2 9633 3636
email: ilee@westernsydney.anglican.asn.au

PROVINCE OF QUEENSLAND
Metropolitan Most Revd Dr Phillip John Aspinall (*Archbishop of Brisbane*)

BRISBANE
Archbishop Most Revd Dr Phillip John Aspinall (*Metropolitan of the Province of Queensland*), GPO Box 421, Brisbane, QLD 4001
Tel: 61 7 3835 2222
Fax: 61 7 3831 1170
email: archbishop@anglicanbrisbane.org.au
Web: www.anglicanbrisbane.org.au

Assistant Bishops
Rt Revd Alison Taylor (*Bishop of the Southern Region*) (*same address*)
Tel: 61 7 3835 2213
Fax: 61 7 3832 5030
email: amtaylor@anglicanbrisbane.org.au
Rt Revd Jonathan C. Holland (*Bishop of the Northern Region*) (*same address*)
Tel: 61 7 3835 2213
Fax: 61 7 3832 5030
email: jholland@anglicanbrisbane.org.au
Rt Revd Robert W. Nolan (*Bishop of the Western Region*), Box 2600, Toowoomba, QLD 4350
Tel: 61 7 4639 1875
Fax: 61 7 4632 6882
email: nolan@anglicanbrisbane.org.au

NORTH QUEENSLAND
Bishop Rt Revd William James (Bill) Ray, PO Box 1244, Townsville, QLD 4810
Tel: 61 7 4771 4175
Fax: 61 7 4721 1756
email: bishopnq@anglicannq.org
Web: www.anglicannq.org

Assistant Bishops
Rt Revd Saibo Mabo (*Assistant Bishop and National Torres Strait Islander Bishop*), PO Box 338, Thursday Island, QLD 4875
Tel: 6 1 7 4069 2747
Fax: 61 7 4969 1960
email: bishopti@anglicannq.org

THE NORTHERN TERRITORY
Bishop Vacancy, PO Box 2950, Darwin, NT 0801
Tel: 61 8 8941 7440
Fax: 61 8 8941 7446
email: ntdiocese@internode.on.net
Web: www.northernterritory.anglican.org

ROCKHAMPTON
Bishop Vacancy, PO Box 710, Central Queensland Mail Centre, Rockhampton, QLD 4702
Tel: 61 7 4927 3188
Fax: 61 7 4927 3188
email: bishop@anglicanrock.org.au
Web: www.anglicanrock.org.au

PROVINCE OF SOUTH AUSTRALIA
Metropolitan Most Reverend Dr Jeffrey William Driver (*Archbishop of Adelaide*)

ADELAIDE
Archbishop Most Reverend Dr Jeffrey William Driver (*Metropolitan of the Province of South Australia*), 18 King William Rd, N Adelaide, SA 5006
Tel: 61 8 8305 9350
Fax: 61 8 8305 9399
email: archbishop@adelaide.anglican.com.au
Web: www.adelaide.anglican.com.au

Assistant Bishop
Bishop Rt Revd Stephen Kim Pickard (*same address*)
email: spickard@adelaide.anglican.com.au

THE MURRAY
Bishop Rt Revd John Ford, PO Box 394, Murray Bridge, SA 5253
Tel: 61 8 8532 2270
Fax: 61 8 8532 5760
email: registry@murray.anglican.org
Web: www.murray.anglican.org

WILLOCHRA
Bishop Rt Revd John Stead, PO Box 96, Gladstone, SA 5473
Tel: 61 8 8662 2249
Fax: 61 8 8662 2027
email: bishop@diowillochra.org.au
Web: www.diowillochra.org.au

PROVINCE OF VICTORIA
Metropolitan Most Revd Dr Philip Leslie Freier (*Archbishop of Melbourne and Primate of the Anglican Church of Australia*)

BALLARAT
Bishop Rt Revd Garry Weatherill, PO Box 89, Ballarat, VIC 3350
Tel: 61 3 5331 1183
Fax: 61 3 5333 2982
email: bpsec@ballaratanglican.org.au
Web: www.ballaratanglican.org.au/

BENDIGO
Bishop Rt Revd Andrew William Curnow AM, PO Box 2, Bendigo, VIC 3552
Tel: 61 3 5443 4711
Fax: 61 3 5441 2173
email: bishop@bendigoanglican.org.au
Web: www.bendigoanglican.org.au

GIPPSLAND
Bishop Vacancy, PO Box 928, Sale, VIC 3853
Tel: 61 3 5144 2044
Fax: 61 3 5144 7183
email: bishop@gippsanglican.org.au
Web: www.gippsanglican.org.au

MELBOURNE

Archbishop Most Revd Dr Philip Leslie Freier (*Metropolitan of the Province of Victoria*), The Anglican Centre, 209 Flinders Lane, Melbourne, VIC 3000 *Tel:* 61 3 9653 4220
Fax: 61 3 9653 4268
email: archbishopsoffice@
melbourne.anglican.com.au
Web: www.melbourne.anglican.org.au/

Assistant Bishops
Rt Revd Paul Raymond White (*Bishop of the Southern Region*) (*same address*) *Tel:* 61 3 9653 4220
Fax: 61 3 9653 4268
email: sthregbishop@melbourne.anglican.com.au
Rt Revd Philip Huggins (*Bishop of the North-Western Region*) (*same address*)
email: phuggins@melbourne.anglican.com.au
Rt Revd Barbara Darling (*Bishop of the Eastern Region*) (*same address*)
email: estregion@melbourne.anglican.com.au

WANGARATTA

Bishop Rt Revd Anthony John Parkes AM, Bishop's Registry, PO Box 457, Wangaratta VIC 3676 *Tel:* 61 3 5721 3484
Fax: 61 3 5722 1427
email: bishop@wangaratta.anglican.org
Web: www.wangaratta.anglican.org

PROVINCE OF WESTERN AUSTRALIA
Metropolitan Most Revd Roger Adrian Herft AM (*Archbishop of Perth*)

BUNBURY

Bishop Rt Revd Allan Bowers Ewing, PO Box 15, Bunbury, WA 6231 *Tel:* 61 8 9721 2100
Fax: 61 8 9791 2300
email: bishop@bunbury.org.au
Web: www.bunbury.org.au

NORTH WEST AUSTRALIA

Bishop Rt Revd Gary Nelson, PO Box 2783, Geraldton, WA 6531 *Tel:* 61 8 9921 7277
Fax: 61 8 9964 2220
email: bishop@anglicandnwa.org
Web: www.anglicandnwa.org

PERTH

Archbishop Most Revd Roger Adrian Herft AM (*Metropolitan of the Province of Western Australia*), GPO Box W2067, Perth, WA 6846
Tel: 61 8 9325 7455
Fax: 61 8 9221 4118
email: archbishop@perth.anglican.org
Web: www.perth.anglican.org

Assistant Bishops
Rt Revd Kay Goldsworthy (*same address*)
email: kgoldsworthy@perth.anglican.org
Rt Revd Tom Wilmot (*same address*)
email: twilmot@perth.anglican.org

TASMANIA

Bishop Rt Revd John Douglas Harrower, OAM, GPO 748, Hobart, TAS 7001 *Tel:* 61 3 6220 2015
Fax: 61 3 6223 8968
email: bishop@anglicantas.org.au
Web: www.anglicantas.org.au/

DEFENCE FORCE

Bishop Rt Revd Ian Lambert (*Anglican Bishop to the Australian Defence Force and Bishop Assistant to the Primate*), Department of Defence, DSG-Duntroon, ACT 2600 *Tel:* 61 2 9265 9935
Fax: 61 2 9265 9959
email: dfc@anglican.org.au
Web: www.anglican.org.au/defence

The Episcopal Anglican Church of Brazil

(Igreja Episcopal Anglicana do Brasil)

The Episcopal Anglican Church of Brazil is the 19th Province of the Anglican Communion, and its work began in 1890 as a result of the missionary work of two north American missionaries in Porto Alegre: James Watson Morris and Lucien Lee Kinsolving. Autonomy from the Episcopal Church in the United States was granted in 1965. The Episcopal Church now has more than a hundred thousand baptized members and a team of more than two hundred clergy, among whom are thirty women priests. It has established communities, and educational and social institutions, in the main urban areas of Brazil. The Brazilian province comprises nine dioceses: Southern, Southwestern, Rio de Janeiro, São Paulo, Recife, Brasília, Pelotas, Curitiba and Amazon. It also has one missionary district: Missionary District West.

Primate Most Revd Francisco de Assis Silva (*Bishop of South Western Brazil*)
email: fassis@ieab.org.br
Web: www.ieab.org.br

Provincial Secretary Revd Arthur Cavalcante

Provincial Offices Praça Olavo Bilac, 63, Campos Elíseos, CEP 01201-050, São Paulo, SP
Tel and *Fax:* 55 11 3 667 8161
email: acavalcante@leab.org.bs

Provincial Treasurer Mrs Silvia Fernandes (*address, etc. as above*) *Tel* and *Fax:* 55 11 3 667 8161
email: silviaieab@gmail.com

CHURCH PAPER
Estandarte Cristão, a bimonthly church journal in Portuguese, published since 1893, which contains general articles and news about the life of the Church at local, national and international level. This journal is the main channel of the Communication Department of the Church. Revdo Felix Batista Filho *Editorial Offices:* Rua Ferreira Lopez, 401-AP 2302, Casa Amarela, Recife, PE, 52060-02

Tel and *Fax:* 55 81 3267 3926/9488 3194
email: fqbfilho@gmail.com

AMAZON
Bishop Rt Revd Saulo Maurício de Barros, Av. Sezerdelo Correia, 514, Batista Campos, 66025–240, Belem, PA   *Tel* and *Fax:* 55 91 3241 9720
email: saulomauricio@gmail.com

BRASÍLIA
Bishop Rt Revd Maurício José Araújo de Andrade, EQS 309/310, sala 1 – Asa Sul, Caixa Postal 093, 70359–970, Brasília, DF
Tel: 55 61 3443 4305
Fax: 55 61 3443 4337
email: brasilia2003@gmail.com
Web: www.dab.ieab.org.br

CURITIBA
Bishop Rt Revd Naudal Alves Gomes, Rua Sete de Setembro, 3927 – Centro, 80250-010 Curitiba, PR
Tel: 55 41 3232 0917
email: naudal@yahoo.com.br

PELOTAS
Bishop Rt Revd Renato da Cruz Raatz, Rua Felix da Cunha, 425 – Centro, Caixa Postal 791, 96001–970 Pelotas, RS   *Tel* and *Fax:* 55 53 3227 7120
email: renatoraatz@terra.com.br
Web: www.dap.ieab.org.br

RECIFE
Bishop Rt Revd João Câncio Peixoto, Rua Alfredo de Medeiros, 60, Espinheiro – 52021–030 Recife, PE   *Tel:* 55 81 3421 1684
email: joao.peixoto1@uol.com.br
Web: www.dar.ieab.org.br

RIO DE JANEIRO
Bishop Rt Revd Filadelfo Oliveira Neto, Rua Fonseca Guimarães, 12 Sta.Teresa, 20240–260, Rio de Janeiro, RJ   *Tel:* 55 21 2220 2148
Fax: 55 21 2252 9686
email: oliveira.ieab@gmail.com
Web: www.anglicana.com.br

SÃO PAULO
Bishop Rt Revd Flávio Borges Irala, Rua Borges Lagoa, 172 – Vila Clementino, 04038–030 São Paulo, SP   *Tel:* 55 11 5549 9086/5579 9011
Fax: 55 11 5083 2619
email: flavioirala@ieab.org.br
Web: https://www.facebook.com/IEAB.DASP?fref=ts

SOUTH WESTERN BRAZIL
Bishop Most Revd Francisco de Assis Silva (*Primate of the Episcopal Anglican Church of Brazil*), Av. Rio Branco, 880/Sub-solo – Centro, Caixa Postal 116, 97010–970 Santa Maria, RS
Tel and *Fax:* 55 55 3221 4328
email: fassis@ieab.org.bs
Web: www.swbrazil.anglican.org

SOUTHERN BRAZIL
Bishop Rt Revd Humberto Maiztegui, Avenida Ludolfo Bohel, 278, Baairro Teresópolis, 91720–150, Porto Alegre, RS
Tel and *Fax:* 55 51 3318 6199
email: dmsec@terra.com.br
Web: www.dm.ieab.org.br

Eglise Anglicane du Burundi

(The Province of the Anglican Church of Burundi)

Members 900,000
There are at least 900,000 Anglicans out of an estimated population of just over 9 million in Burundi. An Anglican presence was established through the work of the CMS in the 1930s and grew rapidly as a result of the East African revival. The former Ruanda Mission (now CMS) set up its first mission stations at Buhiga and Matana in 1935, and Buye in 1936. Activities were mainly focused on evangelism, education and medical work. The first national bishop was consecrated in 1965 and Buye diocese was created, covering the whole country. The Church of the Province of Burundi now consists of six dioceses, and it has been an independent province within the Anglican Communion since 1992. Among the Church's main concerns are peace and reconciliation, repatriation of returnees, community development, literacy, education, and health. It is committed to mission and evangelism with faith in the risen Christ as Lord and Saviour central to its preaching and teaching. It is concerned to support theological education and training for ministry, based on the authority of Scripture.

Primate Most Revd Bernard Ntahoturi (*Archbishop of Burundi and Bishop of Matana*)

Provincial Secretary Vacancy, BP 2098, Bujumbura
Tel: 257 22 224 389
Fax: 257 22 229 129
email: peab@cbinf.com
Provincial Accountant Christine Niyonkuru

Matana Theological Institute (Provincial)
Canon Warner Memorial College, EAB Buye, BP 94 Ngozi
Kosiya Shalita Bible College, EAB Matana, DS 13, Bujumbura *or* BP 447, Bujumbura
Buhiga College, EAB Gitega, BP 23 Gitega
Makamba College, EAB Makamba, BP 96 Makamba
Bujumbura Bible College, EAB Bujumbura, BP 1300 Bujumbura

BUJUMBURA
Bishop Rt Revd Eraste Bigirimana, BP 1300, Bujumbura   *Tel:* 257 22 249 104/5
Fax: 257 22 227 49
email: bigirimanaeraste@yahoo.fr

BUYE
Bishop Rt Revd Sixbert Macumi, BP 94, Ngozi
Tel: 257 22 302 210
Fax: 257 22 302 317
email: buyedioc@yahoo.fr

GITEGA
Bishop Rt Revd Jean Nduwayo, BP 23, Gitega
Tel: 257 22 402 247
email: eab.gitega@cbinf.com

MAKAMBA
Bishop Rt Revd Martin Blaise Nyaboho, BP 96, Makamba   *Tel:* 257 22 508 080
Fax: 257 22 229 129
email: eabdiocmak@yahoo.fr

MATANA
Bishop Most Revd Bernard Ntahoturi (*Archbishop of Burundi*), BP 447, Bujumbura
Tel: 257 79 924 595
Fax: 257 22 229 129
email: ntahober@cbinf.com

MUYINGA
Bishop Rt Revd Paisible Ndacayisaba, BP 55, Muyinga, Burundi   *Tel:* 257 79 700 043
email: ndacp@yahoo.com

RUMONGE
Bishop Rt Revd Pedaculi Birakengana
Tel: 257 79970926
email: birakepeda@yahoo.fr

The Anglican Church of Canada

Members 2,035,500 (2001)

The Anglican witness in Canada started in the eighteenth century with the Church Missionary Society and the United Society for the Propagation of the Gospel. The Eucharist was first celebrated in Frobisher Bay (now Iqaluit) in 1578; the first church building was St Paul's, Halifax in 1750. The Church includes a large number of the original inhabitants of Canada (Indians, Inuit, and Métis) and has been a strong advocate of their rights. A Book of Alternative Services (BAS) was published in 1985. The Church has a strong international role in sustainable development and humanitarian assistance through the Primate's World Relief and Development Fund (PWRDF).

Primate of The Anglican Church of Canada Most Revd Fred J. Hiltz, 80 Hayden St, Toronto, ON, M4Y 3G2   *Tel:* 1 416 924 9192
Fax: 1 416 924 0211
email: primate@national.anglican.ca
Web: www.anglican.ca

General Secretary Ven Dr Michael J. Thompson
email: mthompson@national.anglican.ca

General Synod Treasurer Ms Hanna Goschy
email: hgoschy@national.anglican.ca

Offices of the General Synod and of its Departments 80 Hayden St, Toronto, ON, M4Y 3G2
Tel: 1 416 924 9192
Fax: 1 416 968 7983

National Indigenous Anglican Bishop Rt Revd Mark L. MacDonald (*same address*)
email: mmacdonald@national.anglican.ca

Bishop Ordinary to the Canadian Forces Rt Revd Peter Coffin, 42 Bridle Park Dr., Kanata, ON, K2M 2E2   *Tel:* 1 613 591 7137
Fax: 1 613 232 3995
email: petercoffin@rogers.com

UNIVERSITIES AND COLLEGES OF THE ANGLICAN CHURCH OF CANADA
*Ecumenical
British Columbia
Vancouver School of Theology*, 6000 Iona Dr, Vancouver, BC, V6T 1L4 (Revd Dr Richard R. Topping)   *email:* possibilities@vst.edu

Manitoba
Henry Budd College for Ministry, Box 2518, The Pas MB, R9A IM3 (*Joint Co-ordinators* Ms Marion Jenkins and Revd Paul Sodtke)
email: hbcm@mts.net

ANGLICAN AND PORVOO COMMUNIONS

St John's College, 92 Dysart Rd, Winnipeg, MB, R3T 2M5 (*Warden/Vice Chancellor* Dr Christopher Trott)   *email:* stjohns_college@umanitoba.ca
email: Christopher.trott@ad.umanitoba.ca

Newfoundland
Queen's College, 210 Prince Philip Dr Ste 3000, St John's NL, A1B 3R6 (*Interim Administrator*) Dr Alex Faseruk   *email:* queens@mun.ca
email: afaseruk@mun.ca

Nova Scotia
Atlantic School of Theology*, 660 Francklyn St, Halifax, NS, B3H 3B5 (*President* Dr Dan O'Brien)
email: academicoffice@astheology.ns.ca
email: dobrien@astheology.ns.ca

University of King's College, 6350 Coburg Rd., Halifax, NS, B3H 2A1 (*President* Dr George Cooper)
email: academicoffice@astheology.ns.ca
email: george.cooper@ukings.ca

Nunavut
Arthur Turner Training School *enquiries to* the Diocese of Arctic, Box 190, Yellowknife, NT, X1A 2N2
email (Debra Gill, *Executive Officer* of Diocese of Artic): debra@articnet.org

Ontario
Canterbury College, University of Windsor, 2500 University Ave W, Windsor ON, N9B 2Y1 (*Principal* Dr Gordon Drake)
email: canter@uwindsor.ca
email: gdrake@uwindsor.ca

Huron University College, University of Western Ontario, 1349 Western Rd, London, ON, N6G 1H3 (*Principal* Dr Stephen McClatchie)
email: huron@uwo.ca
email: smcclatchie@huron.uwo.ca

Renison College, University of Waterloo, 240 Westmount Rd N, Waterloo, ON, N2L 3G4 (*Principal* Dr Glenn Cartwright)
email: glenn.cartwright@renison.uwaterloo.ca

Saint Paul University, Anglican Studies Program, 223 Main St, Ottawa, ON, K1S 1C4 (*Director* Kevin Flynn)
email: anglicanstudies@ustpaul.ca
email: kflynn@ustpaul.ca

Thorneloe University, 935 Ramsey Lake Rd, Sudbury, ON, P3E 2C6 (*Provost* Revd Dr Robert Derrenbacker)   *email:* info@thorneloe.ca
email: rderrenbacker@laurentian.ca

Toronto School of Theology, 47 Queen's Park Cres E, Toronto, ON, M5S 2C3 (*Director* Canon Dr Alan Hayes)   *email:* inquiries@tst.edu
email: alan.hayes@utoronto.ca

Trinity College, University of Tornoto, 6 Hoskin Ave, Toronto, ON, M5S 1H8 (*Dean of Divinity* Revd Canon Dr David Neelands)
email: divinity@trinity.utoronto.ca
email: d.neelands@utoronto.ca

Wycliffe College, University of Toronto, 5 Hoskin Ave, Toronto, ON, M5S 1H7 (*Principal* Canon Dr George Sumner)
email: info@wycliffe.utoronto.ca
email: george.sumner@utoronto.ca

Quebec
Bishop's University, 2600 College St, Sherbrooke, QC, J1M 1Z7 (*President* Dr M. Goldbloom/*Registrar* Hans Rouleau)
email: mgoldbloom@ubishop.ca
email: hrouleau@ubishops.ca

Montreal Diocesan Theological College, 3475 University St, Montreal, QC, H3A 2A8 (*Principal* Canon Dr John M Simons)
email: info@dio.mdtc.ca
email: jsimons@montreal.anglican.ca

Saskatchewan
The College of Emmanuel and St Chad, 114 Seminary Cres, Saskatoon, SK, S7N 0X3 (*Principal* Vacancy/*Registrar* Lisa McInnis)
email: emmanuel.stchad@usask.ca

The James Settee College for Ministry, 1308 Fifth Ave E, Prince Albert, SK, S6V 2H7 (*Principal* Mr Gary Graber)   *email:* minden2@hotmail.com

Centre for Christian Studies (Anglican, United) Woodsworth House, 60 Maryland St, Winnipeg, MB, R3G 1K7 (*Principal* Revd Canon Maylanne Maybee)   *email:* info@ccsonline.ca
email: mmaybee@ccsonline.ca

CHURCH PAPERS
Anglican Journal Tabloid format, national church paper with 23 diocesan publications inserted regionally. The paper is under the management of a committee appointed by General Synod.
Editorial Office: 80 Hayden St, Toronto, ON, M4Y 3G2
email: anglican.journal@national.anglican.ca
Web: www.anglicanjournal.com

PROVINCE OF BRITISH COLUMBIA AND YUKON
Metropolitan of the Ecclesiastical Province of British Columbia and Yukon Most Revd John E. Privett (*Archbishop of Kootenay*)

BRITISH COLUMBIA
Bishop Rt Revd Logan McMenamie, 900 Vancouver St, Victoria, BC, V8V 3V7
Tel: 1 250 386 7781
Fax: 1 250 386 4013
email: bishop@bc.anglican.ca
diocesan email: synod@bc.anglican.ca
Web: www.bc.anglican.ca

CALEDONIA
Bishop Rt Revd William (Bill) J. Anderson, 201–4716 Lazelle Ave, Terrace, BC, V8G 1T2
Tel: 1 250 635 6016
Fax: 1 250 635 6026
email: bishopbill@telus.net
diocesan email: caledonia@telus.net
Web: www.caledonia.anglican.ca

CENTRAL INTERIOR, ANGLICAN PARISHES OF
Bishop Rt Revd Barbara J. Andrews, 360 Nicola St, Kamloops, BC, V2C 2P5   *Tel:* 1 778 471 5573
Fax: 1 778 471 5586
email: apcibishop@shaw.ca
diocesan email: apci@shaw.ca
Web: www.apcionline.ca

KOOTENAY
Archbishop Most Revd John E. Privett, 201–380 Leathead Rd, Kelowna, BC, V1X 2H8
Tel: 1 778 478 8310
Fax: 1 778 478 8314
email: bishop@kootenay.info
diocesan email: admin@kootenay.info
Web: www.kootenay.anglican.ca

NEW WESTMINSTER
Bishop Rt Revd Melissa Skelton, 580–410 West Georgia St, Vancouver, BC, V6B 5A1
Tel: 1 604 684 6309
Fax: 1 604 684 7017
email: bishop@vancouver.anglican.ca
Web: www.vancouver.anglican.ca

YUKON
Bishop Rt Revd Larry D. Robertson, PO Box 31136, Whitehorse, YT, Y1A 5P7
Tel: 1 867 667 7746
Fax: 1 867 667 6125
email: synodoffice@klondiker.com
Web: http://anglican.yukon.net

PROVINCE OF CANADA
Metropolitan of the Ecclesiastical Province of Canada Most Revd Percy D. Coffin (*Archbishop of Western Neewfoundland*)

CENTRAL NEWFOUNDLAND
Bishop Rt Revd F. David Torraville, 34 Fraser Rd, Gander, NL, A1V 2E8   *Tel:* 1 709 256 2372
Fax: 1 709 256 2396
email: bishopcentral@nfld.net
Web: www.centraldiocese.org

EASTERN NEWFOUNDLAND AND LABRADOR
Bishop Rt Revd Geoffrey Peddle, 19 King's Bridge Rd, St John's, NL, A1C 3K4
Tel: 1 709 576 6697
Fax: 1 709 576 7122
email: geoffpeddle48@gmail.com
diocesan email: ecrisby@anglicanenl.net
Web: www.anglicanenl.net

FREDERICTON
Bishop Rt Revd David Edwards, 115 Church St, Fredericton, NB, E3B 4C8
Tel: 1 506 459 1801
Fax: 1 506 460 0520
email: edwardsdavid300@gmail.com
diocesan email: diocese@anglican.nb.ca
Web: www.anglican.nb.ca

MONTREAL
Bishop Rt Revd Barry B. Clarke, 1444 Union Ave, Montreal, QC, H3A 2B8   *Tel:* 1 514 843 9443
Fax: 1 514 843 3221
email: bishops.office@montreal.anglican.ca
Web: www.montreal.anglican.ca

NOVA SCOTIA AND PRINCE EDWARD ISLAND
Bishop Rt Revd Ronald W. Cutler, 1340 Martello St, Halifax, NS, B3H 1X3   *Tel:* 1 902 420 0717
Fax: 1 902 425 0717
email: rcutler@nspeidiocese.ca
diocesan email: office@nspeidiocese.ca
Web: www.nspeidiocese.ca

QUEBEC
Bishop Rt Revd Dennis P. Drainville, 31 rue des Jardins, Quebec, QC, G1R 4L6   *Tel:* 1 418 692 3858
Fax: 1 418 692 3876
email: bishopqc@quebec.anglican.ca
diocesan email: synodoffice@quebec.anglican.ca
Web: www.quebec.anglican.org

WESTERN NEWFOUNDLAND
Archbishop Most Rt Revd Percy D. Coffin, 25 Main St, Corner Brook, NL, A2H 1C2
Tel: 1 709 639 8712
Fax: 1 709 639 1636
email: bishop_dsown@nf.aibn.com
Web: www.westernnewfoundland.anglican.org

PROVINCE OF ONTARIO
Metropolitan of the Ecclesiastical Province of Ontario Most Revd Colin R. Johnson (*Archbishop of Toronto and Archbishop of Moosonee*)

ALGOMA
Bishop Rt Revd Dr Stephen G. W. Andrews, Box 1168, Sault Ste Marie, ON, P6A 5N7
Tel: 1 705 256 5061
Fax: 1 705 946 1860
email: bishop@dioceseofalgoma.com
diocesan email: secretary@dioceseofalgoma.com
Web: www.dioceseofalgoma.com

HURON
Bishop Rt Revd Robert (Bob) F. Bennett, 190 Queens Ave, London, ON N6A 6H7
Tel: 1 591 434 6893
Fax: 1 519 673 4151
email: bishops@huron.anglican.ca
Web: www.diohuron.org
Suffragan Bishop Rt Revd Terrance (Terry) A. Dance, Bishop of Norfolk (*as above*)

MOOSONEE (MOOSONEE MISSION AREA)
Archbishop Most Revd Colin R. Johnson, 135 Adelaide St East, Toronto, ON, M5C 1L8
Tel: 1 416 363 6021 ext 250
Fax: 1 416 363 3683
email: cjohnson@toronto.anglican.ca

NIAGARA
Bishop Rt Revd Michael A. Bird, Cathedral Place, 252 James St North, Hamilton, ON, L8R 2L3
Tel: 1 905 527 1316 ext 129
Fax: 1 905 527 1281
email: bishop@niagara.anglican.ca
Web: www.niagara.anglican.ca

ONTARIO
Bishop Rt Revd Michael D. Oulton, 90 Johnson St, Kingston, ON, K7L 1X7
Tel: 1 613 544 4774 ext 129
Fax: 1 613 547 3745
email: moulton@ontario.anglican.ca
diocesan email: synod@ontario.anglican.ca
Web: www.ontario.anglican.ca

OTTAWA
Bishop Rt Revd John H. Chapman, 71 Bronson Ave, Ottawa, ON, K1R 6G6   *Tel:* 1 613 233 7741
Fax: 1 613 232 3995
email: bishopsoffice@ottawa.anglican.ca
Web: www.ottawa.anglican.ca

TORONTO
Archbishop Most Revd Colin R. Johnson, 135 Adelaide St East, Toronto, ON, M5C 1L8
Tel: 1 416 363 6021 ext 250
Fax: 1 416 363 3683
email: cjohnson@toronto.anglican.ca
Web: www.toronto.anglican.ca

Area Bishops
Rt Revd Peter D. Fenty (*York-Simcoe*), PO Box 233, King City, ON, L3B 1A5   *Tel:* 1 905 833 8327
Fax: 1 905 833 8329
email: pfenty@toronto.anglican.ca
Web: www.anglican.toronto.ca
Rt Revd Linda C. Nicholls (*Trent-Durham*), 207–965 Dundas St West, Whitby, ON, L1P 1G8
Tel: 1 905 668 1558
Fax: 1 905 668 8216
email: lnicholls@toronto.anglican.ca
Web: www.anglican.toronto.ca
Rt Revd Patrick T. Yu (*York-Scarborough*), 135 Adelaide St East, Toronto, ON, M5C 1L8
Tel: 1 416 363 6021 ext 253
Fax: 1 416 363 3683
email: pyu@toronto.anglican.ca
Web: www.anglican.toronto.ca
Rt Revd M. Philip Poole (*York-Credit Valley*), 135 Adelaide St East, Toronto, ON, M5C 1L8
Tel: 1 416 363 6021 ext 223
Fax: 1 416 363 3683
email: ppoole@toronto.anglican.ca
Web: www.anglican.toronto.ca

PROVINCE OF RUPERT'S LAND
Metropolitan of the Ecclesiastical Province of Canada
Vacancy

THE ARCTIC
Bishop Rt Revd David W. Parsons, Box 190, 4910 51st St, Yellowknife, NT, X1A 2N2
Tel: 1 867 873 5432
Fax: 1 867 873 8478
email: arctic@arcticnet.org
Web: www.arcticnet.org
Suffragan Bishop Rt Revd Darren J. McCartney, Box 5, Iqaluit, NU, X0A 0H0   *Tel:* 1 867 873 5432
Fax: 1 867 873 8478
email: darren@arcticnet.org
Web: www.arcticnet.org

ATHABASCA
Bishop Rt Revd Fraser W. Lawton, Box 6868, Peace River, AB, T8S 1S6   *Tel:* 1 780 624 2767
Fax: 1 780 624 2365
email: bpath@telusplanet.net
diocesan email: dioath@telusplanet.net

BRANDON
Bishop Rt Revd James (Jim) D. Njegovan, Box 21009, WEPO, Brandon, MB, R7B 3W8
Tel: 1 204 727 7550
Fax: 1 204 727 4135
email: bishopbdn@mymts.net
diocesan email: diobran@mymts.net
Web: www.dioceseofbrandon.org

CALGARY
Bishop Rt Revd Gregory Kerr-Wilson, 180, 1209–59th Ave SE, Calgary, AB, T2H 2P6
Tel: 1 403 243 3673
Fax: 1 403 243 2182
email: gkerrwilson@calgary.anglican.ca
diocesan email: diocese@calgary.anglican.ca
Web: www.calgary.anglican.ca

EDMONTON
Bishop Rt Revd Jane Alexander, 1035 St, Edmonton, AB, T5J 0X5   *Tel:* 1 780 439 7344
Fax: 1 780 439 6549
email: bishop@edmonton.anglican.ca
diocesan email: churched@edmonton.anglican.ca
Web: www.edmonton.anglican.org

KEEWATIN
Diocese exists but has no parishes under its jurisdiction.

MISHAMIKOWEESH, INDIGENOUS SPIRITUAL MINISTRY OF
Bishop Rt Revd Lydia Mamakwa, Box 65, Kingfisher Lake, ON, P0V 1Z0   *Tel:* 1 807 532 2085
Fax: 1 807 532 2344
email: lydiam@kingfisherlake.ca

QU'APPELLE
Bishop Rt Revd Robert Hardwick, 1501 College Ave, Regina, SK, S4P 1B8   *Tel:* 1 306 522 1608
Fax: 1 306 352 6808
email: bishop.rob@sasktel.net
general email: quappelle@sasktel.net
Web: www.quappelle.anglican.ca

RUPERT'S LAND
Bishop Rt Revd Donald D. Phillips, 935 Nesbitt Bay, Winnipeg, MB, R3T 1W6
Tel: 1 204 992 4212
Fax: 1 204 992 4219
email: bishop@rupertsland.ca
diocesan email: general@rupertsland.ca
Web: www.rupertsland.ca

SASKATCHEWAN
Bishop Rt Revd Michael W. Hawkins, 1308 5th Ave East, Prince Albert, SK, S6V 2H7
Tel: 1 306 763 2455
Fax: 1 306 764 5172
email: bishopmichael@sasktel.net
diocesan email: synod@sasktel.net
Web: www.saskatchewan.anglican.org

Diocesan Indigenous Bishop Rt Revd Adam Halkett (*as above*)   *email:* bishopadam@sasktel.net

SASKATOON
Bishop Rt Revd David M. Irving, 1403 9th Ave North, SK, S7K 2Z6   *Tel:* 1 306 244 5651
Fax: 1 306 244 4606
email: bishopdavid @sasktel.net
diocesan email: anglicansynod@sasktel.net
Web: www.saskatoon.anglican.org

The Church of the Province of Central Africa

Members 600,000

The province includes Botswana, Malawi, Zambia and Zimbabwe. The first Anglican missionary to Malawi was Bishop Charles Mackenzie who arrived with David Livingstone in 1861. The province was inaugurated in 1955 and has a movable bishopric. The countries forming the province are very different. Zambia and Botswana suffer the difficulties of rapid industrialization, along with underdevelopment and thinly populated areas. In Malawi 30% of the adult males are away as migrant labourers in other countries at any given time. Zimbabwe is experiencing problems of social adjustment after independence.

Archbishop of the Province Most Revd Albert C. Chama

Provincial Secretary Vacancy

Provincial Treasurer Mr R. Kanja, CPCA, PO Box 22317, Kitwe, Zambia   *Tel:* 260 351 081
260 9719 5368 (Mobile)
Fax: 267 351 668

ANGLICAN THEOLOGICAL COLLEGES
Leonard Kamungu (Anglican) Theological College, PO Box 959, Zomba. Malawi (*Dean* Revd Alinafe Kalemba)   *Tel:* 265 1 525 286
265 8 856 410 (Mobile)
National Anglican Theological College of Zimbabwe (Ecumenical Institute of Theology), 11 Thornburg Ave, Groom Bridge, Mount Pleasant, Harare, Zimbabwe
St John's Seminary, Mindolo, PO Box 20369, Kitwe, Zambia (*Rector* Rt Revd John Osmers)
Tel: 260 2 210960
email: josmers@zamnet.zm

CHURCH PAPER
Link Monthly newspaper for the Dioceses of Mashonaland and Matabeleland giving news and views of the dioceses. *Editorial Offices* Link Board of Management, PO Box UA7, Harare City.

BOTSWANA
Bishop Rt Revd Metlhayotlhe Beleme, PO Box 769, Gaborone, Botswana   *Tel:* 267 395 3779
Fax: 267 395 2075
email: angli_diocese@info.bw

CENTRAL ZAMBIA
Bishop Rt Revd Derek Gary Kamukwamba, PO Box 70172, Ndola, Zambia   *Tel:* 260 2 612 431
email: adcznla@zamnet.zm

CENTRAL ZIMBABWE
Bishop Rt Revd Ishmael Mukuwanda, PO Box 25, Gweru, Zimbabwe   *Tel:* 263 54 221 030
Fax: 263 54 221 097
email: diocent@telconet.co.zw

EASTERN ZAMBIA
Bishop Rt Revd William Muchombo, PO Box 510154, Chipata, Zambia
Tel and *Fax:* 260 216 221 294
email: dioeastzm@zamnet.zm

HARARE
Bishop Rt Revd Chad Gandiya, 9 Monmouth Rd, Avondale, Harare, Zimbabwe
Tel: 263 4 308 042
email: chadgandiya@gmail.com

LAKE MALAWI
Bishop Rt Revd Francis Kaulanda, PO Box 30349, Lilongwe 3, Malawi   *Tel:* 265 1 797 858 (Office)
Fax: 265 1 797 548
email: franciskaulanda@yahoo.com

LUAPULA
Bishop Rt Revd Robert Mumbi, PO Box 710210, Mansa, Luapula, Zambia   *Tel:* 260 2 821 680
email: diopula@zamtel.zm

ANGLICAN AND PORVOO COMMUNIONS

LUSAKA
Bishop Rt Revd David Njovu, PO Box 30183, Lusaka, Zambia *Tel:* 260 1 254 789 (Office)
email: davidnjovu1961@zamnet.zm / davidnjovu1961@gmail.com

MANICALAND
Bishop Rt Revd Julius Makoni, 146 Herbert Chitepo Rd, Mutare, Zimbabwe
Tel: 263 20 8418
email: juliusmakoni@cantab.net

MASVINGO
Bishop Rt Revd Godfrey Tawonezvi, PO Box 1421, Masvingo, Zimbabwe *Tel:* 263 39 362 536
email: bishopgodfreytawonezvi@gmail.com

MATABELELAND
Bishop Rt Revd Cleophas Lunga, PO Box 2422, Bulaweyo, Zimbabwe *Tel:* 263 09 61 370
Fax: 263 09 68 353
email: clunga@aol.com

NORTHERN MALAWI
Bishop Rt Revd Fanuel E. C. Magangani, Box 120, Mzuzu, Malawi, Central Africa *Tel:* 2651312 858
email: magangani@sdup.org.mw

NORTHERN ZAMBIA
Bishop Most Rt Revd Albert Chama (*Archbishop of the Province*), PO Box 20798, Kitwe, Zambia
Tel: 260 2 223 264
Fax: 260 2 224 778
email: chama_albert@yahoo.ca

SOUTHERN MALAWI
Bishop Rt Revd Alinafe Kalemba, PO Box 30220, Chichiri, Blantyre, 3, Malawi
Tel: 265 1 641 218
Fax: 265 1 641 235
email: dean@sdup.org.mw

UPPER SHIRE
Bishop Rt Revd Brighton Vitta Malasa, Private Bag 1, Chilema, Zomba, Malawi
Tel: 265 1 539 203
email: malasab@yahoo.com.uk

The Anglican Church of the Central American Region

(Iglesia Anglicana de la Región Central de América)

Members 15,600
This province of the Anglican Communion is made up of the Dioceses of Guatemala, El Salvador, Nicaragua, Costa Rica and Panama. The Church was introduced by the Society for the Propagation of the Gospel when England administered two colonies in Central America, Belize (1783–1982) and Miskitia (1740–1894). In the later years Afro-Antillean people brought their Anglican Christianity with them. The province is multicultural and multiracial and is committed to evangelization, social outreach, and community development.

Primate Most Revd Armando Román Guerra-Soria (*Bishop of Guatemala*)

Provincial Secretary Rt Revd Hector Monterroso (*Bishop of Costa Rica*) *Tel:* 506 253 0790
Fax: 506 253 8331
email: hmonterroso@episcopalcostarica.org

Provincial Treasurer Mr Harold Charles, Apt R, Balboa, Republic of Panama *Tel:* 507 212 0062
Fax: 507 262 2097
email: iarcahch@sinfo.net

COSTA RICA
Bishop Rt Revd Hector Monterroso, De Plaza Cemaco, 75 Metros Notre Sobre, Calle Paralela, San José, Costa Rica *Tel:* 506 225 0209/253 0790
Fax: 506 253 8331
email: hmonterroso@episcopalcostarica.org

EL SALVADOR
Bishop Most Revd Martin de Jesus Barahona Pascacio, 47 Avenida Sur, 723 Col Flor Blanca, Apt Postal (01), 274 San Salvador, El Salvador
Tel: 503 2223 2252
Fax: 503 2223 7952
email: anglican.es@gmail.com

GUATEMALA
Bishop Rt Revd Armando Román Guerra-Soria (*Primate of the Anglican Church of the Central American Region*), Apt 58A, Avenida La Castellana 40–06, Guatemala City, Guatemala
Tel: 502 2472 0852
Fax: 502 2472 0764
email: agepiscopal@yahoo.com

NICARAGUA
Bishop Rt Revd Sturdie Downs, Apt 1207, Managua, Nicaragua *Tel:* 505 2225 174
Fax: 505 2226 701
email: episcnic@cablenet.com.ni/ episcnic@tmx.com.ni

PANAMA
Bishop Rt Revd Julio Murray, Box R, Balboa, Republic of Panama
Tel: 507 212 0062/507 262 2051
Fax: 507 262 2097
email: iepan@cwpanama.net/anglipan@sinfo.net
Web: www.episcopalpanama.org

The Church of the Province of Congo

Members approximately 500,000

Ugandan evangelist Apolo Kivebulaya established an Anglican presence in the Democratic Republic of Congo (formerly Zaire) in 1896. The Church reached the Katanga (formerly Shaba) region in 1955, but evangelization did not progress on a large scale until the 1970s. Following independence, the Church expanded and formed dioceses as part of the Province of Uganda, Burundi, Rwanda, and Boga-Zaire. The new province was inaugurated in 1992 and changed its name in 1997. On 17 September 2002 the then Archbishop Njojo and many other Congolese citizens had to flee to Uganda because of internal tribal warfare.

Archbishop Most Revd Henri Isingoma Kahwa (*Bishop of Kinshasa*) PO Box 16482 Kinshasa 1 DR Congo   *Tel:* 243 99 3333 090
email: peac_isingoma@yahoo.fr

Provincial Secretary Ven Anthonio Kibwela Kifwambwa   *Tel:* 243 995412138
email: anglicancongo@yahoo.com

Provincial Treasurer and Liaison Office in Kampala Mr Fréderick Ngadjole Badya, PO Box 25586, Kampala, Uganda   *Tel:* 256 77264 7495
email: eac-mags@infocom.co.ug

Provincial Coordinator of Evangelism Revd Desire Mukanirwa Kadorho   *Tel:* 243 99704614
email: peac.evangelisation@gmail.com

THEOLOGICAL COLLEGE
Anglican University of Congo (Universite Anglicane du Congo 'U.A.C.') PO Box 25586, Kampala, Uganda *Rector* Revd Canon Sabiti Tibafa Daniel   *Tel:* 243 99 779 1013
email: email: revdsabiti@yahoo.fr

ARU
Bishop Rt Revd Dr Georges Titre Ande, PO Box 226, Arua, Uganda   *Tel:* 243 81 039 30 71
email: revdande@yahoo.co.uk

BOGA (*formerly* BOGA-ZAIRE)
Bishop Rt Revd William Bahemuka Mugenyi, PO Box 25586, Kampala, Uganda
Tel: 243 99 0668639
email: mugenyiwilliam@yahoo.com

BUKAVU
Bishop Rt Revd Sylvestre Bahati Bali-Busane, Av. Mgr Ndahura, No. Q/Nyalukemba, C/Ibanda, CAC-Bukavu, BP 2876, Bukavu, Democratic Republic of Congo / PO Box 134, Cyangugu, Rwanda   *Tel:* 243 99 401 3647
email: bahati_bali@yahoo.fr

KATANGA
Bishop Rt Revd Corneille Kasima Muno, 1309 Chaussee do Kasenga, Bel-Air, Lubumbashi, PO Box 22037, Kitwe, Zambia
Tel and Fax: 243 81 475 6075
email: kasimamuno@yahoo.fr
Assistant Missionary Bishop from Tanzania based in Kalemie Rt Revd Elisha Tendwa Lawrence
Tel: 243 824621849

KINDU
Bishop Rt Revd Zacharie Masimango Katanda, PO Box 5, Gisenyi, Rwanda   *Tel:* 243 99 891 6258
email: angkindu@yahoo.fr

KINSHASA (Missionary diocese)
Bishop Most Revd Henri Isingoma Kahwa (*Archbishop of the Province*), 11 Ave. Basalakala, Quartier Immocongo Commune de Kalamu, Kinshasa 1, PO Box 16482, DR Congo
email: peac_isingoma@yahoo.fr
Assistant Missionary Bishop based in Congo-Brazzaville Rt Revd Jean Molanga Botola, EAC-Kinshasa, BP 16482, Kinshasa 1, DR Congo
Tel: 243 99 471 3802
email: molanga2k@yahoo.co.uk

KISANGANI
Bishop Rt Revd Lambert Funga Botolome (*Dean of the Province*), Av. Bowane, N°10, Quartier des Musiciens, C/Makiso, PO Box 86, Kisangani, DR Congo *or* c/o PO Box 25586, Kampala, Uganda
Tel: 243 997 252 868 (Mobile)
email: lambertfunga@hotmail.com

NORD KIVU
Bishop Rt Revd Adoplh Muhindo Isesomo, PO Box 322, Butembo, DR Congo *or* PO Box 25586 Kampala, Uganda   *Tel:* 243 99 8854 8601

KASAIS
Bishop Rt Revd Marcel Kapinga Kayibabu wa Ilunga, PO Box 16482, Kinshasa 1, DRCongo
Tel: 243 99 357 0080
email: anglicanekasai2@gmail.com

The Church of England

Baptized members 26,000,000

Covering all of England, the Isle of Man and the Channel Islands; Europe except Great Britain and Ireland; Morocco; Turkey; and the Asian coun-

tries of the former Soviet Union. The Church of England is the ancient national Church of the land. Its structures emerged from the missionary work of St Augustine, sent from Rome in AD 597, and from the work of Celtic missionaries in the north. Throughout the Middle Ages, the Church was in communion with the See of Rome, but in the sixteenth century it separated from Rome and rejected the authority of the Pope. The Church of England is the established Church, with its administration governed by a General Synod, which meets twice a year.

Hong Kong Sheng Kung Hui

(Hong Kong Anglican Church)

Members 30,000
This dynamic province was inaugurated in 1998. The history of the Church in China dates back to the mid-nineteenth century; missionaries were provided by the American Church, the Church of England, the Church of England in Canada, etc. The Province of Chung Hua Sheng Kung Hui (the Holy Catholic Church in China) was established in 1912 of which the Anglican Church in Hong Kong and Macau was an integral part. Chung Hua Sheng Kung Hui ceased to exist in the 1950s and the diocese of Hong Kong and Macau was associated to other dioceses in South East Asia under the custodianship of the Council of Churches of East Asia, until the recent establishment of the diocese as the 38th province of the Anglican Communion. It has parishes in Hong Kong and Macau, which returned to Chinese sovereignty in 1997 and 1999 respectively. It enjoys autonomy and independence as guaranteed by the Basic Law (the mini constitution governing Hong Kong, the Special Administrative Region of China).

Primate Most Revd Paul Kwong, Provincial Office, 16/F Tung Wai Commercial Building, 109–111 Gloucester Road, Wanchai, Hong Kong SAR   *Tel:* 852 2526 5355
Fax: 852 2521 2199
email: office1@hkskh.org
Web: www.hkskh.org

Provincial Secretary General Revd Peter Douglas Koon (*same address*)
email: peter.koon@hkskh.org

Bishop of Hong Kong Island Most Revd Dr Paul Kwong, 71 Bonham Road, Hong Kong SAR
Tel: 852 2526 5366
Fax: 852 2523 3344
email: do.dhk@hkskh.org
Web: http://dhk.hkskh.org

Bishop of Eastern Kowloon Rt Revd Timothy Kwok, Diocesan Office, 4/F Holy Trinity Bradbury Centre, 139 Ma Tau Chung Rd, Kowloon City, Kowloon, Hong Kong SAR   *Tel:* 852 2713 9983
Fax: 852 2711 1609
email: ekoffice@ekhkskh.org.hk
Web: ekhkskh.org.hk

Bishop of Western Kowloon Rt Revd Andrew Chan, Diocesan Office, 11 Pak Po Street, Mongkok, Kowloon, Hong Kong SAR   *Tel:* 852 2783 0811
Fax: 852 2783 0799
email: dwk@hkskh.org
Web: http://dwk.hkskh.org

Bishop of Missionary Area of Macau Most Revd Dr Paul Kwong, 1 andar A, Edf, HuaDu, No. 2 Trav. Do Pato, No. 49–51 Rua do Campo, Macau SAR
Tel: 853 2835 3867
Fax: 853 2832 5314
email: skhmma@macau.ctm.net
Web: www.hkskh.org

The Church of the Province of the Indian Ocean

Members more than 600,000
The Anglican mission was begun in Mauritius in 1812 by the Revd H. Shepherd, and the first Anglican church in the Seychelles was dedicated in January 1856. The first Anglican missionaries went to Madagascar in 1864. The growth of the church was fostered both by the Society for the Propagation of the Gospel and by the Church Missionary Society. The Diocese of Mauritius was created in 1854. The first three dioceses in Madagascar, Antananarivo, Toamasina and Antsiranana, were created in 1969 and Seychelles was established as a diocese in 1973. The dioceses of Madagascar and Mauritius and Seychelles combined in 1973 to create the province, which now comprises eight dioceses.

Archbishop Most Revd Ian Gerald Ernest (*Bishop of Mauritius*), Diocesan Church House, 37th St Paul Rd, Vacoas, Mauritius   *Tel:* 230 686 5158
email: dioang@intnet.mu

Provincial Secretary Revd Canon Samitiana Jhonson Razafindralamo, Dupin Street Rectory, St Clement, Curepipe, Mauritius   *Tel:* 230 676 22 50
email: indian.ocean.psec@gmail.com

Treasurer Mr Bernard Laure (*same address as the Archbishop*)

Chancellor of the Province Mrs Hilda Yerriah, Chancery House, Port Louis, Mauritius
Tel: 230 20 80429 (Office)
230 46 75710 (Home)
email: hilda5885@hotmail.com

Dean of the Province Rt Revd Jean-Claude Andrianjafimanana (*Bishop of Mahajanga*)

St Paul's College, Ambatohararana, Merimandroso, Ambohidratrimo, Madagascar (*Warden* Prof Michel Razafiarivony)

Diocesan Training Centre, Rose Hill, Mauritius (*Warden* Rt Revd Joseph Papatoti)

St Philip's Theological College, La Misère, Seychelles (*Diocesan Trainer* The Revd Peter Raath)

Newsletters of the Province of the Indian Ocean Support Assn. *Editor* The Revd Philip Harbridge, Chaplain, Christ's College, Cambridge CB2 3BY, UK

Seychelles Diocesan Magazine A quarterly newspaper covering diocesan events and containing articles of theological and other interest.

Magazine du Diocèse de Maurice (Le Cordage) A quarterly newspaper covering diocesan events and containing articles of theological and ecumenical interest.

Provincial e-letters: provincial e-news *Le phare* every two months and provincial cycle of prayer every three months.

ANTANANARIVO
Bishop Rt Revd Samoela Jaona Ranarivelo, Évêché Anglican, Lot VK57 ter, Ambohimanoro, 101 Antananarivo, Madagascar   *Tel:* 261 20 222 0827
Fax: 261 20 226 1331
email: eemdanta@dts.mg

ANTSIRANANA
Bishop Rt Revd Oliver Simon, Évêché Anglican, BP 278, 4 rue Grandidier, 201 Antsiranana, Madagascar   *Tel:* 00261 325507774
email: oliversimon45@gmail.com

Bishop Coadjutor Rt Revd Theophile Botomazava

FIANARANTSOA
Bishop Rt Revd Gilbert Rateloson Rakotondravelo, Évêché Anglican Manantsara, BP 1418 Fianarantsoa, Madagascar
Tel: 261 20 75 515 83
261 33 73 067 81 (Mobile)
email: eemdiofianara@yahoo.fr

MAHAJANGA
Bishop Rt Revd Jean-Claude Andrianjafimanana, BP 570, Rue de Temple Ziona, Mahajanga 401, Madagascar   *Tel:* 261 62 23611
261 32 04 55143 (Mobile)
email: andrianjajc@yahoo.fr/eemdmaha@dts.mg

MAURITIUS
Bishop Most Revd Ian Gerald Ernest (*Archbishop of the Province*), Bishop's House, Ave. Nallétamby, Phoenix, Mauritius   *Tel:* 230 686 5158
Fax: 230 697 1096
email: dioang@intnet.mu

SEYCHELLES
Bishop Rt Revd James Richard Wong Yin Song, PO Box 44, Victoria, Mahé, Seychelles
Tel: 248 32 1977/32 3879
248 52 7770 (Mobile)
Fax: 248 22 4043
email: angdio@seychelles.net
Web: www.seychelles.anglican.org

TOAMASINA
Bishop Rt Revd Jean Paul Solo, Évêché Anglican, Rue James Seth, BP 531, Toamasina 501, Madagascar   *Tel:* 261 20 533 1663
261 32 04 55143 (Mobile)
Fax: 261 20 533 1689
email: eemtoam@moov.mg

TOLIARA
Bishop Rt Revd Todd MacGregor, Eklesia Episkopaly, Malagasy, BP 408601, Toliara, Madagascar   *Tel* 261 33 374 2745
Web: peoplereaching.org

The Church of Ireland

According to the 2011 Census figures for the Republic of Ireland the Church of Ireland population has increased in the Republic of Ireland. The Church of Ireland population figures in Northern Ireland are based on the 2011 Census for Northern Ireland.

Members 383,186
Tracing its origins to St Patrick and his companions in the fifth century, the Irish Church has been marked by strong missionary efforts. In 1537 the English king was declared head of the Church, but most Irish Christians maintained loyalty to Rome. The Irish Church Act of 1869 provided that the statutory union between the Churches of England and Ireland be dissolved and that the Church of Ireland should cease to be established by law. A General Synod of the Church, established in 1871 and consisting of archbishops, bishops, and representatives of the clergy and laity, has legislative and administrative power. Irish Church leaders have played a key role in the work of reconciliation in the Northern Ireland conflict.

The Primate of All Ireland and Metropolitan Most Revd Dr Richard Lionel Clarke (Archbishop of Armagh)

The Primate of Ireland and Metropolitan Most Revd Dr Michael Geoffrey, St Aubyn Jackson (Archbishop of Dublin & Bishop of Glendalough)

Central Office of the Church of Ireland Church of Ireland House, Church Ave, Rathmines, Dublin 6, Republic of Ireland   Tel: 353 1 497 8422
Fax: 353 1 497 8821
email: office@rcbdub.org

Chief Officer and Secretary, Representative Church Body Mr Adrian Clements
email: chiefofficer@rcbdub.org

Head of Synod Services and Communications Mrs Janet Maxwell   email: comms@rcbdub.org

THEOLOGICAL INSTITUTE
The Church of Ireland Theological Institute, Braemor Park, Churchtown, Dublin 14, which conducts courses in conjunction with the School of Hebrew, Biblical and Theological Studies, Trinity College, Dublin, Republic of Ireland (Director Revd Dr Maurice Elliott)   Tel: 353 1 492 3506
Fax: 353 1 492 3082
email: admin@theologicalinstitute.ie
Web: theologicalinstitute.ie

CHURCH PAPER
Church of Ireland Gazette (weekly) Deals with items of general interest to the Church of Ireland in a national context and also contains news from the various dioceses and parishes together with articles of a more general nature. Editor/Editorial Offices 3 Wallace Ave, Lisburn, Co Antrim BT27 4AA   Tel: 44 28 9267 5743
Fax: 44 28 9266 7580
email: gazette@ireland.anglican.org

PROVINCE OF ARMAGH
ARMAGH
Archbishop of Armagh (Primate of All Ireland and Metropolitan) Most Revd Dr Richard Lionel Clarke, c/o Church House, 46 Abbey Street, Armagh BT61 7DZ   Tel: 44 28 3752 7144 (Office)
Fax: 44 28 3751 0596
email: archbishop@armagh.anglican.org
Web: http://armagh.anglican.org

CATHEDRAL CHURCH OF ST PATRICK, Armagh
Dean Very Revd Gregory John Orchard Dunstan, The Deanery, Library House, 43 Abbey Street, Armagh BT61 7DY   Tel: 44 28 3752 3142 (Office)
Tel/Fax: 44 28 3751 8447 (Home)
email: dean@armagh.anglican.org

CLOGHER
Bishop Rt Revd Rt Revd Francis John McDowell, The See House, Fivemiletown, Co Tyrone BT75 0QP   Tel and Fax: 44 28 8952 2461
email: bishop@clogher.anglican.org
Web: http://clogher.anglican.org

CATHEDRAL CHURCHES OF ST MACARTAN, Clogher, and ST MACARTIN, Enniskillen
Dean Very Revd Kenneth Robert James Hall, St Macartin's Deanery, 13 Church Street, Enniskillen, Co Fermanagh BT74 7DW
Tel: 44 28 6632 2917 (Office)
Tel: 44 28 6632 2465 (Home)
email: dean@clogher.anglican.org
Web: http://enniskillen.clogher.anglican.org

CONNOR
Bishop Rt Revd Alan Francis Abernethy, Diocesan Office, Church of Ireland House, 61–67 Donegall Street, Belfast BT1 2QH
Tel: 44 28 9082 8870 (Office)
email: bishop@connor.anglican.org
Web: http://connor.anglican.org

CATHEDRAL CHURCH OF CHRIST CHURCH, Lisburn
Dean Very Revd John Frederick Augustus Bond, The Rectory, 49 Rectory Gardens, Broughshane, Ballymena, Co Antrim, BT42 4LF
Tel and Fax: 44 28 2586 1215
email: skerry@connor.anglican.org
Web: http://www.lisburncathedral.org

CATHEDRAL CHURCH OF ST ANNE, Belfast
(Cathedral of the United Dioceses of Down and Dromore and the Diocese of Connor)
Dean Very Revd John Owen Mann, The Deanery, 5 Deramore Drive, Belfast BT9 5JQ
Tel: 44 28 9066 0980 (Home)
44 28 9032 8332 (Cathedral)
Fax: 44 28 9023 8855
email: dean@belfastcathedral.org
Web: http://www.belfastcathedral.org

DERRY AND RAPHOE
Bishop Rt Revd Kenneth Raymond Good, The See House, 112 Culmore Rd, Londonderry, Co Derry BT48 8JF   Tel: 44 28 7126 2440 (Office)
Fax: 44 28 7135 2554
email: bishop@derry.anglican.org
Web: http://derry.anglican.org

CATHEDRAL CHURCH OF ST COLUMB, Derry
Dean Very Revd William Wright Morton, The Deanery, 30 Bishop St, Londonderry, Co Derry BT48 6PP   Tel: 44 28 7126 2746
email: dean@derry.anglican.org
Web: http://www.stcolumbscathedral.org

CATHEDRAL CHURCH OF ST EUNAN, Raphoe
Dean Very Revd Kenneth Arthur Barrett, The Deanery, Raphoe, Co Donegal Tel: 353 74 914 5226
email: dean@raphoe.anglican.org

DOWN AND DROMORE
Bishop Rt Revd Harold Creeth Miller, The See House, 32 Knockdene Park South, Belfast BT5 7AB   Tel: 44 28 9082 8850 (Office)
Fax: 44 28 9023 1902
email: bishop@down.anglican.org
Web: http://down.anglican.org

Anglican and Porvoo Communions

CATHEDRAL CHURCH OF THE HOLY AND UNDIVIDED TRINITY, Down
Dean Very Revd Thomas Henry Hull, Lecale Rectory, 9 Quoile Road, Downpatrick, Co Down BT30 6SE *Tel*: 44 28 4461 3101
Fax: 44 28 4461 4456
Web: http://www.downcathedral.org

CATHEDRAL CHURCH OF CHRIST THE REDEEMER, Dromore
Dean Very Revd Bryan Thomas Kerr, Dromore Cathedral Rectory, 28 Church Street, Dromore, Co Down BT25 1AA *Tel*: 44 28 9269 3968 (Office)
email: cathedral@dromore.anglican.org
Web: http://www.dromorecathedral.co.uk

KILMORE, ELPHIN AND ARDAGH
Bishop Rt Revd Samuel Ferran Glenfield, The See House, Kilmore, Cavan, Co Cavan, Republic of Ireland *Tel*: 353 49 437 1551
email: bishop@kilmore.anglican.org
Web: http://kilmore.anglican.org

CATHEDRAL CHURCH OF ST FETHLIMIDH, Kilmore
Dean Vacancy

CATHEDRAL CHURCH OF ST MARY THE VIRGIN AND ST JOHN THE BAPTIST, Sligo, Republic of Ireland
Dean Very Revd Arfon Williams, The Deanery, Strandhill Road, Sligo, Co Sligo, Republic of Ireland *Tel*: 353 71 915 7993
email: arvonwilliams@eircom.net
Web: http://sligocathedral.elphin.anglican.org

TUAM, KILLALA AND ACHONRY
Bishop Rt Revd Rt Revd Patrick William Rooke, Bishop's House, Breaffy Woods, Cottage Road, Castlebar, Co Mayo, Republic of Ireland
Tel: 353 94 903 5703
email: bishop@tuam.anglican.org
Web: http://tuam.anglican.org

CATHEDRAL CHURCH OF ST MARY, Tuam
Dean Very Revd Alistair John Grimason, Deanery Place, Cong, Co Mayo, Republic of Ireland *Tel*: 353 94 954 6909
email: deantuam@yahoo.co.uk

CATHEDRAL CHURCH OF ST PATRICK, Killala
Dean Very Revd Alistair John Grimason, Deanery Place, Cong, Co Mayo, Republic of Ireland
Tel: 353 94 954 6909
email: deantuam@yahoo.co.uk

PROVINCE OF DUBLIN
CASHEL, WATERFORD, LISMORE, OSSORY, FERNS AND LEIGHLIN
Bishop Rt Revd Michael Andrew James Burrows, Bishop's House, Troysgate, Kilkenny, Republic of Ireland *Tel*: 353 56 77 86633 (Home)
email: cfobishop@gmail.com
Web: http://cashel.anglican.org

CATHEDRAL CHURCH OF ST JOHN THE BAPTIST AND ST PATRICK'S ROCK, Cashel
Dean Very Revd Gerald Gordon Field, The Deanery, Boherclogh Street, Cashel, Co Tipperary, Republic of Ireland *Tel*: 353 62 61232 (Home)
353 62 61944 (Office)

CATHEDRAL CHURCH OF THE BLESSED TRINITY (CHRIST CHURCH), Waterford
Dean Very Revd Maria Patricia Jansson, The Deanery, 41 Grange Park Rd, Waterford, Co Waterford, Republic of Ireland
Tel: 353 51 874119
email: dean@waterford.anglican.org

CATHEDRAL CHURCH OF ST CARTHAGE, Lismore
Dean Very Revd Paul Richard Draper, The Deanery, The Mall, Lismore, Co Waterford, Republic of Ireland *Tel*: 353 58 54105
email: dean@lismore.anglican.org

CATHEDRAL CHURCH OF ST CANICE, Kilkenny
Dean Very Revd Katharine Margaret Poulton, The Deanery, Kilkenny, Republic of Ireland
Tel: 353 56 772 1516
email: dean@ossory.anglican.org

CATHEDRAL CHURCH OF ST EDAN, Ferns
Dean Very Revd Paul Gerard Mooney, The Deanery, Ferns, Enniscorthy, Co Wexford, Republic of Ireland *Tel*: 353 53 936 6124
email: dean@ferns.anglican.org

CATHEDRAL CHURCH OF ST LASERIAN, Leighlin
Dean Very Revd Thomas William Gordon, The Deanery, Old Leighlin, Co. Carlow, Republic of Ireland *Tel*: 353 59 9721570
email: dean.leighlin@gmail.com

CORK, CLOYNE AND ROSS
Bishop Rt Revd Dr William Paul Colton, St Nicholas' House, 14 Cove Street, Cork, Republic of Ireland *Tel*: 353 21 500 5080 (Office)
email: bishop@ccrd.ie
Web: http://cathedral.cork.anglican.org

CATHEDRAL CHURCH OF ST FIN BARRE, Cork
Dean Very Revd Nigel Kenneth Dunne, The Deanery, Gilabbey St, Cork, Republic of Ireland
Tel: 353 21 4318073
email: dean@cork.anglican.org
Web: http://www.cathedral.cork.anglican.org

CATHEDRAL CHURCH OF ST COLMAN, Cloyne
Dean Very Revd Alan Gordon Marley, The Deanery, Midleton, Co Cork, Republic of Ireland
Tel: 353 21 463 1449
email: dean@cloyne.anglican.org
Web: http://cathedral.cloyne.anglican.org/ Cloyne_Union/Welcome_to_Cloyne_ Union.html

CATHEDRAL CHURCH OF ST FACHTNA, Ross
Dean Very Revd Christopher Lind Peters, The Deanery, Rosscarbery, Co Cork, Republic of Ireland   *Tel:* 353 23 48166
email: candjpeters@eircom.net
Web: http://cork.anglican.org/places/ross-union/

DUBLIN AND GLENDALOUGH
Archbishop Most Revd Dr Michael Geoffrey St Aubyn Jackson, The See House, 17 Temple Rd, Dartry, Dublin 6, Republic of Ireland
Tel: 353 1 497 7849
Fax: 353 1 497 6355
email: archbishop@dublin.anglican.org
Web: http://dublin.anglican.org

CATHEDRAL CHURCH OF THE HOLY TRINITY
(COMMONLY CALLED CHRIST CHURCH)
Cathedral of the United Dioceses of Dublin and Glendalough, Metropolitan Cathedral of the United Provinces of Dublin and Cashel

Dean Very Revd Dermot Patrick Martin Dunne, 19 Mountainview Road, Ranelagh, Dublin 6
Tel: 353 1 677 8099 (Cathedral)
Fax: 353 1 679 8991
email: dean@cccdub.ie
Web: http://christchurchdublin.ie/

THE NATIONAL CATHEDRAL AND COLLEGIATE CHURCH OF ST PATRICK, Dublin
(The 'National Cathedral of the Church of Ireland having a common relation to all the dioceses of Ireland')

Dean and Ordinary Very Revd Victor George Stacey, The Deanery, Upper Kevin St, Dublin 8, Republic of Ireland   *Tel:* 353 1 475 5449 (Home)
353 1 475 4817 (Cathedral)
353 1 453 9472 (Office)
Fax: 353 1 454 6374
email: dean@stpatrickscathedral.ie
Web: http://www.stpatrickscathedral.ie

LIMERICK, ARDFERT, AGHADOE, KILLALOE, KILFENORA, CLONFERT, KILMACDUAGH AND EMLY
Bishop Vacancy
Web: http://limerick.anglican.org

CATHEDRAL CHURCH OF ST MARY, Limerick
Dean Very Revd Sandra Ann Pragnell, The Deanery, 7 Kilbane, Castletroy, Limerick, Republic of Ireland   *Tel and Fax:* 353 61 338 697
email: dean@limerick.anglican.org
Web: http://cathedral.limerick.anglican.org/

CATHEDRAL CHURCH OF ST FLANNAN, Killaloe
Dean Very Revd Gary Alexander Paulsen, The Deanery, Abbey Road, Killaloe, Co Clare
Tel: 353 6 137 6687
email: abbeydean2@gmail.com
Web: http://cathedralkillaloe.anglican.org

CATHEDRAL CHURCH OF ST BRENDAN, Clonfert
Dean Vacancy

MEATH AND KILDARE
Bishop Most Revd Patricia Louise (Pat) Storey, Bishop's House, Moyglare, Maynooth, Co Kildare   *Tel:* 353 1 628 9354 (Office)
email: bishop@meath.anglican.org
Web: http://meath.anglican.org

CATHEDRAL CHURCH OF ST PATRICK, Trim
Dean of Clonmacnoise Very Revd Paul David Bogle, St Patrick's Deanery, St Loman's Street, Trim, Co Meath   *Tel:* 353 46 943 6698

CATHEDRAL OF ST BRIGID, Kildare
Dean Very Revd John Joseph Marsden, The Deanery, Morristown, Newbridge, Co Kildare, Republic of Ireland   *Tel:* 353 45 438 158
email: johnmarsden@eircom.net

The Anglican Communion in Japan

(Nippon Sei Ko Kai)

Members 35,000
In 1859 the American Episcopal Church sent two missionaries to Japan, followed some years later by representatives of the Church of England and the Church in Canada. The first Anglican Synod took place in 1887. The first Japanese bishops were consecrated in 1923. The Church remained oppressed during the Second World War and assumed all church leadership after the war.

Primate Most Revd Nathaniel Makoto Uematsu (*Bishop of Hokkaido*)

Provincial Office Nippon Sei Ko Kai, 65 Yarai-cho, Shinjuku-ku, Tokyo 162–0805 (Please use this address for all correspondence)
Tel: 81 3 5228 3171
Fax: 81 3 5228 3175
email: province@nskk.org
Web: www.nskk.org

General Secretary Revd Jesse Shin-ichi Yahagi
email: general-sec.po@nskk.org

Provincial Treasurer Mr Matthias Shigeo Ozaki

Central Theological College, 1–12–31 Yoga, Setagaya-ku, Tokyo 158–0097, for clergy and lay workers

Bishop Williams Theological School, Shimotachiuri-agaru, Karasuma Dori, Kamikyo-ku, Kyoto 602–8332

CHURCH NEWSPAPERS
Sei Ko Kai Shimbun Published on the twentieth of each month in Japanese. Usually eight pages, tabloid format. Subscription through the Provincial Office. Each diocese also has its own monthly paper.

NSKK News English-language newsletter. Published quarterly. Available through the Provincial Office and also on the web page of Anglican Communion.

CHUBU
Bishop Rt Revd Peter Ichiro Shibusawa, 28–1 Meigetsu-cho, 2-chome, Showa-ku, Nagoya 466–0034 *Tel:* 81 52 858 1007
Fax: 81 52 858 1008
email: office.chubu@nskk.org
Web: www.nskk.org/chubu

HOKKAIDO
Bishop Most Revd Nathaniel Makoto Uematsu (*Archbishop of the Province*), Kita 15 jo, Nishi 5-20, Kita-Ku, Sapporo 001-0015 *Tel:* 81 11 717 8181
Fax: 81 11 736 8377
email: hokkaido@nskk.org
Web: www.nskk-hokkaido.jp

KITA KANTO
Bishop Rt Revd Zerubbabel Katsuichi Hirota, 2–172 Sakuragi-cho, Omiya-ku, Saitama-shi, 331–0852 *Tel:* 81 48 642 2680
Fax: 81 48 648 0358
email: kitakanto@nskk.org
Web: www.nskk-kitakanto.org

KOBE
Bishop Rt Revd Andrew Yutaka Nakamura, 5–11–1 Yamatedori, Chuo-ku, Kobe-shi 650–0011 *Tel:* 81 78 351 5469
Fax: 81 78 382 1095
email: aao52850@syd.odn.ne.jp
Web: www.nskk.org/kobe

KYOTO
Bishop Rt Revd Stephen Takashi Kochi, 380 Okakuencho, Shimotachiuri-agaru, Karasuma-dori, Kamikyo-ku, Kyoto 602–8011
Tel: 81 75 431 7204
Fax: 81 75 441 4238
email: nskk-kyoto@kvp.biglobe.ne.jp
Web: www.nskk.org/kyoto

KYUSHU
Bishop Rt Revd Luke Ken-ichi Muto, 2–9–22 Kusakae, Chuo-ku, Fukuoka 810–0045
Tel: 81 92 771 2050
Fax: 81 92 771 9857
email: d-kyushu@ymt.bbiq.jp
Web: http://www1.bbiq.jp/d-kyushu

OKINAWA
Bishop Rt Revd David Eisho Uehara, 3–5–5 Meada, Urasoe-shi, Okinawa 910-2102
Tel: 81 98 942 1101
Fax: 81 98 942 1102
email: office.okinawa@nskk.org
Web: http://anglican-okinawa.jp

OSAKA
Bishop Rt Revd Samuel Osamu Ohnishi, 2–1–8 Matsuzaki-cho, Abeno-ku, Osaka 545–0053
Tel: 81 6 6621 2179
Fax: 81 6 6621 3097
email: office.osaka@nskk.org
Web: www.nskk.org/osaka

TOHOKU
Bishop Rt Revd John Hiromichi Kato, 2-13-15 Kokubun-cho, Aoba-ku, Sendai 980-0803
Tel: 81 22 223 2349
Fax: 81 22 223 2387
email: fujisawa.tohoku@nskk.org
Web: www.nskk.org/tohoku

TOKYO
Bishop Rt Revd Andrew Yoshimichi Ohata, 3-6-18 Shiba Koen, Minato-ku, Tokyo 105-0011
Tel: 81 3 3433 0987
Fax: 81 3 3433 8678
email: general-sec.tko@nskk.org
Web: www.nskk.org/tokyo

YOKOHAMA
Bishop Rt Revd Laurence Yutaka Minabe, 14-57 Mitsuzawa Shimo-cho, Kanagawa-ku, Yokohama 221-0852 *Tel:* 81 45 321 4988
Fax: 81 45 321 4978
email: yokohama.kyouku@nskk.org
Web: anglican.jp/yokohama

ANGLICAN AND PORVOO COMMUNIONS

The Episcopal Church in Jerusalem and the Middle East

Members 10,000

The Church comprises the dioceses of Jerusalem, Iran, Egypt, Cyprus, and the Gulf. The Jerusalem bishopric was founded in 1841 and became an archbishopric in 1957. Reorganization in January 1976 ended the archbishopric and combined the Diocese of Jordan, Lebanon and Syria with the Jerusalem bishopric after a 19-year separation. Around the same time, the new Diocese of Cyprus and the Gulf was formed and the Diocese of Egypt was revived. The Cathedral Church of St George the Martyr in Jerusalem is known for its ministry to pilgrims. St George's College, Jerusalem is in partnership with the Anglican Communion.

THE CENTRAL SYNOD

President-Bishop Most Revd Dr Mouneer Hanna Anis (*Bishop in Egypt with North Africa and the Horn of Africa*)

Provincial Secretary Ms Georgia Katsantonis, 2 Grigori Afxentiou, Nicosia 1515, PO Box 22075, Cyprus   *email:* georgia@spidernet.com.cy

Provincial Treasurer Ven Canon William Schwartz, PO Box 3210, Dohar, Qatar
Tel: 974 4416 5726
email: epiphany@qatar.net.qa

The Jerusalem and the Middle East Church Association acts in support of the Episcopal Church in Jerusalem and the Middle East, the Central Synod and all four dioceses. *Secretary* Mrs Shirley Eason, 1 Hart House, The Hart, Farnham, Surrey GU9 7HA   *Tel:* 01252 726994
Fax: 01252 735558
*email:*secretary@jmeca.eclipse.co.uk

CYPRUS AND THE GULF
Bishop in Rt Revd Michael Augustine Owen Lewis, PO Box 22075, Nicosia 1517, Cyprus
Tel: 357 22 671220
Fax: 357 2 22 674553
email: bishop@spidernet.com.cy/
Web: www.cypgulf.org

EGYPT WITH NORTH AFRICA AND THE HORN OF AFRICA
Bishop in Most Revd Dr Mouneer Hanna Anis (*President Bishop of the Episcopal Church of Jerusalem and the Middle East*), Diocesan Office, PO Box 87, Zamalek Distribution, 11211, Cairo, Egypt   *Tel:* 20 2 738 0829
Fax: 20 2 735 8941
email: bishopmouneer@gmail.com
Web: www.dioceseofegypt.org

Suffragan Rt Revd Grant Lemarquand (*Horn of Africa*) (*same address*)

Assistant Bishop Rt Revd Bill Musk (*North Africa*) (*same address*)
email: billamusk@googlemail.com

IRAN
Bishop in Rt Revd Azad Marshall, St Thomas Center, Raiwind Road, PO Box 688, Lohore, Punjab, 54000, Pakistan   *Tel:* 92 42 542 0452
email: bishop@saintthomascenter.org

JERUSALEM
Bishop in Rt Revd Suheil Dawani, St George's Close, PO Box 1278, Jerusalem 91 019, Israel
Tel: 972 2 627 1670
Fax: 972 2 627 3847
email: bishop@j-diocese.com
Web: www.j-diocese.org

The Anglican Church of Kenya

Members 3,500,000

Mombasa saw the arrival of Anglican missionaries in 1844, with the first African ordained to the priesthood in 1885. Mass conversions occurred as early as 1910. The first Kenyan bishops were consecrated in 1955. The Church became part of the Province of East Africa, established in 1960, but by 1970 Kenya and Tanzania were divided into separate provinces.

Primate Most Revd Dr Eliud Wabukala (*Bishop of All Saints Cathedral Diocese*) PO Box 40502, 00100 Nairobi   *Tel:* 254 2 714 755
Fax: 254 2 718 442
email: archoffice@swiftkenya.com
Web: www.ackenya.org

Provincial Secretary Revd Canon Rosemary Mbogo   *Tel:* 254 20 271 4753
Fax: 254 20 271 8442
email: ackpsoffice@ackenya.org

Provincial Treasurer Dr William Ogara, Corat Africa, PO Box 42493, 00100 Nairobi
Tel: 254 2 890 165/6
Fax: 254 2 891 900/890 481

THEOLOGICAL COLLEGES
ACK Language School and Orientation School, PO Box 47429, Nairobi   *Tel:* 254 2 721893
email: c/o ackenya@insightkenya.com

ACK Guest House, PO Box 56292, Nairobi
Tel: 254 2 723200/2724780
email: ackghouse@insightkenya.com

ACK St Julian's Centre, PO Box 574, Village Market 00621 Tel: 254 66 76221
email: ackstjulians@swiftkenya.com

ACK Guest House Mombasa, PO Box 96170, Likoni, Mombasa
email: ackmsaghouse@swiftkenya.com

Carlile College for Theology & Business Studies, PO Box 72584, Nairobi Tel: 254 2 558596/253
email: Williams@insightkenya.com

St Andrews College of Theology and Development Kabare, PO Box 6, Kerugoya
Tel: 254 60 21256
email: ackstandrewskabare@swiftkenya.com

Berea Theological College, PO Box 1945, Nakuru
Tel: 254 51 51295
email: berea-tc@africaonline.co.ke

St Paul's Theological College, Kapsabet, PO Box 18, Kapsabet Tel: 254 53 2053
email: ackstpaulskapsabet@africaonline.co.ke

St Philip's Theological College Maseno, PO Box 1, Maseno Tel: 254 57 51019

Bishop Hannington Institute Mombasa, PO Box 81150, Mombasa Tel: 254 41 491396
email: ackbhanning-msa@swiftmombasa.com

Provincial TEE Programme (Trinity College), PO Box 72430, Nairobi Tel: 254 2 558655/542607
email: acktrinitycollege@swiftkenya.com

Church Commissioners for Kenya, PO Box 30422, 00100 Nairobi Tel: 254 20 717106
email: churchcom@insightkenya.com
Uzima Press, PO Box 48127, Nairobi
Tel: 254 20 220239/216836
email: uzima@nbnet.co.ke

ALL SAINTS CATHEDRAL DIOCESE
Bishop Most Revd Dr Eliud Wabukala (Archbishop of Kenya), PO Box 40502, 00100 Nairobi
Tel: 254 20 714 755
Fax: 254 20 718 442/714 750
email: archoffice@swiftkenya.com

BONDO
Bishop Rt Revd Johannes Otieno Angela, PO Box 240, 40601 Bondo Tel: 254 57 5 20415
email: ackbondo@swiftkenya.com

BUNGOMA
Bishop Rt Revd George Wafula Mechumo, PO Box 2392, 50200 Bungoma
Tel and Fax: 254 337 30481
email: ackbungoma@swiftkenya.com

BUTERE
Bishop Rt Revd Timothy Wambunya, PO Box 54, 50101 Butere Tel: 254 56 620 412
Fax: 254 56 620 038
email: ackbutere@swiftkenya.com

ELDORET
Bishop Rt Revd Chrisopher K. Ruto, PO Box 3404, 30100 Eldoret Tel: 254 53 62785
email: ackeldoret@africaonline.co.ke

EMBU
Bishop Rt Revd Henry Tiras Nyaga Kathii, PO Box 189, 60100 Embu Tel: 254 68 30614
Fax: 254 68 30468
email: ackembu@swiftkenya.com

KAJIADO
Bishop Rt Revd Gadiel Katanga Lenini, PO Box 203, 01100 Kajiado Tel: 254 301 21201/05
Fax: 254 301 21106
email: ackajiado@swiftkenya.com

KATAKWA
Bishop Rt Revd Zakayo Iteba Epusi, PO Box 68, 50244 Amagoro Tel: 254 55 54079
email: ackatakwa@swiftkenya.com

KERICHO
Bishop Rt Revd Jackson Ole Sapit, c/o PO Box 181, Kericho

KIRINYAGA
Bishop Rt Revd Joseph Kibucha, PO Box 95, 10304 Kutus Tel: 254 163 44221
Fax: 254 163 44 020
email: ackirinyaga@swiftkenya.com

KITALE
Bishop Rt Revd Stephen Kewasis Nyorsok, PO Box 4176, 30200 Kitale Tel: 254 325 31631
email: ack.ktl@africaonline.co.ke

KITUI
Bishop Rt Revd Josephat Mule, PO Box 1054, 90200 Kitui Tel: 254 141 22682
Fax: 254 141 22119
email: ackitui@swiftkenya.com

MACHAKOS
Bishop Rt Revd Joseph Mutungi, PO Box 282, 90100 Machakos Tel: 254 145 21379
Fax: 254 145 20178
email: ackmachakos@swiftkenya.com

MASENO NORTH
Bishop Rt Revd Simon M. Oketch, PO Box 416, 50100 Kakemega Tel and Fax: 254 331 30729
email: ackmnorth@swiftkenya.com

MASENO SOUTH
Bishop Rt Revd Francis Mwayi Abiero, PO Box 114, 40100 Kisumu   *Tel:* 254 35 21297
                               Fax: 254 35 21009
          email: ackmsouth@swiftkenya.com

MASENO WEST
Bishop Rt Revd Joseph Otieno Wasonga, PO Box 793, 40600 Siaya   *Tel:* 254 334 21483
                             Fax: 254 334 21483
          email: ackmwest@swiftkenya.com

MBEERE
Bishop Rt Revd Moses Masambe Nthuka, PO Box 122, 60104 Siakago   *Tel:* 254 162 21261
                             Fax: 254 162 21083
          email: ackmbeere@swiftkenya.com

MERU
Bishop Rt Revd Charles Mwendwa, PO Box 427, 60200 Meru   *Tel:* 254 164 30719
          email: ackmeru@swiftkenya.com

MOMBASA
Bishop Rt Revd Julius R. K. Kalu, PO Box 80072, 80100 Mombasa   *Tel:* 254 41 231 1105
                             Fax: 254 41 231 6361
          email: ackmsa@swiftmombasa.com

Assistant Bishop Rt Revd Lawrence Dena (*same address*)

MOUNT KENYA CENTRAL
Bishop Rt Revd Isaac Maina Ng'ang'a, PO Box 121, 10200 Murang'a   *Tel:* 254 60 30560/30559
                             Fax: 254 60 30148
          email: ackmkcentral@wananchi.com

Assistant Bishop Rt Revd Allan Waithaka (*same address*)

MOUNT KENYA SOUTH
Bishop Rt Revd Timothy Ranji, PO Box 886, 00900 Kiambu   *Tel:* 254 66 22521/22997
                             Fax: 254 66 22408
          email: ackmtksouth@swiftkenya.com

MOUNT KENYA WEST
Bishop Rt Revd Joseph M. Kagunda, PO Box 229, 10100 Nyeri   *Tel:* 254 61 203 2281
          email: ackmtkwest@wananchi.com

MUMIAS
Bishop Rt Revd Beneah Justin Okumu Salala, PO Box 213, 50102 Mumias   *Tel:* 254 333 41476
                             Fax: 254 333 41232
          email: ackmumias@swiftkenya.com

NAIROBI
Bishop Rt Revd Joel Waweru, PO Box 40502, 00100 Nairobi   *Tel:* 254 2 714 755
                              Fax: 254 2 226 259
          email: acknairobi@swiftkenya.com

NAKURU
Bishop Rt Revd Joseph Muchai, PO Box 56, 20100 Nakuru   *Tel:* 254 37 212 155/1
                              Fax: 254 37 44379
          email: acknkudioc@net2000ke.com

NAMBALE
Bishop Rt Revd Josiah M. Were, PO Box 4, 50409 Nambale   *Tel:* 254 336 24040
                             Fax: 254 336 24040
          email: acknambale@swiftkenya.com

NYAHURURU
Bishop Rt Revd Stephen Kabora, PO Box 926, 20300 Nyahururu   *Tel:* 254 365 32179
          email: nyahu_dc@africaonline.co.ke

SOUTHERN NYANZA
Bishop Rt Revd James Kenneth Ochiel, PO Box 65, 40300 Homa Bay   *Tel:* 254 385 22127
                             Fax: 254 385 22056
          email: acksnyanza@swiftkenya.com

TAITA TAVETA
Bishop Rt Revd Samson M. Mwaluda, PO Box 75, 80300 Voi   *Tel:* 254 147 30096
                             Fax: 254 147 30364
          email: acktaita@swiftmombasa.com

THIKA
Bishop Rt Revd Julius Wanyoike, PO Box 214, 01000 Thika   *Tel:* 254 151 21735/31654
                             Fax: 254 151·31544
          email: ackthika@swiftkenya.com

The Anglican Church of Korea

(Daehan Seong Gong Hoe)

Members 14,558
From the time when Bishop John Corfe arrived in Korea in 1890 until 1965, the Diocese of Korea has had English bishops. In 1993 the Archbishop of Canterbury installed the newly elected Primate and handed jurisdiction to him, making the Anglican Church of Korea a province of the Anglican Communion. There are four religious communities in the country as well as an Anglican university.

Primate Most Revd Paul Keun Sang Kim (*Bishop of Seoul*)

Provincial Offices 3 Jeong-dong, Jung-gu, Seoul
100–120   *Tel:* 82 2 738 8952
                                 Fax: 82 2 737 4210
                   email: anglicankorea@gmail.com

Secretary-General Revd Abraham Gwang Joon
Kim (*same address*)   *Tel:* 82 2 738 8952
                                 Fax: 82 2 737 4210
                      email: abgwk@hanmail.net
                          Web: www.skh.or.kr

ANGLICAN UNIVERSITY
(*Sungkonghoe University*) 1–1 Hang-dong, Guro-
gu, Seoul 152–716 (*President* Revd Augustine
Jeong Ku Lee)   *Tel:* 82 2610 4100
                                 Fax: 82 2 737 4210
                        email: jkl@skhu.ac.kr

CHURCH PAPER
Daehan Seonggonghoesinmun This fortnightly
paper of the Anglican Church of Korea is the joint
concern of all three dioceses. Tabloid format.
Printed in Korean. Contains regular liturgical
and doctrinal features as well as local, national
and international church news. *Tel:* 82 2 736 6990
                                 Fax: 82 2 738 1208

BUSAN
Bishop Rt Revd Onesimus Dongsin Park,
Anglican Diocese of Busan, 18 Daecheong-dong
2ga, Jung-gu, Busan 600–092   *Tel:* 82 51 463 5742
                              Fax: 82 51 463 5957
                   email: onesimus63@hanmail.net
                       Web: skhpusan.onmam.com

DAEJEON
Bishop Rt Revd Michael Kwon, Anglican Diocese
of Daejeon, 87–6 Seonhwa 2-dong, Jung-gu,
Daejeon 301–823   *Tel:* 82 42 256 9987
                              Fax: 82 42 255 8918
                       email: tdio@unitel.co.kr
                       Web: www.djdio.or.kr

SEOUL
Bishop Most Revd Paul Keun Sang Kim
(*Presiding Bishop of the Province*), Anglican
Diocese of Seoul, 3 Jeong-dong, Jung-gu, Seoul
100–120   *Tel:* 82 2 735 6157
                              Fax: 82 2 723 2640
                     email: paulkim7@hitel.net
                     Web: www.skhseoul.or.kr

The Church of the Province of Melanesia

Members 250,000
After 118 years of missionary association with
the Church of the Province of New Zealand,
the Church of the Province of Melanesia was
formed in 1975. The province encompasses the
Republic of Vanuatu and the Solomon Islands,
both sovereign island nations in the South
Pacific, and the French Trust Territory of New
Caledonia.

Archbishop of the Province David Vunagi
(*Bishop of Central Melanesia*)

General Secretary Mr Abraham Hauriasi (*same
address*)   *Tel:* 677 20470
                email: hauriasi_a @comphq.org.sb
                        Web: www.acom.org.sb

ANGLICAN THEOLOGICAL COLLEGE
Bishop Patteson Theological College, Kohimarama, PO Box 19, Honiara, Solomon Islands
(trains students up to degree standard) (*Principal*
Revd Atkin Zaku)   *Tel:* 677 29124
                                 Fax: 677 21098
                  email: zakuatkin@yahoo.com.au

BANKS AND TORRES
Bishop Rt Revd Alfred Patteson Worek
                                 Tel: 678 38520
                  email: pattesonworek@gmail.com

CENTRAL MELANESIA
Bishop Most Revd David Vunagi (*Archbishop of the
Province*), PO Box 19, Honiara, Solomon Islands
                                 Tel: 677 26101
                                 Fax: 677 21098
                    email: dvunagi@comphq.org.sb

CENTRAL SOLOMONS
Bishop Rt Revd Ben Seka, PO Box 52, Tulagi, CIP,
Solomon Islands   *Tel:* 677 32006
                                 Fax: 677 32113
                     email: bishopseka@gmail.com

GUADALCANAL
Bishop Rt Revd Nathan Tome, PO Box 19,
Honiara, Solomon Islands   *Tel:* 677 23337
                     email: ntome4080@gmail.com

HANUATO'O
Bishop Rt Revd Alfred Karibongi, PO Box 20,
Kira Kira, Makira Province, Solomon Islands
                                 Tel: 677 50012
                email: bishophanuatoo@solomon.com.sb

MALAITA
Bishop Rt Revd Samuel Sahu, Bishop's House,
PO Box 7, Auki Malaita Province, Solomon
Islands   *Tel:* 677 40125
                     email: sam.malaita@gmail.com

TEMOTU
Bishop Rt Revd George Angus Takeli, Bishop's
House, Lata, Santa Cruz, Temotu Province,
Solomon Islands   *Tel:* 677 53080
                   email: peace.gtakeli@gmail.com

VANUATU
Bishop Rt Revd James Marvin Ligo, Bishop's House, PO Box 238, Luganville, Santo, Republic of Vanuatu   *Tel* and *Fax:* 678 37065/36631
email: dovbishop@vanuatu.com.vu

YSABEL
Bishop Rt Revd Richard Naramana, Bishop's House, PO Box 6, Buala, Jejevo, Ysabel Province, Solomon Islands   *Tel:* 677 35124
email: episcopal@solomon.com.sb

The Anglican Church of Mexico

Members 21,000
The Mexican Episcopal Church began with the political reform in 1857, which secured freedom of religion, separating the Roman Catholic Church from the government and politics. Some priests organized a National Church and contacted the Episcopal Church in the United States, seeking the ordination of bishops for the new church. They adopted the name 'Mexican Episcopal Church'. The Mexican Church became an autonomous province of the Anglican Communion in 1995 with the name Iglesia Anglicana de Mexico.

Archbishop Rt Revd Francisco Manuel Moreno
(*Bishop of Northern Mexico*)

Provincial Secretary Revd Canon Alfonso Walls, Acatlán 102 Oriente, Col Mitras Centro, Monterrey, Nuevo Leon, 64460, Mexico
Tel: 52 81 8333 0992
Fax: 52 81 8348 7362
email: awalls@mexico-anglican.org

Provincial Treasurer C. P. Edgar Gómez-González
email: edgar7911@hotmail.com

CUERNAVACA
Bishop Rt Revd Enrique Treviño Cruz, Calle Minerva No 1, Col. Delicias, CP 62330 Cuernavaca, Morelos, México
Tel: 52 777 315 2870 (Office)
52 777 322 2559 (Home)
email: diocesisdecuernavaca@hotmail.com

MEXICO
Bishop Rt Revd Carlos Touché Porter, Ave San Jerónimo 117, Col. San Ángel, Delegación Álvaro Obregón, 01000 México, D.F.
Tel: 52 55 5616 3193
Fax: 52 55 5616 2205
email: diomex@axtel.net

NORTHERN MEXICO
Bishop Rt Revd Francisco Manuel Moreno (*Archbishop of the Province*), Acatlán 102 Ote, Col. Mitras Centro, CP 64460, Monterrey, NL
Tel: 52 81 8333 0992
Fax: 52 81 8348 7362
email: morenosith@live.com.mx

SOUTHEASTERN MEXICO
Bishop Rt Revd Benito Juárez-Martínez, Avenida de Las Américas #73, Col. Aguacatal, 91130 Xalapa, Veracruz   *Tel:* 52 228 814 6951
Fax: 52 228 814 4387
email: obispobenito.49@gmail.com

WESTERN MEXICO
Bishop Rt Revd Lino Rodríguez-Amaro, Torres Quintero #15, Col. Seattle, 45150 Zapopan, Jalisco   *Tel:* 52 33 3560 4726
Fax: 52 33 3560 4726
email: obispolino@hotmail.com

The Church of the Province of Myanmar (Burma)

Members 60,767
Anglican chaplains and missionaries worked in Burma in the early and mid-nineteenth century. The Province of Myanmar was formed in 1970, nine years after the declaration of Buddhism as the state religion and four years after all foreign missionaries were forced to leave.

Archbishop of the Province Most Revd Stephen Than Myint Oo (*Bishop of Yangon*)

Provincial Secretary Rev Canon Dr Mark Saw Mg Do, PO Box 11191, 140 Pyidaungsu Yeiktha Rd, Dagon, Yangon   *Tel:* 95 1 395279
Tel: 95 1 395350
email: markmgdoe@gmail.com

Provincial Treasurer Daw Myint Htwe Ye (*same address*)

Secretary and Treasurer, Yangon Diocesan Trust Association Daw Pin Lone Soe (*same address*)

ANGLICAN THEOLOGICAL COLLEGES
Holy Cross Theological College, 104 Inya Rd, University PO (11041), Yangon (*Principal* Samuel San Myat Shwe)

CHURCH NEWSLETTER
The province publishes a monthly 36-page *News-letter*. *Editor and Manager* Mr Soe Thein, PO Box 11191, Bishopscourt, 140 Pyidaungsu Yeiktha Rd, Dagon, Yangon

HPA-AN
Bishop Rt Revd Saw Stylo, No (4) Block, Bishop Gone, Diocesan Office, Hpa-an, Kayin State
Tel: 95 58 21696

MANDALAY
Bishop Rt Revd David Nyi Nyi Naing, Bishops-court, 22nd St, 'C' Rd (between 85–86 Rd), Mandalay
Tel: 95 2 34110

MYITKYINA
Bishop Rt Revd John Zau Li, Diocesan Office, Tha Kin Nat Pe Rd, Thida Ya, Myitkyina
Tel: 95 74 23104

SITTWE
Bishop Rt Revd Dr James Min Dein, St John's Church, Paletwa, Southern Chin State, Via Sittwe

TOUNGOO
Bishop Rt Revd Dr Saw (John) Wilme, Diocesan Office, Nat Shin Naung Rd, Toungoo
Tel: 95 54 23 519 (Office)
95 54 24216 (Home)

YANGON
Bishop Most Revd Stephen Than Myint Oo (*Archbishop of the Province*), PO Box 11191, 140 Pyidaungsu-Yeiktha Rd, Dagon, Yangon
Tel: 95 1 395279/395350 (Office)
95 1 381909 (Home)

Assistant Bishop Samuel Htan Oak, 44 Pyi Road, Dagon, Yangon
Tel: 95 1 372300

The Church of Nigeria

(Anglican Communion)

Members 17,500,000

The rebirth of Christianity began with the arrival of Christian freed slaves in Nigeria in the middle of the nineteenth century. The Church Missionary Society established an evangelistic ministry, particularly in the south. The division of the Province of West Africa in 1979 formed the Province of Nigeria and the Province of West Africa. In the 1990s, nine missionary bishops consecrated themselves to evangelism in northern Nigeria. Membership growth has dictated the need for new dioceses year by year. In 1997 the Church of Nigeria was divided into three provinces to enable more effective management. In 1999 another twelve dioceses were created, and in January 2003 the Church was re-organized into ten provinces. There are currently fourteen provinces.

Metropolitan and Primate of All Nigeria Most Revd Nicholas D. Okoh (*Archbishop of the Province of Abuja and Bishop of Abuja*)

Provincial Secretary Ven Michael Olurohunbi, Episcopal House, 24 Douala St, Wuse District, Zone 5, PO Box 212, Abuja, ADCP Garki, Abuja
Tel: 234 9 523 6950
email: mikefarohunbi08@gmail.com
Web: www.anglican-nig.org

Provincial Treasurer Chief O Adekunle, PO Box 78, Lagos
Tel: 234 1 263 3581

THEOLOGICAL COLLEGES
Ezekiel College of Theology, Ujoelen, Ekpoma, Edo State (*Principal* Vacancy)
Tel: 234 08033 859624
email: Aladeinlly2001@yahoo.com

Vining College, PMB 729, Oke Emeso, Akure, Ondo State (*Principal* Ven Dr Steve Fagbemi)
Tel: 234 034 243 031

PROVINCE OF ABA
Archbishop Most Revd Dr Ikechi Nwachukwu Nwosu (*Bishop of Umahia*)

AROCHUKWU-OHAFIA
Bishop Rt Revd Johnson Chibueze Onuoha, Bishopscourt, PO Box 193, Arochukwa, Abia State
Tel: 234 802 538 6407 (Mobile)
email: aroohafia@anglican.ng.org

IKWUANO
Bishop Rt Revd Chigozirim U. Onyegbule, Bishopscourt, PO Box 5, Ahaba-Oloko, Abia State
Tel: 234 803 085 9319 (Mobile)
email: ikwuano@anglican-nig.org

ISIALA NGWA
Bishop Rt Revd Owen Nwankujiobi Aziibuike, Bishopscourt, St George's Cathedral Compound, PNB 2033., Mbawsi, Abia State
Tel: 234 805 467 0528 (Mobile)
email: bpowenazubuike@yahoo.com

ISIALA NGWA SOUTH
Bishop Rt Revd Isaac Nwaobia, St Peter's Cathedral, PO Box 15, Owerrinta, Abia State
Tel: 234 803 711 9317 (Mobile)
email: isialangwasouth@anglican-nig.org

ISIUKWUATO
(Missionary diocese) *Bishop* Rt Revd Manasses Chijiokem Okere, Bishopscourt, PO Box 350, Ovim, Abia State *Tel:* 234 803 338 6221 (Mobile)
email: isiukwuato@anglican-nig.org

UKWA
Bishop Rt Revd Samuel Kelechi Eze, PO Box 20468, Aba, Abia State
Tel: 234 803 789 2431 (Mobile)
email: kelerem53787@yahoo.com

UMUAHIA
Bishop Most Revd Dr Ikechi Nwachukwu Nwosu (*Archbishop of the Province of Aba*), Bishopscourt, PO Box 96, Umuahia, Abia State
Tel: 234 88 221 037
email: ik_nwosu01@yahoo.com

PROVINCE OF ABUJA
Archbishop Most Revd Nicholas D. Okoh (*Metropolitan and Primate of All Nigeria and Bishop of Abuja*)

ABUJA
Bishop Most Revd Nicholas Okoh (*Metropolitan and Primate of All Nigeria and Archbishop of the Province of Abuja*), Episcopal House, 24 Douala St, Wuse District, Zone 5, PO Box 212, Abuja, ADCP Garki
Tel: 234 56 580 682
email: nickorogodo@yahoo.com

BIDA
Bishop Rt Revd Jonah Kolo, Bishop's House, St John's Mission Compound, PO Box 14, Bida
Tel: 234 66 461 694
email: bida@anglican-nig.org

GBOKO
Bishop Rt Revd Emmauel Nyitsse

GWAGWALADA
Bishop Rt Revd Tanimu Samari Aduda, Diocesan Headquarters, Secretariat Road, PO Box 287, Gwagwalada, Abuja
Tel: 234 9 882 2083
email: anggwag@skannet.com.ng

IDAH
Bishop Rt Revd Joseph N. Musa, Bishopscourt's, PO Box 25, Idah, Kogi State
email: idah@anglican-nig.org

KAFANCHAN
Bishop Rt Revd Marcus M. Dogo, PO Box 29, Kafanchan, Kaduna State
Tel: 234 61 20 634

KUBWA
Bishop Rt Revd Duke Timothy Akamisoko, Bishop's House, PO Box 67, Kubwa, Abuja FCT, Nigeria
Tel: 234 0803 451 9437 (Mobile)
email: dukesoko@yahoo.com

KWOI
Bishop Rt Revd Paul Samuel Zamani, Bishop's Residence, Cathedral Compound, Samban Gide, PO Box 173, Kwoi, Kaduna State
Tel: 234 080 651 8160 (Mobile)
email: paulzamani@yahoo.com

LAFIA
Bishop Rt Revd Miller Kangdim Maza, PO Box 560, Lafia, Nasarawa State
Tel: 234 803 973 5973 (Mobile)
email: anglicandioceseoflafia@yahoo.com

MAKURDI
Bishop Rt Revd N. Inyom, Bishopscourt, PO Box 1, Makurdi, Benue State
Tel: 234 44 533 349
email: makurdi@anglican.skannet.com.ng

OTUKPO
Bishop Rt Revd David K. Bello, Bishopscourt, PO Box 360, Otukpo, Benue State
Tel: 234 0803 309 1778
email: bishopdkbello@yahoo.com

ZAKI-BIAM
Bishop Rt Revd Benjamin A. Vanger, Bishopscourt, PO Box 600, Yam Market Road, Zaki-Biam, Benue State
Tel: 234 0803 676 0018
email: rubavia@yahoo.com

ZONKWA (Missionary diocese)
Bishop Rt Revd Jacob W. Kwashi, Bishop's Residence, PO Box 26, Zonkwa, Kaduna State 802002
Tel: 234 0803 311 0252
email: zonkwa@anglican-nig.org

PROVINCE OF BENDEL
Archbishop Most Revd Friday John Imakhai (*Bishop of Esan*)

AKOKO EDO
Bishop Rt Revd Jolly Oyckpen, Bishopscourt, PO Box 10, Igarra, Edo State
Tel: 234 803 470 5941 (Mobile)
email: venjollye@yahoo.com

ASABA
Bishop Rt Revd Justus Nnaemeka Mogekwu, Bishopscourt, PO Box 216, Cable Point, Asaba, Delta State
Tel: 234 802 819 2980 (Mobile)
email: email: justusmogekwu@yahoo.com

BENIN
Bishop Rt Revd Peter O. J. Imasuen, Bishopscourt, PO Box 82, Benin City, Edo State
Tel: 234 52 250 552

ESAN
Bishop Most Revd Friday John Imakhai (*Archbishop of Bendel Province and Bishop of Esan*), Bishopscourt, Ojoelen, PO Box 921, Ekpoma, Edo State
email:
Tel: 234 55 981 079
email: bishopimaekhai@hotmail.com

ETSAKO
Bishop Rt Revd Jacob O. B. Bada, Bishopscourt, PO Box 11, Jattu, Auchi, Edo State

IKA
Bishop Rt Revd Peter Onekpe, St John's Cathedral, PO Box 1063, Agbor, 321001 Delta State
Tel: 234 55 250-14

NDOKWA
Bishop Rt Revd David Obiosa, Bishopscourt, 151 Old Sapele Road, Obiaruka, Delta Square
Tel: 234 803 776 9464 (Mobile)
email: dfao1963@yahoo.com

OLEH
Bishop Rt Revd John Usiwoma Aruakpor, Bishopscourt, PO Box 8, Oleh, Delta State
Tel: 234 53 701 062
email: email: angoleh2000@yahoo.com

SABONGIDDA-ORA
Bishop Rt Revd John Akao, Bishopscourt, PO Box 13, Sabongidda-Ora, Edo State
Tel: 234 57 54 132
email: akaojohn@yahoo.com

SAPELE
Bishop Rt Revd Blessing Erifeta, Bishopscourt, PO Box 52, Sapele, Delta State
Tel: 234 803 662 4282 (Mobile)
email: dioceseofsapele@yahoo.com

UGHELLI
Bishop Rt Revd Cyril Odutemu, Bishopscourt, Ovurodawanre, PO Box 760, Ughelli, Delta State
Tel: 234 53 600 403
email: ughellianglican@yahoo.com

WARRI
Bishop Rt Revd Christian Esezi Ideh, Bishopscourt, 17 Mabiaku Rd, GRA, PO Box 4571, Warri, Delta State   *Tel:* 234 53 255 857
email: angdioceseofwarri@yahoo.com

WESTERN IZON (Missionary diocese)
Bishop Rt Revd Edafe Emamezi, Bishopscourt, PO Box 5, Patani, Delta State
Tel: 234 822 05 6228 (Mobile)
email: anglizon@yahoo.com

PROVINCE OF ENUGU
Archbishop Most Revd Amos Amankechinelo Madu (*Bishop of Oji River*)

ABAKALIKI
Bishop Rt Revd Monday C. Nkwoagu, All Saints' Cathedral, PO Box 112, Abakaliki, Ebonyi State
Tel: 234 43 220 762
email: abakaliki@anglican-nig.org

AFIKPO
Bishop Rt Revd A. Paul Udogu, Bishop's House, Uwana, PO Box 699, Afikpo, Ebonyi State
email: udogupaul@yahoo.com

AWGU-ANINRI
Bishop Rt Revd Emmanuel Ugwu, Bishopscourt, PO Box 305, Awgu, Enugu State
Tel: 234 803 334 9360 (Mobile)
email: afamnonye@yahoo.com

EHA-AMUFU
Bishop Rt Revd Daniel Olinya, St Andrew's Cathedral, Bishopscourt, PO box 85, Eh-Amufu, Enugu State   *Tel:* 234 803 089 2131
email: dankol@yahoo.com

IKWO
Bishop Rt Revd Kenneth Ifemene, Bishop's Residence, Agubia Ikwo, PO Box 998, Abakaliki, Ebonyi State   *Tel:* 234 805 853 4849 (Mobile)
email: bishopikwoanglican.@yahoo.com

NGBO
Bishop Rt Revd Christian I. Ebisike, Bishop's House, PO Box 93, Abakaliki, Ebonyi State
Tel: 234 806 779 4899 (Mobile)
email: vendchris@yahoo.com

NIKE
Bishop Rt Revd Evans Jonathan Ibeagha, Bishopscourt, Trans-Ekulu, PO Box 2416, Enugu, Enugu State   *Tel:* 234 803 324 1387 (Mobile)
email: pnibeagha@yahoo.com

NSUKKA
Bishop Rt Revd Aloysius Agbo, St Cypran's Compound, PO Box 516, Nsukka, Enugu State
Tel: 234 803 932 7840 (Mobile)
email: nsukka@anglican-nig.org

OJI RIVER
Bishop Most Revd Amos Amankechinelo Madu (*Archbishop of the Province of Enugu*), PO Box 123, Oji River, Enugu State
Tel: 234 803 670 4888 (Mobile)
email: amosmadu@yahoo.com

UDI
Bishop Rt Revd Chioke Augustine Aneke, Bishopscourt, PO Box 30, Udi, Enugu State
Tel: 234 806 908 9690
email: bpchijiokeudi@yahoo.com

PROVINCE OF IBADAN
Archbishop Most Revd Dr Segun Okubadejo (*Bishop of Ibadan North*)

AJAYI CROWTHER
Bishop Rt Revd Olugbenga Oduntan, Bishopscourt, Iseyin, PO Box 430, Iseyin, Oyo State
Tel: 234 803 719 8182 (Mobile)
email: ajayicrowtherdiocese@yahoo.com

ETIKI KWARA
Bishop Rt Revd Andrew Ajayi
Tel: 234 803 470 3522 (Mobile)
email: andajayi@yahoo.com

IBADAN
Bishop Most Revd Joseph O. Akinfenwa, PO Box 3075, Mapo, Ibadan   *Tel:* 234 2 810 1400
Fax: 234 2 810 1413
email: ibadan@anglican.skannet.com.ng

IBADAN NORTH
Bishop Most Revd Dr Segun Okubadejo (*Archbishop of the Province of Ibadan*), Bishopscourt, Moyede, PO Box 28961, Agodi, Ibadan
Tel: 234 2 8107 482
email: angibn@skannet.com

IBADAN SOUTH
Bishop Rt Revd Jacob Ademola Ajetunmobi, Bishopscourt, PO Box 166, St David's Compound, Kudeti, Ibadan   *Tel* and *Fax:* 234 2 231 6464
email: jacajet@skannet.com

IFE
Bishop Rt Revd Oluranti Odubogun, Bishopscourt, PO Box 312, Ife, Osun State
Tel: 234 36 2300 46 (Mobile)
email: rantiodubogun@yahoo.com

IFE EAST
Bishop Rt Revd Oluseyi Oyelade, Bishop's House, PMB 505, Modakeke-Ife, Osun State
Tel: 234 802 322 4962 (Mobile)
email: seyioyelade@yahoo.com

IJESHA NORTH EAST
Bishop Rt Revd Joseph Alaba Olusola, PO Box 40, Ipetu Ijesha, Ogun State
Tel: 234 803 942 8275 (Mobile)
email: bpafsola@gmail.com

IJESHA NORTH
Bishop Rt Revd Titus O. B. Fajemirokun, Bishopscourt, PO Box 4, Ijebu-Ijesha, Osun State
Tel: 234 802 344 0333 (Mobile)
email: titusfajemirokun@yahoo.com

ILESA
Bishop Rt Revd Olubayu Sowale, Diocesan Headquarters, Muroko Road, PO Box 237, Iesha, Osun State   *Tel:* 234 36 460 138
email: ilesha@anglican-nig.org

ILESA SOUTH WEST
Bishop Rt Revd Samuel Egbebunmi, Bishopscourt, Cathedral of the Holy Trinity, Imo Ilesa, Osun State   *Tel:* 234 803 307 1876 (Mobile)
email: segbebunmi@yahoo.com

OGBOMOSHO (Missionary diocese)
Bishop Rt Revd Dr Matthew Osunade, Bishopscourt, St David's Anglican Cathedral, PO Box 1909, Ogbomosho, Osun State
Tel: 234 805 593 6164 (Mobile)
email: maaosunade@yahoo.com

OKE-OGUN
Bishop Rt Revd Solomon Amusan, Bishopscourt, PO Box 30, Saki, Oyo State
Tel: 234 802 323 3365 (Mobile)
email: solomonamusan@yahoo.com

OKE-OSUN
Bishop Rt Revd Abraham Akinlalu, Bishopscourt, PO Box 251, Gbongan, Osun State
Tel: 234 803 771 7194
email: abrahamakinlalu@yahoo.com

OSUN
Bishop Rt Revd James Afolabi Popoola, PO Box 285, Osogbo, Osun State   *Tel:* 234 35 240 325
email: folapool@yahoo.com

OSUN NORTH EAST
Bishop Rt Revd Humphery Olumakaiye, Bishopscourt, PO Box 32, Otan Ayegbaju, Osun State
Tel: 234 803 388 2678 (Mobile)
email: bamisebi2002@yahoo.co.uk

OYO
Bishop Rt Revd Williams Oluwarotimi, Bishopscourt, PO Box 23, Oyo, Oyo State
Tel: 234 38 240 225
email: oyo@anglican-nig.org

PROVINCE OF JOS
Archbishop Most Revd Benjamin A. Kwashi (*Bishop of Jos*)

BAUCHI
Bishop Rt Revd Musa Tula, Bishop's House, 2 Hospital Rd, PO Box 2450, Bauchi
Tel: 234 77 546 460
email: bauchi@anglican-nig.org

BUKURU
Bishop Rt Revd Jwan Zhumbes, Bishopscourt, Citrus Estate, Sabon Bariki, PO Box 605, Plateau State

DAMATURU
Bishop Rt Revd Abiodun Ogunyemi, PO Box 312, Damaturu, Yobe State   *Tel:* 234 74 522 142
email: damaturu@anglican-nig.org

GOMBE
Bishop Rt Revd Henry C. Ndukuba, Cathedral Church of St Peter, PO Box 39, Gombe
Tel: 234 72 221 212
email: gombe@anglican-nig.org

JALINGO
Bishop Rt Revd Timothy Yahaya, PO Box 4, Magami, Jalingo, Taraba State
Tel and *Fax:* 234 806 594 4694
email: timothyyahaya@yahoo.com

JOS
Bishop Most Revd Benjamin A. Kwashi (*Archbishop of the Province of Jos*), Bishopscourt, PO Box 6283, Jos, 930001, Plateau State
Tel: 234 73 612 2215
email: benkwashi@gmail.com

LANGTANG

Bishop Rt Revd Stanley Fube, 87 Solomon Lar Road, PO Box 38, Langtang, Plateau State
Tel: 234 803 605 8767
email: stanleyfube@gmail.com

MAIDUGURI

Bishop Most Revd Emmanuel Kana Mani, Bishopscourt, PO Box 1693, Maiduguri, Borno State   *Tel* and *Fax:* 234 76 234 010
email: bishope-45@yahoo.com

PANKSHIN

Bishop Rt Revd Olumuyiwa Ajayi, Diocesan Secretariat, PO Box 24, Pankshin, Plateau State
Tel: 234 803 344 7318
email: olumijayi@yahoo.com

YOLA

Bishop Rt Revd Markus A. Ibrahim, PO Box 601, Jimeta-Yola, Adamawa State   *Tel:* 234 75 624 303
email: marcusibrahim2002@yahoo.com

PROVINCE OF KADUNA

Archbishop Most Revd Edmund E. Akanya (*Bishop of Kebbi*)

BARI

Bishop Rt Revd Idris Zubairu, Bishopscourt, Gidan Mato Bari, Kano State
Tel: 234 808 559 7183 (Mobile)

DUTSE

Bishop Rt Revd Yesufu Ibrahim Lumu, PO Box 67, Yadi, Dutse, Jigawa State   *Tel:* 234 64 721 379
email: dutse@anglican-nig.org

GUSAU

Bishop Rt Revd John Garba Danbinta, PO Box 64, Gusau, Zamfara State   *Tel:* 234 63 204 747
email: gusau@anglican.skannet.com

IKARA

Bishop Rt Revd Yusuf Ishaya Janfalan, Bishops-court, PO Box 23, Ikara, Kaduna State
Tel: 234 803 679 3865 (Mobile)
email: ikara@anglican-nig.org

KADUNA

Bishop Most Revd Josiah Idowu-Fearon, PO Box 72, Kaduna   *Tel:* 234 62 240 085
Fax: 234 62 244 408
email: archbishopfearonk@yahoo.com

KANO

Bishop Rt Revd Zakka Lalle Nyam, Bishopscourt, PO Box 362, Kano   *Tel* and *Fax:* 234 64 647 816
email: kano@anglican.skannet.com.ng

KATSINA

Bishop Rt Revd Jonathan Bamaiyi, Bishop's Lodge, PO Box 904, Katsina
Tel: 234 65 432 718 (Mobile)
234 803 601 5584 (Mobile)
email: bpjonathanbamaiyi@yahoo.co.uk

KEBBI

Bishop Most Revd Edmund E. Akanya (*Archbishop of the Province of Kaduna*), Bishop's Residence, PO Box 701, Birnin Kebbi, Kebbi State
Tel and *Fax:* 234 68 321 179
email: eekanya@yahoo.com

SOKOTO

Bishop Rt Revd Augustine Omole, Bishop's Lodge, 68 Shuni Road, PO Box 3489, Sokoto
Tel: 234 60 234 639
email: akin_sok@yahoo.com

WUSASA

Bishop Rt Revd Ali Buba Lamido, PO Box 28, Wusasa, Zaria, Kaduna State   *Tel:* 234 69 334 594
email: lamido2sl@aol.co.uk

ZARIA

Bishop Rt Revd Cornelius Bello, Bishopscourt, PO Box 507, Zaria, Kaduna State
Tel: 234 802 708 9555
email: cssbello@hotmail.com

PROVINCE OF KWARA

Archbishop Most Revd Michael Akinyemi (*Bishop of Igbomina*)

IGBOMINA

Bishop Most Revd Michael Akinyemi (*Archbishop of the Province of Kwara*), Bishopscourt, PO Box 102, Oro, Kwara State
Tel: 234 803 669 1940 (Mobile)
email: oluakinyemi2000@yahoo.com

IGBOMINA WEST

Bishop Rt Revd James Olaoti Akinola, Bishop's House, PO Box 32, Oke Osin, Kwara State
Tel: 234 803 392 3720 (Mobile)
email: olaotimuyiwa@yahoo.com

JEBBA

Bishop Rt Revd Sunday Adewole, Bishopscourt, PO Box 2, Jebba, Kwara State
Tel: 234 803 572 5298 (Mobile)
email: bishopadewole@yahoo.com

KWARA

Bishop Rt Revd Olusegun Adeyemi, Bishops-court, Fate Rd, PO Box 1884, Ilorin, Kwara State
Tel: 234 31 220 879
email: bishopolusegun@yahoo.com

NEW BUSSA

Bishop Rt Revd Israel Amoo, Bishopscourt, PO Box 208, New Bussa, Niger State
Tel: 234 803 677 3839 (Mobile)
email: bishopamoo@yahoo.com

OFFA

Bishop Rt Revd Akintunde Popoola, Bishop's House, 78–80 Ibrahim Rd, PO Box 21, Offa, Kwara State   *Tel:* 234 805 925 0011 (Mobile)
email: tpopoola@anglican-nig.org

OMU-ARAN
Bishop Rt Revd Philip Adeyemo, Bishop's House, PO Box 244, Omu-Aran, Kwara State
Tel: 234 806 592 4891 (Mobile)
email: rtrevadeyemo@yahoo.com

PROVINCE OF LAGOS
Archbishop Most Revd Adebayo Akinde (*Bishop of Lagos Mainland*)

AWORI
Bishop Rt Revd Johnson Akinwamide Atere, Bishopscourt, PO Box 10, Ota, Ogun State
Tel: 234 803 553 7284 (Mobile)
email: dioceseofawori@yahoo.com

BADAGRY (Missionary diocese)
Bishop Rt Revd Joseph Babatunde Adeyemi, Bishopscourt, PO Box 7, Badagry, Lagos State
Tel: 234 1 773 5546
Mobile: 234 803 306 4601
email: badagry@anglican-nig.org

EGBA
Bishop Rt Revd Emmanuel O. Adekunle, Bishopscourt, Cathedral of St Peter, PO Box 46, Ile-oluji, Ondo State
email: egba@anglican-nig.org/
mowadayo@yahoo.com

EGBA WEST
Bishop Rt Revd Samuel Ogundeji, Bishopscourt, Oke-Ata Housing Estate, PO Box 6204, Sapon, Abeokuta   *Tel:* 234 805 518 4822

IFO
Bishop Rt Revd Nathaniel Oladejo Ogundipe, Bishopscourt, Trinity House KM1, Ibogun Rd, PO Box 104, Ifo, Ogun State   *Tel:* 234 802 778 4377
email: jaodejide@yahoo.com

IJEBU
Bishop Rt Revd Ezekiel Awosoga, Bishopscourt, Ejinrin Rd, PO Box 112, Ijebu-Ode
Tel: 234 37 432 886
email: ijebu@anglican-nig.org/
bishop@ang-ijebudiocese.com

IJEBU NORTH
Bishop Rt Revd Solomon Kuponu, Bishopscourt, PO Box 6, Ijebu-Igbo, Ogun State
Tel: 234 803 457 8506 (Mobile)
email: dioceseofijebunorth@yahoo.com

LAGOS
Bishop Most Revd Ephraim Adebola Ademowo, 29 Marina, PO Box 13, Lagos   *Tel:* 234 1 263 6026
email: adebolaademowo@dioceseoflagos.org

LAGOS MAINLAND
Bishop Most Revd Adebayo Akinde (*Archbishop of the Province of Lagos*), Bishop's House, PO Box 849, Ebute, Lagos   *Tel:* 234 703 390 5522
email: adakinde@gmail.com

LAGOS WEST
Bishop Rt Revd James O. Odedeji, Vining House, 3rd Floor, Archbishop Vining Memorial Cathedral, Oba Akinjobi Road, GRA Ikeja
Tel: 234 1 493 7333
email: dioceseoflagoswest@yahoo.com

REMO
Bishop Rt Revd Michael O. Fape, Bishopscourt, Ewusi St, PO Box 522, Sagamu, Ogun State
Tel: 234 37 640 598
email: remo@anglican-nig.org

YEWA
Bishop Rt Revd Simeon O. M. Adebola, Bishopscourt, PO Box 484, Ilaro, Ogun State
Tel: 234 39 440 695

PROVINCE OF LOKOJA
Archbishop Most Revd Emmanuel Sokowamju Egbunu (*Bishop of Lokoja*)

DOKO
Bishop Rt Revd Uriah Kolo, PO Box 1513, Bida, Niger State   *Tel:* 234 803 590 6327 (Mobile)
email: uriahkolo@gmail.com

IJUMU
Bishop Rt Revd Ezekiel Ikupolati, Bishopscourt, PO Box 90, Iyara-Ijumi Kogi State
Tel: 234 807 500 8780
email: efikupolati@yahoo.com

KABBA
Bishop Rt Revd Steven Akobe, Bishopscourt, Obara Way, PO Box 62, Kabba, Kogi State
Tel: 234 58 300 633

KONTAGORA
Bishop Rt Revd Jonah Ibrahim, Bishop's House, GPA PO Box 1, Kontagora, Niger State
Tel: 234 803 625 2032 (Mobile)
email: jonahibrahim@yahoo.co.uk

KUTIGI
Bishop Rt Revd Jeremiah Ndana Kolo, Bishop's House, St John's Mission Compound, PO Box 14, Bida   *Tel:* 234 803 625 2032 (Mobile)
email: bishopkolo@yahoo.com

LOKOJA
Bishop Most Revd Emmanuel Sokowamju Egbunu (*Archbishop of the Province of Lokoja*) Bishopscourt, PO Box 11, Bethany, Lokoja, Koji State   *Tel:* 234 58 220 588
email: emmanuelegbunu@yahoo.co.uk

MINNA
Bishop Rt Revd Daniel Abu Yisa, Bishopscourt, Dutsen Kura, PO Box 2469, Minna
Tel: 234 803 588 6552 (Mobile)
email: danyisa2007@yahoo.com

OGORI-MAGONGO

Bishop Rt Revd Festus Davies, Bishop's House, St
Peter's Cathedral Ogori, Kogi State
Tel: 234 803 451 0378 (Mobile)
email: fessyoladiran@yahoo.com

OKENE

Bishop Rt Revd Emmanuel Bayo Ajulo, Bishopscourt, PO Box 43, Okene, Kogi State
Tel: 234 803 700 0016 (Mobile)
email: okenediocese@yahoo.com

PROVINCE OF THE NIGER

Archbishop Most Revd Most Revd Christian
Ogochukwo Efobi (*Bishop of Aguata*)

AGUATA

Bishop Most Revd Christian Ogochukwo Efobi
(*Archbishop of the Province of the Niger*),
Bishopscourt, PO Box 1128, Ekwulobia,
Anambra State *Tel:* 234 803 750 1077 (Mobile)
email: christianefobi@yahoo.com

AMICHI

Bishop Rt Revd Ephraim Ikeakor, Bishopscourt,
PO Box 13, Amichi, Anambra State
Tel: 234 803 317 0916 (Mobile)
email: eoikeakor@yahoo.com

AWKA

Bishop Rt Revd Alexander Ibezim, Bishopscourt,
PO Box 130, Awka, Anambra State
Tel: 234 48 550 058
email: chioma1560@aol.com

ENUGU

Bishop Rt Revd Dr Emmanuel O. Chukwuma,
Bishop's House, PO Box 418, Enugu, Enugu
State *Tel:* 234 42 453 804
email: enugu@anglican-nig.org

IHIALA

Bishop Rt Revd Ralph Okafor, Bishopscourt, St
Silas Cathedral, PO Box 11, Ihiala, Anambra
State *Tel:* 234 803 711 2408 (Mobile)
email: raphoka@yahoo.com

MBAMILI

Bishop Rt Revd Henry Okeke, Bishopscourt, PO
Box 2653, Onitsha, Anambra State
Tel: 234 803 644 9780 (Mobile)
email: bishopokeke@yahoo.com

NIGER WEST

Bishop Rt Revd Anthony O. Nkwoka
Tel: 234 803 384 3339 (Mobile)
email: ankwoka@yahoo.com

NNEWI

Bishop Rt Revd Dr Godwin Izundu Nmezinwa
Okpala, Bishopscourt, PO Box 2630, Uruagu-
Nnewi, Anambra State
Tel: 234 803 348 5714 (Mobile)
email: okpalagodwin@yahoo.co.uk

OGBARU

Bishop Rt Revd Samuel Ezeofor, Bishopscourt,
PO Box 46, Atani, Anambra State
email: ezechukwunyere@yahoo.com

ON THE NIGER

Bishop Rt Revd Owen Chidozie Nwokolo,
Bishopscourt, Ozala Rd, Onitsha, Anambra State
Tel: 234 803 726 0548 (Mobile)
email: owenelsie@yahoo.com

PROVINCE OF NIGER DELTA

Archbishop Most Revd Ignatius C. O. Kattey
(*Bishop of Niger Delta North*)

ABA

Bishop Rt Revd Christian Ugwuzor, Bishopscourt, 70–72 St Michael's Rd, PO Box 212, Aba,
Abia State *Tel:* 234 82 227 666
email: aba@anglican-nig.org

ABA NGWA NORTH

Bishop Rt Revd Nathan C. Kanu, Bishopscourt,
All Saints Cathedral, Abayi-Umuocham 1610165,
Owerri Road, PO Box 43, Aba, Abia State
Tel: 234 803 822 4623 (Mobile)
email: odinathnfe@sbcglobal.net

AHOADA

Bishop Rt Revd Clement Nathan Ekpeye,
Bishopscourt, St Paul's Cathedral, PO Box 4,
Ahoada East L.G.A., Rivers State
Tel: 234 803 542 2847 (Mobile)
email: ahoada@anglican-nig.org

CALABAR

Bishop Rt Revd Tunde Adeleye, Bishopscourt,
PO Box 74, Calabar, Cross River State
Tel: 234 87 232 812
email: calabar@anglican-nig.org

ENUGU NORTH

Bishop Rt Revd Sosthenes Eze, Bishopscourt, St
Mary's Cathedral, Ngwo-Enugu
Tel: 234 803 870 9362 (Mobile)
email: bishopsieze@yahoo.com

ETCHE

Bishop Rt Revd Precious Nwala, Bishopscourt,
PO Box 89, Okehi, Etche Rivers State
Tel: 234 807 525 2842 (Mobile)
email: etchediocese@yahoo.com/
precious_model5@yahoo.com

EVO

Bishop Rt Revd Innocent Ordu, Bishopscourt, PO
Box 3576, Port Harcourt, Rivers State
Tel: 234 803 715 2706
email: innocent-ordu@yahoo.com

IKWERE

Bishop Rt Revd Blessing Enyindah, Bishopscourt,
St Peter's Cathedral, PO Box 14229, Port Harcourt,
Rivers State *Tel:* 234 802 321 2824 (Mobile)
email: blessingenyindah@yahoo.com

NIGER DELTA
Bishop Rt Revd Ralph Ebirien, PO Box 115, Port Harcourt, Rivers State
Tel: 234 708 427 9095 (Mobile)
email: revpalph_ebirien@yahoo.com

NIGER DELTA NORTH
Bishop Most Revd Ignatius C. O. Kattey (*Archbishop of the Province of Niger Delta*), PO Box 53, Diobu, Port Harcourt, Rivers State
Tel: 234 803 309 4331 (Mobile)
email: bishopicokattey@yahoo.com

NIGER DELTA WEST
Bishop Rt Revd Emmanuel O. Oko-Jaja, Bishops-court, PO Box 10, Yenagoa, Bayelsa State Tel: 234 803 870 2099 (Mobile)
email: niger-delta-west@anglican-nig.org

NORTHERN IZON
Bishop Rt Revd Anga Fred Nyanabo, Bishops-court, PO Box 705, Yenagoa, Bayelsa State
Tel: 234 803 316 0938 (Mobile)
email: fred_nyanabo@yahoo.co.uk

OGBIA
Bishop Rt Revd James Oruwori, Bishop's House, 10 Queens Street, Ogbia town, Bayelsea State
Tel: 234 803 73 4746
email: jaoruwori@yahoo.com

OGONI (Missionary diocese)
Bishop Rt Revd Solomon S. Gbercgbara, Bishopscourt, PO Box 73, Bori-Ogoni, Rivers State
Tel: 234 803 339 2545
email: ogoni@anglican-nig.org

OKRIKA
Bishop Rt Revd Tubokosemie Abere, Bishopscourt, PO Box 11, Okrika, Rivers State
Tel: 234 803 312 5226 (Mobile)
email: dioceseofokrika@yahoo.com

UYO
Bishop Rt Revd Asuko Antai, Bishopscourt, PO Box 70, Uyo, Akwa Ibom State
Tel: 234 802 916 2305
email: uyo@anglican-nig.org

PROVINCE OF ONDO
Archbishop Most Revd George L. Lasebikan (*Bishop of Ondo*)

AKOKO
Bishop Rt Revd Gabriel Akinbiyi, PO Box 572, Ikare-Akoko, Ondo State   Tel: 31 801 011
email: bishopgabrielakinbiyi@yahoo.com

AKURE
Bishop Rt Revd Simeon O. Borokini, Bishopscourt, PO Box 1622, Akure, Ondo State
Tel and *Fax:* 234 241 572

DIOCESE ON THE COAST (FORMERLY IKALE-ILAJE)
Bishop Rt Revd Joshua Ogunele, Bishopscourt, Ikoya Road, PMB 3, Ilutitun-Osooro, Ondo State
Tel: 234 803 467 1879 (Mobile)
email: joshuaonthecoast@yahoo.ca

EKITI
Bishop Most Revd Christopher Tayo Omotunde, Bishopscourt, PO Box 12, Okesa St, Ado-Ekiti, Ekiti State   Tel: 234 30 250 305
email: adedayoekiti@yahoo.com

EKITI-OKE
Bishop Rt Revd Isaac O. Olubowale, Bishopscourt, PO Box 207, Usi-Ekiti, Ekiti State
Tel: 234 803 600 9582 (Mobile)
email: ekitioke@anglican-nig.org

EKITI WEST
Bishop Rt Revd Samuel O. Oke, Bishop's Residence, 6 Ifaki St, PO Box 477, Ijero-Ekiti
Tel: 234 30 850 314
email: ekitiwest@anglican-nig.org

IDOANI
Bishop Rt Revd Ezekiel Dahunsi, Bishopscourt, PO Box 100 Idoani, Ondo State
Tel: 234 803 384 4029 (Mobile)
email: bolaezek@yahoo.com

ILAJE
Bishop Rt Revd Fredrick Olugbemi, Bishopscourt, PO Box 146, Igbokoda, Ondo State
Tel: 234 806 624 8662 (Mobile)
email: forogbemi@yahoo.com

ILE-OLUJI
Bishop Rt Revd Samson Adekunle, Bishopscourt, Cathedral of St Peter, PO Box 46, Ile-Oluji, Ondo State   Tel: 234 803 454 1236 (Mobile)
email: adkulesamson86@yahoo.co.uk

IRELE-ESEODO
Bishop Rt Revd Felix O. Akinbuluma, Bishops-court, Sabomi Road, Ode Irele, Ondo State
Tel: 234 805 671 2653
email: felixgoke@yahoo.com

ONDO
Bishop Most Revd George L. Lasebikan (*Archbishop of the Province of Ondo*), Bishops-court, College Rd, PO Box 265, Ondo
Tel: 234 34 610 718
email: ondoanglican@yahoo.co.uk

OWO
Bishop Rt Revd James Adedayo Oladunjoye, Bishopscourt, PO Box 472, Owo, Ondo State
Tel: 234 51 241 463
email: bishopoladunjoye@yahoo.co.uk

PROVINCE OF OWERRI

Archbishop Most Revd Caleb A. Maduoma (*Bishop of Ideato*)

EGBU
Bishop Rt Revd Geoffrey E. Okorafor, All Saints' Cathedral, PO Box 1967, Owerri, Imo State
Tel: 234 83 231 797
email: egbu@anglican-nig.org

IDEATO
Bishop Most Revd Caleb A. Maduoma (*Archbishop of the Province of Owerri*), Bishops-court, PO Box 2, Ndizuogu, Imo State
Tel: 234 803 745 4503 (Mobile)
email: bpomacal@hotmail.com

IKEDURU
Bishop Rt Revd Emmanuel C. Maduwike, Bishop's House, PO Box 56, Atta, Imo State
Tel: 234 803 704 4686 (Mobile)
email: emmamaduwike@yahoo.com

MBAISE
Bishop Rt Chamberlain Chinedu Ogunedo, Bishopscourt, PO Box 10, Ife, Ezinihitte Mbaise, Imo State
Tel: 234 803 336 9836 (Mobile)
email: ogunedochi@yahoo.com

OHAJI-EGBEMA
Bishop Rt Revd Chidi Collins Oparaojiaku, Bishop's House, PO box 8026, New Owerri, Imo State
Tel: 234 803 312 1063 (Mobile)
email: chidioparachiaku@yahoo.com

OKIGWE
Bishop Rt Revd Edward Osuegbu, Bishopscourt, PO Box 156, Okigwe, Imo State
Tel: 234 803 724 6374 (Mobile)
email: edchuc@justice.com

OKIGWE NORTH
Bishop Rt Revd Godson Udochukwu Ukanwa, PO Box 127, Anara, Imo State
Tel: 234 803 672 4314 (Mobile)
email: venukanwa@yahoo.com

OKIGWE SOUTH
Bishop Rt Revd David Onuoha, Bishopscourt, Ezeoke Nsu, PO Box 235, Nsu, Ehime Mbano LGA, Imo State *email:* okisouth@yahoo.com

ON THE LAKE
Bishop Rt Revd Chijioke Oti, Bishopscourt, PO Box 36, Oguta, Imo State, Nigeria
Tel: 234 802 788 8738 (Mobile)
email: chijiokeoti72@yahoo.com

ORLU
Bishop Most Revd Bennett C. I. Okoro (*Archbishop of the Province of Owerri*), Bishopscourt, PO Box 260, Nkwerre, Imo State *Tel:* 234 82 440 538
email: anglicannaorlu@yahoo.com

ORU
Bishop Rt Revd Geoffrey Chukwunenye, PO Box 91, Mgbidi, Imo State
Tel: 234 803 308 1270 (Mobile)
email: geoinlagos@yahoo.com

OWERRI
Bishop Rt Revd Dr Cyril C. Chukwunonyerem Okorocha, Bishop's Bourne, PMB 1063, Owerri, Imo State *Tel:* 234 83 230 784
email: owerri_anglican@yahoo.com

The Anglican Church of Papua New Guinea

Members 200,000
The Anglican Church functions mostly in rural areas where mountains and rainforest provide natural barriers to travel. Some 60 per cent of the funding is raised internally; most of the balance comes from grants from Australia, New Zealand, Canada and the UK-based Papua New Guinea Church Partnership. The Church had played an active role in the development of this country, and has a long history of more than a century (120 years, from 1891 to 2011) of providing service throughout its five established Dioceses in PNG (Dogura, Popondota,Port Moresby, Aipo Rongo and New Guinea Islands). The Church's work has expanded over the years into establishing and operating Social Welfare, Education, Health and Economic Development programmes for the most disadvantaged and rural sectors of our communities. The Anglican Church will continue to do this in the years ahead.

Archbishop Most Revd Clyde Igara (*Primate of ACPNG*) *email:* cludemigara@gmail.com

General Secretary Mr Samson Chicki, PO Box 673, Lae, Morobe Province 411 *Tel:* 675 472 4111
Fax: 675 472 1852
email: schicki@acpng.org.pg

Provincial Cellenger Justice Bernard Sakora, Chamber of Justice, Supreme and National Courts of Justice, PO Box 7018, Boroko, NCD, PNG *Tel:* 675 324 5734

Provincial Registrar Mr Goodwin Poole, PO Box 389, Port Moresby, Level 5 Defence House, Crn Hunter St & Champion Pde, National Capital District *Tel:* 675 308 8300
Digicel: 675 720 88300
Fax: 675 308 8399
Web: www.obriens.com.pg

THEOLOGICAL COLLEGE
Newton Theological College, PO Box 162, Popondetta, Oro Province (*Principal* Revd Peter Moi) *Tel (Digicel):* 675 713 95018
email: fr.petermoi@gmail.com

CHURCH PAPER
Family Magazine. Published three times a year. *Editors* Archbishop Most Revd Joseph Kopapa, PO Box 673,, Lae, Morobe Province 411
Tel: 675 472 4111
Fax: 675 472 1852
email: joekopapa@gmail.com

AIPO RONGO
Bishop Rt Revd Nathan Ingen, PO Box 893, Mt Hagen, Western Highlands Province
Tel: 675 542 1151
Mobile: 7696 6345 / 7208 6758
Fax: 675 542 1181
email: bishopnathan2@gmail.com

DOGURA
Bishop Rt Revd Tennyson Bogar, PO Box 19, Dogura via Alotau, Milne Bay Province
Tel: 675 641 1129 / 641 0461

NEW GUINEA ISLANDS
Bishop Rt Revd Allan Migi, Bishop's House, PO Box 806, Kimbe, West New Britain Province
Tel and *Fax:* 675 983 5120
email: AllanRirmeMigi@gmail.com

POPONDOTA
Bishop Rt Revd Lindsley Ihove, Bishop's House, PO Box 26, Popondetta, Oro Province
Tel: 675 629 7194
Fax: 675 629 7476
email: bplindsleyihove@gmail.com

PORT MORESBY
Bishop Vacancy, PO Box 6491, Boroko, NCD
Tel: 675 323 2489
Fax: 675 323 2493
email: acpngpom@global.net.pg/
psramsden.pomanglican@gmail.com
Web: www.portmoresby.anglican.org

The Episcopal Church in the Philippines

Members 170,000
The Philippines is the only Christian nation in Asia. Its 90,000,000 or so population is composed of 75 per cent Roman Catholics while the other 25 per cent are Muslims and other Christian bodies including the Episcopal Church in the Philippines (ECP), which now has seven dioceses. The ECP was first established by the Protestant Episcopal Church in the USA (PECUSA) in 1901 and became an autonomous province of the Anglican Communion in 1991. It continues to maintain a close relationship with PECUSA. Its ministry after gaining autonomy is focused not only in the nurture of the faith of the believers and doing evangelism. It is actively involved in community development projects to help eradicate poverty which is hounding the lives of millions of Filipinos today.

National Office The ECP Mission Center, 275 E Rodriguez Sr Ave, 1102 Quezon City

(*Postal address*) PO Box 10321, Broadway Centrum, 1112 Quezon City *Tel:* 63 2 722 8481
Fax: 63 2 721 1923
email: ecpnational@yahoo.com.ph

Prime Bishop Most Revd Renato M. Abibico (*same address* *email:* reneabibico@yahoo.com

Provincial Secretary Atty. Floyd P. Lalwet (*same address*) *email:* flaw997@gmail.com

Corporate Secretary Ms Laura S. Ocampo (*same address*) *email:* lbso2@yahoo.com

Administrative Assistant Vacancy

National Finance Officer Ms Bridget T. Lacdao
email: bbalitog@yahoo.com

CENTRAL PHILIPPINES
Bishop Rt Revd Dixie C. Taclobao, 281 E. Rodriguez Sr Ave, 1102 Quezon City
Tel: 63 2 412 8561
Fax: 63 2 724 2143
email: taclobaodixie@yahoo.com.ph

DAVAO
Bishop Rt Revd Jonathan L. Casimina, Km. 3 McArthur Highway, Matina, Davao City 8000
Tel: 63 82 299 1511
Fax: 63 82 296 9629
email: episcopaldioceseofdavao@yahoo.com

NORTH CENTRAL PHILIPPINES
Bishop Rt Revd Joel A. Pachao, 358 Magsaysay Ave, 2600 Baguio City *Tel:* 63 74 443 7705
email: bpjoelpachao@yahoo.com

NORTHERN LUZON
Bishop Vacancy, Bulanao, 3800 Tabuk City, Kalinga

NORTHERN PHILIPPINES
Bishop Rt Revd Brent Harry W. Alawas, 2616 Bontoc, Mountain Province
Tel and *Fax:* 63 74 602 1026
email: ednpbrent@yahoo.com

SANTIAGO
Bishop Rt Revd Alexander A. Wandag, Maharlika Highway, 3311 Divisoria Santiago City, Isabela
Tel: 63 78 662 1561
email: alexanderwandag@rocketmail.com

SOUTHERN PHILIPPINES
Bishop Rt Revd Danilo Labacanacruz Bustamante, 186 Sinsuat Ave, 9600 Cotabato City
Tel: 63 64 421 2960
Fax: 63 64 421 1703
email: edsp_ecp@yahoo.com

The Church of the Province of Rwanda

Members 1,200,000
In just over 10,170 square miles there are more than one million Anglicans among a fast-growing population, currently 9.5 million. The former Rwanda Mission (now CMS) established its first station at Gahini in 1925 and grew through the revival of the 1930s and 1940s, with the first Rwandan bishop appointed in 1965. Nine dioceses have up to 306 parishes and 379 clergy, organized in 96 deaconries. Like all strata of Rwandan society, the Church suffered, on many levels, through the genocide, and it is a major priority of the Church to replace clergy through training. The Church has a role as a healing ministry to the many traumatized people in Rwanda and to reconciliation, restoration, and rehabilitation. The Church has also been involved in rural development, medical work, vocational training, and education.

Archbishop Most Revd Dr Onesphore Rwaje (*Bishop of Gasabo*)

Provincial Secretary Revd Francis Karemera, BP 2487, Kigali
Tel: 250 514 160
Fax: 250 516 162
email: egapeer@yahoo.com

Provincial Treasurer Vacancy (*same address*)

BUTARE
Bishop Rt Revd Nathan Gasatura, BP 225, Butare
Tel and *Fax:* 250 530 504
email: nathangasatura@gmail.com

BYUMBA
Bishop Rt Revd Emmanuel Ngendahayo, BP 17, Byumba
Tel and *Fax:* 250 64 242
email: engendahayo@gmail.com

CYANGUGU
Bishop Rt Revd Nathan Amooti Rusengo, BP 52, Cyangugu
Tel and *Fax:* 250 53 7878
email: nathanamooti@gmail.com

GAHINI
Bishop Rt Revd Alexis Bilindabagabo, BP 22, Kigali
Tel and *Fax:* 250 567 422
email: abilindabagabo@gmail.com

GASABO
Bishop Most Revd Dr Onesphore Rwaje (*Archbishop of the Province*),
email: onesphorerwaje@yahoo.fr

KIBUNGO
Bishop Rt Revd Emmanuel Ntazinda, EER Kibungo Diocese, BP 719, Kibungo
Tel and *Fax:* 250 566 194
email: emmanuelntazinda@ymail.com

KIGALI
Bishop Rt Revd Louis A. Muvunyi (*Archbishop of the Province*), BP 61, Kigali
Tel and *Fax:* 250 573 213
email: louismuvunyi@hotmail.com

KIGEME
Bishop Rt Revd Augustin Mvunabandi, BP 67, Gikongoro
Tel: 250 535 086 (Office)
250 535 088 (Secretary)
250 535 087 (Home)
email: dkigeme@rwanda1.com

KIVU
Bishop Rt Revd Augustin Ahimana, BP 166 Gisenyi
Tel: 250 788 350 119
email: aamurekezi@gmail.com

SHYIRA
Bishop Rt Revd Laurent Mbanda, BP 26, Ruhengeri
Tel and *Fax:* 250 546 449
email: mbandalaurent@gmail.com

SHYOGWE
Bishop Rt Revd Jered Kalimba, BP 27, Gitarama
Tel: 250 562 460
Tel and *Fax:* 250 562 469
email: dshyogwe@yahoo.com

The Scottish Episcopal Church

Members 34,119
The roots of Scottish Christianity go back to St Ninian in the fourth century and St Columba in the sixth. After the Reformation, the Episcopal Church was the established Church of Scotland. It was however replaced as the established Church by the Presbyterians at the Revolution in 1689. Penal statutes in force from 1746 to 1792 weakened the Church, although many congregations remained and the bishops maintained

continuity. In 1784 in Aberdeen, the Scottish Church initiated the world-wide expansion of the Anglican Communion with the consecration of the first bishop of the American Church. There was rapid growth in the nineteenth century influenced by the Tractarian movement.

Primus Most Revd David Chillingworth
(*Bishop of St Andrews, Dunkeld & Dunblane*)
email: bishop@standrews.anglican.org
Web: www.standrews.anglican.org

Secretary General Mr John Stuart, 21 Grosvenor Crescent, Edinburgh EH12 5EE
Tel: 0131 225 6357
Fax: 0131 346 7247
email: secgen@scotland.anglican.org
Web: www.scotland.anglican.org

MINISTERIAL TRAINING
The Scottish Episcopal Institute, 21 Grosvenor Crescent, Edinburgh EH12 5EE
Tel: 0131 225 6357
Fax: 0131 346 7247
email: institute@scotland.anglican.org

CHURCH MAGAZINE
Inspires, twenty-eight pages, four issues per year. Magazine format. Produced in-house – contact: *Inspires*, 21 Grosvenor Crescent, Edinburgh, EH12 5EE   *email:* inspires@scotland.anglican.org

ABERDEEN AND ORKNEY
Bishop Rt Revd Dr Robert Gillies, Diocesan Office, St Clement's Church House, Mastrick Drive, Aberdeen, AB16 6UF   *Tel:* 01224 662247
email: office@aberdeen.anglican.org
Web: www.aberdeen.anglican.org

Dean Very Revd Dr A. E. Nimmo, St Margaret's Clergy House, Gallowgate, Aberdeen AB25 JEA
Tel: 01224 644969
email: alexander306@btinternet.com

ST ANDREW'S CATHEDRAL, Aberdeen
Provost Very Revd Richard Kilgour, St Andrew's Cathedral, 28 King Street, Aberdeen AB24 5AX
Tel: 01224 640119
email: provost@aberdeen.anglican.org

ARGYLL AND THE ISLES
Bishop Rt Revd Kevin Pearson, St Moluag's Diocesan Centre, Croft Avenue, Oban, Argyll, PA34 5JJ   *Tel:* 01631 570 870
Fax: 01631 570411
email: office@argyll.anglican.org
Web: www.argyllandtheisles.org.uk

Dean Very Revd A. Swift, Holy Trinity Rectory, 55 Kilbride Road, Dunoon PA23 7LN
email: dean@argyll.anglican.org

ST JOHN THE DIVINE CATHEDRAL, Oban
(The Cathedral of Argyll)
Provost Very Revd Nicola McNelly, The Rectory, Ardconnel Terrace, Oban, PA34 5DJ
Tel: 01631 562323
email: ProvostOban@argyll.anglican.org

COLLEGIATE CHURCH OF THE HOLY SPIRIT, Millport, Cumbrae
(The Cathedral of The Isles)
Warden David Todd   *Tel:* 01475 530353
Fax: 01475 531291
email: Cathedral_Cumbrae@btconnect.com
Web: www.island-retreats.org

BRECHIN
Bishop Rt Revd Dr Nigel Peyton, Diocesan Office. Unit 14 Prospect III, Technology Park, Gemini Crescent, Dundee DD2 1SW
Tel: 01382 562244
email: office@brechin.anglican.org
Web: www.thedioceseofbrechin.org

Dean Very Revd Dr F. Bridger, 3 Wyvis Place, Broughty Ferry DD5 3SX   *Tel:* 01382 562244
email: office@brechin.anglican.org

ST PAUL'S CATHEDRAL, Dundee
Provost Very Revd Jeremy Auld, St Paul's Cathedral, Castle Hill, 1 High Street, Dundee DD1 1TD   *Tel:* 01382 224486
email: provost@saintpaulscathedral.net

EDINBURGH
Bishop Rt Revd Dr John Armes, Diocesan Centre, 21a Grosvenor Crescent, Edinburgh, EH12 5EL
Tel: 0131 538 7044
Fax: 0131 538 7088
email: office@edinburgh.anglican.org
Web: www.edinburgh.anglican.org

Dean Very Revd Susan Macdonald, Diocesan Centre, 21a Grsovenor Crescent, Edinburgh EH12 5EL   *Tel:* 0131 538 7033
email: Dean@dioceseofedinburgh.org

ST MARY'S CATHEDRAL, Edinburgh
Provost Very Revd Dr Graham John Thomson Forbes, Cathedral Office, Palmerston Place, Edinburgh EH12 5AW   *Tel:* 0131 225 6293
Fax: 0131 225 3181
email: provost@cathedral.net

GLASGOW AND GALLOWAY
Bishop Rt Revd Dr Gregor Duncan, Diocesan Centre, 5 St Vincent Place, Glasgow G1 2DH
Tel: 0141 221 6911
email: bishop@glasgow.anglican.org
Web: www.glasgow.anglican.org

Dean Very Revd Ian Barcroft, The Rectory, 4c Auchingramont Road, Hamilton ML3 6JT
Tel: 01698 429895
email: dean@glasgow.anglican.org

ST MARY THE VIRGIN CATHEDRAL, Glasgow
Provost Very Revd Kelvin Holdsworth, St Mary's Cathedral, 300 Great Western Rd, Glasgow G4 9JB
Tel: 0141 339 6691
Fax: 0141 334 5669
email: provost@thecathedral.org.uk

MORAY, ROSS AND CAITHNESS
Bishop Rt Revd Mark Strange, Bishop's House, St Duthac's Centre, Arpafeelie, North Kessock IV1 3XD
Tel: 01463 811333
email: bishop@moray.anglican.org
Web: www.moray.anglican.org

Dean Very Revd Alison Simpson, The New Rectory, 3 Queen Street, Nairn IV12 4AA
Tel: 01667 452458
email: dean@moray.anglican.org

ST ANDREW'S CATHEDRAL, Inverness
Provost Very Revd Alex Gordon, The Rectory, 15 Ardross Street, Inverness, IV3 5NS
Tel: 01463 233 535
email: canonalexgordon@btconnect.com

ST ANDREWS, DUNKELD AND DUNBLANE
Bishop Most Revd David Chillingworth (*Primus*), Diocesan Centre, 28a Balhousie Street, Perth, PH1 5HJ
Tel: 01738 580426
Fax: 01738 443174
email: bishop@standrews.anglican.org
Web: www.standrews.anglican.org

Dean Very Revd Kenneth Rathband, 10 Rosemount Park, Blairgowrie PH10 6TZ
Tel: 01250 874 583
email: abcsaints@btinternet.com

ST NINIAN'S CATHEDRAL, Perth
Provost Very Revd Hunter Farquharson, St Ninian's Cathedral, North Methven Street, Perth PH1 5PP
Tel: 01738 632 053
email: provost@perthcathedral.co.uk
Web: http://www.perthcathedral.co.uk/

The Anglican Church of South America
(Iglesia Anglicana de **Sudamérica**)

Members 22,490
British immigrants brought Anglicanism to South America in the nineteenth century. The South American Missionary Society continues to work effectively among indigenous peoples and today actively supports diocesan initiatives. In 1974 the Archbishop of Canterbury gave over his metropolitical authority for the dioceses of the Southern Cone, and in 1981 the new province was formed. It includes Argentina, Bolivia, Chile, Northern Argentina, Paraguay, Peru and Uruguay.

Presiding Bishop Most Revd Héctor Zavala Muñoz (*Bishop of Chile*)

Provincial Secretary Revd Daniel R. Genovesi, Cro. Gral. Belgrano 946, 1686, Hurlingham, Argentina.
Tel: 5411 4452 7555
email: danielgenovesi@gmail.com

Provincial Treasurer Miss Elisa Aguilar Rojas, Victoria Subercaseux 41 oficina 301, Santiago, Chile
Tel: 56 02 2638 3009
email: eaguilar@iach.cl

Personal Assistant to the Bishop, Mrs. Pamela Santibañez, Victoria Subercaseaux 41 oficina 301, Santiago, Chile
Tel: 56 02 2638 3009
email: psantibanez@iach.cl

THEOLOGICAL EDUCATION
Planned and carried out by a Theological Education Commission which selects candidates, applies grants and sets courses of study, some of which are led by clergy of the diocese. Some students follow courses of theological training 'by extension' and others attend ecumenical seminaries.

ARGENTINA
Bishop Most Revd Gregory James Venables, Rioja 2995, 1636, Olivos, Argentina
Tel: 54 11 4342 4618
Fax: 54 11 4331 0234
email: bpgreg@fibertel.com.ar

BOLIVIA
Bishop Rt Revd Raphael Samuel
Tel and *Fax:* 591 4 440 1168
email: raphaelsamuel@gmail.com
Web: www.bolivia.anglican.org

CHILE
Bishop Rt Revd Héctor Zavala Muñoz (*Presiding Bishop of the Province*), Casilla 50675, Correo Central, Santiago, Chile
Tel: 56 2 638 3009
Fax: 56 2 639 4581
email: tzavala@iach.cl
Web: www.iach.cl

Assistant Bishop Rt Revd Abelino Manuel Apeleo, Casilla de Correo 26-D, Temuco, Chile
Tel and *Fax:* 56 45 910 484
email: aapeleo@iach.cl

NORTHERN ARGENTINA
Bishop Rt Revd Nicholas Drayson, Abraham Cornejo 120, 4400 Salta, Argentina
Tel: 54 3711 420100
email: nicobispo@gmail.com

PARAGUAY

Bishop Rt Revd Peter Bartlett, Casilla de Correo 1124, Asunción, Paraguay   Tel: 595 21 200 933
Fax: 595 21 214 328
email: peterparaguay@gmail.com

Bishop Rt Revd John Alexander Ellison, Iglesia Anglicana de Paraguay, Casilla de Correo 1124, Asunción, Paraguay   Fax: 595 21 214 328
email: jellison@pla.net.py
Web: www.paraguay.anglican.org

PERU

Bishop Rt Revd Harold William Godfrey, Calle Alcala 336, Urb. La Castellana, Santiago de Surco, Lima 33, Peru   Tel: 51 1 422 9160
Fax: 51 1 440 8540
email: diocesisperu@anglicanperu.org/
wgodfrey@amauta.rcp.net.pe
Web: www.peru.anglican.org

Suffragan Bishop Rt Revd Michael Chapman
email: thwmac@juno.com

URUGUAY

Bishop Rt Revd Michele Pollesel, 21 de Setiembre 2875, apto. 903, Montevideo, Uruguay 11300
Tel: 598 2711 7343
email: mfpollesel@rogers.com
Web: https://www.facebook.com/
Iglesia.Anglicana.del.Uruguay

Suffragan Bishop Rt Revd Gilberto Obdulio Porcal Martinez, Reconquista 522, CC 6108, 11000 Montevideo, Uruguay   Tel: 598 2 915 9627
Fax: 598 2 916 2519
email: anglican@netgate.com.uy

The Province of the Anglican Church in South East Asia

Members 224,200
The Anglican Church in South East Asia was originally under the jurisdiction of the Bishop of Calcutta. The first chaplaincy was formed in West Malaysia in 1805; the first bishop was consecrated in 1855. The Diocese of Labuan, Sarawak and Singapore was formed in 1881. A separate Diocese of Singapore was formed in 1909, and in 1962 the Diocese of Jesselton, later renamed Sabah, and the Diocese of Kuching were formed from the former Diocese of Borneo. In 1970 the Diocese of West Malaysia was formed from what had been the Diocese of Malaya and Singapore. Until the inauguration of the Church of the Province of South East Asia, the four dioceses (Kuching, Sabah, Singapore, and West Malaysia) were under the jurisdiction of the Archbishop of Canterbury. Although the province exists under certain social constraints, the Church has experienced much spiritual renewal and has sent out its own mission partners to various parts of the world, especially neighbouring Indonesia, Cambodia, Nepal, Laos, Vietnam and Myanmar.

Primate Most Revd Datuk Bolly Anak Lapok (Bishop of Kuching)

Provincial Secretary Mr Leonard David Shim, Messrs. Reddi & Co. Advocates, REDDI Building, No. 393, Jalan Datuk Abang Abdul Rahim, 93450 Kuching, Sarawak, Malaysia   Office: 60 82 484466
Fax: 60 82 484477
email: leonard.shim@reddi.com.my

Provincial Treasurer Mr Keith Chua, 35 Ford Avenue, Singapore 268714, Singapore
Tel: 65 6235 3344
Fax: 65 6736 1201
email: keithchu@singnet.com.sg

Provincial Chancellor Mr. Andrew Khoo, Messrs Andrew Khoo & Daniel Lo (Advocates & Solicitors), 34, Jalan SS20/26, Damansara Utama, 47400 Petaling Jaya, Selangor, Malaysia
Tel: 60 37 726496
email: andrew_khoo@akdl.com

Provincial Registrar Dato' Benedict Bujang Tembak, Hardin & Co., Advocates, 25, Jalan Tabuan, PO Box 103, 93700 Kuching, Sarawak, Malaysia   Tel: 60 82 252599 Fax: 60 82 429041
email: hardintembak@gmail.com

THEOLOGICAL COLLEGES
House of the Epiphany, PO Box No 347, 93704 Kuching, Sarawak, Malaysia (Warden Revd Canon Michael S. Woods)

Trinity Theological College, 490 Upper Bukit Timah Road, Singapore
678093 (interdenominational)

St Peter's Hall, residential hostel for Anglican students at Trinity Theological College, Singapore (Warden Revd Mervyn Moore)

Seminari Theoloji Malaysia (STM), Lot 3011, Taman South East, Jalan Tampin Lama, Batu 3, Seremban 70100, Negeri Sembilan, Malaysia (Principal Revd Dr Ezra Kok)

KUCHING
Bishop Most Revd Datuk Bolly Anak Lapok, Bishop's House, PO Box 347, 93704 Kuching, Sarawak, Malaysia   Tel: 60 82 240 187
Fax: 60 82 426 488
email: bpofkuching@gmail.com

Assistant Bishops
Rt Revd Aeries Sumping Jingan, PO Box 347, 93704 Kuching, Sarawak, Malaysia   *Tel:* 60 82 429755
Fax: 60 82 426488
email: aersumjin@gmail.com

Rt Revd Solomon Cheong Sung Voon, St Columba's Church, PO Box 233, 98007 Miri, Sarawak, Malaysia   *Tel:* 60 85 417284
Fax: 60 85 435370
email: solomon.cheong@gmail.com

SABAH
Vicar General Rt Revd Melter Jiki Tais, PO Box 10811, 88809 Kota Kinabalu, Sabah, Malaysia
Tel: 60 88 245 846
Fax: 60 88 261 422
email: uskupmjtais@gmail.com

Assistant Bishops
Rt Revd Melter Tais, PO Box 106, 89300 Telupid, Sabah, Malaysia   *Tel and Fax:* 60 89 521448
email: uskupmjtais@gmail.com

Rt Revd John Yeo, 201, Jalan Dunlop, 91000 Tawau   *email:* ad.johnyeo@gmail.com

SINGAPORE
Bishop Rt Revd Rennis Ponniah, St. Andrews Village, No. 1, Francis Thomas Drive, #01–01, Singapore 359340   *Tel:* 65 62 887585
Fax: 65 6288 5574
email: rennis@anglican.org.sg

Assistant Bishops
Rt Revd Low Jee King, St Andrew's Village, No. 1, Francis Thomas Drive, #01–01, Singapore 359340
Tel: 65 6288 8944
Fax: 65 6288 5574
email: lowjeeking@gmail.com

Rt Rev Kuan Kim Seng, St Andrew's Village, No. 1, Francis Thomas Drive, #01–01, Singapore 359340   *Tel:* 65 6288 8944
Fax: 65 6288 5574
email: kuanks@livingstreams.org.sg

WEST MALAYSIA
Bishop Rt Revd Datuk Ng Moon Hing, No. 16 Jalan Pudu Lama, 50200 Kuala Lumpur, Malaysia
Tel: 60 32 031 3213
Fax: 60 2 031 3225
email: canonmoon@gmail.com

Assistant Bishops
Rt Revd Jason Selvaraj, Christ Church, 48, Jalan Gereja, 75000 Melaka, Malaysia   *Tel:* 60 62 848804
Fax: 60 62 848804
email: jasondaphne101@gmail.com

Rt Revd Charles K. Samuel, St George's Church, 1 Lebuh Farquhar, 10200 Penang, Malaysia
Tel: 60 64 2612739
Fax: 60 64 2642292
email: vencan.cs@gmail.com

The Anglican Church of Southern Africa

Members 2,600,000
The province is the oldest in Africa. British Anglicans met for worship in Cape Town after 1806, with the first bishop appointed in 1847. The twenty-eight dioceses of the province extend beyond the Republic of South Africa and include the Foreign and Commonwealth Office (St Helena and Tristan da Cunha), Mozambique (Lebombo and Niassa), the Republic of Namibia, the Kingdom of Lesotho, and the Kingdom of Swaziland. This Church and its leaders played a significant role in the abolition of apartheid in South Africa and in peace keeping in Mozambique and Angola. A mission diocese was inaugurated in August 2002 in Angola. The Diocese of Ukhahlamba was inaugurated in October 2009 and the Diocese of Mbashe was inaugurated in July 2010

Primate Most Revd Dr Thabo Makgoba (*Archbishop of Cape Town and Metropolitan of the Anglican Church of Southern Africa*)

Provincial Executive Officer Revd William Mostert, 20 Bishopscourt Dr, Bishopscourt, Claremont, Western Cape 7708, South Africa
Tel: 27 21 763 1300
Fax: 27 21 797 1329
email: peo@anglicanchurchsa.org.za
Web: www.anglicanchurchsa.org.za

Provincial Treasurer Mr Rob S. Rogerson, PO Box 53014, Kenilworth, 7745, South Africa
Tel: 27 21 763 1300
Fax: 27 21 797 8319
email: rogerson@anglicanchurchsa.org.za

THEOLOGICAL COLLEGE
The College of the Transfiguration, PO Box 77, Grahamstown 6140   *Tel:* 27 46 622 3332
Fax: 27 46 622 3877
email: office@cott.co.za

ANGOLA (Missionary Diocese)
Bishop Rt Revd Andre Soares, Av. Lenini, Travessa D. Antonia Saldanha N.134, CP 10 341, Luanda, Angola   *Tel:* 244 2 395 792
Fax: 244 2 396 794
email: anglicana@ebonet.net/
bispo-Soares@hotmail.com

ANGLICAN AND PORVOO COMMUNIONS

CAPE TOWN
Archbishop Most Revd Dr Thabo Makgoba (*Metropolitan of Southern Africa*), 20 Bishopscourt Dr, Bishopscourt, Claremont, Cape Town 7708, Western Cape, South Africa   *Tel:* 27 21 763 1300
Fax: 27 21 797 1298/761 4193
email: archpa@anglicanchurchsa.org.za
Web: www.anglicanchurchsa.org

Bishop Suffragan
Rt Revd Garth Counsell (*Bishop of Table Bay*), PO Box 1932, Cape Town 8000   *Tel:* 27 21 465 1557
Fax: 27 21 465 1571
email: tablebay@ctdiocese.org.za

CHRIST THE KING
Bishop Rt Revd Peter John Lee, PO Box 1653, Rosettenville 2130, South Africa
Tel: 27 11 435 0097
Fax: 27 11 435 2868
email: bishop@ctkdiocesel.co.za

FALSE BAY
Bishop Rt Revd Margaret Brenda Vertue, PO Box 2804, Somerset West 7129, South Africa
Tel: 27 21 852 5243
Fax: 27 21 852 9430
email: bishopm@falsebaydiocese.org.za

GEORGE
Bishop Rt Revd Brian Melvyn Marajh, PO Box 227, George 6530, Cape Province, South Africa
Tel: 27 44 873 5680
Fax: 27 44 873 5680
email: bishopbrian@george.diocese.co.za

GRAHAMSTOWN
Bishop Rt Revd Ebenezer St Mark Ntlali, PO Box 181, Grahamstown 6140, Cape Province, South Africa   *Tel:* 27 46 636 1996
Fax: 27 46 622 5231
email: bpgtn@intekom.co.za

HIGHVELD
Bishop Rt Revd Hugh Bannerman, PO Box 17462, Benoni West 1503, South Africa
Tel: 27 11 422 2231
Fax: 27 11 420 1336
email: bishophveld@iafrica.com

JOHANNESBURG
Bishop Rt Revd Stephen Mosimanegape Moreo, PO Box 157, Westhoven, Gauteng, South Africa
Tel: 27 11 375 2700
Fax: 27 11 486 1015
email: steve.moreo@anglicanjoburg.org.za

KHAHLAMBA
Bishop Rt Revd Mazwi Ernest Tisani, PO Box 1673 Queenstown, 5320 South Africa
Tel: 27 45 858 8673
Fax: 27 45 858 8675
email: bishopmazwi@mweb.co.za

KIMBERLEY AND KURUMAN
Bishop Rt Revd Oswald Peter Patrick Swartz, PO Box 45, Kimberley 8300, South Africa
Tel: 27 53 833 2433
Fax: 27 53 831 2730
email: oppswartz@onetel.com

LEBOMBO
Bishop Rt Revd Dinis Salomâo Sengulane, CP 120, Maputo, Mozambique
Tel: 258 1 404 364/405 885
Fax: 258 1 401 093
email: bispo_sengulane@virconn.com

LESOTHO
Bishop Rt Revd Adam Andrease Mallane Taaso, PO Box 87, Maseru 100, Lesotho
Tel: 266 22 31 1974
Fax: 266 22 31 0161
email: diocese@ilesotho.com

MATLOSANE
Bishop Rt Revd Stephen Molopi Diseko, PO Box 11417, Klerksdorp 2570, South Africa
Tel: 27 18 464 2260
Fax: 27 18 462 4939
email: diocesematlosane@telkomsa.net
email: mikeomoipinmoye@yahoo.com

MBASHE
Bishop Rt Revd Elliot Sebenzile Williams, PO Box 1184, Butterworth, 4960, South Africa
Tel: 27 47 491 8030
Fax: 27 43 740 4766
email: dioceseofmbhashe@telkomsa.net

MPUMALANGA
Bishop Rt Revd Daniel Malasela Kgomosotho, PO Box 4327, White River 1240
Tel: 27 13 751 1960
Fax: 27 13 751 3638
email: diompu@telkomsa.net

MTHATHA
Bishop Rt Revd Dr Sitembele Tobela Mzamane, PO Box 25, Umtata, Transkei 5100, South Africa
Tel: 27 47 532 4450
Fax: 27 47 532 4191
email: anglicbspmthatha@intekom.co.za

NAMIBIA
Bishop Rt Revd Nathaniel Ndxuma Nakwatumbah, PO Box 57, Windhoek, Namibia
Tel: 264 61 238 920
Fax: 264 61 225 903
email: bishop@anglicanchurchnamibia.com

NATAL
Bishop Rt Revd Rubin Phillip, PO Box 47439, Greyville, 4023 South Africa   *Tel:* 27 31 309 2066
Fax: 27 31 308 9316
email: bishop@dionatal.org.za

Anglican and Porvoo Communions

Bishops Suffragan
Rt Revd Dr Hummingfield Charles Nkosinathi Ndwandwe (*Suffragan Bishop of the South Episcopal Area*) (*same address*)   *Tel:* 27 33 394 1560
          email: bishopndwandwe@dionatal.org.za

Rt Revd Tsietse Edward Seleoane (*Suffragan Bishop of the North West Episcopal Area*), PO Box 463, Ladysmith 3370, South Africa   *Tel:* 27 36 631 4650
          Fax: 27 86 547 1882
          email: bishopseleoane@dionatal.org.za

NIASSA
Bishop Rt Revd Mark van Koevering, CP 264, Lichinga, Niassa, Mozambique
          Tel and *Fax:* 258 712 0735
          email: bishop.niassa@gmail.com

PORT ELIZABETH
Bishop Rt Revd Nceba Bethlehem Nopece, PO Box 7109, Newton Park 6055, South Africa
          Tel: 27 41 365 1387
          Fax: 27 41 365 2049
          email: bpsec@pediocese.org.za

PRETORIA
Bishop Rt Revd Dr Johannes Thomas Seoka, PO Box 1032, Pretoria 0001, South Africa
          Tel: 27 12 322 2218
          Fax: 27 12 322 9411
          email: ptabish@dioceseofpretoria.org

SALDANHA BAY
Bishop The Rt Revd Raphael Bernard Viburt Hess, PO Box 420, Malmesbury 7299, South Africa   *Tel:* 27 22 487 3885
          Fax: 27 22 487 3886
          email: bishop@dioceseofsaldanhabay.org.za

ST HELENA
Bishop Rt Revd Dr Richard David Fenwick, PO Box 62, Island of St Helena, South Atlantic
          Tel: 290 4471
          Fax: 290 4728
          email: richard.d.fenwick@googlemail.com

ST MARK THE EVANGELIST
Bishop Rt Revd Martin Andre Breytenbach, PO Box 643, Polokwane 0700, South Africa
          Tel: 27 15 297 3297
          Fax: 27 15 297 0408
          email: martin@stmark.org.za

SWAZILAND
Bishop Ellinah Ntfombi Wamukoya, Bishop's House, Muir Street, Mbabane, Swaziland
          Tel: 268 404 3624
          Fax: 268 404 6759
          email: bishopen@africaonline.co.sz

THE FREE STATE
Bishop Dintoe Stephen Letloenyane, PO Box 411, Bloemfontein, 9300, South Africa
          Tel: 27 51 447 6053
          Fax: 27 51 447 5874
          email: bishopdintoe@dsc.co.za
          Web: www.cpsa.org.za/bloemfontein

UMZIMVUBU
Bishop Rt Revd Mlibo Mteteleli Ngewu, PO Box 644, Kokstad 4700, South Africa
          Tel and *Fax:* 27 39 727 4117
          email: mzimvubu@futurenet.co.za

ZULULAND
Bishop Rt Revd Dino Gabriel, PO Box 147, Eshowe 3815, South Africa
          Tel and *Fax:* 27 354 742 047
          email: bishopdino@netactive.co.za

The Church of the Province of the Sudan

Members 5,000,000
The Church Missionary Society began work in 1899 in Omdurman; Christianity spread rapidly among black Africans of the southern region. Until 1974, the diocese of Sudan was part of the Jerusalem archbishopric. It reverted to the jurisdiction of the Archbishop of Canterbury until the new province, consisting of four new dioceses, was established in 1976. In 1986 the number of dioceses increased to 11 and in 1992 to 24 dioceses. The doubling of the number of dioceses by 1992 was partly due to leadership crises in the Church and partly due to church growth. Civil and religious strife and a constant flow of refugees have challenged the Church. Its heroic witness to faith in Christ continues to inspire the Anglican Communion and its people.

Archbishop and Primate Most Revd Dr Daniel Deng Bul Yak (*Bishop of Juba*)
          Tel and *Fax:* 249 121212607
          email: ecsprovince@hotmail.com
          archbishopdanieldeng@yahoo.com
          Web: www.sudan.anglican.org

Acting Provincial Secretary John Augustino Lumori, PO Box 110, Juba, South Sudan
          email: provincialsecretary@sudan.anglican.org

Honorary Provincial Treasurer Mr Evans Sokiri
email: sokirik@yahoo.co.uk

THEOLOGICAL COLLEGES
Bishop Gwynne College, PO Box 110, Juba, Sudan (*Acting Principal* Revd David V. Bako)
Tel: 249 9124 54933 (Mobile)
email: davidbako7@hotmail.com

Bishop Alison Theological College, PO Box 1076, Arua, Uganda (*Principal* Dr Oliver Duku)
Tel: 254 77 685 554
email: bat_college@yahoo.com
Shokai Bible Training Institute, PO Box 65, Omdurman, 135 Khartoum, Sudan (*Principal* Revd Musa Elgadi)
Tel: 249 187 564944
email: sbti70@yahoo.com
Renk Bible School, PO Box 1532, Khartoum North, Sudan (*Acting Principal* Revd Abraham Noon Jiel)
Tel: 249 918 068 125 (Mobile)
email: joseph_atem@yahoo.com
Bishop Ngalamu Theological College, PO Box 3364, Khartoum, Sudan (*Principal* Revd Paul Issa)
email: leyeonon@hotmail.com

AKOT
Bishop Rt Revd Isaac Dhieu Ater, c/o CMS Office, PO Box 40360, Nairobi, Kenya

AWEIL
Bishop Rt Revd Abraham Yel Nhial, ECS PO Box 110, Northern Bah el Ghazal, South Sudan
Tel: 211 955 621 584
email: bishop@aweil.anglican.org

BOR
Bishop Rt Revd Ruben Akurdid Ngong, c/o ECS PO Box 110, Juba, South Sudan
Tel: 211 926 572 471
email: ecs_dioceseofbor@yahoo.co.uk

CUEIBET
Bishop Rt Revd Elijah Awate, c/o ECS PO Box 110, Juba, South Sudan   Tel: 211 926 572 471
email: bishop@cuiebet.anglican.org

EL-OBEID
Bishop Rt Revd Ismail Gibriel Abugigin, PO Box 211, El-Obeid, Sudan
Tel: 249 9122 53459 (Mobile)
email: bishop@elobeid.anglican.org

EZO
Bishop Rt Revd John Zawo, c/o ECS PO Box 110, Juba, South Sudan   Tel: 211 926 572 471
email: bishop@ezo.anglican.org

IBBA
Bishop Rt Revd Wilson Elisa Kamani, c/o ECS PO Box 110, Juba, South Sudan
Tel: 211 926 572 471
email: bishop@ibba.anglican.org

JUBA
Bishop Most Revd Dr Daniel Deng Bul Yak (*Archbishop and Primate*), c/o ECS PO Box 110, Juba, South Sudan   Tel: 211 926 572 471
email: dioceseofjuba@yahoo.com

Assistant Bishop Rt Revd Joseph Makor Atot, c/o CMS, PO Box 40360, Nairobi, Kenya

KADUGLI AND NUBA MOUNTAINS
Bishop Rt Revd Andudu Adam Elnail, PO Box 35, Kadugli, Sudan   Tel: 249 631 822898
email: bpkadugli@googlemail.com

KAJO-KEJI
Bishop Rt Revd Anthony Poggo Dangasuk, c/o ECS PO Box 110, Juba, South Sudan
Tel: 211 926 572 471
email: bishopkk@gmail.com

KHARTOUM
Bishop Rt Revd Ezekiel Kondo, c/o ECS PO Box 110, Juba, South Sudan   Tel: 211 926 572 471
email: ecs_bishop_Khartoum@kastanet.org

LAINYA
Bishop Rt Revd Peter Amidi Pitia, c/o ECS PO Box 110, Juba, South Sudan   Tel: 211 926 572 471
email: petamidi@yahoo.com

LUI
Bishop Rt Revd Stephen Dokolo Ismail, c/o ECS PO Box 110, Juba, South Sudan
Tel: 211 926 572 471
email: stephen.dokolo@gmail.com

MALAKAL
Bishop Rt Revd Hilary Garang Deng, PO Box 604, Khartoum, Sudan
email: ecs.malak@live.com

MARIDI
Bishop Rt Revd Justin Badi Arama, ECS Support Office, PO Box 7576, Kampala, Uganda
Tel and Fax: 256 41 343 497
email: ecsmaridi@hotmail.com

MUNDRI
Bishop Rt Revd Bismark Monday Avokaya, c/o ECS PO Box 110, Juba, South Sudan
Tel: 211 926 572 471
email: ecsmundri1984@yahoo.com

PACONG
Bishop Rt Revd Joseph Maker Atot
email: ecs.pacongdiocese@yahoo.com

PORT SUDAN
Bishop Rt Revd Yousif Abdalla Kuku, PO Box 278, Port Sudan, Sudan   Tel and Fax: 249 311 821224
email: ishagkuku@hotmail.com

REJAF
Bishop Rt Revd Enock Tombe, c/o ECS PO Box 110, Juba, South Sudan   *Tel:* 211 926 572 471
email: rejafdioceseecs@yahoo.com

RENK
Bishop Rt Revd Joseph Garang Atem, c/o ECS PO Box 110, Upper Nile State, South Sudan
email: ecs_renk@hotmail.com

ROKON
Bishop Rt Revd Francis Loyo Mori, c/o ECS PO Box 110, Juba, South Sudan   *Tel:* 211 926 572 471
email: bployo@yahoo.co.uk

RUMBEK
Bishop Rt Revd Alapayo Manyang Kuctiel, c/o ECS PO Box 110, Lake State, South Sudan
email: kuctiel@yahoo.com

TEREKEKA
Bishop Rt Revd Micah Dawidi, c/o ECS PO Box 110, Juba, South Sudan   *Tel:* 211 926 572 471
email: bpmicahdawidi@yahoo.com

TORIT
Bishop Rt Revd Bernard Oringa Balmoi, PO Box 26157, Kampala, Uganda   *Tel:* 256 41 343 497
email: ecs.torit@yahoo.org

WAU
Bishop Rt Revd Moses Deng Bol, c/o ECS PO Box 110, Western Bahr El Ghazal, South Sudan
Tel: 254 37 43186
email: mosesdengbol@gmail.com

YAMBIO
Bishop Rt Revd Peter Munde Yacoub, c/o ECS PO Box 110, Wes/Yambio, South Sudan
email: yambio2002@yahoo.com

YEI
Bishop Rt Revd Hilary Luate Adeba, c/o ECS PO Box 110, Juba, South Sudan   *Tel:* 211 926 572 471
email: hill_sherpherd@yahoo.com

YIROL
Bishop Rt Revd Daniel Deng Abil, c/o ECS PO Box 110, Lakes State, South Sudan
email: ecsyiroldicese@yahoo.com

The Anglican Church of Tanzania

Members over 3,000,000
The Universities Mission to Central Africa and the Church Missionary Society began work in 1863 and 1876 in Zanzibar and at Mpwapwa respectively. The province was inaugurated in 1970 following the division of the Province of East Africa into the Province of Kenya and the Province of Tanzania. The 20 dioceses represent both evangelical and Anglo-Catholic Churches.

Archbishop Most Revd Jacob Erasto Chimeledya (*Bishop of Mpwapwa*)

Dean Rt Revd Dr Philip Baji (*Bishop of Tanga*)

Provincial Secretary Revd Canon Dr Dickson Chilongani, PO Box 899, Dodoma
Tel: 255 26 232 4574
Fax: 255 26 232 4565
email: chilongani@anglican.or.tz
Web: www.anglican.or.tz

Provincial Treasurer Rt Revd Hilkah Omindo Deya (*Bishop of Mara*)

Provincial Registrar Justice Augustino Ramadhani, PO Box 20522, Dar es Salaam
Tel: 255 022 211 5418
email: aslramadhani@yahoo.co.uk

THEOLOGICAL COLLEGES
St Philip's Theological College, PO Box 26, Kongwa (*Principal* Rev John Madinda)
Tel: 255 26 232 0096
email: stphilipstz@yahoo.com

St Mark's Theological College, PO Box 25017, Dar es Salaam (*Principal* Canon John Simalenga)
Tel: 255 22 286 3014
email: st-alban@kicheko.com/
jsimalenga@yahoo.com

CHURCH NEWSLETTER
ACT Forum is issued three times a year (April, August, December) in English containing diocesan, provincial and world church news. *Editor* Vacancy

CENTRAL TANGANYIKA
Bishop Vacancy, PO Box 15, Dodoma
Tel: 255 26 232 1714
Fax: 255 26 232 4518
email: bishop@dct-tz.org/mhogolo@pnc.com.au

Assistant Bishop Rt Revd Ainea Kusenha (*same address*)   *email:* ngombe2004@kicheko.com

DAR ES SALAAM
Bishop Most Revd Dr Valentino Mokiwa (*Archbishop*), PO Box 25016, Ilala, Dar-es-Salaam   *Tel:* 255 22 286 4426
email: mokiwa_valentine@hotmail.com

KAGERA
Bishop Rt Revd Aaron Kijanjali, PO Box 18, Ngara
Tel: 255 28 222 3624
Fax: 255 28 222 2518
email: dkagera@googlemail.com

KITETO
Bishop Rt Revd Isaiah Chambala, PO Box 74, Kibaya, Kiteto
Tel: 255 27 255 2106
email: bishopofkiteto@yahoo.com

KONDOA
Bishop Rt Revd Given Gaula, PO Box 7, Kondoa
Tel: 255 26 236 0312
Fax: 255 26 236 0304/0324
email: givenmgaula@yahoo.com

LAKE RUKWA
Bishop Rt Revd Mathayo Kasagara, PO Box 14, Mpanda
email: kasagarajr@gmail.com

LWERU
Bishop Rt Revd Jackton Yeremiah Lugumira, PO Box 12, Muleba
Tel: 255 713 274 085
email: jact@bukobaonline.com

MARA
Bishop Rt Revd Hilkiah Deya Omindo Deya, PO Box 131, Musoma
Tel: 255 28 262 2376
Fax: 255 28 262 2414
email: omindo@anglican.or.tz

MASASI
Bishop Rt Revd Patrick Mwachiko, Private Bag, PO Masasi, Mtwara Region
Tel: 255 23 251 0016
Fax: 255 23 251 0351
email: actmasasi@africaonline.co.tz

MOROGORO
Bishop Rt Revd Godfrey Sehaba, PO Box 320, Morogoro
Tel and Fax: 255 23 260 4602
email: bishopgsehaba@yahoo.com

MOUNT KILIMANJARO
Bishop Rt Revd Stanley Elilekia Hotay, PO Box 1057, Arush
Tel: 255 27 254 8396
Fax: 255 27 254 4187
email: hotaystanley@yahoo.com

MPWAPWA
Bishop Most Revd Jacob Erasto Chimeledya (*Archbishop of the Province*), PO Box 2, Mpwapwa
Tel: 255 26 232 0017/0825
Fax: 255 26 232 0063
email: dmp@do.ucc.co.tz

NEWALA
Bishop Rt Revd Oscar Mnunga, PO Box 92, Newala, Tanzania
email: oscarnewala.diocese@yahoo.com

RIFT VALLEY
Bishop Rt Revd John Lupaa, PO Box 16, Manyoni
Tel: 255 26 254 0013
Fax: 255 26 250 3014
email: act-drv@maf.or.tz

RUAHA
Bishop Rt Revd Joseph Mgomi, PO Box 1028, Iringa
Tel: 255 26 270 1211
Fax: 255 26 270 2479
email: sanbalatchisewo@yahoo.com

RUVUMA
Bishop Rt Revd Dr Maternus Kapinga, PO Box 1357, Songea, Ruvumu
Tel: 255 25 260 0090
Fax: 255 25 260 2987
email: matemask@gmail.com

SHINYANGA
Bishop Rt Revd Charles Kija Ngusa, PO Box 421, Shinyanga
Tel: 255 754 347 746 (Mobile)
email: ckngusa@yahoo.com

SOUTHERN HIGHLANDS
Bishop Rt Revd John Mwela, PO Box 198, Mbeya
Tel: 255 754 266 668 (Mobile)
email: mwelajohn@yahoo.co.uk

SOUTH-WEST TANGANYIKA
Bishop Vacancy, PO Box 32, Njombe
Tel: 255 26 278 2010
Fax: 255 26 278 2403
email: dswt@africaonline.co.tz

TABORA
Bishop Rt Revd Elias Chakupewa, PO Box 1408, Tabora
Tel: 255 26 260 4124
Fax: 255 26 260 4899
email: chakupewalucy@yahoo.com

TANGA
Bishop Rt Revd Maimbo Mndolwa, PO Box 35, Korogwe, Tanga
Tel: 255 27 264 0631
Fax: 255 27 264 0568
email: bajipp@anglican.or.tz

VICTORIA NYANZA
Bishop Rt Revd Boniface Kwangu, PO Box 278, Mwanza
Tel: 255 28 250 0627
Fax: 255 28 250 0676
email: bandmkwangu@yahoo.co.uk

WESTERN TANGANYIKA
Bishop Rt Revd Sadock Makaya, PO Box 13, Kasulu
Tel: 255 28 281 0321
Fax: 255 28 281 0706
email: askofugm@yahoo.com

Assistant Bishops
Rt Revd Naftal Bikaka (*Lake Zone Area of Kigoma District*), PO Box 1378, Kigoma
Tel: 255 28 280 3407
email: bpwbikaka@yahoo.co.uk

Anglican and Porvoo Communions

Rt Revd Marko Badeleya (*Southern Zone Area of Rukwa Region in Sumbawanga*), PO Box 226, Sumbawanga   *Tel:* 255 25 280 0287
          email: bpbadeleya@yahoo.co.uk

ZANZIBAR
Bishop Vacancy, PO Box 5, Mkunazini, Zanzibar
          Tel: 255 24 223 5348
          Fax: 255 24 223 6772
          email: secactznz@zanlink.com

The Church of the Province of Uganda

Members 12,000,000
After its founding in 1877 by the Church Missionary Society, the Church grew through the evangelization of Africa by Africans. The first Ugandan clergy were ordained in 1893 and the Church of Uganda, Rwanda and Burundi became an independent province in 1961. The history of the Church in Uganda has been marked by civil strife and martyrdom. In May 1980 the new Province of Burundi, Rwanda and Zaire was inaugurated; the Province of Uganda has since grown from 17 to 34 dioceses.

Archbishop of the Province Most Revd Stanley Ntagali (*Bishop of Kampala*)

Primatial and Provincial Secretariat PO Box 14123, Kampala   *Tel:* 256 414 270 218
          email: couoffice@gmail.com

Provincial Secretary Revd Amos Magezi (*same address*)
          email: pschurchofuganda@gmail.com

Provincial Treasurer Mr Moses Makasa (*same address*)   *Tel:* 256 414 270 218
          email: coutr@uol.co.ug

THEOLOGICAL COLLEGES
Uganda Christian University, Mukono, PO Box 4, Mukono (*Vice-Chancellor* Revd Canon Dr John Senyonyi)

Bishop Balya College, PO Box 368, Fort-Portal (*Principal* Revd Y. Kule)

Bishop Barham University College (constituent college of Uganda Christian university, Mukono), PO Box 613, Kabale (*Principal* Revd Dr Manual Muranga)

Archbishop Janani Luwum Theological College, PO Box 232, Gulu (*Principal* Revd Sandra Earixson)

Mityana Theological Training College, PO Box 102, Mityana (*Principal* Revd Mukasa-Mutambuze)

Ngora Diocesan Theological College, PO Box 1, Ngora (*Principal* Revd S. Amuret)

Uganda Martyrs Seminary Namugongo, PO Box 31149, Kampala (*Principal* Revd Canon Henry Segawa)

Aduku Diocesan Theological College, PO Aduku, Lira (*Principal* Revd S. O. Obura)

Kabwohe College, PO Kabwohe, Mbarara (*Principal* Revd Y. R. Buremu)

St Paul's Theological College Ringili, PO Box 358, Arua (*Principal* Canon Dr Milton Anguyo)

Bishop Usher Wilson, Buwalasi, Mbale (*Principal* Revd Naphtah Opwata)

Uganda Bible Institute, Mbarara (*Director* Revd Canon Johnson Twinomujuni)

Bishop McAllister College, Kyogyera (*Principal* Revd Paul Jefferees)

Diocesan Training Centre, Duhaga, Hoima (*Principal* Revd Cindy Larsen)

ANKOLE
Bishop Rt Revd Sheldon Mwesigwa, PO Box 14, Mbarara, Ankole   *Tel:* 256 772 770 809
          email: ruharu@utiouline.co.ug

BUKEDI
Bishop Rt Revd Samuel Egesa, PO Box 170, Tororo   *Tel:* 256 775 057 078 (Mobile)
          email: bukedidiocese@yahoo.com

BUNYORO-KITARA
Bishop Rt Revd Nathan Kyamanywa, PO Box 20, Hoima   *Tel:* 256 464 40 128

          256 0776 648 231 (Mobile)
          email: nathan_nathank@yahoo.co.uk

BUSOGA
Bishop Rt Revd Dr Michael Kyomya, PO Box 1568, Jinja   *Tel:* 256 752 649 102 (Mobile)
          email: busogadiocese@gmail.com

CENTRAL BUGANDA
Bishop Rt Revd Jackson Matovu, PO Box 1200, Kinoni-Gomba, Mpigi
          Tel: 256 772 475 640 (Mobile)
          email: bishopmatovu@yahoo.com

EAST RUWENZORI
Bishop Rt Revd Edward Bamucwanira, PO Box
1439, Kamwenge   *Tel:* 256 772 906 236
                email: edward_bamu@yahoo.com

KAMPALA
Bishop Most Revd Stanley Ntagali (*Archbishop of
Uganda*), PO Box 335, Kampala
                Tel: 256 414 279 218
                Fax: 256 414 251 925
                email: abpcou@gmail.com

Assistant Bishop Rt Revd Hannington Mutebi,
PO Box 335, Kampala   *Tel:* 256 414 290 231
                Fax: 256 414 342 601
                email: mutebihanning@yahoo.com

KARAMOJA
Bishop Rt Revd Joseph Abura, PO Box 44, Moroto
                Tel: 256 782 658 502
                email: bishop.abura@yahoo.co.uk

KIGEZI
Bishop Rt Revd George Bagamuhunda, PO Box 3,
Kabale   *Tel:* 256 486 22 003
                Fax: 256 486 22 802
                email: bishopkigezi@infocom.co.ug

KINKIIZI
Bishop Rt Revd Dan Zoreka, PO Box 77,
Kanungu   256 772 507 163 (Mobile)
                email: zorekadan@yahoo.com

KITGUM
Bishop Rt Revd Benjamin Ojwang, PO Box 187,
Kitgum   *Tel:* 256 772 959 924 (Mobile)
                email: ojwangbenjamin@gmail.com

KUMI
Bishop Rt Revd Thomas Edison Irigei, PO Box 18,
Kumi   *Tel:* 256 772 659 460 (Mobile)
                email: kumimothersunion@yahoo.com

LANGO
Bishop Rt Revd John Charles Odurkami, PO Box
6, Lira   *Tel:* 256 772 614 000 (Mobile)
                email: bishoplango@yahoo.com

LUWERO
Bishop Rt Revd Evans Mukasa Kisekka, PO Box
125, Luwero   *Tel:* 256 414 610 048/070
                256 772 421 220 (Mobile)
                Fax: 256 414 610 132/070
                email: kiromas6@yahoo.co.uk

MADI / WEST NILE
Bishop Rt Revd Joel Obetia, PO Box 370, Arua
                Tel: 256 751 625 414 (Mobile)
                email: jobetia@yahoo.com

MASINDI-KITARA
Bishop Rt Revd George Kasangaki, PO Box 515,
Masindi   *Tel:* 256 772 624 461
                email: georgewakasa@gmail.com

MBALE
Bishop Rt Revd Patrick Gidudu, Bishop's House,
PO Box 473, Mbale   *Tel:* 256 45 33 533
                256 782 625 619 (Mobile)
                email: patrickhgidudu@yahoo.com

MITYANA
Bishop Rt Revd Stephen Samuel Kaziimba, PO
Box 102, Mityana   *Tel:* 256 46 2017
                email: sakazimba@yahoo.com

MUHABURA
Bishop Rt Revd Cranmer Mugisha, PO Box 22,
Kisoro   *Tel:* 256 486 30 014/058
                256 712 195 891 (Mobile)
                Fax: 256 486 30 059
                email: cranhopmu@yahoo.co.uk

MUKONO
Bishop Rt Revd James Ssebagala, PO Box 39,
Mukono   *Tel:* 256 41 290 229
                256 712 860 742 (Mobile)
                email: Jamesebagala@yahoo.co.uk

NAMIREMBE
Bishop Rt Revd Wilberforce Luwalira, PO Box
14297, Kampala   *Tel:* 256 414 271 682
                256 712 942 161 (Mobile)
                email: namid@infocom.co.ug

NEBBI
Bishop Rt Revd Alphonse Watho-kudi, PO Box
27, Nebbi   *Tel:* 256 772 650 032 (Mobile)
                email: bpalphonse@ekk.org

NORTH ANKOLE
Bishop Rt Revd John Muhanguzi, c/o PO Box 14,
Rushere-Mbarara, Ankole
                Tel: 256 772 369 947 (Mobile)
                email: nadsrushere@yahoo.com

NORTH KARAMOJA
Bishop Rt Revd James Nasak, PO Box 26, Kotido
                Tel: 256 772 660 228
                email: jnasak@yahoo.com

NORTH KIGEZI
Bishop Rt Revd Patrick Tugume-Tusingwire,
PO Box 23, Rukungiri   *Tel:* 256 486 42 433
                256 772 709 387 (Mobile)
                email: earfchairman@yahoo.com

NORTH MBALE
Bishop Rt Revd Daniel Gimadu, Bishop's House,
PO Box 1837, Mbale   *Fax:* 256 752 655 225
                email: northmbalediocese@yahoo.com/
                petgim2000@yahoo.com

NORTHERN UGANDA
Bishop Rt Revd Johnson Gakumba, PO Box 232,
Gulu   *Tel:* 256 772 601 421 (Mobile)
                email: johnson.gakumba@gmail.com

RUWENZORI

Bishop Rt Revd Reuben Kisembo, Bishop's House, PO Box 37, Fort Portal
Tel: 256 772 470 671 (Mobile)
email: reubenkisembo@gmail.com

SEBEI

Bishop Rt Revd Augusto Arapyona Salimo, PO Box 23, Kapchorwa
Tel: 256 45 51 072
256 772 550 520 (Mobile)
email: augustinesalimo@yahoo.co.uk

SOROTI

Bishop Rt Revd George Erwau, PO Box 107, Soroti
Tel: 256 45 61 795
256 772 653 607 (Mobile)
email: cou.teddo@gmail.com

SOUTH ANKOLE

Bishop Rt Revd Nathan Ahimbisibwe, PO Box 39, Ntungamo
Tel: 256 772 660 636
email: revnathan2000@yahoo.com

SOUTH RUWENZORI

Bishop Rt Revd Jackson T. Nzerebende, PO Box 142, Kasese
Tel: 256 772 713 736 (Mobile)
Fax: 256 483 44 450
email: srdiocese@gmail.com

WEST ANKOLE

Bishop Rt Revd Yona Katoneene, PO Box 140, Bushenyi
Tel: 256 784 829 390 (Mobile)
email: wad@westankolediocese.org

WEST BUGANDA

Bishop Rt Revd Godfrey Makumbi, PO Box 242, Masaka
Tel: 256 772 607 305 (Mobile)
email: westbug@africaonline.co.ug

The Protestant Episcopal Church in the United States of America

(also known as The Episcopal Church)

Members 2,400,000

Anglicanism was brought to the New World by explorers and colonists with the first celebration of the Holy Eucharist in Jamestown, Virginia in 1607. The need for clergy in the colonies was acute and English missionaries provided temporary relief. Though the Bishop of London was responsible for maintaining the church in the colonies, there was no resident bishop for nearly two hundred years, which meant that colonists had to travel to England to be ordained; this caused difficulties when many of the colonial clergy sided with the Crown during the American Revolution. In 1784 the first American bishop (Samuel Seabury of Connecticut) was consecrated in Scotland, and three years later bishops were consecrated in England for the Dioceses of Pennsylvania and New York. In 1785 the first General Convention was held; in 1821 the Domestic and Foreign Missionary Society was formed; and in 1835, by resolution of General Convention, all members of The Episcopal Church were made members of the Missionary Society.

The Episcopal Church today maintains 100 dioceses within the United States plus 10 overseas dioceses (Colombia, the Dominican Republic, Central Ecuador, Litoral Ecuador, Haiti, Honduras, Puerto Rico, Taiwan, Venezuela and the Virgin Islands), the Mission Territory of Micronesia (Guam), the Convocation of American Churches in Europe, and, together with the Anglican Church of Canada and the Church in the Province of the West Indies, is a partner in the Metropolitan Council which oversees the Episcopal Church of Cuba; it is governed by the triennial General Convention consisting of a House of Clergy and Lay Deputies, and a House of Bishops, which includes all serving diocesan, suffragan, coadjutor and assisting bishops. Between General Conventions, church affairs are managed by the Executive Council, whose members are elected in part by the two Houses and in part by the nine regional provinces. The Executive Council meets three times each year (except twice during a General Convention year). The province is a strong base of support to the Anglican Communion and has a significant crisis ministry through Episcopal Relief and Development. Episcopalians are also very active in the areas of social justice and ecumenical and interfaith relations, and witness to their faith in all walks of national life.

Presiding Bishop and Primate Most Revd Dr Katharine Jefferts Schori

Offices of the Episcopal Church and its departments Episcopal Church Center, 815 Second Ave, New York, NY 10017, USA
Tel: 1 212 716 6000
email: via website
Web: www.episcopalchurch.org

President of the House of Deputies Revd Gay C. Jennings (*same address*)
Tel: 1 212 922 5183
email: via website

Executive Officer of the General Convention Revd Canon Michael Barlowe (*same address*)
Tel: 1 212 922 5184
email: via website

Bishop Suffragan for Armed Services and Federal Ministries Rt Revd James Magness, 3504 Woodley Rd NW, Washington DC, 20016, USA
Tel: 1 646 434 0275
email: via website

Bishop of the Office of Pastoral Development Rt Revd F. Clayton Matthews, 2857 Trent Rd, New Bern, NC 28562, USA Tel: 1 252 635 5004
email: via website

Treasurer and Chief Financial Officer Mr N. Kurt Barnes, Episcopal Church Center, 815 Second Ave, New York, NY 10017, USA
Tel: 1 212 922 5296
email: via website
Web: www.episcopalchurch.org

THEOLOGICAL SEMINARIES
California
Church Divinity School of the Pacific, 2451 Ridge Rd, Berkeley, CA 94709-1211, USA (President and Dean Very Revd Dr W. Mark Richardson)
Web: www.cdsp.edu

Connecticut
Berkeley Divinity School at Yale University, 409 Prospect St, New Haven, CT 06511, USA (Dean and President Very Revd Andrew McGowan)
Web: www.berkeleydivinity.net

Illinois
Bexley Seabury, 8785 W Higgins Rd, Chicago, IL 60631, USA (President Revd Dr Roger Ferlo)
Web: www.bexleyseabury.edu

Massachusetts
Episcopal Divinity School, 99 Brattle St, Cambridge, MA 02138, USA (President and Dean Very Revd Dr Katherine Hancock Ragsdale)
Web: www.eds.edu

New York
The General Theological Seminary of The Episcopal Church in the United States, 440 West 21st St, New York, NY 10011, USA (Dean and President Very Revd Kurt H. Dunkle)
Web: www.gts.edu

Ohio
Bexley Seabury, 583 Sheridan Ave, Columbus, OH 43209 (President Revd Dr Roger Ferlo) Web: www.bexleyseabury.edu

Pennsylvania
Trinity School for Ministry, 311 Eleventh St, Ambridge, PA 15003, USA (Dean and President Very Revd Dr Justyn Terry) Web: www.tsm.edu

Tennessee
The School of Theology, Sewanee, The University of the South, 335 Tennesse Ave, Sewanee, TN 37383–0001, USA (Dean Rt Revd J. Neil Alexander)
Web: www.theology.sewanee.edu

Texas
Seminary of the Southwest, 501 E 32nd St, Austin, TX 78768, USA (Dean Very Revd Cynthia Briggs Kittredge) Web: www.ssw.edu

Virginia
Virginia Thelogical, Seminary, 3737 Seminary Rd, Alexandria, VA 22304, USA (Dean and President Very Revd Dr Ian S. Markham) Web: www.vts.edu

Wisconsin
Nashotah House, 2777 Mission Rd, Nashotah, WI 53058, USA (Dean Rt Revd Edward L. Salmon Jr) Web: www.nashotah.edu

CHURCH PAPERS
Episcopal Life An independently edited, officially sponsored monthly newspaper published by the Episcopal Church, 815 Second Ave, New York, NY 10017, USA, upon authority of the General Convention of the Protestant Episcopal Church in the USA. Also see episcopallife online, our electronic news service Web: www.episcopalchurch.org/episcopal_life.htm

The Living Church Weekly magazine. Editorial and Business Offices PO Box 514036, Milwaukee, WI 53203, USA. Contains news and features about Christianity in general and the Episcopal Church in particular.

ALABAMA (Province IV)
Bishop Rt Revd John McKee Sloan, Carpenter House, 521 N 20th St, Birmingham, AL 35203-2611, USA Tel: 1 205 715 2060
Fax: 1 205 715 2060
email: ksloan@dioala.org
Web: www.dioala.org

ALASKA (Province VIII)
Bishop Rt Revd Mark Lattime, 1205 Denali Way Fairbanks, Alaska 99701–4137, USA
Tel: 1 907 452 3040
Fax: 1 907 456 6552
email: mlattime@gci.net
Web: www.episcopalak.org

ALBANY (Province II)
Bishop Rt Revd William Howard Love, 580 Burton Rd, Greenwich, NY 12834, USA
Tel: 1 518 962 3350
Fax: 1 518 692 3350
email: via website
Web: www.albanyepiscopaldiocese.org

ARIZONA (Province VIII)
Bishop Rt Revd Kirk Stevan Smith, 114 West Roosevelt St, Phoenix, AZ 85003–1406, USA
Tel: 1 602 254 0970
Fax: 1 602 495 6603
email: bishop@azdiocese.org
Web: http://azdiocese.org

Assisting Bishop William G. Burrill (*same address*)
email: kburrill@earthlink.net

ARKANSAS (Province VII)
Bishop Rt Revd Larry R. Benfield, 310 West 17th
St, Little Rock, AR 72216–4668, USA
Tel: 1 501 372 2168
Fax: 1 501 372 2147
email: bishopbenfield@mac.com
Web: http://episcopalarkansas.org

ATLANTA (Province IV)
Bishop Rt Revd Robert Wright, 2744 Peachtree
Rd, Atlanta, GA 30305, USA Tel: 1 404 601 5320
Fax: 1 404 601 5330
email: bishopwright@episcopalatlanta.org
Web: www.episcopalatlanta.org

Assistant Bishop Rt Revd Keith Bernard Whitmore
(*same address*)
email: bishopkeith@episcopalatlanta.org

BETHLEHEM (Province III)
Bishop Rt Revd Sean Rowe, 333 Wyandotte St,
Bethlehem, PA 18015–1527, USA
Tel: 1 610 691 5655
Fax: 1 610 691 1682
email: seanrowe@diobeth.org
Web: www.diobeth.org

CALIFORNIA (Province VIII)
Bishop Rt Revd Marc Handley Andrus, 1055
Taylor St, San Francisco, CA 94108, USA
Tel: 1 415 673 5015
Fax: 1 415 673 9268
email: bishopmarc@diocal.org
Web: www.diocal.org

CENTRAL ECUADOR (Province IX)
Bishop Rt Revd Victor Scantlebury, Ofcinas
Diocesanas, Francisco Sarmiento N 39–54
Portete, sector el Batán, Quito, Ecuador
Tel: 2 254 1735
Fax: 2 227 1627

CENTRAL FLORIDA (Province IV)
Bishop Rt Revd Gregory O. Brewer, Diocesan
Office, 1017 E Robinson St, Orlando, FL 32801,
USA
Tel: 1 407 423 3567
Fax: 1 407 872 0006
email: bpbrewer@cfdiocese.org
Web: www.cfdiocese.org

CENTRAL GULF COAST (Province IV)
Bishop Rt Revd Philip Menzie Duncan II, 201 N
Baylen St, Pensacola, FL 32502, USA
Tel: 1 850 434 7337
Fax: 1 850 434 8577
email: staff@diocgc.org
Web: www.diocgc.org

CENTRAL NEW YORK (Province II)
Bishop Rt Revd Gladstone (Skip) Adams, 1020
North St, Liverpool, NY 13088, USA
Tel: 1 315 474 6596
Fax: 1 315 478 1632
email: bishop@cnyepiscopal.org
Web: www.cnyepiscopal.org

CENTRAL PENNSYLVANIA (Province III)
Bishop Rt Revd Robert Gepert, 101 Pine St,
Harrisburg, PA 17101, USA Tel: 1 717 236 5959
Fax: 1 717 236 6448
email: rgepert@diocesecpa.org
Web: www.diocesecpa.org

CHICAGO (Province V)
Bishop Rt Revd Jeffery Lee, 65 E Huron St,
Chicago, IL 60611, USA Tel: 1 312 751 4200
Fax: 1 312 787 5872
email: bishop@episcopalchicago.org
Web: www.episcopalchicago.org

Assisting Bishop Rt Revd C. Christopher Epting
(*same address*) email: ccepting@aol.com

Assisting Bishop Rt Revd John C. Buchanan (*same
address*) email: jbuchanan@episcopalchicago.org

COLOMBIA (Province IX)
Bishop Rt Revd Francisco José Duque Gomez,
Centro Diocesano, Cra6 no 49–85 Piso 2, Bogotá
DC, Colombia Tel: 57 1 288 3167
Fax: 57 1 288 3248
email: obispoduque@iglesiaepiscopal.org.co
Web: www.iglesiaepiscopal.org.co

COLORADO (Province VI)
Bishop Rt Revd Robert John O'Neill, 1300
Washington St, Denver, CO 80203, USA
Tel: 1 303 837 1173
Fax: 1 303 837 1311
email: bishoponeill@coloradodiocese.org
Web: www.coloradodiocese.org

CONNECTICUT (Province I)
Bishop Rt Revd Ian Theodore Douglas, The
Commons, 290 Pratt St, Meriden, CT 061450,
USA Tel: 1 203 639 3501
Fax: 1 203 235 1008
email: itdouglas@episcopalct.org
Web: www.episcopalct.org

Bishops Suffragan
Rt Revd Laura Ahrens (*same address*)
email: lahrens@episcopalct.org

Rt Revd James Elliot Curry (*same address*)
email: jcurry@episcopalct.org

DALLAS (Province VII)
Bishop Vacancy, 1630 N Garrett Ave, Dallas, TX
75206, USA Tel: 1 214 826 8310
Fax: 1 214 826 5968
Web: http://edod.org

Bishop Suffragan Rt Revd Paul Emil Lambert (*same address*) email; plambert@edod.org

DELAWARE (Province III)
Bishop Rt Revd Wayne Parker Wright, 913 Wilson Rd, Wilmington, DE 19803, USA
Tel: 1 302 256 0374
Fax: 1 302 543 8084
email: bishop@dioceseofdelaware.info
Web: www.dioceseofdelaware.net

DOMINICAN REPUBLIC (Province IX)
Bishop Rt Revd Julio Cesar Holguin, Apartado 764, Calle Santiago No 114, Gazcue, DR764, Dominican Republic *Tel:* 1 809 688 7493
Fax: 1 809 688 6344
email: iglepidom@verizon.net.do
Web: www.episcopaldominican.org

EAST CAROLINA (Province IV)
Bishop Rt Revd Peter Lee, 705 Doctors Dr, Kinston, NC 28501, USA *Tel:* 1 252 522 0885
Fax: 1 252 523 5272
email: plee@diocese-eastcarolina.org
Web: www.diocese-eastcarolina.org

EAST TENNESSEE (Province IV)
Bishop Rt Revd George Dibrell Young III, 814 Episcopal School Way, Knoxville, TN 37932, USA
Tel: 1 865 966 2110
Fax: 1 865 966 2535
email: gyoung@dioet.lorg
Web: http://dioet.org

EASTERN MICHIGAN (Province V)
Bishop Rt Revd Steven Todd Ousley, Diocesan Office, 924 N Niagara St, Saginaw, MI 48602, USA *Tel:* 1 989 752 6020
Fax: 1 989 752 6120
email: tousley@eastmich.org
Web: http://eastmich.org

EASTERN OREGON (Province VIII)
Bishop Rt Revd Bavi Edna (Nedi) Rivera, 1104 Church St, Cove, OR 97824, USA
Tel: 1 541 568 4514
Fax: 1 541 568 5000
email: nrivera@episdioeo.org
Web: www.episdioeo.org

EASTON (Province III)
Bishop Rt Revd James Joseph Shand, 314 North St, Easton, MD 21601, USA *Tel:* 1 410 822 1919
Fax: 1 410 763 8259
email: bishopshand@dioceseofeaston.org
Web: http://dioceseofeaston.org

EAU CLAIRE (Province V)
Provisional Bishop Rt Revd William J. Lambert, 510 South Farwell St, Eau Claire, WI 54701, USA
Tel: 1 715 835 3331
Fax: 1 715 835 9212
Web: www.dioec.net

EL CAMINO REAL (Province VIII)
Bishop Rt Revd Mary Gray-Reeves, 1092 Noche Buena St, Seaside, CA 93955, USA
Tel: 1 831 394 4465
Fax: 1 831 394 7133
email: bishopmary@edecr.org
Web: www.edecr.org

EUROPE, CONVOCATION OF EPISCOPAL CHURCHES IN
Bishop in Charge Rt Revd Pierre Welté Whalon, American Cathedral of the Holy Trinity, 23 Avenue George V, 75008 Paris, France
Tel: 33 1 53 23 84 06
Fax: 33 1 49 52 96 85
email: bishop@tec-europe.org
Web: www.tec-europe.org

FLORIDA (Province IV)
Bishop Rt Revd Samuel Johnson Howard, Hamilton West Diocesan Centre, 325 N Market St, Jacksonville, FL 32202, USA *Tel:* 1 904 356 1328
Fax: 1 904 355 1934
email: jhoward @diocesefl.org
Web: www.diocesefl.org

FOND DU LAC (Province V)
Bishop Rt Revd Matthew Alan Gunter, 1051 N Lynndale Drive, Suite 1B, Appleton, WI 54914–3094, USA *Tel:* 1 920 830 8866
Fax: 1 920 830 8761
email: mgunter@diofdl.org
Web: www.episcopalfonddulac.org

FORT WORTH (Province VII)
Provisional Bishop Rt Revd Rayford B. High, 4301 Meadowbank Drive, Fort Worth, TX 76103, USA
Tel: 1 817 534 9000
Fax: 1 817 534 1904
email: bishop@edfw.org
Web: http://episcopaldiocesefortworth.org

GEORGIA (Province IV)
Bishop Rt Revd Scott Anson Benhase, 611 E Bay St, Savannah, GA 31401, USA
Tel: 1 912 236 4279
Fax: 1 912 236 2007
email: bishop@gaepiscopal.org
Web: http://georgia.anglican.org

HAITI (Province II)
Bishop Rt Revd Jean Zaché Duracin, Église Épiscopale d'Haiti, BP 1309, Port-au-Prince, Haiti
Tel: 509 257 1624
email: epihaiti@egliseepiscopaledhaiti.org
Web: egliseepiscopaledhaiti.org

HAWAII (Province VIII)
Bishop Rt Revd Robert LeRoy Fitzpatrick, Diocesan Office, 229 Queen Emma Sq, Honolulu HI 96813–2304, USA *Tel:* 1 808 536 7776
Fax: 1 808 538 7194
email: rlfitzpatrick@episcopalhawaii.org
Web: www.episcopalhawaii.org

Anglican and Porvoo Communions

HONDURAS (Province IX)
Bishop Rt Revd Lloyd Emmanuel Allen, Colonia Trejo 23 Av 21 Calle, San Pedro Sula, Honduras 21105   *Tel:* 504 556 6155
Fax: 504 566 6467
Web: http://honduras.fedigitalis.org

IDAHO (Province VIII)
Bishop Rt Revd Brian James Thom, 1858 Judith Lane, Boise, ID 83705, USA   *Tel:* 1 208 345 4440
Fax: 1 208 345 9735
email: bthom@idahodiocese.org
Web: www.episcopalidaho.org

INDIANAPOLIS (Province V)
Bishop Rt Revd Catherine Elizabeth Maples Waynick, 1100 West 42nd St, Indianapolis, IN 46208, USA   *Tel:* 1 317 926 5454
Fax: 1 317 926 5456
email: bishop@indydio.org
Web: http://indydio.org

IOWA (Province VI)
Bishop Rt Revd Alan Scarfe, 225 37th St, Des Moines, IA 50312–4305, USA   *Tel:* 1 515 277 6165
Fax: 1 515 277 0273
email: ascarfe@iowaepiscopal.org
Web: www.iowaepiscopal.org

KANSAS (Province VII)
Bishop Rt Revd Dean Eliott Wolfe, Bethany Place, 835 SW Polk St, Topeka, KS 66612–1688, USA
Tel: 1 785 235 9255
Fax: 1 785 235 2449
email: dwolfe@episcopal-ks.org
Web: www.episcopal-ks.org

KENTUCKY (Province IV)
Bishop Rt Revd Terry Allen White, 425 S 2nd St, Louisville, KY 40202, USA   *Tel:* 1 502 584 7148
Fax: 1 502 587 8123
email: bishopwhite@episcopalky.org
Web: www.episcopalky.org

LEXINGTON (Province IV)
Bishop Rt Revd Douglas Hahn, 203 E 4th St, Lexington, KY 40508, USA   *Tel:* 1 859 252 6527
Fax: 1 859 231 9077
email: dhahn@diolex.org
Web: http://diolex.org

LITORAL ECUADOR (Province IX)
Bishop Rt Revd Alfredo Morante, Box 0901–5250, Amarilis Fuente 603 entre José Vincento Trujillo y la 'D', Guayaquil, Ecuador
Tel: 593 4 244 6699
Fax: 593 4 244 3088
email: iglesia_litoral@hotmail.com
Web: www.diocesislitoral.org

LONG ISLAND (Province II)
Bishop Rt Revd Lawrence C. Provenzano, 36 Cathedral Ave, Garden City, NY 11530–0510, USA
Tel: 1 516 248 4800
Fax: 1 516 248 1616
email: lprovenzano@dioceseli.org
Web: www.dioceselongisland.org

LOS ANGELES (Province VIII)
Bishop Rt Revd Joseph Jon Bruno, 840 Echo Park Ave, Box 512164, Los Angeles, CA 90051, USA
Tel: 1 213 482 2040
Fax: 1 213 482 5304
email: bishop@ladiocese.org
Web: www.ladiocese.org

Bishops Suffragan
Rt Revd Diane M. Jardine Bruce (*same address*)
email: djbsuffragan@ladiocese.org

Rt Revd Mary Douglas Glasspool (*same address*)
email: mdgsuffragan@ladiocese.org

LOUISIANA (Province IV)
Bishop Rt Revd Morris K. Thompson, 1623 7th St, New Orleans, LA 70115, USA
Tel: 1 504 895 6634
Fax: 1 504 895 6637
email: mthompson@edola.org
Web: www.edola.org

MAINE (Province I)
Bishop Rt Revd Stephen Taylor Lane, Loring House, 143 State St, Portland, ME 04101–3799, USA   *Tel:* 1 207 772 1953
Fax: 1 207 773 0095
email: slane@episcopalmaine.org
Web: http://episcopalmaine.org

MARYLAND (Province III)
Bishop Rt Revd Eugene Taylor Sutton, 4 East University Parkway, Baltimore, MD 21218, USA
Tel: 1 410 467 1399
Fax: 1 410 554 6387
email: esutton@episcopalmaryland.org
Web: www.episcopalmaryland.org

Bishop Suffragan Rt Revd Heather Elizabeth Cook (*same address*)
email: hcook@episcoplamaryland.org

MASSACHUSETTS (Province I)
Bishop Rt Revd Alan McIntosh Gates, 138 Tremont St, Boston, MA 02111–1318, USA
Tel: 1 617 482 5800
Fax: 1 617 482 8431
email: jdrapeau@diomass.org
Web: www.diomass.org

Bishop Suffragan
Rt Revd Gayle Elizabeth Harris (*same address*)
email: msearle@diomass.org

MICHIGAN (Province V)
Bishop Rt Revd Wendell Nathaniel Gibbs Jr, 4800
Woodward Ave, Detroit, MI 48201, USA
Tel: 1 313 833 4000
Fax: 1 313 831 0259
email: bishop@edomi.org
Web: www.edomi.org

MILWAUKEE (Province V)
Bishop Rt Revd Steven Andrew Miller, 804 E
Juneau Ave, Milwaukee, WI 53202–2798, USA
Tel: 1 414 272 3028
Fax: 1 414 272 7790
email: bishop@diomil.org
Web: www.diomil.org

MINNESOTA (Province VI)
Bishop Rt Revd Brian N. Prior, 1730 Clifton Place,
Suite 201, Minneapolis, MN 55403-3242, USA
Tel: 1 612 871 5311
Fax: 1 612 871 0552
email: info@episcopalmn.org
Web: http://episcopalmn.org

MISSISSIPPI (Province IV)
Bishop Rt Revd Brian R. Seage, 118 N Congress
St, Jackson, MS 39225–3107, USA
Tel: 1 601 948 5954
Fax: 1 601 354 3401
email: pjones@dioms.org
Web: www.dioms.org

MISSOURI (Province V)
Bishop Rt Revd George Wayne Smith, 1210
Locust St, St Louis, MO 63103, USA
Tel: 1 314 231 1220
Fax: 1 314 231 3373
email: bishop@diocesemo.org
Web: www.diocesemo.org

MONTANA (Province VI)
Bishop Rt Revd Charles Franklin Brookhart Jr,
515 N Park Ave, Helena, MT 59601–8135, USA
Tel: 1 406 442 2230
Fax: 1 406 442 2238
email: cfbmt@qwestoffice.net
Web: http://diomontana.com

**NAVAJOLAND AREA MISSION (Province
VIII)**
Bishop Rt Revd Rt Revd David Earle Bailey, 1227
Mission Ave, Farmington, NM 87499–0720, USA
Tel: 1 505 326 7194
Fax: 1 505 327 6904
email: via website
Web: http://navajoland.org

NEBRASKA (Province VI)
Bishop J. Scott Barker, 109 N 18th St, Omaha,
NE 68102–4903, USA
Tel: 1 402 341 5373
Fax: 1 402 341 8683
email: sbarker@episcopal-ne.org
Web: www.episcopal-ne.org

NEVADA (Province VIII)
Bishop Rt Revd Dan T. Edwards, 9480 S Eastern
Ave, Suite 1B, Las Vegas, NV 89123–8037, USA
Tel: 1 702 737 9190
Fax: 1 702 737 6488
email: dan@episcopalnevada.org
Web: www.episcopalnevada.org

NEW HAMPSHIRE (Province I)
Bishop Rt Revd A. Robert Hirschfeld, 63 Green
St, Concord, NH 03301, USA
Tel: 1 603 224 1914
Fax: 1 603 225 7884
email: arh@nhepiscopal.org
Web: www.nhepiscopal.org

NEW JERSEY (Province II)
Bishop Rt Revd William H. (Chip) Stokes, 808
West State St, Trenton, NJ 08618–5326, USA
Tel: 1 609 394 5281
Fax: 1 609 394 9546
email: wstokes@newjersey.anglican.org
Web: www.newjersey.anglican.org

NEW YORK (Province II)
Bishop Rt Revd Andrew M. L. Dietsche, Synod
House, 1047 Amsterdam Ave, New York, NY
10025, USA
Tel: 1 212 316 7400
Fax: 1 212 316 7405
email: via website
Web: www.dioceseny.org

Bishop Suffragan Allen K. Shin (*same address*)
email: via website

NEWARK (Province II)
Bishop Rt Revd Mark Beckwith, 31 Mulberry St,
Newark, NJ 07102, USA
Tel: 1 923 430 9900
Fax: 1 923 622 3503
email: mbeckwith@dioceseofnewark.org
Web: www.dioceseofnewark.org

NORTH CAROLINA (Province IV)
Bishop Rt Revd Michael Bruce Curry, 200 West
Morgan St, Suite 300, Raleigh, NC 27601, USA
Tel: 1 919 834 7474
Fax: 1 919 834 7546
email: michael.curry@episdionc.org
Web: http://episdionc.org

Bishop Suffragan Rt Revd Anne Hodges-Copple,
301 N Elm St, Suite 308-C, Greenboro, NC 27401,
USA
Tel: 1 336 273 5770
Fax: 1 336 273 5770
email: bishopanne@episdionc.org

NORTH DAKOTA (Province VI)
Bishop Rt Revd Michael Gene Smith, 3600 S. 25th
St, Fargo, ND 58104–6861, USA
Tel: 1 701 235 6688
Fax: 1 701 232 3077
email: BpNoDak@aol.com
Web: www.ndepiscopal.org

NORTHERN CALIFORNIA (Province VIII)
Bishop Rt Revd Barry Leigh Beisner, 350 University Avenue, Suite 280, Sacramento, CA 95816, USA   *Tel:* 1 916 442 6918
Fax: 1 916 442 6927
email: barry@norcalepiscopal.org
Web: www.norcalepiscopal.org

NORTHERN INDIANA (Province V)
Bishop Rt Revd Edward Stuart Little II, 117 N Lafayette Blvd, South Bend, Indiana 46601, USA
Tel: 1 574 233 6489
Fax: 1 574 287 7914
email: bishop@ednin.org
Web: www.ednin.org

NORTHERN MICHIGAN (Province V)
Bishop Rt Revd Rayford J. Ray, 131 E Ridge St, Marquette, MI 49855, USA   *Tel:* 1 906 228 7160
Fax: 1 906 228 7171
email: rayfordray@chartermi.net
Web: www.upepiscopal.org

NORTHWEST TEXAS (Province VII)
Bishop Rt Revd James Scott Mayer, The Hulsey Episcopal Center, 1802 Broadway Ave, Lubbock, TX 79401, USA   *Tel:* 1 806 763 1370
Fax: 1 806 472 0641
email: diocese@nwtdiocese.org
Web: www.nwtdiocese.org

NORTHWESTERN PENNSYLVANIA (Province III)
Bishop Rt Revd Sean W. Rowe, 145 W 6th St, Erie, PA 16501, USA   *Tel:* 1 814 456 4203
Fax: 1 814 454 8703
email: seanrowe@dionwpa.org
Web: www.dionwpa.org

OHIO (Province V)
Bishop Rt Revd Mark Hollingsworth Jr, 2230 Euclid Ave, Cleveland, OH 44115–2499, USA
Tel: 1 216 771 4815
Fax: 1 216 623 0735
email: mh@dohio.org
Web: www.dohio.org

Assisting Bishops
Rt Revd David C. Bowman (*same address*)
Rt Revd William Dailey Persell (*same address*)
Rt Revd Arthur Williams (*same address*)

OKLAHOMA (Province VII)
Bishop Rt Revd Edward Joseph Konieczny, 924 N Robinson, Oklahoma City, OK 73102, USA
Tel: 1 405 232 4820
email: bishoped@epiok.org
Web: www.epiok.org

OLYMPIA (Province VIII)
Bishop Rt Revd Gregory H. Rickel, 1551 10th Ave, Seattle, WA 98102, USA   *Tel:* 1 206 325 4200
Fax: 1 206 325 4631
email: grickel@ecww.org
Web: www.ecww.org

OREGON (Province VIII)
Bishop Michael Joseph Hanley, 11800 SW Military Lane, Portland, OR 97219, USA
Tel: 1 503 636 5613
Fax: 1 503 636 5616
email: bishop@episcopaldioceseoregon.org
Web: www.dioceseoregon.org

PENNSYLVANIA (Province III)
Bishop Rt Revd Clifton Daniel, 7301 Germantown Ave, 3rd Floor, Philadelphia, PA 19119, USA
Tel: 1 215 627 6434
Fax: 1 215 900 2928
email: cdaniel@diopa.org
Web: www.diopa.org

Assisting Bishops
Rodney Rae Michel   *email:* rodneym@diopa.org
Rt Revd Edward L. Lee
email: bpedwardlee@yahoo.com

PITTSBURGH (Province III)
Bishop Rt Revd Dorsey W. M. McConnell, 4099 William Penn Hwy, Suite 502, Monroeville, PA 15146, USA   *Tel:* 1 412 721 0853
Fax: 1 412 232 6408
email: dmcconnell@episcopalpgh.org
Web: ibwww.epsicopalpgh.org

PUERTO RICO (Province IX)
Bishop Rt Revd Wilfredo Ramos Orench, PO Box 902, St Just, PR 00978–0902, Puerto Rico
Tel: 1 787 761 9800
Fax: 1 787 761 0320
email: obisporamos@episcopalpr.org
Web: www.episcopalpr.org

QUINCY (Province V)
Bishop Rt Revd John Clark Buchanan, c/o St Paul's Cathedral, 3601 N North St, Peoria, IL 61604–1517, USA   *Tel:* 1 309 685 8673
Fax: 1 309 685 8682
email: bishop@dioceseofquincy
Web: www.thedioceseofquincyonline.com

RHODE ISLAND (Province I)
Bishop Rt Revd W. Nicholas Knisely, 275 N Main St, Providence, RI 02903–1298, USA
Tel: 1 401 274 4500
Fax: 1 401 331 9430
email: nicholas@episcopalri.org
Web: www.episcopalri.org

RIO GRANDE (Province VII)
Bishop Rt Revd Michael Louis Vono, 6400 Coors Blvd NE, Albuquerque, NM 87107–4811, USA
Tel: 1 505 881 0636
Fax: 1 505 883 9048
email: bpmichael@dioceserg.org
Web: www.dioceserg.org

ROCHESTER (Province II)
Bishop Rt Revd Prince Grenville Singh, 935 East
Ave, Rochester, NY 14607, USA
                              Tel: 1 585 473 2977
                              Fax: 1 585 473 3195
email: prince@episcopaldioceseofrochester.org
       Web: http://episcopalrochester.org

SAN DIEGO (Province VIII)
Bishop Rt Revd James Robert Mathes, 2083
Sunset Cliffs Blvd, San Diego, CA 92107, USA
                              Tel: 1 619 291 5947
                              Fax: 1 619 291 8362
             email: bishopmathes@edsd.org
                   Web: www.edsd.org

SAN JOAQUIN (Province VIII)
Provisional Bishop Rt Revd David C. Rice, 1528
Oakdale Rd, Modesto, CA 95355, USA
                              Tel: 1 209 576 0104
                              Fax: 1 209 576 0114
     email: bishopdavid@diosanjoaquin.org
           Web: www.diosanjoaquin.org

SOUTH CAROLINA (Province IV)
Bishop Rt Revd Charles vonRosenberg, 98 Went-
worth St, Charleston, SC 29413, USA
                              Tel: 1 843 259 2016
                              Fax: 1 843 723 7628
    email: bishop@episcopalchurchsc.org
         Web: www.episcopalchurchsc.org

SOUTH DAKOTA (Province VI)
Bishop Rt Revd John Thomas Tarrant, 500 S Main
Ave, Sioux Falls, SD 57104–6814, USA
                              Tel: 1 605 338 9751
                              Fax: 1 605 336 6243
email: bishop.diocese@midconetwork.com
               Web: www.diocesesd.org

SOUTHEAST FLORIDA (Province IV)
Bishop Rt Revd Leopold Frade, 525 NE 15 St,
Miami, FL 33132, USA   *Tel:* 1 305 373 0881
                              Fax: 1 305 375 8054
             email: bishopfrade@aol.com
                   Web: www.diosef.org

SOUTHERN OHIO (Province V)
Bishop Rt Revd Thomas Edward Breidenthal, 412
Sycamore St, Cincinnati, OH 45202, USA
                              Tel: 1 513 421 0311
                              Fax: 1 513 421 0315
        email: tbreidenthal@diosohio.org
             Web: www.episcopal-dso.org

SOUTHERN VIRGINIA (Province III)
Bishop Rt Revd Herman (Holly) Hollerith IV, 600
Talbot Hall Rd, Norfolk, VA 23505–4301, USA
                              Tel: 1 757 423 8287
                              Fax: 1 757 440 5354
            email: bishop@diosova.org
                  Web: www.diosova.org

SOUTHWEST FLORIDA (Province IV)
Bishop Rt Revd Dabney T. Smith, 2005 25th St E,
Parrish, FL 34219–9405, USA *Tel:* 1 941 556 0315
                              Fax: 1 941 556 0321
          email: dsmith@episcopalswfl.org
               Web: www.episcopalswfl.org

Assisting Bishops
J. Michael Garrison
Barry R. Howe

SOUTHWESTERN VIRGINIA (Province III)
Bishop Mark Allen Bourlakas, 1002 1st St,
Roanoke, VA 24016, USA   *Tel:* 1 757 423 8287
                              Fax: 1 757 440 5354
           email: bishopmark@dioswva.org
                  Web: www.dioswva.org

SPOKANE (Province VIII)
Bishop Rt Revd James Edward Waggoner Jr, 245
E 13th Ave, Spokane, WA 99202–1114, USA
                              Tel: 1 509 624 3191
                              Fax: 1 509 747 0049
         email: jimw@spokanediocese.org
              Web: www.spokanediocese.org

SPRINGFIELD (Province V)
Bishop Rt Revd Daniel Hayden Martins, 821 S 2nd
St, Springfield, IL 62704, USA
                              Tel: 1 217 525 1876
                              Fax: 1 217 525 1877
      email: bishop@episcopalspringfield.org
           Web: www.episcopalspringfield.org

TAIWAN (Province VIII)
Bishop Rt Revd David Jung-Hsin Lai, 10060
Hangzhou South Rd, Taipei City, Taiwan,
Republic of China   *Tel:* 886 2 2341 1265
              Web: www.episcopaldiotaiwan.org

TENNESSEE (Province IV)
Bishop Rt Revd John Crawford Bauerschmidt,
3700 Woodmont Blvd, Nashville, TN 37215, USA
                              Tel: 1 615 251 3322
                              Fax: 1 615 251 8010
                 email: info@edtn.org
                 Web: http://edtn.org

TEXAS (Province VII)
Bishop Rt Revd Charles Andrew Doyle, 1225
Texas Ave, Houston, TX 77002–3504, USA
                              Tel: 1 713 353 2100
                              Fax: 1 713 520 5723
            email: adoyle@epicenter.org
                 Web: www.epicenter.org

Bishop Suffragan Dena A. Harrison, 510 Rathervue
Place, PO Box 2247, Austin, TX 78768–2247, USA
                              Tel: 1 512 478 0580
                              Fax: 1 512 478 5615
          email: dharrison@epicenter.org

UPPER SOUTH CAROLINA (Province IV)
Bishop Rt Revd W. Andrew Waldo, 1115 Marion St, Columbia, SC 29201, USA
Tel: 1 803 771 7800
Fax: 1 803 799 5119
email: bishopwaldo@edusc.org
Web: www.edusc.org

UTAH (Province VIII)
Bishop Rt Revd Scott B. Hayashi, 75 S 200 E, Salt Lake City, UT 84110–3090, USA
Tel: 1 801 322 4131
Fax: 1 801 322 5096
email: shayashi@episcopal-ut.org
Web: www.episcopal-ut.org

VENEZUELA (Province IX)
Bishop Rt Revd Orlando Guerrero, Colinas de Bello Monte, Caracas 1042-A, Venezuela
Tel: 58 212 751 3046

VERMONT (Province I)
Bishop Rt Revd Thomas Clark Ely, 5 Rock Point Rd, Burlington, VT 05401, USA
Tel: 1 802 863 3431
Fax: 1 802 860 1562
Web: www.diovermont.org

VIRGIN ISLANDS (Province II)
Bishop Rt Revd Edward Ambrose Gumbs, 13 Commandant Gade, Charlotte Amaille, St Thomas, VI 00801, USA
Tel: 1 340 776 1797
Fax: 1 340 777 8485

VIRGINIA (Province III)
Bishop Rt Revd Shannon Sherwood Johnston, 110 W Franklin St, Richmond, VA 23220, USA
Tel: 1 804 643 8451
Fax: 1 804 644 6928
email: sjohnston@thediocese.net
Web: www.thediocese.net

Bishop Suffragan Susan Ellyn Goff (*same address*)
email: sgoff@thediocese.net

Assistant Bishop
Rt Revd Edwin F. (Ted) Gulick, 115 E Fairfax St, Falls Church, VA 22046, USA   *Tel:* 1 703 241 0441
email: tgulick@thediocese.net

WASHINGTON DC (Province III)
Bishop Mariann Edgar Budde, Episcopal Church House, Mount St Alban, Washington, DC 20016–5094, USA
Tel: 1 202 537 6555
Fax: 1 202 364 6605
email: mebudde@edow.org
Web: www.edow.org

WEST MISSOURI (Province VII)
Bishop Rt Revd Martin Scott Field, 420 W 14th St, Kansas City, MO 64105–3227, USA
Tel: 1 816 471 6161
Fax: 1 816 471 0379
email: bishopfield@ediowestmo.org
Web: http://diowestmo.org

WEST TENNESSEE (Province IV)
Bishop Rt Revd Don Edward Johnson, 692 Poplar Ave, Memphis, TN 38105, USA
Tel: 1 901 526 0023
Fax: 1 901 526 1555
email: bishopjohnson@episwtn.org
Web: www.episwtn.org

WEST TEXAS (Province VII)
Bishop Rt Revd Gary Richard Lillibridge, 111 Torcido Dr, San Antonio, TX 78209, USA
Tel: 1 210 824 5387
Fax: 1 210 824 2164
email: gary.lillibridge@dwtx.org
Web: http://dwtx.org

Bishop Suffragan Rt Revd David Reed (*same address*)   *email:* david.reed@dwtx.org

WEST VIRGINIA (Province III)
Bishop Rt Revd William Michie Klusmeyer, 1608 Virginia St E, Charleston, WV 25311, USA
Tel: 1 304 344 3597
Fax: 1 304 343 3295
email: mklusmeyer@wvdiocese.org
Web: www.wvdiocese.org

WESTERN KANSAS (Province VII)
Bishop Rt Revd Michael P. Milliken, 2 Hyde Park, Hutchinson, KS 67502, USA   *Tel:* 1 620 662 0011
Fax: 1 620 662 2930
email: tec.wks2011@gmail.com
Web: http://diowks.org

WESTERN LOUISIANA (Province VII)
Bishop Rt Revd Jacob W. Owensby, 335 Main St, Pineville,LA 71360, USA   *Tel:* 1 318 422 1304
Fax: 1 318 442 8712
email: bishopjake@diocesewla.org
Web: www.diocesewla.org

WESTERN MASSACHUSETTS (Province I)
Bishop Rt Revd Douglas John Fisher, 37 Chestnut St, Springfield, MA 01103, USA   *Tel:* 1 413 737 4786
Fax: 1 413 746 9873
email: communications@diocesewma.org
Web: www.diocesewma.org

WESTERN MICHIGAN (Province V)
Bishop Rt Revd Whayne M. Hougland, Episcopal Center, 5355 Burdick St, Suite 1, Kalamazoo, MI 49007, USA
Tel: 1 269 381 2710
Fax: 1 269 381 7067
email: wmhougland@edwm.org /
edwmorg@edwm.org
Web: www.edwm.org

WESTERN NEW YORK (Province II)
Bishop Rt Revd R. William Franklin, 1064 Brighton Rd, Tonawanda, NY 14150, USA
Tel: 1 716 881 0660
Fax: 1 716 881 1724
email: rwfranklin@episcopalwny.org
Web: http://episcopalwny.org

WESTERN NORTH CAROLINA (Province IV)
Bishop Rt Revd Granville Porter Taylor, 900B
Center Park Drive, Asheville, NC 28805, USA
Tel: 1 828 225 6656
Fax: 1 828 225 6657
email: bishop@diocesewnc.org
Web: www.diocesewnc.org

WYOMING (Province VI)
Bishop Rt Revd John S. Smylie, 123 S. Durbin St,
Casper WY 82601, USA   *Tel:* 1 307 265 5200
Fax: 1 307 577 9939
email: bishopsmylie@wyomingdiocese.org
Web: www.diowy.org

The Church in Wales

Members 56,396
The Church in Wales has been an independent
province since its disestablishment and separation from the Church of England in 1920. It is
practically coterminous with Wales and is the
largest denomination in the country. The major
policy-forming body is the Governing Body and
the Church's inherited assets, including buildings, are held in trust by the Representative Body.

Archbishop Most Revd Barry Cennydd Morgan
(*Bishop of Llandaff*)   *Tel:* 029 2056 2400
Fax: 029 2056 8410
email: archbishop@churchinwales.org.uk

Provincial Secretary and Archbishop's Registrar Mr
John Shirley, 39 Cathedral Rd, Cardiff CF11 9XF
Tel: 029 2034 8218
Fax: 029 2038 7835
email: information@churchinwales.org.uk
Web: www.churchinwales.org.uk

Archbishop's Media Officer Anna Morrell (*same
address*)   *Tel:* 029 2034 8208

THEOLOGICAL COLLEGE
St Michael's Theological College, 54 Cardiff
Road, Llandaff, Cardiff CF5 2YJ (*Acting Principal
and Dean of Residential Training* Revd Dr Mark
Forbes Moreton Clavier)   *Tel:* 029 2056 3379
Fax: 029 2083 8008
email: info@stmichaels.ac.uk

BANGOR
Bishop Rt Revd Andrew Thomas Griffith John,
Ty'r Esgob, Ffordd Garth Uchaf, Bangor,
Gwynedd LL57 2SS   *Tel:* 01248 362895
Fax: 01248 372454
email: bishop.bangor@churchinwales.org.uk
Web: www.churchinwales.org.uk/bangor

CATHEDRAL CHURCH OF ST DEINIOL, Bangor,
Gwynedd
Dean Very Revd Dr Susan Helen Jones, The
Deanery, Cathedral Precinct, Bangor LL57 1LH
Tel: 01248 355530
email: sjones1234jones@btinternet.com

LLANDAFF
Bishop Most Revd Dr Barry Cennydd Morgan
(*Archbishop of the Province*), Llys Esgob, The
Cathedral Green, Llandaff, Cardiff CF5 2YE
Tel: 029 2056 2400
Fax: 029 2056 8410
email: archbishop@churchinwales.org.uk
Web: www.churchinwales.org.uk/llandaff

Assistant Bishop of Llandaff, Rt Revd David
Jeffrey Wilbourne, Llys Esgob, The Cathedral
Green, Cardiff CF5 2YE   *Tel:* 029 20 562400
Fax: 029 2057 7129
email: asstbishop@churchinwales.org.uk

CATHEDRAL CHURCH OF ST PETER AND ST PAUL,
Llandaff, Cardiff
Dean Very Revd Gerwyn Huw Capon, The
Deanery, The Cathedral Green, Llandaff, Cardiff
CF5 2YF   *Tel:* 02920 561545
email: thedean@llandaffcathedral.org.uk

MONMOUTH
Bishop Rt Revd R. E. Pain, Bishopstow, Stow
Hill, Newport NP20 4EA   *Tel:* 01633 263510
email: bishop.monmouth@churchinwales.org.uk
Web: www.churchinwales.org.uk/monmouth

CATHEDRAL CHURCH OF ST WOOLOS, Newport
Dean Very Revd Lister Tonge, The Deanery, Stow
Hill, Newport NP20 4ED   *Tel:* 01633 259627
email: listertonge@gmail.com

ST ASAPH
Bishop Rt Revd Gregory Kenneth Cameron,
Esgobty, Upper Denbigh Road, St Asaph LL17
0TW   *Tel:* 01745 583503
Fax: 01745 584301
email: bishop.stasaph@churchinwales.org.uk
Web: www.churchinwales.org.uk/asaph

CATHEDRAL CHURCH OF ST ASAPH, St Asaph,
Denbighshire

Dean Very Revd Nigel Howard Williams, The
Deanery, Upper Denbigh Road, St Asaph LL17
0RL   *Tel:* 01745 583597
email: nigelwilliams@churchinwales.org.uk

ST DAVIDS

Bishop Rt Revd J. Wyn Evans, Llys Esgob, Abergwili, Carmarthen SA31 2JG
Tel: 01267 236597
Fax: 01267 243381
email: bishop.stdavids@churchinwales.org.uk
Web: www.churchinwales.org.uk/david

CATHEDRAL CHURCH OF ST DAVID AND ST ANDREW, St Davids, Pembrokeshire
Dean Very Revd David Jonathan Rees Lean, The Deanery, St Davids, Haverfordwest SA62 6RH
Tel: 01437 720456
Fax: 01437 721885

SWANSEA AND BRECON

Bishop Rt Revd John David Edward Davies, Ely Tower, Castle Square, Brecon LD3 9DJ
Tel: 01874 622008
Fax: 01874 610927
email: bishop.swanbrec @churchinwales.org.uk
Web: www.churchinwales.org.uk/swanbrec

CATHEDRAL CHURCH OF ST JOHN THE EVANGELIST, Brecon, Powys
Dean Very Revd Dr Paul Alberrt Shackerley, The Deanery, Cathedral Close, Brecon LD3 9DP
Tel: 01874 623344
email: admin@breconcathedral.org.uk

The Church of the Province of West Africa

Members 1,278,000

Church work began in Ghana as early as 1752 and in the Gambia, Guinea, Liberia and Sierra Leone in the nineteenth century. The Province of West Africa was founded in 1951 and was divided to form the Province of Nigeria and the Province of West Africa in 1979.

In September 2012, the Province amended its constitution to create two internal provinces to be headed by two Archbishops, with one of them to be the Primate. The Church exists in an atmosphere of civil strife and Christians remain a minority.

Archbishop and Primate of the Province of West Africa Most Revd. Dr Daniel Yinkah Sarfo (*Bishop of Kumasi and Archbishop of the internal province of Ghana*)

Dean of the Province of West Africa Most Revd Dr Jonathan B. B. Hart (*Bishop of Liberia and Archbishop of the internal province of West Africa*)

Episcopal Secretary of the Province of West Africa Rt Revd Matthias K. Medadues-Badohu (*Bishop of Ho*)

Provincial Secretary Revd Canon Anthony M. Eiwuley, PO Box Lt 226, Lartebiokorshie, Accra, Ghana
Tel: 233 302 257 370
233 27 720 1538 (Mobile)
email: cpwa2014@gmail.com
morkeiwuley@gmail.com

Provincial Treasurer Mr Samuel Atuobi Twum (*same address*)
Tel: 233 21 506 208
233 20 201 7969 (Mobile)
email: atlantichousing@yahoo.co.uk

THEOLOGICAL COLLEGES
Ghana
Trinity College (Ecumenical), PO Box 48, Legon, Ghana

St Nicholas Anglican Theological College, PO Box A 162, Cape Coast, Ghana

Liberia
Cuttington University College, Suacoco, PO Box 10–0277, 1000 Monrovia 10, Liberia

Sierra Leone
Theological Hall and Church Training Centre, PO Box 128, Freetown, Sierra Leone

ACCRA

Bishop Rt Revd Dr Daniel S. M. Torto, Bishops-court, PO Box 8, Accra, Ghana
Tel: 233 302 662 292
233 277 496 479 (Mobile)
email: dantorto@yahoo.com
Web: www.acceaanglican.org

BO

Bishop Rt Revd Emmanuel Josie Samuel Tucker, PO Box 21, Bo, Southern Province, Sierra Leone
Tel: 232 32 648
Fax: 232 32 605
232 76 677 862 (Mobile)
email: bomission@justice.com/
ejstucker@gmail.com

CAMEROON

Bishop Rt Revd Thomas-Babyngton Elango Dibo, BP 15705, New Bell, Douala, Cameroon
Tel: 237 755 58276
email: revdibo2@yahoo.com

CAPE COAST

Bishop Rt Revd Dr Victor R. Atta-Baffoe, Bishopscourt, PO Box A 233, Adisadel Estates, Cape Coast, Ghana
Tel: 233 3321 23 502
233 2065 2319 (Mobile)
Fax: 233 42 32 637
email: victorattabaffoe@yahoo.com

DUNKWA-ON-OFFIN
Bishop Rt Revd Edmund K. Dawson-Ahmoah, PO Box DW42, Dunkwa-on-Offin
233 24 464 4764 (Mobile)
email: papacy11@yahoo.co.uk

FREETOWN
Bishop Rt Revd Thomas Arnold Ikunika Wilson, Bishop's Court, PO Box 537, Freetown, Sierra Leone   *Tel:* 232 22 251 307 (Mobile)

GAMBIA
Bishop Vacancy, Bishopscourt, PO Box 51, Banjul, The Gambia, West Africa   *Tel:* 220 228 405
Web: www.gambiadiocese.com

GUINEA
Bishop Rt Revd Jacques Boston, BP 187, Conakry, Guinea   *Tel:* 224 63 58 79 38 (Mobile)
email: bostonjacques@yahoo.com

HO
Bishop Rt Revd Matthias K. Mededues-Badohu, Bishopslodge, PO Box MA 300, Ho, Volta Region, Ghana   *Tel:* 233 3620 26644 / 233 3620 28606
233 208 162 246 (Mobile)
email: matthoda@ucomgh.com/
matthiaskwab@googlemail.com

KOFORIDUA
Bishop Rt Revd Francis B. Quashie, PO Box 980, Koforidua, Ghana   *Tel:* 233 3420 22 329
Fax: 233 81 22 060
email: fbquashie@yahoo.com

KUMASI
Bishop Most Revd Dr Daniel Yinka Sarfo, Bishop's House, PO Box 144, Kumasi, Ghana
Tel and *Fax:* 233 51 24 117
233 277 890 411 (Mobile)
email: anglicandioceseofkumasi@yahoo.com /
dysarfo2000@yahoo.co.uk

Suffragan Bishop Rt Revd Dr Cyril K. Ben-Smith
(same address)   *Tel:* 233 2477 4308 (Mobile)
email: bishop. mampong@yahoo.co.uk

LIBERIA
Bishop Most Revd Dr Jonathan B. B. Hart, PO Box 10–0277, 1000 Monrovia 10, Liberia
Tel: 231 224 760
231 651 6343 (Mobile)
Fax: 231 227 519
email: jbbhart@yahoo.com /
bishopecl12@yahoo.com
Web: www.liberia.anglican.org

SEKONDI
Bishop Rt Revd Col John Kwamina Otoo, PO Box 85, Sekondi, Ghana   *Tel:* 233 3120 46832
233 208 200887 (Mobile)
email: angdiocesek@yahoo.co.uk

SUNYANI
Bishop Rt Revd Dr Festus Yeboah-Asuamah, PO Box 23, Sunyani, Ghana   *Tel:* 233 3520 23213
233 208 121 670 (Mobile)
Fax: 233 61 712300
email: fyasuamah@yahoo.com

TAMALE
Bishop Rt Revd (Hon) Dr Jacob K. Ayeebo, PO Box 110, Tamale, Ghana   *Tel:* 233 3720 26639
233 243 419 864 (Mobile)
Fax: 233 3729 22906
email: bishopea2000@yahoo.com

WIAWSO
Bishop Rt Revd Abraham Kobina Ackah, PO Box 4, Sefwi, Wiawso, Ghana
Tel: 233 274 005 952 (Mobile)
email: bishopackah@yahoo.com

The Church in the Province of the West Indies

Members 770,000
The West Indies became a self-governing province of the worldwide Anglican Communion in 1883 because of the Church of England missions in territories that became British colonies. It is made up of two mainland dioceses, Belize and Guyana, and six island dioceses including the Bahamas and Turks and Caicos Islands, Barbados, Jamaica and the Cayman Islands, North Eastern Caribbean and Aruba, Trinidad and Tobago, and the Windward Islands. Great emphasis is being placed on training personnel for an indigenous ministry as the island locations and scattered settlements make pastoral care difficult and costly.

Archbishop of the Province Most Revd Dr John Walder Dunlop Holder   *Fax:* 1 246 426 0871

Provincial Secretary Mrs Elenor Lawrence, Provincial Secretariat, Bamford House, Society Hill, St John, Barbados, West Indies
Tel: 1246 423 0842/3/8
Fax: 1 246 423 0855
email: bamford@sunbeach.net

THEOLOGICAL SEMINARIES
Codrington College, St John, Barbados (*Principal* Revd Dr Ian Rock)

United Theological College of the West Indies, PO Box 136, Golding Ave, Kingston 7, Jamaica (*Anglican Warden* Revd Garth Minott)

BARBADOS
Bishop Rt Revd Dr John Walder Dunlop Holder (*Archbishop of the Province*), Mandeville House, Collymore Rock, St Michael, Barbados
Tel: 1 246 426 2761/2
Fax: 1 246 426 0871
email: jwdh@sunbeach.net
Web: www.anglican.bb

BELIZE
Bishop Rt Revd Philip S. Wright, #25 Bishops Thorpe, PO Box 535, Southern Foreshore, Belize City, Belize, Central America
Tel: 501 2 73 029
Fax: 501 2 76 898
email: bzediocese@btl.net
Web: www.belize.anglican.org

GUYANA
Bishop Rt Revd Cornell Moss, The Diocesan Office, PO Box 10949, 49 Barrack St, Georgetown, Guyana, West Indies
Tel: 592 22 64 775
Fax: 592 22 76 091
email: dioofguy@networksgy.com

JAMAICA AND CAYMAN ISLANDS
Bishop Rt Revd Dr Howard Gregory, 2 Caledonia Ave, Kingston 5, Jamaica
Tel: 1 876 920 2712
Fax: 1 876 960 1774
email: bishop.jamaica@anglicandiocese.com
Web: www.anglicandiocesejamaica.com

Bishops Suffragan
Rt Revd Robert McLean Thompson (*Bishop of Kingston*), 3 Duke Street, Kingston, Jamaica, West Indies
Tel: 876 924 9044
Fax: 876 948 5362
email: bishop.kingston@anglicandiocese.com

Vacancy (*Bishop of Mandeville*), Bishop's Residence, 3 Cotton Tree Road, PO Box 84, Mandeville, Jamaica, West Indies
Tel: 1 876 625 6818
Fax: 1 876 625 6819

Vacancy (*Bishop of Montego Bay*), PO Box 346, Montego Bay, Jamaica, West Indies
Tel: 1 876 952 4963
Fax: 1 876 971 8838

THE BAHAMAS AND THE TURKS AND CAICOS ISLANDS
Bishop Rt Revd Laish Z. Boyd, Church House, PO Box N-7107, Nassau, Bahamas
Tel: 1 242 322 3015/6/7
Fax: 1 242 322 7943
email: bishopboyd@bahamasanglican.org

Assistant Bishop Most Revd Drexel Wellington Gomez (*New Providence*) (*same address*)

NORTH EASTERN CARIBBEAN AND ARUBA
Bishop Rt Revd Leroy Errol Brooks, St Mary's Rectory, PO Box 180, The Valley, Anguilla
Tel: 1 264 497 2235
Fax: 1 264 497 8555
email: brookx@anguillanet.com

TRINIDAD AND TOBAGO
Bishop Rt Revd Claude Berkley, Hayes Court, 21 Maraval Road, Port of Spain, Trinidad, Trinidad and Tobago, West Indies
Tel: 1 868 622 7387
Fax: 1 868 628 1319
email: diocesett@tstt.net.tt

WINDWARD ISLANDS
Bishop Rt Revd C. Leopold Friday, Bishop's Court, Montrose, PO Box 502, St Vincent, West Indies
Tel: 1 784 456 1895
Fax: 1 784 456 2591
email: diocesewi@vincysurf.com

Other Churches and Extra-Provincial Dioceses

BERMUDA
(Anglican Church of Bermuda)
This extra-provincial diocese is under the metro-political jurisdiction of the Archbishop of Canterbury.

Bishop Rt Revd Nicholas B. B. Dill
Tel: 1 441 293 1787
email: see Diocesan Office

Diocesan Office, PO Box HM 769, Hamilton HM CX, Bermuda
Tel: 1 441 292 6987
Fax: 1 441 292 5421
email: diocese@anglican.bm
Web: www.anglican.bm

Archdeacon Ven Andrew Doughty, Warwick Rectory, PO Box WK 530, Warwick, WK BX, Bermuda

THE CHURCH OF CEYLON (SRI LANKA)
Members 52,500
The work of the Anglican Church began in Sri Lanka (Ceylon) with the arrival of the British in 1796 and the appointment of the 1st Colonial Chaplain to minister to the British military and civil officials in the colony. Anglican missions in Sri Lanka commenced as far back as 1818 with the arrival of the Church Missionary Society and in 1840, the Society for the Propagation of the Gospel. The Archdeaconry of Colombo was

created in 1818 and the Anglicans in Ceylon were initially within the Diocese of Calcutta and Madras until the Diocese of Colombo was established in 1845 by Letters Patent with the Rt Revd James Chapman DD as first Bishop. The Diocese of Colombo was disestablished in 1886 and was placed under the metropolitical care of the Metropolitan of India in Calcutta. In 1930 the Diocese became part of the newly formed Province of India, Pakistan (from 1947), Burma and Ceylon. In 1950 the Diocese of Colombo was bifurcated and the Diocese of Kurunegala was formed with the Rt Revd Lakdasa de Mel as first Bishop. The Province was dissolved in 1970 with the formation of the Churches of North India and Pakistan and the Province of Myanmar (Burma). Since then the Dioceses of Colombo and Kurunegala have been identified in the Anglican Communion as two extra-provincial Dioceses. In 1998, with the Church of Ceylon (Incorporation) Act passed by the Parliament of Sri Lanka, the Church of Ceylon was legally recognized and classified as a 'National Church' within the Communion. A new Church of Ceylon Constitution was adopted which now governs the Anglican Church in Sri Lanka and has provided for a General Assembly with a Presiding Bishop. The Incorporated Trustees of the Church of Ceylon have responsibility for the financial management of the various properties and Trust funds owned and set up by the Dioceses over the past 165 years. The Dioceses are managed by the Bishops, Archdeacons and the respective Standing Committees.

At present the Bishops of the Church of Ceylon are: Rt Revd Shantha Francis (consecrated 2010), the Bishop of Kurunegala and the Rt Revd Dhiloraj R. Canagasabey (consecrated 2011) the Bishop of Colombo, who as of 2014 is the Presiding Bishop of the Church of Ceylon. Due to the fact that there are only two dioceses the Church of Ceylon is still classified within the Anglican Communion as an extra-provincial church with the Archbishop of Canterbury performing functions as Metropolitan. Representation has been made to the Anglican Consultative Council to explore the possibility of recognizing the Church of Ceylon as a Province, given its unique situation within the Communion.

Clergy, full-time workers and members of the laity are trained at the Ecumenical Theological College of Lanka, Pilimatalawa and at the Cathedral Institute for Education and Formation, Colombo. On the ecumenical journey, both Dioceses remain committed to the goal of a United Church of Lanka and have been members of the National Christian Council of Sri Lanka since 1914 and the Confederation of Christian Churches of Sri Lanka since its formation in 2008. They maintain cordial working relationships with the Roman Catholic Church, the newer Evangelical and Pentecostal churches and other major faith groups prevailing in Sri Lanka. Through a few (11) government approved private Church Schools, the Dioceses are also involved in primary and secondary secular education.

The challenges we face include the training and the empowerment of the people of God for mission and witness in the context of poverty and ethnic and religious tensions within a multi-ethnic and multi-faith context. The Anglican Church in Sri Lanka, in addition to its parochial and evangelistic ministries, is now also engaged in the areas of reconciliation and reconstruction as well as working for peace with justice for all.

THEOLOGICAL COLLEGE
Theological College of Lanka, Pilimatalawa, nr Kandy

COLOMBO
Bishop Rt Revd Dhiloraj R. Canagasabey, 368/3A Bauddhaloka Mawatha, Colombo 7
Tel: 94 1 684 810
Fax: 94 1 684 811
email: anglican@slttalk.net
Secretary Mrs Mary Thanja Peiris (*same address*)
email: sec.diocese.tr@gmail.com

KURUNEGALA
Bishop Rt Revd Shantha Francis, Bishop's House, Cathedral Close, Kurunegala
Tel: 94 37 22 191
Fax: 94 37 26 806
email: bishopkg@sltnet.lk
Secretary Mr Shaantha de Silva, Diocesan Office, 154, D. S. Senanayake Veediya, Kandy
Tel and *Fax:* 94 081 2222016
email: diokg@sltnet.lk
General Assembly of the Church of Ceylon
Presiding Bishop: Rt Revd Dhiloraj R. Canagasabey
Vice President: Rt Revd Shantha Francis
General Secretary: Mrs Barbara Praesoody

EPISCOPAL CHURCH OF CUBA
(Iglesia Episcopal de Cuba)
Members 7,000
The Episcopal Church of Cuba is under a Metropolitan Council in matters of faith and order. Council members include the Primate of Canada, the Archbishop of the West Indies, and the Presiding Bishop of the Episcopal Church of the United States of America or a bishop appointed by the Presiding Bishop.

Diocesan Bishop Rt Revd Maria Griselda Delgado del Carpio, Calle 6 No.273, e/ 11 y 13, Vedado, Plaza, La Habana, CP 10400, Cuba
Tel: 537 832 1120 (Office)
537 833 8003 (Home)
email: griselda@enet.cu

Diocesan Treasurer Lic. Canónigo José Raúl Ortiz Figueredo (*address as above*)
Tel: 537 830 1470 (Office)
email: tesorero@enet.cu

Anglican and Porvoo Communions

Seminario Evangélico de Teología, Matanzas Aptdo. 149, Matanzas (Interdenominational, run in cooperation with the Presbyterian Church)

CHURCH PAPER
Heraldo Episcopal Published three times a year. Contains diocesan, provincial and world news, homiletics, devotional and historical articles.

FALKLAND ISLANDS
In 1977 the Archbishop of Canterbury resumed episcopal jurisdiction over the Falkland Islands and South Georgia which had been relinquished in 1974 to the Church of the Southern Cone of America. In 2006 he appointed Bishop Stephen Venner, then the Bishop of Dover, as his commissary, with the title Bishop for the Falkland Islands. The whole parish covers the Falkland Islands, South Georgia, and the South Sandwich Islands and British Antarctic Territory. Christ Church Cathedral is the most southerly cathedral in the world.

Bishop for the Falkland Islands Rt Revd Nigel Stock (*Bishop to HM Forces*), Lambeth Palace, London SE1 7JU   *Tel:* 020 7898 1200
          email: nigel.stock@lambethpalace.org.uk

Rector Vacancy, The Deanery, PO Box 160, Stanley, Falkland Islands, South Atlantic FIQQ 1ZZ   *Tel:* 00 500 21100
                              Fax: 00 500 21100
          email: christchurch@horizon.co.fk

Associate Minister Revd Kathy Biles (c/o *same address*)   *email:* k.biles@horizon.co.fk

LUSITANIAN CHURCH
(Portuguese Episcopal Church)
Members 5,000
Founded in 1880 by a group of local Roman Catholic priests and lay people as a reaction to a number of dogmas from the first Vatican Council. The Church consisted of Roman Catholic priests who formed congregations in and around Lisbon using a translation of the 1662 English Prayer Book. Its own first Prayer Book of Common Prayer was issued in 1884. A Lusitanian bishop was consecrated in 1958 and in the early 1960s many provinces of the Anglican Communion established full communion with the Church in Portugal. Full integration occurred in 1980 when the Church became an extra-provincial diocese under the metropolitical authority of the Archbishop of Canterbury. It takes seriously its role in the emerging Europe and has a commitment to helping the poor. It has a strong mission emphasis for the many unchurched people in the country, specially by its two diaconal institutions providing services and help to children and the elderly. The Church and its leaders cooperate fully with the Diocese in Europe (Church of England) and the Convocation of American Churches in Europe, assisting in each other's congregation and being a united Anglican voice in an increasingly secular Europe. In 1998 the diocesan synod of the Lusitanian Church approved and accepted the Porvoo Declaration, expressing its desire to be involved in the life of the Porvoo Communion and to cooperate, with interchangeable ministries, with the congregations of the Porvoo Churches in Portugal.

Bishop Rt Revd Dr José Jorge Tavares de Pina Cabral, Rua Afonso de Albuquerque, 86 Mafamude 4430–003 Vila Nova de Gaia, Portugal   *Tel:* 351 22 375 4018
                              Fax: 351 22 375 2016
          email: comunicacao@igreja-lusitana.org
                    Web: www.igreja-lusitana.org

Treasurer Revd Sérgio Filipe de Pinho Alves, Tesouraria Diocesana (*same address*)

SPANISH EPISCOPAL REFORMED CHURCH
Members 5,000
Parishes: 32 self supported, plus a similar number of congregations.
The Spanish Church covers the whole country and is divided into three archdiaconates, with three archdeacons:
Archdiaconate I: Catalonia, Valencia and Balearic islands
Archdiaconate II: Andalusia and Canary islands
Archdiaconate III: Central and Northern Spain
Under the leadership of some former Roman Catholic priests, in 1868 the Spanish Reformed Episcopal Church was established in Gibraltar and was for some years under the pastoral care of the Church of Ireland. The first Bishop was appointed in 1880 and consecrated in 1894 by the Bishop of Meath along with two other Bishops, and the Church of Ireland accepted metropolitan authority. The same year the Church adopted the Mozarabic Liturgy, which was the liturgy of the early Spanish Church. The Church was fully integrated into the Anglican Communion in 1980 under the metropolitical authority of the Archbishop of Canterbury. It has a strong evangelistic and mission commitment and it is organized into departments: youth, women, ecumenism, Christian education, mission and evangelization. The Church also has a very important social programme for immigrants, which was established in many parishes by helping with clothes and food for over 26,000 people per year. The history of the Church has been one of persecution and difficulties, especially during Franco's dictatorship, but it is firm in its cooperation with the Diocese in Europe and the Convocation of American Churches in Europe for a stronger Anglican presence throughout Europe.

Bishop Rt Revd Carlos López Lozano (*Bishop of Madrid*), Spanish Reformed Episcopal Church, Calle Beneficencia 18, 28004 Madrid
Tel: 34 91 445 2560
Fax: 34 91 594 4572
email: eclesiae@arrakis.es
Web: www.anglicanos.org

Treasurer Señor Jesus Diaz Barragan (*same address*)

Regional Councils

COUNCIL OF THE ANGLICAN PROVINCES OF AFRICA

The Council of Anglican Provinces of Africa (CAPA) was established in 1979 in Chilema, Malawi, by Anglican Primates in Africa who saw the need to form a coordinating body that would help to bring the Anglican Communion in Africa together and to articulate issues affecting the Church. The organization was set up with the following aims and objectives:

- to help the Anglican churches in Africa develop beneficial relationships between themselves and with the wider Anglican Communion;
- to provide a forum for the Church in Africa to share experiences, consult and support each other;
- to confer about common responsibilities on the African continent;
- to establish opportunities for collaboration and joint activities;
- to maintain and develop relationships between the Anglican Church in Africa, partners, other denominations, fellowships, national and regional councils.

Today CAPA works with 12 Anglican provinces in Africa and the Diocese of Egypt. These provinces include Nigeria, West Africa, Sudan, Kenya, Uganda, Tanzania, Congo, Rwanda, Burundi, Central Africa, Southern Africa and Indian Ocean.

Chairman Most Revd Ian Ernest (*Primate of Indian Ocean*)

General Secretary The Rev Canon Grace Kaiso, PO Box 10329, 00100 Nairobi, Kenya

Tel: 254 20 3873 283/700
Fax: 254 20 3870 876
email: Generalsec@capa-hq.org
Web: www.capa-hq.org

Administrative Officer Mrs Elizabeth Gichovi (*same address*) *email:* info@capa-hq.org

HIV/AIDS TB & Malaria Programme Coordinator Mr Emmanuel Olatunji (*same address*)
email: olatunji@capa-hq.org/otunuel@yahoo.com

THE COUNCIL OF THE CHURCHES OF EAST ASIA

This Council, whose history began in 1954, has gone through an evolution. With most of the dioceses forming into provinces, the Council is now a fellowship for common action. Its membership includes dioceses in the Province of South East Asia, the Church of Korea, the Philippine Episcopal Church, Hong Kong Sheng Kung Hui, the Diocese of Taiwan (which is associated with the Episcopal Church of the USA), the Province of Myanmar, Nippon Sei Ko Kai (the Holy Catholic Church in Japan), the Philippine Independent Church and the Anglican Church of Australia who are members as a national Church or province.

Chairman Most Revd Dr Paul Kwong, Hong Kong Sheng Kung Hui, Provincial office: 16/F, Tung Wai Commercial Building, No.109–111 Gloucester Road, Wanchai, HK
Tel: 852 2526 5355
Fax: 852 2521 2199
email: Office1@hkskh.org
www.hkskh.org

UNITED CHURCHES IN FULL COMMUNION

CHURCHES RESULTING FROM THE UNION OF ANGLICANS WITH CHRISTIANS OF OTHER TRADITIONS

The population of the countries of South Asia is over 1,000 million and these Churches cover the whole area. The total Christian population is around 22–3 million and Christians of many different traditions, ranging from ancient oriental to pentecostal, are to be found here. The region is undergoing rapid social, economic and political change. There is also a resurgence of some of the great world religions. Although there is a great deal of industrialization and there have been 'green revolutions' in the agricultural sector in many countries, there is still a tremendous inequality in the distribution of wealth and income. In spite of the relatively small numbers of Christians, the Churches have grown steadily and have been responsible for many initiatives in education, medical work and community development. Their influence is out of all proportion to their size. The Church of England continues to relate to these Churches mainly through its mission agencies: CMS, USPG, SPCK and Crosslinks. In addition, the Oxford Mission, the Dublin University Mission to Chota Nagpur and the Religious Communities are doing valuable work. Support in money and personnel also comes from Churches in Canada, from CMS in Australia and New Zealand, from the USA, Holland, Germany, Scandinavia, Japan and Singapore. The Churches themselves are involved in the training and sending of mission personnel both inside and outside India, including the sending of mission partners to the UK. Mission partners from the Church of England work under the authority of the local church or institution to which they have been sent. The Church of North India, the Church of South India and Mar Thoma Syrian Church of Malenkara are in full communion with each other and are members of a joint council to further and deepen their unity. Since 1988, these Churches have become full members of the Lambeth Conference and the Anglican Consultative Council. Their moderators also attend the meetings of Anglican Primates.

The Church of Bangladesh

Members 20,139
Congregations/Pastorates 103
Situated between Burma and India, with the Bay of Bengal in the south, is the small country of Bangladesh. Originally part of India, it gained independence from Britain in 1947, becoming East Pakistan. On 16 December 1971, Bangladesh achieved its sovereign independence, under the leadership of Bangabondhu Sheik Mujibur Rahman, after a bloody liberation war against the Pakistani Army from 26 March in the same year.

The Church of Bangladesh is a church of the Anglican Communion in Bangladesh. It is a united church formed by the union of various Christian churches in the region, principally Anglican and Presbyterian. The Church of Bangladesh came into being as the outcome of the separation from Pakistan. This started as a movement which focused on language and took shape through the liberation war in 1971, which created an independent Bangladesh. The Synod of the Church of Pakistan on 30 April 1974 declared and endorsed a free and independent status for the Church of Bangladesh. The Church of Bangladesh brings together the Anglican and English Presbyterian Churches.

Moderator Rt Revd Paul S. Saker (*Bishop of Dhaka*)

Deputy Moderator Rt Revd Samuel S. Mankhin (*Bishop of Kushtia*)

Hon Synod Secretary Mr Joseph Sudhin Mondal, Church of Bangladesh, 54/1 Barobag, Mirpur 2, Dhaka   *Tel:* 880 2 9025876
                    Fax: 880 2 8053729
    email: cobsynod@churchofbangladesh.org

Hon. Treasurer Mr Avijit Raksam (*same address*)

THEOLOGICAL COLLEGE
St Andrew's Theological College, 54 Johnson Road, Dhaka – 1100, Bangladesh (*Principal* Revd Dr Albert Walters)   *Tel:* 880 2 802 0876

ANGLICAN AND PORVOO COMMUNIONS

DHAKA
Bishop Rt Revd Paul S. Saker (*Moderator of the Church of Bangladesh*), Church of Bangladesh, 54/1 Barobag, Mirpur 2, Dhaka 1216
Tel: 880 2 9025876
Fax: 880 2 8053729
email: sarkerps@gmail.com

KUSHTIA
Bishop Rt Revd Samuel S. Mankhin (*Deputy Moderator of the Church of Bangladesh*), 94 N. S. Road, Thanapara, Kushtia
Tel and *Fax:* 880 71 54618
email: bishop_mankhin@yahoo.com

The Church of North India

Members approx 1.5 million

The Church of North India is part of the One Holy, Catholic and Apostolic Church, the Body of Christ which he is building up out of persons of all generations and races. The Church of North India is what it is as a church by reason of what is has received from God in Christ through bringing together into one life the several traditions of the churches that have united to constitute it. This heritage is the fruit of the continuous working of God's Spirit in his church in all ages from apostolic times through the Reformation and down to our own day.

The churches which united to constitute the Church of North India were all linked with the Church of apostolic times by an essential continuity of doctrine, of experience and allegiance to the Lord Jesus Christ, and by a fellowship in the continued proclaiming of the gospel of salvation through him. In different ways, they had all sought to maintain continuity with the early Church in all matters of order.

The six churches which united on 29 November 1970 in Nagpur to form the Church of North India were:

1. The Council of Baptist Churches in Northern India
2. The Church of the Brethren in India
3. The Disciples of Christ
4. The Church of India (formerly known as the Church of India, Pakistan, Burma and Ceylon)
5. The Methodist Church (British and Australasian Conferences)
6. The United Church of Northern India.

The Church of North India as a united and uniting church together is committed to announcing the Good News of the reign of God inaugurated through the death and resurrection of Jesus Christ in proclamation, and to demonstrating in actions the restoration of the integrity of God's creation through continuous struggle against the demonic powers by breaking down the barriers of caste, class, gender, economic inequality and exploitation of nature.

Moderator Most Revd Dr P. P. Marandih (Bishop of Patna Diocese, CNI)

Deputy Moderator Rt Revd P. K. Samantaroy (Bishop of Amritsar Diocese, CNI)

General Secretary Mr Alwan Masih, CNI Bhavan, 16 Pandit Pant Marg, New Delhi 110 001
Tel: 91 11 4321 4000
email: alwanmasih@cnisynod.org
Web: www.cnisynod.org

Acting Treasurer Mr Prem Masih (*same address and telephone number*) *email:* cnitr@cnisynod.org

CHURCH PAPER
The North India Church Review The official monthly magazine of the CNI. Contains articles, reports, diocesan news, world news and letters. *Editor/Editorial Office* (*same address*) Mr Alwan Masih (*Editor in Chief*), Ms Sushma Ramswami (*Managing Editor*)

AGRA
Bishop Rt Revd Dr Prem Prakash Habil, Bishop's House, 4/116-B Church Rd, Civil Lines, Agra 282 002, Uttar Pradesh *Tel:* 91 562 2854 845
Mobile: 91 9412722501
Fax: 91 562 2520 074
email: doacni@gmail.com/bishopofagra@gmail.com

AMRITSAR
Bishop Rt Revd Pradeep Kumar Samantaroy, 26 R. B. Prakash Chand Rd, Opp Police Ground, Amritsar 143 001, Punjab
Tel and *Fax:* 91 183 222 2910/91 183 2562010
Mobile: 91 9815462121
email: bunu13@rediffmail.com

ANDAMAN AND NICOBAR ISLANDS
Bishop Rt Revd Christopher Paul
Add 1: Cathedral Church Compound, MUS, Car Nicobar 744301
Add 2: Post Box No 19, Port Blair 744 101, Andaman and Nicobar Islands
Tel and *Fax:* 91 3192 231362
Mobile: 91 9476 016029
email: cniportblair@yahoo.co.in

BARRACKPORE
Bishop Rt Revd Brojen Malakar, Bishop's Lodge, 86 Middle Rd, Barrackpore, Kolkata 700120, West Bengal *Telefax:* 91 33 2593 1852
Mobile: 91 9903034609
Fax: 91 33 2592 0147
email: bishop_malakar@rediffmail.com

BHOPAL

Bishop Rt Revd Robert Ali, Masihi Kanya Hr. Sec. School Campus, 9 Boundary Road, Indore 452 001 Madhya Pradesh   *Tel:* 91 731 2492 789
Mobile: 91 99261 86636
email: rev.robertali@gmail.com/
bhopal_diocese@yahoo.com

CHANDIGARH

Bishop Rt Revd Younas Massey, Bishop's House, Mission Compound, Brown Rd, Ludhiana 141 001, Punjab   *Tel* and *Fax:* 91 161 2225 706
Mobile: 91 9915641109
email: bishopdoc2000@yahoo.com
Web: chandigarhdiocesecni.org

CHHATTISHARH

Bishop Rt Revd P. S. Nag, Opp. Raj Bhavan, Gate No. 1, Civil Lines, Raipur 492 001, Chhattisgarh
Tel and *Fax:* 91 771 2210 015
Mobile: 91 812 0118 000
email: revpurnasagar@gmail.com/
bishoppsnag@gmail.com

CHOTA NAGPUR

Bishop Rt Revd B. B. Baskey, Bishop's Lodge, PO Box 1, Church Rd, Ranchi 834 001, Jharkhand
Tel: 91 651 235 0281
Fax: 91 651 235 1184
Mobile: 91 9470193053, 91 7549113206
email: rch_cndta@sancharnet.in/
chotanagpurdiocese@gmail.com

CUTTACK

Bishop Rt Revd Dr Samson Das, Bishop's House, Mission Rd, Cuttack 753 001, Odisha
Tel: 91 671 230 0102
Mobile: 91 986 192 4474
email: bishopsamsondas@gmail.com

DELHI

Bishop Rt Revd Sunil K. Singh, Bishop's House, 1 Church Lane, Off North Ave, New Delhi 110 001
Tel: 91 11 2371 7471/99 1010 3520/
91 11 23358006
Mobile: 91 9911287611
email: bishopsunilsingh@yahoo.com
Web: www.delhidiocese.org

DURGAPUR

Bishop Rt Revd Probal Kanto Dutta, Diocesan Bhavan, Aldrin Path, Bidhan Nagar, Dugapur 713 212, Dist. Burdwan, West Bengal
Tel and *Fax:* 91 343 253 4552 / 91 343 253 6220
email: probaldutta@ymail.com

EASTERN HIMALAYA

Moderator's Commissary, Revd Samuel Lepcha, CNI Diocesan Centre, Gandhi Road, PO Box 4, Darjeeling 734 101, West Bengal
Mobile: 91 9832094806
email: revds127@yahoo.com/
easternhimalaya2010@yahoo.co.in

GUJARAT

Bishop Rt Revd Silvans S. Christian, Bishop's House, I.P. Mission Compound, Ellisbridge, Ahmedabad 380 006, Gujarat
Tel and *Fax:* 91 79 2656 1950
Mobile: 91 74052 27086
email: gujdio@yahoo.co.in /
christiansilvans@yahoo.com

JABALPUR

Bishop Rt Revd Dr Prem Chand Singh, Bishop's House, 2131 Napier Town, Jabalpur 482 001, Madhya Pradesh
Tel : 91 761 2622 109 / 91 761 262 2692
email: bishoppcsingh@yahoo.co.in

KOLHAPUR

Bishop Rt Revd Bathuel Ramchandra Tiwade, Bishop's House, EP School Compound, Nagala Park, Kolhapur 416 001, Maharashtra
Tel and *Fax:* 91 231 2654 832
Mobile: 91 94224 14057
email: kdcdbss@yahoo.com

KOLKATA

Bishop Rt Revd Ashoke Biswas, Bishop's House, 51 Chowringhee Rd, Calcutta 700 071, West Bengal   *Tel:* 91 33 6534 7770
Mobile: 91 97484 56981
Fax: 91 33 2822 6340
email: ashoke.biswas@vsnl.net

LUCKNOW

Moderator's Commissary Revd Daniel Subhan, 25/11 Mahatma Gandhi Marg, Allahabad 211 011, Uttar Pradesh
Tel: 91 532 2427 053/91 532 2427 052
Mobile: 91 9451089682
email: danielsubhan@gmail.com

MARATHWADA

Bishop Rt Revd M. U. Kasab, Bungalow 28 / A, Mission Compound, Cantonment, Aurangabad 431 002, Maharashtra   *Tel:* 91 240 237 3136
Mobile: 91 97648 22888
email: revmukasab@yahoo.co.in /
bishopofmarathwada@rediffmail.com

MUMBAI

Bishop Rt Revd Prakash Dinkar Patole, 19 Hazarimal Somani Marg Fort, Mumbai 400 001
Tel: 91 22 2207 3904
91 98334 80299 (Mobile)
Fax: 91 22 2206 0248
email: cnibombaydiocese@yahoo.com/
bishopprakashpatole@gmail.com

NAGPUR

Bishop Rt Rev Paul Dupare, Cathedral House, Opp. Indian Coffee House, Sadar, Nagpur 440 001, Maharashtra   *Tel* and *Fax:* 91 712 2553351
Mobile: 91 98233 54614
email: nagpurdiocese@rediffmail.com

ANGLICAN AND PORVOO COMMUNIONS

NASIK

Bishop Rt Revd Pradip Lemuel Kamble, Bishop's House, 1 Outram Rd, Tarakpur, Ahmednagar 414 001, Maharashtra   *Tel:* 91 241 241 1806
Mobile: 91 9421099721
Fax: 91 241 242 2314
email: bishopofnasik@rediffmail.com

NORTH EAST INDIA

Bishop Most Revd Dr Purely Lyngdoh, Bishop's Kuti, Shillong, Meghalaya 793 000
Tel: 91 364 2223 155
email: bishopnei15@hotmail.com

PATNA

Bishop Most Revd Dr Philip Phembuar Marandih, Bishop's House, Christ Church Compound, Bhagalpur 812 001, Bihar
Tel: 91 641 2400 033/2300 714
91 94312 13138 (Mobile)
email: cnipatna@rediffmail.com

PHULBANI

Bishop Rt Revd Bijay Kumar Nayak, Bishop's House, Mission Compound, Gudripori, G-udaigiri, Phulbani 762 100, Kandhamal, Odisha 762 001   *Tel:* 91 6847 260569
Mobile: 91 94379 65389
email: bp.bkn@rediffmail.com
Web: www.cniphulbanidiocese.org

PUNE

Bishop Rt Revd A. B. Rathod, 1A, General Bhagat Marg (Stevely Road), Red Bungalow, Pune 411 001, Maharashtra   *Tel:* 91 20 2633 4374
91 98230 37389 (Mobile)
email: rev.andrewrathod@gmail.com, punediocese@yahoo.com

RAJASTHAN

Bishop Rt Revd Warris Masih, 2/10 CNI Social Centre, Civil Lines, Opp. Bus Stand, Jaipur Rd, Ajmer 305 001   *Tel:* 91 145 2420 633
91 80036 02000 (Mobile)
Fax: 91 145 2621 627
email: warrisk.masih@yahoo.in / wkmasih@yahoo.co.in

SAMBALPUR

Bishop Rt Revd Pinuel Dip, Bishop's House, Mission Compound, Bolangir 767 001, Odisha
Tel: 91 6652 230625
91 94383 36476 (Mobile)
email: pinuel_dip@rediffmail.com

The Church of Pakistan

Members approx 1,000,000
One of four United Churches in the Anglican Communion, the Church of Pakistan comprises the Anglican Church of Pakistan, the dioceses of Lahore and Karachi, two conferences of the United Methodist Church, the Scottish Presbyterian Church in Pakistan, and the Pakistan Lutheran Church.

Moderator Rt Revd Samuel Robert Azariah (*Bishop of Raiwind*)

Deputy Moderator Rt Revd Humphrey Sarfaraz Peters (Bishop of Peshawar)

General Secretary Mr Imran Gill, 27 Liaqat Rd, Civil Lines, Hyderabad, Sind   *Tel:* 92 51 289 0420
Mobile: 92 300 655 0074

Treasurer Mr Wilson Massey, Cathedral Close, The Mall, Lahore   *Tel:* 92 423 7233560
Mobile: 92 300 843 3262

FAISALABAD

Bishop Rt Revd John Samuel, Bishop's House, PO Box 27, Mission Rd, Gojra, Distt Toba Tek Sing
Tel: 92 46 351 4689
Mobile: 92 300 655 0074
email: jsamuel@brain.net.pk

HYDERABAD

Bishop Rt Revd Kaleem John, 27 Liaquat Rd, Civil Lines, Hyderabad 71000, Sind
Tel: 92 51 289 0420
Mobile: 92 301 244 5690
email: kaleemjohn@aol.com

KARACHI

Bishop Rt Revd Saddiq Daniel (*Deputy Moderator, COP*), Holy Trinity Cathedral, Fatima Jinnah Rd, Karachi 75530   *Tel:* 92 21 521 6843
Mobile: 92 301 822 2003
email: sadiqdaniel@hotmail.com

LAHORE

Bishop Rt Revd Irfan Jamil (*Moderator, COP*), Bishopsbourne, Cathedral Close, The Mall, Lahore 54000   *Tel:* 92 42 723 3560 (Office)
92 42 7120 766 (Home)
Mobile: 92 333 475 6730
Fax: 92 42 722 1270
email: bishop_Lahore@hotmail.com

MULTAN

Bishop Rt Revd Leo Rodrick Paul, 113 Qasim Rd, PO Box 204, Multan Cantt   *Tel:* 92 61 458 3694
Mobile: 92 300 630 2101
email: bishop_mdcop@bain.net.pk

PESHAWAR
Bishop Rt Revd Humphrey Sarfaraz Peters, *(Deputy Moderator of COP)*, Diocesan Centre, 1 Sir Syed Rd, Peshawar Cantt 2500   *Tel:* 92 91 527 9094
Mobile: 92 300 858 0325
Fax: 92 91 5277499
email: bishopdop@hotmail.com

RAIWIND
Bishop Rt Revd Samuel Azariah, *(Moderator of COP)* 17 Warris Rd, PO Box 2319, Lahore 54000
Tel: 92 42 758 8950
Mobile: 92 300 841 7982
Fax: 92 42 757 7255
email: sammyazariah@yahoo.com

SIALKOT
Commissary Rt Revd Manoo Ramalshah, Lal Kothi, Barah Patthar, Sialkot 2, Punjab
Tel: 92 432 264 895
Mobile: 92 300 839 3725
Fax: 92 432 264 828
email: chs_sialkot@yahoo.com

ARABIAN GULF
Bishop for Rt Revd Azad Marshall *(Area Bishop within the Diocese of Iran)*, PO Box 688, Lahore, Punjab 54000, Pakistan   *Tel:* 92 42 542 0452
email: bishop@saintthomascenter.org

The Church of South India

Members 4,000,000
The Church was inaugurated in 1947 by the union of the South India United Church (itself a union of Congregational and Presbyterian/Reformed traditions), the southern Anglican dioceses of the Church of India, and Burma, and the Methodist Church in South India. It is one of the four United Churches in the Anglican Communion.

Moderator Most Revd Dr G. Dyvasirvadam *(Bishop in Krishna Godavari)*

Deputy Moderator Rt Revd Thomas K. Oommen *(Bishop in Madhya Kerala)*

General Secretary Revd Dr D. R. Sadananda, CSI Centre, 5 Whites Road, Royapettah, Chennai 600 014, India   *Tel:* 91 44 2852 1566/4166 (Office)
2852 3763 (Home)
Fax: 91 44 2852 3528
email: synodcsi@gmail.com, csi@vsnl.com

Honorary Treasurer Adv. C. Robert Bruce, Star Cottage, Saral vilai, Kattathurai, Kanyakumari District, 629 158, India
Tel: 91 44 2852 4166 (Office)
Fax: 91 44 2858 4163
email: treasurercsi@eth.net

OFFICIAL MAGAZINE
CSI Life English Monthly Magazine. Contains articles, reports and news from the dioceses. *Editor:* The General Secretary CSI; published by Dept of Communication on behalf of CSI, 5 Whites Road, Royapettah, Chennai 600 014; Yearly subscription Rs.150/- (£25 in UK, $30 in USA, $ 35 in Australia, $35 in New Zealand, sent by Air Mail).

COIMBATORE
Bishop in Rt Revd Timothy Ravinder, Diocesan Office, 256 Race Course Road, Coimbatore 641 018, Tamil Nadu   *Tel:* 91 422 222 3605
Fax: 91 422 222 3369
email: csi.bpcbe@gmail.com

DORNAKAL
Bishop in Rt Revd Dr Vadapalli Prasada Rao, Diocesan Office, Epiphany Cathedral Compound, Dornakal 506 381, Warangal Dist., Andhra Pradesh
Tel: 91 8719 227 752 (Home)
91 8719 227 535 (Office)
email: dkbpoff@hotmail.com

EAST KERALA
Bishop in Rt Revd Dr K. G. Daniel, Bishop's House, Melukavumattom, Kottayam 686 652, Kerala State   *Tel:* 91 4822 219 044 (Home)
91 4822 220 001 (Office)
Fax: 91 4822 219 044
email: csiekd@gmail.com

JAFFNA
Bishop in Rt Revd Daniel S. Thiagarajah, Bishop's office in Colombo, 17, Frances Road, Colombo 6, Sri Lanka   94 21 225 0827/0826 (Office)
Fax: 94 11 258 2015
email: bishopthiagarajah@gmail.com

KANYAKUMARI
Bishop in Rt Revd Dr G. Devakadasham, CSI Diocesan Office, 71A Dennis St, Nagercoil 629 001, Tamil Nadu   *Tel:* 91 4652 278 920 (Home)
91 4652 231 539 (Office)
Fax: 91 4652 226 560
email: csikkd@bsnl.in

KARIMNAGAR
Bishop Vacancy, *contact* Revd Thomas K. Oommen, Moderator's Commissary, Diocesan Office, 2–8–95 CVRN Road, PO Box 40, Makarampura post, Karimnagar 505 001, Andhra Pradesh   *Tel:* 91 878 2262972 (Office)
97 878 2262971 (Home)
Fax: 91 878 22 62972

ANGLICAN AND PORVOO COMMUNIONS

KARNATAKA CENTRAL

Bishop Vacancy, *contact* Most Revd Dr G. Dyvasirvadam (*Moderator/Bishop-in-charge*), Diocesan Office, 20 Third Cross, CSI Compound, Bangalore 560 027, Karnataka
Tel: 91 80 2222 3766/ 941/91 80 22106953/54 (Office)
email: admin@csikcd.org

KARNATAKA NORTHERN

Bishop in Rt Revd Ravikumar J. Niranjan, Bishop's House, All Saints' Church Compound, Haliyal Road, Dharwad 580 008, Karnataka
Tel: 91 836 244 7733 (Office)
Fax: 91 836 274 5461
email: haradoni.rn@gmail.com

KARNATAKA SOUTHERN

Bishop in Vacancy, Bishop's House, Balmatta, Mangalore 575 001, Karnataka
Tel: 91 824 243 2657 (Office)
Fax: 91 824 243 2363

KRISHNA-GODAVARI

Bishop in Most Revd Dr G. Dyvasirvadam (*Moderator*), Bishop's House, CSI St Andrew's Cathedral Compound, Main Road, Machilipatnam 521 002, Andhra Pradesh
Tel: 91 8672 220 623 (Office)
Fax: 91 8672 220 772
email: bishopkrishna@yahoo.com

MADHYA KERALA

Bishop in Rt Revd Thomas K. Oommen (*Deputy Moderator*), CSI Bishop's House, Cathedral Road, Kottayam 686 001, Kerala
Tel: 91 481 2566 536 (Office)
91 481 2566 531 (Home)
Fax: 91 481 256 6536
email: csimkdbishopsoffice@yahoo.com

MADRAS

Bishop in Vacancy, Diocesan Office, PO Box 4914, 226 Cathedral Rd, Chennai 600 086, Tamil Nadu
Tel: 91 44 2811 3929/3933/7629
Fax: 91 44 2811 0608
Web: www.csimadrasdiocese.org

MADURAI-RAMNAD

Bishop in Rt Revd Dr. M. Joseph, 'Rev.Grub's Garden', No.5 Bhulabai Desai Road, Chokkikulam, Madurai 625 002, Tamil Nadu
Tel: 91 452 2338222 (Office)
Fax: 91 452 2339888
email: csidental@gmail.com

MEDAK

Bishop in Vacancy, *contact* Most Revd Dr G. Dyvasirvadam (*Moderator/Bishop-in-charge*), Diocesan Office, 10–3-65, Church House, Golden Jubilee Bhavan, Old Lancer Lane, Secunderabad – 500 025, Andhra Pradesh
Tel: 94 40 2783 3151/2782 0845 (Office)
Fax: 94 40 2782 0843

NANDYAL

Bishop in Rt Revd E. Pushpalalitha, Bishop's House, Nandyal RS 518 502, Kurnool Dist., Andhra Pradesh *Tel:* 91 8514 222 477 (Office)
email: csibishopnandyal@gmail.com

NORTH KERALA

Bishop in Rt Revd Baker Ninan Fenn, CSI Diocesan Office, PO Box 104, Shoranur 679 121, Palakkad District, Kerala
Tel: 91 466 2224 454 (Office)
91 466 2222 426 (Home)
Fax: 91 466 2222 545
email: csinkd@gmail.com

RAYALASEEMA

Bishop in Rt Revd Dr B.D. Prasada Rao, Bishop's House, R.S.Road, Kadapa, Andhra Pradesh
Tel: 91 8562 325 320 (Office)
91 8562 275 200 (Home)
Fax: 91 8562 275 200
email: lbd_prasad@yahoo.co.in

SOUTH KERALA

Bishop in Rt Revd A. Dharmaraj Rasalam, Bishop's House, LMS Compound, Trivandrum 695 033, Kerala State *Tel:* 91 471 2318662
Fax: 91 471 231 6439
email: bishoprasalam@yahoo.com

THOOTHUKUDI-NAZARETH

Moderator's Commissary Revd Jesu Sagayam, Diocesan Office, Caldwell Hr. Sec. School Campus, Beach Road, Thoothukudi – 628 001
Tel: 91 461 2329408 (Office)
Fax: 91 461 2328408
email: csitnd@bsnl.in

TIRUNELVELI

Bishop in Rt Revd Dr J. J. Christdoss, Bishopstowe, PO Box 118, 16, North High Ground Road, Tirunelveli 627 002, Tamil Nadu
Tel: 91 462 257 8744
Fax: 91 462 257 4525
email: bishopcsitirunelveli@gmail.com

TRICHY-TANJORE

Bishop in Rt Revd Dr G. Paul Vasanthakumar, PO Box 31, 17 VOC Street, Cantonment, Tiruchiarapalli 620 001, Tamil Nadu
Tel: 91 431 2411102 (Home)
91 431 2770172/2771254 (Office)
Fax: 91 431 2418 485/2770172
email: csittd@rediffmail.com

VELLORE

Bishop in Rt Revd Dr A. Rajavelu, CSI Diocesan Office, 3/1, Anna Salai, Vellore 632 001, Tamil Nadu *Tel:* 91 416 2232 160 (Office)
91 416 2216 324 (Home)
Fax: 91 416 2223 835
email: csi.vlrdiocese@gmail.com

THE HOLY CATHOLIC CHURCH IN CHINA

(Chung Hua Sheng Kung Hui)

The Chung Hua Sheng Kung Hui was an important denomination in China and its history dates back to the mid-nineteenth century. Today the CHSKU, as a separate denomination, no longer exists in the People's Republic of China, except for Hong Kong which returned to Chinese sovereignty on 1 July 1997. Under the formula 'one country – two systems' Hong Kong keeps its autonomy for 50 years, including its religious regulations. The same applies to Macao which was returned by Portugal to China at the end of 1999. On the Chinese mainland the denominational Protestant Churches entered into a post-denominational phase under the Three Self Patriotic Movement/China Christian Council in 1953. A united Church is still in the process of being formed and Christians of Anglican inspiration have very much been a part of this process. The most prominent of these, Bishop K. H. Ting, died in December 2012, and his passing marks the end of an era for the China Christian Council and the Nanjing Union Theological Seminary.

Although the CHSKU is no longer in existence, many former Anglicans still share a strong spiritual affinity with other Anglican Churches on matters of belief and liturgical tradition. As the Chinese Protestant Church develops its own ecclesiology and forms of worship, the Anglican traditions are contributing to a richer synthesis.

Relations between the Church in China and the Churches in Britain are facilitated by the World Programmes Desk of Churches Together in Britain and Ireland (CTBI). It provides advice to government, churches and media, and publishes the *China Study Journal*, a documentary review of Chinese religions and government policy. The World Programmes Desk offers the continuity for the ecumenical China Study Project which was established in 1972 by the leading missionary societies, including Anglican organizations such as the CMS, USPG and the Archbishop's China Appeal Fund.

The Friends of the Church in China, an ecumenical association which works closely with the World Programmes Desk of CTBI, takes a more grass-roots approach in relation to Christians in China. It publishes a popular newsletter on China and organizes visits to Chinese churches.

Contact: Christine Elliott, CBTI World Programmes, 39 Eccleston Square, London SW1V 1BX.

Friends of the Church in China (Chairperson, Ms Maggi Whyte) *Web:* thefcc.org.uk

OTHER CHURCHES IN COMMUNION WITH THE CHURCH OF ENGLAND

Old Catholic Churches of the Union of Utrecht

The Old Catholic Churches are a family of nationally organized churches which bound themselves together in the Union of Utrecht in 1889. Most of them owe their origin to Roman Catholics who were unable to accept the decrees of the First Vatican Council in 1870 and left the communion of that Church. The Archbishopric of Utrecht, however (from which the other Old Catholic Churches derived their episcopal orders), has been independent of Rome since the eighteenth century following a complex dispute involving papal and capitular rights of nomination and accusations of Jansenism (until 1910 in the Netherlands only). The Latin Mass continued in use, though all the Old Catholic Churches now worship in the vernacular. Their rites stand within the Western tradition, with various 'Eastern' features.

By the acceptance of the Bonn Agreement on 20 and 22 January 1932, the Convocation of Canterbury established full communion with the Old Catholic Churches by means of the following resolutions:

'That this House approves of the following statements agreed on between the representatives of the Old Catholic Churches and the Churches of the Anglican Communion at a Conference held at Bonn on 2 July 1931:

1. Each Communion recognises the catholicity and independence of the other and maintains its own.
2. Each Communion agrees to admit members of the other Communion to participate in the sacraments.
3. Intercommunion does not require from either Communion the acceptance of all doctrinal opinion, sacramental devotion, or liturgical practice characteristic of the other, but implies that each believes the other to hold all the essentials of the Christian Faith.

'And this House agrees to the establishment of Intercommunion between the Church of England and the Old Catholics on these terms.'

An Anglican–Old Catholic International Coordinating Council was established in 1998.

AUSTRIA
Bishop Rt Revd Dr John Ekemezie Okoro, Schottenring 17/ 1/3/12, A–1010 Vienna
email: kilei@altkatholiken.at
Web: www.altkatholiken.at

CROATIA
Bishop Vacancy, *under the care of Rt Revd* Dr John Ekemezie Okoro, Schottenring 17/1/3/12, 1010 Vienna *email:* bischof.okoro@altkatholiken.at

CZECH REPUBLIC
Bishop Rt Revd Dušan Hejbal, Na Bateriich 27, CZ–162 00 Prague 6 *email:* stkat@starokatolici.cz
Web: www.starokatolici.cz

FRANCE
Bishop Delegate Most Revd Dr Joris Vercammen (*Archbishop of Utrecht*), Kon Wilhelminalaan 3, NL-3818 HN Amersfoort *email:* abvu@okkn.nl
Web: www.vieux-catholique-alsace.com

GERMANY
Bishop Rt Revd Dr Matthias Ring, Gregor–Mendel-Strasse 28, 53115 Bonn, Germany
email: ordinariat@alt-katholisch.de
Web: www.alt-katholisch.de

NETHERLANDS
Archbishop Most Revd Dr Joris Vercammen (*Archbishop of Utrecht and President of the International Bishops' Conference*), Kon Wilhelminalaan, 3, NL–3818 HN Amersfoort
email: buro@okkn.nl
Web: www.okkn.nl/welkom

Bishop of Haarlem Rt Revd Dr Dirk Jan Schoon, Ruysdaelstraat 37, NL-1071 XA Amsterdam
email: djschoon@planet.nl

POLAND (The Polish National Catholic Church)
Prime Bishop Most Revd Prof Dr Wiktor Wysoczanski, ul. Wilcza 31/16c, PL–002–544 Warsaw *email:* polskokatolicki@pnet.pl
Web: www.polskokatolicki.pl

SWEDEN AND DENMARK
Bishop Delegate Rt Revd Dr Dirk Jan Schoon, Ruysdaelstraat 37, NL–1070 XA Amsterdam, Netherlands   *email:* djschoon@planet.nl

SWITZERLAND
Bishop Rt Revd PD Dr Harald Rein, Willadingweg 39, CH–3006 Bern   *email:* bischof@christkath.ch
                                                                              Web: www.christkath.ch

Philippine Independent Church

The Philippine Independent Church is in part the result of the Philippine revolution against Spain in 1896 for religious emancipation and Filipino identity. It was formally established in 1902, declaring its independence from the Roman Catholic Church but seeking to remain loyal to the Catholic Faith. It now derives its succession from the Protestant Episcopal Church in the United States of America (and therefore from Anglican sources), with which full communion was established in September 1961. It has a membership of approximately seven million followers, 34 dioceses with 50 bishops, 600 regular church buildings and 2,000 village chapels served by about 600 priests.

Following the report of a Commission appointed by the Archbishop of Canterbury, full communion on the basis of the Bonn Agreement was established between the Church of England and the Philippine Independent Church in 1963 by the Convocations of Canterbury and York. It is in full communion with all the member Churches in the Anglican Communion.

The Philippine Independent Church is very active in its ecumenical relations. It is the most senior member in the National Council of the Churches in the Philippines, a member of the Council of Churches in East Asia, a member of the Christian Churches in Asia, and an active member of the World Council of Churches.

Supreme Bishop (*Obisbo Maximo*) Most Revd Tomas A. Millamena, 1500 Taft Avenue, Ermita, Manila, Philippines 2801.
                                    Tel: 63 2 523 72 42
                                    Fax: 63 2 521 39 32
                        email: ifiphil@hotmail.com

Mar Thoma Syrian Church of Malabar

The Christian community in South India is very ancient and is believed by its members to have been founded by the Apostle Thomas (Mar Thoma). Over the centuries contact with Christian bodies from outside India has led to the fragmentation of the original community into a number of jurisdictions. During the latter part of the nineteenth century the Christians of the West Syrian (Syrian Orthodox) tradition divided into two over the issue of the removal of non-biblical features from teaching and worship of the Church. The influence of Anglican missionaries of the Church Missionary Society who had been working in Malabar since the beginning of the nineteenth century accelerated the new stance in the Church. The larger section (which itself has subsequently divided into the Indian Orthodox and Jacobite Churches) chose closer links with Antioch and remained 'unreformed'; the smaller group, which eventually adopted the name of Mar Thoma Syrian Church of Malabar, undertook a conservative revision of its rites, removing elements (such as the invocation of saints and prayers for the dead) that were not scriptural practices but had given room for misunderstanding of the gospel. The general form of Mar Thoma worship remains eastern. Its episcopal succession derives from the Patriarchate of Antioch.

The former CIPBC (Church of India, Pakistan, Burma and Ceylon) had partial intercommunion with the Mar Thoma Church from 1937 until 1961 when a Concordat of Full Communion was established. The Mar Thoma Syrian Church of Malabar is now in full communion with the Churches of South India and North India. The union of these three churches is now known as the Communion of Churches in India (CCI), which fosters cooperation in mission, theological training, and formulations and involvement in social issues. The Mar Thoma Church has stated its desire to preserve its eastern traditions and is not willing to merge with the two Western United Churches. A number of Anglican Provinces are in full communion with the Mar Thoma Church, the Church of England having become so in 1974.

The Malabar Independent Syrian Church of Thozhiyoor occupies a unique position in the complex history of the Church in South India. At various times in the past its bishops have consecrated bishops for both the Orthodox and Mar Thoma Churches when the episcopal succession in those churches has died out. The MISC is fully Orthodox in rite and faith. It is in communion with the Mar Thoma Church and its current practice is to extend eucharistic hospitality to Christians of other traditions. The former Metropolitan was an ecumenical participant at the 1998 Lambeth Conference.

ANGLICAN AND PORVOO COMMUNIONS

Other Churches in Communion   **399**

THE MAR THOMA SYRIAN CHURCH OF MALABAR

Metropolitan Most Revd Dr Philipose Mar Chrysostom Mar Thoma, Poolatheen, Tiruvalla 689 101, Kerala, South India

Tel: 91 469 263 0313
Fax: 91 469 260 2626
email: pulathen@md3.vsnl.net.in

Sabha Secretary Revd Dr Cherian Thomas, Mar Thoma Church Headquarters, Sabha Office, SCS Campus, Tiruvalla 689 101, Kerala, South India

Tel: 91 469 263 0449
Fax: 91 469 263 0327
email: marthoma@vsnl.com

THE MALABAR INDEPENDENT SYRIAN CHURCH

Most Revd Cyril Mar Basilios, St George's Cathedral, Thozhiyoor, Thrissur Dt 680 520, Kerala, South India

Maps of the Churches and Provinces of the Anglican Communion

The maps of the Anglican Communion which follow have been supplied by Nicola Lawrence of The Mothers' Union. She will be happy to hear of any changes which need to be made.

ANGLICAN AND PORVOO COMMUNIONS

MAP 1

The Scottish Episcopal Church
1 Moray, Ross and Caithness
2 Argyll and the Isles
3 St Andrews, Dunkeld and Dunblane
4 Aberdeen and Orkney
5 Brechin
6 Glasgow and Galloway
7 Edinburgh

.... Diocesan Boundary

▬ ▬ ▬ ▬ Provincial Boundary

| The Isles of Scilly are included in the Diocese of Truro | The Channel Islands are annexed to the Diocese of Winchester |

The Church of Ireland
Province of Armagh
8 Derry and Raphoe
9 Connor
10 Tuam, Killala and Achonry
11 Kilmore, Elphin and Ardagh
12 Clogher
13 Armagh
14 Down and Dromore

Province of Dublin
15 Limerick and Killaloe
16 Meath and Kildare
17 Cork, Cloyne and Ross
18 Cashel and Ossory
19 Dublin and Glendalough

The Church in Wales
20 Bangor
21 St Asaph
22 St Davids
23 Swansea and Brecon
24 Llandaff
25 Monmouth

The Church of England
Province of York
26 Carlisle
27 Newcastle
28 Durham
29 West Yorkshire and the Dales
30 Blackburn
31 York
32 Manchester
33 Liverpool
34 Chester
35 Sheffield
36 Southwell and Nottingham
37 Sodor and Man

Province of Canterbury
38 Lichfield
39 Derby
40 Lincoln
41 Hereford
42 Worcester
43 Birmingham
44 Coventry
45 Leicester
46 Peterborough
47 Ely
48 Norwich
49 St Edmundsbury and Ipswich
50 Gloucester
51 Bristol
52 Oxford
53 St Albans
54 London
55 Chelmsford
56 Truro
57 Exeter
58 Bath and Wells
59 Salisbury
60 Winchester
61 Portsmouth
62 Guildford
63 Southwark
64 Rochester
65 Chichester
66 Canterbury
Diocese in Europe

Extra-Provincial Dioceses
Bermuda
Lusitanian Church
Spanish Episcopal Reformed Church
The Church of Ceylon
Falkland Islands

Following its approval in draft by the General Synod, the Dioceses Commission made the Bradford, Ripon and Leeds and Wakefield Reorganisation Scheme on 16 July 2013. The Scheme was confirmed by Her Majesty in Council on 9 October 2013. The Scheme dissolved the dioceses of Bradford, Ripon and Leeds and Wakefield with effect from Easter Day 2014 when the new Diocese of Leeds (also to be known as the Diocese of West Yorkshire and the Dales) came into being in their place.

MAP 2

PAPUA NEW GUINEA

The Anglican Church of Australia

Province of Western Australia
1 North West Australia
2 Perth
3 Bunbury

Province of South Australia
4 Willochra
5 Adelaide
6 The Murray

Province of Queensland
7 The Northern Territory
8 North Queensland
9 Rockhampton
10 Brisbane

Province of New South Wales
11 Riverina
12 Bathurst
13 Armidale
14 Grafton
15 Newcastle
16 Sydney
17 Canberra and Goulburn

Province of Victoria
18 Ballarat
19 Bendigo
20 Wangaratta
21 Melbourne
22 Gippsland

23 Tasmania *(extra-provincial)*

The Anglican Church of Papua New Guinea
24 Aipo Rongo
25 Dogura
26 New Guinea Islands
27 Popondota
28 Port Moresby

MAP 3

FIJI

16

The Church of the Province of Melanesia
1 Ysabel
2 Malaita
3 Central Melanesia
4 Hanuato'o
5 Temotu
6 Vanuatu and New Caledonia
7 Banks and Torres
8 Central Solomons

TONGA

The Anglican Church in Aotearoa, New Zealand and Polynesia
9 Auckland
10 Waikato
11 Waiapu
12 Wellington
13 Nelson
14 Christchurch
15 Dunedin
16 Polynesia

Bishopric of Aotearoa
A Hui Amorangi ki te Tai Tokerau
B Hui Amorangi ki te Manawa o te Wheke
C Hui Amorangi ki te Tairawhiti
D Hui Amorangi ki te Upoko o te Ika
E Hui Amorangi ki te Waipounamu

––––––––––––––– Bishopric of Aotearoa

ANGLICAN AND PORVOO COMMUNIONS

The Episcopal Church in the United States of America

Province I
1 Connecticut
2 Maine
3 Massachusetts
4 New Hampshire
5 Rhode Island
6 Vermont
7 Western Massachusetts

Province II
8 Albany
9 Central New York
10 Long Island
11 New Jersey
12 New York
13 Newark
14 Rochester
15 Western New York
Haiti *(see Map 5)*
Virgin Islands *(see Map 5)*
Convocation of American Churches
    in Europe

Province III
16 Bethlehem
17 Central Pennsylvania
18 Delaware
19 Easton
20 Maryland
21 Northwestern Pennsylvania
22 Pennsylvania
23 Pittsburgh
24 Southern Virginia
25 Southwestern Virginia
26 Virginia
27 Washington
28 West Virginia

Province IV
29 Alabama
30 Atlanta
31 Central Florida
32 Central Gulf Coast
33 East Carolina

34 East Tennessee
35 Florida
36 Georgia
37 Kentucky
38 Lexington
39 Louisiana
40 Mississippi
41 North Carolina
42 South Carolina
43 Southeast Florida
44 Southwest Florida
45 Tennessee
46 Upper South Carolina
47 West Tennessee
48 Western North Carolina

Province V
49 Chicago
50 Eau Claire
51 Fond du Lac
52 Indianapolis
53 Michigan
54 Milwaukee
55 Missouri
56 Northern Indiana
57 Northern Michigan
58 Ohio
59 Quincy
60 Southern Ohio
61 Springfield
62 Western Michigan
63 Eastern Michigan

Province VI
64 Colorado
65 Iowa
66 Minnesota
67 Montana
68 Nebraska
69 North Dakota
70 South Dakota
71 Wyoming

Province VII
72 Arkansas
73 Dallas
74 Fort Worth
75 Kansas
76 Northwest Texas
77 Oklahoma
78 Rio Grande
79 Texas
80 West Missouri
81 West Texas
82 Western Kansas
83 Western Louisiana

Province VIII
84 Arizona
85 California
86 Eastern Oregon
87 El Camino Real
88 Idaho
89 Los Angeles
90 Navajoland Area Mission
91 Nevada
92 Northern California
93 Olympia
94 Oregon
95 San Diego
96 San Joaquin
97 Spokane
98 Utah
Hawaii
Alaska *(see Map 6)*
Taiwan *(see Map 14)*
Micronesia

Anglican and Porvoo Communions

MAP 4

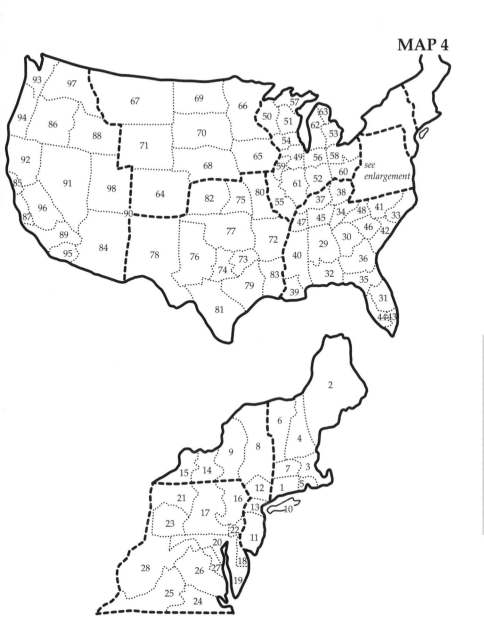

see enlargement

MAP 5

**The Church in the Province
of the West Indies**
32 Belize
33 Jamaica and the Cayman Islands
34 North Eastern Caribbean
   & Aruba
35 Windward Islands
36 Barbados
37 Trinidad and Tobago
38 Guyana
46 Suriname (part of the Diocese
   of Guyana)
47 Cayenne (part of the Diocese
   of Guyana)
39 The Bahamas and the Turks
   and Caicos Islands

Province IX
2 Honduras
6 Litoral Ecuador
7 Central Ecuador
8 Colombia
9 Dominican Republic
11 Puerto Rico
12 Venezuela

The Anglican Church of Mexico
13 Western Mexico
14 Northern Mexico
15 Mexico
16 Cuernavaca
17 Southeastern Mexico

The Anglican Church of the Central American Region
1 Guatemala
3 El Salvador
4 Nicaragua
5 Panama
10 Costa Rica

The Episcopal Anglican Church of Brazil
18 Rio de Janeiro
19 Recife
20 Southern Brazil
21 São Paulo
22 Southwestern Brazil
23 Brasilia
24 Pelotas
44 Curitiba
45 Amazon
48 Missionary District of Oesle-Brasil

Anglican Church of the Southern Cone of America
25 Argentina
26 Chile
27 Northern Argentina
28 Paraguay
29 Peru
30 Uruguay
31 Bolivia

FALKLAND
ISLANDS

**The Episcopal Church
of Cuba**
(Autonomous diocese)
40 Cuba

41 Bermuda (*extra-provincial
   to Canterbury*)
42 Haiti (Province II ECUSA – *see Map 4*)
43 Virgin Islands (Province II ECUSA –
   see Map 4)

Anglican and Porvoo Communions

MAP 6

The Anglican Church of Canada

Province of British Columbia and the Yukon
 1 British Columbia
 2 Caledonia
 3 Anglican Parishes of the Central
   Interior
 4 Kootenay
 5 New Westminster
 6 Yukon

Province of Rupert's Land
 7 The Arctic
 8 Athabasca
 9 Edmonton
10 Calgary
11 Saskatchewan
12 Saskatoon
13 Qu'Appelle
14 Brandon
15 Rupert's Land
16 Keewatin

Province of Ontario
17 Moosonee
18 Algoma
19 Huron
20 Toronto
21 Niagara
22 Ontario
23 Ottawa

Province of Canada
24 Quebec
25 Montreal
26 Fredericton
27 Nova Scotia and Prince Edward Island
28 Western Newfoundland
29 Central Newfoundland
30 Eastern Newfoundland and Labrador

31 Alaska *(in Province VIII of ECUSA)*

ANGLICAN AND PORVOO
COMMUNIONS

MAP 7

The Church of the Province of Southern Africa

1 Niassa
2 Lebombo
3 St Mark the Evangelist
4 Pretoria
5 Highveld
6 Christ the King
7 Johannesburg
8 Matlosane
9 Kimberley and Kuruman
10 Namibia
11 Cape Town
12 George
13 Port Elizabeth
14 Grahamstown

15 Mthatha
16 Umzimvubu
17 Free State
18 Natal
19 Zululand
20 Lesotho
21 Swaziland
40 Angola
45 Mpumalanga
46 False Bay
47 Saldanha Bay
48 Ukhahlamba

St Helena

The Church of the Province of Central Africa

22 Northern Zambia
23 Central Zambia
24 Lusaka
25 Eastern Zambia
26 Lake Malawi
27 Northern Malawi
28 Southern Malawi
29 Harare
30 Manicaland
31 Central Zimbabwe
32 Matabeleland
33 Botswana
41 Upper Shire
43 Masvingo
44 Luapula

The Church of the Province of the Indian Ocean

34 Antsiranana
35 Mahajanga
36 Antananarivo
37 Toamasina
38 Mauritius
39 Seychelles
42 Fianarantsoa

MAP 8

Anglican Church of Kenya
1 Nambale
2 Bungoma
3 Katakwa
4 Maseno North
5 Maseno West
6 Maseno South
7 Southern Nyanza
8 Butere
9 Mumias
10 Nairobi
11 Mount Kenya South
12 Mount Kenya West
13 Nakuru
14 Nyahururu
15 Embu
16 Mbeere
17 Mount Kenya Central
18 Eldoret
19 Kitale
20 Kirinyaga
21 Meru
22 Machakos
23 Kajiado
24 Mombasa
25 Taita Taveta
26 Kitui
44 Thika
45 Bondo
48 All Saints Cathedral
51 Kericho

Anglican Church of Tanzania
27 Morogoro
28 Tanga
29 Zanzibar
30 Ruaha
31 Rift Valley
32 Tabora
33 Western Tanganyika
34 South West Tanganyika
35 Ruvuma
36 Masasi
37 Kagera
38 Victoria Nyanza
39 Mara
40 Mount Kilimanjaro
41 Central Tanganyika
42 Mpwapwa
43 Southern Highlands
46 Kondoa
47 Dar-es-Salaam
49 Shinyanga
50 Lweru
52 Kiteto

ANGLICAN AND PORVOO
COMMUNIONS

MAP 9

The Church of the Province of Uganda
1 Madi and West Nile
2 Northern Uganda
3 Karamoja
4 Nebbi
5 Bunyoro-Kitara
6 Lango
7 Soroti
8 North Mbale
9 Mbale
10 Bukedi
11 Busoga
12 Mukono
13 Kampala
14 Luweero
15 Namirembe
16 Mityana
17 Ruwenzori
18 South Ruwenzori
19 North Kigezi
20 West Ankole
21 Ankole
22 West Buganda
23 Kigezi
24 Muhabura
25 Kinkizi
26 Central Buganda

27 Kitgum
28 Sebei
29 Kumi
30 North Ankole
45 Masindi-Kitara
47 North Karamoja

The Church of the Province of Burundi
31 Bujumbura
32 Buye
33 Gitega
34 Matana
35 Makamba
46 Muyinga

The Church of the Province of Rwanda
36 Byumba
37 Shyira
38 Cyangugu
39 Kigeme
40 Butare
41 Shyogwe
42 Kigali
43 Kibungo
44 Gahini
48 Kivu

MAP 10

The Church of the Province of Sudan
1 Khartoum
2 El Obeid
3 Port Sudan
4 Kadugli and Nuba Mountains
5 Wau
6 Renk
7 Malakal
8 Bor
9 Rumbek
10 Cueibet
11 Yirol
12 Ezzo
13 Yambio
14 Ibba
15 Maridi
16 Mundri
17 Lui
18 Rokon
19 Lainya
20 Yei
21 Kajo-Keji
22 Rejaf

23 Juba
24 Torit
33 Terekeka
34 Pacong
35 Akot
36 Twic East
37 Aweil
38 Wad Medani
39 Nzara

The Church of the Province of the Congo
25 Boga
26 Nord-Kivu
27 Kisangani
28 Kindu
29 Bukavu
30 Katanga (formerly Shaba)
31 Kinshasa
32 Aru

The Church of Nigeria
(Anglican Communion) *(see map overleaf)*

Province of Abuja
7 Minna
9 Abuja
10 Kafanchan
13 Makurdi
48 Lokoja
57 Oturkpo
66 Bida
70 Gwagwalada
71 Lafia
Idah
Kubwa
Zonkwa
Ijumu
Kutigi
Kwoi
Okene
Kotangora

Province of Bendel
19 Benin
26 Asaba
36 Warri
45 Sabongidda-Ora
74 Oleh
75 Ughelli
76 Esan
78 Ikka
Western Izon
Akoko-Edo
Ndokwa

Province of Ibadan
8 Kwara
14 Ibadan
15 Osun
16 Ilesa

30 Ife
46 Oke-Osun
61 Ibadan-North
62 Ibadan-South
64 Offa
65 Igbomina
Ajayi Crowther
New Bussa
Ogbomoso
Oke-Ogun
Oyo
Ekiti Kwara
Ife East
Jebba
Omu-Aran

MAP 11

CAMEROON

see enlargement

**The Church of Nigeria
(Anglican Communion)** *(continued)*

Province of Jos
 4 Maiduguri
 5 Bauchi
11 Jos
12 Yola
54 Jalingo
55 Damaturu
68 Gombe
Langtang
Bukuru
Pankshin

Province of Kaduna
 1 Sokoto
 2 Katsina
 3 Kano
 6 Kaduna
56 Kebbi
58 Dutse
59 Wusasa
69 Gusau
Bari
Zaria

Province of Lagos
31 Ijebu
32 Remo
33 Lagos
34 Yewa
35 Egba
49 Diocese On The Coast
72 Lagos West
Badagary
Ijebu - North
Lagos Mainland
Awori
Egba West
Ifo

Province of The Niger
20 Enugu
24 Awka
25 On the Niger
44 Nsukka
53 Nnewi
60 Abakaliki
73 Oji River
Aguata
Ngbo
Afikpo
Awgu-Aninri
Enugu North
Ihiala
Ikwo
Mbammili
Niger West
Nike
Ogbaru

Province of Niger Delta
21 Calabar
22 Aba
37 The Niger Delta
39 Okrika
42 Ukwa
43 Umuahia
52 Niger Delta North
77 Niger Delta West
79 Okrika
80 Ahoada
Arochukwu Ohafi
Ikwuano
Isuikwuato
Ogoni
Aba Ngwa North
Etche
Ikwerre
Isiala Ngwa
Isiala Ngwa South
Northern Izon
Ogbia

Province of Ondo
17 Ekiti Oke
18 Akoko
27 Owo
28 Akure
29 Ondo
51 Kabba
67 Ekiti West
81 Ekiti

Province of Owerri
23 Orlu
38 Owerri
40 Okigwe North
41 Okigwe South
47 Mbaise
50 Egbu
63 Ideato
Ohaji-Egbema
Oru
On the Lake

A large number of new dioceses have been created in the Church of Nigeria. These are listed above (unnumbered) but unfortunately at the time of going to press it was not possible to confirm the geographical position of these dioceses and so they are not yet represented on the map.

Anglican and Porvoo Communions

MAP 12

The Episcopal Church in Jerusalem and the Middle East
1 Cyprus and the Gulf
2 Iran
3 Egypt
4 Jerusalem

Anglican Communion in Japan (Nippon Sei Ko Kai)
1 Hokkaido
2 Tohoku
3 Kita Kanto
4 Tokyo
5 Yokohama
6 Chubu (Mid Japan)
7 Kyoto
8 Osaka
9 Kobe
10 Kyushu
  Okinawa (*see Map 14*)

The Church of the Province of West Africa
1 The Gambia
2 Guinea
3 Liberia
4 Freetown
5 Bo
6 Tamale
7 Kumasi
8 Koforidua
9 Accra
10 Cape Coast
11 Sekondi
12 Sunyani
13 Ho
14 Wiawso
Cameroon (*see Map 11*)

MAP 1

United Churches in Communion

South India
1 Kanyakumari
2 South Kerala
3 Madhya Kerala
4 East Kerala
5 Tirunelveli
6 Madurai-Ramnad
7 North Kerala
8 Coimbatore
9 Trichy-Tanjore
10 Chennai
11 Vellore
12 Karnataka Central
13 Karnataka South
14 Karnataka North
15 Rayalaseema
16 Nandyal
17 Krishna-Godavari
18 Dornakal
19 Karimnagar
20 Medak
21 Jaffna
59 Thoothukudi-
   Nazareth

North India
22 Kolhapur
23 Mumbai
24 Nasik
25 Nagpur
26 Jabalpur
27 Sambalpur
28 Cuttack
29 Durgapur
30 Calcutta
31 Barrackpore
32 North East India
33 Eastern Himalayas
34 Patna
35 Chota Nagpur
36 Lucknow
37 Bhopal
38 Gujarat
39 Delhi
40 Agra
41 Chandigarh
42 Rajasthan
43 Amritsar
44 Andaman and Nicobar Islands
57 Pune
58 Marathwada

Pakistan
45 Sialkot
46 Lahore
47 Peshawar
48 Faisalabad
49 Multan
50 Raiwind
51 Karachi
52 Hyderabad

Bangladesh
53 Dhaka
54 Kushtia

**The Church of Ceylon
(Sri Lanka)**
55 Colombo
56 Kuranagala

MAP 14

Chung Hua Sheng Kung Hui (China)

Contact is only with the Diocese of Hong Kong and Macao, which is under the temporary Metropolitan Authority of the Council of the Churches of East Asia.

The Anglican Church of Korea
1 Pusan
2 Seoul
3 Taejon

The Province of Myanmar
4 Myitkyina
5 Mandalay
6 Sittwe
7 Yangon
8 Toungoo
9 Hpa-an

The Episcopal Church in the Philippines
10 Northern Luzon
11 North Central Philippines
12 Northern Philippines
13 Central Philippines
14 Southern Philippines

The Province of the Anglican Church in South East Asia
15 Kuching
16 Sabah
17 Singapore
18 West Malaysia

22 Okinawa
(Diocese in the Anglican Communion in Japan)

23 Taiwan
(Diocese in Province VIII of ECUSA)

Hong Kong Sheng Kung Hui
(Hong Kong Anglican Church)
19 Hong Kong Island
20 Eastern Kowloon
21 Western Kowloon

ANGLICAN AND PORVOO COMMUNIONS

THE COMMUNION OF PORVOO CHURCHES

In October 1992 representatives of the four British and Irish Anglican Churches, the five Nordic Lutheran Churches and the three Baltic Lutheran Churches met in Finland for the fourth and final plenary session of their formal Conversations, which had commenced in 1989. They agreed *The Porvoo Common Statement*, named after Porvoo Cathedral, in which they had celebrated the Eucharist together.

The Common Statement recommended that the participating churches jointly make the Porvoo Declaration, bringing them into communion with each other. This involves common membership, a single, interchangeable ministry and structures to enable the Churches to consult each other on significant matters of faith and order, life and work. The implementation of the commitments contained in the Declaration is coordinated by the Porvoo Agreement Contact Group. The Porvoo Panel of the Church of England was established in 2000 to monitor and develop the implementation of the Porvoo commitments in dioceses and sector ministries.

In 1994 and 1995 the Declaration was approved by the four Anglican Churches, four of the Nordic Lutheran Churches and two of the Baltic Lutheran Churches. The General Synod's final approval of the Declaration in July 1995, following a reference to the diocesan synods, was by overwhelming majorities in each House. The Declaration was signed in the autumn of 1996 at services in Trondheim (Norway), Tallinn (Estonia) and Westminster Abbey.

In 1980 the Lusitanian Church (Portuguese Episcopal Church) became an extra-provincial diocese under the metropolitical authority of the Archbishop of Canterbury and in 1998 the diocesan synod of the Lusitanian Church approved and accepted the Porvoo Declaration. Furthermore in 1980 the Spanish Reformed Episcopal Church fully integrated into the Anglican Communion also coming under the metropolitical authority of the Archbishop of Canterbury. Both churches by virtue of coming under the Archbishop of Canterbury's metropolitical authority and accepting the Porvoo Declaration were integrated into the Porvoo Communion.

The Evangelical Lutheran Chuch in Denmark signed the Porvoo Declaration in December 2009 and in 2010 the Estonian Evangelical Lutheran Church Abroad and the Estonian Evangelical Lutheran Church Abroad united.

The Evangelical–Lutheran Church of Latvia has not yet decided to sign the Porvoo Declaration, but continues to participate as an observer.

Along with the Evangelical Lutheran Church of Latvia, the Porvoo Communion is represented by two additional Churches with observer status. They are the Lutheran Church in Great Britain and the Latvian Evangelical Lutheran Church Abroad. The Porvoo Contact Group took the decision to invite both these Churches at its meeting in Madrid in October 2010. At the Porvoo Primates meeting in Reykjavik, Iceland in October 2013, the Primates unanimously agreed to both the Latvian Evangelical Lutheran Church Abroad and the Lutheran Church in Great Britain becoming full members of the Porvoo Communion of Churches. These two churches have followed the process for membership agreed by the Porvoo Primates. Their ecclesiology and polity are along the lines of the Porvoo Agreement. They are committed to a theology of episcopacy and their bishops are being consecrated in historic succession.

The Nordic Lutheran Churches are the historic national Churches of their respective countries. At the Reformation, when they adhered to Lutheranism, they continued to be episcopally ordered, retaining the historic sees. In Sweden and Finland the succession of the laying on of hands at episcopal consecration was unbroken, whereas in Denmark, Norway and Iceland this was not the case. The Estonian and Latvian Lutheran Churches are similarly their countries' historic national Churches, which became Lutheran at the Reformation. Only in the northern part of Estonia was episcopacy retained, and there only until 1710, but it was restored in both Estonia and Latvia in the twentieth century, the bishops being consecrated in the historic succession. The Lithuanian Lutheran Church, which is now a small minority Church, adopted episcopacy in historic succession in 1976.

The Porvoo Agreement supersedes earlier separate agreements dating from the 1920s, 1930s and 1950s with the Churches concerned (except the Lithuanian Lutheran Church). These provided for mutual eucharistic hospitality and (with the Swedish, Finnish, Estonian and Latvian Churches) mutual participation in episcopal consecrations. Because of the Soviet occupation of the Baltic States, however, it was only in 1989 and 1992 respectively that it was possible for an Anglican bishop to participate in a Latvian and an Estonian consecration for the first time.

The Porvoo Declaration commits the signatory Churches 'to regard baptized members of all of our Churches as members of our own'. It also means that clergy ordained by bishops of the signatory Churches are placed in the same position with regard to ministry in the Church of England as those ordained by Anglican bishops overseas.

Further information can be found on the Porvoo website: www.porvoochurches.org, or is available from the European Secretary at the Council for Christian Unity at Church House, Westminster.

The Porvoo Agreement Contact Group

Co-Chairmen
Most Revd Dr Michael Jackson (*Archbishop of Dublin*)   *Tel:* 353 1 497 7849
     email: archbishop@dublin.anglican.org

Rt Revd Peter Skov-Jacobsen (*Bishop of Copenhagen*)   *Tel:* 45 33 47 65 00
     email: kmkbh@km.dk
Co-Secretaries
Ms Beate Fagerli (Nordic and Baltic Churches)
     email: beate.fagerli@kirken.no
Revd Canon Dr Leslie Nathaniel (Church of England Council for Christian Unity)
     email: leslie.nathaniel@churchofengland.org

The Porvoo Panel
Chairman Rt Revd David Hamid (*Diocese in Europe*)

Porvoo Chaplains in England
Denmark
Revd Else Hviid, 4 St Katharine's Precinct, Regent's Park, London NW1 4HH   *Tel:* 020 7935 1723

Estonia
Very Revd Lagle Heinla, Estonian House, 18 Chepstow Villas, London W11 2RB
     Tel: 020 7229 6700

Finland
Revd Teemu Hälli, The Finnish Church in London, 33 Albion Street, London SE16 7JG
     Tel: 020 7237 1261

Iceland
Chaplaincy being carried out by visits at regular intervals from Revd Adda Björnsdottie

Norway
Revd Torbjørn Holt, 1 St Olav's Square, Albion Street, London SE16 7JB   *Tel:* 020 7740 3900

Revd Thomas Wagle (*same address*)

Revd Ingrid Ims, Student Chaplain (*same address*)

Sweden
Very Revd Michael Persson, 6 Harcourt Street, London W1H 2BD   *Tel:* 020 7723 5681

Revd Anders Rune

Churches in the Communion of Porvoo Churches

Note: A more detailed map reflecting all recent changes in the Porvoo Communion is in preparation

NORDIC LUTHERAN CHURCHES

The Evangelical Lutheran Church in Denmark

The Evangelical Lutheran Church in Denmark (ELCD) is the national church in Denmark, with approx. 2000 congregations divided into 10 dioceses, each presided over by a bishop. A bishop is elected by parish council members and pastors in the respective diocese. The role of the bishop is to oversee ministers and congregations in the diocese. The bishop of Copenhagen holds a specific position of honour as *primus inter pares*. There is no office of archbishop. Since 1948 the office has consequently been open to both men and women. In 2010 80.9 per cent of the Danish population (numbering 5.2 million) were members of the ELCD. A vast majority enter into membership as children when they are baptised.

In Denmark there is a strong relationship between the national church and the state. The ELCD is regarded as 'the church of the people' as well as an official national church since the institution of the Danish Constitution of 1849 in which it is particularly mentioned. Every parish council has had its own rights to decide on activities in its local context and to select the pastor of the parish. Thus the local congregation is the cornerstone of the church structure. The queen or king of Denmark is the supreme authority when it comes to organization, liturgy etc. whereas the national parliament (Folketinget) is the *de facto* deciding body with regard to church legislation. Thus, the ELCD is not regulated by a synod, a national church council, as is seen in most other Lutheran churches. The main part of the church budget comes from a membership fee collected by the national tax authorities and ear-marked grants from the state budget. In this way the state contributes to the administration of the church.

The ELCD signed the Porvoo Declaration at a ceremony in Copenhagen Cathedral on 3 October 2010.

General Secretary
Dr Joergen Skov Soerensen, Council on International Relations of the Evangelical Lutheran Church in Denmark, Peter Bangs Vej 1, DK-2000 Frederiksberg   *Tel:* 45 33 11 44 88
Fax: 45 33 11 95 88
email: interchurch@interchurch.dk
Web: www.interchurch.dk

AALBORG
Bishop Rt Revd Henning Toft Bro, Thulebakken 1, 9000 Aalborg   *Tel:* 45 98 18 80 88
email: kmaal@km.dk

AARHUS
Bishop Rt Revd Kjeld Holm, Dalgas Avenue 46, 8000 Aarhus C   *Tel:* 45 86 14 51 00
email: kmaar@km.dk

FYENS
Bishop Rt Revd Tine Lindhardt, Klingenberg 2, 5000 Odense C   *Tel:* 45 66 12 30 24
Fax: 45 66 12 35 24
email: kmfyn@km.dk

HADERSLEV
Bishop Rt Revd Marianne Christiansen, Ribe Landevej 37, 6100 Haderslev   *Tel:* 45 74 52 20 25
Fax: 45 74 53 36 06
email: kmhad@km.dk

HELSINGØR
Bishop Rt Revd Lise-Lotte Rebel, Vor Frue Kloster, Hestemøllestræde 3 A, DK-3000 Helsingør
Tel: 45 49 21 35 00
Fax: 45 49 21 35 16
email: llr@km.dk

KØBENHAVNS
Bishop Rt Revd Peter Skov-Jakobsen, Nørregade 11, DK-1165, København K   *Tel:* 45 33 47 65 00
email: kmkbh@km.dk

LOLLAND-FALSTERS
Bishop Rt Revd Steen Skovsgaard, Bispegården, Østre Allé 2, 4800 Nykøbing F
Tel: 45 54 85 02 11
email: lfstift@km.dk

RIBE
Bishop Rt Revd Elisabeth Dons Christensen, Korsbrødregade 7, 6760 Ribe   *Tel:* 45 75 42 18 00
email: elch@km.dk

ROSKILDE
Bishop Rt Revd Peter Fischer-Møller, Palæet, Stændertorvet 3A, 4000 Roskilde
Tel: 45 46 38 19 20
email: pfm@km.dk

VIBORG
Bishop Rt Revd Karsten Nissen, Domkirkestræde 1, 8800 Viborg   *Tel:* 45 86 62 09 11
email: kmvib@km.dk

The Evangelical Lutheran Church of Finland

The first bishop in the Finnish Church was St Henrik, the Apostle of Finland. According to tradition, St Henrik was an Englishman who accompanied King Erik II of Sweden on a military expedition to south-western Finland in 1155 and was martyred there the following year. From the middle of the thirteenth century until 1809 Finland was part of Sweden, and until the Reformation it formed a single diocese (Turku) in the Province of Uppsala.

In 1554 the Swedish king appointed the Finnish Lutheran Reformer Mikael Agricola (d. 1557) as Bishop of Turku, at the same time founding a second Finnish see, Viipuri (eventually transferred to Tampere). In addition to translating the New Testament and parts of the Old into Finnish, Mikael Agricola compiled the first catechism, liturgy and ritual in Finnish. He is regarded as the father of Finnish as a written language.

A wave of revivals, beginning in the eighteenth century, gave rise in the nineteenth to four mass movements. These remained within the Church of Finland and are still influential on its life today.

In 1809 Finland was annexed by Russia. As a result, the Finnish Church became entirely independent of the Church of Sweden, and from 1817 the Bishop of Turku was styled Archbishop. Finland finally gained its independence in 1917.

Today, roughly 76 per cent of Finns are members of the Evangelical Lutheran Church of Finland, while only 4 per cent are members of other Churches. The ELCF is a 'folk church' (as is the Orthodox Church). The framework for its life is set by the Ecclesiastical Act. Amendments to this state law can only be proposed by the Synod, and Parliament can accept or reject but not amend such proposals. The Church is governed by the Synod, the Church Council and the Bishops' Conference. Although the Archbishop is only *primus inter pares* of the Finnish bishops, he is the President of the Synod and chairs both the Bishops' Conference and the Church Council.

The Church is organized in nine dioceses, one of which consists of the Swedish-speaking parishes (Porvoo). The diocese of Helsinki has recently divided into two, giving rise to the new see of Espoo.

Porvoo Agreement Contact Chief Secretary for Ecumenical Relations and Theology Tomi Karttunen, Department for International Relations, Eteläranta 8, P.O. Box 210, FI-00131 Helsinki
Tel: 358 9 1802 290
Fax: 358 9 1802 350
email: tomi.karttunen@evl.fi
Web: evl.fi/english

ESPOO
Bishop Rt Revd Dr Tapio Luoma, Diocesan Chapter, PO Box 203, FI-02771 Espoo
Tel: 358 9 8050 80
Fax: 358 9 855 4020
email: tapio.luoma@evl.fi

HELSINKI
Bishop Rt Revd Irja Askola, Diocesan Chapter, PO Box 142, FI-00121 Helsinki
Tel: 358 9 2340 3000
Fax: 358 9 2340 3050
email: irja.askola@evl.fi
Web: http://www.helsinginhiippakunta.evl.fi/information_in_english/

KUOPIO
Bishop Rt Revd Dr Jari Jolkkonen, Diocesan Chapter, PO Box 42, FI-70101 Kuopio   *Tel:* 358 17 288 8400
Fax: 358 17 288 8420
email: jari.jolkkonen@evl.fi
Web: www.kuopionhiippakunta.fi

LAPUA
Bishop Rt Revd Dr Simo Peura, Diocesan Chapter, PO Box 60, FI-62101 Lapua   *Tel:* 358 207 630 910
Fax: 358 207 630 911
email: simo.peura@evl.fi
Web: www.lapuanhiippakunta.fi

MIKKELI
Bishop Rt Revd Dr Seppo Häkkinen, Diocesan Chapter, PO Box 122, FI-50101 Mikkeli
Tel: 358 15 3216 00
Fax: 358 15 3216 016
email: seppo.hakkinen@evl.fi
Web: www.mikkelinhiippakunta.evl.fi

OULU
Bishop Rt Revd Dr Samuel Salmi, Diocesan Chapter, PO Box 85, FI-90101 Oulu   *Tel:* 358 8 5358 510
Fax: 358 8 5358 533
email: samuel.salmi@evl.fi
Web: www.oulunhiippakunta.evl.fi

PORVOO
(The Diocese of Porvoo (Borgå) is a non-geographical Swedish-language diocese.)

Bishop Rt Revd Dr Björn Vikström, Diocesan Chapter, PO Box 30, FI-06101 Borgå
Tel: 358 40 142 5213
Fax: 358 19 585 705
email: bjorn.vikstrom@evl.fi
Web: http://www.borgastift.fi/in+english/

Bishop Rt Revd Dr Matti Repo, Diocesan Chapter, Eteläpuisto 2C, FI-33200 Tampere
Tel: 358 3 238 1130
Fax: 358 3 238 1150
email: matti.repo@evl.fi
Web: http://www.tampereenhiippakunta.fi/ english

TURKU
Archbishop of Turku and Finland Most Revd Kari Mäkinen, Diocesan Chapter, PO Box 60, FI-20501 Turku

Tel: 358 2 279 7031
Fax: 358 2 279 7002
email: Arkkipiispa@evl.fi
Web: www.arkkihiippakunta.fi

Bishop of Turku Rt Revd Kaarlo Kalliala (*same address*)
Tel: 358 2 279 7033
Fax: 358 2 2797 001
email: kaarlo.kalliala@evl.fi
Web: www.arkkihiippakunta.fi

The Evangelical Lutheran Church of Iceland

Christianity was adopted at Thingvellir by decree of the legislature in the year 1000. The ancient Icelandic sees of Skálholt and Hólar were founded in 1055 and 1106, respectively. Having previously been under the jurisdiction of Bremen and Lund, from 1153 Iceland belonged to the Province of Nidaros (Trondheim). Part of the Kingdom of Norway from 1262, Iceland eventually came under Danish rule. The Lutheran Reformation was introduced in 1541. From this time onwards until 1908 (with one exception in the late eighteenth century), Icelandic bishops were consecrated by the Bishops of Sealand (Copenhagen).

The two Icelandic sees were united in 1801, but in 1909 they were revived as suffragan sees. Iceland gained its independence from Denmark in 1918, becoming a republic in 1944.

A new Church law came into effect on 1 January 1998, granting the Church considerable autonomy from the state. The Church Assembly is the highest organ of the Church. Today, around 75 per cent of the Icelandic population are members of the Church of Iceland.

Porvoo Agreement Contact: Revd Sigurdur Arni Thordarson, Neskirkja við Hagatorg, 107 Reykjavík
Tel: 354 511 1560
Fax: 354 511 1564
email: s@neskirkja.is

The Church of Iceland comprises a single diocese, with two suffragan bishops in the ancient sees of Hólar and Skálholt.

Bishop of Iceland Rt Revd Agnes M. Sigurdardottir, Laugavegi 31, 150 Reykjavík
Tel: 354 528 4000
Fax: 354 528 4098
email: agnes.m.sigurdardottir@kirkjan.is

Bishop of Skálholt Rt Revd Kristjan Valur Ingolfsson, Skálholt, Biskupshús, Skálholti, 801 Selfoss
Tel: 354 486 8972
Fax: 354 486 8975
email: kristjan.valur.ingolfsson@kirkjan.is

Bishop of Hólar Rt Revd Solveig Lára Gudmundsdottir, Biskupssetur, Hólar, 551 Saudárkrókur
Tel: 354 453 6300
Fax: 354 453 6301
email: srslara@ismennt.is

Contact for ecumenical affairs Revd Thorvaldur Vidisson, Ecumenical Secretary, Bishop´s Office, Laugavegur 31, 150 Reykjavík, Iceland
Tel: 354 528 4000
Fax: 354 528 4099
email: biskupsritari@kirkjan.is

Chairman of committee for ecumenical affairs Revd Steinunn A. Björnsdóttir, Hjallakirkja, Álfaheiði 17, 200 Kópavogur, Iceland
Tel: 354 554 6716
Fax: 354 564 4201
email: steinunn.bjornsdottir@kirkjan.is

The Church of Norway

From around AD 1000 Christianity was brought to Norway by missionaries both from the British Isles and from Germany. Central to the Christianizing of Norway was King Olav Haraldsson. After his death in 1030 he was venerated as St Olav, and his shrine in Nidaros Cathedral (Trondheim) was a centre of pilgrimage. Episcopal sees were established in Nidaros, Bergen, Oslo (by 1100), and in Stavanger (1125) and Hamar (1153). Part of the Province of Lund from 1103, Norway became a separate province when Nidaros was raised to an archiepiscopal see in 1153. In addition to the five Norwegian sees, the Province of Nidaros also included six further dioceses covering Iceland, the Faeroes, Greenland, the Shetland and Orkney Islands, the Hebrides and the Isle of Man. Under Olav IV (1380–87) Norway was united with Denmark.

The Norwegian Reformation of 1537 was imposed by the new King of Denmark, Christian III, with little evidence of popular enthusiasm. New bishops ('superintendents') were ordained to the sees of Nidaros, Bergen and Stavanger by Johannes Bugenhagen, the Superintendent of Wittenberg, in 1537, and Bugenhagen's Danish Church Order was extended to Norway in 1539. Of the pre-Reformation bishops, Bishop Hans Rev of Oslo alone accepted the Reformation, and returned to his see (to which that of Hamar had been united) as Superintendent in 1541. The diocesan structure had been retained, with four of the five historic sees, and the term 'bishop' soon replaced its Latin synonym 'superintendent', but until recent years neither Bishop Rev nor any other bishop consecrated in the historic succession of the laying on of hands participated in the consecration of future bishops. Nidaros ceased to be an archiepiscopal see.

In the eighteenth and nineteenth centuries, pietist movements became influential, but they remained within the Church of Norway, the membership of which still amounts to 77 per cent of the population.

The Church of Norway has an 116-member General Synod, consisting of the members of the eleven diocesan councils (including the bishops), three members representing clergy, laity and lay employees, the moderators of the Sami Church Council and the Council on Ecumenical and International Relations, and three non-voting representatives of the theological faculties. Its executive is the 15-member National Council, which has a lay chair person. Related central bodies include the Bishops' Conference, the Council on Ecumenical and International Relations and the Sámi Church Council.

On 21st May 2012, the Norwegian Parliament passed a constitutional amendment that granted the Church of Norway increased autonomy.

The Parliament's recent decisions loosen historical ties between institutions of State and the majority Lutheran Church, which date back to the sixteenth century. One major consequence is that the responsibility for the appointment of bishops of Church of Norway shifted from the state to the church. A 500-year state-church tradition of the King/the Government appointing bishops has ended. The 116-member General Synod comprising bishops, pastors and lay church members adopted the new order for appointing bishops on 12–17 April 2012. The first bishop appointment following the new order was made by the board of the National Council (15 members elected by the General Synod) in 2012. On January 27 2013, Bishop Stein Reinertsen was consecrated as bishop of the diocese of Agder and Telemark.

Porvoo Agreement Contact Ms Beate Fagerli, Council on Ecumenical and International Relations, PB 799 – Sentrum, N-0106 Oslo
Tel: 47 23 08 12 74
Fax: 47 23 08 12 01
email: beate.fagerli@kirken.no

Presiding Bishop Rt Revd Helga Haugland Byfuglien, Diocesan Centre, Archbishop's House, N-7013 Trondheim/ *Tel:* 47 73 53 91 00
Or:
Church of Norway Bishop's Conference, PB 799 – Sentrum, N-0106 Oslo, *Tel:* 47 23 08 13 90
Fax: 47 23 08 12 01
email: bispemotet@kirken.no

AGDER
Bishop Stein Reinertsen, Diocesan Centre, PB 208, 4662 Krisitansand S *Tel:* 47 38 10 52 20
Fax: 47 38 10 51 21
email: agder.biskop@kirken.no

BJØRGVIN
Bishop Rt Revd Halvor Nordhaug, Diocesan Centre, Strandgt. 198, PB. 1960 Nordnes, 5018 Bergen *Tel:* 47 55 30 64 70
Fax: 47 55 30 64 85
email: bjoergvin.biskop@kirken.no

BORG
Bishop Rt Revd Atle Sommerfeldt, Diocesan Centre, Bjarne Aas gt 9, PB 403, N-1601 Fredrikstad *Tel:* 47 69 30 79 00
Fax: 47 69 30 79 01
email: borg.bdr@kirken.no

HAMAR
Bishop Rt Revd Solveig Fiske, Diocesan Centre, Folkestadgate 52, PB 172, N-2302 Hamar
Tel: 47 62 55 03 50
Fax: 47 62 55 03 51
email: hamar.bdr@kirken.no

MØRE
Bishop Rt Revd Ingeborg Synøve Midtømme, Diocesan Centre, Moldetrappa 1, N-6415 Molde
Tel: 47 71 25 06 70
Fax: 47 71 25 06 71
email: moere.bdr@kirken.no

NIDAROS
Bishop Rt Revd Tor Singsaas, Diocesan Centre, Archbishop's House, N-7013 Trondheim
Tel: 47 73 53 91 00
Fax: 47 73 53 91 11
email: nidaros.bdr@kirken.no

NORD-HÅLOGALAND
Bishop Rt Revd Per Oskar Kjølaas, Diocesan Centre, Conrad Holmboesvei 20, PB 790, N-9258 Tromsø
Tel: 47 77 60 39 60/61
Fax: 47 77 60 39 70
email: nord-haalogaland.bdr@kirken.no

OSLO
Bishop Rt Revd Ole Chr. M. Kvarme, Diocesan Centre, St Halvards plass 3, PB 9307, Gronland, N-0135 Oslo
Tel: 47 23 30 11 60
Fax: 47 23 30 11 99
email: oslo.bdr@kirken.no

SØR-HÅLOGALAND
Bishop Rt Revd Tor Berger Jørgensen, Diocesan Centre, Tolder Holmersvei 11, N-8003 Bodø
Tel: 47 75 54 85 50
Fax: 47 75 54 85 60
email: soer-haalogaland.bdr@kirken.no

STAVANGER
Bishop Rt Revd Erling J. Pettersen, Diocesan Centre, Domkirkeplassen 2, PB 629, N-4003 Stavanger
Tel: 47 51 84 62 70
Fax: 47 51 84 62 71
email: stavanger.bdr@kirken.no

TUNSBERG
Bishop Rt Revd Laila Riksaasen Dahl,Diocesan Centre, Håkon 5.s gt, PB 1253, N-3105
Tel: 47 33 35 43 00
Fax: 47 33 35 43 01
email: tunsberg.bdr@kirken.no

The Church of Sweden

The first to preach the gospel in Sweden was St Ansgar (801–65), the first Archbishop of Hamburg-Bremen, but it was in the eleventh century that the systematic conversion of Sweden was begun, largely by missionaries from England. From 1104 the new Swedish dioceses formed part of the Nordic Province of Lund (which was Danish until 1658), but only until 1164, when Uppsala was raised to an archiepiscopal see. The most celebrated figure of the medieval Swedish Church is St Birgitta of Vadstena (1303–73), foundress of the Brigittine Order.

Under the Lutheran Reformers Olaus Petri (1493–1552) and his brother Laurentius (d. 1573), who became the first Lutheran archbishop in 1531, the Swedish Reformation was gradual, and moderate in character. The Augsburg Confession was adopted in 1593.

The eighteenth and nineteenth centuries saw both latitudinarian and pietist movements, and in the early twentieth century a strong high-church movement developed. Archbishop Nathan Söderblom (1866–1931), one of the leading figures of the Ecumenical Movement, used the concept of 'evangelical catholicity' to describe the Church of Sweden's position. The Conference of Bishops of the Anglican Communion adopted a resolution of altar and pulpit fellowship with the Church of Sweden in 1920. In 1997 Christina Odenberg became the Church of Sweden's first woman bishop, when she was appointed Bishop of Lund.

The Church of Sweden is governed by a General Synod with 251 members and a 15-member Central Board (chaired by the archbishop), together with the Bishops' Conference. The bishops attend the Synod, but are not members of it, although they have all the rights of members except the right to vote. They are *ex-officio* members of the Synod Committee on Church Doctrine.

A separation of Church and State was effected in the year 2000, a year which also was marked by the 1000-year celebration of Christian faith in Sweden at the well of Husaby in the Diocese of Skara.

Porvoo Agreement Contact Revd Jenny Sjögreen, Ecumenical Officer, Church of Sweden, S-751 70 Uppsala
Tel: 46 18 16 95 20
46 70 693 17 10 (Mobile)
Fax: 46 18 16 95 38
email: jenny.sjogreen@svenskakyrkan.se

(**Note:** *The dioceses here are arranged alphabetically. The order traditionally used in Sweden reflects the chronological seniority of the Swedish dioceses.*)

GÖTEBORG

Bishop Rt Revd Dr Per Eckerdal, Stiftskansliet, Box 11937, SE-404 39 Göteborg
Tel: 46 31 771 30 00
Fax: 46 31 771 30 30
email: per.eckerdal@svenskakyrkan.se

HÄRNÖSAND

Bishop Rt Revd Dr Tuulikki Koivunen Bylund, Stiftskansliet, Box 94, SE-871 22 Härnösand
Tel: 46 611 254 00
Fax: 46 611 134 75
email: tuulikki.bylund@svenskakyrkan.se

KARLSTAD

Bishop Rt Revd Esbjörn Hagberg, Stiftskansliet, Box 186, SE-651 05 Karlstad   *Tel:* 46 54 17 24 00
Fax: 46 54 17 24 70
email: esbjorn.hagberg@svenskakyrkan.se

LINKÖPING

Bishop Rt Revd Martin Modéus, Stiftskansliet, Box 1367, SE-581 31 Linköping   *Tel:* 46 13 24 26 00
Fax: 46 13 14 90 95
email: biskopen.linkoping@svenskakyrkan.se

LULEÅ

Bishop Rt Revd Hans Stiglund, Stiftskansliet, Stationsgatan 40, SE-972 32 Luleå
Tel: 46 920 26 47 00
Fax: 46 920 26 47 21
email: hans.stiglund@svenskakyrkan.se

LUND

Bishop Rt Revd Johan Tyrberg, Stiftskansliet, Box 32, SE-221 00 Lund   *Tel:* 46 46 35 87 00
Fax: 46 46 18 49 48
email: johan.tyrberg@svenskakyrkan.se

SKARA

Bishop Rt Revd Åke Bonnier, Malmgatan 14, SE-532 32 Skara   *Tel:* 46 511 262 00
Fax: 46 511 262 70
email: ake.bonnier@svenskakyrkan.se

STOCKHOLM

Bishop Rt Revd Eva Brunne, Stiftskansliet, Box 16306, SE-103 25 Stockholm   *Tel:* 46 8 508 940 00
Fax: 46 8 24 75 75
email: eva.brunne@svenskakyrkan.se

STRÄNGNÄS

Bishop Rt Revd Dr Hans-Erik Nordin, Stiftskansliet, Box 84, SE-645 22 Strängnäs *Tel:* 46 152 234 00
Fax: 46 152 234 56
email: hans-erik.nordin@svenskakyrkan.se

UPPSALA

Archbishop Most Revd Dr Antje Jackelén, SE-751 70 Uppsala   *Tel:* 46 18 16 95 00
Fax: 46 18 16 96 25
email: archbishop@svenskakyrkan.se

Bishop Rt Revd Dr Ragnar Persenius, Box 1314, SE-751 43 Uppsala   *Tel:* 46 18 68 07 00
Fax: 46 18 12 87 62
email: ragnar.persenius@svenskakyrkan.se

VÄSTERÅS

Bishop Rt Revd Thomas Söderberg, Stiftskansliet, V Kyrkogatan 9, SE-722 15 Västerås
Tel: 46 21 17 85 00
Fax: 46 21 12 93 10
email: thomas.soderberg@svenskakyrkan.se

VÄXJÖ

Bishop Rt Rev Jan-Olof Johansson, Box 527, SE-351 06 Växjö   *Tel:* 46 470 77 38 00
Fax: 46 470 72 95 50
email: biskop.vaxjostift@svenskakyrkan.se

VISBY

Bishop Rt Revd Sven-Bernhard Fast, Stiftskansliet, Box 1334, SE-621 24 Visby   *Tel:* 46 498 40 49 00
Fax: 46 498 21 01 03
email: sven-bernhard.fast@svenskakyrkan.se

Further information about the history of the Nordic Lutheran Churches and of their relations with the Church of England can be found in Lars Österlin, *Churches of Northern Europe in Profile. A Thousand Years of Anglo-Nordic Relations* (Norwich, 1995).

BALTIC LUTHERAN CHURCHES

The Estonian Evangelical Lutheran Church

The conversion of Estonia to Christianity began at the end of the tenth century, and the first known bishop was consecrated in 1165. The mission was prosecuted by the Brethren of the Sword, an order founded in 1202 which merged with the Teutonic Order in 1237. In 1219 the Danes conquered the northern area and founded the capital Reval (Tallinn), which became an episcopal see within the Province of Lund. Further sees were established at Dorpat (Tartu) in 1224 and Hapsal (Saare-Lääne) in 1227, within the Province of Riga, the capital of Livonia, which included the southern part of modern Estonia. In some areas secular authority was in the hands of the bishops, while in others the Teutonic Order held sway. The entire area was very much under German dominance.

The Lutheran movement reached Estonia in 1523, and as early as the following year an assembly in Reval decided to adhere to the Reformation. Later in the century, however, the twin provinces of Estonia and Livonia became divided between neighbouring powers. Most of Estonia placed itself under Swedish rule in 1561, but Denmark ruled the island of Oesel (Saarema) from 1560 to 1645 and Livonia was annexed by Poland from 1561 to 1621. In Swedish Estonia, the Church was governed by a bishop and consistory, but Danish ecclesiastical law was introduced in Oesel, while Livonia came under the influence of the Counter-Reformation. Superintendents, rather than bishops, were appointed for these areas after they came under Swedish rule (in 1621 and 1645).

In 1710 both provinces came under Russian rule. In Estonia the office of bishop was replaced with that of superintendent. The consistories were chaired by laymen. In 1832 the Lutheran Churches of all three Baltic provinces were united with Russia's German-speaking Lutheran Church into a Russian Lutheran Church, with a General Consistory in St Petersburg. Each province (and – until 1890 – Reval, Oesel and Riga separately) had its own general superintendent and consistory. The University of Dorpat (Tartu), originally founded in 1632, was refounded in 1802. As the only Protestant theological faculty in the Russian Empire, it was of great importance. Throughout the period up to 1918 the clergy were German, like the ruling elite. The Moravian Church, which was active in Estonia and Livonia from 1736, enjoyed considerable influence over the Estonian peasantry, and by 1854 there were 276 Moravian prayer halls. However, the Moravian authorities blocked the development of this movement into a separate Moravian Church, and the Moravians' adherents remained within the Lutheran Church.

In 1918 Estonia and the Estonian northern part of Livonia became an independent state. The Church too became independent. It remained united, having both German and Estonian clergy and members. The office of bishop was immediately restored, the first bishop being consecrated in 1921 by the Archbishop of Uppsala and a Finnish bishop.

Estonia's independent existence lasted little more than 20 years, however. In 1940 it was occupied by the Red Army. German occupation followed, but Soviet rule was restored in 1944. Archbishop Köpp, who had remained unconsecrated because the war prevented bishops from other countries travelling to Estonia, went into exile with 70 other clergy and tens of thousands of church members. As a result of this the Estonian Evangelical–Lutheran Church Abroad was born. Of the clergy who remained, one-third were eventually deported to Siberia. Not until 1968 was it possible for an archbishop to be consecrated, although the first post-war Archbishop had already been elected in 1949.

In 1988, Estonia began to move towards independence, which was achieved in 1991. This was accompanied by a remarkable blossoming of church life. The Theological Faculty at Tartu, which had been dissolved by the Soviet authorities, was reopened. The Theological Institute of the EELC in Tallinn, which was set up after the war, also continues its work.

The Estonian Evangelical–Lutheran Church still forms one diocese with 167 parishes and congregations, headed by an Archbishop and a Suffragan Bishop. It is governed by a General Synod, the executive organ of which is the seven-member Consistory.

Porvoo Agreement Contact Revd Tauno Teder, Nikolai 22, 80010 Pärnu   *Tel:* 372 56 335 750
email: tauno.teder@eelk.ee

Archbishop of Estonia Most Revd Andres Põder, Consistory of the EELC, Kirikuplats 3, 10130 Tallinn   *Tel:* 372 6 27 73 50
Fax: 372 6 27 73 52
email: konsistoorium@eelk.ee
Web www.eelk.ee

The Evangelical Lutheran Church of Lithuania

Not until 1387 was an episcopal see established in Vilnius, following the baptism the previous year of Grand Duke Jogaila (whose coronation as King of Poland inaugurated a union lasting until 1795), and it was 1418 before the inhabitants of German-dominated Samogitia (covering much of present-day Lithuania) were forced to accept baptism.

A Lutheran congregation was founded in Vilnius as early as 1521, but persecution forced the Lithuanian Reformer Martin Mazvydas to flee to Königsberg. In time the Lithuanian nobility established the Reformed faith on their estates, while the numerous German merchants and craftsmen established Lutheran congregations in the towns from the 1550s. Until the early nineteenth century, the Lutheran Church continued to be a German and urban minority Church.

Sigismund Vasa (1587–1632) successfully restored Roman Catholicism as the religion of the people, and subsequent anti-Protestant policies meant that by 1775, when religious freedom was granted, just 30 Reformed and five Lutheran congregations remained (except those in Prussian-ruled Tauragé/Tauroggen).

In 1795 most of Lithuania was ceded to Russia, and Lithuania's Lutheran congregations were placed under the Consistory of Courland (now southern Latvia). Immigration of Lutheran Letts, Germans and Lithuanians from East Prussia produced new Lutheran congregations, especially in the countryside. The pastors (only nine in 1918) were all Germans.

At independence in 1918, Lithuania's population included 75,000 Lutherans, of whom roughly 30,000 were Germans, 30,000 Lithuanians and 15,000 Letts. In 1920 separate synods had to be formed for the three linguistic groups, and for much of the inter-war period tension between them paralysed the Lutheran Church. By 1939, however, there were 55 congregations with 33 pastors. To these should be added the separate Lutheran Church of the Prussian *Memelgebiet*, which Lithuania annexed in 1923. By 1939 this had 135,000 members (the majority German) in 32 parishes, served by 39 pastors.

Lithuanian Lutheranism was soon to be decimated. In 1941, following the 1940 Soviet annexation of Lithuania, most of the German population, together with a large number of Lithuanian Lutherans, emigrated to Germany. In Memelland and the Vilnius area, both reintegrated into Lithuania and thus the Soviet Union in 1945, the picture was even more stark. All but 30,000 inhabitants fled, while the pastor of the historic Lutheran church in Vilnius emigrated with his entire congregation.

A provisional Lutheran Consistory found itself responsible for 20,000 Lithuanians and Letts in Lithuania proper, together with just 15,000 Lithuanians in Klaipéda (Memelland). There were no pastors in Klaipéda and only six in the rest of the country, three of whom were soon banished to Siberia. After Stalin's death in 1953 and a first post-war synod in 1955, the structures of church life were gradually restored, but several thousand more Protestants emigrated between 1957 and 1965. At a second synod in 1970, Jonas Kalvanas, the only pastor left who had studied theology at university (he was ordained in 1940), was elected to chair the Consistory. It was with his consecration as Bishop by the Archbishop of Estonia in 1976 that his church gained the historic episcopate. He was succeeded in 1995 by his son and namesake, whose early death in 2003 left the see vacant until the consecration in June 2004 of Bishop Mindaugas Sebutis.

In 2014 the Lutheran Church had 56 congregations, with about 20,000 communicant members and twenty-nine clergy.

Porvoo Agreement Contact Revd Dr Darius Petkunas, Sauletekio takas 1, LT-00125 Palanga, Lithuania   *Tel:* +370 611 38226
email: darius.petkunas@liuteronai.lt

Bishop of the Evangelical Lutheran Church of Lithuania Rt Revd Mindaugas Sebutis, Vokieciu 20, LT-01130 Vilnius
Tel: +370 687 95417; +370 5 2626745 (office);
Fax: +370 5 2123792
email: konsistorija@lelb.lt
Web: http://www.liuteronai.lt/eng

NON-SIGNATORY CHURCHES

The Evangelical Lutheran Church of Latvia

The Church of Latvia has not yet voted on the Porvoo Declaration.

Archbishop of Riga and Latvia Most Revd Janis Vanags, M.Pils 4, LV 1050, Riga

Tel: 371 6 225406
email: lelb@lelb.lv / archbishop@ lelb.lv

Porvoo Agreement Contact, Dr Sandra Gintere, Alksnaja iela 3, Riga, LV 1050, Latvia
email: ginteres@gmail.com

There are also Anglican chaplaincies in most of the countries covered by the Porvoo Agreement. These belong to the Archdeaconry of Scandinavia and Germany within the Diocese in Europe. A leaflet giving details is available from the Diocesan Office of the Diocese in Europe, *see below.*

The *Directory of English-speaking Churches Abroad* (£4.00) lists English-speaking churches of Anglican and many other denominations in countries where English is not the first language, and is available from Intercontinental Church Society, Unit 11, Ensign Business Centre, Westwood Way, Westwood Business Park, Coventry CV4 8JA.

Tel: 024 7646 3940
Fax: 024 7767 5868
email: enquiries@ics-uk.org
Web: www.ics-uk.org

Credit card orders accepted by telephone or on the website.

Continental Anglican churches are listed in the *Diocesan Directory* of the Diocese in Europe, available from the Diocesan Office, 14 Tufton St, London SW1P 3QZ

Tel: 020 7898 1155
Fax: 020 7898 1166

Ecumenical   **PART 6**

PART 6   CONTENTS

ECUMENICAL *431*

ECUMENICAL

The Church of England is committed to the search for the full, visible unity of the Christian Church, and to the bodies which promote this at the local, intermediate, national, European and world levels. The Council for Christian Unity advises the General Synod and the Archbishops' Council on inter-church relations and acts as the principal channel of communication between the General Synod and the churches and ecumenical bodies, at the national and international levels. The CCU engages in informal ecumenical dialogue and implements any decisions of the General Synod regarding formal conversations.

ECUMENICAL CANONS
Canon B 43 (Of Relations with Other Churches) and Canon B 44 (Of Local Ecumenical Projects) make provision for sharing in worship and ministry with other churches. Full background information is given in *The Ecumenical Relations Code of Practice* (Church House, 1989). This paper, with its supplements, is now available electronically from http://www.churchofengland. org/about-us/work-other-churches/resources/ the-ecumenical-canons.aspx or by contacting cu@churchofengland.org. A range of useful introductory resource papers is also available from the same address.

CHURCHES DESIGNATED UNDER THE ECUMENICAL RELATIONS MEASURE
The Church of England's legal office maintains the list of the churches that have been designated by the Archbishops of Canterbury and York as churches to which the Church of England (Ecumenical Relations) Measure, and thus Canons B 43 and B 44, apply. An up-to-date list is maintained on the Church of England web site at www.churchofengland.org/about-us/structure/churchlawlegis/canons/section-.b.aspx. The following are currently listed: The Baptist Union, the Methodist Church, the Moravian Church, the Roman Catholic Church in England and Wales, the United Reformed Church, the Congregational Federation, the International Ministerial Council of Great Britain, the Lutheran Council of Great Britain, the Greek Orthodox Archdiocese of Thyateira and Great Britain (Ecumenical Patriarchate), the Council of African and Afro-Caribbean Churches, the Free Church of England, the Southam Road Evangelical Church Banbury, Member Churches of the Evangelical Church in Germany (EKD), the Assemblies of God in Great Britain and Ireland, the New Testament Church of God, the Russian Patriarchal Church of Great Britain being the Orthodox Diocese of Sourozh (Moscow Patriarchate), the Independent Methodist Churches, the Church of the Augsburg Confession of Alsace and Lorraine, the Evangelical–Lutheran Church of France, the Council of Oriental Orthodox Churches of Great Britain and the Republic of Ireland.

Churches Together in England

Churches Together in England is in association with Churches Together in Britain and Ireland. Its basis is as follows:

> Churches Together in England unites in pilgrimage those Churches in England which, acknowledging God's revelation in Christ, confess the Lord Jesus Christ as God and Saviour according to the Scriptures, and, in obedience to God's will and in the power of the Holy Spirit, commit themselves:
> – to seek a deepening of their communion with Christ and with one another in the Church, which is his body; and
> – to fulfil their mission to proclaim the Gospel by common witness and service in the world to the glory of the one God, Father, Son and Holy Spirit.

The Presidents of Churches Together in England are: The Archbishop of Canterbury, the Archbishop of Westminster and Revd Michael Heaney; Archbishop Gregorios (Oecumenical Patriarchate, Archdiocese of Thyateira and GB), who meet together quarterly.

It has forty-two Member Churches: Antiochian Orthodox Church, Apostolic Pastoral Congress, Armenian Orthodox Church, Assemblies of God, Baptist Union of Great Britain, Cherubim and Seraphim Council of Churches, Church of England, Church of God of Prophecy, Church of Scotland (in England), Churches in Communities International, Congregational Federation, Coptic Orthodox Church, Council for African and Caribbean Churches, Council of Oriental Orthodox Christian Churches, Council of Lutheran Churches, Elim Pentecostal Church, Evangelical Lutheran Churches, Exarchate of Orthodox Parishes of the Russian Tradition (Ecumenical Partriarchate), Free Church of England, Ground Level, Ichthus Christian Fellowship, Indian Orthodox Church, Evangelische Synod Deutscher Sprache in Grossbritannien, Independent

Methodist Churches, International Ministerial Council of Great Britain, Joint Council for Anglo-Caribbean Churches, Malankara Orthodox Syrian Church (Indian Orthodox), Mar Thoma Church, Methodist Church, Moravian Church, New Testament Assembly, New Testament Church of God, Oecumenical Patriarchate (Archdiocese of Thyateira and GB), Pioneer, Redeemed Christian Church of God, Religious Society of Friends, Roman Catholic Church, Russian Orthodox Church, Salvation Army, Seventh Day Adventists (observer), Transatlantic and Pacific Alliance of Churches, United Reformed Church, Wesleyan Holiness Church.

The Religious Society of Friends has membership under a clause designed for 'any Church or Association of Churches which on principle has no credal statements in its tradition'.

All substantive decisions are taken by these Member Churches.

Churches Together in England encourages its Member Churches to work together nationally, and provides various means for this purpose. There is an *Enabling Group*, which meets two times a year. Its Convenor is Bishop Christopher Foster and its Deputy Convenor Ruth Bottoms. There is a *Forum* of 300 members, which meets every three years. Its Moderator is Bishop Doyé Agama and its Deputy Moderator Ruth Gee.

- There are 6 *Coordinating Groups* (*see below*).
- There are also a large number of informal or as yet not formally recognized groups and networks.
- Churches Together in England encourages its Member Churches to work together locally. To enable this most counties and metropolitan areas have established ecumenical councils and officers, whose task is to foster and encourage all sorts of ecumenical work locally within their areas. The main task of the two Field Officers (*see below*) is to support those working in counties and metropolitan areas.
- Churches Together in England publishes an ecumenical e-news monthly.

General Secretary Revd Dr David Cornick, Churches Together in England, 27 Tavistock Square, London WC1H 9HH   *Tel:* 020 7529 8131
Web: www.cte.org.uk
Email: firstname.surname@cte.org.uk

Finance Officer Mr Stephen Cutler (*same address*)

Education Officer Ms Sarah Lane Cawte (*same address*)

Training, Resourcing and Events Jenny Bond (*same address*)   *Tel:* 07708 929022

Pentecostal and Multicultural Relations Bishop Joe Aldred (*same address*)   *Tel:* 07775 632288

Evangelisation, Mission and Media Captain Jim Currin (*same address*)   *Tel:* 07837 973214

Inter Faith Relations Celia Blackden (*same address*)   *Tel:* 07926 666218

Administrator Lorraine Shannon (*same address*)   *Tel:* 020 7529 8131

COORDINATING GROUPS
GROUP FOR EVANGELIZATION
Secretary Captain Jim Currin (*address see above*)   *Tel:* 07837 973214
    email: jim.currin@cte.org.uk

CHURCHES COMMITTEE FOR HOSPITAL CHAPLAINCY
Secretary Revd Debbie Hodge   *Tel:* 020 3651 8337
    email: debbie.hodge@freechurches.org.uk

CHURCHES COMMUNITY WORK ALLIANCE
Secretary Nils Chittenden, St Chad's College, North Bailey, Durham DH1 3RH
    Tel: 0191 374 7342
    email: nilsc@ccwa.org.uk

ECUMENICAL LIAISON GROUP FOR MINISTERIAL EDUCATION
Secretary Revd Fiona Thomas, United Reformed Church, 86 Tavistock Place, London WC1H 9RT
    email: fiona.thomas@urc.org.uk

THEOLOGY AND UNITY GROUP
Secretary Revd Dr David Cornick (*CTE address see above*)   *Tel:* 020 7529 8131
    email: david.cornick@cte.org.uk

CHURCHES RURAL GROUP
Convenor Barry Osborne
    email: barry@ruralmissions.org.uk

There are also four *Agencies*:

CHURCHES' MEDIA COUNCIL
(Formerly Churches' Advisory Council for Local Broadcasting)
Administrator Patricia Flynn, Christian Enquiry Agency, Freepost WC2947, South Croydon CR2 8UZ   *Tel:* 020 8144 7177
    email: cea@deogloria.co.uk

CHRISTIAN ENQUIRY AGENCY
Administrator Patricia Flynn, Christian Enquiry Agency, Freepost WC2947, South Croydon CR2 8UZ   *Tel:* 020 8144 7177
    email: cea@deogloria.co.uk

CHRISTIAN AID
PO Box 100, London SE1 7RL   *Tel:* 020 7620 4444
    email: info@christian-aid.org

CAFOD
Director Mr Chris Bain, 2 Romero Close, Stockwell Rd, London SW9 9TY   *Tel:* 020 7733 7900
    email: hqcafod@cafod.org.uk

The following are *Bodies in Association* with Churches Together in England: Action by Christians Against Torture, Association of Inter-Church Families, Bible Society, Christian Council on Ageing, Christian Council on Approaches to Defence and Disarmament, Christian Education, Christians Aware, Church Action on Poverty, Churches Alert to Sex Trafficking Across Europe (CHASTE), Churches Community Work Alliance (CCWA), Churches East–West Europe Relations Network (CEWERN), Churches for All, College of Preachers, Community of Aidan and Hilda, Corrymeela Community, Ecumenical Council for Corporate Responsibility, Ecumenical Society of the Blessed Virgin Mary, Faith in Europe, Feed the Minds, Fellowship of St Alban and St Sergius, Fellowship of Reconciliation, Focolare Movement, Housing Justice, Industrial Mission Association, International Ecumenical Fellowship, Iona Community, Irish School of Ecumenics, L'Arche, Living Stones, MODEM, Oikocredit, Retreat Association, Society for Ecumenical Studies, Student Christian Movement, William Temple Foundation, Women's World Day of Prayer, Young Men's Christian Association, Y Care International.

For addresses, *see* page 438 (under CTBI) or the **List of Organizations** (pages 251–255).

Intermediate County Bodies and Area Ecumenical Councils

Bedfordshire
Churches Together in
  Bedfordshire

Anita Nancollas
email:
  ct.beds@gmail.com

Berkshire
Churches Together in
  Berkshire

Louise Cole
14 Hertford Close
Woose Hill
Wokingham
Berkshire RG41 3BH
Tel: 0118 977 6437
email: ctberks@sky.com

Birmingham (*see also*
  West Midlands)
Birmingham Churches
  Together

Revd Dr Colin Marsh
St George's
  Community Hub
Great Hampton Row
Newtown,
  Birmingham B19 3JG
Tel: 0121 236 3966
email: office@
  birminghamchurches.
  org.uk

Black Country (*see also*
  Staffordshire)
Black Country Churches
  Engaged (BCCE)

Graham Sim
email: graham_sim1@
  btinternet.com

Bristol, Greater
Churches Together in
  Greater Bristol

Jon Doble
162 Pennywell Lane
Bristol BS5 0TX
Tel: 0117 955 7430
email: jon@ccisr.org.uk

Buckinghamshire
Churches Together in
  Buckinghamshire
  (Except Milton Keynes)

Barrie Cheetham
email: barrie@bern
  wodeforest.org.uk

Cambridgeshire
Cambridgeshire
  Ecumenical Council

Mrs Priscilla Barlow
Silverlands, Church St
Litlington
Royston
Herts SG8 0QB
Tel: 01763 852841
email:
  priscilla.barlow@
  keme.co.uk

Cheshire
Churches Together in
  Cheshire

Andrew Taylor
email:
  ceo.ctic@gmail.com

Cornwall
Churches Together in
  Cornwall

David Smith
Chyreene Warra
Rosehill
Marazion
Cornwall TR17 0HB
Tel: 01736 719 432
email: ses.dhs@
  hotmail.co.uk

Coventry *See*
  Warwickshire

Cumbria
Churches Together in
  Cumbria

Helen Boothroyd
email: htctic@
  tiscali.co.uk
Ruth Harvey
Croslands
Beacon Street
Penrith CA11 7TZ
Tel: 074 0363 8339
email: rctic@
  phoencoop.coop

Derbyshire and
  Nottinghamshire
Churches Together in
  Derbyshire and
  Nottinghamshire

Vacancy

ECUMENICAL

Devon
Churches Together in
   Devon

Sue Macbeth
email:
   churchestogether
   devon@gmail.com

Dorset
Churches Together in
   Dorset

Katja Babei
email:
   ctdorset@clara.net

Durham *see* **North-East**
   England

Bill Offler
42 John Street North
Meadowfield
Durham DH7 8RS
Tel: 0191 378 2883
email: william.offler@
   virgin.net

Essex and London, East
Churches Together in
   Essex and East
   London CLG

Vacancy

Gloucestershire
Gloucestershire
   Churches Together

Revd Dr Alison Evans
Britannia Cottage
High Street
Kings Stanley
Stonehouse
GL10 3JD
Tel: 01453 824034
email:
   malcolm.alison@
   btinternet.com

Guernsey
Churches Together in
   Guernsey

Mr Roy Sarre
Le Campère
Les Villets
Forest
Guernsey
Channel Islands
GY8 0HP
Tel: 01481 263930

Hampshire and Isle of
   Wight
Churches Together in
   Hampshire and the
   Isle of Wight

Andrew Wood
4 The Chase
Thornbury Wood
Chandler's Ford
Eastleigh
Hants SO53 5AZ
email:
   Andrew.wood4@
   btopenworld.com

Herefordshire
Churches Together in
   Herefordshire

Anna Nugent
email:
   herefordshireceo@
   gmail.com

Hertfordshire
Churches Together in
   Hertfordshire

Callan Slipper
138 Parkway
Welwyn Garden City
Herts AL8 6HP
Tel: 01707 339 242
email: facilitator@
   ctherts.org.uk

Isle of Man
Churches Together in
   Man

Mrs Mavis Matthewman
Tarnalforn
12 Ballagarey Rd
Glen Vine
Isle of Man
IM4 4EA
Tel: 01624 851693

Isle of Wight *see*
   Hampshire

Jersey
Christians Together in
   Jersey

Martin Dryden
Monte Urbe House
La Rue de la Blinerie
St Clements
Jersey JE2 6QT
email: martin@
   mont-ube.net

Kent
Churches Together in
   Kent

Chris Ruddle
email: CTKentHub@
   yahoo.co.uk

Lancashire
Churches Together in
   Lancashire

Anton Muller
email: antonmuller@
   ctlancashire.org.uk
Revd Steven Hughes
   (Inter Faith Officer)
69 Liverpool Old Rd
Much Hoole
Preston Lancs
PR4 4RB
Tel: 01772 612267
email:
   steven.hughes@
   ctlancashire.org.uk

Leicestershire
Churches Together in
   Leicestershire

Vic Allsop
c/o 14 Church Lane
Hoby
Melton Mowbray
Leicestershire
   LE14 3DR
Tel: 01664 434 697
email: cedo.ctil@
   fsmail.net

Lincolnshire
Churches Together in
   All Lincolnshire

Mel Parkin
   (administrator)
c/o Church House
The Old Palace
Lincoln
LN2 1PU
Tel: 01522 504071
email: ctal@lincoln.
   anglican.org

London, East *see* **Essex**
East London Church
   Leaders Group

Vacancy

London, North *see*
   North Thames

London, North Thames
Churches Together
  North Thames

Wendie Heywood
email: office@
  ctnt.org.uk

London, South
Churches Together in
  South London

John Richardson
c/o St John's Vicarage
Secker Street
London SE1 9UF
Tel: 01462 422502
email: john@
  ctslondon.org.uk

London, West

Vacancy

Manchester, Greater
Greater Manchester
  Churches Together

St John's Rectory
Railton Terrace
Moston
Manchester
  M9 4WE
Tel: 0161 205 8838
Bishop Doyé Agama
  (Acting GMCT
  contact)
email:
  doye@hotmail.com
Seifa Afiesimama
  (Administrator)
email:
  admin@apostolic
  pastors.info

Merseyside
Churches Together in
  the Merseyside
  Region

Revd Ian Smith
Quaker Meeting
  House
22 School Lane
Liverpool L1 3BT
Tel: 0151 709 0125
email: office@
  ctmr.org.uk

Milton Keynes
Mission Partnership of
  the Milton Keynes
  Christian Council

John Robertson
c/o Christian
  Foundation
The Square
Aylesbury Street
Wolverton
MK12 5HX
Tel: 01908 311310
email: admin@mission
  partnership.org.uk

Norfolk
Norfolk and Waveney
  Churches Together

Simon Wilson
The Rectory
Guist Road
Foulsham
Norfolk NR20 5RZ
Tel: 01352 683 275
email: simon.wilson@
  norwich.anglican.
  org

North-East England
North East Christian
  Churches Together
  (NECCT)

Bill Offler
42 John Street North
Meadowfield
Durham DH7 8RS
Tel: 01865 723 801
email: william.offler@
  virgin.net

Nottinghamshire (*see*
Derbyshire)

Oxfordshire
Churches Together in
  Oxfordshire

Revd Peter Ball
c/o Cowley Road
  Methodist Church
Jeune Street
Oxford OX4 1BN
Tel: 01865 723801
email: ctoshire@
  gmail.com

Peterborough (*see*
Shire and Soke)

Shire and Soke
Churches Together in
  Northamptonshire &
  Peterborough

Gill Crow
  (Northamptonshire)
email: gillcrow@
  shireandsoke.org.uk
Philip Hutchinson
  (Peterborough)
email:
  philiphutchinson@
  shireandsoke.org.uk

Shropshire (Except
  Telford)
Churches Together in
  Shropshire

Mr Ged Cliffe
Fern Villa
Four Crosses
Llanymynech
Powys SY22 6PR
Tel: 01691 831374
email: gerard.cliffe@
  btinternet.com

Somerset
Somerset Churches
  Together

Gabrielle Grace
3 Champford Mews
Wellington
  TA21 8JW
Tel: 07811 108 218
email: sctogether@
  phonecoop.coop

Staffordshire
Churches Linked Across
  Staffs & the Potteries
  (CLASP) (*as* **Black
  Country**)

Graham Sim
email: graham_sim1@
  btinternet.com

Suffolk
Churches Together in
  Suffolk

Julie Mansfield
Applegarth
Wilmslow Avenue
Woodbridge
Suffolk
IP12 4HW
Tel: 01394 384370
email: jmmansfield@
  homecall.co.uk

ECUMENICAL

Intermediate County Bodies

Surrey
Churches Together in
  Surrey

Revd Susan Loveday
10 Abbey Gardens
Chertsey
Surrey KT16 8RQ
Tel: 01932 566920
email: sue.loveday.
  ctsurrey@
  lineone.net

Sussex
Churches Together in
  Sussex

Mr Ian Chisnall
85 Hollingbury
  Rise
Brighton
BN1 7HH
Tel: 07976 811654
  (Mobile)
email: ianpchisnall@
  aol.com

Swindon
Swindon Churches
  Together

Vacancy

Telford
Telford Christian
  Council

Andy Smith
Meeting Point House
Southwater Square
Town Centre
Telford TF3 4HS
Tel: 01952 291904
email: andysmith@
  telfordchristian
  council.co.uk

Warwickshire
Churches Together
  in Coventry &
  Warwickshire

Christine Craven
310 Holyhead Road
Coventry
Warwickshire
CV5 8JP
Tel: 02476 599454
email:
  christine.craven9@
  btinternet.com

Waveney *see* **Norfolk**

Wiltshire
Wiltshire Churches
  Together

Liz Overthrow
email:
  liz.overthrow@
  btinternet.com

Worcestershire
Churches Together
  in Worcestershire

Revd David Ryan
4 Daty Croft
Home Meadow
Worcester WR4 0JB
Tel: 01905 616109
email: dpryangb@
  aol.com

**Yorkshire, East
  and Hull**
Kingston upon Hull &
  East Yorkshire
  Churches Together

Vacancy
Key Churches
  Together
Methodist Central
  Hall
King Edward Street
Hull HU1 3SQ
Tel: 01482 328196

**Yorkshire, North York
  Moors**
North York Moors
  Churches Together

Barbara Burke
York & Hull District
  Office
28 The Green
Acomb, York
YO26 5LR
email:
  northyorkschurch@
  hotmail.co.uk

Yorkshire, South
Churches Together in
  South Yorkshire

Erica Dunmow
CTSY Office
C/O SCEC
Montgomery Hall
Surrey Street
Sheffield S1 2LG
email: emdo@
  ctsy.yahoo.co.uk

Yorkshire, Vale of York
ENVOY (Ecumenical
  Network in the Vale
  of York)

Nigel Currey
17 Mayfield Drive
Brayton
Selby
North Yorkshire
YO8 9JZ
Tel: 01757 704892
email: ncurrey1@
  talktalk.net

Yorkshire, West
West Yorkshire
  Ecumenical Council

Clive Barrett
Hinsley Hall
62 Headingley Lane
Leeds LS6 2BX
Tel: 0113 261 8053
Fax: 0113 261 8054
email: clivebarrett@
  wyec.co.uk

Churches Together in Britain and Ireland

Office 39 Ecclestone Square, London SW1V 1BX
Tel: 08456 806851
Fax: 08456 806852
email: gensec@ctbi.org.uk
Web: www.ctbi.org.uk

Churches Together in Britain and Ireland (CTBI) is an umbrella body through which the Churches co-operate on common issues. It works closely with the other 'Churches Together' bodies, which focus separately on England, Wales, Scotland and Ireland. Together they have an important role to witness to the essential unity of the Christian movement. CTBI's core tasks are providing 'structured ecumenical space' for meeting and encounter, facilitating shared study on common issues and fostering relationships – among the Churches and between the Churches and the wider world.

Churches Together in Britain and Ireland (formerly the Council of Churches for Britain and Ireland and the direct successor of the British Council of Churches) was established by its member Churches to enable them to work together for the advancement of the Christian religion, the relief of poverty, the advancement of education and any other charitable purpose. It seeks to further these objects by providing opportunities for representatives of the Churches from the four nations to meet together and to share some of their resources in the pursuance of jointly agreed activities.

Following a review of its work, Churches Together in Britain and Ireland has become an agency serving the churches through the four National Ecumenical Instruments. As a separate charitable company, limited by guarantee, CTBI now relates to the churches, as members, through the ecumenical structures of the nations. It is now more relational and its focus is on working agreed common themes across the different work areas described below. The current themes are:

– environment/climate change
– migration and the movements of people
– culture, identity and the public space

Our principal activities and Networks are:

- Witnessing to and working towards the visible unity of the Christian Churches and providing opportunities for representatives of the Churches to meet and to plan their work together. A **Senior Representatives Forum**, attended by delegates from all member churches and bodies in association, is held in the spring of each year. An annual **Networking Conference** brings together the various Networks which comprise members of the member Chruches, Agencies and Bodies in Association.

- Working on the Churches' behalf on issues of racial justice through the **Churches Racial Justice Network** (formerly known as CCRJ, the Churches' Commission for Racial Justice). The Racial Justice Network is a major vehicle for the Churches' engagement with the complex work of racial justice throughout Ireland, Scotland, Wales and England. Central to the work is the Racial Justice Fund, which supports a wide range of grassroots organizations. These funded groups are invited into a dynamic partnership designed to build their capacity for effective action and to provide first rate information and experience for use in education, lobbying and campaigning. **Racial Justice Sunday,** celebrated ecumenically on the second Sunday in September, gives an opportunity for vital educational work with churches and congregations and raises the media profile of the work of racial justice. Other projects include Capacity Building for Black Churches, the Bail Circle and the Peers project. The recent publication of *Migration Principles*, which in turn is building on the work of *Asylum Principles*, seeks to promote an active discussion and programme around the complex issue of migration. Working with other departments within CTBI, the Racial Justice team are taking forward Migration as a major theme.

- Through the **Churches Network for Mission (CNM),** seeking to serve and assist churches, agencies and the four national ecumenical instruments in our common task of participating in God's mission in the world. GMN is a key point of contact with world ecumenical mission bodies, particularly the World Council of Churches and the Council of European Churches. GMN's current projects include:

  – **Mission Theology Advisory Group,** offering expertise from around the four nations in Mission theology. Publications and web resources are being produced to support the ongoing work of the churches' mission in new contexts.

  – **China** – the China Desk provides a dedicated expert centre maintaining a wide range of relationships in China and undertaking research and analysis on Chinese affairs. It co-ordinates the work of the China Forum which acts as a bridge to Chinese Christians, both Catholic and Protestant, with partnership maintained through a variety of on-going projects.

- Through the **Churches Inter Religious Network,** working with the Churches to engage effectively in relations and dialogue with other faiths in Britain and Ireland. The

ECUMENICAL

Network is a point of reference for the Churches which facilitates an exchange of information and experience among Christians about inter faith relations, whilst enabling critical reflection on the religiously and socially plural society of the four nations. In Scotland, it works through the Churches' Agency for Inter Faith Relations in Scotland. The Network seeks to fulfil its aims by responding to requests by the Churches on inter faith issues, monitoring inter faith relations in the four nations, nurturing links between Christians working in this field, pooling the theological resources of the Churches for ministry and witness in this area, and producing appropriate written or other material to help the Churches. In addition CTBI is a member body, on behalf of the Churches, of the Inter Faith Network for the United Kingdom, which provides a national forum for people from the main faith communities to meet, discuss and share.

- Through the **Churches International Student Network**, supporting international students by networking, education and communication among the Churches and between them, government and other agencies specializing in international students' affairs. The Network seeks to link the varied work of the many church agencies among students and supports the Churches in their response to the needs of international students. It initiated and maintains co-funding from the Foreign Office for denominational and ecumenical scholarships, administers World Council of Churches scholarships in Britain and Ireland and operates a hardship fund for international students for which it raises funding.
- Developing and publishing for the Churches **resources for study and prayer**. This includes printed and web based materials for the Week of Prayer for Christian Unity, which is observed each year from 18 to 25 January, as well as a Lent study programme.
- Through the **Church and Public Issues Network**, supporting and resourcing the Churches in their work on political, social and ethical issues, paying particular attention to:

  - public policy agendas of Westminster, and also Cardiff, Edinburgh, Belfast, Dublin and Brussels
  - the churches' engagement with contemporary social issues
  - moral/ethical issues, especially where there is a distinctive Christian contribution to be made

The Church and Society Forum takes a lead in networking those who work on church and society issues across the four nations, and in sharing and disseminating information and expertise. It represents the Churches jointly, where appropri-

ate, to Government bodies, other agencies and elsewhere. It has one main residential meeting each year, with others as the need arises.

STAFF
Canon Robert Fyffe, *General Secretary*

Revd Peter Colwell, *Deputy General Secretary*
Mr Stephen Cutler, *Director of Business and Finance*
Christine Elliott *Director of World Church Programmes*
Mr Dave Chadwick, *Web Manager*

CTBI MEMBER CHURCHES AND BODIES OF CHURCHES
ANTIOCHIAN ORTHODOX CHURCH
Father George Hackney
Little Portion, Back Lane, Barnby, Newark NG24 2SD   *Tel:* 01636 626417
                    email: fathergeorge@macace.net

BAPTIST UNION OF GREAT BRITAIN
Revd Jonathan Edwards *General Secretary*
Baptist House, 129 Broadway, Didcot OX11 8RT
                    Tel: 01235 517700
                    Fax: 01235 517715
                    email: info@baptist.org.uk
                    Web: www.baptist.org.uk

CATHOLIC BISHOPS' CONFERENCE OF ENGLAND AND WALES
Fr Marcus Stock *General Secretary*
39 Eccleston Square, London SW1V 1BX
                    Tel: 020 7630 8220
                    Fax: 020 7901 4821
                    email: secretariat@cbcew.org.uk
                    Web: www.catholic-ew.org.uk

CATHOLIC BISHOPS' CONFERENCE OF SCOTLAND
Revd Paul Conroy *General Secretary*
64 Aitken St, Airdrie ML6 6LT   *Tel:* 01236 764061
                    Fax: 01236 762489
                    email: GenSec@BpsConfScot.com
Web:
  www.scmo.org/_titles/bishops_conference.htm

CHURCH IN WALES
John Shirley *Provincial Secretary*
39 Cathedral Rd, Cardiff CF11 9XF
                    Tel: 029 2034 8200
                    Fax: 029 2038 7835
     email: johnshirley@churchinwales.org.uk
                    Web: www.churchinwales.org.uk

CHURCH OF ENGLAND
Mr William Fittall *Secretary General of the General Synod and the Archbishops' Council*
Church House, Great Smith St, London SW1P 3AZ   *Tel:* 020 7898 1000
                    Fax: 020 7898 1369
                    email: cofe.comms@c-of-e.org.uk
                    Web: www.cofe.anglican.org

CHURCH OF GOD OF PROPHECY
Bishop Wilton R. Powell *National Overseer*
6 Beacon Court, Birmingham Rd, Great Barr,
Birmingham B43 6NN   *Tel:* 0121 358 2231
Fax: 0121 358 8617
email: admin@cogop.org.uk
Web: www.cogop.org.uk

CHURCH OF IRELAND
Mrs Janet Maxwell *Head of Synod Services and Communications*
Church of Ireland House, Church Avenue, Rathmines, Dublin 6, RoI   *Tel:* ++ 353 (0)1 4125621
Fax: ++ 353 (0)1 4978821
email: janet.maxwell@rcbdub.org
Web: www.ireland.anglican.org

CHURCH OF SCOTLAND
Revd John Chalmers *Principal Clerk*
Principal Clerk's Office, 121 George St, Edinburgh
EH2 4YN   *Tel:* 0131 240 2240
Fax: 0131 240 2239
email: pracproc@cofscotland.org.uk
Web: www.churchofscotland.org.uk

CONGREGATIONAL FEDERATION
Revd Michael Heaney *General Secretary*
8 Castle Gate, Nottingham NG1 7AS
Tel: 0115 911 1460
Fax: 0115 911 1462
email: admin@congregational.org.uk
Web: www.congregational.org.uk

COPTIC ORTHODOX CHURCH
Bishop Angaelos
Coptic Orthodox Church Centre, Shephalbury
Manor, Broadhall Way, Stevenage SG2 8RH
Tel: 01438 745232
Fax: 01438 313879
email: admin@CopticCentre.com
Web: www.CopticCentre.com

COUNCIL OF ORIENTAL ORTHODOX CHURCHES
Bishop Angaelos *President*
c/o Coptic Orthodox Church Centre (*as above*)
email: admin@CopticCentre.com

GERMAN-SPEAKING CONGREGATION
Mr Georg Staab
Council for German Church Work, 35 Craven
Terrace, London W2 3EL   *Tel:* 020 7706 8589
Fax: 020 7706 2870
email: office@ev-synode.org.uk
Web: www.ev-synode.org.uk

INDEPENDENT METHODIST CHURCHES
Mr William Gabb *General Secretary*
Independent Methodist Resource Centre &
Registered Office
Fleet St, Pemberton, Wigan WN5 0DS
Tel: 01942 223526
Fax: 01942 227768
email: resourcecentre@imcgb.org.uk
Web: www.imcgb.org.uk

INTERNATIONAL MINISTERIAL COUNCIL OF GREAT BRITAIN (IMCGB)
Bishop Onye Obika
217 Langhedge Lane, London N18 2TG
Tel: 020 8345 5376
email: imcgb@aol.com
Web: www.imcgb.com

JOINT COUNCIL FOR ANGLO AND AFRICAN-CARIBBEAN CHURCHES
Revd Esme Beswick *President*
141 Railton Rd, London SE24 OLT
Tel and Fax: 020 7737 6542

LUTHERAN COUNCIL OF GREAT BRITAIN
Revd Thomas Bruch *General Secretary*
30 Thanet St, London WC1H 9QH
Tel: 020 7554 2900
Fax: 020 7383 3081
email: enquiries@lutheran.org.uk
Web: www.lutheran.org.uk

MAR THOMA CHURCH
Dr Zac Varghese *Ecumenical Officer*
3 Rose Garden Close, Edgware, London HA8 7RF
Tel: 020 8951 5273
email: zacvarghese@aol.co.uk

METHODIST CHURCH
Revd Dr Martin Atkins *General Secretary*
25 Marylebone Rd, London NW1 5JR
Tel: 020 7467 5143
Fax: 020 7467 5226
email: generalsecretary@methodistchurch.org.uk
Web: www.methodist.org.uk

METHODIST CHURCH IN IRELAND
Revd Donald Ker *General Secretary*
1 Fountainville Ave, Belfast BT9 6AN
Tel: 028 9032 4554
Fax: 028 9023 9467
email: secretary@irishmethodist.org
Web: www.irishmethodist.org

MORAVIAN CHURCH
Jackie Morten
Moravian Church House, 5 Muswell Hill,
London N10 3TJ   *Tel:* 020 8883 3409
Fax: 020 8365 3371
email: office@moravian.org.uk
Web: www.moravian.org.uk

NEW TESTAMENT ASSEMBLY
Revd Nezlin Sterling *General Secretary*
5 Woodstock Ave, London W13 9UQ
Tel: 020 8579 3841
Fax: 020 8537 9253
email: njsterlnta@aol.com

ECUMENICAL

NEW TESTAMENT CHURCH OF GOD
Bishop Donald Bolt
3 Cheyne Walk, Northampton NN1 5PT
Tel: 01604 643311
Fax: 01604 790254
email: bigmove@ntcg.org.uk
Web: www.ntcg.org.uk

OECUMENICAL PATRIARCHATE (ARCHDIOCESE OF
THYATEIRA AND GREAT BRITAIN)
His Eminence Archbishop Gregorios
5 Craven Hill, London W2 3EN
Tel: 020 7723 4787
Fax: 020 7224 9301
email: thyateiragb@yahoo.com
Web: www.nostos.com/church/

PRESBYTERIAN CHURCH OF WALES
Revd Ifan Roberts *General Secretary*
Tabernacle Chapel, 81 Merthyr Road, Whit-
church, Cardiff CF14 1DD   *Tel:* 029 2062 7465
Fax: 029 2061 6188
email: swyddfa.office@ebcpcw.org.uk
Web: www.ebcpcw.org.uk

RELIGIOUS SOCIETY OF FRIENDS
Gillian Ashmore *Chief Recording Clerk*
Friends House, 173 Euston Rd, London NW1 2BJ
Tel: 020 7663 1000
Fax: 020 7663 1001
email: enquiries@quaker.org.uk
Web: www.quaker.org.uk

RELIGIOUS SOCIETY OF FRIENDS IN IRELAND
Mr Ian Woods
40 Castle Grove, Swords, Co Dublin

RUSSIAN ORTHODOX CHURCH (ECUMENICAL
PATRIARCHATE)
Mrs Gillian Crow
6 Maiden Place, London NW5 1HZ
email: gillian@crow.co.uk
Web www.exarchate-uk.org

SALVATION ARMY
Commissioner John Matear *Territorial Commander
UK and RoI*
101 Newington Causeway, London SE1 6BN
Tel: 020 7367 4500
Fax: 020 7367 4728
email: info@salvationarmy.org.uk
Web: www.salvationarmy.org.uk

SCOTTISH EPISCOPAL CHURCH
Mr John Stuart *Secretary General for Synod Office*
21 Grosvenor Crescent, Edinburgh EH12 5EE
Tel: 0131 225 6357
Fax: 0131 346 7247
email: office@scotland.anglican.org
Web: www.scottishepiscopal.com

TRANS-ATLANTIC & PACIFIC ALLIANCE OF
CHURCHES
Archbishop Paul Hackman *President*
281-283 Rye Lane, London SE15 4UA
Tel and Fax: 020 7639 4058
email: tapacglobal@aol.com

UNDEB YR ANNIBYNWYR CYMRAEG/UNION OF
WELSH INDEPENDENTS
Revd Dr Geraint Tudor *General Secretary*
Tŷ John Penri, 5 Axis Court, Riverside Business
Park, Swansea Vale, Swansea SA7 0AJ
Tel: 01792 795888
Fax: 01792 795376
email: Undeb@annibynwyr.org
Web: www.annibynwyr.org

UNITED FREE CHURCH OF SCOTLAND
Revd Andrew McMillan
11 Newton Place, Glasgow G3 7PR
Tel: 0141 332 3435
Fax: 0141 333 1973
email: office@ufcos.org.uk
Web: www.ufcos.org.uk

UNITED REFORMED CHURCH
Revd Roberta Rominger *General Secretary*
86 Tavistock Place, London WC1H 9RT
Tel: 020 7916 2020
Fax: 020 7916 2021
email: urc@urc.org.uk
Web: www.urc.org.uk

ASSOCIATE MEMBER
ROMAN CATHOLIC CHURCH OF IRELAND
Revd Aidan O'Boyle *Executive Secretary*
The Irish Episcopal Conference, Columba Centre,
Maynooth, Co Kildare, Republic of Ireland
Tel: 00 353 1 505 3020
Fax: 00 353 1 629 2360
email: ex.sec@iecon.ie

BODIES IN ASSOCIATION
ACTION BY CHRISTIANS AGAINST TORTURE
Chas Raws, 38 The Mount, Heswello, Wirrall
CH60 4RA
email: uk.acat@googlemail.com
Web: www.acatuk.org.uk

ASSOCIATION OF INTER-CHURCH FAMILIES
Mr Keith Lander (*Executive Officer*), 27 Tavistock
Square, London WC1H 9HH
Tel: 020 7529 8131
Fax: 020 7529 8134
email: info@interchurchfamilies.org.uk
Web: www.interchurchfamilies.org.uk

BIBLE READING FELLOWSHIP
Richard Fisher, 15 The Chambers, Vineyard,
Abingdon OX14 3FE   *Tel:* 01865 319 700
email: enquiries@brf.org.uk
Web: www.brf.org.uk

BIBLE SOCIETY
James Catford (*Chief Executive*), Stonehill Green, Westlea, Swindon SN5 7DG   *Tel:* 01793 418 100
Web: www.biblesociety.org.uk

CHRISTIAN COUNCIL ON AGEING
Mrs Christine Hodgson, 6 The Ridgeway, Market Harborough LE16 7HQ   *Tel:* 01858 432771
email: info@ccoa.org.uk
Web: www.ccoa.org.uk

CHRISTIAN EDUCATION
Peter Fishpool (*Chief Executive*), 1020 Bristol Rd, Selly Oak, Birmingham B29 6LB
Tel: 0121 472 4242
Fax: 0121 472 7575
email: admin@christianeducation.org.uk
Web: www.christianeducation.org.uk

CHRISTIANS AWARE
Mrs Barbara Butler, 2 Saxby St, Leicester LE2 0ND
Tel and *Fax:* 0116 254 0770
email: barbarabutler@christiansaware.co.uk
Web: www.christiansaware.co.uk

CHURCH ACTION ON POVERTY
Mr Niall Cooper (*National Coordinator*), Dale House, 35 Dale St, Manchester M1 2HF
Tel: 0161 236 9321
Fax: 0161 237 5359
email: info@church-poverty.org.uk
Web: www.church-poverty.org.uk

CHURCHES' ALERT TO SEX TRAFFICKING ACROSS EUROPE
Angela Deavall (*Chief Executive*), PO Box 983, Cambridge CB3 8WY   *Tel:* 0845 456 9335
email: contact@chaste.org.uk
Web: www.chaste.org.uk

COLLEGE OF PREACHERS
Ms Marfa Jones (*Administrator*), Chester House, Pages Lane, Muswell Hill, London N10 1PR
Tel: 020 8883 7850
email: administrator@collegeofpreachers.org.uk
Web: www.collegeofpreachers.org.uk

COMMUNITY OF AIDAN AND HILDA
Lindisfarne Retreat, The Open Gate, Holy Island, Berwick-upon-Tweed TD15 2SD
Tel: 01289 389222
email: ca-and-h@demon.co.uk
Web: www.aidanandhilda.org.uk

CORRYMEELA COMMUNITY
Corrymeela House, 8 Upper Crescent, Belfast BT7 1NT   *Tel:* 028 9050 8080
Fax: 028 9050 8070
email: annemcdonagh@corrymeela.org
Web: www.corrymeela.org

ECUMENICAL COUNCIL FOR CORPORATE RESPONSIBILITY
Miles Litvinoff (*Coordinator*), PO Box 500, Oxford OX1 1ZL   *Tel:* 020 8965 9682
email: info@eccr.org.uk
Web: www.eccr.org.uk

ECUMENICAL SOCIETY OF THE BLESSED VIRGIN MARY
Paul Paniccia, 1 Badgers Glade, Burghfield Common, Reading RG7 3RG

FAITH IN EUROPE
Dr Philip Walters (*General Secretary*), 81 Thorney Leys, Witney OX28 5BY   *Tel:* 01993 771778
email: philip.walters@waltfam.freeserve.co.uk
Web: www.faithineurope.org.uk

FEED THE MINDS
Josephine Carlssen (*Director*), Park Place, 12 Lawn Lane, London SW8 1UD
Tel: 020 7592 3900
Fax: 020 7592 3939
email: info@feedtheminds.org.uk
Web: www.feedtheminds.org

FELLOWSHIP OF RECONCILIATION
Revd John Johansen-Berg (*Director*), St James' Church Centre, Beauchamp Lane, Oxford OX4 3LF   *Tel:* 01865 748796
email: office@for.org.uk
Web: www.for.org.uk

FELLOWSHIP OF ST ALBAN AND ST SERGIUS
Revd Stephen Platt, 1 Canterbury Rd, Oxford OX2 6LU   *Tel:* 01865 52991
Fax: 01865 316700
email: gensec@sobornost.org
Web: www.sobornost.org

FOCOLARE MOVEMENT
Celia Blackden, 11 Drummond Avenue, Leeds LS16 5JZ
email: celiablackden@yahoo.co.uk
Web: www.focolare.org.uk

HOUSING JUSTICE
Ms Alison Gelder (*Chief Executive*), 209 Old Marylebone Rd, London NW1 5QT
Tel: 020 7723 7273
Fax: 020 7723 5943
email: info@housingjustice.org.uk
Web: www.housingjustice.org.uk

INDUSTRIAL MISSION ASSOCIATION
Revd Stephen Hazlett, Northumbrian Industrial Mission, 14 The Oaks West, Sunderland SR2 8HZ
Tel: 07900 231360
Web: www.industrialmission.org.uk

ECUMENICAL

INTERNATIONAL ECUMENICAL FELLOWSHIP
David Hardiman, 59 Old St, Headington, Oxford
OX3 9HT   *Tel:* 0191 4566 1643
email: davidhardiman@blueyonder.com
Web: www.uk-ief.co.uk

IONA COMMUNITY
Revd Peter Macdonald, 4th Floor, Savoy House,
140 Sauchiehall St, Glasgow G2 3DH
Tel: 0141 332 6343
Fax: 0141 332 1090
email: admin@iona.org.uk
Web: www.iona.org.uk

IRISH SCHOOL OF ECUMENICS
Prof Linda Hogan, 683 Antrim Rd, Belfast BT15
4EG *and* Bea House, Milltown Park, Dublin 6, RoI
Tel: +44 (0) 28 9077 5010
Fax: +44 (0) 28 9037 3986
email: lhogan2@tcd.ie
Web: www.tcd.ie/ise

L'ARCHE
Ms Lal Keenan, L'Arche Community, 15 North-
wood High St, London SE27 9JU
Tel: 020 8670 6714
Fax: 020 8670 0818
email: info@larche.org.uk
Web: www.larche.org.uk

LIVING STONES
Dr Aziz Nour, 77 Exeter Rd, Southgate, London
N14 5JU
Web: www.livingstonesonline.org.uk

MAGNET RESOURCES
Lynne Ling, PO Box 10378, Bishop's Stortford
CM23 9FT   *Tel:* 0844 7362524
Web: www.ourmagnet.co.uk

MODEM
Mr John Nelson (*National Secretary and Publications Editor*), 24 Rostron Crescent, Formby L37
2ET   *Tel:* 01704 873973
Fax: 01704 871273
email: jrn24rcf2003@yahoo.co.uk
Web: www.modem.uk.com

OIKOCREDIT, ECUMENICAL DEVELOPMENT
COOPERATIVE SOCIETY
Patrick Hynes, UK Support Office, PO Box 809,
Garstang, Preston PR3 1TU
Web: www.oikocredit.org

OPERATION NOAH
Anne Pettifor, Grayston Centre, 28 Charles
Square, London N1 6HT   *Tel:* 0207 324 4761
email: admin@operationnoah.org
Web: www.operationnoah.org

PRISON FELLOWSHIP ENGLAND AND WALES
Tim Diaper, PO Box 945, Maldon, Essex CM9
4EW   *Tel:* 01621 843232
Web: www.prisonfellowship.org

RETREAT ASSOCIATION
Alison MacTier, The Central Hall, 256 Bermond-
sey St, London SE1 3UJ   *Tel:* 020 7357 7736
Fax: 020 7357 7724
email: info@retreats.org.uk
Web: www.retreats.org.uk

SOCIETY OF ECUMENICAL STUDIES
Revd Mark Woodruff (*Secretary*), 26 Daysbrook
Rd, London SW2 3TD   *Tel:* 020 8678 8195
email: ecumenicalstudies@btinternet.com
Web: www.ecumenicalstudies.org.uk

STUDENT CHRISTIAN MOVEMENT
Revd Martin Thompson, Unit 308F, The Big
Peg, 120 Vyse St, Jewellery Quarter, Birmingham
B18 6NF   *Tel:* 0121 200 3355
email: co@movement.org.uk
Web: www.movement.org.uk

WOMEN'S WORLD DAY OF PRAYER MOVEMENT
Jean Hackett, National Office, Commercial Rd,
Tunbridge Wells TN1 2RR   *Tel:* 01892 541411
Fax: 01892 541745
email: office@wwdp-natcomm.org
Web: www.wwdp-natcomm.org

YOUNG MEN'S CHRISTIAN ASSOCIATION (YMCA)
Ms Helen Dennis (*Policy and Parliamentary
Officer*), 53 Parker St, London WC2B 5PT
Tel: 0845 873 6633
email: enquiries@ymca.org.uk
Web: www.ymca.org.uk

Scotland, Wales and Ireland

ACTION OF CHURCHES TOGETHER IN SCOTLAND
7 Forrester Lodge, Inglewood House, Alloa FK10 2HU
Tel: 01259 216980
Fax: 01259 215964
email: ecumenical@acts-scotland.org

General Secretary Revd Matthew Z. Ross

Convenor of the Trustees and ACTS Members' Meeting Mrs Helen Hood

ACTS is the national ecumenical body for Scotland, the expression of the Churches' commitment to cooperation with one another in the service of Christ. ACTS works closely with its partners in England, Wales and Ireland. Its principal body is the Members' Meeting, composed of representatives from the member churches. Further information is available on the ACTS website: www.acts-scotland.org

Member Churches Church of Scotland, Congregational Federation, Methodist Church, Religious Society of Friends, Roman Catholic Church, Salvation Army, Scottish Episcopal Church, United Free Church, United Reformed Church.

CYTÛN: EGLWYSI YNGHYD YNG NGHYMRU
CHURCHES TOGETHER IN WALES
58 Richmond Rd, Cardiff, South Wales CF24 3UR
Tel (main office): 029 2046 4204
Web: www.cytun.org.uk

Chief Executive Revd Canon Aled Edwards OBE
Tel: 029 2046 4375
*email:*aled@cytun.org.uk

Bilingual Office Administrator to the Chief Executive Mrs Sasha Perriam
Tel: 029 2046 4204
email: post@cytun.org.uk

Policy Officer Mr Geraint Hopkins
Tel: 029 2046 4378
email: geraint@cytun.org.uk

Faith and Order Officer Rhian Linecar
Tel: 029 2046 4371
email: rhian@cytun.org.uk

Witness and Publications Officer Mr Ynyr Roberts
Tel: 029 2046 4371
email: ynyr@cytun.org.uk

Cytûn's Basis and Commitment:
CYTÛN unites in pilgrimage those churches in Wales which, acknowledging God's revelation in Christ, confess the Lord Jesus Christ as God and Saviour according to the Scriptures; and, in obedience to God's will and in the power of the Holy Spirit, commit themselves to seek a deepening of their communion with Christ and with one another in the Church, which is his body, and to fulfil their mission to proclaim the gospel by common witness and service in the world, to the glory of the one God Father, Son and Holy Spirit.

Member Denominations The Baptist Union of Wales, the Roman Catholic Church, the Church in Wales, the Congregational Federation, the Covenanted Baptist Churches, the German-speaking Lutheran Church, Indian Orthodox Churches, The Methodist Church, the Presbyterian Church of Wales, the Quakers, the Salvation Army, the Union of Welsh Independents, the United Reformed Church and the South Wales Baptist Association.

Aligned Groupings The Covenanted Churches in Wales, the Free Church Council of Wales.

Cytûn also works in close collaboration with the Commission of the Covenanted Church in Wales and the Free Church Council of Wales.

THE IRISH COUNCIL OF CHURCHES
Inter-Church Centre, 48 Elmwood Ave, Belfast BT9 6AZ
Tel: 028 9066 3145
Fax: 028 9066 4160
email: info@irishchurches.org
Web: www.irishchurches.org

President Revd Dr Donald Watts

Vice-President Rt Revd John McDowell

Hon Treasurer Mr Robert Cochran

Executive Officer Mr Mervyn McCullagh

Administrator Mrs Karen Kelly

Communications and Administration Assistant Ms Alison Meagher

History From 1906 the Presbyterian and Methodist Churches had a joint committee for united efforts. In 1910 the General Assembly of the Presbyterian Church invited other evangelical Churches to set up similar joint committees with it. The Church of Ireland accepted and by 1911 the joint committee of these two Churches was in action. Following a recommendation of the 1920 Lambeth Conference, these joint committees developed in 1922 into the United Council of Christian Churches and Religious Communions

ECUMENICAL

in Ireland including six of the present member churches. In 1966 the United Council changed its name to the Irish Council of Churches. The Council employed its first full-time secretary in April 1972.

Aims The Irish Council of Churches is constituted by Christian Communions in Ireland willing to join in united efforts to promote the spiritual, physical, moral and social welfare of the people and the extension of the rule of Christ among all nations and over every region of life.

Member Churches (14) Antiochian Orthodox Church in Ireland, Greek Orthodox Church, Lutheran Church in Ireland, Methodist Church in Ireland, Irish District of the Moravian Church, Non-Subscribing Presbyterian Church of Ireland, Presbyterian Church in Ireland, Religious Society of Friends in Ireland, Cherubim and Seraphim Church, Redeemed Christian Church of God, Romanian Orthodox Church in Ireland, Russian Orthodox Church in Ireland, Salvation Army (Ireland Division).

Structure The Council consists of 83 members appointed by the member Churches, together with the Heads of the member Churches and up to ten co-opted members, the Executive Secretary, Treasurer and immediate Past President of the Council. There is an Annual Meeting and occasional gatherings. The member Churches appoint an Executive Committee, which meets quarterly and is responsible for the oversight of the work of the Council.

The Council continues to serve both jurisdictions (Northern Ireland and the Republic of Ireland) and comprises 14 member churches (see above). It is an associate member of Churches Together in Britain and Ireland and the Conference of European Churches and has links with the World Council of Churches.

(a) It is currently re-assessing its purpose and direction in the rapidly changing contexts both sides of the border; its ecumenical witness across the island and relationships between and beyond its member churches, and its international links through its Board of Overseas Affairs.

(b) It meets quarterly with the Roman Catholic Church in Ireland through the Irish Inter-Church Committee and every 18 months as the Irish Inter-Church Meeting. The last Meeting was held in Dublin in in October 2010, taking the focus of Baptism.

(c) The Inter-Church Committee on Social Issues (ICCSI), a forum of the Irish Inter-Church Committee, currently employs a Project Officer to working on a parish-based integration programme in the Republic.

(d) It is represented on various regional, national and CTBI bodies concerned with regional equality panels, inter-faith, international, mission, overseas aid, racial justice and TV and radio affairs, and the Week of Prayer for Christian Unity.

(e) It is currently serviced by 3 staff based in the Belfast office (Executive Officer, Administrator and Communications and Administration Assistant).

More information about the Council's work can be obtained from www.irishchurches.org which includes the most recent Annual Report.

Meissen Agreement with the Evangelical Church in Germany

The Evangelical Church in Germany (Evangelische Kirche in Deutschland – EKD) is a Communion of 20 member churches (mostly *Landeskirchen* or territorial churches). Of these, seven are members of the United Evangelical Lutheran Church of Germany – VELKD (eight Lutheran churches were founding members of VELKD). One church in the EKD is purely Reformed, one is predominantly Reformed and twelve today form the Evangelical Church of the Union – UEK (seven churches were founding members of the UEK). One Church (the Evangelische Kirche in Mitteldeutschland) is a member of both VELKD and the UEK. In many of the United churches the Lutheran tradition predominates.

In November 1988 the General Synod welcomed the Meissen Common Statement, *On the Way to Visible Unity*, which called for a closer relationship between the Church of England and the German Evangelical Churches. The Meissen Declaration, which it recommended, was approved by the General Synod in July 1990 without dissent, and solemnly affirmed and proclaimed an Act of Synod on 29 January 1991. The Meissen Declaration makes provision for the Church of England and the Evangelical Church in Germany to live in closer fellowship with one another (though not yet with interchangeable ministries) and commits them to work towards the goal of full visible unity. The member churches of the EKD have been designated as churches to which the Ecumenical Canons apply (*see* **Ecumenical Canons**).

The Meissen Commission (the Sponsoring Body for the Church of England–EKD Relations) exists to oversee and encourage relationships (*see* Council for Christian Unity). Fuller information is contained in *The German Evangelical Churches* (CCU Occasional Paper No 1 £2.95 + 35p p&p) and *Anglo-German Ecumenical Links: An Information Pack* (£1 inc. p&p). The text of the Meissen Agreement can be found in *The Meissen Agreement: Texts* (CCU Occasional Paper No 2 £2.10

inc. p&p). These are all available from the Council for Christian Unity. Most of this material is downloadable from the CCU web site at www.cofe.anglican.org/info/ccu.

Co-Chairmen of the Meissen Commission Bishop Dr Friedrich Weber (*EKD*), Rt Revd Nicholas Baines (*Church of England*)

English Co-Secretary of the Meissen Commission Revd Canon Dr Leslie Nathaniel, Council for Christian Unity, Church House, Great Smith St, London SW1P 3AZ   *Tel:* 020 7898 1474

German Co-Secretary of the Meissen Commission OKR Christoph Ernst, EKD Kirchenamt, Postfach 21 02 20, D – 30402 Hannover, Germany
Tel: 00 49 511 2796 127
Fax: 00 49 511 2796 725
email: christoph.ernst@ekd.de
Web: www.ekd.de

The Reuilly Common Statement: Relations with the French Lutheran and Reformed Churches

Encouraged by the positive reception of the Meissen and Porvoo Agreements, the Anglican Churches of Britain and Ireland engaged in dialogue with the French Reformed and Lutheran Churches, with formal conversations beginning in 1994. These Churches had signalled their desire to enter into closer fellowship with Anglican Churches on the model of the Meissen Agreement, which the Church of England had concluded with the Evangelical Church in Germany (EKD).

The relations between the Anglican and French Churches are steeped in history. Contacts go back to the Middle Ages and took on a new character through the impetus of the Reformation. In later years, at times of turbulence and persecution, churches on both sides of the Channel welcomed those persecuted for their faith.

The conversations involved four participating churches from each side: the four Anglican Churches of the British Isles (the Church of England, the Church of Ireland, the Scottish Episcopal Church and the Church in Wales) and the four French Churches of the Lutheran and Reformed traditions (the Church of the Augsburg Confession of Alsace and Lorraine, the Evangelical Lutheran Church of France, the Reformed Church of Alsace and Lorraine and the Reformed Church of France).

The Reuilly Common Statement which forms the outcome of these conversations takes its name from a community of deaconesses, committed to prayer and meditation. The Statement was approved by the General Synod of the Church of England in November 1999, and the Statement was signed by the participatory Churches in Canterbury and Paris during the summer of 2001.

In common with other ecumenical statements, the Reuilly document first sets the scene, with the history and present context of the participants, and then moves on to current theological issues: the Church as Sign, Instrument and Foretaste of the Kingdom of God; the Church as Communion (*koinonia*); Growth towards Visible Unity; Agreement in Faith and the Apostolicity of the Church and its Ministry.

The Churches declare that they have found a high degree of unity and faith, and outline three areas of future work together: common efforts in witness and service; continuing theological work, particularly on questions of oversight, authority, eucharistic ministry and formally uniting ministries; the practical consequences of the Agreement: prayer, sharing of worship, partnership, and joint ventures across a range of areas.

Within France there have been conversations for greater unity and closer fellowship. The Evangelical Lutheran Church of France (EELF) and the Reformed Church of France (ERF) united in 2013 forming the United Protestant Church of France. The EELF and ERF's move toward unity followed a similar process by the Church of the Augsburg Confession of Alsace and Lorraine (ECAAL) and the Reformed Church of Alsace and Lorraine (ERAL), which in 2004 formed the Union of Protestant Churches in Alsace and Lorraine (UEPAL).

The implementation of the Agreement is coordinated by a Contact Group. The Anglican Co-Chairman is the Bishop of Warwick, the Rt Revd John Stroyan and the French Co-Chairman is Revd Joel Dautheville, President, Communion Protestant Luthéro-Réformée de France.

For information on current links and initiatives, contact:
Revd Canon Dr Leslie Nathaniel, The Council for Christian Unity, Church House, Great Smith Street, London SW1P 3AZ (tel. 020 7898 1474).

The full text of the Reuilly Declaration, together with background articles on the theological issues and the participating Churches, can be found in *Called to Witness and Service*, Church House Publishing (1999), ISBN 0 7151 5757 4.

ECUMENICAL

Conference of European Churches

General Secretary Revd Dr Guy Liagre, Ecumenical Centre, Rue Joseph II 174, 1000 Brussels, Belgium   *Tel:* 32 2 230 17 32 or 33 3 88 15 27 60 (Strasbourg Office)
Fax: 32 2 231 14 13
email: cec@cec-kek.org
Web: ceceurope.org

Born in the era of the 'cold war' 53 years ago, CEC emerged into a fragmented and divided continent. Thus it was that Churches of Eastern and Western Europe felt one priority of their work to be promoting international understanding – building bridges. This CEC has consistently tried to do, always insisting that no 'iron curtain' exists among the Churches.

The supreme governing body of the Conference is the Assembly. Here all 114 member Churches are represented. The first Assembly was in 1959 and further Assemblies were held in 1960, 1962, 1964, 1967, 1971, 1974, 1979, 1986, 1992, 1997, 2003, 2009 and 2013.

CEC initiated the European Ecumenical Assembly 'Peace with Justice' held in Basel in May 1989, co-sponsored with the Council of European Bishops' Conferences (CCEE, Roman Catholic). A second European Ecumenical Assembly was held in Graz, Austria, in 1997 with the theme 'Reconciliation: Gift of God and Source of New Life'. In 2001, CEC and CCEE launched the 'Charta Oecumenica – guidelines for the growing cooperation among the Churches in Europe'. A third European Ecumenical Assembly was held in Sibiu, Romania, in 2007 with the theme 'The light of Christ shines upon all – Hope for renewal and unity in Europe'.

The twenty-member Governing Board oversees the implementation of the decisions of the Assembly.

Since 1 January 1999 the European Ecumenical Commission on Church and Society (EECCS) with offices in Brussels and Strasbourg integrated with CEC, and, together with CEC's existing work, created the new Church and Society Commission of the CEC. A merger is also planned between CEC and the Brussels-based Churches' Commission for Migrants in Europe (CCME).

The Secretariat in Geneva and offices in Brussels and Strasbourg ensure the continuity of the activities.

In July 2013 at its fourteenth General Assembly in Budapest (theme: 'And now what are you waiting for? CEC and its Mission in a Changing Europe'), CEC adopted a renewed and reformulated constitution which included a new vision and mission statement as well as directions for the move of the headquarters from Geneva to Brussels. Rt Revd Christopher Hill was elected as President of CEC.

World Council of Churches

The Church of England has taken its full share in the international ecumenical movement since the Edinburgh Conference of 1910. In 2009 the General Synod made a grant of £108,000 to the General Budget of the World Council of Churches.

Presidium Archbishop Dr Anastasios of Tirana and All Albania (Orthodox Autocephalous Church of Albania), Mr John Taroanui Doom (Maòhi Protestant Church, French Polynesia), Revd Dr Simon Dossou (Protestant Methodist Church in Benin), Revd Dr Soritua Nababan (Protestant Christian Batak Church (HKBP), Indonesia), Revd Dr Ofelia Ortega (Presbyterian-Reformed Church in Cuba), Patriarch Abune Paulos (Ethiopian Orthodox Tewahedo Church), Revd Dr Bernice Powell Jackson (United Church of Christ, USA), Dr Mary Tanner (Church of England)

Moderator of Central Committee Revd Dr Walter Altmann (Evangelical Church of the Lutheran Confession in Brazil)

Vice-Moderators
Metropolitan Prof Dr Gennadios of Sassima (Limouris) (Ecumenical Patriarchate of Constantinople)

Revd Dr Margaretha M. Hendriks-Ririmasse (Protestant Church in the Moluccas, Indonesia)

General Secretary Revd Dr Olav Fykse Tveit (Church of Norway)

Office PO Box 2100, 150 route de Ferney, 1211 Geneva 2, Switzerland   *Tel:* 00 41 22 791 61 11
Fax: 00 41 22 791 03 61
Web: www.oikoumene.com
Cable: Oikoumene Geneva
email: infowcc@wcc-coe.org

The World Council of Churches was brought into formal existence by a resolution of its first Assembly at Amsterdam in 1948.

Member Churches agree to the following basis:

> The World Council of Churches is a fellowship of churches which confess the Lord Jesus Christ as God and Saviour according to the Scriptures and therefore seek to fulfil together their common calling to the glory of the one God, Father, Son and Holy Spirit.

The primary purpose of the fellowship of churches in the WCC is to call one another to visible unity in one faith and in one eucharistic fellowship, expressed in worship and common life in Christ, through witness and service to the world, and to advance towards that unity in order that the world may believe.

In seeking *koinonia* in faith and life, witness and service, the churches through the Council will:

1. promote the prayerful search for forgiveness and reconciliation in a spirit of mutual accountability, the development of deeper relationships through theological dialogue, and the sharing of human, spiritual and material resources with one another;
2. facilitate common witness in each place and in all places, and support each other in their work for mission and evangelism;
3. express their commitment to *diakonia* in serving human need, breaking down barriers between people, promoting one human family in justice and peace, and upholding the integrity of creation, so that all may experience the fullness of life;
4. nurture the growth of an ecumenical consciousness through processes of education and a vision of life in community rooted in each particular cultural context;
5. assist each other in their relationships to and with people of other faith communities;
6. foster renewal and growth in unity, worship, mission and service.

In order to strengthen the one ecumenical movement, the Council will:

1. nurture relations with and among churches, especially within but also beyond its membership;
2. establish and maintain relations with national councils, regional conferences of churches, organizations of Christian World Communions and other ecumenical bodies;
3. support ecumenical initiatives at regional, national and local levels;
4. facilitate the creation of networks among ecumenical organizations;
5. work towards maintaining the coherence of the one ecumenical movement in its diverse manifestations.

The World Council shall offer counsel and provide opportunity for united action in matters of common interest.

It may take action on behalf of constituent churches only in such matters as one or more of them may commit to it and only on behalf of such churches.

The World Council shall not legislate for the churches; nor shall it act for them in any manner except as indicated or as may hereafter be specified by the constituent churches.

The WCC is governed by an Assembly of Member Churches, a Central Committee, and by an Executive Committee and other subordinate bodies as may be established. Assemblies are held every six to eight years and have been as follows:

1. AMSTERDAM, 1948 – theme: 'Man's Disorder and God's Design'
2. EVANSTON, 1954 – theme: 'Christ the Hope of the World'
3. NEW DELHI, 1961– theme: 'Jesus Christ, the Light of the World'
4. UPPSALA, 1968 – theme: 'Behold, I Make All Things New'
5. NAIROBI, 1975 – theme: 'Jesus Christ Frees and Unites'
6. VANCOUVER, 1983 – theme: 'Jesus Christ the Life of the World'
7. CANBERRA, 1991– theme: 'Come, Holy Spirit – Renew the Whole Creation'
8. HARARE 1998 – theme: 'Turn to God – Rejoice in Hope'
9. PORTO ALEGRE 2006 – theme: 'God, in your grace, transform the world'

The Central Committee elected by the Ninth Assembly includes two members of the Church of England: the Rt Revd Thomas Frederick Butler, Bishop of Southwark (now retired), and Dr Mary Tanner, one of the WCC presidents.

The WCC has 349 member churches, including 38 which are associated. Almost every Church of the Anglican Communion is included, together with most of the Orthodox Churches and all the main Protestant traditions. The Roman Catholic Church is not a member but has sent official observers to all main WCC meetings since 1960. It is a full member of the Faith and Order Commission of the WCC.

Regional Conferences

CONFERENCE OF EUROPEAN CHURCHES
See page 446.

Who's Who | **PART 7**

Abbreviations used in the biographies

AABM ..... Archbishops' Adviser for Bishops' Ministry
ABIST .... Associate, British Institute of Surgical Technology
ABM .... Advisory Board of Ministry (now Ministry Division)
AC .... Archbishops' Council
ACA ..... Associate, Institute of Chartered Accountants
ACC .... Anglican Consultative Council
ACCM .... Advisory Council for the Church's Ministry (now Ministry Division)
ACE .... Associateship of the College of Education
Member, Association of Conference Executives
ACGI ... Associate, City and Guilds of London Institute
ACIB .... Associate, Chartered Institute of Bankers (formerly AIB)
ACII .... Associate, Chartered Insurance Institute
ACIS .. Associate, Institute of Chartered Secretaries and Administrators
ACMA .. Associate, Chartered Institute of Management Accountants (formerly ACWA)
ACORA ..... Archbishops' Commission on Rural Areas
ACP .... Associate, College of Preceptors
ACS .... Additional Curates Society
ACertCM .... Archbishop of Canterbury's Certificate in Church Music
AD .... Area Dean
ADipR .... Archbishop's Diploma for Readers
AHA .... Area Health Authority
AIA .... Associate, Institute of Actuaries
AKC .... Associate, King's College London
ALA .... Associate, Library Association
ALCD .... Associate, London College of Divinity
ALCM .... Associate, London College of Music
APR .... Association for Promoting Retreats
ARC .... Anglican-Roman Catholic
ARCIC .... Anglican-Roman Catholic International Commission
ARCM .... Associate, Royal College of Music
ARCO .... Associate, Royal College of Organists
ARCO(CHM) .... Associate, Royal College of Organists with Diploma in Choir Training
ARCS .... Associate, Royal College of Science
ARMIT .... Associate, Royal Melbourne Institute of Technology
ASWA ..... Anglican Society for the Welfare of Animals
ATCL ...... Associate, Trinity College of Music London
ATII .... Associate Member, Institute of Taxation
Aberd .... Aberdeen
Abp .... Archbishop
Aberw .... Aberystwyth
Acad .... Academy
AdDipEd .... Advanced Diploma in Education
Admin . Administration, Administrative, Administrator
Adn .... Archdeacon
Adnry .... Archdeaconry
Adv .... Adviser, Advisory
Agric .... Agricultural, Agriculture
Aid .... Aidan('s)
Alb .... Alban('s)
Andr .... Andrew('s), Andrews
Angl .... Anglican(s)
Ant .... Anthony('s)
Appt .... Appointment(s), appointed
Ascen .... Ascension
Assoc .... Associate, Association
Asst .... Assistant
Assur .... Assurance

Aug .... Augustine('s)
Auth .... Authority
b .... Born
B & W .... (Diocese of) Bath and Wells
BA .... Bachelor of Arts
BAGUPA .... Bishop's Advisory Group on UPAs
BBC .... British Broadcasting Corporation
BCC .... British Council of Churches (now see CCBI)
BCh or BChir Bachelor of Surgery (also see BS and ChB)
BD .... Bachelor of Divinity
BDS .... Bachelor of Dental Surgery
BEd .... Bachelor of Education
BFBS .... British and Foreign Bible Society
BLitt .... Bachelor of Letters
BM .... Board of Mission
BMU .... Board for Mission and Unity
Bmet .... Bachelor of Metallurgy
BMus .... Bachelor of Music (also see MusB or MusBac)
BNC .... Brasenose College
BPS .... British Pharmacological Society
BRF .... Bible Reading Fellowship
BS .... Bachelor of Science (also see BSc), Bachelor of Surgery (also see BCh, BChir and ChB)
BSR .... Board for Social Responsibility
BSc .... Bachelor of Science (also see BS)
BSocSc .... Bachelor of Social Science (also see BSSc)
BTh Btheol .... Bachelor of Theology (also see STB)
BVM&S . Bachelor of Veterinary Medicine and Surgery
BVSc .... Bachelor of Veterinary Science
BYFC .... British Youth for Christ
Bapt .... Baptist('s)
Barn .... Barnabas('s)
Bart .... Bartholomew('s)
Bd .... Board
Bedf .... Bedford
Bibl .... Biblical
Birm .... (Diocese of) Birmingham
Blackb .... (Diocese of) Blackburn
Boro .... Borough
Bp .... Bishop
Br .... British
Bradf .... (Diocese of) Bradford
Bris .... (Diocese of) Bristol
Bucks .... Buckingham(shire)
C .... Curate
C of E .... Church of England
C of I .... Church of Ireland
C-in-c .... Curate-in-charge
CA .... Church Army Member, Institute of Chartered Accountants of Scotland
CAB .... Citizens Advice Bureau
CAC .... Crown Appointments Commission (now Crown Nominations Commission)
CACLB .... Churches Advisory Council for Local Broadcasting (now Churches' Media Council)
CB .... Companion, Order of the Bath
CBE .... Commander, Order of the British Empire
CBF .... Central Board of Finance
CBI .... Confederation of British Industry
CCC .... Corpus Christi College, Council for the Care of Churches
CCCS Commonwealth and Continental Church Society
CCHH .... Churches Council for Health and Healing
CCLA .... Churches, Charities and Local Authorities
CCOM .... Churches' Commission on Mission
CCRJ .... Churches' Commission for Racial Justice
CCU .... Council for Christian Unity

CCYW .... Certificate in Community Youth Work
CD .... Canadian Forces Decoration, Conventional District
CDC .... Clergy Discipline Commission
CEC .... Conference of European Churches
CECC .... Church of England Committee for Communications
CEDR .... Centre for Dispute Resolution
CEEC .... Church of England Evangelical Council
CEIG .... Christian Ethical Investment Group
CEM .... Christian Education Movement
CERT TH .... Certificate in Theology
CF .... Chaplain to the Forces
CFE .... College of Further Education
CHRISM .... Christians in Secular Ministry
CJGS ...... Community of the Companions of Jesus the Good Shepherd
CLASP .. Churches Linked Across Staffs & the Potteries
CME .... Continuing Ministerial Education
CMEAC ...... Committee for Minority Ethnic Anglican Concerns
CMS ... Church Mission Society, Church Music Society
CNC .... Crown Nominations Commission
CPA .... Chartered Patent Attorney
CPAS .... Church Pastoral Aid Society
CPC ...... Certificate of Professional Competence (Road Transport)
CQSW ...... Certificate of Qualification in Social Work
CR .... Community of the Resurrection (Mirfield)
CRAC ... Central Religious Advisory Committee of the BBC and ITA
CRC .... Central Readers Council
CSC .... Community of the Servants of the Cross
CSEM .... Certificate in Special Education Management
CSO .... Central Statistical Office
CSR .... Council for Social Responsibility
CSWG .... Community of the Servants of the Will of God
CTBI .... Churches Together in Britain and Ireland
CTE .... Churches Together in England
CTH .... Certificate in Theology
CTM .... Certificate in Theology for Ministry
CU .... Church Union
CUF .... Church Urban Fund
CYCW ...... Certificate in Youth and Community Work
CYFA .... Church Youth Fellowships Association
Cam .... Cambridge
Cambs .... Cambridgeshire
Can .... Canon
Cant .... (Diocese of) Canterbury
Carl .... (Diocese of) Carlisle
Cath .... Catharine('s)/Catherine('s)
Cathl .... Cathedral
Cchem .... Certified/Chartered Chemist
CdipAF . Certified Diploma in Accounting and Finance
Cen .... Centre, Center, Central
Ceng .... Chartered Engineer
Cert CT .... Certificate in Ceramic Technology
CertEd .... Certificate of Education
CertMBiol .... Certificate of Microbiology
Ch .... Christ('s), Church(es)
Chair .... Chairman, Chairwoman
Chan .... Chancellor
Chapl .... Chaplain(s), Chaplaincy(ies)
ChB .... Bachelor of Surgery (also see BCh, BChir and BS)
Ch Ch .... Christ Church
Chelmsf .... (Diocese of) Chelmsford
Ches .... (Diocese of) Chester
Chich .... (Diocese of) Chichester
Chr .... Christian(s)
Chris .... Christopher('s)
Chu .... Churchill

Cl-in-c .... Cleric-in-charge
Clem .... Clement('s)
Cllr .... Councillor/Counsellor
Cmaths .... Chartered Mathematician
Co .... Company, County(ies)
Co-ord .... Coordinator, Coordinating
Coll .... College
Colleg .... Collegiate
Com .... Community
Commn .... Commission
Commr .... Commissioner
Comp .... Comprehensive
Conf .... Confederation, Conference
Consult .... Consultant/Consultancy
Corp .... Corporation
Coun .... Council
Conv .... Convocation
Cphys ... Chartered Physicist of the Institute of Physics
Cov .... (Diocese of) Coventry
Cstat .... Chartered Statistician
Ctee .... Committee
Cuth .... Cuthbert('s)
DAC Diocesan Advisory Committee, Diploma in Adult Counselling
DBE .... Diocesan Board of Education
DBF .... Diocesan Board of Finance
DCH .... Diploma in Child Health
DCL .... Doctor of Civil Law
DCO .... Diocesan Communications Officer
DD .... Doctor of Divinity
DDO .... Diocesan Director of Ordinands
DDS .... Doctor of Dental Surgery
DHSM .... Diploma in Health Service Management
DHSS .... Department of Health and Social Security
DIC .... Diploma of Membership of Imperial College London
DL .... Deputy Lieutenant
DLC .... Diploma of Loughborough College
DMS .... Diploma in Management Studies
DN .... Diploma in Nursing
DOE .... Department of the Environment
DPA .... Diploma in Public Administration
DPS .... Diploma in Pastoral Studies
DMin .... Doctor of Ministry
DPhil .... Doctor of Philosophy (also see PhD)
DProf .... Doctor in Professional Studies
DRACSC . Deployment, Remuneration and Conditions of Service Committee
DSPT .... Diploma in Social and Pastoral Theology
DSS ... Diploma in Social Studies Department of Social Security
DSc .... Doctor of Science (also see ScD)
DTI .... Department of Trade and Industry
DTS .... Diploma in Theological Studies
DTh .... Doctor of Theology (also see ThD)
DUniv .... Doctor of the University
Dav .... David('s)
Dep .... Deputy
Dept .... Department
Devel .... Development
Dio .... Diocese
Dioc .... Diocesan
Dip .... Diploma
DipAdEd .... Diploma in Advanced Education
DipBA .... Diploma in Business Administration
DipC .... Diploma in Counselling
DipChemEng .... Diploma in Chemical Engineering
DipEd .... Diploma in Education
DipHE .... Diploma in Higher Education
DipLA .... Diploma in Liturgy and Architecture
DipLRM .... Diploma in Leadership, Renewal and Mission Studies
DipMin .... Diploma in Ministry

452   Who's Who

DipN .... Diploma in Nursing
DipPallMed .... Diploma in Palliative Medicine
DipRJ .... Diploma in Retail Jewellery
DipSE .... Diploma in Special Education
DipSW .... Diploma in Social Work
DipSocSc .... Diploma in Social Sciences
DipTh .... Diploma in Theology
Dip UEM .... Diploma in Urban Estate Management
Dir .... Director
Distr .... District
Div .... Divinity, Division
Dn .... Deacon
Dny .... Deanery
Doct .... Doctrinal, Doctrine
Dom .... Domestic
Down .... Downing
Dr .... Doctor
Dss .... Deaconess
Dub .... Dublin
Dur .... (Diocese of) Durham
E .... East, Eastern
EAMTC ...... East Anglian Ministerial Training Course
ECUSA .... Episcopal Church of the United States of
America
EFAC .... Evangelical Fellowship in the Anglican
Communion
EIG . Ecclesiastical Insurance Group (now Ecclesiastical
Insurance)
EJM(RC) .... Ecclesiastical Jurisdiction Measure
(Revision Committee)
EKD .... Evangelische Kirche Deutschland
EPA .... European Patent Attorney
ERMC .... Eastern Region Ministry Course
Eccl .... Ecclesiastical
Ecum .... Ecumenical
Ed .... Editor, Editorial
Edin .... (Diocese of) Edinburgh
Edm .... Edmund('s)
Eds .... Edmundsbury
Educ .... Education
Educl .... Educational
Edw .... Edward('s)
Eliz .... Elizabeth('s)
Em .... Emmanuel('s)
Emer .... Emeritus
Eng .... Engineering
Environ .... Environmental
Engl .... English
Episc .... Episcopal Episcopalian
Eur . (Diocese of) Gibraltar in Europe Europe, European
EurIng .... European Engineer
Eur Phys .... European Physicist
Ev .... Evangelist('s), Evangelists
Evang .... Evangelical, Evangelism
Ex .... (Diocese of) Exeter
Exam .... Examining
Exec .... Executive
FAC .... Fabric Advisory Committee
FASC .... Fellow, Academy of St Cecilia
FBA .... Fellow, British Academy
FBCS .... Fellow, British Computer Society
FCA .... Fellow, Institute of Chartered Accountants
FCAA .... Fellow, Cyprus Association of Actuaries
FCCA .... Fellow, Chartered Association of Certified
Accountants (formerly FACCA)
FCEM .... Fellow, College of Emergency Medicine
FCIM .... Fellow, Chartered Institute of Marketing
(formerly FInstM)
FC INST M ... Fellow, Chartered Institute of Marketing
FCIOB .... Fellow, Chartered Institute of Building
FCIPD .... Fellow, Chartered Institute of Personnel and
Development (formerly FIPD)
FCP .... Fellow, College of Preceptors

FDSRCS .... Fellow in Dental Surgery, Royal College of
Surgeons of England
FE .... Further Education
FGMS .... Fellow, Guild of Musicians and Singers
F&GP .... Finance and General Purposes
FIA .... Fellow, Institute of Actuaries
FIBMS .... Fellow, Institute of Biomedical Sciences
FIHT .... Fellow of the Institution of Highways and
Transportation
FIMA .... Fellow, Institute of Mathematics and its
Applications
FIMgt .... Fellow, Institute of Management
FJMU .... Fellow, Liverpool John Moores University
FKC .... Fellow, King's College London
FLAME .... Family Life and Marriage Education
FOAG .... Faith and Order Advisory Group
FPMI .... Fellow, Pensions Management Institute
FRAI .... Fellow, Royal Anthropological Institute
FRAeS .... Fellow, Royal Aeronautical Society
FRAS .... Fellow, Royal Astronomical Society
FRCO .... Fellow, Royal College of Organists
FRCOG ..... Fellow, Royal College of Obstetricians and
Gynaecologists
FRCOphth . Fellow, Royal College of Ophthalmologists
FRCS .... Fellow, Royal College of Physicians and
Surgeons of England
FRCSE or FRCSEd .. Fellow, Royal College of Surgeons
of Edinburgh
FRHistS .... Fellow, Royal Historical Society
FRICS .... Fellow, Royal Institution of Chartered
Surveyors (formerly FLAS and FSI)
FRIPHH .... Fellow, Royal Institute of Public Health
and Hygiene
FRGS .... Fellow, Royal Geographical Society
FRS .... Fellow, Royal Society
FRSA .... Fellow, Royal Society of Arts
FRSC .... Fellow, Royal Society of Chemistry
(formerly FRIC)
FRSL .... Fellow, Royal Society of Literature
FRSM .... Fellow, Royal Society of Medicine
FSA .... Fellow, Society of Antiquaries
FSCA .... Fellow, Royal Society of Company and
Commercial Accountants
FTII .... Fellow, Institute of Taxation
Fell(s) .... Fellow(s), Fellowship
Fest .... Festival
Fin .... Financial
Fitzw .... Fitzwilliam
Foundn .... Foundation
Fran .... Francis(')
G&C .... Gonville and Caius
GAD .... Government Actuary's Department
GEC .... General Electric Company
GLC .... Greater London Council
GOE .... General Ordination Examination
GP .... General Practitioner
GS .... General Synod
Gabr .... Gabriel('s)
Gd .... Good
Gen .... General
Geo .... George('s)
Gib .... Gibraltar
Glas ..... (Diocese of) Glasgow and Galloway, Glasgow
Glos .... Gloucestershire
Glouc .... (Diocese of) Gloucester
Gov .... Governor
Grp .... Group
Gr .... Grammar
Greg .... Gregorian
Gt .... Great
Guildf .... (Diocese of) Guildford
H .... Holy
H&FE .... Higher and Further Education

HA .... Health Authority
HCC .... Hospital Chaplaincies Council
HDipEd .... Higher Diploma in Education
HE .... Higher Education
HM .... Her (or His) Majesty('s)
HMP .... Her Majesty's Prison(s)
HNC .... Higher National Certificate
HND .... Higher National Diploma
HRH .... Her/His Royal Highness
Hatf .... Hatfield
Hd .... Head
Heref .... (Diocese of) Hereford
Hertf .... Hertford
Herts .... Hertfordshire
Hist .... History
Ho .... House
Hon .... Honorary, Honourable
Hosp(s) .... Hospital(s)
IARCCUM ... International Anglican – Roman Catholic
                      Commission on Unity and Mission
IBA .... Independent Broadcasting Authority
ICI .... Imperial Chemical Industries
ICS .... Intercontinental Church Society
IDC .... Inter-Diocesan Certificate
IMEC .... Initial Ministerial Education Committee
IOM .... Isle of Man
IPR .... Insitute of Public Relations
ITV .... Independent Television
Imp .... Imperial
Inc, Incorp .... Incorporated
Incumb .... Incumbent
Ind .... Industry, Industrial
Info .... Information
Insp .... Inspector, Inspectorate
Inst .... Institute, Institution
Intercon .... Intercontinental
Internat .... International
Ips .... Ipswich
JP .... Justice of the Peace
Jas .... James('s)
Jasp .... Jasper('s)
Jes .... Jesus
Jo .... John('s)
Jos .... Joseph('s)
Jt or jt .... Joint
Jun .... Junior
K .... King('s)
KA .... Knight of St Andrew, Order of Barbados
KCVO ..... Knight Commander, Royal Victorian Order
KHS .... Knight of the Holy Sepulchre
Kath .... Katharine('s), Katherine('s)
LDSRCS(Eng) .... Licentiate in Dental Surgery of the
                      Royal College of Surgeons (of England)
LEA .... Local Education Authority
LEP .... Local Ecumenical Project
LICeram .... Licencicate, Institute of Ceramics
LLAM ...... Licentiate, London Academy of Music and
                                          Dramatic Art
LLB .... Bachelor of Laws
LLD .... Doctor of Laws
LLM .... Master of Laws
LMH .... Lady Margaret Hall
LNSM ... Local Non-stipendiary Minister (or Ministry)
LRAM .... Licentiate, Royal Academy of Music
LRCP .... Licentiate, Royal College of Physicians
LRPS .... Licentiate, Royal Photographic Society
LRSC .... Licentiate, Royal Society of Chemistry
LSE . London School of Economics and Political Science
LTCL ...... Licentiate, Trinity College of Music, London
LTh .... Licentiate in Theology (also see LST)
LVO .... Lieutenant, Royal Victorian Order
Lab .... Laboratory
Lamp .... Lampeter

Lanc .... Lancaster
Lancs .... Lancashire
Laur .... Laurence('s)
Lawr .... Lawrence('s)
Lect .... Lecturer
Leic .... (Diocese of) Leicester
Leics .... Leicestershire
Leon .... Leonard('s)
Legis .... Legislative
Lib .... Librarian, Library
Lic .... Licence, Licensed, Licentiate
Lich .... (Diocese of) Lichfield
Linc .... (Diocese of) Lincoln
Lincs .... Lincolnshire
Liturg .... Liturgical
Liv .... (Diocese of) Liverpool
Llan .... (Diocese of) Llandaff
Lon .... (Diocese of) London
Loughb .... Loughborough
Lt .... Little
Ltd .... Limited
M .... Member
M&AA .... Michael and All Angels
MA .... Master of Arts
MB,BS &MB,ChB .... Conjoint degree of Bachelor of
                      Medicine, Bachelor of Surgery
MBC .... Metropolitan (or Municipal) Borough Council
MBCS .... Member, British Computer Society
MBE .... Member, Order of the British Empire
MCIH .... Corporate Member, Chartered Institute of
                                               Housing
MCIJ .... Member, Chartered Institute of Journalists
MCIM ...... Member, Chartered Institute of Marketing
                                    (formerly MInstM)
MCIPD . Member, Chartered Institute of Personnel and
                      Development (formerly MIPD)
MCLIP .... Member, Chartered Institute of Library
                      and Information Professionals
MCS .... Master of Christian Studies
MCSP .... Member, Chartered Society of Physiotherapy
MCST .... Member, College of Speech Therapists
MCT ..... Member, Association of Corporate Treasurers
MDCT ..... Manager's Diploma in Ceramic Technology
MDiv .... Master of Divinity
MEd .... Master of Education
MIBC .... Member, Institute of Business Counsellors
MICE .... Member, Institution of Civil Engineers
                                    (formerly AMICE)
MIChemE .. Member, Institution of Chemical Engineers
MIEE .... Member, Institution of Electrical Engineers
                              (formerly AMIEE MIERE)
MIMA . Member, Institute of Management Accountants
MIMgt .... Member, Institute of Management
MIOT .... Member, Institute of Operating Theatre
                                             Technicians
MIPD .... Member, Institute of Personnel and
                      Development (now see MCIPD)
MIPR .... Member, Institute of Public Relations
MIStructE ... Member, Institute of Structural Engineers
MInstD .... Member, Institute of Directors
MInstGA .... Member, Institute of Group Analysis
MInstP .... Member, Institute of Physics
MLitt .... Master of Letters
MOD .... Ministry of Defence
MOW .... Movement for the Ordination of Women
MP .... Member of Parliament
MPA .... Mission and Public Affairs
MPhil .... Master of Philosophy
MRCGP .... Member, Royal College of General
                                          Practitioners
MRCS .... Member, Royal College of Surgeons
MRCVS .... Member, Royal College of Veterinary
                                               Surgeons

MRSC	Member, Royal Society of Chemistry
MSc	Master of Science
MTech	Master of Technology
MTh or MTheol	Master of Theology (also see STM and ThM)
MU	Mothers' Union
Magd	Magdalen('s)/Magdalene('s)
Man	(Diocese of) Manchester
Man Dir	Managing Director
Mansf	Mansfield
Marg	Margaret('s)
Mart	Martin('s)
Marlboro	Marlborough
Matt	Matthew('s)
Mert	Merton
Meth	Methodist
Metrop	Metropolitan
Mgr	Manager
Mgt	Management
Mich	Michael('s), Michael and All Angels
Mil	Military
Min	Minister, Ministries, Ministry, Minor
Minl	Ministerial
Miss	Mission('s), Missionary
Missr	Missioner
Mod	Moderator
Movt	Movement
Mss	Manuscripts
Mt	Mount
Mus	Music
MusB or MusBac	Bachelor of Music (also see BMus)
N	North
NACRO	National Association for the Care and Rehabilitation of Offenders
NAHT	National Association of Headteachers
NCA	National Certificate in Agriculture
NCIs	National Church Institutions
NDA	National Diploma in Agriculture
NDD	National Diploma in Design
NEOC	North East Oecumenical Course North East Ordination Course
NHS	National Health Service
NNEB	National Nursery Examination Board
NSM	Non-stipendiary Minister (or Ministry)
NSW	New South Wales (Australia)
NT	New Testament
NTMTC	North Thames Ministerial Training Course
NW	North West/Northwestern
NZ	New Zealand
Nat	National
Newc	(Diocese of) Newcastle
Nic	Nicholas('s)/Nicolas('s)
Nn	Northern
Norf	Norfolk
Norw	(Diocese of) Norwich
Northn	Northampton
Nottm	Nottingham
Notts	Nottinghamshire
Nuff	Nuffield
OAM	Order of Australia Medal
OBE	Officer, Order of the British Empire
OCF	Officiating Chaplain to the Forces
OGS	Oratory of the Good Shepherd
OLM	Ordained Local Minister (or Ministry)
ONC	Ordinary National Certificate
OStJ ...	Officer, Most Venerable Order of the Hospital of St John of Jerusalem
OT	Old Testament
OTC	Open Theology College
OU, Open Univ	Open University
Ord	Ordinand(s), Ordination
Ox	(Diocese of) Oxford
Oxon	Oxfordshire

P	Patron(s), Priest
P in O	Priest in Ordinary
P-in-c	Priest-in-charge
PACTA	Professional Associate, Clinical Theology Association
PCC	Parochial Church Council
PGCE	Postgraduate Certificate in Education
PNG	Papua New Guinea
POT	Post Ordination Training
PPS	Parliamentary Private Secretary
PR	Public Relations
PRCC ..	Policy and Resources Coordinating Committee
PRO	Public Relations Officer
PV	Priest Vicar
PWM	Partnership for World Mission
Par	Parish(es)
Parl	Parliamentary
Pastl	Pastoral
Patr	Patrick('s), Patronage
Pemb	Pembroke(shire)
Perm	Permission
Pet	Peter('s)
Peterb	(Diocese of) Peterborough
Peterho	Peterhouse
PhD	Doctor of Philosophy (also see DPhil)
Phil	Phil(l)ip('s)
Pk	Park
plc	public limited company
Poly	Polytechnic
Portsm	(Diocese of) Portsmouth
Prchr	Preacher
Preb	Prebendary
Prec	Precentor
Prep	Preparatory
Pres	President
Prin	Principal
Pris	Prison(s)
Priv	Private
Prof	Professor, Professorial
Prov	Provost, Provisions
Ptnr	Partner
Pty	Party
pt	part-time
QC	Queen's Counsel
QHC	Queen's Honorary Chaplain
Qu	Queen('s), Queens'
R	Rector, Royal
RAMC	Royal Army Medical Corps
RCHME .	Royal Commission on Historical Monuments of England
RAF	Royal Air Force
RC	Roman Catholic
RCO	Royal College of Organists
RD	Royal Navy Reserve Decoration, Rural Dean
RE	Religious Education
RGN	Registered General Nurse
RHM	Rank Hovis McDougall
RIBA	(Member) Royal Institute of British Architects (formerly ARIBA)
RICS	Royal Institute of Chartered Surveyors
RM	Registered Midwife
RMA or RMC	Royal Military Academy (formerly College), Sandhurst
RMN	Registered Mental Nurse
RN	Royal Navy
RSA	Royal Society of Arts, Republic of South Africa
RSCM	Royal School of Church Music
RSIN	Rural Stress Information Network
Raph	Raphael('s)
Rdr(s)	Reader(s)
Red	Redundant
Relig	Religious
Relns	Relations

Rep(s) .... Representative(s)
Res .... Residential, Residentiary
Resp .... Responsibility
Resurr .... Resurrection
Rev .... Review
Revd .... Reverend
Rich .... Richard('s)
Ripon .... Ripon and Leeds
Roch .... (Diocese of) Rochester
Rsch .... Research
Rt .... Right
Rtd or rtd .... Retired
S .... South, Southern
S&Man .... (Diocese of) Sodor and Man
SAMS .... South American Mission Society
SAOMC .... St Albans and Oxford Ministry Course
SASRA .... Soldiers' and Airmen's Scripture Readers
Association
SBL .... Society of Biblical Literature
SCM .... State Certified Midwife, Student Christian
Movement
SDMTS .... Southern Dioceses Ministerial
Training Scheme
SE .... South East
SEITE ... South East Institute for Theological Education
SOAS .... School of Oriental and African Studies
SOSc .... Society of Ordained Scientists
SPCK ...... Society for Promoting Christian Knowledge
SPI .... Society of Practitioners of Insolvency
SRN .... State Registered Nurse
SRP .... State Registered Physiotherapist
SS .... Saints/Saints', Sidney Sussex
SSC ..... Secretarial Studies Certificate, Societas Sanctae
Crucis (Society of the Holy Cross)
SSF .... Society of St Francis
SSM .... Society of the Sacred Mission
SST .... Society for the Study of Theology
STB .... Bachelor of Theology (also see BTh)
STETS ... Southern Theological Education and Training
Scheme
STh .... Scholar in Theology (also see ThSchol)
STL .... Reader (or Professor) of Sacred Theology
STM ..... Master of Theology (also see MTh or MTheol
and ThM)
SU .... Scripture Union
SW .... South West
Sacr .... Sacrist, Sacristan
Salis .... Salisbury
Sarum .... (Diocese of) Salisbury
Sav .... Saviour('s)
ScD .... Doctor of Science (also see DSc)
Sch(s) .... School(s)
Sec(s) .... Secretary(ies)
Secdry .... Secondary
Selw .... Selwyn
Sem .... Seminary
Sen .... Senior
Sheff .... (Diocese of) Sheffield
Shep .... Shepherd
Shrops .... Shropshire
So .... Souls, Souls'
Soc .... Social, Society
Som .... Somerset
Southn .... Southampton
Sq .... Square
St .... Saint
St Alb .... (Diocese of) St Albans
St And .... (Diocese of) St Andrews, Dunkeld and
Dunblane
St As .... (Diocese of) St Asaph
St D .... (Diocese of) St Davids
St E&I .... (Diocese of) St Edmundsbury and Ipswich

Ste .... Sainte
Steph .... Stephen('s)
Stg .... Standing
Strg .... Steering
Suff .... Suffragan
Supt .... Superintendent
S'wark .... Southwark
S'well .... Southwell
Syn .... Synod
TCert .... Teacher's Certificate
TEFL .... Teacher of English as a Foreign Language
TETC .. Theological Education and Training Committee
TM .... Team Minister (or Ministry)
TR .... Team Rector
TV .... Team Vicar, Television
Tchr .... Teacher
Tdip .... Teacher's Diploma
Tech .... Technical, Technology
Techn .... Technician
Th, Theol .... Theological
ThD .... Doctorate in Theology (also see DTh)
ThM ..... Master of Theology (also see MTh or MTheol
and STM)
Thos .... Thomas('s)
Tm .... Team
Tr .... Trainer
Treas .... Treasurer('s)
Trg .... Training
Trin .... Trinity
UCCF .. Universities and Colleges Christian Fellowship
of Evangelical Unions (formerly IVF)
UCE .... University of Central England
UCL .... University College London
UEA .... University of East Anglia
UMIST ... University of Manchester Institute of Science
and Technology
UPA .... Urban Priority Area (or Areas)
URC .... United Reformed Church
USCL .... United Society for Christian Literature
USPG .... United Society for the Propagation of the
Gospel (formerly SPG, UMCA, and CMD)
UWE .... University of the West of England
UWIST .... University of Wales Institute of Science
and Technology
Univ .... University
V .... Vicar, Virgin('s)
VRSC .... Vocations, Recruitment and Selection
Committee
Vc .... Vice
Ven .... Venerable
Vis .... Visiting
Voc .... Vocational, Vocations
Vol .... Voluntary
W .... West, Western
w .... with
WATCH .... Women and the Church
WCC .... World Council of Churches
WEA .... Workers' Educational Association
WEMTC .. West of England Ministerial Training Course
Wadh .... Wadham
Wakef .... (Diocese of) Wakefield
Warw .... Warwickshire
Westf .... Westfield
Westmr .... Westminster
Wilf .... Wilfred('s), Wilfrid('s)
Wilts .... Wiltshire
Winch .... (Diocese of) Winchester
Wkg .... Working
Worc .... (Diocese of) Worcester
Wrdn .... Warden
YMCA .... Young Men's Christian Association

WHO'S WHO

A Directory of General Synod members, together with those suffragan bishops, deans and archdeacons who are not members of General Synod, and principal staff members of the General Synod, the Archbishops' Council, the Church Commissioners, the Pensions Board and Lambeth Palace, and Church Commissioners who are not members of General Synod. General Synod members are distinguished by the date of their membership, printed at the end of their entry, following the letters GS. Current membership of the General Synod is denoted by the lack of a closing date. The information contained here is supplied by the individuals concerned and no warranty is given as to its accuracy.

ALBAN JONES, Revd Timothy Morris, BA, MBE
The Vicarage Cross Green Soham Ely Cambridgeshire CB7 5DU [ELY] *b* 1964 *educ* Wycliffe Coll; Warwich Univ; Ripon Coll Cuddesdon; *CV* Asst C, Tupsley 1988–93; Chapl St Michael's Hospice, Heref 1990–92; TV Ross Team Ministry 1993–2000; Chapl with Deaf People 1994–2000; Dioc Voc Adv 1995–1999; V Soham and Wicken from 2000; POT Tutor from 2006; M Dioc Voc Panel from 2007; M Dioc Bd of Patronage from 2009; Rural Dean of Fordham and Quy from 2010; Selection Off Bd of Rdrs 2010–12; Wdn of Rdrs from 2012; M DAC from 2014; Chair Dioc Ho of Clergy from 2014; M Bp's Coun from 2014
GS 2010– Tel: 01353 720423
email: vicar@soham.org.uk

ALDERTON-FORD, Revd Jonathan Laurence, B Th
Church Office Christ Church Moreton Hall Symonds Rd Bury St Edmunds IP32 7EW [ST EDMUNDSBURY AND IPSWICH] *b* 1957 *educ* Denes High Sch Lowestoft; Nottm Univ; St Jo Coll Nottm; *CV* C St Faith Gaywood Norw 1985–87; C St Andr Herne Bay 1987–90; Min Ch Ch LEP Moreton Hall from 1990; Chair Mid Anglia New Wine Network; Chair Passion Play for Bury St Edm; Elected M Dioc Commn from 2008; Trustee Premier Christian Radio; Can St Eds Cath from 2008
GS 1999– Tel: 01284 769956 (Home)
01284 725391 (Office)
Fax: 01284 725391
email: minister@ccmh.org.uk

ALEXANDER, Mrs April Rosemary, BA, Cert Ed
59 High Street Bletchingley Redhill Surrey RH1 4PB [SOUTHWARK] *b* 1943 *educ* R Masonic Sch Rickmansworth; Open Univ; Homerton Coll Cam; *CV* Various teaching posts 1964–84; Financial Services Industry 1984–92; Financial Services Authority (formerly Securities and Investments Bd) 1992–99; Exec Dir Occupational Pensions Regulatory Authority 1999–2005; Head of Trustee Educ, The Pensions Regulator 2005–07; Consult The Pensions Regulator and Pensions Ind 2007; Lay Chair Dioc Syn 1996–2006; M DRACSC; M GS Legis Cttee; M Ch Commn Bd of Govs 2009; M Audt Cttee of Ch Commns; M Steering Cttee Clergy Terms of Service 2007; M Rev Cttee

Bps & Ps (Consecration and Ord of Women) Measure 2009
GS 2000– Tel: 01883 7434218
07867 977823
email: april@abalexander.co.uk

ALI, Canon Linda, BA, MA
51 Thief Lane York YO10 3HQ [YORK] *b* 1943 *educ* Bp Anstey Gr Sch Trinidad; Univ of York; *CV* Trade Marks Co-ord, Colgate Palmolive Eur 1970–89; Trade Marks Mgr, Unilever Plc UK 1989–97; Researcher/writer, Nat Archives, Lon from 2002; M York Forum for Racial Concerns; M CMEAC from 2006; Chair of Trustees USPG: Anglicans in World Mission from 2009; M Derwent Dny Syn; M Soc Resp Coun, N Yorks
GS 2005– Tel: 01904 413698
07966 363721 (Mobile)
email: linda@jj26.fsnet.co.uk

ALLAIN CHAPMAN, Ven Dr Justine Penelope Heathcote, BA, AKC, PGCE, DThMin, MDiv
Archdeacon's House Castle Hill Welbourn Lincoln LN5 0NF [ARCHDEACON OF BOSTON; LINCOLN] *b* 1967 *educ* K Coll Lon; Nottm Univ; Linc Th Coll; *CV* Head Rel Studies, South Hampstead High School 1989–91; C Christ Church with St Paul, Forest Hill 1993–96; TV St Paul Clapham 1996–01; V St Paul Clapham 2002–04; Dir Miss & Pastl Studies SEITE 2004–13, Vice Prin 2007–13; PV Roch Cathl 2005–13; Adn of Lindsey from 2013; GS Representative Churches' Commn on Mission 2001–03; S'wark Dioc Liturgical Cttee 1994–2004; Vocations Advisory Panel Min Div 2003–06; Bps' Inspector for Theological Educ from 2010
GS 2000–04 Tel: 01400 273335
07715 077993 (Mobile)
email: justine.allainchapman@
lincoln.anglican.org

ALLAIN CHAPMAN, Dr Thomas Joseph, BA, MA, Ph D
Church House Great Smith St London SW1P 3AZ [PUBLISHING MANAGER, ARCHBISHOPS' COUNCIL] *b* 1969 *educ* Mount St Mary's Coll Sheff; K Coll Lon; *CV* freelance writer and ed 1994–95; Ed, HarperCollins Relig 1995–97; Asst Commissioning Ed, Collins Educ 1997–2000, Commissioning Ed 2000, Publishing Mgr 2000–05; Head of Publishing, Church Ho Publishing 2005–09; Dir

ROOTS for Churches Ltd from 2006; Publishing Mgr AC from 2009   *Tel:* 020 7898 1450
Fax: 020 7898 1449
email: thomas.allain-chapman@churchofengland.org

ALLEN, Mrs (Penelope) Penny, Teaching Cert
12 Cranbrook Grove Perton Wolverhampton WV6 7RY [LICHFIELD] *b* 1950 *educ* Kibworth Beauchamp Gr; Oadby Beauchamp Upper Sch; Leic City Coll of Ed; *CV* Tchr, 1971–2009 in Leics, Wolverhampton, Staffs; Head of RE and PSHCE; M South Staffs District Coun 1989–91; M Perton Parish Coun from 1987; M Ecum Ch Coun Perton; M Trysull Deanery; M Lichf Dioc; M Dioc Fin Cttee; M Bp's Coun; M Patronage Bd
GS 2010–   *Tel:* 01902 756125
email: mrspennyallen@yahoo.co.uk
Web: Online diary for GS:
http://pennyatgeneralsynod.weebly.com

ALLEN, Canon Timothy Edward, MA
Bell House Quay St Orford Woodbridge IP12 2NU [ST EDMUNDSBURY AND IPSWICH] *b* 1944 *educ* Framlingham Coll;Trin Coll Cam; *CV* Bank of England 1966–86; M Haringey Coun Lon 1972–78; Sec to Securities and Investments Bd 1986–97; Sec to Bd of Fin Services Authority 1997–98; M Dioc Syn; M Bp's Coun/DBF; M Agenda Plan and Business Cttee; Chair DAC; M Coun St Eds Cathl 2006–12; M CNC St E and I vacancy 2006–07; M CCC 2006–08; M CBC from 2008; Chair CBC Sculpture and Furnishings Ctee; M Cathl and Ch Bldgs Div Grp; M Fees Advisory Commn 2001–12; M Min Div Fin Panel 2006–12; Chair Revision Cttee on draft Stipends (Cessation of Special Payments) Measure 2004; Chair Revision Cttee on draft Pastl (Amendment) Measure 2004; M Revision Cttee draft Diocs, Pastl and Mission Measure 2006; Chair Revision Cttee on Draft Eccl Fees (Amendment) Measure 2009; Lay Elder Par of Orford from 2001; M Cathl Fabric Comm from 2011; Lay Canon of St Eds Cathl from 2011; M Revision Cttee draft Care of Churches and Ecclesiastical Jurisdiction Measure 2014; M CNC St Eds and Ips vacancy 2014
GS 2000–   *Tel:* 01394 450789
email: tim@bellhouseorford.com

ALLISTER, Rt Revd Donald Spargo, MA, DTh (Hon)
Bishop's Lodging The Palace Peterborough PE1 1YA [BISHOP OF PETERBOROUGH] *b* 1952 *educ* Birkenhead Sch; Peterho Cam; Trinity Th Coll Bris; *CV* C St Geo Hyde, Ches 1976–79; C St Nic Sevenoaks, Roch 1979–83; V Ch Ch Birkenhead, Ches 1983–89; Chaplain Arrowe Park Hosp 1983–85; R St Mary Cheadle, Ches 1989–2002; RD Cheadle 1999–2002; Adn of Chester 2002–10; Bp of Peterborough from 2010; CCU from 2006, Chair from

2013; Abps' Coun Fin Cttee 2011–13; Faith and Order Commn from 2014
GS 2005–   *Tel:* 01733 562492
Fax: 01733 890077
email: bishop@peterborough-diocese.org.uk

ANGAELOS, His Grace Bishop ,
The Coptic Church Centre Shepalbury Manor Broadhall Way Stevenage SG2 8NP [ECUMENICAL REPRESENTATIVE (COPTIC ORTHODOX CHURCH)] *CV* Coptic Orthodox monk, Monastery of Saint Bishoy, Wadi-El-Natroun, from 1990; papal secretary to His Holiness Pope Shenouda III, Monastery of Saint Bishoy 1990–95; parish priest, Coptic Orthodox Church Centre, Stevenage 1995–99; General Bishop, Coptic Orthodox Church in the UK from 1999; Chair Coun Oriental Orthodox Churches UK and Rep of Ireland (pres 2010–12, chair from 2012); Co-chair Anglican-Oriental Orthodox Regional Forum; M Anglican-Oriental Orthodox International Comm; Co-founder and Co-chair Catholic-Oriental Orthodox Regional Forum; Scholar-Consultant Christian-Muslim Forum; Founder and convener Asylum Advocacy Grp (AAG); supporter All Party Parliamentary Grp for International Religious Freedom (APPG) from 2012; Co-founder and Co-chair of the Lausanne-Orthodox Initiative from 2012; Dir Churches Together in England; Moderator Churches Together in Britain and Ireland; Trustee Churches Together in Britain and Ireland; Moderator Churches' Inter-Religious Network for Churches Together in Britain and Ireland (CIRN) from 2004; M Anglican-Oriental Orthodox International Theological Comm; M Global Council United Bible Soc from 2013; M Coptic Delegation World Council of Churches 2013; Ecum Conversations' Team Leader; Patron, Christian Solidarity Worldwide, Christians Aware, Ecum Soc Blessed Virgin Mary, Apostolic Order of St Hadrian of Canterbury, SAT 7 Trust UK, British Egyptian Public Affairs Cttee, Embrace the Middle East, Awareness Foundation
GS 2013–   *Tel:* 020 7993 9001
01438 745232
Fax: 020 7993 2183
email: admin@copticcentre.com
Web: www.copticcentre.com
Twitter: @BishopAngaelos

ANGUS, Dr Christopher John, MA, PhD
Burtholme East Lanercost Brampton Cumbria CA8 2HH [CARLISLE] *b* 1949 *educ* Hampton Sch; Trin Hall, Cam Univ; Newcastle Univ; *CV* Senior Systems Analyst, ICL 1970–75; Consult, Mancos 1975–78; Application Develop Manager, CAD-Centre, Cam 1978–83; Tech Dir, Prosys Technology 1983–89; Dir, Angus Assoc 1989–2000; Software Architect, Shell 2002–03; Chief Architect, Kalido 2003; M Bp's Counc 2006; M Adnry Mapping Cttee from 2001
GS 2010–   *Tel:* 01697 741504
email: chris.angus@btinternet.com

ANNAS, Rt Revd Geoff,
Ash Garth Broughton Crescent Barlaston Stoke-on-Trent ST12 9DD [AREA BISHOP OF STAFFORD; LICHFIELD] *b* 1953 *CV* Area Bp of Stafford from 2010   *Tel:* 01782 373308
    email: bishop.stafford@lichfield.anglican.org

APPLEBY, Revd Janet Elizabeth, BSc, MSc, BA, BA
Battle Hill Vicarage Berwick Drive Wallsend NE28 9ED [NEWCASTLE] *b* 1958 *educ* Bris Univ; Newcastle Poly; Cranmer Hall, Dur; *CV* Planner, London Transport 1984–5; OU Tutor Mathematics 1991–94; Home Educator 1994–2001; AC Holy Cross, Fenham 2003–06; TV, Ch of the Good Shepherd LEP, Battle Hill, Wallsend from 2006; Dioc Ecum Officer from 2012 GS 2010–
    Tel: 01912 627518
    email: janeteappleby@yahoo.com
    Web: www.cogswallsend.btck.co.uk

APPLEGATE, Ven John, Ph D
Southern North West Training Partnership Aiken Hall, University of Chester Crab Lane, Padgate Warrington WA2 0DB [MANCHESTER] *educ* Bris Univ; Trin Coll Bris; *CV* C Collyhurst, Man 1984–87; C Broughton 1987–94; C Higher Broughton 1987–92; C St Clem w St Matthias Lower Broughton 1987–92; C St Jas w St Clem and St Matthias Broughton 1992–94; R Broughton 1994–96; TR Broughton 1996–2002; AD Salford 1997–2002; Hon Rsch Fell and p-t Lect Man Univ from 2000; Adn of Bolton 2002–08; Course Prin Southern Northwest Trg Ptnrship from 2008 GS 2002–ا   *Tel:* 01925 534303
    email: snwtpprincipal@chester.ac.uk

ARDRON, Mrs (Yvonne) Shayne, BSc
93 Letchworth Road Leicester LE3 6FN [LEICESTER] *b* 1966 *educ* Laurence Jackson Sch; Prior Pursglove Coll; Leicester Polytech; *CV* Quality Control Tester 1988-95; Lay Rdr from 2005; mother of 4 from teenage up
GS 2010–   *email:* shayne.ardron.gs@gmail.com

ARMITSTEAD, Col Edward Bradley Lawrence, CBE
Pendomer House Pendomer Yeovil BA22 9PB [BATH AND WELLS] *b* 1946 *educ* Shrewsbury Sch; R Military Academy Sandhurst; Defence Services Staff Coll India; *CV* Army Officer 1967–2001, Rtd from 2001; Preacher and Tchr; M Coun SASRA until 2012; Vice President SASRA from 2012; Rdr; Chair Oak Hill Th Coll Coun
GS 2000–   *Tel:* 01935 862785
    email: e.armitstead@btinternet.com

ARMSTRONG, Very Revd Christopher John, Cert Ed, B Th
The Deanery Preston New Rd Blackburn BB2 6PS [DEAN OF BLACKBURN] *b* 1947 *educ* Dunstable Gr Sch; Dur Univ; Kelham Th Coll; Nottm Univ; *CV* Tchr Dunstable 1969–72; Asst C All SS Maidstone 1975–79; Chapl Coll of St Hild & St Bede Dur 1979–85; Dom Chapl to Abp of York and DDO 1985–91; Incumb St Mart Scarboro 1991–2001; Dean of Blackburn from 2001; Chair, Lancashire CC Fairness Commn from 2014
GS 2003–05   *Tel:* 01254 52502
    01254 503090 (Office)
    Fax: 01254 689666
    email: dean@blackburncathedral.co.uk
    Web: www.blackburncathedral.com

ARORA, Revd Arun, LLB, BA, Solicitor of the Supreme Court of England and Wales
Church House Great Smith Street London SW1P 3AZ [DIRECTOR OF COMMUNICATIONS, ARCHBISHOPS' COUNCIL] *b* 1971 *educ* King Edward VI Five Ways Sch, Birm; Univ of Birm; Cranmer Hall Dur; *CV* Dioc Dir Communications, Birm 2000–04; Asst C St Mark's Harrogate 2006–10; Dir Communications Abp York 2006–09; Team Ldr, Wolverhampton Pioneer Ministries 2010–12; Dir Communications Abp's Coun from 2012
    Tel: 020 7898 1462
    07984 334564
    email: arun.arora@churchofengland.org
    Twitter: @revarun

ASHCROFT, Ven Mark David, BA, MA
14 Moorgate Avenue Withington Manchester M20 1HE [ARCHDEACON OF MANCHESTER] *b* 1954 *educ* Rugby; Worc Coll Ox; Fitzwilliam Coll Cam; Ridley Hall; *CV* Asst C Burnage St Margaret 1982–85; Tutor St Paul Sch of Divinity Kapsabet Kenya 1986–90; Prin St Paul Theol Coll Kapsabet Kenya 1990–95; R Ch Ch Harpurhey, Man 1996–2009; AD N Man 2000–2006; Adn of Man from 2009   *Tel:* 0161 448 1976
    Fax: 0161 445 9458
    email: Archdeaconmanchester@
    manchester.anglican.org

ASHE, Ven (Francis) John, B Met, Cert Th
Hollytree House Whitwell Rd Sparham Norwich NR9 5PN [ARCHDEACON OF LYNN; NORWICH] *b* 1953 *educ* Ch Hosp; Sheff Univ; Ridley Hall Cam; *CV* C Ashtead, Guild 1979–82; P-in-c St Faith Plumstead, Cape Town 1982–87; R Wisley-w-Pyrford, Guild 1987–93; V Godalming, Guild 1993–2001; RD Godalming 1996–2002; TR Godalming 2001–09; M Bp's Coun; Bp's Adv BAP (Pastl) 2002–2009; Hon Can Guild Cathl 2003–2009; Warden of Rdrs, Norw from 2009; Adn of Lynn from 2009
GS 2003–09   *Tel:* 01362 688032
    email: archdeacon.lynn@norwich.anglican.org

ASHFORD, Archdeacon of. See DOWN, Ven Philip Roy

ASHTON, Mr David,
2 Manor Drive Battyeford Mirfield WF14 0ER [WEST YORKSHIRE AND THE DALES] *b* 1941 *educ* Warw Rd Junior Sch; Dewsbury and Batley Tech Sch;

WHO'S WHO

Kitson Eng Coll; *CV* Br Telecom Integrity Mgr; M GS Stg Orders Cttee; M Bp's Coun
GS 1972–   *Tel:* 01924 497996
                    email: david_ashton@hotmail.com

ASHWIN, Mr John Basil Edward Hamilton, MA, PGCE, FRSA
31 Wellington Rd Chichester PO19 6BB [CHICHESTER] *b* 1937 *educ* St Olave's and St Saviour's Sch S'wark; Selwyn Coll Cam; Cam Inst of Educ; *CV* Tchr of Engl then Head of Engl Dept, Emanuel Sch SW Lon 1963–69; Head of Engl Dept then Sen Master, William Morris Sen High Sch, Walthamstow 1969–75; Head, St Dav and St Kath Comp Sch, Hornsey 1975-81; Head, Bp Luffa Sch, Chich 1981–2000; Chair W Sussex Secdry Heads 1995–98; rtd: pt External Adv and Threshold Assessor for schools, Cam Educ Associates; Accredited Section 23 Insp; Mod Rdrs' Trg Chich Dio; Lay Chair Chich Dny Syn; Vc-Chair Govs, Univ Coll Chich; Consult for Secdry Heads; Sec Open Syn Grp from 2011
GS 2002–   *Tel:* 01243 786501
                                            07939 333858 (Mobile)
                    email: johnashwin@tiscali.co.uk

ASHWORTH, Mrs Lorna,
6 Ruston Gardens Southgate London N14 4PF [CHICHESTER] *b* 1970 *CV* Elected to GS 2005
GS 2005–   *email:* lashworth70@gmail.com

ASTON, Archdeacon of. HEATHFIELD, Ven Simon

ASTON, Suffragan Bishop of. [NOT APPOINTED AT TIME OF GOING TO PRESS]

ATKINSON, Very Revd Peter Gordon, MA, Hon DLitt, FRSA
The Deanery 10 College Green Worcester WR1 2LH [DEAN OF WORCESTER] *b* 1952 *educ* Maidstone Gr Sch; St Jo Coll Ox; Westcott Ho Cam; *CV* C Clapham Old Town TM 1979–83; P-in-c Tatsfield 1983–90; R H Trin Bath 1990–91; Prin Chich Th Coll 1991–94; Bursalis Preb Chich Cathl 1991–97; R Lavant 1994–97; Chan Chich Cathl 1997–2007; Dean of Worcester from 2007; Master St Oswald's Hosp Worc from 2007
GS 2000–05   *Tel:* 01905 732909 (Office)
                              01905 732939 (Study)
        email: peteratkinson@worcestercathedral.org.uk

ATKINSON, Rt Revd Richard William Bryant, MA, MA, OBE
Bishop's Lodge Bedford Road Cardington Bedford MK44 3SS [SUFFRAGAN BISHOP OF BEDFORD; ST ALBANS] *b* 1958 *educ* St Paul's Sch Lon; Magd Coll Cam; Cuddesdon Th Coll; Birm Univ; *CV* C Abingdon w Shippon 1984–87; TV Sheff Manor Par 1987–91; Hon M of Staff Cuddesdon Th Coll 1987–92; TR Sheff Manor Par 1991–96; V

All SS Rotherham 1996–2002; Hon Can Sheff Cathl 1998–2002; Adn of Leicester 2002–12; Bp of Bedford from 2012; M CTE and CTBI 1997–2002; Ch Commr 2001–08; M Cen Ch Fund Cttee 1997–2002; CUF Trustee 2003–08; Dep Chair Places for People 1997–2005; Chair Phoenix Enterprises (Rotherham) Ltd 1998–2002; Chair Braunstone New Deal for Communities Programme 2003–06; Chair St Phil Cen for Study and Engagement in Multi Faith Society 2005-12; Chair Launde Abbey Mgt Cttee 2002–08; M Carnegie Trust UK Enquiry into the Future of Civil Society in Britain and Ireland 2007–10; M Presence and Engagement Task Gp; Co-Chair National Hindu Christian Forum from 2010; Near Neighbours Trustee from 2011; Vice-Chair MPA from 2012; Chair St Albans DBE from 2013; Co-Chair Inter Faith Network UK from 2014; Chair Eastern Region Min Course from 2014
GS 1991–2012   *Tel:* 01234 831432
                                Fax: 01234 831484
        email: bishopbedford@stalbans.anglican.org

ATWELL, Very Revd James Edgar, MA, Th M, BD
The Deanery The Close Winchester SO23 9LS [DEAN OF WINCHESTER] *b* 1946 *educ* Dauntsey's Sch; Ex Coll Ox; Harvard Univ; Cuddesdon Th Coll; *CV* C St Jo E Dulwich 1970–74; C Gt St Mary Cam 1974–77; Chapl Jes Coll Cam 1977–81; V Towcester w Easton Neston 1981–95; RD Towcester 1983–91; Prov of St Eds 1995–2000; Dean 2000–06; Dean of Winchester from 2006
                    Tel: 01962 853738 (Home)
                          01962 857205 (Office)
                    Fax: 01962 857264
        email: the.dean@winchester-cathedral.org.uk

ATWELL, Rt Revd Robert Ronald, BA (Hons), M.Litt
The Bishop's Office The Palace Gatehouse Exeter EX1 1HS [BISHOP OF EXETER] *b* 1954 *educ* Wanstead High Sch; St John's Coll Dur; Westcott Ho Cam; *CV* Asst C John Keble Ch Mill Hill 1978–81; Chapl Trinity Coll Cam 1981–87; Benedictine Monk Burford Priory 1987–98; V Par of St Mary-the-Virgin Primrose Hill 1998–2008; Bp Stockport 2008–14; Bp Exeter from 2014; Chair Min Cttee Chester Dioc; Trustee SNWTP; M Working Grp on Discipline in relation to matters of Doctrine, Ritual and Ceremonial; Chair Liturgical Commn from 2014
GS 2014   *Tel:* 01392 272362
                                Fax: 0161 929 0692
        email: bishop.of.exeter@exeter.anglican.org

AUCKLAND, Archdeacon of. See BARKER, Ven Nicholas John Willoughby

AYERS, Revd Paul Nicholas, MA
Vicarage Vicarage Drive Pudsey LS28 7RL [WEST YORKSHIRE AND THE DALES] *b* 1961 *educ* Bradf Gr Sch; St Pet Coll Ox; Trin Coll Bris; *CV* C St Jo Bapt Clayton 1985–88; C St Andr Keighley

1988–91; V St Cuth Wrose 1991–97; V St Lawr and St Paul Pudsey from 1997
GS 1995– *Tel:* 0113 256 4197
email: paul.ayers@tiscali.co.uk

BACK, Mr Robin Philip, AIB, FRSA
The Old Manse Church Lane Guestwick Norfolk NR20 5QJ [NORWICH] *b* 1946 *educ* Uppingham; Geneva Univ; *CV* Standard Chartered Bank in Middle East, India, Indonesia, Thailand and USA 1967–88; MD Backs Electronic Publishing Ltd from 1989; Prime Wdn, Worshipful Co of Dyers of City of Lon 2002–03; M Bp's Coun from 2003; Lay Chair, Dioc Syn 2003–09; Lay Chair, Sparham Dny Syn 1996–2001; M DBF from 2003; Chair Friends of Scott Polar Research Inst, Univ of Cam 2007–10; Dir Wispire Ltd (diocesan trading company) from 2011
GS 2005– *Tel:* 01362 683281
01362 683835
07802 244619
email: robin@bepl.co.uk

BAILEY, Ven David Charles, MA, M Sc, BA
14 Springside Rd Walmersley Bury BL9 5JE [ARCH-DEACON OF BOLTON; MANCHESTER] *b* 1952 *educ* Bradf Gr Sch; Linc Coll Oxf; Nottm Univ; St Jo Coll Nottm; *CV* C St Jo Worksop 1980–83; C Edgware, P-in-c St Andr Broadfields 1983–87; V S Cave and Ellerker w Broomfleet 1987–97; RD Howden 1991–97; Hon Can York Minster 1998–2008; V Beverley Minster 1997–2008; Adn Bolton from 2008 *Tel:* 0161 761 6117
07944 518765 (Mobile)
email: archbolton@manchester.anglican.org

BAIN, Ven (John) Stuart, BA
St Nicholas' Vicarage Hedworth Lane Boldon Colliery NE35 9JA [ARCHDEACON OF SUNDERLAND; DURHAM] *b* 1955 *educ* Blaydon Sec Sch; Durham Univ; Westcott Ho Cam; *CV* C H Trin Washington 1980–84; C St Nic Dunston 1984–86; V St Oswald Shiney Row and St Aid Herrington 1986–92; P-in-c St Paul Spennymoor and Whitworth 1992–97; P-in-c St Jo Merrington 1994–97; AD Auckland 1996–2002; Hon Can Dur 1998; V St Paul Spennymoor, Whitworth and St Jo Merrington 1997–2002; Chair DFW Adoption from 1999; Asst P St Nic Hedworth 2002; P-in-c St Nic Hedworth from 2003; P-in-c St Geo E Boldon from 2009; P-in-c St Nics Boldon from 2010; Adn of Sunderland from 2002 *Tel:* 0191 536 2300
Fax: 0191 519 3369
email: Archdeacon.of.Sunderland@durham.anglican.org

BAINES, Rt Revd Nicholas, BA(Hons)
Hollin House Weetwood Avenue Leeds LS16 5NG [BISHOP OF LEEDS; WEST YORKSHIRE AND THE DALES] *b* 1957 *educ* Holt Comp Sch Liv; Bradf Univ; Trin Coll Bris; *CV* C St Thos Kendal 1987–91; C H Trin Leic 1991–92; V Rothley 1992–2000; RD Goscote 1995–2000; Adn of Lambeth 2000–03;

Broadcaster; Dir EIG 2002–10; Bp of Croydon 2003–10; Angl Co-Chair Meissen Comm; Chair Sandford St Mart Trust from 2009; Bp of Bradf 2011–14; Bp of Leeds from 2014
GS 1995–2003, 2004–05, 2011– *Tel:* 0113 284 4300
email: bishop.nick@westyorkshiredales.anglican.org
Web: nickbaines.wordpress.com
Twitter: @nickbaines

BAKER, Rt Revd Jonathan Mark Richard, MA, M Phil, Hon DD
The Old Deanery Dean's Court London EC4V 5AA [SUFFRAGAN BISHOP OF FULHAM; LONDON] *b* 1966 *educ* Merchant Taylors' Sch Northwood; St Jo Coll Ox; St Steph Ho Th Coll; *CV* C All SS Ascot Heath 1993–96; P-in-c St Mark and H Trin Reading 1996–99; V St Mark and H Trin Reading 1999–2002; Prin Pusey Ho, Ox 2003–13; Bp of Ebbsfleet 2011–13; Bp of Fulham from 2013
GS 2000–11 *Tel:* 020 7932 1130
07881 522669 (Mobile)
email: angela.west@london.anglican.org
2nd email: bishop.fulham@london.anglican.org

BALDRY, Sir Tony, BA, LLB, MA, MP
c/o Parliamentary Unit Church House Westminster SW1P 3az [SECOND CHURCH ESTATES COMMIS-SIONER] *b* 1905 *CV* Barrister at Lincoln's Inn from 1975 *Tel:* 020 7898 1478
Web: http://www.churchofengland.org/our-views/the-church-in-parliament/second-church-estates-commissioner

BANKS, Rt Revd Norman, MA (Oxon); PGCE
Parkside House Abbey Mill Lane St Albans AL3 4HE [BISHOP OF RICHBOROUGH] *b* 1954 *educ* Walllsend Gr; Oriel Coll Ox; Ox Dept Educ; St Stephen's Ho; *CV* C Christ Church with St Ann Newcastle 1982–84; C-in-c St Ann 1984–87; P-in-c Christ Church with St Ann 1987–1990; V Tynemouth St Paul Cullercoats 1990–2000; V Walsingham, Houghton and the Barshams 2000–11; RD Burnham and Walsingham 2008–11; Chapl to HM the Queen 2008–11; Chapl to High Sheriff of Norfolk 2010–11; Bp of Richborough from 2011; M Coun NE Ordination course 1993–2000; ABM Selector 1993–2000; Inspector of Theol Colls and Courses 1995–2000
GS 1990–2000, 2010– *Tel:* 01727 836358
email: bishop@richborough.org.uk

BARBER, Mr John Stephen, BSc
16 Launceston Close Cherry Tree Gardens Oldham OL8 2XE [MANCHESTER] *b* 1971 *educ* The Blue Coat C o fE, Oldham; Oldham Coll, Bolton Univ; *CV* Joiner/Carpenter, Oldham MBC, 1988–96; Bldg Surveyor, Oldham MBC, 1997–2004; Senior Renewal Surveyor, Tameside MBC from 2004
GS 2010– *Tel:* 0161 620 0668
email: johnsbarber@btinternet.com

BARBER, Revd Neil Andrew Austin, BA
*St Giles' Vicarage 16 Browning Street Normanton
Derby DE23 8DN* [DERBY] *b* 1963 *educ* Ealing Coll
of H Ed; Oakhill Coll; NTMTC; *CV* Systems
Eng/Project Mgr, IBM UK, 1986–95; Lay Assoc
Min, St Mary's Basingstoke, Winc 1995–98; C St
Mary's Basingstoke, Winc 1998–2001; Incumb,
St Giles' Normanton by Derby from 2001
GS 2010–   *Tel:* 01332 767483
        email: neil.barber@stgiles-derby.org.uk

BARKER, Ven Nicholas John Willoughby, MA
*Holy Trinity Vicarage 45 Milbank Rd Darlington
DL3 9NL* [ARCHDEACON OF AUCKLAND] *b* 1949
educ Sedbergh Sch; Oriel Coll Ox; Trin Coll Bris;
CV C St Mary Watford 1977–80; TV St Jas and Em
Didsbury 1980–86; TR St Geo Kidderminster
1986–2007; RD Kidderminster 2001–07; Adn of
Auckland from 2007; Hon Can Dur Cathl from
2007
GS 2005–07   *Tel:* 01325 480444
                                     07912 269 364 (Mobile)
                                          Fax: 01325 354027
        email: archdeacon.of.auckland@
                                         durham.anglican.org

BARKER, Ven Timothy Reed, MA
103 Newport Lincoln LN1 3EE [ARCHDEACON OF
LINCOLN; LINCOLN] *b* 1956 *educ* Man Gr Sch;
Queen's Coll Cam; Westcott Ho; *CV* C Nantwich
1980–83; V Norton St Berteline and St Christo-
pher 1983–88; V Runcorn All Saints 1988–94;
Urban Officer Ches 1990–98; Bp of Chester's
Chap 1994–98; P assoc, Ches Cath 1994–98; V
Spalding St Mary and Nicholas 1998–2009; Rural
Dean Elloe West 2000–09; M Linc Cathl Chap
2000–09; Can and Preb of Linc from 2003;
Rural Dean Elloe East 2008–09; P-in-c Spalding
St Paul 2007–09; M DRACS Cttee 2001–05; M
CME Panel 2003–06; M Clergy Terms of Service
Implementation Group 2005–07; M Marriage
Law Working Party 2006; M Marriage (Amend-
ment) Meas Steering Cttee; M Dioc Syn from
1999; Trustee Alcuin Club from 1990; Adn Linc
from 2009
GS 2000–05; 2008–   *Tel:* 01522 504095
                                     07590 950041 (Mobile)
email: archdeacon.lincoln@lincoln.anglican.org

**BARKING, Archdeacon of. See
PERUMBALATH, Ven Dr John**

**BARKING, Area Bishop of. See HILL, Rt Revd
Peter**

BARNEY, Mr Stephen George, B Sc, MBA
The Dower House 77 Brook St Wymeswold LE12 6TT
[LEICESTER] *b* 1950 *educ* Cranfield Univ; *CV* Main
Bd Dir public companies rtd; Rdr; Chair DBF;
Trustee Launde Abbey; Dir SMCP
GS 2005–   *Tel:* 01509 881160
                                     07767 320320 (Mobile)
                                 email: stephen4747@live.co.uk

**BARNSTAPLE, Archdeacon of. EDSON, Ven
Mike (Acting)**

BARRELL, Mrs Anneliese Gledhill, MCSP, Grad
Dip Phys, DSA
47 Whitleigh Ave Crownhill Plymouth PL5 3AU
[EXETER] *b* 1938 *educ* Burlington Sch Lon; Prince
of Wales Gen Hosp Sch of Physiotherapy,
Lon; *CV* Rtd NHS physiotherapy mgr; pt lect,
Plymouth Coll FE; M Dioc Coun for Work with
Children and Young People, Portfolio Holder for
Children, Lay Chair Moorside Deanery Syn;
chwdn St Francis Honicknowle, Foundation
Gov Notre Dame RC Girls Sec Sch Plymouth, PR
Adviser SW Reg Trefoil Guild
GS 2000–   *Tel:* 01752 777053
                                     0754 167115 (Mobile)
                             email: annagb@blueyonder.co.uk

BARTON, Mrs Jennifer Diane,
*The End Game 21 Holland Close Rogerstone Newport
NP10 0AU* [WORCESTER] *b* 1942 *educ* Challney
Secondary Sch, Luton; *CV* Computer Punch Card
Operator, 1958–65; Worc Ed Dept, Spec needs
Children 1986–93; M Dioc Brd Ed 1996–2006;
M Worc Dioc Syn from 1998; M Martley & Worc
West Deanery Syn from 1995
GS 2010–   *Tel:* 01633 891193
                                 email: jdnoumena@aol.com

BASHFORTH, Revd Alan George, MA, B Th
Vicarage 6 Penwinnick Parc St Agnes TR5 0UQ
[TRURO] *b* 1964 *educ* Humphrey Davy Gr Sch; Ox
Univ; Ex Univ; Ripon Coll Cuddesdon; *CV* Police
officer, S Yorks Police 1983–90; nursing auxiliary
1990–93; C Calstock, Truro 1996–98; C St Ives, Truro
1998–2001; V St Agnes and Mithian w. Mount
Hawke from 2001; RD Powder 2004–13; M Bp's
Coun; M DBF; M Dioc Pastl Cttee; Chair Ho of
Clergy from 2009; Hon Can Truro Cathl from 2013
GS 2005–   *Tel:* 01872 553391
                                 email: onepaw@btinternet.com

**BASINGSTOKE, Suffragan Bishop of. See
WILLIAMS, Rt Revd David Grant**

**BATH AND WELLS, Bishop of. See
HANCOCK, Rt Revd Peter**

**BATH, Archdeacon of. See PIGGOTT, Ven
Andy (Andrew John)**

BAYES, Rt Revd Paul, BA, DipTheol
*Bishop's Lodge Woolton Park, Woolton, Liverpool L25
6DT* [BISHOP OF LIVERPOOL] *b* 1953 *educ* Belle Vue
Boys' Sch, Bradf; Univ Birm; Queen's Coll Birm;
CV C Tynemouth Cullercoats St Paul Newc
1979–82; Chapl Qu Eliz Coll Lon 1982–87; Chapl
Chelsea Coll 1985–87; TV High Wycombe Ox
1987–90; TR 1990–94; TR Totton Win 1994–2004; AD
Lyndhurst 2000–04; Nat Miss and Evang Adv
Abps' Coun 2004–10; Hon Can Worc Cathl 2007–
10; Bp of Hertford 2010–14; Bp of Liverpool from
2014   *Tel:* 0151 421 0831
         email: bishopslodge@liverpool.anglican.org

BAYLIS, Revd Sally Anne, BA,MA, PGCE
Daybrook Vicarage 241 Oxclose Lane Daybrook Nottingham NG5 6FB [SOUTHWELL & NOTT] *b* 1955 *educ* Herts & Essex H Sch, Bishop's Stortford; Queen's Coll Lon Univ of Kent; St John's Coll Nott; *CV* Bookseller 1978–85; Freelance editor/translator 1990–2003; Secondary School Tchr 1993–2001; AC All Hallows Gedling 2003–07 P-in-c St Paul's w St Timothy's Daybrook from 2007; M Dioc Syn from 2005
GS 2010– *Tel:* 0115 9262686
07506 441634
email: sally504@btinternet.com

BAYNES, Canon Matthew Thomas Crispin, MA
The Rectory Bredon Tewkesbury GL20 7LT [WORCESTER] *b* 1962 *educ* Orange Hill H Sch, Edgware; MIddx UEA; Cam Univ; Westcott Ho Th Coll; *CV* Nursing Auxillary, St Christopher's Hospice, Sydenham 1983–84; C Ch Ch, Southgate 1987–90; Chapl Southgate Tech Coll 1987–90; P-in-c, All Saints' Berkhamsted 1990–95; Chapl St. Francis Hospice, Berkhamsted 1990–95; V Ch Ch Coseley,1995–99; Assoc Dioc Chapl Agriculture & Rural Life 2002–09; R, Bredon w Bredon's Norton 1999; Rural Dean of Pershore 2005–11; Beckford Grp P 2009; Can Worc 2010; St Alb Dioc Syn; Worc Dioc Syn; Worc Dioc Brd Ed; Worc Dioc Pstrl Cttee
GS 2010– *Tel:* 01684 772237
email: mbaynes@toucansurf.com

BAYNES, Mr Simon Henry Crews, BSc, C Eng, FBCS
4 Pilgrim Close St Albans AL2 2JD [ST ALBANS] *b* 1958 *educ* Orange Hill Boys' Gr Sch, Edgware, Middx; Sheff Univ; *CV* Logica 1979–2009, Dir Simon Baynes Ltd from 2009; Client Dir, Capital Cranfield Trustees Ltd from 2009; M CofE Pensions Board from 2009; Chair, Pension Trustees, Logica 1997–2012; Trustee Cam Univ Press Sen Staff Pension Scheme from 2008; M Nat Audit Office Panel of Pensions Experts from 2011; Trustee, Life Academy (The Pre-Retirement Assoc) 2007–14; Chartered Eng from 1990; M St Alb Dioc Syn from 2003; M St Alb DBF from 2003; M Dny Syn from 2001; M St Alb Cathl Fin Cttee 1997–2007 and from 2010; M Inter-Dioc Fin Forum from 2005; M Bp's Coun from 2007; M CNC (St Alb Vacancy-in-See) 2008–09; Founder and vice-chair St Alb Dioc Penal Affairs Grp from 2008; Chair Nat Conf Stg Grp 'Engaging Churches in Rehabilitation' 2014
GS 2005– *Tel:* 01727 875524 (Home)
01727 875537 (Office)
07860 828711 (Mobile)
email: simon@simonbaynes.fsnet.co.uk

BEACH, Very Revd Mark Howard Francis, BA, MA, DMIN
The Deanery Priors Gate House The Precinct Rochester ME1 1SR [DEAN OF ROCHESTER] *b* 1962 *educ* Ellesmore Coll Shropshire; Univ of Kent; Univ of Nottm; St Stephen's Ho; K Coll Lon; *CV*

C Beeston S'well 1987–90; C Hucknall 1990–93; R Gedling 1993–2001; R Netherfield 1996–2001; Bp's Chapl Wakef 2001–03; TR Rugby Cov 2003–12; Transforming Communities Officer Dioc Cov 2010–12; Chair Warwickshire Community and Voluntary Action; Dean of Roch from 2012; M Cathl Fabric Comm; Chair Medway Healthwatch
GS 2008–12 *Tel:* 01634 202183
Fax: 01634 401410
email: dean@rochestercathedral.org

BEAKE, Ven Stuart Alexander, MA
Archdeacon's House Lime Grove West Clandon Guildford GU4 7UT [ARCHDEACON OF SURREY; GUILDFORD] *b* 1949 *educ* K Coll Sch Wimbledon; Em Coll Cam; Cuddesdon Coll Ox; *CV* C St Mary Hitchin 1974–79; TV St Mary Hemel Hempstead 1979–85; Dom Chapl to Bp of Southwell 1985–87; V Shottery St Andr 1987–2000; RD Fosse Dny 1992–99; DDO Cov Dioc 1995–2000; Hon Can Cov Cathl 1999–2000; Can Res and Sub-Dean Cov Cathl 2000–05; Adn of Surrey from 2005; Can Res Guildf Cathl from 2011
GS 1980–85 *Tel:* 01483 790352 (Office)
01483 211924 (Home)
Fax: 01483 790333 (Office)
01483 223397 (Home)
email: stuart.beake@cofeguildford.org.uk

BEAL, Dr John Frank, PhD, BDS, MFDS(RCSEng), HonMFPH, FRSPH
Oakroyd 4 North Park Road Leeds LS8 1JD [WEST YORKSHIRE AND THE DALES] *educ* Finchley County Gr Sch; Royal Dental Hospital of London; *CV* House Surgeon, Royal Dental Hosp of Lon 1965–66; Lect in Dental Public Health, Birm Univ 1966–76; Senior Dental Officer, Avon Area Health Authority (Teaching) 1977–79; Area Dental Officer, Birm Area Health Authority (Teaching) 1979–83; Consult in Dental Public Health, Leeds Health Authority, 1983–2008; Regional Dental Officer, Yorkshire Regional Health Authority, 1990–2009; Locum Consult in Dental Public Health, Wakefield District Primary Care Trust from 2010; Hospital Chapls Counc 1995–2000; M Bp's Counc, Ripon Dioc from 1990; Vice-chair Brd of Miss and Unity, Ripon Dioc 1987–89
GS 1995–2005; 2010– *Tel:* 0113 294 8795
email: johnfbeal@hotmail.co.uk

BECK, Miss Rachel Gillian, BA
Edward King House Lincoln LN2 1PU [LINCOLN] *b* 1980 *educ* Wales High Sch; Bp Grosseteste Coll; *CV* Receptionist Sheff Dioc Ch Ho 1999–2000; Admin Rotherham Youth Service 2000–01; PA to Asst Dir of Educ, Rotherham 2001–02; Primary Tchr, Linc from 2005–11; Res Cons Dioc Linc from 2011
GS 2000– *Tel:* 07753 634477
email: rgbeck@btinternet.com

BEDFORD, Archdeacon of. See HUGHES, Ven Paul Vernon

BEDFORD, Suffragan Bishop of. See
ATKINSON, Rt Revd Richard William Bryant

BELCHER, Dr William Peter Argent, BSc, PhD
*39 Redgrove Park Cheltenham Gloucestershire GL51
6QY* [GLOUCESTER] *b* 1949 *educ* Framlingham Coll,
Suffolk; Leeds Univ; Cam Univ; *CV* Materials
Eng in Nuclear Electricity Generating Industry,
Nuclear Electric Plc 1988–95; British Energy
Generation Ltd. 1995–2009; Chwrdn, Lay Chair of
PCC; Leadership Team of St Mary w St Matthew
Ch, Cheltenham 2002–08; Materials Eng in
Nuclear Electricity Generating Industry, EDF-
Energy 2009
GS 2010–   *Tel:* 01242 228690
        email: williambelcher@btinternet.com

BELL, Rt Revd James Harold, MA, BA, Cert Theol
Thistledown Main St Exelby Bedale DL8 2HD
[AREA BISHOP OF RIPON; WEST YORKSHIRE
AND THE DALES] *b* 1950 *educ* Appleby Gr Sch; St Jo
Coll Dur; Wycliffe Hall Ox; *CV* Hon C St Mich at
the Northgate, Ox 1975–76; Chapl and lect BNC
Ox 1976–82, Fell 1979–82; R St Mary Northolt,
Lon 1982–93; Area Dean Ealing 1991–93; Adv for
Min, Willesden Area 1993–97; Dir of Min and Tr,
Ripon Dioc 1997–99; Res Can Ripon Cathl 1997–
99; Dir of Mission Ripon Dioc 1999–2004; Hon
Can Ripon Cathl 1999–2004; Bp of Knares-
borough from 2004; M Dioc Syn, DBF, DBE (ex
officio), Chair Rural Affairs Gp of the GS; M
Harrogate Coll Consult Cttee; Gov York St Jo
Univ Coll; Chair Yorks Min Course Coun from
2012
GS 2010–   *Tel and Fax:* 01677 423525
                 email: bishop.james@
              westyorkshiredales.anglican.org

BENFIELD, Revd Paul John, LLB, BTh, Barrister
*St Nicholas Vicarage Highbury Ave Fleetwood FY7
7DJ* [BLACKBURN] *b* 1956 *educ* Cam Gr Sch for
Boys; Newc Univ; Coll of Law, Chancery Lane,
Lon; Chich Th Coll; *CV* Chancery barrister 1978–
86; C Shiremoor, Newc 1989–92; C Hexham,
Newc 1992–93; TV All SS, St Anne, St Mich & St
Thos Lewes, Chich 1993–97; R Pulborough, Chich
1997–2000; V St Nich Fleetwood, Blackb from
2000; M Legal Aid Commn from 2006; M Rev
Cttee on Draft Vacancies in Suffragan Sees and
Other Eccl Offices Meas; M Rev Cttee on Draft
Crown Benefices (Par Representatives) Meas
2008; M Revd Cttee for Draft Pastl and Miss Meas
2009; M Fleetwood Town Coun 2009–11;
M Dioc Commn from 2010; M C of E Pensions
Bd from 2011
GS 2005–   *Tel:* 01253 874402
        email: benfield@btinternet.com

BENNETT, Dr Anthony John, BEd, MA, PhD
1 Merriefield Close, Broadstone Dorset BH18 8DG
[WINCHESTER] *b* 1950 *educ* Nottingham Coll; Univ
of Essex; *CV* Tchr History & US Politics, Royal

Hospital Sch, Ipswich 1974–89; Tchr of US
Politics, Charterhouse, 1989–2009; Under Master,
Charterhouse 1997–2004; Deputy Headmaster,
Charterhouse 2004–09; Bournemouth Deanery
Syn M from 2010
GS 2010–   *Tel:* 01202 252523
              email: ajb44@ymail.com

BENSON, Ven Paddy (George Patrick), MA, BD,
MPhil
3 Hatterall Close Hereford HR1 1GA [ARCHDEACON
OF HEREFORD] *b* 1949 *educ* Benrose Sch Derby;
Leighton Park Sch Reading; Ch Ch Ox; Trin Coll
Bris; All Nations Christian Coll Ware; St John's
Coll Nottm; *CV* Dir Academic Studies St
Andrew's Institute, Kabare, Kenya 1978–87;
Acting Dir Communications, Dioc Mt Kenya East
1987–89; Asst C St Mary Upton, Chester 1991–5;
V Christ Church Barnston, Chester 1995–2010;
Adn of Hereford from 2011   *Tel:* 01432 265659
                                07946 565697
       email: archdeacon@hereford.anglican.org

BENYON, Mr Thomas, DipTh, OBE
*Rectory Farm House 2 Church St Bladon Oxon
OX2O 1RS* [OXFORD] *b* 1942 *educ* Wellington Sch;
RMA Sandhurst; Wycliffe Hall Ox; *CV* Lieut
Scots Guards 1963–67; District Coun AVDC;
Contested Huyton 1974; MP Abingdon 1979–83;
Chair Milton Keynes Health Auth 1989–92; Dir
Buckingham Health Auth 1992–94; Founder
ZANE: Zimbabwe A National Emergency
GS 2005–   *Tel:* 01993 811722
                                07831 859085
       email: tom.benyon@btinternet.com

**BERKSHIRE, Archdeacon of. GRAHAM, Ven
Olivia**

BERRY, Professor Anthony John, B Sc, M Phil, Ph D,
DIC
24 Leafield Rd Disley Stockport SK12 2JF [CHESTER]
b 1939 *educ* Bath Univ; Imp Coll Lon; Seattle
Univ; Man Univ; *CV* Aerodynamicist Br Aircraft
Corp 1962; Aerodynamics Engineer The Boeing
Co Seattle 1965–69; Rsch Fell 1971–73, Lect 1973–
86, Sen Lect 1986–95 in Mgt Devel Man Univ;
Prof Sheff Hallam Univ 1995–2002; Prof emeritus
2002; M Dioc Syn; Rdr
GS 1994–   *Tel:* 01663 762393
                                07759 492318
       email: anthonyberry@btinternet.com

BESSANT, Canon Simon, B Mus, MA
*The Vicarage 25a Mortomley Lane High Green Shef-
field S35 3HS* [SHEFFIELD] *b* 1956 *educ* Francis
Combe Comp Watford; Sheff Univ; St Jo Coll
Nottm; *CV* C St Jo and St Jas Bootle 1981–84;
C Em Holloway 1984–85, P-in-c 1985–81; Ecum
Adv for Bp of Stepney 1990–91; V Ch of the
Redeemer Blackburn 1991–98; RD of Blackburn
1997–98; Dioc Dir for Miss and Evang and Officer
for Dioc Bd for Miss and Unity 1998–2007; Dioc

Dir for CME 1–4 2002–05; V All Saints Ecclesall, Sheff 2007–12; V St Saviour's High Green, Sheff from 2012; P-in-c St Mark's Grenoside from 2014; M Lon Dioc Bd of Educ 1989–91; M Blackb Dioc Bd of Min 1995–2002; M Blackb Dioc Liturg Cttee 1998–2007; Sec to Blackb Dioc, Lancs Coun of Mosques Dialogue Grp 1998–2007; initiator and M Churches Together in Lancs Inter-Faith Forum 1999–2007, Chair 1999–2003; initiator and M Lancs Inter-Faith Forum 2000–2007, Chair 2001–03; GS rep on NEOC Bd 2001–05; M MPA Coun 2003–05; M Presence and Engagement Strg Grp 2004–05; M Follow-up Grp, Strg Cttee and Rev Cttee, Rev of Diocs Pastl and Miss Measure 2004–06; Chair Wkg Party creating code of practice on Miss Initiatives under Diocs, Pastl and Miss Measure from 2006; M Bradf Chs for Dialogue and Diversity Adv Grp from 2006; M AC 2006–07; M C of E Appts Cttee 2006–07; Hon Can Blackb Cath 2006–07; Can Emer Blackb Cath from 2006

GS 2001–07, 2008– Tel: 0114 418 2036
07957 211319
email: simon.bessant@stsaviours.info

BESWICK, Mr David Terence,
1 Vicarage Close Eccleshall Stafford ST21 6BX [LICHFIELD] *b* 1933 *educ* Tarporley C of E Sch; *CV* Chwdn, St Helen Tarporley 1972–77; chwdn, H Trin Eccleshall 1984–2003, lay chair PCC 2003–04, 2011–; lay chair Eccleshall Dny Syn from 2003; M Lich Dioc Syn from 2002, Miss & Pastl Cttee from 2004; M Lich Bp's Coun from 2004; Bp's Visitor from 2011

GS 2005– Tel: 01785 850622
email: dabeswick@btinternet.com

BETTS, Ven Steven James, B Sc, Cert Th
8 Boulton Road Norwich NR7 0DF [ARCHDEACON OF NORFOLK: NORWICH] *b* 1964 *educ* Nottm Blue-coat Gr Sch; York Univ; Cuddesdon Th Coll; *CV* C Bearsted w Thurnham 1990–94; Chapl to Bp of Norw 1994–97; V Old Catton Norw 1997–2005; RD Norw N 2001–05; M Dioc Commn 2001–09; Chair Dioc Ho of Clergy 2003–12; M Bp's Coun from 2003; M DBF Exec from 2003; Bp's Officer for Ord and Initial Trg 2005–12; Hon Can Norw Cathl from 2008; Adn of Norfolk from 2012; M Dioc Bd Educ from 2012; DAC from 2012; Dioc Bd of Patronage from 2012; Dioc Glebe Cttee from 2012, Dioc Investment Policy Grp from 2012; Dioc Asset Management Cttee from 2012; Dioc Property Cttee from 2012; Dir Spire Services from 2012

GS 2000– Tel: 01603 559199
email: archdeacon.norfolk@dioceseofnorwich.org

BEVERLEY, Bishop of. See WEBSTER, Rt Revd Glyn

BIRKENHEAD, Suffragan Bishop of. See SINCLAIR, Rt Revd (Gordon) Keith

BIRMINGHAM, Archdeacon of. See OSBORNE, Ven Hayward John

BIRMINGHAM, Bishop of. See URQUHART, Rt Revd David Andrew

BIRMINGHAM, Dean of. See OGLE, Very Revd Catherine

BISHOP, Ven Ian Gregory, BA, BSc ARICS
57A Sandbach Road Congleton Cheshire CW12 4LH [ARCHDEACON OF MACCLESFIELD; CHESTER] *b* 1962 *educ* Devizes Sch; Portsm Poly; Oak Hill Th Coll; *CV* Surveyor Croydon Counc 1984–86; Estate Mgr Gatwick Airport 1986–88; C Ch Ch Purley S'wark 1991–95; R Tas Valley Team Ministry 1995–2001; R Middlewich & Byley 2001–10; Rural Dean of Middlewich 2004–10; Archdn of Macclesfield from 2011

GS 2010– Tel: 01260 272875
07715 102519
email: ian.bishop@chester.anglican.org

BISHOP, Canon Pamela Elizabeth, BSc, PGCE
250 Nottingham Road Mansfield Notts NG18 4SH [SOUTHWELL & NOTT] *b* 1944 *educ* Staveley Netherthorpe Gr Sch; Nott Univ; *CV* Science Tchr, The Latymer Sch 1967–70; Head of Biology, The Brunts Sch, 1970–77; Deputy Head, The Manor Sch 1977–79; Lect Ed, Nott Univ 1989–2001; Independent Education Consult & Ofsted School Inspector from 2001; Dioc Chair Ho of Laity from 2008; M Bp's Counc from 2006; Deanery Lay Chair from 2007; Lay Can S'well Minster from 2014

GS 2010– Tel: 01623 633494
email: pandpbishop@btopenworld.com

BISSON, Mrs Jane Victoria, FSI, ACIS, MSc
Glenhaven La Rocque Grouville Jersey JE3 9BB [WINCHESTER [CHANNEL ISLANDS]] *b* 1949 *educ* Blancheland Coll; *CV* Legal Trustees (Jersey) Ltd 1988–91; Integro Trust Co 1991–94; Fin Services Commn 1994; Royal Bank of Scotland Internat 1994–2000; Mourant Internat Fin Admin, Legal and Risk Dept from 2005; Regional Mgr KYCOS Ltd, Jersey and Guernsey; M AC Audit Cttee; M Dioc Syn

GS 1995– Tel: 01534 853162
07797 750896 (Mobile)
email: jane.bisson@gmail.com

BLACKBURN, Rt Revd Richard Finn, BA, MA
34 Central Avenue Eccleston Park Prescot Merseyside L34 2QP [BISHOP OF WARRINGTON; LIVERPOOL] *b* 1952 *educ* Aysgarth Sch; Eastbourne Coll; St Jo Coll Dur; Hull Univ; Westcott Ho Th Coll; *CV* NatWest Bank 1976–81; C St Dunstan and All SS Stepney 1983–87; P-in-c St Jo Bapt Isle-worth 1987–92; V St Mark Mosborough w Em

Waterthorpe 1992–99; RD Attercliffe 1996–99; Hon Can Sheff Cathl 1998–99; Can Res Sheff Cathl 1999–2005; M Pensions Bd 2004–09, 2014; Adn of Sheff and Rotherham 1999–2009; Bp of Warrington from 2009
GS 2000–05   *Tel:* 0151 426 1897 (Home)
     0151 705 2140 (Office)
     07887 905970
     email: bishopofwarrington@
     liverpool.anglican.org

BLACKBURN, Archdeacon of. See HAWLEY, Ven John Andrew

BLACKBURN, Bishop of. See HENDERSON, Rt Revd Julian Tudor

BLACKBURN, Dean of. See ARMSTRONG, Very Revd Christopher John

BLOOR, Mrs Anne Felicity,
The Springs Carlton Lane Burton Overy, Leicester LE8 9DF [LEICESTER] *b* 1945 *educ* Malvern Girls Coll;   *Tel:* 0116 259 2440
     Fax: 0116 259 0119
     email: rabloor@gmail.com

BOARDMAN, Ven Jonathan Thomas, MA
Via del Babuino 153 00187 Rome Italy [ARCH-DEACON OF ITALY AND MALTA; EUROPE] *b* 1963 *educ* Bolton Sch; Magd Coll Ox; Magd Coll Cam; Westcott Ho; *CV* C St Mary W Derby, Liv 1990–93; Prec St Alb Abbey 1993–96; TR Catford and Downham, S'wark 1996–99; RD E Lewisham 1998–99; Chapl All SS Rome from 1999; Sen tutor, Angl Cen Rome from 2001; M S'wark Dioc Syn and Bp's Coun 1996–99; M Eur Dioc Syn and Bp's Coun 2004–07; Area Dean Italy and Malta from 2007; Can Dioc Cath Chapter from 2007; Adn Italy and Malta from 2009
GS 2005–09   *Tel:* +39 06 3600 1881
     +39 349 655 8844 (Mobile)
     Fax: +39 06 3600 1881
     email: office@allsaintsrome.org

BOARDMAN, Revd Canon Philippa Jane, MBE, MA
3 Amen Court London EC4M 7BU [LONDON] *b* 1963 *educ* Haberdashers' Aske's Sch for Girls; Jes Coll Cam; Ridley Hall Th Coll; *CV* C St Mary and St Steph Walthamstow 1990–93; Asst Pr St Mary of Eton Hackney Wick 1993–96; P-in-c St Paul w St Mark Old Ford 1996–2003, V 2003–13; Preb St Paul's Cathl 2002–13; Can Treas St Paul's Cathl from 2013
GS 1994–   *Tel:* 020 7248 3312
     email: treasurer@stpaulscathedral.org.uk

BODDINGTON, Ms Caroline Elizabeth, MA (Oxon), MCIPD
The Wash House Lambeth Palace London SE1 7JU [ARCHBISHOPS' SECRETARY FOR APPOINTMENTS] *b* 1964 *educ* Malvern Girls' Coll; Keble Coll Ox; *CV* BG Grp 1986–2003: HR Strategy and Devel

Mgr 1997–99, Hd of Learning and Devel 2000, Hd of HR Operations 2001–03; Abps' Sec for Appts from 2004   *Tel:* 020 7898 1876
     020 7898 1877
     email: caroline.boddington@churchofengland.org

BODMIN, Archdeacon of. See ELKINGTON, Ven Audrey Anne

BOLTON, Archdeacon of. See BAILEY, Ven David Charles

BOLTON, Suffragan Bishop of. See EDMONDSON, Rt Revd Christopher Paul

BONNEY, Very Revd Mark Philip John,
MA(Cantab), MA (Oxon), PGCE
The Deanery The College Ely CB7 2DN [DEAN OF ELY] *b* 1957 *educ* Northgate Gr Sch for Boys, Ipswich; St Catharine's Coll Camb; St Stephen's Ho; *CV* Asst C St Peter's Stockton-on-Tees 1985–88; Chaplain, St Albans Abbey 1988–90; Pre-centor, St Albans Abbey 1990–92; V Eaton Bray with Edlesborough 1992–96; R Great Berkham-sted 1996–2004; RD Berkhamsted 2002–04; Treas and Can Res Salisbury Cathl 2004–12; Dean of Ely from 2012; GS Rep RSCM 1998–2001, 2005–10; Chaplain to GS 2001–05; M Westcott Ho Coun 2002–05; M Lit Commn 2002–05; Ch Salisbury DAC 2007–12   *Tel:* 01353 660316
     07811 466517
     email: m.bonney@cathedral.ely.anglican.org

BOOKER, Revd Michael Paul Montague, BA, MA, PGCE
92 Swaynes Lane Comberton Cambridge CB23 7EF [ELY] *b* 1957 *educ* Cambridgeshire County High Sch; Jesus Coll, Ox; Bris Univ; Trin Coll, Bris; *CV* Tchr, Purley Boys' High Sch 1980–84; C, St Mary Bredin, Cant 1987–91; V, St Mary, Leamington Priors 1991–96; Dir of Miss & Pstrl Studies, Ridley Hall, Cam 1996–2005; P-in-c, Comberton and Toft 2005–10; TR, Lordsbridge Team Ministry from 2010; Chair Dioc Children's Coun 2006–10; RD Bourn Dnry from 2013
GS 2010–   *Tel:* 01223 260095
     email: mikebooker@lordsbridge.org

BOOTH, Mr John David Sebastian, MA, FRSA
Arundel Park West Sussex BN18 9NR [CHICHESTER] *b* 1958 *educ* Huish's Gr Sch Taunton; Mert Coll; *CV* Vc Pres Merrill Lynch 198386; Sen Vc Pres Prudential Bache 198893; Man Dir Bankers Trust Internat 199396; Chair Luther Pendragon Ltd 1992–2006; Chair Link ICAP (subs. of ICAP plc) 1996–2011; Chair Maintel Holdings PLC from 1996; Integrated Asset Mgt PLC from 1998, Jazz FM from 2009; Imaginarium Film Holdings from 2011; Dir Herald Investment Mgmt Ltd; Oldfield and Partners Ltd; Staffcare Ltd; Touchbase Ltd; M AC Fin Cttee 1999–2010 and Investment Review Group 2009–11; Investment Ctte from 2011; M CAC; M DBF; Chair Pensions Measure Review Cttee 2001–2; M Dioc of Europe Measure Steering

Ctte 2011–12; Guardian Nat Shrine of Our Lady of Walsingham; M Chancellor's Court, University of Oxford; M Chancellors Forum, Univ of the Arts Lon; Hon Fellow Mert Coll Ox; Hon Fellow and Vc Coun St Steph Ho, Ox; Gov Pusey Ho, Ox; M Canterbury Cathedral Campaign Board; Chair Queen Victoria Clergy Fund from 2011; M CNC 2013, Chair Chich DBF from 2013; Trustee, Chatsworth House; Pallant House Gallery
GS 1999–   *Tel:* 01798 831344
07767 474343 (Mobile)
email: j@johnbooth.com

BOOYS, Revd Canon Sue (Susan) Elizabeth, BA, Cert Th, PGCE, MA
Rectory Manor Farm Rd Dorchester-on-Thames Wallingford OX10 7HZ [OXFORD] *b* 1956 *educ* Harrow County Girls' Sch; Bristol Univ; Ox Min Course; Heythrop, Lon Univ; *CV* C Kidlington Tm Ox 1995–99; TV Dorchester Tm Ox from 1999, TR from 2005; M Bp's Coun; M GS Business Cttee; Gov Ripon Coll Cuddesdon from 2006; AD Aston and Cuddesdon from 2007
GS 2002–   *Tel:* 01865 340007
07815 609602 (Mobile)
Fax: 01865 340007
email: rector@dorchester-abbey.org.uk

BOSTON, Archdeacon of. See ALLAIN CHAPMAN, Ven Justine Penelope Heathcote

BOUGHTON, Revd Paul Henry, BSc, ACA
The Rectory The Ridgeway Fetcham Surrey KT22 9AZ [TRUSTEE MEMBER, CHURCH OF ENGLAND PENSIONS BOARD] *b* 1955 *educ* Guildford; Imp Coll Lon; Ridley Hall Cam; *CV* Coopers & Lybrand (now PwC) 1977–81; various posts with SGS UK and Swiss head office leading to Chief Financial Officer SGS, UK 1981–9; Asst C Christ Church, Guildf 1991–96; R Fetcham from 1996; voluntary M local authority Standards Committee 2000–05, Vc-Chair 2005–12; M Dioc Worship Cttee from 2001; M Dioc Syn from 2009; Clergy rep C of E Pensions Bd from 2010; Pensions Bd rep on EIAG from 2012   *Tel:* 01372 375000
email: boughtonfamily@yahoo.com

BOURNE, Revd Nigel Irvine, MA(Oxon), MBA, BA
The Vicarage 2A Vicarage Lane Chalk Gravesend Kent DA12 4TF [TRUSTEE MEMBER, CHURCH OF ENGLAND PENSIONS BOARD] *b* 1960 *educ* The Vyne Comprehensive School Basingstoke; Queen Mary's VI Form College Basingstoke; St John's Coll Ox; Trin Coll Bris; OU; *CV* Royal Naval Engineer Officer 1979–89; Royal Naval Reserve Engineer Officer 1989–92; C St Thomas Bedhampton 1992–4; C St John Newport IOW 1994–8, V St Mary Chalk from 1998; M Dioc Syn from 1998; M Fin Cttee Bp's Coun 2003–6, 2014–; M C of E Pensions Bd from 2009; M of Pensions Bd Housing Cttee from 2009; Vice-Chair Churches' Mutual Credit Union from 2014
Tel: 01474 567906
email: vicarofchalk@hotmail.com

BOURNEMOUTH, Archdeacon of. See ROUCH, Ven Peter Bradford

BOYD-LEE, Mr Paul Winston Michael, BA, Dip Th
Manor Barn Horsington Templecombe BA8 0ET [SALISBURY] *b* 1941 *educ* Brighton Coll; Open Univ; Ex Univ; *CV* Theatre Mgr Rank Organization 1963–66; Credit Controller Internat Factors Ltd 1966–72; Dir Bible Truth Publishers from 1972; a Dir of Ch Army 1999–2011; M Ch Army Investment and Remuneration Cttees; M AC from 2005; M Audit Cttee from 2006; M Ethical Investment Adv Gp
GS 1991–   *Tel:* 01963 371137
07710 604777
email: paulbl@btinternet.com

BOYLING, Very Revd Mark Christopher, MA
The Deanery Carlisle CA3 8TZ [DEAN OF CARLISLE] *b* 1952 *educ* K Jas Gr Sch Almondbury, W Yorks; Keble Coll Ox; Cuddesdon Th Coll; *CV* C St Mark Northwood, Kirkby 1977–79; TV 1979–85; Chapl to Bp of Liv 1985–89; V St Pet Formby, Liv 1989–94; Can Res and Prec Liv Cathl 1994–2004; Dean of Carlisle from 2004
GS 2010–   *Tel:* 01228 523335
Fax: 01228 547049
email: dean@carlislecathedral.org.uk

BRACKLEY, Rt Revd Ian James, MA
Dayspring 13 Pilgrims Way Guildford GU4 8AD [SUFFRAGAN BISHOP OF DORKING; GUILDFORD] *b* 1947 *educ* Westcliff High Sch; Keble Coll Ox; Cuddesdon Th Coll; Ecum Inst Geneva; *CV* C St Mary Magd w St Fran Lockleaze Bris 1971–74; Asst Chapl Bryanston Sch 1974–77; Chapl 1977–80; V St Mary E Preston Chich 1980–88; RD Arundel and Bognor 1982–87; TR St Wilf Haywards Heath 1988–96; RD Cuckfield 1989–95; Bp of Dorking from 1996; M Ho of Bps CME Cttee 2001–12; M Bd of Ch Army 2002–11; M CCU 2006–10; Chair Bd of Govs of STETS 1999–2012; Commissary Bp for Portsm Dioc 2009-10; Commissary Bp for Guildf Dioc from 2013
GS 1990–95, 2001–05, 2005–10, 2013–
Tel: 01483 570829
Fax: 01483 567268
email: bishop.ian@cofeguildford.org.uk

BRADFORD, Archdeacon of. See LEE, Ven David John

BRADFORD, Area Bishop of, HOWARTH, Rt Revd Dr Toby

BRADFORD, Dean of. LEPINE, Very Revd Jeremy

BRADLEY, Ven Peter David Douglas, B Th
Rectory 1A College Rd Up Holland Skelmersdale WN8 0PY [ARCHDEACON OF WARRINGTON; LIVERPOOL] *b* 1949 *educ* Brookfield Comp Sch; Nottm Univ; Ian Ramsey Coll; Linc Th Coll; *CV* C Up

Holland 1979–83; V H Spirit Dovecot 1983–94; Sec Dioc Bd of Min 1983–88; Sec Grp for Urban Min and Leadership 1984–88; Asst Dir In-Service Trg 1988–89; Dir CME from 1989; TR St Tho Up Holland from 1994; M BM Mission at Home Cttee; M Dioc Bd of Min; Hon Can Liv Cathl from 2000; Adn of Warrington from 2001/2
GS 1990–2010   *Tel:* 01695 622936
                                 Fax: 01695 625865
email: archdeacon@peterbradley.fsnet.co.uk

BRADLEY, Very Revd Peter Edward, MA
Sheffield Cathedral Church St Sheffield S1 1HA [DEAN OF SHEFFIELD] *b* 1964 *educ* R Belfast Academical Inst; Trin Hall Cam; Ripon Coll Cuddesdon; *CV* C St Mich & All A w St Edm Northampton 1988–90; Chapl Gonville & Caius Coll Cam 1990–95; TV St Mich Abingdon 1995–98; TV All SS High Wycombe 1998–2003, TR 2003; Dean of Sheffield from 2003; Fell Coll of Prchrs, Washington DC from 2006; Chair, Church and Community Fund from 2013   *Tel:* 0114 275 3434
                                      0114 263 6063
                                Fax: 0114 279 7412
email: dean@sheffield-cathedral.org.uk
2nd email: deanpeterbradley@gmail.com
Web: www.sheffield-cathedral.org.uk

BRADWELL, Area Bishop of. See WRAW, Rt Revd John

BRANDON, Revd Dr Beatrice, DD, MA, DMS, FRSA, FRSM
Clopton Manor Clopton Northants NN14 3DZ [ARCHBISHOPS' ADVISER FOR THE HEALING MINISTRY] *b* 1955 *educ* Heythrop Coll Lon; *CV* M Dioc Past Ctee 1992–2005; M Abps Millenium Adv Gp 1996–2000; Dioc Vacancy-in-See Ctee 1996–2003; M Folllow-up Steering Grp to Abps' Commn on the Reorganization of the National Institutions 1996–98; Chair Ho Laity and Lay Vc Chair Dioc Syn Peterb 1997–2003; Convener Ho Bps Healing Min Strg Gp 2000–07; M Cathl Coun Peterb Cathl 2001–05; Chair Chs Together for Healing 2004–08; M Peterb Dioc Bd of Patronage from 2006; Trustee Abp York Youth Trust 2008–11; Abps' Adv for Healing Min from 2007; Dr of Divinity (Lambeth Degree) 2012
GS 1995–2005   *Tel:* 01832 720346
                                 Fax: 01832 720446
email: beatrice@healingministry.org.uk

BRETT, Mr Justin Edward, MA, PGCE
[CHICHESTER] *b* 1971 *educ* Cheltenham Coll; Ex Coll Ox; *CV* Tchr Caldicott Sch 1995–2001; Head of English and RS, Brockhurst Sch 2001–2002; Policy Exec West Berkshire Counc 2003–04; Tchr, St Gabriel's Sch 2004–08; Head of Classics, St Aubyns Sch from 2008; Lay Chair Newbury Deanery 2006–08
GS 2005–   *Tel:* 07876 746074
email: justin.brett@yahoo.co.uk

BREWER, Mrs Rosalind Patricia Anne, BA, RGN
37 Greenstead Road Newby Scarborough YO12 6HN [YORK] *b* 1947 *CV* Qualified RGN 1968; Staff Nurse 1968–70; Night Sister 1972–78; Practice Nursing Sister 1982–90; Family Planning Sister 1984–2006; Senior Practice Nursing Sister/Mgr 1990–2006; Cytology Adv to Primary Care Trust 1995–2006; Nurse Tutor and Assessor 1998–2006; Dioc Prop Sub Cttee from 2010; Archbp's Counc from 2006; Patronage Brd from 2006; Vice Chair Dioc Pstrl & Miss Sub Cttee from 2004;York Dioc Syn from 2006; Lay Chair Scarborough Deanery Syn from 2005
GS 2010–   *Tel:* 01723 369731
email: ros.brewer@btinternet.com

BRIDEN, Rt Worshipful Timothy John, MA, LLB
Lamb Chambers Lamb Building Temple London EC4Y 7AS [VICAR-GENERAL OF CANTERBURY] *b* 1951 *educ* Ipswich Sch; Downing Coll Cam; *CV* Chancellor of Dioc of B&W from 1993; Chancellor of Dioc of Truro from 1998; Vicar-General of Canterbury from 2005; M Legal Adv Commn
GS 2005–   *Tel:* 020 7797 8300
                                 Fax: 020 7797 8308
email: info@lambchambers.co.uk

BRIGHTON AND LEWES, Archdeacon of.
[NOT APPOINTED AT TIME OF GOING TO PRESS]

BRINDLEY, Very Revd David Charles, BD, M Th, M Phil, AKC
The Deanery 13 Pembroke Rd Portsmouth PO1 2NS [DEAN OF PORTSMOUTH] *b* 1953 *educ* Wednesfield Gr Sch; K Coll Lon; *CV* C Epping, Chelms 1976–79; Lect, Coll of St Paul and St Mary, Cheltenham 1979–82; V Quorn and Dir of Clergy Trg, Leic 1982–86; Prin W of Eng Minl Trg Course 1987–94; TR Warwick 1994–2002; Dean of Portsm from 2002; Chair Portsm DAC from 2003; Sec and Treas Assoc of Engl Cathls 2005–09
GS 1985–87, 2004–2005, 2011–
                                 Tel: 023 9282 4400 (Home)
                                 023 9234 7605 (Office)
                                 Fax: 023 9229 5480
email: david.brindley@portsmouthcathedral.org.uk

BRISTOL, Archdeacon of. See FROUDE, Ven Christine Ann

BRISTOL, Bishop of. See HILL, Rt Revd Michael Arthur

BRISTOL, Dean of, see HOYLE, Very Revd Dr David Michael

BRITTON, Mr Andrew James Christie, BA, MSc
2 Shabden Park High Rd, Chipstead Coulsdon, Surrey CR5 3SF [ARCHBISHOPS' COUNCIL] *b* 1940 *educ* R Gr Sch, Newc-upon-Tyne; Oriel Coll Ox; Lon Sch of Economics; *CV* Economist HM Treasury 1968–82; Dir Nat Institute of Economic and Social Research 1982–95; Exec Sec Ch's Enquiry into Unemployment and the Future of Work 1995–97;

Chair S'wark Dioc Bd of Fin 2000–2007; Chair Abps' Coun Fin Cttee from 2007
GS 2007– *Tel:* 01737 553678

BRIXWORTH, Suffragan Bishop of. See HOLBROOK, Rt Revd John Edward

BROADBENT, Rt Revd Pete (Peter Alan) , MA
173 Willesden Lane Brondesbury London NW6 7YN [AREA BISHOP OF WILLESDEN; LONDON] *b* 1952 *educ* Merchant Taylors Sch Northwood; Jes Coll Cam; St Jo Coll Nottm; *CV* C St Nic Dur City 1977–80; C Em Holloway 1980–83; Chapl to N Lon Poly and Hon C St Mary Islington 1983–89; Bp's Chapl for Miss in Stepney 1980–89; Councillor and Chair of Planning Lon Boro of Islington 1982–89; V Trin St Mich Harrow 1989–95; AD Harrow 1994; Adn of Northolt 1995–2001; Bp of Willesden from 2001; M Dioc Commn 1989–92; M Panel of Chairmen GS 1990–92, 2009–14; M C of E Evang Coun 1984–95, from 2006; Chair Vacancy-in-See Cttee Regulation Wkg Pty 1991–93; M GS Stg Orders Cttee 1991–95; M Appts Sub-Cttee 1992–95; M CBF 1991–98; M GS Stg Cttee 1992–98; Chair GS Business Sub-Cttee 1996–98; Chair Elections Review Grp 1996–2000; Chair Lon Dioc Bd for Schs 1996–2006; Chair Memralife Gp (Spring Harvest/ICC); Chair Business Cttee 1999–2000; M AC 1999–2000; M City Parochial Foundn 1999–2003; M Urban Bps Panel from 2001; Trustee CUF 2002–11; Chair Coun St Jo Coll Nottm 2002–10; Pres W Lon YMCA from 2004; Chair Standards Cttee, Lon Boro Harrow 2006–2010; Eden Greater Lon Network from 2010; Bless Network from 2004; Vc Pres CPAS from 2009; Chair Dioc Strategic Policy Cttee from 2009; Acting Bp of Stepney 2010–11
GS 1985–2001; 2004– *Tel:* 020 8451 0189
07957 144674 (Mobile)
Fax: 020 8451 4606
email: bishop.willesden@btinternet.com
Web: Http://bishopofwillesden.blogspot.co.uk /
Facebook: Pete Broadbent
Twitter: @petespurs

BROCK, Mrs Kay (Katharine), BA Hons (Oxon), MBA
Lambeth Palace London SE1 7JU [CHIEF OF STAFF TO THE ARCHBISHOP OF CANTERBURY] *educ* Somerville Coll Ox; London Business Sch;; *CV* MAFF 1975–85 (Private Sec to Perm Sec 1980–81); Cons international trade 1985–88; Spicers Consulting Grp 1988–89; Dir PDN Ltd 1990–91; European Comm External Relations Directorate 1992–95; advisor KnowHow Fund and European Bank for Reconstruction and Development 1995–1999; Asst Private Sec to HM The Queen 1999–2002; Chief of Staff to the Lord Mayor of London 2004–09; Dir Ashridge Strategic Management Centre 2010; Sec for Public Affairs to Abp of Canterbury 2012–13; Chief of Staff to Abp of Canterbury from 2013 *Tel:* 020 7898 1292
email: kay.brock@lambethpalace.org.uk

BROMILOW, Dr Ian Geoffrey, BSc, MSc, Phd
The Old School Hilton Blandford Forum Dorset DT11 0DB [SALISBURY] *b* 1956 *educ* Tower Coll, Rainhill & Scarisbrick Hall Sch, Southport; UCL; ICL; Bris Univ; *CV* Country Chair, Shell Companies in Jordan & Iraq, Amman, Jordan, 2006–09; Country Chair, Shell Iraq, Dubai,UAE, 2005–06; Mging Dir, Shell/BP Kenya Ltd and Shell Tanzania, Nairobi, Kenya 2002–05; Gen Mgr, Shell Uganda and Shell Rwanda, 2000–02; Head Consumer Lubricants, Shell International, London, 1998–2000; Brand Mgr, Shell International, London, 1995–98; Marketing and Sales Mgr, SASLUCO (Shell Joint Venture), Jeddah, Saudi Arabia, 1991–95; Base oil Supply, Demand & Trading, Shell International, 1989–91; Oil Market Analyst, Shell International London, 1986–89; Math, Shell Rsrch, Amsterdam, The Netherlands, 1982–86; Mission and Stewardship Adv, Sarum; Gov, Dunbury Sch, Dorset; Trustee, Longmead Community, Milbourne St Andrew, Dorset
GS 2010– *Tel:* 01258 880044
email: igbromilow@gmail.com

BROMLEY AND BEXLEY, Archdeacon of. See WRIGHT, Ven Dr Paul

BROOKE, Revd David Martin, MA, PGCE
The Rectory Church Lane Redmarshall Stockton-on-Tees TS21 1ES [DURHAM] *b* 1958 *educ* Ferryhill Comp Sch; Selwyn Coll Cam; ULIE; SAOMC; *CV* Asst Master, Bedford Sch 1981–85; Marketing Mngr, Epson UK 1985–92; Marketing Mngr, Dell UK 1992–99; C Luton Lewsey St Hugh St Alb 1999–2000; NSM Sunnyside w Bourne End 2000–02; C 2002–04 V Bishopton w Gt Stainton Dur from 2004; R Redmarshall from 2004; R Grindon, Stillington and Wolviston 2004–13; R Grindon and Stillington 2013–2014; R Stockton Country Parish from 2014; P-in-c Billingham St Mary 2010–13; AD Stockton from 2007
GS 2010– *Tel:* 01740 630810
07967 326085
email: david@revd.co.uk

BROWN, Ven Andrew, BA, MA
St George's Vicarage 16 Devonshire Rd Douglas, Isle of Man IM2 3RB [ARCHDEACON OF MAN; SODOR AND MAN] *b* 1955 *educ* Haslingden Gr Sch; St Peters Coll Oxf; Ridley Hall Cam; *CV* C St Peter's Burnley 1980–83; P-in-c St Francis Brandlesholme 1983–86; P-in-c, V St Peters Ashton-under-Lyne 1986–96; V St Lukes Halliwell 1986–2003; Can Theologian Derby Cathl and Dioc CME Adv 2003–11; Adn of Man and V of St Georges Douglas from 2011
GS 2013– *Tel:* 01624 675430
07624 228100
email: archdeacon@sodorandman.im

BROWN, Mr Andrew Charles, B Sc, FRICS
Church House Great Smith St London SW1P 3AZ [SECRETARY, CHURCH COMMISSIONERS] *b* 1957 *educ* Ashmole Comp Sch; S Bank Poly; *CV* Healey &

Baker 1981–84; St Quintin 1984–94; Dep Sec and Chief Surveyor Ch Commrs 1994–2003, Sec from 2003; M Fin and Invest Ctee, Lionheart from 2007; M Allchurches Trust from 2008; Trustee and Chair the2:67project 2007–10; Trustee William Leech (Foundn) and Dir William Leech (Invest) from 2007; CEDR Accredited Mediator from 2012; Chair CMS Pensions Trust from 2013   *Tel:* 020 7898 1785
Fax: 020 7898 1131
email: andrew.brown@churchofengland.org

BROWN, Revd Dr Malcolm Arthur, MA, PhD, FHEA, FRSA
Church House Great Smith St London SW1P 3AZ [DIRECTOR, MISSION AND PUBLIC AFFAIRS DIVISION, ARCHBISHOPS' COUNCIL] *b* 1954 *educ* Eltham Coll; Oriel Coll Ox; Man Univ; Westcott Ho Cam; *CV* C Riverham w. Dunton Green, Roch 1979–83; TV and Ind Missioner, Southn City Centre, Winch 1983–91; Exec Sec William Temple Foundn 1991–2000; Hon C St Paul Heaton Moor, Man 1993–2000; Prin EAMTC 2000–05; Prin ERMC 2005–07; Dir MPA from 2007; M BSR Ind and Economic Affairs Cttee 1987–91; M BSR Soc, Economic and Ind Affairs Cttee 1997–2002; Th Consult Rev of Diocs, Pastl and Related Measures 2001–04; M Min Div Th Educ and Trg Cttee 2003–07; M Min Div Fin Panel 2006–07; Licensed to Dioc of Ely from 2011   *Tel:* 020 7898 1468
email: malcolm.brown@churchofengland.org

BRUINVELS, Canon Peter Nigel Edward, LLB, FRSA, FCIM, MCIJ, MCIPR
14 High Meadow Close St Paul's Rd West Dorking RH4 2LG [GUILDFORD] *b* 1950 *educ* St Jo Sch Leatherhead; Lon Univ; Inns of Court Sch of Law; *CV* MP Leic E 1983–87; Party Candidate The Wrekin 1997; Prin Peter Bruinvels Associates, Media Mgt and Public Affairs Consults; M Dioc Syn and Dorking Dny Syn from 1974; Freeman of City of Lon 1980; M Dios Commn 1991–96; M Legislative Cttee 1991–96 and from 2000, Dep Chair from 2010; News Broadcaster, Political Commentator and Freelance Journalist; Ch Commr from 1992, Pastl Cttee from 1993, Gov Ch Cmmrs from 1992; Mgt Adv Cttee 1999–2009; Ofsted and Section 48 SIAS RE Sch Insp from 1994; M DSS Child Support and Soc Security Appeals Tribunal 1994–99; Man Ed Bruinvels News & Media, Press and Broadcasting Agents; M Dioc Bd of Educ from 1994; M GS Bd of Educ 1996–2006; Co-opted M Surrey LEA 1997–2007; Gov Univ of York St Jo 1999–2007; Dir Ch Army and Chair Remuneration Cttee 1999–2004; Independent Lay Chair NHS Complaints Tribunal 1999–2004; M Clergy Discipline Review Grp from 1999; Chair Surrey Schs Organisation Cttee 2000–07; Court Member Univ of Sussex 2000–08; M Dearing Implementation Grp from 2001; County Field Officer (Surrey and Sussex) Royal Br Legion 2002–12; Dir E Elmbridge and Mid Surrey Primary Care Trust 2002–07; M Mgt Adv Cttee 1999–2009; Lay Can Guildf Cathl from 2002;

Vc-Pres and Chair Ho of Laity, Dioc Syn 2003–13; Guild CNC from 2003; M SE Veterans and War Pensions Cttee from 2003, Dep Chair from 2013; Chair Surrey Joint Services Charities Cttee from 2004; Chair Guildf Dioc Bd of Educ 2005–08, Vice Chair from 2008; Hon Sec Surrey Military Appeals Cttee from 2002; M Guildf Coll of Cans from 2002; M Cathls Fabric Commn for Eng from 2006; M Guildf Cathl Coun from 2006; Gov Whitelands Coll (Roehampton Univ) from 2007, Chair 2009–12; Dep Chair Nominations & Governance Cttee (Ch Commissioners) 2009–12; M Surrey SACRE from 2013; Regional Fundraiser SE ABF The Soldiers' Charity from 2013; Dir Guildf Dioc Educ Trust (GDET) from 2012; Chief Exec Surrey CC Civilian-Military Partnership Bd from 2013; M Church Commissioners Assets Cttee from 2014
GS 1985–   *Tel:* 01306 887082 (Home)
01306 887680 (Office)
07721 411688 (Mobile)
Fax: 0845 241 4821
email: canonpeterbruinvels@talk21.com
2nd email: pbruinvels@soldierscharity.org
Web: www.soldierscharity.org

BRYANT, Rt Revd Mark Watts, BA
Bishop's House 25 Ivy Lane Gateshead NE9 6QD [SUFFRAGAN BISHOP OF JARROW; DURHAM] *b* 1949 *educ* St Jo Sch Leatherhead; St Jo Coll Dur; Cuddesdon Th Coll; *CV* C Addlestone 1975–79; C St Jo Studley, Trowbridge 1979–83, V 1983–88; Chapl Trowbridge CFE 1979–83; DDO and Dir Vocations and Tr, Cov 1988–96; Hon Can Cov Cathl 1993–2001; TR Cov Caludon 1996–2001; AD Cov E 1999–2001; Adn of Coventry 2001–07; Can Res Cov Cathl 2006–07; Bp of Jarrow from 2007
GS 1998–2008   *Tel:* 0191 491 0917
email: bishop.of.jarrow@durham.anglican.org
Twitter: @BishopMark1

BUCKINGHAM, Archdeacon of. See GORHAM, Ven Karen Marisa

BUCKINGHAM, Area Bishop of. See WILSON, Rt Revd Alan Thomas Lawrence

BUCKLER, Very Revd Philip John Warr, MA
The Deanery 11 Minster Yard Lincoln LN2 1PJ [DEAN OF LINCOLN] *b* 1949 *educ* Highgate Sch; St Pet Coll Ox; Cuddesdon Coll; *CV* C St Pet Bushey Heath 1972–75; Chapl Trin Coll Cam 1975–81; Sacr and Min Can St Paul's Cathl 1981–86; V Hampstead 1987–99; AD N Camden 1993–98; Can Res St Paul's Cathl 1999–2007, Treas 2000–07; Dean of Lincoln from 2007
Tel: 01522 561611
Fax: 01522 561603
email: dean@lincolncathedral.com

BULL, Prof John W, BSc, PhD, DSc, Eur Ing, C Eng, FICE, FIStructE, FCIHT, FIHE, FIMMM
Gable Ends 11 Glebe Mews Bedlington NE22 6LJ [NEWCASTLE] *b* 1944 *educ* Farnborough Gr Sch;

Univ of Chester; Cardiff Univ; *CV* Tchr ILEA 1966–68; Engineer/Chartered Engineer Dur Co Coun 1974–79; Newc Univ 1979–2010, Prof of Civil Eng, Brunel Univ from 2010; M Dioc Syn from 1988; M Bp's Coun from 1988; Vc Pres Dioc Syn 1994–2006; Chair Dioc Bd of Educ 1991–97; Lay Chair Bedlington Dny Syn 1990–97; Dioc Bd of Educ 2004–10; M Coun Nat Soc from 2007
GS 1995–   *Tel:* 01895 267916 (Office)
                                   07710 200416 (Mobile)
                              Fax: 01865 269782
              email: John.Bull@brunel.ac.uk

BULLOCK, Ven Sarah Ruth, BA(Hons), BA(Hons) (Dunelm), PGCert Theol
1 New Lane Huntington York YO32 9NU [ARCH-DEACON OF YORK] *b* 1964 *educ* Fallowfield C of E Sch; Univ of Surrey; Cranmer Hall, St. John's Coll, Dur; *CV* English Tchr, Cheadle Hulme Sch 1986–90; Asst Dioc Yth Off, Man 1986–90; AC St Paul, Kersal Moor w St Andrew, Man, 1993–98; P-in-c St Edmund, Whalley Range 1998–2004; St. James' w St. Clement, Moss Side, 1999–2004; R United Benefice of St. Edmund, Whalley Range & St. James' w St. Clement, Man 2004–13; Hon Can Man Cathl from 2007; Bps Adv Womans Min, Man 2009–13; Dean City & Borough Man 2010–13; M Man Urban Regen & Sem Grp Commiss Urban Life & Faith, 1999–2009; M Bps Adv Grp Sexuality 2004; Chair Discipleship & Min Training Cttee, Man, 2005–13; Bps Adv Womens Min, Man 2009–13; M Man Syn & DBF 2009–13; M Bps Coun 2010; M Min Devlp Review T, Man, 2010–13
GS 2010–13   *Tel:* 01904 758241
                                   07432 289895
              email: adyk@yorkdiocese.org

BURNLEY, Suffragan Bishop of. [NOT APPOINTED AT TIME OF GOING TO PRESS]

BURRAGE, Mr Paul, BSc, FCA
Church House Great Smith St London SW1P 3AZ [DIRECTOR OF ACCOUNTING SERVICES, NATIONAL CHURCH INSTITUTIONS] *b* 1952 *educ* Reading Sch; Sir William Borlase's Sch; Newcastle Univ; *CV* Fin Man to Fin Dir in various internat Freight Forwarding Companies 1979–91; Fin Dir Heating Oil and Petroleum Distributor 1991–92; Consult, Dir of Fin and Resources British Red Cross 1993–2004; Head of Fin Refugee Coun 2005–05; Chief Accountant NCIs 2005–07; (Acting) Dir of Fin Accounting NCIs 2008–09; Dir Accounting Services from 2009   *Tel:* 020 7898 1677
                              Fax: 020 7898 1770
         email: paul.burrage@churchofengland.org

BURRIDGE, Revd Professor Richard Alan, MA, Ph D, PGCE, PGDip Th, FKC
King's College London Strand London WC2R 2LS [UNIVERSITIES, LONDON] *b* 1955 *educ* Bris Cathl Sch; Univ Coll Ox; Nottm Univ; St Jo Coll Nottm; *CV* Classics Master and Ho Tutor Sevenoaks Sch

1978–82; C SS Pet and Paul Bromley 1985–87; Chapl and pt Lect in Depts of Th and Classics & Ancient History Univ of Ex 1987–94; Dean of K Coll Lon from 1994; M Academic Bd NTMTC 1994–2008; Chair Chr Evidence Soc from 1994; Chair Eric Symes Abbott Memorial Fund from 1994; M Studiorum Novi Testamenti Societas from 1995; M SST from 1995; M SBL from 1995; ABM External Moderator to SW Min Tr Course 1995–99; Chair Min Div Educ Validatory Panel 1998–2004; M Min Div TETC 1998–2004; M CECC; Commr to Bp of High Veld 1996–2009; GS Rep PIM Consultation to Province of W Africa 1997; Adv and Writer for Nat Millennium Experience Co and Greenwich Dome 1998–99; M Vote 1 Min Div Wkg Party 1999–2000; M Review Grp on Structure and Funding of Ordination Tr 2000–03; FKC 2002; Chair Bp of S'wark's Theol Grp 2004–2009; rep Abp of Cant and Angl Communion at Second World Congress for Pastl Care of Catholic Foreign Students, Rome, Dec 2005; M Academic Board St Mellitus College from 2008; M Ethical Investment Adv Gp (Ch Commns' rep) from 2008; Prof of Bibl Interpretation at K Coll Lon from 2008; Woods Fell (Visiting Prof) at Virginia Theol Seminary, Alexandria VA, USA 2009; Dep Chr Ethical Investment Adv Gp from 2010; Visiting Fellow Trinity Coll Melbourne Australia from 2013
GS 1994–   *Tel:* 020 7848 2333
              email: richard.burridge@kcl.ac.uk
                   2nd email: dean@kcl.ac.uk
                   Web: www.kcl.ac.uk/dean

BURROWS, Mr Gerald David, B Sc, M Sc, T Cert
3 Hall Rd Fulwood Preston PR2 9QD [BLACKBURN] *b* 1942 *educ* Wellington Gr Sch; Univ Coll of N Wales, Bangor; *CV* Scientific Officer Rutherford High Energy Lab 1967–69; Lect Grimsby Coll of Tech 1969–71; Sen Lect Blackb Coll from 1971
GS 1990–   *Tel:* 01772 719159
         email: gerald.burrows@talk21.com

BURROWS, Rt Revd Peter, BTh
Doncaster House Church Lane Fishlake Doncaster DN7 5JW [SUFFRAGAN BISHOP OF DONCASTER; SHEFFIELD] *b* 1955 *educ* Spondon Ho Sec Sch; Derby Coll of FE; Sarum and Wells Th Coll; *CV* C Baildon 1983–87; R Broughton Astley 1993–93; P-in-c Stoney Stanton w Croft 1993–95; TR Broughton Astley and Croft w Stoney Stanton 1995–2000; RD Guthlaxton I 1994–2000; DDO and Par Development Officer 1996–2000; M Dioc Syn; M Vacancy-in-See Cttee; M DAC; Coord Dioc Tm Forum; M Bp's Coun; Hon Can Leic Cathl; Dep Dir Min from 2002; Dir Min 2003–05; Adn Leeds 2005–11; Hon Can Ripon Cathl 2005–11; Bp of Doncaster from 2012; Chair Min and Training Devel Grp; Chair One City Projects and Oastler Centre; Trustee Children's Internat Summer Villages; M Inst of Directors
GS 2010–12   *Tel:* 01302 846610
         email: bishoppeter@bishopofdoncaster.org.uk

BURTON-JONES, Ven Simon David, MA (Hons); BTh; MA

The Archdeaconry Kings Orchard, The Precinct Rochester, Kent ME1 1TG [ARCHDEACON OF ROCHESTER] *b* 1962 *educ* Fleetwood High Sch; Emmanuel Coll Cam; St John's Coll Nottm; *CV* TC St Peter's Darwen w St Paul's Hoddlesdon 1993–96; C St Mark's Biggin Hill 1996–98; V St Mary's Bromley 1998–2005; R St Nic Chislehurst 2005–10; Adn of Roch from 2010
Tel: 01634 813533 (Home)
01634 560000 (Office)
email: archdeacon.rochester@rochester.anglican.org
Web: www.simonburton-jones.com

BUSH, Very Revd Roger Charles, BA

14 St Mary's Street Truro TR1 2AF [DEAN OF TRURO] *b* 1956 *educ* Fakenham Gr Sch; K Coll Lon; Coll of the Resurr, Mirfield; *CV* C Newbold, Derby 1986–90; TV Parish of the Resurr, Leic 1990–94; TR Redruth w. Lanner & Treleigh, Truro 1994–2004; Can Chan, Truro Cathl 2004–06; Adn of Cornwall 2006–12; Dean of Truro from 2012
GS 2004–
Tel: 01872 276782
Fax: 01872 277788
email: dean@trurocathedral.org.uk

BUTCHER, Dr Jackie (Jacqueline Anne), MA, M Sc, Ph D

10 Vernon Rd Totley Rise Sheffield S17 3QE [SHEFFIELD] *b* 1965 *educ* Wootton Upper Sch; Newnham Coll Cam; Sussex Univ; Leic Univ; *CV* Rsch Associate 1992–95; full-time mother 1995–2000; M Dioc Bd Faith & Justice; Bp's Adv in World Development Issues
GS 2000–
Tel: 0114 262 1293
email: jackie.butcher@cantab.net

BUTLER, Rt Revd Paul Roger, BA (Jt Hons) English and History; BA Oxon Theol

Auckland Castle Bishop Auckland DL14 7NR [BISHOP OF DURHAM] *b* 1955 *educ* Kingston Grammar Sch; Nottm Univ; Wycliffe Hall; *CV* C All Saints w Holy Trinity, Wandsworth 1983–87; Scripture Union Inner Lon Evang 1987–92; Dep Head of Miss 1992–94; NSM St Paul's, East Ham (Chelmsford) 1988–94; P-in-c St Mary w St Stephen Walthamstow (Chelmsford) 1994–97; St Luke, Walthamstow 1994–97; TR of Walthamstow 1997–2004; AD Waltham Forest 2000–04; Can St Paul's Byumba, Rwanda from 2001; Bp of Southampton 2004–2009; Bp of Southwell and Nottm 2009–13; Chair of CMS 2008–10; Jt Chair Churches Safeguarding Advisory Committee from 2011; Pres Scripture Union from 2011; Bp of Durham from 2014Bp of Southwell and Nottingham from 2009
GS 2009–
Tel: 01388 602576 07939 213795
email: bishop.of.durham@durham.anglican.org
Web: bishoppaulbutler.wordpress.com
Twitter: @bishoppaulb

BUTLER, Canon Simon, BSc, DTS, MA

St Mary's Vicarage 32 Vicarage Crescent London SW11 3LD [SOUTHWARK] *b* 1964 *educ* Bourne-

mouth Sch; UEA; Britannia R Naval Coll; St Jo Coll Nottm; *CV* C Chandler's Ford, Winch 1992–94; C St Jos Worker Northolt, Lon 1994–97; V Immanuel and St Andr Streatham, S'wark 1997–2004; AD Streatham 2002–04; P-in-c and acting TR Sanderstead TM, S'wark from 2004, TR 2006–11; V St Mary Battersea from 2011; Chair S'wark Dioc Liturg Cttee; Vice-Chair SEITE Coun
GS 2005–
Tel: 020 7228 8141
07941 552407
email: simon.butler7@gmail.com

BUTTERFIELD, Ven David John, B Mus, Dip Th, DPS

2A Minster Court York YO1 7JJ [ARCHDEACON FOR GENEROUS GIVING AND STEWARDSHIP; YORK] *b* 1952 *educ* Belle Vue Boys Gr Sch Bradf; R Holloway Coll Lon Univ; St Jo Coll Nottm; *CV* C Ch Ch Southport 1977–81; Min St Thos CD Aldridge 1981–91; V St Mich Lilleshall w. St Mary Sheriffhales 1991–2002; V St Mich Lilleshall w. St Jo Muxton and St Mary Sheriffhales 2002–07; M BM 1995–96; RD Edgmond 1997–98; RD Edgmond and Shifnal 1999–2006; M Bp's Coun (Lich) 1994–2006; Chair Dioc Syn Ho of Clergy 2003–06; Adn of E Riding 2007–14; Adn for Generous Giving and Stewardship from 2014; Res Can York Minster from 2014
GS 1990–2005
Tel: 01904 557278
email: archdeacondavid@yorkminster.org

BUTTERY, Revd Graeme, BA, MA

St Oswald's Clergy House Brougham Terrace Hartlepool TS24 8EY [DURHAM] *b* 1962 *educ* Dame Allan's Boys Sch Newc; York Univ; Newc Univ; St Steph Ho Th Coll; *CV* C Peterlee 1988–91; C Sunderland, TM 1991–92; TV Sunderland, TM 1992–94; V St Lawr the Martyr Horsley Hill 1994–2005; V St Oswald Hartlepool from 2005; Can Dur Cathl from 2010
GS 1995–
Tel: 01429 273201
email: G_BUTTERY@sky.com

CAMBRIDGE, Archdeacon of. HUGHES, Ven Alexander

CAMPBELL, Dr (John) Graham, Ph D, B Sc, FCA

18 Eaglesfield Hartford Northwich CW8 1NQ [CHESTER] *b* 1942 *educ* Man Gr Sch, Birm Univ; *CV* Birm Univ Rsch Chemist ICI 1966–71; Student Accountant Worth & Co 1971–74; Audit Sen Spicer & Pegler 1974–76; Accountant then Commercial Mgr Br Nuclear Fuels plc 1976–2003; M Bp's Coun from 1998; M Dioc Fin and Cen Services Cttee from 1997; M Foxhill Dioc Conf Cen Coun from 1998; M C of E Pensions Bd from 2004; Treas C of E Evang Coun 2005–10
GS 2000–
Tel: 01606 75849
email: j.graham.campbell@gmail.com

CANTERBURY, Archbishop of. See WELBY, Most Revd Justin Portal

CANTERBURY, Archdeacon of. See WATSON, Ven Sheila Anne

CANTERBURY, Dean of. See WILLIS, Very Revd Robert Andrew

CAPON, Canon Dr Peter Charles, B Sc, Ph D
137 Birchfields Rd Manchester M14 6PJ [MANCHESTER] *b* 1944 *educ* Kimbolton Sch; Southn Univ; Cam Univ; Man Univ; *CV* Sen Lect in Computer Science Man Univ 1976–2004; rtd; Rdr at H Trin Rusholme, Manch from 1991; Lay Chair Manch Dioc Syn from 2011; Hon Lay Canon Manch Cathl from 2012
GS 1995–   *Tel:* 0161 225 5970
          email: peter.c.capon@gmail.com

CARLISLE, Archdeacon of. See ROBERTS, Ven Kevin Thomas

CARLISLE, Bishop of. See NEWCOME, Rt Revd James William Scobie

CARLISLE, Dean of. See BOYLING, Very Revd Mark Christopher

CARTWRIGHT, Revd Paul, BA, PGCE, MA, MifL
St Peter's Vicarage 1 Osborne Mews Barnsley S70 1UU [WEST YORKSHIRE AND THE DALES] *b* 1971 *educ* Hemsworth H Sch; Leeds Met Univ; Univ of Huddersfield; Leeds Univ; Coll of the Resurrection, Mirfield; *CV* Police Officer, West Yorkshire Police, 1990–2006; Major Incident/Crime Family Liasion Officer, West Yorkshire Police 2002–06; Equalities & Diversity Trainer, West Yorkshire Police 2003–06; Asst Convenor Wakef Fellowship of Vocation from 2008; Barnsley Deanery Vocations Off from 2010; AC St Helen's Church, Athersley 2008–10; AC St John the Evangelist, Carlton 2010–11; P-in-c St Peter the Apostle and St John the Baptist, Barnsley from 2011; Chpl to FE and HE, Barnsley from 2011; Police Chapl to West Yorkshire Police from 2010; GS Rep on CMEAC from 2011
GS 2010–   *Tel:* 01226 282220
                   07852 174303
          email: fr.paul.cartwright@gmail.com

CASTLE, Rt Revd Dr Brian Colin, BA, MA, Ph D
Bishop's Lodge 48 St Botolph's Road Sevenoaks TN13 3AG [SUFFRAGAN BISHOP OF TONBRIDGE; ROCHESTER] *b* 1949 *educ* Wilson's Gr Sch, Camberwell; Univ Coll London; Cuddesdon Coll Ox; Univ of Ox; Univ of Birm; *CV* Asst C St Nic Sutton 1977; Asst C St Pet Limpsfield, S'wark 1977–81; P-in-c Chingola, Chililabombwe and Solwezi, N Zambia 1981–4; Vis Lect Ecum Inst, Bossey, Switzerland 1984–5; V N Petherton and Northmoor Green 1985–92; Vc Prin and Dir of Pastl Studies Ripon Coll Cuddesdon 1992–2001; Bp of Tonbridge and Hon Can Roch Cathl from 2002; Abps' Adv for Alternative Spiritualities

and New Relig Movts; Co-chair Miss Thel Adv Grp; M Faith & Order Commn
                   Tel: 01732 456070
                   Fax: 01732 741449
     email: bishop.tonbridge@rochester.anglican.org

CAWDELL, Preb Simon Howard, BA, MA CTM
The Rectory 16 East Castle Street Bridgnorth Shropshire WV16 4AL [HEREFORD] *b* 1965 *educ* Kings Sch, Worcester; Univ Coll Dur; Kings Coll, Lon; Ridley Hall, Cam; *CV* Investment Analyst; Coast Securities Ltd, Lon 1987–91; C St. Philip, Cheam Common S'wark 1994–98; V Claverley & Tuck Hill 1998–2010; TR Bridgnorth & P-in-c Morville w Aston Ayre, Acton Round& Monkhopton w Upton Cresset from 2010; Rural Dean of Bridgnorth 2009–13; Dioc Syn from 2000–06, from 2009; Chair Ho Clergy form 2012; Bp's Coun from 2012; Dioc Brd Fin from 1999 (Exec M 2007–10), Vice Chair Benefice Bldgs Cttee 2001–07, Chair Dioc Investment Cttee 2007–10; Preb Heref from 2014
GS 2010–   *Tel:* 01746 761573
          email: s.h.cawdell@btinternet.com
     Web: www.bridgnorthteamministry.org.uk

CHAFFEY, Ven Jonathan Paul Michael, BA, MA, QHC
Valiant Building HQ Air Command RAF High Wycombe Bucks HP14 4UE [ARCHDEACON FOR THE ROYAL AIR FORCE] *b* 1962   *Tel:* 01494 493802
     email: airchapservs-chaplaininchief@mod.uk

CHANDLER, Ven Ian Nigel, BD, AKC, CMTh
St Mark's House 46a Cambridge Road Ford Plymouth PL2 1PU [ARCHDEACON OF PLYMOUTH] *b* 1965 *educ* Bishopsgarth Sch Stockton-on-Tees; Stockton Sixth Form Coll; K Coll Lon; Chich Th Coll; *CV* C All SS Hove 1992–96; Dom Chapl to Bp of Chich 1996–2000; V St Rich Haywards Heath 2000–10; RD Cuckfield 2004–06; M Dioc Syn from 2000; M Dioc Fin Cttee 2004–07; Adn of Plymouth from 2010   *Tel:* 01752 202401
          email: archdeacon.of.plymouth@
                   exeter.anglican.org

CHAPMAN, Professor Mark David, MA, DipTh, DPhil
1 Church Close Cuddesdon Oxford OX44 9HD [OXFORD] *b* 1960 *educ* St Bartholomew's Sch, Newbury; Trin Coll Ox; Munich Univ; OMC; *CV* Sir Henry Stephenson Fellow, Univ Sheffield 1989–91; NSM Dorchester Team Ministry, 1994–99; Lect Systematic Th Ripon Coll Cuddesdon from 1992; Vice-Prin, Ripon Coll Cuddesdon from 2001; Visiting Prof, Oxford Brookes Univ from 2009; Rdr Modern Th, Ox Univ from 2008; NSM Assoc P Wheatley Team Ministry w spec respons Cuddesdon, Garsington & Horspath from 1999
GS 2010–   *Tel:* 01865 874310
                   01865 877405
                   07790 524494
          email: mark.chapman@rcc.ac.uk

CHAPMAN, Mrs Mary Madeline, BA;
CHARTERED DIR; DIP CIM
22 Addison Grove London W4 1ER [ARCHBISHOPS'
COUNCIL] *b* 1949 *educ* Sutton High Sch; Univ
Bristol; *CV* Marketing Exec, British Tourist
Authority; Div Dir Nicholas Kiwi; Marketing Dir
L'Oreal UK; Dir Biotherm; Dir Helena Rubenstein;
Dir Personnel Operations and Management
Development L'Oreal UK 1990–93; Chief Exec
Investors in People 1993-98; Chief Exec CMI 1998–
2008; M Coun Girls' Day School Trust from 2004;
Non-exec Dir Royal Mint from 2008; Com-
missioner National Lottery from 2008; Chair Inst
Customer Service from 2009; M Coun Brunel Univ
from 2009; M Min Coun   *Tel:* 020 8994 4934
                                          07919 415994
        email: mary@marychapman.org

CHARING CROSS, Archdeacon of. [NOT
APPOINTED AT TIME OF GOING TO PRESS]

CHARMAN, Canon Jane Ellen Elizabeth, MA
4 The Sidings Downton Salisbury SP5 3QZ [SALIS-
BURY] *b* 1960 *educ* Newtead Wood Sch, Orpington;
St John's Coll Dur; Selwyn Coll Cam; Westcott
House Th Coll; *CV* C, St George's Tuffley w
St Margaret's Whaddon, Glouc, 1985–90; Chapl,
Clare Coll Cam, 1990–95; R Duxford St Peter & V
St Mary & St John Hinxton & St Mary Magdalene
Ickleton, Ely, 1995–2004; Rural Dean Shelford
Deanery, Ely, 2003–04; Dir Lrning for Disciple-
ship and Ministry, Salisbury, from 2004; Dioc
Rep South Central Regional Training Partnership
Management Brd from 2006; Chair South Central
Regional Training Partnership CMD Co-ord Grp
from 2006; Chair South Central Regional Training
Partnership Pioneer Ministry Co-ord Grp from
2008; M National CMD panel from 2009; M
STETS Brd of Studies from 2009; Bp's Advisor for
selection of candidates for ordination from 2012
GS 2010–   *Tel:* 01725 512620
                          07814 899657
        email: jane.charman@salisbury.anglican.org

**CHARTRES, Rt Revd and Rt Hon Richard John
Carew ,** KCVO, DD, FSA
The Old Deanery Dean's Court London EC4V 5AA
[BISHOP OF LONDON] *b* 1947 *educ* Hertf Gr Sch;
Trin Coll Cam; Cuddesdon Th Coll; Linc Th Coll;
CV C St Andr Bedford 1973–75; Bp's Dom Chapl
1975–80; Chapl to Abp of Cant 1980–84; P-in-c
St Steph w St Jo Westmr 1984–85; V 1986–92;
DDO 1985–92; Prof Div Gresham Coll 1986–92;
Six Preacher Cant Cathl 1991–96; Bp of Stepney
1992–95; Bp of Lon from 1995; Dean of HM
Chapels Royal and PC 1996; Chair Ch Heritage
Forum; Ch Commrs from 1999; M Centr Cttee
CEC; M Jt Liaison Grp between CEC and Coun of
Eur Catholic Bps' Confs; Chair Ch Buildings
Cttee from 2003; Acting Chair Ch Commrs Bd
from 1999; Chair Shrink the Footprint from 2004
GS 1995–   *Tel:* 020 7248 6233
                          Fax: 020 7248 9721
        email: bishop@londin.clara.co.uk

CHAVE, Preb Brian Philip, BA (OU)
The Vicarage Vowles Close Hereford HR4 0DF
[HEREFORD] *b* 1951 *educ* Winslade Sch Ex; Seale-
Hayne Agric Coll Devon; Trinity Coll Bris; *CV* C
Cullompton w Kentisbeare and Blackborough,
Ex 1984–87; TV Oakmoor Tm Min, Ex 1987–93;
C for Agric, Heref 1993–96; Comms Officer and
Bp's Staff Officer (Dom Chapl), Heref 1997–2001;
TV W Heref Tm Min from 2001; Chair Bd of Govs
Whitecross High Sch, Heref
GS 2008–   *Tel:* 01432 273086 (Office)
        email: brianchave@btinternet.com

CHEETHAM, Rt Revd Richard Ian, MA, PGCE,
Cert Theol, PhD
*Kingston Episcopal Area Office 620 Kingston Road
Raynes Park SW20 8DN* [AREA BISHOP OF KING-
STON; SOUTHWARK] *b* 1955 *educ* Kingston Gr Sch;
Ch Ch Coll Ox; Ripon Coll Cuddesdon; King;'
Coll London; *CV* C H Cross Fenham 1987–90;
V St Aug of Cant Limbury, Luton 1990–99; RD
Luton 1995–98; Adn of St Alb 1999–2002; Bp of
Kingston from 2002; Co-Chair Nat Chr Muslim
Forum 2010–12; Anglican President Nat Chr
Muslim Forum, 2012 onwards; M Roehampton
Univ Coun 2006–12; ex-Chair C of E Continuing
Ministerial Devel; Chair S'wark Dioc Bd of Educ;
Chair British Regional Committee of St Georges
College Jerusalem 2013 onwards; Whitelands
Professorial Fellow in Christian Theology and
Contemporary Issues, Univ Roehampton; Hon
Research Fellow, King's Coll London; President
YMCA (London South West), Patron Fircroft
Trust   *Tel:* 020 8545 2443
        email: bishop.richard@southwark.anglican.org
        Web: www.bishoprichardcheetham.com

**CHELMSFORD, Bishop of. See COTTRELL,
Rt Revd Stephen Geoffrey**

**CHELMSFORD, Dean of. See HENSHALL,
Very Revd Nicholas James**

**CHELMSFORD, Archdeacon of. LOWMAN,
Ven David**

**CHELTENHAM, Archdeacon of, see
SPRINGETT, Ven Robert,**

**CHESSUN, Rt Revd Christopher Thomas
James,** MA
*Trinity House 4 Chapel Court Borough High Street
London SE1 1HW* [BISHOP OF SOUTHWARK] *b* 1956
educ Hampton Gr Sch; Univ Coll Ox; Westcott
Ho Cam; *CV* Asst C St Mich and AA Sandhurst
1983–87; Sen C St Mary Portsea 1987–99; Chapl
and Min Can St Paul's Cathl 1989–93; R Stepney,
St Dunstan and All SS 1993–2001; AD Tower
Hamlets 1997–2001; Adn of Northolt 2001–05; M
Dioc Syn 2001–05; Bp of Woolwich 2005–11; Bp

for Urban Life and Faith from 2010; Bp of S'wark from 2011 *Tel:* 020 7939 9420 (Office)
020 8769 3256 (Home)
Fax: 0843 2906 894
email: bishop.christopher@
southwark.anglican.org

CHESTER, Archdeacon of, see GILBERTSON, Ven Michael Robert,

CHESTER, Bishop of. See FORSTER, Rt Revd Peter Robert

CHESTER, Dean of. See McPHATE, Very Revd Prof Gordon Ferguson

CHESTERFIELD, Archdeacon of. See WILSON, Ven Christine Louise

CHICHESTER, Archdeacon of. See McKITTRICK, Ven Douglas Henry

CHICHESTER, Bishop of. See WARNER, Rt Revd Martin Clive

CHICHESTER, Dean of. [NOT APPOINTED AT TIME OF GOING TO PRESS]

CLACK, Mr Jeremy William James, MMATH, FIA
62 Whitemoor Road Kenilworth Warwickshire CV8 2BP [TRUSTEE MEMBER OF CHURCH OF ENGLAND PENSIONS BOARD] *b* 1981 *educ* King Edward VI Sch Southampton; Univ of Warwick; *CV* Actuarial consultant; Ch Commisioner from 2012: M C of E Pensions Bd from 2012 *Tel:* 07779 639381
email: jwjclack@gmail.com

CLARK, Rt Revd Jonathan Dunnett, BA, M Litt, MA
St Matthew's House 100 George Street Croydon Surrey CR0 1PE [AREA BISHOP OF CROYDON; SOUTHWARK] *b* 1961 *educ* Ex Univ; Bris Univ; Southn Univ; Trin Coll Bris; *CV* C Stanwix, Carl 1988–92; Chapl Bris Univ 1992–93; Dir of Studies S Diocs Minl Tr Scheme 1994–97; Chapl Lon Metrop Univ 1997–2003; AD Islington 1999–2003; R St Mary Stoke Newington 2003–12; P-in-c Brownswood Park 2004–11; Area Bp Croydon from 2012; M Adv Coun on Relations of Bps and Religious Communities from 2014
GS 2005–2010 *Tel:* 020 8256 9630
020 8686 1822
07968 845698 (Mobile)
Fax: 020 8256 9631
email: bishop.jonathan@southwark.anglican.org
Web: http://clarkinholyorders.wordpress.com
Twitter: @bishopofcroydon

CLARK, Revd Jonathan Jackson, MA
St George's Church Great George Street Leeds LS1 3BR [WEST YORKSHIRE AND THE DALES] *b* 1957 *educ* St Peters Sch, York; Linc Coll, Ox; Ridley, Cam; *CV* C, St Lukes, Princess Drive, Liv 1984–87; C,

St Johns and St Marks, Clacton-on-sea 1987–92; V, St Simon, Shepherds Bush, London 1993–2003; Area Dean, Hammersmith and Fulham 1996–2001; R St George's Leeds from 2003; Chair of St George's Crypt Trustees from 2005
GS 2010– *Tel:* 0113 243 8498
email: jonathan.clark@stgeorgesleeds.org.uk

CLARKE, Very Revd John Martin, MA, BD
The Dean's Lodgings 25 The Liberty Wells BA5 2SZ [DEAN OF WELLS; BATH AND WELLS] *b* 1952 *educ* W Buckland Sch; Hertf Coll Ox; New Coll Edin; Edin Th Coll; *CV* C Ascen Kenton, Newc 1976–79; Prec St Ninian's Cathl, Perth 1979–82; Info Officer and Communications Adv to GS of Scottish Episcopal Ch 1982–87; Philip Usher Memorial Sch, Greece 1987–88; V St Mary Battersea 1989–96; Prin Ripon Coll Cuddesdon 1997–2004; Dean of Wells from 2004
Tel: 01749 670278
email: dean@wellscathedral.uk.net

CLARKE, Canon Professor Michael Gilbert, CBE, DL, BA, MA, DLitt, D Univ
Millington House 15 Lansdowne Crescent Worcester WR3 8JE [WORCESTER] *b* 1944 *educ* Qu Eliz Gr Sch Wakef; Sussex Univ; *CV* Lect in Politics Edin Univ 1969–75; Dep Dir Policy Planning Lothian Regional Coun 1975–81; Dir Local Government Tr Bd 1981–90; Chief Exec Local Government Mgt Bd 1990–93; Hd of Sch of Public Policy Birm Univ 1993–98; Pro-Vc Chan Birm Univ from 1998, Vc-Prin 2003–08; Lay Can and Chapter Member Worc Cathl 2001–10; Canon Emeritus 2010; M Diocs Commn from 2008, Chair from 2011; M Panel of Chairs from 2009
GS 1990–93, 1995– *Tel:* 01905 617634
email: michael.clarkeinworcester@btinternet.com

CLEVELAND, Archdeacon of. [NOT APPOINTED AT TIME OF GOING TO PRESS]

COCHRANE, Revd Philip Andrew, BA
The Parish Office West Street Fareham PO16 0EL [PORTSMOUTH] *b* 1970 *educ* Coleraine Acd Insti; Reading Univ; Trin Coll Bris; *CV* Customer service & sales w Equitable Life & Clerical Medl, 1992–2001; Buckinghamshire County Councillor, 1997–2001; Pensions Consult & Head of Reward Consulting w Jardine Lloyd Thompson Benefit Solutions, 2002–2004; AC, Parish of Holy Trin w St Columba, Fareham 2007–09; Bp Portsm's Adv Porvoo, from 2008; TV Parish of Holy Trin w St Columba, Fareham from 2009; M Dioc Litt & Worship Adv Grp from 2008; M Dioc Syn from 2009; M Bp's Counc from 2010
GS 2010– *Tel:* 01329 318665
email: Philip@scfareham.org.uk

COCKETT, Ven Elwin Wesley, BA
86 Aldersbrook Rd Manor Park London E12 5DH [ARCHDEACON OF WEST HAM; CHELMSFORD] *b* 1959 *educ* St Paul's Cathl Choir Sch; Forest Sch,

Snaresbrook; Aston Trg Scheme; Oak Hill Coll; *CV* C St Chad, Chadwell Heath 1991–94; C-in-c St Paul, Harold Hill 1994–95, P-in-c 1995–97, V 1997–2000; TR Billericay and Little Burstead TM 2000–07; RD Basildon 2004–07; Adn of West Ham from 2007; Club Chapl West Ham United Football Club 1992–2011   *Tel:* 020 8989 8557
Fax: 020 8530 1311
email: a.westham@chelmsford.anglican.org

COCKSWORTH, Rt Revd Dr Christopher John,
BA (Hons), PhD, PGCE, Hon DD
Bishop's House 23 Davenport Rd Coventry CV5 6PW [BISHOP OF COVENTRY] *b* 1959 *educ* Forest Sch for boys, Horsham; Univ of Man; Didsbury Sch of Educ; St John's Coll, Nottm; *CV* Asst C Ch Ch Epsom 1988–92; Chapl Royal Holloway Univ of Lon 1992–96; Dir S Theol Educ and Training Scheme 1996–2001; Prin Ridley Hall Cam 2001–08; Bp Cov from 2008
GS 2008–   *Tel:* 024 7667 2244
Fax: 024 7610 0535
email: bishop@bishop-coventry.org
Web: www.dioceseofcoventry.org

COLCHESTER, Archdeacon of. See COOPER, Ven Annette Joy

COLCHESTER, Area Bishop of. See MORRIS, Rt Revd Roger Anthony Brett

COLES, Preb Stephen Richard, MA, BA
The Cardinal's Hat 25 Romilly Rd Finsbury Park London N4 2QY [LONDON] *b* 1949 *educ* Latymer Upper Sch Hammersmith; Univ Coll Ox; Trin Hall Cam; Leeds Univ; Coll of the Resurrection, Mirfield; *CV* C St Mary Stoke Newington 1981–84; Chapl K Coll Cam 1984–89; V St Thos Finsbury Park from 1989; Preb St Paul's Cathl from 2013
GS 2000–   *Tel:* 020 7359 5741
email: cardinal.jeoffry@btconnect.com
Web: www.stthomaschurch.co.uk

COLLARD, Mr Peter, B Sc
1 Hedben Drive Glossop Derbyshire SK13 8RS [DERBY] *b* 1951 *educ* Durham Chorister Sch; Durham Sch; Univ Edin; *CV* Bp's Coun Derby; Bd of Finance Derby; Parish Share Review Grp   *Tel:* 01457 861435
email: peter@glossop.org

COLLIER, Rt Worshipful Peter Neville, MA, QC
Leeds Crown Court The Courthouse 1 Oxford Row Leeds LS1 3BG [VICAR-GENERAL OF YORK] *b* 1948 *educ* Hymers Coll, Hull; Selw Coll Cam; *CV* Chan Wakef 1992–2006; Chan Linc 1998–2006; Lay Can, York Minster from 2001; Chair York Minster Coun from 2005; Chan York from 2006; Sen Circuit Judge and Hon Recorder of Leeds from

2007; Legal Advisory Comm from 2008; V Gen Province of York from 2008
GS 2008–   *Tel:* 0113 306 2800

COLLINS, Ven Gavin Andrew, MA; MA
Victoria Lodge 36 Osborn Road Fareham Hants PO16 7DS [ARCHDEACON OF THE MEON; PORTSMOUTH] *b* 1966 *educ* Sackville Sch East Grinstead; Trinity Hall Camb; Coll Law Guildford; Trinity Coll Bristol; *CV* AC St Barnabas Cambridge 1997–2002; V Christ Church Chorleywood 2002–11; RD Rickmansworth 2006–11; Hon Canon St Alb Cathl; 2009–11; Adn of the Meon from 2011
GS 2013–   *Tel:* 01329 608895
email: gavin.collins@portsmouth.anglican.org

CONDICK, Mrs Margaret, B Sc, Cert Ed
10 Rectory Lane Kirton Ipswich IP10 0PY [ST EDMUNDSBURY AND IPSWICH] *b* 1944 *educ* Sutton High Sch GPDST; Manch Univ; *CV* Tchr of Physics, Stockport 1967–70; pt tchr of maths, Suffolk 1985–97; Communications Officer, Chs Together in Suffolk 1998–2000; County Ecum Officer for Suffolk 2000–09; Moderator, Churches Together in Felixstowe 2010–13; M Dioc Synod; M Bp's Coun; M CNC St Eds & Ips vacancy 2014
GS 2003–   *Tel:* 01394 448576
email: margaret.condick@btopenworld.com

CONDRY, Rt Revd Dr Edward Francis, BA, BLitt, DPhil, MBA
White Lodge 22 Westbury Road Warminster Wilts BA12 0AW [SUFFRAGAN BISHOP OF RAMSBURY; SALISBURY] *b* 1953 *educ* Latymer Upper Sch Hammersmith; Univ of East Anglia; Exeter Coll, Ox; Univ of Nottm; Lincoln Theol Coll; OU; *CV* Asst C Weston Favell, Peterb 1982–85; V Bloxham, Milcombe and South Newington, Oxford 1985–1993; TR Rugby TM, Coventry 1993–2002; Can Res Cant Cathl 2002–12; Can Librarian 2002–3; Dir IME 4–7 Cant Dioc 2002–07; Can Librarian and Dir of Education 2006–12; Bp of Ramsbury from 2012   *Tel:* 01722 438662
email: edward.condry@salisbury.anglican.org

CONNER, Rt Revd David John , MA; KCVO
The Deanery Windsor Castle Windsor SL4 1NJ [DEAN OF WINDSOR] *b* 1947 *educ* Ex Coll Ox; St Steph Ho Th Coll; *CV* Hon C Summertown Ox 1971–76; Asst Chapl St Edw Sch Ox 1971–73; Chapl 1973–80; TV Wolvercote w Summertown 1976–80; Chapl Win Coll 1980–87; V Gt St Mary w St Mich Cam 1987–94; RD Cam 1989–94; Bp of Lynn 1994–98; Dean of Windsor from 1998; Bp to HM Forces 2001–09   *Tel:* 01753 865561
Fax: 01753 819002
email: david.conner@stgeorges-windsor.org

CONWAY, Rt Revd Stephen David, MA, MA
Bishop's Croft Winterbourne Earls Salisbury SP4 6HJ [BISHOP OF ELY] *b* 1957 *educ* Abp Tenison's Gr Sch Lon; Keble Coll Ox; Selw Coll Cam; Westcott Ho; *CV* C St Mary Heworth 1986–89; C St Mich and

AA Bishopwearmouth 1989–90; DDO 1989–94; Hon C St Marg Dur 1990–94; P-in-c then V St Mary Cockerton 1994–98; Sen Chapl to Bp of Dur and Dioc Communications Officer 1998–2002; Adn of Dur and Can Res Dur Cathl 2002–06; Area Bp of Ramsbury from 2006; M Bps Insp of Th Colls and Courses 1997–2006; Chair of Mental Health Matters from 2004–2010; GS 1995–2000; Chair Dioc Learning, Discipleship and Min Coun from 2006; Warden of Lay Mins from 2006–2010; Trustee Affirming Catholicism 2001–08, Vc-Pres from 2008; Anglican Bishop for LArche from 2010; Bp of Ely from 2010
GS 1995–2000   *Tel:* 01380 729808
Fax: 01380 738096
email: sramsbury@salisbury.anglican.org

COOK, Revd Canon James Christopher Donald, MA (Oxon)
St Agnes's Vicarage 1 Buckingham Avenue Liverpool L17 3BA [LIVERPOOL] *b* 1949 *educ* Bournemouth Sch; Ch Ch Ox; RMA Sandhusrt; St Stephen's House Th Coll; *CV* Regimental Officer 5th Royal Inniskilling Dragoon Guards 1973–78; Asst C Witney 1980–83; Chapl to the Forces 1983–2004; P-in-c St Agnes and St Pancras Toxteth Park 2004–06, V from 2006; Can Wiawso, Ghana from 2009
GS 2010–   *Tel:* 0151 733 1742
email: leoclericus@aol.com
Web: www.stagnes.org.uk

COOK, Revd John Richard Millward, BA
The Vicarage Station Road, Wargrave Reading Berkshire RG10 8EU [OXFORD] *b* 1961 *educ* Repton Sch; St Jo Coll Dur; Wycliffe Hall Th Coll; *CV* C St Peter's Farnborough 1989–92; C and Dir of Tr All Souls, Langham Place, London 1992–98; V of St John w St Andrew, Chelsea 1998–2008; V of St Mary, Wargrave w St Peter's, Knowl Hill, Ox Dico, from 2008
GS 1995–2007; 2010–   *Tel:* 0118 940 2202
0118 940 2300
Fax: 0118 940 1470
email: johnrmcook@btconnect.com

COOPER, Ven Annette Joy, BA, CQSW, Dip RS
63 Powers Hall End Witham CM8 1NH [ARCH-DEACON OF COLCHESTER; CHELMSFORD] *b* 1953 *educ* Lilley and Stone Newark Girls High Sch; Open Univ; Lon Univ Extra-mural Dept; S'wark Ord Course; St John's Coll, Durham; *CV* Local Auth Social Worker; Asst Chapl Tunbridge Wells Health Auth 1988–91; NSM Dn St Pet Pembury 1988; Chapl Bassetlaw Hosp and Community Services NHS Trust 1991–96; Chapl to Center Parcs Sherwood Village 1996–99; Chapl to S'well Dioc MU 1996–99; P-in-c Edwinstowe 1996–2004; Gov St Mary's C of E (Aided) Primary Sch 1996–2004; AD Worksop 1999–2004; Hon Can S'well Minster 2002–04; M Dioc Bd of Educ 1994–97; M Bp's Coun 1999–2004; Vc-Pres/Chair Dioc Ho of Clergy 2001–04; M GS Panel of Chairmen

2003–04, 2006–11; M Discipline Comm 2003–13; Adn of Colchester from 2004; Chelmsf Dioc Bd Fin from 2004; Trustee Dedham Lectureship Trust from 2004; Trustee Lovibond Almshouses from 2004; M Nat Stewardship Cttee 2007–10; Dir Allchurches Trust from 2008' M Appts Cttee from 2011; M Abps' Coun Finance Cttee from 2011; M Clergy Discipline (Amendment) Measure Steering Cttee 2011; Chair George Richards Charity from 2012; Elected Rep (Eastern Region) Ho of Bps from 2013; M Development Advisory Grp from 2014; M Nat Safeguarding Panel from 2014
GS 2000–2004; 2005–2010; 2010–   *Tel:* 01376 513130
Fax: 01376 500789
email: a.colchester@chelmsford.anglican.org
Twitter: @AnnetteAcooper

COOPER, Ms Susan Margaret , B Sc, FIA, DPS
28 Headstone Lane Harrow HA2 6HG [LONDON] *b* 1947 *educ* Harrow Weald Co Gr Sch; Univ Coll of Wales Aberystwyth; Birm Univ; *CV* Legal and Gen Assurance Soc 1969–80; Corporate Business Actuary BUPA 1980–90; Consultant Actuary 1992–2002; Consulting Actuary, GAD 2002–12; Rdr St Jo Bapt Pinner from 1995; M Strg Cttee for Draft Stipends (Cessation of Special Payments) Measure 2003–04; M Br Regional Cttee St Geo Coll Jerusalem from 2003; Hon Sec CHRISM 2006–07, Hon Treas 2008–09; M Strg Ctee for Draft C of E Pensions (Amendment) Measure 2007–08; Appts Cttee from 2011; Ho of Laity Standing Cttee from 2011; Audit Cttee from 2011; Dir Bd of Reference for Heathrow Multifaith Chaplaincy from 2011, M Rev Cttee Misc Prov Measure 2013
GS 2000–   *Tel:* 020 8863 2094 (Home)
07780 708478
email: scooper@hedstone.demon.co.uk

CORNWALL, Archdeacon of. See STUART-WHITE, Ven Bill (William Robert)

CORTEEN, Mrs Christine,
21 Hillside Road Wool Wareham Dorset BH20 6DY [SALISBURY] *b* 1956 *educ* Merchant Taylors' Sch, Liv; Liv Univ; *CV* Local Government Off from 1977; Income and Payments Man, Poole Borough Counc from 1990; Counc Miss, Sarum; St Aldhelm's Miss Fund, Sarum; Learning for Discipleship and Ministry, Sarum
GS 2010–   *Tel:* 01929 462642
email: chriscorteen@gmail.com

COTTON, Canon Robert Lloyd, MA, Dip Th
Holy Trinity Rectory 9 Eastgate Gardens Guildford GU1 4AZ [GUILDFORD] *b* 1958 *educ* Uppingham; Merton Coll Ox; Westcott Ho Cam; *CV* C St Mary Bromley 1983-85; C Bisley & W End 1987–89; P-in-c St Paul E Molesey 1989–96; Prin Guildf Dioc Min Course 1989–96; R H Trin & St Mary

Guildf from 1996; Chair Ho of Clergy 2004–11; Can Dioc of Highveld, S Africa from 2006; Can Guildford Cathl from 2010; Abp's Coun from 2010
GS 2004–ㅤㅤㅤㅤㅤㅤ*Tel:* 01483 575489
ㅤㅤㅤㅤㅤㅤㅤㅤㅤㅤ07710 757248
email: rector@holytrinityguildford.org.uk
Web: www.holytrinityguildford.org.uk/blog

COTTRELL, Rt Revd Stephen Geoffrey, BA
Bishopscourt Main Rd Margaretting Ingatestone Essex CM4 0HD [BISHOP OF CHELMSFORD] *b* 1958 *educ* Belfairs High Sch for Boys; Poly of Central Lon; St Steph Ho; *CV* C Ch Ch & St Paul Forest Hill, S'wark 1984–88; P-in-c St Wilf Parklands, Chich and Asst Dir of Pastl Studies, Chich Th Coll 1988–93; Dioc Missr, Wakef 1993–98; Springboard Missr 1998–2001; Can Pastor Peterb Cathl 2001–04; Bp of Reading 2004–10; Bp of Chelmsford from 2010
GS 2010–ㅤㅤㅤㅤㅤㅤ*Tel:* 01277 352001
ㅤㅤㅤㅤㅤㅤㅤㅤ*Fax:* 01277 355374
email: bishopscourt@chelmsford.anglican.org

COVENTRY, Archdeacon Missioner of. See RODHAM, Ven Morris

COVENTRY, Archdeacon Pastor of. See GREEN, Ven John

COVENTRY, Bishop of. See COCKSWORTH, Rt Revd Dr Christopher John

COVENTRY, Dean of. See WITCOMBE, Very Revd John Julian

COX, Canon Simon John, MA, MA, BSc, PhD
All Hallows Rectory 86 All Hallows Rd Bispham Blackpool FY2 0AY [BLACKBURN] *b* 1953 *educ* Roxeth Manor CSM, South Harrow; Montgomery of Alamein CSM Sch Winchester; Eastleigh Tech Coll; Q Mary Coll London; Univ Liverpool; Ridley Hall Cam; Selwyn Coll Cam; Univ Lancaster; *CV* C Livesey St Andrew 1982–85; C Cheadle Hulme St Andrew i/c Emmanuel 1985–89; V Disley St Mary 1989–94; R Bispham All Hallows from 1994; P-in-c Blackpool South Shore St Peter 2005–07; AD Blackpool from 2004; Hon Can Blackburn from 2008; Vc Chair Dioc Ho of Clergy; M Bp's Coun & Finance Exec, Pastl & Miss Comm; Property Commn; Chair Dioc Patronage Bd; Vc Chair DEF; Chapl TS Penelope Sea Cadet Unit; District Chapl Sea Cadets; Gov, formerly Chair, Bispham Endowed Primary Sch; Nat Chapl Aden Veteran' Assoc; Trustee & Treasurer Fellowship of Word & Spirit
GS 2002–2005, 2009–ㅤㅤㅤ*Tel:* 01253 351886
ㅤㅤㅤㅤㅤ*email:* Drsjcox@yahoo.co.uk

CREDITON, Suffragan Bishop of. See MCKINNEL, Rt Revd Nicholas Howard Paul

CROFT, Rt Revd Dr Steven John Lindsey,
Bishopscroft Snaithing Lane Sheffield S10 3LG [BISHOP OF SHEFFIELD] *b* 1957 *educ* Heath Sch Halifax; Worc Coll Ox; Cranmer Hall, St Jo Coll Dur; *CV* C St Andrew Enfield 1983–1987; V St George's Ovenden 1987–1996; Warden Cranmer Hall 1996–2004; Abps' Missioner and Team Ldr of Fresh Expressions 2004–09; Bp of Sheffield from 2009; Abps' Coun from 2011; House of Bps' Standing Cttee from 2011; Min Coun from 2011, Chair from 2012ㅤㅤㅤㅤㅤㅤ*Tel:* 0114 230 2170
ㅤㅤㅤㅤㅤㅤㅤㅤ*Fax:* 0114 2630110
email: bishop@bishopofsheffield.org.uk
Web: http://bishopofsheffield.blogspot.co.uk
ㅤㅤㅤㅤㅤㅤㅤㅤ*Twitter:* @Steven.Croft

CROFT, Canon William Stuart, MA, BA, MTh
315 Thorpe Road Longthorpe Peterborough PE3 6LU [PETERBOROUGH] *b* 1953 *educ* King Edward VI Sch; Trin Hall, Cam; King's Coll Lon; Ripon Coll Cuddesdon; *CV* AC, St James Friern Barnet 1981–83; Tutor Chich Th Coll 1983–92; V, St Margaret of Antioch Fernhurst 1992 -98; Prec Peterb Cathl 1998–2004; Dioc Dir Ord, Peterb, 1998–2002; P-in-c, St Botolph's, Longthorpe, Peterb from 2004; M Joint Implementation Comm Ang Meth Covenant from 2003
GS 2010–ㅤㅤㅤㅤㅤㅤ*Tel:* 01733 263016
ㅤㅤㅤ*email:* williamsbill_croft@hotmail.com

CROYDON, Archdeacon of. See SKILTON, Ven Christopher John

CROYDON, Area Bishop of. See CLARK, Rt Revd Jonathan Dunnett

CUMBERLAND, Archdeacon of West. See HILL, Ven Colin

CUNLIFFE, Ven Dr Christopher John, MA, D Phil, MA, A R Hist S
Derby Church House Full St Derby DE1 3DR [ARCHDEACON OF DERBY] *b* 1955 *educ* Charterhouse; Ch Ch Ox; Trin Coll Cam; Westcott Ho Cam; *CV* C Chesterfield Par Ch 1983–85; Chapl and Jun Rsch Fell, Linc Coll Ox 1985–89; Chapl City Univ and Guildhall Sch of Music and Drama 1989–91; Selection Sec and Voc Officer, Adv Bd of Min 1991–96; Bp of Lon's Adv for Ord Min 1996–2003; Clerk, All SS Educ Trust 2004; Chapl to Bp of Bradwell 2004–06; Adn of Derby from 2006; Chair Derby Dioc Communications Cttee; Can Res Derby Cathl 2006–08ㅤㅤ*Tel:* 01332 388676
ㅤㅤㅤㅤㅤㅤㅤㅤ*Fax:* 01332 292969
ㅤㅤㅤ*email:* archderby@derby.anglican.org

CURRAN, Ven Patrick Martin Stanley, BA, B Th
British Embassy Jauresgasse 12 Vienna 1030 Austria [ARCHDEACON OF THE EASTERN ARCHDEACONRY; EUROPE] *b* 1956 *educ* Ostsee Gymnasium, Timmendorfer Strand, Germany; Univ of K Coll Halifax,

Nova Scotia, Canada; Southampton Univ; Chich Th Coll; *CV* C Heavitree with Ex St Paul Ex 1984–87; Bp's Chapl to Students, Bradf 1987–93; Chapl Bonn with Cologne, Eur 1993–2000; Can Malta Cathl 2000; Chapl Ch Ch Vienna from 2000; Adn of the Eastern Archdeaconry from 2002; Chair Ho Clergy Eur from 2013

Tel: 00 43 1 7148900
00 43 1 7185902
00 43 699 172 63393
Fax: 00 43 1 7148900
email: office@christchurchvienna.org
2nd email: archdeaconp@gmail.com

CURRIE, Canon Dr Stuart William, MA, PGCE, PhD

St Stephen's Vicarage 1 Beech Avenue Worcester WR3 8PZ [WORCESTER] *b* 1953 *educ* Boteler Gr Sch, Warrington; Hertford Coll Ox; Univ Coll Dur; Fitzwilliam Coll Cam; Westcott Ho; King's Coll Lon; *CV* C Ch Ch Reading 1985–89; V in Banbury TM 1989–94; V Barbourne St Stephen from 1994; Chair Worc Dioc Ho of Clergy; Chair Worc DBE; RD Worcester East GS 2008–   Tel: 01905 452169
email: sw.currie@virgin.net

CUTTING, Ven Alastair Murray, B Ed, MA, L Th, DPS

Woolwich Episcopal Area Office Trinity House, 4 Chapel Court Borough High Street, London SE1 1HW [ARCHDEACON OF LEWISHAM AND GREENWICH; SOUTHWARK] *b* 1960 *educ* Geo Watson's Coll Edin; Lushington (Hebron) Sch Ooty, S India; Watford Boys Gr Sch; Westhill Coll Birm; St Jo Coll Nottm; Heythrop Coll Lon; *CV* C All SS Woodlands, Sheff 1987–88; C Wadsley, Sheff 1989–91; Chapl to The Nave and Town Cen, Uxbridge, Lon 1991–96; V Copthorne, Chich 1996–2010; V Henfield, R Shermanbury and Woodmancote 2010–13; Adn of Lewisham and Greenwich from 2013; M Bp's Coun Chich 1998–2013; Asst RD E Grinstead 2002–10; Chair Ho of Clergy Chich 2009–13; Pro-Prolocutor Prov Cant 2011–13
GS 2005–13   Tel: 020 7979 9408
07736 676106 (Mobile)
Fax: 020 7939 9465
email: alastair.cutting@southwark.anglican.org
Web: www.acutting.org
Twitter: @AlCutting

DAILEY, Miss Prudence Mary Prior, MA

9 Spring Lane Littlemore Oxford OX3 6LF [OXFORD] *b* 1965 *educ* Simon Langton Gr Sch for Girls Cant; K Sch Cant; Mert Coll Ox; *CV* NHS Gen Mgt Trainee and various admin posts in NHS 1988–97; Ox City Coun 1992–96; Sen Business Systems Analyst, Toys 'R' Us 1998–2009; Chairman Prayer Book Soc
GS 2000–   Tel: 01865 236124
07730 516620
email: prudence.dailey@gmail.com

DAKIN, Rt Revd Timothy John, BA, MTh

Wolvesey Winchester SO23 9ND [BISHOP OF WINCHESTER] *b* 1958 *educ* Priory Sch Shrewsbury; St Mary's Sch Nairobi; Henley Sixth Form Coll; St Mark's and St Jo Coll Plymouth; K Coll Lon; Ch Ch Ox; Carlile Coll Nairobi; *CV* Prin Carlile Coll, Nairobi 1993–2000; Hon C Nairobi Cathedral 1994–2000; Gen Sec CMS 2000–11; Can Theol Cov Cathl 2001–11; Assoc P St James Ruscombe & St Marys Twyford 2000–11; M MPA Coun; M PWM Panel; M FAOC; Bp of Winchester from 2011; Lords Spiritual from 2012
GS 2005–   Tel: 01962 854050
email: bishop.tim@winchester.anglican.org
Web: www.winchester.anglican.org

DALES, Mr Martin Paul,

Priory Cottage Old Malton North Yorkshire YO17 7HB [YORK] *b* 1955 *educ* St Dunstan's Coll; Bretton Hall; Open Univ; *CV* Media and PR Adv various inc findclaudia.co.uk and dontdrainus.org; Media Relations Adv RSCM NE Yorks Area (Sec 2000–02); Organist and Choirmaster from 1976, All Saints,Thornton-le-Dale from 2007, also St Leonard & St Mary (RC) Malton from 2013; freelance broadcaster from 1976, BBC Radio York from 1994; Dep Hd, Housemaster and Dir of Music various schs 1976–94; music publisher from 1981; freelance musician, tchr and composer from 1994; Coun Malton Town Coun 1989–99, 2003– (Mayor 1991–92, 1996–97); Chair, Ryedale Cameras in Action; Vice-Chair, Amotherby Sch Govs (Chair 2010–13); M Dioc Syn from 1995; M Coun for Min and Trg 1998–2000; past M Abp's Coun; M Revision Cttee Draft Amending Canon No 22; past M Appts Cttee; past M Ho of Laity Stg Cttee; past M CCU; past M CMEAC; past M CTE Forum and CTBI Assembly; past Chair Chs Together in S Ryedale; M EKD Delegation 2005
GS 1995–   Tel: 01653 600990
07764 985009
email: mpd@martindales.me.uk
Twitter: @martindales

DALLISTON, Very Revd Christopher Charles, MA

The Deanery 26 Mitchell Avenue Newcastle upon Tyne NE2 3LA [DEAN OF NEWCASTLE] *b* 1956 *educ* Diss Gr Sch; Peterhouse Cam; St Steph Ho Ox; *CV* C St Andr Halsead w H Trin and Greenstead Green 1984–87; Dom Chapl to Bp of Chelms 1987–91; V St Edm Forest Gate, Chelms 1991–95; V St Botolp w St Chris Boston 1995–2003; Dean of Newcastle from 2003   Tel: 0191 281 6554
0191 232 1939
email: dean@stnicnewcastle.co.uk

DALLOW, Revd Gillian Margaret, BA, M Ed, PGCE, CEM

26 Baron's Court Road Penylan Cardiff HCF23 9DF [SYNODICAL SECRETARY, CONVOCATION OF CANTERBURY] *b* 1945 *educ* Cathays High Sch Cardiff;

Univ of N Wales Bangor; Bris Univ; Oak Hill Th Coll; W of Eng Univ; *CV* Tchr Mill St Sec Mod Sch Pontypridd 1968–70; Hd of RE Heref High Sch for Girls 1970–73; Hd of RE and Student Counselling Heref Sixth Form Coll 1973–74; Scripture Union Schs Worker S West and Wales 1974–79; Hd of RE Colston's Girls Sch Bris 1979–85; Dioc Educ Adv B & W 1985–91; Dir Tr Lon Bible Coll 1991–98; Adv for Children's Min and P-in-c St Giles Barlestone from 1999; Dioc Dir Under 25s Trg from 2002; Synodical Sec, Conv of Cant from 2006; M C of E Evang Coun from 2006; Sec Eggs (Evangs on GS) from 2009; Perm to Officiate: Dioc of Lon and Dioc of Llandaff; Chapl to Welsh Assembly Government from 2009; Assoc P St Mark's Gabalfa and St Philip's Community Ch Tremorfa Cardiff
GS 2000–05   *Tel:* 0292 0463754
                                      07801 650187 (Mobile)
email: g.dallow@btinternet.com

DAVENPORT, Miss Laura Elizabeth, BA, MA
8 Ashfield Avenue Union Mills Isle of Man IM4 4LN [SODOR AND MAN] *b* 1988 *educ* Queen Elizabeth II High Sch, Isle of Man; Cam Univ; Dur Univ; *CV* Dioc Yth Adv, from 2010; Yth Lder, Braddan Ch, from 2010; Business Analyst, Barclays Wealth from 2010; Dioc Comm Forum 2010
GS 2010–   *Tel:* 01624852167
                                      07624467232
email: laura.elizabeth.davenport@gmail.com

DAVIES, Mr John, PSC, MBIFM, MCIM
Vicarage Cottages Baughurst Road Ramsdell Tadley RG26 5SH [WINCHESTER] *b* 1951 *educ* King Edward's Sch; RMAS; Army Staff Coll; *CV* Regular Army 1969–89; Various commercial appointments 1989–2001; Managing Dir Park Row Consultancy Ltd; Lay Chair Basingstoke Deanery from 2008; Bp's Counc Winc 2009–12; Fin Cttee Winc 2006–09
GS 2005–   *Tel:* 01256 851309
email: johndavies@parkrow.fsnet.co.uk

DAVIES, Very Revd Dr John Harverd, MA, M Phil, PhD
Derby Cathedral Centre 18–19 Iron Gate Derby DE1 3GP [DEAN OF DERBY] *b* 1957 *educ* Brentwood Sch; Keble Coll Ox; Corpus Christi Coll Cam; Lancaster Univ; Westcott Ho; *CV* C Liv Par Ch 1984–87; C Peterb Par Ch and Minor Can Peterb Cathl 1987–90; V St Marg Anfield, Liv 1990–94; Chapl, Fell and Dir of Studies in Theol, Keble Coll Ox 1994–99; V Melbourne and DDO Derby Dioc 1999–2009; Dean of Derby from 2010; M Derby Dioc Bd for Min; M Dioc Syn; M GS Theol Educ and Trg Cttee 2006–07; Chair Industrial Miss in Derbyshire from 2009   *Tel:* 01332 341201
                                      Fax: 01332 203991
email: dean@derbycathedral.org

DAVIES, Rt Revd Mark, BA, Cert PS
The Hollies Manchester Rd Rochdale OL11 3QY [SUFFRAGAN BISHOP OF MIDDLETON; MANCHESTER] *b* 1962 *educ* Hanley High Sch; Stoke-on-Trent Sixth Form Coll; Univ Coll of Ripon and York St Jo; Mirfield Th Coll; *CV* C St Mary Barnsley 1989–92; P-in-c St Paul Old Town Barnsley 1992–95; R Hemsworth from 1995; Asst DDO from 1998; RD Pontefract from 2000; Hon Can Wakef Cathl 2002–06; Adn of Rochdale 2006–08; Bp of Middleton from 2008
GS 2000–06   *Tel:* 01706 358550
email: bishopmark@manchester.anglican.org

DAVIES, Revd Nigel Lawrence, BEd
St Oswald's Vicarage Burneside Kendal Cumbria LA9 6QX [CARLISLE] *b* 1955 *educ* Black Bull Lane Sch; Hutton Gr Sch; St Martin's Coll, Lancaster; Salis and Wells Th Coll; *CV* Dn 1987; P 1988; C St Luke w All Souls, Heywood, Man 1987–91; V Burneside, 1991–07; Tutor Past Studies CBDTI 1992–98; Editor Dioc News 1999–2002; Rural Dean Kendal 2003–08; P-in-c Crosscrake 2004–06; Skelsmergh w Selside and Longsleddale, 2006–07; Hon Canon Carlisle Cathl from 06; TR, Beacon Team. Kendal Deanery, Dioc Carlisle from 2007
GS 2009–   *Tel:* 01539 722015
email: canon.nigel@beaconteam.org.uk

DAWTRY, Ven Dr Anne Frances, BA(Hons), PhD, Dip Min
2 Vicarage Gardens Brighouse West Yorkshire HD6 3HD [ARCHDEACON OF HALIFAX; WEST YORKSHIRE AND THE DALES] *b* 1957 *educ* Westf Coll Lon, Ripon Coll Cuddesdon; *CV* C Corfe Mullen 1993–96; C Parkstone St Pet w Branksea and St Osmund 1996–97; Chapl Bournemouth Univ and Bournemouth and Poole Coll of FE 1997–99; Prin OLM and Integrated Tr 1999–2003; Dir Tr and Prin Dioc OLM Scheme Manchester 2003–06; Course Dir SNWTP 2006–08; C Chorlton-cum-Hardy St Werburgh 2006–08; P-in-c 2008–09; R 209–11; Hon Can Man Cathl 06–11; Adn Halifax from 11; Wdn of Rdrs from 2012: Consultant Liturgical Comm 2000–05; M Liturgical Comm from 2005   *Tel:* 01484 714553 07980 751902
                email: archdeacon.halifax@
                         westyorkshiredales.anglican.org
                Web: www.westyorkshiredales.anglican.org

DERBY, Archdeacon of. See CUNLIFFE, Ven Dr Christopher John

DERBY, Bishop of. See REDFERN, Rt Revd Dr Alastair Llewellyn John

DERBY, Dean of. See DAVIES, Very Revd John Harverd

DOBBIE, Brigadier William Ian Cotter, OBE, BSc(Eng)
5 Richmond Court White Lodge Close Hitchen Hatch Lane, Sevenoaks Kent TN13 3BF [ROCHESTER] *b*

1939 *educ* Wellington Coll; Royal Military Acad Sandhurst; Royal Military Coll of Sc; Army Staff Coll; RAF Staff Coll; *CV* Reg Off 1958–1992; Dep Chief of Staff 3 Armoured Division 1986–88; Comd Engineer HQ BAOR 1988–92; Proj Dir and Adm St Nicholas, Sevenoaks 1992–95; Gen Sec Counc of Vol Welfare Work 1995; Chair Soldiers' and Airmens' Scrip Readers Assoc, 1991; Roch Dioc Bd Patronage
GS 2000–05; 2006–10; 2010–   *Tel:* 01732 465109
email: gensec@cvww.org.uk

DOBSON, Revd Christopher John, BA, MA
25 Ducie Road Staple Hill Bristol BS16 5JZ [BRISTOL] *b* 1962 *educ* Norwich Sch; Aberystwyth Univ; Wycliffe Hall Th Coll;; *CV* Manager HMSO Dept, Norwich 1984–85; Youth Worker Shrewsbury House, Everton 1985–86; C, St Mark, Biggin Hill 1989–92; C, St James and St Philip, Tunbridge Wells 1992–95; R, Alls Souls, Mount Pleasant, Harare 1996–2000; V, St Andrew, Paddock Wood, 2000–08; Bp's Adv Links, Rochester 2004–08; Ecumen and Global Partnership Off Bris from 2008
GS 2010–   *Tel:* 0117 906 0100
                             07530 821641
email: chris.dobson@bristoldiocese.org
Web: www.bristol-uganda.co.uk

DOCHERTY, Mrs Lucy Clare, BA
33 Southampton Road Fareham Hampshire PO16 7DZ [PORTSMOUTH] *b* 1955 *educ* Tavistock Sch; Nott Univ; *CV* Commercial retail & marketing posts 1977–83; Non-exec Dir & Chair NCT Publ Ltd 1996–99; Lay Brd M Fareham Pri Care Grp 1999–2002; Vice Chair National Assoc of Lay People in Pri Care 2000–03; Chair Fareham & Gosport Pri Care Trust 2002–06; Non exec Dir Hampshire Probation Trust from 2007; Elected Gov Portsmouth Hosp Foundn Trust from 2007; Chair Govrs 6th Form Coll from 2010; Chair Rainbow Centre for Conductive Educ 2012, Chair Ho of Laity Portsm from 2006; Chair Portsm Counc Soc Respons from 2006; M Coun Ch House from 2010; Exec M Churches Together in Hampshire, 2000–09; M and one-time Chair Christians Together in Fareham since 1996; Lay Can Portsm Cathl from 2013
GS 2007–   *Tel:* 01329 233602
email: lucy@docherty1.co.uk

DOE, Rt Revd Michael David, BA, LLD (Hon)
405 West Carriage House Royal Carriage Mews Royal Arsenal Woolwich SE18 6GA [PREACHER, GRAY'S INN; HONORARY ASSISTANT BISHOP OF SOUTHWARK] *b* 1947 *educ* Brockenhurst Gr Sch; Dur Univ; Ripon Hall Th Coll; *CV* C St Pet St Helier 1972–76, Hon C 1976–81; Youth Sec BCC 1976–81; V Blackbird Leys LEP Ox 1981–89; RD Cowley 1987–89; Soc Resp Adv Portsm 1989–94; Can Res Portsm Cathl 1989–94; Bp of Swindon 1994–2004; Convenor CTE 1999–2003; Gen Sec USPG 2004–

11; Assistant Bp S'wark from 2004; Preacher Hon Soc Gray's Inn from 2011
GS 1990–94, 2000–04   *Tel:* 020 3259 3841
email: michaeldd@btinternet.com
Web: http://www.graysinn.info/index.php/chapel
Twitter: @GraysInnChapel

**DONCASTER, Archdeacon of. See
WILCOCKSON, Ven Stephen Anthony**

**DONCASTER, Suffragan Bishop of. See
BURROWS, Rt Revd Peter**

DORBER, Very Revd Adrian John, BA, M Th
The Deanery 16 The Close Lichfield WS13 7LD [DEAN OF LICHFIELD] *b* 1952 *educ* St Jo Coll, Dur Univ; K Coll Lon; Westcott Ho Cam; *CV* C Easthampstead, Bracknell, Ox 1979–85; Dny Youth Officer 1982–85; P-in-c St Barn Emmer Green 1985–88; Chapl Portsm Poly 1988–92, Lect 1991–97, Sen Chapl, Public Orator Portsm Univ 1992–97; Hon Chapl Portsm Cathl 1992–97; P-in-c Brancepeth, Dur 1997–2001; Dir Min and Trg 1997–2005; Hon Can Dur Cathl 1997–2005; Dean of Lichfield from 2005; M Dioc Syn and Bp's Coun; M Exec Cttee Assoc English Cathls; M Bd of Governors, Lichfield Cathl Sch; Trustee Lichfield Festival   *Tel:* 01543 306294 (Home)
                             01543 306250 (Office)
                             Fax: 01543 306109
email: adrian.dorber@lichfield-cathedral.org
2nd email: bernice.alexander@lichfield-cathedral.org
Web: www.lichfield-cathedral.org

DORCHESTER, Archdeacon of. FRENCH, Ven Judy

**DORCHESTER, Area Bishop of. See
FLETCHER, Rt Revd Colin William**

DORKING, Archdeacon of. BRYER, Ven Paul

**DORKING, Suffragan Bishop of. See
BRACKLEY, Rt Revd Ian James**

DORMOR, Revd Duncan James, MA, MSc, BA
St John's College Cambridge CB2 1TP [UNIVERSITIES, CAMBRIDGE] *b* 1967 *educ* Sherborne Sch; Magd Coll Ox; Lon Sch of Hygiene and Tropical Medicine; Ripon Coll Cuddesdon; *CV* C Wolverhampton Cen Par, Lich 1995–98; Chapl, St Jo Coll Cam 1998–2002, Dean and Fell from 2002; affiliated lect, Faculty of Div, Cam Univ from 2004; M Coun of Westcott Ho from 2006; M MPA Coun from 2011; Pres, St Jo Coll Cam from 2011; English ARC from 2012
GS 2005–   *Tel:* 01223 338633
email: djd28@cam.ac.uk

DORSET, Archdeacon of. See WAINE, Ven Stephen

DOTCHIN, Revd Andrew Steward, Dip Th (Hons), PG Pstl Th
Whitton Rectory 176 Fircroft Road Ipswich IP1 6PS [ST EDMUNDSBURY AND IPSWICH] *b* 1956 *educ* Royal Hosp Sch, Ipswich; Witwatersrand Technikon, Johannesburg; FedTheo Seminary, Imbali;, Anglia Ruskin Univ; *CV* C and P-in-c, Parish of Standerton with Evander, Jo'burg 1985–87; Asst P St Martin's in the Veld, Rosebank, Jo'burg 1987–88; R St John the Divine, Belgravia Jo'burg, 1989–94; Chapl St Martin's School, Rosettenville, Christ the King 1994–2000; TV: Blyth Valley Team Ministry, Dioc St E&I 2000–04; Editor Third Order Chronicle , Euro Province Third Order Soc St Francis, 2003–10; M House of Clergy, Syn Anglican C of SA 1980–2000; M Prov Elective Assembly Cttee of ACSA, 1993–2000; M ACSA Pub Cttee, 1998–2000; M Exee Cttee SU Independent Sch, 1997–2000; M Dioc HIV/AIDS Cttee, Dioc Jo'burg, 1990–94; R Parish of Whitton w Thurleston and Akenham from 2004; M Dioc Syn from 2002; M Dioc Bd Educ from 2006; M Dioc Bd Patronage from 2006; M Vacancy in See Cttee from 2006; Dioc Chapl to Mothers' Union 2010–14; Chapl 188 (Ipswich) Squadron Air Training Corps from 2005; Chapl Wolsey District Scouts from 2012; Chapl Merchant Navy Assoc Ipswich from 2012; Chapl RBL Ipswich from 2013; Vol Chapl Suffolk Police from 2014
GS 2010–   *Tel:* 01473 741 389
                                               07814 949828
                          email: revdotchin@gmail.com

DOVER, Bishop of. See WILLMOTT, Rt Revd Trevor

DOWN, Ven Philip Roy, MA, M Th, ARMIT, CCPE
The Archdeaconry Pett Lane Charing Ashford TN27 0DL [ARCHDEACON OF ASHFORD; CANTERBURY] *b* 1953 *educ* Lakeside and Watsonia High Sch, Victoria, Australia; R Melbourne Inst of Tech; Melbourne Coll of Div; Hull Univ; *CV* Parish P Brighton, Victoria (Uniting Ch in Australia) 1982–86; Scunthorpe Circuit (Br Meth Conf) 1986–89; C St Mary and St Jas Gt Grimsby, Linc 1989–91, TV 1991–95; R St Steph Cant 1995–2002; AD Cant 1999–2002; Adn of Maidstone 2002;-10; Adn of Ashford from 2010; M DAC; M Dioc Property and Pastl Cttees; M Dioc Framework for Local Church Development; Archbp's Coun, Dioc Syn
GS 2005–   *Tel:* 01233 713140
                                               01233 712649
                                        Fax: 01233 712649
                 email: pdown@archdeacashford.org

DRAPER, Very Revd Dr Jonathan Lee, BA, BA(Hons), PhD
The Deanery 10 Cathedral Close Exeter EX1 1EZ [DEAN OF EXETER] *b* 1952 *educ* Plainfield High Sch, Plainfield NJ, USA; Gordon Coll USA; Univ Dur; Ripon Coll Cuddesdon; *CV* Asst C St John the Divine Brooklands, Manchester 1983–5; Lect Ripon Coll Cuddesdon 1985–92; V Putney, S'wark 1992–2000; Can Theologian York Minster 200–12; Dean of Exeter from 2012
                                     Tel: 01392 285979
              email: dean@exeter-cathedral.org.uk
                 Web: www.exeter-cathedral.org.uk

DRIVER, Ven Penny (Penelope May), MEd, CertEd, MA Adult Ed
The Vicarage Windermere Road Lindale in Cartmel Grange over Sands LA11 6LB [ARCHDEACON OF WESTMORLAND AND FURNESS; CARLISLE] *b* 1952 *educ* All SS Coll Tottenham; Nn Ord Course; Man Univ; *CV* Dioc Youth Adv Newc 1986–88; C St Geo Cullercoats 1987–88; Dioc Youth Chapl Ripon from 1988–96; Min Can Ripon Cathl from 1996; Hon Can Ripon Cathl 1998–2006; Dioc Adv for Women's Mind from 1991; Ass DDO 1996–98; DDO 1998–2006; M CNC from 2003; Adn Exeter 2006–12; Adn Westmorland and Furness from 2012   *Tel:* 01539 534717
    email: archdeacon.south@carlislediocese.org.uk

DRIVER, Revd Canon Roger John, Dip HE, BA (Hons), MA
The Vicarage 70 Merton Road Bootle Liverpool L20 7AT [LIVERPOOL] *b* 1964 *educ* Broadwey Secondary Modern; Weymouth Tech Coll, Liverpool Hope Univ; Trin Coll, Bris; Salis & Wells Th Coll; *CV* AC, St Peter's Much-Woolton, Liv 1990–93; TV, St Paul's, Fazakerley, Liv 1993–2000; TR (designate), Bootle Team Ministry, Liv 2000–03; P-in-c, St Andrew's, Litherland; St Leonard's, Bootle; St Matthew's, Bootle, Liverpool 2000–03; TR, Bootle Team Ministry, Liv from 2003; Civic Link Officer, Sefton Borough from 2004; Area Dean, Bootle, Liv from 2007; Hon Canon, Liv Cathl from 2007; M Bp's Counc, Liv 2001–09
GS 2010–   *Tel and Fax:* 0151 922 3316
                 email: rogerdriver@btinternet.com

DUDLEY, Archdeacon of. GROARKE, Ven Nikki

DUDLEY, Suffragan Bishop of. See USHER, Rt Revd Graham Barham

DUDLEY-SMITH, Revd James, BA, MA, BTh
The Rectory 41 The Park Yeovil BA20 1DG [BATH AND WELLS] *b* 1966 *educ* Fitzw Coll Cam; Wycliffe Hall Ox; *CV* C New Borough and Leigh Sarum 1997–2001; C Hove Bp Hannington Memorial Ch Chich 2001–06; R Yeovil w Kingston Pitney B and W from 2006
GS 2010–   *Tel:* 01935 475352
                          email: jamesds@tesco.net

DUNLOP, Mrs Jennifer Mary, LLB
180a Dowson Rd Hyde SK14 5BW [CHESTER] *b* 1951 *educ* Woking Gr Sch for Girls; Hull Univ; *CV* Solicitor Dukinfield 1975–81; M Dioc Syn from 1988; Family Solicitor in Salford from 1995;

Lay Chair Mottram Dny Syn 1990–2000; Solicitor Salford 1995–2011
GS 2000–   *Tel:* 0161 368 2149
              email: jennydunlop2004@yahoo.co.uk

DUNNETT, Revd John Frederick, MA, MSc, BA, CQSW
39 Crescent Rd Warley Brentwood Essex CM14 5JR [CHELMSFORD] *b* 1958 *educ* K Edw Sch Edgbaston; Sidney Sussex Coll Cam; Worc Coll Ox; Trin Coll Bris; *CV* Rsch Asst and Press Officer to Bp of B&W 1987–88; C Kirkheaton Par Ch 1988–93; V St Luke Cranham Park 1993–2006; Gen Dir CPAS from 2006
GS 2005–   *Tel:* 01277 221419
                 email: jd@johndunnett.co.uk

DUNWICH, Suffragan Bishop of. [NOT APPOINTED AT TIME OF GOING TO PRESS]

DURHAM, Archdeacon of. See JAGGER, Ven Ian

DURHAM, Bishop of. See BUTLER, Rt Revd Paul Roger

DURHAM, Dean of. See SADGROVE, Very Revd Michael

DURLACHER, Mrs Mary Caroline,
Archendines Chappel Road Fordham Colchester CO6 3LT [CHELMSFORD] *b* 1951 *educ* Cranborne Chase Sch; Kent Univ; Moore Coll; *CV* Churchwarden, All Saints Fordham & Eight Ash Green 1999–2005; Foundn Gov, C o E All Saints Fordham Primary Sch from 2005; MM Cathls Fabric Commn from 2011; M Bp's Coun Chelmsf from 2013
GS 2010–   *Tel:* 01206 240627
              email: marydurlacher@hotmail.com

DYER, Mrs Kay, BA, Cert Ed
6 Sycamore Close Stratford-upon-Avon CV37 0DZ [COVENTRY] *b* 1949 *educ* Blakedown High Sch Leamington Spa; Open Univ; Wolverhampton Univ; *CV* County Ecum Officer, Cov and Warw from 2004; OU tutor from 2003; Chair Cov Dioc Youth Initiative 1997–2001; Children's Work Co-ord, St Andrew Shottery, Stratford-upon-Avon from 2005; Lay Rdr from 2011
GS 2005–   *Tel:* 01789 298299
                 email: kay.dyer4@gmail.com

DZIEGIEL, Mrs Julie Patricia, MA(Hons)
239 Chartridge Lane Chesham Bucks HP5 2SF [OXFORD] *b* 1963 *educ* Pynton County High Sch; Newham Coll, Cam; *CV* Arthur Andersen, Chartered Accountants, 1984–88; Chartered Accountant 1988–94; Accountant & Company Sec from 1994; Church Treasurer from 2002
GS 2010–   *Tel:* 01494 773713
              email: julie@stronglg.demon.co.uk

EAGLES, Ven Peter Andrew, BA; AKC; BA; MTh
MoD Chaplains (Army) Army Headquarters, Marlborough Lines Andover, Hants SP11 8HJ [ARCHDEACON FOR THE ARMY] *b* 1959 *educ* RGS Guildford; Sch Slavonic Studies Lon; Uni Heidelberg; St Stephens Ho; *CV* Tchr and translator 1982–86; C St Martin's Ruislip 1989–92; R Army Chapls Dept from 1992; Asst Chaplain General from 2008; Dir Trg and CME 2011; Adn for the Army from 2011; Royal Coll Defence Studies 2013–13; Queen's Hon Chapl from 2013; Dep Chapl Gen HM Land Forces from 2014
GS 2011–   *Tel:* 01264 381836
                                      07747 100944
                                 Fax: 01264 381824
              email: peter.eagles330@mod.uk
              2nd email: paeagles@hotmail.com

EAST RIDING, Archdeacon of, BROOM, Very Revd Andy

EASTERN ARCHDEACONRY (Europe). See CURRAN, Ven Patrick Martin Stanley

EBBSFLEET, Bishop of. See GOODALL, Rt Revd Jonathan

EDMONDSON, Rt Revd Christopher Paul, BA, Dip Th, MA, MBII
Bishop's Lodge Walkden Rd Worsley Manchester M28 2WH [SUFFRAGAN BISHOP OF BOLTON; MANCHESTER] *b* 1950 *educ* Blandford Gr Sch Dorset; Univ of Durham; Cranmer Hall, St John's Coll Dur; *CV* C Kirkheaton Par Ch 1973–79; V Ovenden St George 1979–86; Bp's Adv on Evang 1981–86; Dioc Officer for Evang and P-in-c Bampton, Carl 1986–92; V Shipley St Peter, Bradf 1992–2002; Warden Lee Abbey 2002–08; Bp of Bolton from 2008; Bp's Coun Carl 1989–1992; Chair Bradf Dioc Pastl Cttee 1994–2002; M Bp's Coun Man from 2008; Chair Scargill Movt Coun from 2009; Chair Greater Man Fresh Expressions Area Strategy Tm from 2009; Chair All Saints Centre for MIssion and Ministry from 2011; Pres Archway from 2011; Bp for Fresh Expressions from 2014   *Tel:* 0161 790 8289
                                 Fax: 0161 703 9157
       email: bishopchris@manchester.anglican.org

EDMONDSON, Very Revd Canon Dr John James William, BA, Cert Th, MA, PhD
The Deanery Caldbec Hill Battle TN33 0JY [DEAN OF BATTLE] *b* 1955 *educ* Strode's Sch, Egham; Dur Univ; Cranmer Hall, Dur; *CV* C Gee Cross, Ches 1983–86; C St Paul Camberley, Guildf 1986–88; TV 1988–90; Chapl Elmhurst Ballet Sch, Camberley 1986–90; V Foxton w. Gumley and Laughton and Lubenham, Leic 1990–94; R St Mark Bexhill, Chich 1994–2005; Chich Dioc Vocations Adv 1998–2002; Asst DDO, Chich 2002–05; Dean of Battle, V Battle, Chich from 2005; P-in-c Sedlescombe and Whatlington, Chich 2005–07; Asst RD Battle and Bexhill from 2010; M Dioc Fin Cttee from 2013   *Tel and Fax:* 01424 772693
              email: dean@johnedmondson.org

EDMONTON, Area Bishop of. [NOT APPOINTED AT TIME OF GOING TO PRESS]

EDWARDS, Canon (Diana) Clare, Bth
22 The Precincts Canterbury CT1 2EP [CANTERBURY] *b* 1956 *educ* Nott Univ; Linc Th Coll; *CV* S Wimbledon H Trin and St Peters S'wark 1986–90; Par Dn 1987–90; Par Dn Lingfield and Crowhurst 1990–94; C 1994–94; Chapl St Piers Hosp Sch Lingfield 1990–95; R Bletchingley S'wark 1995–2004; RD Godstone 1998–2004; Hon Can S'wark Cathl 2001–04; Dean of Women's Min 2003–04; Can Res Cant Cathl from 2004
GS 2010–   *Tel:* 01227 865227
    email: canonclare@canterbury-cathedral.org

ELCOCK, Dr Martin, BA, MB, Ch B
The Cottage 3 Digbeth Lane Claverley Wolverhampton WV5 7BP [HEREFORD] *b* 1963 *educ* Oldbury Wells Comp Sch Bridgnorth; Bris Univ; Man Univ; *CV* GP; Chair Good Shepherd Trust (homelessness and social inclusion charity in W Midlands/Derbys); primary sch gov; M Hosp Chapls Counc 2006–10
GS 2000–   *Tel:* 01746 710423
             07971 784639 (Mobile)
    email: m.elcock@btinternet.com

ELKINGTON, Ven Audrey Anne, BA; PhD; MA
4 Park Drive Bodmin Cornwall PL31 2QF [ARCHDEACON OF BODMIN; TRURO] *b* 1957 *educ* King Edward's Sch Witley; St Catherine's Ox; UEA; Durham; St John's Nottm; EA Min Training Course; *CV* D St Mary Monkseaton 1988–91; C St Mary Ponteland 1991–93; AP St Mary Magdalene Prudhoe 1993–2002; Adv Women's Min 2001–11; Bp's Chapl and DDO 2002–11; Adn of Bodmin from 2011   *Tel:* 01208 892811
             07766 822872
    email: audrey@truro.anglican.org

ELY, Bishop of. See CONWAY, Rt Revd Stephen David

ELY, Dean of. See BONNEY, Very Revd Mark Philip John

ETHERINGTON, Revd Ferial Mary Gould, BA
The Vicarage Station Road Flookburgh Grange over Sands LA11 7JY [CARLISLE] *b* 1944 *educ* Liskeard Gr Sch; Coll Law; St Albans MTS; *CV* Legal Exec 1976–93; St Alb Child Protection Off 1997–2004; Selection Conf Secr and Co-ord Ordained Local Min, Min Div, Abps Counc 1997–2004; Carlisle Dioc Ministerial Review Off 2004–11; House-for-Duty TV, Cartmel Peninsula from 2010; M Legal Aid Commn 1991–93; M Rural Affairs Grp in Synod 2011–
GS 1990–93; 2007–   *Tel:* 01539 558751
             07708 958082
    email: ferial.etherington@btinternet.com

EUROPE, Archdeacon in North-West. WILLIAMS, Canon Meurig (Acting)

EUROPE, Bishop of Gibraltar in. INNES, Rt Revd Dr Robert

EUROPE, Suffragan Bishop in. See HAMID, Rt Revd David

EVERITT, Ven Michael John, BD, AKC
6 Eton Park Preston PR2 9NL [ARCHDEACON OF LANCASTER; BLACKBURN] *b* 1968 *educ* Educ Warriner Sch, Bloxham; Banbury Upper Sch; King's Coll Lon; Gregorian Univ Rome; Queen's Coll Birm; Venerable English Coll Rome; *CV* Asst C Cleveleys St Andrew 1992–95; South Africa 1995–98; Succentor Bloemfontein Cathl 1995–96, Precentor 1996–98; Anglican Chaplain Nat Hosp Bloemfontein 1995–98; Anglican Chaplain and Lect in Theology, Univ of the Orange Free State 1996–98; Senior Coll Chaplain; St Martin's Coll Lancaster 1998–2002; Asst Dir of Ordinands, Blackburn Diocese 2000–02; R Standish St Wilfrid 2002–11; AD Chorley Deanery 2005–11; P-in-c Appley Bridge All Saints 2006–10; Hon Can Blackburn Cathl 2010–11; Adn of Lancaster from 2011   *Tel:* 01772 700331
   email: michael.everitt@blackburn.anglican.org

EXETER, Archdeacon of. See FUTCHER, Ven Christopher David

EXETER, Bishop of. See ATWELL, Rt Revd Robert Ronald

EXETER, Dean of. See DRAPER, Very Revd Jonathan Lee

FAULL, Very Revd Vivienne Frances, MA, BA, MBA
Church House 10–14 Ogleforth York YO1 7Jn [DEAN OF YORK] *b* 1955 *educ* Qu Sch Ches; St Hilda's Coll Ox; Nottm Univ; Open Univ Business Sch; St Jo Coll Nottm; *CV* Dss St Matt and St Jas Mossley Hill 1982–85; Chapl Clare Coll Cam 1985–90; Chapl Glouc Cathl 1990–94; Can Pastor Cov Cathl 1994–2000; Vc Prov Cov Cath 1995–2000; Prov of Leic 2000–02; Dean of Leic 2002–12; Chair AEC from 2009; Dean of York from 2012
GS 1987–90, 2004–12   *Tel:* 01904 557202
            Fax: 01904 557204
    email: dean@yorkminster.org
    Web: www.yorkminster.org

FELIX, Revd David Rhys, LLB, Cert Th
Vicarage Daresbury Warrington WA4 4AE [CHESTER] *b* 1955 *educ* Calday Grange County Gr Sch; Univ of Wales; Ripon Coll, Cuddesdon; *CV* C St Barn Bromborough 1986–89; V St Andr Grange, Runcorn 1989–99; Chapl Halton Gen Hosp 1995–99; P-in-c H Trin Runcorn 1996–99; RD Frodsham 1998–99; Ind Missr, Halton 1998–99; V All SS Daresbury from 1999; Sen Ind Missr

Chester Dio 2000–08; M Dioc Adv Bd for Min 1988–90; M Dioc Adoption Services Cttee 1990–92; Dny Ord Chapl 1990–96; M Dioc Pastl Grp 1994–95; M Dioc Syn from 1994; Dir DBF and M Bp's Coun from 1995; M Dioc Bd of Educ and Schs Cttee 1997–2003; M Archidiaconal Pastl Cttee 1992–94 and from 1998; M Eccl Law Soc from 1987 and of Gen Cttee from 2002; M Dioc Cttee for Miss and Unity 2001–08; Hon Can Ches Cathl 2006; Trustee, Southern North West Training from 2010
GS 2002–   *Tel:* 01925 740348
                                07778 859935 (Mobile)
                    email: david.felix@btinternet.com

FERGUSON, Mrs Linda Ann, BA(Hons), ILM L7
Cert. Executive and Leadership Coaching
Church House Great Smith Street London SW1P 3PS
[CHURCH OF ENGLAND PENSIONS BOARD] *educ* Burnham Gr Sch, Univ of Birm; *CV* Inland Revenue 1985–2005; HM Revenue and Customs Sen Policy Adv 2005–08; Head of Complaints Policy 2008–2011; Sen Customer & Strategy Adv 2011–12; Dir Customer Insight and Strategy C of E Pensions Bd from 2012   *Tel:* 020 7898 1833
        email: linda.ferguson@churchofengland.org

FERGUSON, Rt Revd Paul John, MA, FRCO (CHM), PGCE
21 Thornton Road Stainton Middlesborough TS8 9DS [SUFFRAGAN BISHOP OF WHITBY; YORK] *b* 1955 *educ* Birkenhead Sch; New Coll Ox; Westmr Coll Ox; K Coll Cam; Westcott Ho Th Coll; *CV* C St Mary Chester 1985–88; Chapl and Sacr Westmr Abbey 1988–92; Prec Westmr Abbey 1992–95; Prec and Res Can York Minster 1995–2001; Adn of Cleveland 2001–14; Bp of Whitby from 2014; Wdn of Rdrs 2004–14; Sec Ho Bps' Th Grp 1992–2001; M Porvoo Panel from 2009
GS 2010–14   *Tel:* 01642 593273
                                07770 592746
        email: bishopofwhitby@yorkdiocese.org

FIDDES, Revd Professor Paul, MA, D Phil, DD
Regent's Park College Pusey St Oxford OX1 2LB [ECUMENICAL REPRESENTATIVE] *b* 1947 *educ* St Pet Coll, Ox; Regent's Park Coll, Ox; *CV* Principal, Regent's Park Coll, Ox; Prof of Systematic Theol, Ox Univ; Min of Bapt Union of Gt Britain
GS 2005–   *Tel:* 01865 288134
                                    Fax: 01865 288121
            email: paul.fiddes@regents.ox.ac.uk

FIELDEN, Mr Christopher Cameron, MA
Holly Cottage 19 The Street Broughton Giffard Melksham SN12 8PW [SALISBURY] *b* 1939 *educ* Rossall; Lamp; *CV* Pres, Wines & Spirit Assoc of GB and NI from 1990; Chair, Circle of Wine Writers 2006–08
GS 2010–   *Tel:* 01225 782509
            email: winesource@btconnect.com

FINCH, Mrs Sarah Rosemary Ann, BA
97 Englefield Rd Canonbury London N1 3LJ [LONDON] *b* 1945 *educ* Godolphin Sch Sarum; Dur Univ; Ox Univ; *CV* Ed Barrie and Jenkins 1972–75; Trustee BFBS 1978–2005; Chair Exec Cttee BFBS 1991–94; Freelance Non-Fiction Ed from 1986; Gov Sir John Cass's Foundn Primary Sch (C of E) from 1996; M CEEC from 2000; Coun M Latimer Trust from 2003; M Revision Ctee, Common Worship Ordinal; elected M Appts Ctee from 2005; Coun M Oak Hill Theol Coll from 2006; M Angl Mainstream Strg Cttee from 2006; Trustee Latimer Trust from 2007; Dep Chair Latimer Trust Cttee from 2009; M Fin and Gen Purposes Cttee of Oak Hill Theo Coll from 2009
GS 2000–   *Tel:* 020 7226 2803
                                    Fax: 020 7704 2257
                email: sarahrafinch@yahoo.co.uk

FISHER, Ms Alison, CQSW, CMI
[WEST YORKSHIRE AND THE DALES] *b* 1959 *educ* King Edward VI, Devon; Leeds Univ; Univ Coll Cardiff; *CV* Probation Officer 1981–90, Senior Probation Officer from 1990; Non Exec Dir Calderdale & Huddersfield Foundn Trust from 2005; Gen Tching Counc, Lay m from 2007; Diversity Mgr, West Yorkshire Probation Trust from 2008
GS 2010–   *email:* alison.fisher1@ntlworld.com

FITTALL, Mr William Robert, MA
Church House Great Smith St London SW1P 3AZ [SECRETARY GENERAL OF THE GENERAL SYNOD AND THE ARCHBISHOPS' COUNCIL] *b* 1953 *educ* Dover Gr Sch; Ch Ch Ox; *CV* Home Office 1975–80; Ecole Nat d'Administration Paris 1980–81; Home Office 1981–91; Prin Private Sec to N Ireland Sec 1992–93; Home Office 1993–95; Under Sec and Chief of Assessments Staff, Cabinet Office 1995–97; Dir Crime Reduction and Com Programmes, Home Office 1997–2000; Assoc Political Dir, N Ireland Office 2000–02; Sec Gen GS and AC from 2002   *Tel:* 020 7898 1360
                                07738 883712 (Mobile)
                                    Fax: 020 7898 1369
        email: william.fittall@churchofengland.org

FITZSIMONS, Canon Kathryn Anne, Cert Th, Cert Ed; MA
227 Beech Lane Leeds LS9 6SW [WEST YORKSHIRE AND THE DALES] *b* 1957 *educ* Richmond Sch; Bedford Coll of HE; NEOC; Univ of Leeds; *CV* NSM C St Jo Bilton, Harrogate 1990–2002; Soc Resp Officer 1992–99; Dioc Urban Officer 1999–2013; Hon Can Ripon Cathl from 2004; Pres Diaconal Assoc of the C of E 2003–10; P-i-c Church of the Epiphany, Gipton from 2014, P-i-c Oakwood Church from 2015
GS 2004–5, 2005–10, 2010–   *Tel:* 0113 225 6702
            email: kathrynfitzsimons@hotmail.com
                            Twitter: @CanonKathryn

FLACH, Canon Deborah Mary, Dip HE Theol, Dip Counselling
7 rue Leonard de Vinci 59700 Marcq en Baroeul France [EUROPE] *b* 1954 *educ* Beckenham Convent Sch; Trin Coll Bris; Salis and Wells Th Coll; *CV* C St Pet Chantilly, France 1994–96; C H Trin Maisons-Laffitte, France 1996–2004, Asst Chapl 2004–07; M Dioc Syn from 1994; Asst Dir of Ordinands (France) 1997–2010; P-in-c Ch Ch, Lille (Eur) from 2007; Chair House of Clergy 2007–13; Bp's Counc 2007–13; AD Northern France from 2014
GS 2005–   *Tel:* +33 3 28526636
email: chaplain@christchurchlille.com

FLETCHER, Rt Revd Colin William , MA, OBE
Arran House Sandy Lane Yarnton Oxford OX5 1PB [AREA BISHOP OF DORCHESTER; OXFORD] *b* 1950 *educ* Marlboro Coll; Tr Coll Ox; Wycliffe Hall Th Coll; *CV* C St Pet Shipley 1975–79; Tutor Wycliffe Hall and C St Andr Ox 1979–84; V H Tr Margate 1984–93; RD Thanet 1989–93; Dom Chapl to Abp of Cant 1993–2000; Canon Dallas Cathl 1993–2000; Bp of Dorchester from 2000
                                    Tel: 01865 208218
                                    Fax: 01865 849003
email: bishopdorchester@oxford.anglican.org

FLETCHER, Mr Ian Jack, FCA
38 Heaton Grove Heaton Bradford BD9 4DZ [WEST YORKSHIRE AND THE DALES] *b* 1952 *educ* Woodhouse Grove Sch; *CV* Articled Clerk, 1970–74; Chartered Accountant from 1975; Dir D J Fletcher (Insurances) Ltd from 1973; Dir Bradford Churches For Dialogue and Diversity; Dir Wellsprings Together Bradford; Chair Church in the World Dioc Syn Cttee; Lay Canon Bradf Cathl 2001-08; Reader from 2007; Trustee Queen Victoria Clergy Fund from 2010; M Bradf Bps Coun from 2012; Consultant KJA Fletcher Greenwood Ltd from 2013
GS 2010–   *Tel:* 01274 492839
                                    01274 850222
                                    07788 413716
                                    Fax: 01274 725470
email: ijf@fgco.com

FLETCHER, Mr Philip John, CBE, MA
20 Calais St Camberwell London SE5 9LP [APPOINTED MEMBER, ARCHBISHOPS' COUNCIL] *b* 1946 *educ* Marlborough Coll; Trin Coll Ox; *CV* Dir Gen Cities and Countryside Dept of Environment to 1996; Receiver, Metropolitan Police District 1996–2000; Dir Gen Water Services (OFWAT) 2000–06; Chair OFWAT 2006–12; Member Ofqual (Qualifications and Examinations Regulator) Bd from 2010; Chair MPA Coun from 2012
GS 2007–   *Tel:* 020 7733 2200
email: philipjfletcher@yahoo.co.uk

FOLLETT, Mr Samuel (Joseph),
Christ Church Vicarage 5 High Oaks St Albans AL3 6DJ [ST ALBANS] *b* 1990 *educ* St. George's Sch;

Harpenden; Nott Univ; Ridley Hall Camb; *CV* PA to CE, Church Army 2009–10; Dir, Simplicity from 2007
GS 2010–   *Tel:* 07868 258303
                                    07412 555039
                         email: sam@samfollett.co.uk
                    2nd email: sam.follett@gmail.com

FOREMAN, Mrs (Antoinette Joan) Anne, CCYW
5 St Leonards Road Exeter Devon EX2 4LA [EXETER] *b* 1943 *educ* Teignmouth Gr Sch; Bradf & Ilkley Comm Coll; *CV* Yth & Comm Worker, Sutton 1983–85; Senior Yth & Comm Worker, Kingston 1985–88; Asst Prin Yth Off, Sutton 1988–91; National Yth Off Genl Syn Brd Ed 1991–95; Ch House; M GS Brd Miss 2001–03; Lay Chair Okehampton Deanery; 2007–12; M Dioc Syn; M Bps Counc; Vice Chair Dioc Miss & Pstrl Cttee; Chair Vacancy in See Cttee; Bps Adv from 2008; External Exam BEd Fieldwork Placements St. Martins Coll Lan 1992–94; M Adv Counc Comm & Yth Work Course Goldsmiths Coll 1991–94; Dir & Trustee Guildford YMCA 2002–05; M Counc Mngment Univ Coll St. Mark & St. John 2006–10
GS 1999–2005; 2010–   *Tel:* 01392 279859
                                    01392 217020
                         email: anne@anneforeman.co.uk

FORSTER, Rt Revd Dr Peter Robert , MA, BD, Ph D
Bishop's House Abbey Square Chester CH1 2JD [BISHOP OF CHESTER] *b* 1950 *educ* Tudor Grange Gr Sch Solihull; Merton Coll Ox; Edin Univ; Edin Th Coll; *CV* C St Matt and St Jas Mossley Hill Liv 1980–82; Sen Tutor St Jo Coll Dur 1983–91; V Beverley Minster 1991–96; Bp of Ches from 1996; Ch Commr 1999–2004, 2009–13
GS 1985–91,1996–   *Tel:* 01244 350864
                    email: bpchester@chester.anglican.org

FORWARD, Miss Emma Joy, BA, PGCE
24 Whitchurch Ave Exeter EX2 5NT [EXETER] *b* 1984 *educ* St Pet C of E High Sch Ex; St Hugh's Coll Ox; *CV* Trainee tchr from 2005; full time tchr from 2006
GS 2005–   *Tel:* 01392 251617
                    email: emmaforward@yahoo.co.uk

FOSTER, Rt Revd Christopher Richard James, BA, MA (ECON), MA, HonDLitt
Bishopsgrove 26 Osborn Rd Fareham PO16 7DQ [BISHOP OF PORTSMOUTH] *b* 1953 *educ* R Gr Sch Guildf; Dur Univ; Manch Univ; Trinity Hall Cam, Wescott Ho Cam; *CV* Lect in Economics Univ of Dur 1976–77; Asst C Tettenhall Regis TM Wolverhampton 1980–82; Chapl Wadham Col Ox and Asst P St Mary w St Cross and St Pet in the East Ox 1982–86; V Ch Ch Southgate 1986–94; CME Dir Edmonton Area 1988–94; Sub Dean and Res Can St Alb 1994–2001; Bp of Hertford 2001–10; Bp of Portsmouth from 2010
                                    Tel: 01329 280247
                                    Fax: 01329 231538
              email: bishports@portsmouth.anglican.org

FRAIS, Revd Jonathan Jeremy, LLB BA DipTh
The Rectory 11 Coverdale Avenue Little Common East Sussex TN39 4TY [CHICHESTER] *b* 1965 *educ* Judd Gr Sch; Tonbridge; Kingston Poly; Oak Hill Coll; *CV* AC Ch Ch, Orpington 1992–96; Asst Chapl, St Andrew's, Moscow 1996–99; Chapl, Ch Ch, Kyiv, Ukraine 1999–2005; R, St Mark's, Bexhill, from 2005; M Adv Grp Ch Soc 2007–10 GS 2000–05; 2010–   *Tel and Fax:* 01424 843733
email: frais@tiscali.co.uk

FRANCE, Archdeacon of. NAYLOR, Ven Ian

FRANKLIN, Revd Canon Richard Heighway, BA, MPhil
Holy Trinity Vicarage 7 Glebe Close Weymouth Dorset DT4 9RL [SALISBURY] *b* 1954 *educ* Warwick Sch; Southampton Univ; Salis & Wells Th Coll; *CV* C Thame w Towersey 1978–81; Asst chapl Univ of Southampton 1981–83; Tutor & Dir of Studies Chich Th Coll 1983–89; P-in-c Stalbridge 1989–94; V Holy Trinity Weymouth from 1994; Ed journal 'Studies in Christian Ethics' 1987–91; M Dioc Brd of Ch & Soc 1996–2006; RD Weymouth 2004–08
GS 2003–05; 2010–   *Tel:* 01305 760354
email: richardfranklin@iname.com

FREEMAN, Mr John Jeremy Collier, Eur Ing, DLC, B Sc, MIChemE, C ENG
Stable Court 20a Leigh Way Weaverham Northwich CW8 3PR [CHESTER] *b* 1937 *educ* Embley Park Sch; Loughb Univ; *CV* Graduate Chemical Engineer ICI 1961–94 inc Asst to Gen Mgr Magadi Soda Co, Kenya 1975–77; Rtd 1994, now very active in vol sector; M Local Agenda 21 Forum; Par Coun from 1980; Sch Gov from 1980; M Dioc Fin and Central Services Cttee from 1994; M Exec Chs Together in Cheshire from 1995; Chair Dioc PWM Cttee; M Dioc CSR Cttee; Chr Aid activist; Sec Dioc Justice and Devel Educ Grp; M Bp's Coun; M Dioc Syn; Dioc World Devel Adv; M Core Grp Angl World Devel Advs; Treas Open Syn Grp; Companion of the Melanesian Brotherhood
GS 2000–   *Tel:* 01606 852872
Fax: 01606 854140
email: jjcfreeman@talktalk.net

FREEMAN, Rt Revd Robert John, B Sc, MA
Holmcroft 13 Castle Road Kendal LA9 7AU [SUFFRAGAN BISHOP OF PENRITH; CARLISLE] *b* 1952 *educ* Cambs High Sch; St Jo Coll Dur; Fitzw Coll Cam; Ridley Hall Cam; *CV* C St Jo Blackpool 1977–81; TV St Winifred Chigwell 1981–85; V Ch of the Martyrs Leic 1985–99; RD Christianity S (Leic) 1994–98; Hon Can Leic 1994–2003; Nat Evang Adv, AC from 1999; Chair Agenda and Support Cttee of Grp for Evangelisation (CTE) 2000–03; Sec Miss, Evang and Renewal in Eng Cttee, Bd of Mission, AC 1999–2003; Chair rejesus.co.uk from 2000; Dir Just Fairtrade Ltd 2000–03; Adn of Halifax 2003–11; M Chs Regional Commn for Yorkshire and Humber-

side 2004; Chair Chr Enquiry Agency f2006–10; Trustee Simeon and Hyndman's 2007–10; Chair Wakefield Dioc Bd of Finance 2008–11, Bp of Penrith from 2011
GS 1997–99, 2008–11   *Tel:* 01539 727836
07584 684308
email: bishop.penrith@carlislediocese.org.uk
Web: www.rejesus.co.uk
Twitter: @BpRobInCumbria

FRENCH, Mr Philip Colin, MA, MMath, MIET
Arden Five Oak Green Rd Five Oak Green Tonbridge TN12 6TJ [ROCHESTER] *b* 1960 *educ* R Gr Sch Newc; Br Sch Brussels; Churchill Coll Cam; *CV* Rsch Asst, Univ Coll Lon 1984–87; Overseas Career Service Officer, Br Coun 1987–96; (First Sec (Educ & Science), Calcutta 1988–91); Sen Consult, Hewlett-Packard Ltd 1996–99; Tech Dir, Software.com, later Openwave Systems 1999–2003; IT mgt posts in HM Prison Service 2003–06; Chief Information Officer Nat Offender Mgt Service 2006–09; Chief Technology Officer, Min of Justice 2009–12; Non-exec dir and charity trustee, Eduserv from 2011, Chair from 2014; Business Engagement Dir, Steria from 2012; Information Systems Strategy Consultant to Alzheimer's Society; URC elder; Lay Chair Roch Dioc Syn from 2012; Chair, Hands of Compassion (supporting education in Zambia) from 2011
GS 1985–88, 2005–   *Tel:* 01892 838713 (Home)
07952 273253 (Mobile)
email: philip.c.french@btinternet.com
Web: uk.linkedin.com/in/philipfrench

FRITH, Rt Revd Richard Michael Cockayne, MA
The Bishop's House, Hereford HR4 9BN [BISHOP OF HEREFORD] *b* 1949 *educ* Marlboro Coll; Fitzw Coll Cam; St Jo Coll Nottm; *CV* C Mortlake w E Sheen 1974–78; TV Thamesmead 1978–83; TR Keynsham 1983–92; Adn of Taunton 1992–98; Bp of Hull 1998–2014; Bp of Hereford from 2014
GS 1995–98   *Tel:* 01432 271355
Fax: 01432 373346
email: bishop@hereford.anglican.org

FROST, Rt Revd Dr Jonathan Hugh, BD, MTh, DUniv, MSSTh, FRSA
Bishop's House St Mary's Church Close Wessex Lane Southampton SO18 2ST [SUFFRAGAN BISHOP OF SOUTHAMPTON; WINCHESTER] *b* 1964 *educ* KCS Wimbledon; Aberdeen Univ; Nottm Univ; Surrey Univ; Ridley Hall Camb; *CV* C W Bridgford St Giles 1993–97; Police Chapl Trent Div, Notts Constabulary 1994–97; R Ash St Peter 1997–2002; Can Res Guildf Cath 2002–10; Angl Chapl Univ of Surrey 2002–10; Bp's Adv for Inter-Faith Relations 2007–10; Co-ord Chapl Univ of Surrey 2007–10; Tutor Christian Doctrine Local Min Course 1999–2010; Bp of Southampton from 2010
GS 2009–10   *Tel:* 023 8067 2684
email: bishop.jonathan@winchester.anglican.org
Web: www.winchester.anglican.org

FROUDE, Ven Christine Ann, Dip Theol; ACIB
1 Orchard Close Winterbourne Bristol BS36 1BF
[ARCHDEACON OF MALMESBURY AND ACTING
ARCHDEACON OF BRISTOL] *b* 1947 *educ* Llwyn Y
Bryn Girls Gr Swansea; Salisbury and Wells;
CV C St Mary Magdalene Stoke Bishop 1995–99;
Chapl Univ Hosps Bristol NHS Found Children's
Directorate 1999–2001; D of Women's Min 2001–
11; Hon Can Bristol Cathl 2001–11; Adn Malmes-
bury from 2011; Dioc Pastl Managment Ctte; Dioc
Housing and Glebe Ctte; DAC; Dioc Miss and
Pastl Ctte; Dioc Finance Ctte; Acting Adn Bristol
from 2012   *Tel:* 01454 778366
    email: christine.froude@bristoldiocese.org

FROUDE, Canon David Colin, ACIB
1 Orchard Close Winterbourne Bristol BS36 1BF
[BRISTOL] *b* 1949 *educ* Colston's Sch, Bris; *CV*
HSBC Bank (formerly Midland) 1967–2004
retiring as Senior Manager; Par Clerk, St Mary's,
Shirehampton, Bris 2001–11; M Bris Cathl Coun
2002–13; M Provincial Panel Clergy Discipline
Measure from 2003; Chair Bris Dioc Brd Finance
Ltd 2004–11; Chair Bris DBF Fin Cttee 2004–11;
Chair Bris DBF Budget Cttee 2004–11; Chair Bris
DBF Remuneration Cttee 2004–11; M Bris DBF
Audit Cttee 2004–11; M Bris Dioc Syn Agenda
Cttee 2004–11; M Bp's Coun 2004–11; Chair
Trustees Bris DBF Staff Retirement Benefit
Scheme 2004–11; SW Region DBF Chair, M 2004–
11, Convenor 2006–11; C of E Consultative Grp
of DBF Chairs and Dioc Secs, M 2006–11, Chair
2009–11; M C of E Nat Procurement Grp 2007–13;
M Bishop of Bristol Senior Staff 2007–11; M Bris-
tol Dioc Strategic Policy Grp 2007–09; M C of E
Pensions Bd from 2009; Lay Canon Bris Cathl
from 2010; Chair C of E Pensions Bd Audit
Cttee from 2011; Chair Strg Ctte Draft Dioc Eur
Measure 2012; Lay Chair Bris Dioc Syn from
2012; M Bris Bp's Coun from 2012; M Bris Dioc
Syn Agenda Cttee from 2012; Jt Chair Bris Dioc
Appts Cttee from 2012; M RACSC from 2014;
Chair Revision Cttee Draft Canon amend Canon
B12 2014
GS 2010–   *Tel:* 01454 778366
                                     07768 958704
    email: davidfroude@lineone.net
    2nd email: davidcfroude@gmail.com

FRY, Mrs Christine Ann, BA, PG Dip
*25 St Leonards Avenue, Chineham Basingstoke
RG24 8RD* [WINCHESTER] *b* 1964 *educ* Arden Sch;.
Solihull Sixth Form Coll; Southampton Univ;
Middlesex Poly; *CV* Probation Service Off,
Middlesex Probation Area,1986–88; Trainee Pro-
bation Off, Middlesex Probation Area, 1988–90;
Probation Off, Hampshire Probation Area 1990–
93; Youth and Comm Worker, St Mary's Ch,
Eastrop, Basingstoke 1993–95; Court Welfare Off,
Hampshire Probation Area 1995–98; Probation
Off, Hampshire Probation Area, 1998–2001;
Senior Probation Off, Hampshire Probation Area
2001–08; Area Mgr, Hampshire Proabtion Area

2008–09; Business Change Mgr, Hampshire
Probation Trust from 2010; Operations Mgr,
Hampshire Probation Trust from 2013
GS 1995–2000; 2010–   *Tel:* 01256 474466
    email: chrisfry01@yahoo.co.uk

**FULHAM, Suffragan Bishop of. See BAKER,
Rt Revd Jonathan Mark Richard**

FUTCHER, Ven Christopher David, BD, MTh, MA
Emmanuel House Station Road Ide Exeter EX2 9RS
[ARCHDEACON OF EXETER] *b* 1958 *educ* Strode's Gr
Sch, Egham, Surrey; Univ of Edin; Heythrop Coll
Univ of Lon; King's Coll Lon; Westcott Ho; *CV*
Asst C Borehamwood TM 1982–85; Asst C All
Saints Pin Green Stevenage 1985–88; V All Saints
Pin Green Stevenage 1988–96; V St Stephen's
St Albans 1996–2000; R Harpenden 2000–12; Dioc
Ecum Officer 2004–12; Adn of Exeter from 2012;
Wdn of Rdrs from 2013: M English ARC 1991–
2001;   *Tel:* 01392 425577
    email: archdeacon.of.exeter@exeter.anglican.org

GATES, Ven Simon Philip, MA, BA
7 Hoadly Road Streatham London SW16 1AE
[ARCHDEACON OF LAMBETH; SOUTHWARK] *b* 1960
educ Merchant Taylor's Sch, Crosby, Liverpool;
Univ St Andrews; Cranmer Hall; St John's
Coll, Durham;; *CV* C St John's Southall 1987–91;
AM, St Andrew's Kowloon, Hong Kong 1991–95;
V St Stephen's Clapham Park 1996–2006; V St
Thomas with St Stephen Telford Park 2006–13;
AD Lambeth South 2006–13; Adn of Lambeth
from 2013   *Tel:* 020 8545 2440
    email: simon.gates@southwark.anglican.org

GAY, Canon Perran Russell, MA , BA, PGCE, FRGS
Cathedral Office 14 St Mary's Street, Truro TR1 2AF
[TRURO] *b* 1959 *educ* Truro Sch; Cam Univ; Ex
Univ; Ox Univ; Ripon Coll Cuddesdon; *CV* AC
Bodmin w Lanhydrock & Lanivet 1987–90; Bp
Truro's Domestic Chapl 90–94; Truro Dioc Ecum
Offr 1990–93; Dir Ministerial Training, Truro
1993–2001; Can Chan, Truro Cathl 1994–2001;
Can Prec, Truro Cathl from 2001; Dioc Lit Adv,
Truro from 2001; Chapl Epiphany Ho, Truro
2007–12; M Dioc Brd Ed 1988–90 and from 2012;
M Dioc Decade of Evan Steering Cttee 1990–94;
Exec M of Churches Together Cornwall 1990–94;
M CTE Enabling Grp 1992–94; M Praxis Coun
1996–2012; County Chapl, Royal British Legion
from 1998; Chair, Dioc Deaf Ministry Support
Grp 1996–2001; Chair, Dioc Lit Cttee from 2001;
M Dioc Formation Grp 2004–12; Chair, Dioc
Porvoo Link Cttee from 2009; M CFCE from 2011;
Dir Assco English Cathls from 2011; M Liturgical
Commn from 2011; M Joint Liturgical Grp from
2011; M Dioc Bd of Patronage from 2012; M Dioc
Glebe Cttee from 2012; M Planning Cttee
Northern European Cathedrals Conf from 2013
GS 2010–   *Tel:* 01872 245003
                                     Fax: 01872 277788
    email: perran@perrangay.com

GEORGE, Rt Worshipful Charles Richard, MA, QC

Francis Taylor Building Inner Temple London EC4Y 7BY [DEAN OF THE ARCHES AND AUDITOR] *b* 1945 *educ* Bradfield Coll Magdalen Coll Ox; Corpus Christi Coll Cam; *CV* Asst master Eton College 1967–72; Barrister, Francis Taylor Building, Inner Temple (formerly 2 Harcourt Buildings) from 1975; Chancellor Dioc of S'wark 1996–2009; M of Panel of Chairmen of Bps' Disciplinary Tribunals for Provinces of Canterbury and York 2007–09; M of Ho Coun, St Stephen's Ho, Ox 1999–2012; Visiting Lecturer in Environmental Law, KCL from 2006; Dean of the Arches, Auditor of the Chancery Court of York, Master of the Faculties from 2009
GS 2009– *Tel:* 020 7353 8415
Fax: 020 73537622
email: charles.george@ukgateway.net

GERMANY AND NORTHERN EUROPE, Archdeacon of. See POTTER, Ven Peter (Acting)

GIBBS, Rt Revd Jonathan Robert, MA PhD

[AREA BISHOP OF HUDDERSFIELD; WEST YORKSHIRE AND THE DALES] *b* 1961 *educ* The King's Sch; Chester Jesus Coll Ox; Jesus College, Cam; Ridley Hall, Cam; *CV* AC Stalybridge, Holy Trin 1989–92; Chapl, Basel, Switzerland w Freiburg, Germany 1992–98; R, Heswall from 1998; M Bp's Coun from 1999; M Fin and Scrutiny Cttee from 1999; Chair of House of Clergy, Dioc Syn from 2006; Chair Dioc Clergy Chairs Forum from 2011; M Standing Cttee Ho of Clergy GS from 2011; M Coun British Funeral Services from 2012; M Meissen Cttee from 2012; M Clergy Discipline Commn from 2014; Bp of Huddersfield from 2014
GS 1995–98; 2010–14 *email:* bishop.jonathan@westyorkshiredales.anglican.org

GIBRALTAR IN EUROPE, Bishop of. INNES, Rt Revd Robert

GIBRALTAR, Archdeacon of. JOHNSTON, Revd Canon Geoffrey (Acting)

GIBRALTAR, Dean of. See PADDOCK, Very Revd Dr John

GIDDINGS, Dr Philip James, MA, D Phil

5 Clifton Park Rd Caversham Reading RG4 7PD [OXFORD] *b* 1946 *educ* Sir Thos Rich's Sch Glouc; Worc and Nuff Colls Ox; *CV* Lect in Public Admin Ex Univ 1970-72; Sen Lect Politics and Intl Relations, Reading Univ; Rdr; M Dioc Syn from 1974; M Bp's Coun 1979–2006; Lay Vc Pres Dioc Syn 1989–2000; M BSR 1991–96, Exec Cttee 1992–96; M CAC 1992–97; M GS Panel of Chairmen 1995–96; Vc Chair GS Ho of Laity 1995–2000, 2005–10; Chair, GS Ho of Laity from 2010; M AC from 1999; Chair Ch and World Div AC 1999–

2002; M Crown Appts Commn Review Grp 1999–2001; Elected M AC from 2000; Chair Coun of MPA from 2003; Trustee, Angl Mainstream UK from 2003, Chairman and Convenor 2003–14; Dep Chair GS Legislative Cttee 2005–10; M GS Appointments Ctte from 2010, M Coun Wycliffe Hall, Oxford from 2011
GS 1985– *Tel:* 0118 954 3892 (Home)
0118 378 8207 (Office)
Fax: 0118 975 3833
email: philip.j.giddings@gmail.com

GILBERTSON, Ven Dr Michael Robert, MA, BA, PhD

Church House 5500 Daresbury Park Daresbury Warrington WA4 4GE [ARCHDEACON OF CHESTER] *b* 1961 *educ* Stockport Grammar Sch; New Coll Ox; Cranmer Hall Dur; *CV* Dept of Trade and Industry 1982–1991; C St Matthew's Surbiton 1997–2000; V All Saints Stranton 2000–2010; AD of Hartlepool 2002–2010; Hon Can Durham Cathedral 2008–2010; Adn of Chester from 2010 *Tel:* 01928 718834
01244 405253 (Home)
email: michael.gilbertson@chester.anglican.org

GILLEY, Revd Dr Margaret (Meg) Mary, MTheol, PhD

St Chad's Rectory Dunsmuir Grove Bensham Gateshead NE8 4QL [DURHAM] *b* 1954 *educ* Nelson Gr Sch; St And Univ; Dur Univ; NEOC; *CV* Primary Care Devel rsch, Sunderland Health Commn 1991–94; Programmes Mgr, Sunderland Health Auth 1994–96; Locality Dir, Co Durham Health Auth 1996–98; Chief Exec, Darlington Primary Care Grp 1998–2000; C St Jo Birtley 2000–03; V St Mark Stockton & St Jo Elton 2003–2009; Assoc P Lanchester Deanery 2009–11; R Bensham and Teams from 2011
GS 2005– *Tel:* 0191 478 6338
07752 432366 (Mobile)
email: meg.gilley@durham.anglican.org
Twitter: @MegGilley1

GLEDHILL, Rt Revd Jonathan Michael, BA, MA, BCTS, D Univ (Keele)

Bishop's House 22 The Close Lichfield WS13 7LG [BISHOP OF LICHFIELD] *b* 1949 *educ* Strode's Sch Egham; Keele Univ; Bris Univ; Trin Coll Bris; *CV* C All SS Marple 1975–78; P-in-c St Geo Folkestone 1978–83; V St Mary Bredin Cant 1983–96; Tutor/Lect Cant Sch of Min 1983–94; Tutor/Lect SE Inst for Th Educ 1994–96; RD Cant 1988–94; Hon Can Cant Cathl 1992–96; Bp of Southn 1996–2003; M Meissen Commn 1993–96; Chair Angl Old Catholic Internat Co-ordinating Council Coun from 1998; Chair Nat Coll of Evangelists 1998–2010; Bp of Lichfield from 2003; Keele Univ Hon Dr Univ 2007
GS 1995–96, 2003– *Tel:* 01543 306000
Fax: 01543 306009
email: bishop.lichfield@lichfield.anglican.org

GLOUCESTER, Archdeacon of. See SEARLE, Ven Jacqueline Ann

GLOUCESTER, Bishop of. [NOT APPOINTED AT TIME OF GOING TO PRESS]

GLOUCESTER, Dean of, LAKE, Very Revd Stephen David

GNANADOSS, Miss Vasantha Berla Kirubaibai, B Sc
242 Links Rd London SW17 9ER [SOUTHWARK] *b* 1951 *educ* Portsm Gr Sch; Birkbeck Coll Lon; *CV* Commissioner's Secretariat, Metropolitan Police Service
GS 1990–   *Tel:* 020 8769 3515
                                   020 7230 5017
                                   07803 590610 (Mobile)
email: vasanthignanadoss@yahoo.co.uk

GODDARD, Canon Giles William, MA (Cantab); MA Systematic Theology; MA Creative and Life Writing
St John's Vicarage 1 Secker Street London SE1 8UF [SOUTHWARK] *b* 1962 *educ* Lancing Coll Sussx; Clare Coll Camb; King's Coll Lon; S'wark Ordination Course; Goldsmiths Coll Lon; *CV* Asst Buyer John Lewis Partnership 1984–87; Housing Corp 1987–88; Dir Development ASRA Housing Assoc 1988–91; Dir S'wark Dioc Housing Assoc 1991–95; C St Faith's North Dulwich 1995–98; R St Peter's Walworth 1998–2009; AD S'wark and Newington 2001–06; Chair Inclusive Church 2006–11; Hon Can S'wark Cathl from 2008; P-in-c St John's Waterloo; Appts Ctte
GS 2010–   *Tel:* 07762 373674
email: giles@stjohnswaterloo.org

GODDARD, Mrs Madelaine, BSc, SRD
35 Princes Drive Littleover Derby DE23 6DX [DERBY] *b* 1944 *educ* Lewis Sch for Girls; Lon Univ; *CV* Sen Dietitian, Bethnal Green 1967–69; District Dietitian, N Gwent HMC 1969–77; pt tchr, Derby High Sch from 1986; Dioc Pres MU; Tax Commr
GS 2003–   *Tel:* 01332 348077
                                   07817 043257 (Mobile)
email: goddard35@btinternet.com

GODDARD, Mrs Vivienne, BA, PGCE
39 Kearsley Ave Tarleton Preston PR4 6BP [BLACKBURN] *b* 1948 *educ* Roch Girls' Gr Sch; Dur Univ; *CV* RE Tchr, Cleveland Girls Grammar School 1970–74 Supply Tchr 1974–76; Dir Cleveland Lay Training & Foundn Scheme for York Dioc; RE Tchr Bydales School, Marske, 1984–88; Acting Head of Dept, 1988–92; Publishing Manager, Rutherford House, Edinburgh, 1994–95; RE Tchr 1996–97; Local Non-Stipendiary Ministry Officer, Blackb1998; OLM Officer, Blackb 2004; Bp's Officer for LM 1996–2007
GS 1980–88; 2000–   *Tel:* 01772 812532
                                   07779 786141 (Mobile)
email: viviennegoddard@gmail.com

GODFREY, Very Revd Nigel Philip, BA; MA; MBA; MSc; MRTPI
The Deanery Albany Road Peel Isle of Man IM5 1JS [DEAN OF SODOR AND MAN] *b* 1951 *educ* Ripon Coll Cuddesdon; Lon Guildhall Univ; K Coll Lon; *CV* C Kennington St Jo w St Jas S'wark 1979–89; Community of Ch the Servant 1984–93; V Brixton Road Ch Ch S'wark 1989–2001; Prin OLM Scheme 2001–07; Chapl S'wark Cathl 2002–07; V German S & M from 2007; P-in-c Patrick from 2011; Vice-Dean St German's Cathl from 2007; Dean St Germans Cathl from 2011; Leader WMP 2011; V POWC 2012   *Tel:* 01624 844830
                                   email: dean@cathedral.im
                                   Web: www.cathedral.im

GODSALL, Revd Andrew Paul, BA
20 Newport Way Exeter Devon EX1 7SA [EXETER] *b* 1959 *educ* Tudor Grange Gr Sch; Birm Univ; Ripon Coll Cuddesdon; *CV* BBC Studio Mgr 1981–86; BBC Radio Pro 1984–86; AC, St John's Great Stanmore, 1988–91; Assoc V, All Saints Ealing Comm, 1991–94; V, All Saints Hillingdon, 1994–2001; Chair, Willesden Area Litt Resources Grp, 1995–99; DDO, Willesden Area, Lon, 1999–2001; Asst & Chapl Bp Ex, 2001–06; Sec, Patterns of Ministry Working party, Ex, 2002–03 Dir, Coun Worship & Min, 2006; Can Chan, Ex Cathl, 2006; MIssion Community Dev Officer Exeter 2014
GS 2010–   *Tel:* 01392 294920
email: andrew.godsall@exeter.anglican.org

GOLDSMITH, Rt Revd Christopher David (Chris), BA, DPhil
Vounder Tresillian Truro Cornwall TR2 4BW [SUUFFRAGAN BISHOP OF ST GERMANS; TRURO] *b* 1954 *educ* Dartford Gr Sch; York Univ; North Thames Min Tr Course; *CV* AC Pitsea with Nevendon 2000–04; V Warley & Great Warley 2004–13; Bp of St Germans from 2013
                                   Tel: 01872 520192
email: bishopofstgermans@truro.anglican.org

GOODER, Dr Paula Ruth, MA, D Phil
61 Linden Rd Bournville Birmingham B30 1JT [BIRMINGHAM] *b* 1969 *educ* Fallowfield C of E H Sch, Loreto Sixth Form Coll, Manch; Worc Coll Ox; Qu Coll Ox; *CV* Tutor in Biblical Studies, Ripon Coll Cuddesdon 1995–2001; Tutor in NT Studies, Qu Foundn 2001–2007; Freelance Writer and Lecturer Biblical Studies from 2007; Theologian in Residence, Bible Society from 2013; Can Theol Birm Cathl from 2005; Canon Theol Guildf Cathl from 2010; Lay Can Salis Cathl from 2010; Six Preacher Cant Cathl from 2012
GS 2005–   *Tel:* 0121 744 0260
email: prgooder@gmail.com

GORHAM, Ven Karen Marisa, BA, FRSA
Rectory Stone Aylesbury HP17 8RZ [ARCHDEACON OF BUCKINGHAM; OXFORD] *b* 1964 *educ* Mayflower

Sch, Billericay; Trin Th Coll Bris; *CV* C North-allerton w Kirby Sigston 1995–99; P-in-c St Paul Maidstone, Asst DDO and RD Maidstone 1999–2007; Hon Can Cant 2006–07; Adn of Bucking-ham from 2007
GS 2003–07, 2010–   *Tel:* 01865 208264
                          01865 208266
     email: archdbuc@oxford.anglican.org
     Web: ArchdeaconKaren@blogspot.com
             Twitter: @ArchdeaconKaren

GORICK, Ven Martin Charles William,
MA(Cantab)
Archdeacon's Lodgings Christ Church Oxford OX1 1DP [ARCHDEACON OF OXFORD] *b* 1962 *educ* W Bridgeford Comp; Selwyn Coll Camb; Ripon Coll Cuddesdon; *CV* C Birtley, Durham 1987–91; Bp's Chapl, Oxford 1991–4; V Smethwick, Birm 1994–2001; AD Warley 1996–2001; V Stratford-upon-Avon 2001–13; Adn of Oxford from 2013
GS 2011–13   *Tel:* 01865 208263
    email: archdeacon.oxford@oxford.anglican.org
         Web: www.oxford.anglican.org

GOUDIE, Dr Richard Angus, MB BChir MRCGP
197 Gilesgate Durham DH1 1QN [DURHAM] *b* 1951 *educ* Barnard Castle Sch; St John's Coll Cam; Kings Coll Hosp Lon; Newcastle GP Vocational Training Scheme; *CV* GP, Cartington Terrace Medical Grp, Newcastle 1982–1991; GP, Kepier Medical Practice, Tyne and Wear, 1991; PCC m St Nicholas Church Dur & Dur Deanery Syn m from 1996; M Dur Dioc Syn from 2006; M Dur Dioc Syn Miss Cttee 2006–10; M Dur Bps Counc 2010
GS 2010–   *Tel:* 0191 3840013
                 Fax: 0191 5849493
     email: angus.goudie@virgin.net

GOVENDER, Very Revd Rogers Morgan,
BTh, Dip Th
Manchester Cathedral Cathedral Yard, Victoria St Manchester M3 1SX [DEAN OF MANCHESTER] *b* 1960 *educ* Glenover High Sch, Durban, S Africa; Univ of Natal (Pietermaritzburg), S Africa; St Paul's Coll, Grahamstown, S Africa; *CV* C Ch Ch Overport, S Africa 1985–87; R St Mary Greyville, Durban, S Africa 1988–92; R St Matt Hayfields, Pietermaritzburg, S Africa 1993–99; Adn of Pietermaritzburg 1997–99; R St Thos Berea, Durban 1999–2000; P-in-c Ch Ch Didsbury, Man 2001–05; P-in-c St Chris Withington, Man 2003–05; AD Withington 2003–05; Dean of Man from 2006; M Dioc Syn; M Bp's Coun; M AC CMEAC from 2006; M AC Liturg Commn from 2006; Chair Dioc Pastl Cttee
GS 2008–2010   *Tel:* 0161 833 2220
              0161 792 2801 (Home)
              07983 978346 (Mobile)
                Fax: 0161 839 6218
     email: dean@manchestercathedral.org

GRANTHAM, Suffragan Bishop of. [NOT APPOINTED AT TIME OF GOING TO PRESS]

GREEN, Ven John, QHC, BCS
Cathedral and Diocesan Office 1 Hill Top Coventry CV1 5AB [ARCHDEACON PASTOR OF COVENTRY] *b* 1953 *educ* SW Ham County Tech Sch; Hendon Coll of Science and Tech; NE Lon Poly; Linc Th Coll; *CV* Project Eng, Thorn Lighting 1974–77, Sen Eng 1977–80; C St Mich and All Angels, Watford 1983–86; C St Steph w. St Julian, St Alb 1986–91; Chapl RN from 1991; Chapl of the Fleet and Adn for RN 2006–10; Hon Can Portsmouth Cath 2006–10; Adn Pastor of Coventry from 2012
GS 2005–   *Tel:* 024 7652 1337
       email: john.green@covcofe.org

GREENER, Very Revd Jonathan Desmond Francis, MA
The Deanery 1 Cathedral Close Margaret St, Wake-field WF1 2DP [DEAN OF WAKEFIELD] *b* 1961 *educ* Reigate Gr Sch; Trin Coll Cam; Coll of Resurrec-tion Mirfield; *CV* C H Trin w St Matt, Southwark 1991–94; Dom Chapl to Bp of Truro 1994–96; V Ch of Good Shepherd, Brighton 1996–2003; Adn of Pontefract 2003–07; Dean of Wakefield from 2007; Ch Commr from 2011
GS 2003–07   *Tel:* 01924 239308 (Home)
              01924 373923 (Office)
                Fax: 01924 215054
     email: jonathan.greener@wakefield-
                        cathedral.org.uk

GREENWOOD, Mr Adrian Douglas Crispin,
MA, MCIH
91 Lynton Rd Bermondsey London SE1 5QT [SOUTHWARK] *b* 1951 *educ* Judd Sch Tonbridge; Jes Coll Cam; Coll of Law Lon; *CV* M Dioc Syn 1994, Lay Chair 2006; Lay Chair Bermondsey Dny Syn 2004; Chwrdn St James Bermondsey 1983–92, 1995–2004; Lay Chair St James Bermond-sey 1982–2013; Chief Exec Gateway Housing Assoc (formerly Bethnal Green and Victoria Park Housing Assoc Ltd) 1992–2010; Dir Victoria Park Housing Assoc 1975–1992; Trustee Salmon Youth Centre Bermondsey 2000–10, Chair from 2010; Trustee East End Community Foundation 2012; Deputy Chair Dulwich Helpline and S'wark Churches Care from 2012; Trustee Together Southwark from 2012; Chair Mission Housing Assoc from 2014
GS 2000–   *email:* amgreenwood@tiscali.co.uk

GREENWOOD, Mr Nigel Desmond, M Phil, M Ed, C CHEM, FRSC, FIBMS, FRIPH
47 Broomfield Adel Leeds LS16 7AD [WEST YORK-SHIRE AND THE DALES] *b* 1944 *educ* Leeds Gr Sch; Leeds Univ; Leic Univ; *CV* Leeds Public Health Dept 1962–68; Tobacco Rsch Coun 1968–69; United Leeds Hosps 1969–74; Wigston CFE 1974–77; Keighley Tech Coll 1978–80; Airedale and Wharfedale Coll 1981–95; Educ and Trg Consult 1995–99; Dir One City Projects 1999–2011; Con-venor W Yorks Faith in F.E. Gp; Hon Lay Can Ripon Cath from 2009; M Ripon Cathl Coun from 2012; Churchwarden St Chad's Far Headingly,

WHO'S WHO

Leeds from 2012; Trustee Trinity Ch Repair Fund; GS 1990–
Tel: 0113 261 1438
07940 587618 (Mobile)
email: greenwoodnd@aol.com

GREGORY, Rt Revd Clive Malcolm, BA, MA
61 Richmond Rd Wolverhampton WV3 9JH [AREA BISHOP OF WOLVERHAMPTON; LICHFIELD] *b* 1961 *educ* Sevenoaks Sch; Lanc Univ; Qu Coll Cam; Westcott Ho Cam; *CV* C St Jo Bapt Margate 1988–92; Sen Chapl Univ of Warwick 1992–98; TR Coventry East 1998–2007; Hon MA, Univ of Warwick 1999; Assoc DDO Coventry 2001–07; Area Bp of Wolverhampton from 2007
Tel: 01902 824503
Fax: 01902 824504
email: bishop.wolverhampton@
lichfield.anglican.org

GRENFELL, Ven Dr Joanne Woolway, BA, MA, MSt, MA. DPhil
313 Havant Road Farlington Portsmouth PO6 1DD [ARCHDEACON OF PORTSDOWN; PORTSMOUTH] *b* 1972 *educ* Egglescliffe Comp Sch; Oriel College Ox; Univ British Columbia; Westcott Ho; *CV* Adviser to Women Students, Oriel Coll Ox 1995–98, Lect Eng 1997–98; C Kirkby TM 2000–03; P-in-c Sheffield Manor 2003–06; DDO and Res Can Sheff 2006–13; Dean of Women's Ministry Sheff 2009–13; Adn of Portsdown from 2013
Tel: 07833 430140
email: joanne.grenfell@portsmouth.anglican.org
Web: http://joannegrenfell.wordpress.com/

GRIFFITHS, Revd Canon Dr Tudor Francis Lloyd, MA (Oxon), PhD
The Rectory 38 Sydenham Villas Road Cheltenham GL52 6DZ [GLOUCESTER] *b* 1954 *educ* Penlan Comp Sch Swansea; Jes Coll Ox; Leeds Univ; Wycliffe Hall Ox;; *CV* Min Can Brecon Cathl, C Brecon 1979–81; C Swansea St James 1981–83; R Llangattock and Llangynidr 1983–88; CMS Mission Partner and Tutor at Bishop Tucker Theol Coll, Uganda 1989–95; Dioc Missioner Monmouth 1996–2003; R Hawarden 2003–11; R and AD Cheltenham from 2011
GS 2013–
Tel: 01242 234470
07718 906066
email: tudorg@stmstm.org.uk

GRIMSBY, Suffragan Bishop of. COURT, Rt Revd David

GRYLLS, Revd Catherine Anne, MA, MTh, PGCE
15 Raglan Road Edgbaston Birmingham B5 7RA [BIRMINGHAM] *b* 1970 *educ* John Hanson Sch, Andover; Marlborough Coll; Cam Univ, Birm Univ, Ox Univ; Ripon Coll Cuddesdon; *CV* Tm, S'wark Dioc Retreat House 1991–92; Maths and RE Teacher, Saltley Sch, Birmingham, 1993–95; Maths Teacher, Holyhead Sch, Birmingham, 1995–97; Asst C, St Peter's Hall Green Birm 2000–04; P-in-c St Paul Balsall Heath and St Mary & St Ambrose Edgbaston, Birm 2004–05; P-in-C,

Balsall Heath and Edgbaston (SS Mary & Ambrose), Birm 2006–08; Incumbent, Balsall Heath and Edgbaston, Birm from 2008; AD Moseley, Birm from 2013
GS 2010–
Tel: 0121 440 2196
email: gryllsc@btinternet.com

GUERNSEY, Dean of. [NOT APPOINTED AT TIME OF GOING TO PRESS]

GUILDFORD, Bishop of. See WATSON, Rt Revd Andrew John

GUILDFORD, Dean of. GWILLIAMS, Very Revd Dianna

HACKNEY, Archdeacon of. See TREWEEK, Ven Rachel

HADDOCK, Mr Peter,
43 Woodland Way Morden SM4 4DS [SOUTHWARK] *CV* Elected to GS 2005
GS 2005–
email: peterhaddock@rspence.plus.com

HALIFAX, Archdeacon of. See DAWTRY, Ven Anne Frances

HALL, Very Revd John Robert, BA, Hon DD, Hon DTheol, Hon DLitt, FSA, FRSA, Hon FCollT
The Deanery Westminster London SW1P 3PA [DEAN OF WESTMINSTER] *b* 1949 *educ* St Dunstan's Coll Catford; St Chad's Coll Dur; Cuddesdon Th Coll; *CV* Head of RE Malet Lambert High Sch Hull 1971–73; C St Jo Divine Kennington 1975–78; P-in-c All SS S Wimbledon 1978–84; V St Pet Streatham 1984–92; Exam Chapl to Bp of S'wark 1988–92; M GS Bd of Educ 1991–92; Chair FCP 1990–93; Dioc Dir of Educ Blackb 1992–98; Fell Woodard Corp from 1992; M Gov Body, St Mart's Coll Lanc 1992–98; Hon Can Blackb Cathl 1992–94 and 1998–2000; Res Can Blackb Cathl 1994–98; Can Emer from 2000; M Nat Soc Coun 1997–98; Trustee St Gabr's Trust 1998–2006; M Gov Body Cant Ch Ch Univ Coll 1999–2006; Trustee Urban Learning Found 1999–2002; M Gen Teaching Coun 2000–04; Gen Sec Bd of Educ and Nat Soc 1998–2002; CEO, Educ Division and Gen Sec Nat Soc 2003–06; Hon Asst C St Alban S Norwood 2003–06; Gov St Dunstan's Coll 2003–11; Chair of Govs Westmr Sch from 2006; Chair of Govs Harris Westmr 6th Form from 2014; Hon Fell Cant Ch Ch Univ; Hon Fell Coll of Teachers from 2009; Hon Fell St Chad's Coll, Dur from 2009; Fell Society of Antiquaries from 2014; Dean of Westmr from 2006; Dean of the Order of the Bath from 2006; Pro-Chancellor, Roehampton Univ from 2011
GS 1984–92
Tel: 020 7654 4801
020 7654 4803
07973 418859 (Mobile)
Fax: 020 7654 4883
email: john.hall@westminster-abbey.org
Web: www.westminster-abbey.org
Twitter: @deanwestminster

HALL, Mr Robin Michael, LLB, MCIPR
*44 St Margaret's Square Adelaide Avenue London
SE4 1YR* [SOUTHWARK] *b* 1979 *educ* Emmanuel
Gr Sch; Gorseinon Tertiary Coll; Univ Coll, Dur
Univ; *CV* Comm Mgr, London Underground
2007–10; Head of Labour Grp Off, London
Borough of Islington, 2003–07; Caseworker &
Parliamentary Asst, Office of Oona King MP,
2001–03; Ed & Welfare Off, Dur SU 2000–01;
Public Affairs Mgr, Transport for London, from
2010; GS from 2010
GS 2010–   *Tel:* 07779 241322
                              email: robinhall79@googlemail.com

HALLIDAY, Canon Malcolm Keith,
8 Malham Court Silsden Keighley BD20 0QB [WEST
YORKSHIRE AND THE DALES] *b* 1944 *educ* Rutlish
Sch, Merton; *CV* Inland Revenue 1963–1985;
Bradf Dioc Sec 1985–2010; Bradf Dioc Dir Edu
1999–2003; Rdr from 1979; Lay Canon Bradf
Cathl 1999–2010; Lay Canon Emer Bradf Cathl
from 2010
GS 2010–   *Tel:* 01535 656777
                                                    07949 605093
                   email: malcolm.halliday@btinternet.com

HAMID, Rt Revd David, B Sc, M Div, DD
14 Tufton St London SW1P 3QZ [SUFFRAGAN
BISHOP IN EUROPE] *b* 1955 *educ* Nelson High Sch,
Burlington, Canada; McMaster Univ Canada;
Univ of Trin Coll, Toronto, Canada; *CV* C St Chris
Burlington Canada 1981–83; R St Jo Burlington
Canada 1983–87; Miss Co-ord for Latin America/
Caribbean, GS of Angl Ch of Canada 1987–96; Dir
of Ecum Affairs and Studies, Angl Consultative
Coun 1996–2002; Suff Bp in Europe from 2002; ex
officio M FOAG (C of E) 1996–2002; Co-Sec
ARCIC 1996–2002; Co-Sec Angl-Orthodox Theol
Dialogue 1996–2002; Co-Sec Angl-Lutheran
Internat Wkg Grp 1999–2002; Co-Sec Angl-RC
Commn on Unity and Miss 2001–02; Co-Sec
Angl-Baptist Internat Conversations 1999–2002;
Co-Sec Angl-Old Catholic Internat Co-ord
Coun 1998–2002; Co-Sec Angl-Oriental Orthodox
Dialogue 2001–02; Sec Inter-Angl Theol and Doct
Commn 2001–02; Sec Inter-Angl Stg Cttee on
Ecum Relns 2000–02; Consult to Jt Wkg Grp
of WCC and RC Church 2000–06; Consult to
Angl-RC Commn on Unity and Miss 2002–12;
M Angl-Old Catholic Internat Co-ord Coun from
2005; Co-Chair Ang-RC Commn on Unity and
Mission from 2012; Chair Porvoo Panel; Abp of
Cant's Link Bp for Common Word Dialogue w
Muslims 2010–12; Chair Ref Grp for Abp of
Cant's EU rep 2011–13; Trustee CTBI from 2013;
Gov Anglican Centre in Rome from 2013
                                   Tel: 020 7898 1160
                                           07801 449113
                                   Fax: 020 7898 1166
           email: david.hamid@churchofengland.org
                   Web: www.eurobishop.blogspot.com
                                   Twitter: @eurobishop

HAMMOND, Mr Robert Ian, BA, MA, AIWS, FRSA
22 South Primrose Hill Chelmsford CM1 2RG
[CHELMSFORD] *b* 1966 *educ* Hylands Sch Chelmsf;
Open Univ; Heythrop Coll, Lon Univ; *CV*
NatWest Bank 1985–87; HM Customs and Excise
1987–2005; HM Revenue and Customs from 2005,
Senior Prin–Strategic HR Manager; Freelance
Wine and Spirit Educator, Tour Leader and Judge
from 2009; Chelms Dioc Syn from 1996; M Bp's
Coun from 2003; M Chelms Cathl Coun 2003–13;
M MPA Coun 2006–11; M Dioc Bd of Patr 2007–
10; M Dioc Pastl Ctee 2007–10; M C of E
(Eccl Fees) Measure: Steering Ctee 2000–10; M
Dioceses Commn from 2011; Chair of Govs Cathl
Sch Chelmsf 2009–12; Lay Chair Chelmsf North
Deanery
GS 2000–   *Tel:* 01245 269105
                                           07711 672308 (Mobile)
                              email: rihammond@me.com
                                   Twitter: @ChelmsRob

**HAMPSTEAD, Archdeacon of. See MILLER,
Ven Luke Jonathan**

HANCOCK, Rt Revd Peter, MA, BA
The Bishop's Palace Wells Somerset BA5 2PD
[BISHOP OF BATH AND WELLS] *b* 1955 *educ* Price's
Sch Fareham; Selw Coll Cam; Oak Hill Th Coll;
St Jo Coll Nottm; *CV* C Ch Ch Portsdown 1980–
83; C Radipole and Melcombe Regis TM 1983–87;
V St Wilf Cowplain 1987–99; RD Havant 1993–98;
Hon Can Portsm Cathl 1997–99; Adn of The
Meon 1999–2010; Bp of Basingstoke 2010–14; Bp
of Bath & Wells from 2014; Acting Warden of
Rdrs 1999–2000; Acting RD Gosport 2002–03;
Dir of Mission 1999–2006; Chair CPAS Trustees
2004–2010
GS 2005–10, 2014–   *Tel:* 01749 672341
                   email: bishop@bathwells.anglican.org

HANCOCK, Mr Paul, BDS, MSc, Dip HSM, MHSM,
FRSH
*Mamre 3 Arncliffe Drive Burtonwood Warrington
WA5 4NB* [LIVERPOOL] *b* 1946 *educ* K Edw VI Sch
Lich; Man Univ; *CV* Gen dental practitioner
1968–74; Com Dental Officer 1974; Sen Dental
Officer 1974–93; Asst District Dental Officer
1993–97; Asst Dir Dental Services 1997–99; Asst
Clinical Dir Dental Services 1999–2011 (retired);
M Liv Dioc Syn 1997–2003; M Bd of Miss and
Unity 1998–2003; Lay Swanwick Conference
Cttee Sec and Treas 1998–2003; Par Treas 2004–07;
Gift Aid Sec from 2005; M Dny Syn from 2005;
M Dioc Syn from 2008 (ex officio); Winwick Dny
Lay Chair from 2009; Churchwarden from 2012;
M Archidiaconate and Dioc Miss & Pastl Cttees
2012; M DAC 2013
GS 2005–   *Tel:* 01925 292559
                                           07540 331500
                                   Fax: 01925 295988
                              email: hancockpa1@aol.com

HAND, Revd Nigel Arthur, Lth Th
*Birmingham Cathedral Colmore Row Birmingham B3
2QB* [BIRMINGHAM] *b* 1954 *educ* St John's Th Coll,
Nott; *CV* Asst C St Luke 1984–88; Asst C and TV
Walton 1988–97; Asst C Selly Park 1997–2004;
Adn Moseley 2004–07; P-in-c Selly Park 2004–08;
Canon Residentiary and Canon Missioner, Birm
Cathl from 2008
GS 2010–   *Tel:* 0121 262 1856
                                     Fax: 01212 62 1860
email: canonmissioner@birminghamcathedral.com

HANSON, Dr Charles Goring, MA, PhD
*Longlands House Ashgate Lane Wetheral Carlise,
CA4 8HE* [CARLISLE] *b* 1934 *educ* Felsted Sch,
Essex; Trin Hall Cam; *CV* Lect and Senior Lect
Economic, Univ of Newcastle upon Tyne, 1962–
95; Retired
GS 2010–   *Tel:* 01228 560337
     email: charleshansonecon@yahoo.co.uk

HARBORD, Canon (Paul) Geoffrey, MA, LLM
4 Clarke Drive Sheffield S10 2NS [SHEFFIELD] *b* 1956
educ Thornbridge Gr Sch Sheff; Keble Coll Ox;
Chich Th Coll; Cardiff Univ; *CV* C Rawmarsh w
Parkgate 1983–86; C St Geo Doncaster 1986–90;
P-in-c St Edm Sprotbrough 1990–95; V Mas-
brough 1995–2003; JP from 1999; M Legal Aid
Commn; M DAC; M Dioc Worship and Liturg
Cttee; Dom Chapl to Bp of Sheff from 2003; M
Coun Coll of Resurrection, Mirfield; M CDC
2003–06; Hon Can Sheff Cathl 2007; M Steering
Cttee Misc Provisions Measure 2013
GS 2000–   *Tel:* 0114 266 1932
                                            0114 230 2170
                                     Fax: 0114 263 0110
email: geoffrey@bishopofsheffield.org.uk

HARDING, Mr Nick (Nicholas) Andrew, B Ed
8 Belmont Close Mansfield Woodhouse NG19 9GD
[SOUTHWELL AND NOTTINGHAM] *b* 1964 *educ* St
Philip's RC Coll Birm; Ex Univ; *CV* Primary
sch tchr 1985–88; Dir ICIS Trust 1989–94; Educ
Officer, S'well Minster 1995–2002; S'well Dioc
Children's Officer from 2002; M GS Bd of Educ
Children's Panel; M Dioc Liturg Cttee, Bd of
Educ, Lay Min Grp; magistrate
GS 2005–   *Tel:* 01636 817234 (Work)
                                            07827 291694 (Mobile)
                                     Fax: 01623 622272
email: nick@southwell.anglican.org

HARDMAN, Ven Christine Elizabeth, B Sc (Econ),
M Th
7 Foster Close Stevenage Herts SG1 4SA b 1951 *educ*
Qu Eliz Girls' Gr Sch Barnet; City of Lon Poly;
Westmr Coll Ox; St Alb Dioc Minl Trg Scheme;
CV Dss St Jo Bapt Markyate 1984–87; C 1987–88;
Course Dir St Alb Minl Trg Scheme 1988–96; V H
Trin Stevenage from 1996; RD Stevenage from
1999; Adn of Lewisham and Greenwich 2001–12;
M Dioc Syn; M Bp's Coun; Prolocutor Lower Ho

Conv Cant from 2011; M AC from 2011; M Appts
Cttee from 2011; M LAC from 2011
GS 1998–2001, 2004–   *Tel:* 07812 078048
     email: christine.elizabeth.hardman@gmail.com

HARGREAVES-SMITH, Mr Aiden Richard,
MA, LLM, FRSA
23 Battlebridge Court Wharfdale Rd London N1 9UA
[LONDON] *b* 1968 *educ* Batley Gr Sch; Man Univ;
Européenne de Formation Professionnelle, Paris;
Univ of Westminster; Man Metropolitan Univ;
Coll of Law; *CV* Civil Service 1992–95; Tutor St
Anselm Hall 1991–93, Sen Tutor 1993–98, M SCR
from 1991; Trainee Solicitor Winckworth and
Pemberton 1998–2000; Solicitor Winckworth
Sherwood from 2000, Partner from 2007, Head
Eccl and Charities Dep from 2010; Registrar Dioc
in Eur and Bp's Legal Sec from 2009; Registrar
Dioc Chelmsf and Bp's Legal Sec from 2012;
Assoc Fell, Soc for Advanced Legal Studies from
1998; M Law Soc; M Eccl Law Soc from 2002, M
Gen Cttee 2005–11; M Eccl Law Assoc from 2008;
M Exec Cttee from 2012; M Charity Law Assoc; M
Worshipful Company of Parish Clerks; M Soc for
the Maintenance of the Faith from 2002; M Coun
Qu Victoria Clergy Fund from 2003; Gov and
Trustee Pusey Ho, Ox from 2003; M Sen Appts
Review Grp; Assoc M Ecum Coun for Corporate
Responsibility from 2005; M C of E Appts Cttee
from 2005; M Fees Adv Comm (appt by Pres of
Law Soc) 2005–11; M Pastl Meas Appeals Panel
from 2005; M Stg Cttee Ho of Laity from 2005;
M CNC from 2007; Bps'/Abps' advisory groups
for 6 vacancies in Suffragan Sees; Trustee Clergy
Rest Fund from 2011; M Legal Aid Comm from
2011; M Panel of Chairmen of GS from 2012
GS 2000–   *Tel:* 020 7833 9182 (Home)
                                            020 7593 5064 (Office
                                     email: arhs1@tiscali.co.uk

HARLEY, Ven Michael, AKC, Cert Ed, S Th, M Phil
22 St John's Street Winchester Hants SO23 0HF
[ARCHDEACON OF WINCHESTER] *b* 1950 *educ* Qu
Eliz Gr Sch Crediton; K Coll Lon; Ch Ch Coll
Cant; St Aug Coll Cant; Lambeth; Univ of Kent
at Cant; *CV* C St William Walderslade, Roch
1975–78; C-in-charge St Barn Weeke, Winch 1978–
81; V Pear Tree, Southn 1981–86; V Hurstbourne
Tarrant 1986–99; V Chandler's Ford 1999–2009;
Winch Dioc Rural Officer 1991–97; RD Andover
1994–99; Chair Winch Dioc Ho of Clergy 2005–09;
STETS tutor 2003–06; Hon Can Winch Cath from
2007; Par P St Faith Winch, Master St Cross Winch
2009–11; Adn Winch from 2009
GS 2005–   *Tel:* 01962 869442
     email: michael.harley@winchester.anglican.org

**HARLOW, Archdeacon of. See WEBSTER,
Ven Martin Duncan**

**HARPER, Revd Canon (Rosemary Elizabeth)
Rosie,** BA, MA LRAM, DipRAM
*The Rectory Church Street Amersham Bucks HP7
0DB* [OXFORD] *b* 1955 *educ* Blyth G Sch; Birm Univ;

Royal Academy of Music, Lon; Heythrop Coll; NTMTC; *CV* Singer & lect vocal studies; Chapl High Sheriff of Buckingham 2009–10; Acting P-in-c St Leonard's Chesham Bois, 2002–03; AC St Mary's w Coleshill, Amersham, 1990–2002; V Great Missenden w Ballinger & Little Hampden 2003; Chapl Bp Buckingham 2005; Bp's Counc 2006; Dioc Brd Patronage 2006; Hon Can Ch Ch from 2011

GS 2010– *Tel:* 01494 728988
07743 679651
email: rosieswiss@.com

HARRISON, Professor Glynn, MD, FRCPsych
2 Harley Place Clifton Bristol BS8 3JT [BRISTOL] *b* 1949 *educ* Havelock Sch Grimsby; Dundee Univ; *CV* Consult psychiatrist, Nottm 1982–94; Foundation Chair of Com Mental Health, Nottm Univ 1994–97; Norah Cooke Hurle Prof of Mental Health, Bris Univ 1997–2009; Hon Consult Psychiatrist, AWP Trust, Bath 1997–2009; Prof Emeritus of Psychiatry, Bris Univ from 2009; Pres Internat Federation of Psychiatric Epidemiology from 2007; M CNC from 2007

GS 2005– *email:* glynn.harrison9@gmail.com

HARRISON, Dr Jamie (James Herbert), MB, BS, FRCGP, MA
5 Dunelm Court South St Durham DH1 4QX [DURHAM] *b* 1953 *educ* Stockport Gr Sch; Magd Coll Ox; K Coll Hosp Medical Sch Lon; *CV* GP Durham 1990–2014; Dept of Health GP Advisor 2001–06; Specialist GP Advisor, Care Quality Comm from 2014; Sir William Leech Fell in Applied Christian Theology 2012–13; Research Fell St Jo Coll Dur; Rdr; Lay Chair, Dur Dioc Syn; M Clergy Discipline Comm; M Steering Cttee on Women in the Episcopate

GS 1995– *Tel:* 0191 384 8643
Fax: 0191 386 5934
email: dunelm5@btinternet.com

HART, Mr Peter David, Cert. Ed
10 Ashbank Place Crewe Cheshire CW1 3FR [CHESTER] *b* 1949 *educ* Crewe Grammar Sch; Madeley Coll of Edu; *CV* Primary Sch Teacher 1971–2004; Lay Chair Nantwich Deanery Syn; M Archdiaconal Miss and Pastoral Cttee; Lay Chair Foward in Faith Ches Dioc

GS 2010– *Tel:* 01270 216248
07857 500115
email: peter.hart03@talktalk.net

HASLAM, Mrs (Agnes) Lois, Dip Ad Ed, Cert Ed
3 Poplar Close Gatley Cheadle Cheshire SK8 4LU [CHESTER] *b* 1938 *educ* Whalley Range High Sch Man; Man Univ; Totley Hall Coll of Educ; *CV* Tchr St Marg C of E Secdry Sch Man 1959–60; tchr Cheadle Adult Educ Cen 1961–70, 1972–75, Prin 1975–84; tchr Gatley Playgroup 1970–72; Stockport Boro Co-ord for Adult Basic Educ 1984–95; retd 1995; Lay Chair Stockport Dny Syn 2008–14; Dioc Selector for Ordinands; Spiritual Dir; past M Melanesian Wkg Grp; M Dioc Bd of

Educ, Adult Educ and Lay Trg, Cathls Meas 1999 Transitional Coun, Round Tables Future of Educ and Trg; Nat Bp's Selector for 4 years

GS 2005– *Tel and Fax:* 0161 428 2164
email: loishaslam@btinternet.com

HASTINGS, Archdeacon of. See JONES, Ven Philip Hugh

HAWKINS, Revd Canon Clive, MA, Dip Th, DHSM
Eastrop Rectory 2A Wallis Rd Basingstoke RG21 3DW [WINCHESTER] *b* 1953 *educ* Simon Langton Gr Sch for Boys, Cant; St Pet Coll Ox; Trin Th Coll Bris; *CV* C Ch Ch Winch 1982–86; R St Mary Eastrop, Basingstoke from 1986; AD Basingstoke 2000–08; M Bp's Coun, Dioc Stg Cttee, Dioc Syn, N Area Team 2000–08, N Area Pastl Cttee 2000–08; M Strg Cttee Eccl Offices (Terms of Service) Measure; CNC

GS 2005– *Tel:* 01256 830021 (Home)
01256 464249 (Church)
Fax: 01256 330305
email: clive.hawkins@stmarys-basingstoke.org.uk

HAWKINS, Rt Revd David John Leader, B Th, L Th, ALCD
Barking Lodge 35 Verulam Ave Walthamstow London E17 8ES [AREA BISHOP OF BARKING; CHELMSFORD] *b* 1949 *educ* Wrekin Coll Shrops; Nottm Univ; Lon Coll of Div; St Jo Coll Nottm; *CV* C St Andr Bebington 1973–76; Wrdn Bida Bible Trg Cen, Nigeria 1976–82; Can Emer Kaduna, Nigeria 1982; P-in-c St Matt with St Luke Ox 1983–86; V St Geo Leeds 1986–99, TR 1999–2002; Exec Trustee, St Geo's Crypt 1986–2002; Chair Dioc Communications Cttee, Ripon and Leeds 1998–2002; Chapl Yorks Country Cricket Club 1986–2002; Chair of Trustees Leeds Faith in Schs 1993–2002; Dir Ashlar Ho 1986–2002; Area Bp of Barking from 2003; Dioc Hd Bp Miss and Par Devel from 2004; Dioc Hd Bp Youth and Children from 2004; Apb's Hd Bp on Black Majority Ch from 2006; Pres Bardsey Bird and Field Observatory from 2007; Chair Lon Global Day of Prayer 2007

Tel: 020 8509 7377
Fax: 020 8521 4097
email: b.barking@chelmsford.anglican.org

HAWKINS, Revd (Patricia Sally) Pat, MA, BPhil, BTh, CQSW
The Vicarage Lymer Road Oxley Wolverhampton WV10 6AA [LICHFIELD] *b* 1959 *educ* Wygeston Girls Gr Sch, Leic; Lady Margaret Hall, Ox; Exeter Univ;St. Stephen's House Th Coll; *CV* Residential Social worker w adolescents 1980–83; LA Social Worker, Devon 1985–86; M Comm of St. Francis 1986–99; C, P of Stafford 2001–04; Incumbent, P of Oxley 2004; Area Dean, Wolverhampton 2008; M Lichf Dioc Syn 2003–4, from 2006; Preb Lichfield Cathl from 2009; RD Wulfrun from 2011

GS 2010– *Tel:* 01902 783342
email: pathawkins@btinternet.com

HAWLEY, Ven John Andrew, BD, AKC, Cert Theol
19 Clarence Park Blackburn BB2 7FA [ARCHDEACON OF BLACKBURN] *b* 1950 *educ* Ecclesfield Gr Sch; K Coll Lon; Wycliffe Hall Th Coll; *CV* C H Trin Hull 1974–77; C Bradf Cathl 1977–80; V All SS Woodlands, Doncaster 1980–91; TR Dewsbury 1991–2002; Chair Mission Doncaster 1985–2001; M Bp's Coun 1985–91; Vc Chair Wakef Dioc BMU 1991–96; M Action Partners Coun 1992–99; Chair Wakef Dioc Communications 1996–2002; Chair Wakef Dioc Red Chs Uses 1999–2002; Chair Wakef Dioc Ho of Clergy 2000–02; M Pastl Measure Review Grp from 2001; M Misc Provisions Measure Revision Grp from 2000; Adn of Blackburn from 2002; Acting Adn of Lanc from 2010; Vice Chair Abps' Coun Working Grp on House for Duty 2010–12; Bp's Advisor for Hospital and Hospice Chaplaincy from 2013
GS 1996–2002 　　　　　　*Tel:* 01254 262571
　　　　　　01254 503074 (Secretary)
　　　　　　07980 945035 (Mobile)
　　　　　　Fax: 01254 667309
　　email: archdeacon.blackburn@gmail.com

HEALD, Mrs Veronica Mary,
9 West Street Geddington Kettering Northants NN14 1BD [PETERBOROUGH] *b* 1949 *educ* Barnsley Girs High Sch; Barnsley Tech Coll; *CV* NHS Sec from 2009
GS 2010– 　　　　　　*Tel:* 01536 744276
　　　　email: v.heald@talktalk.net

HEDGES, Very Revd Jane Barbara, BA (Hons),
Honorary Doctorate
The Deanery The Close Norwich NR1 4EG [DEAN OF NORWICH] *b* 1955 *educ* Sarisbury Sec Sch; St John's Coll Durham; Cranmer Hall Durham; *CV* D Holy Trin with St Columba, Fareham 1980–83; TV Southampton City Centre 1983–88; Stewardship Advisor Portsm Dioc 1988–93; Res Canon Portsm Cathl 1993–2001; TR Honiton 2001–06; Can Steward/Adn of Westminster 2006–14; Dean of Norwich from 2014; M Bd of Fin Portsm; M Bd of Educ Portsm; Chair Adult Learning Grp Portsm 　　　　　　*Tel:* 01603 218300
　　　　email: dean@cathedral.org.uk

HENDERSON, Rt Revd Julian Tudor, MA
Bishop's House Ribchester Road Clayton-le-Dale Blackburn BB1 9EF [BISHOP OF BLACKBURN] *b* 1954 *educ* Radley Coll; Keble Coll Ox; Ridley Hall Cam; *CV* C St Mary Islington 1979–83; V Em and St Mary in the Castle, Hastings 1983–92; V H Trin Claygate 1992–2005; RD 1996–2001; Chair Dioc Evangelical Fellowship 1997–2001; Hon Can Guild Cathl 2002; Tutor Dioc Min Course from 2003; Adn of Dorking 2005–13; Chair Intercontinental Ch Soc from 2011; Chair Bus Ctte from 2012; Bp of Blackburn from 2013
GS 2004– 　　　　　　*Tel:* 01254 248234
　　email: bishop@bishopofblackburn.org.uk

HENSHALL, Very Revd Nicholas James, MA
(Oxon)
The Dean's House 3 Harlings Grove Waterloo Lane Chelmsford CM1 1YQ [DEAN OF CHELMSFORD] *b* 1962 *educ* Manchester Gr Sch; British Sch of Archaeology, Athens; Wadham Coll Oxf; Ripon Coll Cuddesdon; *CV* C St Mary's Blyth 1988–92; V St Margaret's Scotswood 1992–2002; Can Precentor Derby Cathl 2002–08; presenter BBC Radio Derby 2003–08; V Ch Ch Harrogate 2008–14; Acting Adn Richmond 2013–14; Dean of Chelmsford from 2014; M Bp's Coun from 2014 　　　　　　*Tel:* 01245 294492
　　　　email: nicholas.henshall@
　　　　　　chelmsfordcathedral.org.uk
　　　Web: www.chelmsfordcathedral.org.uk
　　　　　　Twitter: @CCathedral

HEPPLESTON, Mr Michael,
Turnpike House 1 Turnpike Newchurch Lancashire BB4 9DU [MANCHESTER] *b* 1957 *CV* Man Dioc Syn; Man Min & Pstrl Cttee; Organist and Mus Dir St Michael & All Angels Peek Green; Regional Operations Mgr, Media on the Move from 2005
GS 2010– 　　　　　　*Tel:* 01706 220349
　　　email: mheppleston@mediaotm.com

HERBERT, Revd Clare Marguerite, BA, MTh,
CQSW
37 Sydenham Hill London SE26 6SH [LONDON] *b* 1954 *educ* Okehampton Sch; St Hild's Coll, Dur Univ; New Coll, Edinb Univ; Social Work Dept, Bris Univ; Linc Th Coll; *CV* Parish Worker and Asst Univ Chapl , St Paul's Univ Ch, Bris 1981–85; Child and Family Social Worker , North Bris, 1986–89; Paediatric Renal Social Worker, Southmead Hosp, Bris 1989-92; Pastoral Care Adv, Lay Ministry Dept Lon Dioc, 1992–95; C, St Martin-in-the-Fields, 1995–98; R, St Anne w St Thomas and St Peter Soho, 1998–2007; National Coord of Inclusive Church, 2007–10; Lect Inclusive Th at St Martin-in-the-Fields 2010–14; Bp's Staff and Area Counc of the Two Cities Area of the Lon Dioc, 2000–05; Dean of Women for the Two Cities Area; Tutor in Contextual Th and Mission, SEITE from 2014
GS 2010– 　　　　　　*Tel:* 0208 761 3616
　　　　　　0207 766 1143
　　　　　　07504 577210
　　　　　　Fax: 0207 839 5163
　　email: herbert.clare@googlemail.com

HEREFORD, Archdeacon of. See BENSON, Ven Paddy (George Patrick)

HEREFORD, Bishop of. See FRITH, Rt Revd Richard Michael Cockayne

HEREFORD, Dean of. See TAVINOR, Very Revd Michael Edward

HERTFORD, Archdeacon of. See JONES, Ven Trevor Pryce

HERTFORD, Suffragan Bishop of. [NOT APPOINTED AT TIME OF GOING TO PRESS]

HIBBERT, Revd Canon Richard Charles, BA(Hons)
Christ Church Vicarage 115 Denmark St Bedford MK40 3TJ [ST ALBANS] *b* 1962 *educ* Merchant Taylors' Sch Northwood; Trin Coll Bris; *CV* C St Mary Luton 1996–2000; V Ch Ch Bedford from 2000; asst RD Bedford 2004–2010; RD Bedford from 2010; M CEEC 2006–2010; M MPA Coun from 2010; Hon Can St Albans Cathl from 2013
GS 2005–   *Tel:* 01234 359342
                    email: vicar@ccbedford.org
                    Web: www.ccbedford.org

HILL, Rt Revd Michael Arthur,
58a High St Winterbourne Bristol BS36 1JQ [BISHOP OF BRISTOL] *b* 1949 *educ* Wilmslow Gr Sch; NW Cheshire CFE; Man Coll of Commerce; Ridley Hall Cam; Fitzw Coll Cam; *CV* C St Mary Magd Addiscombe 1977–80; C St Paul Slough 1980–83; P-in-c St Leon Chesham Bois 1983–90, R 1990–92; RD Amersham 1989–92; Adn of Berks 1992–98; Bp of Buckingham 1998–2003; Bp of Bristol from 2003
GS 1995–98, 2003–   *Tel:* 01454 777728
                    07808 290908 (Mobile)
                    Fax: 01454 777814
        email: bishop@bristoldiocese.org
        Web: http://www.bristol.anglican.org

HILL, Rt Revd Peter, BSc, PGCE, MTh
Barking Lodge 35A Verulam Avenue London NGE17 8ES [AREA BISHOP OF BARKING; CHELMSFORD] *b* 1950 *educ* Man Univ; Nottm Univ; Wycliffe Hall, Ox; *CV* Schoolteacher 1973–81; C Porchester, S'well 1983–86; V Huthwaite 1986–95; P-in-c Calverton 1995–2004; RD S'well 1997–2001; Chair Dioc Bd of Educ 2001–04 and from 2013; Dioc Chief Exec 2004–07; Hon Can S'well Minster from 2001; Adn of Nottingham 2007–14; M Dearing Commn Church Schools 1999–2001; M Conv Comm on Guidelines for the Professional Conduct of the Clergy 2000–03 and 2012–13; Faiths Advocate Nottingham City Strategic Partnership from 2010; Vc Dioc Commn from 2011; Bp of Barking from 2014
GS 1993–2004, 2010–   *Tel:* 020 8509 7377 (Office)
    email: b.barking@chelmsford.anglican.org
    Web: http://www.chelmsford.anglican.org/
    areas-and-bishops/area-bishops/bishop-of-
                    barking

HILLS, Mr Nicholas Paul, BA
Church House Westminster London SW1P 3AZ [ADMINISTRATIVE SECRETARY, CENTRAL SECRETARIAT] *b* 1964 *educ* Sir Joseph Williamson's Mathematical Sch, Roch; Leic Univ; *CV* 1987–99 Teacher; on staff of Abps' Coun from 1999; Fin Div from 1999; Central Secretariat from 2002; Sec Appts Cttee; Sec Ho of Laity and Ho of Laity Stg Cttee; Asst Sec Abps' Coun   *Tel:* 020 7898 1363
                    Fax: 020 7989 1369
    email: nicholas.hills@churchofengland.org

HIND, Mr Timothy Charles, MA, FCII
Plowman's Corner The Square Westbury-sub-Mendip Wells BA5 1HJ [BATH AND WELLS] *b* 1950 *educ* Watford Boys Gr Sch; St Jo Coll Cam; *CV* Various posts at Sun Life (now AXA) 1972–13; Quality Mgr, AXA UK; Chartered Insurer; M Bp's Coun; Chair Dioc Vacancy-in-See Cttee 1996–98; M Dioc Bd of Educ 1995–97; M Bd of Educ (Schs and Colls) 1995–97; M C of E Pensions Bd 1996–2010; M C of E Pensions Bd Investment and Fin Cttee 1996–97; M ABM 1998; M DRACSC 1999–2008; Lay Vc-Chair Dioc Syn from 1999–2009; Lay Chair Axbridge Dny Syn 1984–91; M Dioc Bd of Patr 1986–94; Vc-Chair Bd of Govs Kings of Wessex Com Sch 1996–99; Churchwarden St Jo Bapt Axbridge 2001–05; Sec OSG 2001–04; Chair OSG 2004–11; Vc Chair C of E Pensions Bd 2010; Vc Ho of Laity from 2011; Legis Cttee from 2011; Standing Orders Cttee from 2011
GS 1995–2000, 2001–   *Tel:* 01749 870356 (Home)
                    07977 580374
            email: tim@hind.org.uk

HINE, Mr Peter Geoffrey, BA
Chapel Howe Sour Nook Sebergham Carlisle CA5 7DY [CARLISLE] *b* 1949 *educ* Wallasey Tech Gr Sch; Dur Univ; *CV* Various posts w Financial Services sector 1972–98; Vol ch and ed worker 1998–2002; Trustee C of E Pension Scheme 1998–2001; Trustee and Dir Worldshare from1999, Chair from 2014; Finance Resources Off Dioc Carlisle 2002–14; Trustee Northern Fells Rural Community Devel Grp
GS 2010–   *Tel:* 01228 815401
                    07584 684297
                    Fax: 01228 815400
        email: phine999@btinternet.com

HM FORCES, Bishop to. See STOCK, Rt Revd (William) Nigel

HOBBS, Revd Christopher John Pearson, BA, BD, Dip.Ed., AKC
St Thomas's Vicarage 2 Sheringham Ave Southgate London N14 4UE [LONDON] *b* 1960 *educ* St Andrew's Cathl Sch, Sydney; Sydney Univ; King's Coll Lon; Wycliffe Hall Th Coll; *CV* Tchr, Hill House International Junior Sch 1983–86; C, Christ Church Barnet 1991–94; Asst Minister, Jesmond Parish Church 1994–97; V St Thomas's Oakwood from 1997
GS 2010–   *Tel:* 020 8360 1749
                    Fax: 020 8360 1749
    email: christopher.hobbs@blueyonder.co.uk

HOBBS, Preb Maureen Patricia, BSc, Dip Bus Admin, CTM
Vicarage 20 Dartmouth Ave Pattingham WV6 7DP [LICHFIELD] *b* 1954 *educ* Wanstead High Sc Lon; Surrey Univ; Warwick Univ; Westcott Ho Cam; *CV* Asst linguist specialist, GCHQ 1976–78; recruitment and mgt consult 1978–95; C St Chad w. St Mary, Shrewsbury 1997–2001; R Baschurch and Weston Lullingfield w. Hordley from 2001;

P-in-c Pattingham w Patshull from 2009; RD Tryshull from 2009; Min Dev Adv for Wolverhampton Episcopal Area; Dioc Adv for Women in Min 2003–11; Preb of Bishopshull from 2012
GS 2005–10; 2010–　　　　　*Tel:* 01902 700257
　　　　　　　　　　07812 805371 (Mobile)
　　email: hobbsmaureen@yahoo.co.uk
　　　　　　　　　　Twitter: @MoHobbs

HODGSON, Mr Charles Christopher, BSc, NCA
3 Marrs Cross Sydling St Nicholas Dorchester DT2 9PG [EXETER] *b* 1945 *educ* St Peter's, Weston-super-Mare; Wellington Coll, Berks; Bristol; *CV* Rtd Eng; hill farmer; M Bp's Dioc Coun Ex; Coun for Church and Society, Ex; Dioc Rural Support Grp, Ex; M Inter Dioc Finance Forum; M GS Rural Affairs Grp
GS 2010–　　　　　　　*Tel:* 01884 861571
　　　　　　　　　　　　0796064023
　　email: charleschodgson@btinternet.com

HOLBROOK, Rt Revd John Edward, MA
Orchard Acre 11 North Street Mears Ashby Northampton NN6 0DW [SUFFRAGAN BISHOP OF BRIXWORTH; PETERBOROUGH] *b* 1962 *educ* Bris Cathl Sch; St Pet Coll Ox; Ridley Hall Cam; *CV* C Barnes St Mary S'wark 86–89; C Bletchley 1989–93; C N Bletchley CD 1989–93; V Adderbury w Milton 1993–2002; RD Deddington 2000–02; R Wimborne Minster 2002–11; P-in-c Witchampton, Stanbridge and Long Crichel etc 2002–11; P-in-c Horton, Chalbury, Hinton Martel and Holt St Jas 2006–11; RD Wimborne 2004–11; Chapl S and E Dorset Primary Care Trust 2002–11; Can and Preb Sarum Cathl 2006–11; Suff Bp of Brixworth Pet from 2011; Can Pet Cathl from 2011
　　　　　　　　　　　Tel: 01733 562492
　　　　　　　　　　　　01604 812318
　　email: bishop.brixworth@peterborough-
　　　　　　　　　　　　diocese.org.uk

HOLLINGHURST, Revd Anne Elizabeth,
BA(Hons); MSt
23 Hall Place Gardens St Albans AL1 3SB [ST ALBANS] *b* 1964 *educ* Range High Sch and Sixth Form, Formby; Univ Bristol; Univ Camb; *CV* Youth worker St Stephen Hyson Green & St Leodegarius Old Basford 1990–93; AC St Saviour Nottingham 1996–99; Chapl Univ Derby 1999–2005; Chapl Derby Cathl 1999–2005; Chapl Bp of Manchester 2005–10; Res Can Manchester Cath 2005–10; V St Peter's St Albans from 2010; Dioc Syn; Ho of Clergy Standing Cttee Canterbury; Bishoprics and Cathedrals Cttee
GS 2011–　　　　　　　*Tel:* 01727 851464
　　email: annehollinghurst@hotmail.co.uk

HOLMES, Mrs Madeleine Ratcliffe,
Le Peladis Rte Pommier 24350 Lisle Dordogne France [EUROPE] *b* 1942 *educ* Knutsford Secondary Sch; Wimslow Eve Class; St John's, Nottm; *CV* Fashion Model 1976–80; Admin/Direct Mail copywriting and PR Perferap Ltd, High

Wycombe 1980–86; Sales & Production Co-ord Communications Direct High Wycombe, 1985–86; PA and PR customers of Software House, Actiontech Ltd, High Wycombe, 1987; PA to Dir Gen Royal Institute of Public Administration 1989–91; Odgers & Co London PA to Management Consult 1989–97; Rder 2006; Dioc Synod Rep 2006–09; Contribtr Chapl Bp's Coun 2006–09; Local Radio Programme for Chapl 2007–12; Archdeaconry sub-cttee 'Building Together in France' 2007; Prayer Chain Coord Chapl from 2008; Dioc Environment Off from 2010; M MPA Team
GS 2010–　　　　　　*Tel:* 00 33 553 04 85 44
　　email: madeleine@peladis.plus.com
　　2nd email: madeleine.holmes13@gmail.com

HOLTAM, Rt Revd Nicholas Roderick, BA; MA;
Hon DCL; BD; FKC
South Canonry 71 The Close Salisbury, Wilts SP1 2ER [BISHOP OF SALISBURY] *b* 1954 *educ* Latymer Gr Sch Edmonton; Collingwood Coll, Dur; King's Coll Lon; Westcott H Camb; *CV* AC St Dunstan and All Saints Stepney 1979–83; Tutor Linc Theol Coll 1983–87; V Christ and St John's with St Luke's Isle of Dogs 1988–95; V St Martin-in the-Fields 1995–2011; Bp of Salisbury from 2011; Trustee Nat Churches Trust from 2008; Vice-Pres RSCM from 2012; Chair Cttee for Ministry of and among Deaf and Disabled People from 2013; Chair *Shrinking the Footprint* from 2014
GS 2011–　　　　　　　*Tel:* 01722 334031
　　　　　　　　　　　Fax: 01722 413112
　　email: bishop.salisbury@salisbury.anglican.org

HORSHAM, Archdeacon of. WINDSOR, Ven Fiona

HORSHAM, Area Bishop of. See SOWERBY, Rt Revd Mark

HOUGHTON, Revd James Robert, AKC, Cert Ed
St Michael's Vicarage 15 Long Acre Close Eastbourne BN21 1UF [CHICHESTER] *b* 1944 *educ* Highgate Sch; K Coll Lon; St Luke's, Ex; *CV* C St Chad E Herrington, Sunderland, Dur 1968–70; Asst Youth Chapl, Bris 1970–72; C St Lawr Heavitree, Ex 1973–78; Mgr Yiewsley and W Drayton Com Cen and Hon C St Mart W Drayton, Lon 1978–80; Chapl and Head of Relig Studies Grey Coat Hosp, Westmr, Lon 1980–88; Chapl and Head of Relig Studies Stonar Sch, Melksham, Salis 1988–96; Chapl and Head of Relig Studies Sch of St Mary and St Anne, Abbots Bromley, Lich 1996–99; R Buxted and Hadlow Down, Chich 1999–2002; V St Mich and All Angels, Eastbourne, Chich from 2002
GS 2005–　　　　　　　*Tel:* 01323 645740
　　email: fatherjamie@btopenworld.com

HOULDING, Preb David Nigel Christopher,
AKC, DD(hc)
All Hallows' House 52 Courthope Rd London NW3 2LD [LONDON] *b* 1953 *educ* K Sch Cant; K Coll

Lon; St Aug Coll Cant; *CV* Lay Chapl Chr Medical Coll Vellore, S India 1976–77; C All SS Hillingdon 1977–81; C St Alb Holborn w St Pet Saffron Hill 1981–85; V St Steph w All Hallows Hampstead from 1985; Preb St Paul's Cath from 2004; Pro-Prolocutor Conv of Cant form 1998; Chair Dioc Ho of Clergy and Vc-Chair Dioc Syn from 2000; AD of N Camden 2001–03; Master SSC from 1997; M Dioc Syn from 1991; M Bp's Coun from 1997; M Edmonton Coun; M Dioc Liturg Grp; M Coun ACS; M Coun of St Steph Ho, Ox from 2001; Ldr, Cath Grp in GS 2000 07; M Adv Panel for Vocations 1997–2002; M Weekday Lectionary and Rules to Order the Service Revision Cttees 1999; M CCRJ 2000–01; M GS Appts Cttee from 2001; M CAC Perry Review Strg Grp 2002–03; M Conv Wkg Grp on Clergy Code of Practice 2000–03; M Clergy Employment Review Grp 2003–05 and Follow-up Grp from 2005; M Meth Cov Impl Grp from 2003; Chair C of E Appts Cttee from 2004, reappointed 2006, 2009; M AC 2004–05, re-elected 2007; Fell Nashotah Ho from 2005; M CCU from 2006; M strg ctee, Clergy Terms of Service; Pres Ch Union from 2012
GS 1995–   *Tel:* 020 7267 7833
020 7267 6317(Office)
07710 403294 (Mobile)
Fax: 020 7267 6317 (Office)
email: fr.houlding@lineone.net

HOWE, Ven George Alexander, BA
1 St John's Gate Threlkeld Keswick CA12 4TZ [CARLISLE] *b* 1952 *educ* Liv Inst High Sch; St Jo Coll Dur; Westcott Ho Th Coll; *CV* C St Cuth Peterlee 1975–79; C St Mary Norton-on-Tees 1979–81; V Hart w Elwick Hall 1981–85; R Sedgefield 1988–91; RD Sedgefield 1988–91; V H Trin Kendal 1991–2000; RD Kendal 1994–99; Adn of Westmorland and Furness 2000–11; Dioc Ecum Offic 2001–11; Chair Ch and Com Fund 2007–13; M CCU from 2006; M Meth/Angl Panel for Unity in Miss from 2010; Bps' Chaplain and Chief of Staff from 2011; DDO from 2011; Adn Emer from 2011
GS 2001–   *Tel:* 01768 779168 (Home)
01768 773430 (Office)
07879 452763
email: george.howe@carlislediocese.org.uk

HOYLE, Very Revd Dr David Michael, MA, PhD
Bristol Cathedral College Green Bristol BS1 5TJ [DEAN OF BRISTOL] *b* 1957 *educ* Watford Boys Grammar Sch; Corpus Christi Coll Cam; Ripon Coll Cuddesdon; *CV* Asst C Good Shepherd Cam1986–1988; Chapl and Fell Magdalene College Cam 1988–1991; Dean and Fell Magadalene Coll Cam 1991–1995; Dir of Studies Magadalene Coll Cam from 1995; V Ch Ch Southgate 1995–2002; Dir POT Edmonton Area 2000–2002; Dir of Mini Dioc of Glos and Can Res Glos Cathl 2002–2010; Dean of Bristol Cathl from

2010; Secretary Ho of Bps Theol Gp 2002–2007
Tel: 0117 926 4879
Fax: 0117 925 3678
email: dean@bristol-cathedral.co.uk

HUBBARD, Ven Julian Richard Hawes, MA
(Cantab, Oxon)
Church House Westminster London SW1P 3AZ [DIRECTOR OF MINISTRY, ARCHBISHOPS' COUNCIL] *b* 1955 *educ* K Edw VI Gr Sch Chelms; Em Coll Cam; Wycliffe Hall Ox; *CV* C St Dionis Parsons Green Lon 1981–84; Chapl Jesus Coll Ox 1984–89; Tutor Wycliffe Hall Ox 1984–89; Selection Sec ACCM 1989–91; Sen Selection Sec ABM 1991–93; V St Thos on the Bourne Guildf 1993–99; RD Farnham 1996–99; Guidf Dioc FE Officer 1993–97; Dir Minl Trg Guidf Dioc 1999–2005; Res Can Guidf Cathl 1999–2005; Adn Oxf and Res Can Ch Ch 2005–11; Dir of Min, AC from 2011
Tel: 020 7898 1390
email: julian.hubbard@churchofengland.org

HUDDERSFIELD, Area bishop of. See GIBBS, Rt Revd Jonathan Robert

HUGHES, Ven Paul Vernon, Dip UEM, Cert Theol Oxon
17 Lansdowne Rd Luton LU3 1EE [ARCHDEACON OF BEDFORD; ST ALBANS] *b* 1953 *educ* Pocklington Sch, E Yorks; Poly Cen Lon; Ripon Coll Cuddesdon; *CV* Res Property Surveyor, Chestertons 1974–79; C Chipping Barnet w Arkley 1982–86; TV Dunstable Tm Min 1986–93; V Boxmoor 1993–2003; RD Hemel Hempstead 1996–2003; Adn of Bedford from 2003; M DBF Cttees, DAC, Dioc Pastl and Miss Cttee, Closed Chs Uses Cttee, Bd for Ch and Soc, New Devel Areas, Bp's Staff, Bp's Staff Deployment Grp   *Tel:* 01582 730722
Fax: 01582 877354
email: archdbedf@stalbans.anglican.org

HULL, Suffragan Bishop of. [NOT APPOINTED AT TIME OF GOING TO PRESS]

HUMPHREYS, Mrs Jennifer Ann, BA
34 Riverside Banwell North Somerset BS29 6EE [BATH AND WELLS] *b* 1951 *educ* Wesley Coll Bristol; *CV* World Mission Adviser Bath and Wells from 1998
GS 2010–   *Tel:* 01934 822052
01749 670777
email: jenny@humphreys.eclipse.co.uk
2nd email: jenny.humphreys@
bathwells.anglican.org

HUMPHREYS, Ms Jacqueline Louise, MA, LLM
St John's Chambers 101 Victoria St Bristol BS1 6PU [BRISTOL] *b* 1970 *educ* Churchill Comp Sch; Worc Coll Ox; Inns of Court Sch of Law; Cardiff Univ; *CV* Barrister from 1994; M Family Law Bar Assoc from 1998; M Eccles Law Soc from 1999; M Legis Cttee from 2000; M Legal Adv Commn from

2000; M Rules Cttee from 2004, M Legal Aid Cttee from 2006
GS 2000– Tel: 0117 921 3456
Fax: 0117 929 4821
email: jacqueline.humphreys@stjohnschambers.co.uk

HUNGERFORD, Miss Priscilla Mary Louise, MBE
Pamber Place Pamber End Tadley, Hants RG26 5QJ [WINCHESTER] *b* 1944 *educ* St Catherine's Bramley; La Colline. Vevey. Switzerland; *CV* Parliament Office, Ho of Lords 1967–2005; Hon Steward Westminster Abbey from 1991; Chwdn St James's church Bramley from 2008
GS 2009–2010, 2010– Tel: 01256 850934

HUNTINGDON AND WISBECH, Archdeacon of. See McCURDY, Ven Hugh Kyle

HUNTINGDON, Suffragan Bishop of. See THOMSON, Rt Revd David

HURLEY, Mr Robert Michael, BA
Nursery House 38 Furlong Road Bourne End Bucks SL8 5AA [OXFORD] *b* 1987 *educ* John Hampden Gr Sch; Sir William Borlase's Gr Sch; Nott Univ; *CV* Info Analyst, Enfield PCT; Senior Comm Analyst, North West Lon Hosp NHS Trust; Database Adminstrator (DBA), North West Lon Hosp NHS Trust
GS 2008– Tel: 01628 524214
07845 564464
email: rmh@rmhurley.com

HUTCHINSON, Revd Canon Karen Elizabeth, MA (Oxon), MA, Ox Dip Min
2 Middle Avenue Farnham Surrey GU9 8JL [GUILD-FORD] *b* 1964 *educ* Surbiton High Sch; Lady Margaret Hall Ox; Guildford Coll of Law; Univ of Kent; Wycliffe Hall Oxf;; *CV* C St Lawrence Alton 2001–06; V Crondall and Ewshot 2006–12; V United Benefice of The Bourne and Tilford from 2012; Hon Can Guildford Cathl from 2013; Dioc Advr in Women's Ministry from 2010
GS 2013– Tel: 01252 715505
email: vicar@thebourne.org.uk

HUTCHINSON-CERVANTES, Revd Canon Ian Charles, BSc, MSc, MA, GDip Th
St George's Anglican Church Calle Nunez de Balboa 43 28001 Madrid Spain 28001 [EUROPE] *b* 1962 *educ* St Thomas' Sch, Malaysia; St Paul's Coll NZ; Amazon Valley Acad, Brazil; Cant Univ NZ; Reading Univ; Cam Univ; Cardiff Univ; Westcott House Th Coll; *CV* Asst C, St Mary the V, Ox, 1989–92; LT St Marys Pro-Cathl, Dioc Venezuela 1993; P-in-c St Andrews w St Barnabbas, Dioc Belize, 1993–97; Miss Personnel Prog Off & Regional Dask Off Latin America and Caribbean, USPG 1997–2004; Chapl St George's Ch, Madrid, Dioc Euro from 2004; Bp's Nom USPG Counc;

Bp's Rep PWM; Dioc Obs IERE Syn; Hon Can St John the Baptist, Dioc Argentina 2002; Hon Can Cathl of the Redeemer, Pelotas, Brazil from 2006; Can Cathl Holy Trinity, Gib from 2010
GS 2010– Tel: +34915765109
email: chaplain@stgeorgesmadrid.com

INESON, Revd Dr Emma Gwynneth, BA, MPhil, PhD
The Vicarage Mariners Drive Stolke Bishop Bristol BS9 1QjJ [BRISTOL] *b* 1969 *educ* Bryntirion Comp Schl, Bridgend, Wales; Birm Univ; Trin Coll Bris; *CV* Tching Asst Eng Lang, Birm Univ, 1993–97; Asst C, Dore, Sheffield 2000–03; Chapl, Lee Abbey Devon 2003–06; Tutor Prac Th, Trin Coll Bris 2007–13; NS Asst C and Assoc Min from 2010, St Matthew and St Nathanael, Kingsdown, Bris from 2006; M Bris Dioc Remun Cttee from 2008; Bp's Chapl Bris from 2013; Principal Trin Coll Bris from 2014
GS 2010– Tel: 0117 968 2803
email: inesone@trinity-bris.ac.uk
2nd email: principal@trinity-bris.ac.uk
Web: www.trinity-bris.ac.uk

INGE, Rt Revd Dr John Geoffrey, BSc, PGCE, MA, PhD, Hon DLitt
Bishop's Office The Old Palace Deansway Worcester WR1 2JE [BISHOP OF WORCESTER] *b* 1955 *educ* Kent Coll Cant; Dur Univ; Keble Coll Ox; Coll of the Resurrection Mirfield; *CV* Asst Chapl Lancing Coll 1984–86; Jun Chapl Harrow Sch 1986–89, Sen Chap 1989–90; V Wallsend St Luke, Newc 1990–96; Res Can Ely Cathl 1996–2003, Vice Dean 1999–2003; Bp of Huntingdon 2003–07; M Coun Ridley Hall from 2004; Trustee, Common Purpose from 2005, Trust Protector from 2011; Bp of Worcester from 2007; Visitor, Com of the Holy Name from 2007; Visitor Mucknell Com from 2009; Chair Coll of Evangelists from 2010; M Faith and Order Commn from 2010; Hon DLitt Univ Worc 2011; Chair Coun Abp's Examination in Theology from 2012 Tel: 01905 731599
Fax: 01905 739382
email: bishop.worcester@cofe-worcester.org.uk

IPGRAVE, Rt Revd Michael Geoffrey, PhD, MA, OBE
37 South Road London SE23 2UJ [BISHOP OF WOOLWICH; SOUTHWARK] *b* 1958 *educ* Magd Coll Sch, Brackley; Oriel Coll Ox; St Chad's Coll Dur; SOAS, Lon Univ; Ripon Coll Cuddesdon; *CV* Dn 1982; P 1983 (Peterb); C All SS Oakham w. Hambleton and Egleton, and Braunston w. Brooke, Peterb 1982–85; Asst P The Resurrection, Chiba, Yokohama, Japan 1985–87; TV The Ascension, Leic 1987–90; TV The Holy Spirit, Leic 1990–94; P-in-c St Mary de Castro, Leic 1994–95; TR The Holy Spirit, Leic 1995–99; Dioc Adv on Inter Faith Relns 1990–99; Bp's Chapl 1990–99; Hon Asst P The Presentation, Leic 1999–2004; Hon Can Leic Cathl 1994–2004; Inter Faith Relns Adv,

AC 1999–2004; Sec Chs Commn on Inter Faith Relns 1999–2004; Adn of Southwark 2004–12; Can Miss S'wark Cathl 2010–12; Bp of Woolwich from 2012   *Tel:* 020 7939 9407
email: bishop.michael@southwark.anglican.org

IRELAND, Revd Mark Campbell, M Theol, MA
35 Crescent Rd Wellington Telford TF1 3DW [LICHFIELD] *b* 1960 *educ* Bromsgrove High Sch; Oban High Sch; St Jo Sch Marlborough; St Andr Univ; Wycliffe Hall Ox; Cliff Coll, Sheff Univ; *CV* Tchr, Murree Chr Sch, Pakistan 1981–82; C St Gabriel Blackb 1984–87; C Lancaster Priory 1987–89; Chapl HM Prison, Lancaster 1987–89; V Baxenden, Accrington 1989–97; Dioc Missr, Lich 1998–2007; TV St Matt Walsall 1998–2007; Tm Leader, Miss Div, Lich Dioc 2002–06; M Bp's Coun 2000–03; V All SS Wellington w. St Cath Eyton from 2007; M Abps' Coun from 2011
GS 1995–98; 2005–   *Tel:* 01952 641251 (Home)
                   01952 248554 (Office)
email: markcireland@gmail.com

ISLE OF MAN, Archdeacon of. See BROWN, Ven Andrew

ISLE OF WIGHT, Archdeacon of the. SUTTON, Ven Peter

ISON, Very Revd David John, BA, PhD, DPS
The Deanery 9 Amen Court London EC4M 7BU [DEAN OF ST PAUL'S; LONDON] *b* 1954 *educ* Brentwood Sch; Leic Univ; Nottm Univ; St Jo Coll Nottm; K Coll Lon; *CV* C St Nic w. St Luke Deptford, S'wark 1979–85; Tutor, Ch Army Trg Coll 1985–88; V St Phil Potters Green, Cov 1988–93; Dioc Officer for CME, Ex 1993–2005; Res Can Ex 1995–2005; Dean of Bradf 2005-12; Dean of St Paul's from 2012
GS 1990–93, 2010–12, 2013–   *Tel:* 020 7236 2827
email: dean@stpaulscathedral.org.uk
Web: www.stpauls.co.uk
Twitter: @deansouthwark

ITALY AND MALTA, Archdeacon of. See BOARDMAN, Ven Jonathan Thomas

JACKSON, Rt Revd Richard Charles, MA, MSc, DipHE
The Vicarage Cowfold Road Bolney Haywards Heath RH17 5QR [AREA BISHOP OF LEWES; COLCHESTER] *b* 1961 *educ* Latymer Upper Sch; Ch Ch, Ox; Cranfield Univ; Trin Coll Bris; *CV* Senior Agronomist, Cleanacres Ltd 1985–92; C All Saints, Lindfield 1994–98; Archdnry Wdn of Rdrs 1999–2004; Dioc Rdrs Cttee 1999–2004; V Rudgwick 1998–2009; RD Horsham, 2004–09; Dioc Adv Miss and Renewal 2009–14; Bp of Lewes from 2014
GS 2010–14   *Tel:* 01273 421021
              01444 881301
email: bishop.lewes@chichester.anglican.org
Web: www.chichester.anglican.org

JAGGER, Ven Ian, MA, MA
15 The College Durham DH1 3EQ [ARCHDEACON OF DURHAM] *b* 1955 *educ* Huddersfield New Coll; K Coll Cam; St Jo Coll Dur; *CV* C St Mary Virgin Twickenham Lon 1982–85; P-in-c Willen, Milton Keynes Ox 1985–87; TV Willen, Stantonbury LEP 1987–94; Chapl Willen Hospice 1985–94; Dir Milton Keynes Chr Trg Scheme 1986–94; TR Fareham H Trin Portsm 1994–98; Ecum Officer Portsm Dio 1994–96; RD Fareham 1996–98; Can Res Portsm Cathl and Dioc Missr 1998–2001; Adn of Auckland 2001–06; Adn of Durham and Can Res Dur Cathl from 2006
GS 2002–   *Tel:* 0191 384 7534
           Fax: 0191 386 6915
email: archdeacon.of.durham@
durham.anglican.org

JAMES, Rt Revd Graham Richard , BA
Bishop's House Norwich NR3 1SB [BISHOP OF NORWICH] *b* 1951 *educ* Northampton Gr Sch; Lanc Univ; Cuddesdon Th Coll; *CV* C Christ Carpenter Peterb 1975–78; C Digswell 1978–82; TR Digswell 1982–83; Selection Sec and Sec for CME ACCM 1983–85; Sen Selection Sec 1985–87; Chapl to Abp of Cant 1987–93; Bp of St Germans 1993–99; Bp of Norw from 1999; M Bd of Countryside Agency 2001–06; Chair Rural Bps Panel 2001–06; Chair CRAC, BBC and Ofcom 2004–08; M AC from 2006; Chair Min Div 2006–12; Chair Stg Conf on Relig and Belief, BBC 2009–11; M HoL Selection Cttee on Communications from 2011
GS 1995–   *Tel:* 01603 629001
           Fax: 01603 761613
email: bishop@dioceseofnorwich.org
Web: www.dioceseofnorwich.org

JAMES, Mr Philip John, B SocSc
Church House Great Smith St London SW1P 3AZ [HEAD OF (RESOURCE) STRATEGY AND DEVELOPMENT UNIT, CHURCH COMMISSIONERS AND ARCHBISHOPS' COUNCIL] *b* 1967 *educ* Bris Gr Sch; Birm Univ; *CV* On staff of Ch Commrs from 1988; Hd of Policy Unit from 1999; Head of (Resource) Strategy and Development Unit, Ch Commrs and AC from 2009   *Tel:* 020 7898 1671
email: philip.james@churchofengland.org

JARROW, Suffragan Bishop of. See BRYANT, Rt Revd Mark Watts

JEANS, Ven Alan Paul, B Th, MIAS, MIBC, MA
Herbert House 118 Lower Rd Salisbury SP2 9NW [ARCHDEACON OF SARUM; SALISBURY] *b* 1958 *educ* Bournemouth Sch; Dorset Inst of HE; Southn Univ; Sarum and Wells Th Coll; Univ Wales Lamp; *CV* C Parkstone Team 1989–93; P-in-c Bp Cannings, All Cannings and Etchilhampton 1993–98; Dioc Adv for Par Develt 1998–2005;

M DAC; Adn of Sarum from 2003; Asst DDO 2005–07; RD Alderbury 2005–07; DDO 2007–13 GS 2000–05, 2010–   *Tel:* 01722 336290 (Home) 01722 438662 (Office) *Fax:* 01722 411990 *email:* adsarum@salisbury.anglican.org *Web:* www.salisbury.anglican.org *Twitter:* @alanpjeans

JENKINS, Ven Dr David Harold, MA, PhD
Sudbury Lodge Stanningfield Road Bury St Edmunds IP30 0TL [ARCHDEACON OF SUDBURY; ST EDMUNDS-BURY AND IPSWICH] *b* 1961 *educ* Belfast Royal Academy; Sidney Sussex Coll Cam; Ripon Coll Cuddesdon; Univ Wales: Lampeter; *CV* Asst C Good Shepherd Cambridge 1989–1991; Asst C St Peter's Earley Reading 1991–1994; V St Michael & All Angels Blackpool 1994–1999; V St John Baptist Broughton Preston 1999–2004; DDE Dioc of Carlisle 2004–2010; Residentiary Can Carlisle Cathl 2004–2010; Adn of Sudbury from 2010 *Tel:* 01284 386942 *email:* archdeacon.david@cofesuffolk.org

JENKINS, Canon Gary John, BA, PGCE, BA, MTh
4 Thurland Road London SE16 4AA [SOUTHWARK] *b* 1959 *educ* Sir Walter St John's School, Battersea University of York Oak Hill; *CV* C St Luke's, West Norwood 1989–94; V St Peter's, St Helier, 1994–2001; V, Holy Trin, Redhill 2001–12; M Bps S'wark Th Issues Grp, 2005–10; M S'wark Dioc Syn from 2001; AD Reigate 2012; V St James & St Anne, Bermondsey from 2012 GS 2010–   *Tel:* 020 7394 6449 *email:* garyjjenkins@outlook.com

JEPSON, Dr Rachel Margaret Elizabeth, B Ed (Hons), MA, PhD, TEFL, FIMA
56a Upland Rd Selly Park Birmingham B29 7JS [BIRMINGHAM] *b* 1967 *educ* Edgbaston CE Coll for Girls; Univ Coll of St Mart Lanc; Univ of Glos w Trin Coll Bris; St Jo Coll Dur; *CV* Tchr Grove Sch Handsworth 1993–98; Res Tutor St Jo Coll Dur 1998–2002; M Dioc Bd of Educ to 2006; GS Rep, CTE Forum and CTBI Assembly; Appt M Revision Cttee Care of Cathls Measure 2002; Appt M Additional Collects Revision Cttee 2003; M Birm Dioc Bp's Coun; M Birm Stg Adv Coun for Relig Educ; Tchr (Phase Leader, RE Co-ord), Rookery Sch, Handsworth from 2007; Appt Revision Cttee C of E (Misc Provisions) Meas 2008; Vc-Chair PCC St Martin-in-the-Bull Ring Birm Par Ch 2008–11; Appt M Governing Body Queen's Found Birm 2012; CCU 2013; M Steering Cttee Clergy Discipline and Safeguarding Meas 2013 GS 2000–   *Tel:* 0121 472 2064 *email:* rachel.jepson@tiscali.co.uk

JERSEY, Dean of. See KEY, Very Revd Robert Frederick

JOHN, Very Revd Jeffrey Philip Hywel, MA, D Phil
The Deanery Sumpter Yard St Albans AL1 1BY [DEAN OF ST ALBANS] *b* 1953 *educ* Tonyrefail Gr Sch; Hertf Coll Ox; BNC Ox; Magd Coll Ox; St Steph Ho; *CV* C St Aug Penarth 1978–80; Asst Chapl Magd Coll Ox 1980–82; Chapl and lect BNC Ox 1982–84; Fell and Dean of Divinity Magd Coll Ox 1984–91; V H Trin Eltham 1991–97; Dir of Trg S'wark Dioc and Can Theol and Chanc S'wark Cathl 1997–2004; M GS Stg Cttee 1996–2000; M GS Appts Cttee 1995–2000; M S'wark Dioc Syn, Bp's Coun 1997–2004; Dean of St Alb from 2004   *Tel:* 01727 890202 *Fax:* 01727 890227 *email:* dean@stalbanscathedral.org

JOHNS, Mrs Sue (Susan Margaret), HNC, M Phil
8 Dragonfly Lane Norwich NR4 7JR [NORWICH] *b* 1955 *educ* Thorpe Gr Sch; Norw City Coll; Leeds Univ; *CV* Analytical Chemist, Public Analyst's Lab 1973–80; Housewife and Mother; Food Scientist MAFF CSL Food Science Lab Norw 1991–98; Joint Food Safety and Standards Grp 1998–2000; Food Standards Agency 2000–09, Health & Safety Exec 2009–13; Head of Corporate Governance Office for Nuclear Regulation from 2013 GS 1990–   *Tel:* 01603 607509 07714 764618 *email:* sue1326@hotmail.com

JOHNSTON, Mrs Mary Geraldine, BA, AKC, CMCIPD
56 Fairlawn Grove Chiswick London W4 5EH [LONDON] *b* 1939 *educ* Barking Abbey Sch; K Coll Lon; *CV* Personnel Dept ICI 1961–66; Personnel Admin and Employee Relations Singer Co New York 1966–68; American Express New York 1968–70; Asst Personnel Mgr and Staff Devel Mgr Guinness Overseas 1970–80; M Lon and S'wark Dioc Jt Prisons and Penal Concerns Grp 1995–2008; M Coun Corp Church Ho 1999–2008; M Revision Comm Clergy Terms of Service; Dir Affirming Catholicism; Convenor of Affirming Catholics in Synod; M CNC GS 1995–   *Tel:* 020 8995 6427 *email:* marygjohnston@btinternet.com

JONES, Canon Joyce Rosemary, MA
Oakfield 206 Barnsley Road, Denby Dale Huddersfield HD8 8TS [WEST YORKSHIRE AND THE DALES] *b* 1954 *educ* King Edward VI H Sch Birm; Cam Univ; Newnham Coll; NOC; *CV* AC All Saints Pontefract 1997–2000; Vocations Adv, Asst Chapl Kirkwood Hospice & AC Cumberworth Denby and Denby Dale 2000–01; P-in-c Shelley and Shepley from 2001; Bp's Adv for Prayer and Spirituality 2005–11; RD Kirkburton from 2011 GS 2010–   *Tel:* 01484 862350 *Fax:* 01484 862350 *email:* joycerjones@aol.com

JONES, Ven Philip Hugh, Dip Chr Theol & Min, Solicitor
27 The Avenue Lewes BN7 1QT [ARCHDEACON OF HASTINGS; CHICHESTER] *b* 1951 *educ* Leys Sch Cam; Chich Theol Coll; *CV* C St Mary V Horsham 1994–97; V H Innocents Southwater 1997–2005; RD Horsham 2002–05; Adn of Lewes & Hastings from 2005   *Tel:* 01273 479530
                                                 Fax: 01273 476529
        email: archlandh@chichester.anglican.org

JONES, Canon Sharon Ann, BA, CERT TH
St Andrew's Vicarage Arm Road Dearnley OL15 8NJ [MANCHESTER] *b* 1960 *educ* St Kath Coll Liv; Cranmer Hall Dur; *CV* DSS 1985 D 1987 P 1994. Rubery Birm 1985–89; Par Dn 1987–89; C-in-c Chelmsley Wood St Aug CD 1989–92; Perm to Offic Newc 1992–93; Chapl HM Pris Acklington 1993–97; Chapl HM YOI Castington 1997–2000; Chapl HM Pris Forest Bank 2000–06; AD Salford 2003–06; P-in-c Dearnley Man from 2006; AD Rochdale from 2006
GS 2010–   *Tel:* 01706 378466
                                                       07738 96627
        email: dearnleyvicarage@yahoo.com

JONES, Ven Dr Trevor Pryce, B Ed, B Th, LL M, DThM, Cert Ed, ACP
Glebe House St Mary's Lane Hertingfordbury Hertford SG14 2LE [ARCHDEACON OF HERTFORD; ST ALBANS] *b* 1948 *educ* Dial Stone Sch Stockport; St Luke's Coll Ex; Southn Univ; Sarum and Wells Th Coll; Univ of Wales, Cardiff Law Sch; St Jo Coll Dur; *CV* C St Geo Glouc 1976–79; Warden Bp Mascall Centre Ludlow and M Heref Dioc Educ Tm 1979–84; DCO 1981–96; Sec Heref-Nurnberg Eur Ecum Partnership 1982–87; M Bp's Coun 1987–87; M Dioc Ecum Cttee 1985–87, Chair 1996–97; TR Heref S Wye TM 1984–97; OCF 1985–97; Preb Heref Cathl 1993–97; M Dioc Pastl/Minl Cttee 1996–97; Adn of Hertford from 1997; Hon Can St Alb Cathl 1997; M Beds and Herts Historic Churches Trust Coun 1997; Chair St Alb and Ox Min Course 1998–2007; Chair Reach Out Projects Mgt Coun from 1998, Reach Out Plus from 2010; Bp's Selector 2001–08; Chair Rural Strategy Grp from 2001; Vc-Chair ERMC from 2004; Chair Hockerill Educ Foundn 2005–11; M Legal Adv Commn 2006–10; M GS Rule Cttee from 2013; M Camb Theol Fed Coun from 2013
GS 2000–05; 2005–10   *Tel:* 01992 581629
                                                 Fax: 01992 535349
        email: archdhert@stalbans.anglican.org

JUDKINS, Mrs Mary, BA, PGCE, MA
Old Vicarage 3 Church Lane East Ardsley Wakefield WF3 2LJ [WEST YORKSHIRE AND THE DALES] *b* 1951 *educ* Leominster Gr Sch; Bris Univ; St Mary's Coll Cheltenham; Open Univ; *CV* Tchr in Bris and E Grinstead 1984–94; Supply Tchr; Homemaker/Mother; Lay Chair Dioc Syn; GS Rep SAMS 1995–2005; M CCU; M CMEAC 2000–05; delegate WCC 9th Assembly 2006; vol co-ord N Kirklees Chr Faith Cen, Dewsbury Minster from 2005; Educ Officer Interfaith Kirklees (Schools) 2007–13; Independent Consultant from 2013
GS 1995–   *Tel:* 01924 826802
                                   email: elephantmj@aol.com

KAJUMBA, Ven Daniel Steven Kimbugwe, BA, HND, Dip Th, Dip IMBM, LAMDA
84 Higher Drive Purley CR8 2HJ [ARCHDEACON OF REIGATE; SOUTHWARK] *b* 1952 *educ* Christian Life Coll; Bournemouth Univ; Open Univ; S'wark Ord Course; Lond Univ; *CV* C St Alb Goldington 1985–87; pt Chapl Bedford Prison; Uganda 1987–98: Man Dir Transocean; Gen Man Rio Holdings Internat; Kingdom of Buganda Sec Gen, Cabinet Min PR, Functions and Protocol, Min Foreign Affairs; TV St Fran Horley 1999–2001; Adn of Reigate from 2001; M Dioc Syn; M Bp's Coun; M Business Cttee; M Fin Cttee; M Exec and Glebe Cttee; M Stipends and Budget Cttee; M Parsonages and Property Maintenance Cttee; M Fairer Shares Cttee; M Sites/Advisory and Red Churches Uses Cttee; M CMEAC; M Croydon Area Coun   *Tel:* 020 8660 9276 (Home)
                                     020 8681 5496 (Work)
                                     07949 594460 (Mobile)
                               Fax: 020 8660 9276 (Home)
                                     020 8686 2074 (Work)
        email: daniel.kajumba@southwark.anglican.org

KEARON, Canon Kenneth Arthur, BA, MA, M Phil, DD
Anglican Communion Office St Andrew's House 16 Tavistock Crescent London W11 1AP [SECRETARY GENERAL, ANGLICAN COMMUNION] *b* 1953 *educ* Mountjoy Sch Dub; Trin Coll Dub; Cam Univ; Irish Sch of Ecumenics; *CV* Dn 1981; P 1982; C All SS Raheny and St Jo Coolock, Dioc of Dublin and Glendalough 1981–84; Dean of Residence Trin Coll Dub 1984–91; R Tullow, Dub 1991–99; Dir Irish Sch of Ecumenics 1999–2004; M Chapter of Ch Ch Cathl, Dub from 1995, Chan 2002–04; Sec Gen Angl Communion from 2005; Hon Can St Paul's Cathl Lon, St Geo Cathl Jerusalem, Ch Ch Cathl Cant; Ch Ch Cathl Cape Coast W Africa   *Tel:* 020 7313 3905
                                       Fax: 020 7313 3999
        email: kenneth.kearon@anglicancommunion.org

KELLY, Mr Declan Gerard, MSc, BSc, MCLIP
Church House Great Smith St London SW1P 3AZ [DIRECTOR OF LIBRARIES AND ARCHIVES, CHURCH COMMISSIONERS] *b* 1960 *educ* St Hugh's Coll Nottm; Qu Mary Coll Lon; Sheffield Univ; *CV* Rsch Centre Mgr, BBC World Service 1993–97; Intake and Acquisitions Mgr, BBC Archives 1997–99, Rsch Services Mgr 2000–03, Output Services Mgr 2003–05; Dir of Libraries, Archives and IT, Ch Commrs from 2005
                                         Tel: 020 7898 1432
        email: declan.kelly@churchofengland.org
        Web: www.lambethpalacelibrary.org

KEMP, Mr David Stephen,
11 Ham Shades Lane Whitstable Kent CT5 1NT
[CANTERBURY] *b* 1947 *educ* Simon Langton Gr Sch,
Cant;; *CV* Sec Herne Bay Bldg Soc 1978–86; Dep
CEO, Kent Reliance Bldg Soc 1986–90; Dioc Sec,
Cant 1990–2007; Gov Cant Ch Ch Univ 2006;
Chair Cant Dioc Child Protection Management
Gp from 2007
GS 2010–   *Tel:* 01227 272470
            email: kemps11@btinternet.com

KENNY, Miss Bernadette, LLB (Hons), Barrister
29 Great Smith Street London SW1P 3PS [CEO,
CHURCH OF ENGLAND PENSIONS BOARD] *educ*
Chichester High Sch for Girls; Univ Man; Inns
of Court Sch of Law; Barrister, Lincoln's Inn; *CV*
Lord Chancellor's Dept 1980–1991; Dep Circuit
Adm SE Circuit 1991–93; Head of Agency Team,
Court Service 1993–94, Head of Personnel and
Training, 1994–99, Dir Operational Policy 1999–
2002; Dir Dept Constitutional Affairs 2002–04;
CEO Royal Parks 2005; Dir Gen Personal Tax,
HM Revenue and Customs 2005–11; CEO Church
of England Pensions Bd from 2011
                        Tel: 020 8898 1807
email: bernadette.kenny@churchofengland.org

**KENSINGTON, Area Bishop of. See
WILLIAMS, Rt Revd Paul Gavin**

KENT, Mr Ian David,
*Brightmanshayes Petrockstowe Okehampton EX20
3EY* [EXETER] *b* 1980 *educ* Gt Torrington Sch;
Plymouth Coll of Art and Design; *CV* Printer
from 1996; M Dioc Syn from 2000
GS 2000–2010   *Tel and Fax:* 01409 281281
email: ian.kent@brightmanshayes.freeserve.co.uk

KEY, Very Revd Robert Frederick, BA, DPS
The Deanery David Place St Helier Jersey JE2 4TE
[DEAN OF JERSEY] *b* 1952 *educ* Alleyn's Sch
Dulwich; Bris Univ; Oak Hill Th Coll; *CV* C
St Ebbe Ox 1976-80; Min St Patr Wallington 1980–
85; V Eynsham and Cassington 1985–91; V St
Andr Ox 1991–2001; M Coun Wycliffe Hall
1985–2010; M Coll of Evangelists; Gen Dir CPAS
2001–05; Canon Preacher dioc Rio Grande from
2004; Dean of Jersey from 2005
GS 1995–2005, 2010–   *Tel and Fax:* 01534 720001
                          07700 711952
            email: robert_f_key@yahoo.com

KEY, Mr Simon Robert, MA, Cert Ed, FSA
4 Old St Salisbury SP2 8JL [SALISBURY] *b* 1945 *educ*
Salis Cathl Sch; Sherborne Sch; Clare Coll Cam;
CV Master, Loretto Sch Edin 1967–69; Harrow
Sch 1969-83; Min for Local Government and
Inner Cities 1990–92, for Nat Heritage 1992–93,
for Transport 1993–94; Shadow Min for Defence
1997–99, for Internat Devel 1999–2001, for Science
2003–05; MP for Salis 1983–2010; M Salis Dioc
Syn from 2003; M Coun of Salis Cathl from 2002;

Fellow Soc of Antiquaries from 2006; Lay Can
Salis Cath from 2008; M Eccl Cttee of Parliament
2005–10; M Defence Select Cttee 2005–10; Chair,
Salisbury Magna Carta 2015 Project from 2011;
Chair, Ho of Laity, Sarum from 2011
GS 2005–   *Tel:* 01722 326622
                          07770 940782
            email: srobertkey@hotmail.com

KIDDLE, Canon John, MA, MTh
19 Stanbury Avenue Watford Herts WD17 3HW
[ST ALBANS] *b* 1958 *educ* Monkton Combe Sch;
Queens' Coll Cam; Heythrop Coll UL; Ridley
Hall, Cam; *CV* AC, Ormskirk Parish Church,
1982–86; V, St Gabriel's Church Huyton Quarry,
1986–91; V, St Luke's Church Watford, 1991–08;
Rural Dean of Watford, 1999–04; Hon Can St Alb
Cathl 2005–10; Off Miss and Devlp, St Alb from
2008; Residentiary Can St Alb Cathl from 2010;
Dir Miss St Alb from 2011; M Dioc Syn 1986–89;
Sec Brd Miss and Unity 1986–89; M Dioc Syn
1997–00; M Dioc Pstrl Cttee 1997–00; M Bedford
Deanery Review 1999–00; Chair Luton Deanery
Review Grp 2003–04; Chair Dioc Vision for
Action Grp 2004–06; Exec Off Brd Ch and Soc
from 2008
GS 2010–   *Tel:* 01923 460083
                          01727 818146
                          07590 636966
            email: john.kiddle@stalbans.anglican.org

KILLWICK, Canon Simon David Andrew, BD,
AKC, Cert Th
*Christ Church Rectory Monton St Moss Side Man-
chester M14 4GP* [MANCHESTER] *b* 1956 *educ*
Westmr Sch; K Coll Lon; St Steph Ho Th Coll; *CV*
C St Mark Worsley 1981–84; TV St Mary
Ellenbrook 1984–97; P-in-c Ch Ch Moss Side from
1997, R from 2006; Exam Chapl to Bp of Man
2002–07; Hon Can Manch from 2004; AD Hulme
2007–12
GS 1998–   *Tel:* 0161 226 2476
            email: frskillwick@btinternet.com

KING, Ven Robin, MA
*The House The Street Bradwell Braintree Essex CM77
8EL* [ARCHDEACON OF STANSTED; CHELMSFORD]
b 1959 *educ* King's Sch Cant; Dundee Univ; Ridley
Hall; *CV* C St Augustines, Ipswich 1989–92;
V Bures with Assington & Little Cornard 1992–
2013; RD Sudbury 2006–13; Hon Can St Eds Cathl
2009–13; Adn of Stansted from 2013
                        Tel: 01376 563662
email: a.stansted@chelmsford.anglican.org

KINGS, Rt Revd Graham Ralph, MA, DipTh, PhD
*Sherborne House Tower Hill Iwerne Minster Bland-
ford Forum DT11 8NH* [SUFFRAGAN BISHOP OF
SHERBORNE; SALISBURY] *b* 1953 *educ* Buckhurst
Hill County Sch; RMA Sandhurst; Hertford Coll
Ox; Ridley Hall Cam; Selwyn Coll Cam; *CV* Asst
C St Mark Harlesden 1980–84; CMS Mission

Partner Kenya 1985–91; Dir Studies and Vc Prin St Andrew's Coll Kabare 1985–91; Hon Can St Andrew's Cath Kerugoya Kenya 1991; Overseas Advr Henry Martyn Trust Cam 1992–95; Lect Mission Stud 1992–2000; Dir Henry Martyn Centre for Mission studies in World Christianity 1995–2000, Cambridge Theological Federation; V St Mary Islington 2000–09; M MTAG 1996–2005; Trustee Anvil 1998–2004; M Lit Comm from 2002; Manager Ang Comm Network for Inter faith Concerns from 2007; Theol Sec Fulcrum from 2003; Area Bp of Sherborne from 2009

Tel: 01202 659427
Fax: 01202 691418
email: gsherborne@salisbury.anglican.org
Web: www.salisbury.anglican.org

KINGSTON, Area Bishop of. See CHEETHAM, Rt Revd Richard Ian

KIRK, Revd Gavin John, BTh, MA
The Precentory Minster Yard Lincoln LN2 1PX [LINCOLN] *b* 1961 *CV* Asst C, Seaford-cum-Sutton 1986–89; Succentor Rochester Cathl 1989–91; Head of Classics and Asst Chapl, The King's Schl, Rochester, 1991–98; Can Res & Precentor Portsmouth Cathl 1998–2003; Canon Residentiary & Precentor, Lincoln Cathl from 2003; Chair Portsmouth Bp's Adv Grp for Worship 1998–2003; Trustee NTMTS 2001–03; Warden Com Holy Cross from 2006; Chair Lincoln Dioc Lit Cttee from 2008; Ch Bp's Advisory Grp for Prayer and Spirituality from 2011
GS 2000–03; 2010–   *Tel:* 01522 561632
email: precentor@lincolncathedral.com

LAKE, Very Revd Stephen David, BTh, MA
The Deanery 1 Miller's Green Gloucester GL1 2BP [DEAN OF GLOUCESTER] *b* 1963 *educ* Homefield Sch Dorset; Chich Th Coll; *CV* C Sherborne Abbey 1988-92; V St Aldhelm Branksome 1992–2001; RD Poole 2000–01; Can Res and Sub Dean St Albans Cathl 2001–11; Dean of Gloucester from 2011; Trustee Scout Assoc; Chair, Gloucester Regeneration Advisory Bd
GS 2003–10   *Tel:* 01452 524167
07900 988646
email: dean@gloucestercathedral.org.uk
Web: www.gloucestercathedral.org.uk

LAMBETH, Archdeacon of. See GATES, Ven Simon

LAMBETH, Bishop at. See STOCK, Rt Revd (William) Nigel

LANCASTER, Archdeacon of. See EVERITT, Ven Michael John

LANCASTER, Suffragan Bishop of. See PEARSON, Rt Revd Geoffrey Seagrave

LANGSTAFF, Rt Revd James Henry, MA (Oxon), BA (Nottm)
Bishopscourt St Margaret's Street Rochester ME1 1TS [BISHOP OF ROCHESTER] *b* 1956 *educ* Cheltenham Coll; Ox Univ; Nottm Univ; St Jo Coll Nottm; *CV* C St Pet Farnborough, Guildf 1981–86, P-in-c 1985–86; P-in-c St Matt Duddeston & St Clem Nechells, Birm 1986, V 1987–96; RD Birm City 1995–96; Chapl to Bp of Birm 1996–2000; R H Trin Sutton Coldfield, Birm 2000–04; Area Dean of Sutton Coldfield 2002–04; Bp of Lynn 2004–10; Bp of Rochester from 2010; Chair Flagship Housing Grp 2006–10; M E of England Regional Assembly 2007–10; Chair Housing Justice from 2008; Bp to Prisons from 2013
GS 2010–   *Tel:* 01634 842721
07551 007560
email: bishop.rochester@rochester.anglican.org

LEAFE, Mrs Susannah Mary, BSc PGCE
6 Troy Court Daglands Road Fowey PL23 1JX [TRURO] *b* 1971 *educ* Wimbledon H Sch; Bris Univ; Nott Univ; *CV* Head of Geography, Clifton H Sch 1996–2008; Tchr Geography, Queen Elizabeth's Hosp 2008; FLAME coord, Truro Dioc 2009–10; Women's Ministry Facilitator, Fowey Parish Ch 2008–13; Dir Reform from 2013
GS 2010–   *Tel:* 01726 832413
07753 690120
email: ds.leafe@gmail.com

LEE, Ven David John, B Sc, MA, PhD, Dip Theol, Dip Miss Studies
47 Kirkgate Shipley W Yorkshire BD18 3EH [ARCHDEACON OF BRADFORD; WEST YORKSHIRE AND THE DALES] *b* 1946 *educ* Wolverhampton Gr Sch; Bris Univ; All Nations Chr Coll; Lon Univ; Cam Univ; Birm Univ; Ridley Hall, Cam; *CV* Sch Master, Lesotho 1967–68; Sch Master, Walsall 1968–77; C St Marg Putney, S'wark 1977–80; Lect in NT and Theol, Bp Tucker Coll Uganda 1980–86; Lect in Biblical Studies and Missiology, Selly Oak Colls, Tutor Crowther Hall, Selly Oak 1986–91; R Middleton and Wishaw 1991–96; Dir for Miss and Res Can Birm Cathl 1996–2004; Adn of Bradford from 2004; sometime involvement with Angl Ch Planting Initiatives, Nat Coun for Chr Unity (Local Unity Panel), Grace Houses, Birm (internat student work), Chaplaincy Plus, Birm (work-based chaplaincy and mission), Samuel White Charities, Middleton (almshouse trust); Bradf Chs for Dialogue and Diversity (miss educ); Gov Imm C of E Com Coll, Idle, Bradf; Chair Wellsprings Together Brdf; Chair Bradf Diocesan Academies Trust
GS 2005   *Tel and Fax:* 01274 200698
07711 671351
email: david.lee@
westyorkshiredales.anglican.org
2nd email: david.lee@bdat-academies.org

LEE, Revd John, B Sc, M Sc, MInstGA, FRSM
Church House Great Smith Street London SW1P 3AZ
[CLERGY APPOINTMENTS ADVISER] *b* 1947 *educ*
St Dunstan's Coll Catford; Univ Coll Swansea;
Inst of Grp Analysis Lon; Ripon Hall Th Coll;
CV Experimental Officer R Australian Navy
Rsch Laboratory Sydney 1971–73; pt Nursing
Auxiliary Chu Hosp Ox 1973–75; C Cockett 1975–
78; P-in-c St Teilo Cockett 1976–78; Pr/Counsellor
St Botoloph Aldgate 1978–84; Hon Psycho-
therapist Dept of Psychological Medicine St
Bart's Hosp Lon 1980–86; Course Consultant
St Alb Minl Tr Scheme 1980–85; P-in-c
Chiddingstone w Chiddingstone Causeway
1984–89; R 1989–98; Tutor in Individual and Grp
Psychotherapy Dept of Psychological Medicine
St Bart's Medical Sch 1987–92; Staff Consult
Richmond Fell 1989–98; Psychotherapist and
Grp Analyst in private practice 1987–98; Clergy
Appointments Adv from 1998; Chapl to HM the
Queen from 2010   *Tel:* 020 7898 1898
                                   Fax: 020 7898 1899
email: admin.caa@churchofengland.org

LEE, Revd (John Charles) Hugh Mellanby, MA,
M Tech, FRSA
64 Observatory Street Oxford OX2 6EP [OXFORD]
b 1944 *educ* Marlboro Coll; Trin Hall Cam; Brunel
Univ; Ox NSM Course; *CV* Operational Rsch
Scientist Nat Coal Bd 1966–76; Coal Supply Tm
Leader Internat Energy Agency 1976–84; Dep
Hd of Economics Br Coal 1984–91; Dir Coal and
Electricity Consulting WEFA Energy (now IHS
Global Insight) 1992–95; NSM Amersham-on-
the-Hill 1981–88; NSM St Aldate Ox 1988–93;
NSM Wheatley 1993–95; pt Work and Economic
Life Missr Berks, Bucks and Oxon 1995–2002;
NSM House for Duty P-in-c, St Mich at the
North Gate, Ox and City R 2002–09; SSM Beckley,
Forest Hill with Shotover, Horton-cum-Studley
and Stanton St John from 2013; pt Consult Energy
Economist from 1995; Treas and Trustee Chs
Media Trust 1994–2001; Dir EBICO from 1998,
Chair from 2003; founding trustee Ox Industrlal
Chapl from 1998; Moderator CHRISM 1998–2001
and 2009–12; Convenor WATCH GS Task
Force from 2010; married Anne Mellanby 1967;
children Kate born 1971, Alexander born 1973;
M DRASCS 2004–06; M Conv Cant Standing
Cttee from 2011
GS 2000–   *Tel:* 01865 316245
                                   07879 426625
email: hugh.lee@btinternet.com

LEEDS, Archdeacon of. See HOOPER, Ven Paul

**LEEDS, Bishop of. See BAINES, Rt Revd
Nicholas**

**LEICESTER, Archdeacon of. See STRATFORD,
Ven Timothy Richard**

**LEICESTER, Bishop of. See STEVENS, Rt Revd
Timothy John**

**LEICESTER, Dean of. See MONTEITH,
Ven David Robert Malvern**

LENNOX, Mr Lionel Patrick Madill, LLB
*Provincial and Diocesan Registry Stamford House
Piccadilly York YO1 9PP* [REGISTRAR OF PROVINCE
AND DIOCESE OF YORK; REGISTRAR OF CONVOCA-
TION OF YORK; REGISTRAR OF TRIBUNALS FOR
PROVINCE OF YORK] *educ* St Jo Sch Leatherhead;
Birm Univ; Leeds Metropolitan Univ; *CV*
Solicitor from 1973; In private practice 1973–80;
Asst Legal Adv GS 1981–87; Sec Abp of Cant's
Grp on Affinity 1982–84; Sec Bp of Lon's Grp on
Blasphemy 1981–87; Sec Legal Adv Commn
1986–89; Registrar Province and Dioc York, Legal
Secretary to the Archbp of York, Registrar York
Conv and Eccl Notary from 1987 and Ptnr
Denison Till (York) Solicitors from 1987; M Legal
Adv Commn from 1987; Notary Public from
1992; M Eccll Rule Cttee from 1992; Registrar of
Tribunals from 2006; Trustee Yorks Hist Chs
Trust; Trustee St Leon Hospice York 2000–09;
City of York Under Sheriff 2006–07; Pres York-
shire Law Soc 2007–08   *Tel:* 01904 623487
                                   01904 611411
                                   Fax: 01904 561470

**LEWES, Area Bishop of. See JACKSON,
Rt Revd Richard Charles**

LEWIS, Mr Paul, BA, Postgrad Dip (Environmental
Planning)
Church House Great Smith St London SW1P 3AZ
[PASTORAL AND CLOSED CHURCHES SECRETARY,
BISHOPRICS AND CATHEDRALS SECRETARY, CHURCH
COMMISSIONERS] *b* 1952 *educ* Cantonian High
Sch, Cardiff; Liv Univ; *CV* Asst Planner Chorley
Borough Coun 1974–85; Appeals Officer Mon-
mouth Borough Coun 1985–91; Asst Borough
Planning Officer Hastings Borough Coun 1991–
95, Borough Planning Officer/Chief Planner
1995–2004; Pastl and Closed Chs Sec Ch Commrs
from 2004; Bishoprics and Cathls Sec Ch Commrs
from 2009   *Tel:* 020 7898 1741
                                   07894 930474
                                   Fax: 020 7898 1873
email: paul.lewis@churchofengland.org

**LEWISHAM AND GREENWICH, Archdeacon
of. See CUTTING, Ven Alastair Murray**

**LICHFIELD, Archdeacon of. BAKER, Ven
Simon**

**LICHFIELD, Bishop of. See GLEDHILL,
Rt Revd Jonathan Michael**

**LICHFIELD, Dean of. See DORBER, Very Revd
Adrian John**

LILLEY, Canon Christopher Howard, Dip CM, FTII
*The Chrysalis 12 Hillside Ave Sutton on Sea Mable-
thorpe LN12 2JH* [LINCOLN] *b* 1951 *educ* K Sch
Grantham; St Jo Coll Nottm; *CV* Hon C Skegness

and Winthorpe 1985–93; C Gt Limber w Brock-lesby 1993–96; P-in-c Middle Rasen Grp 1996–97; R Middle Rasen Grp 1997–02; V Scawby with Redbourne and Hibaldstow and P-in-c Wadding-ham, Snitterby and Bishop Norton 2002–10; RD Yarborough 2002–09; M Bp's Coun 2001–09; Dioc Ecum Officer 2001–09; Ch Commr 1997–98; M AC Fin Cttee 1999–2001 and 2004–07; M Ch Commrs Bishoprics and Cathls Cttee 1999–2006; P-in-c Kirton w. Lindsey and Grayingham 2006–10; M CCU 2007–11; Miss Enabler (NSM) Mablethorpe and Sutton on Sea Gps of Par from 2010; Acting Dioc Warden of Rdrs from 2011
GS 1996–   *Tel:* 01507 440039
                email: c.lilley@btinternet.com

LINCOLN, Archdeacon of. See BARKER, Ven Timothy Reed

LINCOLN, Bishop of. See LOWSON, Rt Revd Christopher

LINCOLN, Dean of. See BUCKLER, Very Revd Philip John Warr

LINDISFARNE, Archdeacon of. See ROBINSON, Ven Peter John Alan

LIVERPOOL, Archdeacon of. See PANTER, Ven Ricky (Richard) James Graham

LIVERPOOL, Bishop of. See BAYES, Rt Revd Paul

LIVERPOOL, Dean of. See WILCOX, Very Revd Peter Jonathan

LLOYD, Canon Nigel James Clifford, MA, BTh, STh
St John's Vicarage 5 Macaulay Road Broadstone Poole BH18 8AR [SALISBURY] *b* 1951 *educ* Lancing Coll; Nottm Univ; Linc Th Coll; Sarum Coll; *CV* C Sherborne Abbey 1981–84; R Lytchett Matravers 1984–92; TR Lower Parkstone 1992–12; V Broad-stone from 2012; Area Ecum Officer 1994–99; Dioc Ecum Officer 1999–2001; Asst RD Poole 2000–01, RD 2001–09; non-res Can and Preb of Salis Cathl from 2002; M CCU 2001–05; M Bp's Coun 2000–05; Bd M Lewis Manning Hospice 2005–12; Surrogate from 2010; Bd M Poole Mission Communities from 2011
GS 2000–   *Tel:* 01202 694109 (Home)
                         07940 348776 (Mobile)
             email: canon.nigel@gmail.com

LONDON (ST PAUL'S), Dean of. See ISON, Very Revd David John

LONDON, Archdeacon of. See MEARA, Ven David Gwynne

LONDON, Bishop of. See CHARTRES, Rt Revd and Rt Hon Richard John Carew

LORDING, Canon Rosemary Kathleen, BA
93 Kings Acre Rd Hereford HR4 0RQ [HEREFORD] *b* 1947 *educ* Eliz Newcomen Sch, Lon; Mid Essex Tech Coll, Chelms; Herefordshire Coll of Tech; *CV* Catering mgt 1968–73; Personnel and trg mgr, retail 1988–96; Gen Mgr, Three Counties Trg 1996–99; Trg and Devel Mgr, Herefordshire Primary Care Trust 1999–2001; voluntary worker; M Bp's Coun, Dioc Policy and Resources Cttee, DBF Revenue Cttee; additional M Heref Cathl Chapter; Chair Ho of Laity Heref Dioc; Can Heref Cathl from 2010
GS 2004–   *Tel:* 01432 340050
             email: rk.lording@virgin.net

LOUGHBOROUGH, Archdeacon of. See NEWMAN, Ven David Maurice Frederick

LOWSON, Rt Revd Christopher, M Th, STM, LLM, AKC
Bishop's Office The Old Palace Minster Yard Lincoln LN2 1PU [BISHOP OF LINCOLN] *b* 1953 *educ* Newc Cathl Sch; Consett Gr Sch; K Coll Lon; St Aug Coll Cant; Pacific Sch of Religion Berkeley California (WCC Scholar); Heythrop Coll Lon; Cardiff Law Sch; *CV* C St Mary Richmond 1977–82; P-in-c H Trin Eltham 1982–83, V 1983–91; Chapl Avery Hill Coll 1982–85; Chapl Thames Poly 1985–91; V Petersfield and R Buriton 1991–99; RD Petersfield 1995–99; Vis Lect Portsm Univ 1998–2006; Adn of Portsm Jan-Nov 1999; Adn of Portsdown 1999–2006; Chair Bd of Min; Bp of Portsm's Adv to Hosp Chaplaincy; Dioc Rep on Inter-Diocesan Fin Forum 1999–2006; Dir of Min, AC 2006–11; PV Westmr Abbey 2006–11; Bp of Lincoln from 2011
GS 2000–05, 2011–   *Tel:* 01522 504090
                                        01522 504050
   email: bishop.lincoln@lincoln.anglican.org
               Web: www.lincoln.anglican.org

LUDLOW, Archdeacon of. See MAGOWAN, Rt Revd Alistair James

LUDLOW, Suffragan Bishop of. See MAGOWAN, Rt Revd Alistair James

LUNN, Councillor Robin Christopher, BA
Little Hambledon 10 Malthouse Crescent Inkberrow WR7 4EF [WORCESTER] *b* 1968 *educ* Ditcham Park Sch; Univ of Kent; *CV* Independent Financial Adviser; County Councillor for Redditch N from 2005
GS 2004–   *Tel:* 01386 792073
                         07785 305849 (Mobile)
                           Fax: 01386 791531
             email: rlunn47@gmail.com

LYNAS, Preb Stephen Brian, B Th, MBE, PGCE
Bishops' Office The Palace Wells Somerset BA5 2PD [BATH AND WELLS] *b* 1952 *educ* Borden Gr Sch, Kent; St Jo Coll Nottm; Trin Hall Cam; *CV* C Penn, Lich 1978–81; Relig Progr Org BBC Radio

Stoke-on-Trent 1981–84; C Hanley 1981–82; C Edensor 1982–84; Relig Progr Producer BBC Bris 1985–88; Relig Progr Sen Producer BBC S and W Eng 1988–91; Hd Relig Progr TV South 1991–92; Com and Relig Affairs Ed Westcountry TV from 1992; Abps' Officer for Millennium 1996–2001; P Resources Adv, B&W Dioc 2001–07; Sen Chapl and Adv to Bps of B & W and Taunton from 2007; M Ho of Clergy Standing Cttee from 2010; pro-Prolocutor Cant from 2013
GS 2005–   Tel: 01749 672341
                            Fax: 01749 679355
    email: chaplain@bathwells.anglican.org
    Web: http://bathwellschap.wordpress.com
                        Twitter: @bathwellschap

LYNN, Archdeacon of. See ASHE, Ven (Francis) John

LYNN, Suffragan Bishop of. See MEYRICK, Rt Revd (Cyril) Jonathan

LYON, Mrs Rosemary Jane, BA, MA, PGCE
13 New Acres Newburgh Wigan WN8 7TU [BLACK-BURN] *b* 1962 *educ* Ormskirk Grammar Sch; St Aidan's Coll Dur Univ; York Univ; Lon Univ; *CV* Teacher Cardinal Vaugh Mem Sch 1985–88; Vol Pastoral Asst Dioc Argentina 1988–89; Cowley High Sch 1989–90; Chester Catholic High Sch 1990–92; Tarporley County Sch 1992–93; Ormskirk Grammar Sch 1993–94; Maricourt Catholic High Sch from 2002; St Mary's Catholic Pri Sch from 2010; M W Dev Gp Blackb
GS 2010–   Tel: 01257 464541
                        email: rosie.jl46@.co.uk

MACCLESFIELD, Archdeacon of. See BISHOP, Ven Ian Gregory

MacLEAY, Revd Angus Murdo, MA, M Phil
St Nicholas Rectory Rectory Lane Sevenoaks TN13 1JA [ROCHESTER] *b* 1959 *educ* The Vyne Basingstoke; Qu Mary's Sixth Form Coll Basingstoke; Univ Coll Ox; Wycliffe Hall Ox; *CV* C H Trin Platt, Man 1988–92; V St Jo Houghton w. St Pet Kingmoor, Carl 1992–2001; R St Nich Sevenoaks from 2001; M Angl-Meth Formal Conversations 1998–2001; M Dioc Syn; M Revision Cttee for Consecration and Ordination of Women Measure; M Ho of Bps' Code of Practice Working Grp Concerning Women Bishops
GS 1995–2001; 2005–   Tel: 01732 740340
                            Fax: 01732 742810
    email: angus.macleay@stnicholas-sevenoaks.org

MAGOWAN, Rt Revd Alistair James, B Sc, Dip HE, M Th (Oxon)
Bishop's House Corvedale Road Craven Arms SY7 9BT [SUFFRAGAN BISHOP OF LUDLOW AND ARCH-DEACON OF LUDLOW; HEREFORD] *b* 1955 *educ* K Sch Worc; Leeds Univ; Trin Coll Bris; Westmr Coll Ox;

CV C St Jo Bapt Owlerton 1981–84; C St Nic Dur 1984–89; Chapl St Aid Coll Dur 1984–89; V St Jo Bapt Egham 1989–2000; RD Runnymede 1993–2000; Chair Guidf Dioc Bd of Educ 1996–2000; Adn of Dorset 2000–09; Suff Bp of Ludlow from 2009; Adn of Ludlow from 2009; Chair Salis DBE 2004–09
GS 1995–2000, 2004–10   Tel: 01588 673571
            email: office@bishopofludlow.co.uk

MAIDSTONE, Archdeacon of, TAYLOR, Ven Stephen

MAIDSTONE, Suffragan Bishop of. [NOT APPOINTED AT TIME OF GOING TO PRESS]

MALCOURONNE, Mr Keith Robert, MA, FCA, CF
20 Riverside Rd Staines-upon-Thames Middlesex TW18 2LE [GUILDFORD] *b* 1959 *educ* Sutton Manor Gr Sch; New Coll Ox; *CV* Managing Partner Financial Professional and Strategy Services LLP from 2008; Chair Insight Management and Systems Consultants Ltd 2005–09; Fin Partner BC technologies LLP from 2000; Fin Dir The Specialist Washing Company Ltd from 2007; Managing ptnr, Bolton Colby Chartered Accountants 1993–2005; Man Dir Heathrow Corporate Consulting Ltd from 2005; Dir and Chair Bd Fin and Audit Ctee, World Vision UK; Chartered Accountant, corporate financier and bus consult with KPMG 1983–91; Nat Chair of Crusaders 1991–97; Chair Berega Relief Equipment and Devel Trust from 2001; Treas Ox Cen for Miss Studies; Vc-Chair AC Audit Cttee from 2006; M Diocese Commn from 2010; M Guildf Dioc Bp's Coun and DBF exec, Dioc Audit Cttee; Lay Chair Runnymede Dny
GS 2005–   Tel: 01784 455501
                                07990 511905
                email: keith@bc-group.co.uk

MALLARD, Canon Zahida, Dip Mgt Studies, PG Dip Diversity Mgt
17 The Crescent Crossflatts Bingley BD16 2EU [WEST YORKSHIRE AND THE DALES] *b* 1968 *educ* Westborough High Sch Dewsbury; Dewsbury and Batley Tech and Art Coll; Wulfrun Coll Wolverhampton; Wolverhampton Poly; Bradf Univ; Queen's Birm Th Coll; *CV* Welfare Rights Officer Bradf Coun from 1992, Welfare Rights Manager 2000–09, Interpreting and Translation Service Manager 2006, Development Officer: Equalities and Diversity 2009; M DBE; M Dioc Bd for Ch in Society; Dioc Link Person to CMEAC; M MPA Coun; M Bradf Com Legal Services Advice Partnership Bd; Common Purpose Graduate; Bp's Counc Bradf from 2003; Brd Edu 2006–09; Lay Canon from 2010; Trustee Bd of Social Aid and Bradf Hate Crime Alliance
GS 2000–   Tel: 01274 562640 (Home)
                            01274 435174 (Office)
                            07931 761202 (Mobile)
            email: zahidamallard@yahoo.co.uk

MALLETT, Revd Canon Dr Marlene Rosemarie, BA, PhD

St John's Vicarage 49 Wiltshire Road London SW9 7NE [SOUTHWARK] *b* 1959 *educ* Foxford Comp Sch; Sussex Univ; Warwick Univ; SEITE; *CV* AC Ch Ch North Brixton 2004–07; C Exec Off, Brent Mental Health Consortium 200204; Rsrch Sociologist, Med Rsrch Counc 1991–2002; Academic Co-ord, Centre for Caribbean Med, Guys, Kings & St. Thomas' Med Sch, 2001–02; Hon. Lect, Dept. of Legal, Political & Social Sciences, South Bank Univ 1995–97; Rsrch Fellow Institute of Social & Economic Rsrch, Univ of the West Indies, Cave Hill Campus, 1989–90; Rsrch Consult, Swedish International Development Agency, Addis Ababa 1988; Project Admin Rsrch Co-op Adv Grp, 1987–88; Rsrch Consult Women & Development Project, Commonwealth Secr HQ, 1986–87; Rsrch Asst, Institute of Development Studies, 1985–86; Rsrch Admin, Institute of Development Studies, 1983–85; Rsrcher/Admin Eastern & Southern African Universities Rsrch Project, ESAURP, Univ of Dar es Salaam, 1982–83; P-in-c St. John the Evan, Angell Town from 2007; M Dioc Syn from 2005; Convenor of Kingston Area Minority Ethnic Anglican Concerns Cttee 2006; M Dioc Minority Ethnic Anglican Concerns Cttee 2006; M Kingston Area Forum 2007; M Dioc Litt Cttee from 2008; M Liturgical Comm from 2011; M S'wark Cathl Chapter from 2012; V St John the Evangelist, Angell Town from 2013; ADO S'wark from 2013; Hon Can S'wark Cathl from 2013

GS 2010– *Tel:* 020 7733 0585
email: rosemarie.mallett@gmail.com
Web: Http://about.me/rosemarie.mallett
Twitter: @rosemariemallet

MALMESBURY, Archdeacon of. See FROUDE, Ven Christine Ann

MAN, Archdeacon of. See BROWN, Ven Andrew

MANCHESTER, Archdeacon of. See ASHCROFT, Ven Mark David

MANCHESTER, Bishop of. See WALKER, Rt Revd David Stuart

MANCHESTER, Dean of. See GOVENDER, Very Revd Rogers Morgan

MANDELBROTE, Mr Giles Howard, MA, FSA
Lambeth Palace Library London SE1 7JU [LIBRARIAN AND ARCHIVIST, LAMBETH PALACE LIBRARY] *b* 1961 *educ* Eton Coll; St John's Coll Ox; *CV* Editor Quiller Press (publishers) 1989–92; Curatorial Officer, Royal Commission on Historical Manuscripts 1992–95; Curator, British Collections 1501–1800, British Library 1995–2010; Librarian and Archivist, Lambeth Palace Library from 2010 *Tel:* 020 7898 1266
Fax: 020 7898 7932
email: giles.mandelbrote@churchofengland.org
Web: www.lambethpalacelibrary.org/
lambethpalacelibrary.wordpress.com

MANSELL, Ven Clive Neville Ross, LLB, Dip HE
3 The Ridings Blackhurst Lane Tunbridge Wells TN2 4RU [ARCHDEACON OF TONBRIDGE; ROCHESTER] *b* 1953 *educ* City of Lon Sch; Leic Univ; Coll of Law; Trin Coll Bris; *CV* Solicitor (no longer practising); C Gt Malvern Priory 1982–85; Min Can Ripon Cathl 1985–89; R Kirklington w Burneston, Wath and Pickhill 1989–2002; AD Wensley 1998–2002; Archdeacon of Tonbridge from 2002; M Revision Cttee on the Draft Churchwardens Measure; M Legal Aid Commn from 1996; Ch Commr from 1997–2008 (M Ch Commissioners' Assets Cttee, Red Chs Cttee); M Revision Cttee on Draft Amending Canon No 22; M Revision Cttee on Draft C of E (Misc Provisions) Measure and Draft Amending Canon No 23; Chair Strg Cttee C of E Pensions (Amendment) Measure; M Strg Cttee, Common Worship Ordinal, Chair Dioc Bd of Educ; M Dioc Bd of Patronage; M Dioc Rural Adv Grp; Chair Ch in Society; M Bp's Coun; formerly Chair of Dioc Bd for Mission, Ecumenism and Parish Devt, M Eccl Law Soc; Dep Prolocutor N Province/Prov of York 2001–02; M Appeal Panel for Internal Syn Elections and Elections of Convocations; M of Appeal Panel constituted under Schedule 4 of the 1983 Pastoral Measure; M GS Panel of Chairmen 2003–10, Ch Revision Cttee on Draft Bps and Ps (Consecration and Ord of Women) Measure; Chair Strg Cttee Ecclesiastical Property Measure; M Nat Adns Forum 2003–10; Chair of Adns on GS; Simeon's Trustee from 2003; Foundation Fell Univ of Gloucestershire
GS 1995– *Tel:* 01892 520660
email: archdeacon.tonbridge@
rochester.anglican.org

MANTLE, Dr Richard John, DMus (Hon) FRSA
Cleveland House Barrowby Lane Kirkby Overblow Yorkshire HG3 1HQ [WEST YORKSHIRE AND THE DALES] *b* 1947 *educ* Tiffin Sch; Ealing Coll of Higher Ed; *CV* Deputy Managing Dir, ENO 1979–85; Managing Dir Scottish Opera 1985–91; Gen Dir Edmonton Opera Canada, 1991–94; Guardian of the Holy House, Shrine of Our Lady of Walsingham from 1999; Treasurer, College of Guardians, Dir WCTA Ltd; Gen Dir Opera North from 1994; Dir and Trustee, Nat Opera Studio from 1995; M Coun Coll of the Resurrection Mirfield from 2010; M Abps' Coun Fin Cttee from 2011; M Advisory Bd, Music Dept Univ York from 2012
GS 2010– *Tel:* 01423 81592
email: richard.mantle@operanorth.co.uk

MARSHALL, Dr Edmund Ian, MA, Ph D
37 Roundwood Lane Harpenden Herts AL5 3BP [ST ALBANS] *b* 1940 *educ* Humberstone Foundn Sch Clee; Magd Coll Ox; Liv Univ; *CV* Univ Lect Liv and Hull 1962–66; Mathematician in Industry 1967–71; MP Goole 1971–83; Lect in Management Science Bradf Univ 1984–2000; Vc-Pres Meth Conf 1992–93; M Wakef Dioc Syn from 1996; M Bp's Coun 1997–2007; M Dioc Pastl Cttee 1998–2007; Bp's Adv for Ecum Affairs Wakef 1998–2007; Chair Wakef Cathl Com Cttee 2000–07; Rdr 1994–2007; M Wakef Cathl Chap 2003–07; M CCU 2006–11; Chair Rev Ctee for Diocs Pastl and Miss Measure 2006; Reader St Alb Dioc from 2008; Chair rev Cttee for C of E (Naming of Dioceses) Measure 2014
GS 2000–   *Tel:* 01582 461236
        email: edmund.marshall@btinternet.com

MARSHALL, Mr Lee, BSc, MBA
Church House Great Smith Street London SW1P 3PS [CHIEF OF STAFF, CHURCH OF ENGLAND PENSIONS BOARD] *b* 1961 *educ* Tunbridge Wells Gr Sch for Boys; Univ of Lancaster; Univ Manchester (Business Sch); *CV* On staff of Ch Commissioners from 1983, holding various posts including Asset Accountant; SAP Project Business Change Mgr; Chief of Staff, C of E Pensions Bd from 2009   *Tel:* 020 7898 1681
        email: lee.marshall@churchofengland.org

MARTIN, Mrs (Bridget Elizabeth) Anne, BEd, MMus, MPhil, LTCL
8 Woodberry Close Chiddingfold GU8 4SF [GUILDFORD] *b* 1949 *educ* Whyteleafe Gr Sch; Homerton Coll Cam; Lon Univ Inst of Educ; Surrey Univ; Trin Coll of Music; *CV* Primary sch music specialist in state (inc ch schs) and private sectors in Suffolk, Cambs and Germany 1972–79; lect in music, Basford Hall FE Coll Nottm 1982–84; head of music, St Ives Prep Sch, Haslemere 1988–96; rsch Renaissance music Surrey Univ 1996–98; music tchr, Tormead Sch Guildf 1998–2001; Head of Music, St Teresa's Prep Sch 2001–04; Guildf Dioc Lay Chair 2012; M Godalming Dny Syn 2005 and Guildf DBE from 2006; Guildf Bp's Coun 2009; M Rural Affairs GP from 2011; longserving M of ch choir; involved with Chr Aid locally for 20 yrs; Musical dir Annual festival of Soc of Recorder Players 2012; currently selfemployed specialist recorder tchr, accompanist, arranger, writer, adjudicator and conductor
GS 2005–   *Tel:* 01428 683854
        07789 992979
        email: be_anne_martin@hotmail.com

MASON, Canon Dr John Philip, MA PhD CChem FRSC
3 Flaxyards Eaton Lane Tarporley CW6 9GL [CHESTER] *b* 1959 *educ* King George V Sch; Ch Coll Cam; Birm Univ; *CV* Rsrch Scientist, Harwell Laboratory 1980–85; Rsrch & Business Mgr, AEA Technology 1986–94; Programme/Business Mgr, Laboratory of the Government Chemist (LGC)

1994–2002; Dir LGC Grp Holdings plc 2002–06; Dioc Sec, Chester 2006–10; Lay Canon Chester Cathl from 2008; Sec Historic Cheshire Churches Preservation Trust from 2010; Dioc Chair Ho of Laity from 2012; Dir NanoFlex from 2014
GS 2010–   *Tel:* 01829 733971
        email: johnpmason@gmail.com

MAURICE, Rt Revd Peter David, BA, Dip Th
The Palace Wells BA5 2PD [SUFFRAGAN BISHOP OF TAUNTON; BATH AND WELLS] *b* 1951 *educ* Purley Gr Sch; St Chad's Coll Dur; Mirfield Th Coll; Westmr Coll Ox; *CV* C St Paul Wimbledon Park 1975–79; TV All SS East Sheen 1979–85; V H Trin Rotherhithe 1985–96; RD Bermondsey 1991–96; V All SS Tooting 1996–2003; Adn of Wells 2003–06; Bp of Taunton from 2006   *Tel:* 01749 672341
        Fax: 01749 679355
        email: bishop.taunton@bathwells.anglican.org
        Twitter: @tauntonbish

McCURDY, Ven Hugh Kyle, BA(Hons)
Whitgift House The College Ely CB7 4DL [ARCHDEACON OF HUNTINGDON AND WISBECH; ELY] *b* 1958 *educ* Geo Abbot Sch Guild; Portsm Poly; Cardiff Univ; Trin Coll Bris; *CV* C St Jo Egham 1985–88; C St Jo Woking 1988–91; V St Andr Histon 1991–2005; P-in-c St Andr Impington 1998–2005; RD N Stowe 1994–2005; Adn of Huntingdon and Wisbech from 2005; M DAC, Pastl Cttee, Bp's Coun; Trustee Cambridgeshire ACRE; Gov Wisbech Grammar Sch; M Cam Theol Federation Coun; M Coun Ridley Hall Th Coll; Pres Huntingdonshire Soc for the Blind; Trustee Bedfordshire and Cambridgeshire Rural Support Grp
GS 2010–   *Tel:* 01353 658404
        01353 652709 (Office)
        email: archdeacon.handw@ely.anglican.org

McDONOUGH, Canon Philip Michael James, BSc
28 Washbrook Close Barton-le-Clay MK45 4LF [ST ALBANS] *b* 1939 *educ* Wandsworth Tech Coll Lon; Imp Coll Lon; *CV* Asst Chapl Luton and Dunstable Hosp 1996–2004; Rdr from 1985; Sec St Alb Dioc Rdrs Assoc 1995–2004; M CRC Exec 1999–2004; M AC Min Div VRSC 2000–05; M C of E Hosp Chapl Coun, Coun St Alb Cathl 2001–09; Lay Chair Ampthill Dny Syn 2002–10; Hon Can St Alb Cathl 2002–09, Emeritus 2009; Associate Sec CRC 2004–05; Trustee Br Red Cross Soc Staff Pension Fund from 2006; M St Alb Bd for Christian Dev from 2007; Lay Chair Ampthill & Shefford Dny Syn 2011
GS 2000–2005; 2005–2010; 2010–
        Tel: 01582 881772
        07759 444879
        email: canonpmcdonough@btinternet.com

McFARLANE, Ven Janet (Jan) Elizabeth, B Med Sci, BA, Dip Min Std
31 Bracondale Norwich NR1 2AT [ARCHDEACON OF NORWICH] *b* 1964 *educ* Blythe Bridge High Sch

Stoke-on-Trent; Sheff Univ; Dur Univ; Cranmer Hall Dur; *CV* Speech therapist 1987–90; C Stafford TM, Lich 1993–96; Chapl and Min Can, Ely Cathl 1996–99; Norw Dioc Communications Officer 1999–2009; Chapl to Bp of Norw 2001–09; Hon PV Nor Cath 2000–09; M Bp's Coun, Dioc Syn; Adn Norwich from 2009; Dioc Dir of Communications from 2009
GS 2005–   *Tel:* 01603 620007
email: archdeacon.norwich@ dioceseofnorwich.org
Web: www.dioceseofnorwich.org
Twitter: @AdnNorwich

McGINLEY, Revd John Charles, BSocSci, BA
5 Ratcliffe Road Leicester LE2 3TE [LEICESTER] *b* 1969 *educ* Hewett Comp Sch, Norwich; Birm Univ; Trinity Coll Bris; *CV* Asst Buyer, Harrods Ltd, 1990–93; Asst C Holy Trinity w St Paul, Hounslow 1996–2000; TV Holy Trinity w St John, Hinckley 2000–05; TR Holy Trinity w St John, Hinckley 2005–09; V Holy Trinity Leic from 2009; Regional Dir New Wine Midlands and East
GS 2010–   *Tel:* 0116 2548981
                            0116 2448867
email: vicar@holytrinityleicester.org
Twitter: @johnmcginleyht1

McGREGOR, Revd and Worshipful Alexander Scott, MA
Legal Office Church House Great Smith St London SW1P 3AZ [DEPUTY LEGAL ADVISER TO THE ARCH-BISHOPS' COUNCIL AND THE GENERAL SYNOD] *b* 1972 *educ* John Lyon Sch Harrow; Ch Ch Ox; Coll of Law; Inns of Court Sch of Law; St Albans and Ox Min Course; *CV* Barrister in independent practice 1996–2005; Legal Adviser in the Legal Office of the NCIs 2006-08; Deputy Legal Adviser to the Archbishops' Coun and the GS from 2009; M The Honourable Soc of Lincoln's Inn from 1994; M Dacorum Boro Coun 1999–2007; Assistant C (NSM) St Mary Harrow 2006–09; Assistant C (NSM) St Barnabas Pimlico and St Mary Bourne Street from 2009; Deputy Chancellor Dioc of Ox 2007–13; Chancellor Dioc of Oxford from 2013   *Tel:* 020 7898 1748
email: alexander.mcgregor@churchofengland.org

McINTYRE, Revd Eva, MA (Oxon)
The Vicarage Church Avenue Stourport on Severn DY13 9DD [WORCESTER] *b* 1960 *educ* Parkstone Grammar Sch Girls; Worcester Coll Ox; St Stephen's Ho; Birm Sch of Acting; *CV* Dss St James Devizes 1984–6; Dn Oakdale team Ministry 1986–8; Producer Religious Programmes BBC Radio Leeds 1988–90; Producer BBC 1990–1; Area Co-ordinator Christian Aid 1992–8; Freelance writer; R Bangor Monachorum and Worthenbury, Church in Wales 1998–2003; Co-ordinating Chaplain HMP Brockhill 2003–06; V Stourport on Severn and Wilden from 2006; Co-ordinator of Mental Health Matters from 2011; member of CMDDP (cttee of the Abps'

Coun) from 2011; Dir Green Blade Theatre Co from 2012   *Tel:* 01299 822041
email: evacymru@btinternet.com
Web: www.mentalhealthmatters-cofe.org www.greenbladetheatre.org

McISAAC, Mrs Debrah, BA, LLB/D. Jur. Law Soc of Eng & Wales
Parsonage Farm House White Way Pitton Wiltshire SP5 1DT [SALISBURY] *b* 1953 *educ* Marian High Sch, Saskatchewan; Canada Univ of Regina; Univ of Saskatchewan, Canada; Osgoode Hall, York Univ, Canada; Wycliffe Hall; Ripon Coll Cuddesdon; *CV* Adv, Off of the Ombudsman, Province of Saskatchewan 1973; Spec Adv Minister of Justice, Ottawa 1975; Barrister and Solicitor, Edmonton, Alberta, Canada admitted 1976; Barrister and Solicitor, Law So of Upper Canada admitted 1983; Solicitor, Law Soc of England and Wales admitted 1985; Solicitor Durrant Piesse, Lon 1985–86; Solicitor, Freshfields, Lon 1986–88; Dir Prof Devlp, Lovells, Lon 1989–2000; Chief Monitor, Training Contracts, Law Soc of Eng & Wales 2000–06; Principal, D Ball Consulting 2000–10; Legal Ed and Training Grp: Treasurer,1994–96; Chair, 1996–98; Lord Chancellor's Adv Cttee Ed & Conduct Standing Conf 1994–99; Advocacy Sub-cttee of Law Soc's Training Cttee 1998–2008; Counc of the Law Soc of Eng & Wales: Counc M 2005–08; Chair, Ed & Training Cttee 2005–08; M Regulatory Affairs Grp 2005–07; M, Regulatory Affairs Bd 2007–08; Governor, Old Sarum School 2012; M Dioc Syn Sarum from 2009; M Sarum Archdeaconary Miss & Pstrl Cttee from 2010; Lay Chair, Alderbury Dny Syn from 2010; Alderbury Deanery Standing & Pstrl Cttee from 2005; Lay Chair Clarendon Team from 2011
GS 2010–   *Tel:* 01722 712758
                            01722 712940
                            07879 662188
email: debbie@dball.com

McKINNEL, Rt Revd Nicholas Howard Paul, MA(Cantab), MA(Oxon), Hon DD (Plymouth)
32 The Avenue Tiverton Devon EX16 4HW [SUFFRAGAN BISHOP OF CREDITON; EXETER] *b* 1954 *educ* Marlborough Coll; Queens' Coll Cam; Wycliffe Hall Ox; *CV* C St Mary's, West Kensington 1980–83; Angl Chaplain Liverpool Univ 1983–87; R Hatherleigh, Meeth, Exbourne and Jacobstowe 1987–94; TR St Andrew's Plymouth and St Paul's, Stonehouse 1994–2012; Prb Exeter Cathl 2002; Bp of Crediton from 2012
                      Tel: 01884 250002
email: bishop.of.crediton@exeter.anglican.org

McKITTRICK, Ven Douglas Henry, BTh
2 Yorklands Dyke Rd Avenue Hove BN3 6RW [ARCHDEACON OF CHICHESTER] *b* 1953 *educ* John Marley Comp Sch, Newcastle-upon-Tyne; St Steph Ho Ox; *CV* C St Paul Deptford, S'wark 1977–80; C St Jo Tuebrook, Liv 1980–81; TV St

Steph Grove St, Liv 1981–89; V St Agnes Toxteth Pk, Liv 1989–97; V St Pet with Chapel Royal Brighton, Chich from 1997; RD of Brighton from 1998; Can and Preb of Chich Cathl from 1998; Archdeacon of Chichester from 2002; M DAC, Bd of Educ, DBF, Pastl Cttee, Parsonages Cttee; Bp's Adv Hosp Chaplaincy; Coun M Additional Curates Soc 2005; M Hosp Chapl Coun 2006; Bp's Adv on Ecumenism; M Eccl Law Soc; M Nikaean Club
GS 2004–   Tel: 01273 505330 (Home)
                  01273 421021 (Office)
                  Fax: 01273 421041
email: archchichester@chichester.anglican.org

McLEAN, Revd Canon (Margaret Anne) Maggie, MA
Battyeford Vicarage 107A Stocks Bank Road Mirfield WF14 9QT [WEST YORKSHIRE AND THE DALES] *b* 1962 *educ* Greenhead Gr Sch; Birm Univ; Heythrop Coll; Cranmer Hall Dur; *CV* C All Saints Church, Bedford 1991–94; Chapl St Albans High Sch for Girls 1994–98; Assoc P St Alb Abbey; Asst Social Responsibility Adv 1998–99; Anglican Chapl, Univ of Huddersfield 1999–2002; P-in-c St Philip and St James, Scholes and St Luke and Whitechapel, Cleckheaton 2002–09; Christ the King, Battyeford from 2009; Dioc Training Off; Canon Wakefield Cathl from 2011
GS 2010–   Tel: 01924 493277
                  07791 880691
email: m.a.mclean@btinternet.com
Web: www.christthekingbattyeford.org
Twitter: @CTKMaggie

McMULLEN, Canon Christine Elizabeth, BA, Dip Ad Ed, MA
Farm Cottage Montpelier Place Buxton SK17 7EJ [DERBY] *b* 1943 *educ* Homelands Sch Derby; R Holloway Coll Lon; Nott Univ; Derby Univ; *CV* Rdr from 1986; Chair Buxton Dny from 2005; Lay Can Derby Cathl from 2010; Dir Pastl Studies, Nn Ord Course 1994, Vice Prin 1995–2009; M Lit Comm from 2011
GS 1990–   Tel: 01298 73997
email: christine.mcmullen@hotmail.com

McPHATE, Very Revd Prof Gordon Ferguson, BA, MA, M Th, M Sc, MB, Ch B, MD, FRCP
The Deanery 7 Abbey St Chester CH1 2JF [DEAN OF CHESTER] *b* 1950 *educ* Perth Gr Sch; Cam Univ; Aberd Univ; Edin Univ; Surrey Univ; Westcott Ho Cam; *CV* Lect in Physiology, Guy's Hosp Lon 1979–84; Hon C Sanderstead, S'wark 1978–80; Hon PV and Sacrist, S'wark Cathl 1980–86; Registrar in Chemical Pathology, Guildf Hosps 1984–86; Lect and Sen Lect in Pathology, Univ of St Andr 1986–2002; Hon Angl Chapl, Univ of St Andr 1986–2002; Consult Chemical Pathologist, Fife Hosps 1993–2002; Dean of Chester from 2002; Vis Prof of Theol, Univ of Chester from 2003
GS 2004–05   Tel: 01244 500971
email: dean@chestercathedral.com

McPHERSON, Mrs Katherine, MBA, BA
59 Mycenae Rd London SE3 7SE [APPOINTED MEMBER, ARCHBISHOPS' COUNCIL] *b* 1964 *educ* P. L. Meth Girls' Sch Singapore; Temasek Jun Coll Singapore; Nat Univ of Singapore; Univ of Kent; *CV* Exec Consult, Ernst and Young Singapore 1987–92; Sen Mgr, Ernst and Young Lon 1992–95; Lon Hd of Sales and Marketing (Media & Resources), Ernst and Young 1996–98; Nat Hd of Sales and Marketing (Telecoms, Media & Entertainment), Ernst and Young 1998–99; Project Dir (secondment), BBC Mar-Nov 1999; Managing Consult, Cap Gemini Ernst and Young 1999–2001; Operations Dir, YMCA Lambeth, Lewisham and S'wark 2001–2002; Dir Business Devel and Marketing, EMEA, White and Case 2002–04; Apptd M AC 2003–09; Head of Bus Devel, Corporate Div, Herbert Smith 2004–05; Head of Bus Devel, Europe, Herbert Smith 2005–07; Head Winning Business, Global Markets, KPMG 2007–10; Dir Global Markets, KMPG 2010–13
GS 2003–10   Tel: 020 8858 1856 (Home)
                    07984 046149 (Mobile)
email: mcpherson.katherine@gmail.com
2nd email: mcpehrson.katherine@gmail.com

MEARA, Ven David Gwynne, MA, S.Th, FSA
Rectory St Brides Church Fleet St London EC4Y 8AU [ARCHDEACON OF LONDON] *b* 1947 *educ* Merchant Taylor's Sch Northwood; Oriel Coll Ox; Cuddesdon Theol Coll; *CV* C Ch Ch Reading 1973–77; Chapl Univ of Reading 1977–82; V Basildon Aldworth and Ashampstead 1982–94; RD Bradfield 1990–94; R Buckinham 1994–2000; AD Buckingham 1994–2000; Chair Ox Dioc Adv Gp on Miss 1990–2000; R St Bride's Fleet St from 2000; Adn of Lon from 2009; Hon Can Ch Ch Ox; M Lon DAC from 2009; M Dioc Syn from 2009
                    Tel: 020 7427 0133
                    020 7236 7891
                    Fax: 020 7583 4867
email: archdeacon.london@london.anglican.org

MEON, Archdeacon of The. See COLLINS, Ven Gavin Andrew

MEYRICK, Rt Revd (Cyril) Jonathan, MA (Oxon), DEd(Hon)
The Old Vicarage Castle Acre King's Lynn PE32 2AA [SUFFRAGAN BISHOP OF LYNN; NORWICH] *b* 1952 *educ* Lancing Coll; St Jo Coll Ox; Salis & Well Th Coll; *CV* C Bicester, Ox 1976–78; Bp's Chapl, Ox 1978–81; OT tutor, Codrington Coll, Barbados 1981–84; TV Burnham Team, Ox 1984–90; TR Tisbury, Salis 1990–98; RD Chalke, Sarum 1997–98; Res Can Roch 1998–2005; acting Dean of Roch 2002–04; Dean of Exeter 2005–2011; Chair Coun for Miss & Unity 2005–2011; Bp of Lynn from 2011
GS 2013–   Tel: 01760 755553
                  01760 755085
email: bishop.lynn@norwich.anglican.org
Web: www.norwich.anglican.org

MIDDLESEX, Archdeacon of. See WELCH, Ven Stephan John

MIDDLETON, Suffragan Bishop of. See DAVIES, Rt Revd Mark

MILLAR, Revd Dr Sandra, BA; MA; PhD; DipTh; DipMin
Church House Great Smith Street London SW1P 3AZ [HEAD OF PROJECTS AND DEVELOPMENT, ARCHBISHOPS' COUNCIL] *b* 1957 *educ* Rugby High Sch for Girls; Univ Coll, Cardiff; Warwick Univ; Ripon Coll, Cuddesdon; *CV* Product mgr, Boots Company,1979–84; Product mgr, Coop 1984–88; Sales/Marketing Mgr, Windsor Foods 1989–91; Sales/Marketing Mgr, SU 1991-93; National Dir Kings Kids England 1994–98; AC, Chipping Barnet w Arkley 2000–03; TV, Dorchester Team and tutor at Ripon Coll Cuddesdon 2003–07; Children's Off, Glouc from 2007; Brd for Christian Devlp, St Alb 2000–03; Dioc Syn, St. Alb 2000–03; Gov of SAOMC 2001–06; M Miss Initiatives Grp, from 2007; M Bps Worship, Prayer and Spirituality Grp from 2007; Head of Projects and Development, Abps' Coun from 2013
GS 2010–13   *Tel:* 020 7898 100
    email: sandra.millar@churchofengland.org

MILLER, Ven Geoff (Geoffrey Vincent), BEd, MA
80 Moorside North Fenham Newcastle-upon-Tyne NE4 9DU [ARCHDEACON OF NORTHUMBERLAND; NEWCASTLE] *b* 1956 *educ* Sharston High Sch, Manch; Dur Univ; St Jo Coll Nottm; Newc Univ; *CV* C Jarrow 1983–86; TV St Aidan Billingham 1986–92; Dioc Urban Devel Officer 1991–99; Com Chapl Stockton-on-Tees 1992–94; P-in-c St Cuth Darlington 1994–96, V 1996–99; Dioc Urban Officer and Res Can Newc Cathl 1999–2005; Adn of Northumberland from 2005; M DAC; M Dioc Pastl Cttee; M Fin, Pastl, Parsonages cttees and Strat Dev Grp Bp's Coun; M Dioc Safeguarding Cttee; M Shepherd's Dene, Sons of Clergy, Ch Inst, Hosp of God at Greatham, Lord Crewe Trust; Chair Bp Cttee of French Protestant Industrial Miss; Chair Strategic Dev Grp Bp's Coun; Chair Shepherd's Dene Trustees; Special Trustee Newc Healthcare Charity; Newc Fairness Commn 2012   *Tel:* 0191 273 8245
                    Fax: 0191 226 0286
    email: g.miller@newcastle.anglican.org

MILLER, Ms Loraine, BA (Hons)
Church House Great Smith Street London SW1P 3PS [HEAD OF HOUSING, CHURCH OF ENGLAND PENSIONS BOARD] *b* 1957 *educ* The Skinners' Company's Sch for Girls; Queen Mary Coll; *CV* Nat Trng Mgr, English Ch Housing Grp 1984–89; Supported Housing Bus Mgr, English Ch Housing Grp 1989–2007; Dep Housing Mgr C of E Pensions Bd 2007–09; Head of Housing, C of E Pensions Bd from 2009   *Tel:* 020 7898 1852
    email: loraine.miller@churchofengland.org

MILLER, Ven Luke Jonathan, MA (Cantab); MA (Oxon)
The Archeaconry House 39 Bounds Green Road Wood Green, London N22 8HE [ARCHDEACON OF HAMPSTEAD; LONDON] *b* 1966 *educ* Haileybury Coll; Sidney Sussex Coll Camb; St Stephen's Ho; *CV* AC St Matthew Oxhey 1991–94; AC St Mary the Virgin Tottenham 1994–95; V St Mary the Virgin Tottenham 1995–2011; AD East Haringay 2005–11; Acting Adn Hampstead 2009-10; Adn Hampstead from 2011; Dioc Syn 1998–2005, 2009–; M Edmonton Area Coun from 2005; M Dioc Strategic Planning Com from 2008; M Stephen's Ho Coun from 2008 and Chair Fin and Gen Purposes Ctte from 2008; Chair Area Fin Ctte from 2011; DAC; M St Stephen's Ho; Chair Faith Sector Panel, London Resilience Forum from 2014; M Faith Forum for London 2014
                    Tel: 020 7932 1190
                    07742 104065
    email: archdeacon.hampstead@
                    london.anglican.org
    Twitter: @ArchdeaconLuke

MILLS, Mr David John, MBE
51 Greenways Over Kellet Carnforth LA6 1DE [CARLISLE] *b* 1937 *CV* Senior Probation Officer (Rtd); Rdr; Bp's Adv CDC; M Dioc Bd of Educ
GS 1985–   *Tel:* 01524 732194
    email: david.j.mills@btinternet.com

MITCHELL, Revd Canon Richard John Anthony, BA (Hons), Cert Th, PGCE
The Vicarage School Lane Shurdington Cheltenham GL51 4TF [GLOUCESTER] *b* 1964 *educ* Trinity Comp Sch Carlisle; St Martin's College; Univ of Lancaster; Salis and Wells Theol Coll;; *CV* AC Holy Trinity Kendal 1991–95; TV Kirkby Lonsdale Team Ministry 1995–2003; AD Gloucester North 2004–09; V Badgeworth, Shurdington and Witcombe with Bentham from 2004; AD Severn Vale from 2009; Chair Ho of Clergy Gloucester from 2011; M Carlisle Dioc Bd Educ 2001–03; M Gloucester Dioc Bd Educ from 2006; M Bp's Coun Gloucester from 2011 GS 2013–   *Tel:* 01242 702911
    email: richard.mitchell@talk21.com
    Web: www.bswbchurches.co.uk

MONCKTON, Mrs Joanna Mary,
Horsebrook Hall Brewood Stafford ST19 9LP [LICHFIELD] *b* 1941 *educ* Oxton Ho Sch Kenton Exeter; *CV* High Sheriff of Staffordshire 1995–96; Dir Penk (Holdings) Ltd and Penk Ltd; Farm Partner; Housewife; Chairman Lichf Branch Prayer Book Soc 1982–2001; Shannon Trust rep for HMYOI Brinsford until 2010
GS 1990–   *Tel:* 01902 850288
    email: jmm@strettonestate.com

MONTEITH, Very Revd David Robert Malvern, BSC, BTh, MA
St Martins House 7 Peacock Lane Leicester LE1 5PZ [DEAN OF LEICESTER] *b* 1968 *educ* Portora Royal Sch, Enniskillen; St John's Coll, Univ Durham;

St John's Coll Nottm; *CV* AC All Saints' Kings Heath, Birm 1993–97; AC St Martin-in-the-Fields 1997–2002; P-in-c Holy Trinity, South Wimbledon 2002–09; AD Merton 2004–09; TR Merton Priory Team Ministry, S'thwk 2009; Can Chanc, Leic Cathl 2009–13; Dean of Leicester from 2013
Tel: 0116 261 5356
email: david.monteith@leccofe.org
Web: www.leicestercathedral.org

MORGAN, Mr David Geoffrey Llewelyn,
25 Newbiggen St Thaxted CM6 2QS [CHELMSFORD] *b* 1935 *educ* St Jo Sch Leatherhead; *CV* Non-practising Solicitor; Chair Dioc Bd of Patr 1998–2013; M Dioc Fin Cttee 1988–2013; Dioc Rep Victoria Clergy Fund from 1989; Chair Nat CU Coun from 1998–2013; Gen Sec Guild of All Souls from 2003
GS 1990–
Tel: 01371 830132
email: dgllm@btinternet.com

MORGAN, Ven Ian David John, BAHons, LTCL
Glebe House The Street Ashfield cum Thorpe Stowmarket Suffolk IP14 6LX [ARCHDEACON OF SUFFOLK; ST EDMUNDSBURY AND IPSWICH] *b* 1957 *educ* Educ Wallingford Sch; Univ of Hull; Ripon Coll Cuddesdon; *CV* C Holy Trinity Hereford 1983–86; C St Nicolas and St Mary de Haura, Shoreham by Sea 1986–88; Presenter, Producer, Senior Producer BBC Network and Local Radio 1988–92; V All Hallows Ipswich 1992–95; R South West Ipswich Team Ministry 1995–12; CUF Link Officer from 2006; RD Ipswich 2008–12; Hon Canon, St Edmundsbury Cathedral from 2009; Adn of Suffolk from 2012
Tel: 01728 685497
email: archdeacon.ian@stedmundsbury.anglican.org
Web: www.st edmundsbury.anglican.org

MORRIS, Revd Jane Elizabeth, BA, MSc, PGCE
156 Anson Road London NW2 6BH [LONDON] *b* 1960 *educ* Ealing Gr Sch; York Univ; NEOC; *CV* Tchr, Science at Tadcaster Gr Sch 1972–74; Head of Science at the Mount Sch, York 1974–92; Head of Science and Chapl, Queen Margaret's Sch, Escrick 1992–95; AC St Michael-le-Belfrey Church, York 1992–95; Assoc V St George's Church, Leeds 1995–2005; Brd of Studies, NEOC 1998–2002; Lder West Yorkshire New Wine Network 2003–05; M New Wine North Leadership 2003–05; V St Gabriel's Church, Cricklewood from 2005; Healing Ministry Adv in the Willesden Episcopal Area until 2013; M New Wine Leadership Team for Lon and the South East 2005–10; Resource Church Leader for the Alpha Course
GS 2010–
Tel: 020 8452 6305
email: jane.morris@st-gabriels.org

MORRIS, Rt Revd Roger Anthony Brett, BSc (Hons), ARCS, MA (Cantab)
1 Fitzwalter Road Colchester CO3 3SS [AREA BISHOP OF COLCHESTER; CHELMSFORD] *b* 1968 *educ* Chipping Sodbury Sch; Filton Tech Coll; Imperial Coll Lon; Trin Coll Cam; Ridley Hall Cam; *CV* Asst C Northleach, W Hampnett and Farmington, Cold Aston, W Notgrove and Turkdean 1993–96; R Sevenhampton w Charlton Abbotts, Hawling and Whittington, Dowdeswell w Andoversford, The Shiptons and Salperton, and Withington 1996–2003; Dir Par Devel and Evang, Cov 2003–08; Adn of Worc 2008–14; Bp of Colchester from 2014
Tel: 01206 576648
email: b.colchester@chelmsford.anglican.org

MOUNTFORD, Mr Roger Philip, BSc(Econ), MS(Management)
Hookstile House Byers Lane Godstone Surrey RH9 8JH [TRUSTEE MEMBER, CHURCH OF ENGLAND PENSIONS BOARD] *b* 1948 *educ* Kingston Gr Sch; Lon Sch Econ; Stanford Bus Sch; *CV* Merchant banker 1971–2000, followed by various directorships; Gov Lon Sch Econ; M C of E Pensions Bd
Tel: 01342 893198
07799 662601
email: mountford.roger@btinternet.com

MUNRO, Revd Dr Robert Speight, B Sc, BA, Dip Ap Th, PGCE, D Min
Rectory 1 Depleach Rd Cheadle SK8 1DZ [CHESTER] *b* 1963 *educ* William Hulme's Gr Sch Man; Bris Univ; All Souls Coll Lon; Man Univ; Oak Hill Th Coll; Refrmd Th Sem US; *CV* Teach Math and PE Hazel Grove HS 1987–1990; C St Jo Bapt Hartford 1993–97; R St Wilf Davenham 1997–2003; R St Mary Cheadle from 2003; M Bp's Coun from 2000
GS 2005–
Tel: 0161 428 3440
0161 428 8050
Fax: 0161 428 3440
0161 428 8050
email: rob@munro.org.uk

NAGEL, Mrs Mary Philippa, B Ed
Aldwick Vicarage 25 Gossamer Lane Bognor Regis PO21 3AT [CHICHESTER] *b* 1954 *educ* Worthing High Sch; Lon Univ; *CV* Section 23 Insp of Schs until 2005
GS 1990–
Tel: 01243 262049
07947 145962
email: mary@nagel.me.uk

NEIL-SMITH, Mr (Noel) Jonathan, MA
Church House Great Smith St London SW1P 3AZ [ADMINISTRATIVE SECRETARY, CENTRAL SECRETARIAT] *b* 1959 *educ* Marlboro Coll; St Jo Coll Cam; *CV* On staff of Ch Commrs from 1981; Bishoprics Officer 1994–96; Seconded to GS from 1997; Asst Sec Ho of Bps 1997–98; Sec Ho of Bps 1998–2011; Sec Diocs Comm from 2011; Sec Ho of Clergy from 2011; Hon Lay Can Guildf Cathl from 2002
Tel: 020 7898 1373
Fax: 020 7898 1369
email: jonathan.neil-smith@churchofengland.org

NEWARK, Archdeacon of. See PICKEN, Ven David Anthony

NEWCASTLE, Assistant Bishop of. See WHITE, Rt Revd Frank (Francis)

NEWCASTLE, Bishop of. [NOT APPOINTED AT TIME OF GOING TO PRESS]

NEWCASTLE, Dean of. See DALLISTON, Very Revd Christopher Charles

NEWCOMBE, Dr Lindsay Kathleen, BEng, PhD
Holy Trinity Vicarage 3 Bletchley Street London N1 7QG [LONDON] *b* 1980 *educ* Purbeck Sch, Wareham; UCL; *CV* Research Fell, Dept of Mech Eng, UCL 2001–06, PhD research in bioengineering 2006–09; Tech Specialist (Orthopaedics), BSI from 2009
GS 2010–   *Tel:* 020 7253 4796
email: lindsaynewcombe@gmail.com

NEWCOME, Rt Revd James William Scobie, MA
Bishop's House Ambleside Road Keswick CA12 4DD [BISHOP OF CARLISLE] *b* 1953 *educ* Marlboro Coll; Trin Coll Ox; Selw Coll Cam; Ridley Hall Th Coll; *CV* C All SS Leavesden 1978–82; Min Bar Hill LEP Ely 1982–94; Tutor Ridley Hall Cam 1983–88; V Dry Drayton 1990–94; RD N Stowe 1993–94; DDO Ches 1994–2000; Res Can Ches Cathl 1994–2002; Dioc Dir of Min 1996–2002; Suff Bp of Penrith 2002–09; Bp Carlisle from 2009; M Bps CME Cttee; Chair Nat Stewardship Cttee; M SAGE Grp; Lead Bp on Healthcare; Dir Univ Cumbria; Lead Bishop for URC; Pres St John's Coll Dur
GS 2000–02   *Tel:* 01768 773430
email: bishop.carlisle@carlislediocese.org.uk

NEWEY, Mr (Sidney) Brian, MA
Chestnut Cottage The Green South Warborough OX10 7DN [OXFORD] *b* 1937 *educ* Burton-upon-Trent Gr Sch; Worc Coll Ox; *CV* With Br Rail from 1960, Gen Mgr W Region 1984–87; Dir Regional Railways 1987–90; Asst to Chief Exec Br Rail 1990–93; Consult in transport 1993–96; rtd; M AC Fin Cttee; M AC Audit Cttee; M DRACSC; M Nat Soc Investment Cttee; Chair Ox DBF and assoc cttees
GS 2005–   *Tel:* 01865 858322
                            Fax: 01865 858043

NEWMAN, Rt Revd Adrian, B Sc, Dip Th, M Phil, Doctor of Civil Law
63 Coborn Road London E3 2DB [AREA BISHOP OF STEPNEY; LONDON] *b* 1958 *educ* Rickmansworth Comp Sch; Bris Univ; Trin Coll Bris; *CV* C St Mark Forest Gate 1985–89; V Hillsborough and Wadsley Bridge, Sheff 1989–96; R St Mart in the Bull Ring, Birm 1996–2004; Dean of Roch 2005–11; Bp of Stepney from 2011; Hon Fell Cant Ch Ch Univ   *Tel:* 0207 932 1140
                            07805 213319
email: bishop.stepney@london.anglican.org

NEWMAN, Ven David Maurice Frederick, BA, MA
St Martin's House 7 Peacock Lane Leicester LE1 5FX [ARCHDEACON OF LOUGHBOROUGH; LEICESTER] *b* 1954 *educ* The Leys Sch Cam; Hertf Coll Ox; St John's Nottm; *CV* Asst C Christ Church Orpington 1979–83; Asst C St Mary's Bushbury 1983–86; V All Saints Ockbrook and St Stephen's Borrowash 1986–1997; TR Emmanuel Loughborough and St Mary-in-Charnwood, Nanpanton 1997–2009; AD Akeley East deanery 1999–2006; Chair Ho Clergy Leic Dioc 2006–09; Adn of Loughborough from 2009
                            Tel: 0116 261 5321
                            07817 664189
email: dmfnewman@talktalk.net

NEWTON, Canon Sandra Clare, MSc, BSc, BA
50 Broomgrove Road Sheffield South Yorkshire S10 2NA [VICE CHAIR AND TRUSTEE MEMBER, CHURCH OF ENGLAND PENSIONS BOARD] *b* 1951 *educ* Minchenden Gr Sch; Lon Sch Econ; OU; *CV* Hon Can Sheffield Cathl from 2006; Chair Sheffield Dioc Bd of Fin from 2008; M C of E Pensions Bd from 2010; M Abp's Coun Fin Cttee from 2011   *Tel:* 0114 266 1079
email: sandracnewton@aol.com

NORFOLK, Archdeacon of. See BETTS, Ven Steven James

NORTH, Revd Philip John, MA
The Rectory 191 St Pancras Way London NW1 9NH [LONDON] *b* 1966 *educ* The Latymer Sch, Edmonton; York Uni; St Stephen's House, Ox; *CV* AC S Mary and S Peter, Sunderland 1992–96; V Holy Trin, Hartlepool 1996–2002; Area Dean of Hartlepool 2000–02; P Administrator of the Shrine of Our Lady of Walsingham 2002–08; TR of the Parish of Old St Pancras from 2008
GS 2010–   *Tel:* 020 7485 5791
                            07919 180788
email: philip.north@mac.com
                    Twitter: @FrPhilipNorth

NORTH-WEST EUROPE, Archdeacon in. WILLIAMS, Canon Meurig (Acting)

NORTHAMPTON, Archdeacon of. See ORMSTON, Ven Richard Jeremy

NORTHOLT, Archdeacon of. See GREEN, Ven Duncan

NORTHUMBERLAND, Archdeacon of. See MILLER, Ven Geoff (Geoffrey Vincent)

NORWICH, Archdeacon of. See McFARLANE, Ven Janet Elizabeth

NORWICH, Bishop of. See JAMES, Rt Revd Graham Richard

NORWICH, Dean of. See HEDGES, Very Revd Jane

NOTTINGHAM, Archdeacon of. CLARK, Ven Sarah

NUNN, Very Revd Andrew Peter, BA, BA
Southwark Cathedral London Bridge London SE1 9DA [DEAN OF SOUTHWARK] *b* 1957 *educ* Guthlaxton Upper Sch Wigston, Leic; Leic Poly; Leeds Univ; Coll of Resurr Mirfield; *CV* C St Jas Manston, Ripon 1983–87; C Leeds Richmond Hill 1987–91, V 1991–95; Chapl Agnes Stewart C of E High Sch, Leeds 1987–95; Personal Asst to Bp of S'wark 1995–99; Vice-Provost, Prec and Can Res S'wark Cathl 1999–2000; Sub-Dean, Prec and Can Res S'wark Cathl 2000–11, Dean of S'wark from 2012; M Dioc Syn; CNC from 2011
GS 2005–10, 2010–   *Tel:* 020 7367 6727
                            07961 332051
                 Fax: 020 7367 6725
email: andrew.nunn@southwark.anglican.org
          Web: www.southwarkcathedral.org

O'BRIEN, Mr Gerald Michael, B Sc, DMS
Chestnuts 14 Oakhill Rd Sevenoaks Kent TN13 1NP [ROCHESTER] *b* 1948 *educ* Dulwich Coll; Bris Univ; *CV* Promotions Sec, ICS 1994–97; Dir of Communications, Crosslinks 1997–2002; M CEEC 1988–92, from 1996; M CPAS Coun 1999–2004; GS Appts Cttee 1997–2000; Bus Cttee from 2005
GS 1980–85, 1987–   *Tel:* 01732 453894
                 07711 938517 (Mobile)
         email: gmobrien@btinternet.com

OAKHAM, Archdeacon of. See STEELE, Ven Gordon John

OGLE, Very Revd Catherine, BA, MPhil, MA, MA
38 Goodby Road Moseley Birmingham B13 8NJ [DEAN OF BIRMINGHAM] *b* 1961 *educ* Perse Sch for Girls, Cam; Univ of Leeds; Fitzwilliam Coll Cam; Westcott Ho Cam; Univ Leeds; *CV* AC St Mary Middleton, Leeds 1988–91; Relig Programmes Ed BBC Leeds 1991–95; NSM St Margaret & All Hallows, Leeds 1991–95; P-in-c Woolley w W Bretton 1995–2001; Ed Wakef Dioc Magazine 1995–2001; V Huddersfield 2001–2010; Dean of Birmingham from 2010; M Wakef Dioc Liturgy Gp, Communications Gp, Dioc Syn; M Coun Coll of the Resurrection, Mirfield 2008–10; Hon Can Wakef Cathl from 2008   *Tel:* 0121 262 1840
                 Fax: 0121 262 1860
       email: dean@birminghamcathedral.org
         Web: www.birminghamcathedral.org

OLDHAM, Mr Gavin David Redvers, MA (Cantab)
Ashfield House St Leonards Tring HP23 6NP [OXFORD] *b* 1949 *educ* Eton; Trin Coll Cam; *CV* Wedd Durlacher Mordaunt 1975–86, Partner 1984–86; Secretariat Barclays De Zoete Wedd (BZW) 1984–88; Chief Exec Barclayshare Ltd 1986–89, Chair 1989–90; Chief Exec The Share Cen Ltd 1990–13; Chief Exec Share plc 2000–13, Chair 2014; Chair The Share Foundn from 2005; MD Share Radio from 2013; Chair Wider Share Ownership Council from 2014; Ch Commr 1999–

2013; M Fin Cttee AC 2001–11; M Ethical Investment Adv Grp 1999–2013
GS 1995–   *Tel:* 01494 758348 (Home)
                 01296 439100 (Office)
                 07767 337696 (Mobile)
                 Fax: 01296 414410
          email: gdro@btconnect.com
                 Web: www.gdro.net

ORMSTON, Ven Richard Jeremy, BA, MTh
Westbrook 11 The Drive Northampton NN1 4RZ [ARCHDEACON OF NORTHAMPTON; PETERBOROUGH] *b* 1961 *educ* Stamford Sch; Roehampton Inst; Oak Hil Theol Coll; *CV* AC Rodbourne Cheney, Swindon 1987–91; R Collingtree w Courteenhall and Milton Malsor 1991–2001; RD Wootton 1996–2011; V Oundle w Ashton and Benefield w Glapthorn 2001–14; RD Oundle 2002:13; Adn of Northampton from 2014
                 Tel: 01604 714015
                 Fax: 01604 792016
     email: archdeacon.northampton@
          peterborough-diocese.org.uk
     Web: www.peterborough-diocese.org.uk

OSBORNE, Mrs Emma Charlotte, MA
Lawn Farm Milton Lilbourne Pewsey SN9 5LQ [CHURCH COMMISSIONER] *b* 1964 *educ* Redland High Sch, Bris; Ch Ch Ox; *CV* County NatWest 1985–89; Lloyds Investment Mgrs 1989–91; Credit Suisse/CSFB 1991–97; Investment Mgr, Chubb Insurance from 1997   *Tel:* 01672 563459
                 020 7956 5362
       email: emma.osborne@lawnfarm.co.uk

OSBORNE, Ven Hayward John, MA, PGCE
Church of England Birmingham 1 Colmore Row Birmingham B3 2BJ [ARCHDEACON OF BIRMINGHAM] *b* 1948 *educ* Sevenoaks Sch; New Coll Ox; Westcott Ho Th Coll; *CV* C St Pet and St Paul Bromley 1973–77; C Halesowen 1977–80, TV 1980–83; TR St Barnabas Worc 1983–88; V St Mary Moseley 1988–2001; AD Moseley 1994–2001; Hon Can Birm Cathl from 2000; Adn of Birm from 2001
GS 1998–   *Tel:* 0121 426 0441 (Office)
       email: hs.osborne@btinternet.com

OSBORNE, Very Revd June, BA (Econ) Hons, M Phil, Cert Theol, DL
The Deanery 7 The Close Salisbury SP12EF [DEAN OF SALISBURY] *b* 1953 *educ* Whalley Range Gr Sch, Manch; Manch Univ; St Jo Coll Nottm; Wycliffe Hall Ox; Birm Univ; *CV* C St Mart-in-the-Bullring and Chapl, Birm Children's Hosp 1980–84; St Mark Old Ford 1984–89; St Paul w St Steph and St Mark Old Ford 1989–95; Can Treas Salis Cathl 1995–2004; Dean of Salis from 2004; M Bd of Soc Resp 1985–90; M Stg Cttee GS 1990–95; Sen Insp of Theol Educ 1994–2004; Chair DAC 2003–07; Deputy Lieut of Wilts from 2006
GS 1985–95; 2004–05   *Tel:* 01722 555110
                 07771 743760
                 Fax: 01722 555155
          email: thedean@salcath.co.uk

OXFORD (CHRIST CHURCH), Dean of, PERCY, Very Revd Martyn William

OXFORD, Archdeacon of. See GORICK, Ven Martin Charles William

OXFORD, Bishop of. [NOT APPOINTED AT TIME OF GOING TO PRESS]

PADDOCK, Very Revd Dr John Allan Barnes, BA, MA, PhD, PGCE, FRSA
The Deanery Bomb House Lane Gibraltar [DEAN OF GIBRALTAR; EUROPE] *b* 1951 *CV* Dean of Gibraltar from 2008
Tel: 00350 200 78377
Fax: 00350 78463
email: deangib@gibraltar.gi

PANTER, Ven Ricky (Richard) James Graham, Cert Ed, GOE
115 Papillon Drive Fazakerley Liverpool L9 9HL [ARCHDEACON OF LIVERPOOL] *b* 1948 *educ* Monkton Combe Sch Bath; Worc Coll of Educ; Oak Hill Th Coll; *CV* RE tchr, Chatham Tech High Sch for Boys 1970–71; primary tchr, Boscombe C of E Primary 1971–73; C H Trin Rusholme, Man 1976–80; Asst V St Cyprian w Ch Ch Toxteth 1980–85; V St Andr Clubmoor 1985–96; V St Jo and St Jas Orrell Hey, Bootle 1996–11; AD Bootle 1999–2002; Adn of Liverpool from 2002; M Dioc BMU Ecumenism Cttee 1985–90; M Dioc Pastl Cttee 1991–96
Tel: 0151 705 2154 (Office)
07540 300842
email: ricky.panter@liverpool.anglican.org
2nd email: rickypanter@gmail.com

PARKER, Ven Matthew John, BA. BA
39 The Brackens Clayton Newcastle under Lyme ST5 4JL [ARCHDEACON OF STOKE-UPON-TRENT; LICHFIELD] *b* 1963 *educ* BP Wand C of E Sec Sch. Sunbury-on-Thames; Manch Univ; Camb Univ; Ridley Hall Camb; *CV* AC St Mary's Twickenham 1988–91; AC St George's Stockport 1991–93; Chapl Stockport Gr Sch 1991–94; P-in-c St Mark's Edgeley, Stockport 1993–95; TV Stockport South West 1995–2000; TR Leek and Meerbrook TM 2000–13; RD Leek 2007–13; Adn of Stoke-on Trent from 2013
Tel: 01782 663066
email: archdeacon.stoke@lichfield.anglican.org

PARSONS, Revd Canon Dr Michael William Semper, MA, DPhil
6 Spa Villas Montpellier Gloucester GL1 1LB [GLOUCESTER] *b* 1947 *educ* Hul GS; St Catherine's Coll, Ox; Selwyn Coll Cam; Ridley Hall Cam; *CV* Prin Lect Th, Univ Glouc 2009–10; DDO and Dir C Training, Glouc 2000–04; DDO & P-in-c, Hempsted,Glouc 1996–2000; TR, Walbrook Epiphany, Derby 1995–96; , Derby St Augustine, Derby 1985–95; Vocations Adv, Derby 1987–96; SPCK Fellow, NEICE & Hon Lect Th, Univ Dur 1984–85; SPCK Viewdata Fellow, Dept Th, Univ Dur 1981–84; AC, Edmonton All Saints, Lon 1978–81; Univ Tching Fellow, Dept Physics, Univ

Nott 1973–75; Lect Physics, St Catherine's Coll, Ox 1972–73; Prin, WEMTC 2004–11; Exec Dir, Ian Ramsey Centre, Th Fac, Ox Univ 1999; P-i-C St Oswald, Glos from 2011; Hon Can Glos Cathl from 2003; Bd of Educ 2011
GS 2003–05; 2010–
Tel: 01452 524550
Fax: 01452 564889
email: mwsp@btinternet.com
2nd email: mike.parsons@stoswaldconeyhill.com
Web: www.stoswaldconeyhill.com

PATERSON, Rt Revd Robert Mar Eskine, BA, MA, DipTh
Thie yn Aspick 4 The Falls Douglas Isle of Man IM4 4PZ [BISHOP OF SODOR AND MAN] *b* 1949 *educ* King Henry VIII Sch, Cov; St John's Coll Dur Univ; Cranmer Hall Dur; *CV* C Harpurhey Man 1972–73; C Sketty Swansea 1973–78; R Llangattock and Llangynidr 1978–83; V Gabalfa Cardiff 1983–94; TR Cowbridge Llandaff 1994–2000; Prin Officer Ch in Wales Coun for Miss and Min 2000–06; Chapl and Researcher to Abp of York 2006–08; Bp Sodor and Man from 2008; Vc Chair Liturg Commn; Chair Central Rders Coun; M Min Coun
Tel: 01624 622108
07624 450633
email: bishop@sodorandman.im
Web: www.sodorandman.im

PATTERSON, Revd Neil Sydney, MA
The Rectory Weston-under-Penyard Ross-on-Wye HR9 7QA [HEREFORD] *b* 1979 *educ* Haberdashers' Aske's Boys Sch, Brasenose Coll Ox; Ripon Coll Cuddesdon; ; *CV* C Cleobury Mortimer with Hopton Wafers etc, 2004–08; R Ariconium from 2008; M Bp's Coun Hereford from 2012
GS 2012–
Tel: 01989 567229
email: pattersonneil@hotmail.com

PAVER, Canon Elizabeth Caroline, FRSA
113 Warning Tongue Lane Bessacar Doncaster DN4 6TB [SHEFFIELD] *b* 1944 *educ* Doncaster Girls High Sch; St Mary's Coll Cheltenham; *CV* In Primary Educ 28 years; Hdtchr Crags Rd Nurs/Inf Sch 1976–80; Hdtchr Askern Nurs/Inf Sch Littlemoor 1980–86; Hdtchr Intake Nursery and First Sch Doncaster from 1986; M Nat Coun NAHT from 1991; Centenary Nat Pres 1997–97; NAHT Appointee to Gen Teaching Coun from 2000; past M Panel of Chairmen GS; Lay Chair Dioc Syn; M Bp's Coun; M Dioc Bd of Educ Tr Cttee; apptd M AC 1999–2002; Lay Can Sheff Cathl from 2000; Ch Commr from 2004
GS 1991–
Tel: 01302 530706
Fax: 01302 360811
email: johnpaver@btinternet.com

PEARSON, Rt Revd Geoffrey Seagrave, BA
Shireshead Vicarage Whinney Brow Forton Preston PR3 0AE [SUFFRAGAN BISHOP OF LANCASTER; BLACKBURN] *b* 1951 *educ* St Jo Coll Dur; Cranmer Hall Dur; *CV* C Kirkheaton, Wakef 1974–77; C-in-c Redeemer, Blackb 1977–82, V 1982–85;

WHO'S WHO

Asst Home Sec GS Bd for Miss and Unity 1985–89; Hon C Forty Hill, Lon 1985–89; Exec Sec BCC Evang Cttee 1986–89; V Roby, Liv 1989–2006; AD Huyton 2002–06; Hon Can Liv Cathl 2003–06; Bp of Lancaster from 2006

Tel: 01524 799900
07809 618385 (Mobile)
Fax: 01524 799901
email: bishoplancaster@gmail.com

PENFOLD, Revd Canon Dr Susan, BA, MA, PhD
The Vicarage Church Lane Great Harwood BB6 7PU [BLACKBURN] *b* 1952 *educ* York Univ; Bris Univ; Selwyn Coll Cam Univ; Ridley Hall Th Coll; *CV* Rsrch Asst, Dept Biochemistry, Bris Univ, 1976–77; Travelling Sec, Universities and Colleges Christian Fellowship, 1977–81; Deaconess, Buckhurst Hill, Chelmsf 1984–87; C, Parish of Greenside, Dur 1987–90; C Cononley w Bradley, Bradf 1990–97; Assoc DDO, Bradf 1996–2001; Dioc Dir Ordinands and Dean of Ministry, Wakef 2001–08; Dir Ministry and Residentiary Canon, Blackb from 2008; M Coun Coll of the Resurrection, Mirfield, 2001–08; M Ministry Division FinPanel 2003–08; Assessor for the Lower House of the Convocation of York 2005–08, 2010
GS 2005–08; 2010–   *Tel:* 01254 658919
07753 987777
email: sue.penfold@blackburn.anglican.org
Twitter: @PenfoldSue

PENRITH, Suffragan Bishop of. See FREEMAN, Rt Revd Robert John

PERUMBALATH, Ven Dr John, MA, MTh, PhD
11 Bridgefields Close Hornchurch RM11 1GQ [ARCHDEACON OF BARKING; CHELMSFORD] *b* 1966 *educ* Calicut Univ; Osmania Univ; North West Univ; Serampore Th Coll; *CV* Lect in New Testament, Serampore Coll 1993–95; V St James' Church, Calcutta 1995–2000; V St Thomas' Church, Calcutta 2000–01; Asst P St George's Church, Beckenham 2002–05; T Northfleet and Rosherville 2005–08; V All Saints Church, Gravesend 2008–13; Dioc Urban Officer 2008–13; M Bp's Coun from 2007; M Adv Coun for Ministry and Training 2007–10; Tutor, Coll of Preachers from 2008; Trustee USPG from 2009; Adn of Barking from 2013
GS 2010–   *Tel:* 01708 474951
email: a.barking@chelmsford.anglican.org

PETERBOROUGH, Bishop of. See ALLISTER, Rt Revd Donald Spargo

PETERBOROUGH, Dean of. See TAYLOR, Very Revd Charles William

PHILIPS, Dr Jacqui (Jacqueline Louise), MA(Cantab), MA(Durham), DPhil(Oxon)
Church House Great Smith Street London SWP 3AZ [CLERK TO THE SYNOD AND DIRECTOR OF CENTRAL SECRETARIAT] *b* 1971   *Tel:* 0207 898 1385
email: jacqui.philips@churchofengland.org

PHILPOTT, Preb Sam (Samuel), MBE
21 Plaistow Crescent Plymouth PL5 2EA [EXETER] *b* 1941 *educ* R Naval Hosp Sch Holbrook; Kelham Th Coll; *CV* C St Mark Swindon 1965–70; C St Martin Torquay 1970-73; TV All SS Exmouth 1973–76; V Shaldon 1976–78; P-in-c St Pet Plymouth 1978–80, V from 1980; RD Plymouth Devonport 1985–91 and 1995–2001; Preb Ex Cathl 1991–13; Preb Emer 2013; Acting P-in-c St Thomas N Keyham from 1997, P-in-c from 1999; P-in-c St Peter and the Holy Apostles 2009–13; Chapl to Bp of Plymouth 2013; Chair of Govs St Peter's C of E VA Primary Sch from 1978; Gov of All Saints C of E Academy Plymouth 2010; Gov St George C of E Academy Plymouth 2013; Chair Dioc Ho of Clergy 2000–09; M Bp's Coun; M Dioc Bd of Educ (Vc Chair of DBE); M Dioc Budget Assess Grp 2000–09; M DBF Stg Cttee 2000–09; M Dioc Vacancy-in-See Cttee; M Bp of Plymouth's Adv Grp for Plymouth city; M Drake Foundn Plymouth; Chair Community Cttee and Grants Cttee, Grass Roots Panel 2009–11; Dir and Chair Millfields Comm Economic Devel Trust Plymouth; Bp of Ebbsfleet's Coun of Priests; Bp of Ebbsfleet's Rep to the Bp of Truro 2014; M Nat Coun and Exec Cttee Forward in Faith; Regional Dn Tamar 1999–2014; Forward in Faith; Trustee of Confraternity of the Blessed Sacrament; Chapl to Lord Mayor of Plymouth 2012–13; M Plymouth Fairness Commn 2013; Chapl to Plymouth Area Bus Coun 2012; M Plymouth City Coun Cross Party Working Party on Child Poverty and Chair Plymouth Child Poverty Standing Conversation 2013
GS 1990–   *Tel:* 01752 298502
07770 504415
email: frphilpott@gmail.com

PICKEN, Ven David Anthony, BA(Hons), MA, PGCE
22 Rufford Road Edwinstowe Notts NG21 9HY [ARCHDEACON OF NEWARK; SOUTHWELL] *b* 1963 *educ* Kingsmead; Lon amd Nottm Univs; Ch Ch Cant; Lincoln Theol Coll; *CV* Asst C Worth TM 1990–3; TV St Clare's and Hospital Chapl 1993–97; TR Wordsley 1997–2004; AD Kingswinford 2001–04; TR High Wycombe 2004–11; AD Wycombe 2008–11; Adn of Newark from 2012; M Bp's Coun; Chair Liturgical Cttee; M DAC; M Fin Cttee; M Church closure working group; M Design Team for 2020 planning; BAP adviser; Dioc LIstening Process Convenor; Chair Dioc Bd Educ; Chair First Appointments Grp; M Coun St John's Theological Coll   *Tel:* 01636 817206
07917 690576
email: archdeacon-newark@
southwell.anglican.org

PIGGOTT, Ven Andy (Andrew John), B Sc (Econ), Dip Th, PGCE
56 Grange Rd Saltford Bristol BS31 3AG [ARCHDEACON OF BATH; BATH AND WELLS] *b* 1951 *educ* Thornes Ho Gr Sch Wakef; Holly Lodge Gr Sch

Smethwick; Q Mary Coll Lon; Nottm Univ; St Jo Coll Nottm; *CV* C St Phil w. St Jas Dorridge, Birm 1986–89; TV St Chad Kidderminster w. St Geo Team, Worc 1989–94; V St Lawr Biddulph, Lich 1994–99; CPAS Min & Vocations Adv 1999–2001; acting Gen Dir 2000–01, Patr Sec 2001–05; Adn of Bath from 2005; GS 2010–
GS 2010–   *Tel:* 01225 873609
                                              Fax: 01225 874610
            email: adbath@bathwells.anglican.org

PILGRIM, Revd (Colin) Mark, BA, MA, CertEs
St Peter's Vicarage 17 The Drive Henleaze Bristol BS9 4LD [BRISTOL] *b* 1956 *educ* St John's Sch, Leatherhead; Kingston Poly; Geneva Univ; W of Eng Univ; Westcott House Th Coll; *CV* C, Chorlton-cum-Hardy, Man 1984–87; C, Ecum P Whitchurch, 1987–89; V, St Oswald's, Bedminster Down 1989–95; Dioc Child and Y Off, Bris 1995–2001; V, St Peter, Henleaze from 2001; Area Dean, Bris West Deanery from 2006; Chair Dioc Lit and Wor Cttee 2004–08; M Bp's Counc from 2010
GS 2009–   *Tel:* 0117 962 0636
            email: markpilgrimis@aol.com

PLAYLE, Mrs Kathleen (Kathy),
136 Abbs Cross Lane Hornchurch Essex RM12 4XT [CHELMSFORD] *b* 1950   *Tel:* 01708 442211
            email: kathyplayle@btconnect.com

PLYMING, Revd Dr Philip James John, BA, MA, PhD
The Vicarage Church Road Claygate Esher KT10 0JP [GUILDFORD] *b* 1974 *educ* Oakmeeds Comm Sch; Haywards Heath VIth Form Coll; Cam Univ; Dur Univ; Edin Univ; Cranmer Hall Dur; *CV* C Ch Ch Chineham 2001–06; V, Holy Trin Claygate from 2006; M Guildf Dioc Syn from 2007; M RACSC from 2011; RD Emly from 2012; Sec EGGS (Evangelical Group of General Synod) from 2011
GS 2009–   *Tel:* 01372 463603
email: philipplyming@holytrinityclaygate.org.uk
                              Twitter: @philipplyming

PLYMOUTH, Archdeacon of. See CHANDLER, Ven Ian Nigel

PLYMOUTH, Suffragan Bishop of. [NOT APPOINTED AT TIME OF GOING TO PRESS]

PONTEFRACT, Archdeacon of. See TOWNLEY, Ven Peter Kenneth

PORTER, Rt Revd Anthony, MA (Oxon), MA (Cantab)
Dunham House 8 Westgate Southwell NG25 0JL [SUFFRAGAN BISHOP OF SHERWOOD; SOUTHWELL AND NOTTINGHAM] *b* 1952 *educ* Aire Boro Gr Sch; Don Valley High Sch; Gravesend Sch for Boys; Hertford Coll Ox; Ridley Hall Cam; *CV* C Edgware, Lon 1977–80; C St Mary Haughton,

Manch 1980–83; P-in-c Ch Ch Bacup 1983–87, V 1987–91; R Rusholme 1991–2006; Bp of Sherwood from 2006; M Dioc Syn, Bp's Coun; M Coll of Evangs 2009   *Tel:* 01636 819133
    email: bishopsherwood@southwell.anglican.org

PORTSDOWN, Archdeacon of. See GRENFELL, Ven Dr Joanne Woolway

PORTSMOUTH, Bishop of. See FOSTER, Rt Revd Christopher Richard James

PORTSMOUTH, Dean of. See BRINDLEY, Very Revd David Charles

POTTER, Ven Peter Maxwell, MA
St Ursula's Church Jubilaumsplatz 2 3000 Bern 6 Switzerland [ARCHDEACON OF SWITZERLAND; EUROPE; ARCHDEACON OF GERMANY AND NORTHERN EUROPE (ACTING); EUROPE] *b* 1946 *educ* County Grammar Sch Crewe; Univ Coll Swansea; Univ of British Columbia; Salisbury and Wells Theol Coll; *CV* C Bradford-on-Avon 1985–88; C Harnham 1988–91; P-in-c N Bradley, Southwick and Heywood 1991–96; V St Anne's Sale 1996–2000; R St Columba's Largs 2000–08; Chapl St Ursula's Berne w Neuchatel from 2008; Adn of Switzerland from 2009
                              Tel: 0041 31 351 0343
                     email: berne@anglican.ch

POUNDS, Mrs Sylvia Lynn, RGN, RDN, FD Ministry
3 Woodlands Louth Lincolnshire LN11 0WS [LINCOLN] *b* 1950 *educ* Cheadle County Gr Sch; Trent Polytech; Coll of St Mark and St John Plymouth, Lincoln Sch of Th and Min Studies; *CV* Nursing and Nurse Management Posts 1976–1990; Dir of Nursing and Health Visiting 1990–92; Sector Manager Comm Health Care NHS 1992–94; Nurse Non-Exec Dir 1992–95; Gen Manager Adult and Older Peoples Mental Health 1994–2000; Dir Goole Development Trust 1997–98; Head of Specialist Child and Adolescent Mental Health, 2000–10; Student of Theology from 2010; Rdr from 2013
GS 2010–   *Tel:* 07771 549947
            email: spounds@btconnect.com

PRATT, Ven Richard David, MA (Oxon), BCS, PhD (Birmingham)
50 Stainburn Road Workington Cumbria CA14 1SN [ARCHDEACON OF WEST CUMBERLAND] *b* 1955 *educ* Ranelagh School, Bracknell; Lincoln Coll, Ox; Nottingham Univ; Lincoln Theol Coll; Birm Univ; *CV* C All Hallows Wellingborough 1984–87; TV Kingsthorpe 1987–92; V St Benedict's Hunsbury 1992–7, P-in-c St Cuthbert's Carlisle and DCO Carlisle Diocese 1997–2008; Adn West Cumbria from 2009   *Tel:* 01900 66190
                                              07788 728508
    email: archdeacon.west@carlislediocese.org.uk

PRATT, Revd Stephen Samuel, BA, DipH.E, BA, PGCE
The Rectory 203 St Michaels Road Chell Stoke on Trent ST6 6JT [LICHFIELD] *b* 1967 *educ* St Margarets Aigburth Liv; Univ Coll Chester, Keele Univ; Oak Hill Th Coll; *CV* Maths Tchr & Head of Year at St Edwards C of E, Romford 1989–98; C All Saints, Goodmayes 2000–03; TV Chell Team Ministry 2003–07; P-in-c St Michael Chell w Ch of the Saviour Chell Heath 2007–08; V St Michael Chell w Ch of the Saviour Chell Heath from 2008; Chapl to TA Forces from 2005; Voc Advisor from 2008
GS 2010–   *Tel:* 01782 838708
                                    07951 027290
                  email: stephen_pratt@sky.com

PRESLAND, Mr Andrew Roy, B Sc
58 Harborough Rd Rushden NN10 0LP [PETER-BOROUGH] *b* 1966 *educ* Rushden Boys' Sch; Leic Univ; *CV* Asst Statistician, DOE 1989–95; Statistician DOE, later DETR 1995–99; Sen Lib Clerk (Statistics), Ho of Commons Lib (second-ment) 1999–2001; Statistician, Office of Dep Prime Min (local govt finance) 2001–06, DCLG 2006–11 (strategy and performance), and from 2011 (homelessness and planning statistics); Lay Chair, Higham Dny Syn; Treas E Northants Faith Grp 2005–13, Sec from 2013; M Bp's Coun from 2006; M AC Fin Cttee 2006–11; M DBF 2006–08; Gov Whitefriars Jun Sch Rushden from 2012; GS rep Coun Ridley Hall Camb from 2014
GS 2003–   *Tel:* 01933 316927
                  email: andrewpresland@
harboroughroad58.freeserve.co.uk
                  Web: www.dirtyhands.co.uk
                  Twitter: @AndrewPresland

PRESTON, Dr John Philip Harry, BSc, PHD
Church House Great Smith St London SW1P 3AZ [NATIONAL STEWARDSHIP AND RESOURCES OFFICER, ARCHBISHOPS' COUNCIL] *b* 1965 *educ* Lakes Sch; Exmouth Sch; Lancs Univ; *CV* Market-ing Mgr Procter and Gamble 1989–2000; Grp Marketing Dir S Staffordshire Grp 2000–02; Marketing, Sales and NPD Mgr, Freshway Foods 2002–05; Nat Stewardship and Resources Officer from 2005   *Tel:* 020 7898 1540
         email: john.preston@churchofengland.org

PRITCHARD, Miss Heather Anne, IBDIP
[CHURCH OF ENGLAND YOUTH COUNCIL REPRE-SENTATIVE] *b* 1994 *educ* Perse Sch for Girls Senior; Stephen Perse Found Sixth Form Coll, Cam; Univ Warwick;; *CV* Ldr numerous children's holiday clubs (2007–12); Manager two Social Enterprise projects 2010–11; Head Girl Chorister, Great St Mary's Camb 2011–12; Co-Manager 2000-person capacity Spa Pavilion and its stewards at Whitby Folk Week 2012; Pres Warwick Chaplaincy Charity Ball 2013; Leader Scripture Union Norfolk Broads Sailing Cruises 2013; Under-graduate Student from 2012; Coventry Dioc Children and Youth Auditor from 2013; Senior Ambassador at Warwick Welcome Service including a coordinating role of ambassadors at university open days from 2013; Dioc of Ely Youth Council Vice-Chair 2010–12; M Bp's Coun and Dioc Synod Ely 2011–12; M Bp's Coun Coventry from 2012
GS 2013–

PROUD, Rt Revd Andrew John, BD, MA, AKC
Bishop's House Tidmarsh Lane Tidmarsh, Reading RG8 8HA [AREA BISHOP OF READING; OXFORD] *b* 1954 *educ* K Coll Lon; SOAS;.Linc Th Coll; *CV* C Stansted Mountfitchet Chelmsf 1980–83; TV Borehamwood St Alb 1983–90; C Bp's Hatfield 1990–92; R E Barnet 92–2001; Chapl Adis Ababa St Matt Ethiopia 2002–07; Area Bp Ethiopia and Horn of Africa 2007–11; Area Bp of Reading from 2011   *Tel:* 0118 984 1216
                              Fax: 0118 984 1218
         email: bishopreading@oxford.anglican.org

PYE, Mr Christopher Charles, BA, M Sc
140 Hinckley Rd St Helens WA11 9JY [LIVERPOOL] *b* 1946 *educ* Grange Park Sch St Helens; Open Univ; Manchester Univ; *CV* Technologist in Glass Industry from 1963; Rtd Occupational Hygiene Mgr; Lay Chair St Helens Dny Syn 1986–2014; Lay Chair Dioc Syn 1991–2003; Rdr
GS 1985–90, 1992–   *Tel:* 01744 609506
                  email: chrispye@blueyonder.co.uk

RAMSBURY, Suffragan Bishop of. See CONDRY, Rt Revd Edward Francis

RAYFIELD, Rt Revd Dr Lee Stephen, B Sc (Hons), PhD, CTM
Mark House Field Rise Swindon SN1 4HP [SUFFRAGAN BISHOP OF SWINDON; BRISTOL] *b* 1955 *educ* Thos Bennett Comp Sch, Crawley; Crawley Coll of Tech; Southn Univ; St Mary's Hosp Medical Sch, Lon Univ; Ridley Hall, Cam; *CV* C All SS w. St Andr Woodford Wells, Chelmsf 1993–97; P-in-c St Pet w. St Mark Hosp Ch Furze Platt, Ox 1997–2004, V 2004–05; AD Maidenhead & Windsor, Ox 2000–05; Bp of Swindon from 2005; M UK Gene Therapy Adv Cttee 2000–09; M Soc of Ordained Scientists from 1995; M Fell of Par Evang from 1995; Coun M Evang Alliance from 2007; M Ho of Bps CME Cttee from 2007 (CMD Cttee from 2012); M Ethical Investment Adv Grp from 2007; M Human Embryology and Fertilisa-tion Authority from 2012   *Tel:* 01793 538654
                              Fax: 01793 525181
         email: bishop.swindon@bristoldiocese.org
Web: www.bristol.anglican.org/news/microblog

RAZZALL, Revd Charles Humphrey, MA
St Michael's Rectory 198 Ford Lane Crewe CW1 3TN [CHESTER] *b* 1905 *educ* St Paul's Sch, Lon; Worchester Coll Ox; Westcott House Th Coll; *CV* Asst C Catford and Downham T, 1979–83; V St Hilda w St Cyprian, Crofton Park 1983–87;

TV Oldham 1987–2001; Area Dean Oldham 1992–99; Hon Can Man Cathl 1998–2001; R St Michael Coppenhall, Crewe from 2001
GS 1995–2000; 2010–   *Tel:* 01270 215151
          email: razzall@angelfields.eclipse.co.uk

READ, Revd Charles William,
42 Heigham Road Norwich NR2 3AU [NORWICH] *b* 1960 *educ* King Edward VI Sch, Lichfield; Man Univ; Man Poly; St John's Coll, Nott; *CV* Head of RS, Audenshaw High School 1982–86; C, Oldham Team Ministry, 1988–90; C, St.Clement Urmston 1990–93; Goodshaw & Crawshawbooth 1993–94; P-in-c & TV Broughton Team Ministry 1994–99; Lect Lit & Doc, Cranmer Hall, Dur 1999–2006; Vice-Prin & Dir Studies Norwich Dioc Ministry Course from 2007; Eucharistic Prayers Steering Cttee 1998–2000; Thl Ed & Training Cttee 2005–06
GS 1997–2000; 2005–06; 2010–   *Tel:* 01603 729813
          email: charlesread@norwich.anglican.org

READING, Area Bishop of. See PROUD, Rt Revd Andrew John

REDFERN, Rt Revd Dr Alastair Llewellyn John, MA, MA, Ph D
The Bishop's House 6 King St Duffield Belper DE56 4EU [BISHOP OF DERBY] *b* 1948 *educ* Bicester Sch; Ch Ch Ox; Trin Coll Cam; Westcott Ho Th Coll; Bris Univ; *CV* C Tettenhall 1976–79; Lect in Ch Hist, Dir of Pastl Studies and Vc-Prin Cuddesdon Th Coll 1979–87; C All SS Cuddesdon 1983–87; Can Res Bris Cathl 1987–97; Can Theologian and Dir of Tr 1987–97; Mod of Par Resource Tm 1995–97; M ABM Initial Minl Educ Cttee; Mod Abps Dip for Rdrs; Bp of Grantham 1997–2005; Dean of Stamford 1998–2005; Chair Fin Panel, Min Div; M Theol, Educ and Trg Cttee; M Bp's Cttee for Min; M Bp's CME Cttee; M Legal Aid Commn; Bp of Derby from 2005; M Ho of Bps Th Gp; M Bd Trustees Christian Aid
GS 2005–   *Tel:* 01332 840132
          email: bishop@bishopofderby.org

REED, Ven John Peter Cyril, BD, AKC, Cert Th (Oxon)
2 Monkton Heights West Monkton Taunton TA2 8LU [ARCHDEACON OF TAUNTON; BATH & WELLS] *b* 1951 *educ* Monkton Combe Sch; K Coll Lon; Cuddesdon Th Coll; *CV* Asst C Croydon Par Ch 1979–82; Prec St Alb 1982–86; R Timsbury and Priston 1986–93; Chapl for Rural Affairs Bath Adnry 1987–93; TR Ilminster and District TM 1993–99; Adn Taunton from 1999; Dioc Warden of Rdrs   *Tel:* 01823 413315
          07971 440990 (Mobile)
          email: adtaunton@bathwells.anglican.org

REES, Mrs Christina (Henking Muller), BA, MA, FRSA
Churchfield Pudding Lane Barley Royston Herts SG8 8JX [ST ALBANS] *b* 1953 *educ* Hampton Day Sch; Pomona Coll; Wheaton Graduate Sch; K Coll Lon; *CV* Researcher IBA 1980; Asst Public Relns

Officer The Children's Society 1985–87; Writer from 1980; Broadcaster from 1990; Consultant and Trainer from 1995; Coach from 2003; M Strg Cttee and Initiation Services Revision Cttee 1996–98; M CECC 1996–98; M ABM 1996–98; Chair WATCH 1996–2010; Trustee, Li Tim-Oi Foundn from 1997; Elected M AC 1999–2000; Convenor, Church and Media Consultation 2000, 2005, 2010; Trustee, Chr Evidence Soc 2000–05; M Theol Educ and Trg Cttee 2000–05; GS rep, Bd Govs Ripon Coll Cuddesdon from 2000; co-opted Bd Govs Tr Coll Bris 2000–05; M CMEAC 1999–2004; Dir Churchfield Trust; M CRAC; Dip in Coaching (Coaching Futures/OCR) 2003; elected M AC from 2005; Trustee Chr Assoc of Business Execs; M Bus Cttee from 2011; Consultant, Ernst and Young from 2011
GS 1990–   *Tel:* 01763 848472
          01763 848822
          07768 151646
          Fax: 01763 848774
          email: christina@mediamaxima.com

REES, Canon (Vivian) John (Howard), MA, LLB, M Phil
16 Beaumont St Oxford OX1 2LZ [JOINT REGISTRAR, PROVINCE OF CANTERBURY] *b* 1951 *educ* Skinners' Sch Tunbridge Wells; Southn Univ; Ox Univ; Leeds Univ; Wycliffe Hall Th Coll; *CV* Solicitor and Eccl Notary (Admitted 1975); C Moor Allerton TM 1979–82; Chapl and Tutor Sierra Leone Th Hall, Freetown 1983–86; Ptnr Winckworth Sherwood Solicitors from 1986; Treas Eccl Law Soc from 1995; Jt Registrar Ox Dioc from 1998; Jt Registrar Prov of Cant from 2000; Registrar, Court of Arches from 200; Legal Adv ACC from 1998; Vc-Chair Legal Adv Commn from 2001; Provincial Can Cant Cathl from 2001; Registrar, Clergy Discipline Tribunals Prov of Cant from 2006
GS 1995–2000   *Tel:* 01865 297200 (Office)
          01865 865875 (Home)
          07973 327417 (Mobile)
          Fax: 01865 726274
          email: jrees@wslaw.co.uk
          2nd email: vjhrees@btinternet.com
          Web: www.wslaw.co.uk

REID, Canon Jenny (Jennifer), BA
Healam 9 Poplars Rd Linthorpe Middlesbrough TS5 6RL [YORK] *b* 1943 *CV* University lecturer, rtd
GS 2000–   *Tel:* 01642 823127 (Home)
          01642 782095 (Office)
          email: jennyreid@ntlworld.com

REIGATE, Archdeacon of. See KAJUMBA, Ven Daniel Steven Kimbugwe

RENSHAW, Canon Elizabeth, MBE, Adv Dip Bus Man & Admin Man
82 Ennisdale Drive West Kirby Wirral CH48 9UA [CHESTER] *CV* Bus Man 1991–2008; Proj Co-ordinator 2008–11; Church Commissioners;

Bishoprics & Cathls Commn; DBF Chairs rep, Eccls Fees Comm; Chair, Chester Dioc Bd Finance; Bp's Coun; Chair, Finance and Scrutiny, HR and Staffing Review Cttes; Lay Canon Chester Cathl; Cathl Council; Par Giving Officer; Dir Chester DBE & Chester Academies Trust; Secondary Sch Gov; Trustee Educational Trust; Trustee Community Trust
GS 2010–   *Tel:* 0151 625 5044
              email: betty.renshaw@gmail.com

REPTON, Suffragan Bishop of. See SOUTHERN, Rt Revd Humphrey Ivo John

RICE, Dr Philip, BSc MSc, PhD,MICE C.Eng, MEI
23 Christchurch Square Homerton London E9 7HU [LONDON] *b* 1949 *educ* Doncaster Gr Sch; LSE, UCL; *CV* Rsrch Fellow Transport Section, Imperial Coll 1978–85; Direct Entrant Economist Civil service, 1985; Economic Adv, Dept of Energy, Energy Forecasts and Oil Prices, 1985–91; Economic Adv, Inland Revenue, Statistics and Economics Division, Oil & Financial Sector and Capital Gains Tax 1991–98; Senior Economist, Inland Revenue, Team Leader, Direct Business Taxes & Anti-Avoidance, from 1998; Lay Chair of Hackney Deanery, Lon Dioc 2000–06; M Bp's Counc Lon Dioc from 2006
GS 2010–   *Tel:* 020 8985 1914
email: phillip@christopherrice.orangehome.co.uk

RICHBOROUGH, Bishop of. See BANKS, Rt Revd Norman

RICHMOND AND CRAVEN, Archdeacon of. See SLATER, Ven PAUL

RICHMOND, Revd Dr Patrick Henry, MA(Oxon), DPhil
161 Newmarket Road Norwich NR4 6SY [NORWICH] *b* 1969 *educ* Marlborough Coll, Wilts; Balliol Coll; Green Coll, Ox; Wycliffe Hall Th Coll; *CV* C, Church of the Martyrs, Leic 1997–2001; Chapl & Fellow, St Catharines Coll, Cam 2001–06; Dean of Chapel, St Catharines Coll, Cam 2006–07; V, Ch Ch, Eaton, Norwich from 2007
GS 2010–   *Tel:* 01603 2508449
                            07982 785765
            email: phr@eatonparish.com
            Web: www.eatonparish.com

RIPON, Area Bishop of. See BELL, Rt Revd James Harold

RIPON, Dean of. DOBSON, Very Revd John

ROBERTS, Canon (John) Mark Arnott, AKC, PGCE
Rectory Knightrider St Sandwich CT13 9ER [CANTERBURY] *b* 1954 *educ* Caterham Sch; K Coll Lon Univ; Ch Ch Coll Cant; Chich Th Coll; *CV* C St Mary V, Ashford, Kent 1977–82; V and R St Mary's Bay, St Mary in the Marsh, Ivychurch 1982–91; P-in-c Worth from 2004; Eastry, Northbourn and Tilmanstone 2010–12; R Sandwich and Worth from 2012; AD of Sandwich 2000–06; M Dioc Syn; Hon Can Cant Cathl from 2003; Chair Dioc Syn Ho of Clergy 2006–12
GS 2003–   *Tel:* 01304 613138
            email: revdmarkroberts@supanet.com

ROBERTS, Ven Kevin Thomas, MA, BA
2 The Abbey Carlisle CA3 8TZ [ARCHDEACON OF CARLISLE] *b* 1955 *educ* Guisborough Grammar Sch; Prior Pursglove Coll; Queens' Coll Cam; Univ Nottm; St John's Coll Nottm; *CV* C Beverley Minster 1983–86; C St James Woodley 1986–91; V Meole Brace 1991–2009; RD Shrewsbury 1998–2008; Preb Lichfield Cathl 2002–09; Res Can Carlisle Cathl from 2009; Adn Carlisle from 2009; Ox Dioc Syn 1988–91; Lich Dioc Syn 1992–2009; Bps Coun Lich 1997–2006; Lich Vacancy-in-See Comm 1998–2003; Chair Carlisle Bd of Educ from 2009; Dir DBE Services from 2009; Trustee ReSource from 2014   *Tel:* 01228 523026 (Home)
                            01228 815408 (Office)
                            07584 684300 (Mobile)
email: archdeacon.north@carlislediocese.org.uk

ROBERTS, Ven Stephen John, BD, MTh
2 Alma Rd Wandsworth London SW18 1AB [ARCHDEACON OF WANDSWORTH; SOUTHWARK] *b* 1958 *educ* Newcastle-under-Lyme High Sch; K Coll Lon; Westcott Ho Cam; Heythrop Coll Lon; *CV* C St Mary Riverhead w. St Jo Dunton Green, Roch 1983–86; C St Martin-in-the-Fields, S'wark 1986–89; V St Geo Camberwell and Wrdn Trin Coll Centre, S'wark 1989–2000; Sen DDO and Can Res, S'wark Cathl 2000–05; Adn of Wandsworth from 2005   *Tel:* 020 8874 8567 (Home)
                        020 8785 1985 (Work)
                        Fax: 020 8785 1981
email: stephen.roberts@southwark.anglican.org

ROBILLIARD, Mr David John,
Le Petit Gree Torteval Guernsey GY8 0RD [CHANNEL ISLANDS] *b* 1952 *educ* Guernsey Gr Sch for Boys; *CV* Clearing and Internat Banking 1969–82; HM Dep Greffier 1982–87; Prin Asst Chief Exec Guernsey Civil Service 1987–94; Hd of Constitutional Affairs States of Guernsey 1994–2007; Prin Officer States Assembly and Constitution Cttee 2008–13; Dep Clerk Guernsey States of Deliberation from 2010; Private Sec to Bailiff of Guernsey from 2013; M GS Standing Orders Cttee; Treas & Trustee Guernsey Dny Syn; chwdn of Torteval
GS 1998–   *Tel:* 01481 264344 (Home)
                            01481 749507 (Office)
                            07781 164344 (Mobile)
                            Fax: 01481 713861
                email: villula@cwgsy.net

ROBINSON, Rt Revd Anthony William, Cert Ed
*Pontefract House 181a Manygates Lane Wakefield
WF2 7DR* [AREA BISHOP OF WAKEFIELD; WEST
YORKSHIRE AND THE DALES] *b* 1956 *educ* Bedf
Modern Sch; Bedf Coll of HE; Sarum and Wells
Th Coll; *CV* C St Paul Tottenham 1982–85; TV
Resurr Leic 1985–89, TR 1989–97; RD Christianity
N 1992–97; Hon Can Leic Cathl from 1994; M CBF
1995–97; M CMEAC 1996–97; Adn of Pontefract
1997–2003; Bp of Pontefract 2002–14; Bp for the
Area of Wakefield and Acting Bp of Huddersfield
2014; Bp for the Area of Wakefield from 2014
GS 1995–97, 2000–02   *Tel:* 01924 250781
                         email: bishop.tony@
                      westyorkshiredales.anglican.org

ROBINSON, Ven Peter John Alan, BA, MA, PhD
4 Acomb Close Morpeth NE61 2YH [ARCHDEACON
OF LINDISFARNE; NEWCASTLE] *b* 1961 *educ*
St Jo Coll Camb; St Jo Coll Durham; *CV* C
North Shield 1995–99; Dir Urban Ministry and
Theology Project, Newc East Deanery; P-in-c
Byker St Martin 1999–2008; P-in-c Byker St
Michael w St Lawrence 2001–08; Hon Can
Newcastle Cathl 2007–08; Adn of Lindisfarne
from 2008; Chair William Temple Foundation
from 2009   *Tel:* 01670 503810
                                           07786 642124
                                  Fax: 01670 503 469
email: p.robinson@newcastle.anglican.org

**ROCHDALE, Archdeacon of. See VANN,
Ven Cherry Elizabeth**

**ROCHESTER, Archdeacon of. See BURTON-
JONES, Ven Simon David**

**ROCHESTER, Bishop of. See LANGSTAFF,
Rt Revd James Henry**

**ROCHESTER, Dean of. See BEACH, Very Revd
Mark Howard Francis**

RODGERS, Mrs Sue (Susan Elizabeth),
13 Rowlands Ave Waterlooville PO7 7RT [PORT-
SMOUTH] *b* 1954 *educ* Haywards Heath Sec Sch;
CV WRNS 1971–79; Night Staff St Mary's Hosp
Portsm; Bereavement Cllr; Co-ord Bereavement
Grp; Par Asst/Administrator St Wilf Cowplain
until 2001; Lay Can Portsm Cath from 2008; M
Educ Admission Appeal Panel 2008; Port Rep
Southampton Docks 2009
GS 2000–   *Tel:* 023 9225 3091
                             07974 570414 (Mobile)
                       email: Sue@Rodgersuk.com

RODHAM, Ven Morris, MA, PGCE, BA, DipHE
3 The Gardens Thurlaston Rugby CV23 9LS [ARCH-
DEACON MISSIONER, DIOCESE OF COVENTRY] *b* 1959
educ RGS Newcastle; Durham Univ Hatfield
College; Bristol Univ; Trinity Coll Bristol; *CV*
Regular Army (Royal Artillery) 1978, 1981–84;

Tchr Warwick Schl (Classics, CCF, Hockey)
1985–90; C St Mark's Leamington 1993–1997;
V St Mary's Leamington 1997–2010; RD Warwick
and Leamington 2006–10; Adn Missioner from
2010   *Tel:* 02476 521337
            email: morris.rodham@covcofe.org

ROSE, Revd Susan Margaret, B Ed
*The Vicarage Station Road Cheddar Somerset BS27
3AH* [BATH AND WELLS] *b* 1959 *educ* Stoud Girls
High Sch; Keswick Grammar Sch; Westminster
Coll Higher Ed; SAOMC; *CV* Teacher, 1981–98;
C,North Petherton w Moorland, 1998–2000;
Rector, The Alfred Jewel Benefice, 2000–09; P-in-
c, Cheddar; Rodney Stoke w Draycott, 2009; Sec
Cttee Ministerial Review, 2000–04; Design team
Bps Course for Rdrs, 2003–05; Vocations Chapl
2004–06; Rural Dean 2006–09; M Dioc Patronage
Brd from 2009
GS 2010–   *Tel:* 01934 740394
                 email: rev.suerose@virgin.net

ROSEMARY CHN, Sister , MA, MA, PGCE, Dip Pastl
Th (APU)
*Convent of the Holy Name Morley Rd Oakwood
Derby DE21 4QZ* [RELIGIOUS COMMUNITIES
(SOUTH)] *b* 1944 *educ* Barr's Hill Sch Cov;
Newnham Coll Cam; Hughes Hall Cam;
St Mary's Coll Dur Univ; Westcott Ho Cam;
CV Various teaching posts, 1967–76; Community
of the Holy Name from 1976; Dn 1998; P 1999
(Derby Dioc); C St Osmund, Derby 1998–2001;
Perm to officiate, Derby and S'well Diocs from
2001; Assoc P, Morley, Smalley and Loscoe
(Derby) 2010–14; Assoc P Morley and Smalley
from 2014
GS 2003–   *Tel:* 01332 671716
            email: rosemarychn@yahoo.co.uk
                           Web: chnderby.org

ROUCH, Ven Dr Peter Bradford, MA (Oxon); MA
(Cantab); PhD (Manch)
*22 Bellflower Way Chandler's Ford Hampshire
SO53 4HN* [ARCHDEACON OF BOURNEMOUTH;
WINCHESTER] *b* 1966 *educ* Sir Joseph Williamson's
Mathematical Sch Rochester; Brasenose Coll Ox;
Peterhouse Cam; Univ Manchester;
GS 240513   *Tel:* 01962 710962
                                           02380 260955
    email: peter.rouch@winchester.anglican.org

ROY, Mr Anirban, BA
*1 Wilton Lodge 45 New Dover Road Canterbury Kent
CT1 3AT* [LONDON] *b* 1977 *educ* Tiffin Sch; Trin
Coll, Cam; Open Univ; *CV* Corporate Finance
Consult, Arthur D. Little, 1999–2002; Strategy
Consult Solving International, 2002–04; Policy
Manager, Head of Regulatory Compliance, Prin-
cipal Ofcom 2004–11; Head of Regulatory Affairs
Arquiva from 2011
GS 2010–   *Tel:* 07968 173 213
                 email: urbanroy@gmail.com
                          Twitter: @Suburbanroy

RUOFF, Mrs Alison Laura, SRN, SCM, DN
The White House 75 Crossbrook St Cheshunt EN8 8LU [LONDON] *b* 1942 *educ* Sutton Coldfield Girls High Sch; Nightingale Sch of Nursing, St Thos Hosp; Br Hosp for Mothers and Babies; Nursing Inst Worc; RCNursing; *CV* VSO India 1961–62; Night Sister St Thos Hosp 1966–67; Asst Dir of Nursing Internat Grenfell Assoc Newfoundland 1968–70; Admin Sister St Thos Hosp Grp 1970–72; Nursing Officer/Sen Nursing Officer Univ Coll Hosp 1972–74; Housewife and mother; JP 1979–2003; M Dioc Bp's Coun; CEEC 1995–2013; Lay Chair Lon DEF; M Coun Church Society; speaker and broadcaster
GS 1995– *Tel:* 01992 623113
07956 569323 (Mobile)
email: alison_ruoff@hotmail.com

RUSSELL, Ven Brian Kenneth, MA, PhD
26 George Rd Edgbarton Birmingham B15 1PJ [ARCHDEACON OF ASTON; BIRMINGHAM] *b* 1950 *educ* Bris Gr Sch; Trin Hall Cam; Birm Univ; Cuddesdon Ox; *CV* C St Matt Redhill 1976–79; P-in-c St Jo Kirk Merrington, Dur and Dir of Studies NEOC 1979–83; Dir of Studies and Lect in Chr Doct, Linc Theol Coll 1983–86; Sec Cttee for Theol Educ and Selection Sec, ACCM/ABM 1986–93; Bp's Dir for Min, Birm Dioc 1993–2005; sch gov; Hon Can Birm Cathl from 1999; M Vol and Continuing Educ Cttee, GS Bd of Educ 1994–99; Bp's Sen Selector from 1998; Bp's Sen Insp for Theol Colls and Courses from 2001; M Bps' Inspections Wkg Pty from 2003; Bp's Exam Chapl, Birm from 1996; Chair Birm Dioc Ministries Forum from 2005; Gov Q Foundn for Theol Educ, Birm from 1994; Adn of Aston from 2005 *Tel:* 0121 426 0428
0121 454 5525
Fax: 0121 428 1114
email: b.russell@birmingham.anglican.org

RUSSELL, Mrs Victoria Christine, Cert Ed
47a Theobalds Way Frimley Camberley Surrey GU16 9RF [OXFORD] *b* 1948 *educ* Badminton Sch; Whitelands Coll of Ed; *CV* Tchr, 1970–76; Head of RE & Geography, Gateway School, Bucks, 1989–1996; Head of RE & Geography, Maltman's Green School, Bucks, 1996–2006; M Ox Healing Team
GS 2010– *Tel:* 01276 64110
07765 951 021 (Mobile)
email: vcrussell@gmail.com

RUTHERFORD, Revd Rosalind Elizabeth,
BA PGCE
45 Beaconsfield Road Basingstoke Hampshire RG21 3DG [WINCHESTER] *b* 1952 *educ* King's H Sch for Girls, Warwick; St Hugh's Coll, Ox; Goldsmiths' Coll, UL; STETS; *CV* Field Officer, Third World First 1974–76; Toy Library Organiser, Manchester Youth and Community Service1976–77; Tchr, Parliament Hill Sch for Girls 1998–80; Tchr Burlington Danes Sch 1980–84; Adult Education

tutor Reading Adult Coll 1987–2003; C St Peter's Earley 2003–06; TV Basingstoke Team Ministry from 2006
GS 2010– *Tel:* 01256 464616
email: vicar@allsaintsbasingstoke.org.uk

RYLANDS, Rt Revd Mark James, MA
Athlone House 68 London Road Shrewsbury SY2 6PG [AREA BISHOP OF SHREWSBURY] *b* 1961 *CV* Area Bp of Shrewsbury from 2009
Tel: 01743 235867
email: bishop.shrewsbury@lichfield.anglican.org
Twitter: @shrewsbishop

SADGROVE, Very Revd Michael, MA, FRSA, DL
The Deanery Durham DH1 3EQ [DEAN OF DURHAM] *b* 1950 *educ* Univ Coll Sch Lon; Ball Coll Ox; Trin Coll Bris; *CV* Lic to Offic Ox dio 1975–76; Lect OT Sarum & Wells Th Coll 1977–82; Vc-Prin 1980–82; V Alnwick 1982–87; Can Res, Prec and Vc-Provost Cov Cathl 1987–95; Provost of Sheff 1995–2000, Dean 2000–03; Dean of Durham from 2003; M Dur Univ Coun; R St Chad's Coll Dur *Tel:* 0191 384 7500 07828 516198
Fax: 0191 386 4267
email: michael.sadgrove@durhamcathedral.co.uk
Web: www.durhamcathedral.co.uk
Blog http://decanalwoolgatherer.blogspot.com
Twitter: @sadgrovem

SALFORD, Archdeacon of , see SHARPLES, Ven David

SALIMI, Ms Saira Alia, MA (Oxon), MA (Open),
Solicitor
Legal Office Church House Great Smith Street London SW1P 3AZ [DEPUTY OFFICIAL SOLICITOR TO THE CHURCH COMMISSIONERS] *b* 1974 *educ* The Lady Eleanor Holles Sch; Corpus Christi Coll Oxf; *CV* Solicitor in private practice 1999–2003; Asst Parliamentary Counsel, Cabinet Office, 2003–08; Sen Asst Parliamentary Counsel, Cabinet Office 2008–11; Dep Official Solicitor Church Commissioners from 2011 *Tel:* 020 7898 1717
email: saira.salimi@churchofengland.org

SALISBURY, Bishop of. See HOLTAM, Rt Revd Nicholas Roderick

SALISBURY, Dean of. See OSBORNE, Very Revd June

SALOP, Archdeacon of. See THOMAS, Ven Paul Wyndham

SARUM, Archdeacon of. See JEANS, Ven Alan Paul

SAXBY, Revd Canon Martin Peter, BA, DipTh
St George's Vicarage St John's Avenue Rugby CV22 5HR [COVENTRY] *b* 1952 *educ* Wandsworth Comp Sch; St. John's Coll, Dur; Cranmer Hall; *CV* AC St Mary Magdalene, Peckham 1978–81; AC Ramsey

w St Peter's Upwood & Ramsey St. Mary's 1981–84; Incumb Mattishall w Mattishall Burgh, Welborne and Yaxham 1984–90; Incumb St Matthew's Rugby 1990–2007; Incumb St Matthew's & St Oswald's Rugby 2008–13; AD Rugby 2005–13; Healthy Churches Development Mentor for Dioc Cov from 2013; M Bp's Coun 2004–12; Joint Chair Dioc Miss Fund 2010–11; Chair Dioc Miss Links Cttee from 2011; Hon Can Coventry Catheral from 2011
GS 2010–
                            Tel: 01788 330790
             07944 670288 (Mobile)
                 Fax: 07053 480 079
    email: martin.saxby@covcofe.org
    Web: www.healthychurches.org.uk
             Twitter: @martinsaxby

SAXBY, Canon Steven Michael Paul, BA, MA, ADVDIP, MA, MA
St Barnabas' Vicarage St Barnabas Road London E17 8JZ [CHELMSFORD] *b* 1970 *educ* Fitzw Coll Cam; Univ of East London; Heythrop Coll Lon; Univ Coll Lon; Aston Tr Scheme; Linc Th Coll; Westcott Ho;; *CV* C East Ham with Upton Park 1998–2000; C Barking St Margaret with St Patrick 2000–02; Waltham Forest Dny Dev Officer 2002–07; NSM Walthamstow 2002–03; V Walthamstow St Peter-in-the-Forest 2003–09; P-in-c Walthamstow St Saviour 2011–13; AD Waltham Forest 2007–12; P-in-c Walthamstow St Barnabas and St James the Greater from 2009; Executive Officer London Church Leaders/London Churches Social Action from 2013; Hon Can Philippines from 2014; M Church Buildings Comm from 2014
GS 2013–
                 Tel: 020 8520 5323
    email: stevensaxby@btinternet.com

SCOTT, Mrs Angela Mary, MTh, Cert Ed
The Stead Willow Grove Chislehurst Kent BR7 5BU [ROCHESTER] *b* 1950 *educ* Portsmouth High Sch; Bedord Coll of Phys Ed; Spurgeon's Th Coll; *CV* Tchr, Stratford House Sch, Kent 1972–75; Home Maker 1975–99; Part-time Tchr, Marjory McClure Sch, Kent 1984–87; Supply Tching, Bromley 1987–92; Church Admin, 1992–98; Dioc Pastoral Asst from 2000; Dioc Tutor, 2000–08
GS 2000–05; 2010–
                 Tel: 020 8467 3589
                 07809 438737
    email: a@5scotts.freeserve.co.uk

SCOWEN, Mr Clive Richard, LLB
69 Brooke Ave Harrow HA2 0ND [LONDON] *b* 1958 *educ* John Lyon Sch Harrow; Bris Univ; Inns of Court Sch of Law; *CV* Called to bar (Inner Temple) 1981; law reporter, Incorporated Coun of Law Reporting 1983–90; Dep Ed Weekly Law Reports 1990–2000; Joint Ed, Law Reports Consolidated Index from 2000; Man Ed, Weekly Law Reports 2006–07; Ed Law Reports and Weekly Law Reports from 2008; Councillor, Lon Boro of Harrow 1990–2002; Rdr from 1991; M Bris Univ Court from 1980; Dir Glencoe Trust Ltd; Dir Soul Survivor Harrow; Trustee, Charles Gardner

Meml Fund; Trustee, Maseno Project Trust; M MPA Coun; M GS Stg Orders Cttee; M Lon Dioc Bp's Coun; Dir Lon Dioc Fund; M Willesden Area Coun; M Bp of Lon's Miss Fund Bd; M Harrow Dny Stg Cttee
GS 2005–
                 Tel: 020 8422 1329
            07771 780805 (Mobile)
    email: clivescowen@onetel.com

SEARLE, Ven Jacqueline Ann, MA, BEd, Dip Th
2 College Green Gloucester GL1 2LY [ARCHDEACON OF GLOUCESTER] *b* 1960 *educ* Talbot Heath, Bournemouth; Whitelands Coll, Lon; Trin Coll Bris; *CV* Tchr 1982–90; C Ch Ch Roxeth 1992–94; C St Stephen's Ealing 1994–96; Tutor Applied Th & Dean of Women Trin Coll Bris 1996–2003; Dean of Women's Ministry Derby 2007–10; Incumb St Peter's, Littleover, Derby from 2003; RD Derby South 2010–12; Adn of Glos from 2012; Can Res Glos Cathl from 2012
GS 2010–12
                 Tel: 01452 835594
                 Fax: 01452 381528
    email: archdglos@glosdioc.org.uk

SEDDON, Mr (William Trevor) Bill, BSc, ASIP
20 Carpenters Wood Drive Chorleywood Rickmansworth Herts WD3 5RJ [ST ALBANS] *b* 1952 *educ* Grove Park Boys' Gr Sch, Wrexham; UCL; *CV* Asst Investment Man, Central Fin Brd Methodist Ch, 1985–87; Investment Man, Dominion Insurance 1980–85; Asset Manager Paine Webber 1977–80; Asst Investment Man, White Weld 1975–77; Trainee Investment Man, Central Brd Fin C of E 1973–75; Investment M & CE, Central Fin Brd Methodist Ch and Epworth Investment Management Ltd from 1987.
GS 2010–
                 Tel: 01923 285727
                 Fax: 0207 496 3631
    email: bill.seddon@cfbmethodistchurch.org.uk

SELBY, Suffragan Bishop of. THOMSON, Rt Revd John

SELVARATNAM, Revd Christian Nathan, BSc, DipTheol
52 The Gallops York YO24 3NF [YORK] *b* 1968 *educ* Wolfreton Sch; Univ of Warwick; Cranmer Hall Th Coll; *CV* Holy Trin Ch, Coventry, Head Verger 1990–92; Copyzone Printers, Bishop's Stortford, Mgr & Graphic designer 1992–96; Comm Ch, Bishop's Stortford, Asst Pastor 1994–99; York City Ch, Senior pastor, 1999–2004; Alpha International, Dir of Alpha in the North of England from 2004; G2 (Fresh Expression of Church), P-in-c from 2008; St Michael le Belfrey, Head of Discipleship and New Initiatives from 2010
GS 2010–
                 Tel: 01904 624190
    email: christian.selvaratnam@gmail.com

SENTAMU, Most Revd and Rt Hon Dr John Tucker Mugabi , LLB, MA, Ph D, LLD (Hon), DD (Hon), FRSA, Privy Counsellor
Bishopthorpe Palace Bishopthorpe York YO23 2GE [ARCHBISHOP OF YORK] *b* 1949 *educ* Makerere Univ

Kampala; Selw Coll Cam; Ridley Hall Th Coll; *CV* Asst Chapl Selw Coll Cam 1979; Chapl HM Remand Cen Latchmere Ho 1979–82; C St Andr Ham 1979–82; C St Paul Herne Hill 1982–83; P-in-c H Trin Tulse Hill; Par Priest St Matthias 1983–84; V H Trin and St Matthias Tulse Hill 1985–96; P-in-c St Sav Brixton 1987–89; Bp of Stepney 1996–2002; M NACRO Young Offenders Cttee 1986–95; M Abp's Adv Grp on UPAs 1986–92; M ABM Coun from 1985; M Stg Cttee GS Ho of Clergy 1985–96; M GS Stg Cttee 1988–96; M GS Policy Cttee 1990–96; Chair Dioc Ho of Clergy 1992–96; M Decade of Evang Strg Grp and Springboard Exec 1991–96; M Turnbull Proposals Strg Grp; M Strg Grp Women (Priests) Ordination Measure; Pro-Prolocutor Conv of Cant 1990–94; Chair CMEAC 1990–99; Prolocutor Conv of Cant 1994–96; M The Stephen Lawrence Judicial Inquiry 1997–99; Pres and Chair Lon Marriage Guidance Coun 2000–04; Chair Damilola Taylor Murder Review 2002; Fell Univ Coll Ch Ch Cant 2001; Fell Qu Mary Coll Univ of Lon 2001; Hon Dr OU 2001; D Phil (Hon) Univ of Glos 2002; DD (Hon) Univ of Birm 2003; M Birmingham Hospitals NHS Trust 2002; Chair ECI NDC 2002–04; Chair NHS Sickle Cell and Thalassaemia Screening Programme 2001–13; Bp of Birmingham 2002–05; Midlander of the Year 2003; Vc-Chair Commn on Urban Life and Faith; Pres Youth for Christ, Eng from 2004 and Nat YMCA from 2005; Abp of York from 2005; LLD (Hon), Univ of Leic 2005; Hon Fell Selw Coll Cam 2005; Chan York St Jo Univ from 2006; Freeman City of Lon 2000; DD (Hon) Univ of Hull 2007; DL (Hon) Univ of Sheff 2007; Yorkshire Man of the Year 2007; Speaker of the Year 2007; Master Bencher (Hon) Gray's Inn 2007; Freeman City of Montego Bay 2007; DL (Hon) Univ of the West Indies 2007; Chan Univ of Cumbria from 2007; Hon Dr Birm City Univ 2008; DD (Hon) Univ of Cam 2008; DCL (Hon) Northumbria Univ 2008; DD (Hon) Univ of Nottm 2008; DD (Hon) Wycliffe Coll Toronto 2009; LLD (Hon) Teesside University 2009; DTheol (Hon) Univ of Chester 2009; Hon Dr Univ of York 2010; LLD (Hon) Univ of Leeds 2010; DD (Hon) Sewanee (University of the South) Tennessee 2010; DD (Hon) Univ of London 2010; York Tourism Awards 'York Ambassador' 2010; Sponsor York Fairness Comm 2011–12; DD (Hon) Huron Univ Coll Ontario 2013; DD (Hon) Univ of Aberdeen 2013; Harold Turner Visiting Fell, Univ of Otago 2014; Hon Fell St Margaret's Coll Dunedin 2014; Chair Living Wage Comm 2013–14
GS 1985–96; 2002– 	*Tel:* 01904 707021
Fax: 01904 772389
email: office@archbishopofyork.org
Web: www.archbishopofyork.org

SHAND, Mr John Alexander Ogilvie, MA, LIB
(Cant), MA (Birm)
1 Old Barnhouse Mews Hill Top Longdon Green, Rugeley Staffordshire, WS15 4GA [LICHFIELD]

b 1942 *educ* Nottingham High Sch; Queen's Coll Cam; Centre for Reformation and Early Modern Studies Univ Birm; *CV* Barrister Midland and Ox Circuit, 1965–69, 1972–81; Tutor and Fellow Queen's Coll Cam 1969–72; Chair Ind Tribunal 1981–88; Circuit Judge 1988–2005; Chan Dioc of Lich and S'well
GS 2010– 	*Tel:* 01543 492662
email: jandvshand@btinternet.com

SHARPLES, Ven David,
2 The Walled Gardens Ewhurst Avenue Swinton M7 0FR [ARCHDEACON OF SALFORD; MANCHESTER]
b 1958 *CV* Adn of Salford from 2010
Tel: 0161 794 2331
0161 708 9366
email: archdeaconsalford@manchester.anglican.org

SHEFFIELD AND ROTHERHAM, Archdeacon of. CHAMBERLAIN, Ven Malcolm

SHEFFIELD, Bishop of. See CROFT, Rt Revd Dr Steven John Lindsey

SHEFFIELD, Dean of. See BRADLEY, Very Revd Peter Edward

SHELLEY, Dr (John Richard) Jack, MA, MB BChir, MRCGP
Shobrooke Park Crediton Devon EX17 1DG [EXETER]
b 1943 *educ* King's Sch, Cam Univ; St Mary's Univ; Ex Univ; SWMTC Rdr Cert; *CV* Chair Devon Local Med Cttee 1999–2002; Partner South Molton Health Centre 1974–2003; Farmer 1974; Med Prac 1967; Rdr Ex 2009; M Ex Dioc Syn from 2002; M Counc Worship & Min Ex from 2003; Lay Chair Cadbury Deanery from 2005; Rdr from 2009
GS 2009– 	*Tel:* 01363 775153
07971 136901
email: jack@shobrookepark.com

SHERBORNE, Archdeacon of. See TAYLOR, Ven Paul Stanley

SHERBORNE, Suffragan Bishop of. See KINGS, Rt Revd Graham Ralph

SHERIFF, Canon Suzanne, BA
78 Station Rd Tadcaster LS24 9JR [YORK] *b* 1963 *educ* Dorchester Gr Sch for Girls; Trin Coll Bris; *CV* Par Dn St Nich Hull 1987–91; Par Dn/C St Aidan Hull 1991–96; TV Marfleet 1996–2000; TR Marfleet 2000–07; M York Dioc Syn; M Coll of Cans York Minster from 2001; V Tadcaster and Newton Kyme from 2007; P-i-c St John's Kirkby Wharfe w Ulleskelf and St Mary's Church Fenton from 2010
GS 2005– 	*Tel:* 01937 833394
email: sue.sheriff@virgin.net

SHERWOOD, Suffragan Bishop of. See PORTER, Rt Revd Anthony

SHOREY, Mr Kenneth John, BA, Cert Ed
30 Pool Road Hartley Wintney Hook RG27 8RD
[WINCHESTER] *b* 1947 *educ* Greenford Gr Sch;
Borough Road Coll; OU; *CV* Headteacher, Court
Moor Sch, Hampshire, 1987–2005; Chief Exec
Positive Parenting Publ & Programmes, 2006–09;
Project Dir Care for the Family, 2009–10; Pre-
senting Officer (Admission Appeals) Hampshire
CC Children's Serv from 2005
GS 2010–   *Tel:* 01252 843803
                                        07931 511849
        email: ken@shoreyfamily.co.uk

**SHREWSBURY, Area Bishop of. See
RYLANDS, Rt Revd Mark**

SINCLAIR, Rt Revd (Gordon) Keith, MA, BA
Bishop's Lodge 67 Bidston Rd Prenton CH43 6TR
[SUFFRAGAN BISHOP OF BIRKENHEAD; CHESTER]
b 1952 *educ* Trin Sch Croydon; Ch Ch Ox;
Cranmer Hall Dur; *CV* C Ch Ch Summerfield
1984–88; pt Chapl, Children's Hosp Birm; V SS
Pet & Paul Aston juxta Birm 1988–2001; AD
Aston 2000–01; V H Trin Cov 2001–06; Bp of
Birkenhead from 2007; M Bp's Coun and Dioc
Syn, Ches; Trustee/Chair Ches DBE; Gov Bp's
High Sch Ches; Trustee Historic Cheshire
Chs Preservation Trust; Trustee Chs Together in
Merseyside; Chair Gov Body for Bp's High Sch;
Chair CPAS Coun of Reference; Trustee, Five
Talents; Coun of Reference True Freedom Trust
                                  Tel: 0151 652 2741
                                  Fax: 0151 651 2330
    email: bpbirkenhead@chester.anglican.org

SINCLAIR, Revd John Robert,
16 Towers Avenue Jesmond Newcastle NE2 3QE
[NEWCASTLE] *b* 1958 *educ* Walbottle High Sch; Oak
Hill Th Coll; *CV* C Ponteland S Mary Newcastle
1992–96; V Longbenton St Mary Magdalene
Newcastle 1996–2001; V Newburn St Michael &
All Angels Newcastle from 2001; AD Newcastle
West from 2007; Hon Can Newcastle Cathl from
2008; Chair House of Clergy from 2009; M Evang
Task Group 2001; M Dioc Fin Strategy Grp 2009;
Proctor in Convocation 2010; Res Can Newcastle
Cathl and Local Evangelism Officer from 2011
GS 2010–   *Tel:* 0191 281 9375
                                        07746 743857
        email: johnsinclair247@aol.com

SKILTON, Ven Christopher John, MA, Cert Theol,
MA (Miss & Min)
*St Matthew's House 100 George Street Croydon CR0
1PE* [ARCHDEACON OF CROYDON; SOUTHWARK]
b 1955 *educ* Latymer Upper Sch Hammersmith;
Magd Coll Cam; Wycliffe Hall Ox; *CV* C St Mary
Ealing 1980–84; C Newborough w Leigh St Jo
Wimborne 1984–88; TV St Paul Gt Baddow
1988–95; TR Sanderstead 1995–2003; RD Croydon
S 2000–03; Adn of Lambeth 2004–13; Adn of
Croydon from 2013   *Tel:* 020 8256 9633
                                        07903 704506
    email: chris.skilton@southwark.anglican.org

SLACK, Mr Stephen, MA
Church House Great Smith Street London SW1P 3AZ
[REGISTRAR AND CHIEF LEGAL ADVISER TO THE
GENERAL SYNOD, JOINT REGISTRAR OF THE
PROVINCES OF CANTERBURY AND YORK, CHIEF
LEGAL ADVISER TO THE ARCHBISHOPS' COUNCIL
AND OFFICIAL SOLICITOR TO THE CHURCH COM-
MISSIONERS] *b* 1954 *educ* Aylesbury Gr Sch;
Ch Ch Ox; *CV* Solicitor in private practice 1979–
84; Sen Lawyer Charity Commn Liv 1984–89; Hd
Legal Section Charity Commn Taunton 1989–
2001; Hd Legal Office and Chief Legal Adv to AC
and GS from 2001, Registrar GS, Jt Registrar
Provinces Cant and York, M Legal Adv Commn
from 2001; Official Solicitor to Ch Commrs from
2009   *Tel:* 020 7898 1366
                                    Fax: 020 7898 1718
                                          020 7898 1721
    email: stephen.slack@churchofengland.org

SLATER, Mr Colin Stuart, MBE, MA (Honorary)
11 Muriel Rd Beeston Nottingham NG9 2HH
[SOUTHWELL AND NOTTINGHAM] *b* 1934 *educ* Belle
Vue Gr Sch Bradf; *CV* Chief PRO Notts Co Coun
1969–87, Severn Trent Water 1987–89, Notts Co
Cricket Club 1989–95; Chair BBC Radio Nottm
Adv Coun 1975–79; former Chair Soc of Co PROs
and IPR Local Govt Grp; M Coun Inst of PR
1986–90; JP 1977–2004; Chair Nottingham
Magistrates 2003 and 2004; Chair Notts Courts
Bd 2005–07; Chair Notts-Derbys Courts Bd 2007–
12; PR Consult and freelance broadcaster
from 1995; M Bp's Coun, Fin Cttee; Vc-Chair
Chr Stewardship Cttee of AC 1999–2012; M Coun
St Jo (Nottm) Coll from 2006 and its Stg Ctee from
2008, Vc Chair from 2010; awarded Freedom of
Borough of Broxtowe (Notts) 2010
GS 1990–   *Tel and Fax:* 0115 925 7532
                                    07919 008788 (Mobile)
                email: colinslater@mac.com

SLATER, Ven Paul John, MA, BA
*Woodlands Netherghyll Lane Cononley Keighley
BD20 8PB* [ARCHDEACON OF RICHMOND AND
CRAVEN; WEST YORKSHIRE AND THE DALES] *b* 1958
educ Bradf Gr Sch; Corpus Christi Ox; St Jo
Dur; *CV* C St Andr Keighley 1984–88; P-in-c St Jo
Cullingworth 1988–93; Dir Lay Trg Foundn
Course 1988–93; PA to Bp of Bradf 1993–95; Wdn
of Rdrs 1992–96; R St Mich Haworth 1995–2001;
Bp's Officer for Min 2001;-14 Adn of Craven
2005–13; Adn of Richmond 2014; Adn of
Richmond and Craven from 2014
GS 2013–   *Tel:* 01535 635113 (Home)
                                    01535 650533 (Office)
                                  Fax: 01535 635113
                              email: paul.slater@
                  westyorkshiredales.anglican.org

SLATER, Mrs Susan Gay, Cert Ed, DGA
3 Church St Spalding PE11 2PB [LINCOLN] *b* 1944
educ Ox High Sch; Homerton Coll Cam; *CV*
Admin trainee/Higher Exec Officer, DHSS

1967–74; domestic admin and voluntary work 1974–94; PA to Nat Dir Leprosy Mission England and Wales 1994–2005; rtd 2005; Gen Adv S Holland CAB from 2005; M Linc Dioc HR Cttee 2005–10; Sec Elloe W Dny Syn 2005–10; M Ch & Com Fund Cttee 2005–10; Chair S Holland Fairtrade Steering Gp 2008–10; Rdr in Training, Linc Theol Sch from 2010
GS 2005–   *Tel:* 01775 768286
                           email: sueslater@d-lweb.net

SMALLMAN, Ven Wilhemina, BEd, BA(Hons)
[ARCHDEACON OF SOUTHEND; CHELMSFORD] *b* 1956 *educ* Aylestone High Sch; Paddington Coll; North Thames Min Tr Course; *CV* Head Drama and 2nd in English 1989–92; Head Expressive Arts Faculty 1993–2000; Asst Prin Sec Educ 2000–03; TV Ch Ch Thames View Barking; M Dioc Syn Chelmsf; Adn of Southend from 2013
                           email: minaexp@hotmail.com

SMITH, Rt Revd Dr Alan Gregory Clayton, BA, MA, Ph D, Hon DD (Birm)
Abbey Gate House Abbey Mill Lane St Albans AL3 4HD [BISHOP OF ST ALBANS] *b* 1957 *educ* Trowbridge High Sch for Boys; Birm Univ; Wycliffe Hall Th Coll; Univ of Wales, Bangor; *CV* C St Lawr Pudsey 1981–82, w St Paul 82–84; Chapl Lee Abbey 1984–90; Dioc Missr and Exec Sec Lichf Dioc BMU 1990–97; TV St Matt Walsall 1990–97; Adn of Stoke-upon-Trent 1997–2001; Canon of Lichfield Cathedral, 1997–2009; Bp of Shrewsbury 2001–09; Chair Shrops Strategic Ptnrship 2006–09; M Rural Bps Panel 2006–09; Joint Chair Angl Meth Working Party on the Ecclesiology of Emerging Expressions of Ch from 2009; Bp of St Albans from 2009; M Ho of Lords from 2013
GS 1999–2001, 2009–   *Tel:* 01727 853305
                                   Fax: 01727 846715
          email: bishop@stalbans.anglican.org

SMITH, Mr Graham William, BSc, DMS
20 Parklands Wotton-under-Edge GL12 7LT [GLOUCESTER] *b* 1943 *educ* Mundella Gr Sch; Aston Univ; *CV* Principal Eng, Project Management Dept, Nat Power plc until 1992; Bursar and Clerk to Govs, Katharine Lady Berkeley's Sch 1993–96; rtd 1996; M Bp's Coun; M Dioc Syn; M IDFF; M Queen Victoria Clergy Fund; Trustee Bishop Monk Horfield Trust; M Company of St Kyneburga
GS 2005–   *Tel:* 01453 842618
                           email: smithgra@supanet.com

SMITH, Ven Jonathan Peter,
6 Sopwell Lane St Albans Herts AL1 1RR [ARCHDEACON OF ST ALBANS] *b* 1955 *educ* Ipswich Sch; King's Coll London; Queens' Coll Cam; Westcott Ho Cam; *CV* Asst C All Saints' Gosforth 1980–82; Asst C Waltham Abbey 1982–85; Chapl The City Univ 1985–88; R Harrold and Carlton w Chellington 1988–97; V St John's Harpenden

1997–2008; Rural Dean Wheathampstead 1999–2008; Adn St Alb from 2008; St Alb Bp's Counc; St Alb Brd Patronage; St Alb Brd Fin; St Alb Miss & Pstrl Cttee; St Alb Brd Ed; St Alb Adv Cttee; St Alb Urban Forum; Residentiary Can Cathl and Abbey Ch of St Alb
GS 2010–   *Tel:* 01727 818121
                                   Fax: 01727 844469
   email: archdstalbans@stalbans.anglican.org

SMITH, Mr Peter Reg, FRICS
48 The Mowbrays Framlingham Woodbridge IP3 9DL [ST EDMUNDSBURY AND IPSWICH] *b* 1946 *educ* K Edw VI Sch Southn; Coll of Estate Mgt; *CV* M Coun USPG 1991–2011; Chair Dioc Overseas Miss Grp 1997–2004; Chair Dioc Ho of Laity 1997–2000; M Bd of Miss 2001–03; M Bp's Coun and Pastl Cttee; M Vacancy-in-See Cttee; M Revision Cttee, Common Worship Ordinal; M Revision Cttee, Pastl (Amendment) Measure; M CFCE 2006–11; Lay Can St Eds Cathl 2005–11; Trustee, Queen Victoria Clergy Fund; M Dioc Bd of Patronage
GS 1993–   *Tel:* 01728 727489
                                   07790 596502 (Mobile)
               email: happyhackers@usa.net

SNOW, Rt Revd Martyn James, BSc, BTh, MA
Bishop's House Staverton Cheltenham GL51 0TW [SUFFRAGAN BISHOP OF TEWKESBURY; GLOUCESTER] *b* 1968 *educ* Newcastle Royal Gr; Sheffield Univ; Wycliffe Hall Ox; St John's Durham; *CV* C St Andrew's Brinsworth with St Mary's Catcliffe 1995–98; 1999–2001 CMS Mission Partner Dioc Guinea; 2001–10 V Christ Church Pitsmoor; Adn of Sheffield and RotherhaM 2010–13; Bp of Tewkesbury from 2013   *Tel:* 01242 680188
                                   Fax: 01242 680233
         email: bshptewk@glosdioc.org.uk

SODOR AND MAN, Bishop of. See PATERSON, Rt Revd Robert Mar Erskine

SODOR AND MAN, DEAN OF. See GODFREY, Very Revd Nigel Philip

SOUTHAMPTON, Suffragan Bishop of. See FROST, Rt Revd Jonathan

SOUTHEND, Archdeacon of. See SMALLMAN, Ven Wilhemina

SOUTHERN, Rt Revd Humphrey Ivo John, MA
Repton House Church St, Lea Matlock DE4 5JP [SUFFRAGAN BISHOP OF REPTON; DERBY] *b* 1960 *educ* Harrow Sch; Ch Ch Ox; Ripon Coll Cuddesdon; *CV* C St Marg Rainham, Roch 1986–89; C Walton-on-the-Hill, Liv 1989–92; V Hale, TR Hale w Badshot Lea, Guildf 1992–99; Guildf Dioc Ecum Officer 1993–99; TR Tisbury, TR Nadder Valley Tm Min, Sarum 1999–2007; RD Chalke 2000–07; Hon Can Salis Cathl 2006–07; Bp of Repton from 2007; M Guildf Dioc Syn 1992–99;

M Sarum Dioc Syn 2000–07; Chair Ho of Clergy, Sarum Dioc Syn 2004–07; M Sarum Dioc Pastl Cttee 2000–07; Chair Derby Dioc Pastl Cttee from 2007; Chair Dioc Bd of Educ from 2013

Tel: 01629 534644
email: bishop@repton.free-online.co.uk

SOUTHWARK, Archdeacon of. See STEEN, Ven Dr Jane Elizabeth

SOUTHWARK, Bishop of. See CHESSUN, Rt Revd Christopher Thomas

SOUTHWARK, Dean of. See NUNN, Very Revd Andrew Peter

SOUTHWELL AND NOTTINGHAM, Bishop of. INWOOD, Rt Revd Richard (Acting)

SOUTHWELL AND NOTTINGHAM, Dean of.
[NOT APPOINTED AT TIME OF GOING TO PRESS]

SOWERBY, Rt Revd Mark Crispin Rake, BD, AKC, MA
Bishop's House 21 Guildford Rd Horsham W Sussex RH12 1LU [AREA BISHOP OF HORSHAM; CHICHES-TER] *b* 1963 *educ* Barnard Castle Sch; St Aidan & St Jo Fisher's United Sixth Form Harrogate; K Coll Lon; Lanc Univ, Coll of Resurrection, Mirfield; *CV* C Knaresborough 1987–90; C St Cuth Darwen w. St Steph Tockholes 1990–92; V St Mary Magd Accrington 1992–97; Chapl St Christopher's CE Hich Schl Accrington 1992–97; Chapl Accrington Victoria Hosp 1992–97; Asst DDO Blackb 1993–96; M Blackburn Dioc Syn; Selection Sec/Vocations Officer ABM/Min Div of AC 1997-2001; Sec Vocations Adv Sub-Cttee (ABM) then Voc Panel (Min Div); Staff M VRSC and Candidates Cttee/Panel 1997–2001; V St Wilf Harrogate 2001–04, TR from 2004; M Ripon Dioc Syn 2001–09; Asst DDO Ripon 2005–09; Dio Minl Rev Adv from 2008; M Mirfield/NOC Jt Monitoring Body 2001–09; Bp's Insp of Colls and Courses; M Coun Coll of Ressurrection, Mirfield; Frere Trustee (Mirfield); M VRSC 2006–07; M Min Coun from 2008; TR St Wilfrid's Harrogate; M Ripon Dioc Dyn 2002–09; M Mirfield/NOC Jt Monitoring Body 2001–09; M Coun Coll of Resurrection Mirfield 2005–09; Area Bp of Horsham from 2009
GS 2005–09
Tel: 01403 211139
Fax: 01403 217349
email: bishop.horsham@chichester.anglican.org

SPENCER, Mrs Caroline Sarah, BA, PGCE
Little Eggarton, Eggarton Lane Godmersham Canterbury CT4 7DY [CANTERBURY] *b* 1953 *educ* Wycombe Abbey Sch; St Hilda's Coll Ox; Lon Univ Inst of Educ; *CV* Asst Tchr Hist Sydenham High Sch 1976–80; pt Tutor Westmr Tutors Ltd 1981–84; Mother and Vol Worker for Ch and Com from 1980; M Dioc Abp's' Coun; Lay Member,

Chapter of Cant Cathl; Chair, Dioc Licensed Ministries Framework; Chair Open Syn Grp
GS 1995–
Tel: 01227 731170
07947 045025 (Mobile)
email: caroline@eggarton.eclipse.co.uk

SPENCER, Dr Jonathan Page, CB, MA, DPhil
Little Eggarton, Eggarton Lane Godmersham Canterbury CT4 7DY [CHAIR, CHURCH OF ENGLAND PENSIONS BOARD] *b* 1949 *educ* Bournemouth Sch; Univ Camb; Univ Ox; *CV* DTI 1974–2002 (Principal Private Secretary 1982–3, Dir Insurance 1991–7, Dir Gen 1997–2002); LCD/DCA 2002–5 (Dir Gen Policy); Chair C of E Pensions Bd form 2009; Dep Chair, East Kent Hospitals Trust from 2007; M Gibraltar Fin Services Commn 2011; M Solicitors Regulatory Authority 2005–9; company director from 2006
GS 2009–
Tel: 01227 731170
email: jspencer@eggarton.eclipse.co.uk

SPIERS, Revd Canon Peter Hendry, BA, Cert Th
St Luke's Vicarage 71 Liverpool Rd Great Crosby Liverpool L23 5SE [LIVERPOOL] *b* 1961 *educ* Liv Coll; St Jo Coll Dur; Ridley Hall Th Coll; *CV* C St Luke Princess Drive 1986–90; TV St Pet Everton 1990–95; V St Geo Everton 1995–2005; P-in-c St Luke's Great Crosby 2005–13; V St Luke' Great Crosby from 2013; AD Sefton from 2009
GS 2000–
Tel: 0151 924 1737
07590 690780
email: pete@spiersfamily.eclipse.co.uk

SPRINGETT, Ven Robert, BTh, MA
Abbey Cottage Stables 1 Gloucester Rd Tewkesbury Gloucestershire GL20 5SS [ARCHDEACON OF CHEL-TENHAM; GLOUCESTER] *b* 1962 *educ* Brentwood Sch; Nottm Univ; Kings Coll Lon; Lincoln Theol Coll; *CV* C St James Colchester 1989–92; C St Martin Basildon 1992–94; P-in-c South Ockendon and Belhus Park 1994–2001; AD Thurrock 1998–2001; R Wanstead 2001–10; Area Dean of Redbridge 2008–10; Adn of Cheltenham from 2010; M DAC Bd of Educ
Tel: 01684 300067 (Home)
01452 835581 (Office)
07962 273544
email: archdchelt@glosdioc.org.uk

ST ALBANS, Archdeacon of. See SMITH, Ven Jonathan Peter

ST ALBANS, Bishop of. See SMITH, Rt Revd Alan Gregory Clayton

ST ALBANS, Dean of. See JOHN, Very Revd Jeffrey Philip Hywel

ST EDMUNDSBURY AND IPSWICH, Bishop of. See THOMSON, Rt Revd David (Acting)

ST EDMUNDSBURY, Dean of. See WARD, Very Revd Frances Elizabeth Fearn

ST GERMANS, Suffragan Bishop of. See GOLDSMITH, Rt Revd Christopher David

ST PAUL'S, Dean of. See ISON, Very Revd David John

STAFFORD, Area Bishop of. See ANNAS, Rt Revd Geoff

STANSTED, Archdeacon of. See KING, Ven Robin

STEADMAN, Revd Mark John, LLB, MA
Trinity House 4 Chapel Court, Borough High Street London SE1 1HW [SOUTHWARK] *b* 1974 *educ* Horndean Comm Sch; Univ of Southampton; Inns of Court Sch of Law; Cam Univ; Westcott Ho Th Coll; *CV* AC S. Mary's Portsea 2002–05; P-in-c S. Philip with S. Mark Camberwell 2005–11; Area Dean Bermondsey 2008–11; Acting Area Dean Camberwell 2009–11; Chapl to Bp of Southwark from 2011; M Dioc IME Staff Team from 2005; M Legal Advisory Commn from 2011; M Porvoo Panel 2012
GS 2010–   *Tel:* 0207 939 9420
     07870 266553
     Fax: 08432 906294
email: mark.steadman@southwark.anglican.org

STEELE, Ven Gordon John, MA
The Diocesan Office The Palace Peterborough PE1 1YB [ARCHDEACON OF OAKHAM; PETERBOROUGH] *b* 1955 *educ* Owen's Gr Sch Lon, Univ Kent, Worcester Coll Ox, Coll of the Resurrection, Mirfield; *CV* Diocesan Treasurer, Tanzania 1977–80; C St John the Baptist, Greenhill, Harrow 1984–88; part-time Chapl to Bp of Willesden 1987–92; TV, St Andrew's, Uxbridge 1988–94; V St Alban's, Northampton 1994–2001; V St John the Baptist, Peterb 2001–12; RD Peterb 2004–10; Hon Canof Peterb Cathl from 2004; Adn of Oakham from 2012   *Tel:* 01733 887017
     Fax: 01733 555271
email: archdeacon.oakham@peterborough-diocese.org.uk
Web: www.peterborough-diocese.org.uk

STEEN, Ven Dr Jane Elizabeth, MA, PhD
Trinity House 4 Chapel Court Borough High Street London SE1 1HW [ARCHDEACON OF SOUTHWARK] *b* 1964 *educ* The Old Palace; Univ Camb; Westcott Ho; *CV* AC Chipping Barnet w Arkley, St Albans 1996–99; Dom Chapl, Bp of S'wark 1999–2005; Can Chanc, S'wark Cathl; Can Theologian and DME, S'wark 2005–13; Adn of S'wark from 2013; M Jt Implementation Cttee, Anglican-Methodist Covenant from 2012   *Tel:* 020 7939 9409
     Fax: 020 7939 9465
email: jane.steen@southwark.anglican.org

STEPNEY, Area Bishop of. See NEWMAN, Rt Revd Adrian

STEVENS, Mr Robin Michael, B Sc
3 Aldeburgh Way Chelmsford CM1 7PB [CHELMS-FORD] *b* 1945 *educ* Chigwell Sch; Birm Univ; *CV* Eng Marconi Communication Systems 1967–79; eng Thames Television 1979–91; Nat Stewardship Officer, AC 1992–2005; Chelmsf Borough councillor 2005–11; Dep Mayor Chelmsf 2010–11; Rdr from 1990
GS 2005–   *Tel:* 01245 268042
     07721 046991
     email: rms@ukgateway.net

STEVENS, Rt Revd Timothy John, MA, DCL, DLitt
Bishop's Lodge 10 Springfield Rd Leicester LE2 3BD [BISHOP OF LEICESTER] *b* 1946 *educ* Chigwell Sch; Selw Coll Cam; Ripon Coll Cuddesdon; *CV* C E Ham TM 1976–79; TV St Alb Upton Park 1979–80; TR Canvey Island 1980–88; Bp of Chelmsf's Urban Officer 1988–91; Adn of West Ham 1991–95; Bp of Dunwich 1995–99; Bp of Leic from 1999; Chair Urban Bps Panel 2001–06; Chair Children's Soc 2004–10; M AC 2006–10; M Ho of Bps Standing Cttee 2006–10; Chair Westcott Ho Coun 2007–12; M Jt Cttee on Lords Reform 2011–12; Convenor of Lords Spiritual Ho of Lords from 2009; Chair Common Purpose UK from 2013; Trustee United Learning from 2013
GS 1987–95, 1999–   *Tel:* 0116 270 8985
     07860 692258
     email: bishop.tim@leccofe.org

STOCK, Rt Revd (William) Nigel , BA, Dip Theol
Lambeth Palace London SE1 7JU [BISHOP AT LAMBETH] *b* 1950 *educ* Dur Sch; Dur Univ; Ripon Coll Cuddesdon; *CV* C St Pet Stockton 1976–79; P-in-c St Pet Taraka, PNG 1979–84; V St Mark Shiremoor 1985–91; TR N Shields 1991–98; RD Tynemouth 1992–98; Hon Can Newc Cathl 1997–98; Res Can Dur Cathl 1998–2000; Bp of Stockport 2000–07; Bp of St E & I from 2007; M Ho of Bps CME Cttee 2002–09; M Appts Cttee of C of E 2003–13; Chair Local Unity Panel (CCU) 2007–09; M Min Coun from 2008; M Dioc Commn from 2008; Co-Chair Meth Angl Panel for Unity in Miss from 2009; Chair Melanesian Miss from 2009; M Ho of Lords from 2011; Bp at Lambeth from 2013; Bp to HM Forces from 2014; Bp for the Falkland Islands from 2014
GS 2003–   *Tel:* 020 7898 1200
     Fax: 020 7401 9886
     Web: www.archbishopofcanterbury.org

STOCKPORT, Suffragan Bishop of. [NOT APPOINTED AT TIME OF GOING TO PRESS]

STOKE-UPON-TRENT, Archdeacon of. See PARKER, Ven Matthew

STOKOE, Father (Wayne) Jeffrey, Dip HE
17 Heaton Gardens Edlington DN12 1SY [SHEF-FIELD] *b* 1956 *educ* Trin Ho Navigation Sch, Hull; Coll of the Resurrection, Mirfield; *CV* C

St Catherine of Siena Sheff 1996–98; V St Jo the Baptist Edlington from 1999; Hon Chapl 103 (Doncaster) sqdrn ATC from 2003
GS 2009– *Tel:* 01709 858358
email: wjs@stokoej.freeserve.co.uk

STORKEY, Dr Elaine, BA, MA, DD, Ph D (Hon)
The Old School High St Coton Cambridgeshire CB23 7PL [ELY] *educ* Ossett Gr Sch; Univ Coll of Wales Abth; McMaster Univ Ontario; York Univ; *CV* Tutor in Philosophy Man Coll Ox 1967–68; Rsch Fell in Sociology Stirling Univ 1968–69; Tutor Open Univ 1976–80; Vis Lect Calvin Coll USA 1980–81; Covenant Coll USA 1981–82; Lect in Philosophy Oak Hill Th Coll 1982–87; Lect in Faculty of Social Science Open Univ 1987–91; Dir Inst for Contemporary Christianity 1992–98; Vis Lect in Theol K Coll Lon 1996–2001; Ext Mod Birkbeck Coll Lon from 1998; Scriptwriter for BBC OU; Assoc Ed 'Third Way' from 1984; Broadcaster BBC from 1987; M ACORA 1988–90; M Crown Appts Commn 1990; Vc-Pres UCCF 1987–93; M Abps' Commn on Cathl 1992–94; M Lausanne Wkg Pty on Th 1992–97; M CRAC 1993–98; Examiner Sociology of Religion Lon Univ from 1993; Trustee C of E Newspaper from 1994; Vc-Pres Cheltenham and Glouc Coll of HE from 1994; M Forum for the Future 1995–98; M Orthodox-Evang Dialogue WCC from 1996; New Coll Scholar Univ of NSW Sydney 1997; Pres Tear Fund from 1997; M Wkg Pty on Chr-Jewish Relns from 1998; Lambeth DD 1998; M John Ray Inst from 1999; Sen Rsch Fell Wycliffe Hall, Ox 2003–07; M CNC 2002–07; Visiting Prof Messiah Coll, Pennsylvania, USA summer 2005; Chair Fulcrum from 2006; columnist for Swedish newspaper 'Dagen' from 2006; Chair Ch Army Ord and Commn Review Gp 2007–08; Examiner Univ of Wales 2008
GS 1987– *Tel:* 01954 212381
07969 354673 (Mobile)
email: elaine@storkey.com

STOW AND LINDSEY, Archdeacon of. [NOT APPOINTED AT TIME OF GOING TO PRESS]

STRAIN, Revd Christopher Malcolm, LLB, Solicitor, Cert Theol (Oxon)
St Luke's Vicarage 2 Birchwood Rd Parkstone Poole BH14 9NP [SALISBURY] *b* 1956 *educ* Aldwickbury Prep Sch; Bedford Sch; Southn Univ; Guildf Coll of Law; Wycliffe Hall; *CV* Solicitor and CMS Volunteer Nigeria pre-ordination; C St Jo w. Em Werrington, Peterb 1986–89; C-in-charge St Steph Broadwater, Worthing, Chich 1989–1994; TV Hampreston and Stapehill, Wimborne, Salis 1994–2000; V St Luke Parkstone from 2000; Sch gov; Chapl to Scouts and Cubs, Poole; Surrogate for Marriages; Chair Ch Together in Poole 2008–13; Asst RD Poole from 2010
GS 2005– *Tel:* 01202 741030
email: cmstrain@tiscali.co.uk

STRATFORD, Ven Dr Timothy Richard, B Sc, PhD
St Martins House 7 Peacock Lane Leicester LE1 5PZ [ARCHDEACON OF LEICESTER] *b* 1961 *educ* Knowsley Hey Comp Sch; York Univ; Wycliffe Hall Th Coll; Univ of Sheff; *CV* C Mossley Hill 1986–89; C St Helens St Helen 1989–91; Chapl to Bp of Liv 1991–94; V Gd Shep W Derby 1994–2003; TR Kirkby and TV St Chad Kirkby 2003–12; M Liturg Commn from 2006; Adn of Leicester from 2012
GS 2000–13 *Tel:* 0116 261 5309
0116 270 4441
Fax: 0116 261 5220
email: tim.stratford@leccofe.org
Web: www.leicester.anglican.org

STROYAN, Rt Revd John Ronald Angus, M Theol, MA
Warwick House 139 Kenilworth Rd Coventry CV4 7AP [SUFFRAGAN BISHOP OF WARWICK; COVENTRY] *b* 1955 *educ* Harrow Sch; St Andr Univ; Q Coll Birm; Ecum Inst, Bossey, Switzerland; Univ of Wales; *CV* C St Pet Hillfields, Cov E Tm 1983–87; V St Matt w. St Chad Smethwick, Birm 1987–94; V Bloxham, Milcombe & S Newington, Ox 1994–2005; AD Deddington, Ox 2002–05; Bp of Warwick from 2005; Pres Com of the Cross of Nails UK from 2007; Sec W Midlands Regional Gp from 2008; M Rural Bps' Panel from 2009; Co-Moderator Chs Together in Cov and Warwickshire 2009–12; M Internat Commn for Angl-Orthodox Theol Dialogue from 2009; M Ho of Bps Working Grp on Human Sexuality 2012–14; Co-chair Reuilly Contact Grp from 2013
Tel: 024 7641 2627
Fax: 024 7641 5254
email: bishop.warwick@CovCofE.org

STUART-WHITE, Ven Bill (William Robert), MA(Oxon), BA
10 The Hayes Bodmin Road Truro TR1 1FY [ARCHDEACON OF CORNWALL; TRURO] *b* 1959 *educ* Winchester Coll; Merton Coll Ox; Trin Coll Bris; *CV* AC Upper Armley 1986–91; P-in-c Austrey 1991–92; P-in-c Warton 1991–92; V Austrey and Warton 1992–98; R Camborne 1998–2006; P-in-c Stoke Climsland 2006–09; P-in-c Linkinhorne 2006–09; P-in-c St Breoke and Egloshayle 2009–12; Rural Link Officer 2006–12; Adn of Cornwall from 2012
Tel: 01872 242374
email: bill@truro.anglican.org

STURGESS, Canon Sheridan Jane, MA (Cantab) FCA
Holywell Gables Pengover Road Liskeard Cornwall PL14 3NW [TRURO] *b* 1955 *educ* Kidderminster H Sch; Newnham Coll, Cam; *CV* Dioc Sec, Truro, 2002–10; Stewardship Adv, Truro 1997–2002; Parish Admin, St Martins Ch, Liskeard 1994–97; Self-employed Chartered Accountant, Sheridan Sturgess & Co 1983–94; M Fin Cttee 2008–10 and from 2011; M Ch & Comm Fund 2005–09; M Inter-Dioc Fin Forum 2002–10; Dioc Lay Char

Truro from 2012; Lay Can Truro Cathl from 2013; M Steering Cttee Misc Provisions Measure
GS 2010–   Tel: 01579 346411
                                                      07793 805685
          email: sheri.sturgess@gmail.com

SUDBURY, Archdeacon of, JENKINS, Ven Dr David Harold

SUFFOLK, Archdeacon of. See MORGAN, Ven Ian David John

SUGDEN, Canon Dr Christopher Michael Neville, MA, M Phil, PhD
36 North Hinksey Village Oxford OX2 0NA [OXFORD] *b* 1948 *educ* K Sch Roch; St Pet Coll Ox; Nottm Univ; Westmr Coll Ox; St Jo Coll Nottm; *CV* C St Geo Leeds 1974–77; relig programmes producer, BBC Radio Leeds 1977; Asst Presbyter St Jo Bangalore, Ch of S India 1978–83; Asst Dir Assoc for Theol Educ by Extension, India 1978–83; Assoc Dir EFICOR Education and Training Unit, India 1979–83; Registrar and Dir of Academic Affairs, Ox Cen for Miss Studies 1983–2001; Exec Dir OCMS 2001–04; Exec Sec Angl Mainstream Internat from 2004; Trustee/Chair of Trustees of Traidcraft 1986–2007; M MPA Coun 2006–10; Can St Luke's Cathl, Jos, Nigeria from 2001; Trustee and Sec Angl Internat Devel from 2008; Dir and Sec Fell of Confessing Angls UK and Ireland from 2009; Dir and Sec Oxford Centre for Religion and Public Life from 2009; Dir and Sec Oxford Centre for Training, Reseach, Advocacy and Dialogue from 2009; Dir and Sec St Augustine's Soc from 2010; Dir Anglican Mainstream from 2003, Convenor from 2014; Hon Can St Anselm's Cathl, Sunyani, Ghana from 2010; Bp's Commissary for Diocs of NE Caribbean and Aruba, West Indies and Sunyani, Ghana, West Africa
GS 2005–2010, 2011–   Tel: 07808 297043
           email: csugden@ocrpl.org
           Web: www.ocrpl.org

SULLIVAN, Ven Nicola Ann, BTh, SRN, RM
6 The Liberty Wells BA5 2SU [ARCHDEACON OF WELLS; BATH AND WELLS] *b* 1958 *educ* Ips Convent of Jesus and Mary; Mills Gr Sch, Framlingham; St Bart's Hosp; Bris Maternity Hosp; Wycliffe Hall Ox; *CV* C St Anne Earlham, Norw 1995–99; Assoc V Bath Abbey 1999–2002; Subdean Wells Cathl 2003–07; Bp's Chapl and Pastl Asst 2002–07; Adn of Wells and Res Can Wells Cathl from 2007; M Norw Dioc Syn 1997–99; M B & W Dioc Syn, Bp's Coun, DBF   Tel: 01749 685147
                                                  Fax: 01749 679755
     email: adwells@bathwells.anglican.org

SUNDERLAND, Archdeacon of. See BAIN, Ven (John) Stuart

SURREY, Archdeacon of. See BEAKE, Ven Stuart Alexander

SUTCLIFFE, Mr Tom (James Thomas), MA
12 Polworth Rd Streatham London SW16 2EU [SOUTHWARK] *b* 1943 *educ* Prebendal Sch Chich; Hurstpierpoint Coll; Magd Coll Ox; *CV* Engl tchr Central Tutorial Sch for Young Musicians (now Purcell Sch) 1964–65; Countertenor lay-clerk Westmr Cathl 1966–70; Mgr Musica Reservata 1966–69; performer with Schola Polyphonica, Pro Cantione Antiqua, Musica Reservata, Concentus Musicus, Vienna and Darmstadt Opera 1966–70; Advertisement Mgr and Ed 'Music and Musicians' magazine 1968–73; Sub-ed, opera critic, dep arts ed, dep obits ed 'Guardian' 1973–96; Opera Critic 'Evening Standard' 1996–2002; Leverhulme Fell 1991, 2005; Hon Fell Rose Bruford Coll from 2006; M Exec Cttee Affirming Catholicism 1996–2002; Chair Music Section of Critics' Circle 1999–2009; Pres of Critic's Circle 2010–12; dramaturg in Brussels and Vienna from 1998; M Cathls Fabric Commn for Eng 2002–11; M Editorial Advisory Board of The Bridge (Southwark) since 1995; columnist in New Directions since 2010
GS 1990–   Tel: 020 8677 5849
                                                      020 8677 7939
                                                      07815 101314
                                              Fax: 020 8677 7939
          email: tomsutcliffe@email.msn.com

SUTTON, Mrs Debbie (Deborah Margaret), BSc, PG Dip Dietetics
2 Taswell Rd Southsea PO5 2RG [PORTSMOUTH] *b* 1957 *educ* Walthamstow Hall, Sevenoaks; Chelsea Coll, Lon Univ; *CV* Dietitian, Portsm Hosps NHS Trust; Project Coodinator, Patient Safety
GS 2005–10, 2010–   Tel: 023 9275 6926
          email: deb2tas@hotmail.com

SWINDON, Suffragan Bishop of. See RAYFIELD, Rt Revd Dr Lee Stephen

SWINSON, Mrs Margaret Anne, MA, ACA, CTA
46 Glenmore Ave Liverpool L18 4QF [LIVERPOOL] *b* 1957 *educ* Alice Ottley Sch Worc; Liv Univ; *CV* Accountant (Tax Specialist); M (Vc-Chair) CCU from 2006; Mod CTBI from 2006; M ACC from 2012; GS Stg Cttee 1991–97; M BSR 1990–95; Chair Race and Com Relns Cttee 1990–95; Trustee CUF 1987–97; M CTBI; C of E Delegate to WCC Canberra 1991; M CBF 1996–98; M Bd of Miss 2001–03; M CCU from 2006; Mod CTBI from 2006
GS 1985–   Tel: 0151 724 3533
          email: maggie@swinsonfamily.net

SWITZERLAND, Archdeacon in. See POTTER, Ven Peter Maxwell

SYKES, Mr John Nicholas, MA
Tower Place West London EC3R 5BU [CHURCH COMMISSIONER] *b* 1959 *educ* Bradford Gr Sch; Jes Coll Ox; *CV* Investment Consult; Baillie, Gifford & Co Ltd 1980–84; Baring Asset Mgt 1984–97;

Sen Consult William M Mercer Investment from 1997; Ch Commr from 2001; M Assets Cttee and Securities Grp   *Tel and Fax:* 020 7178 3268
                                    email: nick.sykes@mercer.com

TAN, Dr Chik Kaw, B Pharm, MSc, PhD, MRPharmS, PGCMedEd
12 Montfort Place Westlands Newcastle-under-Lyme ST5 2HE [LICHFIELD] *b* 1956 *educ* Anglo-Chinese Sch, Ipoh, Malaysia; Bath Univ; Aston Univ; Keele Univ; *CV* Pres Bath Univ Chr Union 1979–80; Adv Bris Chinese Chr Fellowship 1981–86; Prayer Grp leader, Newcastle-under-Lyme OMF Prayer Grp 1986–95; M OMF Internat 1996–2002; Assoc Pastor, Surabaya (Indonesia) Internat Chr Fellowship 2001–02; M Preaching Tm, St Jas Audley from 1987; Hon Sen Lect Keele Univ from 2005; M Newc Dny Syn; M Lich Dioc Syn; M N Staffs Local Rsch Ethics Cttee 2202–2008; GS 2008–2010
GS 2005–   *Tel:* 01782 441604
                                    email: ck11x@yahoo.ie

TANN, Professor Jennifer, BA; PhD
Thanet House High Street Chalford Stroud GL6 8DH [GLOUCESTER] *b* 1939 *educ* Badminton Sch; Man Univ; Leic Univ; *CV* Prof Innovation, Birm Univ, 1989–2008; Dir Continuing Ed, Univ Newcastle 1986–89; R Aston Univ 1974–86; Lec Aston Univ 1969–74; Prof Emerita, Birm Univ from 2008; Management Consultant, Caret Ltd from 1992
GS 2010–   *Tel:* 01453 884142
                          email: innovation.jt@btinternet.com

TATTERSALL, Worshipful Canon Geoffrey Frank, MA, QC
2 The Woodlands Lostock Bolton BL6 4JD [MAN-CHESTER] *b* 1947 *educ* Man Gr Sch; Ch Ch Ox; *CV* Barrister; Called to Bar Lincoln's Inn 1970; Bencher 1997; In practice Nn Circuit from 1970; Recorder Crown Court from 1989; QC from 1992; Called to Bar NSW 1992; SC from 1995; Judge of Appeal IOM from 1997; Deputy High Court Judge from 2003; Lay Chair Bolton Dny Syn 1993–2002; Chair Ho of Laity Dioc Syn 1994–2003; M Fees Adv Commn from 1995; M Strg Cttee Clergy Discipline Measure from 1996; M Bp's Coun; M DBF and Trust and Fin Cttee till 2004; Chair Stg Orders Cttee GS from 1999; Panel of Chairmen of GS from 2011; Chan of Carl Dioc from 2003; Hon Lay Can Manch Cathl 2003; Chan Manch Dioc from 2004; Dep V-Gen S & Man 2004–08, 2014–; External Reviewer of decisions of Dir of Fair Access 2005–13; Chair Disciplinary Tribunals, Clergy Discipline Measure from 2006; Chair Revision Cttee, draft C of E Marriage Measure 2006–07; Chair Revision Cttee, draft Eccl Officer (Terms of Service) Measure 2007–08; Chair Revision Cttee, draft Convocations (Elections to Upper House) (Amendment), Clergy Representation Rules (Amendment) and Church Representations Rules

(Amendment) Resolutions 2014; M Strg and Revisions Cttee for draft C of E Bps and Ps (Consecration and Ord of Women) Measure 2009–12; M Worshipful Co of Par Clerks from 2009; Par Clerk St George-in-the-East
GS 1995–   *Tel:* 01204 846265
                                    Fax: 01204 849863
                                    email: gftqc@hotmail.co.uk

TAUNTON, Archdeacon of. See REED, Ven John Peter Cyril

TAUNTON, Suffragan Bishop of. See MAURICE, Rt Revd Peter David

TAVINOR, Very Revd Michael Edward, MA, MMus, MTh, ARCO, PGCE
The Deanery College Cloisters Cathedral Close Hereford HR1 2NG [DEAN OF HEREFORD] *b* 1953 *educ* Bishopshalt Sch Hillingdon, Middx; Univ Coll Dur; Em Coll Cam; K Coll Lon; Ripon Coll Cuddesdon; Univ Wales: Lampeter; *CV* C St Pet Ealing Lon 1982–85; Prec, Sacrist and Min Can Ely Cathl 1985–90; P-in-c Stuntney Ely 1987–90; V Tewkesbury with Walton Cardiff Glouc 1990–2002; V Twyning Glos 1999–2002; Hon Can Glouc Cathl 1997–2002; Dean of Hereford from 2002; M Dioc Syn from 2002; Pres Ch Music Soc 2005; Hon Fell Guild of Ch Musicians from 2006
                                    Tel: 01432 374203
                                    Fax: 01432 374220
                          email: dean@herefordcathedral.org

TAYLOR, Very Revd Charles William, BA, MA, Hon FGCM
The Deanery Minster Precincts Peterborough PE1 1XS [DEAN OF PETERBOROUGH] *b* 1953 *educ* St Paul's Cathl Choir Sch; Marlborough Coll; Selwyn Coll Cam; Cuddesdon Coll Ox; Ch Divinity Sch of Pacific, Graduate Theol Union, Berkeley, Calif USA; *CV* C Cen Wolverhampton TM 1976–79; Chapl Westmr Abbey (Minor Can) 1979–84; V Stanmore w. Oliver's Battery, Winch 1984–90; R N Stoneham & Bassett, Southn 1990–95; Can Res and Prec, Lich Cathl 1995–2007; Dean of Peterb from 2007; M Lich Dioc Liturg Cttee 1976–79; M Winch Dioc Liturg Cttee 1984–95; Chair Lich Dioc Worship Team 1995–2006; M Cathls Liturg and Music Cttee 1996–2007; Gov King's Sch Peterb, Oakham Sch, Uppingham Sch from 2007; M Peterb City Com Cohesion Bd 2008–13; Dir Peterb Culture & Leisure Trust from 2010; Chair Cathedrals Plus from 2011
                                    Tel: 01733 355315
                  email: dean.pa@peterborough-cathedral.org.uk

TAYLOR, Ven Paul Stanley, B Ed, M Th
Aldhelm House Rectory Lane West Stafford Dorchester DT2 8AB [ARCHDEACON OF SHERBORNE; SALISBURY] *b* 1953 *educ* Lodge Farm Co Sec Sch; Redditch Co High Sch; Westmr Coll Ox; Westcott Ho Cam; *CV* C St Steph Bush Hill Park 1984–88;

WHO'S WHO

V St Andr Southgate 1988–97; Asst Dir POT 1987–94, Dir 1994–2000, 2002–04; V St Mary & Ch Ch Hendon 1997–2004; AD W Barnet 2000–04; Assoc Tutor NTMTC 2001–04; Adn of Sherborne from 2004
Tel: 01305 269074
07796 691203 (Mobile)
Fax: 01305 269074
email: adsherborne@salisbury.anglican.org

TERRETT, Group Captain Paul Everard, OBE, LLB
Idle Cottage Sharptor Liskeard PL14 5AT [TRURO] *b* 1934 *educ* Cotham Gr Sch; Bris Univ; *CV* Dny lay Chair from 1996; Can Emer Truro Cathl; Chair Truro DBF 2003–06, Vc-Chair from 2006; M Bp's Coun, DBF, Patr, Pastl and Glebe Ctees, DBE
GS 2005–
Tel: 01579 362741
email: terretts@sharptor.co.uk

TEWKESBURY, Suffragan Bishop of. See SNOW, Rt Revd Martyn James

THEODORESON, Mr Ian, FCA
Church House Great Smith St London SW1P 3AZ [CHIEF FINANCE OFFICER, NATIONAL CHURCH INSTITUTIONS] *CV* Sen Mgr Ernst & Young 1977–87; Fin Dir Save the Children 1987–95; Dir Corporate Resources Barnardo's 1995–2009; Chief Finance Officer, NCIs from 2009
Tel: 020 7898 1795
email: ian.theodoreson@churchofengland.org

THETFORD, Suffragan Bishop of. See WINTON, Rt Revd Alan Peter

THOMAS, Ven Paul Wyndham, BA; MA; BA; Cert Theol
Archdeacon's House The Vicarage Tong, Shifnal TF11 8PW [ARCHDEACON OF SALOP] *b* 1955 *educ* Cardiff High Sch; Oriel Coll Ox; Wycliffe Hall Ox; *CV* C Llangynwyd with Maesteg 1979–85; TV Langport Area churches 1985–90; P-in-c Thorp Arch W Walton and Clergy Training Off Dioc York 1990–93 V Nether w Upper Poppleton 1993–2004; Doxey and Par Dev Adv 2004–11; Adn of Salop from 2011; DAC; Bldngs and Benefices Cttee; Glebe Cttee; Bp's Coun; Dioc Syn
Tel: 01902 372622
Fax: 01902 374060
email: archdeacon.salop@lichfield.anglican.org

THOMAS, Preb Rod (Roderick Charles Howell), B Sc, Cert Th
St Matthew's Vicarage 3 Sherford Rd Elburton Plymouth PL9 8DQ [EXETER] *b* 1954 *educ* Ealing Gr Sch for Boys; LSE; Wycliffe Hall Th Coll; *CV* Dir Employment Affairs CBI 1987–91; C St Paul Stonehouse Plymouth 1993–95; C St Andr Plymouth 1995–99; P-in-c St Matt Elburton 1999–2005, V from 2005, Preb from 2012; Chair Reform; M BM 2001–03; M Wkg Pty on Sen Ch Appts

from 2005; M CPAS Coun of Reference from 200; M Stg Cttee on Women in the Episcopate Legislation 2013–14
GS 2000–
Tel: 01752 402771
email: rod.thomas@elburtonchurch.com

THOMAS-BETTS, Dr Anna, MBE, MA, Ph D
68 Halkingcroft Langley Slough SL3 7AY [OXFORD] *b* 1941 *educ* Christava Mahilalayam, Alwaye, S India; Madras Chr Coll, Madras Univ; Keele Univ; *CV* Lect in Physics Madras Chr Coll 1960–62; Post-Doctoral Rsch Asst Imp Coll Lon 1966–74; Lect in Geophysics Imp Coll Lon 1974–92, Sen Lect 1992–2001; Coll Tutor 1998–2010; M CCU 1991–96; M CBF 1996–99; M BSR 2000–02; M MPA from 2003; M Gov Body of Ripon Coll Cuddesdon from 2006; Founder M of Oxf Dioc Cttee for Interfaith Concerns, Chair 2012; Chair Independent Monitoring Bd, Colnbrook Immigration Removal Cen 2004–09; Chair Forum of Chairs of Independent Monitoring Bds at Immigration Removal Cen 2007–08; Rep for immigration detention estate on Nat Coun IMBs from 2009
GS 1990–
Tel: 01753 822013 (Home)
email: anna.t_b@btinternet.com

THOMSON, Canon Celia Stephana Margaret, MA
3 Miller's Green Gloucester GL1 2BN [GLOUCESTER] *b* 1955 *educ* St Swithun's Winch 1967–71; Ox Univ; Salisbury and Wells Theol Coll; *CV* C St Barnabas Southfields, S'wark 1991–95; V Ch Ch W Wimbledon, S'wark 1995–2003; Tutor in Ethics, SEITE 1995–2000; Vocations Adv Lambeth Adnry 1995–2000; Bp's Adv from 2007; Can Pastor Glouc Cath from 2003; M CDC and Cathls Fabric Commn for England from 2011
GS 2008–
Tel: 01452 415824
email: cthomson@gloucestercathedral.org.uk

THOMSON, Rt Revd David, MA, D Phil, FRSA, FSA, FRHistS
14 Lynn Road Ely CB6 1DA [SUFFRAGAN BISHOP OF HUNTINGDON; ELY; ACTING BISHOP OF ST EDMUNDSBURY AND IPSWICH] *b* 1952 *educ* K Edw VII Sch Sheffield; Keble Coll Ox; Selwyn Coll Cam; Westcott Ho Cam; *CV* C Maltby 1981–84; TV Banbury 1984–94; TR Cockermouth 1994–2002; Chair Dioc Children and Young People's Cttee; Bp's Adv for Healthcare Chapl, Team and Grp Mins and Deliverance Min; Archdeacon of Carlisle and Can Res Carl Cathl 2002–08; Bp Huntingdon from 2008; Hon Can Ely Cathl from 2008; Interim Bp St Eds and Ipswich from 2013; Vice-Chair National Society and Board of Education from 2013
Tel: 01353 662137
07771 864550 (Mobile)
Fax: 01353 669357
email: bishop.huntingdon@ely.anglican.org
2nd email: bishops.orrice@cofesuffolk.org
Web: bpdt.wordpress.com

THORNTON, Rt Revd Tim (Timothy) Martin,
BA, MA
Lis Escop Feock Truro TR3 6QQ [BISHOP OF TRURO]
b 1957 *educ* Devonport High Sch for Boys;
Southn Univ; St Steph Ho Ox; K Coll Lond;
CV C Todmorden 1980–82; P-in-c Walsden
1982–85; Chapl 1985–86; Sen Chapl 1986–87; Bp's
Chapl Wakef 1987–91; DDO Wakef 1988–91; Bp's
Chapl Lon 1991–94; Dep P in O 1992–2001; Prin
N Thames Minl Tr Course 1994–98; V Kensington
St Mary Abbots w S Geo, Gov St Mary Abbots C
of E Primary Sch, Chair Campden Charities
1998–2001; AD Kensington 2000–01; K Coll Theol
Trustee; Area Bp of Sherborne 2001–08; Bp Truro
from 2009; Chair The Children's Society
Tel: 01872 862657
Fax: 01872 862037
email: bishop@truro.anglican.org

TICEHURST, Mrs Carol Ann,
35 South Park Lincoln LN5 8ER [LINCOLN] *b* 1938
educ Sincil Girls' Sch Lincoln; Lincoln Coll; *CV*
Medical Sec; hdmaster's PA; Pres R Br Legion
Lincs Women's Section and caseworker from
1998; M GS Catholic Grp; M Forward in Faith
GS 1995– Tel: 01522 580728
email: xxcaticehurst@virginmedia.com

**TONBRIDGE, Archdeacon of. See MANSELL,
Ven Clive Neville Ross**

**TONBRIDGE, Suffragan Bishop of. See
CASTLE, Rt Revd Dr Brian Colin**

TOOKE, Mr Stephen Edgar,
*The Haven 21 Wisbech Road March Cambridgeshire
PE15 8ED* [ELY] *b* 1946 *educ* Queen's Sch; Isle of
Ely Coll; *CV* Police Superintendent 1989–96;
National Co-ord SPCK Worldwide 1996–99; Area
Fundraising Mgr The Children's Soc 1999–2001;
Lay Chair Ely Dioc Syn 1996– 2009; Rdr from
1997; Lay Chair Deanery Syn from 2002; M Ely
Dioc Bp's Counc; M Vacancy in See Cttee and
CNC. 2001 and 2010; M Coun for Min
GS 1995–2005; 2010– Tel: 01354 652844
email: stooke@havenmarch.plus.com

**TOTNES, Archdeacon of. COHEN, Ven Clive
(Acting)**

TOWNLEY, Ven Peter Kenneth, BA, DSPT
The Vicarage Kirkthorpe Wakefield WF1 5SZ [ARCH-
DEACON OF PONTEFRACT; WEST YORKSHIRE AND
THE DALES] *b* 1955 *educ* Moston Brook High Sch
Man; Sheff Univ; Man Univ; Ridley Hall Th Coll;
CV C Ch Ch Ashton-under-Lyne 1980–83; P-in-c
St Hugh's CD Oldham 1983–88; R All SS Stretford
1988–96; V St Mary-le-Tower Ipswich 1996–2008;
M Meissen Commn 1991–2001; RD of Ipswich
from 2001; Hon Can from 2003; M Porvoo
Panel from 2003; M Inter-dioc Fin Forum; Adn
Pontefract from 2008; Chair Meissen Library

Management Cttee in Durham; Chair Dioc Bd
Educ 2008–13; Chair Dioc Academies Trust from
2011
GS 1992–95, 2000–08 Tel: 01924 434459 (Office)
01924 896327 (Home)
Fax: 01924 364834 (Office)
01924 896327 (Home)
email: peter.townley@
westyorkshiredales.anglican.org

TREWEEK (nee Montgomery), Ven Rachel,
BA, BTh
*St Andrew's House 35 St Andrew's Hill London
EC4V 5DE* [ARCHDEACON OF HACKNEY; LONDON]
b 1963 *educ* Broxbourne Sch; Reading Univ;
Wycliffe Hall Ox; *CV* Paediatric Speech and
Language Therapist, Gospel Oak Health Cen,
Hampstead Health Auth 1985–87; Speech and
Language Therapist, Child Devel Team,
Hampstead Health Auth 1987–89; Clinical Mgr
for Paediatric Speech and Language Therapists in
Health Cens, Bloomsbury, Hampstead & Isling-
ton Health Auths 1989–91; C St Geo Tufnell Park,
Lon 1994–97, Assoc V 1997–99; V St Jas the Less
Bethnal Green, Lon 1999–2006; Adn of Northolt
2006–11; Adn of Hackney from 2011; CME
Officer, Stepney Area, Lon Dioc 1999–2001; Bp's
Visitor, Stepney Area 2004–06
GS 2010– Tel: 020 7932 1145
email: archdeacon.hackney@london.anglican.org

TROTT, Revd Stephen, BA, BA, MA, LLM
*The Rectory 41 Humfrey Lane Boughton Northamp-
ton NN2 8RQ* [PETERBOROUGH] *b* 1957 *educ* Bp
Vesey's Gr Sch Sutton Coldfield; Hull Univ;
Fitzw Coll Cam; Cardiff Univ; Westcott Ho Th
Coll (Cam Federation of Th Colls); *CV* C Hessle
1984–87; C St Alb Hull 1987–88; R Pitsford w
Boughton from 1988; Sec CME 1988–93; Vis
Chapl Pitsford Sch from 1991, Gov and Dir from
2001; Surrogate for Marriage Licences from 2001;
M Dioc Syn from 1990; M Vacancy-in-See Cttee
from 1995; Clerical Vc-Pres Dioc Syn and Chair
Dioc Ho of Clergy 2000–03; M Peterb Cathl Coun
2001–04 and from 2013; M of DBF and Bishop's
Council from 2010; Chair Church Buildings Cttee
from 2010; FRSA 1986; M Eccl Law Soc from 1988;
M Legis Cttee 1995–2000, 2005–10; M Legal Adv
Commn 1996–2006; M CCBI and CTE 1996–99;
M Revision Cttee on Calendar, Lectionary
and Collects 1996; Ch Commr from 1997, Bd
of Govs from 1999; M Pastl Cttee 1998–2012;
Closed Chs Cttee from 2004, Dep Chair from
2009; M Nominations and Governance Cttee
from 2009–2012; M DRACSC 1999–2001; M
Revision Cttee on Clergy Discipline Measure
1999–2000; GS Rep on Gov Body of SAOMC
2001–06; C of E Delegate to Conf of Eur Chs,
Trondheim, 2003; M Pastl (Amendment) Measure
Revision Cttee from 2004; M Follow-up Grp,
Review of Diocs, Pastl & Related Measures from
2004; M Panel of Reference, Angl Communion

from 2005; M Strg Cttee Diocs Pastl and Miss Measure 2005–06; Stg Cttee, Conv of Cant from 2006–2010; M Revision Cttee, Eccl Fees Meas 2011; Synodical Sec, Convocation of Cant from 2010; M Council of Christians and Jews from 2011; Fees Advisory Commn from 2013
GS 1995– 	*Tel:* 01604 845655
07712 863000
email: revstrott@btinternet.com
Web: www.pitsford.org.uk
Twitter: @revstrott

TRURO, Bishop of. See THORNTON, Rt Revd Tim (Timothy) Martin

TRURO, Dean of. See BUSH, Very Revd Roger Charles

TURNER, Canon (Thelma) Ann, B Sc
Grote Steenweg 47/42 2600 Berchem Belgium [EUROPE] *b* 1948 *educ* Wintringham Gr Sch, Grimsby; Univ of Kent at Cant; *CV* Hd of Science, Upminster Comp Sch 1972–78; Scientific Engl trainer 1985–91; written communication trainer from 1991; M Adnry of NW Eur Stg Cttee; Vc-Chair Ho of Laity, Dioc in Eur; M Dioc Communications Cttee, Dioc OLM Wkg Party, Dioc PIM Consultation, Bp's Coun; Lay Can (Gibraltar) from 2009
GS 2005– 	*Tel:* 0032 3440 2581
0032 477 626 184 (Mobile)
email: ann@turner.be

URQUHART, Rt Revd David Andrew, BA(Hons); Hon DD; Hon DUniv
Bishop's Croft, Old Church Road Harborne Birmingham B17 0BG [BISHOP OF BIRMINGHAM] *b* 1952 *educ* Rugby Sch; Ealing Business Sch; Wycliffe Hall Th Coll; *CV* C St Nic Hull 1984–87; TV Drypool Hull 1987–92; V H Trin Cov 1992–2000; Bp of Birkenhead 2000–06; Chair CMS Trustees 1994–2007; Prelate of Order of St Mich and St Geo from 2005; Abp of Cant's Episcopal Link with China from 2006; Bp of Birm from 2006; Chair Ridley Hall Coun from 2010; Lords Spiritual from 2010
GS 2006– 	*Tel:* 0121 427 1163
email: bishop@birmingham.anglican.org
Web: www.cofebirmingham.com
Twitter: @David_Urq

USHER, Rt Revd Graham Barham, BSC, BA MA
Bishop's House, Bishop's Walk, Cradley Heath B64 7RH [SUFFRAGAN BISHOP OF DUDLEY; WORCESTER] *b* 1970 *educ* Edin Univ; Ch Ch Cam; Westcott Ho; St Nic Th Coll Ghana; *CV* C Nunthorpe, York 1996–99; V N Ormesby 1999–2004; R Hexham Newc 2004–14; AD Hexham 2006–11; Bp of Dudley from 2014; Hon Can Kumasi Ghana from 2007
	Tel: 0121 550 3407
Fax: 0121 550 7340
email: bishopsofficedudley@cofeworcester.org.uk
Twitter: @bishopdudley

VANN, Ven Cherry Elizabeth, GRSM, ARCM, Dip RS, Cert in Counselling, Br Sign Lang Level 3
57 Melling Rd Oldham OL4 1PN [ARCHDEACON OF ROCHDALE; MANCHESTER] *b* 1958 *educ* Lutterworth Upper Sch; R Coll of Music; Westcott Ho; *CV* C St Mich, Flixton 1989–92; Chapl Bolton Coll of HE and FE and C Bolton Par Ch 1992–98; Chapl among Deaf People and TV E Farnworth and Kearsley 1998–2004; TR E. Farnworth & Kearsley 2004–08; Bp's Adv in Women's Min 2004–09; AD Farnworth 2005–08; Hon Can Man Cathl 2007; Adn Rochdale from 2008; Prolocutor Lower Ho Conv York from 2013
GS 2003– 	*Tel:* 0161 678 1454
07803 139274 (Mobile)
email: archrochdale@manchester.anglican.org

VINCE, Mr Jacob Peter, MA, DBA, MRICS
3 High St Horam Heathfield TN21 0EJ [CHICHESTER] *b* 1960 *educ* Latymer Upper Sch; Univ of Wales; City Univ; *CV* Dir and Charterer Surveyor from 1996; M Bp's Coun; Ch Commr; M Ch Buildings (Uses and Disposals) Cttee
GS 2005– 	*Tel:* 01453 812623
01435 813700
Fax: 01435 813732
email: jacob.vince@btconnect.com

VINCENT, Mr Adrian, BA, MA
16 Faris Barn Drive Woodham Surrey KT15 3DZ [GUILDFORD] *b* 1970 *educ* George Abbot Sch; Dur Univ; Kings' Coll Lon; *CV* ITT Lon and Edinb Insurance Grp 1993–95; Asst Grants Sec, Adv Brd Min 1995–97; Archbps' Commission on the Organisation of the C of E 1997–98; Statistics Unit, Archbps' Counc 1999–2000; Exec Off, House of Bps Dept of the Central Sec 2000–07; Policy Off, The Gen Counc of the Bar 2007–08; Head of Remuneration and Policy, The Gen Counc of the Bar from 2008
GS 2010– 	*Tel:* 01932 349335
email: avwebsite@hotmail.co.uk
Web: www.adrianvincent.org.uk

WAINE, Ven Stephen,
28 Merriefield Drive Broadstone BH18 8BP [ARCHDEACON OF DORSET; SALISBURY] *b* 1959 *CV* Adn of Dorset from 2010 	*Tel:* 01202 659427
Fax: 01202 691418
email: addorset@salisbury.anglican.org

WAKEFIELD, Area Bishop of. See ROBINSON, Rt Revd Anthony William

WAKEFIELD, Dean of. See GREENER, Very Revd Jonathan Desmond Francis

WALKER, Canon Anthony (Tony) Charles St John, MA
St Saviour's Vicarage 31 Richmond Rd Retford DN22 6SJ [SOUTHWELL AND NOTTINGHAM] *b* 1955 *educ* Brentwood Sch; Tr Coll Ox; Wycliffe Hall Ox; *CV* C Bradf Cathl 1981–84; C St Ann w. Em

Nottm 1984–88; V St Saviour Retford 1988–2001; P-in-c St Swithun E Retford 2001; TR Retford 2002–11; TR Retford Area Team Ministry from 2011; AD Retford 2000–09; Hon Can Southwell Minster 2004–11; Can Emeritus Southwell Minster from 2011; M Dioc Syn, Bp's Coun
GS 2004–   *Tel:* 01777 703800
    email: tony@tonywalker.f9.co.uk

WALKER, Rt Revd David Stuart , MA, FRSA
Bishopscourt Bury New Road Manchester M7 4LE [BISHOP OF MANCHESTER] *b* 1957 *educ* Man Gr Sch; K Coll Cam; Qu Th Coll Birm; *CV* C Handsworth 1983–86; TV Maltby 1986–91; Ind Chapl Maltby 1986–91; V Bramley and Ravenfield 1991–95; TR Bramley and Ravenfield w Hooton Roberts and Braithwell 1995–2000; Hon Can Sheff Cathl 2000; Bp of Dudley 2000–13; M Adv Coun on Relns of Bps and Relig Coms from 2002, Chair from 2008; FRSA 2007; M CUF from 2008; M C of E Min Coun from 2013; Church Commissioner from 2013: Bp of Manchester from 2013; Chair Greater Manchester Police Ethics Cttee from 2014; M C of E Ethical Investments Advisory Cttee from 2014
GS 2005–   *Tel:* 0161 792 2096
    email: bishop.david@manchester.anglican.org

WALKER, Mrs (Pauline) Debra, B Pharm, MRPharmS
Willow Lodge Church Lane Lydiate L31 4HL [LIVERPOOL] *b* 1960 *educ* Ormskirk Gr Sch; Bradf Univ; *CV* Pharmacist qualified 1982
GS 2010–   *Tel:* 0151 520 2496
    email: debrawalker@btinternet.com

WALKER, Revd Ruth Elizabeth, BA, PGCE
The Vicarage 5 Howard Close Bidford-on-Avon Warwickshire B50 4EL [COVENTRY] *b* 1958 *educ* Hayes Sch; St.John's Coll, Dur; Hughes Hall, Cam; St.John's Coll Nott; *CV* RE Tchr The Embrook School, Wokingham, Berks 1980–83; RE Tchr, Ranelagh School, Bracknell, Berks 1983–86; Parish Dn St. Mary's Princes Risborough w Ilmer, Ox 1988–90; AC & Congregational Chapl Bradf Cathl 1990–93; AC P of West Swindon & the Lydiards, Bris1993–94; NSM P of West Swindon & the Lydiards, Bris 1994–96; AC St. John the Baptist & St. Andrew Parks & Walcot, Bris 1996–98; Hon.Ce PTO P of Ch Ch Swindon, Bris 1999; Assoc Minr Keresley w Coundon & C-in-C Keresley Village Comm Ch, Cov 1999–2010; AD Cov North Deanery 2004–10; Assoc Min Heart of England Parishes, Cov 2010
GS 2010–   *Tel and Fax:* 01789 772217
    email: ruth@heartparishes.org.uk

WALSALL, Archdeacon of. [NOT APPOINTED AT TIME OF GOING TO PRESS]

WANDSWORTH, Archdeacon of. See ROBERTS, Ven Stephen John

WARD, Very Revd Dr Frances Elizabeth Fearn, M Theol; PhD
Deanery The Great Churchyard Bury St Edmunds Suffolk IP33 1RS [DEAN OF ST EDMUNDSBURY] *b* 1959 *educ* King's Sch Ely; Univ of St Andrews; Royal Lon Hospital; Univ of Cam; Univ of Man; Univ of Bradf; Westcott Ho Cam; *CV* Par Deacon St Bartholomew, Westhoughton 1989–93; Tutor Practical Theol, Northern Coll (URC & Cong. Fed) 1993–98; Hon C St George, Unsworth 1998–99; V St Peter, Bury 1999–2005; Bp's Advisor on Women's Min 2002–04; Hon C St Stephen and all Martyrs' Leverbridge 2005–06; Residentiary Can Bradf Cathl 2006–2010; Dean of St Edmundsbury from 2010
    Tel: 01284 748722
    Fax: 01284 768655
    email: dean@stedscathedral.org

WARD, Mr John Selwyn, LLB
[LONDON] *b* 1971 *educ* Abbey Gate Coll Ches; Bris Univ; Katholieke Universiteit Leuven; Coll of Law, Ches; *CV* Solicitor; trainee solicitor, S J Berwin, Lon 1994–96; Stagiaire, Directorate Gen for Competition, Eur Commn 1996–97; asst solicitor, S J Berwin, Brussels 1997; Sen Legal Adv, Office of Fair Trading 1997–2003; Sen Legal Adv, DEFRA 2003–07 and 2010–13; Legal Sec to the Advocate Gen for Scotland 2007–10; Dep Dir Home Office Legal Adviser's Branch from 2013; M PCC Emm Ch W Hampstead from 1999; M N Camden Dny Syn from 2002; Convener GS Human Sexuality Grp 2006–14
GS 2005–   *Tel:* 07734 080573 (Mobile)
    email: jward.anglican@zen.co.uk

WARD, Revd Dr Kevin, MA, Ph D
Theology & Religious Studies University of Leeds Leeds LS2 9JT [UNIVERSITIES, NORTHERN] *b* 1947 *educ* Pudsey Gr Sch; Edin Univ; Trin Coll Cam; Bp Tucker Th Coll, Mukono, Uganda; *CV* CMS Miss Ptnr (Tutor Bp Tucker Th Coll, Ch of Uganda) 1975–91; Tutor Qu Coll Birm 1991; Par Min Halifax, Wakef Dio 1991–95; Sen Lect in African Studies, Sch of Th and Relig Studies, Leeds Univ from 1995; NSM St Mich Headingley, Ripon Dio; M Ripon Dioc Wkg Grp in Human Sexuality; Trustee CMS 2003–10; Newsletter Editor, Uganda Church Association from 1993
GS 2003–05; 2005–   *Tel:* 0113 343 3641
    email: trskw@leeds.ac.uk

WARNER, Rt Revd Martin Clive, BA, MA, PhD
The Palace Chichester West Sussex PO19 1PY [BISHOP OF CHICHESTER] *b* 1958 *educ* K Sch Roch; Maidstone Gr Sch; St Chad's Coll Dur; St Steph Ho; *CV* C St Pet Plymouth 1984–88; TV Resurr Leic 1988–93; P Admin Shrine of Our Lady of Walsingham 1993–2002; Can Pastor, St Paul's Cathl from 2003; Treasurer, St Paul's Cathl 2008–09; Bp of Whitby 2009–12; Bp of Chichester from 2012
    Tel: 01243 782161
    Fax: 01243 531332

WARREN, Dr Yvonne, MA, PhD, UKCP, BACP
Cornerston 6 Hillview Stratford Upon Avon Warwick-shire CV37 9AY [COVENTRY] *b* 1938 *educ* Beford High Sch; *CV* Nurse 1957–61; Relate Supervisor 1980–95; Psychotherapist from 1996; Bp's Adv from 1990; Candidates Panel from 1994; R from 1996; Bp's Visitor 1990–2006; Lay Rep GS Ridley Hall Th Coll 2000–07; Act Dioc Adv Pastoral Care and Counselling until 2011; Abps' Assessor from 2011
GS 2000–05; 2005–07; 2010– *Tel:* 01789414255
email: ywarren@hotmail.co.uk

WARRINGTON, Archdeacon of. See BRADLEY, Ven Peter David Douglas

WARRINGTON, Suffragan Bishop of. See BLACKBURN, Rt Revd Richard Finn

WARWICK, Suffragan Bishop of. See STROYAN, Rt Revd John Ronald Angus

WATSON, Rt Revd Andrew John, MA
Willow Grange Woking Road Guildford Surrey GU4 7QS [BISHOP OF GUILDFORD] *b* 1961 *educ* Win Coll; CCC Cam; Ridley Hall Th Coll; *CV* C St Pet Ipsley 1987–90; C St Jo and St Pet Notting Hill 1990–95; V St Steph E Twickenham from 1995; M Bp's Coun; M MPA Coun from 2006; AD Hampton 2003–08; Bp of Aston from 2008; M Bd Queen's Foundation, Birminghamfrom 2011; M Bd Abps' College of Evangelists from 2011; Chair of Trustees CPAS 2013; Chair of Panel for World Mission and the Anglican Communion 2013
GS 2000–08 *Tel:* 01483 590500
Fax: 01483 590501
email: bishop.guildford@cofeguildford.org.uk

WATSON, Ven Sheila Anne, MA, M Phil, DD
29 The Precincts Canterbury CT1 2EP [ARCH-DEACON OF CANTERBURY] *b* 1953 *educ* Ayr Acad; St And Univ; Corpus Christi Coll Ox; Coates Hall Th Coll Edin; *CV* Dss St Sav Bridge of Allan and St Jo Alloa, St And 1979–80; Dss St Mary Monkseaton Newc 1980–84; Officer for Miss and Min Kensington Episc Area Lon 1984–87; Hon C St Luke and Ch Ch Chelsea Lon 1987–96; Selection Sec ABM 1992–93, Senior Selection Sec 1993–96; Adv in CME Salis 1997–2002; Dioc Dir of Min Salis 1998–2002; Hon Can Salis 2000; Adn of Buckingham 2002–07; Adn of Canterbury from 2007 *Tel:* 01227 865238
Fax: 01227 785209
email: archdeacon@canterbury-cathedral.org

WEBSTER, Rt Revd Glyn Hamilton, SRN
Holy Trinity Rectory Micklegate York YO1 6LE [BISHOP OF BEVERLEY] *b* 1951 *educ* Darwen Sec Tech (Gr) Sch; St Jo Coll Dur; *CV* C All SS Huntington York 1977–81; V St Luke Ev York and Sen Chapl York District Hosp 1981–92; Sen Chapl York Health Services NHS Trust 1992–99; Can

and Preb York Minster 1994–99; RD York 1997–2004; Can Res and Treas York Minster from 1999; Can Pastor from 2000; Prolocutor of York from 2000; M AC from 2000; Chair Dioc Ho of Clergy; Chan York Minster from 2004; Assoc DDO from 2005; M GS Business Cttee from 2005; M Hosp Chapl Coun from 2005; Bp of Beverley from 2012
GS 1995– *Tel:* 01904 628155
email: office@seeofbeverley.org.uk

WEBSTER, Ven Martin Duncan, BSc, Dip Th
Glebe House Church Lane Sheering Bishops Stortford CM22 7NR [ARCHDEACON OF HARLOW; CHELMS-FORD] *b* 1952 *educ* Dury Falls Sec Modern Sch; Abbs Cross Tech High Sch; Nottm Univ; Linc Th Coll; *CV* C St Pet and St Mich Thundersley, Chelmsf 1978–81; TV Canvey Island 1981–86; V All SS and St Giles Nazeing 1986–99; AD Harlow 1989–99; NSM Officer 1995–99; TR Waltham Abbey 1999–2009; Adn Harlow from 2009
GS 2005–2010 *Tel:* 01297 734524
email: a.harlow@chelmsford.anglican.org

WELBY, Most Revd Justin Portal, MA, BA
Lambeth Palace London SE1 7JU [ARCHBISHOP OF CANTERBURY] *b* 1956 *educ* Eton Coll; Trin Coll Cam; St Jo Coll Dur; Cranmer Hall; *CV* Mgr Project Finance, Soc Nationale Elf Aquitaine, Paris 1978–83; Treas Elf UK plc, Lon 1983–84; Grp Treas Enterprise Oil plc, Lon 1984–89; C All SS Chilvers Coton and St Mary V, Astley, Nuneaton, Cov 1992–95; R St Jas Southam and St Mich & All Angels Ufton, Cov 1995–2002; Dir of Internat Min and Res Can Cov Cathl 2002–05; Sub-Dean and Can for Reconciliation Min, Cov Cathl 2005–07; P-in-c H Trin Cov 2007; Dean of Liv 2007–11; Bp of Durham 2011–12; Abp of Canterbury from 2012 *Tel:* 020 7898 1200
email: contact@lambethpalace.org.uk
Web: www.lambethpalace.org.uk

WELCH, Ven Stephan John, BA, DipTheol, MTh
98 Dukes Ave Chiswick London W4 2AF [ARCH-DEACON OF MIDDLESEX; LONDON] *b* 1950 *educ* Luton Gr Sch; Luton Sixth Form Coll; Hull Univ; Birm Univ; Heythrop Coll, Lon Univ; Qu Coll Birm; *CV* C Ch Ch Waltham Cross, St Alb 1977–80; P-in-c and V St Mary Reculver & St Bart Herne Bay, Cant 1980–92; V St Mary Hurley & St Jas the Less Stubbings, Ox 1992–2000; V St Pet Hammersmith, Lon 2000–06; AD Hammersmith and Fulham 2001–06; Adn of Middlesex from 2006; Chair Lon Dioc Bd for Schs; M DAC, DBF, Bp's Coun *Tel:* 020 8742 8308
07780 704059 (Mobile)
email: archdeacon.middlesex@london.anglican.org

WELLS, Archdeacon of. See SULLIVAN, Ven Nicola Ann

WELLS, Dean of. See CLARKE, Very Revd John Martin

WEST CUMBERLAND, Archdeacon of. See PRATT, Ven Richard

WEST HAM, Archdeacon of. See COCKETT, Ven Elwin Wesley

WESTMINSTER, Dean of. See HALL, Very Revd John Robert

WESTMORLAND AND FURNESS, Archdeacon of. See DRIVER, Ven Penny (Penelope May)

WHEATLEY, Ven Ian James, BTh
Naval Chaplaincy Service Navy Command HQ, Mp 1–2 Leach Building Whale Island Portsmouth PO2 8BY [ARCHDEACON FOR THE ROYAL NAVY] *b* 1962 *educ* Royal Grammar Sch Worc; Chich Theol College;; *CV* Royal Navy 1981–91; C Braunton 1994–97; Chapl Royal Navy from 1997; Royal Navy Prin Denominational Chapl (Anglican) and Deputy Chapl of the Fleet
GS 2013–   *Tel:* 0239 2625193
                                       Fax: 0239 2625134
                   email: ian.wheatley928@mod.uk

WHITBY, Suffragan Bishop of. See FERGUSON, Rt Revd Paul John

WHITE, Mr David Peter, AMusLCM, BSc, FCMA, DChA, CGMA
Church House Great Smith St London SW1P 3AZ [HEAD OF FINANCIAL POLICY AND PLANNING, FINANCE AND RESOURCES, NATIONAL CHURCH INSTITUTIONS] *b* 1966 *educ* Dartford Gr Sch; LSE; *CV* On staff of Church Commissioners since 1990, Head of Fin Planning, Ch Crs 2002–07, Head of Fin Policy and Planning, AC and Ch Crs 2007–11, Head of Fin Policy and Planning, National Church Instutions from 2011   *Tel:* 020 7898 1684
                                       Fax: 020 7898 1131
        email: david.white@churchofengland.org

WHITE, Rt Revd Frank (Francis), BSc, DipTh
Bishop's House 29 Moor Rd South Newcastle Upon Tyne NE3 1PA [ASSISTANT BISHOP OF NEWCASTLE] *b* 1949 *educ* St Cuth Gr Sch Newc; Consett Tech Coll; UWIST Cardiff; Univ Coll Cardiff; St Jo Coll Nottm; *CV* Dir Youth Action York 1971–73; Detached Youth Worker Man Catacombs Trust 1973–77; C St Nic Dur 1980–84; C St Mary and St Cuth Chester-le-Street 1984–87; Chapl to Dur HA Hosps 1987–89; V St Jo Ev Birtley 1989–97; RD Chester-le-Street 1993–97; Hon Can Dur Cathl 1997–2002; Adn of Sunderland 1997–2002; Bp of Brixworth from 2002–2010; Hon Can Peterb Cathl 2002–10; Fell Univ of Northampton from 2010; Asst Bp of Newc from 2010; Hon Can Newc Cathl from 2010
GS 1987–2000   *Tel:* 0191 285 2220
                                       Fax: 0191 284 6933
      email: bishopfrank@newcastle.anglican.org
            Web: www.newcastle.anglican.org

WHITE, Mrs Margaret Joan, MBE, CQSW
The White House 6 Blayney Row Heddon Station Newcastle NE158QD [NEWCASTLE] *b* 1933 *educ* Skerry's Coll; Walbottle Gr Sch; Rutherford Coll of F Ed; Sunderland Poly; *CV* Shorthand Typist 1948–52; Sec Thos. Cook 1952–54; Secy Lon & Lanc Insurance Co. 1954–56; Sec Assoc Anaesthetists, Winnipeg, 1956–60; Sec Chipman Chemicals, Winnipeg 1960–61; Sec Med Rsrch Counc,Newcastle 1961–62; Sec Transport & Genl Workers' Union 1962–65; Sec Westlands Special Sch 1965–74; Ed Welfare Off, Newcastle LEA, 1974–92; Dioc Apptmt, AFIA Rep MU from 1990
GS 2010–   *Tel:* 0191 2674569
        email: heddonstation@btinternet.com

WHITE, Canon Bob (Robert Charles), MA, Cert Th
St Mary's Vicarage Fratton Rd Portsmouth PO1 5PA [PORTSMOUTH] *b* 1961 *educ* Portsmouth Gr Sch; Mansfield Coll Ox; St Steph Ho Ox; *CV* C St Jo Forton 1985–88; C St Mark North End with special responsibility for St Fran Hilsea 1988–92; V St Clare Warren Park 1992–2000; V St Fran Leigh Park 1994–2000; RD Havant 1998–2000; V St Mary Portsea from 2000; AD Portsmouth from 2011; M Bp's Coun; Dioc Adv on Urban Ministry; CUF Link Officer; Chair Dioc Ho of Clergy
GS 1995–2000, 2004–   *Tel:* 023 9282 2687
              email: revrcwhite@aol.com

WHITEHEAD, Revd Canon Dr Hazel, BD, AKC, MA, D. MIN
The Rectory 5 The Spinning Walk Shere Surrey GU5 9HN [GUILDFORD] *b* 1954 *educ* Fryerns Gr; King's Coll Lon; NTMTC, Lambeth; *CV* Tchr 1989–95; AC St Mary Oatlands 1993–1997; Prin Guild Dioc Min 1994–2005; Dioc Dir Min Training 2005; Archbp's CMD Assesor BAP Adv; Co-Chair South Central Regional Training Partnership from 2008; M TETC and EVP 1994–2004; Chair CAEIMT 2003–05
GS 2010–   *Tel:* 01483 709307
                                          01483 202394
                                          07824 556043
                                       Fax: 01483 790333
    email: hazel.whitehead@cofeguildford.org.uk

WHITTAM SMITH, Mr Andreas, MA, CBE
154 Campden Hill Rd London W8 7AS [FIRST CHURCH ESTATES COMMISSIONER] *b* 1937 *educ* Birkenhead Sch; Keble Coll Ox; *CV* Founder & Ed 'The Independent' 1986–94; Dir Independent Print Limited); Pres Br Bd of Film Classification 1997–2002; Chair Fin Ombudsman Service Ltd 1999–2003; Chair The Children's Mutual 2005–10; Vc-Pres Nat Coun for One-Parent Families; Chair Ch Commrs Assets Cttee; M Ch Commrs Bd of Govs; M AC from 2002
GS 2002–   *Tel:* 020 7221 8354
              email: andreasws@mac.com

WHITWORTH, Mrs Ruth,
4 Cravenwood Close Weeley Heath Clacton-on-Sea CO16 9DG [CHELMSFORD] *b* 1952
GS 1990–99; 2005–10; 2010–   *Tel:* 01255 426175
email: ruth@greenend.com

WIGHT, Archdeacon of the Isle of. See BASTON, Ven Caroline Jane

WILCOCKSON, Ven Stephen Anthony,
MA(Oxon), BA
14 Armthorpe Lane Doncaster South Yorkshire DN2 5LZ [ARCHDEACON OF DONCASTER; SHEFFIELD] *b* 1951 *educ* Park High Sch Birkenhead; Nottm Univ; Ox Univ; Wycliffe Hall; *CV* C St Lawrence Pudsey 1976–78; Sen C All Saints w Holy Trinity Wandsworth 1978–81; V St Peter Rock Ferry 1981–86; V St Mark, Lache cum Saltney 1986–95; V St Paul, Howell Hill 1995–2009; RD Epsom 2000–07; Par Dev Officer Chester Dioc 2009–12; Adn of Doncaster from 2012   *Tel:* 01302 325787
01709 309110
email: steve.wilcockson@sheffield.anglican.org

WILCOX, Very Revd Dr Pete (Peter Jonathan),
BA, MA, DPhil
1 Cathedral Close Liverpool L1 7BR [DEAN OF LIVER-POOL] *b* 1961 *educ* Worksop Coll; St John's Coll Durham; Robinson Coll Cam; St John's Coll Ox; Ridley Hall Cam; *CV* C All Saints', Preston on Tees 1987–1990; Asst P St Margaret's with St Philip and St Giles Ox 1990–93; TV St Edmund's Chapel Gateshead and Dir Cranmer Hall Urban Mission Centre 1993–98; P-in-c St Paul's Church at the Crossing, Walsall 1998–2006; Can Chancellor Lichfield Cathl 2006–12; Dean of Liverpool from 2012   *Tel:* 0151 702 7220
email: dean@liverpoolcathedral.org.uk
Web: www.liverpoolcathedral.org.uk

WILLESDEN, Area Bishop of. See BROADBENT, Rt Revd Pete (Peter Alan)

WILLIAMS, Sister Anne, Dip EvS
Good Shepherd Clergy House Forest Rd Ford Estate Sunderland SR4 0DX [DURHAM] *b* 1946 *educ* A J Dawson Gr Sch Wellfield; Wilson Carlile Coll of Evang; *CV* Civil Servant 1964–70; Fin Office Admin 1971–93; Communications/PR Support for Third World charity 1993–96; Dep Bursar Dur High Sch for Girls 1996–2002; Vc-Chairman Forward in Faith from 1994; Ch Army Ev in trg 2003–04; Com Missioner from 2004; Miss Enabler pt-time 2004–09; Regional Devel Officer CLCGB from 2009
GS 1990–   *Tel:* 0191 5656 870 (Home)
07715 178654 (Mobile)
email: sranneca@aol.com

WILLIAMS, Rt Revd David Grant, BSc Soc Sci
Bishop's Lodge Old Alresford Place Colden Lane Alresford SO24 9DY [SUFFRAGAN BISHOP OF BASINGSTOKE; WINCHESTER] *b* 1961 *educ* Newport Free Gr Sch; Bris Univ; Crowther Hall, Birm; Wycliffe Hall Th Coll; *CV* Deputy Headteacher (CMS Mission Partner), Kitui District, Kenya 1983–85; Lay Asst, Christ Ch Clifton, Bris 1985–86; AC Ecclesall, Sheffield Dioc 1989–92; V Ch Ch Dore, Sheffield Dioc 1992–2002; AD, Eccesall Deanery, Sheffield Dioc 1997–2002; Chapl, Aldine House Secure Unit, Sheffield 1998–2002; V Ch Ch Winc 2002–14; Hon Can Winc Cthl from 2012; Chair Dioc Ho Clergy 2012–14; Bp of Basingstoke from 2014
GS 2010–14   *Tel:* 01962 737330
01962 737350
07889 547095
email: bishop.david@winchester.anglican.org

WILLIAMS, Rt Revd Paul Gavin, BA
Dial House Riverside Twickenham TW1 3DT [AREA BISHOP OF KENSINGTON; LONDON] *b* 1968 *educ* Court Fields Sch Wellington; Grey Coll Univ Dur; Wycliffe Hall Ox; *CV* C St James Muswell Hill 1992–95; Asst V Christ Ch Clifton 1996–99; R St James Gerrards Cross w Fulmer 1999–2009; Area Bp of Kensington from 2009; Chair Trustees CPAS 2011–14   *Tel:* 020 7932 1180
email: bishop.kensington@london.anglican.org

WILLIAMS, Revd Dr Rowan Clare,
St Lawrence Vicarage 11 Newland Park Close York YO10 3HW [YORK] *b* 1967 *educ* K Coll Cam; Jes Coll Cam; Westcott Ho Cam; *CV* C Leic Resurr 2005–08; Chapl Univ Hosps Leic NHS Trust 2008–10; Chapl York Univ from 10; M Bd Educ from 2013
GS 2013–   *Tel:* 01904 415460
07919 861912
email: rcw514@york.ac.uk

WILLIS, Very Revd Robert Andrew, DL
The Deanery The Precincts Canterbury CT1 2EP [DEAN OF CANTERBURY] *b* 1947 *educ* Kingswood Gr Sch; Warw Univ; Worc Coll Ox; Cuddesdon Th Coll; *CV* C St Chad Shrewsbury 1972–75; V Choral Sarum Cathl 1975–78; TR Tisbury and RD Chalke 1978–89; V Sherborne 1987–92; RD Sherborne 1991–92; Dean of Heref 1992–2001; Dean of Cant from 2001; M PWM Cttee 1990–2001; M Cathls Fabric Commn from 1993; M Liturg Commn 1994–98; Chair Deans' Conf from 1999
GS 1985–92, 1994–   *Tel:* 01227 762862
01227 865200
Fax: 01227 865222
email: dean@canterbury-cathedral.org

WILLMOTT, Rt Revd Trevor, MA, Dip Theol
The Bishop's Office Old Palace Canterbury CT1 2EE [BISHOP OF DOVER AND BISHOP IN CANTERBURY; ASSISTANT BISHOP OF WINCHESTER] *b* 1950 *educ* Plymouth Coll; St Pet Coll Ox; Fitzw Coll Cam; Westcott Ho Th Coll; *CV* C St Geo Norton 1974–77; Asst Chapl Oslo w Trondheim 1978–79; Chapl Naples w Capri, Bari and Sorrento 1979–

83; R Ecton and Wdn Peterb Dioc Retreat Ho 1983–89; DDO and Dir of POT 1986–97; Can Res and Prec Peterb Cathl 1989–97; Adn of Dur and Can Res Dur Cathl 1997–2002; Suff Bp of Basingstoke 2002–2010; Bp of Dover from 2010; M GS Business Sub-cttee from 2005; M Ho of Bps Stg Cttee from 2005; Trustee Foundn for Chr Leadership; M Rural Bps Panel from 2004; Patr Cross Borders YMCA from 2005; Trustee St Michael's Coll, Llandaff; Visitor to the Sisters of Bethany; Asst Bp of Winchester

GS 2000–   *Tel:* 01227 459382
                         Fax: 01227 784985
         email: trevor.willmott@bishcant.org

WILSON, Rt Revd Alan Thomas Lawrence,
MA, D Phil

Sheridan Grimms Hill Great Missenden HP16 9BG [AREA BISHOP OF BUCKINGHAM; OXFORD] *b* 1955 *educ* St Jo Coll Cam; Ball Col Ox; Wycliffe Hall Ox; *CV* Hon C Eynsham, Ox 1979–81, C 1981–82; C Caversham and Mapledurham 1982–89; V St Jo Caversham 1989–92; Angl substitute Chapl, HMP Reading, 1990–1992; R Sandhurst 1992–2003; RD Sonning 1998–2003; Area Bp of Buckingham from 2003; M Coun, Wycombe Abbey Sch from 2008; Chair Ox Dioc Bd of Educ from 2010; Univ of Buckingham Visiting Prof in Theol from 2010

                      Tel: 01494 862173
                 07525 655756 (Mobile)
                      Fax: 01494 890508
    email: bishopbucks@oxford.anglican.org

WILSON, Mr Brian Kenneth, MA FIA

84 Albert Road Epsom Surrey KT17 4EL [SOUTHWARK] *b* 1947 *educ* Lewes Co Sch for Boys; Univ Oxford; *CV* Sch Master, Dulwich Coll 1971–74; Sch Master, King's Sch Cant 1974–76; Asst Actuary, Bacon & Woodrow 1976–83; Partner, Bacon & Woodrow 1983–2002; Prin, Hewitt Assoc 2002–10; Prin, Aon Hewitt 2010; rtd 2010; M C of E Pensions Bd from 2011; M Remuneration and Conditions of Service Cttee of AC from 2011

GS 2010–   *Tel:* 01372 740155
     email: brian.k.wilson@btinternet.com

WILSON, Ven Christine Louise, Dip Th

The Old Vicarage Baslow Derbyshire DE45 1RY [ARCHDEACON OF CHESTERFIELD; DERBY] *b* 1958 *educ* Margaret Hardy Sch, Brighton; SDMTS; *CV* C Henfield w. Shermanbury and Woodmancate, Chich 1997–2002; TV Hove 2002–08; V Goring by Sea 2008–10; Adn Chesterfield from 2010; Chich Dioc Overseas Cttee 2007–09; Adv Cttee, Derby from 2010; Bd of Finance, Derby from 2010; Bd of Edu, Derby from 2010; Pastoral Cttee, Derby from 2010; Parsonages Cttee, Derby from 2010; Chair Peak Centre from 2010; Glebe Ctte, Derby from 2010

GS 2010–   *Tel:* 01246 583023
   email: archchesterfield@derby.anglican.org

WILSON, Mr John, MIH, MIF

49 Oakhurst Lichfield WS14 9AL [LICHFIELD] *b* 1946 *educ* Polytechnic of North London; *CV* HM Forces 1961–76; Deputy Area School Meals Advisor, Cambridgeshire County Council 1977–78; Regional Sales and marketing Manager, Bateman Catering 1978 -83; Dir of Training, Mantislight Ltd, 1983–87; Dir Operations, Deansbury Ltd, 1987–92; Charity Management Consult, Charity Support Services, 1992–97; National Fundraising and Marketing Advisor, Age Concern England, 1997–2001; Charity Management Consult, Charity Support Services, 2001–06; Chief Exec, Line Line, 2006–10; M Dioc Syn from 1989; M Dioc Pastoral Cttee from 2000; M Bp's Coun from 2000; M Brd of Patronage from 2003; Dioc Chair of Ho of Laity from 2009; Lay Chair of Lichf Deanery from 1987; Treasurer Church House Deaneries Group (The National Deaneries Network) from 2003; Chair Board of Directors/Trustees Link Line Community Services from 2010; Managing Director Church Jobs Ltd (www.churchjobfinder.co.uk) from 2010

GS 2005–   *Tel:* 01543 268678
                         07785 334077
                      Fax: 01543 411685
    email: charity.services@btclick.com

WILSON-RUDD, Miss Fay (Felicity),

3 Old School Place North Grove Wells BA5 2TD [BATH AND WELLS] *b* 1941 *educ* Filton High Sch; *CV* Asst Stewardship Adv St Alb Dio 1981–84; Resources Adv B & W 1984–2001; pt Chapl Co-ord Somerset NHS Ptnrship and Soc Care Trust from 1999

GS 1993–   *Tel and Fax:* 01749 677286 (Home)
                     07712 581903 (Mobile)
         email: faywilsonrudd@msn.com

WILTS, Archdeacon of. WORSLEY, Ven Ruth

WINCHESTER, Archdeacon of. See HARLEY, Ven Michael

WINCHESTER, Bishop of. See DAKIN, Rt Revd Timothy John

WINCHESTER, Dean of. See ATWELL, Very Revd James Edgar

WINDSOR, Dean of. See CONNER, Rt Revd David John

WINTER, Revd Canon Dr Dagmar, Dr Theol

The Vicarage Kirkwhelpington Newcastle upon Tyne NE19 2RT [NEWCASTLE] *b* 1963 *educ* Gesamtschule Oberursel; Erlangen Univ; Aberd Univ; Heidelberg Univ; Herborn Th Coll; *CV* C St Mark Bromley 1996–99; Assoc V and Dny Trg Officer Hexham Abbey 1999–2006; P-in-c Kirkwhelpington w Kirkharle & Kirkheaton, and Cambo and Dioc Officer for Rural Affairs from 2006; AD

Morpeth 2010–12; Hon Can Newc Cathl from 2011;Bp's Adviser for Women's Ministry from 2012; Hon Fell Dur Univ from 2014
GS 2005–
email: dagmar.winter@btinternet.com
Twitter: @DagmarKirk

WINTON, Rt Revd Alan Peter, BA, PhD
The Red House 53 Norwich Rd Stoke Holy Cross Norwich NR14 8AB [SUFFRAGAN BISHOP OF THETFORD; NORWICH] *b* 1958 *educ* Chislehurst and Sidcup Gr Sch; Trin Coll Bristol; Univ Sheff; Linc Theol Coll; *CV* Asst C Christ Ch Southgate 1991–95; P-in-c St Paul's Walden w Preston 1995–99; CME Officer Dioc St Albans 1995–99; R Welwyn w Ayot St Peter 1999–2005; TR Welwyn 2005–09; Bp of Thetford from 2009; Chair Discipleship and Min Forum Dioc Norw
Tel: 01508 491014
email: bishop.thetford@dioceseofnorwich.org

WISBECH, Archdeacon of. [NOT APPOINTED AT TIME OF GOING TO PRESS]

WITCOMBE, Very Revd John Julian, MA, MPhil
1 Hill Top Coventry CV1 5AB [DEAN OF COVENTRY] *b* 1959 *educ* Bramcote Hills Gr Sch; Nott High Sch; Emman Colle, Cam; Nott Univ; St. John's Coll, Nott; *CV* C, St John's Birtley, Dur 1984–87; C-in-C, St. Barnabas' Inham Nook, S'well 1987–91; V, St. Luke's Lodge Moor, Sheff, 1991–95; TR, Uxbridge, Lon, 1995–98; Dean, St John's Coll Nott, 1998–2005; Off Min & Dir of Ordinands, Glouc, 2005–2010; Dir, Dept of Disicipleship and Ministry, Glouc 2010–12; Res Can Glouc Cathl 2010–12; Dean of Coventry from 2012
GS 2010–
Tel: 024 7652 1223
Web: www.coventrycathedral.org.uk

WITTS, Mrs Susan Anne, BA
20 Amber Drive Chorley PR6 0LA [BLACKBURN] *b* 1958 *educ* Mather Colll Man; Edge Hill Univ; Church Coll Cert Sch Work St Martin's Lanc;; *CV* Primary Sch Tchr 1979–2005; Asst Dir Children's Work, Bd Edu; Blackb Dioc from 2005; Dioc Blackb bd Edu Liturg Ctee; Elected to GS 2010
GS 2010–
Tel: 01254 503070
email: susan.witts@blackburn.anglican.org

WOLSTENHOLME, Canon Carol, OBE, FCIPD
12 Ashleigh Crescent Denton Newcastle upon Tyne NE5 2AE [NEWCASTLE] *b* 1943 *educ* Rutherford High Sch Newc; *CV* Dept Work and Pensions Human Resources 1960-2003; Mgt Consult from 2000; Rdr 2006; Cathl Coun 2006; Chair Newc Dioc Miss and Pastl Ctee from 2006; M Newc Dioc Strategical Devel Gp from 2007; Bp's Coun from 2007; Chair Deaneries Dev Task Grp 2009; Trustee Lindisfarne Reg Trg Partnership 2012; Lay Chair Dioc Syn 2012
GS 2009–
Tel: 0191 2745144
email: cawol43@aol.com

WOLVERHAMPTON, Area Bishop of. See GREGORY, Rt Revd Clive Malcolm

WOLVERSON, Revd Marc Ali Morad, BA, Dip Min
Vicarage 85 Buxton Rd High Lane Stockport SK6 8DS [CHESTER] *b* 1968 *educ* St Louis Country Day Sch, USA; Loyola Univ, USA; Kansas Univ, USA; Ripon Coll Cuddesdon; *CV* C St Mary Nantwich 1996–99; Asst R and sch Chapl, St Luke's Episcopal Ch and Sch, Baton Rouge, Louisiana 1999–2000; Assoc V St Mich and All Angels Bramhall 2000–04; V St Thos High Lane from 2004; M Ches Dioc Syn; Dioc Spiritual Dir, Cursillo
GS 2005–
Tel: 01663 762627
email: frmarc@onetel.com

WOOD, Canon Frances Mary, BA(Hons)
8 Butts Lane Egglescliffe Stockton-on-Tees TS16 9BT [DURHAM] *b* 1946 *educ* Harrogate Gr Sch; Univ Reading
Tel: 01642 782113
07742 732019
email: fran.wood3@gmail.com

WOOD, Canon (Nicholas) Martin, AKC, MTh
101 London Road Bowers Gifford Basildon Essex SS13 2DU [CHELMSFORD] *b* 1951 *educ* Brentwood Sch; Mid Essex Tech Coll; Kings Coll Lon; St Augustine's Coll, Cant; Univ of Wales Lampeter; *CV* C East Ham Team Ministry 1975–78; C in C, St. Luke, Leyton 1978–81; V Rush Green 1981–91; Chapl Barking Coll 1981–91; TR Elland 1991–2005; Rural Dean of Brighouse & Elland 1996–2005; Hon can Wakef Cathl 2001–05; P Develp Adv Bradwell Episcopal Area of Chelms from 2005; Hon can Chelms Cathl from 2008; Chelms Dioc Brd Miss 1983–84; Chelms Dioc Pstrl support & develp grp 1985–88; Wakef Dioc Syn 1991–05; Wakef Bp's Counc 1997–2005; Wakef Dioc Brd Min & Training sub cttee 1991–94; Wakef Dioc clergy ed and training grp 1994–98; Wakef Min Scheme Counc & ed sub grp 1996–2005; Wakef Min Adv Grp 1994–2005; Chair Wakef Dioc Family Life grp FLAME 1998–2005; Chelms Miss and P Develop Adv Grp from 2005; Chelms Dioc Syn from 2009; Chair Ho of Clergy Dioc Syn Chelmsf from 2010; Chapl to Bp of Bradwell and Parish Dev Adv (Bradwell Area) 2011–12; Miss and Min Adv (Bradwell Area) from 2012
GS 2010–
Tel: 01268 552219
07814 909976
email: mwood@chelmsford.anglican.org
Web: www.chelmsford.anglican.org/mwood

WOOLWICH, Area Bishop of. See IPGRAVE, Rt Revd Michael Geoffrey

WORCESTER, Archdeacon of. JONES, Ven Robert

WORCESTER, Bishop of. See INGE, Rt Revd Dr John Geoffrey

WORCESTER, Dean of. See ATKINSON, Very Revd Peter Gordon

WRAW, Rt Revd John Michael, BA
Bishop's House Orsett Rd Horndon-on-the-Hill SS17 8NS [AREA BISHOP OF BRADWELL; CHELMSFORD] *b* 1959 *educ* K Sch Chester; Lincoln Coll Ox; Fitzwilliam Coll Cam; Ridley Hall Cam; *CV* C St Pet Bromyard, Heref 1985–88; TV Sheff Manor Team 1988–92; V Clifton St Jas, Sheff 1992–2001; P-in-c Wickersley St Alb, Sheff 2001–04; Adn of Wilts 2004–12; Bp of Bradwell from 2012
Tel: 01375 673806
07702 296701
Fax: 01375 674222
email: email: b.bradwell@
chelmsford.anglican.org
Twitter: @johnwraw

WRIGHT, Ven Dr Paul, BD, MTh, DMin, AKC
The Archdeaconry The Glebe Chislehurst BR7 5PX [ARCHDEACON OF BROMLEY AND BEXLEY; ROCHESTER] *b* 1954 *educ* Crayford Sch; K Coll Lon; Heythrop Coll Lon; Ripon Coll, Cuddesdon; Lampeter Univ of Wales; *CV* C St Geo Beckenham, Roch 1979–83; C St Mary w St Matthias & St Jo, S'wark 1983–85; Chapl Ch Sch Richmond, S'wark 1983–85; V St Aug Gillingham, Roch 1985–90; R St Paulinus Crayford, Roch 1990–99; RD Erith 1993–97; Hon Can Roch Cathl 1998–2003; V St Jo Evang Sidcup, Roch 1999–2003; Adn of Bromley and Bexley from 2003; M Bp's Coun; M Dioc Bd of Patr; M Eccl Law Soc
Tel and Fax: 020 8467 8743
07985 902601 (Mobile)
email: archdeacon.bromley@
rochester.anglican.org

WYNNE, Mrs Alison,
88 Balcarres Rd Leyland PR25 3ED [BLACKBURN] *b* 1961 *educ* Pleckgate High Sch, Blackb; *CV* Wages clerk, MOD 1979–83; Computer Programmer, MOD 1983–86; Computer Applications Programmer, Lancs Constabulary 1986–87; IT Systems Programmer, Lancs Constabulary 1987–89; Chr outreach worker from 2001; Orthopaedic support worker Lancashire Teaching Hospitals from 2009; Ch Min Asst from 2012
GS 2005–
Tel: 01772 454209
07719 727527 (Mobile)
email: alison@wynne.org.uk

WYTHE, Mr John Michael, BSc, FRICS
Woodpeckers Ashwood Rd Woking GU22 7JN [CHURCH COMMISSIONER] *b* 1956 *educ* Woking Gr Sch for Boys; Reading Univ; *CV* Dir and Head of Fund Management at Prudential Property Investment Managers until 2010; Ch Commissioner from 2007; M Assets Cttee; current bd, cttee, advisory and Trustee roles with Norges Bank, CBRE Global Investors, DTZ Investment Management, The Portman Estate, Pollen Estate, AIA and Sue Ryder
Tel: 01483 726710
email: jm.wythe@gmail.com

YEOMAN, Revd Ruth Jane, MA, BSc, MSc
Vicarage 12 Fairfax Gardens Menston Ilkley LS29 6ET [WEST YORKSHIRE AND THE DALES] *b* 1960 *educ* Nottm Bluecoat Sch; Sheff Univ; Ripon Coll Cuddesdon; *CV* C St Pet and St Paul Coleshill w. Maxstoke, Birm 1991–95; Asst P St Phil and St Jas Hodge Hill and Adv for Children's Work, Birm Dioc 1995–2000; Houseleader, L'Arch Lambeth Com 2001–02; V St Jo Divine Menston w. Woodhead from 2003; Assoc DDO Bradf from 2006; NADAWM representative Bradf from 2009
GS 2005–
Tel: 01943 877739
07752 912646 (Mobile)
email: ruthjyeoman@hotmail.com

YORK, Archbishop of. See SENTAMU, Most Revd and Rt Hon Dr John Tucker Mugabi

YORK, Archdeacon of. See BULLOCK, Ven Sarah Ruth

YORK, Dean of. See FAULL, Very Revd Vivienne Frances

INDEX

Note: Names of dioceses appear in *italics*; page references in **bold** type indicate maps. Names beginning 'St' are filed as if spelled 'Saint'. Hyphens and apostrophes are ignored for filing purposes.

Index